UNIX®

THIRD EDITION

Robin Burk, et al.

SAMS

EXECUTIVE EDITOR
Jeff Koch

AQUISITIONS EDITOR
Jane Brownlow

DEVELOPMENT EDITOR
Mark Cierzniak

MANAGING EDITOR
Brice Gosnell

PROJECT EDITOR
Katie Purdum

COPY EDITORS
Geneil Breeze
Michael Dietsch

INDEXER
Kelly Talbot

PROOFREADERS
Andrew Beaster
Jennifer Earhart

TECHNICAL EDITORS
Eric C. Richardson
Nalneesh Gaur

INTERIOR DESIGN
Gary Adair

COVER DESIGN
Aren Howell

LAYOUT TECHNICIANS
Ayanna Lacey
Heather Miller
Amy Parker

Contents at a Glance

Table of Contents

About the Lead Author

Robin Burk has been fooling around with computers for more years than she would like to admit. A successful executive in entrepreneurial companies, she had led teams in the development of operating systems, network protocol stacks, language tools, and multimedia applications. She holds an undergraduate degree in physics and an MBA in finance and operations.

For relaxation, Robin breeds, trains, and shows dogs. She founded the Internet discussion list for English Cocker Spaniels and can be reached at robink@wizard.net.

About the Contributing Authors

Bill Ball, author of *Sams Teach Yourself Linux in 24 Hours* and Que's *Using Linux*, is a technical writer, editor, and magazine journalist. A reformed Macophile, he broke down and bought a PC after using Apple computers for nearly 10 years. Instead of joining the Dark Side, he started using Linux! He has published more than a dozen articles in magazines such as *Computer Shopper* and *MacTech Magazine*, and first started editing books for Que in 1986. He is forever grateful to Dale Puckett for lessons in how to use casts and code tight loops in 6800 assembler—and to William Boatman for lessons in how to cast and throw tight loops on the stream. An avid fly fisherman, Bill builds bamboo fly rods and fishes on the nearby Potomac River. He lives in the Shirlington area of Arlington County, Virginia.

Chris Byers is currently a consultant for a major credit card company. As a consultant and former disaster recovery specialist, he has many years of experience in the wide world of UNIX. He lives in South Jersey with his wife, his son (plus another child on the way), and their cat Amelia. He can be reached at southst@voicenet.com.

Lance Cavener is cofounder of Senarius. His function is to provide support to employers in eastern Canada. He is also the president and senior network Administrator of ASCIO Communications, a subsidiary of Senarius. He provides the public and businesses with Internet-related services. Lance has been actively involved in UNIX since 1990 as an administrator for corporate networks at various companies in eastern Canada. His work includes working with BIND/DNS, Sendmail, Usenet setup, Web servers, and

UNIX security. He has also written various programs for SunOS, MS-DOS, MS Windows, and VMS.

Matt Coffey performs UNIX systems administration on SunOS, Solaris, IBM AIX, and HP systems. He has been responsible for a Sun Parallel Database Server that supported users nationwide. Currently he is supporting Sun legacy systems and an IBM SP2 Frame comprised of over 30 individual nodes.

David B. Horvath, CCP, is a senior consultant in the Philadelphia, Pennsylvania area. He has been a consultant for over 14 years and is also a part-time adjunct professor at local colleges teaching topics that include C programming, UNIX, and database techniques. He is currently pursuing an M.S. degree in dynamics of organization at the University of Pennsylvania (the degree should be received on December 22, 1998). He has provided seminars and workshops to professional societies and corporations on an international basis. David is the author of *UNIX for the Mainframer* (Prentice-Hall PTR), contributing author to *UNIX Unleashed Second Edition: System Administration Edition* and *Internet Edition* volumes (with cover credit), contributing author to *Red Hat Linux Second Edition*, contributing author to *Using UNIX Second Edition* (Que), and has written numerous magazine articles. When not at the keyboard, he can be found working in the garden or soaking in the hot tub. He has been married for over 11 years and has several dogs and cats. David can be reached at unx3@cobs.com for questions related to this book. No spam please!

For the past 15 years, **Chris Negus** has written or contributed to dozens of books on the UNIX system, computer networking, and the Internet. As a consultant, Chris worked at AT&T Bell Laboratories and UNIX System Laboratories on UNIX System V development teams. Later he worked with Novell's UnixWare system development. He was a contributing author for previous editions of *Using UNIX*, *UNIX Unleashed*, and *Microsoft Office Administrator's Desk Reference* for Macmillan Computer Publishing. Chris lives in Salt Lake City, Utah with Sheree, Caleb, and Seth.

William Pierce is an MIS director at DSI-CSS in Indianapolis, Indiana. His background includes system administration and very basic Oracle database administration on SMP UNIX systems. He has programmed in C, C++, COBOL, Scripting, Awk, and Assembler. He graduated from Ball State University in Muncie, Indiana in 1976. He currently lives in Anderson, Indiana with his wife, Jody, and their son, Jonathan.

Steve Shah is a systems/network administrator at the Center for Environmental Research and Technology at the University of California, Riverside. In a parallel life he does research in the area of network bandwidth control algorithms and is hoping he can contribute his thesis back into Linux. Sadly, this leaves little time for his better half and personal cheerleader, Heidi, but he is adamant about rectifying the situation as soon as he gets his master's degree next year. Steve is also a contributing author of *Unix Unleashed, System Administrator's Edition* and *Red Hat Linux Unleashed, Second Edition*.

Sriranga Veeraraghavan has worked at Cisco Systems, Inc. in the area of network management since 1996. He enjoys developing software in C, C++, Java, Perl, and Shell on Linux and Solaris. He has contributed to several UNIX and Linux books. He takes pleasure in listening to classical music, reading classical literature, mountain biking, and playing Marathon on the home network with his brother, Srivathsa. Sriranga earned a bachelor's degree in engineering from the University of California at Berkeley in 1997 and is currently working toward a master's degree at Stanford University. He can be reached at `ranga@soda.berkeley.edu`.

Daniel J. Wilson is a senior principal consultant with Oracle Corporation and works out of the Indianapolis, Indiana practice. His background includes UNIX systems administration and Oracle database administration in both SMP and Clustered environments. He has extensive experience in UNIX systems and Oracle database performance tuning and troubleshooting. He has programmed in C, C++, COBOL, and SQL. He graduated from Ball State University in Muncie, Indiana in 1984. He currently resides just outside of Indianapolis with his wife, Angela, and their two children, Timothy and Emily. Many thanks to Linda Billingsley at PRC and to Ron James at Hewlett-Packard for providing the best support ever!

William D. Wood works at Software Artistry, Inc., as a support specialist on UNIX systems. He supports the Expert Advisor software it runs on SunOS, HP-UX, and IBM AIX. He has specialized in multi-systems and remote systems support since 1985, when he started work at the Pentagon. He has solely supported infrastructures that span the world and others that span just the U.S. He has also supported up to 80 UNIX machines at one time.

About the Technical Editors

Eric C Richardson (`eric@rconsult.com`) is a professional Webmaster with nine years Internet experience and over two decades of work with computers under his belt. He has worked as a college instructor, writer, consultant, and author in the Internet field. He currently oversees the Web sites and related extranet for Nabisco Incorporated. He is a member of the World Organization of Webmasters and serves on their national accreditation board. He enjoys spending time with his wife, Stacie, and their daughter, Katie. He has written or coauthored eight books about the Internet and has worked as editor on nearly a dozen.

Nalneesh Gaur works for TimeBridge Technologies as a systems engineer. His current work involves UNIX/Windows NT integration, Web design, and Internet/intranet security.

Dedication

To Roger and the Laurelwood English Cocker Spaniels, all of whom were patient and supportive while I took time for this book.

Robin Burk

Acknowledgements

I'd like to begin by thanking the staff of Macmillan for the hard work that they contribute to their books. As with past book projects, they have been invaluable in assembling the chapter authors, responding to the inevitable project glitches and getting this book out to the UNIX community. Beginning with Jane Brownlow,—the acquisitions editor for this project—through the development, layout, and distribution staff, it's been a pleasure to work with you all.

I'd also like to acknowledge the special contribution of David Horvath to this edition. David and I worked together on the second edition of *UNIX Unleashed* and I was pleased to have him back on the team for this edition as well.

The support of my husband, Roger, has been invaluable as I've juggled book efforts, work responsibilities, and my dog hobby. Between keyboard and kennel, I'm often distracted in one project or another. Thanks, Love, for putting up with all this and buying groceries in the meanwhile. Yes, we *will* have a chance to take a weekend off together now that the book is finished!

Finally, I'd like to acknowledge the companionship of my dogs, the Laurelwood English Cocker Spaniels. Show dogs, hunters, couch potatoes, and accomplished beggars, they spent hours at my feet while I wrote and edited. Right now I'm surrounded by Haley, an AKC Champion of Record who will have her first litter of puppies soon and who gave up beloved walks by the lake for this book; by Fancy, who gave up field work; and by Bogie, who looks to be our next young Champion and who wants you to know he doesn't get nearly enough treats. <smile>

—*Robin Burk*

Tell Us What You Think!

As the reader of this book, *you* are our most important critic and commentator. We value your opinion and want to know what we're doing right, what we could do better, what areas you'd like to see us publish in, and any other words of wisdom you're willing to pass our way.

As an Executive Editor for the Operating Systems team at Sams Publishing, I welcome your comments. You can fax, email, or write me directly to let me know what you did or didn't like about this book—as well as what we can do to make our books stronger.

Please note that I cannot help you with technical problems related to the topic of this book, and that due to the high volume of mail I receive, I might not be able to reply to every message.

When you write, please be sure to include this book's title and author as well as your name and phone or fax number. I will carefully review your comments and share them with the author and editors who worked on the book.

Fax: 317-817-7070

E-mail: feedback@sampublishing.com

Mail: Jeff Koch
       Sams Publishing
       201 West 103rd Street
       Indianapolis, IN 46290 USA

Introduction

by Robin Burk

Welcome to the third edition of *UNIX Unleashed*!

Who Should Read This Book

As with previous editions, this book is written to be useful to a wide range of readers:

- People new to UNIX
- Anyone using UNIX that wants to learn more about the system and its utilities
- Programmers looking for a tutorial or reference guide to C, C++, Perl, GUI environments, and UNIX shells
- Systems administrators concerned about security and performance on their machines
- Anyone who wants to bring his or her UNIX skills and knowledge base up-to-date

UNIX continues to evolve as the user community widens. Expansive growth of the Internet and the World Wide Web has brought UNIX into mainstream corporations, Internet Service Providers, and desktop workstations around the world. If you are a technical professional, chances are that you will either work directly with UNIX or interact with a UNIX-based system regularly.

What's New in This Edition

Our highly popular first edition brought comprehensive, up-to-date information on UNIX to a wide audience. As use of UNIX exploded along with the Internet, we offered a successful second edition in two volumes, one for Internet programming (server- and client-side) and the other for systems administrators. The second edition offered specific help in using the many variants of UNIX (many of them vendor-specific) that had emerged into use.

This third edition continues our tradition of providing timely information on the evolving world of UNIX. We've updated this edition of UNIX Unleashed to provide you current information regarding:

- The most frequently used UNIX variants and shells, including the updated version of bsh
- Updated information on security issues and technologies you can use to protect your system

- The most popular Graphical User Interfaces (GUIs) and editors
- How to create and deploy useful programs of your own
- On-line, Internet and journal sources for more information about UNIX

The ongoing evolution of UNIX into the mainstream of computing has brought a certain degree of consolidation regarding the variants, shells and third party utilities which proliferated during the mid-1990's. UNIX lovers still have a wide variety of choices in these matters; however, this consolidation has allowed us to return to our popular, single volume format for *UNIX Unleashed.*

How *UNIX Unleashed, Third Edition* Is Organized

Part I, "Introduction to UNIX," is designed to get you started using UNIX. It provides you with general information regarding the organization of the UNIX operating system, how and where to find files, the standard commands and general information on networking and communicating with other systems. Part I also covers graphical user interfaces, and using vi and emacs to edit text.

Part II, "UNIX Shells," provides you with information regarding your choices for a user interface with UNIX. The most popular shells: Bourne, Bourne Again (BASH), Korn and C, are covered, as well as a comparison between them. In addition to providing your basic user interface, shells allow you to customize your computing environment in powerful ways.

Part III, "Programming," introduces the most popular program development languages: awk, Perl, C, C++. This section also discusses the make utility, a powerful rule-based method for controlling program compilation, as well as the standard utilities for managing source code libraries and controlling code revisions.

Part IV, "System Administration," covers the tasks needed to install, administer and manage UNIX on single-user or shared systems. In this section you will find solid advice from experienced administrators on topics ranging from the duties of a systems administrator through user account management, periodic maintenance tasks, performance monitoring and optimization, security matters and managing UNIX upgrades. UNIX systems administrators have a number of very useful third-party utilities which are discussed here as well.

Part V, "UNIX and the Internet," introduces the communications protocols, programming tools and concepts used with the World Wide Web. Here you will find information on HTML (used to program Web pages) and HTTP (the protocol used by Web servers). This section also contains information on administering Web servers and monitoring server performance.

Conventions Used In This Volume

This book uses the following typographical conventions:

- Menu names are separated from the individual menu options with a vertical bar (|). For example, "File|Save" means select the File menu and then choose the Save option.

- New terms appear in *italic*.

- All code appears in `monospace`. This includes pseudocode that is used to show a general format rather than a specific example.

- Words that you are instructed to type appear in **`bold monospace`**.

- Placeholders (words that stand for what you actually type) appear in *`italic monospace`*.

- Line of code that are too long to fit on one line in this book are broken at a conveinent place and continued on the next line. A code continuation character ➥ precedes the new line. All code that contains this character should be entered as one long line without a line break.

- An elipsis … in code indicates that some code has been omitted for the sake of brevity.

Introduction to UNIX

PART

I

IN THIS PART

## CHAPTER 1

The UNIX Operating System

by Robin Burk and Rachel and Robert Sartin

IN THIS CHAPTER

Welcome to the world of UNIX. Once the domain of wizards and gurus, today UNIX has spread beyond the university and laboratory to find a home in global corporations and small Internet servers alike. This capability to scale up or down, to accommodate small installations or complex corporate networks with little or no modification, is only one of the characteristics that have won UNIX its popularity and widespread use.

As you'll see through the course of this book, UNIX is a rich and complex system built on simple, powerful elements. Although many more recent operating systems have borrowed concepts and mechanisms from UNIX, those who are most familiar with legacy mainframe environments, or whose experience is mostly limited to single-user personal computers, may find UNIX to be a bit intimidating at first. The best advice we can give is to take it slowly, but don't give up. As you read through these chapters and begin to use some of the features and utilities described in this book, you'll find that once-foreign ideas have taken clear and concrete shape in your mind.

> **NOTE**
>
> One distinctive characteristic of UNIX compared to other operating systems is the fact that there are several flavors, or variants, of the operating system. Because the source code of the early versions was made available to a variety of computer manufacturers and third parties, many slightly different forms of UNIX coexist. Some are specific to a given hardware manufacturer; others differ in the utilities, configuration methods, or user interfaces they offer. This book points out the differences between the most commonly used UNIX variants.

> **TIP**
>
> Throughout this book you will find specific details regarding how to accomplish tasks in each of the most popular versions of UNIX.

At its base, UNIX is both simple and elegant, with a consistent architecture that, in turn, underlies and guides the design of its many application programs and languages. If you are new to UNIX, we're a bit jealous of the fun you'll have as you begin to explore this fascinating environment for the first time. If you are a more experienced UNIX user, administrator, or programmer, this revised edition of *UNIX Unleashed* contains a wealth of information that can help you extend your UNIX use to Internet and World Wide Web applications, guard against hackers and other unauthorized intruders, and fine-tune your system management skills.

What Is UNIX?

UNIX is:

- A trademark
- A multitasking, multiuser operating system
- The name given to a whole family of related operating systems and their most common application, utility, and compiler programs
- A rich, extensible, and open computing environment

Let's take these one at a time. To begin with, UNIX is a trademark, which means that there is intellectual property associated with UNIX that is not in the public domain. Some versions of UNIX require a paid license for their use.

The term *UNIX* also refers to a powerful multitasking, multiuser operating system.

Once upon a time, not so long ago, everyone knew what an operating system (OS) was. It was the complex software sold by the maker of your computer system, without which no other programs could function on that computer. Application (user) programs asked the operating system to perform various functions; users seldom talked to the OS directly.

Today those boundaries are not quite so clear. The rise of graphical user interfaces, macro and scripting languages, suites of applications that can exchange information seamlessly, and the increased popularity of networks and distributed data all have blurred the traditional distinctions. Today's computing environments consist of layers of hardware and software that interact together to form a nearly organic whole.

At its core (or, as we say in UNIX, in the kernel), however, UNIX does indeed perform the classic role of an operating system. Like the mainframe and minicomputer systems that came before, UNIX enables multiple people to access a computer simultaneously and multiple programs and activities to proceed in parallel with one another.

Unlike most proprietary operating systems, however, UNIX has given birth to a whole family of related, or variant, systems. Some differ in functionality or origin; others are developed by computer vendors and are specific to a given line of machines; still others were developed specifically as shareware or even freeware. Although these various flavors of UNIX differ from one another to some degree, they are fundamentally the same environment. All offer their own version of the most common utilities, application programs, and languages. Those who use `awk`, `grep`, the Bourne shell, or `make` in one version of UNIX will find their favorites available on other UNIX machines as well.

Those who do not care much for these programs, however, are free to substitute their own approach for getting various computing jobs done. A salient characteristic of UNIX is that it is extensible and open. By extensible, I mean that UNIX allows the easy definition of new commands, which can then be invoked or used by other programs and terminal users. This is practical in the UNIX environment because the architecture of the UNIX kernel specifically defines interfaces, or ways that programs can communicate with one another without having been designed specifically to work together.

Understanding Operating Systems

An operating system is an important part of a computer system. You can view a computer system as being built from three general components: hardware, operating system, and applications (see Figure 1.1). The hardware includes physical pieces such as a central processing unit (CPU), keyboard, hard drive, and printer. Applications are why you use computers; they use the rest of the system to perform the desired task (for example, play a game, edit a memo, send electronic mail). The operating system is the component that on one side manages and controls the hardware and on the other manages the applications.

FIGURE 1.1.
Computer system components.

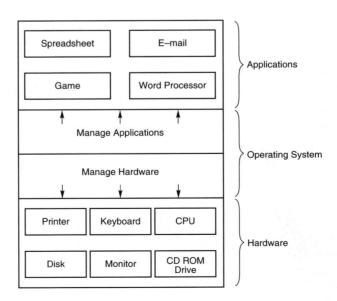

When you purchase a computer system, you must have at least hardware and an operating system. The hardware you purchase can use (or run) one or more different operating systems. You can purchase a bundled computer package, which includes the hardware, operating system, and possibly one or more applications. The operating system is necessary to manage the hardware and the applications.

When you turn on your computer, the operating system performs a series of tasks, presented in chronological order in the next few sections.

Hardware Management, Part 1

One of the first things you do, after successfully plugging together a plethora of cables and components, is turn on your computer. The operating system takes care of all the starting functions that must occur to get your computer to a usable state. Various pieces of hardware need to be initialized. After the startup procedure is complete, the operating system awaits further instructions. If you shut down the computer, the operating system also has a procedure that makes sure that all the hardware is shut down correctly. Before turning off your computer again, you might want to do something useful, which means that one or more applications are executed. Most boot ROMs do some hardware initialization but not much. Initialization of I/O devices is part of the UNIX kernel.

Process Management

After the operating system completes hardware initialization, you can execute an application. The operating system's job is to manage execution of the application. When you execute a program, the operating system creates a new process or instance of a thread of logic executing within the computer and its main memory. Many processes can exist simultaneously, but only one process actually engages the CPU at a given moment. The operating system switches between your processes so quickly that it can appear that the processes are executing simultaneously. This concept is referred to as *time-sharing* or *multitasking*.

When you exit your program (or it finishes executing), the process terminates, and the operating system manages the termination by reclaiming any resources that were being used.

Most applications perform some tasks between the time the process is created and the time it terminates. To perform these tasks, the program makes requests to the operating system, and the operating system responds to the requests and allocates necessary resources to the program. When an executing process needs to use some hardware, the operating system provides access for the process.

Hardware Management, Part 2

To perform its task, a process may need to access hardware resources. The process may need to read or write to a file, send data to a network card (to communicate with another computer), or send data to a printer. The operating system provides such services for the process. This is referred to as *resource allocation*. A piece of hardware is a resource, and the operating system allocates available resources to the different processes that are running.

Table 1.1 shows a summary of different actions and what the operating system (OS) does to manage them.

TABLE 1.1. OPERATING SYSTEM FUNCTIONS.

Action	*OS Does This*
You turn on the computer.	Hardware management
You execute an application.	Process management
Application reads a tape.	Hardware management
Application waits for data.	Process management
Process waits while other process runs.	Process management
Process displays data onscreen.	Hardware management
Process writes data to tape.	Hardware management
You quit; the process terminates.	Process management
You turn off the computer.	Hardware management

From the time you turn on your computer until you turn it off, the operating system is coordinating the operations. As hardware is initialized, accessed, or shut down, the operating system manages these resources. As applications execute, request, and receive resources, or terminate, the operating system takes care of these actions. Without an operating system, no application can run, and your computer is just an expensive paperweight.

The UNIX Operating System

The previous section looked at operating systems in general. This section looks at a specific operating system: UNIX. Traditionally used on minicomputers and workstations in the academic community, UNIX is now available on personal computers, and the business community has started to choose UNIX for its openness. This section looks at how UNIX fits into the operating system model.

UNIX, like other operating systems, is a layer between the hardware and the applications that run on the computer. It has functions that manage the hardware and functions that manage executing applications. What characterizes UNIX is its internal implementation and the interface that is seen and used by users. For the most part, this book ignores the internal implementation. If you want to know these details, many texts cover them. This book describes the interface in detail. The majority of UNIX users need to be familiar with the interface and need not understand the internal workings of UNIX.

The UNIX system is actually more than strictly an operating system. Beyond the traditional operating system components, a standard UNIX system includes a set of libraries and a set of applications. Figure 1.2 shows the components and layers of UNIX. Sitting above the hardware are two components: the file system and process control. Next is the set of libraries. On top are the applications. The user has access to the libraries and to the applications. These two components are what many users think of as UNIX because together they constitute the UNIX interface.

FIGURE 1.2.

The layers of UNIX.

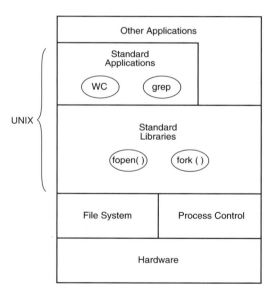

The part of UNIX that manages the hardware and the executing processes is called the kernel. In managing all hardware devices, the UNIX system views each device as a file (called a device file). This allows the same simple method of reading and writing files to be used to access each hardware device. The file system manages read and write access to user data and to devices, such as printers, attached to the system. It implements security controls to protect the safety and privacy of information. In executing processes the

UNIX system allocates resources (including use of the CPU) and mediates accesses to the hardware.

One important advantage that results from the UNIX standard interface is the capability of a single application to be executed on various types of computer hardware without being modified. This can be achieved if the application uses the UNIX interface to manage its hardware needs. UNIX's layered design insulates the application from the different types of hardware. UNIX goes beyond the traditional operating system by providing a standard set of libraries and applications that developers and users can use. This standard interface allows application portability and facilitates user familiarity with the interface.

The History of UNIX

How did a system such as UNIX ever come to exist? UNIX has a rather unusual history that has greatly affected its current form.

The Early Days

In the mid-1960s, AT&T Bell Laboratories (among others) was participating in an effort to develop a new operating system called Multics. In 1969, Bell Labs pulled out of the Multics effort, and members Ken Thompson, Dennis Ritchie, and others developed and simulate what later evolved into the UNIX file system.

As the team continued to experiment, they deployed their work to do text processing for the patent department at AT&T. Shortly afterward, the now famous C programming language was developed on and for UNIX, and the UNIX operating system itself was rewritten into C. This then radical implementation decision is one of the factors that enabled UNIX to become the open system it is today.

As a then-regulated telephone company, AT&T was not allowed to market computer systems. Nonetheless, the popularity of UNIX grew through internal use at AT&T and licensing to universities for educational use. By 1977, commercial licenses for UNIX were being granted. Later versions developed at AT&T (or its successor, UNIX System Laboratories) included System III and several releases of System V. The two most recent releases of System V, Release 3 (SVR3.2) and Release 4 (SVR4) remain popular for computers ranging from PCs to mainframes. All versions of UNIX based on the AT&T work require a license from the current owner, UNIX System Laboratories.

Berkeley Software Distributions

In 1978, the research group turned over distribution of UNIX to the UNIX Support Group (USG), which had distributed an internal version called the Programmer's Workbench. In 1982, USG introduced System III, which incorporated ideas from several different internal versions of and modifications to UNIX, developed by various groups. In 1983, USG released the original UNIX System V, and thanks to the divestiture of AT&T, was able to market it aggressively. A series of later releases continued to introduce new features from other versions of UNIX, including the internal versions from the research group and the Berkeley Software Distribution.

The Computer Science Research Group at the University of California at Berkeley (UCB) developed a series of releases known as the Berkeley Software Distribution, or BSD. The original PDP-11 modifications were called 1BSD and 2BSD. Support for the Digital Equipment Corporation VAX computers was introduced in 3BSD. VAX development continued with 4.0BSD, 4.1BSD, 4.2BSD, and 4.3BSD, all of which (especially 4.2 and 4.3) had many features (and much source code) adopted into commercial products.

UNIX and Standards

Because of the multiple versions of UNIX and frequent cross-pollination between variants, many features have diverged in the different versions of UNIX. With the increasing popularity of UNIX in the commercial and government sector came the desire to standardize the features of UNIX so that a user or developer using UNIX could depend on those features.

The Institute of Electrical and Electronic Engineers (IEEE) created a series of standards committees to create standards for "An Industry-Recognized Operating Systems Interface Standard based on the UNIX Operating System." The POSIX.1 committee standardizes the C library interface used to write programs for UNIX. The POSIX.2 committee standardizes the commands available for the general user.

In Europe, the X/Open Consortium brings together various UNIX-related standards, including the current attempt at a Common Open System Environment (COSE) specification. X/Open publishes a series of specifications called the X/Open Portability. The MOTIF user interface is one popular standard to emerge from this effort.

The United States government has specified a series of standards based on XPG and POSIX. Currently, FIPS 151-2 specifies the open systems requirements for federal purchases.

UNIX for Mainframes and Workstations

Many mainframe and workstation vendors make a version of UNIX for their machines. We discuss several of these variants (including Solaris from SunSoft, AIX from IBM, and HP-UX from Hewlett Packard) throughout this book.

UNIX for Intel Platforms

Thanks to the great popularity of personal computers, many UNIX versions are available for Intel platforms. Unfortunately, the UNIX industry has not settled on a complete binary standard for the Intel platform.

Source Versions of "UNIX"

Several versions of UNIX and UNIX-like systems have been made that are free or inexpensive and include source code. These versions have become particularly attractive to the modern-day hobbyist, who can now run a UNIX system at home for little investment and with great opportunity to experiment with the operating system or make changes to suit his or her needs.

An early UNIX-like system was MINIX, by Andrew Tanenbaum. His book *Operating Systems: Design and Implementations* describes MINIX and includes a source listing of the original version.

The most popular source version of UNIX is Linux (pronounced ì*lin nucks*.î Linux was designed from the ground up by Linus Torvalds to be a free replacement for UNIX, and it aims for POSIX compliance. Linux has emerged as the server platform of choice for small to mid-sized Internet service providers and Web servers.

Introduction to the UNIX Philosophy

UNIX has its roots in a system that was intended to be small and supply orthogonal common pieces. Although most UNIX systems have grown to be fairly large, and monolithic applications are not uncommon, the original philosophy still lives in the core commands available on all UNIX systems. There are several common key items throughout UNIX:

- Simple, orthogonal commands
- Commands connected through pipes
- A (mostly) common option interface style
- No file types

Simple, Orthogonal Commands

The original UNIX systems were very small, and the designers tried to take every advantage of those small machines by writing small commands. Each command attempted to do one thing well. The tools could then be combined (either with a shell script or a C program) to do more complicated tasks. One command, called wc, was written solely to count the lines, words, and characters in a file. To count all the words in all the files, you would type wc * and get output like that in Listing 1.1.

LISTING 1.1. USING A SIMPLE COMMAND.

```
$ wc *
351     2514    17021 minix-faq
1011    5982    42139 minix-info
1362    8496    59160 total
$
```

Commands Connected Through Pipes

To turn the simple, orthogonal commands into a powerful toolset, UNIX enables the user to use the output of one command as the input to another. This connection is called a *pipe*, and a series of commands connected by pipes is called a *pipeline*. For example, to count the number of lines that reference MINIX in all the files, one would type grep MINIX * ¦ wc and get output like that in Listing 1.2.

LISTING 1.2. USING A PIPELINE.

```
$ grep MINIX * ¦ wc
105     982     6895
$
```

A (Mostly) Common Option Interface Style

Each command has actions that can be controlled with options, which are specified by a hyphen followed by a single letter option (for example, -l). Some options take option arguments, which are specified by a hyphen followed by a single letter, followed by the argument (for example, -h Header). For example, to print on pages with 16 lines each all the lines in the file minix-info that mention Tanenbaum, you would enter wc minix-info ¦ pr -l 16 and get output like that in Listing 1.3.

LISTING 1.3. USING OPTIONS IN A PIPELINE.

```
$ grep Tanenbaum minix-info ¦ pr -l 16


Feb 14 16:02 1994    Page 1


 [From Andy Tanenbaum <ast@cs.vu.nl> 28 August 1993]
The author of MINIX, Andrew S. Tanenbaum, has written a book describing
Author:      Andrew S. Tanenbaum
subjects.ast (list of Andy Tanenbaum's
Andy Tanenbaum since 1987 (on tape)
Version 1.0 is the version in Tanenbaum's book, "Operating Systems: Design


$
```

No File Types

UNIX pays no attention to the contents of a file (except when you try to run a file as a command). The meaning of the characters in a file is entirely supplied by the command(s) that uses the file. This concept is familiar to most PC users but was a significant difference between UNIX and other earlier operating systems.

Summary

UNIX has a long history as an open development environment. More recently, it has become the system of choice for both commercial and some personal uses. UNIX performs the typical operating system tasks, but also includes a standard set of commands and library interfaces. The building-block approach of UNIX makes it an ideal system for creating new applications.

Getting Started:
Basic Tutorial

*by Robin Burk, Rachel and
Robert Sartin, and Fred Trimble*

In This Chapter

UNIX is a multiuser, multitasking environment. Unlike personal computers, UNIX systems are inherently designed to allow simultaneous access to multiple users.

Whether you are working with UNIX on a large, multiuser system or have a dedicated UNIX-based workstation on your desk, the multiuser, multitasking architecture of the operating system influences the way you will work with the system and the requirements it will place on you as a user and a system administrator.

The purpose of this chapter is to acquaint you with the basics of UNIX from the user's point of view. Not all UNIX systems actually support multiple users with keyboards or terminals of their own. Some workstations are dedicated to a single person, and others function as servers that support multiple remote computers rather than end users. In all cases, however, UNIX operates as if it might be called on to furnish a fully multiuser, multitasking capability. For the purpose of this tutorial, we'll assume that you have a dedicated UNIX workstation on your desk.

Logging In to the System

Several people can be using a UNIX-based computer at the same time. For the system to know who you are and what resources you can use, you must identify yourself. In addition, because UNIX expects to communicate with you over a terminal (or a PC running terminal-emulation software), you must establish the ground rules that will govern the transfer of information. The process of establishing the communications session and identifying yourself is known as *logging in*.

> **Note**
>
> UNIX actually distinguishes between a communications session and a login session, in that it is possible to log in as one user, log out, and log in again as another user without disrupting the communications session. Because an increasing number of people access UNIX systems from a PC, and for purposes of simplicity in this tutorial, we've treated the communications and login sessions as identical in this chapter. As you become more familiar with the UNIX environment and with utilities such as `telnet`, this distinction will become more important.

User Account Setup

After a UNIX system is booted, you cannot simply start using it as you do a PC. Before you can access the computer system, someone—usually the system administrator—must configure the computer for your use. If you are running UNIX on your PC at home, you will most likely need to do these things for yourself. If you are a UNIX novice trying to set up your home computer system, you can refer to Chapter 21, "UNIX Installation Basics."

No matter who sets up your computer account, you must know two things before you can use the system: your username and your password. If you don't know what these are, you must stop and find out what has been assigned to you. The username is a unique name that identifies you to the system. It is often related to your real name, such as your first name, your last name, or a combination of first initial and last name (for example, "frank," "brimmer," or "fbrimmer," respectively). If you get to request a username, try to choose something that makes others think of you alone and is not vague or common enough to cause confusion with others. The system administrator will verify that no one else on your system has this name before allowing you to have it. The password that you request or that has been assigned to you is a temporary string that allows you to initially access the computer system. The initial password isn't of any real importance because you should change it to something of your choice the first time you log in to the system (see "Managing Your Password" later in this chapter).

Logging In to the System

Now that you know your username (say it's "brimmer") and password (say it's "new_user"), you can access the system. When you sit down in front of a UNIX work-station, you are expected to log in to the system. This is true whether you are local to your UNIX system or are accessing a remote machine using a remote service such as `telnet`. The system prompts (asks) you for your username by displaying `login:`. You should then enter your username. Next, UNIX prompts you for your password by displaying `Password:`. Enter your password. As you type your password, don't be alarmed if the characters you type are not displayed on your screen. This is normal and is for your protection. No one else should know your password, and this way no one can look at your screen and see your password when you log in.

```
login: brimmer
Password:
Please wait...checking for disk quotas

Marine biology word of the day:
Cnidaria (n.) Nigh-DARE-ee-uh (L. a nettle)  - a phylum of basically
radially symmetrical marine invertebrates including corals, sea
anemones, jellyfish and hydroids. This phylum was formerly known
as Coelenterata.
$
```

TIP

Some keyboards have a key labeled Return. Some have a key labeled Enter. If your keyboard has both, Return is probably the correct key to use.

TIP

On some systems, erase is #, and kill is @. On others, erase is Backspace or Delete, and kill is Control+U or Control+X.

If you typed everything correctly and the system administrator has everything set up correctly, you are now logged in and may use the system. If you get a message saying Login Incorrect, you may have typed your username or password incorrectly. If you make a mistake while entering your username, the Backspace key and the Delete key may not undo this mistake for you. The easiest thing to do is start over by pressing Enter twice to get to a new login: prompt.

Other error messages you might receive are No Shell, No Directory, or Cannot Open Password File. If you see any of these messages, or if multiple attempts at logging in always produce the Login Incorrect message, contact your system administrator for help.

TIP

The No Shell message means that UNIX is not able to start the command interpreter, which was configured when your account was set up. Depending on the UNIX system, your login may complete successfully, and the default shell will be used. If this happens, you can use the chsh command, which changes the shell specified in your account. See Part II, "UNIX Shells," for more information about various shells. The No Directory message means that UNIX cannot access your home directory, which was specified when your account was set up. Again, depending on the system, your login may complete successfully, placing you in a default directory. You may need to then enlist the help of the system administrator to create your home directory or change the home directory value for your account. See Chapter 3, "The UNIX File System," regarding directories and, specifically, your home directory. The Cannot Open Password File message means that UNIX is having a problem accessing the system password file, which holds the account information (username, password, user ID, shell, group, and so on) for each user. If there is a problem with this file, no user can log in to the system. Contact your system administrator if you see this message.

If your system is configured to use a graphical user interface (GUI), you probably have a login screen. This screen performs the same function as the command-line prompts but is presented as a graphical display. The display probably has two boxes for you to fill in, each with a label. One box is for your username, and the other is for your password.

After Login Succeeds

After a successful login, several messages appear on your screen. Some of these may be the date and time of your last login, the system's informative message (called the "Message of the Day"), and a message informing you whether you have (electronic) mail. The Message of the Day can be an important message to watch because it is one way that administrators communicate with the system users. The next scheduled down time (when no one can use the system) is an example of information that you might see here.

After all the messages scroll by, the system is ready and waiting for you to do something. This ready-and-waiting condition is signified by a prompt followed by a cursor. Typical prompts are $ or %. The dollar-sign prompt is commonly used by Bourne and Korn shells, and the percent sign by C shells. The value of this prompt (your primary prompt) can be changed if you want. The person who set up your account may have already configured a different prompt value. To change this prompt, you need to change the value of the environment variable PS1 (for Bourne and Korn) or prompt (for C shell). (See the section "Configuring Your Environment" in this chapter for details on environment variables.) The cursor (the spot on the screen where the next character you type is displayed) is commonly an underline (_) or a box, either of which can be blinking. The cursor you see may vary from system to system.

Different Privileges for Different Users

If you are administering your own personal system, it is still important for you to set up a personal account for yourself, even though your system will come configured with some type of administrative account. This account should be used to do systemwide administrative actions. Be careful when using this account because it has special privileges. UNIX systems have built-in security features. Most users cannot set up a new user account or do other administrative procedures. The user "root" is a special user, sometimes called superuser, which can do anything at all on the system. This high degree of power is necessary to fully administer a UNIX system, but it also allows its user to make a mistake and cause system problems. For this reason, you should set up a personal account for yourself that does not have root privilege. Then, your normal, day-to-day activities will affect only your personal environment, and you will be in no danger of causing systemwide problems. In a multiuser, nonpersonal environment, you will most likely have only user (and not superuser) privileges. This security is even more important when more than one person is involved because one mistake by the root can affect every user and the entire system.

UNIX also has security to help prevent different users from harming each other on a multiuser system. Each user "owns" his or her environment and can selectively let groups or all others have access to this work. If you are doing private work in one area that no one else should be allowed to see, then you should restrict access to the owner (you). If you and your team members are working on a group project, you can restrict access to the owner (you) and everyone in your group. If this work should be shared with many or all people on the system, then you should allow access to everyone.

Logging Out

When you are done using the system, you should log out. This prevents other people from accidentally or intentionally getting access to your files. It also makes the system available for their use.

The normal way to log out from almost any shell is to type exit. This causes your shell to exit, or stop running. When you exit from your login shell, you log out. If you are using csh, you can also type logout; if you are in a login shell, then csh logs you out. Some shells, depending on your configuration, also log you out if you type the end-of-file character (typically Control+D; see "Working on the System" later in this chapter).

If you have a graphical user interface, your logout procedure may be different. Consult your manuals or online help to learn about logging out of your GUI.

Using Commands

During the login process, described in the "Logging In to the System" section, UNIX performs several actions that prepare you and the system for each other. These include performing system accounting, initializing your user environment, and starting a command interpreter (commonly called a *shell*). Commands are how you tell the system to do something. The command interpreter recognizes these commands and passes the information off to where it is needed. UNIX systems originally came with a command interpreter called the Bourne shell (usually referred to as sh, though some systems ship Korn or POSIX as sh—see the Note that follows). This shell is still available on most UNIX computer systems. A newer shell that is common to most UNIX systems is the C shell (referred to as csh). Another commonly used, but not as pervasive, shell is the Korn Shell (referred to as ksh). Among different shells, there is some variation of the commands that are available. Refer to Part II for details on these UNIX shells.

NOTE

There are a number of different common shells on various UNIX operating systems. The most common are as follows:

sh   The Bourne shell is the most common of all the shells. (May be installed as bsh.)

ksh   The Korn shell is a derivative of the Bourne shell, which adds history and command-line editing. (Sometimes installed as sh.)

sh   The POSIX shell is much like the Korn shell. The POSIX standard requires it to be installed as sh. Some vendors install it as /bin/sh. Some put it in a special directory and call it sh, leaving the Bourne shell as /bin/sh.

csh   The C shell is based on the popular C language.

bash The Bourne Again shell is less common.

tcsh This is a version of the C shell with interactive command-line editing.

What Is a Command?

A UNIX command is a series of characters that you type. These characters consist of words that are separated by whitespace. *Whitespace* is the result of typing one or more Space or Tab keys. The first word is the name of the command. The rest of the words are called the command's *arguments*. The arguments give the command information that it might need, or specify varying behavior of the command. To invoke a command, simply type the command name, followed by arguments (if any); to indicate to the shell that you are finished typing and are ready for the command to be executed, press Enter.

Try it out. Enter the date command. The command's name is "date," and it takes no arguments. Therefore, type date and press Enter and see what happens. You should see that the computer has printed the current date and time. If the date or time does not match reality, ask the system administrator to fix it. How about trying a command that has arguments? Try the echo command. The name of the command is "echo," and it takes a series of arguments. The echo command then writes, or echoes, these arguments out to your screen. Try creating a command that writes your first and last names on the screen. Here is what these commands and output look like on our system:

```
$ date
Sat Aug  5 11:11:00 EST 1997
$ echo MyName
MyName
$
```

> **NOTE**
>
> Some commands such as echo are part of the particular shell you are using. These are called built-ins. In this case, the commands are not standard from one shell to another. Therefore, if you learn one shell and then later have to (or want to) switch to using a different shell, you may have to learn new commands (and unlearn others). Other commands are standard UNIX commands and do not depend on what shell you are using. These should be on every UNIX system. The remaining commands are nonstandard UNIX and may or may not be on a particular UNIX system.

UNIX commands use a special type of argument called an *option*. An option commonly takes the form of a dash (made by using the minus sign key) followed by one or more characters. The options provide information to the command. Most of the time, options are just a single character following a dash. Two of the other lesser used forms are a plus sign rather than a minus sign, and a word following a dash rather than a single character. The following paragraph shows a common command with two of its common options. The ls command lists the files in your current directory.

First, try the ls command with no arguments. Then, try it with the -a option and note that the directory listing contains a few files that start with a period. These hidden files get listed by the ls command only if you use the -a option. Next, try the ls command with the -l option. This option changes the format of the directory listing so that each file is displayed along with some relevant details. Finally, try the ls command with both of these options, so that your command is as follows: ls -a -l.

```
$ ls
visible
$ ls -a
.           ..          .hidden   visible
$ ls -l
total 0
-rw-rw-rw-   1 sartin    uu                 0 Mar  5 12:58 visible
$ ls -a -l
total 16
drwxrwxrwx   2 sartin    uu              1024 Mar  5 13:03 .
drwxr-xr-x  37 sartin    uu              3072 Mar  5 13:03 ..
-rw-rw-rw-   1 sartin    uu                 0 Mar  5 12:58 .hidden
-rw-rw-rw-   1 sartin    uu                 0 Mar  5 12:58 visible
$
```

A command developer often tries to choose option letters that are meaningful. Regarding the ls command, you might think of the -a as meaning that "all" files should be listed (including the special files starting with period). And you might think of the -l option as meaning a "long" directory listing because the format is changed so that each line contains one file along with its details. This makes for a longer listing.

Redirecting Input and Output

One pervasive concept in UNIX is the redirection of commands' input and output. Before looking at redirection, though, it is a good idea to look at input and output without modification. UNIX uses the word *standard* in this subject to mean the default or normal mode. Thus, UNIX has the term *standard input*, which means input coming from the default setting, and the term *standard output*, which means output going to the normal place. When you first log in to the system, and your shell executes, your standard input is set to be what you type at the keyboard, and your standard output is set to be your display screen. With this in mind, follow along with the example.

The cat command takes any characters from standard input and then echoes them to standard output. For example, type the cat command, with no arguments. Your cursor should be sitting on the next line without a prompt. At this point, the cat command is waiting for you to enter characters. You can enter as many as you want, and then you should specify that you are finished. Type a few words and then press Return. Now type the special character, Control+D (hold down the Control key while typing the D key). This is the "eof" control character. (See "Working on the System" later in this chapter for a description of control characters.) The words you typed should be on your screen twice—once caused by you entering them from the keyboard, and next as the cat command outputs them to your screen. This first step used standard input (from you typing on the keyboard), and standard output (the command results being printed on the screen).

```
$ cat
s
A few words
<CTRL><D>
A few words
$ cat > scotty
Meow, whine
meow
<CTRL><D>
$ cat < scotty
Meow, whine
meow
$ cat scotty
Meow, whine
meow
$
```

Although this simple case may not seem terribly useful yet, wait to see its use as you add redirection.

UNIX shells have special characters that signify redirection. Only the basics are covered here. Refer to Part II for details on each shell's redirection syntax. Output redirection is signified by the > character, and input redirection is signified by the < character. Output is commonly redirected to and input is redirected from a file. Now, continue with the rest of the example.

Next, try the `cat` command using output redirection, leaving standard input alone. Enter `cat > filename`. The `filename` is a name of your choice. Once again, the `cat` command should be waiting for input (coming from standard input, which is your keyboard) at the beginning of the next line. Enter a few words, as you did before, press Return, and then, at the start of the next line, press Control+D. The words you typed didn't show up on your screen because you redirected the output of the `cat` command. The output was directed to go to the file `filename`. But how do you know it is there? To verify this, use the `cat` command with input redirection—which is the next order of business.

CAUTION

`<Ctrl><D>` must be specified as the first character of an input line for it to be seen as "eof."

To see the contents of the file `filename`, you want the input of the `cat` command to come from that file, and the output to go to the screen so that you can see it. Therefore, you want to redirect standard input and leave the output alone. Enter `cat < filename`. This time, the `cat` command did not wait for you—because you were not supplying the input. The file supplied the input. The `cat` command printed the contents of the file to the screen.

TIP

Note the subtle distinction between these two commands: `cat > filename` and `cat < filename`. You can remember the difference by verbalizing which way the sign points; does it point into the command or out of the command? Into the command is input redirection, and out of the command is output redirection.

The `cat` command allows you to specify a filename to use as input. Try showing the contents of the file this (more common) way: enter `cat filename`. Many commands are designed similarly—they have an argument that is used to specify a file as the input.

Because of this common command design, redirecting input in this way is not nearly as common as redirecting the output.

UNIX was developed with the philosophy of having simple commands that do well-defined, simple things. Then, by combining these simple commands, the user could do powerful things. Pipes are one of the ways UNIX allows users to combine several commands. The pipe is signified by the vertical bar (¦) symbol. A pipe is a means of taking the output of one command and redirecting it as the input of another command.

Say that you want to know how many files you have in your current directory. Recall that the `ls` command lists all the files in your current directory. You could then count the number of files. But UNIX has a command that counts the number of characters, words, and lines of input and displays these statistics. Therefore, you can combine these two commands to give you the number of files in your directory.

One way you could do this is as follows: `ls -l ¦ wc -l`. Analyzing this command, you can see that the first part is something familiar. The `ls -l` command gives a directory listing in long format. In fact, it prints one file per line. The `wc -l` command gives the number of lines that are in the input. Combining the two commands via a pipe takes the output of the first command (the long directory listing) and gives it to the input of the second command. The output of the second command (which is not redirected—it goes to standard output) is displayed on your screen.

These basic forms of redirection allow you to be versatile as you learn a few commands at a time. Try to learn a command and use it with various options and arguments, then add redirection of input and output. And finally, combine commands with pipes. This approach should help you to feel comfortable with the commands and their varied uses.

Configuring Your Environment

To make using the shell easier and more flexible, UNIX uses the concept of an environment. Your environment is a set of values. You can change these values, add new values, or remove existing ones. These values are called environment variables—environment because they describe or define your environment, and variables because they can change.

Viewing and Setting Environment Variables

Every user's environment looks a little different. Why don't you see what your environment looks like? Type the `env` command with no arguments. The output formatting and variable names depend on which shell you are using and how your system is configured. A typical environment might include some of the following:

```
$ env
HOME=/u/sartin
LOGNAME=sartin
MAIL=/usr/mail/sartin
MANPATH=/usr/man:/usr/contrib/man:/usr/local/man
PATH=/bin/posix:/bin:/usr/bin:/usr/contrib/bin:/usr/local/bin
SHELL=/bin/sh
TERM=vt100
TZ=CST6CDT
$ echo $HOME
/u/sartin
$
```

Sometimes the number of variables in your environment grows quite large, so much so that you don't want to see all the values displayed when you are interested in just one. If this is the case, you can use the echo command to show an environment variable's current value. To specify that a word you type should be treated differently—as a value of an environment variable—you immediately precede the variable name with a dollar sign ($). Be careful not to type any whitespace between the $ and the word. One of the variables in the example is HOME. You probably have this variable in your environment, too. Try to display its value using echo.

> **NOTE**
>
> If you use csh, some environment variables are automatically copied to and from csh variables. These include HOME, TERM, and PATH, which csh keeps in home, term, and path.

You can create a new environment variable by simply giving it a value. If you give an existing variable a value, the old value is overwritten. One difficulty in setting environment variables is that the way you set them depends on the shell you are using. To see how to set environment variables, look at the details about the shell you are using in Part II.

For your screen to display the output correctly, the environment variable TERM needs to have a reasonable value. This variable name comes from the times when terminals were used as displays (before PCs and graphics displays were common). Different terminals supported varying output control. Therefore, UNIX systems have various terminal types that they support. These are not standard, so you need to find out which terminal type to use from your support personnel. If you are using a PC to connect to a UNIX system, your PC is running a terminal emulation tool. Most of these tools have the capability to emulate several types of terminal. The important point here is to make sure that your emulator and your TERM variable are the same (or compatible). Start by seeing what your TERM variable is set to by entering echo $TERM. Refer to your PC terminal emulation manual and ask your system administrator for help to make sure that this is set up correctly.

> **TIP**
>
> Many terminal emulators (including the Microsoft Windows "Terminal" program) support either "VT100" or ANSI standard terminal control sequences. Try setting TERM to vt100 or ansi for this type of terminal emulator.

Using Shell Startup Files

Where do all these environment variables come from? Well, the system sets up various ones for you. And each user commonly sets up others during the login process. Yes, you may be doing this without even knowing it. During the startup, which happens at login, a shell is started. This shell automatically looks in a special place or two for some startup information. One of these places is in your home directory. The startup information in your home directory is found in special files. The specific shell you are using determines the name of the particular file. When the shell starts up, it examines this file and performs whatever actions are specified. One of the common actions is to give values to environment variables. This action is called *initializing* or setting the values.

One environment variable that is commonly set in a user's shell startup file is the PATH variable (or lowercase path for C shell users). This variable's value is a list of places (directories) on the system where the shell should look to locate a command. Each command you type is physically located as a file somewhere on your file system. It is possible for the same command name to be located in different places (and to have either the same or different behavior when executed). Say that you have a program called my_program that is stored in your home directory, and your friend has a program called my_program, which is in her home directory. If you type my_program at the prompt, the shell needs to know where to look to find the storage location of my_program. The shell looks at the value of the PATH variable and uses the list of directories as an ordered directory search list. The first directory that has a my_program stops the search, and the shell executes that file. Because all files within a single directory must be unique, this gives a straightforward and sufficient method for finding executables (commands).

You probably want $HOME/bin to be toward the beginning of your PATH directory list, whereas you may want your friend's binary directory to be toward the end, or not listed at all. This way, when you type my_program, you will execute your my_program rather than hers. You can do all types of things in shell startup files in addition to setting environment variable values. If you want, you can add an `echo` command that prints out a greeting or reminds you to do something. One common item that is configured inside a shell startup file is the setup of your control characters. (See "Working on the System" later in this chapter.) These startup files are a powerful tool for you, the user of the shell, to configure the behavior of the shell automatically. Shell startup files are covered in more detail in Part II, "UNIX Shells."

> **TIP**
>
> It is a good idea to create a `bin` directory in your HOME and store executables there. Include `$HOME/bin` in your path.

Configuring with `rc` files

The idea of having a file that is read on startup is not only used by the shells. In fact, many commands have special files containing configuration information that the user can modify. The general class of files is called `rc` files. This comes from the naming convention of these files. Most of these files end with the letters *rc*. Some of the more common files are `.exrc`, `.mailrc`, and `.cshrc`. These are all dot files; that is, they begin with a period (dot). The significance of starting a filename with a dot is that this file is not displayed during normal directory listing. If you want to see these files, use the `-a` option to the `ls` command. The `.exrc` file is used by the `vi` and `ex` editors (see Chapter 7, "Text Editing with `vi` and `Emacs`"). The `.mailrc` file is used by various electronic mail tools (see Chapter 6, "Communicating with Others"). The `.cshrc` file is the C shell startup file just discussed. The `rc` files are normally found in your home directory; that is, the default location for most of these files. Look at which `rc` files you have in your home directory (use the `ls -a` command). Then examine the contents of one of the files (use the `cat `*`filename`* command).

Your environment has a great effect on the use of your system. It is initialized during login with a shell startup file, and it grows and changes as you create new variables and change existing ones. Your environment affects every command you execute. It is important to get your environment set up to make your common actions easy. Spend the time to do this now, and you will be glad you did later.

Managing Your Password

During login, UNIX asks you to enter your password. If this is your first time on this computer, your password was configured by the system administrator. One of the first things you should do after logging in is change your password so that no one, not even the system administrator, knows what it is. You can do this via the `passwd` command. But before you do this, you should put some thought into what you want your password to be. Here are some points to consider:

1. It should be easy for you to remember. If you forget what your password is, no one, not even the system administrator, can look it up for you. The only thing the system administrator can do is to reset your password to a value. This wastes the administrator's time as well as yours.

2. It shouldn't be easy for anyone to figure out. Do not make it anyone's name or birth date, your username, or any of these spelled backwards. It is also wise to avoid something that appears in a dictionary. A good idea would be to include at least one nonalphabetic character (for example, a period or a dollar sign).

3. Make it a reasonable length. Some systems impose a minimum number of characters for a password. At least five characters is adequate. There isn't usually a limit as to the maximum number of characters, but only the first eight are significant. The ninth character and after are ignored when checking to see whether you typed your password correctly.

4. Change your password once in a while. Some systems check the last time you changed your password. If a time limit has been reached, you will be notified that your password has expired as you log in. You will be prompted to change it immediately and won't be allowed to log in until you successfully get it changed. This time limit is system imposed. Changing your password every few months is reasonable.

5. Don't write it down or tell it to anyone. Don't write it on scraps of paper. Don't tell your mother. Don't write it in your calendar. Don't write it in your diary. Don't tell your priest. Don't put it in a dialup terminal configuration file. Nowhere. Nobody. Maybe in your safe deposit box.

After you have thought about what you want your password to be, you can change it with the `passwd` command. Try it now; you can change your password as often as you want. Enter `passwd`. First, a prompt asking you to enter your old password is displayed. Type your old password and press Return. Next, you are prompted for your new password. Type it in and press Enter. Finally, you are prompted to re-enter your new password. This confirmation helps avoid changing your password if you made a typing error. If you make a mistake entering your old password, or if the two new password entries are not identical, then no change is made. Your old password is still in effect. Unless you make the same mistake both times that you enter the new password, you are in no danger of erroneously changing your password.

Working on the System

Most keys on the keyboard are fairly obvious. If you type the S key, an s character appears on your screen. If you hold down the Shift key and type the S key, a capital s character (S) appears on your screen. In addition to the letters and digits, the symbols, some of which are above the digits, are familiar—such as the percent sign (%) and the comma (,). There are some UNIX and system-specific special characters in addition to these, with which you should become familiar. They help you manage your work and typing more effectively. The general type of character is called a *control character*. The name comes from the way in which you type them. First, locate the Control key—there should be one or maybe two on your keyboard. It may be labeled Ctrl or some other abbreviation of the word Control. This key is used like the Shift key. You press it but don't release it. While the Control key is pressed, you press another key, often a letter of the alphabet. If you press the Q key while holding down the Control key, this is called Control+Q and is commonly written ^Q (the caret symbol, which is found above the digit 6, followed by the alphabetic character).

NOTE

When you see the notation ^Q, this does not mean to hold down Control and Shift while pressing Q. All you do is to hold down the Control key while pressing Q.

UNIX uses these control keys for various common keyboard actions. They can come in very handy. But the hard part is that different systems have different default Control key settings for these actions. Therefore, first you should find out what your current settings are, and then you can change them if you want. To look at what your current settings are, use the stty command. Enter stty -a at your command prompt and look at the results. Refer to the next example for an output of this command.

TIP

If you're typing and nothing is showing on your screen, a ^S (or stop control character) inadvertently may have been typed. Try typing ^Q (or start control character) and see whether your typed characters now appear.

```
$ stty -a
speed 28800 baud; line = 0; susp <undef>; dsusp <undef>
rows = 44; columns = 120
intr = ^C; quit = ^\; erase = ^H; kill = ^X; swtch <undef>
eof = ^D; eol = ^@; min = 4; time = 0; stop = ^S; start = ^Q
-parenb -parodd cs8 -cstopb hupcl cread -clocal -loblk -crts
-ignbrk -brkint -ignpar -parmrk -inpck -istrip -inlcr -igncr icrnl -iuclc
ixon -ixany -ixoff -rtsxoff -ctsxon -ienqak
isig icanon iexten -xcase echo echoe echok -echonl -noflsh
opost -olcuc onlcr -ocrnl -onocr -onlret -ofill -ofdel -tostop tab3
$
```

Referring to the preceding example of `stty` output, look for the section that has the words `erase`, `kill`, and `eof`. Associated with each word is a control character. Find the similar part of your `stty` output. Keep this handy as you read the next topics.

Erase

Look at the word `erase` in the `stty` output. Next to this word is `^H` (verbalized as Control+H). Therefore, on my system, Erase, which means to back up over the last character typed, is done by typing `^H`. The Erase key is how you can fix your typing errors. Remember to look at your `stty -a` output because your system may be configured differently from this example. Try it out on your system. First, type a character you want to erase, say, an A. Now type your Control, Backspace, or Delete key associated with your Erase. If everything goes right, your cursor should have backed up to be on top of your A, and the next key you type will be where the A was. Try typing a correct series of keys, say `date<Return>`, to make sure that the control character actually worked. If you get a message similar to `A^Hdate not found`, then Erase is not working. To make it work correctly, pick the key you want associated with Erase and input the following (assuming that you have picked the Backspace key):

```
$ stty erase '^H'
$
```

Now, try entering the date command again and deleting the A in dAte and replacing it with a.

NOTE

Depending on your display, erasing characters may not actually make the character disappear. Instead, it may reposition the cursor so that the next keystroke overwrites the character.

The Erase key is one of the most used control keys because typing without mistakes is difficult. Therefore, most keyboards have one or more special keys that are suited to this job. Look for keys labeled "Delete" or "Backspace." One of these usually works as an erase key. Try typing some characters and seeing what happens when you then press Backspace or Delete. Normally the Backspace key is set up to be ^H, so, if your erase is configured to be ^H, Backspace most likely will work.

Kill

The Kill control character is similar to the Erase control character, in that it allows you to back up over typing mistakes. Whereas Erase backs up one character at a time, Kill backs up all the way to the prompt. Therefore, if you are typing a really long command and you realize, toward the end, that you forgot to do some other command first, you can start over by typing the control character associated with Kill. If you can't see what your Kill is set to, redo the `stty` command. In the `stty` output example, the system has kill set to ^X. Again, remember that your system can be configured differently from this example. Now, try typing several characters followed by your Kill control character and see what happens. All the characters should be erased, and your cursor should be after the prompt.

Stop and Start

Two other commonly used control characters are Stop and Start. Their normal values are ^S and ^Q, respectively. Stop allows you to temporarily pause what is happening on your screen, and Start allows you to resume activity following a stop. This is useful if text is scrolling on your screen too fast for you to read. The Stop control character pauses the scrolling indefinitely so that you can read at your leisure. You might try this during your next login while the Message of the Day is scrolling by (see the section earlier in this chapter called "Logging In to the System"). But remember to be prepared and be swift because that text can scroll by quite quickly. Try to stop the scrolling, and then don't forget to continue the scrolling by typing your Start control character.

> **NOTE**
>
> On modern GUIs and high-speed connections, Stop and Start give poor control of output. This is because the output is so fast an entire screen may go by before you type the Stop character.

eof

The eof control character is used to signal the end of input. The letters eof come from end of file. The normal value of the eof control character is ^D, but be sure to verify this using the stty command. You can see how the eof character is used in the section called "Redirecting Input and Output" earlier in this chapter.

There are several other control characters that we will not look at here. Refer to the stty command in your system documentation for information. Or better yet, keep reading because we will show you how to find information about commands via the UNIX online help facility.

The stty command is also used to set the value of control characters. You can simply enter stty erase '^H' to change your Erase character to Backspace. Do not enter a Control+H here; rather, enter '^H'. Some shells, including the original Bourne shell, treat the caret specially, so you may need the quotes. (Double quotation marks would also work in this example.) Try changing the value of your Erase control character and then use the stty -a command to make sure that it happened.

TIP

Remember that typing the end of file character to your shell might log you out of the system!

Where to Find Information About Using UNIX

One of the most important things to know about UNIX or any computer system is how to get help when you don't know how to use a command.

Some information is available online. For instance, most UNIX commands give you a usage message if you incorrectly enter the command. This message shows you the correct syntax for the command. This can be a quick reminder of the arguments and their order. For many commands, you can get the usage message by using the option -?. The usage message often does not give you any semantic information.

The UNIX command man is another powerful tool that gives you complete online access to the UNIX manuals.

Finally, a number of books, such as this one, and technical publications can be helpful. Also, because the UNIX operating system has had a profound impact on the development of the Internet, many Internet and Web sites exist that provide information on many facets of UNIX. In addition to identifying some important Web sites, this chapter identifies some key newsgroups, user groups, and publications to help you become a UNIX guru.

UNIX Manual Pages

Each UNIX system comes with a set of printed documentation. Most UNIX system administrators configure their systems to make this information available to their users. They are often referred to as *man pages*, because they are accessed with the man command. The man command is discussed later in this section. If the manual pages are not available on your system, see your system administrator.

Manual Page Organization

The manual pages are divided into eight sections. They are organized as follows:

1. Commands — This section provides information about user-level commands, such as ps and ls.

2. UNIX System Calls — This section gives information about the library calls that interface with the UNIX operating system, such as open for opening a file, and exec for executing a program file. These are often accessed by C programmers.

3. Libraries — This section contains the library routines that come with the system. An example library that comes with each system is the math library, containing such functions as fabs for absolute value. Like the system call section, this is relevant to programmers.

4. File Formats — This section contains information on the file formats of system files, such as init, group, and passwd. This is useful for system administrators.

5. File Formats — This section contains information on various system characteristics. For example, a manual page exists here to display the complete ASCII character set (ascii).

6. Games — This section usually contains directions for games that came with the system.

7. Device Drivers — This section contains information on UNIX device drivers, such scsi and floppy. These are usually pertinent to someone implementing a device driver, as well as the system administrator.

8. System Maintenance   This section contains information on commands that are useful for the system administrator, such as how to format a disk.

At first, knowing which section to search can seem bewildering. After a little practice, however, you should be able to identify the appropriate section. In fact, certain man page options allow you to span sections when conducting a search.

The Manual Page Command

The man command enables you to find information in the online manuals by specifying a keyword. You can use it to do so in the following ways:

- List all entries whose one-line summary contains the keyword.
- Display all one-line descriptions based on the specified keyword.
- Display the complete manual page entry for the specified keyword.
- Search only the specified section, as outlined previously, for the specified keyword.

The simplest way to invoke the man command is to specify a keyword without any options. For example, if you want more information on the finger command, invoke the man finger command. On an HP system running the HP-UX version of UNIX, the following output is displayed:

FIGURE 2.1.

Output to man finger *command on an HP-UX machine.*

```
NAME
     finger-user information lookup program

SYNOPSIS
     finger [options] user_name...

DESCRIPTION
     By default, finger lists for each user_name on the system:

          +Login name,
          +Full given name,
          ...

OPTIONS
     finger recognizes the following options:

          -b       Suppress printing the user's home directory and shell.
          ...

WARNINGS
     Only the first line of the .project file is printed.

FILES
     /etc/utmp    who file

SEE ALSO    who(l)
```

Notice that the man page is divided into a number of sections, such as NAME, SYN-OPSIS, and DESCRIPTION. Depending on the manual page, there are other sections, including DIAGNOSTICS, FILES, and SEE ALSO.

If you have a particular subject that you want to investigate in the online documentation but don't know where to start, try invoking the man command with the -k option. This searches all the descriptions in all eight of the manual page sections and returns all commands where there is a match. For example, suppose that you want to find out information related to terminals, but you aren't sure which command you should specify. In this case, specify the command man -k terminal. The following is sent to your screen:

```
clear (1) - clear terminal screen
ctermid (3s) - generate file name for terminal
getty (8) - set terminal mode
gettytab (5) - terminal configuration database
lock (1) - reserve a terminal
lta (4) - Local Area Terminal (LAT) service driver
pty (4) - pseudo terminal driver
script (1) - make typescript of terminal session
```

You can then use the man command to find more information on a particular command.

Unfortunately, not all systems are configured to use this option. To use this feature, the command /usr/lib/whatis must be in place. If it is not in place, see your system administrator.

Finally, when you invoke the man command, the output is sent through what is known as a pager. This is a command that lets you view the text one page at a time. The default pager for most UNIX systems is the more command. You can, however, specify a different one by setting the PAGER environment variable. For example, setting it to pg allows you to use features of the pg command to go back to previous pages.

Web Sites

The World Wide Web has an abundance of sites with useful information on UNIX. This section presents a survey of some helpful ones and provides the sites' URLs (Uniform Resource Locator) for access through a Web browser, along with a brief description of the kinds of information you'll find.

Book Lists

http://www.amsoft.ru/unixbooks.html

This site gives a bibliography of UNIX books. It also includes comments for some of the books. Most of the titles came from misc.books.technical faq.

`http://www.cis.upenn.edu/~lwl/unix_books.html`

This site provides a list of UNIX titles, along with a brief review of the book.

`http://wwwhost.cc.utexas.edu/cc/docs/unix20.html`

This site also contains a list of recommended UNIX titles, along with a discussion of the book contents. Its contents include books on introductory UNIX, text editing and processing, networking topics, advanced UNIX programming, and UNIX system administration.

Frequently Asked Questions (FAQ)

`http://www.cis.ohio-state.edu/hypertext/faq/usenet/unix-faq/faq/top.html`

This site contains the Usenet FAQ for questions in the `comp.unix.questions` and `comp.unix.shell` newsgroups. Due to its size, it is divided here into seven sections.

`gopher://manuel.brad.ac.uk/11/.faq/.unix`

This gopher site contains links to the FAQs for many UNIX-related topics, such as `rcs`, `sccs`, shells, and UNIX variants.

Finally, many UNIX FAQs have been reproduced and appear at the end of the *Internet Edition*.

Tutorials

`http://www.tc.cornell.edu/Edu/Tutor`

This page contains a link called "UNIX Basics." It includes sections on basic UNIX concepts for beginners, as well as tutorials on `vi`, `emacs`, and `ftp`.

`http://www.cs.indiana.edu/eip/tutorial.html`

This site contains a tutorial for the `emacs` editor and the `elm` mail program, along with a brief overview of some UNIX commands.

`http://www.cco.caltech.edu/cco/refguide/unixtutorial.html`

This site contains an extensive tutorial on UNIX, including logging in, manual pages, file and directory structure, mail, and job control. It ends with a summary of useful UNIX file commands.

`http://www.eos.ncsu.edu/help/tutorials/brain_tutorials`

Here, you will find a wide variety of practical tutorials, covering `vi`, `emacs`, email, `ftp`, `tar`, remote system access, network newsreader, advanced UNIX commands, and more.

`http://www.cs.indiana.edu/usr/local/www`

From this page, check out the UNIX link. It contains links to scores of other UNIX-related Web pages. Here, you will find information on Usenet FAQs, UNIX shell FAQs, IBM AIX, HP-UX, UNIX for PCs, Sun Systems, X Window, networking, security, Linux, UNIX humor, and much more.

`http://www.physics.orst.edu/tutorial/unix`

This site provides an excellent interactive UNIX tutorial called "Coping With UNIX: An Interactive Survival Kit." It is sponsored by the Northwest Alliance for Computational Science and Engineering. The tutorial runs best on a Web browser that supports frames and is Java-enabled.

`http://www.towson.edu/~michele/GUIDES/dirstruc.html`

This page contains an overview of the UNIX directory structure.

`http://www.uwsg.indiana.edu/uhelp/tutorials/toc.html`

This page contains a list of UNIX tutorials that can be found on systems at Indiana University and on outside systems as well. This page contains five links: beginning tutorials, intermediate tutorials, advanced topics and tutorials, quick references, and other references. Each link contains a number of UNIX references.

`gopher://hp.k12.ar.us/11/classes/unixbasics`

This gopher site contains five introductory UNIX lessons. Each lesson can be downloaded to your system.

`http://goophy.physics.orst.edu/~maestri/work/book.html`

This tutorial is named "Coping With UNIX, A Survival Guide." It covers UNIX basics with a sense of humor.

`http://wsspinfo.cern.ch/file/doc/unixguide/unixguide.html`

This UNIX tutorial is extensive, containing information about many UNIX commands and utilities. It also contains information about the Internet and the World Wide Web.

`http://albrecht.ecn.purdue.edu/~taylor/4ltrwrd/html/unixman.html`

This tutorial, entitled "UNIX is a Four Letter Word, and vi is a Two Letter Abbreviation," contains a humorous look at some basic UNIX commands and the vi editor.

`http://www.cs.curtin.edu.au/units/cg252-502/src/notes/html/contents.shtml`

This tutorial contains an outline of X Window programming concepts.

```
http://www.uwsg.indiana.edu/usail/
```

This tutorial is entitled USAIL, which stands for UNIX System Administration Independent Learning. It is designed to be an independent study course for prospective UNIX system administrators. It contains information on typical system administrator tasks, including installation, network administration, maintaining mail, backup and restore, and system performance. It contains a self-evaluating quiz.

```
http://www.bsd.org/unixcmds.html
```

This page contains a summary of UNIX commands.

```
http://www.indiana.edu/~ucspubs/b017
```

This site also contains a summary of UNIX commands.

```
http://www.bsd.org
```

This site contains many interesting links, including FAQ lists for most popular UNIX vendors, a DOS-to-UNIX command information sheet, and a number of links to other interesting sites.

```
http://www.nda.com/~jblaine/vault
```

This site, named "Jeff's UNIXVault." contains many links to interesting UNIX sites. Topics include "unices" (links to sites that focus on different flavors of UNIX), windowing systems on UNIX, shells, security, shell scripting, organizations, publications, UNIX and PCs, and UNIX newsgroups.

```
http://www.perl.com
```

As the name implies, this site contains a link to "The Perl Language Home Page." It gives information on how to download the latest version of Perl, as well as documentation, a Perl FAQ, and Perl bug reports. It also contains links to other Perl sites, Perl mailing lists, Perl security information, and "The Perl Journal," a newsletter dedicated to Perl.

```
http://wagner.princeton.edu/foldoc
```

While working with UNIX, you are likely to come across terms that you haven't seen before. This site provides a free online dictionary of computing that will help you discover the meaning of such terms. It even provides a search mechanism for ease of use.

```
http://rossi.astro.nwu.edu/lentz/misc/unix/home-unix.html
```

This site contains a number of links to other interesting sites. It contains links to sites that cover networking issues, UNIX organizations, and various UNIX utilities, such as Perl, Tcl/Tk, Python, elm, and pine.

`http://alabanza.com/kabacoff/Inter-Links/guides.html`

Here, you will find many links to Internet guides. The site also contains a couple of UNIX-specific links.

`http://www.python.org`

Python is a portable, interpreted, object-oriented language that runs on many UNIX systems. This site contains a wealth of information, including links to other relevant sites.

`http://athos.rutgers.edu/~patra/unix.html`

This site contains many links to a wide variety of sites, including UNIX FAQ, UNIX security, Perl, UNIX system administration, and C and C++ programming.

`http://www.intersource.com/faqs/unix.html`

Here, you find descriptions of many UNIX and Internet commands.

FTP Sites

`ftp://ftp.gnu.ai.mit.edu`

This site contains all the programs available from the GNU Software Foundation.

`ftp://ftp.x.org`

This site contains a great deal of X Window software.

`ftp://src.doc.ic.ac.uk/computing/systems/unix`

Here, you find many UNIX utilities for programmers and system administrators alike.

Newsgroups

The UNIX operating system has played a major role in the development of the Internet and the World Wide Web. Consequently, a number of newsgroups are dedicated to various aspects of UNIX. For more information on how to participate in a newsgroup on the Internet, see Chapter 6, "Communicating with Others." Here is a listing of various UNIX discussion groups, in alphabetical order:

`cern.security.unix`	This newsgroup holds discussions on UNIX security at CERN. CERN is the European Particle Physics Laboratory and is where the World Wide Web originated.
`comp.lang.c`	Discussion about the C programming language.

`comp.lang.perl`	Discussion of the Perl programming language.
`comp.os.linux.advocacy`	These groups discuss the benefits of Linux, compared to other operating systems.
`comp.os.linux.answers`	This is a moderated discussion group that includes FAQs on Linux.
`comp.os.linux.hardware`	This group discusses Hardware compatibility and Linux.
`comp.os.linux.misc`	General information about Linux that is not covered in the other group.
`comp.os.linux.setup`	Linux installation and system administration.
`comp.security.unix`	Discussion of UNIX security.
`comp.sources.unix`	This contains postings of complete UNIX-oriented source code (moderated).
`comp.std.unix`	Discussion for the P1003 UNIX committee (moderated).
`comp.unix.admin`	This newsgroup discusses any topic related to UNIX system administration.
`comp.unix.aix`	This group is dedicated to discussions of IBM's flavor of UNIX (AIX).
`comp.unix.amiga`	Discussion of UNIX on the Commodore Amiga.
`comp.unix.aux`	Discussion of UNIX on the Apple Macintosh II computer.
`comp.unix.internals`	Discussions on UNIX internals.
`comp.unix.large`	UNIX on mainframes and on large networks.
`comp.unix.misc`	UNIX topics that seem to fit other groups.
`comp.unix.programmer`	This is a question and answer forum for people who program in a UNIX environment.
`comp.unix.questions`	This group is appropriate for newcomers to UNIX, with general questions about UNIX commands and system administration. It is one of the most widely used newsgroups on the Internet.
`comp.unix.shell`	This group discusses using and programming shells, including the Bourne shell (`sh`), Bourne Again shell (`bash`), C Shell (`csh`), Korn shell (`ksh`), and restricted shell (`rsh`).
`comp.unix.solaris`	Discussion of Sun's solaris variant of UNIX.
`comp.unix.sys5.r4`	Discusses UNIX System V Release 4.

`comp.unix.ultrix`	This group is dedicated to discussions of DEC's flavor of UNIX (ultrix).
`comp.unix.unixware`	Discussion about Novell's UnixWare products.
`comp.unix.user-friendly`	Discussion of UNIX user-friendliness.
`comp.unix.xenix.misc`	This group discusses general questions about Xenix, not including SCO.
`comp.unix.xenix.sco`	This group discusses Xenix from SCO (Santa Cruz Operation).
`comp.unix.wizards`	This is a moderated discussion group for advanced UNIX topics.
`comp.windows.x`	This is a discussion group for the X Window system.
`info.unix-sw`	UNIX software that is available via anonymous ftp.

UNIX User Groups

Joining a UNIX user group can be a great way to learn about UNIX. Many groups sponsor meetings, which often include a guest speaker as well as a forum to share ideas and experiences. Literally hundreds of UNIX user groups are in existence worldwide, so to list them here would not be practical. However, an excellent listing of UNIX user groups can be found by visiting `http://www.sluug.org/~newton/othr_uug.html`.

Professional Associations

Many professional associations are dedicated to the discussion and advancement of UNIX and Open Systems. This section gives information about some of the larger groups.

The Electronic Frontier Foundation

The Electronic Frontier Foundation (EFF) is a nonprofit organization dedicated to privacy and free expression, including social responsibility, for online media. For anyone interested in encryption, the Internet, and legal issues, this site is a must.

For more information, including membership, contact them at `http://www.eff.org`, or at the following:

The Electronic Frontier Foundation
1550 Bryant Street, Suite 725
San Francisco CA 94103-4832 USA
Phone: (415) 436-9333

Fax: (415) 436-9993

Email: ask@eff.org

The Open Group

The Open Group, consisting of X/Open and the OSF (Open Software Foundation), is an international consortium of vendors and end users from many disciplines, including industry, government, and academia. It is dedicated to the advancement of multivendor information systems. The group is actively involved in creating UNIX standards that incorporate widely accepted practices. For more information about The Open Group, including membership information, see its Web site at http://www.osf.org.

USENIX

USENIX is the advanced computing system's technical and professional association. Since 1975, Usenix has supported the presentation and discussion of advanced developments in all aspects of computing. Each year, the association sponsors a number of conferences, symposia, and workshops covering a wide variety of topics. Their conferences are usually well attended and are aimed at the UNIX developer and researcher. USENIX also has a number of programs for colleges and universities, including student research grants, undergraduate software projects, scholarship programs, and student stipends so that students can attend USENIX events. They also provide a discount to students for the yearly dues.

USENIX also sponsors a technical group called SAGE (System Administrator's Guild). SAGE is an organization dedicated to the system administration profession. They publish a number of excellent booklets and pamphlets with practical information on system administration. They also publish a bi-monthly newsletter with useful tips for system administrators.

For more information, you can contact USENIX at http://www.usenix.org. In addition to membership information, you will find a number of useful articles from their publication, ";login:," as well as papers published at previous conferences.

You can also contact USENIX with the following information:

The USENIX Association

2560 Ninth Street, Suite 215

Berkeley, CA 94710 USA

Email: office@usenix.org

Phone: (510) 528-8649

Fax: (510) 548-5738

UniForum

UniForum is a professional association aimed at promoting the benefits and practices of open systems. Its members come from a wide variety of backgrounds, including engineers, developers, system administrators, system integrators, MIS directors, and CIOs. One of its stated goals is to provide a vendor-neutral approach to the evaluation and development of open systems. Each year, it sponsors a number a high-quality conferences and seminars. It also provides a number of technical publications that help you to understand open systems technologies. For example, you can access its online newsletter "UniNews Online," through its Web site (`http:/www.uniforum.org`). The association has a number of excellent technical articles on its Web site as well. Perhaps its most popular publication is the Open Systems Products Directory. It contains a description of thousands of open systems products and services and is free of charge to members.

For more information about UniForum, including how to become a member, contact them at `http://www.uniforum.com`, or at the following address or phone number:

> UniForum Association
> 10440 Shaker Drive, Suite 203
> Columbia, MD 21046
> (410) 715-9500
> (800) 255-5620 (US Only)

The X Consortium

This group was recently incorporated into The Open Group. It is dedicated to the X Window desktop environment and its role in the UNIX environment. It is a nonprofit organization for developing user interface standards and graphics technology in an open systems environment. For more information, including membership, visit its Web site at `http://www.x.org`.

Publications

Several useful UNIX-related publications are available. Some are available free of charge for qualified individuals.

UNIX Review

UNIX Review is a monthly magazine that covers the latest in UNIX technologies. It contains useful information for both UNIX developers and administrators. The magazine covers many aspects of UNIX-based systems, including software, hardware, peripherals, and support services. You can subscribe to *UNIX Review* by filling out an online qualification form at its Web site (`http://www.unixreview.com`). In fact, you may qualify for a free subscription.

UNIX World

UNIX World is a subscription-free Web-based magazine. It provides practical tutorials on a wide variety of subjects. It contains a handy online search facility for searching for articles in its archives. You can find UNIX World at
`http://www.unixworld.com/uworld`.

Sys Admin

Sys Admin magazine focuses on UNIX system administration. It provides in-depth coverage of multiple versions of UNIX on a variety of platforms. It covers a number of topics, including system monitoring, system security, backup and recovery, crash recovery, shell scripting, and X Window. You can subscribe to Sys Admin by filling out the subscription form on its Web page at `http://www.samag.com`.

Sun World

This is an online magazine with a focus on Sun products and services. Each month, it contains many practical articles for users and system administrators alike, such as the column "UNIX 101." It also provides a means to search for back issues by keyword. You can access the magazine at `http://www.sun.com/sunworldonline/index.html`.

SunExpert

This is another magazine dedicated to the Solaris flavor of UNIX. Monthly columns include "Ask Mr. Protocol," "UNIX Basics," and "System Administration." It recently merged with another UNIX publication entitled *RS/magazine*. It is free of charge to qualified readers. For subscription information, visit
`http://www.netline.com/sunex/sunex.main.html`.

Summary

This chapter presented a basic tutorial in using UNIX and listed a number of additional resources for learning UNIX.

Because it was designed as a multiuser, multitasking operating system, UNIX provides a rich set of commands and capabilities. One characteristic of UNIX is that commands typically do simple tasks and can be combined in flexible, powerful ways.

The UNIX manual pages are accessible online and are a good place to start in learning how to use UNIX. In addition to books such as this one, a number of other resources are available to help you become a UNIX expert. The Internet contains a great deal of information, including tutorials, newsgroups, UNIX FAQ lists, and online publications. There are also a number of user groups and organizations dedicated to UNIX topics.

The UNIX File System

by Robin Burk and Sanjiv Guha

Nearly all computers reference and use information that is stored but changeable. This information, whether it is executable instructions, a document, or other data, is organized into files.

In some older operating systems, it was common for the operating system itself to know something about the internal structure and purpose of the information in a file. UNIX treats every file the same way, as a stream of bytes (also known as characters) encoded in ASCII.

Of course, from the point of view of commands and other programs, the data within a UNIX file can and usually does have an internal structure beyond being a byte stream. A few of these structures, such as executable programs, are native to UNIX; that is, UNIX knows about the internal structure and typically has commands that interpret or manipulate them. However, the information in some files can't be processed by native UNIX commands. For example, a file containing data for a third-party database such as Oracle needs special programs to be processed, viewed, and so on. UNIX still can move, copy, and report on these files but won't be able to manage the information within them.

A file can reside on different media. A file can also be a permanent file on disk, a temporary file in the memory, or a file displaying or accepting data from the terminal The functions usually performed on a file include the following:

- Opening a file for processing
- Reading data from a file for processing
- Writing data to a file after processing
- Closing a file after all the necessary processing has been done

File System Organization

As with most contemporary operating systems, UNIX supports the capability to organize files to make finding and naming them more feasible.

The most common file system organization, and the one adopted by UNIX, is called a *tree structure*. To follow the metaphor for a moment, a tree has a main trunk, which branches into subtrunks, which branch again, and so on until the final elements are the leaves themselves. Similarly, the file system on a UNIX machine has a root organization, or directory, which may be subdivided into subdirectories, each of which in turn may be subdivided into sub-subdirectories and so on. The final elements are individual files.

Just as the subtrunks of a tree do not necessarily branch and subdivide into exactly the same final pattern, so too the main subdirectories may support different numbers of sub-subdirectories. And, just as even a main trunk can directly grow leaves in many tree species, so too in UNIX a directory can hold files themselves as well as sub-subdirectories.

If you start at the root of a tree and trace it upwards as the trunk branches, and branches again, you will trace the path from the ground to a given leaf. Similarly, we speak of pathnames or paths as a shorthand way to trace the subdivisions of the UNIX file structure, which take us to a given file or files.

Naming Files and Directories

The pathname of a file is given in the following form

`/Directory/subdirectory/sub-subdirectorym …… / filename`

The *root directory* begins all other pathnames and is denoted by a single / (forward slash). Figure 3.1 shows a typical directory tree structure. In a curious twist on the metaphor, it has become common to draw tree structures with the "root node" at the top of the picture.

FIGURE 3.1.

A directory tree.

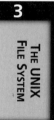

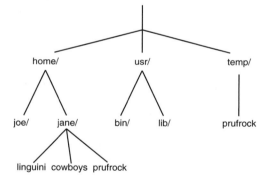

UNIX is flexible regarding the naming of directories and specific files. By convention, however, a number of names are generally used for certain kinds of information, and most distributions of UNIX assume some or all of these names unless configured otherwise. Table 3.1 provides a list of standard directory names in the UNIX file system. This list is not exhaustive. A complete list would depend on the UNIX system you are working with.

TABLE 3.1. LIST OF STANDARD UNIX DIRECTORIES.

Directory name	*Details about the directory*
/	Root directory. This is the parent of all the directories and files in the UNIX file system.
/bin	Command-line executable directory. This directory contains all the UNIX native command executables.
/dev	Device directory containing special files for character- and block-oriented devices such as printers and keyboards. A file called null existing in this directory is called the bit bucket and can be used to redirect output to nowhere.
/etc	System configuration files and executable directory. Most of the administrative, command-related files are stored here.
/lib	The library files for various programming languages such as C are stored in this directory.
/lost+found	This directory contains the in-process files if the system shuts down abnormally. The system uses this directory to recover these files. There is one lost+found directory in all disk partitions.
/u (or) /home	Conventionally, all the user home directories are defined under this directory.
/usr	This directory has a number of subdirectories (such as adm, bin, etc, and include. For example, /usr/include has various header files for the C programming language.

Because the full pathname is required to fully specify a file in UNIX, it is acceptable (and often desirable) for subdirectory and filenames to be duplicated in various portions of the tree. For example, if you kept mail received by month and day, you could create directories named january, february, march, and so on. Under each of these directories, you could create files such as day01, day02, and day03. The same holds true for directories. That is, you can have the same directory name under different directories.

Although the file tree in most UNIX machines is complex, typically you will be working in one local area of it at any given time. UNIX provides a way to identify the local region you're working in by differentiating between the current directory and pathnames relative to that directory, on the one hand, and absolute pathnames on the other hand.

The current directory is that fully specified pathname whose contents (subdirectories or data files) are considered local to you, and which are considered to be the location of any files to which you might (explicitly or implicitly) refer while executing programs or issuing commands.

Absolute pathnames give the full path, beginning at the root. The current directory is a node in the tree whose contents you are examining or manipulating. For example, if you were in the directory named january and you executed the command

```
ls -l day01
```

you would get the attributes of the file day01 under the january directory, which means that UNIX looked in the directory you were currently in to find out whether the file you specified was present. All the commands in UNIX use the current directory to resolve the filename if the filename does not have directory information.

The relative pathname is simply a shorthand way of specifying a pathname in terms of its location relative to the current directory you are in.

For example, if you were in the directory january and wanted to get the attributes of file day01 in directory february, you could specify the absolute pathname of the file:

```
ls -l /home/username/february/day01
```

However, the current directory might exist at several levels of subdirectory from the root, in which case this would be awkward to remember and type. UNIX uses the special characters .. (two consecutive periods) as a relative pathname to indicate the parent directory, or the directory of which the current directory is an immediate subdivision. For example, if you were in the directory /home/username/january, .. (two consecutive periods) would be a shorthand way to refer to the /home/username directory (which is the parent directory of /home/username/january), and ../.. in the relative pathname would indicate the /u directory. This convention provides an easy way to refer to nodes that are nearby the current directory.

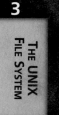

File Types

This section discusses the various file types available in UNIX. You might be familiar with some of these types of files, such as text documents and source files.

Regular Files

Regular files are permanent in nature and contain data such as source code for a program, mail received from the boss, and a letter you are writing to a friend. These files almost always contain text information. In these files, the data is organized into *records* delimited by the newline character. Most UNIX commands support text processing. However, keep in mind that text files are not the only type of regular files. Some files have a stream of bytes without any newline characters. Although UNIX is built to process text documents, the data in these files cannot be processed by UNIX.

The following are examples of some of the regular files:

- `prog.c` is a file containing a C source program.
- `prog.cbl` is a file containing a COBOL source program.
- `prog.exe` is a file containing executable code for a program.
- `invite.doc` is a file containing an invitation to a party from a coworker.

> **NOTE**
>
> The examples provided here follow the usual UNIX file naming conventions. However, these are just conventions, not the rules. So, it is possible for someone to name a file `prog.c`, even though it contains a letter to his or her boss.

Files have attributes or characteristics that are known to UNIX. The attributes of a file can be displayed using the `ls` command:

```
ls -al testfile
```

The result is

```
rwxr-xr-x   2 username    staff       1012 Oct 30 18:39 testfile
```

UNIX keeps track of the file attributes using a data structure called *inode*. Each inode in the system is identified by a number called the *inode number*. Each file in the system has an associated inode that contains information such as the following:

- Ownership details of a file
- Permission details of a file
- Time stamps of a file (date and time of creation, date and time of modification, and so on)
- Type of file

A number of time stamps are associated with a file. These times are

- Last access time
- Last modification time
- Last inode modification time

The last access time changes whenever you perform any operation on a file. The last modification date changes when the contents of the file are modified. The last inode modification time is when any of the information stored in the inode changes.

> **NOTE**
>
> Some UNIX versions, for instance, AIX, do not modify the last access time when you execute them.

Directory Files

A *directory file* is a special file that contains information about the various files stored in the directory, such as file locations, file sizes, times of file creation, and file modifications. This special file can be read only by the UNIX operating system or programs expressly written to do directory processing. You may not view the content of the directory file, but you may use UNIX commands to inquire about these attributes of the directory. When you ask UNIX to process a filename, UNIX consults (and may modify) the specified directory to obtain information about the file. In each directory, you always find two files:

1. . (single period)
2. .. (two consecutive periods)

The single period (.) refers to the current directory, and the two consecutive periods (..) refer to the directory one level up (sometimes referred to as parent directory).

An example of the directory attributes of a `testdir` are presented here:

```
drwxr-xr-x   2 username    writer      512 Oct 30 18:39 testdir
```

`rwxr-xr-x` defines the permissions of `testdir` created by a user called `username` belonging to a group called `writer`. The size of the directory entry `testdir` is 512 bytes. The directory was last modified on October 30 at 6:39 p.m.

A directory is treated as a file by UNIX, but it has some special characteristics. A directory has at least two names. For example, if the current directory were `/home/username` and you created a subdirectory called `testdir`, two links would be created:

- `/home/username/testdir`
- `/home/username/testdir/.`

The entry `/home/username/testdir` is created in the directory `/home/username`, and the entry `/home/username/testdir/.` is created in the directory `/home/username/testdir`.

First, the entry `/home/username/testdir` is created as an empty directory and then is linked to `/home/username/testdir/.` (single period). Both these links exist during the life of the directory and are deleted when you delete the directory.

Character and Block Device Files

The character special files are used for unbuffered I/O to and from a device, and the block special files are used when data is transferred in fixed-size packets. The character special files do I/O on one character at a time mode whereas the block special files use a buffer chaching mechanism to increase the efficiency of data transfer by keeping in-memory copy of the data. Some examples of these files are

- Floppy disk device—character or block special file
- Tape device—character special file
- Terminal—character special file

UNIX treats the keyboard and the monitor (terminal) as files. The keyboard is considered an input file, also referred to as a *standard input file* (*stdin* in UNIX terminology). The terminal is considered an output file, also referred to as the *standard output file* (*stdout* in UNIX terminology).

An important corollary of the standard input and output is referred to as *I/O redirection*. In UNIX, using I/O redirection makes it possible to change the standard input file from keyboard to a regular file, and change the standard output file from terminal to a new or existing regular file.

All UNIX commands, by default, accept input from standard input, display output on standard output, and send error messages to standard error output. By using I/O redirection, it is possible to control the source and destination of the command input and output, respectively. It is possible to direct the output of a command to a different file than the standard output. Similarly, it is possible to accept the input from a file rather than standard input. It is also possible to direct error messages to a file rather than the standard output. This gives you the flexibility to run commands in the background, where these special files—that is, standard input, standard output, and standard error output—are not available. You can use regular files to redirect these input, output, or error messages when you are running commands in the background.

Another interesting special file is the *bit bucket*. This is defined as the file /dev/null. If you redirect the output of a command to /dev/null, the output is produced but immediately discarded and not seen at all. Suppose that you wanted to run a command and were interested only in finding out whether the command execution generated errors. You would redirect the standard output to /dev/null. When you do so, the output is not produced for the command.

Sockets

A *socket* is an application programming interface (API), which is used to communicate between two host computers. In other words, the socket performs network I/O. The abstraction of socket has been designed similar to files, but a socket is not a real file. To use a socket in a program, create a socket and configure the socket with the required addresses of the local and remote hosts. After the socket is connected, the program can use the socket to communicate with the remote hosts. However, there are ways to communicate between hosts using connectionless sockets. A connected socket transfers data between two points between which connection has been established. In the case of a connectionless socket, for each transfer the destination address has to be specified; that is, transfer is not limited between two points. A connectionless socket can be used to communicate between any two computers in a network.

A network program communication has typically two parts: a client and server. Client programs usually actively seek to connect to the server; server programs passively listen for incoming requests from clients. UNIX I/O does not have passive capabilities. So, the sockets, although similar to files, are not exactly identical to files. Sockets have extra system functions to handle capabilities needed by servers, such as passively listening and waiting for client requests.

The files with which most people are familiar reside on hard disks and have fixed addresses. Although an address may be modified by moving the file to a new location, this does not happen during operations on the file. This concept is suited for fixed-connection network communications. However, computers might need to communicate without fixed addresses, using connectionless communication. For connectionless communication, the UNIX concept of a file does not work because the point-to-point connection is not achieved. For this purpose, sockets have a number of special APIs.

Let us see how a connectionless communication is achieved. The program specifies the destination address to which the data has to be delivered. However, the program does not actually deliver this data; instead, it passes the data to the network to do the actual delivery.

The following is a list of socket API functions to transmit data:

- `send`: Transmits data through a connected socket
- `write`: Transmits data through a connected socket using a simple data buffer
- `writev`: Transmits data through a connected socket (using noncontiguous memory locations)

3

**THE UNIX
FILE SYSTEM**

- `sendto:` Transmits data through an unconnected socket
- `sendmsg:` Transmits data through an unconnected socket using a special data structure

The following is a list of functions used for receiving data using a socket:

- `recv:` Reads data through a connected socket
- `read:` Reads data through a connected socket using simple buffer
- `readv:` Reads data through a connected socket (using noncontiguous memory locations)
- `recvfrom:` Reads data through an unconnected socket
- `recvmsg:` Reads data through an unconnected socket using a special data structure

A socket has a number of arguments associated with it. These arguments must be specified during socket creation. The first argument is the communication protocol family to be used to communicate. Many protocols are available, of which the Internet's TCP/IP is the most popular. While working with the protocol families, you should also know about the address families. Each network has a different format for the address of computers attached to it. The second argument is the type of the communication to be used. This data can be sent as a stream of bytes, as in a connection-oriented communication or as a series of independent packets (called datagrams), as in a connectionless communication. The last argument is the actual protocol to be used, which is part of the protocol family specified as the first argument.

Named Pipes

A *named pipe* is a file created to do interprocess communication. That is, it serves as a go-between for data between two programs. The sending process writes data to the named pipe, and the receiving process reads data from the named pipe. It is a temporary file that lasts as long as the processes are communicating. The data is processed in a FIFO (first-in, first-out) basis from the named pipe.

Symbolic and Hard Links

Links create pointers to the actual files, without duplicating the contents of the files. That is, a link is a way of providing another name to the same file. There are two types of links to a file:

- Hard link
- Symbolic (or soft) link; also referred to as *symlink*

With hard links, the original filename and the linked filename point to the same physical address and are absolutely identical. There are two important limitations of a hard link. A directory cannot have a hard link, and it cannot cross a file system. (A *file system* is a physical space within which a file must reside; a single file cannot span more than one file system, but a file system can have more than one file in it.) It is possible to delete the original filename without deleting the linked filename. Under such circumstances, the file is not deleted, but the directory entry of the original file is deleted, and the link count is decremented by 1. The data blocks of the file are deleted when the link count becomes zero.

With symbolic or soft links, there are two files: One is the original file, and the other is the linked filename containing the name of the original file. An important limitation of the symbolic link is that you may remove the original file, and it will cause the linked filename to be there, but without any data. However, a symbolic linked filename can cross file systems.

Be careful about symbolic links. If you are not, you will be left with files that do not point anywhere because the original file has been deleted or renamed.

An important feature of the symbolic link is that it can be used to link directories as well as files.

If you have a file called `origfile` in the directory `/home/username`, whose characteristics are

```
-rw-r—r—  2 username   writer    30 Nov  8 01:14 origfile
```

a file called `hlinkfile`, which has been hard linked to `origfile`, will have the following characteristics:

```
-rw-r—r—  2 username   writer    30 Nov  8 01:20 hlinkfile
```

The 2 before `username` signifies that there are two files linked to the same physical address (`origfile` and `hlinkfile`).

A file called `slinkfile`, which has been soft linked to `origfile`, will have the following characteristics

```
lrwxrwxrwx 1 username   writer     8 Nov  8 01:18 slinkfile -> origfile
```

The link is evident in the filename. In this case, if you delete `origfile`, `slinkfile` is rendered useless.

3

**THE UNIX
FILE SYSTEM**

Naming Files and Directories

Each file is identified by a name, which is a sequence of characters. The older versions of UNIX had limitations on the number of characters that could be used in a filename. All the newer versions of UNIX have removed this limitation. Be careful when naming the files, though. Although UNIX allows most characters to be used as part of the filename, some of the characters have special meaning in UNIX and can pose some problems.

For example, the character > is used as an output redirection operator in UNIX. If you wanted to create a file named x>y, you would use the `touch` command:

```
touch x>y
```

You would then get two files: one named x and one named y.

To circumvent this problem, use a special character (\) (in Korn and C shell) and use the `touch` command, as follows:

```
touch x\>y
```

> ### CAUTION
>
> Using special characters such as asterisks (*) and dollar signs ($) as part of the filename doesn't work because the shell interprets these characters differently. The presence of these characters can trigger the shell to interpret the filename as a command and execute it.

The following is a list of characters that may be used as part of the UNIX filenames:

- A through Z or a through z
- Numerals 0 through 9
- Underscore (_)
- Period (.)

The underscore can separate words in a filename, thus making the filename easier to read. For example, instead of naming a file `mytestfile`, you could name it `my_test_file`.

A period may be used to append an extension to a filename in a way similar to DOS file-names. For example, a C language source file containing a program called `prog` may be named `prog.c`. However, in UNIX you are not limited to one extension. Keep in mind that a period (.), when used as the first character in a filename, has a special meaning. The period as the first character gives the file a hidden status. For example, if you have the files x and .x in your current directory, issuing an `ls` command shows you only the file x. To list both the files, use `ls -a`.

> **CAUTION**
>
> UNIX is case-sensitive. For example, a file named abc is different from a file named ABC.
>
> Some of the system files that begin with a . (period), also called hidden files, will not be displayed until special flags are used—for example, the `.profile` file.

Table 3.2 provides a list of characters or combination characters that should be avoided because they have special meanings. This list is not exhaustive and depends on the UNIX shell you are running.

TABLE 3.2. MEANING OF SOME SPECIAL CHARACTERS.

Character	Meaning
$	Indicates the beginning of a shell variable name. For example, $var will look for a shell variable named var.
¦	Pipes standard output to next command.
#	Starts a comment.
&	Executes a process in the background.
?	Matches one character.
*	Matches one or more characters.
$#	Number of arguments passed to a shell script.
$*	Arguments passed to a shell script.
$?	Returns code from the previous executed command.
$$	Process identification number.
> (greater-than symbol)>)>	Output redirection operator.
<	Input redirection operator.
` (backquote)	Command substitution.
>>	Output redirection operator (to append to a file).

continues

TABLE 3.2. CONTINUED

Character	Meaning
[ ]	Lists a range of characters. [a-z] means all characters a through z. [a,z] means characters a or z.
. *filename*	Executes the file *filename*
:	Directory name separator in the path.

Working with Directories

When you log in to a UNIX system, the directory you are placed in is known as your home directory. Each user in the system has his or her own home directory, and, by convention, it is /home/username. The Korn and C shells use a special character tilde (~) as a shortcut to identify the home directory of a user. For example, if *username* is the user currently logged in, the following would hold true:

- ~ refers to the home directory of username.
- ~friend refers to the home directory of a user friend.

Listing Files and Directories with ls

You can use ls (with its various options) to list details about one or more files or directories on the system. For example, executing the command in the current directory /home/username

```
ls -l
```

shows the following:

```
-rwxrwxrwx   1 username     staff          7161 May  8 15:35 example.c
drwxrwxrwx   3 username     staff          1536 Oct 19 00:54 exe
-rw-r—r—     2 username     staff            10 Nov  3 14:28 file1
-rw-r—r—     2 username     staff            10 Nov  3 14:28 file112
```

The details about a file include the following:

- Permission attributes of the file
- Number of links
- User
- Group of the user who created the file
- Size of the file date and time when the file was last modified
- Name of the file

The previous example shows that the current directory has a directory called exe and three files—example.c, file1, and file2. For the directory exe, the number of links shown is three, which can be counted as one to the parent directory /home/username, one that is the directory entry exe itself, and one more that is to a subdirectory under exe. The number of links for the file example.c is one because that file does not have any hard links. The number of links in files file1 and file2 are two because they are linked using a hard link.

As mentioned, be careful about hidden files. You will not know they exist if you do not use the option -a for ls. In the previous example, if you use

```
ls -al
```

you will see two more entries, . (single period) and .. (two consecutive periods), which are the directory and the parent directory entries.

In the previous examples, the first character before the permissions (for example, d in drwxrwx——) provides information about the type of the file. The file-type values are as follows:

- d: The entry is a directory.
- b: The entry is a block special file.
- c: The entry is a character special file.
- l: The entry is a symbolic link.
- p: The entry is a first-in, first-out (FIFO) special file.
- s The entry is a local socket.
- -: The entry is an regular file.

Creating and Deleting Directories: mkdir and rmdir

When you are set up as a user in a UNIX operating system, you usually are set up with the directory /home/username as your home directory. You will need to organize your directory structure. As with the files, you can use relative or absolute pathnames to create a directory. If your current directory is /home/username,

```
mkdir temp
```

create a subdirectory called temp under the directory temp whose absolute pathname is /home/username/temp.

```
mkdir /home/username/temp
```

can also be used to have the same effect as the previous command.

```
mkdir ../temp
```

can be used to create the directory /home/temp. This example uses .. (two consecutive periods) as part of the relative pathname to indicate that the directory temp will be created under the directory one level up, which is /u. Using mkdir, it is possible to create more than one directory at a time. For example, from your current directory, issue the following command:

```
mkdir testdir1 /home/username/temp/testdir2
```

which creates testdir1 in the current directory and testdir2 under /home/username/temp (assuming it exists). In this example, testdir1 uses a relative pathname, and /home/username/temp/testdir2 uses an absolute pathname.

If the directory is already present, UNIX displays an error stating that the directory already exists.

To create a directory, you must have write permission to the parent directory in which you are creating the subdirectory, and the parent directory must exist. However, many UNIX systems provide an option -p with mkdir so that the parent directory is also created if it does not already exist.

After you are finished using a directory or you run out of space and want to remove a directory, you can use the command rmdir to remove the directory.

If your current directory is /home/username, and directory temp is under it, to remove the directory temp, use the following command:

```
rmdir temp
```

When you execute this command, you might get an error message stating Directory temp is not empty, which means that you still have files and directories under the temp directory. You can remove a directory only if it is empty (all the files and directories under it have been removed). As with mkdir, it is possible to specify multiple directory names as part of the rmdir command. You cannot delete files using the rmdir command. For deleting files, you need to use the rm command instead.

Using the find Command

If you are working on multiple projects at the same time, it might not be possible for you to remember all the details about the various files you are working with. The find command comes to your rescue. The basic function of the find command is to find the filename or directory with specified characteristics in the directory tree specified.

The most basic form of the `find` command is as follows:

```
find . -print
```

You can specify a number of arguments with the `find` command for different attributes of files and directories.

- `name`: Finds files with certain naming conventions in the directory structure
- `modify date`: Finds files that have been modified during the specified duration
- `access date`: Locates files that have been accessed during the specified duration
- `permission`: Locates files with certain permission settings
- `user`: Locates files that have specified ownership
- `group`: Locates files that are owned by specified group
- `size`: Locates files with specified size
- `type`: Locates a certain type of file

Using the `find` command, it is possible to locate files and directories that match or do not match multiple conditions, for example:

- a to have multiple conditions ANDed
- o to have multiple conditions ORed
- ! to negate a condition
- `expression` to satisfy any complex condition

The `find` command has another group of arguments used for specifying the action to be taken on the files or directories that are found, for example:

- `print` prints the names of the files on standard output.
- `exec command` executes the specified command.

The most common reason for using the `find` command is to utilize its capability to recursively process the subdirectories.

3

THE UNIX
FILE SYSTEM

> **NOTE**
>
> Always use the `-print` option of the `find` command. If you do not, the `find` command will execute but, depending on your version of UNIX, may not generate any output. For example, to find all files that start with "t" in the current directory or subdirectories under that, you should use `find . -name "t*"-print` rather than `find . -name "t*"`.

If you want to obtain a list of all files accessed in the last 24 hours, execute the following command:

```
find . -atime 0 -print
```

If the system administrator wants a list of .profile (this file has special use while logging in to the UNIX system) used by all users, execute the following command:

```
find / -name .profile -print
```

You can also execute the find command with multiple conditions. If you want to find a list of files that have been modified in the last 24 hours and have a permission of 777, execute the following command:

```
find . -perm 777   -a -mtime 0 -print
```

Reviewing Disk Utilization with du and df

Until now, this chapter has discussed files and directories but not the details of their physical locations and limitations. This section discusses the physical locations and limitations of the files and directories.

In UNIX, the files and directories reside on what are called *file systems*. File systems define the attributes of the physical devices on which the files reside. UNIX imposes restrictions on the file system size. A file cannot span across file systems; a file cannot exceed the size of a file system. A UNIX system has multiple file systems, each of which has files and directories. To access files in a file system, a file system must be mounted. Another important concept is that of a network file system (NFS), which is used to access files on a physically different computer from the local computer. Similar to the local file system, NFS also must be mounted for you to access the files in it.

The command df is used to obtain the attributes of all or specified file systems in the system. Typically, the attributes displayed by the df command are as follows:

- file system: Name of the file system
- kbytes: Size of the file system in kilobytes
- used: Amount of storage used
- avail: Amount of storage still available
- iused: Number of inodes used
- capacity: Percentage of the total capacity used
- %iused: Percentage of the available inodes already used
- mounted on: The name of the top-level directory

If you are in your home directory and execute the following command

```
df .
```

which returns the following

```
File system     Total KB    free %used    iused %iused Mounted on
/dev/hd1          151552    41828   72%     5534    14% /u
```

it means that your home directory is on a file system called `/dev/hd1`, and the top-level directory in the file system is called `/u`. For this example, you get the same result regardless of what your current directory is, as long as you are in a directory whose absolute pathname starts with `/u`.

You can execute the `df` command without any arguments to obtain a list of all the file systems in your system and their attributes. You can provide an absolute or a relative pathname for a directory to find out the file system attributes of the file system to which it belongs.

The `du` command displays the number of blocks for files and directories specified by the file and directory arguments and, recursively, for all directories within the specified directory argument.

You can execute the following command from your current directory:

```
du or du .
```

and obtain the following result

```
8           .
```

which means that the file system on which the current directory is present has only the current directory in it and it has taken up eight blocks. If there were more directories in that file system, all of them and their sizes would have been displayed.

Determining the Nature of a File's Contents with `file`

The command `file` can be used to determine the type of the file the specified file is. The `file` command actually reads through the file and performs a series of tests to determine the type of the file. The command then displays the output in standard output.

If a file appears to be ASCII, the `file` command examines the first 512 bytes and tries to determine the language. If a file does not appear to be ASCII, the `file` command further attempts to distinguish a binary data file from a text file that contains extended characters.

If the file argument specifies an executable or object module file and the version number is greater than 0, the `file` command displays the version stamp.

The `file` command uses the `/etc/magic` file to identify files that have some sort of a magic number—that is, any file containing a numeric or string constant that indicates type.

For example, if you have a file called `letter` in your current directory and it contains a letter to your friend, executing the command

```
file letter
```

displays the following result:

```
letter:   commands text
```

If you have a file called `prog` and it is a executable program (and you are working on IBM RISC 6000 AIX version 3.1), executing the command

```
file prog
```

displays the following result:

```
prog:         executable (RISC System/6000 V3.1)
```

If you are in the `/dev` directory, which contains all the special files, executing the command

```
file hd1
```

for a file called `hd1` (a disk on which a file system has been defined) displays the following result:

```
hd1:          block special
```

You learn more about the options to be used with the `file` command in Chapter 4.

File and Directory Permissions

Earlier in this chapter, you saw that the `ls` command with the option `-al` displays the permissions associated with a file or a directory. The permissions associated with a file or a directory tell who can or cannot access the file or directory, and what the user can or cannot do.

In UNIX, each user is identified with a unique *login ID*. Additionally, multiple users can be grouped and associated with a *group*. A user can belong to one or more of these groups. However, a user belongs to one *primary group*. All other groups to which a user belongs are called *secondary groups.* The user login ID is defined in the /etc/passwd file, and the user group is defined in /usr/group file. The file and directory permissions in UNIX are based on the user and group.

All the permissions associated with a file or a directory have three types of permissions:

- Permissions for the owner: This identifies the operations the owner of the file or the directory can perform on the file or the directory

- Permissions for the group: This identifies the operations that can be performed by any user belonging to the same group as the owner of the file or the directory.

- Permissions for world: This identifies the operations everybody else (other than the owner and members of the group to which the owner belongs) can do.

Using the permission attributes of a file or directory, a user can selectively provide access to users belonging to a particular group and users not belonging to a particular group. UNIX checks on the permissions in the order of owner, group, and other (world)—and the first permission that is applicable to the current user is used.

Here is an example of a file called testfile in the current directory, created by a user called username belonging to a group called staff. The file is set up so that only the user username can read, modify, or delete the file; users belonging to the group can read it, but nobody outside the group can access it. Executing the following command from current directory

```
ls -al testfile
```

displays the permissions of the file testfile:

```
-rw-r— —-   1 username    staff        2031   Nov 04 06:14 testfile
```

Be careful when setting up permissions for a directory. If a directory has read permissions only, you might be able to obtain a list of the files in the directory, but you will be prevented from doing any operations on the files in that directory.

For example, if you have a directory called testdir in the current directory, which contains a file called testfile, and the group permission for testdir is read-only, executing the following command

```
ls testdir
```

displays the following result:

```
testfile
```

However, if you want to see the content of the file testfile using the following command:

```
cat testdir/testfile
```

you get the following error message:

```
cat: testdir/testfile permission denied
```

To perform any operation on `testfile` in `testdir`, you must have the execute permission for `testdir`.

If you want all the members in your group to know the names of the files in a particular directory but do not want to provide any access to those files, you should set up the directory using only read permission.

The owner of a file is determined by the user who creates the file. The group to which the file belongs is dependent on which UNIX system you are working on. In some cases, the group is determined by the current directory. In other cases, you might be able to change to one of your secondary groups (by using the `newgrp` command) and then create a file or directory belonging to that group.

Similarly, if you set up a directory with just execute permission for the group, all members of the group can access the directory. However, without read permission, the members of the group cannot obtain a list of directories or files in it. However, if someone knows the name of a particular file within the directory, he or she can access the file with the file's absolute pathname.

For example, assume that you have a subdirectory `testdir` under `/home/username` that has a file called `testfile`. Assume that the subdirectory `testdir` has been set up with 710 permission (that is execute permission for the group). In such a case, if a member of the group executes the `ls` command on `testdir`, the following is the result:

```
ls -l testdir
```

```
testdir unreadable
```

```
total 0
```

Whereas if someone is aware of the file `testfile` and executes the following command:

```
ls -l testdir/testfile
```

```
-rw-r—r—   1 username    staff        23 Jul  8 01:48 testdir/testfile
```

then he or she gets all the information about the file `testfile`.

In UNIX, there is a special user who has blanket permission to read, write, and execute all files in the system regardless of the owner of the files and directories. This user is known as `root`.

The Permission Bits

You know that files and directories have owners and groups associated with them. The following are three sets of permissions associated with a file or directory:

- Owner permission
- Group permission
- World (other) permission

For each of these three types of permissions there are three permission bits associated. The following is a list of these permission bits and their meanings for files:

- Read (r): The file can be read.
- Write (w): The file can be modified, deleted, and renamed.
- Execute (x): The file can be executed.

The following is a list of these permissions and their meanings for directories:

- Read (r): The directory can be read.
- Write (w): The directory can be updated, deleted, and renamed.
- Execute (x): Operations can be performed on the files in the directory. This bit is also called the *search bit* because execute permission in a directory is not used to indicate whether a directory can be executed but whether you are permitted to search files under the directory.

Let us examine the directory permissions more closely. Suppose that there is a subdirectory called testdir under the directory /home/username with the following permissions:

```
drwxrws—-   3 username    staff      1536 Nov  4 06:00 testdir
```

Also, a file called testfile is in the directory testdir with the following permission:

```
-rwxr—-—-   1 username    staff      2000 Nov  4 06:10 testfile
```

This means that the user username can read, modify, and rename the directory and files within the directory. Any member of the group staff also has access to the directory. The file testfile is set up with read permissions only for all members of group staff. However, because all members of staff have read, write, and execute permissions on testdir, anyone belonging to group staff may modify, delete, and rename the file testfile.

3

**THE UNIX
FILE SYSTEM**

CAUTION

If a user has write permissions to a directory containing a file, the permissions of the files in that directory are overridden by permissions of the directory.

Permissions (for owners, groups, and others) are stored in the UNIX system in octal numbers. An octal number is stored in the UNIX system using three bits so that each number can vary from 0 through 7. Following is how an octal number is stored:

- Bit 1, value 0 or 1 (defines read permission)
- Bit 2, value 0 or 1 (defines write permission)
- Bit 3, value 0 or 1 (defines execute permission)

The first bit (read) has a weight of 4, the second bit (write) has a weight of 2, and the third bit (execute) has a weight of 1. For example, a value of 101 is 5. (The value of binary 101 is (4 * 1) + (0 * 1) + (1 * 1) = 5.)

Let us now examine how to use the octal number to define the permissions. For example, you might want to define the following permissions for the file testfile in the current directory:

- Owner read, write, and execute
- Group read and execute
- Others—no access at all

This can be defined as (using binary arithmetic):

- Owner 111 = 7
- Group 101 = 5
- Others 000 = 0

Thus, the permission of the file testfile is 750.

Some versions of UNIX provide an additional bit called the *sticky bit* as part of a directory permission. The purpose of the sticky bit is to allow only the owner of the directory, owner of the file, or the root user to delete and rename files.

The following is a convention for setting up permissions to directories and files. For private information, the permission should be set to 700. Only you will have read, write, and execute permissions on the directory or file.

If you want to make information public but you want to be the only one who can publish the information, set the permission to 755. Nobody else will have write access, and nobody else will be able to update the file or directory.

If you do not want the information to be accessed by anybody other than you or your group, set the permission for other 0. The permission may be 770 or 750.

The following is an example of where you can set up permissions to deny permissions to a particular group. Assume that there is a directory called `testdir` in the current directory owned by a group called `outsider`. If you execute the following command in the current directory, the group `outsider` cannot perform any function on the directory `testdir`:

```
chmod  705 testdir
```

Default Permissions: `umask`

When a user logs in to a UNIX system, she is provided with a default permission. All the files and directories the user creates have the permissions defined in `umask`.

You can find out what default permissions you have by executing the following command:

```
umask
```

It might display the following result:

```
022
```

`umask` is stored and displayed as a number to be subtracted from 777. 022 means that the default permissions are

```
777 - 022 = 755
```

That is, the owner can read, write, and execute; the group can read and execute; and all others can also read and execute.

The default `umask`, usually set for all users by the system administrator, may be modified to suit your needs. You can do that by executing the `umask` command with an argument, which is the mask you want. For example, if you want the default permissions to be owner with read, write, and execute (7); group with read and write (5); and others with only execute (1), `umask` must be set to 777 - 751 = 026. You would execute the command as follows:

```
umask 026
```

Changing Permissions: `chmod`

You have just seen how the default permissions can be set for files and directories. There might be times when you want to modify the existing permissions of a file or directory to suit your needs. The reason for changing permissions might be that you want to grant or deny access to one or more individuals. This can be done by using the `chmod` command.

With the `chmod` command, you specify the new permissions you want on the file or directory. The new permissions can be specified using one of the following two ways:

- In a three-digit, numeric octal code
- In symbolic mode

You are already familiar with the octal mode. If you wanted the file `testfile` to allow the owner to read, write, and execute; the group to read; and others to execute, you would need to execute the following command:

```
chmod 741 testfile
```

When using symbolic mode, specify the following:

- Whose (owner, group, or others) permissions you want to change
- What (+ to add, - to subtract, = to equal) operation you want to perform on the permission
- The permission (`r`, `w`, `x`)

Assuming that the current permission of `testfile` is `740` (the group has read-only permission), you can execute the following command to modify the permissions of `testfile` so that the group has write permissions also:

```
chmod g+w testfile
```

Another example of symbolic mode is when you want others to have the same permissions as the group for a file called `testfile`. You can execute the following command:

```
chmod o=g testfile
```

Another example of symbolic mode is when you want to modify the permissions of the group as well as the world. You can execute the following command to add write permission for the group and eliminate write permission for the world:

```
chmod  g+w, o-w testfile
```

Changing Owner and Group: `chown` and `chgrp`

If you wanted to change the owner of a file or directory, you could use the `chown` command.

> **CAUTION**
>
> On UNIX systems with disk quotas, only the root user may change the owner of a file or directory.

If the file `testfile` is owned by user `username`, to change the ownership of the file to a user `friend`, you would need to execute the following command:

```
chown friend testfile
```

If you wanted to change the group to which the file belongs, you may use the `chgrp` command. Assume that user `username` owns the file `testfile` and the group of the file is `staff. username` To change the owner of `testfile` from `staff` to `devt`, execute the following command:

```
chgrp devt testfile
```

Setuid and Setgid

When you execute some programs, it becomes necessary to assume the identity of a different user or group. It is possible in UNIX to set the `SET USER ID(setuid)` bit of an executable so that when you execute it, you assume the identity of the user who owns the executable. For example, if you are executing a file called `testpgm`, which is owned by `specialuser`, for the duration of the execution of the program, you will assume the identity of `specialuser`. Similarly, if `SET GROUP ID(setgid)` of a executable file is set, executing that file results in you assuming the identity of the group that owns the file during the duration of execution of the program.

Here is an example of how the `SET USER ID` bit is used. Suppose that you want a backup of all the files in the system to be done by a night-shift operator. This usually is done by the root user. Create a copy of the backup program with the `SET USER ID` bit set. Then, the night-shift operator can execute this program and assume the identity of the root user during the duration of the backup.

Summary

This chapter discussed what files are, the various types of files, and how to organize the files in different directories. You learned how to define permissions on files and directories. You also saw some of the commands used on files, such as `ls` to list files and its details, `chmod` to change permissions on files and directories, `chown` to change the ownership of a file or directory, `chgrp` to change the group ownership of a file, `umask` to display and change default permission settings for the user, and `du` or `df` to find out about utilization of disk space. You learn more about various UNIX commands in Chapter 4.

General Commands

by Robin Burk and Sanjiv Guha

CHAPTER 4

UNIX offers a particularly rich command environment with which you can accomplish a variety of computing tasks. As you will see later in this book, UNIX allows you to treat a variety of programs as if they were native commands (that is, as if they were built into UNIX). It also allows you to create a shorthand, or alias, for commands and options you use regularly.

This chapter describes the basic native UNIX commands. Although commands differ to some degree among UNIX variants and shell environments, a core set of common commands exists. These are described in this chapter.

UNIX commands can be invoked from a command line or within shell scripts. Most commands accept flags that control the details of their operation, and many accept or require arguments as well. The general form of a command is as follows:

```
command [flags] [argument1] [argument2] ...
```

Flags are preceded by a hyphen. Several flags can be specified together with only one hyphen. For example, the following two commands are equivalent:

```
ls -a -l

ls -al
```

Depending on the command, the arguments can be optional or mandatory. All commands accept inputs from the standard input, display output on the standard output, and display error message on the standard error. You can use UNIX redirection capabilities to redirect one or more of these. *Standard input* is where UNIX gets the input for a command, *standard output* is where UNIX displays output from a command, and *standard error* is where UNIX displays any errors as a result of the execution of a command.

All commands, when executed successfully, return a zero return code. However, if the command is unsuccessful or partially successful, it returns a non-zero return code. The return codes can be used as part of control logic in shell scripts.

CAUTION

Use the man command to verify how command flags and options work on your own system.

User-Related Commands

User-related commands allow you to establish and end UNIX sessions on a given system and within a given user account.

login

Each user in a UNIX system has a unique login ID that identifies the user and any characteristics associated with the user. User IDs are established by the system administrator. When you first connect to a UNIX system, the login prompt usually asks for the following information:

```
login:
password:
```

You are allowed into a system, if, and only if, you enter the login ID and password correctly. When the login is successful, you get information such as the last unsuccessful login, the last successful login, whether you have any mail, messages from the system administrator, and more. Following is an example of a successful login:

```
**********************************************************************
*                                                                    *
* You are now logged on to the host1 computer                        *
*                                                                    *
**********************************************************************
Last unsuccessful login: Thu Nov  7 22:32:41 1996 on tty1
Last login: Fri Nov  8 01:17:04 1996 on tty1
/u/testuser:>>
```

Most users interact with UNIX through one of the common shells, which provide richer and more friendly command environments. *Shells* typically run a script file associated with your ID when you log in. The Bourne shell executes the `.profile` file in your home directory. The Korn shell executes the file pointed to by the environment variable ENV.

The purpose of these files is to set up a standard computing environment for your login sessions. For example, you can set the search path, the terminal type, and various environment variables or run special programs depending on your requirements. Following is an example of a Korn shell's `.profile` file for user `testuser`. Here, the PATH variable is set to include directories that user `testuser` uses for daily work, and the mail is being checked.

```
PATH=$PATH:/u/testuser:/u/testuser/exe:/u/testuser/script
PATH=/usr2/cdirect/local:$PATH
export PATH
```

4

rlogin

UNIX provides you with the `rlogin` command to let you move between various computers in a network. The `rlogin` command is similar to the `telnet` command described in the following section.

To be allowed access to a remote host, you must satisfy the following conditions:

- The local host is included in the `/etc/hosts.equiv` file of the remote host, the local user is not the `root` user, and the `-l User` option is not specified.
- The local host and user name are included in the `$HOME/.rhosts` file in the remote user account.

Once logged in, you can execute commands and programs on that system. When you log out of the session on the remote host, you are back on the local host.

If you execute the `rlogin` command without specifying a user ID, the user ID for the remote host is assumed to be the same as that of the user ID logged in to the local host. For example, if `testuser` is logged in currently on `box1`, UNIX assumes that you are issuing the `rlogin` command for `testuser` on `box2`.

If, however, your user ID is different on `box2` than on `box1`, you can use another option of the `rlogin` command:

```
rlogin box2 -l testusernew
```

With this option, you tell `rlogin` that the user ID to be used for the remote host is `testusernew`.

telnet

If you are in an environment in which you work with multiple UNIX computers networked together, you will have to work on different machines from time to time. The `telnet` command provides you with a facility to log in to other computers from your current system without logging out of your current environment. The `telnet` command is similar to the `rlogin` command described earlier in this section.

The `hostname` argument of `telnet` is optional. If you do not use the host computer name as part of the command, you are placed at the `telnet` prompt, usually, `telnet>`. A number of subcommands are available from the `telnet>` prompt. Some of these subcommands are as follows:

Subcommand	Description
`exit`	Closelose the current connection and return to the `telnet>` prompt if the subcommand `open` was used to connect to the remote host. If, however, `telnet` was issued with the `host-name` argument, the connection is closed, and you return to where you invoked the `telnet` command.
`display`	Display operating arguments.
`open`	Open a connection to a host. The argument can be a host computer name or address.
`quit`	Exit `telnet`.
`set`	Set operating arguments.
`status`	Print status information.
`toggle`	Toggle operating arguments (`toggle ?` for more).
`?`	Print help information.

If, for instance, you are currently logged in on `box1`, you can execute the following command to log in to `box2`:

```
telnet box2
```

As a response to this command, `box2` responds with a login screen at which you can enter your user ID and password for `box2`. After completing your work on `box2`, you can come back to `box1`.

passwd

When your user ID is first set up in a computer, the system or security administrator will assign you a temporary password. The first time you try to log in, the system will ask you to change your password; you will use the new password for all subsequent logins.

As a security precaution, it is a good practice to modify your password frequently using the `passwd` command. `passwd` prompts you for your current password, and then prompts you twice more to enter the new password. The new password must follow the rules set up at your installation; these rules typically specify the following:

- The minimum number of alphabetic characters.
- The maximum number of times a single character can be used in a password.
- The minimum number of weeks that must elapse before a password can be changed.
- The maximum number of weeks after which the password must be changed. The system will prompt you to modify the password when this happens.

Passwords control access to your account and your files. Select your password carefully to prevent it from being guessed or from being easily generated by an automated hacker attack.

- Avoid using proper nouns (such as personal names) or strings of characters followed by numbers (such as `xyz01`).
- Use both uppercase and lowercase letters mixed with numbers.
- Use at least 7 characters.
- Don't write down your password.
- Choose a password that you can type quickly.

exit

When you log in to a UNIX system, you are always placed in a shell. The `exit` command allows you to exit the current shell.

You can also exit your current shell by pressing Ctrl+D. (Hold down the Ctrl key and the D key together.) If you are on the command line and press Ctrl+D, you will be logged off.

Locating Commands

Most commands are executed by programs stored in executable or script files. Each user has a *search path*—a list of directories in the order to be searched for locating commands.

The default search paths set by the installation usually include standard directories such as `/bin`, `/usr/bin`, and other installation specific directories. You can modify the search path for your environment as follows:

- Modify the `PATH` statement in the `.profile` file (Korn shell and Bourne shell).
- Modify the `set path=(....)` statement in the `.cshrc` or `.login` file (C shell).

Add the directory that contains your commands, or any commands you have modified, to the beginning of the path. They will be found first and executed first.

which

The `which` command can be used to find and report the directory in which a particular command exists. For example, to find out where the `which` command resides, enter this command:

```
which which
```

The system responds with the following message, meaning that the command `which` exists in the directory `/usr/bin`:

```
/usr/bin/which
```

whence

The Korn shell offers the `whence` command, which supports a flag `-v` to produce output in a verbose form.

```
whence -v which
```

The preceding command produces the following output:

```
which is /usr/bin/which
```

However, if you have aliased commands, this command shows the underlying command string behind the alias.

where

The `where` command is used to obtain the full path name of one or more files or directories. No flags are associated with the `where` command. For example, to find the path name of the current directory, issue the following command:

```
where
```

Assuming that you are in the directory `/u/testuser`, the preceding command results in this output:

```
box1:/u/testuser
```

Determining Command Usage

UNIX provides you with online help to learn about various commands and their options and flags. You may be familiar with the most often used commands and their various options, but to find out about less popular commands or command usage, you can use the online help provided by UNIX.

man

The man command is used to display the online UNIX manual page for a given command, file, subroutine, and so on. If you do not know the full name of the item for which you want help, you can use the UNIX wildcard to specify the object name. Following are some of the flags and arguments you can use with the man command:

Flag	Meaning
-k keyword	Provide a list of summary information about manual sections in the keyword database for the specified keyword.
-f command	Provide details associated with the specified command. The root user must set up the file /usr/man/whatis before you can use this option.
-M path	Specify the search path for the man command.

The following is a list of sections in the manual page that can be specified:

- 1—Commands
- 2—System calls
- 3—Subroutines
- 4—File formats
- 5—Miscellaneous
- 7—Special files
- 8—Maintenance

For example, if you want to find out about the find command, execute the following command:

```
man find
```

To find out about file system related keywords, execute the following command:

```
man -k filesystem
```

Administration

Only the UNIX system administrator can perform certain functions such as starting the system, shutting down the system, setting up new user accounts, monitoring and maintaining various file systems, installing new software on the system, and more. The following sections discuss the commands necessary to fulfill these duties.

install

The `install` command is used to install new versions of current software programs or brand new software programs. The basic function of the `install` command is to copy the binary executable and any associated files to the appropriate directories.

> **NOTE**
>
> For new software, the default permissions are set to 755 with owner and group both set to `bin`. The default directories searched to find whether the command is present are `/usr/bin`, `/etc`, and `/usr/lib`—in that order.

Following are some of the flags that can be used for the `install` command:

Flag	Meaning
-c directory	Install the files in the specified directory, if, and only if, the command does not already exist.
-f directory	Install the files in the specified directory, even if the command already exists in that directory.
-G group	Set the group of installed files to the specified group instead of the default group `bin`.
-O owner	Setet the ownership of the installed files to the specified user instead of the default owner `bin`.
-o	Save the current version with the prefix `OLD`; that is, if the name of the file is `sample`, it is saved as `OLDsample`.
-i	Specify that you do not want to search the default directories but want to search the command line specified directories.
-n directory	Specify that you want to install the files in the specified directory if they are not found in the search directories.

4

GENERAL COMMANDS

You can execute the following command to install the file `sample_program` in the directory `/usr/bin` (default directory):

```
install sample_program
```

Assuming that `sample_program` already exists in the `/u/testuser/exe` directory, you can install the new version by executing the following command:

```
install -f /u/testuser/exe sample_program
```

shutdown

To shut down the machine in an orderly fashion, use the `shutdown` command from the `root` user. By default, this command brings down the system to single-user mode from multiuser mode. Following is a list of some of the flags that can be used with the `shutdown` command:

Flag	Meaning
-h	Halt the operating system completely.
-i	Display interactive prompts to guide the user through the shutdown.
-k	Simulate a system shutdown.
-m	Bring the system down to maintenance (single user) mode.

It is also possible to specify the time when restart is to be done by specifying a future date or relative time. In that case, the system sends messages to the users periodically about the impending shutdown.

ulimit

The `ulimit` command, available in the Korn and Bourne shells, sets limits on certain resources for each process. The corresponding command in the C shell is `limit`. There are two types of limits:

- *Hard limits* are those defined in the resources on a system-wide basis and can be modified only by `root` authority.
- *Soft limits* are the default limits applied to a newly created process. Soft limits can be increased to a system-wide hard limit.

Following are the flags that can be used with the `ulimit` command:

Flag	Meaning
-a	Show the soft limits.
-Ha	Showhow the hard limits.
-c *size*	Set the `coredumpsize` in blocks.
-t *size*	Set the CPU time in seconds.
-f *size*	Set the maximum file size in blocks.
-d *size*	Set the maximum size of the data block in kilobytes.
-s *size*	Set the maximum size of the stack in kilobytes.
-m *size*	Set the maximum size of the memory in kilobytes.

To obtain the current setting of the hard limits, execute the following command:

```
ulimit -Ha
time(seconds)     unlimited
file(blocks)      4097151
data(kbytes)      unlimited
stack(kbytes)     unlimited
memory(kbytes)    unlimited
coredump(blocks)  unlimited
```

To obtain the current setting of the soft limits, execute the following command:

```
ulimit -a
time(seconds)     unlimited
file(blocks)      4097151
data(kbytes)      2048576
stack(kbytes)     82768
memory(kbytes)    909600
coredump(blocks)  102400
```

umask

The umask command is used by the system administrator to set the default permissions to be assigned to each file created by a user. You, as a user, can modify this default setting.

Three groups of permissions are associated with a file or directory: owner, group, and world (sometimes referred to as others). The permissions for these three groups are assigned using octal numbers—one octal number for each group. The values for each group depend on the following three bits:

- read bit (0 or 1)
- write bit (0 or 1)
- execute bit (0 or 1)

Using binary arithmetic, the value can vary from 0 (all bits having a value of zero) to 7 (all bits having a value of 1).

The value associated with umask can be used to derive the value of the default permission by subtracting it from 777. For example, if the value of umask is 022, then the value of the permission is 777 – 022 = 755 (read, write, execute for owner; read, execute for group; and read, execute for the world).

To obtain the default value of the umask, execute the following command:

```
umask
```

For example, to set the value of the permission to 751, you set umask to the value 026 (777 – 751), like this:

```
umask 026
```

Process-Related Commands

In UNIX, a *process* is a program that has its own address space. Simple commands such as umask have only one process associated with them; a string of commands connected by pipes has multiple processes associated with it.

Processes can be categorized into the following broad groups:

- *Interactive processes* are invoked at the terminal and run either in the foreground or in the background. In a *foreground process*, the input is accepted from standard input, output is displayed to standard output, and error messages are sent to standard error. While executing a process in the background, the terminal is detached from the process so that it can be used for executing other commands. It is possible to move a process from the foreground to the background and vice versa.

- *Batch processes* are not submitted from terminals. They are submitted to job queues to be executed sequentially.

- *Daemons* are never-ending processes that wait to service requests from other processes.

In UNIX, each process has a number of attributes associated with it. Following is a list of some of these attributes:

- *Process ID* is a unique identifier assigned to each process by UNIX.
- *Real User ID* is the user ID of the user who initiated the process.
- *Effective User ID* is the user ID associated with each process and determines the process's access to system resources. Under normal circumstances, the Real User ID and the Effective User ID are one and the same.

- *Real Group ID* is the group ID of the user who initiated the process.

- *Effective Group ID* is the group ID that determines the access rights. The Effective Group ID is similar to the Effective User ID.

- *Priority (Nice Number)* is the priority associated with a process relative to the other processes executing in the system.

kill

The `kill` command is used to send signals to nonforeground processes. The `kill` command terminates the process unless the process has the appropriate logic to accept the signal and respond differently. Unless you are logged in as the `root` user, you can kill only the processes initiated by you.

The flags associated with the `kill` commands are as follows:

Flag	Meaning
`-l`	Obtain a list of all the signal numbers and their names that are supported by the system.
`-signal number`	The signal number to be sent to the process. You can also use a signal name in place of the number. The strongest signal you can send to a process is `9` or `kill`.

The argument to the `kill` command is the Process ID (PID). You can specify more than one PID as arguments to kill more than one process. The value of the PID can be one of the following:

- PID greater than zero to kill specified processes.

- PID equal to zero to kill all processes whose Process Group ID is the same as the Process Group ID of the user initiating the `kill` command.

- PID equal to -1 to kill all processes owned by the Effective User ID of the user initiating the `kill` command.

- PID equal to a negative number but not -1 to kill processes whose PID is equal to the absolute value of the number specified.

Use the `kill` command carefully because it immediately ends any specified processes.

If you are running a command in the background and think it has gone into a loop, you will want to terminate it. If the process number is, for example, 2060, execute the following command:

```
kill 2060
```

4

GENERAL COMMANDS

If, for some reason, this command does not kill it, use the stronger version:

```
kill -kill 2060
```

The preceding command is the same as the `kill -9 2060` command.

nice

Each process has a relative priority that governs the resources allocated to it by the operating system. The `nice` command is used to lower priorities, typically for background or batch processes. You can also raise priorities if you have `root` privileges.

A negative number signifies a higher priority than a positive number. The value is usually in the range –20 to 20.

If you want to find, at a lower priority in background, all the C source files in the current directory or its subdirectories, execute the following command:

```
nice find . -name *.c -print &
```

This command sets the process to a default `nice` priority, which may be 10. To run the process at an even lower priority, execute the following command:

```
nice 16 find . -name *.c -print &
```

ps

The `ps` command is used to find out which processes are currently running. Depending on the options you specify, you can find all processes or only those initiated by your user ID. When the `ps` command is executed without any flags or arguments, it lists all processes (if any) initiated from the current terminal.

Following is a list of some of the flags that determine what processes are listed by the `ps` command:

Flag	*Meaning*
-A	List details of all processes running in the system.
-e	List details of all processes, except kernel processes.
-k	List all the UNIX kernel processes.
-p *list*	List details of all processes specified in the list.
-t *list*	List details of all processes initiated from the terminals specified in the list.
-U *list* (-u *list*)	List details of all processes initiated by the users specified in the list.

Flag	*Meaning*
a	List details of all processes that have terminals associated with them.
g	List details of all processes.
x	List details of all processes that do not have any terminal associated with them.

> **NOTE**
>
> Some of the flags used by the ps command are not preceded by a hyphen (-).

Following is a list of some of the flags for the ps command that determine which details are displayed for each process listed:

Flag	*Meaning*
-l	Generate the listing in a long form.
-f	Generate a full listing.
-F *format*	Generate a formatted output.

The following details are displayed if formatting flags are not used:

- Process ID of the process.
- Terminal ID associated with the process. Hyphen (-) if no terminals are associated.
- CPU time consumed by the process.
- Command being executed as part of the process.

By using the formatting command, some of the details that can be obtained are as follows:

- User ID of the user who initiated the process.
- Process ID of the process.
- Parent Process ID of the process.
- CPU utilization of the process.
- Start time of the process. If the process has been started on the same day, it shows the time; otherwise, it shows only the date.
- Terminal ID associated with the process. It display a hyphen (-) if there are no terminals associated with the process.
- CPU time consumed by the process.
- Commands being processed as part of the process.

4

GENERAL COMMANDS

To display the processes initiated by the current user at the current terminal, execute the following command:

```
ps
```

The result is displayed as follows:

```
  PID   TTY  TIME CMD
66874     2  0:00 -ksh
71438     2  0:00 ps
```

The two processes displayed here are the login shell (in this case, the Korn shell) and the ps command itself.

If you want more details, execute the following command:

```
ps -f
```

This generates the following display:

```
  USER     PID   PPID  C   STIME     TTY  TIME CMD
testuser  66874      1  1 22:52:26     2  0:00 -ksh
testuser 480076  66874  6 00:21:33     2  0:00 ps -f
```

If you want to know all the processes executing at terminal tty2, execute the following command:

```
ps -f -t tty2
```

Here is the result:

```
  USER     PID   PPID  C   STIME     TTY  TIME CMD
testuser  66874      1  1 22:52:26     2  0:00 -ksh
testuser 703277  66874  6 00:24:17     2  0:00 ps -f -t tty2
```

jobs

In UNIX, there is a subtle difference between a *process* and a *job*. A *job* is typically one command line of commands, which can be a single command, a shell script, or a chain of piped commands. In a chain of piped commands, each command has a unique process ID, but all have the same job ID.

The C shell and some versions of the Korn and Bourne shells offer the jobs command. You can use the jobs command to find out the details about active jobs. Once you have the job ID, you can start using it to do primitive job controls.

You use the % (percent sign) in front of the job number to indicate that the number is a job number rather than a process ID.

For instance, if you want to bring job number 5 from the background to the foreground, execute the following command:

```
fg %5
```

If you have one job called `sample_job` running in the background, execute the following command to get the details of the job:

```
jobs
```

The resulting display looks like this:

```
[1] +  Running                     nohup sample_job > sample_log &
```

If you use the `-l` option, the process number is also displayed as follows:

```
[1] + 270384      Running                  nohup sample_job > sample_log &
```

wait

You can use the `wait` command to wait for completion of jobs. This command takes one or more process IDs as arguments. The `wait` command is useful during shell programming when you want one process to finish before the next process is invoked. If you do not specify a process ID, UNIX will wait for termination of all processes spawned by the current environment.

To find out whether the process ID 15060 has completed, execute the following command:

```
wait 15060
```

The return code from the `wait` command is zero if you invoked the `wait` command without any arguments. If you invoked the `wait` command with multiple process IDs, the return code depends on the return code from the last process ID specified.

nohup

Executing processes under UNIX can be running in the foreground or the background. In a foreground process, you are waiting at the terminal for the process to finish. Under such circumstances, you cannot use the terminal until the process is finished. However, you can put the foreground process into the background as follows:

```
Ctrl-z
bg
```

The processes in UNIX will be terminated when you log out of the system or exit the current shell whether they are running in foreground or background. The only way to ensure that the process currently running is not terminated when you exit is to use the `nohup` command.

4

GENERAL COMMANDS

The `nohup` command has default redirection for the standard output. It redirects the messages to a file called `nohup.out` under the directory from which the command was executed. That is, if you want to execute a script called `sample_script` in the background from the current directory, use the following command:

```
nohup sample_script &
```

The & (ampersand) tells UNIX to execute the command in the background. If you omit the &, the command is executed in the foreground. In this case, all the messages will be redirected to `nohup.out` under the current directory. If the `nohup.out` file already exists, the output is appended to it. If the permissions of the `nohup.out` file are set up so that you cannot write to that file, UNIX creates or appends to the `nohup.out` file in your home directory.

When you initiate the `nohup` command in the background (by using & at the end of the command line), UNIX displays the process ID associated with it. You can later use this information with commands such as `ps` to find out the status of the execution.

For example, to find the string `sample_string` in all the files in the current directory, execute the following command:

```
nohup grep sample_string * &
```

UNIX responds with the following message:

```
[2]     160788
Sending output to nohup.out
```

The first line of the display is the process ID; the second line is the informational message about the output being directed to the default `nohup.out` file. You can later go into the file `nohup.out` to find out the result of the `grep` command. To redirect the output to a file called `mygrep.out`, execute the following command instead:

```
nohup grep sample_string * > mygrep.out &
```

sleep

If you want to wait for a certain period of time between execution of commands, use the `sleep` command. Use this command in cases where you want to check for, say, the presence of a file every 15 minutes. The argument is specified in seconds.

Communication

UNIX has several commands used to connect to another host, to transfer files between host computers, and so on without logging into a user session on the remote system.

cu

The cu command allows you to connect to another host computer, either directly or indirectly. That is, if you are currently on host1 and you use cu to connect to host2, you can connect to host3 from host2, so that you are connected directly to host2 and indirectly to host3.

Following is a list of some of the flags that can be used with cu command:

Flag	*Meaning*
-d	Print diagnostic messages.
-lLine	Override the default device to be used for communication.
-n	Prompt for the telephone number rather than accepting it as part of the command line.
-sSpeed	Specify the speed (in bauds) of the line to be used for communication between hosts.
-Tseconds	Specify the length of time UNIX will try to connect to the remote host.

The following arguments can be specified with the cu command:

- System Name is the name of the system to which you want to connect. This name must be defined in the /etc/uucp/Systems file. Also defined in this file are parameters, such as telephone number, line speed, and more, which are used to connect to the remote host. If you are using System Name, you should not use the -l and -s option.

- Telephone Number is the telephone number to be used to connect to the remote host. The number can be local or long distance.

After making the connection, cu runs as two processes: The transmit process reads data from the standard input and—except for lines beginning with ~ (tilde)—passes the data to the remote system. The receive process accepts data from the remote system and—except for lines beginning with ~ (tilde)—passes it to the standard output.

Once you are able to successfully log in to the remote host, you can use several subcommands, listed here. Remember to prefix the ~ with a \ so that UNIX does not apply special meaning to ~.

4

GENERAL
COMMANDS

Subcommand	*Meaning*
~.	Disconnect from the remote host.
~!	Disconnect from the remote host.
	To activate an interactive shell on the local host, you can toggle between interactive shells of local and remote hosts using ~! and Ctrl+D.
~!*Command*	Execute *Command* at the local host.
~%cd *directory*	Change the directory on the local host to the specified directory.
~%put *From [To]*	Copy an ASCII text file on the local system to a file on the remote system. If the *To* variable is not specified, the local file is copied to the remote system under the same filename.
~%take *From [To]*	Copy an ASCII text file from the remote system to a file on the local system. If the *To* variable is not specified, the remote file is copied to the local system under the same filename.
~$*Command*	Run, on the local system, the command denoted by the *Command* variable and send the command's output to the remote system for execution.

For example, if remote2 is defined in the /etc/uucp/Systems file, you can execute the following command:

cu remote2

If you want to connect to a specific device, tty1, on a remote host at a specified line speed, 2400, execute the following command:

cu -s 2400 -l tty1

After you are in the remote host, you can execute any of the cu subcommands. To the directory /u/testuser on the local host, execute this command:

\~%cd /u/testuser

If you have a file called `local_file` from directory `/u/testuser` on the local host, you can copy it to the current directory in the remote host with the same name by executing the following command:

```
\~%put /u/testuser/local_file
```

To execute the `ls` command on the local system, execute the following command:

```
\~!ls
```

ftp

You can use the `ftp` command to transfer files between two host computers. You cannot copy files from directories recursively using a single `ftp` command. Instead, you must transfer each file or directory individually. You should also be aware that `ftp` can be used between different types of systems, which means that system-dependent file attributes may not be preserved when files are transferred.

While using the `ftp` command, you need to use a login and password to log in to the remote host. However, it is possible to log in to the remote host without a password if the home directory has a `.netrc` file and that file contains the macro necessary for logging in to the remote host.

If a login ID and password are needed, the `ftp` command prompts for that information. In such a case, you cannot proceed until you are able to successfully log in using the correct user ID and password.

After you log in successfully, the `ftp` command displays an `ftp>` prompt. From the `ftp>` prompt, you can use a number of subcommands to perform file transfers.

You can specify the host name as part of the `ftp` command or open a connection to a host in the `ftp>` prompt. If you specify the host name as part of the command line, you are prompted for the login ID and password before you are see the `ftp>` prompt. For example, if you execute the following command, you will be prompted for a user ID and password:

```
ftp box2
```

Some of the flags that can be used with the `ftp` command are as follows:

Flag	Meaning
-i	If you do not want to be prompted with filenames in case more than one file is being transferred using a single command.

continues

4

GENERAL
COMMANDS

Flag	Meaning
-d	For debug information.
-n	To prevent automatic login in case a .netrc file is present.
-v	To display the messages from the remote host on the terminal.

Once you are at the ftp> prompt, you can use several subcommands:

Subcommand	Meaning
!	Invoke the interactive shell on the local host. Optionally, you can invoke a command with arguments by specifying the command and arguments after the ! sign.
?	Display a list of subcommands available. Optionally, a subcommand can be specified after the ? to get information specific to that subcommand.
type	Set the file transfer mode. Valid modes are ASCII for text files, binary for files that may contain special files so that the data is transferred without any translation, and EBCDIC to transfer files in EBCDIC code.
cd	Change to the home directory on the remote host. If a directory is specified, the current directory is changed to the specified directory on the remote host.
pwd	Print the current working directory on the remote host.
ls	Print a list of the files on the remote host. If no directory is specified, files and directories in the specified directory are printed. You can direct the list of files to a file on the local host by specifying a local filename.

Subcommand	*Meaning*
mkdir *directory*	Make a new directory under the current directory on the remote host.
dir	Generate a list of files. Similar to the ls command, but produces a detailed list.
rmdir *directory*	Remove the specified directory on the remote host, provided that the directory is empty.
rename *oldname newname*	Rename a file from *oldname* to *newname* on the remote host.
delete *filename*	Delete the specified file on the remote host.
get *filename*	Transfer a file from the remote host to the local host. The name of the file is not altered. Optionally, you can specify a local *filename* to which the file from the remote host will be copied.
mget	Transfer multiple files from the remote host to the local host. You can specify a filename using a wildcard, which is expanded by UNIX. If the prompt option is set, you will be prompted for each filename for confirmation. If a prompt option is not set, all files are copied without any confirmation.
put *filename*	Transfer a file from the local host to the remote host. The name of the file is not altered. Optionally, you can specify a local filename to which the file from the remote host will be copied.
mput	Transfer multiple files from the local host to the remote host. You can specify a filename using a wildcard, which is expanded by UNIX. If the prompt option is set, you will be prompted for each filename for confirmation. If the prompt option is not set, all files are copied without confirmation.

4

GENERAL
COMMANDS

continues

Subcommand	Meaning
mdelete	Delete multiple files by specifying wildcard filenames.
append *filename*	Append a local file to the end of a file on the remote host. Optionally, you can specify a filename on the remote host to append at the end of the specified file. If the remote filename is not specified, the local filename is used by default.
open	Open a connection to a remote host by specifying a remote host name.
close	Close the existing connection to the remote host.
bye or quit	Quit the ftp session.
lcd	Change to the home directory on the local host. If a directory is specified, the current directory is changed to the specified directory on the local host.

Examples

To open an ftp session on a remote host named otherhost, execute one of the following commands:

```
ftp otherhost

ftp
ftp> open otherhost
```

In both cases, you are prompted to enter the user ID and password, if you are not set up in the .netrc file with the user ID and password. The prompts and messages appear as follows:

```
Connected to otherhost.
220 otherhost FTP server (Version 4.14 Fri Oct 10 13:39:22 CDT 1994)
ready.
Name (otherhost;testuser): testuser
331 Password required for testuser.
Password:
230 User testuser logged in.
```

After you are at the `ftp>` prompt, you can execute the `ftp` subcommands. If you want to find out which directory you are in on the remote host, execute the following subcommand:

```
ftp> pwd
257 "/home/testuser" is current directory.
```

To copy a file called `testfile` from `otherhost` to the local host, execute the `get` subcommand. Following is the subcommand and its response:

```
ftp> get testfile
200 PORT command successful.
150 Opening data connection for testfile (73 bytes).
226 Transfer complete.
80 bytes received in 0.02583 seconds (3.025 Kbytes/s)
```

Similarly, to copy a file called `testfile` from the local host to the remote host, `otherhost`, use the `put` subcommand. Following is the subcommand and its response:

```
ftp> put testfile
200 PORT command successful.
150 Opening data connection for testfile.
226 Transfer complete.
142 bytes sent in 0.02954 seconds (4.695 Kbytes/s)
```

Following is a series of commands and responses that copy a file called `testfile` in binary mode from the `/u/testuser` directory on the local host to a directory called `/u/testuser/testdir` on the remote host `otherhost`.

```
ftp otherhost
Connected to otherhost.
220 otherhost FTP server (Version 4.14 Fri Aug 5 13:39:22 CDT 1994) ready.
Name (otherhost;testuser): testuser
331 Password required for testuser.
Password:
230 User testuser logged in.
ftp> lcd /u/testuser
Local directory now /u/testuser
ftp> cd /u/testuser/testdir
250 CWD command successful.
ftp> binary
200 Type set to I.
ftp> put testfile
200 PORT command successful.
150 Opening data connection for testfile.
226 Transfer complete.
46197 bytes sent in 0.03237 seconds (1394 Kbytes/s)
ftp> quit
221 Goodbye.
```

4

GENERAL COMMANDS

Here are some more examples of transferring multiple files, listing files, and deleting multiple files:

```
ftp otherhost
Connected to otherhost.
220 otherhost FTP server (Version 4.14 Fri Aug 5 13:39:22 CDT 1994) ready.
Name (otherhost;testuser): testuser
331 Password required for testuser.
Password:
230 User testuser logged in.
ftp> mput file*
mput file1? y
200 PORT command successful.
150 Opening data connection for file1.
226 Transfer complete.
46197 bytes sent in 0.03323 seconds (1358 Kbytes/s)
mput file2? y
200 PORT command successful.
150 Opening data connection for file2.
226 Transfer complete.
44045 bytes sent in 0.01257 seconds (3422 Kbytes/s)
mput file3? y
200 PORT command successful.
150 Opening data connection for file3.
226 Transfer complete.
41817 bytes sent in 0.01172 seconds (3485 Kbytes/s)
ls -l
200 PORT command successful.
150 Opening data connection for /bin/ls.
total 176
-rw-r-----   1 testuser    author       1115 Dec 15 11:34 file1
-rw-r-----   1 testuser    author      43018 Dec 15 11:34 file2
-rw-r-----   1 testuser    author      40840 Dec 15 11:34 file3
226 Transfer complete.
mdel file*
mdel file1? y
250 DELE command successful.
mdel file2? y
250 DELE command successful.
mdel file3? y
250 DELE command successful.
```

mailx

In UNIX, you can send mail to other users in the system and receive mail from them by using the mailx commands. The mailx commands provide subcommands to facilitate saving, deleting, and responding to messages. The mailx command also provides facilities to compose and edit messages before finally sending it to one or more users.

The mail system on UNIX uses mailboxes to receive mail for a user. Each user has a system mailbox in which all mail for that user is received pending action by the user. The user can read, save, and delete the mail after the mail is received. When the user has read mail, the mail can be moved to a secondary, or personal, mailbox. The default secondary mailbox is called the mbox. The mbox is usually present in the home directory of the user. However, the user can specify the name of a file as a secondary mailbox. All messages saved in the mailbox mbox are save indefinitely until moved to other secondary mailboxes, which are sometimes known as *folders*. You can use folders to organize your mail. For example, you can organize folders by subject matter and save all mail pertaining to a subject in a particular mailbox.

You can send messages to one or more users using the mailx command. This command allows you to send mail to users on the same host or on other hosts in the network to which the local host is connected. You do not get a positive acknowledgment if the mail delivery is successful, but if the mail cannot be delivered, you are notified.

Following is a list of some of the flags that can be used with the mail command:

Flag	*Meaning*
-d	Display debug information.
-f	Display a list of messages in the default mailbox mbox. Optionally, you can specify the name of a folder in which you have saved your mail previously.
-s *subject*	Associate a subject for the mail to be created.
-v	Display detailed information by the mailx command.

Each mail has information associated with it. The following is a list of this information:

- status indicates the status of a mail. Following is a list of the various statuses of a mail item:

M	Indicates that the message will be stored in your personal mailbox.
>	Indicates the current message.
N	Indicates that the message is a new message.
P	Indicates that the message is to be preserved in the system mailbox.

4

GENERAL COMMANDS

R	Indicates that you have read the message.
U	Indicates an unread message. An unread message is one that was a new message at the last invocation of `mailx` but was not read.
*	Indicates that the message has been saved or written to a file or folder.

A message without a status indicates that the message has been read but has not been deleted or saved.

- *number* indicates a numerical ID of the message by which it can be referred to.
- `sender` indicates the user who sent the message.
- `date` indicates when the mail was received in the mailbox.
- `size` indicates the size of the message in number of lines and number of bytes.
- `subject` indicates the subject matter of the mail if the sender has associated a subject with the mail. This may or may not be present, depending on whether the mail has an associated subject.

Following is a list of subcommands you can use from the `mail>` prompt:

Subcommand	Meaning
q	Apply mailbox commands entered this session.
x	Quit.
!*command*	Start a shell, run a command, and return to the mailbox.
cd	Place you in the home directory. Optionally, you can specify a directory name to place you in the specified directory.
t	Display the current message. Optionally, you can specify a message list to display messages in that list.
n	Display the next message.
f	Display headings of the current message. Optionally, you can specify a message list and display all headings in that message list.

Subcommand	*Meaning*
e	Edit the current message. Optionally, you can specify a message number to modify that message.
d	Delete messages or the current message. Optionally, you can specify a message list to delete the message in the message list.
u	Restore deleted messages.
s *file*	Append the current message, including its heading, to a file. Optionally, you can specify a message list between s and *file* to append the specified messages to the file.
w *file*	Append the current message, excluding its heading, to a file. Optionally, you can specify a message list between w and *file* to append the specified messages to the file.
pre	Keep messages in the system mailbox. Optionally, you can specify a list of messages to keep them in system mailbox.
m *addresslist*	Create or send a new message to addresses in the *addresslist*.
r	Send a reply to senders and recipients of messages. Optionally, you can specify a list of messages to send a reply to senders and recipients of all messages in the list.
R	Send a reply only to senders of messages for the current message. Optionally, you can specify a list of messages to send reply to senders of the messages.
a	Display a list of aliases and their addresses.

Examples

You can invoke the `mailx` command by itself to display the `mail>` prompt, from which you can use the subcommands. You can get to the `mail>` prompt only if you have mail.

4

GENERAL
COMMANDS

Otherwise, you will get a message similar to you have no mail. If you have mail, prompts similar to the following are displayed:

```
mailx
Mail [5.2 UCB] Type ? for help.
"/usr/spool/mail/testuser": 1 message 1 new
>N  1 testuser     Sat Nov 16 22:49  285/9644
&
```

If you now quit the mailx command using the quit subcommand (which can be abbreviated as q), the mail is saved in your personal mailbox (the mbox file in your home directory).

To see the mail, use the mailx -f command, which results in the following dialog:

```
mailx -f
Mail [5.2 UCB] Type ? for help.
"/u/testuser/mbox": 1 message
>   1 testuser     Sat Nov 23 00:11   162/5175
&
```

To save mail in a folder from in the mailx command, execute the following subcommand:

```
& save 1 /u/testuser/folder1/file1
```

This command creates file1 from the first message in the directory /u/testuser/folder1.

If you invoke the mailx command to read the file /u/testuser/folder1, it results in the following dialog:

```
mailx -f /u/testuser/folder1
Mail [5.2 UCB] Type ? for help.
"/u/testuser/folder1": 1 message
>   1 testuser     Sat Nov 23 00:11   162/5175
&
```

Once you are in mailx, you can execute the subcommand m to create and send mail to other users as follows:

```
& m friend1
Subject: Testing mailx command
This is test of the mailx command
Here we are trying to send a mail to user friend1 with cc to friend2
Cc: friend2
&
```

The body of the mail is terminated by pressing Ctrl+D. You can send mail to multiple users using the m subcommand.

talk

You can converse with another user in real time using the `talk` command if the other user is logged on. Using the `talk` command, you can converse with users on the local host or on a remote host.

The `talk` command takes one mandatory argument: the user name or user and host name. You can optionally provide a second argument that specifies the TTY onto which the user is logged.

The user on the remote host can be specified in one of the following formats:

- *username@host*
- *host!username*
- *host.username*
- *host;username*

When you execute the `talk` command, it opens two windows—one for sending messages and one for receiving messages. The command waits for the other user to respond.

Examples

Suppose that you execute the following command to converse with the user `friend`:

```
talk friend
```

You will get the following screen:

```
[Waiting for your party to respond]

- - - - - - - - - - - - - - - - - - - - - - - - - - - - - - - - - - - - - - - - - - - - - - - - - -

```

One half of the screen is used to send messages, and other half is used to receive messages. If the specified user is not logged on, you get a message similar to `Your party is not logged on`.

The user `friend` gets the following message:

```
Message from Talk_Daemon@host1 at 0:46 ...
talk: connection requested by testuser@host1.
talk: respond with:  talk testuser@host1
[Waiting for your party to respond]
```

To start the conversation, the user `friend` has to respond with the following command:

```
talk testuser@host1
```

To quit the talk session, press Ctrl+C.

4

vacation

If you want to notify a mail sender that you are on vacation, you can use the `vacation` command. The message sent can be a customized message if you create the message in a file called `.vacation.msg` in your home directory. If this file does not exist, a system default message is sent. By default, the system message is sent only once a week to a user who sends mail to you.

The `vacation` command can be used to forward messages you receive during vacation to other users by using the `.forward` file in your home directory. Include the user names of all the users to whom you want the messages to be forwarded. The entry in the `.forward` file is of the following format:

```
testuser, "¦/usr/bin/vacation testuser"
```

The `vacation` command also lets you store the names of users who sent messages to you while you were on vacation. These user names are stored in the `.vacation.dir` and `.vacation.pag` files in your home directory.

The `vacation` command has one option flag, `-i`, which is used to initialize the `.vacation.dir` and `.vacation.pag` files before the start of your vacation.

The `.forward` file in your home directory is used by the system to identify that you are on vacation. When you come back, you should delete or rename the `.forward` file.

Before you go on vacation, use the following command to initialize the `.vacation.dir` and `.vacation.pag` files in your home directory:

```
vacation -I
```

This should be followed by the creation of the `.forward` and `.vacation.msg` files.

write

You can use the `write` command to hold a conversation with another user in the local host or remote host, just as you can with the `talk` command. To hold a conversation with another user, the following must be true:

- The user must be logged on.
- The user must not have denied permission by using the `mesg` command.

A message consists of all the characters you type until you press the Enter key. Both you and the other user can send messages this way. To end the conversation, press Ctrl+D.

Following is a list of some of the flags that can be used with the `write` command:

Flag	Meaning
-h *Handle,Reply*	Reply to a message sent by a utility or shell script using write with the reply option. The *handle* is a number generated by the system. The *reply* can be ok, cancel, or query.
-nHost	Specify a remote host if you want to hold conversation with a user on a remote host. It is also possible to specify user at a remote host as *username@host*.
-q	Find out about messages awaiting replies from users on a host and display them with their handles.

Examples

If you want to hold a conversation with a user called friend, execute the following command:

```
write friend
```

If user friend is not logged on, you get a message similar to the following:

```
friend is not logged on.
```

If the user friend has used the mesg command to turn the permission off for conversations, you will get a message similar to the following:

```
write: permission denied
```

If the write command succeeds, the user gets a message similar to the following:

```
Message from testuser on mainhost(pts/3) [Fri Nov 22 19:48:30 1996] ...
```

You can use the UNIX input redirection operator to send long messages from a file called, for example, long_message:

```
write friend < long_message
```

To start the conversation, the other user must also use the write command as follows:

```
write testuser
```

If you want to hold a conversation with user friend on the remote host otherhost, execute either of the following two commands:

```
write friend@otherhost
```

```
write -n otherhost friend
```

4

GENERAL COMMANDS

File Comparison

The following sections describe some of the commands you can use for comparing the contents of files. These commands compare the contents and, depending on various options, generate outputs of the differences between the files. There are also commands that can be used to compare the contents of directories.

cmp

The `cmp` command compares the contents of two files and generates output into standard output. Although it is possible to have one of the files be standard input, both files cannot be. You can use a - (hyphen) to indicate that the file is standard input, which is terminated using Ctrl+D. Use the `cmp` command for nontext files to find out whether they are identical. For text files, use the `diff` command, discussed later.

Following are the outputs generated by the `cmp` command:

- No output if the files are exactly identical.
- Displays the byte number and line number of the first position where the files are different.

Here are the flags that can be used with `cmp` command:

Flag	Meaning
-l	Display, for each difference, the byte number in decimal and the differing bytes in octal.
-s	Return only an exit value without generating any output. The values of the return code are 0 for identical files, 1 if the files are different, or 2 if the `cmp` file is not successful in comparing the files.

Examples

If you want to compare the new version of an executable file with the old version of the executable file, execute the following command:

```
cmp new_prog1 old_prog1
```

If the files are identical, no output will be generated. If the files are different, output similar to the following will be generated:

```
new_prog1 old_prog1 differ: byte 6, line 1
```

If you are using the cmp command in a shell script, you can use the -s flag to determine whether two files are identical. Following is part of a shell script that uses the -s command:

```
ret_code='cmp -s new_prog1 old_prog1'
if [[ $ret_code -eq 0 ]] then
   echo "Files are identical ..."
else
   echo "Files are different ..."
fi
```

If the files are identical except that one file has extra bytes at the end, use of the -l flag will generate the following output:

```
cmp -l new_prog1 old_prog1
    18   12   63
cmp: EOF on new_prog1
```

comm

If you have files that are sorted and you want to compare them, use the comm command. The comm command can be used to either exclude or include the common lines between the two files. You can use a - (hyphen) to indicate that one of the files is to be accepted from standard input.

The default output is generated on the standard output in three columns, which are as follows:

- Lines that exist only in the first file.
- Lines that exist only in the second file.
- Lines that exist in both files.

Following is a list of flags that can be used with the comm command:

Flag	Meaning
-1	Suppress the display of the first column.
-2	Suppress the display of the second column.
-3	Suppress the display of third column.

Examples

Assume that you have two files named file1 and file2. The content of the files has been displayed using the more command as follows:

4

GENERAL
COMMANDS

```
more file1
line 1
line 2
line 3
line 5
line 6
line 7
line 8
line 9

more file2
line 1
line 2
line 3
line 4
line 5
line 6
line 7
line 9
```

If you compare the two files file1 and file2, you get the following output:

```
comm file1 file2
                line 1
                line 2
                line 3
        line 4
                line 5
                line 6
                line 7
line 8
                line 9
```

The output shows that file1 has one line that is not in file2 (in column 1); file2 has one line that is not in file1 (in column 2); there are seven lines that exist in both file1 and file2 (in column 3).

If you are interested only in the differences, you can drop column 3 as follows:

```
comm -3 file1 file2
        line 4
line 8
```

If you are interested only in finding out which lines are identical in file1 and file2, you can drop columns 1 and 2 as follows:

```
comm -12 file1 file2
line 1
line 2
line 3
```

```
line 5
line 6
line 7
line 9
```

diff

Although you can compare text files with the `diff` command, you cannot compare non-text files. You can use `diff` to compare individual files or multiple files with identical names in different directories. To compare individual files, use a - (hyphen) to indicate that one of the files is to be accepted from standard input.

The group of output lines of the `diff` command is preceded by an information line containing the following information:

- Lines that are different in the first file. This may a single line number or two line numbers separated by a comma (which refers to the lines within that range).

- Action code, for which valid values are a (for lines added), c (for lines modified), and d (for lines deleted).

- Lines that are different in the second file. This may a single line number or two line numbers separated by a comma (which refers to the lines within that range).

The `diff` command generates `ed` commands. The `ed` commands can be applied to the first file; doing so makes the second file identical to the first file.

The following three forms of output are generated by the `diff` command:

- `Number1aNumber2,Number3`, which means that line `Number2` through line `Number3` in the second file must be added to the first file after line `Number1` to make the files identical. This form is followed by the actual lines from the second file preceded by a > (greater-than sign).

- `Number1dNumber2`, which means that line `Number1` through line `Number2` must be deleted from the first file to make the files identical. This form is followed by the actual lines from the first file preceded by a < (less-than sign).

- `Number1,Number2cNumber3,Number4`, which means that line `Number1` through line `Number2` in the first file must be modified by the lines `Number3` through `Number4` in the second file to make the files identical. This form is followed by the actual lines from the first file, each preceded by < (less-than sign), and then actual lines from the second file, each preceded by > (greater-than sign).

Following is a list of some of the flags that can be used with the `diff` command:

Flag	Meaning
-b	Ensure that more than one space or tab character is considered as one. However, leading space or tab characters are processed as-is.
-C LINE	Produce the output in a format different from the default format. The output first identifies the files being compared along with their creation date and time. Each modified group of lines is separated by a line with an * (asterisk) followed by lines from the first file and lines from the second file. The lines removed from the first file are designated with a - (hyphen). The lines added to the second file are designated with a + (plus sign). Lines that exist in both files but differ are designated with an ! (exclamation point). Changes that lie within the specified context lines of each other are grouped together as output.
-c LINE	Produce the output in a format different from the default format. The LINE parameter is optional. The output first identifies the files being compared along with their creation date and time. Each modified group of lines is separated by a line with an * (asterisk) followed by lines from the first file and lines from the second file. The lines removed from the first file are designated with a - (hyphen). The lines added to the second file are designated with a + (plus sign). Lines that exist in both files but differ are designated with an ! (exclamation point). Changes that lie within the specified context lines of each other are grouped together as output.
-D String	Create a merged version of the first and second files on the standard output. The C preprocessor controls are included so that a compilation of the results, without defining String, is equivalent to compiling the first file. Defining String compiles the second file.
-e	Generate output that can be input to ed to produce the second file from the first file.

Flag	*Meaning*
`-f`	Create output that is the reverse of what is produced by the `-e` flag.
`-i`	Compare the two files ignoring case of letters.
`-l`	Generate formatted output. This flag also generates a summary at the end.
`-n`	Generate output in the reverse order of the `-e` flag. Additionally, this flag generates the count of lines added and deleted.
`-r`	Execute the `diff` command on all identically named subdirectories of the specified directory.
`-s`	Generate output to obtain a list of identical files along with differences between identically named files. This flag also generates a list of files that are only in one of the directories.
`-S FILE`	Ignore files. This option can be used while comparing directories to ignore filenames that collate less than that of the specified `FILE`.
`-t`	Preserve the original indentation of the lines. The indentation of lines in the output can be modified by the use of the > (greater-than sign) or the < (less-than sign) in the output.
`-w`	Ignore all space and tab characters. That is, treat them identically for comparison purposes.

4

GENERAL COMMANDS

Examples

Assume that you have two files, `file1` and `file2`. The contents of the files are shown using the `more` command:

```
more file1
This is the first line
This is the second line
This is the fourth line
```

```
This is the fifth line
This is the sixth line
This is the seventh              line
This is the eighth line
This is the NINTH line
```

more file2
```
This is the first line
This is the second line
This is the third line
This is the fourth line
This is the sixth line
This is the seventh line
This is the eighth              line
This is the ninth line
```

The plain-vanilla `diff` command on `file1` and `file2` generates output as follows:

diff file1 file2
```
2a3
> This is the third line
4d4
< This is the fifth line
6,8c6,8
< This is the seventh              line
< This is the eighth line
< This is the NINTH line
---
> This is the seventh line
> This is the eighth              line
> This is the ninth line
```

This means add `This is the third line` to `file1`, delete `This is the fifth line` from `file1`, and modify lines 6 and 7 to `This is the seventh line` and `This is the eighth              line` in `file1` to make `file1` identical to `file2`.

If you do not care about space and tab characters, use the `-b` flag in the following command:

diff -b file1 file2
```
2a3
> This is the third line
4d4
< This is the fifth line
8c8
< This is the NINTH line
---
> This is the ninth line
```

As you can see, lines 6 and 7 are not displayed because the only reason these lines are different is the existence of extra space and tab characters.

You can display the output in special format using the -C or -c flag in the following command:

```
diff -C 0 file1 file2
*** file1          Thu Nov 28 22:15:23 1996
--- file2          Thu Nov 28 18:05:59 1996
***************
*** 2 ****
--- 3 ----
+ This is the third line
***************
*** 4 ****
- This is the fifth line
--- 4 ----
***************
*** 6,8 ****
! This is the seventh            line
! This is the eighth line
! This is the NINTH line
--- 6,8 ----
! This is the seventh line
! This is the eighth            line
! This is the ninth line
```

The output contains the filenames being compared and their creation dates and times; the output has a format different from the default diff format.

If you want to generate output in a format that can be input to ed, use the -e flag as in the following command:

```
diff -e file1 file2
6,8c
This is the seventh line
This is the eighth             line
This is the ninth line
.
4d
2a
This is the third line
.
```

This output can then be input to ed to be applied to file1 to make it identical to file2. This can be used to maintain a base version and incremental changes so that any version can be created by applying the changes to the base version. Following is an example that shows how we can make file1 identical to file2 using the -e command.

Let's redirect the output of the diff command to a file called diffout as in the following command:

```
diff -e file1 file2 > diffout
```

If you execute the `more` command on `diffout`, you will get the following output:

```
more diffout
6,8c
This is the seventh line
This is the eighth              line
This is the ninth line
.
4d
2a
This is the third line
.
```

Let's now add an extra command line at the end of the file `diffout`. The command is `w`, which ensures that when the file is input to `ed`, the output is written back to the file on which it is applied. If we now execute `more` on the file `diffout`, you can see the extra line at the end:

```
more diffout
6,8c
This is the seventh line
This is the eighth              line
This is the ninth line
.
4d
2a
This is the third line
.
w
```

To update `file1` and see the result, we use the following commands:

```
ed - file1 < diffout
more file11
This is the first line
This is the second line
This is the third line
This is the fourth line
This is the sixth line
This is the seventh line
This is the eighth              line
This is the ninth line
```

If you do not want to update the original file, use the command `1,$p` instead of `w`. This command generates the output to the standard output instead. You can also redirect the output to a file as follows:

```
ed - file1 < diffout > file1.new
```

To generate output in reverse order from that specified by -e, execute the following command with the -f flag:

```
a2
This is the third line
.
d4
c6 8
This is the seventh line
This is the eighth          line
This is the ninth line
.
```

If you do not care about whether the files have lowercase or uppercase letters, use the -i flag to execute a case-insensitive diff command as in the following command:

```
diff -i file1 file2
2a3
> This is the third line
4d4
<Ti s the fifth line
6,7c6,7
< This is the seventh          line
< This is the eighth line
- - -
> This is the seventh line
> This is the eighth
```

Notice that the lines This is the NINTH line in file1 and This is the ninth line in file2 are evaluated to be equal when we use the -i flag.

If you want to know the number of lines affected by each insertion or deletion, use the -n flag as in the following command:

```
diff -n file1 file2
a2 1
This is the third line
d4 1
d6 3
a8 3
This is the seventh line
This is the eighth              line
This is the ninth line
```

The information in this output is with respect to file1. It tells you that one line is to be inserted after line 2 and then shows the lines to be inserted, one line is to be deleted at line 4, three lines are to be deleted at line 6, and three lines are to be inserted after line 8 and then lists the lines to be inserted.

4

GENERAL COMMANDS

To ignore all tab and space characters, use the -w flag. The difference between the -b flag and the -w flag is that -b ignores all space and tab characters except leading ones, while -w ignores all space and tab characters. Following is an example of the use of the -w flag:

```
diff  -w file1 file2
2a3
> This is the third line
4d4
< This is the fifth line
8c8
< This is the NINTH line
---
> This is the ninth line
```

So far, we have seen the actions of the diff command for comparing two files. Now let's look at some examples of comparing two directories. Assume that the two subdirectories testdir1 and testdir2 exist under the current directory. Now let's see what files exist under these directories:

```
ls -R test*

testdir1:
file1     file2     file3     file4     file5     file6     testdir3

testdir1/testdir3:
filea  fileb  filec  filed  filee

testdir2:
file2     file4     file5     file7     file8     testdir3

testdir2/testdir3:
fileb  filed  filee  filef  fileg
```

The simplest form of the diff command (without any flags to compare the two directories) results in the following output:

```
diff testdir1 testdir2
Only in testdir1: file1
Only in testdir1: file3
Only in testdir1: file6
Only in testdir2: file7
Only in testdir2: file8
Common subdirectories: testdir1/testdir3 and testdir2/testdir3
```

In this example, the diff command does not go through the subdirectory testdir3 under the directory testdir1 and testdir2. If you want the diff command to traverse the subdirectory under the specified directories, use the -r flag as in the following command:

```
diff -r testdir1 testdir2
Only in testdir1: file1
Only in testdir1: file3
Only in testdir1: file6
Only in testdir2: file7
Only in testdir2: file8
Only in testdir1/testdir3: filea
Only in testdir1/testdir3: filec
Only in testdir2/testdir3: filef
Only in testdir2/testdir3: fileg
```

If you want a list of all files in the directories that are identical, use the -s command as in the following command:

```
diff -rs testdir1 testdir2
Only in testdir1: file1
Files testdir1/file2 and testdir2/file2 are identical
Only in testdir1: file3
Files testdir1/file4 and testdir2/file4 are identical
Files testdir1/file5 and testdir2/file5 are identical
Only in testdir1: file6
Only in testdir2: file7
Only in testdir2: file8
Only in testdir1/testdir3: filea
Files testdir1/testdir3/fileb and testdir2/testdir3/fileb are identical
Only in testdir1/testdir3: filec
Files testdir1/testdir3/filed and testdir2/testdir3/filed are identical
Files testdir1/testdir3/filee and testdir2/testdir3/filee are identical
Only in testdir2/testdir3: filef
Only in testdir2/testdir3: fileg
```

If you do not want to process all files whose names collate before the specified filename (in this case file2), use the -S flag as in the following command:

```
diff -r -S file2  testdir1 testdir2
Only in testdir1: file3
Only in testdir1: file6
Only in testdir2: file7
Only in testdir2: file8
Only in testdir1/testdir3: filea
Only in testdir1/testdir3: filec
Only in testdir2/testdir3: filef
Only in testdir2/testdir3: fileg
```

diff3

The diff command compares two files. If you want to compare three files at the same time, use the diff3 command. The diff3 command writes output to the standard output that contains the following notations to identify the differences:

- ==== means all three files differ.
- ====1 means the first file differs.
- ====2 means the second file differs.
- ====3 means the third file differs.

Following is a list of flags that can be used with the `diff3` command:

Flag	Meaning
-3	Produce an edit script that contains only lines containing the differences from the third file.
-E, -X	Produce an edit script in which the overlapping lines from both files are inserted by the edit script, bracketed by <<<<<< and >>>>>> lines.
-e	Create an edit script that can be input to the `ed` command to update the first file with differences that exist between the second and third files (that is, the changes that normally would be flagged with ==== and ====3).
-x	Produce an edit script to incorporate only changes flagged with ====.

The format of the generated output is as follows:

- `File Id;Number1 a` means that lines are to be added after line `Number1` in the file `File Id`. The `File Id` can be 1, 2, or 3, depending on the file it is referring to. This is followed by the lines to be added.
- `File Id;Number1[,Number2]c` means that lines in the range `Number1` through `Number2` are to be modified. This is followed by the lines to be modified.

Examples

Assume that we have three files: `file1`, `file2`, and `file3`. The contents of these three files are shown using the `more` command:

```
more file1
This is the first line in first file
This is the second line
This is the third line
This is the fourth line
This is the fifth line
```

```
This is the sixth line
This is the seventh line
This is the eighth line
This is the ninth line
```

more file2
```
This is the first line
This is the second line
This is the third line
This is the 3.5th line
This is the fourth line
This is the sixth line in second file
This is the seventh line
This is the eighth line
This is the ninth line
```

more file3
```
This is the first line
This is the second line
This is the third line
This is the fourth line
This is the sixth line in third file
This is the seventh line
This is the eighth line
This is the ninth line
This is the tenth line
This is the eleventh line
```

Now execute diff3 on these three files without using any flag, as in this command:

diff3 file1 file2 file3
```
====1
1:1c
  This is the first line in first file
2:1c
3:1c
  This is the first line
====2
1:3a
2:4c
  This is the 3.5th line
3:3a
====
1:5,6c
  This is the fifth line
  This is the sixth line
2:6c
  This is the sixth line in second file
3:5c
  This is the sixth line in third file
====3
1:9a
```

4

GENERAL COMMANDS

```
2:9a
3:9,10c
  This is the tenth line
  This is the eleventh line
```

The first group of lines starting with ====1 show that line 1 in `file1` is different from line 1 in `file2` and `file3`. The lines starting with ====2 show that line 4 in `file2` should be inserted after line 3 of `file1` and `file3` to make all three files identical. The lines starting with ==== show that lines 5 and 6 of `file1`, line 6 of `file2`, and line 5 of `file3` are all different. The lines starting with ====3 show that lines 9 and 10 of `file3` should be inserted after line 9 of `file1` and `file2` to make all three files identical.

If you are interested in finding only the differences in `file3`, use the `-3` flag as in the following command:

```
diff3 -3 file1 file2 file3
9a
This is the tenth line
This is the eleventh line
.
w
q
```

This output tells you that there are two lines (lines 9 and 10) that are present in `file3` but are not in `file1` or `file2`.

If you want to apply changes between `file2` and `file3` to `file1`, use the `-e` flag to create an edit script as in the following command:

```
diff3 -e file1 file2 file3
9a
This is the tenth line
This is the eleventh line
.
5,6c
This is the sixth line in third file
.
w
q
```

This output means that `file3` has two extra lines at line 9 and that line 6 of `file2` has been replaced by line 5 of `file3`. If, however, you are interested in changes, use the `-x` flag as in the following command:

```
diff3 -x file1 file3 file2
5,6c
This is the sixth line in second file
.
w
q
```

dircmp

If you want to compare the contents of two directories, use the `dircmp` command. This command compares the names of the files in each directory and generates a list of file-names that exist in only one of the directories followed by filenames that exist in both and whether they are identical or not.

Following is a list of flags that can be used with `dircmp` command:

Flag	Meaning
-d	Generate a list of files that exist in either of the directories followed by a list of files that exist in both directories; specify whether they are identical or different. This information is further followed by the output of the `diff` command on pairs of files that are different.
-s	Generate a list of files that exist in either of the directories followed by a list of files that are different.

Examples

Assume that the there are two subdirectories, `testdir1` and `testdir2`, in the current directory. The list of files in these directories are as follows:

```
ls testdir1
file1   file2   file3   file4   file5   file6

ls testdir2
file2   file3   file5   file6   file7   file8
```

If you want to do a plain-vanilla `dircmp` between these two directories, execute the following command:

```
dircmp testdir1 testdir2

Fri Nov 29 22:51:34 1996 testdir1 only and testdir2 only Page 1

./file1         ./file7
./file4         ./file8

Fri Nov 29 22:51:34 1996 Comparison of testdir1 and testdir2 Page 1

directory       .
different       ./file2
same            ./file3
same            ./file5
same            ./file6
```

The first part of this report lists on the left the files present only in testdir1; on the right, it lists the files found only in testdir2. The second part of the report shows a comparison of the directories and also shows which files are identical and which are different. If you want further information about the differences between the files in these directories, use the -d flag as in the following command:

testdir -d testdir1 testdir2

```
Fri Nov 29 22:56:01 1996 testdir1 only and testdir2 only Page 1

./file1          ./file7
./file4          ./file8

Fri Nov 29 22:56:01 1996 Comparison of testdir1 and testdir2 Page 1

directory        .
different        ./file2
same             ./file3
same             ./file5
same             ./file6

Fri Nov 29 22:56:01 1996 diff of ./file2 in testdir1 and testdir2 Page 1

1c1
< This file is in testdir1
---
> This file is in testdir2
```

If you only want a list of the files that are unique to each directory and the files that are different, use the -s flag as in the following command:

dircmp -s testdir1 testdir2

```
Fri Nov 29 23:39:59 1996 testdir1 only and testdir2 only Page 1

./file1          ./file7
./file4          ./file8

Fri Nov 29 23:39:59 1996 Comparison of testdir1 and testdir2 Page 1

different        ./file2
```

If you want to suppress the display of identical files, but you want a list of the files that are different and the difference between these files, execute the dircmp command with both -s and -d flags.

sdiff

The command sdiff compares two files and displays output on the standard output in a side-by-side format. Following is the detail of the display format:

- If the two lines are identical, the command displays each line of the two files with a series of spaces between them.
- If the line exists in only the first file, a < (less-than sign) is displayed at the end of the line.
- If the line exists in only the second file, a > (greater-than sign) is displayed at the beginning of the line.
- If the lines from the two files are different, a ¦ (vertical bar) is displayed between the lines.

The flags that can be used with `sdiff` command are as follows:

Flag	Meaning
-s	If you do not want to display the identical lines.
-w *number*	Set the width of the display to *number*.
-1	Display only the line from the first file if the lines from the two files are identical.
-o *file*	Create a merged file from the first and second file depending on a number of subcommands you can specify.

Examples

Assume that we have two files, `file1` and `file2`, whose contents are displayed using the more command:

```
more file1
This is the first line in first file
This is the second line
This is the third line
This is the fourth line
This is the fifth line
This is the sixth line
This is the seventh line
This is the eighth line
This is the ninth line

more file2
This is the first line
This is the second line
This is the third line
This is the 3.5th line
This is the fourth line
This is the sixth line in second file
```

```
This is the seventh line
This is the eighth line
This is the ninth line
```

If we execute `sdiff` command on the two files `file1` and `file2`, we get the following result:

```
sdiff file1 file2
This is the first line in first file                    |  This is the f
irst line                                                  irst line
This is the second line                                    This is the s
econd line                                                 econd line
This is the third line                                     This is the t
hird line                                                  hird line
                                                        >  This is the 3

.5th line
This is the fourth line                                    This is the f
ourth line                                                 ourth line
This is the fifth line                                  |  This is the s
ixth line in second file                                   ixth line
This is the sixth line                                  <
This is the seventh line                                   This is the s
eventh line                                                eventh line
This is the eighth line                                    This is the e
ighth line                                                 ighth line
This is the ninth line                                     This is the n
inth line                                                  inth line
```

If, however, you do not want to display the identical lines, use the -s flag as in the following command:

```
sdiff -s file1 file2
This is the first line in first file                    |  This is the f
irst line                                                  irst line
                                                        >  This is the 3
.5th line
This is the fifth line                                  |  This is the s
ixth line in second file                                   ixth line
This is the sixth line                                  <
```

You can use the -1 flag to display only the line from the first file if the lines are identical so that the other lines stand out:

```
sdiff -l  file1 file2
This is the first line in first file                    |  This is the f
irst line                                                  irst line
This is the second line
This is the third line
                                                        >  This is the 3

.5th line
This is the fourth line
```

```
This is the fifth line                              ¦   This is the s
ixth line in second file
This is the sixth line                              <
This is the seventh line
This is the eighth line
This is the ninth line
```

File-Manipulation Commands

The following sections discuss several commands you can use to manipulate various attributes of one or more files, as well as to copy and move files from one location to another. The various attributes that can be manipulated include modification time, permission, and more.

touch

The `touch` command can be used for a number of purposes depending on whether or not a file already exists. If a file does not exist, the `touch` command creates it (if you have write access to the directory). If a file is already present, the `touch` command modifies the last modification time of the file.

Examples

To create a file called `testfile` in the current directory, execute the following command:

```
touch testfile
```

To create `testfile` in the `/u/testuser/testdir`, execute the following command:

```
touch /u/testuser/testdir/testfile
```

chmod

You may have to modify the permission of a directory or files to either secure them or to make them accessible to others. You can use the `chmod` command to modify the permission for files and directories. The permission in UNIX is specified in an octal number (0 thorough 7). Permission for a file or directory can be specified for the following:

- Owner: The user who created the file.
- Group: The group to which the owner belongs.
- World or others: Users other than the owner and users in the group to which the owner belongs.

For each of these entities, one octal number is specified to designate the permission granted. The permission granted to the owner, group, and world is derived from three bits associated with read, write, and execute authority for the file. That is, the bit for read has a value of 1 if read permission is to be granted; the bit for write has a value of 1 if write permission is to be granted, and the bit for execute has a value of 1 if execute permission is to be granted.

You should be aware that the execute bit functions differently for directories than it does for files. The execute permission for a directory is used to designate whether you can access that directory.

The combination of these three bits is expressed as an octal number and is used to designate the permission. The weight associated with the read bit is 4, the weight associated with the write bit is 2, and the weight associated with the execute bit is 1. The value of the permission is derived as follows:

```
(4 * value of read bit) + (2 * value of write bit) +
③(1 * value of execute bit)
```

The value of the permission can vary from 0 (no read, write, or execute permission) to 7 (read, write, and execute permission).

For example, if you want to provide read and write permission but no execute permission, the value to be used is calculated as follows:

```
(4 * 1) + (2 * 1) + (1 * 0) = 6
```

Remember that execute permission for a directory means that the directory can be accessed. That is, operations can be performed on files residing in that directory. If you provide write permissions to a directory, the user can read, write, delete, and execute all files in that directory, regardless of the permissions associated with the individual files.

With the chmod command, you can specify the new permissions you want on the file or directory. The new permission can be specified in one the following ways:

- As a three-digit numeric octal code
- As symbolic mode

Examples

Suppose that you want the file testfile to have these permissions:

- Owner with read, write, and execute permission
- Group with read only permission
- Others with execute only permission

To assign these permissions, you must execute the following command:

```
chmod 741 testfile
```

If you are using the symbolic mode, the following must be specified:

- Whose permission (owner, group, or others) you want to change.
- What operation—+ (add), – (subtract), or = (equals)—you want to perform on the permission.
- The permission (r, w, x, and so on).

If you want to set up the permission for testfile owned by you in the current directory so that only you and users in your group can read and write the file, execute the following command using absolute permissions:

```
chmod 660 testfile
```

If you want to add write permission for the group for testfile in the current directory (assuming that currently testfile has 741 permission), execute the following command:

```
chmod g+w testfile
```

Similarly, if you want to revoke the read permission for others for testfile in the current directory, execute the following command:

```
chmod o-r testfile
```

If you want to grant the same permissions to the world (others) as the group for testfile in the current directory has, execute the following command:

```
chmod o=g testfile
```

> **NOTE**
>
> Modifying the permissions does not have any effect on the root user. The root user has access to all files and directories regardless of the permissions you may have granted.

4

GENERAL
COMMANDS

chgrp

If you want to change the group to which the file belongs, use the chgrp command. The group must be one of the groups to which the owner belongs. That is, the group must be either the primary group or one of the secondary groups of the owner.

Examples

Assume that user `testuser` owns the file `testfile`, and the group of the file is `staff`. Also assume that `testuser` belongs to the groups `staff` and `devt`. To change the owner of `testfile` from `staff` to `devt`, execute the following command:

```
chgrp devt testfile
```

chown

If you want to change the owner of a file or directory, use the `chown` command.

> **CAUTION**
>
> On UNIX systems with disk quotas, only the `root` user can change the owner of a file or directory.

Examples

If the file `testfile` is owned by the user called `testuser`, you can change the ownership of the file to user `friend` by executing the following command:

```
chown friend testfile
```

rm

When you are done with a file and do not want to use it any more, you may want to remove the file to regain the disk space used by the file. The `rm` command lets you do this by removing files permanently from the disk. If an entry is the last link to a file, the file is deleted. To remove a file from a directory, you do not need either read or write permission to the file, but you do need write permission to the directory containing the file. The `rm` command is usually used to remove files, but it provides a special flag `-r` to remove files in a directory recursively, including the directory and its subdirectories.

Following is a list of some of the flags that can be used with the `rm` command:

Flag	Meaning
`-i`	Interactively remove the files.
`-f`	Remove the files without any messages. This flag does not generate any messages for cases in which a file does not exist or you do not have permission to remove one or more files.

Flag	Meaning
-r	Remove files within a directory and directories themselves recursively.

The native version of the rm command does not ask for confirmation before removing files. You should be careful when using wildcards with the rm command.

Examples

If you want to remove all files starting with test in the current directory, execute the following command:

```
rm test*
```

However, if you make a typing mistake and type rm test *, you will remove all the files because of the asterisk (*).

> **CAUTION**
>
> Be careful when using wildcards with the rm command. Be sure that you have typed the command correctly before you remove a file; once a file is removed, it cannot be recovered.

To avoid disastrous mistakes, use the -i flag to indicate that you want to execute the rm command in interactive mode. In this mode, the system asks you for confirmation before removing files. Only if you confirm the prompt by pressing Y will the system remove the file. Following is the dialog you can have with the system if you want to remove two files in the current directory: testfile1 and testfile2, using the -i flag with the rm command:

```
rm -i testfile*
Remove file testfile1? y
Remove file testfile2? y
```

You can use the -f flag with the rm command if you do not want to see any messages from the command. Usually, rm displays a message if a file is not present (for example, if you provide an incorrect filename). However, using the -f flag forces rm to not display any messages. Suppose that you execute the following command:

```
rm -f testfile
```

The file testfile is deleted if it is present, and no action is taken if testfile is not present. In either case, you will not see any message from the rm command. Also, the rm -f command always has a return code of 0 (zero).

4

GENERAL
COMMANDS

You can use the `-r` flag to remove files in directories recursively, including directories and subdirectories. If there is a directory called `testdir` under the current directory that, in turn, has the files `testfile1` and `testfile2`, you can execute the following command to remove the files `testfile1` and `testfile2` as well as the directory `testdir`:

```
rm -r testdir
```

It is advisable that you set up an alias for the `rm` command as `rm -i` in your environment so that you have to confirm before deleting any files.

The `rm` command processes a hard-linked file in a different way. If you have a `testfile1` file in your current directory, execute the following command to create a file called `testfile2` that is hard-linked to the file `testfile1`:

```
ln testfile1 testfile2
```

This command, in effect, creates two identical files: `testfile1` and `testfile2`. Suppose that you now execute the following command:

```
ls -l testfile*
```

You get the following result:

```
-rw-r--r--   2 testuser     staff          10 Nov  3 14:28 testfile1
-rw-r--r--   2 testuser     staff          10 Nov  3 14:28 testfile2
```

In this example, both `testfile1` and `testfile2` show the number of links as 2 because they are linked using a hard link. Now suppose that you remove the file `testfile1` using the `rm` command as follows:

```
rm testfile1
```

The system must take two actions—to remove the file `testfile1` and to decrease the link count of the file `testfile2` from 2 to 1. If you repeat the `ls` command, you get the following display:

```
-rw-r--r--   1 testuser     staff          10 Nov  3 15:38 testfile2
```

Notice that the number of links for `testfile2` is 1.

mv

If you are not satisfied with a filename, you may want to name the file differently. The `mv` command lets you do that. In addition, the `mv` command allows you to move files from one directory to another, retaining the original filename. This action is equivalent to copying the files from the source directory to the destination directory and then removing the file from the source directory. You may choose to move files if you are reorganizing your files. When you are moving files or directories, the target file or directory gets the permission of the source file or directory, regardless of whether or not the target file or directory already exists.

Following is a list of some of the flags that may be used with the `mv` command:

Flag	Meaning
`-i`	Move or rename files interactively.
`-f`	Move or rename files without any messages. Use of this flag suppresses messages when you are trying to rename a nonexistent file or you do not have permission to rename a file.

The `mv` command takes two arguments. The first argument is the source file or directory name; the second argument is the destination file or directory. However, the behavior of the `mv` command depends on whether the destination file or directory name exists.

If you move files within the same file system, all links to other files are retained. But if you move the files across file systems, the links are not retained.

Examples

To rename a file in the current directory, use the following command:

```
mv source_file dest_file
```

If the file `dest_file` does not exist, a new `dest_file` is created by copying `source_file` into it; the original `source_file` is removed. If `dest_file` exists and you have write permission to it, `source_file` is copied to `dest_file` and removed. On the other hand, if you do not have permission, the `mv` command does not take any action.

To move `source_file` from the current directory to the `/u/testuser/target_dir` directory, retaining the name, execute one of the following commands:

```
mv source_file /u/testuser/target_dir
```

```
mv source_file /u/testuser/target_dir/.
```

If the file already exists in `/u/testuser/target_dir`, the existing file is overwritten.

To move `source_file` from the current directory to the `/u/testuser/target_dir` directory with the name `target_file`, execute the following command:

```
mv source_file target_dir/target_file
```

If you are not sure whether the file `target_file` exists, use the `-i` flag as follows:

```
mv -i source_file target_dir/target_file
```

If the file `target_file` exists, the system prompts you to confirm whether you want to move the file.

The . (period) as the target filename indicates that the source filename is to be retained. This convention is especially useful if you want to move multiple files to another directory. If you want to move all files with names beginning with `test` to the `/u/testuser/target_dir` directory, execute the following command:

```
mv test* /u/testuser/target_dir/.
```

To rename the directory `source_dir` to the `/u/testuser/target_dir` directory, execute the following command:

```
mv /u/guahs/source_dir /u/testuser/dest_dir
```

If the directory `dest_dir` does not exist, the directory `/u/testuser/source_dir` is renamed to `/u/testuser/dest_dir`. If `/u/testuser/dest_dir` exists and you have write permissions to it, all the files and subdirectories under `/u/testuser/source_dir` are moved to `/u/testuser/dest_dir`.

cp

The `cp` command can be used to make a copy of the contents of one or more source files as specified target files. If the target file already exists, it is overwritten with the contents of the source file. The behavior of the `cp` command varies depending on whether the source and the target are files or directories.

Following is a list of some of the flags that can be used with the `cp` command:

Flag	Meaning
-p	Retain the modification date and time as well as permission modes of the source file.
-i	Execute the copy command in interactive mode so that it asks for confirmation if the target file already exists.
-h	Follow the symbolic links.
-r	Copy files under the specified directories and their subdirectories. Treat special files, such as linked files, the same way as regular files.

Examples

You can execute the following `cp` command (its simplest form) to copy `source_file` to `target_file` under the current directory:

```
cp source_file target_file
```

If you want to copy `source_file` to the `/u/testuser/target_dir` directory retaining the filename, execute the following command:

```
cp source_file /u/testuser/target_dir/.
```

To copy all files in `/u/testuser/source_dir` to the `/u/testuser/target_dir` directory while retaining the filenames, the last modification date and time, and permissions, execute the following command:

```
cp -p /u/testuser/source_dir/* /u/testuser/target/dir/.
```

This command does not copy any subdirectories or files under those subdirectories. To copy all the files in a directory, as well as its subdirectories and files in those subdirectories, while retaining the last modification date and time and permissions for all files and subdirectories, use the following command:

```
cp -r /u/testuser/source_dir /u/testuser/target_dir/.
```

If you are not sure whether the target file already exists, use the `-i` flag. Following is the dialog for copying `testfile` from the current directory to the `/u/testuser/testdir` directory assuming that `testfile` already exists in the `/u/testuser/testdir` directory:

```
cp -i testfile /u/testuser/testdir/.
overwrite /u/testuser/testdir/testfile? y
```

cat

You have seen that the `cp` command allows you to copy one file into another file. It does not allow you, however, to copy multiple files into the same file. To concatenate multiple files into a single file, use the `cat` command. By default, the `cat` command generates output into the standard output and accepts input from standard input. The `cat` command takes in one or more filenames as its arguments. The files are concatenated in the order they appear in the argument list.

Following is a list of some of the flags that can be used with the `cat` command:

Flag	Meaning
-b	Eliminate line numbers from blank lines when used with the -n flag.

continues

4

GENERAL COMMANDS

Flag	Meaning
-e	Display a $ (dollar sign) at the end of each line, when specified with the -v flag.
-n	Display output lines preceded by line numbers, numbered sequentially from 1.
-q	Suppress messages if the cat command cannot find one or more of the input files.
-v	Display nonprintable characters in the file as printable characters.

CAUTION

If you are using the output redirection operator (>) to redirect the standard output of the cat command, be careful not to use one of the input filenames as the output filename. If you do that, the input filename is overwritten. Some UNIX versions may give you an error message when you try to do that but will overwrite the file anyway.

If you are accepting input from the standard input, you should press Ctrl+D to indicate the end of the input.

Examples

In its most simple form, you can just type the command cat, which puts you in entry mode. In this mode, you can type multiple lines; press Ctrl+D to signal the end of the input. The cat command will display the lines you have just entered:

```
cat
This is test line 1
This is test line 1
This is test line 2
This is test line 2
Ctrl+D
```

You should be aware that the cat command does not provide any prompt, as is shown in the preceding example.

If you want display a file called testfile in the current directory on your terminal, execute the following command:

```
cat testfile
```

This command produces output such as the following:

```
This is a test file
This does not contain anything meaningful
This is for demo only
```

Be careful if the file is big. A large file will scroll by on your terminal, and you will see only the last few lines. You can get around this by piping the output to either the more or pg command as follows:

```
cat testfile ¦ more
```

To concatenate multiple files for display on the terminal, use the following command:

```
cat testfile1 testfile2 testfile3
```

If you want to concatenate these files into a file called testfile, use the redirection operator > as follows:

```
cat testfile1 testfile2 testfile2 > testfile
```

If the file testfile already exists, it is overwritten with the concatenated files testfile1, testfile2, and testfile3. If testfile already exists and you want to concatenate at the end of the existing file, instead of using the redirection operator >, use the >> operator (two consecutive greater-than signs) as follows:

```
cat testfile1 testfile2 testfile2 >> testfile
```

If you try to concatenate a file or a number of files but one or more files do not exist, cat concatenates all the available files and, at the end, generates a message about the nonexistent files. Suppose that you want to concatenate two files, testfile1 and testfile2, into the file testfile in the current directory, but you mistype testfile2 as testtile2 while executing the following command:

```
cat testfile1 testtile2 > testfile
```

In this example, you will get a message similar to the following, and testfile will have only the contents of testfile1:

```
cat: cannot open testtile2
```

If you use the -q flag, you will not see the error message.

If you have testfile in the current directory containing the following lines (note that the last line contains special characters), cat shows the following:

```
This is a test file

This file does not contain anything meaningful
This file is for demo only
^F^F^F^F^F
```

If you execute the `cat` command with the `-n` flag, `cat` will display lines with line numbers, but the last line with special characters will be displayed as a blank line:

```
cat -n testfile
     1  This is a test file
     2
     3  This file does not contain anything meaningful
     4  This is for demo only
     5
```

If you want to be sure that the blank lines displayed actually do not contain any characters other than nonprintable ones, use the `-v` flag with the `cat` command. This flag ensures that the nonprintable characters are displayed as printable characters:

```
cat -v testfile
This is a test file

This file does not contain anything meaningful
This is for demo only
^F^F^F^F^F
```

rcp

So far, we have seen a number of commands that move or copy files between directories within the local host. If you need to copy files from one host to another, you can use the `rcp` command to copy files between the same or different hosts. You can execute the `rcp` command on a local host to copy files between the local host and a remote host or between two remote hosts.

The filename on the remote host is preceded by the remote host ID as `hostname:/dirname/filename`. The colon (`:`) is used as a delimiter between the host name and the filename.

It is also possible to specify the user name at the remote host as `username@hostname:/dirname/filename`. The @ (at sign) is used as a delimiter between the user name and the host name. The user name, however, is optional. If not specified, the user name at the remote host is the same as user name at the local host.

If neither the source nor the target file specifies the host name, the `rcp` command behaves the same way as the `cp` command.

If the filename on the remote host is not qualified fully, starting with the root directory, the filename or directory name is assumed to start with the home directory of the remote user.

If the files do not already exist on the remote host, they are created with the default permission of the remote user. If the files already exist on the remote host, the permissions of the target files are preserved.

As you can with the `cp` command, you can use the `rcp` command to copy directories and files within directories.

Following is a list of some of the flags that can be used with the `rcp` command:

Flag	Meaning
-p	Create the target file with the modification date and time of the source file as well as the permission of the source file.
-r	Copy files recursively while copying directories.

> **NOTE**
>
> To use the `rcp` command to transfer files from or to a remote host, you must have the local host name defined in the `/etc/hosts.equiv` file at the remote host, or the local host name and the user name defined in the `.rhosts` file in the user's home directory on the remote host.

Examples

If you want to copy `testfile` from the current directory to `testfile` in the directory `testdir` under the home directory on the remote host called `otherhost`, execute the following command:

```
rcp testfile otherhost;testdir/testfile
```

If the user name on the local host is `testuser`, this command will assume that the user name on the remote host is `testuser`. If the user name `testuser` does not exist on the remote host and you must use the user name `newtestuser` on the remote host, execute the following command:

```
rcp testfile newtestuser@otherhost;testdir/testfile
```

If you must transfer `testfile` from a remote host `otherhost1` to another remote host `otherhost2`, and you want to preserve the modification date and time as well as the permissions, execute the following command:

```
rcp -p testuser1@otherhost1:testfile testuser2@otherhost2:testfile
```

This command copies `testfile` from the home directory of user `testuser1` on the remote host `otherhost1` to `testfile` in the home directory of `testuser2` on remote host `otherhost2`.

4

GENERAL COMMANDS

If you want to copy all the files in the directory `/u/testuser/testdir` from the remote host `otherhost` to the current directory on the local host, execute the following command:

```
rcp testuser@otherhost:/u/testuser/testdir/* .
```

This command does not copy any subdirectories you may have in `testdir` or any files in those subdirectories. To copy all the subdirectories and files in those subdirectories, use the following command:

```
rcp -r testuser@otherhost:/u/testuser/testdir/* .
```

ln

Sometimes, you have to provide alternate names for a file. This task can be achieved by linking a filename to another filename using the `ln` command. It is possible to link a file to another name in the same directory or to the same name in another directory.

When linking a filename to another filename, you can specify only two arguments: the source filename and the target filename. When linking a filename to a directory, you can specify multiple filenames to be linked to the same directory.

If you are linking using hard links, you cannot link to a file in another file system. If you are using soft links, however, you can link filenames across file systems.

The flags that can be used with the `ln` command are as follows:

Flag	Meaning
-s	Create a soft link to another file or directory. In a soft link, the linked file contains the name of the original file. When an operation on the linked filename is done, the name of the original file in the link is used to reference the original file.
-f	Ensure that the destination filename is replaced by the linked filename if the file already exists.

By default, the `ln` command creates a hard link.

Examples

If you want to link `testfile1` to `testfile2` in the current directory, execute the following command:

```
ln testfile1 testfile2
```

This command creates a hard-linked `testfile2`, linking it to `tesftfile1`. In this case, if one of the files is removed, the other will remain unaltered.

If `testfile` is in the current directory and is to be linked to `testfile` in the directory `/u/testuser/testdir`, execute the following command:

```
ln testfile /u/testuser/testdir
```

To create a symbolic link of `testfile1` in the current directory, execute the following command:

```
ln -s testfile1 testfile2
```

This command creates a linked `testfile2`, which contains the name of `testfile1`. If you remove `testfile1`, you are left with an orphan `testfile2`, which points nowhere.

If you want to link all the files in the current directory to another directory, `/u/testuser/testdir`, execute the following command:

```
ln * /u/testuser/testdir/.
```

Directory-Manipulation Commands

When you are set up as a user in a UNIX operating system, you usually are set up with the directory `/u/`*username* as your home directory. To organize your files, you must set up directories of your liking. The following sections present the commands to create and remove directories.

mkdir

To create a directory, use the `mkdir` command. The `mkdir` command accepts multiple directory names for creation at the same time. As you did with files, you can use a relative path name or an absolute path name to create a directory. To create a directory, you must have write permission for its parent directory. UNIX uses the current permission settings (refer to the `umask` command) to set the permission for the directory.

Following is a list of the flags that can be used with the `mkdir` command:

Flag	Meaning
-p	Create all the directories in the part name of the specified directory if they do not exist.
-m	Permission to specify permission for the directory to be created.

Examples

If your current directory is /u/testuser, you can use the following command to create a directory called temp under the directory /u/testuser, whose absolute path name is /u/testuser/temp:

```
mkdir temp
```

You can also use the following command to have the same effect as the previous one:

```
mkdir /u/testuser/temp
```

Use this command to create the /u/temp directory:

```
mkdir ../temp
```

In this example, we used .. (two consecutive periods) as part of the relative path name to indicate that the directory temp will be created under the directory one level up, that is, /u.

To create testdir1 and testdir2 in the current directory, use the following command:

```
mkdir testdir1 /u/testuser/temp/testdir2
```

This command creates testdir1 in the current directory and creates testdir2 in /u/testuser/temp (assuming that it exists). In this example, testdir1 uses a relative path name and /u/testuser/temp/testdir2 uses an absolute path name.

If the directory testdir is already present and you try to create the directory again, you get a message similar to the following:

```
mkdir: cannot create testdir.
testdir: File exists
```

If you want to create the directory testdir under the current directory and grant the access 770 to it, execute the following command:

```
mkdir -m 770 testdir
```

If you want to create the directory testdir under the current directory and create the subdirectory temp under testdir, create both of them using a single command as follows:

```
mkdir -p testdir/temp
```

rmdir

When you are done with a directory or you run out of space and want to remove a directory, use the rmdir command. You can remove a directory only if it is empty, that is, if all the files and directories in it have been removed. You can specify multiple directory names as arguments to `rmdir` command. To remove a directory, you must have write permission to the parent directory.

You can use the `-p` flag with the `rmdir` command. The `-p` flag removes all the directories in the specified path name.

Examples

If your current directory is `/u/testuser`, and it contains the `temp` subdirectory, you can remove `temp` with this command:

```
rmdir temp
```

If the directory `temp` is not empty, you will get a message similar to the following:

```
rmdir: Directory temp is not empty.
```

Assume that you are in the directory `/u/testuser` and that it contains a subdirectory `testdir`; also assume that the subdirectory `testdir` contains a subdirectory `temp`. To remove the directory `testdir` in the current directory and the subdirectory `temp` under `testdir`, execute the following command (assuming that all the files and directories under them have been removed):

```
rmdir -p testdir/temp
```

File Information Commands

Each file and directory in UNIX has several attributes associated with it. UNIX provides several commands to inquire about and process these attributes.

ls

The `ls` command can be used to inquire about the various attributes of one or more files or directories. You must have read permission to a directory to be able to use the `ls` command on that directory and the files under that directory. The `ls` command generates output to standard output, which can be redirected to a file using the UNIX redirection operator >.

You can provide the names of one or more filenames or directories to the `ls` command. The file and directory names are optional. If you do not provide them, UNIX processes the current directory.

Be default, the list of files within a directory is sorted by filename. You can modify the sort order by using some of the flags discussed later.

4

GENERAL COMMANDS

You should be aware that files starting with a . (period) are not processed unless you use the -a flag with the ls command. This means that entries starting with . (single period) and .. (two consecutive periods) are not processed by default.

Following is a list of some of the flags that can be used with the ls command:

Flag	Meaning
-A	List all entries in a directory except . (single period) and .. (two consecutive periods).
-a	List all entries in a directory including hidden files (filenames starting with a . (period)).
-b	Display nonprintable characters. The characters are displayed in an octal (\nnn) notation.
-c	Use the time of the last modification of the i-node. When used with the -t flag, the output is sorted by the time of last modification of the i-node. When used with the -l flag, the time displayed is the last modification time of the i-node. This flag must be used with the -t or -l flag.
-C	Sort output vertically in a multiple column format. This is the default method when output is to a terminal.
-d	Restrict the information displayed to that of only the directory specified. By default, the information about the files or subdirectories under a directory is also displayed.
-e	Display the following information for each specified file or directory:

- Permission associated with the files and directories
- Number of links
- Owner
- Group
- Size (in bytes)
- Time of last modification

Flag	Meaning
	• Name of each file. For a special file, the size field contains the major and minor device numbers. If the file is a symbolic link, the path name of the linked-to file is printed preceded by a -> (a minus sign followed by a greater-than sign). The attributes of the symbolic link are displayed.
-f	List the name in each slot for each directory specified in the directory parameter. This flag turns off the -l, -t, -s, and -r flags and turns on the -a flag. The order of the listing is the order in which entries appear in the directory.
-F	Put special characters before different file types as follows: • / (slash) after each directory • * (asterisk) if the file is executable • = (equal sign) if the file is a socket • ¦ (pipe sign) if the file is a FIFO • @ (at sign) for a symbolic link
-g	Display the following information for files and directories: • Permission • Number of links • Group • Size (in bytes) • Time of last modification
-i	Display the i-node number in the first column of the report for each file.
-l	Display the following information about specified files and directories: • Permission • Number of links

4

GENERAL COMMANDS

continues

Flag	Meaning
	• Owner
	• Group
	• Size (in bytes)
	• Time of last modification
-m	Display the output in a comma-separated format.
-n	Display the following information for specified files and directories:
	• Permission
	• Number of links
	• Owner ID
	• Group ID
	• Size (in bytes)
	• Time of last modification
-o	Display the following information about specified files and directories:
	• Permission
	• Number of links
	• Owner ID
	• Size (in bytes)
	• Time of last modification
-p	Put a slash (/) after each directory name.
-q	Display nondisplayable characters in filenames as a ? (question mark).
-r	Reverse the order of the sort. If the list is to be displayed in name order, it will be displayed in reverse name order. If the list is to be displayed in descending time order (using the -t flag, that is, the latest one first), the list will be displayed in ascending time order (oldest one first).
-R	List all subdirectories recursively under the specified directory.

Flag	Meaning
-s	Provide the size of files and directories in kilobytes.
-t	Sort the list of entries by time of last modification (latest first) instead of by name.
-u	Use the time of last access instead of the time of last modification. If used with -l, the time of last access is displayed instead of the time of last modification. If used with -t, the output is sorted by the time of last access instead of last modification. This flag must be used with the -l and -t flags.
-x	Sort the output horizontally in a multiple-column format.
-1	Display the output as one entry per line.

The permission details displayed by the ls command when certain flags are used (such as -l) consists of 10 characters, details of which are as follows:

- **Byte 1:** d designates a directory, b designates a block special file, c designates a character special file, l designates a symbolic link, p designates a first-in, first-out (FIFO) special file, s designates a local socket, designates an ordinary file (for example, one that contains text).

- **Byte 2:** r if read permission for owner has been granted, - (hyphen) if read permission for owner has not been granted.

- **Byte 3:** w if write permission for owner has been granted, - (hyphen) if write permission for owner has not been granted.

- **Byte 4:** x if execute permission for owner has been granted, - (hyphen) if execute permission for owner has not been granted, s if the file has set-user-ID mode.

- **Byte 5:** r if read permission for group has been granted. - (hyphen) if read permission for group has not been granted.

- **Byte 6:** w if write permission for group has been granted, - (hyphen) if write permission for group has not been granted.

- **Byte 7:** x if execute permission for group has been granted, - (hyphen) if execute permission for group has not been granted, s if the file has setgroup-ID mode.

- **Byte 8:** r if read permission for others has been granted, - (hyphen) if read permission for others has not been granted.

4

GENERAL COMMANDS

- **Byte 9:** w if write permission for others has been granted, - (hyphen) if write permission for others has not been granted.
- **Byte 10:** x if execute permission for others has been granted, - (hyphen) if execute permission for others has not been granted.

The execute permission for a file means that the file is an executable file. But the execute permission for a directory means that you can execute searches on the specified directory to locate one or more files.

Examples

Assume that the following files and directories are present in the current directory: .dot1, test1, test2, test3, and test4. Also assume that test2 is a directory.

The simplest form of the ls command can be used to get the list of files and directories in the current directory as follows:

```
ls
test1   test2 test3   test4 test5
```

In this list, the entry .dot1 is not displayed because the file .dot1 is a hidden file. To display all the entries including the hidden files, execute the following command:

```
ls -a
. .. .dot1 test1   test2 test3   test4 test5
```

From this output, you cannot see details about any entry. To get a detailed list of all the files and directories, execute the following command:

```
ls -la
total 56
drwxrwx---   3 testuser    author    3072 Nov 24 17:35 .
drwxr-xr-x  36 root        system    2048 Nov 23 19:51 ..
-rw-r--r--   1 testuser    author       0 Nov 24 14:54 .dot1
-rw-r--r--   1 testuser    author      10 Nov 24 17:36 test1
drwxr-xr-x   2 testuser    author     512 Nov 24 17:32 test2
-rw-r--r--   1 testuser    author       0 Nov 24 14:58 test3
-rw-r--r--   1 testuser    author       0 Nov 24 17:33 test4
-rw-r--r--   1 testuser    author   11885 Nov 24 11:50 test5
```

Use of the -a flag displays the two special entries that are present in all directories: . (a single period) to identify the specified directory and .. (two consecutive periods) to identify the parent directory of the specified directory. In the preceding example, . (a single period) identifies current directory; .. (two consecutive periods) identify the parent directory.

If you just want to have a list of directories, execute the following command with the -d flag:

```
ls -ald
drwxrwx---    3 testuser    author        3072 Nov 24 17:15 .
```

As you have seen in these examples, the list of files and directories are ordered by name. If you want to get a list of the entries by time of last modification so that you know which files you worked on last, execute the following command:

```
ls -lat
total 56
drwxrwx---    3 testuser    author     3072 Nov 24 17:37 .
-rw-r--r--    1 testuser    author       10 Nov 24 17:36 test1
-rw-r--r--    1 testuser    author        0 Nov 24 17:33 test4
drwxr-xr-x    2 testuser    author      512 Nov 24 17:32 test2
-rw-r--r--    1 testuser    author        0 Nov 24 14:58 test3
-rw-r--r--    1 testuser    author        0 Nov 24 14:54 .dot1
-rw-r--r--    1 testuser    author    11885 Nov 24 11:50 test5
drwxr-xr-x   36 root        system     2048 Nov 23 19:51 ..
```

Until now, we have not specified any file or directory name in the ls command. If you want to search for all entries that start with test, specify test* as the entry name, as in this example:

```
ls -la test*
-rw-r--r--    1 testuser    author       10 Nov 24 17:36 test1
-rw-r--r--    1 testuser    author        0 Nov 24 14:58 test3
-rw-r--r--    1 testuser    author        0 Nov 24 17:33 test4
-rw-r--r--    1 testuser    author    11885 Nov 24 11:50 test5

test2:
total 16
drwxr-xr-x    2 testuser    author      512 Nov 24 17:32 .
drwxrwx---    3 testuser    author     3072 Nov 24 17:41 ..
-rw-r--r--    1 testuser    author        0 Nov 24 17:45 test21
-rw-r--r--    1 testuser    author        0 Nov 24 14:58 test22
```

Notice that the entries . (single period), .. (two consecutive periods), and .dot1 are not displayed because the wildcard * (asterisk) does not match the . (period) character.

If you want to obtain a comma-separated list of file and directory names in the current directory, execute the following command with the -m flag:

```
ls -am
., .., .dot1, test1, test2, test3, test4, test5
```

4

GENERAL COMMANDS

If you want to obtain a list of entries while being able to identify the directories with / (slash), execute the following command with the -p flag:

```
ls -ap
./                    test1                 test4
../                   test2/                test5
.dot1                 test3
```

A similar output can be obtained using the -F flag. -F is more versatile than the -p flag because -F can also identify executable files, symbolic links, and so on.

If you want to get the list of entries in the reverse order of name, execute the following command with the -r flag:

```
ls -rla
total 56
-rw-r--r--    1 testuser     author       11885 Nov 24 11:50 test5
-rw-r--r--    1 testuser     author           0 Nov 24 17:33 test4
-rw-r--r--    1 testuser     author           0 Nov 24 14:58 test3
drwxr-xr-x    2 testuser     author         512 Nov 24 17:32 test2
-rw-r--r--    1 testuser     author          10 Nov 24 17:36 test1
-rw-r--r--    1 testuser     author           0 Nov 24 14:54 .dot1
drwxr-xr-x   36 root         system        2048 Nov 23 19:51 ..
drwxrwx---    3 testuser     author        3072 Nov 24 18:00 .
```

To obtain a list of all files in the current directory as well as all files under all the subdirectories, execute the following command with the -R flag:

```
ls -lR
total 40
-rw-r--r--    1 testuser     author          10 Nov 24 17:36 test1
drwxr-xr-x    2 testuser     author         512 Nov 24 17:32 test2
-rw-r--r--    1 testuser     author           0 Nov 24 14:58 test3
-rw-r--r--    1 testuser     author           0 Nov 24 17:33 test4
-rw-r--r--    1 testuser     author       11885 Nov 24 11:50 test5

./test2:
total 0
-rw-r--r--    1 testuser     author           0 Nov 24 17:45 test21
-rw-r--r--    1 testuser     author           0 Nov 24 14:58 test22
```

Following are examples of the ls command with and without the -u flag. The list without the -u flag displays the time of last modification; the list displayed with the -u flag displays the time of last access:

```
ls -lu
total 40
-rw-r--r--    1 testuser     author          10 Nov 24 17:34 test1
drwxr-xr-x    2 testuser     author         512 Nov 24 18:19 test2
-rw-r--r--    1 testuser     author           0 Nov 24 14:58 test3
-rw-r--r--    1 testuser     author           0 Nov 24 17:33 test4
-rw-r--r--    1 testuser     author       11885 Nov 24 17:56 test5
```

```
ls -l
total 40
-rw-r--r--    1 testuser    author        10 Nov 24 17:36 test1
drwxr-xr-x    2 testuser    author       512 Nov 24 17:32 test2
-rw-r--r--    1 testuser    author         0 Nov 24 14:58 test3
-rw-r--r--    1 testuser    author         0 Nov 24 17:33 test4
-rw-r--r--    1 testuser    author     11885 Nov 24 11:50 test5
```

find

If you are not sure where a particular file is stored, use the `find` command to search for the particular file. The `find` command gives you the flexibility to search for a file by various attributes, such as name, size, permission, and so on. Additionally, the `find` command allows you to execute commands on the files that are found as a result of the search.

The format of the `find` command is as follows:

```
find directory-name search-expression
```

The `directory-name` can be a full path name or a . (single period) for the current directory.

Following is a list of terms that can be used with the `find` command:

- `-name filename` to specify the name of the file (including wildcards) to be used for searching. You also use a range as part of the wildcards. If you want to use wildcard characters, you must specify them within quotes. For example, `"test*"` finds all files starting with the letters `test`. If you specify, `"test[1-2]"`, you will find files that start with `test` and have 1 or 2 as the last characters such as `test1` and `test2`.

- `-size Number` to specify the size of the file to be used for searching. The file size specified is in blocks. To specify that you want to match the size of files less than the specified size, use a – (minus sign) in front of the size; to match the size of files greater than the specified size, use a + (plus sign) in front of the size. Note that the size of a file while matching is always rounded up to the next nearest block. For example, `-size 5` matches files that have size of 5 blocks, `-size -5` matches files that have size of less than or equal to 5 blocks, and `-size +5` matches files that have size of more than 5 blocks.

- `-size Numberc` to specify the size of the file to be used for searching. That is, specify a c at the end of the number. The file size is then taken to be specified in number of bytes. To specify that you want to match the size of files less than the specified size, use a – (minus sign) in front of the size; to match the size of files

4

GENERAL
COMMANDS

greater than the specified size, use a + (plus sign) in front of the size. For example, `-size 50c` matches files that have a size of 50 bytes, `-size –50c` matches files that have a size of less than or equal to 50 bytes, and `-size +50c` matches files that have a size of more than 50 bytes.

- `-prune` to restrict the `find` command not to process directories recursively. By default, `find` recursively processes all the directories and subdirectories under the specified directory.

- `-atime` *number* to search for files that have been accessed in the specified number of 24-hour periods. The number of 24-hour periods is computed by adding 1 to the number specified. 0 means the last 24 hours.

- `-mtime` *number* to search for files that have been modified in the specified number of 24-hour periods. The number of 24-hour periods is computed by adding 1 to the number specified. 0 means the last 24 hours.

- `-ctime` *number* to search for files whose i-node has been modified in the specified number of 24-hour periods. The number of 24-hour periods is computed by adding 1 to the number specified. 0 means the last 24 hours.

- `-type` *filetype* to search for a specific type of file. Following is a list of types that can be used:

b	Block special file
c	Character special file
d	Directory
f	Regular file
l	Symbolic link
p	FIFO (a named pipe)
s	Socket

- `-user` to search for files whose owner matches the specified user name.

- `-perm` *permission* to search for files with a specified permission. The *permission* is specified as an octal number of up to three digits. If the permission is not preceded by a - (hyphen), an exact match of the permission specified is made with the file permissions. If permission is preceded by a - (hyphen), file permission is ANDed with the specified permission. For example, if you want to search for files with owner read permission, use `-perm -400`.

- -newer *filename* to search for files that have a time of modification later than that of the specified filename.
- -group *groupname* to search for files that belong to the specified group.
- -inum *Number* to search for files whose i-node number matches the specified i-node number
- -links *Number* to search for files with a specified number of links. To specify that you want to match the number of links less than the specified number of links, use a – (minus sign) in front of the number of links; to match a number of links greater than the specified number of links, use a + (plus sign) in front of the number of links.
- -ls to print the current path name along with the following attributes:
    - i-node number
    - Size in kilobytes (1024 bytes)
    - Protection mode
    - Number of hard links
    - User
    - Group
    - Size in bytes
    - Modification time
- -exec *command* to execute the command. To execute the command on the list of files found by the find command, use {} followed by \; (a backslash followed by a semicolon).
- -ok *command* to execute the command. To execute the command on the list of files found by the find command, use {} followed by \; (a backslash followed by a semicolon). UNIX asks for confirmation before executing the command.
- -print to print the output generated as a result of the search.

These operators can be specified in conjunction with each other to form complex criteria for searches. You can combine several operators as follows:

- *operator* -a *operator* to search for files that satisfy both the specified conditions.
- *operator* -o *operator* to search for files that satisfy either of the specified conditions.
- !*operator* to search for files that do not satisfy the specified condition.

4

GENERAL COMMANDS

Examples

Assume that the following files exist in the current directory:

```
ls -al
total 64
drwxrwx---    3 testuser    author        3072 Nov 25 00:41 .
drwxr-xr-x   36 root        system        2048 Nov 23 19:51 ..
-rw-r--r--    1 testuser    author           0 Nov 24 14:54 .dot1
-rw-------    1 testuser    author          10 Nov 24 17:36 test1
drwxr-xr-x    2 testuser    author         512 Nov 24 17:32 test2
-r-x------    1 testuser    author           0 Nov 24 14:58 test3
-rw-r--r--    1 testuser    author           0 Nov 24 17:33 test4
-rw-r--r--    1 testuser    author       15647 Nov 24 18:32 test5
```

You can execute the following find command (in its simplest form) to get a list of all the files in the current directory and its subdirectories:

```
find . -print
.
./test5
./test1
./test3
./test4
./test2
./test2/test21
./test2/test22
./.dot1
```

If you want to search for all the files in the current directory that have been modified in the last 24 hours, use the -mtime operator as follows:

```
find . -mtime 0 -print
.
./test5
./test1
./test3
./test4
./test2
./test2/test21
./test2/test22
./.dot1
```

To search for a file whose permission is 600 (only owner has read and write permissions), execute the following command using the -perm operator:

```
find . -perm 600  -print
./test1
```

In this case, only the file that has permission of exactly `600` is displayed. However, if you want to search for a file with owner read and write permission, execute the following command using a `-`(hyphen) in front of `600`:

```
find . -perm -600  -print
.
./test5
./test1
./test4
./test2
./test2/test21
./test2/test22
./.dot1
```

If you are interested in searching only for directories, use the `-type` operator and execute the following command:

```
find . -type d -print
.
./test2
```

To get more information about the files that are found as a result of the search, use the `-ls` operator and execute the following command:

```
find . -ls
    2    4 drwxrwx---  3 settlea  eod       3072 Nov 25 01:11 .
   16   16 -rw-r--r--  1 testuser author     647 Nov 24 18:32
./test5
   18    4 -rw-------  1 testuser author      10 Nov 24 17:36
./test1
   19    0 -r-x------  1 testuser author       0 Nov 24 14:58
./test3
   20    0 -rw-r--r--  1 testuser author       0 Nov 24 17:33
./test4
67584    4 drwxr-xr-x  2 testuser author     512 Nov 24 17:32
./test2
67585    0 -rw-r--r--  1 testuser author       0 Nov 24 17:45
./test2/test21
67586    0 -rw-r--r--  1 testuser author       0 Nov 24 14:58
./test2/test22
   22    0 -rw-r--r--  1 testuser author       0 Nov 24 14:54
./.dot1
```

To search for all filenames that start with `test`, use the `-name` operator and execute the following command:

```
find . -name "test*" -print
./test5
./test1
./test3
./test4
```

4

GENERAL COMMANDS

```
./test2
./test2/test21
./test2/test22
```

As you can see, the `find` command traversed the subdirectory `test2` to obtain the file-names in that directory as well. If you want to restrict the search to only the current directory and leave out the subdirectories, use the operator `-prune` and execute the following command:

`find . -name "test*" -prune -print`
```
./test5
./test1
./test3
./test4
./test2
```

To find a list of files in the current directory that are newer than the file `test1`, use the operator `-newer` and execute the following command:

`find . -newer test1   -print`
```
./test5
./test2/test21
```

On the other hand, if you want to find a list of files older than the file `test1`, use the negation operator ! in conjunction with the operator `-newer`, as in the following command:

`find . ! -newer test1   -print`
```
.
./test3
./test4
./test2
./test2/test22
./.dot1
```

If you want a list of all files that are exactly 10 bytes in size, use the `-size` operator and execute the following command:

`find . -size 10c   -print`
```
./test1
```

If you want to create a list of all files that are less than 10 bytes in size, execute the following command (the command is exactly the same as the preceding one except for the hyphen in front of the 10):

`find . -size -10c -print`
```
./test3
./test4
./test2/test21
./test2/test22
./.dot1
```

If you want a list of all the files that have zero size, execute the `find` command with the `-exec` parameter as follows:

```
find . -size 0c -exec ls -l {} \;
-r-x------  1 testuser    author          0 Nov 24 14:58 ./test3
-rw-r--r--  1 testuser    author          0 Nov 24 17:33 ./test4
-rw-r--r--  1 testuser    author          0 Nov 24 17:45 ./test2/test21
-rw-r--r--  1 testuser    author          0 Nov 24 14:58 ./test2/test22
-rw-r--r--  1 testuser    author          0 Nov 24 14:54 ./.dot1
```

If you want to remove all the files with zero size but want to confirm the delete before you actually remove them, execute the following command with the `-ok` operator:

```
find . -size 0c -ok rm {} \;
< rm ... ./test3 > (yes)?     y
< rm ... ./test4 > (yes)?     n
< rm ... ./test2/test21 > (yes)?    y
< rm ... ./test2/test22 > (yes)?    y
< rm ... ./.dot1 > (yes)?    y
```

In this example, we decided not to remove the file `test4`.

All the examples we have seen so far have used one operator at a time. It is possible to execute the `find` command with complex conditions by combining multiple operators and by using `or` or `and` conditions. If you want to find all the files that start with `test` and have a size of zero, execute the following command:

```
find . -name 'test*' -size 0c -print
./test3
./test4
./test2/test21
./test2/test22
```

In this example, we combined two different operators. It is possible to use the same operator multiple times and combine it with `and` or `or` operators. If you want to search for all files in the current directory that have a size of more than zero bytes *and* less than 50 bytes and whose names start with `test`, use the following command:

```
find . -size +0c -a -size -50c -name 'test*' -exec ls -l {} \;
-rw-------  1 testuser    author         10 Nov 24 17:36 ./test1
```

file

The `file` command can be used to determine the type of the specified file. The `file` command actually reads through the file and performs a series of tests to determine the type of the file. The command then displays the output as standard output.

If a file appears to be ASCII, the `file` command examines the first 512 bytes and tries to determine its language. If a file does not appear to be ASCII, the `file` command further attempts to distinguish a binary data file from a text file that contains extended characters.

If the `File` argument specifies an executable or object module file and the version number is greater than 0, the `file` command displays the version stamp.

The `file` command uses the `/etc/magic` file to identify files that have some sort of a magic number; that is, any file containing a numeric or string constant that indicates type.

Examples

If you have a file called `letter` in your current directory that contains a letter to your friend, you can execute the following command:

```
file letter
```

This command displays the following result:

```
letter:  commands text
```

If you have an executable program in a file called `prog`, and you are working on IBM RISC 6000 AIX version 3.1, you can execute this command:

```
file prog
```

This command displays the following result (if you are on a RISC 6000 system):

```
prog:        executable (RISC System/6000 V3.1)
```

If you are in the `/dev` directory, which contains all the special files, you can execute this command for a file called `hd1` (which is a disk on which a file system has been defined):

```
file hd1
```

This command displays the following result:

```
hd1:          block special
```

File Content-Related Commands

The following sections discuss some of the commands you can use to look at the contents of a file (or parts of the file). You can use these commands to look at the top or bottom of a file, search for strings in the file, and so on.

more

The `more` command can be used to display the contents of a file one screen at a time. By default, the `more` command displays one screen's worth of data at a time. However, the number of lines displayed can be modified. The more command pauses at the end of each page of display. Press the spacebar to display the next page; press the Return or Enter key to display the next line. The more command is typically used when output from other commands is piped to the more command for display.

Following is a list of flags that can be used with the more command:

Flag	Meaning
-d	Prompt to quit, continue, or get help.
-f	Count logical lines in the file.
-number	Set the size of the display window to *number*.
-p	Disable scrolling. This flag results in the more command clearing the screen at the start of each page.
-s	Display only one blank line when multiple contiguous blank lines are present in the file.
-u	Display lines without special attributes if lines in the file have special attributes.
-v	Prevent display of nondisplayable characters graphically.
-w	Allow you to go back in a file after reaching end-of-file. The default for more is to exit when end-of-file is reached.
+number	Start display at line *number* in the file.
+g	Start at the end of the file and be able to go backwards.
+/pattern	Start in the file at the line number where *pattern* occurs first.

As has already been stated, the more command pauses at the end of each page of display. There are several subcommands you can use when more pauses to control further behavior of the more command. These subcommands are as follows:

4

GENERAL COMMANDS

Subcommand	Action
`number`spacebar	Page forward by *number* and by one screen if *number* is not specified.
`number`d	Page forward by a default number of lines (usually 11) if *number* is not specified and by *number* of lines if *number* is specified.
`number`z	Page forward by the specified number of lines if *number* is specified; otherwise, page forward by one screen page.
`number`s	Skip a specified number of lines and display one screen page. If *number* is not specified, the next line is displayed.
`number`f	Skip forward the specified *number* of screens. If *number* is not specified, the next screen is displayed.
`number`b	Skip backward the specified number of screens. If *number* is not specified, the previous screen is displayed.
`number`Ctrl-B or `number`Ctrl-b	Skip backward the specified *number* of screens. If *number* is not specified, the previous screen is displayed.
q	Quit the more command.
v	Invoke the vi editor.
`number`/`expression`	Search for the expression and its position for the number of occurrences specified by *number*. If the

Subcommand	Action
	file has less than the specified number of occurrences of the expression, the display remains unaltered.
*number*n	Search forward for the specified occurrence of the last expression entered. If *number* is not specified, the next occurrence is searched for and that screen is displayed.
!command	Start *command* with the filename as an argument if command is specified. If command is not specified, you return to the shell prompt. You can then use the exit command to get back to the more command.
number;n	Skip to the specified file following the current file if you have invoked the more command with multiple files. If the specified relative file *number* is invalid, more skips to the last file.
number;p	Skip to the specified file before the current file if you have invoked the more command with multiple files. If the specified relative file number does not exist, more skips to the first file.
:f (followed by Return key)	Display the filename of the current file being displayed and the current line number being displayed at the top of the screen.
:q or :Q (followed by the Return key)	Quit the more command.
. (single period)	Repeat the last command executed.

4

GENERAL COMMANDS

Examples

Assume that we have a file called `file1` in the current directory. The content of the file is shown here:

```
This is the line 1
This is the line 2
This is the line 3
This is the line 4
This is the line 5
This is the line 6
This is the line 7
This is the line 8
This is the line 9
This is the line 10
This is the line 11
This is the line 13
This is the line 14
This is the line 15
This is the line 16
This is the line 17
This is the line 18
This is the line 19
This is the line 20
This is the line 21
This is the line 22
This is the line 23
This is the line 24
This is the line 25
```

If you want to display `file1`, use the following command:

```
more file1
This is the line 1
This is the line 2
This is the line 3
This is the line 4
This is the line 5
This is the line 6
This is the line 7
This is the line 8
This is the line 9
This is the line 10
This is the line 11
This is the line 13
This is the line 14
This is the line 15
This is the line 16
This is the line 17
This is the line 18
This is the line 19
This is the line 20
```

```
This is the line 21
This is the line 22
This is the line 23
--More--(91%)
```

This command has a disadvantage because after the end-of-file is reached, the `more` command is exited. If do not want to exit from the `more` command even when the end-of-file is reached, use the `-w` flag. This flag is especially useful if you are looking at a file that is in the process of being created. The following command shows the use of the `-w` flag:

```
more -w file1
```

If you want to start from the bottom of the file rather than at the top of the file and go backwards, use the `+g` flag as in the following command:

```
more +g file1
This is the line 3
This is the line 4
This is the line 5
This is the line 6
This is the line 7
This is the line 8
This is the line 9
This is the line 10
This is the line 11
This is the line 12
This is the line 13
This is the line 14
This is the line 15
This is the line 16
This is the line 17
This is the line 18
This is the line 19
This is the line 20
This is the line 21
This is the line 22
This is the line 23
This is the line 24
This is the line 25
--More--(EOF)
```

If you want to start the display of the file at line number 20 of `file1`, use the following command:

```
more +20 file1
This is the line 20
This is the line 21
This is the line 22
This is the line 23
This is the line 24
This is the line 25
```

If you want to display the five files `file1`, `file2`, `file3`, `file4`, and `file5`, execute the following command:

```
more file1 file2 file3 file4 file5
```

less

The `less` command is one more in the family of commands to view the contents of a file. This command may not be available by default on all UNIX systems. The `less` command behaves similarly to the `more` command, except that the `less` command allows you to go backward as well as forward in the file by default.

Following is a list of subcommands that can be used from the `less` command:

Subcommand	Action
h	Display a list of the subcommands that can be used.
spacebar or Ctrl+v or Ctrl+f or f	Go forward in the file one screen. If preceded by a number, move forward by the specified number of lines.
Return key or Ctrl+N or Ctrl+E or e or j	Move forward by one line. If preceded by a number, move forward by the specified number of lines.
Ctrl+B or b	Go backward in the file by one screen. If preceded by a number, move backward by the specified number of lines.
Ctrl+D or d	Go forward by a half screen (the default of 11 lines). If preceded by a number, move forward by the specified number of lines. The new number is then registered as the new default for all subsequent d or u commands.
g	Go the top of the file by default. If preceded by a number, the file is positioned at the line specified by the number.
G	Go the bottom of the file by default. If preceded by a number, the file is positioned at the line specified by the number.
p or %	Go to the top of the file by default. If preceded by a number between 0 and 100, positions the screen at the percentage of the file specified by the number.

Subcommand	Action
Ctrl+P or Ctrl+K or Ctrl+Y or k or y	Go backward by one line. If preceded by a number, move backward by the specified number of lines.
Ctrl+U or u	Go backward by a half screen (the default of 11 lines). If preceded by a number, move backward by the specified number of lines. The new number is registered as the new default for all subsequent d or u commands.
Ctrl+L or Ctrl+R or r	Redraw the current screen.
m*lowercaseletter*	Mark the position with the *lowercaseletter* marker for use later.
'*lowercaseletter*	Go to the position marked with *lowercaseletter* using the m subcommand. If ' is followed by ^ (caret), less displays the top of the file. If ' is followed by $ (dollar sign), less displays the bottom of the file.
number/*pattern*	Position the file in the specified occurrence of the *pattern* in the file. You can use the following special characters to indicate special actions:

- ! to search for lines that do not contain the specified *pattern*.
- * to search multiple files if invoked with multiple files.
- @ to start the search at the top of the first file if invoked with multiple files.
- n to repeat the last search executed. If the subcommand is preceded by a number, the file is positioned to the specified occurrence of the *pattern* previously specified. You can use the N subcommand to search in the reverse direction.

continues

4

GENERAL COMMANDS

Subcommand	Action
:e filename or : E filename	Execute the less command for a specified filename and add it to the list of files for subsequent use.
:n	Execute the less command on the next file on the list of files. The list of files can be specified by invoking less with multiple files, or added to the list by using the :e subcommand. Similarly, you can use the :p subcommand for the previous file in the list.
:numberx	Execute the less command on the first file in the list if *number* is not specified. If *number* is specified, the less command is executed on the file in that position in the list.
= or :f	Get information about the file and the current position in the file.
q or Q	Exit the less command.
v	Invoke the vi editor with the current filename.
!command	Execute a shell command. If command is omitted, you are put into a shell prompt. You can exit the shell by using the exit command to go back to the less command.

Example

To invoke the less command for a file named file1, use the following command:

```
less file1
```

tail

You can use the tail command to display a file, on standard output, starting at a specified point from the top or bottom of the file. Whether the tail command starts at the top of the file or at the end of the file depends on the parameter and flags used. One of the flags, -f, can be used to look at the bottom of a file continuously as it grows in size. By default, tail displays the last 10 lines of the file.

Following is a list of flags that can be used with the `tail` command:

Flag	Meaning
-c *number*	Start from the specified character position *number*.
-b *number*	Start from the specified 512-byte block position *number*.
-k *number*	Start from the specified 1024-byte block position *number*.
-n *number*	Start display of the file at the specified line *number*.
-r *number*	Display lines from the file in reverse order.
-f	Display the end of the file continuously as it grows in size.

With all these flags, the *number* you specify can be a number prefixed by a + (plus sign) or a – (minus sign). If you specify a +, the `tail` command starts processing from the top of the file. If you specify a – or do not specify any sign, `tail` starts processing from the bottom of the file.

Examples

Assume that we have a file called `file1` that contains 30 lines. The contents of the file are displayed here:

```
This is the line 1
This is the line 2
This is the line 3
This is the line 4
This is the line 5
This is the line 6
This is the line 7
This is the line 8
This is the line 9
This is the line 10
This is the line 11
This is the line 12
This is the line 13
This is the line 14
This is the line 15
This is the line 16
This is the line 17
This is the line 18
This is the line 19
```

4

GENERAL
COMMANDS

```
This is the line 20
This is the line 21
This is the line 22
This is the line 23
This is the line 24
This is the line 25
This is the line 26
This is the line 27
This is the line 28
This is the line 29
This is the line 30
```

If you want to see the last 10 lines of the file, execute the `tail` command without any flags as follows:

```
tail file1
This is the line 21
This is the line 22
This is the line 23
This is the line 24
This is the line 25
This is the line 26
This is the line 27
This is the line 28
This is the line 29
This is the line 30
```

In the preceding example, the last 10 lines of `file1` are displayed. If you want to skip 27 lines from the start of the file, execute the following example:

```
tail +27 file1
This is the line 28
This is the line 29
This is the line 30
```

In this example, the display starts at the 28th line from the top of the file. If you want to start from a specified byte position in the file instead of at a particular line position, use the `-c` flag as follows:

```
tail -c +500 file1
the line 27
This is the line 28
This is the line 29
This is the line 30
```

In this example, the display starts at the 500th byte from the top of the file. If you want to specify an absolute line number from which to display the file, use the `-n` flag as in the following example:

```
tail -n -5 file1
This is the line 26
```

```
This is the line 27
This is the line 28
This is the line 29
This is the line 30
```

In this example, the display starts at the 5th line from the bottom. If you want to display the lines of file1 in reverse order, use the -r flag as in the following example:

```
tail -r -n -5 file1
This is the line 30
This is the line 29
This is the line 28
This is the line 27
This is the line 26
```

In this example, the last five lines are displayed in reverse order, with the last line first.

head

The head command displays a file on the standard output. The head command starts at the top of the file and displays the specified number of bytes or lines from the top of the file. By default, head displays 10 lines.

Following are the flags that can be used with the head command:

Flag	Meaning
-c *number*	Display the *number* of bytes from the top of the file.
-n *number*	Display the *number* of lines from the top of the file.

The *number* can be specified without any sign or can be preceded by a – (minus sign), both of which mean the same thing.

Examples

Assume that we have a file file1 whose contents are the same as the one shown in the examples for the tail command, in the preceding section.

If you want to display a specified number of lines from the top, use the -n flag as in the following example:

```
head -3 file1
This is the line 1
This is the line 2
This is the line 3
```

In this example, the first three lines of file1 are displayed. If you want to display the first specified number of bytes from the top of the file, use the -c flag as in the following example:

4

```
head -c 29 file1
This is the line 1
This is th
```

In this example, the first 29 bytes of `file1` are displayed.

WC

The `wc` command counts the number of bytes, words, and lines in specified files. A *word* is a number of characters stringed together and delimited by either a space or a newline character.

Following is a list of flags that can be used with the `wc` command:

Flag	Meaning
-l	Count only the number of lines in the file.
-w	Count only the number of words in the file.
-c	Count only the number of bytes in the file.

You can use multiple filenames as arguments to the `wc` command.

Examples

If you want to know the number of bytes, words, and lines in `file1`, execute the following command:

```
wc file1
      25      125      491 file1
```

This example shows that `file1` has 25 lines, 125 words, and 491 bytes. If you want to find only the number of words in `file1`, use the `-w` flag as in the following example:

```
wc -w file1
      125 file1
```

If you want to get the word count on `file1` and `file2`, execute the following command:

```
wc -w file1 file2
      125 file1
      463 file2
      588 total
```

Notice that if you use multiple files, the `wc` command displays an extra line in the output that lists the total of all files.

read

The read command is used in shell scripts to read each field from a file and to assign it to a shell variable. A *field* is a string of bytes separated by spaces or newline characters. If the number of fields read is less than the number of variables specified, the rest of the fields are unassigned.

You can use the -r flag with the read command. Use -r to treat a \(backslash) as part of the input record and not as a control character.

Examples

Following is a piece of shell script code that reads the first name and last name from the namefile file and prints them:

```
while read -r lname fname
do
        echo $lname","$fname
done < namefile
```

od

The od command can be used to display the contents of a file in a specified format. Usually, this command is used to look at executable files or other files that are not text, which most UNIX commands cannot process. You can also specify the offset from which you want the display of the file to start.

Following is a list of the flags that can be used with the od command:

Flag	Meaning
-d	Display the output as a signed decimal number.
-i	Display the output as an unsigned decimal number.
-f	Display the output as a floating number.
-b	Display the output as an octal value.
-h	Display the output as a hexadecimal value.
-c	Display the output as ASCII characters.

After the filename, you can specify the offset of the byte at which you want to start the display. If the offset is preceded by 0x, the offset is interpreted as a hexadecimal number. If the offset is preceded by 0, the offset is interpreted as an octal number. The offset can

4

GENERAL COMMANDS

be suffixed by b for bytes, k for kilobytes (1024 bytes), or m for megabytes (1024 × 1024 bytes).

Examples

To display the contents of file1, execute the following command:

```
od file1 ¦ more
0000000   000737 000007 031147 104407 000000 000000 000000 000000
0000020   000110 010007 000413 000001 000002 024250 000001 056674
0000040   000012 030504 000001 052320 000000 001000 000000 000000
0000060   000001 055020 000004 000002 000004 000004 000007 000005
```

This command displays file1 in decimal format. If you want to display the file in hexa-decimal format, use the -h flag as in the following example:

```
od -h file1 ¦ more
0000000   01df 0007 3267 8907 0000 0000 0000 0000
0000020   0048 1007 010b 0001 0002 28a8 0001 5dbc
0000040   000a 3144 0001 54d0 0000 0200 0000 0000
0000060   0001 5a10 0004 0002 0004 0004 0007 0005
```

If you want to start the display at byte position 40 and display it in ASCII format, use the following command:

```
od -c file1 +40 ¦ more
0000040   \0  \n   1   D  \0 001    T 320  \0  \0 002  \0  \0  \0  \0  \0
0000060   \0 001    Z 020  \0 004  \0 002  \0 004  \0 004  \0 007  \0 005
```

It is possible to display the contents of file1 in octal, ASCII, and hexadecimal format all at once, using the following command:

```
od -bch file1 ¦ more
0000000   001 337 000 007 062 147 211 007 000 000 000 000 000 000 000 000
          001 337  \0 007   2   g 211 007  \0  \0  \0  \0  \0  \0  \0  \0
              01df     0007     3267     8907     0000     0000     0000     0000
0000020   000 110 020 007 001 013 000 001 000 002 050 250 000 001 135 274
           \0   H 020 007 001 013  \0 001  \0 002   ( 250  \0 001   ] 274
              0048     1007     010b     0001     0002     28a8     0001     5dbc
0000040   000 012 061 104 000 001 124 320 000 000 002 000 000 000 000 000
           \0  \n   1   D  \0 001   T 320  \0  \0 002  \0  \0  \0  \0  \0
              000a     3144     0001     54d0     0000     0200     0000     0000
0000060   000 001 132 020 000 004 000 002 000 004 000 004 000 007 000 005
           \0 001   Z 020  \0 004  \0 002  \0 004  \0 004  \0 007  \0 005
              0001     5a10     0004     0002     0004     0004     0007     0005.
```

pg

The pg command displays the contents of a file one page at a time, just like the more and less commands do. The pg command pauses at the end of each screen display so that you can enter a number of subcommands that can search for a string in the file, go backward or forward in the file, and so on.

Following is a list of flags that can be used with the `pg` command:

Flag	*Meaning*
-c	Clear the screen at the end of each page of display and start the display at the top of the screen.
-e	Continue to the next file at the end of one file, if the `pg` command is invoked with multiple files. Usually, `pg` pauses at the end of each file.
-f	Truncate lines that are longer than the width of the screen display.
-p *string*	Display the *string* as the `pg` command prompt. The default prompt is : (colon). If the `string` specified is %d, the page number is displayed at the prompt.
-s	Highlight all messages and prompts issued by the `pg` command.
+*number*	Start the display at the specified line number in the file.
-*number*	Set the size of the display screen to the specified number of lines.
+/pattern/	Search for the `pattern` in the file and start the display at that line.

A number of subcommands can be used with the `pg` command when it pauses at the end of each screen of display. You must press the Return key after entering each subcommand. Following is a list of some of these subcommands:

Subcommand	*Action*
-*number*	Go backward the number of pages specified by *number*.
+*number*	Go forward the number of pages specified by *number*.
l	Go forward in the file by one line.

continues

4

GENERAL
COMMANDS

Subcommand	Action
*number*l	Start the display in the file at the line specified by *number*.
+*number*l	Go forward in the file the number of lines specified by *number*.
-*number*l	Go backward in the file the number of lines specified by *number*.
d	Go forward by a half screen.
-d	Go backward by a half screen.
-n	Indicate to pg that it should interpret and execute the subcommands as they are entered without waiting for the newline character to be entered.
Ctrl+L	Redraw the current screen.
$	Go to the last page of the file.
number/*pattern*/	Search forward for the *pattern* in the file starting at the beginning of the next page. If *number* is specified, pg searches for the specified occurrence number of *pattern*. The search does not wrap around. If you want to search backward, use ? (question mark) instead of / (slash).
*number*p	Start executing the pg command on the previous file if *number* is not specified. If *number* is specified, start at the file whose position in the list of files is *number* before the current file.
*number*n	Start executing the pg command on the next file if *number* is not specified. If *number* is specified, start at the file whose position in the list of files is *number* after the current file.
s*filename*	Save the current file being processed in the specified filename.
q or Q	Quit the pg command.

Examples

Assume that we have a file `file1` whose content is the same as that shown in the `tail` command example, earlier in this chapter.

To change the number of lines to be displayed by the `pg` command, prefix the size by a – (minus sign) as in the following example:

```
pg -7 file1
This is the line 1
This is the line 2
This is the line 3
This is the line 4
This is the line 5
This is the line 6
This is the line 7
:
```

In this example, the number of lines displayed is modified to 7. If you want to start the display at the 7th line, prefix the number with a + (plus sign) as in the following example:

```
pg +7 file1
```

If you want to modify the default prompt of : (colon) with a personalized prompt, use the `-p` flag as in the following example:

```
pg -7 -s -p "Enter Subcommand -> " file1
This is the line 1
This is the line 2
This is the line 3
This is the line 4
This is the line 5
This is the line 6
This is the line 7
Enter Subcommand ->
```

In this example, the default prompt has been replaced by the `Enter Subcommand ->` prompt. If you want to start the file with the line on which the pattern `line 5` appears, execute the following command:

```
pg +/"line 5"/ file1
```

tee

If you want to execute a command and want its output redirected to multiple files in addition to the standard output, use the `tee` command. The `tee` command accepts input from the standard input, so it is possible to pipe another command to the `tee` command.

4

GENERAL COMMANDS

You can use the -a flag with the `tee` command. Use -a to append to the end of the specified file. The default of the `tee` command is to overwrite the specified file.

Examples

If you want to use the `cat` command on `file1` to display it on the screen, but you want to make a copy of `file2`, use the `tee` command as follows:

```
cat file1 ¦ tee file2 ¦ more
```

If you want to append `file1` to the end of an already existing `file2`, use the flag -a as in the following example:

```
cat file1 ¦ tee -a file2 ¦ more
```

vi

The `vi` command can be used to edit one or more files using full-screen mode. If a filename is not provided, UNIX creates an empty work file without any name. If a filename is provided but the file does not exist, UNIX creates an empty work file with the specified name. The `vi` command does not modify existing files until the changes are saved.

CAUTION

The `vi` command does not lock a file while editing it. It is possible that more than one user can edit the file at the same time. The version of the file saved last is the one that is retained.

Following is a list of some of the flags that can be used with the `vi` command:

Flag	Meaning
-c *subcommand*	Execute the specified *subcommand* before placing the specified file in editing mode.
-r filename	Recover the specified `filename`.
-R	Place the specified file in editing mode with the read-only option so that any modifications made cannot be saved.
-y*number*	Set the editing window to a size with *number* of lines.

Here is a list of the modes the vi editor has:

- *Command mode* is the default mode when you enter vi. In this mode, you can enter various subcommands to manipulate the lines, such as deleting lines, pasting lines, moving to a different word, moving to a different line, and so on.
- *Text input mode* is the mode in which you can modify the text in the lines or enter new lines. You enter this mode from command mode by using the subcommand a, i, or c. To return to command mode, press the Esc key.
- *Command entry mode* is the mode in which you can enter certain subcommands that require additional parameters. Two of these subcommands are w (which requires a filename) and / (which requires entry of a pattern). You can use the Esc key to return to command mode.

Following is a quick reference of subcommands that can be used in command mode for *moving within the same line*:

Subcommand	Action
h	Move the cursor left to the previous character in the same line.
l	Move the cursor right to the next character in the same line.
j	Move the cursor down to the next line in the same column.
k	Move the cursor up to the previous line in the same column.
w	Move the cursor to the start of next small word in the same line.
W	Move the cursor to the start of the next big word in the same line.
b	Move the cursor to the start of the previous small word in the same line.
B	Move the cursor to the start of the previous big word in the same line.

4

GENERAL
COMMANDS

continues

Subcommand	Action
e	Move the cursor to the end of the next small word in the same line.
E	Move the cursor to the end of the previous big word in the same line.
fc	Move the cursor to the next character *c* in the same line.
Fc	Move the cursor to the previous character *c* in the same line.
tc	Move the cursor to one column before the next character *c* in the same line.
Tc	Move the cursor to one column after the previous character *c* in the same line.
number ¦	Move the cursor to the specified column *number*.

Following is a quick reference of subcommands that can be used in command mode for *moving across the lines*:

Subcommand	Action
+ or Enter	Move the cursor to the next line's first nonblank character.
–	Move the cursor to the previous line's first nonblank character.
0	Move the cursor to the first character of the current line.
$	Move the cursor to the last character of the current line.
H	Move the cursor to the top line of the screen.
L	Move the cursor to the last line of the screen.
M	Move the cursor to the middle of the screen.

Following is a quick reference of subcommands that can be used in command mode for *redrawing the screen*:

Subcommand	Action
z-	Make the current line the last line of the screen and redraw the screen.
z.	Make the current line the middle line of the screen and redraw the screen.
Ctrl+L	Redraw the screen.
/pattern/z-	Find the next occurrence of *pattern* and make that the last line of the screen.

Following is a quick reference of subcommands that can be used in command mode for *scrolling across pages*:

Subcommand	Action
Ctrl+F	Move forward by one screen.
Ctrl+D	Move forward by one-half screen.
Ctrl+B	Move backward by one screen.
Ctrl+U	Move backward by one-half screen.
Ctrl+E	Scroll the window down by one line.
Ctrl+Y	Scroll the window up by one line.

Following is a quick reference of subcommands that can be used in command mode for *searching for patterns in the file*:

Subcommand	Action
/pattern	Search for the specified *pattern* in the forward direction. If end-of-file is reached, the search wraps around.
?pattern	Search for the specified *pattern* in the backward direction. If the top-of-file is reached, the search wraps around.

continues

4

GENERAL COMMANDS

Subcommand	Action
n	Repeat the last search in the same direction as was specified in the last search.
N	Repeat the last search in the opposite direction of what was specified in the last search.
/pattern/+number	Position the cursor the specified *number* of lines after the line in which the *pattern* has been found.
/pattern/-number	Position the cursor the specified *number* of lines before the line in which the pattern has been found.
%	Find the matching braces or parenthesis.

Following is a quick reference of subcommands that can be used to **enter text in text-entry mode**. You can terminate text entry at any time by pressing the Esc key.

Subcommand	Action
a	Start entering text after the cursor position.
A	Start entering text at the end of the line.
i	Start entering text before the cursor position.
I	Start entering text before the first nonblank character in the line.
o	Insert an empty line after the line in which the cursor is positioned.
O	Insert an empty line before the line in which the cursor is positioned.

Following is a quick reference of subcommands that can be used to **modify text from command mode**. You can terminate text entry at any time by pressing the Esc key.

Subcommand	Action
cc or S	Change a complete line.
C	Change the contents of a line after the cursor position.
cw	Change the word at which the cursor is positioned.

Subcommand	Action
dd	Delete the current line.
D	Delete the rest of the line beyond where the cursor is positioned.
dw	Delete part of the word in which the cursor is positioned.
J	Join the contents of the next line to the end of the current line.
rc	Replace the character at the cursor position with the character c.
R	Overwrite the contents of the current line.
u	Undo the last modification.
x	Delete the character at the cursor position.
X	Delete the character to the left of the cursor position.
~ (tilde)	Change uppercase letter to lowercase letter or vice versa.
.	Repeat the last change.
<<	Shift the current line to the left.
>>	Shift the current line to the right.

Following is a quick reference of subcommands that can be used to *move or copy text from one part of the file to another*:

Subcommand	Action
p	Paste the contents of the undo buffer (as a result of deleting or yanking) after the cursor position.
P	Paste the contents of the undo buffer (as a result of deleting or yanking) before the cursor position.

4

GENERAL COMMANDS

continues

Subcommand	Action
"*b*d	Delete text into the named buffer *b*.
"*b*p	Paste the contents of the named buffer *b*.
yy	Yank the current line into the undo buffer.
Y	Yank the current line into the undo buffer.
yw	Yank the word from the current cursor position into the undo buffer.

Following is a quick reference of subcommands that can be used to *save a file*:

Subcommand	Action
:w	Save the changes to the original file.
:w *filename*	Save the changes to the specified *filename* if the file *filename* does not exist. If you try to save an already existing file using this subcommand, you will get an error.
!w *filename*	Save the changes to the specified *filename* if the file filename already exists.

Following is a quick reference of subcommands that can be used to *move between various files* if you have invoked vi with multiple files:

Subcommand	Action
:n	Start editing the next file in the list of files specified when vi was invoked.
:n *filenames*	Specify a new list of files to be edited.

Following is a quick reference of subcommands that can be used to *move between the current file and the alternate file*:

Subcommand	Action
:e *filename*	Invoke vi and make *filename* the alternate file.
:e!	Load the current file again. If changes have been made to the current file, those changes are discarded.

Subcommand	Action
`:e + filename`	Invoke `vi` with `filename` and start editing at the end of the file rather than at the beginning.
`:e + number filename`	Invoke `vi` with `filename` and start editing at the specified line number.
`:e #`	Start editing the alternate file.

Following is a quick reference of subcommands that can be used to *add lines to the current file from other sources*:

Subcommand	Action
`:r filename`	Read the complete `filename` and add it after the current line.
`:r !command`	Execute the specified `command` and add the output after the current line.

Following is a quick reference of some of the *miscellaneous subcommands* you can use with `vi`:

Subcommand	Action
Ctrl+G	Get information about the current file being edited.
`:sh`	Start the shell so that commands can be executed. You can return by using the `exit` command or by pressing Ctrl+D.
`:!command`	Execute the specified `command`.
`!!`	Reexecute the last `:!command`.
`:q`	Quit `vi`. If you try to quit using this subcommand and you have made modifications to the file, UNIX does not allow you to quit.
`:q!`	Quit `vi` regardless of any changes made to the file.
ZZ or `:wq`	Save changes to the original file and exit `vi`.

You can use a special file called `.exrc` in which you can specify *special vi subcommands*. To use these subcommands in a `vi` session, use a : (colon) in front of the command. Some of these subcommands are as follows:

4

GENERAL COMMANDS

Subcommand	Action
`Ab abb ph`	Abbreviate `ph` to `abb`.
`unab` *abbreviation*	Turn the abbreviation off.
`map m seq`	Map a sequence of `vi` commands to a character or key.

File Content Search Commands

We have seen that we can use the `find` command to search for filenames in a directory. To search for a pattern in one or more files, use the `grep` series of commands. The `grep` commands search for a string within the specified files and display the output on standard output.

egrep

The `egrep` command is an extended version of `grep` command. This command searches for a specified pattern in one or more files and displays the output to standard output. The pattern can be a regular expression in which you can specify special characters to have special meaning, some of which are as follows:

Character	Meaning
.	Match any single character.
*	Match one or more single characters that precede the asterisk.
^	Match the regular expression at the beginning of a line.
$	Match the regular expression at the end of a line.
+	Match one or more occurrences of a preceding regular expression.
?	Match zero or more occurrences of a preceding expression.
[ ]	Match any of the characters specified within the brackets.

Following is a list of flags that can be used with the `egrep` command:

Flag	Meaning
-b	Display the block number at the start of each line found.
-c	Display the count of lines in which the pattern was found without displaying the lines.
-f *filename*	Specify a *filename* that contains the patterns to be matched.
-h	Suppress the filenames as part of the display if more than one file is being searched.
-i	Search, ignoring the case of the letter.
-l	List just the filenames in which the specified pattern has been found.
-n	Display the relative line number before each line in the output.
-q	Suppress all output.
-s	Display an error message if an error occurs.
-v	Find lines not matching the specified pattern.
-w	Search for specified patterns as words.
-x	Match the patterns exactly to a line.

The `egrep` command has some special features for the patterns you can specify. The features are as follows:

- You can specify a + (plus sign) at the end of a pattern that matches one or more occurrences of the pattern.
- You can specify a ? (question mark) at the end of a pattern that matches zero or one occurrence of the pattern.
- You can specify a ¦ (vertical bar or pipe) between two patterns to match either one or both patterns (`or` operator).

- You can specify a pattern within a left and a right parentheses to group the patterns.

Examples

Assume that we have a file called `file1` whose contents are shown here using the `more` command:

```
more file1
*****  This file is a dummy file *****
which has been created
to run a test for egrep
grep series of commands are used by the following types of people
    programmers
    end users
Believe it or not, grep series of commands are used by pros and novices
alike
*****  THIS FILE IS A DUMMY FILE *****
```

If you want to find all occurrences of `dummy`, use the following command:

```
egrep dummy file1
*****  This file is a dummy file *****
```

If you want to find all occurrences of `dummy`, regardless of the case of the letters, use the `-i` flag as in the following example:

```
egrep -i dummy file1
*****  This file is a dummy file *****
*****  THIS FILE IS A DUMMY FILE *****
```

If you want to display the relative line number of the line that contains the pattern being searched, use the `-n` flag as in the following example:

```
egrep -i -n dummy file1
1:*****  This file is a dummy file *****
8:*****  THIS FILE IS A DUMMY FILE *****
```

If you are just interested in finding the number of lines in which the specified pattern occurs, use the `-c` flag as in the following example:

```
egrep -i -c dummy file1
2
```

If you want to get a list of all lines that do not contain the specified pattern, use the `-v` flag as in the following example:

```
egrep -i -v dummy file1
which has been created
to run a test for egrep
grep series of commands are used by the following types of people
    programmers
```

```
      end users
Believe it or not, grep series of commands are used by pros and novices
alike
```

If you are interested in searching for a pattern that you want to search as a word, use the
-w flag as in the following example:

egrep -w grep file1
```
grep series of commands are used by the following types of people
Believe it or not, grep series of commands are used by pros and novices
alike
```

Notice that the search did not find the pattern egrep because that word contains e before
the pattern grep. The use of the -w flag forced egrep to search for the pattern grep
delimited by spaces or newline characters.

If you want to search for a pattern that is the only string in a line, use the -x command as
in the following example:

egrep -x "   end users" file1
```
    end users
```

Now, let's examine some of the special features of egrep. If you want to find out where
either of two specified patterns occur, use the ¦ (vertical bar) to separate the two patterns:

egrep "(dummy¦pro)" file1
```
*****  This file is a dummy file *****
    programmers
Believe it or not, grep series of commands are used by pros and novices
alike
```

In this example, the lines that contain either the pattern dummy or the pattern pro are displayed. In case you are interested in searching for either pros or programmers, use the ?
(question mark) at the end of the pattern as in the following example:

egrep "pro(grammer)?s" file1
```
    programmers
Believe it or not, grep series of commands are used by pros and novices
alike
```

In this example, the pattern matches both pros and programmers because (grammar)?
matches zero or one occurrence of grammar with the zero occurrence (for the pros line)
and with the one occurrence (for the programmers line).

To search for lines containing only capital letters C, D, E, or F, use regular expressions as
follows:

egrep [C-F] file1
```
*****   THIS FILE IS A DUMMY FILE *****
```

4

GENERAL COMMANDS

fgrep

As do `egrep` and `grep`, `fgrep` also searches one or more files for a specified string and displays output on standard output. The `fgrep` command is supposed to be the faster version of the `grep` command, but in reality may not be. Please notice that the `fgrep` command is used to search for a specified *string* and not a pattern (a string is a regular expression in which special characters can be used to indicate special meaning).

Following is a list of flags that can be used with the `fgrep` command:

Flag	Meaning
-b	Display the block number at the start of each line found.
-c	Display the count of lines in which the pattern was found without displaying the lines.
-f *filename*	Specify the *filename* that contains the patterns to be matched.
-h	Suppress the filenames as part of the display if more than one file is being searched.
-i	Search, ignoring the case of the letter.
-l	List just the filenames in which the specified pattern has been found.
-n	Display the relative line number before each line in the output.
-q	Suppress all output.
-s	Display an error message if an error occurs.
-v	Find lines not matching the specified pattern.
-w	Search for specified patterns as words.
-x	Match the patterns exactly with a line.

Examples

Assume that we have a file called `file1` whose contents are shown here using the `more` command:

```
more file1
*****  This file is a dummy file *****
which has been created
to run a test for egrep
grep series of commands are used by the following types of people
   programmers
   end users
Believe it or not, grep series of commands are used by pros and novices
alike
*****  THIS FILE IS A DUMMY FILE *****
```

If you want to find all occurrences of dummy, use the following command:

```
fgrep dummy file1
*****  This file is a dummy file *****
```

If you want to find all occurrences of dummy regardless of the case of the letters, use the -i flag as in the following example:

```
fgrep -i dummy file1
*****  This file is a dummy file *****
*****  THIS FILE IS A DUMMY FILE *****
```

If you want to display the relative line number of the line that contains the pattern being searched, use the -n flag as in the following example:

```
fgrep -i -n dummy file1
1:*****  This file is a dummy file *****
8:*****  THIS FILE IS A DUMMY FILE *****
```

If you are just interested in finding the number of lines in which the specified pattern occurs, use the -c flag as in the following example:

```
fgrep -i -c dummy file1
2
```

If you want to get a list of all lines that do not contain the specified pattern, use the -v flag as in the following example:

```
fgrep -i -v dummy file1
which has been created
to run a test for egrep
grep series of commands are used by the following types of people
   programmers
   end users
Believe it or not, grep series of commands are used by pros and novices
alike
```

If you are interested in searching for a pattern that you want to search as a word, use the -w flag as in the following example:

```
fgrep -w grep file1
grep series of commands are used by the following types of people
Believe it or not, grep series of commands are used by pros and novices
alike
```

Notice that the search did not find the pattern egrep because that word contains e before the pattern grep. The use of the -w flag forced fgrep to search for grep delimited by spaces or newline characters.

If you want to search for a pattern that is the only string in a line, use the -x command as in the following example:

```
fgrep -x "    end users" file1
   end users
```

grep

The grep command can be used to search for a specified pattern in one or more files; it displays the matching output on standard output.

Following is a list of flags that can be used with grep command:

Flag	Meaning
-b	Display the block number at the start of each line found.
-c	Display the count of lines in which the pattern was found without displaying the lines.
-E	Indicate that the grep command behaves as the egrep command.
-F	Indicate that the grep command behaves as the fgrep command.
-f *filename*	Specify *filename* that contains the patterns to be matched.
-h	Suppress the filenames as part of the display if more than one file is being searched.
-i	Search, ignoring the case of the letter.
-l	List just the filenames in which the specified pattern

Flag	Meaning
	has been found.
-n	Display the relative line number before each line in the output.
-q	Suppress all output.
-s	Display an error message if an error occurs.
-v	Find lines not matching the specified pattern.
-w	Search for specified patterns as words.
-x	Match the patterns exactly with a line.

Examples

Assume that we have a file called file1 whose contents are shown here using the more command:

```
more file1
*****  This file is a dummy file *****
which has been created
to run a test for egrep
grep series of commands are used by the following types of people
    programmers
    end users
Believe it or not, grep series of commands are used by pros and novices
alike
*****  THIS FILE IS A DUMMY FILE *****
```

If you want to find all occurrences of dummy, use the following command:

```
grep dummy file1
*****  This file is a dummy file *****
```

If you want to find all occurrences of dummy regardless of the case of the letters, use the -i flag as in the following example:

```
grep -i dummy file1
*****  This file is a dummy file *****
*****  THIS FILE IS A DUMMY FILE *****
```

If you want to display the relative line number of the line that contains the pattern being searched, use the -n flag as in the following example:

```
grep -i -n dummy file1
1:*****  This file is a dummy file *****
8:*****  THIS FILE IS A DUMMY FILE *****
```

4

If you are just interested in finding the number of lines in which the specified pattern occurs, use the `-c` flag as in the following example:

```
grep -i -c dummy file1
2
```

If you want to get a list of all lines that do not contain the specified pattern, use the `-v` flag as in the following example:

```
grep -i -v dummy file1
which has been created
to run a test for egrep
grep series of commands are used by the following types of people
    programmers
    end users
Believe it or not, grep series of commands are used by pros and novices
alike
```

If you are interested in searching for a pattern that you want to search as a word, use the `-w` flag as in the following command:

```
grep -w grep file1
grep series of commands are used by the following types of people
Believe it or not, grep series of commands are used by pros and novices
alike
```

Notice that the search did not find the pattern `egrep` because that word contains e before the pattern `grep`. The use of the `-w` flag forced `grep` to search for the pattern `grep` delimited by spaces or newline characters.

If you want to search for a pattern that is the only string in a line, use the `-x` command as in the following example:

```
grep -x "    end users" file1
    end users
```

Now, let's examine some of the special features of `grep`. If you want to find out which lines start with a capital letter A through C, use the following command:

```
grep "^[A-C]" file1
Believe it or not, grep series of commands are used by pros and novices
alike
```

In this example, the ^ (caret) indicates that the following character is searched for at the beginning of each line. If you are interested in searching for all lines that do *not* start with capital letters A through F, use the following command:

```
grep "^[^A-F]" file1
*** This file is a dummy file *****
which has been created
to run a test for egrep
```

```
grep series of commands are used by the following types of people
    programmers
    end users
*****   THIS FILE IS A DUMMY FILE *****
```

In this example, the ^ (caret) outside the [ ] (square brackets) searches for the following character at the beginning of the line; the ^ (caret) inside the [ ] indicates that the match should be made where the character does not match A through F (meaning that all lines that do not have A through F at the beginning of the line are matched).

To search for lines containing only the capital letters C, D, E, or F, use regular expression as follows:

```
grep [C-F] file1
*****   THIS FILE IS A DUMMY FILE *****
```

strings

The strings command can be used to search for strings in executable files. A *string* consists of four or more printable characters terminated by a null or newline.

Following is a list of some of the flags that can be used with the strings command:

Flag	Meaning
-a or -	Search the entire file, not just the data section.
-o	List each string preceded by its offset in the file (in octal).
-Number	Specify a minimum string length other than the default of 4.

Examples

To see the strings that exist in the strings command executable file, execute the following command in a directory that contains the command:

```
strings strings
¦@(#)56
1.17  com/cmd/scan/strings.c, cmdscan, bos320, 9227320b 5/7/92 10:21:20
Standard input
strings.cat
/usr/mbin/strings
Usage: strings [ -a ] [ -o ] [ -# ] [ file ... ]
%7o
%7o
```

If you also want the offset of the strings in the executable file for the `strings` command, use the -o flag as follows:

```
strings -o strings
   6017 ¦@(#)56
   6027 1.17  com/cmd/scan/strings.c, cmdscan, bos320, 9227320b 5/7/92
10:21:20
   6140 Standard input
   6164 strings.cat
   6200 /usr/mbin/strings
   6224 Usage: strings [ -a ] [ -o ] [ -# ] [ file ... ]
   6314 %7o
   6330 %7o
```

If you want to limit your search to only, say, 15 characters or more in size in the `strings` command executable, execute the following command:

```
strings -o -15 strings
   6027 1.17  com/cmd/scan/strings.c, cmdscan, bos320, 9227320b 5/7/92
10:21:20
   6200 /usr/mbin/strings
   6224 Usage: strings [ -a ] [ -o ] [ -# ] [ file ... ]
```

Printing

You may have several documents that you want to print, and you may have several printers attached to your computer with which you can print. The following sections discuss some of the commands that direct the printing of specified documents to specified printers and determine the status of the printers. We will also discuss commands to cancel specified printing jobs.

In a UNIX system, you can have multiple printers but only one of the printers can be set up as the default printer to which all the print requests are sent if a printer name is not specified.

cancel

If you have queued up requests to print one or more documents using the `lp` command, and you want to cancel those requests, use the `cancel` command. By using the `cancel` command, you can either cancel a specified job or cancel all queued requests to a specified printer queue. If you are an ordinary user, you can cancel only the jobs that have your user ID.

With the `cancel` command, you can specify either one or more job IDs or a printer name.

Examples

To cancel a print job with ID 734, use the following command:

```
cancel 734
```

To cancel all queued requests that you have queued up in the printer our_printer, use the following command:

```
cancel our_printer
```

lp

To print one or more files to a specified printer, use the lp command. By default, the lp command accepts input from the standard input. If more than one file is specified, the files are printed in the order of their appearance in the command. The files you are printing should exist until they are printed because the lp command does not make copies of the file while printing (unless you use the -c flag).

Following is a list of flags that can be used with the lp command:

Flag	Meaning
-c	Make a copy of the file so that the file can be deleted or modified while the printing is still going on.
-d*printqueue*	Specify the *printqueue* where the print request is to be directed.
-m	Notify the requesting user at successful completion of the print request by mail.
-n*copies*	Specify the number of copies to be printed.
-t*title*	Print the specified title on the banner page.

Examples

To print the file file1, execute the following command:

```
lp file1
```

In this example, file1 will be printed on the default line printer. However, if you want to print on the specific printer our_printer, use the -d flag as in the following example:

```
lp -dour_printer file1
```

4

GENERAL
COMMANDS

If `file1` is big and you want to get notification after the print job is successfully completed, use the `-m` flag as in the following example:

```
lp -m -dmain_printer file1
```

If you want to print multiple copies of `file1` for distribution to your colleagues, use the `-n` flag as in the following example:

```
lp -n15 -dour_printer file1
```

This example prints 15 copies of `file1` on the printer called `our_printer`. If you want to print a title `urgent memo` in the banner page, use the `-t` flag as in the following example:

```
lp -n15 -t"urgent memo" -dour_printer file1
```

This example prints 15 copies of `file1` on `our_printer` with the title `urgent memo` printed on the banner page.

pr

The `pr` command accepts input from the standard input and generates output on the standard output by default. This command formats the output into pages with the name of the file, date, time, and page numbers. If the line length is longer than the page width, the line is truncated. As the `pr` command formats and paginates the output, you can pipe the output of the `pr` command to a print command such as `lp` to print the output.

Following is a list of some of the flags that can be used with the `pr` command:

Flag	Meaning
`-d`	Generate the output with double spacing.
`-f` or `-F`	Use a form-feed to a new page instead of a sequence of line-feed characters.
`-h "heading"`	Print *heading* instead of the filename as header on each page.
`-l pagelength`	Set the number of lines to be printed on each page to *pagelength* instead of the default of 66.
`-n`	Specify the width of the line number to be printed in front of each line. Optionally, you can specify a character to be printed between the line number and the contents of the line.
`-oindent`	Indent each line by *indent* columns.

Flag	Meaning
-p	Pause after each page if the output is being directed to standard output. To continue, press the Enter key.
-r	Suppress diagnostic messages.
-t	Suppress printing of page headers and page footers.
-w*width*	Set the width of each page to *width* instead of the default of 72.
+*pagenumber*	Specify that the display should start at page number *pagenumber* instead of 1.

Examples

Assume that we have a file `file1` in the current directory, the contents of which are shown here using the `more` command:

```
more file1
This is a test file for pr command
We will use it to show the usage of various flags of pr command
```

The plain-vanilla use of the `pr` command is as follows:

```
pr file1
Wed Dec  4 00:40:14 1996 file1 Page 1


This is a test file for pr command
We will use it to show the usage of various flags of pr command
```

If you want to display the output in double spacing, use the `-d` flag as in the following example:

```
pr -d file1
Wed Dec  4 00:40:14 1996 file1 Page 1


This is a test file for pr command

We will use it to show the usage of various flags of pr command
```

If you want to print a title other than the filename, use the `-h` flag as in the following example:

```
pr -h "TEST FILE FOR pr COMMAND" file1
Wed Dec  4 00:40:14 1996 TEST FILE FOR pr COMMAND Page 1
```

```
This is a test file for pr command
We will use it to show the usage of various flags of pr command
```

If you do not want to print the headers, use the -t flag as in the following example:

pr -t file1
```
This is a test file for pr command
We will use it to show the usage of various flags of pr command
```

If you want to print the line numbers in front of each line and you want to print a - (hyphen) between the line number and the line, use the -n flag as in the following example:

pr -n-5 file1
```
Wed Dec  4 00:40:14 1996 file1 Page 1


    1-This is a test file for pr command
    2-We will use it to show the usage of various flags of pr command
```

lpstat

You can use the lpstat command to display the current status of all line printers. If the lpstat command is executed without any flags, it displays the status of each printer with the entries queued by the lp command.

Following is a list of some of the flags that can be used with the lpstat command:

Flag	Meaning
-a*queue* or -c*queue* or -p*queue*	Display status as well as information on jobs in the specified list of *queue*.
-d	Display the default line printer information.
-o*queue* or -o*jobnumber*	Display the status of the specified *queue* or to display the status of the specified *jobnumber*.
-r	Display status and job information for all queues.
-s	Display summary information about all queues.

Flag	Meaning
-t	Display detailed status information for all queues.
-u*username*	Display the status of print requests started by the specified *username*.
-v*printername*	Display a list for the specified *printername*.

Examples

If you want to find out about all the printers in your system, use the `lpstat` command without any flags as in the following example:

```
lpstat ¦ more
Queue   Dev   Status    Job Files         User     PP %   Blks  Cp Rnk
------- ----- --------- --- --------------- ------- ---- -- ----- --- ---
m_prt   lp0   READY
prt_01  bshde READY
prt_02  lp0   READY
```

If you want to get information about the default line printer, use the -d flag as in the following example:

```
lpstat -d
Queue   Dev   Status    Job Files         User     PP %   Blks  Cp Rnk
------- ----- --------- --- --------------- ------- ---- -- ----- --- ---
m_prt   lp0   READY
```

If you are printing `file1` on `printer_01` and want to find out about the status of the printer and the job, use the -a flag as in the following example:

```
lpstat -aprinter_01
Queue   Dev   Status    Job Files         User     PP %   Blks  Cp Rnk
------- ----- --------- --- --------------- ------- ---- -- ----- --- ---
systems lpprt READY
prt_01: prt_01 is ready and printing
prt_01: Rank    Owner     Job  Files                  Total Size
prt_01: active testuser       735  file1                   156486
bytes
```

Scheduling

UNIX gives you the ability to schedule scripts and commands for execution at some later time. You can specify the exact time when the command should be run. UNIX also provides a way of reporting on the scheduled jobs and removing them if you do not want to execute them.

at

The at command allows you to do the following:

- Schedule a command for execution at a specified time.
- Display a list of scheduled jobs.
- Remove jobs from the scheduled jobs list.

You can schedule jobs by specifying either the absolute time or a time relative to the current time.

Following is a list of some of the flags that can be used with the at command:

Flag	Meaning
-l	Display a list of jobs scheduled by you.
-m	Mail a report of successful execution of the job.
-t *date*	Schedule a job to be executed at the specified date and time.
-r joblist	Remove the jobs specified in the job list from the queue.

You are allowed to execute the at command provided that at least one of the following is true:

- The system has an at.allow file and your user name appears in the at.allow file.
- The system has an at.deny file and your name does not appear in the at.deny file.

The exact location of the at.allow and at.deny files depends on the UNIX system you are working with.

The at command accepts the time, day, and relative increments in a variety of formats. Some of the formats are as follows:

- 1830 December 4
- 6:30 pm December 4
- 6:30 P December 4
- now + 2 hours
- tomorrow 1830
- 1830 next week
- 1830 Tuesday next week

Examples

If you want to schedule a job called my_job at 11:00 P.M. today assuming that the current time is 9:30 P.M., execute any one of the following commands:

```
at 2300 my_job
```

```
at 23:00 my_job
```

```
at 11:00 pm my_job
```

```
at 11:00 P my_job
```

```
at 2300 today my_job
```

If the time currently is 11:30 P.M., the job will be scheduled at 11:00 P.M. the next day.

To schedule my_job 6 hours from now, use the following command:

```
at now + 6 hours my_job
```

To schedule my_job at 6:30 P.M. next week, use the following command:

```
at 6:30 pm next week my_job
```

In the preceding example, if today is Thursday and the current time is 5:30 P.M., my_job will be scheduled for 5:30 P.M. next Thursday. If the current time is 7:30 P.M., my_job will be scheduled for 6:30 P.M. next Friday.

To list the jobs scheduled, use the -l flag as in the following example:

```
at -l
testuser.850519800.a      Fri Dec 13 18:30:00 1996
testuser.849858400.a      Fri Dec  6 02:46:40 1996
```

To remove a scheduled job, use the -r command as in the following example:

```
at -r testuser.850519800.a
at file: testuser.850519800.a deleted
```

atq

The atq command can be used to list the jobs scheduled at a later time. The jobs are displayed in the order of the time scheduled with the earlier-scheduled jobs displayed first.

Following is list of flags that can be used with the atq command:

Flag	Meaning
-c	Display a list of jobs in order of time at which the at command was executed to schedule the jobs.
-n	Display the number of scheduled jobs.

4

GENERAL
COMMANDS

Examples

To list all the jobs scheduled using the at command, use the following command:

```
atq
testuser.849915000.a      Fri Dec  6 18:30:00 1996
testuser.850519800.a      Fri Dec 13 18:30:00 1996
```

If you want to list all the jobs scheduled according to the time the corresponding at command was run rather than according to when the scheduled jobs are supposed to run, use the -c flag as in the following example:

```
atq -c
testuser.850519800.a      Fri Dec 13 18:30:00 1996
testuser.849915000.a      Fri Dec  6 18:30:00 1996
```

If you want to find out the number of jobs currently scheduled, use the -n flag as in the following example:

```
atq -n
2 files in the queue
```

crontab

UNIX systems have a daemon running all the time that can run jobs at regularly scheduled intervals. You can specify the jobs that the crontab command will execute in a file, and the cron daemon will check it when the cron daemon is initialized or when additions or modifications are made to the file.

The entries you can make in the crontab file consist of the following fields (separated by spaces or tab characters):

- minute
- hour
- day (of the month)
- year
- day of the week
- command

Each of these fields can have more than one discrete value (separated by commas), a range of values, or an * (an asterisk, meaning that all values are to be matched).

Following is a list of flags that can be used with the `crontab` command:

Flag	Meaning
-l	List your `crontab` file.
-e	Edit or create the `crontab` file.
-r	Remove your `crontab` file.
-v	List the status of the `crontab` jobs.

Examples

If you want to display the string `Time to go for lunch` at 12:30 P.M. every day, set up the following:

```
30 12 * * * echo "Time to go for lunch"
```

If you want to execute `my_job` on Friday at 4:00 P.M. every week, set up the following:

```
0 16 * * 5 my_job
```

Storage

The following sections discuss a number of commands that can be used for file management. There are commands to back up files to different media, to restore files from different media, to compress files to save disk space, to uncompress files to restore them, and so on.

compress

You can use the `compress` command to reduce the size of a file. A file created by the `compress` command has a `.Z` appended to its name. The compressed file retains the permission and time attributes of the original file.

Following is a list of flags that can be used with the `compress` command:

Flag	Meaning
-d	Force the `compress` command to act as an uncompress command.
-c	Compress the file to standard output (which can be redirected to another file) so that the original file is intact.

4

GENERAL
COMMANDS

Flag	Meaning
-f or -F	Compress the file and overwrite the compressed file if it already exists.
-v	Display the compression percentage.
-V	Display the current version and compile options.

Examples

To compress file1, execute the following command:

```
compress file1
```

If you want the compression statistics, use the -v flag as in the following example:

```
compress -v file1
file1: Compression: 50.85%  -- replaced with file1.Z
```

cpio

You can use the cpio command to copy files to archival medium from disk or to restore files from archival medium to disk. There are three major forms of the cpio command:

- cpio -o to read standard input for path names and copy them to standard output.
- cpio -i to read from standard input archival files and create disk files.
- cpio -p to read standard input for the path name and copy to the specified directory.

Following is a list of some of the flags that can be used with the cpio command:

Flag	Meaning
a	Modify the access time of the copied files to that of the current file.
B	Indicate that cpio should do block I/O.
d	Create a directory if the specified directory does not exist.
f	Copy files that do not match the specified pattern.
r	Copy files interactively with the option of modifying the filename.

Flag	Meaning
t	Create a list of files without actually copying a file.
u	Overwrite a file if it already exists.
v	List the filenames being copied.

Examples

If you have a list of files that you want to copy to a diskette, execute the following command:

```
ls *.txt ¦ cpio -ov > /dev/rfd0
file1.txt
file2.txt
55 blocks
```

This example copies all files that have an extension of .txt and displays the filenames being copied.

If you want to list the files on the diskette, use the t and v flags as in the following example:

```
cpio -itv < /dev/rfd0
100644 testuser     13771 Dec 07 00:13:38 1996 file1.txt
100644 testuser     13947 Dec 07 00:13:30 1996 file2.txt
55 blocks
```

If you want to copy the files from the diskette and rename them while copying, use the r flag as in the following command:

```
cpio -ir "*.txt" < y
Rename <file1.txt>
file3.txt
Rename <file2.txt>
file4.txt
55 blocks
```

In the preceding example, file1.txt is renamed to file3.txt and file2.txt is renamed to file4.txt.

If you want to copy all files from the current directory as well as all the files in its subdirectories, use the -p flag. Additionally, you can use the d flag so that all the needed directories are created. You can execute the commands as follows:

```
find . -print ¦ cpio -pd /u/testuser/cpiodir
```

4

GENERAL COMMANDS

dd

The dd command can be used to read data from the standard input and copy it to the standard output after converting the data according to specified conversion parameters. Along with the data conversion, the physical attributes, such as block size, can also be modified by specifying appropriate parameters.

Following is a list of flags that can be used with the dd command:

Flag	*Meaning*
bs=*blocksize*	Specify the block size of the input and output file. This flag overrides the ibs and obs flags.
if=*filename*	Specify the input *filename* to be copied.
ibs=*blocksize*	Specify the block size of the input file.
fksip=*numberofeof*	Specify the number of end-of-file markers to be skipped in the input file before starting the copy.
files=*numberoffiles*	Specify the number of files to be copied (such as from a tape containing multiple files).
count=*numberofblocks*	Specify the number of blocks to copy from the input file.
skip=*nummberofblocks*	Skip the specified number of blocks in the input file before starting the copy.
of=*filename*	Specify the output *filename* to be created.
obs=*blocksize*	Specify the block size of the output file.
seek=*recordnumber*	Specify the record number in the output file at which to start copying the input file.
conv=*conversionparameter*	Specify the type of conversion to be used. Some of the values of this parameter can be ASCII, EBCDIC, block, unblock, lcase, and ucase.

Examples

If you have a file from a system that stores data in EBCDIC format and you want to convert the data to ASCII, use the following command:

```
dd if=file1 of=file2 conv=ascii
```

This command reads `file1` and converts each character of this file to ASCII and copies the characters to `file2`.

If you want to copy `file1` on disk to a tape with a block size of 1024, use the following command:

```
dd if=file1 of=/dev/rmt0 bs=1024 conv=sync
```

If you want to copy the third file on a tape to a file called `file1`, use the following command:

```
dd if=/dev/rmt0 fskip=2 of=file1
```

If you want to print a memo in capital letters, use the following command to convert `file1` to `file2` and then print `file2`:

```
dd if=file1 of=file2 conv=ucase
lp -dmain_printer file2
```

pack

If you want to save disk space, use the `pack` command to compress a file in a way similar to the `compress` command. The `pack` command compresses a file and generates a new file with `.z` appended to the filename. The original file is removed. The amount of space saved depends on the contents of the file. Usually, you can get from 30 to 50 percent compression for text files. By default, the `pack` command does not compress if it cannot reduce the size of the file.

Following is a list of flags that can be used with the `pack` command:

Flag	Meaning
-	Display statistics about compression.
-f	Force packing.

Examples

If you have a file called `file1` that you want to compress, use the following command:

```
pack file1
pack: file1: 41.7% Compression
```

If you want more information about the compression, use the - (hyphen) flag as in the following example:

```
pack - file1
pack: file1: 41.7% Compression
        from 28160 to 16404 bytes
        Huffman tree has 15 levels below root
        102 distinct bytes in input
        dictionary overhead = 124 bytes
        effective  entropy  = 4.66 bits/byte
        asymptotic entropy  = 4.62 bits/byte
```

In some cases, pack may not compress the file and will give you an error as it does in the following example:

```
pack file1
pack: file1: no saving
        - file unchanged
```

In such a case, you can force compression by using the -f flag as in the following example:

```
pack -f  file1
pack: file1: 40.8% Compression
```

pcat

The pcat command can be used to uncompress a file to the standard output. This command does not have any flags.

Examples

If you want to uncompress a file called file1.z that you have earlier created by using the pack command on file1, use one of the following commands:

```
pcat file1
```

```
pcat file1.z
```

tar

The tar command is used to copy files from disk to an archival medium (usually tape) or vice versa. The tar command does not provide any recovery from tape errors.

Following is a list of some of the flags that can be used with the tar command:

Flag	Meaning
-c	Create a new archive and write the file details at the beginning of the archive.

Flag	Meaning
-t	Generate a list of files in the archive.
-x	Obtain one or more files from an archive. If you specify a directory name, all the files in the directory are extracted. If no file or directory is specified, all the files in the specified archive are extracted. If one or more files extracted do not exist, they are created with the original user ID if you have root authority; otherwise, they are created with your user ID.
-m	Use the time of extraction from the archive as the modification time of the extracted file.
-p	Restore the files with their original permission, ignoring the current setting of the umask.
-f *archive*	Use the specified *archive* as the archive name instead of the system default.
-v	Display the name of each file as it is processed.

Examples

If you want to extract all the files in the /u/testuser directory from the archive file on the /dev/rmt1 tape device, use the following command:

```
tar --xvf /dev/rmt1 /u/testuser
```

If you want to archive a file to an archive on the default tape drive, use the following command:

```
tar -c file1
```

uncompress

The uncompress command can be used to uncompress a file that has earlier been compressed using the compress command. By default, the uncompress command uncompresses a file in place; that is, the compressed file is deleted and the uncompressed file—without the .Z suffix—is created in its place. The uncompressed file retains the permission and modification time attributes of the compressed file, but the user and the group of the file are changed to that of the user who is uncompressing the file.

Following is a list of some of the flags that can be used with the `uncompress` command:

Flag	Meaning
-f or -F	Force the uncompress even though a file by the name of the uncompressed file may already exist.
-c	Uncompress the specified by file to the standard output, retaining the original compressed file.
-v	Display a message with the uncompressed filename.
-q	Suppress display of compression statistics from the uncompress command.

Examples

If you want to uncompress `file1.Z`, use either of the following commands:

```
uncompress file1
```

```
uncompress file1.Z
```

If you want to uncompress `file1.Z` to standard output and retain the original compressed file, use the `-c` flag as in the following example:

```
uncompress -c file1
```

unpack

The `unpack` command can be used to uncompress files that have the `.z` extension and that have been compressed using the `pack` command. The uncompressed file is created at the same place as the compressed file, and the compressed file is removed. The uncompressed file retains the attributes (such as the user, group, permission, access, and modification time) of the compressed file. The `unpack` command does not uncompress the file if a file by the name of the uncompressed file already exists.

If you want to uncompress `file1.z`, use either of the following two commands:

```
unpack file1
```

```
unpack file1.z
```

zcat

The `zcat` command can be used to uncompress a file that has been compressed using the `compress` command to the standard output, retaining the compressed file. You can redirect the standard output to another file to get an expanded version of the compressed file. This command works the same way as the uncompress command with the -c flag.

Examples

If you want to create a copy of the uncompressed version of a file without destroying the compressed file, use the following command:

```
zcat file1.Z > file2
```

This example creates file2, which is an uncompressed version of file1.Z, and at the same time retains file1.Z.

Status Commands

The following sections discuss several commands that display the status of various parts of the system. These commands can be used to monitor the system status at any point in time.

date

You can use the date command to display the current date and time in a specified format. If you are the root user, use the date command to set the system date.

To display the date and time, you must specify a + (plus) sign followed by the desired format. The format can be as follows:

Format	Appearance of Date
%A	Display the date complete with weekday name.
%b or %h	Display a short month name.
%B	Display the complete month name.
%c	Display default date and time representation.
%d	Display the day of the month as a number from 1 through 31.
%D	Display the date in mm/dd/yy format.
%H	Display the hour as a number from 00 through 23.
%I	Display the hour as a number from 00 through 12.

continues

4

GENERAL
COMMANDS

Format	Appearance of Date
%j	Display the day of the year as a number from 1 through 366.
%m	Display the month as a number from 1 through 12.
%M	Display minutes as a number from 0 through 59.
%p	Display AM or PM appropriately.
%r	Display 12-hour clock time (01-12) using the AM/PM notation.
%S	Display seconds as a number from 0 through 59.
%T	Display the time in hh;mm;ss format for a 24-hour clock.
%U	Display the week number of the year as a number from 1 through 53 (counting Sunday as first day of the week).
%w	Display the day of the week as a number from 0 through 6 (with Sunday counted as 0).
%W	Display the week number of the year as a number from 1 through 53 (counting Monday as first day of the week).
%x	Display the default date format.
%X	Display the time format.
%y	Display the last two digits of the year from 00 through 99.
%Y	Display the year with the century as a decimal number.
%Z	Display the time-zone name, if it is available.

Examples

If you want to display the date without formatting, use `date` without any formatting descriptor as follows:

```
date
Sat Dec  7 11:50:59 EST 1996
```

If you want to display only the date in `mm/dd/yy` format, use the following command:

```
date +%m/%d/%y
12/07/96
```

If you want to format the date in `yy/mm/dd` format and the time in `hh;mm;ss` format, use the following command:

```
date "+%y/%m/%d %H:%M:%S"
96/12/07 11:57:27
```

Following is another way of formatting the date:

```
date +%A","%B" "%d","%Y
Sunday, December 15,1996
```

If you want the Julian date, use the following command:

```
date +%j
350
```

If you want to find the week number for the current week, you have two options: the `W` and `U` flags, as shown in the following commands:

```
date +%W
49
date +%U
50
```

env

The env command can be used to display the current environment or to change one or more of the environment variables and run a specified command. The changes are effective only during the execution of the command.

You can use the `-i` flag with the env command. Use `-i` to indicate that only the variables set up as part of the env command are used for the specified command; all the current variable setups are ignored.

Examples

If you want to display the current environment, use the following command:

```
env
```

Assume that we have a script called `my_job` that displays the current setting of the variable called `LANG`. If you execute the script `my_job` as part of the `env` command without modifying the `LANG` variable, you get the following result:

```
env PATH=/u/testuser/jobs:$PATH my_job
LANG = C
```

If you modify the `LANG` variable as part of the `env` command, you get the following result:

```
env LANG=C++ PATH=/u/testuser/jobs:$PATH my_job
LANG = C++
```

If you use the `-i` flag and do not modify `LANG` as part of the `env` command, that variable is not available to `my_job`; you get the following result:

```
env -i PATH=/u/testuser/jobs:$PATH my_job
LANG =
```

iostat

The `iostat` command can be used to obtain statistics about the CPU, disks, and TTY of a system. The first time you run `iostat` after you boot the system, `iostat` provides the statistics since that boot. Subsequent executions of this command provide statistics since the last execution of the `iostat` command.

The `iostat` command displays the following details:

- TTY and CPU header
- TTY and CPU statistics detail
- Physical volume header
- One line for each physical volume

Following is a list of data items displayed for TTY and CPU statistics:

- `tin` displays the number of characters read by the system for all TTYs.
- `tout` displays the number of characters written by the system for all TTYs.
- `%user` displays the utilization percentage of the CPU at the application level.
- `%system` displays the utilization percentage of the CPU at the system level.
- `%idle` displays the utilization percentage of the CPU while it was idling (this represents the unused utilization of the CPU).
- `%iowait` displays the idling percentage of the CPU while waiting for the I/O request.

Following is a list of data items displayed as part of the physical volume utilization:

- %tm_act displays the active utilization percentage of the physical volume.
- Kbps displays the number of kilobytes transferred per second to or from the physical volume.
- tps displays the number of physical I/O requests to the physical volume.
- msps displays average number of milliseconds required for each seek of the physical volume.
- Kb_read displays the number of kilobytes read from the physical volume.
- Kb_wrtn displays the number of kilobytes written to the physical volume.

Following is a list of flags that can be used with the iostat command:

Flag	Meaning
-d	Display only the physical volume utilization report. This flag cannot be used with -t flag.
-t	Display only the TTY and CPU utilization report. This flag cannot be used with the -d flag.

Examples

If you want to display only the TTY and CPU utilization, use the -t flag as in the following example:

```
iostat -t
```

```
tty:     tin        tout      cpu:   % user    % sys    % idle    % iowait
         0.5        78.7             32.6      25.2      35.7       6.4
```

If you want to display only the utilization of the physical volume of disk1, use the -d flag as in the following example:

```
iostat -d disk1
```

```
Disks:      % tm_act     Kbps      tps    Kb_read    Kb_wrtn
disk1            6.7      4.3       5.0    2339721    4048758
```

sar

You can use the sar command to get a report about system information. The sar command allows you to save the information report. By default, the sar command generates the CPU utilization reports, but you can use various flags to collect information about other system activities.

Following is a list of some of the flags that can be used with the sar command:

Flag	Meaning
-A	Report data on all system activities.
-a	Report data on the use of the file system access routine.
-b	Report buffer activities.
-c	Report system calls such as forks, execs, and so on.
-e optionally followed by time in hh;mm;ss format	Specify the time at which data accumulation should be terminated.
-f *file*	Extract data from the specified *file*.
-i *seconds*	Extract data from the file for the closest time closest in *seconds*.
-k	Report on kernel activity.
-m	Report on semaphore and message activities.
-o *file*	Save the activity data in the specified *file*.
-r	Report on paging statistics.
-s optionally followed by time in hh;mm;ss format	Specify the time at which to start the data accumulation.
-v	Report on process and i-node activity.
-y	Report on TTY activity.

uname

The uname command displays details about the operating system and the computer system on the standard output. You can use certain flags to set the system name.

Following is a list of some of the flags that can be used with the uname command:

Flag	Meaning
-m	Display the machine ID.
-r	Display the release number of the operating system.
-s	Display the system name.
-v	Display the operating system version.
-S *name*	Modify the system name.
-a	Display the machine ID, the release number of the operating system, and the system name.

Examples

If you want to display details about the hardware and operating system, you can use the -a flag as in the following example:

```
uname -a
AIX main_system 2 3 000010000526
```

In this example, the information displayed is as follows:

Operating system name	AIX
Machine name	main_system
Operating system release number	2
Operating system version number	3
Machine ID	000010000526

uptime

The uptime command displays the following information:

- The current time
- The length of time the system has been up
- The number of users currently logged on
- The number of jobs executing in the system

4

GENERAL COMMANDS

vmstat

The vmstat command can be used to get information about the processes, virtual memory, physical volumes, and CPU activity. The information includes the CPU utilization, virtual memory, and physical volume. This information can be used to monitor the load on the system.

The first invocation of vmstat displays the statistics since the system startup; subsequent invocations display statistics since the last invocation. You can specify a count and an interval parameter to control the number of reports generated and an interval between the reports.

The details displayed by vmstat are as follows:

- Processes
- Virtual memory
- Page
- Faults
- CPU

The details displayed for the *processes* are as follows:

- r displays the number of processes placed in the queue and ready to execute.
- b displays the number of processes placed in the queue and waiting for execution.

The details displayed for the *memory* are as follows:

- avm displays the number of pages being consumed (the pages are from the page space).
- fre displays the number of pages in the free list.

The details displayed for *page* are as follows:

- re displays the number of page reclaims per second observed in the specified interval.
- pi displays number of pages brought in from the page space in the specified interval.
- po displays the number of pages swapped out to page space in the specified interval.
- fr displays the number of pages freed in the specified interval.
- sr displays the number of page examined to determine whether they can be freed in the specified interval.
- cy displays the number of clock revolutions per second.

The details displayed for *faults* are as follows:

- in displays the number of interrupts per second in the specified interval.
- sy displays the number of system calls per second in the specified interval.
- cs displays the number of context switches per second in the specified interval.

The details displayed for *CPU* are as follows:

- us displays the percentage utilization of CPU at the application level during the specified interval.
- sy displays the percentage utilization of CPU at the system level during the specified interval.
- id displays the percentage utilization of CPU idling during the specified interval without any I/O wait.
- wa displays the percentage utilization of CPU idling during the specified interval caused by disk I/O requests.

You can specify up to four physical volume names to get the number of transfers that occurred in those disks in the specified interval.

You can use the -s flag with the vmstat command. Use -s to display the statistics since the system initialization.

Examples

If you want to display the statistics five times, at intervals of five seconds, execute the following command:

```
vmstat 5 5
procs     memory              page                 faults          cpu
----- -----------   -------------------------   -------------   -----------
 r  b    avm    fre   re  pi  po   fr    sr   cy   in    sy   cs  us sy id wa
 1  0  44036    120    0   0   0   125   275   0   366  1458 391  33 25 36  6
 1  0  44036    120    0   0   0   542   938   0   446  4932 246  65 24  0 12
 1  0  44036    121    0   0   0   624  1116   0   453  5848 259  64 25  0 11
 1  0  44037    124    0   0   0   512  1010   0   434  4812 266  59 25  0 16
 0  0  44037    121    0   0   0   564  1109   0   426  4838 265  64 24  0 11
```

Text Processing

UNIX provides several commands to process the contents of a text file.

4

GENERAL
COMMANDS

cut

You can use the cut command to extract data from each line of a text file. This command can be used for a file that contains data records so that each line consists of one or more fields separated by tab characters.

Following is a list of some of the flags that can be used with the cut command:

Flag	Meaning
-c*characterlist*	Specify a list of characters to be cut from each line.
-f*fieldlist*	Specify a list of fields to be cut from each line. You can additionally specify the flag -d*character* to override the character to be interpreted as the field delimiter. You can also specify the flag -s to suppress lines that do not have the specified delimiter character.

Examples

Assume that we have a file called file1 whose contents are as follows:

```
more file1
Misty      Ghosh
Saptarsi        Guha
Sanjiv  Guha
```

In this file, the fields are separated by tab characters.

If you want to extract the first field, use the following command:

```
cut -f1 file1
Misty
Saptarsi
Sanjiv
```

If you want to cut the characters 2 to 6, use the following command:

```
cut -c2-5 file1
isty
apta
anji
```

If you want to cut all characters in the first field up to the first s character, use the following command:

```
cut -d"s" -f1   file1
Mi
Saptar
Sanjiv  Guha
```

You will notice that the third line is cut completely. To suppress lines that do not contain the s character, use the -s flag as in the following example:

```
cut -d"s" -s -f1   file1
Mi
Saptar
```

ex

The ex command invokes the ex editor to edit one or more files.

Following is a list of some of the flags that can be used with the ex command:

Flag	Meaning
-c *subcommand*	Perform the specified *subcommand* on the specified file before invoking the ex command.
-R	Disallow updating the file.
-w*size*	Set the window to the number of lines equal to *size*.
-v	Invoke the vi editor.
-r *file*	Do the recovery on the specified *file*.

Once you are in the ex editor, you can use the following subcommands to move around in the file and edit the file:

Subcommand	Action
z	Invoke full-screen mode.
u	Undo the last change made.
n	Move to the next file if you have invoked the ex editor with multiple files.
/*pattern*/	Find a *pattern* in the file.
d	Delete one or more lines.
a	Append.

4

GENERAL
COMMANDS

The ex operates in the following modes:

- *Command mode:* When the ex editor starts, it is in command mode, which displays a : (colon) prompt at which you can enter a subcommand.
- *Text input mode:* In this mode, you can add or change text in the file. You can enter text using the a, I, or c subcommand. The use of these subcommands allows you to enter text in the buffer. You can return to command mode by entering a . (a single period) as the first character of the text buffer.

fmt

The fmt command can be used to format files to a 72-character line by default. The fmt command preserves the blank lines in the input file as well as the spacing between words. You can modify the line length using the -Width flag.

Examples

Assume that we have file1 whose contents are shown here:

```
more file1
This is a test file for fmt

The fmt command      formats a file
for mail command
```

Notice that we have a blank line in the file and that the spacing between command and formats on the third line is more than one character. Let's format file1 using the fmt command to create file2 as in the following command:

```
fmt file1 > file2
```

Now let's see the contents of file2 using the more command as follows:

```
more file2
This is a test file for fmt

The fmt command      formats a file for mail command
```

In this example, the blank line and interword spacing have been preserved.

fold

The fold command can be used to generate multiple lines from a single line by splitting the line at the specified position. By default, the line length is 80 bytes. A newline character is inserted at the end of the line.

Following is list of flags that can be used with the `fold` command:

Flag	Meaning
-b	Specify the position in bytes.
-s	Split a line after the last space at a position that is less than or equal to the specified width.
-w *width*	Specify the line width.

Examples

Assume that we have `file1` containing one line of 129 characters which is shown here:

```
more file1
The fold command can be used on files which have line lengths more than 80
bytes
, it breaks the line into multiple 80 byte lines
```

If you want to split the line at byte position 40, use the following command:

```
fold -w 40  file1 > file2; more file2
The fold command can be used on files wh
ich have line lengths more than 80 bytes
, it breaks the line into multiple 80 by
te lines
```

In this example, the split happens in the middle of words. If you do not want to split words, use the -s flag as in the following example:

```
fold -w 40 -s  file1 > file2; more file2
The fold command can be used on files
which have line lengths more than 80
bytes, it breaks the line into multiple
80 byte lines
```

join

The `join` command can be used to merge two files (one can be standard input) to create a third file (which can be standard output). Each line in the file is merged on the basis of a field that has the same value in both input files to create one line in the output file. The fields in each file are separated by either a space or the tab character.

4

GENERAL COMMANDS

Following is a list of flags that can be used with the `join` command:

Flag	Meaning
`-1` *field* or `-j1` *field*	Specify that the join should be made on the basis of the *field* in the first file.
`-2` *field* or `-j2` *field*	Specify that the join should be made on the basis of the *field* in the second file.
`-e` *string*	Specify that blank fields in the output file be replaced by the specified *string*.
`-o` *fileid.fieldnumber*	Specify that the output should consist of the specified fields. You can specify multiple fields by separating them with commas.
`-t` *character*	Modify the field separator *character* from the default value of the space.
`-a` *fileid*	Generate an output line for each line in the file specified by the *fileid* parameter for lines that cannot be matched to the lines in the other file using the join field. The output lines are produced in addition to the default output.
`-v` *fileid*	Generate an output line for each line in the file specified by the *fileid* parameter for lines that cannot be matched to the lines in the other file using the join field. The default output is not produced.

Examples

Assume that we have two files, `file1` and `file2`, whose contents are shown as follows:

```
more file1
computer1 16MB 1.2GB 17inch CDROM
computer2 8MB 840MB 14inch
computer3 12MB 1.6GB 17inch
computer4 4MB 270MB 14inch

more file2
computer1 1stfloor office5
computer3 2ndfloor office9A
computer4 1stfloor office2
computer5 3rdfloor office1
```

If you want to join the two files and display only the matching lines, execute the following command:

```
join file1 file2
computer1 16MB 1.2GB 17inch CDROM 1stfloor office5
computer3 12MB 1.6GB 17inch 2ndfloor office9A
computer4 4MB 270MB 14inch CDROM 1stfloor office2
```

If you want to join the two files and display the matching lines as well as the nonmatching lines from the specified file, use the -a flag as in the following example:

```
join -a1 file1 file2
computer1 16MB 1.2GB 17inch CDROM 1stfloor office5
computer2 8MB 840MB 14inch
computer3 12MB 1.6GB 17inch 2ndfloor office9A
computer4 4MB 270MB 14inch CDROM 1stfloor office2
```

This example displays the line with computer2 from file1 because it does not have a matching line in file2. If you want to display only the lines that do not match lines from the specified file, use the -v flag as in the following example:

```
join -v2 file1 file2
computer5 3rdfloor office1
```

This example displays the line with computer5 from file2 because it does not have a matching line in file1.

If you want to display only certain fields from the input files to the output file, use the -o flag as in the following example:

```
join -o 1.1 2.2 2.3 1.5 file1 file2
computer1 1stfloor office5 CDROM
computer3 2ndfloor office9A
computer4 1stfloor office2 CDROM
```

In this example, the line with computer3 is displayed with one field short because that field is not present in the input file. You can insert a fixed legend in the empty field in the output by using the -e flag as in the following example:

```
join -o 1.1 2.2 2.3 1.5 -e"NO CDROM" file1 file2
computer1 1stfloor office5 CDROM
computer3 2ndfloor office9A NO CDROM
computer4 1stfloor office2 NO CDROM
```

paste

The paste command can be used to paste lines from one or more files (one of them can be the standard input) to the standard output, which can be redirected to a file. The paste command concatenates the line from each input file to the output file, separating them by default with the tab character.

Following is a list of flags that can be used with the `paste` command:

Flag	Meaning
`-dlist`	Specify characters that will be used to separate corresponding lines from the input files in the output file. You can specify multiple characters if you have multiple input files.
`-s`	Merge subsequent lines from the input file for each input file, one at a time, separated by the specified delimiter character.

Examples

Assume that we have two files, `file1` and `file2`, whose contents are shown here:

```
more file1
computer1 16MB 1.2GB 17inch CDROM
computer2 8MB 840MB 14inch
computer3 12MB 1.6GB 17inch
computer4 4MB 270MB 14inch
```

```
more file2
computer1 1stfloor office5
computer3 2ndfloor office9A
computer4 1stfloor office2
computer5 3rdfloor office1
```

If you want to merge `file1` and `file2`, use the following command:

```
paste file1 file2
computer1 16MB 1.2GB 17inch CDROM        computer1 1stfloor office5
computer2 8MB 840MB 14inch        computer3 2ndfloor office9A
computer3 12MB 1.6GB 17inch        computer4 1stfloor office2
computer4 4MB 270MB 14inch        computer5 3rdfloor office1
```

The lines from `file1` and `file2` are separated by tab characters.

If you want to modify the default separator from the tab character to, for example, the / (slash), use the `-d` flag as in the following example:

```
paste -d"/" file1 file2
computer1 16MB 1.2GB 17inch CDROM/computer1 1stfloor office5
computer2 8MB 840MB 14inch/computer3 2ndfloor office9A
computer3 12MB 1.6GB 17inch/computer4 1stfloor office2
computer4 4MB 270MB 14inch /computer5 3rdfloor office1
```

If you want to merge the lines from within each input file, use the -s flag as in the following example:

```
paste -d"/" -s file1 file2
computer1 16MB 1.2GB 17inch CDROM/computer2 8MB 840MB 14inch/computer3
③12MB 1.6G
B 17inch/computer4 4MB 270MB 14inch
computer1 1stfloor office5/computer3 2ndfloor office9A/computer4
③1stfloor office
2/computer5 3rdfloor office1
```

sort

The sort command is used to sort one or more files in the specified order by the specified key. It can also be used to merge files that have already been sorted. When more than one file is used, the sort command concatenates these files before sorting according to the specifications.

Following is a list of some of the flags that can be used with the sort command:

Flag	Meaning
-k*key*	Specify the *key* on which to sort. The specification for the key includes the starting field and column position and the end field and column position.
-A	Specify that sorting be done according to ASCII sequence.
-c	Check whether the specified files are sorted according to the specified key and order.
-d	Sort according to dictionary order.
-f	Change all letters to uppercase before the sort.
-i	Ignore nondisplayable characters for comparison.
-m	Merge presorted input files.
-n	Sort according to numeric value.
-o*file*	Redirect the output to the specified *file* instead of to the standard output.

4

GENERAL
COMMANDS

continues

Flag	Meaning
-r	Sort the output in the reverse order of the specified order.
-u	Create only one line in the output for lines that sort identically.

Examples

Assume that we have a file called file1 whose contents are shown here:

more file1
```
disk drive
memory
video memory
monitor
[tape drive]
CD-ROM
3.5inch diskette
modem
monitor
sound blaster
```

If you want to sort file1, use the following command:

sort file1
```
3.5inch diskette
CD-ROM
[tape drive]
disk drive
memory
modem
monitor
monitor
sound blaster
video memory
```

If you want to sort in the reverse order, use the -r flag as in the following example:

sort -r file1
```
video memory
sound blaster
monitor
monitor
modem
memory
disk drive
[tape drive]
CD-ROM
3.5inch diskette
```

If you want to sort according to alphabetic order, use the `-d` flag as in the following example:

```
sort -d file1
3.5inch diskette
CD-ROM
disk drive
memory
modem
monitor
monitor
sound blaster
[tape drive]
video memory
```

In this example, the line `[tape drive]` is sorted as `tape drive` because the `[` and `]` are ignored by the `-d` flag.

If you want only one line to be retained in case more than one line is sorted equally, use the `-u` flag as in the following example:

```
sort -u file1
3.5inch diskette
CD-ROM
[tape drive]
disk drive
memory
modem
monitor
sound blaster
video memory
```

In this example, the line `monitor` appears only once, even though there are two such entries in the file.

If you want to sort `file1` according to the uppercase-letter sort order, use the `-f` flag as in the following example:

```
sort -f file1
3.5inch diskette
CD-ROM
disk drive
memory
modem
monitor
monitor
sound blaster
video memory
[tape drive]
```

tr

You can use the `tr` command to translate or delete characters from standard input to generate standard output. Following are the details of the main functions of the `tr` command:

- Translate specified characters in the input to new specified characters in the output.
- Delete specified characters in the input from the input to generate the output.
- Delete all but the first occurrence of the specified characters.

Following is a list of some of the flags that can be used with the `tr` command:

Flag	Meaning
-c	Translate all but the specified characters using the specified new character.
-d	Delete the specified characters.
-s	Delete all but the first occurrence of the specified characters.

You can specify the input and output sequence of characters in certain special ways as follows:

- [*character1-character2*] to specify a range of characters including `character1` and `character2`.
- [*character*number*] to specify *number* occurrences of *character*.
- [*character**] to specify the use of as many occurrences as are needed of *character* so that the input string of characters to be translated matches the output characters.
- [:*characterlist*:] to specify a list of characters as the input or output string. The *characterlist* can be `upper`, `lower`, `alpha`, `space`, `digit`, and so on.

Examples

Assume that we have `file1` whose contents are shown as follows:

```
more file1
"this        is a test file
for tr command"
"it has 4 lines
but should be 1 line"
```

If you want to change the double quotes to spaces, use the following command:

```
tr '\"' ' ' < file1
 this        is a test file
for tr command
 it has 4 lines
but should be 1 line
```

If you want to change all lowercase letters to uppercase letter, use the following command:

```
tr [:lower:] [:upper:] < file1
"THIS         IS A TEST FILE
FOR TR COMMAND"
"IT HAS 4 LINES
BUT SHOULD BE 1 LINE"
```

If you want to delete all the newline characters from this file, use the -d flag as in the following example:

```
tr -d '\n' < file1
"this         is a test file for tr command""it has 4 lines but should
be 1 line"
```

If you want to delete all but the first occurrence of a space and replace the space with a - (hyphen), use the -s flag as in the following example:

```
tr -s ' ' '-' < file1
"this-is-a-test-file-
for-tr-command"
"it-has-4-lines-
but-should-be-1-line"
```

uniq

The uniq command can be used to eliminate duplicate adjacent lines from a file or from standard input to generate standard output or another file. This is the default operation of the uniq command. However, it is possible to compare only part of a line for comparison by using certain flags.

Following is a list of some of the flags that can be used with the uniq command:

Flag	Meaning
-c	Precede each line with a number while displaying the output (the number specifies the number of occurrences of the line in the input file).

continues

4

GENERAL
COMMANDS

Flag	Meaning
-d	Display only the lines that occur multiple times adjacent to each other in the input file.
-u	Display only the lines that appear only once in the input file.
-s *numberofcharacters* or +*numberofcharacters*	Specify the number of characters from the start of a line that will be ignored while comparing adjacent lines.
-*numberoffields* or -f *numberoffields*	Specify the number of fields from the start of a line that will be ignored while comparing adjacent lines.

Examples

Assume that we have file1 whose contents are displayed as shown here:

```
more file1
This is line 1
This is line 1
This is line 2
This is line 3
THIS IS line 3
This is line 4
```

If you want to find the unique lines in file1, use the following command:

```
uniq file1
This is line 1
This is line 2
This is line 3
THIS IS line 3
This is line 4
```

In this example, the first line has been dropped because it is identical to the second line. If you want to display only the duplicate lines, use the -d flag as in the following example:

```
uniq -d file1
This is line 1
```

If you want to display the lines that appear only once in file1, use the -u flag as in the following example:

```
uniq -u file1
This is line 2
This is line 3
THIS IS line 3
This is line 4
```

In this example, the first two lines are not displayed because they are identical. If you want to skip the first two fields while comparing adjacent lines, use the -f flag as in the following example:

```
uniq -f 2 file1
This is line 1
This is line 2
This is line 3
This is line 4
```

sed

You can use the sed command to edit a file using a script. In the script, you can specify commands to edit one or more lines according to rules specified as part of one or more commands.

Following is a list of some of the flags that can be used with the sed command:

Flag	Meaning
-e *command*	Use the specified sed *command* to edit the file.
-f *filename*	Use the *filename* as the editing script to edit the file.
-n	Suppress messages from sed.

The sed command uses two different areas while performing editing:

- The *pattern area* holds selected lines for editing.
- The *hold area* temporarily holds the lines.

The sed subcommands can affect either all of the lines or only the specified lines.

Following is a list of some of the subcommands that affect the ***pattern area*** used by the sed command:

Subcommand	Action
#	Specify the start of comments. Everything in a line following the # is treated as a comment.
:*label*	Specify an addressable *label* that can be used in the script.
[/*pattern*/]=	Write to output the line number of each line that contains the specified *pattern*.

continues

Subcommand	Action
[*address*]a*textstring*	Append *textstring* to each line specified by the *address*.
[*address1*][,*address2*]c\ *textstring*	Replace the lines in the specified address the *textstring*.
[*address1*][,*address2*]d	Delete the lines in the specified address range.
[*address*]i*textstring*	Insert *textstring* before each specified line.
[*address1*][,*address2*]p	Print the lines in the specified address range.
[*address1*][,*address2*]n	Specify that the current line be displayed and that the next line be made the current line.
[*address1*][,*address*]N	Specify that the current line be appended to the contents of the pattern area separated by a newline character.
[*address*]q	Exit when the specified address is encountered.
[*address1*][,*address2*]s/ *old pattern*/*new pattern*/ [*flag*]	Change the *old pattern* to *new pattern* in the specified range. The behavior of the replacement can be modified by specified *flag*s.
[*address1*][,*address2*] w *file*	Write the contents of the specified range to the specified *file*.
[*address1*][,*address2*]y/ *old character list* /*new character list*/	Modify each character in the *old character list* by the corresponding character in the *new character list*.

Following is a list of some of the subcommands that affect the ***hold area*** used by the sed command:

Subcommand	Action
`[address1][,address2]g`	Copy the contents of the hold area to the pattern area, which then becomes the new content of the pattern area.
`[address1][,address2]G`	Append the contents of the hold area to the pattern area following the specified address.
`[address1][,address2]h`	Copy the contents of the pattern area to the hold area, which then becomes the new contents of the hold area.
`[address1][,address2]H`	Append the contents of the pattern area to the hold area following the specified address.
`[address1][,address2]x`	Exchange the contents of the pattern and hold areas.

Examples

Assume that we have `file1` whose contents are displayed as shown here:

```
more file1
This file is a test file for sed command
- - - - - - - - - - - - - - - - - - - - - - - - - - - - - - - - - - - - -
The sed command is used for stream editing files
- - - - - - - - - - - - - - - - - - - - - - - - - - - - - - - - - - - - - - -
The sed command a number of sub-commands which may be used to do the
- - - - - - - - - - - - - - - - - - - - - - - - - - - - - - - - - - - - - - - - - - - - - - - - - - - -
editing in specified line
- - - - - - - - - - - - - - - - - -
```

If you want to print the line numbers of the line in which a specified pattern is found, use the following command:

```
sed -e "/sed/=" file1
1
This file is a test file for sed command
- - - - - - - - - - - - - - - - - - - - - - - - - - - - - - - - - - - - -
3
The sed command is used for stream editing files
- - - - - - - - - - - - - - - - - - - - - - - - - - - - - - - - - - - - - - -
5
The sed command a number of sub-commands which may be used to do the
- - - - - - - - - - - - - - - - - - - - - - - - - - - - - - - - - - - - - - - - - - - - - - - - - - - -
```

```
editing in specified line
- - - - - - - - - - - - - - - - - - - - - - -
```

In this example, the line numbers are displayed for the lines containing the pattern sed. If you want to add a specified text after each specified line, use the following command:

sed -f sfile file1
```
This file is a test file for sed command
+++++++++++++++++++++++++++++++++++
- - - - - - - - - - - - - - - - - - - - - - - - - - - - - - - - - - - -
The sed command is used for stream editing files
+++++++++++++++++++++++++++++++++++
- - - - - - - - - - - - - - - - - - - - - - - - - - - - - - - - - - - - - - - -
The sed command a number of sub-commands which may be used to do the
+++++++++++++++++++++++++++++++++
- - - - - - - - - - - - - - - - - - - - - - - - - - - - - - - - - - - - - - - - - - - - - - - - - - -
editing in specified line
- - - - - - - - - - - - - - - - - - - - - - -
```

In this example, the file sfile contains the following line:

```
/sed/a\
+++++++++++++++++++++++++++++++++++
```

In this example, a string of + (plus signs) is printed after each line containing the string sed. If you want to delete lines containing a specified string, use the following command:

sed -f sfile file1
```
This file is a test file for sed command
The sed command is used for stream editing files
The sed command a number of sub-commands which may be used to do the
editing in specified line
```

In this example, sfile contains the following:

```
/---/d
```

In this example, all lines that contain the string - - - are deleted. If you want to change all occurrences of a particular string to another string, use the following command:

sed -f sfile file1
```
This file is a test file for sed command
++++++++++++++++++++++++++++++++++++++++
The sed command is used for stream editing files
- - - - - - - - - - - - - - - - - - - - - - - - - - - - - - - - - - - -
The sed command a number of sub-commands which may be used to do the
- - - - - - - - - - - - - - - - - - - - - - - - - - - - - - - - - - - - - - - - - - - - - - - - - - -
editing in specified line
- - - - - - - - - - - - - - - - - - - - - - -
```

In this example, `sfile` contains the following:

```
1,3s/----/++++/g
```

In this example, all occurrences of `----` are replaced by `++++` for lines 1 through 3. If you want to insert a specified string before each line containing a specified string, use the following command:

`sed -f sfile file1`
```
++++
This file is a test file for sed command
----------------------------------------
++++
The sed command is used for stream editing files
------------------------------------------------
++++
The sed command a number of sub-commands which may be used to do the
-------------------------------------------------------------------
editing in specified line
-------------------------
```

In this example, `sfile` contains the following:

```
/sed/i\
++++
```

In this example, a string `++++` is printed before each line in which the string `sed` appears. If you want to change each occurrence of a character to another character, use the following command:

`sed -f sfile file1`
```
This file is A test file for sed commAnd
++++++++++++++++++++++++++++++++++++++++
The sed commAnd is used for streAm editing files
------------------------------------------------
The sed command a number of sub-commands which may be used to do the
-------------------------------------------------------------------
editing in specified line
-------------------------
```

In this example, `sfile` contains the following:

```
1,3s/-/+/g
```

In this example, each occurrence of a - (hyphen) is modified to a + (plus sign), and each occurrence of a is modified to A for lines 1 through 3, inclusive. If you want to delete all lines but the ones in which the specified pattern occurs, use the following command:

`sed -f sfile file1`
```
This file is a test file for sed command
The sed command is used for stream editing files
The sed command a number of sub-commands which may be used to do the
```

In this example, `sfile` contains the following:

```
/sed/!d
```

In this example, the ! (exclamation mark) is used to denote that all lines except those that contain the string `sed` are to be processed.

Miscellaneous Commands

The following sections discuss some of the commands available to do miscellaneous operations in UNIX.

banner

You can use the `banner` command to print one or more characters in a large size.

Example

If you want to print the word `banner` in a large size on the standard output, use the following command:

banner banner

```
#####     ##     #     #  #     #  ######  #####
#    #   #  #    ##    #  ##    #  #            #
#####   #    #   # #   #  # #   #  #####     #
#    #  ######  #  #  #  #  #  #  #        #####
#    #  #    #  #   ## #  #   ## #        #    #
#####   #    #  #    # #  #    # #  ######  #    #
```

bc

If you want to perform simple arithmetic expressions in UNIX, use the `bc` command. By default, all the numbers are assumed to be decimal numbers, but you can also perform operations on octal or hexadecimal numbers. You can also scale decimal numbers. The `bc` command accepts input first from the specified file and then from standard input. You can, however, use input redirection to accept input only from a file.

The arguments that can be used with the `bc` commands are as follows:

- Variable name (one letter)
- Variable array name (letter[expression])
- A literal such as `scale`

Some of the other operands that can be used with the bc command are as follows:

- \+ for adding
- \- for subtracting
- / for division
- * for multiplication
- % for percentage
- ++ for adding 1 to the preceding variable
- \-\- for subtracting 1 from the preceding variable
- = to assign a value
- sqrt for square root computation
- length for getting length of a number
- scale for specifying the number of digits after the decimal

You can also use C program-like statements, expressions, and functions. You can use some special arithmetic functions with bc; these functions include the following:

- s(x) for sine of x
- c(x) for cosine of x
- l(x) for log of x

Following is a list of flags that can be used with the bc command:

Flag	Meaning
-c	Compile the bc program parameters but do not execute them.
-l	Include the library of math functions.

Examples

Assume that we have file1 which contains the following bc command parameters:

```
more file1
b=5
c=10
a=b+c
a
```

If you want to compile the contents of file1 without executing them, use the -c flag as in the following example:

```
bc -c < file1
  5sb
```

```
 10sc
lblc+sa
laps.
q
```

If you want to execute the contents of `file1`, use the following command:

bc < file1
15

Now assume that we have `file1` whose contents are displayed as shown here:

```
a=0
j=50
for (i=1; i<=j; i++) a=i+a;
a
```

If we execute the bc command with this file as input, bc will add all the numbers from 1 through 50 and display the total as follows:

bc < file1
1275

cal

You can use the `cal` command to display the calendar for one or more months on standard output. If you do not specify any arguments, `cal` displays the calendar for the current month. You can specify the month and year for which you want to display the calendar. If you specify only one argument, `cal` displays a calendar for all 12 months of the specified year.

Examples

If you want to display the calendar of the current month, execute the following command:

cal
```
        December 1996
Sun Mon Tue Wed Thu Fri Sat
  1   2   3   4   5   6   7
  8   9  10  11  12  13  14
 15  16  17  18  19  20  21
 22  23  24  25  26  27  28
 29  30  31
```

If you want to display the calendar for January 1995, use the following command:

cal 1 1995
```
        January 1995
Sun Mon Tue Wed Thu Fri Sat
```

```
 1   2   3   4   5   6   7
 8   9  10  11  12  13  14
15  16  17  18  19  20  21
22  23  24  25  26  27  28
29  30  31
```

If you want to obtain calendars for all 12 months of 1997, use the following command:

cal 1997

```
                              1997

            January                         February
Sun Mon Tue Wed Thu Fri Sat     Sun Mon Tue Wed Thu Fri Sat
              1   2   3   4                               1
  5   6   7   8   9  10  11       2   3   4   5   6   7   8
 12  13  14  15  16  17  18       9  10  11  12  13  14  15
 19  20  21  22  23  24  25      16  17  18  19  20  21  22
 26  27  28  29  30  31          23  24  25  26  27  28

             March                           April
Sun Mon Tue Wed Thu Fri Sat     Sun Mon Tue Wed Thu Fri Sat
                          1               1   2   3   4   5
  2   3   4   5   6   7   8       6   7   8   9  10  11  12
  9  10  11  12  13  14  15      13  14  15  16  17  18  19
 16  17  18  19  20  21  22      20  21  22  23  24  25  26
 23  24  25  26  27  28  29      27  28  29  30
 30  31
              May                            June
Sun Mon Tue Wed Thu Fri Sat     Sun Mon Tue Wed Thu Fri Sat
              1   2   3           1   2   3   4   5   6   7
  4   5   6   7   8   9  10       8   9  10  11  12  13  14
 11  12  13  14  15  16  17      15  16  17  18  19  20  21
 18  19  20  21  22  23  24      22  23  24  25  26  27  28
 25  26  27  28  29  30  31      29  30

             July                           August
Sun Mon Tue Wed Thu Fri Sat     Sun Mon Tue Wed Thu Fri Sat
          1   2   3   4   5                           1   2
  6   7   8   9  10  11  12       3   4   5   6   7   8   9
 13  14  15  16  17  18  19      10  11  12  13  14  15  16
 20  21  22  23  24  25  26      17  18  19  20  21  22  23
 27  28  29  30  31              24  25  26  27  28  29  30
                                 31
           September                        October
Sun Mon Tue Wed Thu Fri Sat     Sun Mon Tue Wed Thu Fri Sat
      1   2   3   4   5   6               1   2   3   4
  7   8   9  10  11  12  13       5   6   7   8   9  10  11
 14  15  16  17  18  19  20      12  13  14  15  16  17  18
 21  22  23  24  25  26  27      19  20  21  22  23  24  25
 28  29  30                      26  27  28  29  30  31
```

4

GENERAL
COMMANDS

```
            November                      December
   Sun Mon Tue Wed Thu Fri Sat   Sun Mon Tue Wed Thu Fri Sat
                             1           1   2   3   4   5   6
     2   3   4   5   6   7   8     7   8   9  10  11  12  13
     9  10  11  12  13  14  15    14  15  16  17  18  19  20
    16  17  18  19  20  21  22    21  22  23  24  25  26  27
    23  24  25  26  27  28  29    28  29  30  31
    30
```

calendar

You can use the `calendar` command to get reminders from messages stored in a special file named `calendar` in the current directory. The messages are stored in the following format:

- `date message`
- `message date`

In these formats, `date` can be in a variety of formats such as these:

- March 7
- Mar 7
- mar 7
- march 7th
- 3/7
- */7 (7th of each month)

On Friday, the `calendar` command displays the messages for four days: Friday, Saturday, Sunday, and Monday.

clear

You can use the `clear` command to clear the screen of your workstation. This command checks the terminal type to determine how to clear the screen.

Examples

To clear the screen on your terminal, use the following command:

```
clear
```

time

You can use the `time` command to obtain the execution time of a script, command, or program. The execution time is displayed with the following three times:

- Real
- User
- System

Examples

If you want to find out the execution time of the script `sample`, use the following command:

```
time sample
real    0m6.49s
user    0m0.02s
sys     0m0.03s
```

xargs

You can use the `xargs` command to group multiple arguments and then input them to a command. `xargs` passes as many arguments to the command as necessary to ensure that the maximum size limit for command-line arguments is not exceeded.

Following is a list of some of the flags that can be used with the `xargs` command:

Flag	Meaning
`-eendoffilecharacter`	Specify the character to be used to terminate the argument string. The default is the _ (underline) character
`-istring`	Use each line as a single parameter in place of the *string* variable specified as part of the command line. The default *string* is {}.
`-lnumber`	Specify the number of nonempty lines to be used as arguments to the command for each invocation. The last invocation can use fewer than the specified *number*.
`-nnumber`	Specify the number of arguments to be used in each invocation. The last invocation can use fewer than the specified *number*.
`-p`	Ask for confirmation before executing the command.

continues

Flag	Meaning
`-ssize`	Set the maximum size of the argument list for each invocation.
`-t`	Echo the constructed command to the standard error.

Examples

Assume that we have `xfile` whose contents are shown here:

```
more xfile
file1 file2 file3
file4 file5 file6
file7 file8 file9
```

If you want to pass only two arguments to the `ls` command at a time, use the `-n` flag as in the following example:

```
xargs -n2 ls  < xfile
file1   file2
file3   file4
file5   file6
file7   file8
file9
```

If you want to pass two lines at a time to the `ls` command, use the `-l` flag as in the following example:

```
xargs -l2 ls  < xfile
file1   file2   file3   file4   file5   file6
file7   file8   file9
```

If you want to confirm the command to be executed before actually executing the command, use the `-p` flag as in the following example:

```
xargs -l2 -p ls  < xfile
sfile1file2 file3 file4 file5 file6 ?...y
file1   file2   file3   file4   file5   file6
ls file7 file8 file9 ?...y
file7   file8   file9
```

In this example, you have to press the y key to confirm that the command should be executed. If you want to rename all the files that start with the name `file` (`file1` through `file9`), use the `-i` flag as in the following example:

```
ls file* | xargs -t -i cp {} {}.old
cp file1 file1.old
cp file2 file2.old
cp file3 file3.old
```

```
cp file4 file4.old
cp file5 file5.old
cp file6 file6.old
cp file7 file7.old
cp file8 file8.old
cp file9 file9.old
```

In this example, the -t flag forces the display of the constructed command to the standard error.

Regular Expression

A *regular expression* in UNIX is a string of one or more characters and metacharacters. The commands that accept regular expressions must first expand the expression to get the specified pattern before matching it to the input. The matching is done on a character-by-character basis.

> **CAUTION**
>
> The regular expression looks similar to the file-matching pattern used by some commands such as the find command. But the regular expression is not the same as the file-matching pattern.

A regular expression contains the following:

- *Character set*, which matches one or more characters at the specified position.
- *Count*, which specifies the number of the previous character to be repeated. This can be an * (asterisk) to specify that zero or more of the previous characters should be repeated.
- *Position specifier*, which is a set of special characters to indicate certain fixed positions such as the start of a line, the end of a line, and so on.
- *Metacharacters* to specify special meaning.

Character Set

A *character set* is a list of one or more specified characters. The character set can be specified as follows:

- *Range of characters*, which can be specified as two characters separated by a hyphen enclosed within square brackets. This set matches one occurrence of a character within the specified range. If you specify a ^ (caret) in front of the range, the matching is reversed, that is, all characters *except* those in the specified range will be matched.

- *List of characters*, which can be a list of individual characters enclosed within square brackets. This list matches one occurrence of one of the characters in the list. You can specify a ^ (caret) in front of one or more characters to match all characters *except* those.

Position Specifier

UNIX allows the use of a number of special characters to specify certain special positions in a line. Following is a list of these special characters:

- ^ at the start of a regular expression to specify the beginning of a line.
- $ at the end of the regular expression to specify the end of a line.

Metacharacters

A *metacharacter* is a character that, when used as part of a regular expression, has a special meaning. Following is a list of metacharacters:

- . to match all characters except the newline character.
- * to match zero or more of the preceding characters or regular expressions.
- ^ to match the regular expression following this metacharacter at the beginning of the line (for this to work, you must specify ^ as the first character of the regular expression).
- $ to match the regular expression preceding this metacharacter at the end of the line (for this to work, you must specify $ as the last character of the regular expression).
- [ ] to match exactly one of the enclosed characters. The characters enclosed can be a range or a list of individual characters.
- \{n1,n2\} to match a minimum of n1 and a maximum of n2 occurrences of the preceding character or regular expression.
- \ to interpret the following character as a regular character rather than as a metacharacter.
- \(\) to save the enclosed regular expression for later use. This expression can then be reused by using \1 through \9.
- \< to match the following regular expression at the beginning of a word.
- \> to match the preceding regular expression at the end of a word.

- ? to match zero or one instance of the preceding regular expression.
- + to match one or more instances of the preceding regular expression.

Examples

Assume that we have a file called `file1` whose contents are shown here:

```
more file1
This is a test
THIS IS A TEST
This is really a test
Believe it, this is really a test
This is a test, better believe it
```

You can specify a string of characters as a regular expression. If you want to find the string `really` in `file1`, use the following command:

```
grep really file1
This is really a test
Believe it, this is really a test
```

If you want to find the string `THIS` at the beginning of a line, use the `^`(caret) at the beginning of a regular expression as in the following example:

```
grep ^THIS file1
THIS IS A TEST
```

If you want to find the string `it` at the end of a line, use the `$` (dollar sign) at the end of a regular expression as in the following example:

```
grep it$ file1
This is a test, better believe it
```

If you want to find both `believe` and `Believe`, use the following command:

```
grep [Bb]elieve file1
Believe it, this is really a test
This is a test, better believe it
```

In this example, `[Bb]` matches the single character B or b. If you want to find characters other than the specified one, use the following command:

```
grep [T][^h] file1
THIS IS A TEST
```

In this example, the `[^h]` matches anything *other than* h. Hence, `[T][^h]` matches anything that starts with T and is followed by any character *other than* h. If you want to match any six-character string preceded and followed by a space, use the following command:

```
grep " ...... " file1
This is really a test
```

4

```
Believe it, this is really a test
This is a test, better believe it
```

In this example, the " `......` " matches a string such as `really` or `better` preceded and followed by a space. If you want to modify all strings that start with a t, that have a t at the end, and that have any two characters in the middle, use the following command:

sed "s/\(t\)..\1/ − − /g" file1
```
This is a ----
THIS IS A TEST
This is really a ----
Believe i----his is really a ----
This is a ----, better believe it
```

In this example, `\(t\)` saves the character t; `\1` uses the t at the specified position. If you want to find one or more instances of a regular expression, use the following command:

egrep it+ file1
```
Believe it, this is really a test
This is a test, better believe it
```

In this example, `it+` tells egrep to find one or more instances of the string it. If you want to find whether a regular expression is repeated a specified number of times, use the following command:

egrep tt\{1,4\} file1
```
This is a test, better believe it
```

In this example, at least one—and a maximum of four—repetitions of the expression it are matched. If you want to modify all characters other than letters, use the following command:

sed "s/[^a-zA-Z]/:/g" file1
```
This is a test
THIS IS A TEST
This is really a test
Believe it: this is really a test
This is a test: better believe it
```

In this example, all characters—other than a through z, A through Z, and spaces—are replaced by a : (colon).

Executing Commands

There are several ways to execute the commands you have learned about in this chapter. In this section, you learn about some of the ways you can execute command in isolation and in conjunction with other commands.

By default, UNIX accepts input from *standard input* (which is the keyboard) and displays output on *standard output* (which is the terminal). You can, however, use the UNIX redirection facility to redirect the input from a file or redirect the output to a file.

You can execute a command in the foreground or in the background. When you invoke a command, by default it executes in the foreground. You can force a command to the background by using the & (ampersand) sign. You can start a command in the foreground and then force it into the background. To achieve this, press Ctrl+Z to suspend the command and then use the bg command to put it in the background.

Because all UNIX commands accept input from standard input and generate output to standard output, there is a convenient way of passing output from one command to the next command: the ¦ (pipe) character. You can have a string of commands, each connected to the next using a pipe.

Summary

In this chapter, you learned about various UNIX commands. Most of these commands should work on different UNIX systems as described here, but you may find that some of the commands or flags behave differently. Following is a list of some of the activities you can do using various UNIX commands:

- Log in to related activities using commands such as login, rlogin, and passwd.
- Create, rename, delete, and copy files and directories using commands such as cp, rm, rmdir, and mkdir.
- Search for text in files using commands such as grep.
- Grant access to files and directories for users using commands such as chmod and chgrp.
- Modify contents of files using commands such as vi and sed.
- Display contents of files using commands such as more, tail, head, and pg.

Getting Around the Network

by David B. Horvath, CCP, and
Rachel and Robert Sartin

IN THIS CHAPTER

The "information superhighway" has received a lot of attention recently. Much of this "network of the future" is with us today. This chapter introduces you to the basic UNIX software used today to connect hundreds of thousands of machines together on the Internet and locally within organizations.

Connecting machines in a network gives you even more computing and information resources than you can get from simply having a computer at your desk or in your computing center. A network of machines connected together enables you to share data files with coworkers, send electronic mail, play multiuser games with people from all over the world, read Usenet news articles, contribute to worldwide discussions, perform searches for software or information you need, and much more. In this chapter, you learn about the two most common ways to connect UNIX machines together in a network: UUCP and TCP/IP. On this simple base exists a worldwide network of machines and services that has the potential to greatly increase your productivity. By learning to use these services effectively, you open the door to new possibilities using your computer. This chapter only begins to probe the extent of available software and resources. Refer to the Sams Publishing book *Internet Unleashed* for even more information on this topic.

What Is a Network?

A *network* is a system of two or more computers connected to one another. In this chapter, you learn about some common ways to network UNIX machines together. At the simplest end of the scale, a network can be two UNIX machines connected to each other using a serial line (typically through a modem) and running *UUCP*, the UNIX-to-UNIX Copy Program. More complicated network configurations run *TCP/IP*, the Transmission Control Protocol/Internet Protocol, the common name for the protocol family used on the Internet, a collection of networks that allows you to connect your computer to hundreds of thousands of other computers.

UUCP—The Basic Networking Utilities

Early in the history of UNIX, it became apparent that connecting UNIX machines would be advantageous so that they could share resources. One attempt to connect machines together resulted in the UUCP protocol, which allows you to connect two UNIX machines to each other using a serial line (often with a modem attached). The primary focus of UUCP is to allow files to be copied between two UNIX machines, but services built on top of UUCP allow execution of certain commands, such as news and mail commands, thus enabling more sophisticated processing. You can use UUCP to send electronic mail between two UNIX machines and to transmit and receive Usenet news articles. The most common release of UUCP available now is often called either *BNU*, the

Basic Networking Utilities—the System V version of UUCP—or HoneyDanBer (HDB). There are other freely available and commercial implementations of UUCP. Although UUCP originated on UNIX and was designed specifically for copying between UNIX machines, there are now versions of UUCP that run on MS-DOS and other platforms.

 Just in case your UNIX machine does not include UUCP, there is a freely available version of UUCP (1.06.1) on the CD-ROM. You can build this version on your UNIX machine, and it will interoperate with HDB UUCP.

> **NOTE**
>
> Although UUCP comes with most UNIX versions and is also available for most other systems, its use is rapidly declining in favor of TCP/IP.
>
> At one time, there was a National Network in the United States (and in some other countries) based in UUCP where one system would call another, which would call another, and so on. Systems would store and forward data (email, Usenet news, data files) as it moved around from the source machine to the destination machine over what could be many different hops.
>
> ftp is used to transfer files over TCP/IP (more about this later in this chapter) today.

TCP/IP—LAN, WAN, and the Internet

In the 1970s, the United States Department of Defense began a research program called ARPA, the Advanced Research Projects Administration. One of the efforts of ARPA was to create an *Internet*, an interconnected set of networks, that would allow research labs across the country to interact. This network was called the ARPAnet, and the protocol that ran the interconnections was and is called *IP*, or Internet Protocol. Since the original ARPAnet, internetworking has grown incredibly, and there is now a huge and difficult-to-define thing called the Internet that allows interconnections between computers all over the world. The Internet includes hundreds of thousands of machines (because of the amorphous nature of the Internet, it is difficult even to get an accurate count) connected through a series of public and private networks.

> **NOTE**
>
> At some point in the mid-1980s, the "Defense" was added on to the name (Defense Advanced Research Projects Agency) resulting in DARPA.

The Internet Protocol allows the sending of packets between any two computers that are connected to the Internet. IP supplies only a primitive service, and further levels of protocol exist that use IP to perform useful functions. Two common protocols are *TCP/IP* and *UDP/IP*. TCP/IP connects two programs in much the same way a serial line connects two computers. UDP/IP, the User Datagram Protocol/IP, supplies a simple way of sending short messages between two programs. Most interesting user programs that use IP networking use TCP to create a connection, so "TCP/IP" is often used to refer to the interconnection protocol on the Internet.

Names and Addresses

To use machines and resources on the network, you need to locate them. Hostnames use a hierarchical naming space that allows each hostname to be unique, without forcing it to be obscure or unpronounceable. For example, `ftp.uu.net` is the name of one host on the Internet. IP itself uses *Internet addresses*, unique identifiers of Internet hosts, which are usually written in *dot notation*, four numbers (each between 0 and 255), separated by periods. For example, `192.48.96.9` is the address (as of this writing) of the host `ftp.uu.net`, which is covered in the section "Transferring Files—`rcp`, `ftp`, and `uucp`."

What's in a Name?

Hostnames on the Internet are a series of "words" separated by periods, or *dots*. The dots separate different parts of the name.

The naming system used is called the *domain naming system* (DNS) because it separates responsibility for unique names into administrative domains. The administrator of each domain is responsible for managing and assigning unique names within that domain. The management of the *top-level* or *root* domain, the extreme right word in a hostname, is responsible for the naming conventions. The best way to understand hostnames is to start out by reading them right to left, one word at a time.

Look at the hostname `ftp.uu.net`. Reading right to left, the first word is `net`, which means that the hostname is a network service provider; see Table 5.1 for explanations of this and other top-level names. The next word is `uu`. Within `.net`, `uu` belongs to UUNET Communications, a company that supplies networking services. Elsewhere in the domain naming space, the name `uu` may mean something else.

TABLE 5.1. TOP-LEVEL DOMAINS.

Domain	Meaning
EDU	Educational. Colleges and Universities.
ORG	Organizations. Nonprofit and not-for-profit.

Domain	Meaning
NET	Networks. Networking services providers (some under COM).
COM	Commercial. Businesses.
GOV	Government. United States Federal government offices.
MIL	Military. The U.S. Armed Forces.
cc	Countries. *cc* is an ISO country code.
US	An example of a country code. The United States.

> **NOTE**
>
> Due in part to the history of the ARPAnet, most hosts in the United States (and some international organizations and businesses) are under EDU, ORG, NET, COM, GOV, or MIL. Many hosts in other countries are under a top-level domain that is the two-character ISO country code for the country. To further confuse things, the United States has a U.S. zone that includes local organizations, primary and secondary schools, and local governments.
>
> This all may change in the future; various groups are working to change the top-level domain structure to remove the special status of domains in the United States.

Look at the hostnames conch.newcastle.org and conch.austin.tx.us. The org means that the name belongs to an organization. The newcastle means that Newcastle Associates is the owner. Finally, conch is a particular host in Newcastle's network. In the second name, us means the United States, tx means Texas, austin means the city Austin, and conch is a particular hostname. Note that the two machines are completely different machines with different owners. They happen to share one component of their name, but that is not a problem because of the hierarchical namespace presented by DNS.

In fact, there are many repetitions of names. Many machines on the Internet have ftp as the first part of their domain names, and many have www as the first part of their names. The advantage of using the DNS is that these repetitions are not in conflict. It has been said about names that "all the good ones are taken," but the DNS allows you to reuse some of the good ones in a different context.

5

GETTING AROUND THE NETWORK

NOTE

In addition to having an official name, some hosts have aliases as well. The alias is simply another name for the host. For example, `ftp.x.org` is actually an alias for the current machine being used for `ftp` by `x.org`.

Using Shorter Names

Usually, the DNS is configured to use a *search path* for hostnames that don't end in a dot. This lets you use shorter names for hosts in your search path. Typically, your DNS is configured to search your domain and then search progressively up to the root domain. Check your system documentation to see whether you can change the DNS search path. If you were on `cnidaria.newcastle.org` and used the name `newcstle.net`, it would try the following names, matching the first one that exists:

1. `newcstle.net.newcastle.org`
2. `newcstle.net.org`
3. newcstle.net

TIP

Because of the search algorithm, you may see faster network access if you use full names ending in a dot for machines outside your local domain.

Decoding Addresses and Ports

Although DNS names are a reasonably convenient way for humans to refer to hosts, the Internet Protocol needs to use a 32-bit Internet address to find a host on the network. For example, as of this writing the host `ftp.uu.net` has the Internet Address `192.48.96.9`. Internet addresses are usually written using *dot names*, with four numbers between 0 and 255, separated by dots. Note that each of the four numbers is 8 bits, so you end up with a 32-bit Internet address.

It is not enough just to connect to the correct machine. You also need to connect to the correct program. TCP/IP and UDP/IP use *ports* to specify where a connection goes. To make a connection to a remote computer, there has to be some program listening on the correct port. If you think of IP addresses as being like phone numbers, a *port number* is like an extension. When your IP message reaches the correct machine, the port number enables it to be delivered to the correct program.

When a new protocol is adopted as a standard, it is assigned a port number that always is used for that protocol. For example, the `login` protocol used to implement `rlogin` is assigned port 513, and `telnet` is assigned port 23. You can examine the assignments of ports to protocols by looking at the file `/etc/services` on your machine. If you are running NIS (the Network Information System, formerly called the Yellow Pages), you can run the command `ypcat services` to look at the map.

Look at what happens when you run the command `rlogin remotehost`. If `remotehost` is willing to accept `rlogin` requests, there is a program waiting for connections on port 513 on `remotehost`; this program (called `inetd`) handles all the work on `remotehost` that needs to be performed to allow you to use `rlogin` (`inetd` does this by handing the incoming connection to a program called `rlogind`, which implements the protocol). The `rlogin` program on your host attempts to open a connection to port 513 on the `remotehost`. The program monitoring port 513 on `remotehost` accepts the connection and lets your `rlogin` program perform the setup necessary to perform a login.

Converting Names to Addresses

You have seen what hostnames look like and what the low-level Internet address and port numbers are, but you still need to learn how names get converted to addresses.

Hostname conversion is usually handled by the domain naming system, which, in addition to specifying what hostnames look like, specifies a protocol for translating hostnames to addresses. First look at a hostname conversion of the name `ftp.x.org`. When your local host tries to convert the name `ftp.x.org` to an IP address, it contacts a *name server*, a machine that has DNS mappings loaded and is prepared to answer questions about them. Your name server is also configured with information about how to contact other name servers so that it can look up names that it doesn't already know.

A Brief Introduction to NIS

When implementing a network, one common problem that arises is management of `passwd` and group files. Some organizations want to have a common user and group list for all or most hosts in a network. The Network Information Service, introduced by Sun Microsystems, is one way to solve this problem. NIS allows sharing of `passwd`, group, and other information between hosts that share administrative control. Other (commercial and freely available) solutions to this problem exist, but none have yet become as widespread as NIS.

If you are running NIS, use the command `ypcat passwd` to examine the `passwd` information on your system. The actual `/etc/passwd` file does not list all the users who can log in to a machine running NIS. If you are using NIS to manage `passwd` files, your password is the same on any machine in your network that runs NIS. NIS may also be used to create an environment where you can share files transparently between systems. This is done using the network file system, NFS, which enables you to mount a file system from a mount computer and access it as if it were local. Some computing environments configure NIS so that your HOME is always the same directory, no matter what machine you use. This means that your files will be accessible no matter what machine in the network you are using. Check with your system administrators to find out whether NIS is running and whether it is being used to handle automounting of home (and other) directories.

Connecting to Other Systems— rlogin, telnet, and cu

With the three services rlogin, telnet, and cu, you can connect to a remote computer over the network. rlogin uses the login service to connect using the TCP/IP protocol over the network, telnet uses the telnet service to connect using the TCP/IP protocol over the network, and cu connects over a phone line.

Before Using rlogin, rsh, and rcp

Before you use rlogin, some user configuration may be needed. The same configuration is used for rsh and rcp. Refer to these details when reading the next section as well. For reference, *loc-host* is used as the local machine name and *rem-host* is the name of the remote machine.

Two files on the remote machine affect your remote access capability: /etc/hosts.equiv and .rhosts in the remote user's home directory. The hosts.equiv file contains a list of hostnames. Each machine in this list is considered to be a trusted host. Any user who has an account on both *loc-host* and *rem-host* is allowed to access the remote machine from the local machine without question. The "without question" is important and means that the user does not have to supply a password for access.

> **TIP**
>
> System administrators should seriously consider disabling the rlogin and rexec protocols on machines directly connected to the Internet because the authentication used on these protocols is very weak. At the very least, be extremely careful about entries in /etc/hosts.equiv and any .rhosts files.

The .rhosts file in the remote user's home directory contains a list of trusted host and user pairs. This is similar to the trusted hosts of the hosts.equiv file but gives a finer grain of control. Each entry grants trusted access to one particular user on a particular host rather than to all common users on a particular host. Lines in .rhosts that name only a machine grant access to a user with the same login name. The user on *loc-host* can access *rem-host* without question (that is, without specifying a password). The user authentication is done by the protocol.

Usually only the system administrator can change the values in the /etc/hosts.equiv file. Because file allows many users access, this is a system configuration file. But each user can set up his or her own .rhosts file. This file must live in the user's home directory and be owned by the user (or by root). The ownership restrictions are security measures preventing a user from gaining access to another user's account.

Listing 5.1 and Listing 5.2 show examples of the hosts.equiv and .rhosts files. These two files are located on the machine called flounder, and the .rhosts file is owned by user rob and is located in his home directory. The two hosts listed in the /etc/hosts.equiv file, manatee and dolphin, are trusted hosts to flounder. Any user with an account on manatee and flounder may remotely access flounder from manatee without specifying a password. Likewise, any user with an account on dolphin and flounder may remotely access flounder from dolphin without specifying a password.

LISTING 5.1. /ETC/HOSTS.EQUIV AND $HOME/.RHOSTS FILES.

```
manatee
dolphin
```

LISTING 5.2. /USERS/ROB/.RHOSTS ON MACHINE FLOUNDER.

```
french-angel
rob yellowtail
rob dolphin
rob dolphin
root dolphin
diane stingray
rob stingray
root flying-gurnard
root
```

> **CAUTION**
>
> Check your local documentation for the exact format of these files; some sys-
> tems require a wildcard symbol when the username is specified without a
> remote system name.

The `.rhosts` file of the user `rob` contains a list of users on a remote machine who may access `flounder` as user `rob` without specifying a password. That sentence packed sever-al important points together that need expanding:

- The `.rhosts` file of user `rob`—This implies that the machine `flounder` has a user account, with `rob` as the username. The home directory of user `rob` (the example implies it is `/users/rob`) has a file named `.rhosts` that is owned by `rob`.

- Users on a remote machine who may access `flounder`—Each entry in the list is a pair of names—the machine name and the associated username. This pair of names describes one particular user who may access `flounder`. That user must be access-ing `flounder` from the specified machine. It is not enough for the user to simply have an account on the machine; the remote access must be initiated from that machine (by that user).

- As user `rob`—This is probably the most subtle of all the points, so be careful here. Any of the users who are in the list may access `rob`'s account on `flounder`, as `rob`. They "become" `rob` on `flounder` even if they were a different user on the initiating machine. This is effectively the same as giving `rob`'s password on machine `flounder` to this user. Because of this, be extremely selective about entries in your `.rhosts` files.

- Without specifying a password—Some services (`rlogin`) allow for the possibility of a password prompt. If the user authentication was not successful via the equiva-lence files, the service can fall back on the prompt method of authentication. So the capability to access a remote host without specifying a password may not be need-ed. Other services (`rsh` and `rcp`) do not have a way to prompt for a password. To use these services, the access must be configured so that specifying a password is unnecessary.

Using Listing 5.2, for each of the following scenarios, decide whether the user would be able to access `flounder`—as `rob`—without a password. Assume that each user has an account on the local machine in the question, as well as on `flounder`.

1. User `root` on machine `stingray`?
2. User `root` on machine `manatee`?

3. User `root` on machine `french-angel`?

4. User `frank` on machine `dolphin`?

5. User `frank` on machine `stingray`?

6. User `frank` on machine `tarpon`?

7. User `diane` on machine `manatee`?

8. User `diane` on machine `dolphin`?

9. User `diane` on machine `flying-gurnard`?

10. User `rob` on machine `yellowtail`?

11. User `rob` on machine `dolphin`?

12. User `rob` on machine `manatee`?

13. User `rob` on machine `flying-gurnard`?

The answers are as follows:

1. Yes; rob's `.rhosts` file has an entry `stingray root`.

2. No; rob's `.rhosts` file does not have an entry `manatee root`. However, `root` from manatee could access `flounder`—as root—without a password because manatee is listed in /etc/hosts.equiv.

3. No; rob's `.rhosts` file does not have an entry `french-angel root`.

4. No; rob's `.rhosts` file does not have an entry `dolphin frank`. However, `frank` from dolphin could access `flounder`—as frank—without a password because `dolphin` is listed in `/etc/hosts.equiv`.

5. No; rob's `.rhosts` file does not have an entry `stingray frank`.

6. No; rob's `.rhosts` file does not have an entry `tarpon frank`.

7. No; rob's `.rhosts` file does not have an entry `manatee diane`. However, `diane` from manatee could access `flounder`—as diane—without a password because manatee is listed in `/etc/hosts.equiv`.

8. Yes; rob's `.rhosts` file has an entry `stingray diane`.

9. No; rob's `.rhosts` file does not have an entry `flying-gurnard diane`.

10. Yes; rob's `.rhosts` file has an entry `yellowtail rob`.

11. Yes; the `/etc/hosts.equiv` file has an entry `dolphin`. Note that if the system administrator removed this entry, this answer would still be yes because of the `dolphin rob` entry in his `.rhosts` file.

12. Yes; the `/etc/hosts.equiv` file has an entry `manatee rob`.

13. No; the `/etc/hosts.equiv` file does not have an entry `flying-gurnard` nor does rob's `.rhosts` file have an entry `flying-gurnard rob`.

Using `rlogin`

If you need or want to be logged in to a computer that is away from your current location, `rlogin` can help you. The `rlogin` application establishes a remote login session
from your machine to another machine that is connected via the network. This machine
could be next door, next to you on your desk, or even on a different continent. When you
successfully execute an `rlogin` from your screen, whether it is a terminal, or one window of your graphical display, the shell that prompts you and the commands you enter
are executing on the remote machine just as if you sat down in front of the machine and
entered login.

Establishing a `rlogin` Connection

The `rlogin` command takes a mandatory argument that specifies the remote host. Both
the local and remote host must have `rlogin` available for a connection to be established.
If this is the case, the local `rlogin` connects to the specified remote machine and starts a
login session.

During a nonremote login, the login process prompts you for two things: your username
and your password. Your username identifies you to the computer, and your password
authenticates that the requester is really you. During an `rlogin`, the `rlogin` protocol
takes care of some (or even all) of this identification/authorization procedure for you.
The `rlogin` protocol initiates the login session on the remote host for a particular user.
By default, this user is the same as the local user (that is, you). In this case, you never
have to type in your username. However, if you want to log in to the remote host as a
different user, you may override the default username by using the `-l` option to specify a
username.

The `rlogin` protocol may even take care of the authentication for you. If you (or your
system administrator) have made the proper entry in the `/etc/hosts.equiv` or your
`$HOME/.rhosts` file, no authentication is necessary (that is, you are not prompted for
your password). If these files do not have entries for your host and username, a password
prompt is printed just like in a local login attempt.

A few examples follow. Assume that your username is `rachel`, and the local machine to
which you're logged in is called `moray-eel`.

To log in as yourself on machine `flounder`, you would enter:

```
$ rlogin flounder
```

The connection to `flounder` would take place, and a login session would be initiated for
user `rachel` (and fail if user `rachel` doesn't exist on `flounder`). Next, the `rlogin`

protocol checks the special files to see whether authentication is necessary. If `moray-eel` is listed in the file `/etc/hosts.equiv` or in `~rachel/.rhosts`, no authentication is needed.

To log in to `flounder` as user `arnie`, you would enter:

```
$ rlogin -l arnie flounder
```

Here the login session is initiated with the username `arnie`. If user `arnie` exists on `flounder`, the special files are checked for authentication. Because the username for the remote login is different from the local username, the `/etc/hosts.equiv` file does not provide authentication. If the file `~arnie/.rhosts` has an entry `moray-eel rachel`, no authentication is necessary (that is, login succeeds without password). If this entry does not exist, the password prompt appears, and you must enter the password associated with user `arnie`. This is not a prompt for your password.

Failed Connect

Several things might go wrong when you try to connect to a remote machine via `rlogin`. Some of these are problems that are out of your control. In these instances, you should contact a system administrator to help you solve the problem.

In cases where authentication is necessary, you might enter the password incorrectly. If this happens, the result is the same as in a local login attempt. The login process lets you try again by prompting first for your username and then your password. Note that this is the only situation in which you must supply your username if you're trying to `rlogin` as yourself.

For most other problems, you need your system administrator's help. See the section "Troubleshooting TCP/IP" for ways to identify the cause of the problem. Any details about the problem symptoms will help the person responsible for fixing the problem. Some of the problems you might see are the following:

- The user account does not exist on the remote.
- Your local host is not connected to the remote via the network.
- The remote host is down.
- The remote host does not support rlogin.
- The network between the local and remote hosts is having problems.

Using the Remote Login Session

After a successful remote login, the `rlogin` protocol initiates your session using some information from your local session. This saves you the trouble of having to initialize your environment totally from scratch. Your terminal type (the value of the TERM environment variable) is propagated. Other information, such as baud rate and your screen (window) size, may also be propagated, depending on what the local and remote hosts support.

Then the login process proceeds as if you were actually directly connected to this machine. All the information and files are taken from the remote. The remote password file contains the user account information, including the login shell to be executed and the starting (HOME) directory. All shell startup files (found on the remote) execute, which further initializes your environment. When the startup completes, the shell prompt you see is the shell running on the remote host.

> **NOTE**
>
> In some LAN environments, the network is configured such that your HOME directory is on a remote file server that is mounted on each machine you access. In this case, you actually have just one physical HOME directory, and thus just one set of dot files (for example, .login). This results in the same login environment for you on each machine. However, this makes writing your dot files a little more complicated because you need to take into account all the different machines to accommodate.

> **TIP**
>
> Because the remote prompt and local prompt might look alike, you might want to include hostname in your prompt variable (PS1). If you're ever in doubt about what host the shell prompt is coming from, use the hostname command.

When you see the remote prompt, you can enter any commands you would in a local environment. The rlogin protocol transfers input and output between the local and remote hosts. This transfer is transparent to you. Sometimes you might notice slow performance, depending on the network speed and load.

During your remote session, you might want to access your local machine. You could just exit your remote session, at which point you would be back at your local prompt. But if you aren't finished using the remote, using exit followed by another rlogin, possibly multiple times, is tedious. There is a better way—using the escape character.

Using the Escape Character

The `rlogin` protocol provides an escape character that, when typed as the first character on the command line, is treated specially. The default escape character is the tilde (~) character, but you may change this on the `rlogin` command line via the `-e` option. If the character immediately following the escape character is one that the local `rlogin` process recognizes, it performs the function associated with this character. Otherwise, the escape character (and the remaining characters) are executed on the remote.

The `~.` character sequence is the command to disconnect from remote. This is not a graceful disconnect, as in an exit. It immediately disconnects from the remote. This should only be used when, for some reason, you are unable to execute the `exit` command.

If the local `rlogin` was executed by a job-control shell (C shell or Korn shell), then you can suspend the `rlogin` by the escape sequence ~susp, where `susp` is your suspend control character, usually Ctrl+Z. This is very convenient. It saves the multiple `exit` command followed by another `rlogin` sequence you would otherwise need for accessing the local machine. In a graphical user interface environment, having two windows—one for the `rlogin` and one locally—solves this problem as well.

It is possible to `rlogin` to one machine and then `rlogin` from there to another machine. You can use multiple escape characters to denote any one of the machines in this chain. For example, say that you are locally logged in to Host A. You are using a job-control shell with `suspend` set to Ctrl+Z. From Host A, you `rlogin` to Host B. From there, you log in to Host C. And from there, you rlogin to Host D. At this point, everything you enter is going all the way to D to execute. To reach any host in the chain, just associate one escape character with each host. You must start with your local host and then go in the same order as the `rlogins`. In this example, a single ~ refers to Host A, ~~ refers to Host B, and ~~~ refers to Host C.

To suspend the `rlogin` from Host B to Host C, type ~~^Z. This leaves you in your original shell on Host B. To return to `rlogin`, use the `fg` command as with any suspended process.

To disconnect the `rlogin` from Host C to Host D, type ~~~..

One common escape sequence, which is not supported on all platforms, is the shell escape, `~!`. Typing this sequence causes the `rlogin` to give you a subshell on the machine that is referred to by ~. You can use multiple escape characters to denote any host within a chain of `rlogins`. To return to the `rlogin`, simply exit the subshell.

> **NOTE**
>
> There is a difference between ~susp and ~!. The suspend command puts rlogin in the background and lets you interact with your original shell (the one from which you ran rlogin). The shell escape starts a new shell as a child of rlogin.

> **TIP**
>
> telnet does not require configuration on the remove system (.rhosts and /etc/hosts.equiv) like rlogin does.

Using telnet

The telnet service is used to communicate with a remote host via the telnet protocol. Invoking telnet with the remote host as an argument causes telnet to connect to that host. The remote telnet server usually initiates a login just as you would get on a terminal connected to the machine. After your login name and password are entered and verified, you see the shell prompt on the remote machine. All commands and input you enter go to the remote; all output you receive comes from the remote.

If you want to enter telnet command mode while you are connected to a remote, type the escape character. The default escape character is Ctrl+], but this can be changed via the set command. To return to the remote connection, simply execute a command. A set command will do this. If you have nothing you want to send or set, do a send nop. The nop argument stands for *no operation*.

If you enter telnet without any arguments, you start up the telnet service in command mode. You see a special telnet prompt (telnet>). You can enter any of the telnet commands. Table 5.2 provides a list of some of the most common telnet commands you might use. Refer to your system's manual for telnet, for a complete list.

TABLE 5.2. COMMON TELNET COMMANDS.

Command	Description
open	Connects to specified host.
close	Disconnects from host and returns to command mode.
quit	Closes the connection (if one exists) and exits telnet.
set	Changes the value for a given argument.
send	Sends a command to the remote and returns to remote connection.

Command	Description
display	Shows current setting of telnet configuration.
status	Shows current status of telnet connection.
?	Gives help.

The following sections look at some of these commands in a bit more detail.

open

The open command takes two parameters, host and port. The host, which is mandatory, can be a hostname or an IP address. This specifies the remote host to which a connection is to be established. This remote host must be reachable via the network and must support the telnet service. The port, which is optional, specifies the port number to use in connecting to the remote host. By default, the port to which telnet connects is the well-known telnet port (23). When a connection on the remote comes in on the telnet port, the remote's telnet service handles the connection. The remote telnet service assumes that the local connector wants to log in and invokes the login process on this connection. You can use this feature to do certain kinds of debugging and troubleshooting. For example, to connect to the mail server on a machine, you could enter telnet *hostname* smtp (or replace smtp with 25 if the first doesn't work). This connects you directly to the Simple Mail Transfer Protocol on hostname, and you can use this connection to troubleshoot mail problems. Sometimes network services are offered by telnet to a specific port number. For example, many gopher and WWW providers offer a special port for telnet access to the service.

In this default mode, a telnet open command is somewhat like an rlogin. A remote login is initiated on the remote host. But the telnet protocol, unlike rlogin, does not perform any conveniences for you. It does not propagate any of your local environment. It does not perform any part of the login procedure (user identification and authentication).

If the first thing you use telnet for is an open command, you do not need to enter telnet command mode at all. On the telnet command line, you can enter a host followed optionally by a port number. This causes telnet to immediately do an open with the command-line arguments.

close

The close command terminates the open connection (if one exists). On some versions of telnet, this does not exit telnet command mode. So if you are connected to Host B but decide you really want to be connected to Host C, enter close and then enter an open B command.

quit

The `quit` command should be used when you are finished using `telnet`. This command performs a `close` on the open connection (if one exists). Then it terminates the `telnet` service, returning you to your local shell prompt.

set

`telnet` has several internal variables used for configuration. You can use the `set` command to change these values. To see the current variable values, use the `display` command. The `telnet` escape character can be changed via `set`.

> **TIP**
>
> You can set certain special characters (such as `erase`) with `telnet`, but these settings may only work if you run `telnet` in line mode. Line mode is often used for connecting to remote machines that have line-oriented user interfaces and allows you to compose an entire line of text input before sending it to the remote (when you press Enter). You should probably not use line mode when connecting to a UNIX machine because interactive commands (such as `vi`), job control, and some shell history (`ksh` interactive command editing) rely on receiving characters as they are typed.

?—The Question Mark

The question mark (?) is a `telnet` command that, without arguments, gives a list of all the `telnet` commands. This is useful if you've forgotten the name of a command. To get help about a specific command, use ? with the command as an argument. The ? can also be used as an argument to the `set`, `send`, and `toggle` commands to list the valid arguments of the command.

Before Using cu

Before you can use `cu`, your system administrator needs to configure the appropriate devices and machines for UUCP access. Check your system's UUCP documentation for information on how to do this.

Using cu

The `cu` service calls up another system. This service is used only to connect two computers via phone lines. Your local host must have an outgoing modem, and the remote host must have a modem that supports incoming calls.

Your system administrator may have configured the parameters necessary to call up certain systems. This configuration is kept in the file /etc/uucp/Systems.

> **NOTE**
>
> The actual file depends on which version of UUCP you have. This is correct for SVR4. Because the location may vary, consider this the "systems" file.

You can enter cu *system-name* to dial the remote host. If the remote host has not been configured in the */etc/uucp/Systems* file, you can specify the necessary parameters on the command line. The cu *phone-number* command calls up the specified phone number. For example, cu 9=14085551212 calls using the ad device and gives it the phone number 914085551212. The equals sign specifies that a pause is desired before the next digit is dialed.

You can also call up using a local device by specifying it with the -l option. You can use the -l option to specify the device to use for making the connection. This is generally used only for hard-wired connections: cu -l *dev* dir connects directly to the line named dev.

Transferring Files—rcp, ftp, and uucp

Files are the basis for everything you do in UNIX. When you execute a command (aside from shell built-ins), the associated file contains the executing instructions. When you store or retrieve information, the data is kept in one or more files. The UNIX interface to hardware devices is through device files. Files are pervasive. Therefore, having the necessary files within your reach is extremely important.

Sometimes files you need are not stored on your local machine. Client-server environments are designed to provide a means of sharing files among many machines. When machines on a LAN are configured to share files (via the network), many more files become reachable to you. If you are using NFS, some directories on your system are mounted from remote machines. These directories and files are available as part of the normal UNIX file system, and you need no special techniques to access them.

Not all UNIX environments are configured this way. Even those that are might not share all file systems of all machines. Many files exist outside a local LAN environment. In these cases, you might want to obtain a copy of a file from somewhere other than your local environment. You could use the tools in I'm on the wire to remotely log in and access them. But if you need to execute the file locally, or want to have your own copy of the file, you need to copy the remote file to your local system.

The next section presents several tools to do remote copies. Your local configuration, the remote configuration, the way the remote and local configurations are connected, as well as your personal preference will determine which tool you choose.

Using `rcp`

You might want to review the section "Before Using `rlogin`, `rsh`, and `rcp`" before reading this section. For `rcp` to work, you must configure the remote machine(s) so that user authentication is not necessary. For each remote you access via `rcp`, an entry in one or both of `/etc/hosts.equiv` and `$HOME/.rhosts` is mandatory. This is because `rcp` does not have a mechanism for in-process authentication (unlike `rlogin`).

After the configuration is complete, you can use `rcp` in much the same way you use the `cp` command. Each command basically says to "copy File A to Location B." The `rcp` command adds some syntax that enables you to specify remote machines and users.

Specifying a Remote File

You can specify a remote file in several different ways. In general, unless a hostname is specified, the file is considered local. If the character string has a colon (:) before any slashes (/), the string before the colon specifies the remote host, and the string after the colon specifies the file path. Here are three forms of the complete remote file specification:

- *hostname:filepath*
- *user@hostname:filepath*
- *user@hostname.domain:filepath*

The file path in each can be an *absolute* path, a *relative* path, or blank. If it is relative, it is relative to the remote user's HOME directory. The remote user is considered the same as the local user unless explicitly included in the remote specification. In the preceding second and third forms, the remote user is explicitly included.

If the file path is absolute, this is an absolute path on the remote system. If the file path is blank, the user's HOME directory is assumed.

The hostname can be a simple name or an alias of the remote machine, or it can be a host domain name as in the third form shown previously.

If you want to use a different user account on the remote machine, you can specify the remote file, including the username. The username must refer to an account on the remote machine, and the user's `$HOME/.rhosts` file must contain the proper entry for your local machine.

Understanding the `rcp` Command-Line Syntax

The `rcp` command line is flexible; to support this flexibility, there are a few variations of the command line:

- `rcp single-file dest`—In this variation, the first argument, `single-file`, is a single file. This file is copied to the destination `dest`. If `dest` is an existing directory, the file `dest/single-file` is created. If `dest` is an existing file, `dest` is overwritten with `single-file`. Otherwise, the file `dest` is created by copying `single-file`.

- `rcp sources dest`—In this variation, the first argument, `sources`, is one or more files or directories. `dest` must be a directory. Only the members of `sources` that are files are copied to the destination `dest`. If `dest` is an existing directory, the files are copied under directory `dest`. It is unwise to specify a `dest` directory that does not exist with this form of the `rcp` command. The results vary from system to system. See the next form for copying a single directory.

- `rcp -r sources dest.` By adding the option `-r`, the files in `sources` as well as the directories (and all their subdirectories) are copied to `dest`.

- If `sources` is a single directory, it is okay to specify a destination `dest` that doesn't exist. The directory is created for you. This is probably what you want. Beware of this situation because if `dest` *does* exist, the copied directory is placed as a subdirectory of `dest`.

- If `sources` is multiple directories or files, `dest` must be an existing directory. If it doesn't exist, the results are not specified and differ from one UNIX system to another.

- Each version of the `rcp` command line supports an additional option, `-p`. This option causes `rcp` to preserve the modification times as well as the modes when the copy is made.

Using `ftp`

The `ftp` service is the interface to the file transfer protocol. This service provides a connection service to a remote computer along with file manipulation functions including sending and receiving files. It also provides user authentication, unlike `rcp`. It supports different file types.

To connect with a remote host, you can simply type `ftp` *hostname*. The *hostname* can either be a hostname or an Internet address. If you do not specify a remote host on the command line, you enter `ftp` command mode. Then you can use the `open` command to initiate a connection.

By default, when a connection is initiated via `ftp`, the remote `ftp` server starts up the login process. You must enter a valid username and password to access the remote system. After you have been authenticated, you are connected to the remote `ftp` server, and it awaits your commands.

The `ftp` service has many commands. Table 5.3 lists several common commands. For complete details, refer to your system's manual for `ftp`.

TABLE 5.3. COMMON FTP SERVICE COMMANDS.

Command	Description
Connection-Related Commands	
open	Open a connection to specified host.
close	Close current open connection.
quit	Close current open connection and exit `ftp`.
File Transfer-Related Commands	
binary	Change the file representation type to binary.
ascii	Change the file representation type to ascii.
put	Transfer a single file from the local to the remote host.
mput	Transfer multiple files from the local to the remote host.
get	Transfer a single file from the remote to the local host.
mget	Transfer multiple files from the remote to the local host.
File and Directory Management Commands	
cd	Change remote's current working directory (UNIX `cd`).
lcd	Change the local's current working directory (UNIX `cd`).
cdup	Change remote's current working directory to be the parent directory (UNIX `cd ..`).
dir	List the remote's current working directory (UNIX `ls`).
pwd	Print the remote's current working directory (UNIX `pwd`).
mkdir	Make a new directory on the remote (UNIX `mkdir`).
rmdir	Delete a directory on the remote (UNIX `rmdir`).
rename	Change the name of a remote file or directory (UNIX `mv`).

Command	Description
File and Directory Management Commands	
delete	Delete a remote file (UNIX rm, with one file specified).
mdelete	Delete multiple remote files (UNIX rm, with multiple files).
Miscellaneous Commands	
?	Obtain help about ftp.
!	Escape shell.

Connection-Related Commands

The ftp connection-related commands are fairly straightforward. The open command tries to connect to the ftp server on the specified remote host. The close command terminates the open connection (if one exists) and then returns to command mode. This is usually used when you want to connect to a different host, so you will commonly follow it with an open command. The quit command closes the connection and then exits ftp.

File Transfer-Related Commands

The ftp service defines several file representation types for transfer. The two most common are ascii and binary. By default, the type is set to ascii. Any file that is plain ASCII text can be transferred using ascii type. Binary files, like a compiled and linked executable file, must be transferred using binary type. Be sure to set the correct type before transferring any files.

TIP

Transferring ASCII text files between UNIX machines is slightly faster with binary type, but using binary type to transfer an ASCII text file between a UNIX and a non-UNIX machine might corrupt the file.

TIP

If you are having trouble decoding or executing a binary file you got elsewhere, check to make sure that you used binary type transfer.

5

GETTING AROUND THE NETWORK

The `get` and `mget` commands transfer files from the remote to the local host. The `put` and `mput` commands transfer files from the local to the remote host. Both `get` and `put` transfer one file per command. On both of these commands, you may specify the destination for the file copy. If the destination is not specified, the file is placed in the current working directory. Both `mget` and `mput` transfer multiple files per command. The files are placed in the current working directory.

File and Directory Management Commands

The file and directory management commands are analogous to UNIX file and directory commands. In Table 5.3, the UNIX command that is analogous to the `ftp` command is given in parentheses. Remember that all these commands, except `lcd`, operate on the remote file system. If you need to perform more in-depth local file management, use the shell escape command (`!`) to escape to a local shell prompt.

Miscellaneous Commands

The `?` command provides help about `ftp` commands. If you want help about a specific command, you can specify this command as the first argument to the `?`. The shell escape command (`!`) is used to start a subshell on the local machine. This is useful if you need to perform some operations on your local host while you are connected to a remote `ftp` server. After you are finished working on the local host, simply exit the (sub)shell, and you will return to `ftp`.

Configuring with `.netrc`

The `ftp` command can automatically perform the login to remote `ftp` servers and initialize your connection. It does this by reading in the `.netrc` file in your home directory. You can configure the login, password, and account (some `ftp` servers allow or require an extra account specification at authentication time) to use for a particular machine. In the following example from the `.netrc` file, automatic login is included as anonymous for several popular servers:

```
machine dg-rtp.rtp.dg.com login anonymous password sartin@pencom.com
machine town.hall.org login anonymous password sartin@pencom.com
machine ftp.uu.net login anonymous password sartin@pencom.com
machine rtfm.mit.edu login anonymous password sartin@pencom.com
machine ftp.x.org login anonymous password sartin@pencom.com
machine prep.ai.mit.edu login anonymous password sartin@pencom.com
machine ftp.ncsa.uiuc.edu login anonymous password sartin@pencom.com
machine emx.cc.utexas.edu login anonymous password sartin@pencom.com
machine boombox.micro.umn.edu login anonymous password sartin@pencom.com
machine rs.internic.net login anonymous password guest
```

> **TIP**
>
> Most versions of ftp use your .netrc for password information only if the file is readable by you only. For password security, this file should be unreadable by others or, better yet, should contain no sensitive passwords.

Anonymous `ftp`

A special login for ftp allows you to anonymously access files on part of a remote machine. Anonymous access is not entirely anonymous because some machines log the connection, the password used, and all files retrieved. To use anonymous ftp, you use the login anonymous (on some machines, the login ftp works) and supply any nonempty string for the password.

> **TIP**
>
> Some machines do password validation on anonymous logins. Most require that you supply a valid email address.

After you have successfully logged in as anonymous, you are granted limited access to the anonymous ftp subtree on the remote machine. All the commands described in this section can be used. Some sites have a directory called /incoming (or a directory named incoming somewhere in the ftp tree) where you can put files. Many sites put the publicly accessible files under /pub.

Using `uucp`, `uuto`, and `uupick`

The file copying tools uucp, uuto, and uupick are part of the Basic Networking Utilities software release. These might not be on your UNIX system. Even if they are, more recent networking services (for example, ftp and rcp) are preferred. If you are interested in using the uu tools, check your system documentation to see whether they are supported.

Following, for the sake of completeness, is a brief summary of these tools. For details, check your system's manual entry for each command.

uucp

The uucp service copies one or more files from one UNIX machine to another UNIX machine. Use the uuname command to see what remote machines you can reach via uucp. uucp uses an older host naming scheme in the form *hostname!filepath*. To copy a local file, `myfile`, to remote machine *rem-host* to directory `/tmp`, enter the command `uucp myfile` *rem-host*`!/tmp/`.

uuto and *uupick*

The `uuto` tool sends a file to a specific user on a remote UNIX host. The file is deposited in a special place on the specified remote host. For the remote user to receive this file, she must use the `uupick` tool. The remote host and user are specified by the syntax *rem-host*`!`*username*. To send the local file `myfile` to user `arnie` on machine `sturgeon`, enter the command `uuto myfile sturgeon!arnie`.

Then user `arnie` must use the `uupick` tool to receive the file.

When you are ready to receive files that were sent via `uuto`, simply enter the `uuto` command without any arguments. Each file that has been sent to you is displayed, one at a time. As each is displayed, you have the choice of skipping it, moving it, deleting it, or printing it.

Other Networking Services

This section gives an abbreviated introduction to some other services currently available on the Internet. These services give you access to the wealth of information available on the Internet, including source code, current weather information, financial data, computer conferences on a wide variety of topics, and some more frivolous programs, including a computerized tarot reader.

CAUTION

These programs are useful to you only if you are connected to the Internet and have a gateway that allows you to make outgoing connections. Check your local network configuration to be sure.

CAUTION

These programs can be addictive. Make sure that you get enough sleep and social activity between your net surfing excursions.

archie

The `archie` program offers access to a large list of files available via anonymous `ftp`. When you run an `archie` string search, the server searches for a name that is an exact match for the string in its list of archives and returns the matches to you. You can modify the search behavior by specifying one of the following:

- `-c`—Case-sensitive substring search
- `-r`—Regular expression search
- `-s`—Case-insensitive substring match

For example, if you were looking for the source to `xmosaic`, you could enter `archie -s xmosaic`. The output lists many sites that have `xmosaic` available via anonymous `ftp`. Here is part of the response from that command:

```
Host ftp.engr.ucf.edu
    Location: /pub/linux-mirrors/tsx11/binaries/usr.bin.X11.nomirror
         FILE -rw-r--r--    497473  Dec 26 18:06   xmosaic-
1.2.term.tar.z
```

For each host that had a match of the string, there is a list of locations that had matches. The best way to use `archie` output is to look for a host "near" you (for example, your service provider, someone in the same city/state as your service provider, someone in the same country) and use `ftp` to retrieve the desired files.

gopher

The University of Minnesota has developed a program called `gopher`, that you can use to retrieve information over the Internet. They report (in the `00README` file available by anonymous `ftp` from `boombox.umn.edu` in `/pub/gopher/00README`):

The internet Gopher uses a simple client/server protocol that can be used to publish and search for information held on a distributed network of hosts. Gopher clients have a seamless view of the information in the gopher world even though the information is distributed over many different hosts. Clients can either navigate through a hierarchy of directories and documents -or- ask an index server to return a list of all documents that contain one or more words. Since the index server does full-text searches every word in every document is a keyword.

If you want to test a gopher client without setting up your own gopher server you should configure the client to talk to "gopher.micro.umn.edu" at port 70. This will allow you to explore the distributed network of gopher servers at the University of Minnesota. You can try the Unix client by telneting to consultant.micro.umn.edu and logging in as "gopher".

World Wide Web

In 1991, the European Laboratory for Particle Physics began a project that turned into the World Wide Web, also known as WWW or W3. WWW is fairly difficult to pigeonhole, and the best way to become familiar with it is to explore it. WWW is a set of software, conventions, servers, and a protocol (HTTP) for organizing information in a hypertext structure. It allows linking of pictures (both still and moving), sounds, and text of various kinds into a web of knowledge. You can start at any place (a particularly good place to start is the default home page at NCSA or a copy of it, using `xmosaic`) and choose the links that interest you. Information is located using a *Uniform Resource Locator* (URL), which generally looks like this:

`protocol://hostname/path`

The `protocol` tells how to access the data (and is often `http`, which indicates the Hypertext transfer protocol). The `hostname` tells the name of the host to access. The `path` gives a host-specific location for the resource; paths often look like normal UNIX filenames. A big difference between an URL path and a filename is that an URL path often points to information that is generated on-the-fly (for example, a current weather report), and the actual data returned might depend on what features your WWW client supports. By exploring the Web, you can find information ranging from your personal biorhythms to common questions about the PowerPC to an archive of scuba diving destination reports.

The National Center for Supercomputing Applications at the University of Illinois has developed World Wide Web interfaces called Mosaic. The UNIX version runs with Motif widgets using X11 and is called `xmosaic`.

Troubleshooting TCP/IP

Sometimes you might find that your attempts at making network connection are not working. Some common errors for each command were covered in the sections "Connecting to Other Systems—`rlogin`, `telnet`, and `cu`" and "Transferring Files—`rcp`, `ftp`, and `uucp`." This section covers some system-level troubleshooting you might want to try if you are having trouble making network connections using TCP/IP (`rlogin`, `telnet`, `rcp`, `ftp`, and the commands mentioned in the section "Other Services"). The suggestions here help solve simple problems and help classify problems. See Chapter 26, "Networking," for more information on troubleshooting network problems.

`nslookup` to Check Address Mapping

One common failure in trying to make network connections is either having the wrong hostname or encountering an error or delay in the name service. One way to check the validity of the hostname is to try using the `nslookup` command. The simplest way to run the `nslookup` command is `nslookup` hostname:

```
$ nslookup ftp.uu.net.
Name Server:  lazerus.pencom.com
Address:  198.3.201.57

Name:    ftp.uu.net
Address:  192.48.96.9

$ nslookup no.such.name.org
Name Server:  lazerus.pencom.com
Address:  198.3.201.57

*** lazerus.pencom.com can't find no.such.name.org: Non-existent domain
$
```

This queries the DNS for the name of hostname (`ftp.uu.net` in the first example, `no.such.name.org` in the second).

> **TIP**
>
> When a machine is newly added to the DNS, it might take a while before the name servers learn about it. During that time, you may get "unknown host" errors. The person who adds a new host to the DNS should be able to give an estimate of how long to wait before a DNS failure should be considered an error.

Is There Anybody Out There? (ping)

If you can find the address of a host but your connections are failing, it might be because the host is unreachable or down. Sometimes you might get a `"host unreachable"` or `"network unreachable"` error. You get these messages when the software that manages interconnections determines that it could not send a packet to the remote host. The network routing software has internal tables that tell it how to reach other networks and hosts, and these error messages indicate that there is no table entry that lets you reach the desired network or host.

5

GETTING AROUND
THE NETWORK

When a host is simply down, you might get connection timeouts. You might want to try using the `ping` command to test whether a host is running. The `ping` command sends a special kind of message called an *Internet control echo request message* or *ICMP echo request* (ICMP is the Internet control message protocol). This message asks the remote computer to send back an echo reply that duplicates the data of the echo request message. The low-level networking software of the remote computer handles responding to an echo request, so a machine should be able to respond to a `ping` as long as the network software is running.

The following example uses `ping` to check the status of two hosts:

```
$ /etc/ping conch 100 10
PING conch.pencom.com: 100 byte packets
100 bytes from 198.3.200.86: icmp_seq=0. time=3. ms
100 bytes from 198.3.200.86: icmp_seq=1. time=4. ms
100 bytes from 198.3.200.86: icmp_seq=2. time=3. ms
100 bytes from 198.3.200.86: icmp_seq=3. time=5. ms
100 bytes from 198.3.200.86: icmp_seq=4. time=4. ms
100 bytes from 198.3.200.86: icmp_seq=5. time=8. ms
100 bytes from 198.3.200.86: icmp_seq=6. time=3. ms
100 bytes from 198.3.200.86: icmp_seq=7. time=3. ms
100 bytes from 198.3.200.86: icmp_seq=8. time=3. ms
100 bytes from 198.3.200.86: icmp_seq=9. time=3. ms

conch.pencom.com PING Statistics--
10 packets transmitted, 10 packets received, 0% packet loss

round-trip (ms)  min/avg/max = 3/3/8

$ /etc/ping brat 100 10
PING brat.pencom.com: 100 byte packets

--brat.pencom.com PING Statistics--
10 packets transmitted, 0 packets received, 100% packet loss
$
```

In the first example, the 100 says to use 100 bytes of data in each message, and the 10 says to use 10 messages. All 10 messages were returned. The second example shows what happens when you attempt to `ping` a host that is not up.

After you determine that the remote host is not responding, you can either attempt to get the machine back up or wait until later to use it. If the machine is on your LAN, it should be fairly easy to go to it and start it running or talk to a local administrator. If the machine is somewhere remote, you might need to phone or email someone to get assistance. If the machine is a resource on the Internet that is offered by some other school or company, you should probably just wait until it is running again unless your need is urgent (for both you and the remote administrator).

Summary

In this chapter, you learned how UNIX machines are networked and how to take advantage of that networking. You have learned to log in to remote machines, copy files, begin to surf the Internet, and troubleshoot minor problems. By using these network services, you can perform useful work on networked systems and explore the "information superhighway."

Communicating with Others

by Chris Byers, Ron Dippold, and Fred Trimble

In This Chapter

From its inception, the purpose of the Internet has been to facilitate communication among people. It was originally developed by the military to provide a vast distributed communications network capable of continued operation in case of a nuclear attack. Its designers wanted a distributed network to eliminate the possibility of a "vulnerable central node." They also wanted a communications protocol that would be independent of any particular physical media. Despite its military roots, it has become characterized by the general public as the "Infobahn," "Information Superhighway," and "Cyberspace." Today, some 20 years later, the benefits of the Internet are being realized by many groups of people, including schools, home users, and private industry. The Internet infrastructure was originally designed to support applications such as electronic mail and file transfer. Although electronic mail is still the most popular application on the Internet, other networking hardware and protocols continue to evolve so that they can support other types of communication, including real-time audio and video.

Throughout the history of the Internet, UNIX has certainly played a major role. Most early UNIX systems provided built-in support for the Internet's main protocol: TCP/IP (Transmission Control Protocol). Therefore, this chapter covers the following topics, with an emphasis on UNIX facilities where appropriate:

Email	Electronic mail allows you to exchange messages with other people all over the world. Many electronic mail programs have extended features, such as the capability to attach binary files.
Usenet	Usenet is the world's largest electronic discussion forum. One of the most popular features of the Internet, it allows people all over the world to discuss topics and exchange ideas on a wide variety of subjects.
Talk	The `talk` command allows two people to exchange text messages in real-time.
IRC	Internet Relay Chat extends the capabilities of the `talk` command. It provides a real-time multiple-person discussion forum, much like a CB radio channel.
Multimedia	The Internet allows real-time audio and video to be transmitted.
The future	This section provides a glimpse into the future of the Internet.

Electronic Mail (Email)

Electronic mail is the most widely used application on the Internet. It is known as an asynchronous type of communication system because after a mail message has been sent, it resides on the recipient's computer until the recipient logs on and retrieves the message. This section focuses on many facets of email, including the structure of a mail message, sending binary data (such as a graphics file) with a mail message, email addressing, how messages are sent over the Internet, and common end-user mail programs.

Components of a Mail Message

A mail message consists of two main sections: a message header and a message body. The header contains information such as who sent the message and when it was sent. The body contains the actual message text. Some people finish their messages with an optional third part known as a "signature." Each of these mail message sections is described in detail in the following sections.

Message Headers

The message header consists of several lines at the top, formatted as *"keyword: value"* pairs. Messages sent to a user who is located on the same local UNIX host using the `mail` or `mailx` program have a simple structure. For example:

```
From smithj Thu Apr 24 00:42 EDT 1997
To: jonest
Subject: Code Review Meeting
Status: R


Please plan on attending the code review
meeting tomorrow at 10:00am.
```

The message header of a mail message that ends up going over the Internet, however, is much more complex. For example:

```
From nihil@eniac.seas.void.edu Thu Apr  24 08:15:01 1997
Flags: 000000000015
Received: from phones.com (phones.com [229.46.62.22]) by
happy.phones.com (8.6.5/QC-BSD-2.1) via ESMTP;
id IAA13973 Thu, 24 Apr 1997 08:14:59 -0800 for
<rdippold@happy.phones.com>
Received: from linc.cis.void.edu (root@LINC.CIS.VOID.EDU
[230.91.6.8]) by phones.com (8.6.5/QC-main-2.3) via ESMTP;
id IAA14773 Thu, 24 Apr 1997 08:14:56 -0800 for
<rdippold@phones.com>
Received: from eniac.seas.void.edu (nihil@ENIAC.SEAS.VOID.EDU
[230.91.4.1]) by linc.cis.void.edu (8.6.5/VOID 1.4) with
```

```
ESMTP id LAA17163 for <rdippold@phones.com>
Thu, 24 Apr 1997 11:14:45 -0500
Received: from localhost by eniac.seas.void.edu
id LAA24236; Thu, 24 Apr 1997 11:14:44 -0500
From: nihil@eniac.seas.void.edu [B Johnson]
Sender: nihil@ocean.void.edu
Reply-To: nihil@void.edu,nihil@freenet.com
Cc: group-stuff@uunet.UU.NET
Cc: james@foobar.com
Message-Id: <199302011614.LAA24236@eniac.seas.void.edu>
Subject: Re: Apple IIe/IIgs Software and books for SALE...
To: rdippold@phones.com (Ron Dippold)
Date: Thu, 24 Apr 97 11:14:44 EST
In-Reply-To:      <CMM.342342.rdippold@happy.phones.com>;
from "Ron Dippold" at Apr 24, 97 1:00 am
X-Mailer: ELM [version 2.3 PL11-void1.13]
Mime-Version: 1.0
Content-Type: text/plain; charset=US-ASCII
Content-Transfer-Encoding: 7bit
Content-Length: 10234
```

Message headers are constructed for you automatically by mail software known as *mail user agents* (MUA) and *mail transport agents* (MTA). In fact, the presence of certain items in the header, such as carbon copies and receipt notification, depend on the sophistication of the mail software itself. These components of an electronic mail system are discussed in detail in a later section. Some header information is intuitive. Other sections require some explanation.

Here's the first line from the previous example:

```
From nihil@eniac.seas.void.edu Thu Apr  24 08:15:01 1997
```

This line was added by the MTA on the local system (sendmail). It is used as a quick message summary, noting who sent the message and when. Because many mail systems store all of a user's mail messages in a single text file, such summary lines are also used to separate messages within the file. This provides a way to tell the end of one message from the start of the next. For most mail programs, this is the text From at the start of a line. This also means that if you try to place a From at the start of a line of text in your actual message, your mail program should place a > or some other character before it, so that it doesn't falsely indicate the start of a new message.

```
Flags: 000000000015
```

The Flags field, which is specific to Berkeley mail and mailx, was also added by the local mail program. Each message can have several different statuses, such as deleted, unread, and flagged for further attention. This varies with the sophistication of the mail program.

```
Received: from phones.com (phones.com [229.46.62.22]) by
happy.phones.com (8.6.5/QC-BSD-2.1) via ESMTP;
id IAA13973 Thu, 24 Apr 1997 08:14:59 -0800 for
<rdippold@happy.phones.com>
```

Each system that receives mail adds its own received header on top of the message. Because this is the first such header in the message, it must indicate the last mail transfer. The machine `happy.phones.com` (where my mail is located) received the message from `phones.com` (our company gateway) on April 24, 1997. The transfer was done using `sendmail` 8.6.5 (although you can't tell from this header that it was `sendmail`), and the protocol used was ESMTP. The intended recipient is listed last. This can change as the message goes through gateways, so it's helpful for tracking mail problems.

```
Received: from linc.cis.void.edu (root@LINC.CIS.VOID.EDU
[230.91.6.8]) by phones.com (8.6.5/QC-main-2.3) via ESMTP;
id IAA14773 Thu, 24 Apr 1997 08:14:56 -0800 for
<rdippold@phones.com>
```

RFC 822, which documents the standard format for Internet text messages, contains information about the header format.

An alternative to `sendmail` is UUCP. RFC 976 explains the UUCP mail protocol, which is a store-and-forward mechanism. Instead of making a direct connection like a phone circuit, host A makes a temporary connection to send mail to host B, which stores it temporarily and forwards it to host C, the final recipient. UUCP is a pain in the neck, not to mention a serious security hole; avoid it if you can.

NOTE

Throughout this chapter, reference will be made to RFCs. RFC stands for Request For Comments and is the means by which the research and development community has documented the standards that form the basis of the Internet. For example, RFC 821 documents the SMTP protocol for sending mail.

The Message Body

The message body is separated from the message header by a single blank line. The message body contains the actual text of the message. Here, you are free to type whatever you want to the recipient.

Signatures

Some email messages conclude with an optional signature. A signature is a brief description of who sent the message, such as full name, telephone and fax numbers, and email address. This is stored in the user's `.sig` file and can be modified with `vi`. Some signatures try to embellish this information with a picture drawn with ASCII characters. It is considered good practice to limit your signature to five lines or less. Most modern mail programs can be configured to automatically append your signature to the end of your message.

Sending Binary Data

The protocol for sending email over the Internet (SMTP) allows only for the transmission of ASCII text characters. Therefore, binary files, such as audio or video files, are not directly supported. The preferred method for sending binary data is to use a mail program that supports Multipurpose Internet Mail Extensions (MIME). This is discussed in a later section. Before the advent of MIME, a technique used to circumvent this restriction is to encode such data as ASCII text before sending it with a mailer program, such as `elm` or `mailx`. On UNIX systems, use the `uuencode` program to convert a binary file to ASCII text. On the receiving end, use the `uudecode` program to convert the data back to binary.

Mail programs such as `mailx` are also discussed in more detail later in the chapter.

Addressing Remote Systems

To send a message over the Internet, you need to specify a specially formatted Internet address. It is composed of two major sections separated by an @ sign. The part of the address to the left of the @ sign is the Internet account that will receive the mail message. This is usually the login name of the mail recipient. The part of the address to the right of the @ sign is known as the domain name. It uniquely identifies a host on the Internet. All domain names on the Internet comprise the Domain Name System, which is a hierarchy that divides the Internet into logical groups (domains). The domain is read from right to left and specifies a series of progressively smaller logical domain names. Each part of the domain name is separated with a period. For example, note the following Internet address:

`ccarter@minn.com`

The rightmost portion of the domain, `.com`, indicates that this is a commercial site. The following list shows the most popular domains for the United States:

com	commercial
edu	education
gov	government

mil	military
net	network
org	organization

Outside of the United States, sites can be registered to `.com`, `.net`, and `.org`. In addition, the two-letter ISO country code can also be used. For example, "ca" for Canada, "uk" for the United Kingdom, and so on.

To the left of the highest level domain name (`.edu`, `.org`, and so on) can appear any number of logical subdomains. These are used to specify, in greater detail, the name of the host where the mail recipient can be found. By Internet convention, capitalization in the domain name is ignored. Therefore, the following Internet addresses are equivalent: `ccarter@Minn.com`, `ccarter@MINN.com`, and `ccarter@MINN.COM`). Most modern mail software ignores case in the username portion of the address for consistency. However, this is not a requirement. Therefore, it is considered good practice to preserve case for the username, just in case the recipient's system is using older mail software.

An older type of addressing scheme is known as a UUCP bang-path address (*bang* is computer jargon for an exclamation point). It is unlikely that you will see an address in this format, though, and is mentioned here for historical reasons. In this type of scheme, you must indicate each system you want the mail to pass through. For example, note the following address for user `katherine`:

`comp01!comp02!comp03!katherine`

This indicates that you want the mail to pass through systems named `comp01`, `comp02`, and `comp03`. After the message has been delivered to `comp03`, it will be delivered to `katherine`.

How Messages Are Routed Over the Internet

Before an Internet address in *username@domain* format can be used for transmission, it must be converted into an IP address. An IP address consists of four numbers, separated by dots, which uniquely identify a host on the Internet. For example, "128.254.17.7" is an example of an IP address. Translating an Internet address to an IP address is the province of systems on the Internet known as name servers.

When a mail message is sent over the Internet, it is sent as a stream of packets, each containing a portion of the message. Each packet also contains the IP address of the destination. The packets are sent over the Internet using the IP protocol. Specialized networking systems on the Internet, known as routers, examine the IP address in each packet, and route it to the appropriate host. Many factors, such as network traffic volume, on various Internet backbones are taken into consideration to determine the best possible path. In fact, packets from the same mail message may take different routes. All packets are combined in the correct order on the receiving host using the TCP protocol.

Sending Mail to Other Networks

In addition to sending email over the Internet, it is possible to send mail to other networks, such as online services.

Internet Email Gateways

In theory, the Internet is a competitor with all the existing services such as AT&T Mail, CompuServe, and the rest. In practice, it's a neutral competitor. It's not some guided, malevolent entity that is trying to do away with any of the other services. Rather, it competes just by its existence; it offers more information and more connectivity than most of the services can ever hope to offer. Smart information services finally realized that this could be put to their advantage. Anyone who cares to can join the Internet, and a service that joins the Internet has advantages over its competitors.

One huge advantage is connectivity. As soon as a mail service adds a computer (known as a *gateway*) that can transfer from its system to the Internet and vice versa, its users can exchange mail with anyone on the service or with anyone on the Internet. That's a lot of people. So, many services are now offering some sort of mail gateway. Even Prodigy, which was somewhat late to grasp the possibilities, has one now.

Instead of GEnie needing to install a special gateway to talk to Prodigy, and one to CompuServe, and one to SprintMail, and one to BubbaNet, it can set up and maintain just one gateway to the Internet, through which everything flows. Given the glacial speed with which most of the online services implement upgrades like this, requiring only a single gateway is a good thing.

So now anyone can send email anywhere! Well, not exactly.

Addressing Issues

It turns out that the services that connect to the Internet keep their same old account names and horrible mail systems. CompuServe's octal account addresses are as much an anachronism as punch cards, but because of the company's current investment, it isn't going to change them. And you can't just send a mail message to a CompuServe account using an Internet-style address. A CompuServe ID looks something like this:

```
112233,44
```

In Internet addressing, a comma separates members of a list so you can't use the comma in the CompuServe address. There's a way around that (use a period instead of a comma), but you have to know that in advance. Someone trying to send mail to a system has to deal with those quirks. Hence this section, which details the translation that has to be done between the major networks.

Again, an Internet email address looks something like this:

```
user@machine.site.domain
```

Any address to a mail gateway is going to be some variation (minor or major) on this theme.

X.400 Addressing

The Internet uses what is formally known as RFC-822 addressing. Many large commercial services specializing in electronic mail use something known as an X.400 gateway to talk to the Internet. Those addresses look something like this:

```
/A=value/B=value/C=value
```

This style is usable from the Internet because RFC 822 allows slashes and equals signs. In fact, there's the opposite problem: RFC 822 allows many characters to be used in addressing that cause an X.400 gateway to go into convulsions, including the @ sign. Because this appears in all Internet-style mail addresses, there's an obvious problem.

Whenever the Internet address has a special character, you need to use the following translation table:

Internet	X.400
@	(a)
%	(p)
!	(b)
"	(q)
_	(u)
(	(l)
)	(r)

For any other special character, such as #, substitute (*xxx*), where *xxx* is the three-digit decimal ASCII code for the character. For #, you would use (035).

For example, to convert the Internet address

```
oldvax!Mutt#Jeff@cartoon.com
```

into something that can be sent from an X.400 service such as MCI Mail, you need to turn it into this:

```
oldvax(b)Mutt(035)Jeff(a)cartoon.com
```

Gateway Translation Specifics

Using the following instructions should be fairly easy. To send mail to CompuServe from an Internet mail account, see the translation instructions in the "CompuServe" section later in this chapter.

Parts of the address that you have to replace with appropriate information are given in

> **NOTE**
>
> The ! is replaced with (b) because computer users like short names, and refer to an exclamation point as a *bang*.

italics. For instance, with

`userid@aol.com`

you need to replace *userid* with the recipient's account name or number. *domain* is the part of the Internet address after the @.

If you are sending mail from one service to another through the Internet, for example from WWIVNet to CompuServe, you have to do two translations. First, check the "CompuServe" section and see how to translate the ID "From Internet." Then check the "WWIVNet" section and see how to translate that address "To Internet." If you do this from one strange network to another, the name may be a crawling horror, but at least it should be possible.

America Online

America Online (AOL) is a major commercial information system that recently joined the Internet (although it has had Internet email for a while). Its Internet email is seamless from an Internet point of view.

From Internet: America Online looks just like any other normal Internet site.

`userid@aol.com`

Example: `jjones@aol.com`

To Internet: There's no need to do anything special; just use the regular Internet format.

`userid@domain`

Example: `bsmith@wubba.edu`

6

To Others: America Online lets you use special abbreviated domains for mail to AppleLink, CompuServe, or GEnie. Send your mail to *userid*@applelink, *userid*@cis, or *userid*@genie, respectively.

Example: `11111.2222@cis`

AT&T Mail

From Internet: Use standard Internet addressing:

userid@attmail.com

To Internet: Use the following. Note the backward order here—this is the old bang-path type addressing. Oh well.

Example: `internet!wubba.edu!bsmith.`

CompuServe

CompuServe is a large commercial system. Although it finally bowed to the pressures of Internet standardization, CompuServe still allows the format shown in the next section.

From Internet: Use standard Internet addressing with one difference: CompuServe IDs are in the form *77777,7777*. Because the Internet dislikes commas in addresses, you need to change the comma to a period:

77777.7777@compuserve.com

Example: `12345.677@compuserve.com`

To Internet: You need to add a prefix to the standard Internet addressing:

`>INTERNET;`*userid*@*domain*

Example: `>INTERNET;bsmith@wubba.edu`

EasyLink

This is a set of commercial Internet services from AT&T.

For more information on AT&T's EasyLink, you can contact them at `http://www.att.com/easycommerce/easylink/mail.html`.

FidoNet

FidoNet is a large international BBS network—sort of the Internet for the BBSing crowd. It's not as fast as the Internet, but access is usually very cheap, and chances are there's a FidoNet BBS in your area.

Because it's run over phone lines, the BBS operators will rack up long-distance charges for any mail transferred, so please don't send large messages to FidoNet sites. Many sites even chop your messages to 8,000 or 16,000 bytes, so much of your message won't get through.

From Internet: First, you need to know the network address of the BBS your recipient is on. It will be in a form such as `Z;N/F.P`. Then send the mail to the following address:

`userid@pP.fF.nN.zZ.fidonet.org`

If the network address of the BBS doesn't have a `P` component, leave the `pP.` part out of the address. For the `userid` replace any nonalphanumeric characters (such as spaces) with periods (`.`).

Example: `Jim_Jones@p4.f3.n2.z1.fidonet.org`

To Internet: Use standard Internet addressing with a suffix:

`userid@userid ON gateway`

The `gateway` is a special FidoNet site that acts as a gateway to the Internet. You can use `1:1/31` unless you find a better one.

Example: `bsmith@wubba.edu ON 1:1/31`

Prodigy

Prodigy is a large commercial service, Prodigy Information Services (jointly developed by Sears and IBM).

From Internet: Use standard Internet addressing:

`domain@prodigy.com`

Example: `jone45a@prodigy.com`

To Internet: When online, `Jump` to `ABOUT MAIL MANAGER` and proceed from there.

SprintMail

Hmm…AT&T and MCI have commercial mail services. Sprint has to have one, if only for the principle of the matter. Actually, to be fair, Sprint has always been one of the more network-oriented phone companies. You may have used their Telenet network.

From Internet: Use this addressing:

`/G=first/S=last/O=organization/ADMD=TELEMAIL/C=US/@sprint.com`

`first` and `last` are the recipient's first and last names, of course, and `organization` is the recipient's SprintMail organization name.

Example: `/G=Chris/S=Smith/O=FooInc/ADMD=TELEMAIL/C=US/@sprint.com`

To Internet: Use this addressing:

`C;USA,A;TELEMAIL,P;INTERNET,"RFC-822":<`*userid*`(a)`*domain*`>) DEL`

Again, refer to the section "X.400 Addressing" earlier in the chapter, to see how to handle nonstandard characters in addresses.

Example: `C;USA,A;TELEMAIL,P;INTERNET,"RFC-822":<bsmith(a)wubba.edu>) DEL.`

Other Gateways

There are other gateways, and more are sure to appear. Most services offering this type of gateway should have at least some clue of how the address translation needs to be done—ask the service if you need to know.

Finding Addresses

Many places on the World Wide Web keep track of people's names and their corresponding email addresses. Many sites also provide a nice "front end" to these databases, allowing you to search for someone's email address.

One such site is `http://www.four11.com`. It allows you to narrow your search based on geographic regions, such as country and state. It also has a handy "smart name" feature, that expands a search for certain variations in a name (for instance, Robert = Bob). It currently contains more than 6.5 million listings. Other worthwhile sites include `http://www.iaf.net` and `www.bigfoot.com`. Finally, be sure to check out `http://www.starthere.com/index.html`. It has links and descriptions of many sites, which, in turn, do the actual email address searches on the Web.

To find someone in the communications field, try RPI's address server. Send mail to Internet address `comserve@vm.its.rpi.edu` with `help` as the body of the message.

UNINNETT of Norway maintains an X.500 address registry service. Send mail to Internet address `directory@uninett.no` with `help` as the body of the message.

PSI runs an X.500 service at Internet address `whitepages@wp.psi.com` with `help` as the message body.

Usenet Address Server

MIT keeps track of every person who has ever posted an article to Usenet since the late 1980s (many Usenet readers would be shocked to know this). This includes those from other networks who use a news gateway. If the person you are looking for has posted an article to Usenet since then, he or she might be in this database.

Send mail to the Internet address `mail-server@rtfm.mit.edu`. In the body of the message, put this:

```
send usenet-addresses/key1 key2 key...
```

The keys should include all the words you think might appear in the address, usually parts of the person's name. In many cases, you will use only *key1*. The keys are case insensitive.

You can try the following:

```
send usenet-addresses/dippold
```

to return several entries. The server returns only 40 matches, so if your keys are overly general (Smith) you will need to give more keys, such as a first name, to narrow the search.

You can do several searches at once by placing several `send usenet-addresses/keys` lines in the message.

Mail Programs

Three main components are involved in sending mail. First there's the *link level transport layer*. Directly above the transport layer is the mail transport agent (MTA). This layer is responsible for the movement and delivery of mail messages. An MTA has several components, including routing mechanisms, a local delivery agent, and a remote delivery agent. The MTA for most UNIX systems is the `sendmail` program. An MTA that takes liberties in modifying the contents of a message is known as a hostile MTA. Finally, the mail user agent (MUA) provides the user interface. It allows you to read, send, and otherwise manipulate mail messages. This is what people usually mean when they talk about a *mail program*. This is covered in more detail in Chapter 30, "Mail Administration."

There are many mail programs from which to choose. The next section covers the elements common to them all.

Using Mail Programs

As mentioned earlier, there are many mail programs, each with its own quirks. But they try to accomplish the same task and tend to present the messages in a similar format.

To learn more about the many common UNIX mail programs available and their various features, see Chapter 30, "Mail Administration."

SMTP—Simple Mail Transfer Protocol

Simple Mail Transfer Protocol (SMTP), or some variation of it (such as Extended SMTP) is used by computers on the Internet that handle mail to transfer messages from one machine to another. It's a one-way protocol—the SMTP client contacts the SMTP server and gives it a mail message.

Most mail client programs support SMTP for sending outgoing mail, simply because it's easy to implement. Few mail clients support SMTP for incoming mail because normally your mail computer can't contact your personal computer at will to give it mail. It's possible if your personal computer happens to be permanently networked to the mail computer via Ethernet, for instance, or if your mail computer knows how to use a modem to call your personal computer, but in most cases this isn't done.

POP3 (Post Office Protocol 3)

The standard protocol used by most mail clients to retrieve mail from a remote system is the post office protocol POP3. This protocol enables your mail client to grab new messages, delete messages, and do other things necessary for reading your incoming mail. POP only requires a rather "stupid" mail server in the sense that your mail client needs to have most of the intelligence needed for managing mail. It's a simple protocol and is offered by most mail clients.

POP3 is somewhat insecure in that your mail client needs to send your account name and password every time it calls. The more you do this, the greater the chance that someone with a network snooper might get both. (We're not trying to scare you, but it's possible.) An extension known as APOP uses a secure algorithm known as MD5 to encrypt your password for each session.

Finally, note that standard POP3 has no way to send mail back to the mail server. There is an optional extension to POP3 known as XTND XMIT that allows this, but both the client and the server have to support it. Generally, a mail client uses SMTP to send messages and POP3 to retrieve them.

Mailing Lists

With email, you can carry on a conversation with another person. But why not with three others? Easy enough—just use the Cc header or specify multiple recipients on the To header. What about hundreds? Well, that might be tough. But what if there were enough interest in something (such as the band REM) that someone agreed to serve as a central dispatch point? All mail to that account would be sent to all other people in the discussion. This is known as a mailing list, and they are quite popular. The REM list mentioned has more than 800 subscribers.

The first thing you have to realize is that when you join (subscribe to) a mailing list, all of a sudden you're going to have a lot of messages in your mailbox. Can you handle the extra time it's going to take to read these new messages? Are you paying for mail? Many people don't comprehend exactly what they're getting into when they sign up for a mailing list. Remember to save the instructions on how to unsubscribe from the group, so you don't send your unsubscribe request to all the members of the group and feel like a fool.

Finding Lists

First you need to find some lists. Every month several informative postings are made to the Usenet group `news.answers`, describing hundreds of mailing lists and how to subscribe to them. For example, Stephanie da Silva posts "Publicly Accessible Mailing Lists." If you have Usenet access, `news.answers` is your best bet. Perhaps some of the people you correspond with know of some lists.

If neither approach works, you can use the `uga.cc.uga.edu` mail server described in the following paragraph.

LISTSERVers are nifty automatic programs that handle much of the drudgery involved in maintaining a mailing list. There are several such LISTSERVs, but you need only one to get started. We suggest you use `listserv@uga.cc.uga.edu`. Others include `listserv@mizzou1.missouri.edu`, `listserv@jhuvm.bitnet`, `listserv@vm1.nodak.edu`, `listserv@ucsd.edu`, `listserv@unl.edu`, `LISTSERV@PSUVM.PSU.EDU`, and `LISTSERV@SJSUVM1.SJSU.EDU`.

Commands to these sites are simple. You can give a new instruction on each line of the body if you want, although generally most of your requests consist of a single line.

To start with, try sending mail to `listserv@uga.cc.uga.edu` with only the text `help` in the body of the message (the subject doesn't matter). You should get back a list of valid commands. Probably the most interesting for you will be `listserv refcard`, which returns a reference card, and `lists global`, which returns a big list of all known mailing lists on many LISTSERVers—it's more than 300,000 bytes. You're in mailing list heaven! If that's too big, try just `lists`.

Joining and Dropping

If your mailing list is managed by a LISTSERVer, joining a list is easy. Send mail to `listserv@domain`, with the following message line:

`SUB LISTNAME Firstname Lastname`

`LISTNAME` is the name of the list, such as HUMOR. `Firstname` and `Lastname` are your first and last names.

To sign off the list, use this:

`SIGNOFF ` *`LISTNAME`*

Do not send your unsubscribe request to the mailing list itself. You'll just irritate people, and they'll laugh at you.

If you would rather get one mailing a day—consisting of all the posts to the mailing list in one big chunk—rather than receiving dozens of little messages during the day, use this:

`SET ` *`LISTNAME`*` DIGEST`

To get each piece as it is sent, use this:

`SET ` *`LISTNAME`*` MAIL`

There are other commands—the `help` command should get them for you.

If the mailing list isn't being handled by a LISTSERVer, you're at the mercy of the mailing list maintainer as to how subscriptions are handled.

Generally, the address to send messages to for a mailing list is this:

`listname@domain`

The address to send messages to for subscribing and unsubscribing is this:

`listname-request@domain`

However, you can't always count on these. In this case, you have to rely on the instructions for the specific list, which you need to get from the maintainer or a friend.

Automatic Mail Sorting

We're not going to go into too much detail about mail sorting because it's a rather complex subject, but sometimes you get to the point where you can't treat your incoming mail file as a single entity.

We get literally hundreds of messages a day, and we would go insane if we didn't use a program known as a mail filter. These look at your incoming mail, and based on criteria you set regarding the contents of header items or message text, they sort the mail into several mailboxes before you even see them.

For instance, Ron subscribes to several mailing lists. He routes messages from each of these into a separate mailbox for reading at his leisure. He has Usenet voting ballots arriving all the time—these go into a special voting file for processing by the voting software. Everything that's left goes into a general mailbox for normal reading.

Actually, mail filters can often do more than this. You can use them to selectively forward mail to other users, or to send automatic responses to certain messages. You can even have them send only a single informational message to anyone who mails you while you're on vacation, no matter how many messages they send you during that time.

The drawback to a filter program is that it can be tough to set up, unless you're using a mail client with the capability built in (for example, Eudora). Carefully check your configuration files to make sure that you aren't accidentally dropping messages on the floor!

procmail

procmail is probably the most popular of the mail filters. You have quite a bit of control over your messages and can even pass them through other programs, such as a formatter, before they are saved. It can execute other programs on demand and can be used to run simple mailing lists or mail servers. It's been extensively tested, it is stable, and it is fast. Be careful, though, that you don't accidentally tell it to send some of your mail into a black hole.

You can get the latest version by anonymous ftp to `ftp://ftp.informatik.` `rwth-aachen.de` as `/pub/packages/procmail`.

deliver

Although procmail is the king of the hill for mail filter programs, we personally like deliver. You write shell scripts to handle all incoming messages. This requires more work on your part, usually, than would procmail, but it's very clean, almost infinitely flexible, and limits what you can do with your email only to how well you can program scripts. The speed shouldn't be too much of a concern on that fast machine of yours.

We found deliver by anonymous ftp at `sunsite.unc.edu` as `ftp://sunsite.unc.edu/pub/Linux/distributions/slackware/contrib/deliver.tgz`.

mailagent

mailagent is another well-known email filter. This one is written in the Perl language, which again means that you can do anything with your email by extending mailagent yourself (if you know Perl). It comes with quite a few built-in features. We suggest this if you know Perl. Anonymous ftp to `ftp://ftp.foretune.co.jp` and get `/pub/` `network/mail/mailagent`.

elm

elm comes with a support program named filter, which does mail filtering.

Usenet

As described in the introduction, Usenet is the world's largest electronic discussion forum. One of the most popular features of the Internet, Usenet allows people all over the world to discuss topics and exchange ideas on a wide variety of subjects.

One way to describe Usenet is in terms of email. Think of your mailbox, with all its new and old messages. Imagine what it might be like if everyone on the Internet could read that mailbox, enter new messages, and leave replies. Now imagine having 20,000 mailboxes. This is analogous to how Usenet works.

Usenet is a huge public messaging system. It is divided into thousands of discussions of different subjects—each separate piece is known as a newsgroup, or group. When someone enters a message while "in" a group, that message goes to all other Usenet sites in the world, and people reading that same group can read the message and reply to it if they want. Generally, dozens of different conversations (also known as *threads*) are going on in any particular group—each is distinguished by a subject name, much like the Subject in a mail message. Thousands of new messages are posted each day.

Usenet is commonly thought of as being the same thing as the Internet, but they're not the same thing. The Internet is an international network of computers tied together via dedicated lines. Usenet is just one service that uses the Internet. If you're familiar with bulletin board systems (BBSes), you might think of the Internet as the BBS hardware, and Usenet as the message bases.

Not all computers on the Internet have Usenet (it can take a lot of space!). Not all computers carrying Usenet groups are on the Internet—like email, some systems call Internet systems to exchange Usenet messages.

USENET Is Usenet Is NetNews

Frankly, capitalization standards on Internet are quite relaxed. You can call it USENET, you can call it Usenet, you can call it UseNet. People will know what you mean. If you call it UsEnEt, people will start edging nervously for the exits. You can even refer to it by the ancient moniker Netnews (or NetNews). People will understand what you mean.

Usenet Messages

Usenet messages are much like the Internet mail messages described earlier in this chapter. They consist of a header, which has information about the message, and the body, which has the actual message. They even use the same format as mail messages, and most of the same headers are valid. There are a few new ones, which are covered in the following sections.

The Usenet Distribution Model

Every computer that gets Usenet keeps a database of Usenet messages. When a new message is entered, it is sent to neighboring Usenet sites using NNTP (Network News Transfer Protocol). These distribute the post to other sites, until it is on every machine on Usenet. Various mechanisms prevent a message from showing up on the same machine more than once, which we don't need to get into here. Only occasionally does a broken machine (usually a FidoNet gateway) regurgitate old articles back onto the Net.

We said that all machines get all posts. Well, sort of—because Usenet is so huge, many sites only carry a subset of all the available groups. A site won't get posts for groups it doesn't care about, or if it does, it won't keep them. In addition, there's something called a Distribution header that you can put in your message to try to restrict its distribution to a geographical area, such as San Diego. This is useful for messages that affect only San Diego.

Newsgroup Names

Newsgroups are named like this:

```
comp.sys.ibm.pc.games.action
```

This is a hierarchy reading down from left to right. Reading the group name, you have a computer group for computer systems from IBM, the PCs to be exact. You're talking about games for those systems, more specifically action games.

Here's another one:

```
talk.politics.guns
```

You have a group for talk about politics, more specifically gun control. We'll talk more about these hierarchies later.

The newsgroup with which your post is associated is given in the header of the message, in the Newsgroups item. It looks like this:

```
Newsgroups: news.announce.newgroups
```

Unlike traditional bulletin board systems, each post can go in multiple groups. If we do this:

```
Newsgroups: alt.usenet.future,news.groups
```

my post appears in both groups. This is known as *crossposting*. Although you should know it is possible, you shouldn't actually do this until you've looked around a while, because frivolous crossposting is frowned on.

In fact, another header can be used to send any replies back to a specific group. For instance, you might make a wide informational post to several groups but specify that the discussion (if any) should be only in a single group. This is the `Followup-To` header. Together, the headers look like this:

```
Newsgroups: rec.arts.comics.misc,rec.arts.comics.strips,
rec.arts.comics.animation
Followup-To: rec.arts.comics.animation
```

Remember from the email header discussion that one header can spread over several lines, as long as succeeding lines are indented. That's what you did to split `Newsgroups` over two lines. All replies to the post go to `rec.arts.comics.animation`, unless the person replying overrides that.

Crossposting can be abused, but more on that later.

Threads

An original post and all the replies to it are considered to be a single "thread" of conversation. This can actually look more like a Christmas tree than a straight line, as there are replies to replies, and replies to those replies, which branch off until each sub-branch dies of finality or boredom.

Each Usenet message has a Subject associated with it that is supposed to summarize the contents of the message (although this is often not the case). One way to track a thread is to note the message subjects, which those who reply to the post are supposed to preserve until the discussion wanders too far from the original subject. The only way to fully keep track of threads is to use a threaded newsreader, which is discussed in the next section.

Newsreaders

The first item of business is which program you will use to read Usenet. Your choice of these programs (known as newsreaders) can hugely impact how you read the Net, how much information you get out of it, and how much garbage you have to sludge through.

rn (readnews)

rn is free, so there's a good chance the system you use to read mail has it, and a good chance that it will be offered to you as your default newsreader. Avoid using it if you can.

Back when rn was first written, one person could read every single message posted to Usenet and still have time for a life. It reflects those simpler times—its default is to dive in and show you all the messages in the group, one at a time.

This sounds reasonable, but it's a fact that the majority of the posts on most newsgroups you read are of no interest to you. There will come a time when you no longer want to slog through every post on the group and become choosy about which posts you read. rn does not let you do this easily. Because popular groups can get more than 100 messages a day, rn's preference for showing you every single message really wastes your time.

Message Overview and Threading

Just how much of your time rn wastes is evident the first time you run another news program that first gives you an overview of the group. It provides you with a summary line for each post, just as a mail program does—it gives you the poster's name, the subject, and possibly the message size. Scroll through the pages of summaries and choose which posts look interesting. When you're done choosing, read the posts you've selected.

Now we'll add another concept to that—the newsreader should keep track of which posts are related to each other and group them, so that you can select or ignore whole groups of posts at once. It can do this by noticing the threads and subject names mentioned before.

These two changes account for an almost unbelievable difference in speed between a good threaded newsreader and something like rn. When you've gotten good at determining which threads look promising and which don't, you can read Usenet literally 100 times faster than you could before. We'll recommend some right after this....

Kill Files

In a group where more than half the discussion is about something you don't care about (for instance, a particular author on a fantasy group), having the newsreader kill all articles relating to that author can save you time and make you less likely to lose valuable articles in the crush.

There's also the opposite of a kill file. If you know you want to read every posting on a particular subject or from a particular person, a selection file lets you have the newsreader automatically mark them for reading. This isn't quite as common as the kill file.

NN (No News)

NN is fast, flexible, and configurable; has nice kill and selection options; sorts messages in several ways, and offers several ways to manage the old messages. It even has its own group, news.software.nn. This is definitely worth a look.

Other UNIX Readers

Other UNIX readers that are worth looking at (if your site offers them) are TRN, STRN, and TIN. TIN happens to have the largest number of UNIX readers at this time. They meet or exceed the criteria given. You can also read the Usenet group `news.software.readers` for the latest information.

Netscape

The Netscape Web browser provides facilities for tracking, replying to, and initiating user group postings. To access a particular newsgroup, invoke the File and Open Location menu items, and enter the URL for the newsgroup. The URL for a newsgroup consists of the word news, followed by a colon (`:`) and the name of the group. For example, to access the Oracle database newsgroup, enter `news;comp.databases.oracle`. You can even use an asterisk (`*`) to display all items at a particular level in the hierarchy. For example, the URL `news;comp.databases.*` would list all database discussion groups.

When you have opened a particular group, a set of command buttons that perform some common Usenet functions appears. For example, buttons are available to subscribe/unsubscribe to groups, as well as initiate and receive postings.

When you subscribe to a newsgroup, the entry is maintained for future use by the Netscape software. The list of all your newsgroups can be accessed by selecting the Directory and Go To Newsgroups menu options.

Other Readers

For other systems, you should be reading the Usenet groups `comp.os.msdos.mail-news` and `news.software.readers`. There are, most likely, programs out there for your system. For instance, there's Trumpet for DOS and WinTrumpet for Windows. If you have a complete TCP/IP package, you might want to see whether it includes a mail reader (other than `rn`).

Offline Readers

Just as you can use a mail client to do your mail processing offline, you can use an offline reader to do your Usenet processing offline. This is useful if you're paying by the minute for your connect time. See the group `alt.usenet.offline-reader` for help with these.

Finding Your Groups

You can participate in literally thousands of newsgroups. This section helps you find the groups in which you are interested.

The Hierarchies

As mentioned earlier, group names are arranged in hierarchies from left to right. The left item is known as the top-level of the hierarchy. In the case of a group such as this:

`alt.tv.animaniacs`

it is said that the group is "in the `alt` hierarchy" (or "`alt.` hierarchy"). The Net is organized into eight major hierarchies, one anarchic hierarchy, and a bunch of smaller, less important hierarchies.

The Big Eight Hierarchies

The big eight hierarchies are the following:

`comp.`	Computer topics—This ranges from programming to hardware to peripherals to folklore. Most popular computer systems and operating systems have their own set of groups here.
`misc.`	Miscellaneous—When nobody can figure out where to put a new group, it often ends up under `misc.`. For example, the `misc.jobs` groups don't clearly belong in any of the other six hierarchies, so they go under `misc.`.
`news.`	The business of USENET—This is where people talk about Usenet administration, propose new groups, and argue about when Usenet is going to die of its own excesses.
`rec.`	Recreational topics—This is where most of the hobbyist stuff, such as `rec.crafts.jewelry`, goes. It also contains artistic and music discussions, crafts, and more in that vein.
`sci.`	Science—This is where the math and physics types hang out. Medical, too, such as `sci.med.radiology`.
`soc.`	Social topics—This is a grab bag of many cultural groups for different regions, such as `soc.culture.chile`, social research groups, religious discussion groups, and alternative lifestyle groups. It's something of a milder version of the talk hierarchy.
`talk.`	Heated debate—Incredibly vicious personal attacks by people (most of whom seemingly haven't even heard of the concept of "critical thinking") that go on interminably about all the things you would expect—politics and religion. See `talk.politics.mideast`, for example. No debate here is ever really ended.

| `humanities.` | Literature and fine arts—This hierarchy contains a wealth of discussion regarding music, philosophy, and fine art. For example, see `humanities.lit.author.shakespeare`. |

These hierarchies are sometimes known as Usenet proper and are considered by many news administrators to be the only "real" hierarchies. For a new group to be created in any of these eight hierarchies, it has to go through a group interest polling procedure that discourages overly frivolous group creation. More on this later.

Where Do I Go?

Back to your original question—how do you know where to go for a particular subject? There are several ways.

First, your newsreader might be smart enough to find part of a group name. If I tell NN to go to group `beer`, for instance, it asks me whether I mean `alt.beer` or `rec.food.drink.beer`. In this way, I just found two groups, and if I look for brewing, I'll find more.

Dave Lawrence posts "List of Active Newsgroups" and "Alternative Newsgroup Hierarchies" to `news.groups` and `news.answers`. This is the mother lode—all "official" groups (although with `alt.` "official" doesn't mean much), each with a short description. Get it if you can.

Your newsreader probably has a way to show you a list of all groups. This might take some digging to find. (It's `:show groups all` in NN.)

Next, you can look through a file your newsreader leaves in your home directory, named `.newsrc` or something similar. This is just a list of group names, but they might give you some hints.

You can always ask for help on the group `news.groups.questions`, which is just for this sort of question.

Signature Files

Most newsreaders enable you to attach a signature to every post you make. It takes the contents of the file `.signature` in your home directory and attaches it to the end of the post. This is intended to be used for identification purposes—perhaps your name and place of work if it's not obvious from the header. Or sometimes it's used for disclaimers.

By far, the most common use is as a small personality statement—this usually involves your name, Internet address, a favorite quote, and maybe a small picture drawn with text characters.

Read the FAQ!

One day, the people of Usenet noted that new users all tended to ask the same few questions. They decided to create a Frequently Asked Questions List (FAQ—the L just didn't sound good), which would present the answers to these questions and prevent them from being asked over and over.

That worked pretty well, and now many groups have FAQs. This means that if you pop up on a group and ask a question that is in the FAQ, you're going to get some negative responses ("Read the FAQing FAQ!") If you enter a new group for the purpose of asking a question, make sure that you look for a post with "FAQ" in the title. If you find any, read them first. Your answers (and answers to questions you hadn't even thought of yet) may be in there.

If you're looking for information in general, most FAQs are posted to `news.answers`. You can go there and browse all the beautiful FAQs.

Talk

Talk is a program that allows two users to communicate in real-time using a split screen interface. A user "talks" to another user by typing text in one area of the split screen and "listens" as the other user's text appears in another area of the screen. It can be used for users on the same system, or over a TCP/IP network.

Before initiating a talk session, you need the other person's address. If the user is connected to the same local machine as you, the login name will suffice.

Next, you need to make sure that the other user is logged in. You can find out with the `finger` command. For example:

```
$ finger userid
leibniz 24: finger trimblef
Login name: trimblef                    In real life: Frederick Trimble
Directory: /users/leibniz/INFO780-543/trimblef  Shell: /bin/csh
On since Apr 28 00:21:37 on pty/ttys0 from ts2.noc.drexel.e

No Plan.
$
```

In the preceding example, the `finger` command indicates that user `trimblef` is logged on to the system on pseudo-terminal `pty/ttys0`. The `finger` command can also determine whether a remote user is logged in by specifying a remote address. For example:

```
finger userid@domain
```

After you verify that the user with whom you want to speak is logged on, he must agree to talk with you. To initiate a talk session, first issue the `talk` command:

```
talk userid@domain
```

The talk initiator's screen clears, and the talk header appears at the top of the screen:

```
[Waiting for connection...]
```

On the other screen, the following text appears:

```
talk: connection requested by username@host
talk: respond with: ntalk username@host
```

After the user responds with the appropriate message, the connection is established. Everything typed at this point appears on the other terminal, until the connection is terminated. The talk session is terminated when one of the users presses Control+C.

In certain situations, receiving a talk connect request can be disrupting. You can use the following command to disable any such request from a remote user:

```
mesg n
```

To enable such requests, use the `mesg` command with the `y` option:

```
mesg y
```

To see the current status of your talk request mode, use the `mesg` command with no options.

The `talk` command is based on a set of protocols that allow communication to take place. There are two protocols for the `talk` command: One is based on version 4.2 BSD UNIX, and the other on version 4.3 BSD UNIX. Unfortunately, these versions are not compatible. Therefore, you cannot establish a talk session between UNIX systems whose `talk` command is based on different versions of the protocol.

Another variation of the `talk` command is the `ytalk` command. The most interesting feature of `ytalk` is that it allows more than two users to partake in a conversation. In addition, it supports both versions of talk protocols. Therefore, the `ytalk` command can establish a connection with either version of the `talk` command.

To establish a `ytalk` session with multiple users, type the address of each user on the command line. For example:

```
ytalk mary@gwyned.edu fred@drexel.edu katherine@nova.edu
```

The `ytalk` command then splits the screen into several panes. Each screen is labeled with the corresponding user, so you always know who is typing.

If you need assistance with any `ytalk` options, simply press the ESC key. A small menu of `ytalk` commands appears as follows:

```
################################################
# a) add a new user to session                #
# b) delete a user from session               #
# c) output a user to a file                  #
# Your choice:                                 #
################################################
```

Internet Relay Chat (IRC)

Each day, thousands of people worldwide hold "keyboard conversations" using Internet Relay Chat (IRC). Like the `ytalk` facility, IRC allows multiple people to converse at the same time. When it is your turn to type, the characters appear on all other workstations that are logged in to the same channel.

> **TIP**
>
> Because typing is slow compared to real conversation, it can be annoying watching the other party backspacing over misspelled words. If you feel the other party should be able to figure out the intention of the misspelled word, it is considered acceptable to continue typing after a spelling mistake.
>
> Also, it is not uncommon for more experienced users to abbreviate commonly used phrases. Here is a list of abbreviations that you may encounter:
>
> | | |
> |------|-------------------------|
> | BCNU | Be seeing you |
> | BRB | Be right back |
> | BTW | By the way |
> | BYE | Good-bye |
> | CU | See you |
> | CUL | See you later |
> | FYI | for your information |
> | FWIW | For what it's worth |
> | GA | Go ahead and type |
> | IMHO | In my humble opinion |
> | IMO | In my opinion |
> | JAM | Just a minute |
> | O | Over |

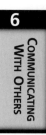

OO	Over & out
OBTW	Oh, by the way
ROTFL	Rolling on the floor laughing
R U THERE	Are you there
SEC...	Wait a second
WRT	With respect to

Basic IRC Structure

IRC uses a client-server model. The IRC "universe" consists of hundreds of channels with names such as #initgame. Users join (using their client software) in a channel that interests them and are then in conversation with everyone else who is on that same channel. You can talk with everyone or direct your comments to certain individuals. This is a flexible format that allows something as free-form as a general babble to many pairs of private conversations to a game of IRC Jeopardy, which plays much like the TV show. Some channels are private.

> **NOTE**
>
> During the attempted Communist coup in Russia in 1993, an IRC channel was set up to relay eyewitness accounts of the event. IRC channels have also been set up during other natural disasters, such as earthquakes and hurricanes.

In addition, IRC users have their own nicknames and become quite attached to them (because your reputation goes with your nickname, this is understandable).

Getting IRC Clients

Before you can do anything, you need an IRC client. You need to grab the source code appropriate for your machine and compile it.

You can get the UNIX IRC client by pointing your Web browser to ftp://cs-ftp.bu.edu. The software is located in the irc/clients directory. Look to see which file the symbolic link CURRENT points to—it will be linked to the latest UNIX source code for ircII.

A PC client running under MS-DOS, OS/2, or Windows can anonymous ftp to ftp://cs-ftp.bu.edu and look under /irc/clients/pc. You have your choice of several for each operating system. MIRC is now the most popular client for the Windows environment.

A Mac client can also anonymous `ftp` to `ftp://cs-ftp.bu.edu` and look under `/irc/clients/macintosh`. Grab the latest version of `Homer` you find there.

Connecting to a Server

After you have your client, you need to figure out which IRC server you will be talking to. Anonymous `ftp` to `cs.bu.edu` and look under `/irc/support`. There should be a file named `servers.950301` (the last number is the date, so that part will change). Grab this and look for a server that's close to you.

Then tell your client to connect to this server. With luck, it'll talk back to you, and you'll be in the world of IRC.

Choosing Channels

After you get on an IRC server, all commands start with a `/`.

`/help` gives you a list of commands. To get the new user help, do `/help intro` and then `/help newuser`.

`/list` shows all the current IRC channels. It looks something like this, except that there will be many more channels:

```
*** Channel    Users  Topic
*** #wubba     3      Wherefore the wubba?
*** #hoffa     5      i know where the body is
*** #litldog   2      where oh where has he gone
```

`/names` might be more interesting. It shows who's logged on each channel and whether it's a private or public channel:

```
Pub: #wubba      @wubba jblow jdoe
Prv: *     marla donald ivana bill hillary
Pub: #litldog    @yakko dot
```

Then use `/join channel` to participate on *channel*. Here you might do a `/join #wubba`.

`/nick nickname` enables you to change to a new nickname in case your old one is too stodgy.

`/msg nickname message` enables you to send a private *message* to *nickname*. Use the `/query nickname` to enter a private conversation with *nickname*. Use `/query` to exit it.

If you get ambitious and create a channel (using `/join` on a nonexistent channel creates it), be sure to look at the `/mode` command, which lets you determine the behavior of the channel.

Need Help?

`/join #Twilight_zone` is where IRC operators often hang out, and some are willing to help. Just ask your question—don't announce that you need to ask a question first.

Bad Moves

Don't use someone else's nickname if you can help it—people are very protective about them.

Never type anything that someone asks you to type if you aren't sure what it does. You might find that you've just given someone else control of your client!

Don't abuse the `telnet` server. If you're going to IRC a lot, get your own client.

Further Info

More information on IRC can be found via anonymous `ftp` on `ftp://cs-ftp.bu.edu` in the `/irc/support` directory. IRC also has several `alt.` groups dedicated to it: `alt.irc.corruption`, `alt.irc.ircii`, `alt.irc.lamers`, `alt.irc.opers`, `alt.irc.questions`, `alt.irc.recovery`, and `alt.irc.undernet`.

Multimedia

Multimedia is defined as the presentation of information in which more than one medium is used at a time. Using animation and sound in addition to ordinary text is such an example. By using more than one medium, multimedia enhances our ability to communicate and understand one another. The advent of powerful desktop computers equipped with high-resolution color monitors and stereo sound has increased the demand.

Internet Infrastructure

Delivering multimedia to the desktop over the Internet presents several obstacles. First, the Internet and its supporting protocols were designed to transmit 7-bit ASCII text to support email and file transfer. Second, the original NSFNET was made up of 56KB data communication lines. (The Internet backbone has been upgraded in recent years with higher network speeds.) Although this was sufficient for its original purpose of supporting email and file transfer, it is not adequate for supporting the growing demand for multimedia.

Files containing multimedia data require large amounts of disk space. When such files are transferred across a network, they require large amounts of network bandwidth. When a router handles a packet of data, it has no knowledge of data flow. It only sees individual packets and handles them separately. When transferred across a network using a connectionless oriented protocol like IP, individual packets of data may arrive out of order. The TCP protocol is responsible for reassembling the packets before they are made available to an application. There is also no priority information specified in the IP packet, so that real-time data could take precedence over other types of data with a lower priority. This type of protocol was fine for supporting applications such as email and text-based chat sessions. It is not acceptable, however, for packets of data that are sensitive to time delay, such as real-time audio and video. Thus, to support large-scale multimedia, fundamental changes in the Internet infrastructure are necessary, including the data communication lines, routers, and protocols.

Delivering Multimedia Over the Internet

As mentioned previously, the current Internet infrastructure is not adequate for supporting multimedia. This section examines two attempts at updating the infrastructure to deliver large-scale multimedia.

RTP/RSVP

The connectionless nature of the IP protocol does not lend itself to the time-sensitive nature of data packets carrying real-time audio and video. The Real-Time Transport Protocol (RTP) and the ReSerVation Setup Protocol (RSVP) protocols are currently being developed by the IETF (Internet Engineering Task Force) to make such multimedia support a reality. One of the major challenges of this effort is to minimize the amount of change in the existing Internet infrastructure to support them.

The initial specification of RSVP defines four levels of Quality of Service (QoS) without requiring wholesale changes to the Internet:

- Guaranteed delay
- Controlled delay
- Predictive service
- Controlled load

Although these QoS specifications vary in the priority in which they are handled, each adds a higher degree of determinism to the time in which packets are routed. RSVP/RTP advocates claim that this is sufficient for meeting the needs of multimedia applications.

The fundamental idea behind RSVP is to create a reservation with each router through which the data packets pass. This reservation consists of a flow identifier, to identify the data stream, and a flow specification, which identifies the QoS that must be provided to the data flow. In essence, the reservation defines a contract for service between the network and the requesting application.

Multimedia applications access these protocols by using a WINSOCK version 2 compliant application programming interface (API). The interface calls even allow specification of the QoS. Changing the API to support new features, while minimizing the amount of changes that need to be made to existing software will not be easy.

Another issue that must be resolved is payment for additional services. How will users be billed for specifying a higher level of service?

Multicast Backbone

As previously mentioned, the backbone of the Internet consists of high-speed data communication lines. Many experiments are being conducted to find ways of upgrading the physical hardware to support the transmission of real-time audio and video. One such experiment is known as the Multicast Backbone (MBONE). MBONE is not separate from the Internet. Rather, it is a set of Internet sites with powerful hosts and high-speed connections between them.

Unfortunately, MBONE can handle the display of only three to five frames per second. Full-motion video, on the other hand, requires the display of 30 frames per second. Although its potential does not approach broadcast quality, it is sufficient for a number of useful applications, such as teleconferencing. For more information, you can visit the `http://www.mbone.com` website.

Audio Over the Internet

At this time, there are two methods for handling audio data over the Internet. The first technique requires that an audio data file be transferred to a workstation, which is then handled by the appropriate audio player. The second technique does not require the complete file to be transferred before the file can begin to be played.

> **NOTE**
>
> On July 20th, 1996, the National Science Foundation and NASA sponsored a live broadcast over the MBONE. The presentation, given to commemorate the 20th anniversary of the Mars Viking Landings, discussed the Mars Pathfinder and Mars Global Surveyor missions.

Audio File Transfer

Many sound files are on the Internet in a variety of formats. Each format has a unique file extension associated with it, such as .wav or .au. The following list shows file extensions that you are likely to see, along with their associated platform:

File Extension	Platform
AU	UNIX
SND	Macintosh
WAV	PC
AIF, AIFF	Macintosh
RA (RealAudio)	Macintosh, PC, UNIX

Each file type requires a special "player" utility. In most cases, these utilities can be configured to work with your favorite Web browser, so that they can be played automatically when referenced within the browser. These are known as "helper" applications in Web terminology.

The major disadvantage of this technique, however, is the amount of time it takes to transfer the files. Even though the files are usually compressed, they are still large.

Streaming Audio

A technique known as *streaming audio* was developed to improve the performance of the plain file transfer method. This method allows the file to be played at the same time that the file is being transferred. To utilize this technique, you must use audio files and a player application capable of supporting streaming audio. The most popular audio streaming technology today is RealAudio.

While the audio file is being played, the audio server and audio player exchange information about the connection. If it is a low-speed connection, a smaller version of the file is sent. If it is a high-speed connection, a larger, higher quality version of the file is used.

To reduce the amount of time necessary to transfer the data over the Internet, the file is compressed. The User Datagram Protocol (UDP) is used in conjunction with the IP protocol to transfer the data packets. Unlike TCP, UDP does not resend packets if problems in the transmission occur. If this were the case, the sound player would not be able to play the file due to frequent interruptions.

Phone Calls Over the Internet

Another form of audio over the Internet is making phone calls. Technically speaking, you can call anyone who has an email address. All that is needed are a speaker and microphone for your desktop computer, along with software to interpret the digitized packets of data. A number of competing companies make phone products for the Internet, including WebTalk by Quarterdeck, NetPhoneby Electric Magic, and Internet Phonefrom VocalTec.

The main benefit of making phone calls over the Internet is the price. The only charge incurred is the cost of an Internet connection. The main disadvantages are voice quality and compatibility between Internet phone products. Other users must have the same exact software as you to have a phone conversation.

Video Over the Internet

Just like audio, there are two primary methods for handling video data over the Internet. The first technique requires that a video data file be transferred to a workstation, which is then handled by the appropriate video player. The second technique does not require the complete file to be transferred before the file is processed.

Video File Transfer

Many video files are on the Internet in a variety of formats. Each format has a unique file extension associated with it. The following list shows file extensions for video files that you are likely to see, along with their associated platform:

File Extension	Platform
QT (QuickTime)	Macintosh, PC
AVI	PC
MPG, MPEG	Macintosh, PC, UNIX
MOV	Macintosh, PC

Just like audio files, there are corresponding "player" applications for each file type. Even when compressed, they suffer from the same problem as audio files: They are simply too large.

Streaming Video

Conceptually, streaming video works in the same way as streaming audio. That is, compressed files are transferred over the Internet using the UDP/IP protocol. The user actually sees the file being played before the file transfer is complete. This can deliver reasonable performance when sent over a high-speed network, such as the MBONE.

The first attempt at implementing streaming video over the Internet is a product called VDOLive. Just like RealAudio, it tries to adjust the quality of the video based on speed of the connection. VDOLive can deliver 10 to 15 frames per second on a two-inch section of the screen over a 28.8 Kbps line. Over an ISDN line, 30 frames per second are possible. Before video data is transmitted, it must be compressed. Therefore, it does not lend itself to live broadcasts. Despite these limitations, VDOLive has a lot of potential.

Two newer products are RealPlayer and Streamworks. They combine both audio and video.

Videoconferencing

An application that uses both audio and video over the Internet is videoconferencing. In addition to a specially equipped workstation, including a microphone and a video camera, special software is needed.

The most popular videoconferencing software in use to date is a product called CU-SeeMe. This technology works much like streaming audio and video. When someone wants to participate in a videoconference, he first must log in to a special system on the Internet known as a *reflector*. A reflector hosts many videoconferences that you can join. After you log in, voice and video data are digitized and compressed before transport over the Internet. For efficiency reasons, the UDP protocol is used rather than TCP. Any missing packets are ignored by the application.

CU-SeeMe also tries to reduce the amount of network bandwidth needed by only sending relevant portions of the images. For example, if someone is speaking, but rarely makes any motion in the field of the camera, only the changes from previous video frames need to be sent.

It is also possible to have a videoconference without a reflector site. If you know the other person's IP address, you can contact them directly and have a two-way conference.

> **NOTE**
>
> NASA has quite a few reflector sites from which live videos can be seen using CU-SeeMe. They also have an excellent collection of audio and video clips that are available for downloading. See `http://www.nasa.gov` for details.

Summary

The Internet, also known as the Information Superhighway, is still evolving. It was built to support applications such as email and file transfer. For it to support multimedia, such as audio and video, the infrastructure needs to be upgraded. Researchers are busy at work trying to figure out how to upgrade the infrastructure without requiring a major overhaul. Efforts such as RSVP/RTP are promising but are still on the horizon.

A more compelling problem is the data communications structure in place that connects to our homes and schools. To support multimedia, more bandwidth is needed at this juncture. This is known as the "last mile" problem.

It spite of these physical limitations, technology is still growing by leaps and bounds. When these bottlenecks are removed, a whole new world of possibilities for communicating with others will be at our fingertips.

Text Editing with vi and Emacs

by David B. Horvath, CCP, and Jeffrey A. Simon

A text editor is one of the most common and useful tools found in any computer system. It is a program used to create and modify text or other data-type objects, usually interactively by the user at a terminal. It is distinguished from a word processor or desktop publishing program in that a text editor is generally expected to produce plain ASCII text files that do not have embedded formatting information. Those other programs are intended to produce more complex documents that contain much more formatting information. For example, a typical word processor has a graphical user interface and is capable of producing "what-you-see-is-what-you-get" (abbreviated as WYSIWYG) printed output.

Common uses of a text editor are to produce simple ASCII text files, program source code, email, and so on. Therefore, text editors are often extended to provide features that assist with specific aspects of such tasks, such as the formatting of a specific programming language. For example, such extended modes exist for C++, Lisp, and HTML, to name only a few. Detailed examples of some of these features are described later in this chapter.

This chapter examines two of the most popular and widely used editors in the UNIX world, vi and Emacs. In addition to being useful tools, each of these editors has its own group of devoted users, ready to "sing praises" to the virtues of using their favorites. In any case, you can get a lot of work done with either of these tools.

Full-Screen Editors Versus Line Editors

A full-screen editor displays on the user's terminal a view of all or a portion of the document he or she is working on. For example, on a 25-line display, the user sees a 24-line section of the document. When using an editor, you are not actually making edits to the file that is stored on the hard disk. When the editor is commanded to begin working with a particular file, a working copy of that file is made. This working copy is often called the *buffer*. Adding, changing, and deleting of text ("editing") is done only within the buffer until the file is saved. You often hear the advice to "save your work." This advice is applicable to using a full-screen editor as well as any other computer work that uses a buffer in the same way.

You can think of the screen as a movable viewport into the buffer. This viewport is also often called a *window*. Editing actions take place at or relative to a specific point on the screen referred to as the *cursor*. The cursor is usually indicated on the screen by some sort of highlighting, such as a underscore or a solid block, which may or may not be blinking. Edits to the buffer are shown on the screen as soon as they are entered. This type of user-interface makes simple editing functions convenient for the user.

In contrast, a line editor does not attempt to show the appearance of a continuous section of the document being edited. It concentrates on editing one line at a time. Thus, its user interface is more primitive. The type of editing that you would naturally do in a full-screen editor becomes more cumbersome under such an arrangement.

However, do not be misled into thinking that the primitive user interface of the line editor means that a line editor lacks power or that all line editors are obsolete. (A great many line editors are obsolete; the trick is recognizing those that are not!)

Certain powerful editing functions are most easily executed by using a line editor. For example, if you had to reverse the order of the lines in a file, you could do that with eight keystrokes in vi! So it might be a good thing if there was an editor that could take advantage of the power of both the full-screen and line-oriented modes.

What Is vi?

vi (usually pronounced *vee-eye*) is a full-screen text editor that comes with nearly every UNIX system. Many versions of vi or similar programs have been made for other operating systems. Such versions exist for Amiga, Atari, Macintosh, MS-DOS, OS/2, Windows 3.1/95/NT, and probably many other operating systems.

The Relationship of vi and ex

vi is "closely" related to the line editor ex. (In fact, they are one and the same.) vi is the visual (or open) mode of ex. This means that you could start editing a file with the ex editor. At any time, you can invoke the visual mode of ex. Voila`—you are in vi! From vi, you can at any time "drop down into ex" because all ex commands are available from within vi. Thus you can easily go back and forth between the visual and line-oriented modes, executing the particular editing operation you need from the mode in which it is most effectively accomplished. Later in this chapter, you see examples of such operations.

Why Would I Be Interested in Using vi?

Many computer users are familiar with the powerful word processing programs widely available on personal computers. If you are used to such a tool, you might be disappointed to find out that vi is not a WYSIWYG word processor. However, it is rare that such a word processing program is available on the typical UNIX system. vi on the other hand is nearly always available. One of the strongest reasons for knowing at least the rudiments of vi is the fact that it is nearly always available on any UNIX system. It becomes particularly invaluable to those who have to periodically go into a UNIX environment away from their everyday system.

Although the lack of a graphical user interface might be a hindrance to the novice, many "power users" believe that the fastest and most productive interaction with online tools is through command-based interfaces. This is also true of vi. After the keystrokes of the commands become second nature, the productivity of a vi user is not easily surpassed. In fact, the apprehension of the uninitiated toward command-based interfaces is probably due to the following common misconception: People think they have to memorize an obtuse, counter-intuitive set of command keys when, in fact, it is more a matter of finger training than memorization.

For example, suppose that you want to move the cursor (the point where actions on the text take place) down one line. After learning to use vi and becoming comfortable with it, there is no mental process (such as "Move down—let's see that's a "j"). Rather it is a physical motion (such as "Move down—finger motion to press the "j" key). Think of it as like learning to drive a car. After having mastered the process, if you see a ball bouncing into the road ahead, you do not have a mental process (such as "Ball—child—STOP! Let's see, which pedal is it? Where's the instruction manual?!). Rather, your body reacts instantly to press the brake pedal. It is the same way with a command-based interface. After you learn it, your fingers effectively execute the command.

Starting Up and Exiting vi

The first thing to learn with any new program is how to start it and how to get out of it. The simplest way to start vi is to type its name along with the name of the file you want to edit. If no name is specified, vi responds with an empty screen, except for a column of tildes along the left side. Your screen looks similar to the following:

At the bottom of the screen there may be nothing at all (yet another example of the terseness of UNIX!), or "Empty buffer," depending on your version of vi. The tildes (~, which is the name of the "squiggly-line" character) indicate that the line is empty. There are as many tildes as needed to fill your monitor's screen, leaving one line at the bottom that is used to display status information (as shown in the previous example), or to enter commands. In this chapter, the line at the bottom of the screen is referred to as the command line.

~
~
~
~
~
~
~
~
~
~
~
~
~
~
~
~
~
~
~
~
~
~
~
~
~
~
Empty buffer

> **TIP**
>
> If the TERM environment variable has not been set or vi does not recognize the terminal, it starts up in ex mode. You will see a message about not recognizing the terminal and one line from the file. You will also see just a colon (:) as a prompt.
>
> If that happens, exit vi by pressing q and Enter. Then set the environment variable to something that vi understands on the system you are using. Most terminal emulators support vt100 mode (if the number is higher than 100—such as, 220 or 320, don't worry; it is just a super-vt100. At the UNIX prompt, enter:
>
> ```
> export TERM=vt100
> ```
>
> And start vi again.

If you entered a file name, the first lines of that file are displayed until the screen is full. If there are not enough lines to fill the screen, once again, tildes are displayed on the empty lines. In addition, the name of the file and the number of lines are displayed at the bottom of the screen. For example, your screen may look like the following example of a vi screen after loading a text file. (The reader may recognize this text as taken from Sun Tzu, *The Art of War.*)

```
     If wise, a commander is able to recognize changing circumstances and to
act expediently.  If sincere, his men will have no doubt of the certainty of
rewards and punishments.  If humane, he loves mankind, sympathizes with others,
and appreciates their industry and toil.  If courageous, he gains victory by
seizing opportunity without hesitation.  If strict, his troops are disciplined
because they are in awe of him and are afraid of punishment.
     Shen Pao-hsu ... said: 'If a general is not courageous he will be unable
to conquer doubts or to create great plans.'
~
~
~
~
~
~
~
~
~
~
~
~
~
~
~
"art1"  8 lines, 576 characters
```

The second most important thing to know about operating a program is how to get out of it. There are several useful ways to get out of vi, depending on what you want to do with your buffer. All of them must be executed from command mode (described later in this chapter), so to be sure you are in command mode, press the Esc (for Escape) key until you hear a beep before trying the following commands while you are learning.

NOTE

In the preceding paragraph, the Escape key is mentioned. You do not type the letters E-s-c-a-p-e, you look for the key with the word "Escape" or "Esc" on it.

Entering the command ZZ saves your file and exits. The other ways of exiting involve ex mode commands. To enter ex mode, enter the colon character :. The screen display changes so that a colon is displayed on the bottom line of the screen, and the cursor is positioned immediately to the right of this colon, waiting for your command.

The :q key "quits" the file, if no changes have been made since the last save of the file. If a change has been made, you are prevented from exiting, and the following warning is displayed: No write since last change (use ! to override). The command wq can be used to handle this situation, by writing the file before exiting. Or you can go ahead and use the :q! as the message indicates, to go ahead and quit anyway, abandoning all your edits since the last save of the file. (It's good to keep in mind the :q! command for those cases in which you have truly messed up and want to get rid of your mess.)

Table 7.1 summarizes the exiting commands presented so far.

TABLE 7.1. EXITING COMMANDS.

Keystrokes	Result
ZZ	Save file and immediately exit
:wq	Save file and immediately exit (same as ZZ)
:q	Exit; prevented if file not saved
:q!	Exit; forced exit whether saved or not

Getting Started with vi: The Big Picture

Let's look at some pieces of the big picture that give vi its character.

vi Has Modes

vi was created back when the keyboard and screen method of interaction with computers was new. In those primitive days, keyboards did not have all the useful function keys that are now familiar. Therefore, vi was designed to allow you to enter and modify text using only the typewriter keys plus the Escape key. With newer versions, other key sequences are sometimes recognized, such as the cursor control keys.

Although it might seem like a limitation not to take advantage of the many additional keys available on the modern keyboard, the "silver lining" of this limitation is that all functions can be executed without taking your hands away from the touch-typing position. The result makes for efficient and rapid typing.

To enable the many editing functions necessary for interactive, full-screen editing, vi is operated in three modes. The insert mode is used for entering text. While in insert mode, every typewriter key pressed is displayed on the screen and entered into your text. The command mode is used for most editing functions. While in command mode, nearly every typewriter key pressed causes some action other than the direct entry of text, such as moving around to different points in your text, deleting blocks of text, copying blocks of text, and so on. A third mode, called ex mode is used to execute additional functions, such as searching, global replacement, manipulation of multiple files, and many more. The ex mode is based on the underlying ex editor and is described in greater detail later in the section "Using the Power of ex from vi."

TIP

vi has the capability of showing the mode it currently is in. On the screen, you can type the following:

```
:set showmode
```

This enables the display of the insert status for this editing session only. Not all versions of vi support this capability. See the "Changing vi Settings" section of this chapter for more information on the settings and how to save them permanently.

Starting vi

When vi is started up, the default mode is command mode. Test this out: start vi by typing in the program name only:

```
$ vi
```

vi can also be started with the view command, which starts vi in a read-only mode (preventing you from saving any changes). Some versions of UNIX have a vedit command, which is a novice version of vi. One nice feature of vi is that it tracks changes to a file until you save it. If the system goes down or you are disconnected, you can recover your changes using vi -R *yourfilename*.

You see something similar to the following:

```
~
~
~
~
~
~
~
~
~
~
~
~
~
~
~
~
~
~
~
~
~
~
~
Empty buffer
```

> **TIP**
>
> Most UNIX systems send you email reminding you to use vi -R to recover your
> file.

i—Insert

Now press the i key to enter insert mode. The "i" character does not echo (that is, it is
not displayed on your screen). Thereafter, every key you press is displayed as it is
entered into the buffer. Now begin to enter some text. Let's assume that you are entering
some text from *The Art of War* by Sun Tzu, and that the passage you have selected
results in your screen looking as follows. Note that the cursor position is indicated in the
example by an underscore under the period at the very end of the passage:

```
    If wise, a commander is able to recognize changing circumstances and to
act expediently.  If sincere, his men will have no doubt of the certainty of
rewards and punishments.  If humane, he loves mankind, sympathizes with others,
and appreciates their industry and toil.  If courageous, he gains victory by
seizing opportunity without hesitation.  If strict, his troops are disciplined
because they are in awe of him and are afraid of punishment.
    Shen Pao-hsu ... said: 'If a general is not courageous he will be unable
to conquer doubts or to create great plans.'
~
~
~
~
~
~
~
~
~
~
~
~
~
~
~
~
```

Esc—Cancel

When you have entered enough, press the Esc key to return to command mode. If you are already in command mode when you press Esc, you hear a beep. The Esc key is used to cancel an incomplete command as well as to terminate any type of insert mode. After pressing Esc, the cursor backs up over the last character you typed. Leave it there for now.

Unfortunately, there is no readily visible indication of which mode you are in unless you enable showmode. However, it is pretty easy to see what mode you are in. If the keystrokes go into the text, you are in insert mode; if your screen jumps around wildly, beeps, and all kinds of weird things are happening, you are probably in command mode. If you are unsure of what mode you are in, just press Esc twice to get the beep confirming that you are in command mode.

Moving Around and Simple Editing

It's time to look at the most basic movement commands, the ones that you must train your fingers to execute automatically.

The Most Important Movement Keys

Editing commands in vi are composed of objects and commands. Objects are used by themselves to move around, or "navigate," in the buffer. A single object keystroke either causes the cursor position to move on the screen, or to reposition the "viewport" in the buffer. Let's see how the various movement commands affect the cursor position in our sample text.

h—Cursor Left

First, move the cursor back five positions by pressing the h key five times (if you see five h's go into the text, you forgot to press the Esc key). The cursor should now be under the "p" of "plans" (see the following example):

```
        If wise, a commander is able to recognize changing circumstances and to
act expediently.  If sincere, his men will have no doubt of the certainty of
rewards and punishments.  If humane, he loves mankind, sympathizes with others,
and appreciates their industry and toil.  If courageous, he gains victory by
seizing opportunity without hesitation.  If strict, his troops are disciplined
because they are in awe of him and are afraid of punishment.
        Shen Pao-hsu ... said: 'If a general is not courageous he will be unable
to conquer doubts or to create great plans.'
~
~
~
~
~
~
~
~
~
~
~
~
~
~
```

k—Cursor Up

Now let's move the cursor up five lines using the k key. As you might expect, there is a shortcut for pressing the key five times. Just prefix the object (or action) portion of the command with a number. Instead of pressing the k key five times, you have the same result by typing 5k. Try this now. The cursor should now be under the "e" of "he" (see the following example):

```
    If wise, a commander is able to recognize changing circumstances and to
act expediently.  If sincere, his men will have no doubt of the certainty of
rewards and punishments.  If humane, he loves mankind, sympathizes with others,
and appreciates their industry and toil.  If courageous, he gains victory by
seizing opportunity without hesitation.  If strict, his troops are disciplined
because they are in awe of him and are afraid of punishment.
    Shen Pao-hsu ... said: 'If a general is not courageous he will be unable
to conquer doubts or to create great plans.'
~
~
~
~
~
~
~
~
~
~
~
~
~
~
~
~
```

There is a limit to the effect of the object you can use. For example, if the h or l keys are used with an object that would go beyond either the beginning or the end of the line the cursor is on, the cursor stays at the beginning or end of the line, and the beep sounds.

Other commands work like the h and k keys. Table 7.2 describes their functions. The best way to get used to how they work is to practice using them. Table 15.2 shows the most frequently used movement keys.

TABLE 7.2. FREQUENTLY USED MOVEMENT KEYS.

Keystroke(s)	*Moves*
h	one character left
j	one line down
k	one line up
l	one character right
w, W	one word forward (W ignores punctuation)
b, B	one word backward (B ignores punctuation)
$	to end of line

Keystroke(s)	Moves
^	to first non-space character of line
0	to beginning of line
G	to top of buffer
nG	where n is a whole number, to line n

The upper- and lowercase versions of the word movement commands have a subtle difference. The lowercase version counts most punctuation marks as "words." The uppercase version skips over them as if they were not present.

Practice moving around in your sample text, using the previously described commands. Although they might seem awkward at first, you will soon get used to them as your fingers are trained.

The Most Important Editing Procedures

Let's look at some of the simplest and most often used editing procedures:

Changing Text

Nobody is perfect. Sooner or later you will want to change some text that you have created. In fact, more text editing time is probably spent modifying existing text than in entering brand-new text, so you need some easy ways of changing text. This section shows how.

x—Delete Character

The simplest way to delete text is with the x command. This command causes the character that the cursor is over to be deleted, and the remaining characters on the line to be shifted one character to the left. You can think of "x-ing" out the text you want to get rid of. If the character deleted is the last one on the line, the cursor moves one character to the left, so as not to be over nonexistent text. If there is no more text on the line, the beep sounds.

d—Delete Object

The delete command requires a text object on which to operate. A text object, or object for short, is the block of text that would be traversed by the use of a movement command. For example, w advances to the next word. So dw deletes to the beginning of the next word. 5w advances to the beginning of the fifth word (remember, punctuation symbols count as "words" to the w command). So 5dw (or alternatively d5w) deletes to the beginning of the fifth word. Both forms work because 5dw mean "do five delete-words"; d5w means "do delete five words."

dd—Line Delete

One of the most often used forms of the d command is the special version, dd, which deletes an entire line. As before, 5dd deletes five lines.

D—Big Delete

The uppercase form D is used to delete from the cursor position to the end of the line. It has the same action as d$.

u—Undo After learning how to do deletes, the first thing I want to know is whether there is an undo function. There is. It is invoked naturally by the u command. The u command undoes the most recent change to the file (not only deletes, but any edits). The cursor does not need to be at the location of that most recent change.

> **CAUTION**
>
> Unfortunately, standard vi has only one level of undo. After a second change is made, you cannot undo the first. If you press u a second time, it will "undo the undo," which is sometimes known as "redo." Repeated presses of the u key toggles the text back and forth between the two versions.
>
> This also applies for U—the big undo.

U—Big Undo

The "big brother" of the u command, the U command undoes all changes made to the line that the cursor is on, since the cursor was last moved on to that line. After the cursor is moved off a line, the U command no longer works on the edits that have already been made to that line.

.—Repeat

Repeats the last editing command.

How Commands Are Formed

By now you have probably noticed that there is a pattern to the structure of the vi commands. First, the commands are fairly mnemonic, which means that the letter of the command should remind you of the function being executed. Second, many commands have an uppercase version, which is usually a modified form of the basic, lowercase command. Third, all commands can be multiplied by a repeat count, entered as a prefix.

Table 7.3 shows the easiest ways to see how the commands are formed. You can see that there are several ways of combining command elements to get the result you want.

To repeat a command, just enter the repeat count prior to the command itself, as in the previous examples of cursor motion and deletion.

TABLE 7.3. HOW vi COMMANDS ARE FORMED.

General form of vi *commands*	
{count}{command}{object}	All parts are optional (see the following).
	The {count}, if present, causes the command to be executed *count* number of times.
	The {command}, if present, causes some action to take place. If absent, the cursor is moved according to the object.
	The {object} is used together with the command to indicate what portion of the text is to be affected.
Specific Forms of vi *Commands*	
{count}	Position the cursor *count* lines down, if terminated with return or +; position the cursor *count* line up if terminated with -.
{command}	Execute the command.
{object}	Move the cursor over the indicated block.
{count}{command}	Execute the command *count* times.
{count}{object}	Move the cursor over *count* indicated blocks.
{command}{object}	Execute the *command* over the indicated block.

Table 7.4 shows examples of combining some of the commands that you already know.

TABLE 7.4. EXAMPLES OF COMBINING COMMANDS.

Command	Result
h	Move cursor left one character
3h	Move cursor left three characters
dd	Delete one line
3dd	Delete three lines
w	Move cursor forward one word
dw	Delete one word
3dw	Delete three words

You now have the basic editing commands that will enable you to get started. You might want to start practicing these commands right away. With these commands, you could do any text editing project. But you wouldn't want to. By adding some additional commands, you can make your work much faster and easier. The whole point of computers is to make work easier, so why not use the power of vi to have the computer do what it is good at!

Other Useful Editing Commands

a—Append

The a command is used to append text. It is almost identical to the i command. The slight difference is that the i command inserts text at the cursor position; the a command appends text immediately after the cursor position. To illustrate the difference, we will use both commands to insert the phrase "is able to" into the sample text. For example, suppose that your screen looks like the following example, with the cursor at the "r" of "recognize." We want to insert the missing phrase "is able to" between the words "commander" and "recognize":

```
If wise, a commander recognize changing
~
~
~
~
~
~
~
~
~
~
~
~
~
~
~
~
~
~
~
~
~
~
~
~
```

Type the following to use the i command to insert text:

```
iis able to <Esc>
```

There is a blank between the word "to" and the Esc key. Your screen should look like this after inserting "is able to":

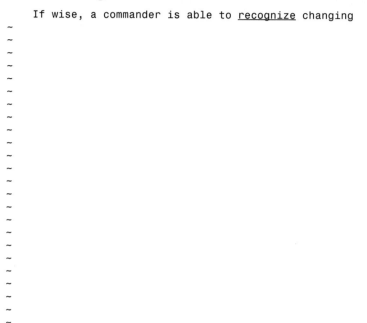

```
If wise, a commander is able to recognize changing
~
~
~
~
~
~
~
~
~
~
~
~
~
~
~
~
~
~
~
~
~
```

Now restore the text to the way it was by executing an undo command. Press the u key. (If a "u" is inserted into your text, you forgot to press Esc after the first insert.) Now before trying the a command, move the cursor back one character with the h key. Your screen should now look like the following:

TIP

You can insert a repeated string sequence by using one of the insert or append commands with a repeat count. For example, to insert 78 asterisk characters, you could type **78i*Esc**.

```
        If wise, a commander recognize changing
~
~
~
~
~
~
~
~
~
~
~
~
~
~
~
~
~
~
~
~
~
~
~
```

Type the following:

```
ais able to <Esc>
```

As you can see, the action of the i and a commands differ by where the insertion begins.

A—Big Append

The A command is like the a command but begins the append at the end of the line.

c—Change Object

To change text, you can use the c command. The c command takes an object to indicate the block of text that will be changed. The c command works like the d command followed by the i command. That is, it first performs the deletion that would be performed by the d command with the same object and then allows the insert of any amount of text (including line feeds) until the Esc key is pressed. This behavior makes it especially useful in such situations where you want to change the text from the position of the cursor to the beginning of the line (using c0) or to the end of the line (using c$).

cc—Change Line

In a similar vein, the cc command works like the dd command followed by an i command. It deletes the line the cursor is on and then inserts all keystrokes typed until the Esc key is pressed.

c—Big Change

The C command works like the D command followed by the i command; it deletes the text from the cursor position to the end of the line; then enters insert mode. The C command has the same action as c$.

r—Replace Character

The r command replaces the single character where the cursor is placed. After the r key is pressed, no change is seen on the screen. The next key typed replaces the character at the cursor position and then vi returns to command mode. It is a simple way to change just one character.

When used with a numeric count, the same replacement occurs over count characters. For example, suppose that the screen looks like the following, with the cursor under the "c" of "commander":

```
If wise, a commander recognize changing
~
~
~
~
~
~
~
~
~
~
~
~
~
~
~
~
~
~
~
~
~
~
~
~
~
```

Now suppose that you type **4rx**. The screen now looks like the following, and vi is in command mode. Note that the cursor has moved to the end of the replaced text:

```
        If wise, a xxxxander is able to recognize changing
~
~
~
~
~
~
~
~
~
~
~
~
~
~
~
~
~
~
~
~
~
```

R—Big Replace

The uppercase version of the r command differs from the r command by the same pattern that the uppercase versions of the d command and the c command differ from their lowercase versions. The R command allows the replacement of the text from the cursor position to the end of the line. Any text entered after typing R until the Esc key is pressed overlays the existing text on the screen, up to the end of the line. Thereafter, text entered is appended to the end of the line.

When used with a numeric count, the same replacement occurs *count* times. This use of the R command may not produce what you are expecting.

o—Open Line

The o command opens up a new line below the line the cursor is on and goes into insert mode.

O—Big Open Line

The O command opens up a new line above the line the cursor is on and goes into insert mode.

A Copy Is a "Yank"

Many text editors have features known as "cut and paste" or "copy and paste." vi calls the copy part of "copy and paste" a *yank*. You can use the yank command to save any block of text in the undo buffer. The undo buffer is a special place that vi keeps internally. You can't directly see the contents of this buffer. The contents of this buffer can be put into the text with the p command.

Each use of the y command overwrites the contents of the undo buffer, as does any delete command. There is a more advanced version of the yank command explained in the section "How To Use Buffers," which can be used to save text in multiple named buffers.

y—Yank

The yank command works with an object in the same way as the c and d commands. You can yank a word with yw, yank to the end of the line with y$, yank three lines with 3yy.

Y—Big Yank

There is an exception to the pattern, however. For some reason, the Y command does not take its action to the end of the line as C and D do. Instead, it yanks the whole line and is therefore identical to yy.

Copying Text

The commands discussed in the following sections are used to copy text.

p—Put

The p command takes whatever is in the undo buffer and inserts it into the text after the cursor position.

P—Big Put

The P command takes whatever is in the undo buffer and inserts it into the text before the cursor position.

Moving Text

In addition to text that you specifically yank being placed in the undo buffer, each portion of text that is deleted goes into the same undo buffer, replacing the previous contents each time. So to perform a cut and paste, you would use any delete function, move the cursor to the desired insertion point, and then use one of the put commands to insert the text. You have to pay attention to the location of the cursor and whether to use the p or P commands to get exactly what you want.

For example, suppose that your screen appears as shown in the following example:

```
     If wise, a commander is able to recognize changing circumstances and to
act expediently.  If sincere, his men will have no doubt of the certainty of
rewards and punishments.  If humane, he loves mankind, sympathizes with others,
and appreciates their industry and toil.  If courageous, he gains victory by
seizing opportunity without hesitation.  If strict, his troops are disciplined
because they are in awe of him and are afraid of punishment.
     Shen Pao-hsu ... said: 'If a general is not courageous he will be unable
to conquer doubts or to create great plans.'
~
~
~
~
~
~
~
~
~
~
~
~
~
~
~
~
```

Now suppose that you want to change the order of the paragraphs so that the paragraph beginning with "Shen Pao-hsu" comes first. First, move the cursor on to any character in the first line of the "Shen Pao-hsu" paragraph, as shown here:

```
     If wise, a commander is able to recognize changing circumstances and to
act expediently.  If sincere, his men will have no doubt of the certainty of
rewards and punishments.  If humane, he loves mankind, sympathizes with others,
and appreciates their industry and toil.  If courageous, he gains victory by
seizing opportunity without hesitation.  If strict, his troops are disciplined
because they are in awe of him and are afraid of punishment.
     Shen Pao-hsu ... said: 'If a general is not courageous he will be unable
to conquer doubts or to create great plans.'
~
~
~
~
~
~
~
~
~
~
~
~
~
~
~
~
```

Then press 2dd to delete the second paragraph. Your screen appears as in the following example:

```
    If wise, a commander is able to recognize changing circumstances and to
act expediently.  If sincere, his men will have no doubt of the certainty of
rewards and punishments.  If humane, he loves mankind, sympathizes with others,
and appreciates their industry and toil.  If courageous, he gains victory by
seizing opportunity without hesitation.  If strict, his troops are disciplined
because they are in awe of him and are afraid of punishment. ~
~
~
~
~
~
~
~
~
~
~
~
~
~
~
~
~
~
```

Now move the cursor to any character on the top line (1G takes you to the first line), as shown here:

```
    If wise, a commander is able to recognize changing circumstances and to
act expediently.  If sincere, his men will have no doubt of the certainty of
rewards and punishments.  If humane, he loves mankind, sympathizes with others,
and appreciates their industry and toil.  If courageous, he gains victory by
seizing opportunity without hesitation.  If strict, his troops are disciplined
because they are in awe of him and are afraid of punishment.
~
~
~
~
~
~
~
~
~
~
~
~
~
~
~
~
~
~
```

7

TEXT EDITING WITH vi AND Emacs

Now use the p command to put the text. Oops! Your screen looks like this:

```
     If wise, a commander is able to recognize changing circumstances
and to
     Shen Pao-hsu ... said: 'If a general is not courageous he will be unable to
act expediently.  If sincere, his men will have no doubt of the certainty of
rewards and punishments.  If humane, he loves mankind, sympathizes with others,
and appreciates their industry and toil.  If courageous, he gains victory by
seizing opportunity without hesitation.  If strict, his troops are disciplined
because they are in awe of him and are afraid of punishment. ~
~
~
~
~
~
~
~
~
~
~
~
~
~
~
```

This is not what we intended! To fix it, first press u to undo; then press P to put before the cursor. After a little practice, you will get used to easily accomplishing what you want to do.

You probably noticed during this exercise that you were able to use the put command repeatedly to put the same text. You can do this because the put command does not change the contents of the undo buffer. This feature sometimes comes in handy.

Searching for Patterns

/, //, ?, ??, n, and N—Search

One of the more useful ways of moving around in your text is to search for a pattern. You might be editing a long source code file and want to go back to a routine that you remember contains a specific instruction. You can do this by using /, the forward search command, or ?, the backward search command. As soon as you type the slash or question mark while in command mode, the cursor moves to the command line. You then type the pattern that you want to find. This pattern can be a literal text string, which is the exact character sequence you want to find. Or it can be a regular expression, described in detail in the "Regular Expressions" section.

After pressing the Return key, the text is repositioned so that the line containing the first occurrence of the pattern is displayed approximately in the center of the screen (assuming there is enough surrounding text to permit this), and the cursor is positioned to the first character of the matched text. If the pattern is not found, the message "Pattern not found: pattern" is displayed on the command line.

You use the / command to search forward in the text (that is, from the cursor's position to the end of the buffer). You use the ? command to search backward in the text (that is, from the cursor's position to the top of the buffer). You can repeat either forward or backward searches without reentering the pattern by using the two search again commands (/ and ? without any search text—// and ?? also work). You must also press the Return key after these search again commands. After a pattern has been entered, you can intermix the forward and backward search commands.

Another variation on repeating search commands is to use the n command, which repeats the previous search in the same direction, whether forward or backward. The N command repeats the previous search in the opposite direction.

vi searches "wrap around" the top and bottom of the buffer. When searching for the pattern, if vi hits one end of the buffer, a message displays on the command line notifying you of this fact. For example, the message "search hit BOTTOM, continuing at TOP" may appear. At this point, you may press Return to continue the search. This behavior can be changed; refer to the "For the Power User: Customizing vi" section to see how you can use special settings to change vi's default behavior.

> **TIP**
>
> Because there are different versions of vi, the behavior you see might be different. Look at the man page and check your personal vi settings.

\How To Use Buffers

The undo buffer contains only the most recent yanked or deleted text. This means that if you were intending to yank some text and copy it in somewhere, but before you put the text you performed any other deletion, you would be disappointed with the result. To keep various text snippets available for putting, you have to use named buffers.

Named Buffers

Named buffers allow you to keep up to 26 separate places where text can be deleted or yanked. Using the named buffers allows you to overcome the problem of intermediate deletes replacing the text that you have yanked or deleted. The contents of a named buffer remain unchanged until the end of your vi session, unless you use commands to deliberately change it.

Buffers are named by using a " followed by a lowercase letter. So the buffers are named from "a to "z. To yank or delete into a named buffer, prefix the yank or delete command with the name. For example, to yank two lines from the cursor position into buffer z, you would use the following keystrokes: "z2yy. To put from the named buffers, the key sequence is the buffer name followed by the p command. Table 7.5 shows some examples of using named buffers (some of these object commands have not been introduced yet; they will be explained further):

TABLE 7.5. EXAMPLES OF USING NAMED BUFFERS.

Keystrokes	*Result*
"a2dw	Delete next two words into named buffer a
"jD	Delete from cursor to end of line into named buffer j
"jp	Put the contents of named buffer j after the cursor
"by)	Yank from cursor position to end of sentence into named buffer b

As with a normal yank into the regular (unnamed) undo buffer, the action of the yank or delete into the named buffer replaces the previous contents of that buffer. If, instead, you want to collect text in a named buffer by appending it to what is already there, you may do this by uppercasing the letter of the buffer's name. Yanks and deletes can be intermixed when using the appending method, as shown in the sequence in Table 7.6.

TABLE 7.6. INTERMIXED SEQUENCE OF YANKS AND A DELETE.

Keystrokes	*Result*
"a2yy	Yank two lines into named buffer a, discarding the previous contents
"Ad4w	Delete the next four words and append them into buffer a
"Ay)	Yank from the cursor to the end of the sentence and append into buffer a

CAUTION

In executing such a sequence, do not forget to use the capital letter. If you forget, the previous contents are obliterated, and your careful work is lost. For this reason, I seldom use this technique, and when I do use it, I do it carefully!

Delete Buffers

In addition to the named buffers, vi provides numbered delete buffers. A normal undo can only undo the last delete and only if it was the last edit. However, vi saves the most recent nine deletes in buffers numbered from 1 to 9. The most recent delete is kept in buffer 1, the next most recent in buffer 2, and so on. To recover the contents of one of these buffers, use the number as the buffer name with the p command, as in "2p to put from the second delete buffer.

TIP

How do you know what is in each of the delete buffers? A special feature of the . (repeat) command (described later in the "Recovering Deleted Text: Cutting and Pasting" section) allows you to easily choose from among the numbered buffers. When the repeat command is used after a command referencing a numbered buffer, the buffer number is incremented.

Thus you can put from numbered buffer 1, see the text that is inserted, use the u command to undo the put, and then just press . (the *repeat* command) to see the next buffer's contents. Continuing this process with a series of u commands and . (*repeat*) commands quickly scans through the nine most recent deletions. (When you get to the ninth one, continued key presses "stick" on the ninth buffer's contents.) This is another technique that is much easier to do than to describe.

The Complete Guide to Movement and Editing: Command Reference Tables

By this point, you have seen the most commonly used vi commands. However, many useful and powerful movement and editing commands that, although less frequently used, might become invaluable to you as you learn to use them. Some of them are likely to be included in your repertoire of often-used commands, sooner or later. This section is intended to provide complete coverage of the movement, editing, and other commands, for easy reference.

7

TEXT EDITING
WITH vi AND EMACS

Note that some commands are shifted commands. Commands represented by uppercase letters are entered by holding down the Shift key while the alphabetic letter is pressed.

> **NOTE**
>
> So called Control-key commands are entered in a similar fashion, with the Ctrl key held down while the other key is pressed. Ctrl-key commands are indicated in the vi sections by prefixing the command with a caret symbol (^), or alternatively, by the sequence Ctrl+key. So, for example, when you see in the text the symbol ^A, you are to hold down the Ctrl key while you press the letter a.
>
> Later, in the Emacs sections, the standard Emacs way of indicating control keys will be used—do not let this confuse you.

Be aware that all the commands shown in Table 7.7 can be combined in the ways described in Table 7.3. That is, you can amplify the effect of commands by using a count or an object or both, as appropriate.

Some commands included here have not been introduced yet. They will be explained in detail in the advanced editing section.

Movement

In Table 7.7 the following words in the command column have the specified meaning: *char* means any character; *number* (or *nbr*) is a whole number; *pattern* is a string of characters or a regular expression.

In the description column, a small word is a word that can be either a string of alphanumeric characters (plus the underscore) or a string of punctuation characters, delimited by whitespace (spaces, tabs, and line feeds); a big word is a sequence of nonblank characters. These precise but technical definitions are saying, in effect, that small words consider the punctuation to be separate "words"; big words include the punctuation as part of the word. The easiest way to see the difference is first to try a repeated sequence of moves using the lowercase version of a command; then try the uppercase version of the command.

TABLE 7.7. MOVEMENT COMMANDS.

Single character cursor motion

Command	Result
h	Moves one character left

Single character cursor motion

Command	Result
^H	
left-arrow	
j	Moves one line down
^J	
^N	
down-arrow	
k	Moves one line up
^P	
up-arrow	
l	Moves one character right
right-arrow	

Movement within a line

Command	Result
^	Moves to first nonspace character on the line
0	Moves to beginning of the line
$	Moves to end of line
f*char*	Moves to next occurrence of character *char*
F*char*	Moves to previous occurrence of character *char*
t*char*	Moves to character before next occurrence of character *char*
T*char*	Moves to character after previous occurrence of character *char*
;	Repeats previous f, F, t, or T command; same direction
,	Repeats previous f, F, t, or T command; opposite direction

Motion to a specified line

Command	Result
Enter	Moves to next line
+	Moves to next line (usually used with preceding count)

continues

7

TEXT EDITING WITH vi **AND EMACS**

TABLE 7.7. CONTINUED.

Motion to a specified line

Command	Result
-	Moves to previous line (usually used with preceding count)
*number*G	Moves to line *number*
number¦	Moves to column *number*

Screen positioning

Command	Result
H	Moves to top line displayed onscreen
L	Moves to bottom line displayed onscreen
M	Moves to middle line displayed onscreen
^D	Scrolls down one-half screen
number^D	Scrolls down *number* lines
^U	Scrolls up one-half screen
number^U	Scrolls up *number* lines
^F	Scrolls forward one screen
^B	Scrolls backward one screen
^E	Scrolls down one line
^Y	Scrolls up one line

Lexical object positioning

Command	Result
w	Moves forward one small word
W	Moves forward one big word
b	Moves backward one small word
B	Moves backward one big word
e	Moves to end of next small word
E	Moves to end of next big word
(	Moves to beginning of previous sentence
)	Moves to beginning of next sentence
{	Moves to beginning of previous paragraph
{	Moves to beginning of next paragraph
[[	Moves to beginning of next section
]]	Moves to beginning of previous section

Screen redrawing

Command	Result
z	Redraws screen with current line at top of the screen
z-	Redraws screen with current line at bottom of the screen
z.	Redraws screen with current line at center of the screen

Positioning by pattern searching

Command	Result
/pattern	Moves to next line containing pattern
?pattern	Moves to previous line containing pattern
/	Repeats last search forward
?	Repeats last search backward
n	Repeats last search in same direction
N	Repeats last search in opposite direction
/pattern/+nbr	Moves to *nbr* lines after next line containing *pattern*
?pattern?-nbr	Moves to *nbr* lines before previous line containing *pattern*
/pattern/z-	Redraws screen with next line containing pattern at bottom of the screen
	(Other z options give the corresponding positioning)
%	Moves to parenthesis or brace matching the one at the current cursor position

Positioning to marked text locations

Command	Result
m*char*	Marks the current cursor position with the letter *char*
\`*char*	Moves to mark specified by *char*
'*char*	Moves to beginning of line containing mark specified by *char*
\`\`	Moves to previous location of the current line (after a cursor movement)
' '	Moves to beginning of line containing previous location of current line (after a cursor movement)

7

TEXT EDITING
WITH vi AND EMACS

> **NOTE**
>
> Some versions of `vi` do not allow you to use the arrow keys on the keyboard for cursor movement. This is typically an operating system or terminal (terminal emulator) issue, not really a `vi` problem.
>
> The other cursor movement keys will work.

Editing

In Table 7.8, the words in the command column have the specified meaning: *object* means an object command from Table 7.7; *letter* means one of the 26 alphabetic characters from a to z. All editing commands can take nearly any movement command as an object. The text insertion commands cause entry into *insert* mode; `vi` then stays in that mode until you press the Esc key.

TABLE 7.8. EDITING COMMANDS.

Inserting text

Command	Result
i	Inserts text before the cursor
I	Inserts text before first nonblank character of line
a	Inserts text after the cursor
A	Inserts text at the end of the line
o	Adds an empty line below the current line and enters insert mode there
O	Adds an empty line above the current line and enters insert mode there

Changing text while in insert mode

(Note: These commands are only available while in insert mode.)

Command	Result
^H	Backspaces and erases the previous character (only since insert began)
^W	Backspaces over and erases the previous small word (only since insert began)
\	Quotes the erase and kill characters
Esc	Ends insert mode and goes back to command mode

Changing text while in insert mode

Command	Result
^D	Goes back to previous auto-indent stop
^^D	(Caret followed by Ctrl+D) no auto-indent on current line only
0^D	Moves cursor back to left margin
^V	Enters any character into text (do not interpret control characters)

Changing text

Command	Result
c*object*	Changes the text object to the text inserted until the Esc key is pressed
C	Changes the rest of the line to the text insert until the Esc key is pressed (same as c$)
cc	Changes the whole line to the text inserted until the Esc key is pressed
r*char*	Replaces the character the cursor is on with *char*; then returns to command mode
R	Overwrites text until the Esc key is pressed; if you go past the end of the line, appends new text to the end of the line
s	Substitutes characters (same as c1)
S	Substitutes lines (same as cc)

Deleting text

Command	Result
x	Deletes the character under the cursor
X	Deletes the character before the cursor
d*object*	Deletes the text object
D	Deletes the reset of the line (same as d$)
dd	Deletes the line

Using buffers

Command	Result
u	Undoes the last change
U	Restores the current line to the state it was in when the cursor was last positioned to it

Table 7.8. continued.

Using buffers

Command	Result
`yobject`	Places the text of the object into the undo buffer
`yy`	Places the line the cursor is on into the undo buffer
`Y`	Places the line the cursor is on into the undo buffer (same as `yy`, which is a departure from the pattern set up by `C` and `D`)
`p`	Inserts the text in the undo buffer after the cursor
`P`	Inserts the text in the undo buffer before the cursor
`"letterdobject`	Deletes the object into the letter buffer
`"letteryobject`	Yanks (copies) the object into the letter buffer
`"letterp`	Inserts the text in the letter buffer after the cursor
`"numberp`	Inserts the *number*-th last delete of a complete line or block of lines

Other editing commands

Command	Result
`.`	Repeats the last editing command (and increments n in a `"np` command)
`~`	Changes the case of the letter under the cursor and moves cursor to the left one character (does not support a count in standard `vi`)
`J`	Joins two lines
`>>`	Shifts line *shiftwidth* characters to the right (use `:set sw` to change the *shiftwidth*)
`>L`	Shifts all lines from the line the cursor is on to the end of the screen *shiftwidth* characters to the right (use `:set sw` to change the *shiftwidth*)
`<<`	Shifts line *shiftwidth* characters to the left (use `:set sw` to change the *shiftwidth*)
`<L`	Shifts all lines from the line the cursor is on to the end of the screen *shiftwidth* characters to the left (use `:set sw` to change the *shiftwidth*)

Other `vi` Commands

In Table 7.9, commands that start with : (colon) are `ex` commands. If these are being executed from within the `ex` editor, you do not need the colon. When the ! modifier is included with a command, some form of override is performed. Not all combinations that include the ! are shown.

In the command column, the following words have the specified meaning: *file* means the name of a disk file; *number* or *nbr* means a positive whole number; *command* or *cmd* means a UNIX shell command; *tag* means a function identifier created using the *ctags* program; *addr* means an `ex` line address (defined in the "Using the Power of `ex` from `vi`" section following).

TABLE 7.9. OTHER `vi` COMMANDS.

Saving the buffer to a file

Command	Result
:w	Writes (saves) the buffer to disk, using the original file name
:w *file*	Writes the buffer to disk, to file
:w!	Writes the buffer to disk, overwriting file

Exiting commands

Command	Result
ZZ	Writes the buffer to disk and exits the program
Q	Enters the `ex` editor (same as typing :)
:q	Quits `vi`, unless you have an unsaved buffer
:q!	Always quits `vi`, overriding warning about an unsaved buffer
:wq	Writes the buffer to disk and exits the program (same as ZZ)

Editing other files

Command	Result
:e *file*	Edits *file*, unless you have an unsaved buffer
:e!	Discards any changes and starts over with the last saved version of the file from disk
:e + *file*	Edits *file*, unless you have an unsaved buffer; places cursor on bottom line

continues

7
TEXT EDITING
WITH VI AND EMACS

TABLE 7.9. CONTINUED.

Editing other files

Command	Result
`:e +nbr file`	Edits file, unless you have an unsaved buffer; places cursor on line *nbr*
`:e #`	Edits alternate file
`:n`	Edits the next file (applies when a list of files was entered on the command line)
`:n file file file`	Sets up a new list of files to edit
`:r file`	Reads (inserts) contents of file into the buffer on the line below the cursor
`:r !command`	Runs the shell command and inserts the output of the command on the line below the cursor
`^G`	Displays information about the current file (filename, current line number, number of lines in file, percentage through the file)
`:ta tag`	Jumps to the file and the location in the file specified by *tag* (before you can use this function, you must use the *ctags* program to create the *tags* file. Refer to the section on the *:ta* command for details.)

Redrawing the screen

Command	Result
`^L`	Redraws the screen (implementation depends on terminal type)
`^R`	Redraws the screen; eliminates blank lines marked with @ (implementation depends on terminal type)
`znumber`	Sets screen window to *number* lines

UNIX shell commands

Command	Result
`:sh`	Executes a shell; remain in shell until shell exit command given (^D)
`:!command`	Executes the shell command and returns to vi (After the ! command, certain special characters are expanded. # is expanded to the alternate file name; % is expanded to the current file name; ! is expanded to the previous shell command.)

UNIX shell commands

Command	Result
`:!!`	Repeat the previous shell command
`!object cmd`	Executes the shell *cmd*; replaces the text object with the shell *cmd* output. If the shell *cmd* takes standard input, the designated text object is used.
`nbr!!cmd`	Executed the shell *cmd*; replaced *nbr* lines beginning at the current line with the shell *cmd* output. If *nbr* is missing, 1 is assumed. If the shell *cmd* takes standard input, the designated lines are used.

ex *editing commands*

Command	Result
`:vi`	Enters visual mode from the `ex` command line
`:addrd`	Deletes the lines specified by `addr`
`:addrmnbr`	Moves the lines specified by *addr* after line *nbr*
`:addrconbr`	Copies the lines specified by *addr* after line *nbr*
`:addrtnbr`	Copies the lines specified by *addr* after line *nbr* (same as `co` command)

Advanced Editing with `vi`: Tips and Techniques

You may be ready for the any of the topics included in this section at any time while you are learning `vi`. Do not let the title of the section deter you from browsing for features that interest you. Although some `vi` commands are less often used, the real power of the `vi` editor will not be fully yours until you are comfortable with at least some of these features.

Using the Power of `ex` from `vi`

As mentioned earlier, `vi` is actually the visual mode of the `ex` editor. As such, all the power and features of the `ex` editor are available at any time while editing in `vi`, without leaving your place in the file. `vi` commands that are actually `ex` commands are shown in the command reference tables and elsewhere in this chapter prefixed with a : (colon).

You can think of this prefix in either of two ways: (1) as a prefix to a special vi command; or, (2) the command that takes the editor into ex mode, at which time the screen display changes so that a colon is displayed on the bottom line, and the cursor is placed immediately to the right of the colon. Thereafter, the editor acts exactly the same as if you were in the ex editor, except that you still have the vi screen displayed on all lines but the bottom line. Certain commands return you to the vi mode; others leave you in the ex mode. To return explicitly to the vi mode, just enter the :vi command.

The real power of using ex commands from within vi is that certain specific editing functions are provided in this way that are usually not available in most text editors. (The power of such operations is approached by macro languages included with PC-based word processing programs; however, the simplicity and elegance of the ex commands are not.)

The types of operations that are available only from the ex command line are using basic ex commands to manipulate blocks of text, search and replace operations, global search and replace with regular expressions, and edit multiple files.

Using Basic ex Commands to Manipulate Blocks of Text

ex has its own versions of delete, copy, and move commands. Sometimes these commands are preferable to the vi versions, particularly when you want to manipulate the file as a whole. The main ex commands for these operations are covered here.

First, let's look at the general form of an ex command. An ex command is composed of an object and an operation to perform on the lines in the file that are selected by the object. The general form is

`:object command` Return

where Return means to press the Return or Enter key. All ex commands require the Return key (which is labeled Enter on a PC keyboard) to be pressed. The spaces shown in the preceding example can be used if desired for readability, but they are not necessary.

Rather than using the vi concepts of a full-screen display with the cursor position to indicate where actions take place, ex has the concept of a current line. This concept means that ex takes its action on or relative to that line.

Both the *object* and *command* are optional. If the *object* is missing, the default is to apply the *command* to the current line. If the *command* is missing, the default is the ex print command, which displays the selected lines on the screen. Spaces between the parts of the command are also optional. In the examples, spaces are included for clarity.

When using the ex editor from the command line (that is, you are not running from within vi), ex responds to each command by displaying the lines affected. In the examples that follow, the behavior of the ex editor is shown with the assumption that you are using it from the command line, rather than from within vi. You might want to get a feel for the pure ex mode of interaction by trying it from the command line. When operating from within vi, the effect on the text you are editing is shown, just as if you executed the equivalent vi command. The screen display is repositioned if necessary.

The ex editor can be entered from within vi to edit the file you are currently editing by typing :. It can also be started from the command line with the name of the file you want to edit. If you start from the command line in this way, you might see the following on your screen (assuming that you are editing the same sample file that we have been using all along):

```
$ex art1
"art" 8 lines, 576 characters
:
```

Selecting Lines to Edit

Sets of lines may be selected in several ways. Because you already know that ex is a line editor, it is not surprising that line addresses refer to lines in the file without regard to content. The simplest way to address a line is with its number. For example, to print line three of your file, you could enter the following command:

```
:3p
rewards and punishments. If humane, he loves mankind, sympathizes with
others,
```

Another way to give an address is with a pattern search. A pattern search is indicated by surrounding the exact character string you are looking for with forward slashes. For example, to display on the screen the first line of your file containing the word "general," you could enter the following command:

```
:/general/p
Shen Pao-hsu ... said: 'If a general is not courageous he will be unable
```

In both of these preceding two examples, you could leave off the p command because as mentioned already, the p command is the default.

You may also specify a range of lines by entering two addresses separated by commas, as in the following example:

```
:3,6p
rewards and punishments. If humane, he loves mankind, sympathizes with others,
and appreciates their industry and toil.  If courageous, he gains victory by
seizing opportunity without hesitation.  If strict, his troops are disciplined
```

7

TEXT EDITING
WITH vi AND Emacs

Patterns also work in range selection, as in the following example:

```
:/humane/,/hesitation/p
rewards and punishments. If humane, he loves mankind, sympathizes with others,
and appreciates their industry and toil.  If courageous, he gains victory by
seizing opportunity without hesitation.  If strict, his troops are disciplined
```

You can mix patterns and line numbers too:

```
:4,/awe/p
and appreciates their industry and toil.  If courageous, he gains victory by
seizing opportunity without hesitation. If strict, his troops are disciplined
because they are in awe of him and are afraid of punishment.
```

Special ex line addressing symbols can be used as addresses. Line addressing takes on greater flexibility when you add these capabilities to the ones you already know. The special symbols are shown in Table 7.10:

TABLE 7.10. SPECIAL ex LINE ADDRESSING SYMBOLS.

Command	Result
.	The current line
$	The last line of the file
%	Every line in the file

Another feature to allow greater flexibility in line addressing is line number arithmetic. This feature allows you to use the + and - symbols along with numbers to refer to offsets from the position specified. For example, to refer to 20 lines from the current line number, you would use .+20.

When using two line addresses, the second address cannot be less than the first address. Sometimes when you try to use search patterns to select a line or line number arithmetic, you may get the error message ex: The first address cannot exceed the second address. This is because both line addresses are determined relative to the current line. In this case, you get an error message. What you really wanted was to have the second address be determined relative to the first address. ex has a feature that causes the second line address to be relative to the first. You use this feature by using a semicolon between the two addresses instead of a comma.

Table 7.11 shows several examples of the various methods of line addressing presented so far.

TABLE 7.11. VARIOUS METHODS OF LINE ADDRESSING.

Command	Result
1,5	Lines 1 through 5
.,20	From the current line to line 20
.,.+20	20 lines beginning at the current line
.,+20	Another way of specifying 20 lines beginning at the current line (the second . is optional)
.,$	From the current line to the end of the file
1,$	All lines in the file (same as %)
8,/pattern/	From line 8 to the next line containing *pattern*
5;.+20	From line 5 to 20 lines beyond line 5

Basic ex Commands

ex has the property that every command has a name. You can enter the full name of the command, or any length abbreviation of the command that sufficiently distinguishes it from all other commands. As new ex commands are introduced in this chapter, the full command name will be used first. However, the examples will use the shortest possible abbreviation of the command because that is the way you will want to use them. Table 7.12 shows a few of the basic ex commands:

TABLE 7.12. BASIC EX COMMANDS.

Command	Result
d	Delete
m	Move
co	Copy
t	Copy (synonym for co)

Table 7.13 presents examples of various ex editing commands. It summarizes the information given in this section on manipulating blocks of text.

TABLE 7.13. EXAMPLES OF EX EDITING COMMANDS.

Command	Result
1,5d	Deletes lines 1 through 5
.,20m$	Moves the current line through line 20 to the end of the file
.,.+20co0	Copies 20 lines beginning at the current line to the top of the file
8,/pattern/t.	Copies from line 8 to the next line containing *pattern* to the point after the current line

In this section, some basic ex commands that are useful to extend the power of vi were introduced. Several additional ex commands provide an alternative way of doing various editing tasks. However, these tasks are more easily done by using the features of vi. Therefore, such commands are not covered here.

Search and Replace

One of the main uses for ex commands from within vi (in addition to working with files and exiting the program) is to execute search and replace operations. In this section, basic search and replace operations are introduced. The next section introduces the topic of regular expressions. Regular expressions are extraordinarily powerful tools to search for text. If you are familiar with so-called "wildcard" searches offered by certain text manipulation tools, you can think of regular expressions as "wildcards on steroids"! The use of regular expressions for searching is covered in the second section following this one.

Simple search and replace operations are done in ex (and, therefore, in vi) by using the substitute command. Unless line addressing is used (see the following), the substitute command operates on the current line, so it is necessary to move the cursor to the line you want to edit first. The following example assumes that you want to substitute the word "opportunities" for the word "plan" in line 8 of the sample text. Note that the final slash is required:

```
:8                          Position to line 8 of the buffer
:s/plans/opportunities/     Replace "plans" with "opportunities" on the
                            current line
```

You can also perform search and replace operations on the entire file, or a selected range of lines. Table 7.14 shows examples of using the substitute command to operate on all lines in the buffer, or a selected range of lines.

TABLE 7.14. USING THE SUBSTITUTE COMMAND.

Command	Result
`:%s/warrior/general/g`	Replaces every occurrence of `warrior` in the buffer with `general`.
`:.,.+20s/warrior/general/`	Replaces the first occurrence of `warrior` with `general` on 20 lines beginning with the current line.

Another way to search is to use the global command, as shown here:

`:g/plans/command`

When used in this way, the command is performed on all lines that match the pattern. To negate the action of the search (that is, to act on all lines that do not match the pattern), use `:g!`.

If the global command is used without the final slash and the command, the cursor is positioned to the last line in the file that contains the pattern (or does not contain the pattern, if ! is used). If no match is found, the screen does not change, and the cursor stays where it is. (There is little point to using the global command to search in this way—use the `vi`, `/`, or `?` instead.)

You can use the global command with line addressing to limit the scope of its action. Table 7.15 shows examples of using the global command with other commands.

TABLE 7.15. USING THE GLOBAL COMMAND WITH OTHER COMMANDS.

Command	Result
`:g/22/d`	Deletes all lines containing 22
`:g/plans/p`	Displays all lines containing `plans`
`:g!/22/d`	Deletes all lines not containing 22.
`:8,12g/plans/p`	Displays all lines between lines 8 and 12 containing `plans`.

The global command can also be used to perform replacements. However, the real power of this command for replacements does not emerge until you begin to use it with regular expressions, which are explained in the next section.

Regular Expressions

Regular expressions are patterns used in search and replace operations that vastly extend the power and flexibility of the editing you can do. Regular expressions include in addition to literal characters, combinations of so-called *metacharacters,* which have special properties. Table 7.16 shows all the metacharacters available for use within vi. (Although a number of UNIX tools can operate on regular expressions such as grep, sed, and awk, certain metacharacters shown in the table are not implemented for these other tools. Such vi-and-Emacs-only metacharacters are indicated by the comment "editors only.")

TABLE 7.16. METACHARACTERS AVAILABLE WITH VI.

Metacharacter	Matches
.	Any single character, except a newline.
*	Zero or more occurrences of the previous character.
^	When the first character of the regular expression, the beginning of a line.
$	When the last character of the regular expression, the end of a line.
\<	The first character of a word (editors only).
\>	The last character of a word (editors only).
\	The escape character; alters ("escapes from") the standard interpretation of the following character. For example, to search for the literal presence of a metacharacter, you must escape the character by preceding it with a backslash.
[ ]	Any single character within the brackets; ranges may be used with a hyphen. For example, [a-z] matches all lowercase letters, [a-zA-Z] matches both lower- and uppercase characters. When metacharacters (other than ^) appear within square brackets, they do not need to be escaped. The literal hyphen can be included by placing it as the first character after the left square bracket.
[^]	Any single character not within the brackets.
\(\)	In a search pattern, saves the text matched within the escaped parenthesis in a numbered buffer for later "replaying." (The number is the position in the line as it is scanned from left to right; the first occurrence of this metacharacter pair is numbered 1, the second occurrence 2, and so on).

Metacharacter	*Matches*
\n	In a replacement pattern, where *n* is a digit from 1 to 9, "replays" the text saved by the escaped parenthesis.
&	Uses the entire search pattern which produced the match; used to save typing.
\u or \l	In a replacement pattern, causes the next character to be either upper- or lowercased.
\U or \L	In a replacement pattern, causes the rest of the replacement pattern (or until a \e or \E is scanned) to be upper- or lowercased.
\e or \E	In a replacement pattern, terminates the action of \U or \L.
~	Matches the search pattern of the last regular expression search.

CAUTION

The use of metacharacters might vary in different contexts. The shells use metacharacters for filename expansion; however, the interpretation of the metacharacters by the shells is slightly different from the interpretation by the utilities and text editors.

A shell is the name given to the UNIX command processor. There are several common versions of shell programs. The most common are sh, csh, ksh, and bash. Refer to Part II, "UNIX Shells" for an extensive discussion on this topic.

This can be a source of confusion, especially to the newcomer. To make matters worse, the implementation of metacharacters differs between different UNIX versions.

TIP

All regular expression matches are limited to a single line. That is, a match that "wraps around" from the end of one line to the beginning of the next is not allowed.

> **TIP**
>
> All regular expression searches are case sensitive. You have to explicitly use the features of the metacharacters to perform case-insensitive searches. For example, if you want to perform a search for the word "general" that is case-insensitive on the initial "g," you should use /[Gg]eneral/ for the search string.

> **TIP**
>
> Regular expressions are usually delimited by forward slash (/) characters. However, any nonalphanumeric character other than ", ¦, or # can be used. This is especially helpful when the slash is one of the characters in the search string and you don't want to escape the slash.

Global Search and Replace with Regular Expressions

You have already seen how to perform searches from vi using the / and ? commands. As mentioned earlier, you can use these commands with regular expressions as well as with literal text strings. There are two ways to use regular expressions to perform search and replace operations. Both methods work from the ex command line, and both are extensions of commands you have been exposed to in the "Search and Replace" section. One way is to use the substitute command; the other way is through the use of the global command.

Using the Substitute Command with Regular Expressions

When you want to make a global replacement, you can use the substitute command with line addressing and regular expressions. A commonly used form is to use the % addressing symbol to refer to all lines in the file. The general form of such a command is as follows:

`:address s/searchexpression/replaceexpression/options`

(The space after address in the preceding example is for clarity and is optional.) The *options* refer to one of the options shown in Table 7.17.

TABLE 7.17. SUBSTITUTE OPTIONS.

Command	Result
g	Makes the substitution global. (Without this option, the substitution only occurs on the first occurrence in the line; with it, all occurrences on the line are substituted. Do not confuse this option to the substitute command, which is placed at the far right of the command, with the global command itself, which occurs on the left of the command line near the colon.)
c	Confirm. vi displays each line found and indicates the text to be substituted with ^ symbols as follows:

```
this is some text                    ^ ^ ^ ^
```

You must enter a "y" to make the substitution; any other response causes the substitution not to be made. (Note: Some versions of vi handle this a little differently, using text highlighting to indicate the pattern matched and allowing additional choices at each step.)

You may combine both of these options into one substitute command.

Using the Global Command with Regular Expressions

The global command becomes very powerful when combined with the substitute command. One interesting way to use this combination is to use the global command to select the lines and then use the substitute command to cause a change on the lines that does not directly relate to the text that caused the line to be selected.

In effect, the global command provides a two-step editing function. First, a set of lines is selected using several of various techniques (line addressing and pattern matching). Then another command is used on the lines selected. When the global command was first introduced in this chapter, it was used in a simple way with other commands to display or delete text. In fact, the global command can be used with most any other command. (Some creative techniques, indeed, have been invented that use the global command. Some are shown in the examples of Table 7.18.)

The best way to show how the substitute command works and how the global and substitute commands can be used together is to present some examples. Table 7.18 shows a few of the types of search and replace operations that can be done. (Note: For clarity, the bolded lowercase letter b is used to indicate a single blank space.)

TABLE 7.18. EXAMPLES OF SEARCH AND REPLACE WITH THE s AND g COMMANDS.

Command	Result
`:%s/ex/vi/g`	Substitutes every occurrence of `ex` in the buffer with `vi`.
`:.,$s/ex/vi/c`	Substitutes the first occurrence of `ex` with `vi` on every line from the current line to the end of the buffer, confirming each substitution.
`:%s/\<author\>/contractor/g`	Substitutes the word `contractor` for each occurrence of the full word `author` in the buffer; note that text objects containing "author" as a substring, such as "authority" will not be substituted.
`:g/editor/s/line/full-screen/g`	Substitutes every occurrence of `line` with `full-screen` on all lines containing the pattern editor.
`:g/editor/s//word-processor/g`	Substitutes every occurrence of `editor` with `word-processor`; note that when the second search string is missing, the first search string is used; in this case, the string editor.
`:%s/bb*/b/g`	Substitutes a single space for every occurrence of one or more spaces (note: the b stands for a single space).
`:%s/[:.]bb*\([a-z]\)/\.bb\u\1/g`	Searches for all occurrences of a colon or a period followed by one or more spaces and a lowercase letter; substitutes a period, two spaces, and the uppercase form of the letter.
`:g/^$/d`	Deletes all blank lines (lines that have only a beginning followed immediately by the end).
`:g/^/m0`	Reverses all the lines in the buffer.
`:g!/Complete/s/$/ To be done/`	Appends `To be done` to all lines not containing the string `Complete`.

Working with Files

The basic commands for saving files were introduced in the "Starting Up and Exiting vi" section. This section more fully explains these commands and shows how to use them to work with more than one file at a time.

Saving Changes to a File

:w—Write

The w command is used to write the buffer to the current disk file. The current disk file is the one most recently loaded for editing, either from the command line when vi was started, or using the :e command. If there is no current disk file (perhaps because vi was loaded without specifying a file to edit), vi displays an error message and no action occurs. In this case, you can give a name to the current disk file with the version of the :w presented next.

Until the buffer is written to disk, all edits to the file are only stored temporarily. It is, therefore, a good habit to save your work frequently during your session to minimize the inconvenience of a system failure or major editing error that may occur.

> **CAUTION**
>
> You need to have write permission to the file you are changing. vi does not warn you when you start, only when you try to save.

:w *filename*—Write to *filename*

This version of the write command saves the buffer to the named *filename*. If there was previously no current file defined, the *filename* becomes the current file. Otherwise, the current file remains the same as it was before the :w *filename* command was issued.

If the *filename* file already exists, as usual vi warns you of this fact with an error message and gives advice on how to override the warning, as follows for a file name art1:

    "art1" ex: The file already exists. Use w! art1 to force the write.

If you do in fact want to overwrite the existing version, you can use the syntax :w! *filename*.

:*address* w *filename*—Write addressed lines to *filename*

This version of the write command further refines the action of the :w *filename* version. The difference is that only the lines selected by the address are written. The same caveat regarding existing files applies.

:*address* w >> *filename*—Append addressed lines to *filename*

This version of the write command uses the UNIX redirect and append operator to add the addressed lines on to the end of an existing *filename* file. As you would expect, if you omit the address portion, the full buffer is appended.

Editing a Different File

:e *filename*—Edit file

Begins to edit the *filename* file. If the file does not exist, then a new file is started, and *filename* becomes the current file. (That is, a subsequent :w command writes the *filename* file.)

If the current file has been changed since the last time it was saved, the :e *filename* command is not allowed. Instead, vi gives the usual warning about the unsaved file, which may look as follows:

```
ex: No write since the file was last changed. The edit! command will force
the action.
```

Once again, you could use :e! *filename* "to force the action."

:e!—Revert

This special use of the edit command forces the last saved version of the current file to be loaded for editing. This has the effect of reverting back to the last saved version, discarding all edits you made since then. (If you omit the exclamation point, in effect you are telling vi to begin editing the current file. If there were no changes yet, vi would oblige; however, this is a useless function. If there were changes, vi would do its normal routine of warning you that there has been "no write, etc." So the only useful version of this command is with the exclamation point.)

:e + *filename*—Edit *filename* at end

This command edits the *filename* file and places the cursor at the end of the file.

:e + *number filename*—Edit *filename* at line number

This command edits the *filename* file and places the cursor on line *number*.

:*address* r *filename*—Import (read) *filename*

The read command allows you to import the full contents of another file into the buffer. If the optional address is present, the *filename* file's lines are imported immediately after the line selected by the address. If the address is omitted, the lines are imported immediately after the line the cursor is presently on. The address can be a line number (with 0 indicating the top of the file), $ to indicate the last line of the file, or a search pattern.

Editing More Than One File

:n—Next file

When vi is started, more than one file can be listed on the command line. For example, to edit the three files art1, art2, and art3, you would enter the following shell command:

$vi art1 art2 art3

vi loads the file art1 as usual, and you may begin editing it. After saving the file, you can go on to the next file with the :n command. If you try to use the next command before you have saved the current file, you get the usual warning, which can be overridden in the usual way (yes, you guessed it—with n!). There is no "previous file" command.

Alternating Between Two Files

vi keeps two filenames available via special symbols for use with ex commands. These are # for the alternate file, and % for the current file. After you have switched files with the :e command, the previous ("alternate") file can be referenced via the # symbol. You can toggle back and forth between the two files by just typing :e# each time you want to switch.

The % symbol is mainly used to save typing within shell commands.

Moving Text Between Files

You can use named buffers to copy or move text from one file to another. The method is just like copying or moving text from one part of a single file to another part of that file using the buffers as already described in the "How To Use Buffers" section. The difference is that after (say) a yank is done, an :e or :n command is used to change to another file. Then the put is done into the new file.

This technique works because when you change files with the :e or :n commands, the contents of all the buffers are retained. This is still a single vi session, which is why text can be moved between files using the named buffers.

Using the Power of UNIX from Within vi

You may have already seen in Chapter 4, "General Commands," the general UNIX strategy for combining the functions of single-purpose or specialized tools to achieve results. vi shares in the capability to interact with the shell, filters, and utilities, and, in general, with any program that reads from the standard input and writes to the standard output. This section explains the various vi commands that make this possible.

:sh—Shell

This :sh command invokes the shell. The shell that is run depends on your UNIX environment but can be controlled with the sh setting (see the "Changing vi Settings" section). You use this command when you want to temporarily leave vi to enter the shell and then return to the vi session at the point where you left off. You would usually enter the shell to run one or more shell commands, staying within the shell between each command. Any output to the terminal from the command you type is displayed normally, and the display of the vi session scrolls upward.

To return to your vi session, press ^D (or use the proper convention for the shell that you are using). You are then returned to vi, with the screen still showing the output of your shell session. In addition, at the bottom of the screen, the text "Press return to continue" is displayed. After pressing Return, the screen is cleared and redrawn. You are then at the exact point in your editing session where you left off.

:!—Shell

In some versions of vi, this command is the same as the :sh command. Other versions give an error message prompting you to use the :sh form.

:!*shellcommand*—Shell Command

This command executes the *shellcommand* and returns to vi. Note that in the shell command, the ex special symbols for files (introduced in the section "Editing Multiple Files") are expanded. These are % for the current file, and # for the alternate file. If you want to prevent these from being expanded, you must escape them with a \ (backslash). The role of the escape character is explained in detail next, under "Repeat Shell Command."

:!!—Repeat Shell Command

This command repeats the last :!*shellcommand*. Note that any unescaped ! that follows the :! command is expanded to the last shell command issued via :!. For example, if you enter the following sequence, you get a result similar to what follows (the text in *italics* are my comments):

```
:!ls                                  to display your directory
     art1 art2 !test1 lsefair         contents of the directory
                                       (perhaps)

[Press return to continue]
:!ls -l !*                            attempt display of long listing
                                       for all files starting with !
    -rw-rw-rw-  1 jas      system     2886 Nov  3 10:07 lsefair
[Press return to continue]            not what you wanted!
```

When you entered `:!ls -1 !*`, the final exclamation point was expanded to the last command issued. Because the last command issued was `ls`, the actual command passed to the shell was `ls -1 ls*`, where the `!` was replaced with `ls`. To prevent expansion of the `!`, you must escape it by preceding it with a `\` (backslash). The correct way to enter the command is `:!ls -1 \!*`.

`:address!shellcommand`—Filtering text through a shell command (`ex`)

This command works with `ex` line addressing to select some text to send to a shell command. The output of the command then replaces the selected lines. You could use this command, for example, to sort a section of your text. The following example shows how to sort lines 100 to 108:

`:100,108!sort`

Note that if the shell command does not take any standard input, then the selected lines are just replaced.

`!object shellcommand`—Filtering text through a shell command (`vi`)

You can also select `vi` objects to filter, using certain of the keystrokes that are used to select objects. This technique does not work on anything less than a whole line, so you must either use keystrokes that cover more than a line, or use a count prefix to extend the object selected. The following example shows how to uppercase the next paragraph using the `tr` filter:

`!}tr '[a-z]' '[A-Z]'`

When you use this technique, note that `vi` responds in a special way. First, when you type the initial exclamation point, nothing is displayed on the screen. After the keystrokes are typed to select an object, an exclamation point appears on the command line, but the keystrokes for the selected object do not. At this point, you can type the shell command, as shown previously. In addition, certain special features are available. If you type another exclamation point, it is expanded to the text of any previous shell command. So for example, if you wanted to continue to move around in your file and uppercase various text objects after typing the string in the previous example, you could just type `!object!` each time after positioning to the chosen spot.

`count!!shellcommand`—Filtering text through a shell command

`!count!shellcommand`

These two commands are equivalent. They are variations on the preceding `vi` text filtering command. They apply to `count` number of lines relative to the line the cursor is on. The `count` is optional; if absent, the current line is processed.

> ## TIP
>
> You can test a script that you've just written and saved (assuming that the file already has execute permissions) by using the following command:
>
> ```
>     :!%
> ```
>
> `vi` substitutes the current filename for the percent sign (%).

Marking Your Position

It is often necessary when editing larger files to move back and forth between specific points. Many editors implement the concept of a *bookmark*, which is a mechanism for marking a place in your buffer and then allowing an easy way to return to that exact place. In `vi`, this concept is implemented in several ways.

mx—Mark

This command marks the position that the cursor is presently at with the letter *x*, where *x* is any letter. The mark is not visible on the screen.

`x (back quote)—Move to mark *x*

The `x (back quote) command moves the cursor to the exact position marked by the letter *x*.

'x (apostrophe)—Move to beginning of line of mark *x*

The 'x (apostrophe) command moves the cursor to the beginning of the line marked by the letter *x*.

`` (two back quotes)—Move to previous location

This command moves to the exact position before the previous repositioning of the cursor via pattern search, `G` command, or move to a mark.

'' (two apostrophes)—Move to beginning of line of previous location

Moves to the beginning of the line of the cursor position before the previous repositioning of the cursor via pattern search, `G` command, or move to a mark. You can also use marks with addresses such as:

```
:'a,+20w foo
```

For the Power User: Customizing `vi`

If you have stuck with this chapter this far, you are probably looking for the "Power User" features. Here they are!

Automation of Common Chores

As you become more familiar with an editor, you may find yourself seeking to automate certain keystroke sequences that seem to be occurring over and over. There are two ways to do this in `vi`: abbreviations and key mappings. Both of these methods are described in the following sections.

Abbreviations

`vi` has the built-in capability of using abbreviations that you set up. For example, suppose that you are often found typing the phrase "SAMS Publishing, an imprint of Macmillan Computer Publishing USA." You could abbreviate this phrase for example as SAMS, with the following command:

`:ab SAMS SAMS Publishing, an imprint of Macmillan Computer Publishing USA`

`vi` expands the abbreviation while you are in insert mode into the full text after you have typed the abbreviation plus either a space or a punctuation character. Note that the abbreviation is case-sensitive, so you can retain the capability to omit the expansion by a judicious choice of upper- and lowercase characters in the abbreviation.

To see all the abbreviations currently in effect, just enter `:ab` with no arguments (that is, by itself). To eliminate an abbreviation (perhaps so that you can include the literal characters of the abbreviation itself), use the `:unab` command.

> **TIP**
>
> Although the abbreviation feature is used primarily to save retyping common strings, another useful technique can be used with the feature: correcting common mistakes. Just set up as an abbreviation the mistyped word.
>
> For example, because I am in the habit of typing "wrok" when I mean "work," and "flies" when I mean "files." I could set both of these as abbreviations and see `vi` automatically change my mistake into the correct word.
>
> However, do not overdo this—as you can see, if I used "flies" as an abbreviation for "files," then I lose the ability to use the word "flies."

Creating Macros with the `:map` Command

The `:map` command is used in a similar way as an abbreviation. The `:map` command allows you to assign command mode keystroke sequences to a single (or multiple) keystroke sequence. Such commands are often called keyboard macros. Often `:map` commands are used to assign keystrokes available on your keyboard (such as the cursor control arrow keys) to the desired `vi` commands (h, j, k, and l).

A `:map` command is entered just like an abbreviation. For example, to map the command sequence `dwelp` (which reverses the order of two adjacent words) to the letter "v," enter this command:

```
:map v dwelp
```

To use a control character in the mapping, you must precede the entry of that control character with a `^V`. Otherwise, `vi` immediately tries to interpret the control character you are typing. The `^V` tells `vi`, in effect, "do not interpret the next character, just enter it into text." When you type the `^V`, only the ^ (caret) shows. For example, when you want to insert an Esc character into the mapping, you would type `^V` followed by the Esc key. Suppose that you wanted to map the "v" key to the Esc key. What you would see on the screen after typing the `^V` would be the following:

```
:map v ^
```

Then when you pressed the Esc key, your screen would look like this:

```
:map v ^[
```

After pressing Return, your mapping would be in effect.

To remap certain keys that might be on your keyboard to the equivalent function in `vi`, you may not even need to know what character sequence is assigned to your keyboard. Just use the `^V` key; then type the key that you want to assign. This might not work, depending on the terminal mapping in effect at your terminal. See your system administrator for help if you are having trouble setting up your keyboard mappings.

It is useful to see what keys are not already used by `vi` and are, therefore, available for mappings without losing any functions (there are, in fact, a few keys left unused). They are as follows: g, K, q, V, v, ^A, ^K, ^O, ^T, ^W, ^X, _, *, \, =.

> **NOTE**
>
> The = key is not available if the lisp setting is in effect.

To remove the mapping, use the :unmap command. To see all mappings currently in effect, use the :map command with no arguments.

Other creative uses for the map command are shown in Table 7.19, which shows several examples of both the :ab and :map commands.

TABLE 7.19. SOME EXAMPLES OF THE AB AND MAP COMMANDS.

Command	Result
:ab L1 Level One	Sets L1 to expand to "Level One"
:ab	Displays all abbreviations
:unab L1	Removes the expansion of L1
:map v dwelp	Reverses two adjacent words (not at the end of a line)
:map ^A i"^[ea"^[	Surrounds a word with quote characters

Changing vi Settings

Until this section, I have been describing the default behavior of vi under various circumstances. You can modify these default behaviors by changing the vi settings. The easiest way to understand these settings is with an example. One such default behavior is what vi does while you are inserting text, and you get to the end of the line. The default behavior is to continue adding text to the line; however, the display gives the appearance of wrapping to the next line. You can confirm this by using the 0 and $ commands from command mode to see where vi considers lines to begin and end. You can alter this default behavior to suit your requirements.

> **TIP**
>
> In addition to using the 0 and $ commands to see where lines begin and end, you can also use line numbering with :set nu to see how vi is assigning line numbers. Another technique that might help is using :set list, which shows tabs and line ends with ^I and $, respectively.

If you are typing the text of a memo for example, you might want vi to automatically wrap lines. By using the setting wrapmargin, (abbreviated as wm), you can cause vi to insert a line feed automatically when you get close to the end of the line (the behavior of the wm setting is described later). If, on the other hand, you are editing a source code file, most likely you would want there to be no such wrapping, so the default behavior is what you want.

The `vi` settings can be modified in four ways, as shown in Table 7.20.

TABLE 7.20. WAYS TO MODIFY DEFAULT `vi` CHARACTERISTICS.

Command	*Result*
`set commands`	Executed during a `vi` session to temporarily change the characteristic, until they are explicitly changed again or the `vi` session ends.
`.exrc` *file*	Changes included in the `.exrc` file go into effect whenever the editor is started, until overridden during the session by a set command.
`EXINIT`	An environment variable that can be used just like the `.exrc` file. (If the same setting is changed by both an entry in an `.exrc` file and the `EXINIT` environment variable, the setting from the `.exrc` file takes precedence.)

The methods are listed in precedence order, from highest to lowest. This means that any of the commands overrides the effect of the same command of a type shown lower in the table. For example, a set command overrides the same command from the `.exrc` file, which in turn overrides the effect of the same command from the `EXINIT` environment variable).

There are two types of `vi` settings. The first is a toggle setting, which may be either on or off. To put the setting into effect, you would use the command `:set` *option*, where *option* is the desired setting to put into effect. To remove the setting from effect, you use the command `:set` *nooption*, where *nooption* is the same name as you would use to put it into effect with the characters "no" preceding the name.

The other type of setting is a numeric setting, which has a numeric value. For example, the `wrapmargin` setting may have a value of 10. To use a numeric setting, you would use the command `:set` *option*=x, where *option* is the name of the setting, and *x* is the numeric value. For example, use `:set wrapmargin=10` to set the `wrapmargin` setting to a value of 10.

Many of the settings have abbreviations. For example, you have already been introduced to the `wrapmargin` abbreviation of `wm`.

The `.exrc` file is a plain text file located in the user's home directory. It consists of `set`, `ab`, and `map` commands, entered one per line. (The ab and map commands were described in the "Automation Of Common Chores" section.) If such a file exists, `vi` reads it immediately after starting and the commands it contains will be placed into effect just as if you had typed them from the ex command line before starting to edit. The following shows an example of an .exrc file:

```
set wrapmargin=10 nowrapscan
ab SAM SAMS Publishing
```

With the preceding example as your .exrc file, the wrapmargin is set to 10, wrapscan is turned off, and an abbreviation is created every time you start vi. In addition to reading the .exrc file in your home directory, vi tries to read an .exrc file in the current directory you are in when you start vi. If such a file is found, the entries there are added to the ones put into effect from the .exrc file in your home directory. This feature allows you to have your preferred settings for all vi sessions, plus special tailoring for separate projects.

> **NOTE**
>
> In System V UNIX, the feature to look for an .exrc file in the current directory is only enabled if the exrc setting is enabled (it is off by default). This setting is a security feature. An attack on the security of a system could be made by planting an .exrc file in a directory that causes some unintended and undesirable action.

You can see what settings you have placed in effect by entering :set without any options. By entering :set all, the value of all settings is displayed.

Table 7.21 shows the most useful vi settings. A number of additional settings are not shown, falling into two categories: (1) settings rarely used that should be considered obsolete (for example, several settings are intended for slow line speeds such as 300 baud and under); and (2) settings that are particular to specific vi implementations.

The first column shows the name of the setting. The second column shows the minimum abbreviation for the setting as well as for deactivation of the setting. If there is a default value for a setting, it is shown in the third column, using abbreviations wherever they exist. The fourth column contains the description of the setting.

TABLE 7.21. THE MOST USEFUL vi SETTINGS.

Setting	Abbreviation	Default	Description
autoindent	ai	noai	Inserted new lines of text are indented to the same distance as the preceding line.

continues

TABLE 7.21. CONTINUED.

Setting	Abbreviation	Default	Description
noai			
autowrite	aw	noaw	Automatically saves a changed file before opening the next file with :n or using a shell command with :!.
noaw			
directory	dir	/tmp	Directory in which buffer files are stored.
edcompatible		noedcompatible	When substituting act like the ed editor
errorbells	eb	eb	Sound the bell
noeb			(usually called a "beep") when an error occurs.
exrc	ex	noex	Allows an .exrc file in the current directory to override the .exrc file in the user's home directory.
*noex			
lisp		nolisp	Helps formatting for editing lisp source code files.
			Changes the behavior of indenting; the following commands are modified: ( ),{},[[,]].
list		nolist	Displays on the screen special characters: tabs show as ^I; ends of lines are marked with a $.
magic		magic	The .,*, and [ ] characters act as wildcards in pattern searches.
mesg		mesg	System messages are allowed when vi is running.
number	nu	nonu	Display line numbers. These numbers are not saved in the file when the buffer is written to disk.

Setting	Abbreviation	Default	Description
nonu			
paragraph	para	IPLPPPQP LIpplpipbp	Defines paragraph moves using nroff macros, for use with { and } commands
readonly	ro	noro	Buffer may not be written to a file unless ! override is used.
noro			
redraw	re	nore	After each edit, the screen is redrawn. By turning this option off, performance can be improved when you have a slow line speed.
nore			When text is inserted with nore, the new characters appear to overwrite existing characters until the Esc key is pressed. When lines are deleted with nore, the space taken by the lines is not closed up; instead an @ character is displayed on the line. The main reason to be aware of this setting is to be able to disable it if your terminal has it enabled.
remap		remap	Map commands may be nested.
report		5	When an edit affects more lines than this setting, a message is displayed.
scroll		half-window	Number of screen lines to scroll.
sections	sect	SHNHH HUnhsh	Defines section moves using nroff macros, for use with [[and]].
shell	sh	/bin/sh	Defines the shell to use for shell commands. Different UNIX variants may provide a different default.

continues

7

TEXT EDITING WITH vi AND Emacs

TABLE 7.21. CONTINUED.

Setting	Abbreviation	Default	Description
shiftwidth	sw	8	Number of spaces to use for ^D back tabs.
showmatch	sm	nosm	When a) or } is typed, the cursor is briefly positioned to the matching character. Helps while programming in C or lisp.
nosm			
showmode		noshowmode	Indicates type of Insert mode. Only available in certain UNIX variants.
tabstop	ts	8	The number of spaces the tab character moves over.
taglength	tl	0	The number of characters that are significant in tags.
tags		/usr/lib/tags	The default tags file path.
term			Defines the terminal in use.
terse		noterse	Shorter error messages are displayed.
timeout	to	to	When to is in effect during the typing of a multikey sequence that is mapped (for example, :map xxx d} to delete the next paragraph), vi waits one second to get the next keystroke. If longer than one second occurs, vi does not consider the mapped sequence to have been typed. For example, three x characters must be typed with less than a one-second interval between them for vi to consider the mapped sequence to have occurred.
noto			When noto is in effect, vi waits indefinitely between keystrokes before making the determination.
warn		warn	Gives a warning message when a shell command is issued but the buffer has been changed.

Setting	Abbreviation	Default	Description
wrapscan	ws	ws	Searches reaching an end of the buffer wrap around to the other end.
nows			
wrapmargin	wm	0	When set to a number other than zero, carriage returns are inserted automatically when the cursor gets to within that number of spaces from the right edge of the screen. Very useful for normal text editing (not for source code).
writeany	wa	nowa	Allows writing to any file without using the ! override.
nowa			

(Note: This setting is only available in System V; in other UNIX variants, the setting does not exist, but the override is allowed; that is, the behavior is as though the **exrc setting was in effect.)*

Other Advanced Editing Techniques

Although we have definitely scratched the surface of the power of vi, more is available. The capabilities mentioned briefly in this section are here to let you know they exist. You will only be able to get maximum benefit from them by using them yourself.

@ Functions

An @ function executes the content of a named buffer as a vi command. So another way to build a macro command is to type the text of a command that you want to use repeatedly, escaping each control character with a ^V and then deleting that text into a named buffer. You may then execute the command in that buffer using the @*x* command, where *x* is the named buffer.

Using autoindent

The autoindent commands and settings are indispensable when editing source code files. When the autoindent setting is enabled, each new line is indented to the same distance as the previous line, which makes for easy structuring of source code. There are several commands you can use in conjunction with autoindent.

^D—Backtab (with autoindent)

This backs up to the previous autoindent stop, as specified by the shiftwidth setting. To use this most effectively, you should coordinate the shiftwidth setting with the tabstop setting.

^^D—End Autoindent, One Line Only

This command is the caret character, followed by a Ctrl+D. It causes autoindent to be suspended for the current line only. The cursor moves back to the left margin. On the next line, the autoindent resumes at the previous position.

0^D—Cursor to left margin

This command moves the cursor back to the left margin.

Using Tags

:ta *tag*—Jump to Tag

The :ta command is of interest only to C programmers. This command allows you to easily work with a number of C source code files. It removes the need for you to keep track of which C function is contained in which source code file.

Before you can use this command, you must first use the ctags program to create a database of source code filenames and function names. Refer to the documentation of the ctags program (you can use the man ctags command).

If the tags file has been created with the ctags program, the command :ta *tag* jumps to the file containing the tag function and positions the cursor to that function. The tags file is first searched for in the location given by the tags setting and then in the current directory.

What Is Emacs?

Emacs is one of the most powerful text editing environments available today. It is a mature tool, having evolved over more than 20 years; it is still evolving today. Emacs has a reputation for being formidable and difficult to learn. Although it is true that Emacs is a large program (and that some say that it has more features than can be possibly be assimilated fully by any one individual), that does not mean that it actually is difficult to learn or use. In fact, after having used it, you probably will wonder why such a fuss is made.

Comparison to vi

Because Emacs and vi are both text editors, they share many of the general characteristics of text editors. For example, the concept of buffers pertains to both programs, although Emacs has a more fully developed implementation of the concept. Therefore, general advice such as "save your work often" applies equally to both editors.

Like vi, Emacs is a full-screen editor. However, Emacs does not have a separate mode for entering commands and inserting text. (Emacs does have its own version of modes; see "The Big Picture" section.) You are always able to enter text and commands without the annoyance of having to switch modes. This feature alone first convinced me to give Emacs a try. The way Emacs handles commands is to make all commands either shifted keys or escape sequences. The way this works is described in detail in the "Basic Editing with Emacs: Getting Started" section.

One key advantage of Emacs is integration. Emacs goes beyond providing text editing capabilities—it actually has so many built-in tools and utilities that you may not need to acquire or learn several other tool suites to do all of your work, as you would in other computing environments. The real payoff of this high degree of integration is the great convenience and time savings that you get. If Emacs is available to you, it is well worth your effort to check it out.

Emacs is also *extensible*. This means that you are not limited to the built-in capabilities provided with the editor, as you are with vi. If you are familiar with the *lisp* programming language, you can even add your own commands to Emacs.

How To Get Emacs

A major difference between vi and Emacs is that whereas vi is provided with nearly every UNIX implementation, Emacs must be obtained and installed separately. For this reason alone, many have missed out on the opportunity to sample its power and convenience. However, if you do not have access to Emacs at present, that is no great hurdle because it is readily available over the Internet at no out-of-pocket cost, most notably in the GNU Emacs version, which is a product of the Free Software Foundation. Or you can just load GNU Emacs version 20.3, which is provided with this book on the included CD-ROM.

If you are obtaining the Emacs files electronically, be prepared for a 10 megabyte file transfer; then be prepared to sacrifice more than 100 megabytes of your hard disk space.

Why Would I Be Interested in Using Emacs?

As already mentioned, Emacs can be a comprehensive work environment. If you like powerful, integrated tools, you might find learning Emacs to be one of the better investments of your time.

Starting Up and Exiting the Program

Starting Emacs is just like starting vi. Enter the name of the program (which may vary, depending on the version you have), optionally followed by one or more filenames. If you omit the filename, Emacs creates a new file for you. Emacs starts up with some general information about the help system. As soon as you begin to type, this information is cleared, and everything you type is displayed on your screen. After typing some text, your screen looks like the following:

```
If wise, a commander is able to recognize changing circumstances and to
act expediently. If sincere, his men will have no doubt of the certainty of
rewards and punishments. If humane, he loves mankind, sympathizes with others,
and appreciates their industry and toil.  If courageous, he gains victory by
seizing opportunity without hesitation.  If strict, his troops are disciplined
because they are in awe of him and are afraid of punishment.
     Shen Pao-hsu ... said: 'If a general is not courageous he will be unable
to conquer doubts or to create great plans.'
```

```
-----Emacs: art1            (Text)--All-------------------------------------
Wrote /home/jas/art1
```

If you have entered a filename on the command line, the file is opened and loaded into the editor. To exit from Emacs, use the sequence C-x C-c.

Basic Editing with Emacs: Getting Started

When learning an editor, it is only necessary to learn some of the basic features before you can be productive with the tool. As when learning vi, the learning process is more a matter of training your fingers and reflexes than it is of memorization. Also as in vi, there are certain patterns to the structure of the commands that become comfortable after you gain familiarity with the program.

Control and Meta Key Sequences

All editing commands in Emacs have a name and can be executed by using that name. However, it would be tedious and inefficient to have to use a long command name every time you wanted to do something as simple as moving the cursor forward one character. So all the commonly used commands are "bound" to more easily used keystroke sequences. Thus, the term *binding* is used in Emacs to refer to the association of specific keystroke sequences to editing commands.

To distinguish commands from text that is to be inserted, Emacs uses shift-key sequences. A shift-key sequence is entered by holding down the designated shift key while pressing another key. The shift keys used by Emacs are the Ctrl key and the Meta key. In Emacs literature and in the Emacs online help system, these keys are abbreviated as C-*x* and M-*x*, where x is any other key name.

On most terminals, the Meta key is not present. To get the effect of the Meta key on terminals where it is not provided, you have to instead first press the Esc key as a separate keystroke, followed by the second key.

> **TIP**
>
> On some terminals, the Alt key takes the function of the Meta key, operating as a shift key. If you have an Alt key, be sure to try it to see whether works because it is a lot more convenient to be able to press and hold down the Alt key during the pressing of the other keys, especially during multiple shift-key sequences, than it is to have to press Esc before every keystroke.
>
> This is not typically the case with terminal emulators running on PCs. If you are running Emacs on your PC, the Alt key *might* work.

There is a general pattern to the way that Emacs binds keystrokes to functions. The shifted and Esc key sequences fall into five forms. First, the most common commands are entered as C-*, where * is any key. Second, the next most common commands are entered as ESC * (the Esc key followed by any key; because most terminals do not have the Meta key, from this point on, I will indicate an M-* sequence using the Esc key notation).

Next, commands that are somewhat frequently used are entered as C-x *, where C-x is the Control-*X* sequence, and * is any other command, including shifted-key sequences. Then there are the least frequently used commands or commands used in specialized modes that are entered as C-c *, where C-c is the Control-C sequence and * is once again any other command.

> **NOTE**
>
> Where Emacs commands are shown in this chapter as C-x * or ESC *, the space preceding the * is only present for clarity. You should not type any spaces before the *. When Emacs echoes the command in the mini-buffer, it also puts in the space, even though you have not typed one.

Finally, there is a set of commands that do not have a key binding at all—you must use the long command name. Such commands are entered by the following sequence: ESC x *commandname*, where *x* is the literal "x" character, and *commandname* is the long command name (actually any command may be entered in this format—it's just easier to use the key bindings after your fingers learn them). Entering the long *commandname* is not as bad as it sounds: Emacs has a completion feature (type a few characters of the name and press Tab; Emacs either completes the command name or gives you a menu of choices, which is described further in the "Completion" section) that makes this quite simple.

These command forms are summarized in Table 7.22.

TABLE 7.22. COMMAND FORMS IN EMACS.

Form	*Description*
C-*	Most commonly used commands
ESC *	Next most commonly used commands
C-x * file-related commands)	Somewhat frequently used commands (such as
C-c *	Infrequent or specialized commands
ESC x *commandname*	Any command may be entered in this form; mandatory for those that do not have key bindings

The most important key bindings are shown in this chapter in tables. In these tables, there are certain key name abbreviations, as shown in Table 7.23.

TABLE 7.23. KEY NAME ABBREVIATIONS USED IN THIS CHAPTER.

Abbreviation	Key
C-x	Control-X
ESC x	Escape X or Meta-X
RETURN	Return or Enter key
DEL	Delete or Del key
INS	Insert or Ins key
SPACE	Spacebar
SHIFT	Shift key
TAB	Tab key

In addition to the defined commands that are built in to Emacs, you may also create your own command bindings.

> **NOTE**
>
> Another word used in Emacs documentation is the term *point*, which you can often think of as synonymous with *cursor*. In fact, there is a slight technical difference between the two terms. The cursor is the highlighted character position on your screen where the next text insertion or editing action takes place. The point is the position in the buffer that is analogous to the cursor, but is actually between the character positions.
>
> So, for example, when you see the cursor on your screen on top of the letter "h" in the word "the," the point is actually between the "t" and the "h." Sometimes thinking about the point as between two characters helps to understand the editing action that Emacs takes.

The Big Picture

Before getting into the details of working with Emacs commands, there are several general attributes of Emacs with which you should be familiar. Emacs is X Window compatible. If you are running a version of X, Emacs runs in an X client window. When running in this way, the usual features of X are available to control the size and placement of the window, as well as window and mouse controls to move around in the text. (Emacs has numerous special functions available only when running under X Window, but they are not covered here.)

The Emacs Screen

Beginning with version 19.30 of Emacs, even the text-based version (non-X-Window) has menus, as can be seen at the top of the following example.

```
Buffers Files Tools Edit Search Help
     If wise, a commander is able to recognize changing circumstances and to
act expediently.  If sincere, his men will have no doubt of the certainty of
rewards and punishments. If humane, he loves mankind, sympathizes with others,
and appreciates their industry and toil.  If courageous, he gains victory by
seizing opportunity without hesitation.  If strict, his troops are disciplined
because they are in awe of him and are afraid of punishment.
     Shen Pao-hsu ... said: 'If a general is not courageous he will be unable
to conquer doubts or to create great plans.'
```

```
-----Emacs: art1            (Text)--All----------------------------------------
```

You will notice several key features about this screen. First, at the top of the screen (if you are running Emacs version 19.30 or later) there is a set of menu choices (that is, Buffers, Files, Tools, Edit, Search, Help). All the Emacs commands are available from the pull-down menu as well as from the traditional keyboard bindings. In addition, some features are only available from the menus. These are pointed out in the appropriate contexts.

On the second line from the bottom is a status line, which contains the following information: "Emacs," the filename, the current major mode (described later) in parentheses, file size, and relative position in the file.

The last line of the screen is blank. This line is called the mini-buffer.

Modes

As already mentioned, Emacs does not have a separate command mode and insert mode as does vi. However, Emacs makes a great use of modes to simplify your work. A major mode is simply a set of editing characteristics and commands that are appropriate for a particular type of work. There are modes for common tasks. For example, text mode is used for creating letters, memos, and documents. It has characteristics that help in that task, namely recognizing text elements such as sentences and paragraphs. There are modes for creating source code files for popular languages. For example, C++ mode is used for editing C++ source code; it has characteristics specific to that task, namely assisting with indenting for C++. There are even modes for emulating other text editors and word processors, such as vi and Wordstar.

Each buffer is in exactly one mode at all times. Table 7.24 lists the most important major modes.

TABLE 7.24. EMACS MAJOR MODES.

Major mode	Description
Fundamental	Most basic mode; standard Emacs defaults only.
Text	For writing general text.
Indented text	Provides additional support for automatically indenting text.
Outline	Allows selective hiding and display of levels of text.
Picture	Allows drawing simple pictures from characters; repeats characters in a straight line in one of eight selected "compass directions."
Dired	Provides file manager like functions for copying, deleting, and renaming files, and many more.
View	Provides read-only file access; for use with dired mode.
Shell	Allows executing a UNIX shell within an Emacs buffer; you can edit the command line with all Emacs capabilities.
Mail	Assists with formatting and sending email over the Internet.
RMAIL	For reading and managing email you receive.
Telnet	For using telnet from within Emacs to log in to another system.
Ange-ftp	Extends Emacs find-file command to work with ftp to find files over the Internet.

continues

TABLE 7.24. CONTINUED.

Major mode	Description
FORTRAN	Assists with editing and formatting FORTRAN source code.
C	Assists with editing and formatting C source code.
C++	Assists with editing and formatting C++ source code.
LISP	Assists with editing and formatting LISP source code.

Minor modes can be toggled on or off individually. They act independently of one another. The simplest example of a minor mode may be overwrite mode, which is used to overwrite existing text. (Normally Emacs inserts new text into the buffer.) Overwrite mode is toggled into by pressing the Ins key, or by using the ESC x overwrite-mode RETURN sequence. Because this mode is a toggle, it is deactivated by entering the command a second time.

Table 7.25 describes the most important minor modes.

TABLE 7.25. THE MOST IMPORTANT EMACS MINOR MODES.

Minor mode	Description
Abbrev	Enables the word abbreviation feature (similar to vi abbreviations)
Auto-fill	Enables word wrap (similar to vi wrapmargin setting)
Auto-save	Enables automatic timed saving of your work
Line number	Displays line numbers (similar to vi number setting)
Overwrite	Entered text types over existing text, rather than being inserted
VC	Provides an interface to several version control systems

Completion

Emacs implements a feature known as completion. This very helpful feature can save a lot of time, so you are strongly encouraged to experiment with it. Completion is used when you are required to enter a string of text in the mini-buffer, either to give a long command name, or to enter a filename. In either case, after a portion of the string is entered, you can press the TAB key, and Emacs automatically completes the entry of the full name. (So the long commands are not so burdensome after all!) Or the rest of the file name is provided.

When Emacs cannot fully resolve the command or filename, a menu of choices is provided from which you may select your choice.

Emacs Is an Environment

The attractiveness of Emacs is largely from the degree of integration that it offers. Emacs includes within it numerous features and functions that are often provided in separate programs. By having all these programs integrated into one, you may develop a working style that offers greater convenience and simplicity than having to use a lot of tools separately.

Emacs has so many built-in features and extensions, that it is impossible to cover them all within the scope of this chapter. Therefore, the coverage from this point forward is intended to give you an overview of the many features, and to convince you of the power of the program.

Moving Around and Simple Editing

One of the most user-friendly features of Emacs is that is has a built-in help system, which includes a tutorial. The tutorial is geared for the complete novice and is nicely done. So rather than present complete keystroke-by-keystroke details as to the basic tasks of editing in Emacs, the best service I can give you here is to point you towards this tutorial. The tutorial is entered by typing the command sequence C-h t. Other elements of the Emacs help system are covered later.

The Most Important Navigation Keys

Even in simple moving around there are differences between the way Emacs looks at the world and the way vi does. Movement forward and backward by characters in vi is restricted to a single line. When you get to the end of the line and try to go farther, all you get is a beep. Emacs is a little more friendly here. When you attempt to go off the end of a line, Emacs obligingly moves the cursor to the beginning of the next line. When you attempt to go off the beginning of a line, the cursor is likewise positioned at the end of the previous line.

The most important navigation commands are in Tables 7.26 and 7.27. In these tables, the commands are separated into two subcategories to help you get familiar with the way commands are structured. So-called "physically oriented" commands in Table 7.26 are oriented towards physical elements of the text: characters, lines, screens, pages, and buffers. So-called "lexically oriented" commands in Table 7.27 are oriented toward lexical (or language-related) elements of the text: words, sentences, paragraphs. (If this distinction escapes you, no big deal—just ignore it!)

TABLE 7.26. PHYSICALLY ORIENTED MOVEMENTS.

Binding	Function name	Move
C-f	forward-char	One character forward
C-b	backward-char	One character backward
C-n	next-line	Next line
C-p	previous-line	Previous line
C-a	beginning-of-line	Beginning of line
C-e	end-of-line	End of line
C-v	scroll-up	Next screen
ESC v	scroll-down	Previous screen
C-x]	forward-page	One page forward
C-x[	backward-page	One page backward
ESC >	end-of-buffer	End of buffer
ESC <	beginning-of-buffer	Beginning of buffer

TABLE 7.27. LEXICALLY ORIENTED MOVEMENTS.

Binding	Function name	Move
ESC f	forward-word	One word forward
ESC b	backward-word	One word backward
ESC a	forward-sentence	Beginning of sentence
ESC e	backward-sentence	End of sentence
ESC }	forward-paragraph	One paragraph forward
ESC {	backward-paragraph	One paragraph backward

The Most Important Editing Procedures

The most important editing procedures involve working with files and with the procedures for deleting text, cutting and pasting text, and undoing edits.

Working with Files

Before you can do much editing, you need to know the commands that Emacs uses to manipulate files. Table 15.28 shows the most important commands for working with files.

TABLE 7.28. EMACS FILE COMMANDS.

Binding	Function name	Description
C-x C-f	find-file	Opens and loads a file
C-x C-v	find-alternate-file	Looks for a different file
C-x i	insert-file	Inserts a file into the buffer
C-x C-s	save-file	Writes (saves) buffer to original file (see following Caution)
C-x C-w	write-file	Writes (saves) buffer as file (defaults to original file)

CAUTION

You might have trouble using the C-x C-s command if your terminal communications environment is using XON/XOFF flow control. In such a case, the C-s key (also known as "XOFF") is interpreted by the communications software to mean "stop sending characters." If you press this key, your terminal appears to freeze up. The corresponding keystroke needed to re-enable communications to your terminal is the C-q key (also known as "XON"), which in Emacs is normally the quoted-insert function (which allows the following keystroke typed to be inserted into the text rather than interpreted as a command).

Because of this common situation, Emacs also provides the flow-control command, which is executed as ESC x flow control, which when invoked, causes the functions normally bound to C-s and C-q to be replaced with C-\ and C-^. That is, when flowcontrol is in effect, the command for saving a file is C-x C-\; the command for quoted-insert is C-^.

Deleting Text

There are several simple delete commands. The DEL key deletes the character to the left of the point. C-d deletes the character the cursor is on (that is, to the right of the point). ESC d deletes the next word.

> **CAUTION**
>
> The action of the DEL key is similar to the action of the backspace key in many word processing programs. However, the backspace key is usually bound to the character used to invoke the Emacs help system. If you press the backspace key inadvertently and your screen is split in a way you did not expect to open the help buffer, press C-g (quit) to get back.

To delete the line the cursor is on, use the C-k command. This command operates in an unusual way. The first time C-k is pressed, the text on the line the cursor is on is deleted, leaving a blank line. It takes a second C-k command to delete the blank line.

To delete a particular portion of your text that is not a specific text element such as a word, sentence, or line, you can use the mark command to mark a region of text upon which to operate. The mark command C-@ (or alternatively C-SPACE) is used as follows: first position the cursor to one end of the region you want to mark. Press one of the mark commands. Then move the cursor to the other end of the region. From this point, any command that operates on a region takes effect on all the text between the mark point and the current cursor position. For example, to delete the text in the marked region, use the C-w (or alternatively, SHIFT+DEL) command.

The commands shown in Table 7.29 are used to delete text.

TABLE 7.29. DELETE COMMANDS.

Binding	Function name	Description of text deleted
DEL	delete-backward-char	The character to left of point (the one just typed)
C-d	delete-character	The character the cursor is on
C-k	kill-line	The line cursor is on
ESC d	kill-word	The next word
ESC DEL	backward-kill-word	The previous word
ESC k	kill-sentence	The next sentence
C-x DEL	backward-kill-sentence	The previous sentence
C-@	set-mark-command	Marks one end of a region
C-SPACE	set-mark-command	Marks one end of a region (same as C-@)
C-w	kill-region	Marked region
SHIFT-DEL	kill-region	Marked region (same as C-w)

Recovering Deleted Text: Cutting and Pasting

There are two ways to get back text that has been deleted: (1) yanking from the kill ring; (2) the Emacs undo function.

CAUTION

There are some terminology differences between Emacs and vi. vi calls its buffers where deletions are kept the undo buffers. Emacs calls its equivalent the kill buffers.

In Emacs, a yank is conceived in the opposite way as it is in vi. In vi, a yank copies from your text to an undo buffer; in Emacs, a yank is the reverse action of copying from the kill buffer back to the text.

Emacs keeps all killed text in internal buffers called the *kill ring*. Text that is deleted, not killed, is not saved in the kill ring. For example, single characters deleted with DEL or C-d are not saved there.

To recover recently deleted text from the kill ring, you use two commands together. First you must perform a yank with the C-y command (SHIFT-INS is a synonym). This command yanks back the most recent deletion. If this is not the deleted text you want, successive uses of the ESC y command recovers the previous deletions in order, similar to the vi sequence of the "np command followed by the repeat (.) command. The first time ESC y is used, the first previously killed text is inserted. The next ESC y replaces the yanked text with the next most recent deletion. (After you have gone back to the limit of the number of deletions saved, the most recent deletion is yanked in. That is where the term *ring* comes from. The initial default size of the kill ring is 20.) After you get used to the actions of these commands, it becomes simple to rearrange text by a series of kill commands followed by yank commands.

Table 7.30 shows the yank commands.

TABLE 7.30. YANK COMMANDS.

Binding	Function name	Description
C-y	yank	Inserts text from the start of the kill ring
ESC y	yank-pop	Replaces yanked text with previous kill

Another Method of Deleting and Pasting

As you can see from the discussion of the delete and yank commands, one of the simplest ways of moving text around in Emacs is via the menu commands for select and paste. When you use this command, a window is displayed with the first line of each of the most recent deletions. You can paste into your text any one of the displayed choices.

Undoing Edits

The Emacs undo functions are very powerful. Repeated applications of the undo function C-x u (or alternatively, C-_ or C-\, unless you have remapped this binding) will successively undo each edit you have done, eventually taking you back to the beginning of your editing session. The undo function undoes every editing change, not just deletions.

You can also redo edits that you have undone. To redo one of the edits you have undone, you have to move the cursor, and then execute another undo command. Now each time you undo, you instead are redoing edits. To switch directions again, just move the cursor again.

Other Useful Editing Functions

As you would expect, there are numerous useful commands in Emacs that go beyond the most basic editing requirements. Examples of such commands are those to undo edits, reformat text, transpose text, and modify capitalization.

The commands of this section are summarized the Table 7.31.

TABLE 7.31. OTHER USEFUL EDITING COMMANDS.

Binding	Function name	Reformat
ESC q	fill-paragraph	Paragraph, rewrapping the lines

Binding	Function name	Transpose
C-t	transpose-chars	Two adjacent characters
ESC t	transpose-words	Two adjacent words
C-x C-t	transpose-lines	Two adjacent lines

Binding	Function name	Capitalize
ESC c	capitalize-word	First letter of word
ESC u	upcase-word	Uppercase whole word
ESC l	downcase-word	Lowercase whole word

Binding	Function name	Repeating commands
ESC *x*	digit-argument	Repeats the next command *x* times, where *x* is a whole number
C-u	universal-argument	Repeats the next command four times; often used in a series (C-u C-u for 16 repetitions, C-u C-u C-u for 64 repetitions, and so on)
C-u *x*		Repeats the next command *x* times (same as ESC *x*)

Command Reference Tables

In this section, the most important editing commands are summarized. Note that the commands presented here in Tables 7.32 and 7.33 only scratch the surface of Emacs. No commands are shown that are particular to the specialized modes listed in Tables 7.24 and 7.25. (Some of the modes have literally dozens of their own specialized commands and operations.)

Navigation Commands

TABLE 7.32. COMMAND REFERENCE SUMMARY: NAVIGATION.

Binding	Function name	Move (Physical)
C-f	forward-char	One character forward
C-b	backward-char	One character backward
C-n	next-line	Next line
C-p	previous-line	Previous line
C-a	beginning-of-line	Beginning of line
C-e	end-of-line	End of line
C-v	scroll-up	Next screen
ESC v	scroll-down	Previous screen
C-x]	forward-page	One page forward
C-x [	backward-page	One page backward
ESC >	end-of-buffer	End of buffer
ESC <	beginning-of-buffer	Beginning of buffer

continues

TABLE 7.32. CONTINUED.

Binding	Function name	Move (Lexical)
ESC f	forward-word	One word forward
ESC b	backward-word	One word backward
ESC a	forward-sentence	Beginning of sentence
ESC e	backward-sentence	End of sentence
ESC }	forward-paragraph	One paragraph forward
ESC {	backward-paragraph	One paragraph backward

Binding	Name	Description
C-x C-f	find-file	Open a file and load
C-x C-v	find-alternate-file	Look for a different file
C-x i	insert-file	Insert a file into the buffer
C-x C-s	save-file	Write (save) buffer to original file (see following Caution)
C-x C-w	write-file	Write (save) buffer as file (defaults to original file)

Editing Commands

TABLE 7.33. COMMAND REFERENCE SUMMARY: EDITING.

Binding	Function Name	Delete
DEL	delete-backward-char	Character to left of point (the one just typed
C-d	delete-character	The character the cursor is on
C-k	kill-line	The line cursor is on
ESC d	kill-word	The next word
ESC DEL	backward-kill-word	The previous word
ESC k	kill-sentence	The next sentence
C-x DEL	backward-kill-sentence	Previous sentence
C-@	set-mark-command	Mark one end of a region
C-SPACE	set-mark-command	Mark one end of a region (same as C-@)
C-w	kill-region	Marked region
SHIFT-DEL	kill-region	Marked region (same as C-w)

Binding	Function name	Description
C-y	yank	Insert text from the start of the kill ring
ESC y	yank-pop	Replace yanked text with previous kill

Binding	Function name	Reformat
ESC q	fill-paragraph	Paragraph, rewrapping the lines

Binding	Function name	Transpose
C-t	transpose-chars	Two adjacent characters
ESC t	transpose-words	Two adjacent words
C-x C-t	transpose-lines	Two adjacent lines

Binding	Function name	Capitalize
ESC c	capitalize-word	First letter of word
ESC u	upcase-word	Uppercase whole word
ESC l	downcase-word	Lowercase whole word

Advanced Editing with Emacs: Tips and Techniques

This section introduces some of the powerful things you can do with Emacs.

Search and Replace

Emacs has an abundance of different ways in which you can search for and replace text. In the following discussion of the various search types, the term *target* refers to both the text that you are looking for, as well as the matching text that Emacs has found. The term *replacement* refers to the replacement string that you want to substitute for the target. The following are the five different search methods you can use:

1. Simple search. This type of search is the easiest to understand. Emacs looks for a fixed string of characters, placing the cursor after the first matching string if one is found.

To execute a simple search, use the command C-s RETURN *target* RETURN. The search may be repeated by simply entering C-s. To search backward, use the command C-r RETURN *target* RETURN. To search backward again, just enter C-r. To use the simple search with replacement of all text found with a replacement string, use the command ESC x replace-string RETURN *target* RETURN *replacement* RETURN, where the text replace-string is literally typed as it is the name of the command.

In many cases, it is not a good idea to use the simple search and replace method for replacing text, as such an action on any substantial amount of text will invariably result in numerous replacements that are not wanted. For example, in a contract referring to the authorship of a work for hire, you might want to change all references to the author into references to the contractor. If there are other uses of the string author in the buffer, such as the word authority, you would end up with the word *contractority*, clearly not what you want.

2. Query-replace. The query-replace overcomes the some of the problems of the simple search and replace. As you might have guessed, the query search operates by asking for your permission before making each replacement. To execute a query-replace, enter the command ESC %. You are then prompted in the mini-buffer for a search string. Enter the search string and press RETURN. Next you are prompted for a replacement string. Enter the replacement string and again press RETURN. When Emacs finds a match, you are then prompted as to your desired action. You have many choices after each match has been found. Table 7.34 shows the responses you may make.

TABLE 7.34. QUERY-REPLACE RESPONSES.

Response	Meaning
y	Replace and find next
SPACE	Replace and find next (same as y)
n	Do not replace; find next
DEL	Do not replace; find next (same as n)
.	Replace and quit searching
,	Replace but show the result before continuing search (requires confirmation before continuing)
!	Replace all without further prompting
q	Quit query-replace
RETURN	Quit query-replace (same as q)

RECURSIVE EDIT

A wonderful feature that Emacs provides as part of query-replace is the capability to temporarily suspend the search and replace operation to allow you to do some editing. This feature is called a *recursive edit*. I have numerous times hankered after this feature while using various other editors.

In fact, I could almost state it as a rule, that just about every time I have to execute a search and replace in a document of any size at all, that during the query-replace type of operation, I see something near a found target string that I want to edit. So without having the recursive edit feature, I either have to try to remember to come back to the point in question later, which will then often not occur, or I have to abandon the query-replace and restart it later.

Table 7.35 shows the commands needed in conjunction with the recursive edit feature.

TABLE 7.35. RECURSIVE EDIT COMMANDS (ONLY AVAILABLE DURING QUERY-REPLACE).

Binding	Action
C-r	Begin a recursive edit
C-w	Delete the target string and begin a recursive edit
ESC C-c	End the recursive edit and resume the query-replace
C-]	End both recursive edit *and* query-replace

3. Incremental search. An incremental search is a unique feature among text editors, although it is often implemented in applications that provide some sort of list box processing or table lookup functions. An incremental search takes place on-the-fly as you type in the target string. This works as follows: after invoking an incremental search command, you start typing in the characters of the search string. You type the first letter, and Emacs searches for the first matching target to that letter. You type the next letter, and Emacs searches further for the first matching target to the two letters you have typed so far. This process continues until Emacs has either found the target you are seeking, or no such match exists.

To execute an incremental search, use the C-s command. Then start typing in the characters of the target string. If you find the target string you are seeking, press RETURN, and the search stops. You can continue searching for more matching targets without typing in the search string again, by just entering the C-s command again.

> **NOTE**
>
> Searching again for the same target is done via the C-s command whether the original search was a simple search or an incremental search. After Emacs has located the target, the repeated search action no longer depends on how the original search was performed.
>
> If the immediately prior action was a search, then C-s (or C-r for a reverse search) immediately jumps to the next target. If there were intervening commands, such as cursor positioning, the C-s (or C-r) command must be entered twice: once to start the search, and the second time to tell Emacs to use the same target as the last search.

One advantage to an incremental search is that you may find the target you are seeking without having to type the whole string. Table 7.36 lists the commands needed with an incremental search.

TABLE 7.36. COMMANDS NEEDED FOR INCREMENTAL SEARCHING.

Binding	Function name	Action
C-s	isearch-forward	Begin incremental search forward
C-r	isearch-backward	Begin incremental search backward (reverse)
DEL		Remove last character typed from search string (search backs up to previous matching target)
RETURN		Quit incremental search after finding target
C-g		Quit incremental search while it is in progress

4. Word search. A word search is another special type of search. A word search only matches a complete word or phrase, ignoring spaces, punctuation, and line breaks. You can use it to avoid the type of problem described previously that simple searching has. A word search is the only search type that can wrap around lines because it ignores line breaks. Because the other search types are confined to a single line, they often miss the target if a phrase is the target because the target might be spread over two lines. To perform a word search, enter the command C-s RETURN C-w *target* RETURN, where *target* is a word or a phrase.

5. Regular expression searches. Regular expressions were introduced while discussing

their use in vi. You can use this powerful tool in your Emacs search and replace operations as well. Regular expressions can be used with query-replace searches and incremental searches and also in a global form to affect the whole buffer with no prompting. Table 7.37 shows the commands to execute regular expression searches.

TABLE 7.37. COMMANDS FOR REGULAR EXPRESSION SEARCH AND REPLACE.

Binding	Function name	Action
ESC C-s RETURN	re-search-forward	Search forward for a regular expression
ESC C-r RETURN	re-search-backward	Search backward for a regular expression
query-replace-regexp		Query-replace for a regular expression
ESC C-s	isearch-forward-regexp	Incremental search forward for a regular expression
ESC C-r	isearch-backward-regexp	Incremental search backward for a regular expression
(none)	replace-regexp	Search and replace using regular expressions

Using Multiple Buffers

The relationship of files and buffers, which were discussed in the introductory section of this chapter entitled "Full-screen Editors Versus Line Editors," applies to Emacs. That section used the terms *buffer*, *cursor*, *viewport*, and *window* to describe how to think about your file and the display on your screen.In Emacs, these concepts are more fully developed than in vi. Emacs has the capability to maintain several buffers in memory at the same time. You can easily switch back and forth between several buffers to edit more than one file at a time. Further, you can display several buffers at the same time on your screen, each in its own window. When you use the Emacs help function, you are in fact using this capability. The following example shows how a screen with two buffers displayed in separate windows might look:

```
          If wise, a commander is able to recognize changing circumstances and to
      act expediently.  If sincere, his men will have no doubt of the certainty of
      rewards and punishments. If humane, he loves mankind, sympathizes with others,
      and appreciates their industry and toil.  If courageous, he gains victory by
      seizing opportunity without hesitation.  If strict, his troops are disciplined
      because they are in awe of him and are afraid of punishment.
          Shen Pao-hsu ... said: 'If a general is not courageous he will be unable
      to conquer doubts or to create great plans.'




-----Emacs: art1          (Text)--All-------------------------------------
          If wise, a commander is able to recognize changing circumstances and to
      act expediently.  If sincere, his men will have no doubt of the certainty of
      rewards and punishments. If humane, he loves mankind, sympathizes with others,
      and appreciates their industry and toil.  If courageous, he gains victory by
      seizing opportunity without hesitation.  If strict, his troops are disciplined
      because they are in awe of him and are afraid of punishment.
          Shen Pao-hsu ... said: 'If a general is not courageous he will be unable
      to conquer doubts or to create great plans.'




-----Emacs: art1          (Text)--All-------------------------------------
```

This function becomes more powerful as you use it in your own way. The following are some of the most useful things you can do with multiple window displays: (1) load a secondary text not to edit but for reference purposes; (2) easily copy and paste sections of text between several files; (3) compare the text of two or more files. There are special commands in Emacs that enhance your capability to perform these tasks.

Working with Buffers

When you load a file with C-x C-f when you already have an open buffer, Emacs creates a new buffer for the file that you are loading. It does not lose the original buffer. You can change between buffers using the buffer command C-x b. This command allows you to choose by name the buffer you want to switch to. The name of the buffer is the name displayed on the status line and is usually the name of the file that you are editing. Or you can create a new buffer that is not associated with a file by using a new name. You can also use completion with the buffer command (type a few characters of the name and press TAB; Emacs either completes the buffer name or gives you a menu of choices).

Table 7.38 shows the most important commands for working with buffers.

TABLE 7.38. COMMANDS FOR WORKING WITH BUFFERS.

Binding	Function name	Action
C-x b	switch-to-buffer	Switch to the selected buffer
C-x C-b	list-buffers	Open a the buffer list window
C-x k	kill-buffer	Delete the current buffer
C-x s	save-some-buffers	Buffer by buffer prompt to save each buffer

A powerful way to work with buffers is through the buffer list. You can use the buffer list to manipulate buffers via a set of commands that are active when the buffer list is the active window. The following example shows what your screen might look like when the buffer list is displayed.

```
        If wise, a commander is able to recognize changing circumstances and to
act expediently.  If sincere, his men will have no doubt of the certainty of
rewards and punishments. If humane, he loves mankind, sympathizes with others,
and appreciates their industry and toil.  If courageous, he gains victory by
seizing opportunity without hesitation.  If strict, his troops are disciplined
because they are in awe of him and are afraid of punishment.
        Shen Pao-hsu ... said: 'If a general is not courageous he will be unable
to conquer doubts or to create great plans.'




-----Emacs: art1            (Text)--All-------------------------------------
  MR Buffer       Size  Mode         File
  -- ------       ----  ----         ----
  .   art1        576   Text         /home/jas/art1
      *scratch*   0     Fundamental
  *   *Buffer List* 180 Fundamental




--%%-Emacs: *Buffer List*    (Buffer Menu)--All-----------------------------
```

Working with Windows

When you have more than one window visible on your Emacs editing screen, there are certain properties which pertain to each window. There is only one cursor in an Emacs session; it can be in only one window at a time. The window that contains the cursor is said to be the active window. However, each buffer maintains its own point. So when you switch between different windows, the cursor appears at the point in that buffer where you were last working.

You can use both vertical and horizontal windows in `Emacs`, and combinations of both. The following example shows three windows, with one horizontal split and one vertical split, with the same sample text in each window:

```
        If wise, a commander is able to $¦       If wise, a commander is able to$
act expediently.  If sincere, his men $¦act expediently.  If sincere, his men$
rewards and punishments.  If humane, h$¦rewards and punishments.  If humane, $
and appreciates their industry and toi$¦and appreciates their industry and to$
seizing opportunity without hesitation$¦seizing opportunity without hesitatio$
because they are in awe of him and are$¦because they are in awe of him and ar$
        Shen Pao-hsu ... said: 'If a gen$¦        Shen Pao-hsu ... said: 'If a ge$
to conquer doubts or to create great p$¦to conquer doubts or to create great $
                                       ¦
                                       ¦
                                       ¦
-----Emacs: art1        (Text)--A -----Emacs: art1        (Text)--A
        If wise, a commander is able to recognize changing circumstances and to
act expediently.  If sincere, his men will have no doubt of the certainty of
rewards and punishments. If humane, he loves mankind, sympathizes with others,
and appreciates their industry and toil.  If courageous, he gains victory by
seizing opportunity without hesitation.  If strict, his troops are disciplined
because they are in awe of him and are afraid of punishment.
        Shen Pao-hsu ... said: 'If a general is not courageous he will be unable
to conquer doubts or to create great plans.'




-----Emacs: art1        (Text)--All-------------------------------------
```

Table 7.39 shows the most important commands to work with windows.

Table 7.39. Commands to work with windows.

Binding	Function name	Action
C-x 2	split-window-vertically	Splits the current window into two windows, one on the top and one on the bottom, with each taking the full width of the current window
C-x 3	split-window-vertically	Splits the current window into two windows, one on the top and one on the bottom, with each taking the full width of the current window

Binding	Function name	Action
C-x o	other-window	Switch to "next" window (clockwise)
C-x 1	delete-other-windows	Make the current window the only window
C-x 0	delete-window	Delete the current window (redraw others)
C-x >	scroll-right	Scroll the contents of the current window right
C-x <	scroll-left	Scroll the contents of the current window left
(none)	compare-windows	Compare the contents of the buffers associated with the current window and the next window (clockwise); cursor stops at the next difference

Bookmarks to Mark Your Position

Emacs provides a bookmark function that goes far beyond the text marking capabilities of vi. When you set up a bookmark, Emacs creates a file in your home directory in which to keep a permanent record of all your bookmarks. Each bookmark keeps track of the full path and name of the marked file and the marked position in that file. Thereafter, each time you start an Emacs session, this bookmark file is loaded. You can use a special set of commands to find any of the points in any of the files you have been working with. When you are working on a large project or dealing with multiple buffers, this full-featured bookmark capability can become a great time-saver.

Emacs allows you to work with your bookmark list with a similar interface as provided to work with buffers: you can display the bookmark list in a window and then issue specialized commands to directly manipulate the bookmarks. Once again, you can use the Emacs completion feature to select a bookmark (type a few characters of the name and press TAB; Emacs either completes the bookmark name or gives you a menu of choices). Table 7.40 shows the most important commands for working with bookmarks and the bookmark list.

TABLE 7.40. COMMANDS FOR WORKING WITH BOOKMARKS.

Binding	Function name	Action
C-x r m	bookmark-set	Record the current cursor position as a bookmark
C-x r b	bookmark-jump	Jump to the bookmark
C-x r l	bookmark-menu-list	Display the bookmark list (various subcommands are available)

Formatting for Various Languages

Emacs provides programmers with assistance in writing source code. There are a number of major modes for common computer languages. Some of the well-known (and obscure) languages that Emacs supports with built-in modes are Assembly, AWK, C, C++, FOR-TRAN, LISP, modula-2, Pascal, Perl, Prolog, Scheme, and SGML.

The types of features Emacs offers for each language differs. In general, Emacs "understands" the syntax of the language in a basic way. When Emacs is in text mode, it recognizes the boundaries of certain text structures such as words, sentences, and paragraphs, so that cursor movement commands can be executed and so forth. In the same way, when in one of the language modes, Emacs recognizes the basic building blocks of that language. These building blocks are such language elements as identifiers, grouping symbols, terminators, and so on. When Emacs recognizes such an element, the mode is set up to perform a suitable action, such as automatically inserting a line feed, or indenting a specified amount.

One of the main features of each language is help with setting the indent for various code blocks and sub-blocks. While in C mode, for example, there are even options for formatting according to several different styles (namely, GNU, K&R, BSD, Stroustrup, Whitesmith, and Ellemtel). Or if you are handy with the LISP language (in which Emacs is implemented), you can modify and extend these modes to implement your own personal coding style.

Emacs as an Integrated Development Environment

To assist programmers even further, Emacs provides additional support in the form of an integrated development environment. The main components of this support are an interface facility, the capability to execute a compiler in a window, the capability to manipulate the error output of the compiler to jump to the point of the error in the source file, and the capability to execute a shell in a window, for testing and general utility purposes. Several commands work in connection with each of these features.

A special feature that will be of interest to C and C++ programmers is the etags facility. This facility is similar to the tags function of vi, described in the vi section. The purpose of this facility is to use a database of source code filenames and program function names that was created by the separate etags program. As usual, the Emacs version of this feature is more powerful than the equivalent function used within vi—more commands can be used to work with the tags.

Using Emacs as an Environment

I hope by now you are convinced that Emacs provides a full array of tools that cover nearly all aspects of anything to do with text. In case you are not convinced, this section is going to cover yet additional facilities tightly integrated into Emacs. Giving a thorough enough description to actually show you how to use these tools is beyond the scope of this chapter. Hopefully, the richness of Emacs as an environment is sufficient to tempt you into trying it out for yourself.

This section introduces some of the extensions of Emacs into a wide variety of tools. This section is by no means comprehensive but merely a sampling.

Using Emacs as a File Manager

The dired ("directory editor") mode was listed in Table 7.24 as one of the major modes of Emacs. This mode can be started in several ways. One way is to start Emacs with the name of a directory instead of a file. A second way is to use the usual find-file command but to supply a directory name instead of a filename. The third way is to directly issue the dired command by typing C-x d and then providing a directory name.

When you are in dired mode, the buffer appears similar to the output of the ls command. From this buffer, you can perform many file-related actions. You can copy, move, delete, rename, compress, view, and edit individual files. You can create directories. You can execute other UNIX commands on files. You can also mark a set of files for these same manipulations. You can select files for manipulation using regular expressions. It is often when operating on such sets of files that the greatest productivity gains occur. For example, you can query-replace on a set of files all at once.

Although it is true that you cannot do anything under dired mode that you could not do by individually executing shell commands, I can definitely state as one who has long experience with both shell operations and using the dired file manager-like methods, that there can be a great gain in productivity, depending on your working style. I routinely run into situations where an operation that otherwise would have taken hours is reduced to minutes.

Using Emacs with Shell Buffers

Shell mode in Emacs can be explained simply. After starting a shell buffer by entering the command ESC x shell, Emacs opens up buffer in which you can execute normal UNIX shell commands. However, Emacs provides the capability to use many of its editing capabilities on text you are entering, including the completion feature, and screen history-like functions (the capability scroll back through a "transcript" of your shell session to examine the output of commands, and even to re-execute commands that are in the buffer without retyping them).

One of the best hidden treasures of shell mode is the capability to run multiple simultaneous visible shell sessions, while also keeping the output of each session from interfering with each other. In fact, before X Window became popular, many Emacs users had similar functionality just by using the Emacs shell mode.

Using Emacs Like a Word Processor

In addition to being a pretty good text editor, Emacs also can dress up your documents somewhat when you want it to. Although not presuming to be a real word processor, you can perform a limited set of simple formatting tasks. These tasks include working with fonts and colors on your screen, alignment of text, indentation of text, adding page breaks, working with columns, and working with outlines.

Using Emacs to Mark Up Text

With the World Wide Web gaining widespread adoption, the concept of a markup language has become more widely known. The language of the Web is HTML, which stands for Hypertext Markup Language. HTML is a form of text that contains ASCII characters as well as special tags, which are interpreted by a browser to produce a polished effect, depending on the capabilities of the browser. The special tags have a fairly simple structure. You could use any standard editor to create an HTML document; however, when an editor is extended to understand the HTML tags, it can help you to get the job done more easily.

There are major modes and packages that implement HTML and other types of markup languages. The common ones provided with Emacs are for troff (the standard UNIX text formatter) and nroff (a version of troff for character-based terminals), TEX, and LATEX.

Using Emacs with the Internet

There are several Internet activities for which Emacs provides direct support. You can use Emacs as an operating environment with features that interface directly to email, including sending, receiving, and managing your correspondence. You can use Telnet from within Emacs to log on to another system and keep a transcript in an Emacs buffer of your session; you can extend the find-file command with Ange-ftp mode to work with FTP to find and download files. You can also use the Gnus newsreader (a separate program) directly from within Emacs through the built-in interface.

Abbreviation Mode

As was hinted at in the section on minor modes, there is an abbreviation feature in Emacs that can be enabled. The uses of this mode were covered in the vi section, so I will only briefly mention that Emacs has such a mode, with a few more features than vi.

To enable the abbreviation mode, use the command `ESC x abbrev-mode RETURN`. To set up an abbreviation, first type the abbreviation you want to use into your text and then enter the command `C-xaig`. When `Emacs` asks you for the expansion, type the full text that you want to have inserted when you type the abbreviation and then press `RETURN`. The abbreviation you just typed is expanded. It is expanded every time you type it followed by a space or punctuation mark.

Using Macros

`Emacs` provides a complete macro facility. An `Emacs` macro is a series of keystrokes recorded for later playback. By playing back keystrokes, you can accomplish a series of repetitive tasks easily. Many editors and word processors provide a macro facility. The `Emacs` capability is especially powerful because virtually any series of keystrokes and commands can be used. You can then multiply the number of times the macro is executed by preceding the command with one of the multiplier commands, such as `C-u` to repeat the macro four times, or `C-u C-u` to repeat it 16 times, and so on.

There are two ways to execute a macro. You can either execute the most recently recorded macro (the current macro), with the `C-x e` command. Or you can name your macros and execute them by name. To name a macro, use the `name-last-kbd-macro` function (there is no standard key binding for this command). When you record macros, they are available only during the current `Emacs` session. (The current macro is only available until you record another one; so if you want to keep it around, you will have to name it as just described, so that you can record another one.)

To make your macros permanent, you have to save them in a file. You can either save them in a special file, which you can then explicitly load when you want to use the macros it contains, or you can set them up to load automatically every time you start `Emacs` (see the following section, "Configuring `Emacs` to your Tastes").

Table 7.41 shows the commands used for working with macros.

TABLE 7.41. COMMANDS FOR WORKING WITH MACROS.

Binding	Function name	Action
`C-x (`	start-kbd-macro	Begin recording a macro
`C-x )`	end-kbd-macro	End recording a macro
`C-x e`	call-last-kbd-macro	Play back the current macro
`ESC n C-x e`	digit-argument	Play back the current macro *n* times followed by call-last-kbd-macro
(none)	name-last-kbd-macro	Assign a name to the current macro

continues

TABLE 7.41. CONTINUED.

Binding	Function name	Action
(none)	insert-last-kbd-macro	Write the last named macro into a file
(none)	*macroname*	Play back the *macroname* macro
(none)	load-file	Activate all the macros in the specified file

Configuring Emacs to Your Tastes

As I am sure you have guessed by now, Emacs is extensively customizable. The primary types of customization are (1) to create your own key bindings for functions that have no standard bindings but you find that you are using frequently; or (2) to remap function keys provided by your terminal to common Emacs functions. Both of these customizations are effected through the use of the .Emacs file in your home directory.

For example, to bind the help function to the sequence C-x ? and to bind the backspace function to C-h, you could enter the following in your .Emacs file (note the pair of double quotes and the single appearance of the single quote):

```
(global-set-key "\C-x?" 'help-command)
(global-set-key "\C-h" 'backward-char)
```

Another type of customization that is beyond the scope of this chapter is to actually add functions to Emacs via coding in Emacs LISP, which is the implementation language for Emacs (only the most basic part of Emacs is written in C; the rest is written in Emacs LISP). With this latter approach, you could truly say that Emacs is infinitely flexible.

Command Summary vi and Emacs

For your convenience, this section provides a quick reference of the major commands for vi in Table 7.42 and for Emacs in Table 15.43. For explanations of the symbols and conventions used in the tables, refer to the text accompanying Tables 15.7, 15.8, 15.9, 15.32, and 7.33.

TABLE 7.42. QUICK REFERENCE TO vi COMMANDS.

Single character cursor motion

Command	Result
h	One character left
^H	
left-arrow	

Single character cursor motion

Command	Result
j	One line down
^J	
^N	
down-arrow	
k	One line up
^P	
up-arrow	
l	One character right
right-arrow	

Movement within a line

Command	Result
^	First non-space character on the line
0	Beginning of the line
$	End of line
f*char*	To next occurrence of character *char*
F*char*	To previous occurrence of character *char*
t*char*	To character before next occurrence of character *char*
T*char*	Ro character after previous occurrence of character *char*
;	Repeats previous f, F, t, or T command; same direction
,	Repeats previous f, F, t, or T command; opposite direction

Motion to a specified line

Command	Result
Enter	To next line
+	To next line (usually used with preceding count)
-	To previous line (usually used with preceding count)
*number*G	To line *number*
number¦	To column *number*

continues

Table 7.42. CONTINUED.

Screen positioning

Command	Result
H	To top line displayed onscreen
L	To bottom line displayed onscreen
M	To middle line displayed onscreen
^D	Scroll down one-half screen
number^D	Scroll down number lines
^U	Scroll up one-half screen
number^U	Scroll up number lines
^F	Scroll forward one screen
^B	Scroll backward one screen
^E	Scroll down one line
^Y	Scroll up one line

Lexical object positioning

Command	Result
w	Forward one small word
W	Forward one big word
b	Backward one small word
B	Backward on big word
e	To end of next small word
E	To end of next big word
(	To beginning of previous sentence
)	To beginning of next sentence
{	To beginning of previous paragraph
{	To beginning of next paragraph
[[	To beginning of next section
]]	To beginning of previous section

Screen redrawing

Command	Result
z	Redraws screen with current line at top of the screen

Screen redrawing

Command	Result
z-	Redraws screen with current line at bottom of the screen
z.	Redraws screen with current line at center of the screen

Positioning by pattern searching

Command	Result
/*pattern*	Moves to next line containing *pattern*
?*pattern*	Moves to previous line containing *pattern*
/	Repeats last search forward
?	Repeats last search backward
n	Repeats last search in same direction
N	Repeats last search in opposite direction
/*pattern*/+*nbr*	To *nbr* lines after next line containing *pattern*
?*pattern*?-*nbr*	To *nbr* lines before previous line containing *pattern*
/*pattern*/z-	Redraws screen with next line containing *pattern* at bottom of the screen (other z options will give the corresponding positioning)
%	To parenthesis or brace matching the one at the current cursor position

Positioning to marked text locations

Command	Result
m*char*	Marks the current cursor position with the letter *char*
`*char*	To mark specified by *char*
'*char*	To beginning of line containing mark specified by *char*
``	To previous location of the current line (after a cursor movement)
''	Ro beginning of line containing previous location of current line (after a cursor movement)

TABLE 7.42. CONTINUED.

Inserting text

Command	Result
i	Inserts text before the cursor
I	Inserts text before first non-blank character of line
a	Inserts text after the cursor
A	Inserts text at the end of the line
o	Adds an empty line below the current line and enters insert mode there
O	Adds an empty line above the current line and enters insert mode there

Changing text while in insert mode

(Note: These commands are only available while in insert mode.)

Command	Result
^H	Backspaces and erases the previous character (only since insert began)
^W	Backspaces over and erases the previous small word (only since insert began)
\	Quotes the erase and kill characters
Esc	Ends insert mode and go back to command mode
^D	Back to previous auto-indent stop
^^D	(Caret followed by Ctrl-D) no auto-indent on current line only
0^D	Moves cursor back to left margin
^V	Enters any character into text (do not interpret control characters)

Changing text

Command	Result
cobject	Changes the text object to the text inserted until the Esc key is pressed
C	Changes the rest of the line to the text insert until the Esc key is pressed (same as c$)
cc	Changes the whole line to the text inserted until the Esc key is pressed

Changing text

Command	Result
r*char*	Replaces the character the cursor is on with *char*; then return to command mode
R	Overwrites text until the Esc key is pressed; if you go past the end of the line, append new text to the end of the line
s	Substitutes characters (same as c1)
S	Substitutes lines (same as cc)

Deleting text

Command	Result
x	Deletes the character under the cursor
X	Deletes the character before the cursor
d*object*	Deletes the text object
D	Deletes the reset of the line (same as d$)
dd	Deletes the line

Using buffers

Command	Result
u	Undo the last change
U	Restores the current line to the state it was in when the cursor was last positioned to it
y*object*	Places the text of the object into the undo buffer
yy	Places the line the cursor is on into the undo buffer
Y	Places the line the cursor is on into the undo buffer (same as yy, which is a departure from the pattern set up by C and D)
p	Inserts the text in the undo buffer after the cursor
P	Inserts the text in the undo buffer before the cursor
"*letter*d*object*	Deletes the object into the letter buffer
"*letter*y*object*	nks (copies) the object into the letter buffer
"*letter*p	Inserts the text in the letter buffer after the cursor
"*number*p	Inserts the *number*-th last delete of a complete line or block of lines

continues

TABLE 7.42. CONTINUED.

Other editing commands

Command	Result
.	Repeats the last editing command (and increments n in a "np command)
~	Changes the case of the letter under the cursor and moves cursor to left one character (does not support a count in standard vi)
J	Joins two lines
>>	Shifts line *shiftwidth* characters to the right (use :set sw to change the *shiftwidth*)
>L	Shifts all lines from the line the cursor is on to the end of the screen *shiftwidth* characters to the right (use :set sw to change the *shiftwidth*)
<<	Shifts line *shiftwidth* characters to the left (use :set sw to change the *shiftwidth*)
<L	Shifts all lines from the line the cursor is on to the end of the screen *shiftwidth* characters to the left (use :set sw to change the *shiftwidth*)

Saving the buffer to a file

Command	Result
:w	Writes (saves) the buffer to disk, using the original filename
:w *file*	Writes the buffer to disk, to file
:w!	Writes the buffer to disk, overwriting *file*

Exiting commands

Command	Result
ZZ	Writes the buffer to disk and exits the program
Q	Enters the ex editor (same as typing :)
:q	Quits vi, unless you have an unsaved buffer
:q!	Always quits vi, overriding warning about an unsaved buffer
:wq	Writes the buffer to disk and exits the program (same as *ZZ*)

Editing other files

Command	Result
:e *file*	Edits file, unless you have an unsaved buffer
:e!	Discards any changes and starts over with the last saved version of the file from disk
:e + *file*	Edits *file*, unless you have an unsaved buffer; places cursor bottom line
:e +*nbr* *file*	Edits *file*, unless you have an unsaved buffer; places cursor on line *nbr*
:e #	Edits alternate file
:n	Edits the next file (applies when a list of files was entered on the command line)
:n *file file file*	Sets up a new list of files to edit
:r *file*	Reads (inserts) contents of file into the buffer on the line below the cursor
:r !*command*	Runs the shell command and inserts the output of the command on the line below the cursor
^G	Displays information about the current file (filename, current line number, number of lines in file, percentage through the file)
:ta *tag*	Jumps to the file and the location in the file specified by *tag* (before you can use this function, you must use the *ctags* program to create the *tags* file. Refer to the section on the :ta command for details.)

Redrawing the screen

Command	Result
^L	Redraws the screen (implementation depends on terminal type)
^R	Redraws the screen; eliminates blank lines marked with @ (implementation depends on terminal type)
z*number*	Sets screen window to *number* lines

continues

7

TEXT EDITING WITH VI AND EMACS

TABLE 7.42. CONTINUED.

UNIX shell commands

Command	Result
:sh	Executes a shell; remain in shell until shell exit command given (^D)
:!*command*	Executes the shell command and returns to vi (after the ! command, certain special characters are expanded. # is expanded to the alternate file name; % is expanded to the current file name; ! is expanded to the previous shell command)
:!!	Repeat the previous shell command
!*object cmd*	Execute the shell *cmd*; replace the text *object* with the shell *cmd* output. If the shell *cmd* takes standard input, the designated text object is used.
nbr!!*cmd*	Execute the shell *cmd*; replace *nbr* lines beginning at the current line with the shell *cmd* output. If *nbr* is missing, 1 is assumed. If the shell *cmd* takes standard input, the designated lines are used.

ex editing commands

Command	Result
:vi	Enters visual mode from the ex command line
:*addr*d	Delete the lines specified by *addr*
:*addr*m*nbr*	Move the lines specified by *addr* after line *nbr*
:*addr*co*nbr*	Copy the lines specified by *addr* after line *nbr*
:*addr*t*nbr*	Copy the lines specified by *addr* after line *nbr* (same as *co* command)

TABLE 7.43. QUICK REFERENCE TO EMACS COMMANDS.

Binding	Function name	Move (Physical)
C-f	forward-char	One character forward
C-b	backward-char	One character backward
C-n	next-line	Next line
C-p	previous-line	Previous line
C-a	beginning-of-line	Beginning of line

Binding	Function name	Move (Physical)
C-e	end-of-line	End of line
C-v	scroll-up	Next screen
ESC v	scroll-down	Previous screen
C-x]	forward-page	One page forward
C-x[	backward-page	One page backward
ESC >	end-of-buffer	End of buffer
ESC <	beginning-of-buffer	Beginning of buffer

Binding	Function name	Move (Lexical)
ESC f	forward-word	One word forward
ESC b	backward-word	One word backward
ESC a	forward-sentence	Beginning of sentence
ESC e	backward-sentence	End of sentence
ESC }	forward-paragraph	One paragraph forward
ESC {	backward-paragraph	One paragraph backward

Binding	Function Name	Description
C-x C-f	find-file	Open a file and load
C-x C-v	find-alternate-file	Look for a different file
C-x i	insert-file	Insert a file into the buffer
C-x C-s	save-file	Write (save) buffer to original file (see caution below)
C-x C-w	write-file	Write (save) buffer as file (defaults to original file)

Binding	Function name	Delete
DEL	delete-backward-char	Character to left of point (the one just typed
C-d	delete-character	The character the cursor is on
C-k	kill-line	The line cursor is on
ESC d	kill-word	The next word
ESC DEL	backward-kill-word	The previous word
ESC k	kill-sentence	The next sentence
C-x DEL	backward-kill-sentence	Previous sentence

continues

TABLE 7.43. CONTINUED.

Binding	Function name	Delete
C-@	set-mark-command	Mark one end of a region
C-SPACE	set-mark-command	Mark one end of a region (same as C-@)
C-w	kill-region	Marked region
SHIFT-DEL	kill-region	Marked region (same as C-w)

Binding	Function name	Description
C-y	yank	Insert text from the start of the kill ring
ESC y	yank-pop	Replace yanked text with previous kill

Binding	Function name	Reformat
ESC q	fill-paragraph	Paragraph, rewrapping the lines

Binding	Function name	Transpose
C-t	transpose-chars	Two adjacent characters
ESC t	transpose-words	Two adjacent words
C-x C-t	transpose-lines	Two adjacent lines

Binding	Function name	Capitalize
ESC c	capitalize-word	First letter of word
ESC u	upcase-word	Uppercase whole word
ESC l	downcase-word	Lowercase whole word

Summary

In this chapter, two of the most important UNIX text editors were introduced: vi and Emacs. The important roles these tools play have been put into perspective, and detailed instruction on their use has been presented. These two editors have been compared to each other, to give you a feeling for the particular strengths of each.

The discussion of vi has covered nearly every feature. Differences between UNIX variants of vi have been pointed out where necessary. The important role of the ex editor and how it relates to the vi editor has also been covered. A moderately detailed presentation of regular expressions was presented to enable the reader to quickly get up to speed in using them within both vi and Emacs.

The role of Emacs as an integrating environment for uses such as file management, email, and shell programming, has been emphasized. The basics of its operation as well as a selection of details on some of the more advanced features have been covered.

Finally, more advanced uses of both editors have been presented, including methods of customizing their use to your preferences.

GUIs for End Users

by Chris Negus

CHAPTER 8

What Is a GUI?

A graphical user interface (GUI) provides a visual, intuitive way for a person to use a computer. With a GUI, computer files, folders, and devices can be represented by icons. You can use a mouse to click buttons, icons, or windows to start applications or organize how your work appears on the screen (which is sometimes referred to as the workspace or desktop).

The first UNIX systems were completely command driven. UNIX would show you a command prompt (often $ or #), and you would have to know the name of the program you wanted to run, what options it needed, and where the files you wanted to work on were located. As GUIs were added to the UNIX system, UNIX became a better platform for application programs that needed to be run by users who required an easier interface.

Figure 8.1 shows an example of a GUI providing a UNIX user with the controls needed to use a computer. The figure shows icons and windows that might appear on a typical GUI workspace. (The GUI is an X Window system and Motif window manager.)

FIGURE 8.1.

GUIs simplify how users operate computers.

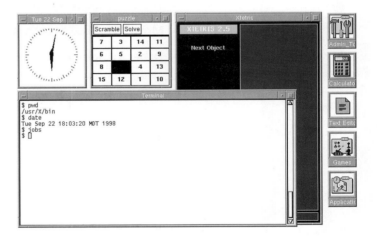

Although several GUIs have been created for the UNIX system, today nearly every major UNIX GUI is based on the *X Window system.* The X Window system (usually referred to as X or X11) creates a foundation for running graphical applications. Unlike other windowing systems, X was designed to be used in a networked environment. So, applications can be run on one computer in a network and be displayed and worked with on another.

The standard version of the X Window system is maintained by the Open Group (`http://www.opengroup.org`). The latest version of X (released March 31, 1998) is referred to as X11R6.4. A public domain version of X, called XFree86, is available free of charge from sites on the Internet and is included in most Linux distributions.

On top of X, a user can choose from a variety of *window managers*. A window manager provides the look and feel of the graphical interface. For example, different window managers will have different pull-down menus, different uses for mouse buttons, and different ways of arranging icons and setting screen colors. Motif is a popular standard window manager, and FVWM is a widely used public-domain window manager that is available on UNIX (and UNIX look-alikes).

You can customize how your UNIX GUI appears and behaves. With the Motif window manager, nearly every item of the interface (background, window borders, buttons, and so on) has attributes (such as color and font), which are called resources. Methods for changing resources and tailoring the look and feel of your GUI are described later in this chapter.

Although a GUI is all well and good, without application programs a GUI is a frame without a picture. Thousands of applications have been developed for X, many of which are used exclusively by large companies to manage their information. However, a variety of X utilities are freely available. These include things such as `xterm` (a terminal emulator that opens a UNIX shell on the desktop) and `xclock` (that enables you to place a running clock on your desktop).

The X Window System

If you are using a GUI on a UNIX system, chances are the GUI is running on an X Window system server. X is described as a portable, network-transparent window system. The portable part means that X can run on a variety of platforms (mostly UNIX, but also Microsoft Windows systems and others). The network-transparent part means that an application may be running from another computer on the network as you use the application from your own screen, mouse, and keyboard.

X is designed to be used with a window manager. If you were to use X without a window manager, X applications would still appear on your desktop. However, no pull-down menus would be available for starting applications, and no borders would appear around applications to control their size and placement on the desktop. Motif is the most popular commercial window manager, although many free window managers are available.

The words client and server are often used in describing the X Window system. If you have heard those terms before, you should be aware that the X Window system uses them in the opposite way than you are used to. For example, when you use email, the mail reader (mail client) that runs on your computer retrieves your mail from your remote ISP (mail server). With X, the X server typically runs on your local computer, but the X clients that appear on your screen can be running remotely from another computer on the network.

Figure 8.2 should help clarify the relationship between the X server and X clients. The X server controls your mouse, keyboard, and screen; it manages the client processes that can appear there. Clients represent applications that typically appear as windows on the screen. A client could be a word processor, a terminal window, or a graphics program, to name a few.

FIGURE 8.2.

The X server manages client programs from anywhere on the network.

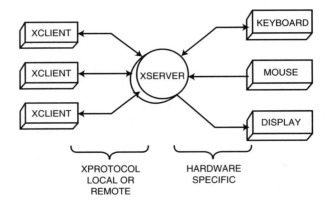

Setting up X to work on your computer is often the job of your company's network administrator. Your first view of X might be when you turn on your computer. A graphical `login` screen may appear. When you log in, X and a window manager (complete with icons to run company programs) may appear on your screen. If you are configuring X yourself, you can refer to descriptions of `xdm` and `xinit` programs later in this chapter.

To make your X server behave as you would like, you can use several configuration files. Files such as `.Xresources` and `.xinitrc` can be added to your home directory to define how X will initially appear when you start it. These and other configuration files are described in detail later.

For the user, the focus of the X Window system is the user's display screen, keyboard, and mouse. The location of these items, however, doesn't have to be the computer's console terminal (as is the case with GUIs on most PCs). The DISPLAY variable can be used to identify where the X display and clients appear. (See the sidebar, "Identifying the X Display," for more information.)

All this power of sharing application on networks may make you wonder how secure X is. Although it is true that X allows applications to be run on one computer and appear on another, security tools control how this is done. For example, X tools such as *xhost* enable you to indicate which host computers can and can't run applications on your X server.

CAUTION

Before you set up X, you should know some information about your video adapter and your monitor. For your monitor, you should know the horizontal and vertical sync frequency options and the bandwidth. For the video adapter, you should know the driving clock frequency. Setting information improperly, such as a frequency rate that is too high, can damage your monitor.

IDENTIFYING THE X DISPLAY

When an X server process is launched from a UNIX system, the process is directed to the display identified by the DISPLAY variable set for the current shell. Because X allows displays to be anywhere on the network, display names can include the host name of the X display, as well as a number identifying the display (and the screen within the display).

The simplest—and most common—display name is :0, which identifies the display as the first screen (0) of the console terminal (0) on the current host. (The screen and host are taken as default.) The full display name is in the form:

```
hostname:displaynumber.screennumber
```

So, for example, the full display name identifying the first screen (screen 0) on the third display (display 2) on a computer named snowbird would appear as follows: snowbird:2.0. (For DECnet addresses, use two colons after the host name.) Usually, you can drop the screen number unless multiple monitors are associated with a single keyboard and mouse.

Before you launch an X server or application from a shell, you can check the current DISPLAY value by typing:

```
echo $DISPLAY
```

To change the DISPLAY value, you can set it as you would any other variable. Some shells use the form *DISPLAY=host:0.0;export DISPLAY*, for example, but others require you to type *setenv DISPLAY host:0.0*. After the DISPLAY value is set, output from subsequent X commands is directed to that display.

continues

8

**GUIs FOR
END USERS**

To use X over a network, computers must be connected to a supported network (such as TCP/IP or DECnet). If you log in to a remote computer to start your X server, you will most likely need to set the DISPLAY manually. This can be done by creating a shell script to set the display and launch X or by adding those entries to a login configuration file (so it executes automatically).

New X Features (Version X11R6.4)

The X Window system has always had a strong base of support for UNIX features. With the X version called X11R6.4 (released March 31, 1998) the X Window system has made advances toward integrating X with the World Wide Web. The following are some of the most recent features available in the X Window system that are designed to make it Internet-ready:

- Universal Access—By allowing the X Window system clients to interact with HTTP protocols, X applications can now be found, launched, and used over the World Wide Web.

- Low-Bandwidth X (LBX)—The X Window system was first designed to be run over high-bandwidth networks (such as LANs). Using many new optimizing techniques, such as compression and caching, X is becoming a viable product to use over common dial-up connections to Internet Service Providers.

- Reduced X Server Memory Footprint—For users who require thin client applications, an X server with a 20% to 50% size reduction is optionally available.

- Easy Resource Configuration (ERC)—Changing resources for X applications can now be done on-the-fly, without having to restart the application.

- Xinerama—With this feature, you can drag applications between multiple screens or allow a multiheaded system to behave as one large screen.

- Remote Execution—This feature enables users to run remote applications from within a Web browser. It was designed to enable Web users to have the power that has been available to UNIX users with such commands as rsh (remote shell) or rlogin (remote login).

- Web Browser Plug-in—To make X Window system Web integration features accessible to less sophisticated users, a browser plug-in has been created. With this plug-in, users can find and launch X clients from within their browser window.

- Security—Keeping in line with the Web model, new security features have begun to separate security models between Trusted and Untrusted classes of applications.

Those applications that are Trusted exist behind the organization's firewall and have a less stringent set of security measures. Untrusted applications, however, are those that come from outside the firewall; these are treated more carefully.

Because X11R6.4 is a fairly new release, it may not yet be available on the computer systems you use today. Check the Open Group Web site (`http://www.opengroup.org`) for information on availability of this and later releases of X technologies. Also, check out the Broadway/Xweb Information and Resource Center (`http://www.broadway info.com`) for more information about X Window system Web integration.

Obtaining X

If you purchased a UNIX system, it probably includes X. Commercial UNIX systems provided X software based on source code obtained from the Open Group. Public domain UNIX systems tended to use the free XFree86 implementation of X.

TIP

To see if X is installed on your computer, check for `/usr/X` or `/usr/X11R6` directories. Executables for X should be in bin subdirectories for those directories. If you run X manually, you might want to add the X bin directory to your PATH.

Although the X Window system was given away until recently, this is no longer the case. As of release X11R6.3, the free and commercial versions of X have diverged. For X11R6.4, the Open Group (`http://www.opengroup.org`), which now maintains X, has begun charging licensing fees. For that reason, The XFree86 Project decided to continue development of XFree86 based on X11R6.3.

If you don't have X on your computer, or if you want a different or later version of X, try one of the following two sites:

- XFree86 Home Page (`http://www.xfree86.org`)—This site provides information about the XFree86 implementation of the X Window system. The site also contains links to documentation, the XFree86 distribution, and software patches.

- The Open Group X Window Page (`http://www.camb.opengroup.org/x`)—From this page, follow links to ordering information for the X Window system. Although X is no longer free for commercial use, you can currently get a copy of the latest X version (X11R6.4) without cost for noncommercial use. Try this site to download X11R6.4:

  `http://www.camb.opengroup.org/tech/desktop/onlineorder/xdownload.htm`

8

GUIs FOR
END USERS

If you are curious about how the X Window system has evolved from a university project to the de facto standard for graphical display software on UNIX systems, see the "History of the X Window System" sidebar.

HISTORY OF THE X WINDOW SYSTEM

Development of the X Window system was begun in 1984 by Bob Scheifler at the MIT Laboratory for Computer Science. As its popularity grew, the MIT X Consortium (formed in 1988) was replaced by the X Consortium (formed in 1993).

The X Consortium was a not-for-profit organization that developed the X user interface and underlying technology standards. There were more than sixty members of the consortium, including many computer and other technology companies. The X Consortium added development of Common Desktop Environment (CDE) and Motif to its charter in 1995.

By encouraging cooperation across the computer industry, the X Consortium was able to create a graphical architecture that became the most widely accepted in the UNIX industry. X design principles of being device independent, network transparent, and able to support multiple applications concurrently made it a viable, portable solution for many computer platforms.

In 1997, the X Consortium transferred responsibility for developing and maintaining the X Window system to the Open Group. The Open Group added X development to its charter of developing Common Desktop Environment (CDE) and Motif technologies. With this change also came a change in X licensing. For the first time, a licensing fee is charged for X Window system source code.

Starting X

Although it is possible to start up an X process by itself, the more common way to start X is through the xdm or xinit utilities. Both xdm and xinit start the X process, set some initial values used by X, and begin processes that are specified by the user. When each utility is done, you should have a working GUI with the preferences set and initial application running on the X display.

In general, xdm (the X display manager) is most appropriate for a computer that begins X at start-up time. The xdm utility can boot up to a graphical login screen and can manage several X Window sessions. When the xdm utility starts, it presents the user with a graphical login prompt; then, after the user is authenticated, the user-specific session is started. Besides being able to manage several X Window sessions for local users, xdm can also manage remote X servers that may be running on an X terminal.

The xinit utility is most useful for starting X manually. This may be useful if a computer runs several windowing systems or if the user only wants to run X windows on occasion. Like xdm, xinit can read a configuration file that is specific to the user who is running xinit so specific preferences can be set and selected programs can start automatically.

The following sections describe how to use the xdm and xinit utilities to start X.

> **NOTE**
>
> For X to work properly for the video card your display is using, you probably have to run a setup utility. Depending on the UNIX system you are using, the utility may be setvgamode (UNIX System V), XF86Setup (XFree86 versions of X), or some other utility. Without running one of these utilities, you may not be able to take advantage of higher resolution capabilities and the maximum video RAM available with your video card.

Starting X at Boot Time (xdm)

Using the xdm utility, you can set up your UNIX system to start X when the computer boots. With GUIs becoming the more preferred interface, many UNIX systems come with xdm configured to start automatically. The system boots and the first thing the user sees is a graphical login screen.

> **TIP**
>
> The xdm utility doesn't work well on computers that use multiple windowing systems. For that reason, you should use xinit to start X if you need multiple windowing systems on your computer.

Checking Whether xdm Is Configured

One way to have xdm start automatically is to have it configured to run at a particular boot level. For example, you could add the xdm command to the /etc/inittab file or to a shell script in one of the run level files. When the computer enters that initialization state, the console and any other displays that are configured see the graphical login screen.

Your computer may already have an xdm script ready to run, but that requires a small change to activate. First, look in the inittab file (usually /etc/inittab) to see if any reference exists to xdm. In some systems, xdm runs automatically when the system is booted to state 5. By changing the initdefault value to the state noted by xdm (for example, id:5:initdefault), the next time the system boots, it will start in the state needed to run xdm. The entry in inittab that actually starts xdm may look like the following:

```
x:5:respawn:/usr/bin/X11/xdm ñnodaemon
```

This line shows an entry that is tagged by the letter x. The command is started when init state 5 is begun. If the xdm command is terminated for some reason, it should be restarted (respawn). The last part of the line shows the command that is run (/usr/bin/X11/xdm ñ nodaemon). You can add numbers to the second field to have xdm start in different init states, and you can add or change xdm options by changing the end of the line.

If xdm isn't noted in the inittab file, look in the /etc/init.d or /etc/rc.d directories. If, for example, a file called xdm is in /etc/init.d, you could link that file to an rc.d directory to have it run automatically. For example, linking the file to /etc/rc3.d/S90xdm would cause the xdm script to be started when the system enters state 3.

Setting the xdm Configuration (Administrator)

When xdm runs, a set of configuration files are read, and several scripts are run. Many of these files are controlled by the system administrator, but others are maintained by each individual user.

Most of the administrative configuration files used by xdm are contained in the xdm directory. The xdm directory is in different places on different UNIX systems, such as /usr/X11/xdm, /usr/X11R6/lib/X11/xdm, or /usr/X/lib/xdm.

The xdm-config file is the first configuration file to check. Within xdm-config, the locations of all the other xdm files are set. The following are examples of entries in the xdm-config file:

```
DisplayManager.errorLogFile:    /usr/X/lib/X11/xdm/xdm-errors
DisplayManager.pidFile:         /usr/X11R6/lib/X11/xdm/xdm-pid
DisplayManager.accessFile:      /usr/X11R6/lib/X11/xdm/Xaccess
DisplayManager*resources:       /usr/X/lib/X11/xdm/Xresources
DisplayManager.servers:         /usr/X/lib/X11/xdm/Xservers
DisplayManager*session:         /usr/X/lib/X11/xdm/Xsession
DisplayManager._0.setup:        /usr/X/lib/X11/xdm/Xsetup_0
DisplayManager._0.startup:      /usr/X/lib/X11/xdm/GiveConsole
DisplayManager._0.reset:        /usr/X11R6/lib/X11/xdm/TakeConsole
DisplayManager._0.authorize:    true
```

The xdm-error file is where error messages for xdm are sent. If you have problems starting xdm, check this file for information. The xdm-pid stores the number of the xdm process so it can be retrieved and used to kill the X session later. You can change the locations of these files, although no other configuration is needed. Other configuration files (Xaccess, Xresources, Xservers, and Xsession) can be modified and are described later.

Also with xdm-config, several entries are used to set the location of configuration files that apply to the console terminal. At startup, the GiveConsole shell script sets the ownership of the console device to that of the person who has logged in, and TakeConsole changes the ownership back to root. The Xsetup_0 configuration file is described later.

The xdm configuration files you can modify are described in the following paragraphs:

> **TIP**
>
> These configuration files will apply to all displays that start the X Window system from your computer using xdm. Because of this, these files offer an excellent opportunity to configure a particular look or set of applications for all the computer's users.

8

GUIs FOR
END USERS

- Xaccess—This file contains information that controls which hosts and X terminals can have access to the xdm services. Entries define the responses xdm should make to Direct and Broadcast queries, as well as Indirect queries. An administrator can list the names of hosts that are allowed or disallowed access. In the case of X terminals, this file can contain chooser entries that offer host menus to selected X terminals.

  The following are examples of entries in an Xaccess file. A pound sign (#) indicates that the remainder of the line is interpreted as a comment.

  ```
  chris.twostory.com      # Direct/broadcast service is allowed for this
  display
  !john.twostory.com      # Direct/broadcast service is not allowed for
  this display
  *.handsonhistory.com    # Direct/broadcast service is okay for all
  displays in the domain
  x.twostory.com          y.twostory.com      # Cause indirect query from
  x to be directed to y
  !z.twostory.com         dummy               # Disallow indirect access
  by z
  %HOSTS                  a.handsonhistory.com b.handsonhistory.com
  c.handsonhistory.com.
  *.handsonhistory.com    %HOSTS              # Displays in the domain
  choose from HOSTS.
  ```

- Xresources—Before the authentication widget starts up (which typically prompts for a login and password), resources are set from values included in the Xresources file. Resources set in the Xresources file can include

  - xlogin resources—The xlogin widget is used to authenticate the user when on the first window presented by xdm. Resources for this widget can set such things as the login prompt, the greeting, login failure message, and various color and border resources.

NOTE

You can set more than a dozen xlogin resources. They are described in detail in the xdm manual page. About half of these resources are already set in the Xresources file.

  - xconsole resources—If an xconsole window appears on the initial screen (so that important system messages can appear), resources can set the size, fonts, and other characteristics of this window.
  - chooser resources—If the authentication process includes the capability to present a set of choices to X terminal users as to where they log in (using the chooser process), the characteristics of that process and how it is displayed can be changed by these resources. These resources can set where the XDMCP Host Menu is taken from (usually the local host), the size of the menu window, and the fonts used.

  By default, the Xresources file sets the Ctrl+R key sequence to abort the initial display. Using this key sequence, you can leave the initial xdm authentication screen and go right to a shell login prompt. This is valuable if, for some reason, the graphical display screen is garbled or if you need a nongraphical login (such as when you are using telnet or rlogin to log in).

- Xservers—Use this configuration file to identify the X server used for each display that starts up the X Window system via xdm. The following is how the entry should look for the console terminal (display 0):

  ```
  :0   local   /usr/X/bin/X
  ```

  Entries in Xservers can apply to remote displays, such as those from X terminals, as well.

- Xsession—This configuration file provides you with the opportunity to add those clients and set resources that you want to appear on every display that starts X on your computer using xdm. This file also identifies the personal configuration files each user can create. By default, personal configuration files include .xsession and .Xresources in each user's home directory. Those entries might appear in the Xsession file as follows:

```
startup=$HOME/.xsession          resources=$HOME/.Xresources
if [ -f "$startup" ]; then       exec "$startup"
elif [ -f "/usr/X/wmconfig/xsessionrc" ]; then
    exec "/usr/X/wmconfig/xsessionrc"
else      if [ -f "$resources" ]; then      xrdb -load "$resources"
fi
exec xsm
fi
```

In this example, the startup variable is set to the .xsession file, and resources is set to the .Xresources file in the user's home directory. If a user has an .xsession file, the information in that file is used to configure the session. Otherwise, a default session file is used (xsessionrc). Likewise, if resources are defined in a user's .Xresources file, then those resources are loaded using the xrdb utility. (See the description of setting the xdm configuration for end users for descriptions of these files.)

NOTE

In case of failure, Xsession contains a failsafe mode. This mode opens an xterm window so you can type shell commands, for example, to fix your .xsession file or manually kill the X process.

- Xsetup_0—This configuration is an example of one that is specific to a particular display. In this case, the file applies to display 0 (the console). This file is executed each time someone signs on from the console terminal, regardless of who the user is. One entry this file might contain is an xconsole command, so console messages can appear on the display (instead of being lost).

Setting the xdm Configuration (End User)

Although the X Window system provides default settings so users can begin with a usable display, users have ways of tailoring their X displays to their own needs and preferences. In particular, the users can create a .xsession and .Xresources file in their home directories to define how their display looks, feels, and works.

- $HOME/.xsession—In this file, users can indicate the type of window manager they want to use and the default programs they want to start up. The following are a few things you should remember about this file:

- It should be executable. The user should be the file owner. A viable set of permissions would be rwxr-xr-x, so only you can change it, but anyone else can read or execute it.

- Put ampersands at the end of each command. This runs each command in the background. In this way, after launching the command, the `.xsession` can continue on to the next line.

People often start with an existing `.xsession` file and modify it to suit their needs. A sample `.xsession` may be delivered with your UNIX system. (For example, an xsessionrc file may exist that you could copy and modify.)

The following is an example of what may be contained in a `.xsession` file:

```
mwm&
xeyes&
xterm -geometry 80x24-0-0 &
```

This example shows the Motif window manager starting up (`mwm`), the `xeyes` utility being run, and a terminal window (`xterm`) opening.

- `$HOME/.Xresources`—Using this file, you can set a variety of resources that change such things as colors, fonts, and sizes of the windows and other items on your X display. For details on the resources you can add to this file, see the section "Customizing X Resources" later in this chapter.

Starting X Manually (`xinit`)

If starting X automatically (such as through `xdm`) is not appropriate for your situation, you may want to start X using the `xinit` utility. With `xinit`, an individual user can start X from a UNIX shell after he or she has logged in. You may want to start X manually for the following reasons:

- Several windowing systems are available on your computer, so you want the users on your computer to be able to choose their own.

- Users sometimes may want to use a nongraphical shell when they log in.

- Users may want to start X from a remote display that is unknown to your computer. In this case, when users start X with `xinit`, they can identify their display (using the `DISPLAY` variable or the `-display` option).

Running `xinit`

To start `xinit`, the user simply types `xinit` from the shell, along with any desired options. To configure the desktop, `xinit` executes the user's `$HOME/.xinitrc` file. If no `.xinitrc` file is available, `xinit` simply starts X with a single terminal window (`xterm`) open and no window manager running. Of course, the preferred way is to have a `.xinitrc` file configured.

On the command line, you can specify a different client process or server process to be used instead of the default. You could, for example, start a window manager as the client process from the xinit command line as follows:

```
xinit /usr/X/bin/mwm
```

To start a different X server process, you add two dashes to the xinit command line, followed by the path to the X server process. (This is one way to test X programs that were created for different screen resolutions.) You can specify both client and server processes on the xinit command line as follows:

```
xinit /usr/X/bin/mwm -- /usr/bin/X11/XF86_Mono
```

> **NOTE**
>
> When you specify client and server processes on the xinit command line, you must give a full path (/) or a relative path (./) to the location of the program. Otherwise, xinit assumes you are entering options to be used by the default client of server programs.

Instead of different clients or servers, you can add options to be passed to the existing client (xterm) or server (X). In the following example, the geometry option sets the size and location of the xterm client, and the X display is set to :1 (instead of :0). (Remember that the server command or options are set after two dashes.)

```
xinit -geometry 60x20+1+1 -- :1
```

If you run xinit often with the same options, you may want to create a shell script containing the full command line.

Creating a .xinitrc File

A sample .xinitrc file is probably delivered with your UNIX system. Users should copy that file into their home directories, then modify the file to suit their needs. A .xinitrc file typically contains the following:

- Locations of the resources files and key/pointer maps files for the system and for the particular user
- Commands that read the resources and key/pointer maps files
- A command that starts the selected window manager
- Several useful commands that start such things as terminal windows, clocks, and other commonly used utilities

The following is an example of the resources and modmap files identified in a `.xinitrc` file:

```
userresources=$HOME/.Xresources
usermodmap=$HOME/.Xmodmap
sysresources=/usr/X/lib/X11/xinit/.Xresources
sysmodmap=/usr/X/lib/X11/xinit/.Xmodmap
```

The first two lines identify the user's resources (`$HOME/.Xresources`) and modmap files (`$HOME/.Xmodmap`), and the next two lines identify those items for the whole system. The contents of those files are interpreted using the `xrdb` command (for setting resources) and `xmodmap` (for setting key and pointer maps). See "Customizing X Resources" later in this chapter for information in setting up your `.Xresources` and `.Xmodmap` files.

After all resources are set, the last lines in the `.xinitrc` files should start the window manager and some useful utilities. The following are some examples:

```
xtetris &
xclock -geometry 60x60-1+1 &
twm
```

These utilities start the window manager that comes with X (`twm`), start the X version of the tetris game, and run a clock on the display (`xclock`). Of course, you can add any utilities that are appropriate for you, so they start up when `xinit` is run. With the exception of the last program, all programs run from the `.initrc` file must be followed by "&" to run in the background.

The last program in the `.xinitrc` file must NOT be run in the background because as soon as the last program exits, X exits as well. Usually, you will want to run the window manager last so that when you are ready to end your X session, you can simply exit from the window manager.

CAUTION

Remember, the last program in your `.xinitrc` file must not be run in the background, but all others must be run in the background. If all programs are run in the background, X will start and exit immediately. If a program early in `.xinitrc` is run in the foreground, no later programs in the file will run.

Customizing X Resources

To control the way X clients appear and behave in X, you can set a variety of resources. Some resources are general in nature, controlling such things as colors and fonts. Other resources can be quite specific to an application, such as how a prompt should appear in an X client.

X resources are typically set during X startup time by automatically running a program called xrdb. For users customizing X resources, the most common thing to do is to create .Xdefaults files in their home directories ($HOME/.Xdefaults). Resources relating to particular clients and the window manager can be added to this file.

The format for specifying resources is

```
client*resource: value
```

where client is the name of the X client or window manager, resource is the resource being set, and value is what the resource is being set to. So if you wanted to set the background of xterm terminal windows to green, for example, you would add the following to your .Xdefaults file:

```
Xterm*background: green
```

With this concept in mind, you can use many resources to change the appearance and actions of a particular client. Resources that are specific to a particular client are usually listed on the client's manual page. Resources that apply to all clients are usually set by modifying resources for the window manager. The following are some of the changes you can make to window manager resources that can apply to the client windows that will appear on your workspace.

Setting Font Resources

The fonts that appear in places associated with windows on the desktop can be specified by setting several resources. To specify a particular font to be used by all Motif windows, you can set the fontList resource. To specify a font to be used only on the window menu, you can set the menu*fontlist resource. The following are examples of setting each resource for the Motif window manager:

```
Mwm*fontList: -adobe-times-bold-r-normal--*-120-*-*-*-*-*-*
Mwm*menu*fontList: -adobe-courier-bold-r-normal--*-120-*-*-*-*-*-*
```

Setting Decoration Resources

With decoration resources, you can define what elements appear on each window frame. You can define a different set of elements to appear on the more permanent windows (clientDecoration) than the ones that appear on transient windows (transientDecoration), such as dialog boxes. The following are the decorations you can have on or off:

- all—Turns on all decorations
- border—The window border
- menu—The window menu button
- maximize—The maximize button
- minimize—The minimize button
- none—Turns off all decorations
- resizeh—The resize handles
- title—The title bar

The standard windows (clientDecoration) contain all decorations by default. Transient windows (transientDecoration), however, only include menu, resizeh, and title decorations. The following are some examples of window decoration resources set for Motif:

```
Mwm*clientDecoration: -minimize -maximize
Mwm*transientDecoration: menu title
```

The first line removes the minimize and maximize buttons from all standard windows that are displayed by Motif. The second line defines the transient windows as containing only the Menu button and the Title bar.

Setting Color Resources

Colors can be redefined for most of the elements controlled by the Motif window manager. For example, you can set different foreground and background colors for window frames and menus. In fact, you can assign different colors to be applied to window frames depending on whether the current window is active or inactive. The following are some examples of setting color resources:

```
Mwm*menu*background: gold
Mwm*menu*foreground: black
Mwm*background: grey
Mwm*foreground: white
Mwm*activeBackground: black
Mwm*activeForeground: red
```

In this example, the window menu will have a gold background (menu*background) and black foreground (menu*foreground). The window itself will be grey (background) and white (foreground) while the window is inactive. When the window is active, the background (activeBackground) will be black and the foreground (activeForeground) will be red.

Working with X Clients

Every X Window system is delivered with a variety of client programs you can run. Although most of these clients are simple, you can try a few of them to help understand generally how to start X clients, how to control remote access to clients, and to understand some of the standard options available for using X clients.

Starting X Clients

A few dozen X client programs are delivered with every X Window system. These clients are things such as calculators (`xcalc`), clocks (`xclock`), and terminal windows (`xterm`). Although most companies that use X to develop their in-house applications will offer much more complex applications, you can try out these simple X utilities to get a feel for how X works.

Unlike GUIs that are associated with the Macintosh or with Windows 95, the X Window system's design as a network application environment, built on an operating system such as UNIX, offers a more powerful and flexible application environment. As a result, there are more ways of running programs and more responsibilities for controlling how applications are run. For example:

- X clients can appear on your local display after being launched from your computer—or potentially any computer—on your network.
- Access control features make it possible for the person using the X display to control which hosts can launch applications that appear on the display.
- By setting a variety of options for the X clients you run, you can control such things as how each application appears (for example, its window size, colors, fonts, and so on), as well as how each application behaves (for example, how text scrolls or wraps within the application).

The following paragraphs describe the different issues related to launching X clients locally, launching them remotely, and using a variety of options to modify how X applications behave. Several popular X clients, such as `xconsole`, `xterm`, `xlock`, `bitmap`, and others are also described.

Launching X Clients Locally

If you are using X from the console display on a UNIX system, running an X client application is quite simple. Depending on the window manager you are using, a Desktop window or a pull-down menu may exist that enables you to start X applications. From a shell command line, you can run X clients so they appear on your display.

Assuming that your X display is already running, you can start an X client by typing the command into a Terminal window (`xterm`) from the local display. (Most X configurations will either have started an xterm window automatically or offer an icon or pull-down menu to open one.) Try running the following command:

`xclock&`

The `xclock` utility should appear on your display screen. (The `xclock` utility is described later in this chapter.) If the command fails to execute and appear on your display, this may have occurred for the following reasons:

- Client is not in `PATH`. Client programs delivered with the X Window system are usually in a directory in the shell's `PATH`. If not, you can probably find X clients (such as `xclock`) in `/usr/X/bin`, `/usr/bin/X11`, or `/usr/X11R6/bin`. After you find which directory exists on your computer, either add it to your `PATH` or type the full path to the client.

- `DISPLAY` is set wrong. The `DISPLAY` variable in the shell you are using should be set to indicate your current display. Type echo $DISPLAY from the shell to see what is set for the current display. If the `DISPLAY` is not set properly, change it and rerun the command. (See the sidebar "Identifying the X Display" for further information.)

Another way to run X clients is from items on the GUI itself. Most X Window systems are delivered not only with a window manager, but with a desktop interface. The desktop interface typically contains a set of icons and menus that enable you to select useful functions and utilities. It also contains a file manager that enables you to open folders and select files.

Double-clicking icons that represent X clients will typically start those clients on the desktop. Look for folders named "Programs" or "Games" to find X clients. Or browse the file system for the bin containing X clients and start up ones that look interesting.

Most X-based desktop interfaces will enable you to define how an application behaves from the GUI. Select an application, then look for a menu option that enables you to change its properties or run actions. You might be able to configure what options are used when the icon is run, what icon represents the application, and what occurs when drag-and-drop is used with the application.

Often the most popular utilities, such as those that open terminal windows, simple editors, or basic administration, will be available from a desktop menu. Click either the right or left mouse buttons in an open area of the display background (not in a window), and a menu should appear that enables you to select the application you want to run.

Using Remote X Clients

Running remote X client processes, which means those that are launched from a computer other than the one that is running your X server, opens up a whole new set of opportunities and potential security issues.

When you run a remote X client, you are taking advantage of the remote computer's processing power. The remote X client is run as a particular user on that computer, giving the X client access to any files, directories, devices, or other resources to which the user would have access. Although the X server is running somewhere else, the X client has the same permission as a person logging in directly to the remote host.

In general, to run a remote client on your local display, you need the following:

- A transport provider—For a remote X client to be displayed on the local X server, the client and server must be connected by some sort of transport provider. A transport provider is a type of computer network service that provides end-to-end delivery of messages between host computers. TCP/IP is the most popular transport provider. However, DECnet and other transport providers are supported. (See Chapter 26, "Networking" for information on how to set up TCP/IP.)

- Remote access—By default, only the same computer that is running the X server can launch a client to run on the display. For you to allow X clients from other computers to appear on your display, you can open access to your display to all hosts or to selected hosts, as well as to specific users from those hosts. (See "Controlling Client Access" later in this chapter for information on how to allow remote client access to your X display.)

- A way of launching the client— Several ways of launching remote X clients are possible. One way is to log in to the remote computer containing the X client (using `rlogin` or `telnet`) from your xterm window. Then you can change the `DISPLAY` variable to that of your local X server and run the X client program (probably in the background). The X client will appear on your local display (given that access control is open to the remote host).

  Another possibility is to use some sort of application launcher. Some X window desktops, such as those that come with UNIX SVR4, come with an Application Sharing window. Using that window, host computers can add X applications to a list of those being shared; then users can launch those applications from X displays on other computers.

After your X display is up and running, you can start remote X client processes using the following procedure. This procedure assumes that you have a TCP/IP connection configured between the client and server computers. For this example, the remote X clients will run on a computer named brighton, and the local X server is using display 0 on a computer named snowbird.

1. From the X display, open a terminal window (`xterm`).

2. From the terminal window, type the following to allow the remote host (`brighton`) access to the local display:

```
$ xhost brighton
brighton being added to access control list
$
```

3. Log in to the remote host (`brighton`) using a remote login command (in this case, `rlogin`) as the user name you want to use (`john`):

```
$ rlogin -l john brighton
Password:
```

After you log in, any command you run will be assigned to the user you logged in as.

4. Set the `DISPLAY` variable to direct output of X clients to the local X server (in this case, snowbird). Depending on your shell, you will use one of the following two commands:

```
$ DISPLAY=snowbird:0;export DISPLAY
or
$ setenv DISPLAY snowbird:0
```

5. Run the X client in the background (`&`) that you want to appear on your local display (in this case, `xclock`). If the command is not in your `PATH`, you may need to type the full pathname to the command.

```
$ xclock &
```

The remote X client (`xclock` from `brighton`) will appear on the local display (`snowbird:0`).

Although you would be working from a display on snowbird, all actions of the application (in this case, `xclock`) are associated with brighton. So, for example, the `xclock` program would show the time based on `brighton`'s clock time. If the client were something that used the file system, such as a text editor, changes and saves of files would all be associated with the file system on brighton.

> **TIP**
>
> If you open xterm windows on remote hosts and display them locally, you should make sure the command line prompt reflects the host name. It's very easy to start working on the wrong computer if you have several terminal windows open locally and remotely.

The xon command is another way to start a remote X client to be displayed locally. To use xon you can simply type xon, followed by the remote host and X client. For example:

```
$ xon brighton xterm
```

runs the xterm command on the host named brighton and returns the output to the local display. The drawback to using xon is that you can use it only between Trusted computers. A local host would have to be added to the remote user's .rhosts file so that no password was required to complete the transaction.

Controlling Client Access

As an X Window system user, you can add or remove access to your display by X clients started from remote computers. The most common—though not the most secure—X security method is host access method, where access is restricted by the host computer. Other, more secure, methods use cookies or public keys to control X client access.

To find the current host access associated with your display and to change it, you can use the xhost command. To run xhost, you should first open a Terminal window. The Terminal window should be running on the same computer as the server or, with an X terminal, from the login computer. In the Terminal window, type the following:

```
$ xhost
access control enabled, only authorized clients can connect
INET: snowbird
INET: brighton
INET: solitude
LOCAL:
```

Running xhost without options shows the current access control state. In this case, access control is enabled; therefore, only X clients from those hosts listed can appear on the local display. So, local clients can appear on the display, as can TCP/IP (INET) clients run from hosts named snowbird, brighton, and solitude.

To open access control so any computer can show X clients on your display, type:

```
$ xhost +
access control disabled, clients can connect from any host
```

8

GUIs FOR
END USERS

CAUTION

By opening up your display to any host, you become vulnerable to being spoofed. Spoofing is when software pretends to be one thing but is really another. For example, a malicious person could create a window that looks like

continues

> a login screen and have it appear on your display. If you type in your login and password, thinking that you are just entering the information locally, you might actually be giving away your login and password to the person who sent the spoofed window.

Using `xhost +` to completely open your display might open your display to unwanted security risks. More often, you will want to open your display only to selected hosts. For example:

```
$ xhost + snowbird
```

adds the host snowbird to the current access control list (the + is optional). To remove the same host from the list, you could type the following

```
$ xhost - snowbird
```

Although the host access method of X security is a common security method, it is not the most secure. In fact, that security method is only recommended on Trusted networks (such as LANs in a workplace) where each machine is used by only one user.

The following are examples of other security methods that can be used with the X Window system (X11R6). Each of these methods relies on data stored in the `.Xauthority` file in the user's home directory.

- MIT Magic Cookie-1—With this method, the `xdm` utility creates 128-bit magic cookies that are transmitted by the X client to the server for authentication. Users store this information in their `$HOME/.Xauthority` files.

  This form of authentication is useful for computers that are running several X server sessions at the same time because it helps avoid client access to the wrong displays. Because the cookie is not encrypted, some risk exists of the cookie being discovered by someone monitoring the physical network.

- XDM Authorization-1—This is a DES-based access control method that works by storing a key in the user's `$HOME/.Xauthority` file. The key is made up of a 56-bit DES encryption key and 64 bits of random data. The later part is used for authentication.

  To become authenticated, the application creates a 192-bit packet that is encrypted with the DES key, sent to the server computer, and then decrypted by the X server to verify the application. The packet contains the current time (in seconds) and a 48-bit identifier (such as the TCP/IP address and port). Because this information is encrypted, this method is considered more secure than the magic cookie method.

- SUN DES-1—This method, created for SunOS versions of UNIX, enables you to authenticate X client processes by user name as well as by host name. It combines features from NIS and Secure RPC to allow access based on the user name associated with the client process.

  Access is allowed by adding user name/NIS domain information with the xhost command. For example, to add the user john from the domain named snowbird.com from the server computer, you could type

  ```
  xhost + john@snowbird.com
  ```

  The user must then add the user running the server process to his or her $HOME/.Xauthority file. This is done with the xauth command. This method can only be used when the users on both the client and server sides have set up the public and private key pairs on their systems.

- MIT Kerberos-5—This method provides authentication of X clients by having a third party verify both sides of the client/server connection. When xdm starts, the X server process uses the user's password to get Kerberos tickets from a Kerberos server. Those tickets allow that user access to network services.

  To enable or disable authorization by the user running the X display to users running client processes, the X display user runs the xhost command. For example, the following command allows access by the user named bill from the Kerberos realm named sundance:

  ```
  xhost krb5:john@sundance
  ```

For each of the nonhost access methods of X access control, you need to use the xauth program to create and modify the contents of the .Xauthority file. At connection time, the contents of the .Xauthority file is passed to the X server process. That information can then be used to authenticate the client requests that arrive at the server.

Useful X Clients

Regardless of which UNIX system you are using, you are sure to have several X clients available on your computer. The most common client is probably xterm, which opens a terminal window to allow you to type shell commands. Other useful X clients include a calculator (xcalc), a screen lock program (xlock), and a bitmap editor (bitmap).

The following sections describe some useful X clients. Most of these clients use standard options to change such things as window size, fonts, colors, and so on. See "Common X Client Options" for information about these options.

8

**GUIs FOR
END USERS**

Terminal Window (`xterm`)

The `xterm` client opens a terminal window on the computer on which the client is run. The terminal window provides a shell interface to the UNIX system while emulating a particular character terminal (such as a VT100 or Tektronix 4014 terminal). The terminal window is useful for those who need to use shell commands during X sessions and for launching applications that require a character interface.

Figure 8.3 shows an example of an `xterm` client.

FIGURE 8.3.

The xterm client provides a command-line interface in X.

The xterm client accepts many standard X Toolkit command line options and resources for changing such things as window sizes and colors. However, you can modify some resources for `xterm` that are specific to certain types of terminal emulation.

Console Monitor Window (`xconsole`)

When you are running an X Window session from the console terminal, important system messages that are directed to that terminal can be lost. When the computer's system state changes, for example, messages relating to the processes that are started or stopped appear on the console. The `xconsole` client is a way of having console messages appear on the X desktop.

> **NOTE**
>
> Console messages are those that are sent to the `/dev/console` device.

Figure 8.4 shows an example of a console monitor (`xconsole`) window.

FIGURE 8.4.

Display console messages with the xconsole console monitor.

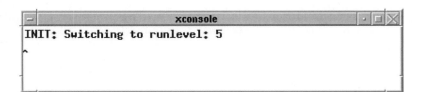

Besides monitoring the console, xconsole can be used to monitor messages output to other devices as well. To monitor a device other than /dev/console, add the option **-file** *filename*, where *filename* is replaced by the name of the device you want to monitor.

Calculator (xcalc)

Using the xcalc scientific calculator client, you can emulate a TI-30 or HP-10C calculator on the X desktop. Figure 8.5 shows an example of an xcalc window.

FIGURE 8.5.

Use scientific calculator functions with xcalc.

By default, the calculator will emulate a TI-30 calculator. To emulate an HP-10C calculator, add the -rpn option to the xcalc command line.

Bitmap Editor (bitmap)

The bitmap client is used to create and edit simple, rectangular bitmap images. The bitmaps are stored in C language code fragments. Programmers can use them to create icons or cursors. Figure 8.6 shows an example of a bitmap editor.

FIGURE 8.6.

Create simple images with bitmap editor.

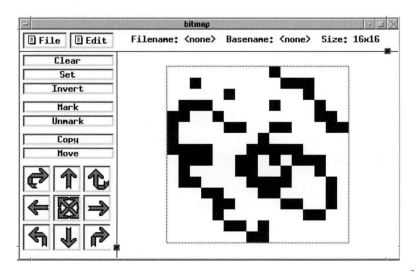

8

GUIs FOR
END USERS

With editing commands on the bitmap editor window, you can move, flip, rotate, and perform a variety of other functions. Using the `bmtoa` and `atobm` utilities, you can convert bitmap images to and from ASCII strings.

X Display Lock (`xlock`)

With the `xlock` utility, you can lock your X window session until you enter a password to restore it. When `xlock` is on, the mouse is disabled, client connections are rejected, and the desktop is covered with a changing pattern.

When you are ready to unlock your display, click any key from the keyboard. The `xlock` utility will prompt you for a password, as shown in Figure 8.7.

FIGURE 8.7.

Lock an X display with `xlock`.

Name: root
Password:
Enter password to unlock; select icon to lock.

You can choose from more than 60 display modes to use with `xlock`. To use a display mode with `xlock`, use the **-mode** *name* option. The following is an example of `xlock` in a bouncing ball mode:

```
xlock -mode ball
```

The following are a few of the other modes you can use with `xlock`:

bat	Flying bats
blot	Rorschach's ink blot
braid	Random braids and knots
dclock	Floating digital clock
eyes	Eyes following a bouncing grelb
fract	Fractals
image	Random logos
life3d	Bay's game of 3D life
maze	Random maze solver
puzzle	Puzzle being scrambled and solved
star	Twisting star field
world	Spinning earths

If you don't choose a mode, `xlock` switches between modes randomly.

Clock (`xclock`)

To display time in either analog or digital format, you can use the `xclock` utility. By default, time is displayed in analog format (with a clock face and hands). Time is updated every 60 seconds, so by default, no second hand is displayed.

Figure 8.8 shows the default `xclock` display.

FIGURE 8.8.

Time can be displayed in analog format (shown here) or digital format with `xclock`*.*

To change the clock to digital, use the `-digital` option. To change how often the clock is updated, use the `-update` option. For example, to show a digital clock that updates every second, type the following:

```
xclock -digital -update 1 &
```

Other options with `xclock` include the `-chime` and `-hands` options. By adding `-chime` to the command line, the clock chimes once on the half hour and twice on the hour. With the **-hands** *color* option, you can replace *color* with the name of a color to have the hands be displayed in that color.

X Eyes (`xeyes`)

With the `xeyes` utility, you can always tell where your mouse pointer is located. As you move your mouse around the screen, the eyes follow it. Figure 8.9 shows the `xeyes` utility.

Fish Tank (`xfishtank`)

The `xfishtank` is just one of several X clients that can make your desktop more fun to watch. When you start `xfishtank`, it places fish on your desktop and has them swim slowly across the screen. The fish swim behind your windows, so not to disrupt your work. Figure 8.10 shows an example of the `xfishtank` on a desktop.

FIGURE 8.9.

Eyes follow your mouse with the xeyes utility.

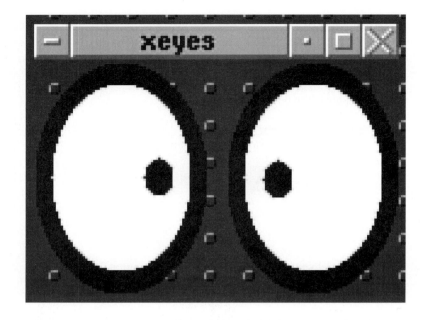

FIGURE 8.10.

Fish swim across the desktop with xfishtank.

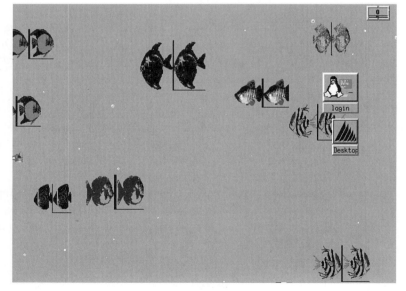

Common X Client Options

By learning a few options that are available on most X client utilities, you can save yourself the trouble of looking up options for each X client you come across. The following are a few of the most common X client options:

Changing the Display

By default, an X client connects to the X server that is identified in the $DISPLAY variable. Most X clients enable you to direct the client to another display using the option

`-display displayname`

The *displayname* value is in the form *host*:0.0 or :0. Of course, if the display is set to a value other than the local display, the remote X server must grant the X client permission to connect to the server. (See "Controlling Client Access" for details.)

Setting Window Size and Location

Using the **-geometry** option, you can specify the size and location of the main window the client creates on the X display. The width and height values are noted in either pixels or characters, depending on the application. The form of the -geometry option is

-geometry widthxheight+xoff+yoff :

The xoff value indicates where the window begins in relation to the left side of the screen. The yoff value indicates the location of the window, based on the top edge of the screen. Both negative and positive values for xoff and yoff are valid. The following geometry value would open a window that is 40 pixels wide and 40 pixels high and that begins 20 pixels from the left and 10 pixels from the top:

`-geometry 40x20+20+10`

Adding geometry options to the utilities that start in a start-up file (such as .xinitrc) enable you to start your X session with the set of utilities you like on the screen and arranged on your desktop the way you prefer.

Assigning Window Colors

Color attributes are associated with different parts of the windows of X clients. You can use a common set of X client options to change the colors on the window border, its background, and its foreground (typically the text that appears in a window). These options are -bg (background), -fg (foreground), and -bd (border).

8

**GUIs FOR
END USERS**

The following is an example of an `xterm` command line with the background set to black, the foreground set to white, and the border set to green.

```
xterm -bg black -fg white -bd green &
```

> **NOTE**
>
> The window manager you use may override some of the color attributes you set on the X client's command line. Most window managers will replace the border, for example, so the border color you set won't appear.

Colors can be indicated using either words (blue, green, yellow, and so on) or numbers representing combinations of red, green, and blue (`rgb:0/0/0`) to form colors. These words and numbers are defined in a color database file, the text version of which is usually contained in the `rgb.txt` file in the `<XROOT>/lib/X11` directory. Check the `rgb.txt` file for a full list of color names and numbers

The following is a list of eight primary colors, along with the rgb number you would use to represent each color. The numbers separated by the slashes represent the values of red, green, and blue, respectively. (Instead of the hex number, you could use a decimal number. So, for example, instead of `ffff`, you could use `255`.)

```
Black       rgb:0/0/0
White       rgb:ffff/ffff/ffff
Red         rgb:ffff/0/0
Green       rgb:0/ffff/0
Blue        rgb:0/0/ffff
Cyan        rgb:0/ffff/ffff
Magenta     rgb:ffff/0/ffff
Yellow      rgb:ffff/ffff/0
```

More than 700 colors are listed in the `rgb.txt` file. In addition to the primary colors, such colors as `DeepPink1`, `DarkGoldenrod1`, and `PaleGreen1` are available. A good way to try them out is to launch an `xterm` window with different background and foreground colors set.

> **NOTE**
>
> Because many video cards are monochrome or support only a few colors, you may be limited in which colors you can use. For example, a basic color video card may support only 16 or 256 colors.

Changing Fonts

Hundreds of fonts are delivered with each X Window system. X clients can use these fonts within their applications. As a user, you can change the font used for displaying text on may X clients. Font families that are often available include Courier, Helvetica, New Century Schoolbook, Times Roman, Utopia, Lucinda, and several symbol fonts.

To change the text font used on some X clients (such as xterm), you can use the **-fn** *font* option. The following is an example of a command line that includes the -fn option:

```
xterm -fn '*courier-bold*240*' &
```

Because font names can be quite long, you will probably use wildcards to indicate the font you want. An asterisk (*) can be replaced by any number of characters, and a question mark (?) can be replaced with a single character. When you use wildcards, surround the font in single quotes to prevent the wildcards from being interpreted by the shell.

> **NOTE**
>
> For a font to be used, it must be available on the X server system. Although you may indicate a font to use from a remote client's system, the font won't appear unless the server has it.

If you are not sure which fonts are available (or what their full names are), you can use two programs to check available fonts on your system. The xlsfonts utility is a shell command that lists the fonts available on the server. The xfontsel program is an X client that provides a friendly, GUI-oriented way of displaying available fonts.

Because xlsfonts produces a long list of fonts, the best way to use it is to either search for a particular pattern or pipe it through a paging command (such as more or pg). By default, xlsfonts lists all X fonts available on the computer. To search for a pattern, use the -fn option as follows:

```
xlsfonts -fn '*courier*' ¦ more
```

This example displays all font names that include the word Courier. Notice that asterisks are used as wildcards and that the whole string is surrounded by single quotes.

The xfontsel program enables you to pull down menus to view and select the available fonts. When a font is selected, a character set of the font is displayed in the window. Click the fndry button to select the foundry group of fonts (such as adobe or sun) to choose from. Then select the family of fonts (such as Helvetica or Courier). Continue to select font attributes (such as point size and slant) until you see a font you like. Figure 8.11 shows an example of an xfontsel window.

FIGURE 8.11.

Use xfontsel to view available X fonts.

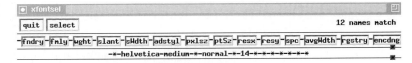

Changing the Title

You can change the name that appears across the title bar of an X window client using the -title option. This option is very handy if you want to indicate something special about the client process that is running. For example, if you want to indicate from where the client is running, you can add the name of the client's host on the title bar as follows:

```
xterm -title "Terminal Window from Snowbird"
```

This kind of use of the -title option helps you remember where you are working. (Remember, the X client will reference the client's host for the file system, devices, and other resources rather than the X server's host.)

Motif Window Manager

Motif is the most widely used window manager for commercial UNIX systems. Besides providing the look and feel of the graphical user interface, Motif includes toolkits that allow application developers to create GUI-based applications that can run without modification across a variety of computer platforms that employ the X Window system.

To the end user, Motif provides the window controls (borders, buttons, window menu, scroll bars, and title bar), mouse controls, keyboard controls, icons, and root window menu. Motif also offers mechanisms for automatically launching applications and customizing every aspect of how the interface works.

Features that distinguish Motif from other window managers are its three-dimensional appearance and its use of widgets. Motif window borders are shadowed to give the windows an appearance of depth. Widgets help standardize the look and feel of Motif by providing a standard look to common features, such as pull-down menus and dialog boxes.

The latest release of Motif is Motif 2.1. The Motif specification and source code are currently being maintained by the Open Group (http://www.opengroup.org). Besides maintaining Motif, the Open Group also maintains the Common Desktop Environment (CDE) and X Window system specification, as well as other standards that are of interest to the UNIX community. See the sidebar "Motif 2.0 and 2.1 Features" for information about new Motif features.

NOTE

Most commercial UNIX systems come with X and Motif installed and ready to use. If your version of UNIX doesn't have Motif, third-party versions are available. The following are a few Motif products: Bluestone MWM (http://www.bluestone.com), Metro Link Motif (http://www.metrolink.com/products/motif/index.html), SCO Premier Motif (http://www.premier.sco.com), Red Hat Motif (http://www.redhat.com), and UniPress Motif for Sun (http://www.unipress.com/cat/motif.html).

Because Open Group charges a fee, no free versions of Motif officially exist. However, LessTif is a free window manager that claims to be source-compatible with Motif. (See the description of LessTif later in this chapter.)

MOTIF 2.0 AND 2.1 FEATURES

If you are currently using an older version of Motif, you may be interested in new features in Motif 2.0 and 2.1. Changes to the Motif user interface include

- Support for printing using a print server based on X protocol. Supported output formats include Postscript, PCL, and Raster.
- Improved drag-and-drop between Motif clients. Motif supports drag-and-drop between different applications, for example, even those running between different hosts.
- Virtual window management and workspace management improvements.
- Internationalization enhancements that enable users to work with text and character sets in their native languages. Text strings in windows can be localized for Asian and European languages. Vertical text is supported for some Asian languages.
- Widgets that support new or PC-style functions, such as drop-down lists, combo boxes, containers, and notebooks.
- Updated menu bar and menu selections.

Starting Motif Window Manager

If you are running a standard UNIX system, your X Window system will automatically be configured to start the Motif window manager when the user starts up an X session. If you want to start the Motif window manager directly, you need to run the mwm command after the X Window session has started.

Working with Motif Windows

You can use the Motif window manager with a mouse and/or keyboard, although the mouse is used most often. Using the mouse, you can move the pointer and click mouse buttons to select, move, resize, drag-and-drop, and open objects. The objects you can manipulate include windows, icons, text, menus, and buttons.

Although almost all Motif features can be customized, Motif begins with a default set of definitions for how windows appear and how mouse and keyboard actions are used. Also, many client programs include Motif widgets, which further standardizes the Motif look and feel.

Figure 8.12 shows a window being managed by the Motif window manager.

FIGURE 8.12.
Motif window controls enable you to manipulate client windows.

The client application controls the center area of the window. The Motif window manager controls the outside part of the window. The following are descriptions of each part of the window managed by Motif:

- Title Area—Shows the title of the window. You can move the window by selecting the title area and moving the mouse.

- Resize Handles—Select any side of the window to resize the window vertically or horizontally.

- Resize Corners—Select any corner to vertically and horizontally resize the window simultaneously.

- Window Menu button—Click this button to display the window menu. Selections on the window menu enable you to move or modify the window. (See the description "Using the Window Menu.")

- Minimize button—Reduces the window to an icon on the desktop.

- Maximize button—Expands the window to fill the entire screen.

Although you would typically use the mouse to select these window buttons and resize areas, keyboard equivalents are also available for selecting these items. (See the "Using the Keyboard" section for more information about manipulating windows using the keyboard.)

Using the Window Menu

When you select the Window Menu button on a Motif window, you can choose from the following selections:

- Restore—When a window has been reduced to an icon, this function enables you to restore that window to its original size. Likewise, you can also restore a maximized window.

- Move—Begins a window move operation. Complete the move by moving the mouse and clicking the mouse button.

- Size—Begins a window resize operation. Move the mouse to complete the resize operation.

- Minimize—Reduces the window to an icon on the desktop.

- Maximize—Enlarges the window to fill the screen.

- Lower—Lowers the window so it is behind any windows it is currently covering.

- Close—Kills the client process and removes the window.

Navigating with the Mouse

Motif assumes that you are using a 3-button mouse to navigate the workspace. If you have only a 2-button mouse, you can use the mouse in combination with certain keys to get the functions of the third button. The following are the general uses for each mouse button:

- Button 1 (left button)—This button is used most often. It can select, open, or drag-and-drop an item.
- Button 2 (middle button, not available on a 2-button mouse)—This button is used to transfer data.
- Button 3 (right button)—This button is used to open pull-down menus for items.

As you move the mouse on the Motif workspace, the mouse pointer changes depending on the current activity. As it moves around the workspace, the pointer is an arrow. In a text area, the pointer looks like an I-beam. If Motif is waiting for a process to finish, the pointer may be an hourglass. When the pointer is being used to resize or move a window, one of several arrow pointers appears.

> **TIP**
>
> When you first start the GUI, your mouse pointer may be in an "X" shape. This means that the X session has begun, but Motif has not started yet. Motif should start soon. If it doesn't, you may need to run mwm manually from an xterm window.

Clicking the pointer over a window or icon may make that item active (depending how certain resources are set). Single-clicking the left button selects the window or icon being pointed to. Single-clicking buttons may start a function or display a pull-down menu. Double-clicking opens the icon or maximizes the window.

Pressing and holding the left mouse button can be used in several ways. On a resize handle or resize corner, holding and moving the mouse causes the window to resize. On an object (such as an icon), you can hold and move the mouse to drop the object on another application. In a text area, holding and moving the mouse can be used to select a text area.

Navigating with the Keyboard

To navigate the Motif workspace without a mouse, you can use keystrokes. These keystrokes enable you to change focus from one window to the next or navigate within a window.

Because some applications can consist of several windows, navigation keys can either take you among the windows in a single application or among the windows of different applications. As you change focus, the new, current window is highlighted. The following are some keystrokes you can use to focus on the window you want:

- Windows within an application—When an application is represented by several windows, to move to the next window within that application, press Alt+F6 (forward) or Alt+Shift+F6 (backward).

- Windows of different applications—To go to the next application, press Alt+Tab (forward) or Alt+Shift+Tab (backward). If the application has several windows, focus returns to the last window in the group to have focus.

After a window or icon is selected, you can select the window's menu button using Shift+Esc. You can then select any function from the menu: Restore (Alt+F5), Move (Alt+F7), Size (Alt+F8), Minimize (Alt+F9), Maximize (Alt+F10), Lower (Alt+F3), and Close (Alt+F4).

To move around within a window, many of the keystrokes are intuitive. Arrow keys can move the cursor up, down, left, and right within a text area. Page Up and Page Down can move among different pages in a scrollable display. To move to different fields in a window, use Ctrl+Tab (next field) or Ctrl+Shift+Tab (previous field).

Using the Root Menu

A set of functions apply to the Motif workspace as a whole. These functions are accessible via the root menu. To display the root menu, click the right mouse button on an open part of the workspace. Then select one of the following functions:

- New Window—This selection starts and opens a new xterm window so you can type shell commands.

- Shuffle Up—When several windows are on top of each other on the workspace, this selection moves the bottom window to the top.

- Shuffle Down—When several windows are on top of each other on the workspace, this selection moves the top window to the bottom.

- Refresh—Redisplays all the windows and icons on the entire display.

- Pack Icon—Organizes all the icons in an orderly way.

- Restart—Restarts the Motif window manager. (The most common reason for restarting Motif is to have any resources you changed go into effect.)

You can add your own items to the root menu. This is described in the next section, "Customizing Motif."

Customizing Motif

Almost everything about how Motif appears and acts can be customized to suit your preferences. You can define what menus appear by selecting mouse buttons, then define what actions occur from choosing each menu item. Likewise, you can change the look and feel of many aspects of the user interface.

Most of the look-and-feel changes to Motif can be done by adding resources to each user's $HOME/.Xdefaults file. This is where you would set values that apply to all X clients as well as the Motif window manager. Examples of Motif resources that you can add to .Xdefaults are described in the section "Customizing X Resources."

Changes to Motif menus, mouse button actions, and key sequences can be defined in a configuration file that is specific to Motif. This configuration file is named .mwmrc and can be added to each user's home directory ($HOME/.mwmrc).

One way to create your own .mwmrc file is to copy the system.mwmrc file, make the changes you want, then copy it to $HOME/.mwmrc. Mostly what you want to do in this file is define what happens when mouse buttons or key sequences are pressed in different circumstances. In particular, you want to define personalized menus that result in the actions you choose.

The following is an example of the contents of a .mwmrc file. The contents define several menus, then bind those menus to particular mouse buttons. The first part defines the root menu:

```
Menu DefaultRootMenu
{
        "My Menu"       f.title
        separator       f.separator
        "Programs"      f.menu apps
        "Refresh"       f.refresh
        "Pack Icon"     f.pack_icons
        "Restart"       f.restart
}
```

In this example, the root menu (DefaultRootMenu) is named "My Menu," followed by a separator. The Programs menu item was added to open a submenu called apps. The rest of the menu offers standard Motif functions (Refresh, Pack Icon, and Restart).

```
Menu apps
{
        "Programs"      f.title
        "Eyes"          f.exec "xeyes"
        "Xv"            f.exec "xv"
        "Terminal"      f.exec "xterm"
}
```

The apps menu, called Programs, is displayed when someone clicks Programs from the root menu. At that point, the menu displays three entries (Eyes, Xv, and Terminal) that can launch individual programs (xeyes, xv, and xterm).

```
Buttons DefaultButtonBindings
{
        <Btn1Down>      icon|frame       f.raise
        <Btn2Down>      root             f.menu  apps
        <Btn3Down>      icon|frame       f.post_wmenu
        <Btn3Down>      root             f.menu  DefaultRootMenu
}
```

Mouse buttons are defined to provide different functions. When button 1 is pressed on an icon or a frame, the selected window is raised to the top of the window stack (f.raise). When button 2 is pressed on the workspace (root), the Programs menu (apps) is displayed. When button 3 is pressed on an icon or a frame, the window menu appears. Finally, when button 3 is pressed on the workspace, the root menu (DefaultRootMenu) appears.

```
Keys DefaultKeyBindings
{
        Shift<Key>Escape        window|icon          f.post_wmenu
        Alt<Key>space           window|icon          f.post_wmenu
        Alt<Key>Tab             root|icon|window     f.next_key
        Alt Shift<Key>Tab       root|icon|window     f.prev_key
        Alt<Key>Escape          root|icon|window     f.circle_down
        Alt Shift<Key>Escape    root|icon|window     f.circle_up
        Alt Shift Ctrl<Key>exclam root|icon|window   f.set_behavior
        Alt<Key>F6              window               f.next_key
transient
        Alt Shift<Key>F6        window               f.prev_key
transient
}
```

The Keys DefaultKeyBindings entry shows the default key sequences that are defined for Motif in this example. The first two lines (Shift+Esc and Alt+space) result in the window menu being displayed. The next two lines change the focus to the next or previous windows. The next two lines lower or raise the current window in the stack, respectively. The next line restarts the window manager. The last two lines move the focus to the next transient window in the stack.

Other Window Managers

Because the X Window system is so widely deployed in UNIX systems, most new GUIs for UNIX have been done by creating window managers that work with X. Often the intent of these window managers is to enable users who are comfortable with a particular type of GUI to be able to have that look and feel while using UNIX.

Most of the window managers described here are shareware or freeware. Although Web sites that contain descriptions of each window manager are noted in the following text, several sites provide access to information about several window managers. In particular, check out the Window Managers for X page (`http://www.PLiG.org/xwinman`) and the Sunsite window managers ftp directory (`http://www.sunsite.unc.edu/pub/Linux/X11/window-managers`).

TWM Window Manager

The Tab Window Manager (TWM) is one of the early window managers available for the X Window system. It is a simple but functional window manager, allowing standard features for reshaping windows, adding title bars, and offering pull-down menus.

Using the main pull-down menu (right-click anywhere on the desktop), you can select a function, then apply that function to a client window by clicking it. The following items are available on the main TWM pull-down menu:

- Iconify—Reduces the client window to an icon.
- Resize—Enables the selected window to be resized.
- Move—Enables the selected window to be moved.
- Raise—Raises the window so it is displayed in front of the other windows.
- Lower—Lowers the window so it is displayed behind the other windows.
- Focus—Makes the selected window the current window (without raising or lowering its position).
- Unfocus—Removes focus from the selected window.
- Kill—Kills the selected client window.
- Delete—Removes the selected client window from the screen.

From the TWM menu, you can also select Show Iconmgr (which displays a list of running clients) or Hide Iconmgr (which removes the list from the screen). By selecting the Restart function, you restart all the running xclients

Configuration files for TWM can include: $HOME/twmrc.*X* (where *X* is replaced by the screen number), $HOME/.twmrc, and `system.twmrc` (in `<XRoot>/lib/X11/twm`). The first two configuration files apply to the individual user, and the third file applies to anyone using TWM on the window manager's computer.

FVWM Window Manager

FVWM is perhaps the most popular window manager used on Linux systems. Designed to appear like the Motif window manager, FVWM was actually a redesigned TWM window manager that was intended to improve memory consumption and add a 3D look.

To improve Motif compatibility, FVWM can recognize Motif mwm hints. The buttons on each window also look and behave like Motif. So, for example, the leftmost button displays a window menu, and three right buttons iconify the window, maximize the window, and delete the window, respectively.

Left-click an open desktop area and a workplace menu appears. This menu enables you to choose from a variety of applications, shells, games, desktop features, configuration selections or help items. Right-click the desktop to view and select from a menu of active clients.

Figure 8.13 shows an example of an FVWM window manger. This example is running on a Caldera Open Linux system.

FIGURE 8.13.

FVWM is a free window manager with similarities to Motif.

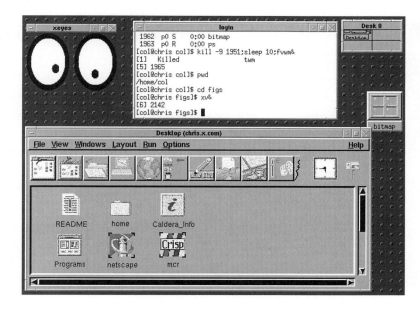

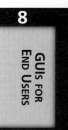

8

GUIs FOR END USERS

For more information about FVWM, see the Official FVWM Homepage
(`http://www.hpc.uh.edu/fvwm`).

AfterStep Window Manager

For users who like the interface provided with NeXTSTEP computers, the AfterStep window manager provides much of the same look and feel of NeXTSTEP in an X Window system environment. AfterStep is based on the FVWM window manager, with several differences.

To behave more like NeXTSTEP, AfterStep adapted the title bar, buttons, corners, and borders to appear as they do in NeXTSTEP. Menus on the root window are done in the NeXTSTEP style. The initialization file used with AfterStep is `.bowmanrc`.

For more information on AfterStep, you can visit the Official AfterStep Site (`http://www.afterstep.org.`).

AmiWm Window Manager

For users who like the user interface on Amiga computers, the AmiWm window manager offers a similar look and feel. With AmiWm, users can drag multiple screens and assign different backdrops to each.

To obtain the AmiWm window manager, you can visit the AmiWm home page (`http://www.lysator.liu.se/~marcus/amiwm.html`).

CTWM Window Manager

The CTWM window manager is really an extension to the TWM window manager. Using a workspace manager, CTWM enables you to switch between up to 32 virtual screens (referred to as workspaces). Each workspace can have a separate customized set of attributes, such as names, colors, and buttons.

Figure 8.14 contains an example of a CTWM window manager. The boxes numbered one through eight are buttons you can click to display any of the eight (default) virtual screens.

FIGURE 8.14.
Select from multiple virtual screens with CTWM.

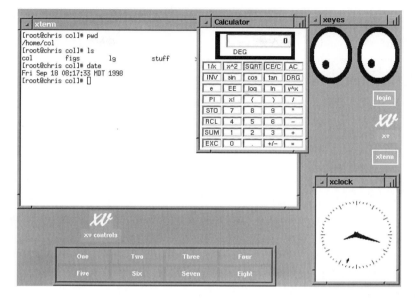

LessTif Window Manager

The LessTif window manager is a Motif lookalike that is based on the FVWM window manager. LessTif's greatest feature is that it is source compatible with OSF/Motif 1.2. Therefore, source code that compiles in Motif should work the same in LessTif.

LessTif was created by Chris Toshok and the Hungry Programmers. It contains a clone of the Motif Window manager, as well as libraries needed to run popular Motif applications. Netscape Communicator, for example, relies on Motif libraries to run, as does the Open Inventor model building software from SGI.

To get more information on LessTif along with links to LessTif download sites, go the LessTif home page at http://www.lesstif.com.

OLVWM Window Manager

The OLVWM window manager is a partial implementation of the OpenLook graphical user interface. At one time, OpenLook was the major competitor to Motif for domination of the UNIX desktop interface. OpenLook was developed by Sun Microsystems, although Sun has also moved to Motif as the standard GUI.

The OLVWM window manager is compliant with the Xview toolkit. Included with the window manager are such features as pushpins (for pinning menus on the workspace), as well as distinctive OpenLook buttons, icons, and window borders.

8

GUIs FOR
END USERS

wm2 Window Manager

The wm2 window manager was designed to be simple in its features and fast to operate. There are no icons, configuration options, virtual desktops, toolbars, or root menus you can extend. This is a bare-bones window manager.

What wm2 does include is most everything you need to efficiently use the desktop. You can move and resize windows, hide and restore windows, and then delete them when you are done. Descriptions and download information for wm2 is available from the wm2 home page at `http://www.all-day-breakfast.com/wm2`.

Summary

Nearly all graphical user interfaces (GUIs) used with UNIX today are based on the X Window system. In addition to providing a mechanism for displaying and managing client programs, the X Window system is designed to easily allow client applications from anywhere on the network to be used on the local display.

Although X provides the framework for the GUI, it is the window manager that offers the controls, as well as the look and feel of the GUI. X allows many different window managers to be used; however, Motif is the most popular window manager for commercial UNIX systems. Motif offers many ease-of-use features as well as a powerful set of tools for creating graphical applications.

For users who want a different look and feel for their GUI, several inexpensive or public domain window managers are available. Most provide features that are similar to GUIs in other computer environments. For example, the AmiWm window manager causes the GUI to behave like the GUI on an Amiga computer, and the AfterStep window manager behaves like the NeXTSTEP computing environment.

UNIX Shells

PART

II

IN THIS PART

What Is a Shell?

by Robin Burk and William A. Farra

CHAPTER 9

Nearly every human-usable invention has an interface point with which you interact. Whether you are in the front seat of a horse and buggy, in the cockpit of a plane, or at the keyboard of a piano, this position is where you manipulate and manage the various aspects of the invention to achieve a desired outcome. The human interface point for UNIX is the shell, which is a program layer that provides you with an environment in which to enter commands and parameters to produce a given result. As with any invention, the more knowledge and experience you have with it, the greater the accomplishment you make with it.

To meet varying needs, UNIX has provided different shells. Discussed in Chapters 10 through 13 are Bourne, Bourne Again, Korn, and C shells. Each of these offers features and ways to interact with UNIX. The following topics are discussed in this chapter:

- How shells works with you and UNIX
- The features of a shell
- Manipulating the shell environment

How the Kernel and the Shell Interact

When a UNIX system is brought online, the program unix (the Kernel) is loaded into the computer's main memory, where it remains until the computer is shut down. During the bootup process, the program init runs as a background task and remains running until shutdown. This program scans the file /etc/inittab, which lists what ports have terminals and their characteristics. When an active, open terminal is found, init calls the program getty, which issues a login: prompt to the terminal's monitor. With these processes in place and running, the user is ready to start interacting with the system.

UNIX Calls the Shell at Login

Figure 9.1 shows the process flow from the kernel through the login process. At this point, the user is in an active shell, ready to give commands to the system.

During login, when you type your username, getty issues a password: prompt to the monitor. After you type your password, getty calls login, which scans for a matching entry in the file /etc/passwd. If a match is made, login proceeds to take you to your home directory and then passes control to a session startup program; both the username and password are specified by the entry in /etc/passwd. Although this might be a specific application program, such as a menu program, normally the session startup program is a shell program such as /bin/sh, the Bourne shell.

FIGURE 9.1.

*How a shell is
started from login.*

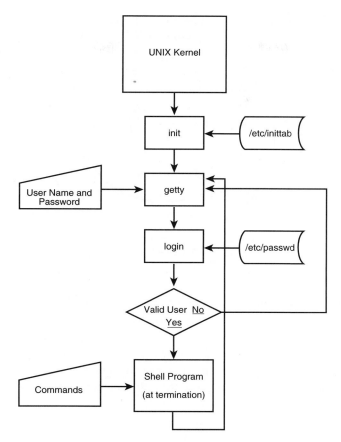

From here, the shell program reads the files /etc/profile and .profile, which set up the system-wide and user-specific environment criteria. At this point, the shell issues a command prompt such as $.

When the shell is terminated, the kernel returns control to the init program, which restarts the login process. Termination can happen in one of two ways: with the exit command or when the kernel issues a kill command to the shell process. At termination, the kernel recovers all resources used by the user and the shell program.

The Shell and Child Processes

In the UNIX system, there are many layers of programs starting from the kernel through a given application program or command. The relationship of these layers is represented in Figure 9.2.

9

WHAT IS A
SHELL?

FIGURE 9.2.
UNIX system layers.

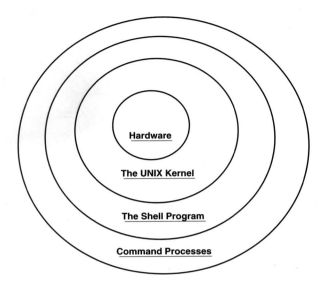

After you finish logging on, the shell program layer is in direct contact with the kernel, as shown in Figure 9.2. As you type a command such as $ ls, the shell locates the actual program file, /bin/ls, and passes it to the kernel to execute. The kernel creates a new child process area, loads the program, and executes the instructions in /bin/ls. After program completion, the kernel recovers the process area and returns control to the parent shell program. To see an example of this, type the following command:

```
$ps
```

This lists the processes you are currently running. You see the shell program and the ps program. Now type the following:

```
$sleep 10 &
$ps
```

The first command creates a sleep child process to run in the background, which you see listed with the ps command. Whenever you enter a command, a child process is created and independently executes from the parent process or shell. This leaves the parent intact to continue other work.

Auto-Execution of the Shell

Some UNIX resources, such as cron, can execute a shell program without human inter-action. When using this feature, the user needs to specify which shell to run in the first line of the shell program, like this:

```
#! /bin/sh
```

This specifies the Bourne shell.

You should also redirect any output because no terminal is associated with auto-execution. This is described in the "File Handling: Input/Output Redirection and Pipes" section later in this chapter.

The Functions and Features of a Shell

It doesn't matter which of the standard shells you choose because they all have the same purpose: to provide a user interface to UNIX. To provide this interface, all the shells offer the same basic characteristics:

- Command-line interpretation
- Reserved words
- Shell metacharacters (wildcards)
- Access to and handling of program commands
- File handling: input/output redirection and pipes
- Maintenance of variables
- Environment control
- Shell programming

Command-Line Interpretation

When you log in, starting a special version of a shell called an interactive shell, you see a shell prompt, usually in the form of a dollar sign ($), a percent sign (%), or a pound sign (#). When you type a line of input at a shell prompt, the shell tries to interpret it. Input to a shell prompt is sometimes called a command line. The basic format of a command line is

command arguments

command is an executable UNIX command, program, utility, or shell program. *arguments* are passed to the executable. Most UNIX utility programs expect arguments to take the following form:

options filenames

For example, in the command line

```
$ ls -l file1 file2
```

there are three arguments to `ls`; the first is an option, and the last two are filenames.

One thing the shell does for the kernel is eliminate unnecessary information. For a computer, one type of unnecessary information is whitespace; therefore, it is important to know what the shell does when it sees whitespace. Whitespace consists of space characters, horizontal tabs, and newline characters. Consider this example:

```
$ echo part A    part B    part C
part A part B part C
```

Here, the shell has interpreted the command line as the echo command with six arguments and has removed the whitespace between the arguments. For example, if you were printing headings for a report and wanted to keep the whitespace, you would have to enclose the data in quotation marks, as in the following:

```
$ echo 'part A    part B    part C'
part A    part B    part C
```

The single quotation mark prevents the shell from looking inside the quotes. Now the shell interprets this line as the `echo` command with a single argument, which happens to be a string of characters including whitespace.

Reserved Words

All shell versions have words that have special meaning. In shell programming, words such as `do`, `done`, `for`, and `while` provide loop control—and `if`, `then`, `else`, and `fi` provide conditional control. Each shell version has different reserved word pertaining to its specific features.

Shell Metacharacters (Wildcards)

All shell versions have metacharacters, which allow the user to specify filenames. The following are wildcards:

Wild Card	Description
*	Matches any portion
?	Matches any single character
[]	Matches a range or list of characters

Wildcards can be useful when processing a number of specific files. The following are some examples:

```
$ls t*
```

This lists all files starting with t.

```
$ls test?5.dat
```

This lists all files starting with test followed by any single character and ending with `5.dat`.

```
$ls [a-c]*
```

This lists all files starting with a through c.

```
$ls [e,m,t]*
```

This lists all files starting with e, m, or t.

Program Commands

When a command is typed, the shell reads the environment variable `$path`, which contains a list of directories containing program files. The shell looks through this set of directories to find the program file for the command. The shell then passes the true filename to the kernel.

File Handling: Input/Output Redirection and Pipes

In previous chapters, you learned about standard input and output. Unless otherwise specified with arguments, most UNIX commands take input from the terminal keyboard and send output to the terminal monitor. To redirect output to a file, use the > (greater-than) symbol. For example,

```
$ls > myfiles
```

lists the files in your current directory and places them in a file called `myfiles`. Likewise, you can redirect input with the < symbol. For example,

```
$wc -l < myfiles
```

feeds the command wc with input from the file `myfiles`. Although you could obtain the same output by having the filename as an argument, the need for input redirection becomes more apparent in shell programming.

To string the output from one command to the input of the next command, you can use the | (pipe) symbol. For example,

```
$ls -s ¦ sort -nr ¦ pg
```

9

WHAT IS A SHELL?

This lists the files in the current directory with blocksize and then pipes the output to the sort, which sorts the files in numeric descending order and pipes that output to the paging command pg for final display on the terminal's monitor. The pipe command is one of the most useful tools when creating command constructs.

Command Substitution

Command substitution is similar to redirection except that is used to provide arguments to a command from the output of another. For example,

```
$grep `wc -l myfiles` *
```

takes the number of lines in the file myfiles from the wc command and places the number as an argument to the grep command to search all files in the current directory for that number.

Maintenance of Variables

The shell is capable of maintaining variables. Variables are places you can store data for later use. You assign a value to a variable with an equal (=) sign:

```
$ LOOKUP=/usr/mydir
```

Here, the shell establishes LOOKUP as a variable and assigns it the value /usr/mydir. Later, you can use the value stored in LOOKUP in a command line by prefacing the variable name with a dollar sign ($). Consider these examples:

```
$ echo $LOOKUP
/usr/mydir
$ echo LOOKUP
LOOKUP
```

To make a variable available to child processes, you can use the export command—for example:

```
$ LOOKUP=/usr/mydir
$export LOOKUP
```

NOTE

Assigning values to variables in the C shell differs from doing so in the Bourne and Korn shells. To assign a variable in the C shell, use the set command:

```
% set LOOKUP = /usr/mydir
```

Notice that spaces precede and follow the equal sign.

Like filename substitution, variable name substitution happens before the program call is made. The second example omits the dollar sign ($). Therefore, the shell simply passes the string to echo as an argument. In variable name substitution, the value of the variable replaces the variable name.

For example, in

```
$ ls $LOOKUP/filename
```

the ls program is called with the single argument /usr/mydir/filename.

Shell Startup—Environment Control

When a user begins a session with UNIX and the shell is executed, the shell creates a specified environment for the user. The following sections describe these processes.

Shell Environment Variables

When the login program invokes your shell, it sets up your environment variables, which are read from the shell initialization files /etc/profile and .profile. These files normally set the type of terminal in the variable $TERM and the default path that is searched for executable files in the variable $PATH. Try these examples:

```
$ echo $TERM
$ echo $PATH
```

You can easily change the variables the same way you assign values to any shell variable.

> **NOTE**
>
> C shell assigns values to environment variables using the setenv command:
>
> ```
> % setenv TERM vt100
> ```

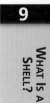

Shell Startup Files

The file .profile is the local startup file for the Bourne shell. The Korn shell uses .kshrc, and the C shell uses .cshrc. You can edit these files to manipulate your startup environment. You can add variables as the need arises. You also can add shell programming to have conditional environment settings, if necessary.

Shell Startup Options

When invoking the shell either from /etc/passwd or the command line, you can set several options as arguments to the shell program. For example, the Bourne shell has a -x option that displays commands and their arguments before they are executed. This is useful for debugging a shell program. These options are described in detail in the following chapters.

Shell Programming

You've seen that the shell is used to interpret command lines, maintain variables, and execute programs. The shell is also a programming language. You can store a set of shell commands in a file. This is known as a shell script or shell programming. By combining commands and variable assignments with flow control and decision making, you have a powerful programming tool. Using the shell as a programming language, you can automate recurring tasks, write reports, and build and manipulate your own data files. The remaining chapters in Part II of this book discuss shell programming in more detail.

Summary

The shell provides an interface between the user and the heart of UNIX—the kernel. The shell interprets command lines as input, makes filename and variable substitution, redirects input and output, locates the executable file, and initiates and interfaces programs. The shell creates child processes and can manage their execution. The shell maintains each user's environment variables. The shell is also a powerful programming language.

Although this chapter gives an overview of the UNIX shell, Chapters 8 through 12 describe in detail the various shells, their features, and language specifics. Also described are the fundamentals of shell programming and execution. Continued reading is highly recommended.

The Bourne Shell

by Robin Burk, William A. Farra, and Richard E. Rummel,

IN THIS CHAPTER

This chapter presents the fundamentals and many useful specifics of the Bourne shell, currently the most popular of the UNIX shells for execution of application programs. The chapter also describes the steps to organize and script shell commands to produce a program that you can run by name at the shell prompt, or other UNIX methods of program initiation.

The following topics are discussed in this chapter:

- Shells Basics
  - Invocation
  - Environment
  - Options
  - Special Characters
- Shell Variables
  - User-Defined Variables
  - Environment Variables
  - Positional Variables or Shell Arguments
- Shell Script Programming
  - Conditional Testing
  - Repetition and loop control
- Customizing The Shell

Shell Basics

Stephen Bourne wrote the Bourne shell at Bell Laboratories, the development focal point of UNIX. Since then, many system corporations have produced hardware specific versions of UNIX, but have remarkably kept Bourne Shell basics consistent.

> **NOTE**
>
> $man sh or $man bsh on most UNIX systems lists the generalities of the Bourne Shell and details the specifics to that version of UNIX. It is recommended that you become familiar with the version you are using before and after reading this chapter.

The Shell Invocation and Environment

The first level of invocation occurs when a user logs on to a UNIX system and is specified by his entry into /etc/passwd file. For example:

```
farrawa:!:411:102:William Farra, Systems
Development,x385:/home/farrawa:/bin/bsh
```

This entry (which is : delimited) has the login ID, encrypted password (denoted by !), user ID #, default group ID #, comment field, home directory, and startup shell program. In this case, it is the Bourne shell. As the shell executes, it reads the system profile /etc/profile. This may set up various environment variables, such as PATH, that the shell uses to search for executables and TERM, the terminal type being used. Then the shell continues to place the user into the associated home directory and reads the local .profile. Finally, the shell displays the default prompt $.

> **NOTE**
>
> On UNIX systems, the superuser, also referred to as root, is without restriction. When the superuser logs in, she sees the pound sign (#) as a default prompt. It is a reminder that as superuser some of the built-in protections are not available and that extra care is necessary in this mode. Because the superuser can write to any directory and can remove any file, file permissions do not apply. Normally, the root login is only used for system administration and adding or deleting users. Experienced users often create a regular user account for themselves even on a single-user machine, to guard against disastrous slips of the keyboard.

Shell Invocation Options

When invoking or executing the Bourne shell, you can use any of several options. The following is a list of Bourne shell options available on most versions of UNIX.

-a	Tag all variables for export.
-c "string"	Commands are read from string.
-e	Noninteractive mode.
-f	Disable shell filename generation.
-h	Locate and remember functions as defined.
-i	Interactive mode.
-k	Put arguments in the environment for a command.

-n	Reads commands but does not execute them (test for syntax).
-r	Restricted mode.
-s	Commands are read from the standard input.
-t	A single command is executed, and the shell exits (use for debugging).
-u	Unset variables are an error during substitution.
-v	Verbose mode, displays shell input lines.
-x	Trace mode, displays commands as they are executed.

Many combinations of these options work together. Some obviously do not, such as -e, which sets noninteractive mode, and -i, which sets interactive mode. However, experience with options gives the user a multitude of alternatives in creating or modifying his shell environment.

The Restricted Shell

bsh -r or /bin/rsh or /usr/bin/rsh.

Depending on the version of UNIX, this command invokes the Bourne shell in restricted mode. With this option set, the user cannot change directories (cd), change the PATH variable, specify a full pathname to a command, or redirect output. This ensures an extra measure of control and security to the UNIX system and is typically used for application users (who never see a shell prompt) and dialup accounts (where security is a must). Normally, a restricted user is placed, from login, into a directory in which she has no write permission. Not having write permission in this directory does not mean that the user has no write permission anywhere. It does mean that he cannot change directories or specify pathnames in commands. Also, he cannot write a shell script and later access it in his working directory.

> **NOTE**
>
> If the restricted shell calls an unrestricted shell to carry out the commands, the restrictions can be bypassed. This is also true if the user can call an unrestricted shell directly. Remember that programs such as vi and more allow users to execute commands. If the command is sh, again it is possible to bypass the restrictions.

Changing Shell Options with set

When the user is at the command prompt $, she can modify her shell environment by setting or unsetting shell options with the set command. To turn on an option, use a -

(hyphen) and option letter. To turn off an option, use a + (plus sign) and option letter. For example:

```
$set -xv
```

This enables the trace mode in the shell so that all commands and substitutions are printed. It also displays the line input to shell.

```
$set +u
```

This disables error checking on unset variables when substitution occurs. To display which shell options have been set, type the following:

```
$echo $-
is
```

This indicates that the shell is in interactive mode and taking commands from standard input. Turning options on and off is useful when debugging a shell script program or testing a specific shell environment.

The User's Shell Startup File: `.profile`

Under each Bourne shell user's home directory is a file named `.profile`, which is used to specify permanent modifications to that userís shell environment. For example, to add a directory to the existing execution path, just add the following as line into `.profile`:

```
PATH=$PATH:/sql/bin ; export PATH
```

With this line in `.profile`, from the time the user logs in, the directory `/sql/bin` is searched for commands and executable programs. Other modifications can also be made via `.profile`.

Shell Environment Variables

UNIX systems offer environment variables whose values govern execution of programs. The following are among the most common are:

CDPATH	Contains search path(s) for the cd command.
HOME	Contains the user's home directory.
IFS	Internal field separators, normally space, tab, and newline.
MAIL	Path to a special file (mail box), used by UNIX email.
PATH	Contains search path(s) for commands and executables.
PS1	Primary prompt string, by default $.
PS2	Secondary prompt string, by default >.
TERM	Terminal type being used.

10

THE BOURNE SHELL

If the restricted mode is not set, these variables can be modified to accommodate the user's various needs. The syntax for modifying environment variables is as follows:

```
$variable="value" ; export variable
```

To display the value(s) in any given variable, type the **echo** command, space, and a **$** followed by the variable name.

```
$echo $MAIL
/usr/spool/mail/(user id)
```

Use caution when modifying environment variables. Incorrect modifications to shell environment variables may cause commands either not to function or not to function properly. If this happens, logging out of the session and logging back in restores the default values.

Special Characters and Their Meanings

The Bourne shell uses many nonalphanumeric characters to define specific shell features. Most of these features fall into four basic categories: special variable names, filename generation, data/program control, and quoting/escape character control.

Special Characters for Shell Variable Names

There are special characters that denote special shell variables, automatically set by the shell:

$#	The number of arguments supplied to the command shell.
$-	Flags supplied to the shell on invocation or with set.
$?	The status value returned by the last command.
$$	The process number of the current shell.
$!	The process number of the last child process.
$@	All arguments, individually double quoted.
$*	All arguments, double quoted.
$n	Positional argument values, where *n* is the position.
$0	The name of the current shell.

To display the number of arguments supplied to the shell, type the following:

```
$echo $#
0
```

This indicates that no arguments were supplied to the shell on invocation. These variables are particularly useful when writing a shell script.

Special Characters for Filename Generation

The Bourne shell uses special characters or metacharacters to indicate pattern matches with existing filenames. The following are those characters:

*	Matches any string or portion of string
?	
[-,!]	Range, list or not matched

To match files with a prefix of invoice, any middle character, and a suffix of dat, type the following:

```
$ls invoice?dat
```

To match files starting with the letter a through e, type the following:

```
$ls [a-e]*
```

To match files starting with a, c, and e, type the following:

```
$ls [a,c,e]*
```

To exclude a match with the letter m, type following:

```
$ls [!m]*
```

Special Characters for Data/Program Control

The Bourne shell uses special characters for data flow and execution control. With these characters, the user can send normal screen output to a file or device or as input to another command.

>(file)	Redirect output to a file.
>>(file)	Redirect and append output to the end of a file.
<(file)	Redirect standard input from a file.
;	Separate commands.
¦	Pipe standard output to standard input.
&	Place at end of command to execute in background.
``	Command substitution, redirect output as arguments.

Special Characters for Quoting and Escape

The Bourne shell uses the single quotes, ' ', and double quotes, " ", to encapsulate special characters or space delineated words to produce a single data string. When using double quotes, variable and command substitution is active as well as the escape character.

10

THE BOURNE SHELL

```
$echo "$HOME $PATH"
$/u/farrawa /bin:/etc:/usr/bin:
```

This example combines the values of $HOME and $PATH to produce a single string.

```
$echo '$HOME $PATH'
$$HOME $PATH
```

This example simply prints the string data enclosed. The shell escape character is a backslash \, which is used to negate the special meaning or shell function of the following character.

```
$echo \$HOME $PATH
$$HOME /bin:/etc:/usr/bin:
```

In this example, only the $ of $HOME is seen as text, and the variable meaning the shell is negated, $PATH, is still interpreted as a variable.

How the Shell Interprets Commands

The first exposure most people have to the Bourne shell is as an interactive shell. After logging on the system and seeing any messages from the system administrator, the user sees a shell prompt. The default prompt for the interactive Bourne shell is a dollar sign ($), indicating that the interactive shell is ready to accept a line of input, which it interprets.

The shell sees a line of input as a string of characters terminated with a newline character, which is usually the result of pressing Enter on your keyboard, and causes the shell to begin to interpret the line.

Entering Simple Commands

The most common form of input to the shell is the simple command, in which a command name is followed by any number of arguments. In the example

```
$ ls file1 file2 file3
```

ls is the command, and *file1*, *file2*, and *file3* are the arguments. The command is any UNIX executable. It is the responsibility of the command, not the shell, to interpret the arguments. Many UNIX commands, but certainly not all, take the following form:

```
$ command -options filenames
```

The shell does not interpret the arguments of the command but does process special characters to redirect input and output, start a different command, search the directories for filename patterns, substitute variable data, and substitute the output of other commands.

Substitution of Variable Data

Many of the previous examples in this chapter have used variables in the command line. Whenever the shell sees (not quoted or escaped) a dollar sign $, it interprets the subsequent text as a variable name. Whether the variable is environmental or user defined, the data stored in the variable is substituted on the command line. For example, the command

```
$ ls $HOME
```

lists the contents of the user's home directory, regardless of what the current working directory is. You can substitute variable names anywhere in the command line, including for the command name itself.

Redirection of Input and Output

When the shell sees the input (<) or output (>) redirection characters, the argument following the redirection symbol is sent to the subshell that controls the execution of the command. When the command opens the input or output file that has been redirected, the input or output is redirected to the file.

```
$ ls -l >dirfile
```

In this example, the only argument passed on to `ls` is the option `-l`. The filename `dirfile` is sent to the subshell that controls the execution of `ls`.

Entering Multiple Commands on One Line

The shell special character—the semicolon, ;,—indicates that the preceding command text on a line is ended, and the following is a new command. For example, the command line

```
$ who -H; df -v; ps -e
```

is the equivalent of

```
$ who -H
$ df -v
$ ps -e
```

In the second case, however, the results of each command appear between the command input lines. Commands are executed in sequence. If there is an error, the shell stops executing the command line where the error occurred.

Linking Multiple Commands with Pipes

One of the most powerful features of the Bourne shell is its capability to take standard output from one command and use it as standard input to another. This is accomplished

10

THE BOURNE
SHELL

with the pipe symbol, ¦. When the shell sees a pipe, it executes the preceding command and then creates a link to the standard input of the following command in the order the commands are on the command line. For example:

```
$who ¦ grep fred
```

This takes the list of users logged in from the who command and searches the list for the string fred using the grep. This creates output only if user fred is logged in.

Any UNIX command that takes input from standard input and sends output to standard output can be linked using the pipe.

Entering Commands to Process in Background

To take advantage of the UNIX multitasking capability, the shell allows commands to be processed in background. This is accomplished by placing the ampersand symbol, &, at the end of a command. For example:

```
$find / -name "ledger" -print > find.results 2>/dev/null &
```

This command line searches the entire file system for files named ledger, sends its output to a local file named find.results, eliminates unwanted errors, and processes this command independent of the current shell (in background).

> **NOTE**
>
> If a user has processes running in the background and she logs off, most UNIX systems terminate the processes owned by that login. Also when you enter a command to process in background, the shell returns and displays the process ID number.

Substituting the Results of Commands in a Command Line

Sometimes it is useful to pass the output or results of one command as arguments to another command. You do so by using pairs of the shell special character, the back quotation mark (`` ` ``), to delineate the command to be executed and whose output will be substituted at that point in the script. You most commonly use this method to store the results of command executions in variables. To store the five-digit Julian date in a variable, for example, you use the following command:

```
$ julian=`date '+%y%j'`
```

The back quotation marks cause the date command to be executed before the variable assignment is made. Back quotation marks can be extremely useful when you're performing arithmetic on shell variables.

Shell Variables

Variables are symbolic names that stand for some value. Earlier in this chapter, you saw how the variable HOME stood for the name of a user's home directory. If you enter the change directory command, cd, without an argument, cd takes you to your home directory. Variables are useful in any computer language because they allow you to refer to a piece of information without knowing its value. The Bourne shell has four types of variables: user-defined variables, positional variables or shell arguments, predefined or special variables, and environment variables.

Storing Data or User-Defined Variables

Variable names are comprised of alphanumeric characters and the underscore character, with the provision that variable names do not begin with one of the digits 0 through 9 and are case sensitive. Variables take on values when they appear in a command line to the left of an equal sign (=). For example, in the following command lines, COUNT takes on the value of 1, and NAME takes on the value of Stephanie:

```
$ COUNT=1
$ NAME=Stephanie
```

> **TIP**
>
> Because most UNIX commands are lowercase words, shell programs have traditionally used all capital letters in variable names to make them easy to identify.

To access the value of a variable, precede the variable name by a dollar sign ($):

```
$ NAME=John
$ echo Hello $NAME
Hello John
```

You also can assign variables to other variables, as follows:

```
$ JOHN=John
$ NAME=$JOHN
$ echo Goodbye $NAME
Goodbye John
```

You can assign more than one variable in a single line by separating the assignments with whitespace, as follows:

```
$ X=x Y=y
```

The variable assignment is performed from right to left:

```
$ X=$Y Y=y
$ echo $X
y
$ Z=z Y=$Z
$ echo $Y

$
```

An undefined variable has the null value. Values can be removed by using the unset command.

Conditional Variable Substitution

The Bourne shell requires that you enclose the name of a variable in curly braces ({ }) if substitution of its value at that point is to be made conditional.

Substituting Default Values for Variables

To establish default values for variable substitution, use the following form:

```
${variable:-value}
```

where *variable* is the name of the variable, and *value* is the default substitution. For example:

```
$ echo Hello $UNAME
Hello
$ echo Hello ${UNAME:-there}
Hello there
```

When you use this type of variable substitution, the default value is substituted in the command line, but the value of the variable is not changed. To substitute the default value and also assign the default value to the variable, use the following:

```
${variable:=value}
```

which causes *variable* to be assigned *value* after the substitution has been made.

The substitution value need not be literal; it can be a command in back quotation marks.

A third type of variable substitution substitutes the specified value if the variable has been set, as follows:

```
${variable:+value}
```

If *variable* is set, then *value* is substituted; if *variable* is not set, then nothing is substituted.

Conditional Variable Substitution with Error Checking

Another variable substitution method allows for error checking during variable substitution:

```
${variable:?message}
```

If variable is set, its value is substituted; if it is not set, *message* is written to the standard error file. If the substitution is made in a shell program, the program immediately terminates.

Positional Variables or Shell Arguments

When the shell's command-line interpreter processes a line of input, the first word of the command line is considered to be an executable file, and the remainder of the line is passed as arguments to the executable. If the executable is a shell program, the arguments are passed to the program as positional variables $1, $2, and so on up to $9. The positional variable $0 always contains the name of the executable.

Preventing Variables from Being Changed

If a variable has a value assigned, and you want to make sure that its value is not subsequently changed, you may designate a variable as a read-only variable with the following command:

```
readonly variable
```

From this point on, *variable* cannot be reassigned.

Making Variables Available to Subshells with export

When a shell executes a program, it sets up a new environment for the program to execute in, called a *subshell*. In the Bourne shell, variables are considered to be local variables and are not recognized outside the shell in which they were assigned a value. You can make a variable available to any subshells you execute by exporting it using the export command. Your variables can never be made available to other users.

When a variable has been made global in this way, it remains available until you log out of the parent shell. You can make an assignment permanent by including it in your .profile.

Shell Script Programming

The Bourne shell allows you to combine commands, including conditional logic and flow control, to generate powerful tools customized to your own needs. This section covers the most useful elements of shell scripting.

What Is a Program?

When you enter a complex command like

```
$ ls -R / ¦ grep myname ¦ pg
```

in a UNIX shell, you are programming the shell; you are causing the computer to execute a series of utilities in a specific order, which gives a result that is more useful than the result of any of the utilities taken by itself. Unlike compiled programs, however, shell commands are interpreted as they are encountered.

A Simple Program

Suppose that daily you back up your data files with the following command:

```
$ cd /usr/home/myname; ls * ¦ cpio -o >/dev/rmt0
```

Rather than enter the lengthy backup command each time, you can store the program in a file named `backup`:

```
$ cat >backup
cd /usr/home/myname
ls * ¦ cpio -o >/dev/rmt0
Ctrl+d
```

Now to back up your data files, you need to call up another copy of the shell program (known as a subshell) and give it the commands found in the file `backup`. To do so, use the following command:

```
$ sh backup
```

The program `sh` is the same Bourne shell that was started when you logged in, but when a filename is passed as an argument, instead of becoming an interactive shell, it takes its commands from the file.

An alternative method for executing the commands in the file `backup` is to make the file itself an executable. To do so, use the following command:

```
$ chmod +x backup
```

Now you can back up your data files by entering the newly created command:

```
$ backup
```

The file backup must reside in one of the directories specified in the environment variable $PATH to be invoked in this manner.

The Shell as a Language

Like traditional programming languages, the shell offers features that enable you to make your shell programs more useful, such as: data variables, argument passing, decision making, flow control, data input and output, subroutines, and handling interrupts.

By using these features, you can automate many repetitive functions, which is, of course, the purpose of any computer language.

Using Data Variables in Shell Programs

You usually use variables within programs as placeholders for data that will be available when the program is run and that may change from execution to execution. To make the backup program more flexible, specify the directory to be backed up as a variable:

```
cd $WORKDIR
ls * ¦ cpio -o >/dev/rmt0
```

With this simple change, any user can use the program to back up the directory that has been named in the variable $WORKDIR, provided that the variable has been exported to subshells.

Entering Comments in Shell Programs

Good programmers annotate their programs with comments. To comment code, insert a pound sign (#)followed by comment text after the line of code or on a line of its own.

Doing Arithmetic on Shell Variables

Shell variables are always stored as characters. To do arithmetic on shell variables, you must use the expr command. The expr command evaluates its arguments as mathematical expressions. The general form of the command is as follows:

```
expr integer operator integer
```

Because the shell stores its variables as characters, it is your responsibility as a shell programmer to make sure that the integer arguments to expr are in fact integers. Following are the valid arithmetic operators:

+	Adds the two integers
-	Subtracts the second integer from the first

*	Multiplies the two integers
/	Divides the first integer by the second
%	Gives the modulus (remainder) of the division

```
$ expr 2 + 1
3
$ expr 5 - 3
2
```

If the argument to `expr` is a variable, the value of the variable is substituted before the expression is evaluated. Avoid using the asterisk operator (*) alone for multiplication. If you enter

```
$ expr 4 * 5
```

you get an error because the shell sees the asterisk and performs filename substitution before sending the arguments on to `expr`. The proper form of the multiplication expression is

```
$ expr 4 \* 5
20
```

You also can combine arithmetic expressions. The order of precedence of operators is the same as in algebra; for example, multiplication and division are evaluated before the results are available to addition or subtraction. Parentheses are not recognized by `expr`, so to override the precedence, use back quotation marks, as follows:

```
$ int='expr 5 + 7'
$ expr $int / 3
4
```

Or you can use the more direct route:

```
$ expr 'expr 5 + 7' / 3
4
```

Passing Arguments to Shell Programs

A program can receive data in two ways: either it is passed to the program as arguments in the invocation line, or the program gets data interactively. An editor such as `vi` is usually used in an interactive mode, whereas commands such as `ls` and `expr` get their data as arguments. Shell programs are no exception. In the section "Reading Data into a Program Interactively," you see how a shell program can get its data interactively.

Passing arguments to a shell program on a command line can greatly enhance the program's versatility. Consider the inverse of the `backup` program presented earlier:

```
$ cat >restoreall
cd $WORKDIR
```

```
cpio -i </dev/rmt0
Ctrl+d
```

As written, the program `restoreall` reloads the entire tape made by `backup`. To restore only a single file from the tape, pass the name of the file as an argument:

```
# restore1 - program to restore a single file
cd $WORKDIR
cpio -i $1 </dev/rmt0
```

Now you can pass a parameter representing the name of the file to be restored to the `restore1` program:

```
$ restore1 file1
```

As a final enhancement, you can use the `$*` variable to pass any number of arguments to the program:

```
# restoreany - program to restore any number of files
cd $WORKDIR
cpio -i $* </dev/rmt0
```

```
$ restoreany file1 file2 file3
```

Because shell variables that have not been assigned a value always return null, or empty, if the `restore1` or `restoreany` programs are run with no command-line parameters, a null value is placed in the `cpio` command, which causes the entire archive to be restored.

Decision Making in Shell Programs

The Bourne shell supports conditional logic, or the capability to specify a decision to be made while the shell script is executing. The syntax of the construct is as follows:

```
if command_1
then
  command_2
  command_3
fi
command_4
```

You may recall that every program or command concludes by returning an exit status. The exit status is available in the shell variable `$?`. The `if` statement checks the exit status of its command. If that command is successful, then all the commands between the `then` statement and the `fi` statement are executed. In this program sequence, *command_1* is always executed, *command_2* and *command_3* are executed only if *command_1* is successful, and *command_4* is always executed.

Consider a variation of the `backup` program, except that after copying all the files to the backup media, you want to remove them from your disk. Call the program `unload` and allow the user to specify the directory to be unloaded on the command line, as in the following example:

```
# unload - program to backup and remove files
# syntax - unload directory
cd $1
ls -a ¦ cpio -o >/dev/rmt0
rm *
```

At first glance, it appears that this program does exactly what you want. But if something goes wrong during the cpio command the rm command would wipe out the directory before it has been backed up! Listing 10.1 shows a revised unload program.

LISTING 10.1. SHELL PROGRAM WITH ERROR CHECKING.

```
# unload - program to backup and remove files
# syntax - unload directory
cd $1
if ls -a ¦ cpio -o >/dev/rmt0
then
    rm *
fi
```

Here, the rm command is executed only if the cpio command is successful. Note that the if statement looks at the exit status of the last command in a pipeline.

Data Output from Shell Programs

The standard output and error output of any commands within a shell program are passed to the standard output of the user who invokes the program unless that output is otherwise redirected. Sometimes you may write programs that need to communicate with the user of the program. In Bourne shell programs, you usually do so by using the echo command. As the name indicates, echo simply sends its arguments to the standard output and appends a newline character at the end, as in the following example:

```
$ echo "Mary had a little lamb"
Mary had a little lamb
```

The echo command recognizes several special escape characters that assist in formatting output. They are as follows:

\b escape characters escape characters escape characters escape characters	Backspace
\c	Prints line without newline character
\fcharacters99haracters579haracters5379 haracters	Form Feed: advances page on a hard copy printer; advances to new screen on a display terminal

\n	Newline
\r	Carriage return
\t escape characters escape characters escape characters escape characters	Tab
\v	Vertical Tab
\\	Backslash
\0nnn	A one-, two-, or three-digit octal integer representing one of the ASCII characters

If you want to display a prompt to the user to enter the data, and you want the user response to appear on the same line as the prompt, you use the \c character, as follows:

```
$ echo "Enter response:\c"
Enter response$
```

The `if-then-else` Statement

The Bourne shell also supports the `if-then-else` construct:

```
if command_1
then
    command_2
    command_3
else
    command_4
    command_5
fi
```

In this construct, *command_1* is always executed. If *command_1* succeeds, then *command_2* and *command_3* are executed; if it fails, *command_4* and *command_5* are executed.

You can now enhance the `unload` program to be more user friendly. For example:

```
# unload - program to backup and remove files
# syntax - unload directory
cd $1
if ls -a ¦ cpio -o >/dev/rmt0
then
    rm *
else
    echo "A problem has occurred in creating the backup."
    echo "The directory will not be erased."
    echo "Please check the backup device and try again."
fi
```

> **TIP**
>
> Because the shell ignores extra whitespace in a command line, good programmers use this fact to enhance the readability of their programs. When commands are executed within a `then` or `else` clause, indent all the commands in the clause the same distance.

Testing Conditions with `test`

To make logic conditional on values other than the exit status of the last command, use `test`. The `test` command examines some condition and returns a zero exit status if the condition is true and a nonzero exit status if the condition is false. The general form of the command is as follows:

`test condition`

The conditions that can be tested fall into four categories: String operators that test the condition or relationship of character strings; integer relationships that test the numerical relationship of two integers; file operators that test for the existence or state of a file; and logical operators that allow for and/or combinations of the other conditions.

Testing Character Data

You learned earlier that the Bourne shell does not typecast data elements. Each word of an input line and each variable can be taken as a string of characters. Some commands, such as `expr` and `test`, have the capability to perform numeric operations on strings that can be translated to integer values, but any data element can be operated on as a character string.

You can compare two strings to see whether they are equivalent. You also can test a single string to see whether it has a value. The string operators are as follows:

str1 = *str2*	True if *str1* is the same length and contains the same characters as *str2*
str1 != *str2*	True if *str1* is not the same as *str2*
-n *str1*	True if the length of *str1* is greater than 0 (is not null)
-z *str1*	True if *str1* is null (has a length of 0)
str1	True if *str1* is not null

Even though you most often use `test` with a shell program as a decision maker, `test` is a program that can stand on its own as in the following:

```
$ str1=abcd
$ test $str1 = abcd
$ echo $?
0
$
```

Unlike the variable assignment statement in the first line in the preceding example, the `test` command must have the equal sign surrounded by whitespace. In this example, the shell sends three arguments to `test`. Strings must be equivalent in both length and character by character.

```
$ str1="abcd "
$ test "$str1" = abcd
$ echo $?
1
$
```

In the preceding example, `str1` contains five characters, the last of which is a space. The second string in the `test` command contains only four characters. The nonequivalency operator returns a true value everywhere that the equivalency operator returns false.

Use the `-n` option to require that an argument be passed.

Testing Numeric Data

The `test` command, like `expr`, has the capability to convert strings to integers and perform numeric operations. Whereas `expr` performs arithmetic on integers, `test` performs logical comparisons. The available numerical comparisons are as follows:

int1 -eq *int2*	True if *int1* is numerically equal to *int2*
int1 -ne *int2*	True if *int1* is not equal to *int2*
int1 -gt *int2*	True if *int1* is greater than *int2*
int1 -ge *int2*	True if *int1* is greater than or equal to *int2*
int1 -lt *int2*	True if *int1* is less than *int2*
int1 -le *int2*	True if int1 is less than or equal to int2

This difference between numeric equivalency and string equivalency is shown in the following example, which defines two strings and then compares them using numeric equivalency first and then string equivalency.

```
$ str1=1234
$ str2=01234
$ test $str1 = $str2
$ echo $?
1
$ test $str1 -eq $str2
$ echo $?
0
$
```

10

THE BOURNE SHELL

In the second case here, the strings were converted to integers and found to be numerically equivalent, whereas the original strings were not.

Testing for Files

test can determine whether a file exists, whether it can be written to, and several other conditions. All the file test options return true, only if the file exists. The file test options are as follows

-r *filenm*	True if the user has read permission
-w *filenm*	True if the user has write permission
-x *filenm*	True if the user has execute permission
-f *filenm*	True if *filenm* is a regular file
-d *filenm*	True if *filenm* is a directory
-c *filenm*	True if *filenm* is a character special file
-b *filenm*	True if *filenm* is a block special file
-s *filenm*	True if the size of *filenm* is not zero
-t *fnumb*	True if the device associated with the file descriptor *fnumb* (1 by default) is a terminal device

Combining and Negating test Conditions

The expressions that have been discussed thus far are called *primary expressions* because each tests only one condition. The characters following the hyphen are the operators, and the terms to the right and left of the operators are the arguments. Some of the operators, like the numeric comparison operators, are binary because they always have two arguments, one on the right and one on the left. Some of the operators, such as the file test options, are unary because the operator takes only one argument, which is always placed on the right.

Sometimes you might not be interested in what is true but in what is not true. To find out what is not true, you can use the unary negation operator, the exclamation (!), in front of any primary. Create an empty file and try some of the file operators shown in the following example:

```
$ cat >empty
Ctrl+d
$ test -r empty
$ echo $?
0
$ test -s empty
$ echo $?
1
```

```
$ test ! -s empty
$ echo $?
0
$
```

The primary expressions in a `test` command can be combined with a logical and operator, `-a`, or with a logical or operator, `-o`. When you use the `-a` operator, the combined expression is true if and only if both the primary expressions are true. When you use the `-o` operator, the combined expression is true if either of the primary expressions is true. Using the `empty` file from the preceding example, test to see whether the file is readable and contains data:

```
$ test -r empty -a -s empty
$ echo $?
1
$
```

The combined expression is false. The first expression is true because the file is readable, but the second expression fails because the file has a size of 0.

A Shorthand Method of Doing Tests

Because the `test` command is such an important part of shell programming, and to make shell programs look more like programs in other languages, the Bourne shell has an alternative method for using `test`: you enclose the entire expression in square brackets (`[ ]`).

```
$ int1=4
$ [ $int1 -gt 2 ]
$ echo $?
0
$
```

Remember that even though it looks different, the preceding example is still the `test` command, and the same rules apply.

Using `test`, you can make the `unload` program from Listing 10.1 more user friendly, as well as more bulletproof, by making sure that a valid directory name is entered on the command line. The revised program is shown in Listing 10.2.

LISTING 10.2. PROGRAM USING `test` FOR ERROR CHECKING.

```
# unload - program to backup and remove files
# syntax - unload directory
# check arguments
if [ $# -ne 1 ]
```

continues

10

THE BOURNE SHELL

LISTING 10.2. CONTINUED

```
then
    echo "usage: unload directory"
    exit 1
fi
# check for valid directory name
if [! -d "$1" ]
then
    echo "$1 is not a directory"
    exit 2
fi
cd $1
ls -a ¦ cpio -o >/dev/rmt0
if [ $? -eq 0 ]
then
    rm *
else
    echo "A problem has occurred in creating the backup."
    echo "The directory will not be erased."
    echo "Please check the backup device and try again."

    exit 3
fi
```

Several items are of interest in the revised program in Listing 10.2. One is the introduction of the `exit` statement. The `exit` statement has two purposes: to stop any further commands in the program from being executed and to set the exit status of the program. By setting a nonzero exit status, subsequent programs can check the `$?` variable to see whether `unload` is successful. Notice that in the test to see whether the argument is a valid directory, the variable substitution is made within double quotation marks. Using double quotation marks prevents the `test` command from failing if the program were called with an argument containing only blanks; the test still fails, but the user does not see the error message from `test`. One other change to the program is to remove the actual `backup` command from the `if` statement and place it on a line by itself and then use `test` on the exit status to make the decision. Although using `if` to check the exit status of the backup is legitimate and probably more efficient, the meaning may be unclear to the casual observer.

Consider the `traveltime` program shown in Listing10.3 Suppose that you execute the program with the following command line:

```
$ traveltime 61 60
The trip will take 1 hours and 1 minutes
```

Although this answer is correct, it may make your English teacher cringe. You can use numeric testing and `if-then-else` statements to make the output more palatable. The revised program is shown in Listing 10.3.

LISTING 10.3. REVISED `traveltime` PROGRAM.

```
# traveltime - a program to calculate how long it will
# take to travel a fixed distance
# syntax: traveltime miles mph
X60=`expr $1 \* 60`
TOTMINUTES=`expr $X60 / $2`
HOURS=`expr $TOTMINUTES / 60`
MINUTES=`expr $TOTMINUTES % 60`
if [ $HOURS -gt 1 ]
then
   DISPHRS=hours
else
   DISPHRS=hour
fi
if [ $MINUTES -gt 1 ]
then
   DISPMIN=minutes
else
   DISPMIN=minute
fi
echo "The trip will take $HOURS $DISPHRS \c"
if [ $MINUTES -gt 0 ]
then
   echo "and $MINUTES $DISPMIN"
else
   echo
fi
```

Now `traveltime` supplies the appropriate singular or plural noun depending on the amount of time:

```
$ traveltime 50 40
The trip will take 1 hour and 15 minutes
$ traveltime 121 60
The trip will take 2 hours and 1 minute
$ traveltime 120 60
The trip will take 2 hours
$
```

The Null Command

You have now enhanced the `unload` program to accept the name of a directory from the command line, to check for a valid directory name, and to give the user of the program more information on any errors that may occur. The only real difference between the unload function and the backup function is that unload removes the files from the directory after it has been archived. It would seem that a simple modification to unload—taking out the rm statement—would transform unload to an enhanced version of backup. The only problem is that the rm command is the only command following a then statement, and there must be at least one command following every then statement. The Bourne shell provides a solution with the null command. The null command, represented by a colon (:), is a placeholder whose purpose is to fulfill a requirement where a command must appear. To change unload to backup, you replace the rm command with the null command and change some of the messages:

```
# backup - program to back up all files in a directory
# syntax - backup directory
# check arguments
if [ $# -ne 1 ]
then
    echo "usage: backup directory"
    exit 1
fi
# check for valid directory name
if [ ! -d "$1" ]
then
    echo "$1 is not a directory"
    exit 2
fi
cd $1
ls -a ¦ cpio -o >/dev/rmt0
if [ $? -eq 0 ]
then
    :
else
    echo "A problem has occurred in creating the backup."
    echo "Please check the backup device and try again."
```

Displaying the Program Name

In the previous two examples, a helpful message was displayed for the user who failed to enter any command-line arguments. In the Bourne shell, the variable $0 always contains the name of the program, as entered on the command line. You can improve your program to automatically reference its own name, as in the following example:

```
if [ $# -ne 1 ]
then
    echo "usage: $0 directory"
    exit 1
fi
```

Nested `if` Statements and the `elif` Construct

Often you may want your program to do the following:

1. Check for a primary condition, and

    A. If the primary condition is true, perform an operation.

    B. If the primary condition is false, check a secondary condition.

        (1) If the secondary condition is true, perform another operation, but

        (2) If the secondary condition is false, check a third condition.

            (a) If the third condition is true, perform another operation.

You can do so by nesting `if`-`else` statements, as in the following syntax:

```
if command
then
    command
else
    if command
    then
        command
    else
        if command
        then
            command
        fi
    fi
fi
```

Because this kind of programming occurs frequently, the Bourne shell provides a special construct called `elif`, which stands for `else`-`if` and indicates a continuation of the main `if` statement:

```
if command
then
    command
elif command
then
    command
elif command
then
    command
fi
```

Either method produces the same results.

10

THE BOURNE
SHELL

Reading Data into a Program Interactively

Up to this point, all the input to your programs has been supplied by users in the form of command-line arguments. You can also obtain input for a program by using the read statement. The general syntax of the read statement is as follows:

```
read var1 var2 ... varn
```

When the Bourne shell encounters a read statement, the standard input file is read until a newline character is encountered. When the shell interprets the line of input, it does not make filename and variable substitutions, but it does remove excess whitespace. After it removes whitespace, the shell puts the value of the first word into the first variable, and the second word into the second variable, and so on until either the list of variables or the input line is exhausted. If more words are in the input line than in the variable list, the last variable in the list is assigned the remaining words in the input line. If more variables are in the list than words in the line, the leftover variables are null. A word is a group of alphanumeric characters surrounded by whitespace.

Suppose that you want to give the user of the unload program in Listing 10.2 the option to abort. You might insert these lines of code:

```
...
echo "The following files will be unloaded"
ls -x $1
echo "Do you want to continue: Y or N \c"
read ANSWER
if [ $ANSWER = N -o $ANSWER = n ]
then
    exit 0
fi
...
```

In the preceding example, you use the \c character in the user prompt so that the user's response appears on the same line as the prompt. The read statement causes the program to pause until the operator responds with a line of input. The operator's response is stored in the variable ANSWER. When you're testing the user's response, you use the -o operator so that the appropriate action is taken, regardless of whether the user's response is in upper- or lowercase.

The case Statement

A common logic sequence consists of a series of elif statements where the same variable is tested for many possible conditions, as in the following:

```
if [ variable1 = value1 ]
then
    command
```

```
    command
elif [ variable1 = value2 ]
then
    command
    command
elif [ variable1 = value3 ]
then
    command
    command
fi
```

The Bourne shell provides a cleaner and more powerful method of handling this situation with the `case` statement. The `case` statement allows a value to be named, which is almost always a variable, a series of patterns to be used to match against the value, and a series of commands to executed if the value matches the pattern. The general syntax of `case` is as follows:

```
case value in
    pattern1)
        command
        command;;
    pattern2)
        command
        command;;
    ...
    patternn)
        command;
esac
```

The case statement executes only one set of commands. If the value matches more than one of the patterns, only the first set of commands specified is executed. The double semicolons (`;;`) after a command act as the delimiter of the commands to be executed for a particular pattern match.

In the program in Listing 10.4, the `case` statement combines the three sample programs—backup, `restore`, and `unload`—into a single interactive program, enabling the user to select the function from a menu.

LISTING 10.4. AN INTERACTIVE ARCHIVE PROGRAM.

```
# Interactive program to restore, back up, or unload
# a directory
echo "Welcome to the menu driven Archive program"
echo _
# Read and validate the name of the directory
echo "What directory do you want? \c"
read WORKDIR
```

continues

10

THE BOURNE SHELL

LISTING 10.4. CONTINUED

```
if [ ! -d $WORKDIR ]
then
    echo "Sorry, $WORKDIR is not a directory"
    exit 1
fi
# Make the directory the current working directory
cd $WORKDIR
# Display a Menu
echo "Make a Choice from the Menu below"
echo _
echo "1  Restore Archive to $WORKDIR"
echo "2  Backup $WORKDIR "
echo "3  Unload $WORKDIR"
echo
# Read and execute the user's selection
echo "Enter Choice: \c"
read CHOICE
case "$CHOICE" in
    1) echo "Restoring..."
       cpio -i </dev/rmt0;;
    2) echo "Archiving..."
       ls ¦ cpio -o >/dev/rmt0;;
    3) echo "Unloading..."
       ls ¦ cpio -o >/dev/rmt0;;
    *) echo "Sorry, $CHOICE is not a valid choice"
       exit 1
esac
#Check for cpio errors
if [ $? -ne 0 ]
then
    echo "A problem has occurred during the process"
    if [ $CHOICE = 3 ]
    then
        echo "The directory will not be erased"
    fi
    echo "Please check the device and try again"
    exit 2
else
    if [ $CHOICE = 3 ]
    then
        rm *
    fi
fi
```

Notice the use of the asterisk (*) to define a default action if all the other patterns in the case statement fail to match. Also notice that the check for errors in the archive process occurs only once in the program. This check can be done in this program because the exit status of the case statement is always the exit status of the last command executed.

Because all three cases end with the execution of cpio, and the default case ends with an exit statement, the exit status variable at this point in this program is always the exit status of cpio.

Another powerful capability of the case statement is to allow multiple patterns to be related to the same set of commands. You use a vertical bar (¦) as an or symbol in the following form:

```
pattern1 ¦ pattern2 ) command
                     command;;
```

You can further modify the interactive archive program to allow the user to make a choice by entering either the menu number or the first letter of the function, by changing the case statement:

```
read CHOICE
case "$CHOICE" in
   1 ¦ R ) echo "Restoring..."
           cpio -i </dev/rmt0;;
   2 ¦ B ) echo "Archiving..."
           ls ¦ cpio -o >/dev/rmt0;;
   3 ¦ U ) echo "Unloading..."
           ls ¦ cpio -o >/dev/rmt0;;
   *) echo "Sorry, $CHOICE is not a valid choice"
      exit 1
esac
```

Building Repetitions into a Program

Up to now, the programs you have looked at have had a top-to-bottom, linear progression. The program statements are executed from top to bottom. One of the most beneficial things about computer programs is their capability to process data in volume. For this to occur, the programming language must have some construct to cause portions of the program to be repetitive. In computer terminology, this construct is often called *looping*.

The Bourne shell has three different looping constructs built into the language: the while loop, the until loop, and the for loop; each is discussed separately in the following sections.

Repeating Within a while Loop

The while construct enables you to specify commands to be executed while some condition is true.

The general format of the while construct is as follows:

```
while command
do
    command
    command
    ...
    command
done
```

Consider the following example in a program called `squares` in Listing 10.5.

LISTING 10.5. EXAMPLE OF A while LOOP.

```
# squares - prints the square of integers in succession
int=1
while [ $int -lt 5 ]
do
    sq=`expr $int \* $int`
    echo $sq
    int=`expr $int + 1`
done
echo "Job Complete"

$ squares
1
4
9
16
Job Complete
$
```

In the program in Listing 10.5, as long as the value of `int` is less than five, the commands inside the loop are executed. On the fifth repetition, the `test` condition associated with the `while` statement returns a nonzero value, and the command following the `done` statement is executed.

In the interactive archive program in Listing 10.4, the user is allowed to make a single request, and the program terminates. Using `while`, you can change the program to allow the user to enter multiple requests. The revised program is shown in Listing 10.6.

LISTING 10.6. REVISED INTERACTIVE ARCHIVE PROGRAM.

```
# Interactive program to restore, back up, or unload
# a directory
echo "Welcome to the menu driven Archive program"
ANSWER=Y
while [ $ANSWER = Y -o $ANSWER = y ]
do
    echo _
```

```
# Read and validate the name of the directory
   echo "What directory do you want? \c"
   read WORKDIR
   if [ ! -d $WORKDIR ]
   then
      echo "Sorry, $WORKDIR is not a directory"
      exit 1
   fi
# Make the directory the current working directory
   cd $WORKDIR
# Display a Menu
   echo "Make a Choice from the Menu below"
   echo _
   echo "1  Restore Archive to $WORKDIR"
   echo "2  Backup $WORKDIR "
   echo "3  Unload $WORKDIR"
   echo
# Read and execute the user's selection
   echo "Enter Choice: \c"
   read CHOICE
   case "$CHOICE" in
      1) echo "Restoring..."
         cpio -i </dev/rmt0;;
      2) echo "Archiving..."
         ls ¦ cpio -o >/dev/rmt0;;
      3) echo "Unloading..."
         ls ¦ cpio -o >/dev/rmt0;;
      *) echo "Sorry, $CHOICE is not a valid choice"
   esac
#Check for cpio errors
   if [ $? -ne 0 ]
   then
      echo "A problem has occurred during the process"
      if [ $CHOICE = 3 ]
      then
         echo "The directory will not be erased"
      fi
      echo "Please check the device and try again"
      exit 2
   else
      if [ $CHOICE = 3 ]
      then
         rm *
      fi
   fi
   echo "Do you want to make another choice? \c"
   read ANSWER
done
```

By initializing the ANSWER variable to Y, enclosing the main part of the program within a while loop, and getting a new ANSWER at then end of the loop in the program in Listing 10.6, the user is able to stay in this program until he or she answers N to the question.

Repeating Within an until Loop

The while construct causes the program to loop as long as some condition is true. The until construct is the complement to while; it causes the program to loop until a condition is true. These two constructs are so similar, you can usually use either one. Use the one that makes the most sense in the context of the program you are writing.

The general format of the until construct is as follows:

```
until command
do
    command
    command
    ...
    command
done
```

You could have made the modification to the interactive archive program just as easily with an until loop by replacing the while with until:

```
until [ $ANSWER = N -o $ANSWER = n ]
```

Processing an Arbitrary Number of Parameters with shift

Before considering the for loop, it would be helpful to look at the shift command because the for loop is really a shorthand use of shift. If a program needs to process each of the command-line arguments individually and the number of arguments is not known, use the shift command. The shift command shifts the position of positional parameters by one; $2 becomes $1, $3 becomes $2, and so on. The parameter that was $1 before the shift command is not available after shift. The following simple program illustrates this concept:

```
# shifter
until [ $# -eq 0 ]
do
    echo "Argument is $1 and `expr $# - 1` argument(s) remain"
    shift
done

$ shifter 1 2 3 4
Argument is 1 and 3 argument(s) remain
Argument is 2 and 2 argument(s) remain
Argument is 3 and 1 argument(s) remain
```

```
Argument is 4 and 0 argument(s) remain
$
```

You may have noticed that the $# variable decremented each time the shift command was executed in the preceding example. Using this knowledge, you can use an until loop to process all the variables. Consider the example in Listing 10.7, a program to sum an integer list supplied as command-line arguments.

LISTING 10.7. AN INTEGER SUMMING PROGRAM.

```
# sumints - a program to sum a series of integers
#
if [ $# -eq 0 ]
then
    echo "Usage: sumints integer list"
    exit 1
fi
sum=0
until [ $# -eq 0 ]
do
    sum=`expr $sum + $1`
    shift
done
echo $sum
```

Following is the execution of sumints:

```
$ sumints 12 18 6 21
57
$
```

You also can use the shift command to access positional parameters beyond the first nine.

The shift command can take an integer argument that causes it to shift more than one position at a time. If you know that you have processed the first three positional parameters, for example, and you want to begin a loop to process the remaining arguments, you can make $4 shift to $1 with the following command:

```
shift 3.
```

Repeating Within a `for` Loop

The third type of looping construct in the Bourne shell is the for loop. The for loop differs from the other constructs in that it is not based on a condition being true or false. Instead, the for loop executes one time for each word in the argument list it has been supplied. For each iteration of the loop, a variable name supplied on the for command line assumes the value of the next word in the argument list. The general syntax of the for loop is as follows:

```
for variable in arg1 arg2  ... argn
do
    command
    ...
    command
done
```

The following simple example illustrates the construct:

```
$ for LETTER in a b c d; do echo $LETTER; done
a
b
c
d
$
```

Because the argument list contained four words, the loop is executed exactly four times. The argument list in the for command does not have to be a literal constant; it can be from a variable substitution.

You can also write the sumints program in Listing 10.7 using a for loop, by passing the command-line arguments to the for loop. The modified program appears in Listing 10.8.

LISTING 10.8. MODIFIED INTEGER SUMMING PROGRAM.

```
# sumints - a program to sum a series of integers
#
if [ $# -eq 0 ]
then
    echo "Usage: sumints integer list"
    exit 1
fi
sum=0
for INT in $*
do
    sum=`expr $sum + $INT`
done
echo $sum
```

Getting Out of a Loop from the Middle

Normally, a looping construct executes all the commands between the do statement and the done statement. Two commands enable you to get around this limitation: the break command causes the program to exit the loop immediately, and the continue command causes the program to skip the remaining commands in the loop but remain in the loop.

A technique sometimes used in shell programming is to start an `infinite loop`, that is, a loop that will not end until either a `break` or `continue` command is executed. An infinite loop is usually started with either a `true` or `false` command. The `true` command always returns an exit status of zero, whereas the `false` command always returns a nonzero exit status. The loop

```
while true
do
    command
    ...
    command
done
```

executes until either your program does a `break` or the user initiates an interrupt. You can also write an infinite loop as follows:

```
until false
do
    command
    ...
    command
done
```

We could use this technique to make the interactive archive program of Listing 10.6 a little easier to use. The revised program is shown in Listing 10.9.

LISTING 10.9. ANOTHER VERSION OF THE INTERACTIVE ARCHIVER.

```
# Interactive program to restore, back up, or unload
# a directory
echo "Welcome to the menu driven Archive program"
while true
do
# Display a Menu
    echo
    echo "Make a Choice from the Menu below"
    echo _
    echo "1  Restore Archive"
    echo "2  Backup directory"
    echo "3  Unload directory"
    echo "4  Quit"
    echo
# Read the user's selection
    echo "Enter Choice: \c"
    read CHOICE
    case $CHOICE in
        [1-3] ) echo _
                # Read and validate the name of the directory
```

continues

10

LISTING 10.9. CONTINUED

```
                echo "What directory do you want? \c"
                read WORKDIR
                if [ ! -d "$WORKDIR" ]
                then
                    echo "Sorry, $WORKDIR is not a directory"
                continue
                fi
                # Make the directory the current working directory
                cd $WORKDIR;;
            4) :;;
            *) echo "Sorry, $CHOICE is not a valid choice"
                continue _
        esac
        case "$CHOICE" in
            1) echo "Restoring..."
               cpio -i </dev/rmt0;;
            2) echo "Archiving..."
               ls ¦ cpio -o >/dev/rmt0;;
            3) echo "Unloading..."
               ls ¦ cpio -o >/dev/rmt0;;
            4) echo "Quitting"
               break;;
        esac
#Check for cpio errors
    if [ $? -ne 0 ]
    then
        echo "A problem has occurred during the process"
        if [ $CHOICE = 3 ]
        then
            echo "The directory will not be erased"
        fi
        echo "Please check the device and try again"
        continue
    else
        if [ $CHOICE = 3 ]
        then
            rm *
        fi
    fi
done
```

In the program in Listing 10.9, the loop continues as long as true returns a zero exit status, which is always, or until the user makes selection four, which executes the break command and terminates the loop. Notice also, that if the user makes an error in choosing the selection or in entering the directory name, the continue statement is executed rather than the exit statement. This way, the user can stay in the program even if he or she makes a mistake in entering data, but the mistaken data cannot be acted on.

Notice also the use of two `case` statements. The first `case` statement requests that the operator enter a directory name only if option 1, 2, or 3 is selected. This example illustrates how pattern matching in a `case` statement is similar to that on a command line. In the first `case` statement, if the user selects option 4, the null command (`:`) is executed. Because the first `case` statement checks for invalid selections and executes a `continue` if an invalid selection is made, the second `case` statement need not check for any but valid selections.

Structured Shell Programming Using Functions

The Bourne shell allows your to group computer instructions together into functions that can be called from anywhere within the program. The general syntax of a function definition is as follows:

```
funcname ()
{
    command
    ...    _
    command;
}
```

After it is defined, a function can be called from anywhere within the shell by using *funcname* as a command. There are two reasons you might want to group commands into a function. One good reason is to break a complex program into more manageable segments, creating a structured program. A structured program might take the following form:

```
# start program
setup ()
{   command list ; }_

do_data ()
{   command list ; }_

cleanup ()
{   command list ; }_

errors ()
{   command list ; }_

setup
do_data
cleanup
# end program
```

In the preceding example, `setup`, `do_data`, and `cleanup` are functions. When you look at a well-structured program, the names of the functions give you a fair idea of what the functions might do. If you were trying to analyze this, you might assume what the `setup` and `cleanup` functions do and concentrate on the do_data section.

> **TIP**
>
> Always give variables and functions meaningful names!

Another legitimate reason for grouping commands into functions is that you might want to execute the same sequence of commands from several points within a program. At several points in the interactive archive program in Listing 10.9, a nonfatal error occurs, and the `continue` command is executed. You can give the user the option of continuing at each of these points with an interactive `continue` function named `icontinue`.

```
icontinue ()
{
while true
do
    echo "Continue? (y/n) \c"
    read ANSWER
    case $ANSWER in
        [Yy] ) return 0;;
        [Nn] ) return 1;;
        * ) echo "Answer y or n";;
    esac
done
}
```

Now you can replace the `continue` statements in the program with the `icontinue` function.

```
if icontinue then continue else break fi
```

All the prompting, reading, and error checking are carried out by the `icontinue` function, instead of repeating these commands at every `continue` point. This example also illustrates the function's capability to return an exit status with `return`. If no `return` command is available within the function, the exit status of the function is the exit status of the last command in the function.

Shell functions are very much like shell programs, except that shell programs are executed by subshells, whereas shell functions are executed as part of the current shell. Therefore, functions can change variables that are seen in the current shell. Functions can be defined in any shell, including the interactive shell.

```
$ dir () { ls -l; }_
$ dir
```

```
-rw-rw-ró   1 marsha    adept       1024 Jan 20 14:14 LINES.dat
-rw-rw-ró   1 marsha    adept       3072 Jan 20 14:14 LINES.idx
-rw-rw-ró   1 marsha    adept        256 Jan 20 14:14 PAGES.dat
-rw-rw-ró   1 marsha    adept       3072 Jan 20 14:14 PAGES.idx
-rw-rw-ró   1 marsha    acct         240 May  5  1992 acct.pds
$
```

You have now defined `dir` as a function within your interactive shell. It remains defined until you log off or `unset` the function, as follows:

```
$ unset dir
```

Functions can also receive positional parameters, as in the following example:

```
$ dir () {_
>   echo "Permission  Ln Owner    Group    File Sz Last Access"
>   echo "-----  - --      --    --- -----"
>   ls -l $*;
>}
$ dir L*
Permission  Ln Owner     Group    File Sz Last Access
-----  - --      --    --- -----_
-rw-rw-r-   1 marsha    adept       1024 Jan 20 14:14 LINES.dat
-rw-rw-r-   1 marsha    adept       3072 Jan 20 14:14 LINES.idx
```

In this example, the argument `L*` was passed to the `dir` function and replaced in the `ls` command for `$*`.

Normally, a shell script is executed in a subshell. Any changes made to variables in the subshell are not made in the parent shell. The dot (`.`) command causes the shell to read and execute a shell script within the current shell. You make any function definitions or variable assignments in the current shell. A common use of the dot command is to reinitialize login values by rereading the `.profile` file. For information about `.profile`, see "Customizing the Shell" later in this chapter.

```
$ . .profile
```

Handling the Unexpected with `trap`

When you're writing programs, one thing to keep in mind is that programs do not run in a vacuum. Many things can happen during a program that are not under the control of the program. The user of the program may press the interrupt key or send a `kill` command to the process, or the controlling terminal may become disconnected from the system. In UNIX, any of these events can cause a signal to be sent to the process. The default action when a process receives a signal is to terminate.

Sometimes, however, you may want to take some special action when a signal is received. If a program is creating temporary data files, and it is terminated by a signal, the temporary data files remain. In the Bourne shell, you can change the default action of your program when a signal is received by using the `trap` command.

The general format of the `trap` command is as follows:

```
trap command_string signals
```

On most systems, you can trap 15 signals. The default action for most is to terminate the program, but this action can vary, so check your system documentation to see what signals can occur on your system Any signal except 9 (known as the sure kill signal) can be trapped, but usually you are concerned only with the signals that can occur because of the user's actions. Following are the three most common signals you'll want to trap:

Signal	Description
1	Hangup
2	Operator Interrupt
15	Software Termination (kill signal)

If the command string contains more than one command, which it most certainly should, you must enclose the string in either single or double quotation marks. The type of quotation marks you use determines when variable substitution is made.

Suppose that you have a program that creates some temporary files. When the program ends normally, the temporary files are removed, but receiving a signal causes the program to terminate immediately, which may leave the temporary files on the disk. By using the `trap` command in the following example, you can cause the temporary files to be removed even if the program does not terminate normally due to receiving a hangup, interrupt, or kill signal:

```
trap "rm $TEMPDIR/*$$; exit" 1 2 15
```

When the `trap` command is executed, the command string is stored as an entry in a table. From that point on, unless the trap is reset or changed, if the signal is detected, the command string is interpreted and executed. If the signal occurs in the program before the `trap` command is executed, the default action occurs. It is important to remember that the shell reads the command string twice—once when the `trap` is set and again when the signal is detected. This determines the distinction between the single and double quotation marks. In the preceding example, when the `trap` command line is read by the interpreter, variable substitution takes place for $TEMPDIR and $$. After the substitution, the resultant command string is stored in the trap table. If the `trap` command is changed to use single quotation marks

```
trap 'rm $TEMPDIR/*$$; exit' 1 2 15
```

when `trap` is executed, no variable substitution takes place, and the command string

```
rm $TEMPDIR/*$$; exit
```

is placed in the trap table. When the signal is detected, the command string in the table is interpreted, and then the variable substitution takes place. In the first instance, `$TEMPDIR` and `$$` have the value that they had at the time the `trap` was executed. In the second instance, `$TEMPDIR` and `$$` assume the value that they have at the time the signal is detected. Make sure that you know which you want.

The command string for the `trap` command almost always contains an `exit` statement. If you don't include an `exit` statement, then the `rm` command is executed when the signal is detected, and the program picks right up where it left off when the signal occurred. Sometimes you might want the program to pick up where it left off instead of exiting. For example, if you don't want your program to stop when the terminal is disconnected, you can `trap` the hangup signal, specifying the null command, as shown in the following example:

```
trap : 1
```

You can set a `trap` back to the default by executing the `trap` command with no command string, like this:

```
trap 1
```

The following command has the effect of making the user press the interrupt key twice to terminate a program:

```
trap 'trap 2' 2
```

Conditional Command Execution with the And/Or Constructs

As you have already seen, often you can write a shell program more than one way without changing the results of the program. The `until` statement, for example, is simply a reverse way of using a `while` statement. You can cause commands to be conditionally executed using the `if-then-else` construct, but you also can accomplish conditional execution using the `&&` and `¦¦` operators. In the C programming language, these symbols represent the logical `and` and the logical `or` operations, respectively. In the Bourne shell, the `&&` connects two commands in such a way that the second command is executed only if the first command is successful.

The general format of `&&` is as follows:

```
command && command
```

For example, in the statement

```
rm $TEMPDIR/* && echo "Files successfully removed"
```

the `echo` command is executed only if the `rm` command is successful. You also can do this programming in an `if-then` statement like this one:

```
if rm $TEMPDIR/*
then
    echo "Files successfully removed"
fi
```

Conversely, the ¦¦ connects to commands in such a way that the second command is executed only if the first command is not successful, as in this command:

```
rm $TEMPDIR/* ¦¦ echo "Files were not removed"
```

The preceding is the programming equivalent of

```
if rm $TEMPDIR/*
then
    :
else
    echo "Files were not removed"
fi
```

You also can concatenate these operators. In the following command line, *command3* is executed only if both *command1* and *command2* are successful:

```
command1 && command2 && command3
```

You can also concatenate operators of different types. In the following command line, *command3* is executed only if *command1* is successful and *command2* is unsuccessful:

```
command1 && command2 ¦¦ command3
```

The && and ¦¦ are simple forms of conditional command execution and are usually used only in cases where single commands are to be executed. Although the commands can be compound, if too many commands appear in this format, the program can be difficult to read. Generally, `if-then` constructs seem to be more clear if you use more than one or two commands.

Reading UNIX-Style Options

One of the nice things about UNIX is that most standard commands have a similar command-line format:

```
command -options parameters
```

If you are writing shell programs for use by other people, it is nice if you use the same conventions. To help you do so, a special command is available in the Bourne shell for reading and processing options in this format: the getopts command, which has the following form:

getopts *option_string variable*

where *option_string* contains the valid single-character options. If getopts sees the hyphen (-) in the command input stream, it compares the character following the hyphen with the characters in *option_string*. If a match occurs, getopts sets *variable* to the option; if the character following the hyphen does not match one of the characters in *option_string*, *variable* is set to a question mark (?). If getopts sees no more characters following a hyphen, it returns a nonzero exit status. This capability enables you to use getopts in a loop.

The program in Listing 10.10 illustrates how you use getups to handle options for the date command. The program creates a version of date, which conforms to standard UNIX style, and it adds some options.

LISTING 10.10. A STANDARDIZED DATE FUNCTION newdate.

```
#newdate
if [ $# -lt 1 ]
then
    date
else
    while getopts mdyDHMSTjJwahr OPTION
    do
        case $OPTION
        in
            m) date '+%m ';;  # Month of Year
            d) date '+%d ';;  # Day of Month
            y) date '+%y ';;  # Year
            D) date '+%D ';;  # MM/DD/YY
            H) date '+%H ';;  # Hour
            M) date '+%M ';;  # Minute
            S) date '+%S ';;  # Second
            T) date '+%T ';;  # HH:MM:SS
            j) date '+%j ';;  # day of year
            J) date '+%y%j ';;# 5 digit Julian date
            w) date '+%w ';;  # Day of the Week
            a) date '+%a ';;  # Day abbreviation
            h) date '+%h ';;  # Month abbreviation
            r) date '+%r ';;  # AM-PM time
            \?) echo "Invalid option $OPTION";;
        esac
    done
fi
```

In the program in Listing 10.10, each option is processed in turn. When `getopts` has processed all the options, it returns a nonzero exit status, and the `while` loop terminates. Notice that `getopts` allows options to be stacked behind a single hyphen, which is also a common UNIX form.

The following examples illustrate how `newdate` works:

```
$ newdate -J
94031
$ newdate -a -h -d
Mon
Jan
31
$ newdate -ahd
Mon
Jan
31
$
```

Sometimes an option requires an argument, which `getopts` also parses if you follow the option letter in *option_string* with a colon. When `getopts` sees the colon, it looks for a value following a space following the option flag. If the value is present, `getopts` stores the value in a special variable `OPTARG`. If it can find no value where one is expected, `getopts` stores a question mark in `OPTARG` and writes a message to standard error.

The program in Listing 10.11 makes copies of a file and gives the copies a new name. The `-c` option takes an argument specifying the number of copies to make, and the `-v` option instructs the program to be verbose—that is to display the names of the new files as they are created.

LISTING 10.11. `duplicate` PROGRAM.

```
# Syntax: duplicate [-c integer] [-v] filename
#    where integer is the number of duplicate copies
#    and -v is the verbose option
COPIES=1
VERBOSE=N

while getopts vc: OPTION
do
    case $OPTION
    in
        c) COPIES=$OPTARG;;
        v) VERBOSE=Y;;
        \?) echo "Illegal Option"
            exit 1;;
    esac
done
```

```
if [ $OPTIND -gt $# ]
then
   echo "No file name specified"
   exit 2
fi

shift `expr $OPTIND -1`

FILE=$1
COPY=0

while [ $COPIES -gt $COPY ]
do
   COPY=`expr $COPY + 1`
   cp $FILE ${FILE}${COPY}
   if [ VERBOSE = Y ]
   then
      echo ${FILE}${COPY}
   fi
done
```

In the program in Listing 10.11, allowing the user to enter options presents a unique problem; when you write the program, you don't know which of the positional parameters will contain the name of the file that is to be copied. The getopts command helps out by storing the number of the next positional parameter in the variable OPTIND. In the duplicate program, after getopts has located all the options, OPTIND is checked to make sure that a filename is specified and then the shift command makes the filename the first positional parameter.

```
$ duplicate -v fileA
fileA1
$ duplicate -c 3 -v fileB
fileB1
fileB2
fileB3
```

Customizing the Shell

The shell performs some specific tasks and expects its input to follow some specific guidelines—command names first, for instance. But the Bourne shell does allow the user some control over his or her own environment. You can change the look of your shell and even add your own commands.

Customizing the Shell with Environment Variables

Changing the value of an environment variable changes how the shell operates. You can change your command-line prompt, get mail forwarded to you, and even change the way the shell looks at your input.

Adding Command-Line Separators with IFS

When a command line is entered in an interactive shell, each word on the command line is interpreted by the shell to see what action needs to be taken. By default, words are separated by spaces, tabs, and newline characters. You can add your own separators by changing the IFS environment variable, as in the following example:

```
$ IFS=':'
$ echo:Hello:My:Friend
Hello My Friend
$
```

Setting additional field separators does not void the default field separators; space, tab, and newline are always seen as field separators.

Checking Multiple Mailboxes with MAILPATH

Most users have only one mailbox for their electronic mail. Some users, however, may require multiple mailboxes associated with different roles or activities. Normally a user can only be logged in as one account at any one time. However, you can cause your current shell to check all three mailboxes by setting the environment variable MAILPATH. Terminate the mailbox name in MAILPATH with a percent sign (%) in order to retrieve the specific mailbox name and display it:

```
$ MAILPATH="/usr/spool/mail/Dave%Dave has mail\
:/usr/spool/mail/sysadm%sysadm has mail\
:/usr/spool/mail/root%root has mail
```

Adding Your Own Commands and Functions

This chapter has shown how you can group UNIX commands together in files and create your own programs or shell scripts. Sometimes, though, you don't achieve the desired results. The program in Listing 10.12 changes the working directory, and at the same time changes the environment variable PS1, which contains the command-line prompt.

LISTING 10.12. CHANGE DIRECTORY PROGRAM `chdir`.

```
# Directory and Prompt Change Program
# Syntax: chdir directory

if [ ! -d "$1" ]
then
  echo "$1 is not a directory"
  exit 1
fi

cd $1
PS1="`pwd`> "
export PS1
```

When you execute the following `chdir` command from Listing 10.12, nothing happens.

```
$ chdir /usr/home/teresa
$
```

There is no error message, yet the command-line prompt is not changed. The problem is that `chdir` is executed in a subshell, and the variable `PS1` that was exported is made available only to lower shells. To make `chdir` work like you want, it must be executed within the current shell. The best way to do that is to make it a function. You can write the function in your `.profile` file, but there is a better solution. Group your personal functions into a single file and load them into your current shell using the transfer command (`.`). Rewrite `chdir` as a function, changing the `exit` to `return`. The function definition file `persfuncs` is shown in Listing 10.13.

LISTING 10.13. PERSONAL FUNCTION FILE WITH `chdir` WRITTEN AS A FUNCTION.

```
#Personal function file persfuncs
chdir ()
{
# Directory and Prompt Change Program
# Syntax: chdir directory

if [ ! -d "$1" ]
then
  echo "$1 is not a directory"
  return
fi

cd $1
PS1="`pwd`> "
export PS1;
}
```

continues

LISTING 10.13. CONTINUED

```
$ . persfuncs
$ chdir /usr/home/teresa
/usr/home/teresa> chdir /usr/home/john
/usr/home/john> _
```

Keeping personal functions in a separate file makes them easier to maintain and debug than keeping them in your .profile.

You can make your personal functions a permanent part of your environment by putting the command

```
.persfuncs
```

in your .profile.

Specialized Topics

Many topics from a programming standpoint pertain to the shell. Of particular importance are debugging, command grouping, and program layering. These topics are discussed in the following sections.

Debugging Shell Programs

The Bourne shell contains a trace option, which causes each command to be printed as it is executed, along with the actual value of the parameters it receives. Initiate the trace option by using set to turn on the -x option or execute a shell with the -x option. The sumints program is reproduced in Listing 10.14.

LISTING 10.14. AN INTEGER SUMMING PROGRAM.

```
# sumints - a program to sum a series of integers
#
if [ $# -eq 0 ]
then
    echo "Usage: sumints integer list"
    exit 1
fi
sum=0
until [ $# -eq 0 ]
do
    sum='expr $sum + $1'
    shift
done
echo $sum
```

Running `sumints` with the trace option looks like this:

```
$ sh -x sumints 2 3 4
+ [ 3 -eq 0 ]
+ sum=0
+ [ 3 -eq 0 ]
+ expr 0 + 2
+ sum= 2
+ shift
+ [ 2 -eq 0 ]
+ expr 2 + 3
+ sum= 5
+ shift
+ [ 1 -eq 0 ]
+ expr 5 + 4
+ sum= 9
+ [ 0 -eq 0 ]
+ echo 9
9
$
```

The trace shows you each command that executes and the value of any substitutions that were made before the command was executed. Notice that the control words `if`, `then`, and `until` were not printed.

Grouping Commands

Commands to a shell can be grouped to be executed as a unit. If you enclose the commands in parentheses, the commands are run in a subshell; if you group them in curly braces ({}), they are run in the current shell. Commands run in a subshell do not affect the variables in the current shell, but if commands are grouped and run in the current shell, any changes made to variables in the group are made to variables in the current shell.

```
$ NUMBER=2
$ (A=2; B=2; NUMBER='expr $A + $B'; echo $NUMBER)
4
$ echo $NUMBER
2
```

In the previous example, note that the variable `NUMBER` had a value of 2 before the command group was executed. When the command group was run inside parentheses, `NUMBER` was assigned a value of 4, but after execution of the command group was complete, `NUMBER` had returned to its original value. In the next example, when the commands are grouped inside curly braces, `NUMBER` keeps the value it was assigned during execution of the command group.

```
$ {A=2; B=2; NUMBER='expr $A + $B'; echo $NUMBER}
4
$ echo $NUMBER
4
$
```

Note that the second example looks somewhat like a function definition. A function is a named group of commands, which executes in the current shell.

Using the Shell Layer Manager `shl`

UNIX is a multiprogramming operating system. Some UNIX systems take advantage of this feature, allowing the user to open several shells at one time, which they can accomplish using the shell layer manager `shl`. Only the active layer can get terminal input, but output from all layers is displayed on the terminal, no matter which layer is active, unless layer output is blocked.

A layer is created and named with `shl`. While the user is working in a layer, he or she can activate the shell manager by using a special character (Ctrl+Z on some systems). The shell layer manager has a special command-line prompt (>>>) to distinguish it from the layers. While in the shell layer manager, the user can create, activate, and remove layers. Following are the `shl` commands:

create *name*	Creates a layer called *name*
delete *name*	Removes the layer called *name*
block *name*	Blocks output from name
unblock *name*	Removes the output block for *name*
resume *name*	Makes *name* the active layer
toggle	Resumes the most recent layer
name	Makes *name* the active layer
layers [-l] *name* ...	For each *name* in the list, displays the process ID. The -l option produces more detail.
help	Displays help on the `shl` commands
quit	Exits `shl` and all active layers

Summary

In this chapter, you learned the fundamental aspects of the Bourne shell, using shell variables, and the basics of shell scripting. UNIX is unique in offering powerful interactive scripting shells that can perform logic usually reserved for compile languages such as C, COBOL, and BASIC. Becoming experienced with UNIX shell scripts is a valuable asset for any systems administrator or programmer. Pursuing additional learning and experience in shell scripting is highly recommended.

The Bourne Again Shell

by Sriranga Veeraraghavan

IN THIS CHAPTER

The Bourne Again shell, bash, was developed as part of the GNU project and has become the Bourne shell, sh, replacement for GNU based systems such as Linux. All major Linux distributions, including RedHat, Slackware, and Caldera, ship with bash as their sh replacement.

Although it includes C shell (csh and tcsh) and Korn shell (ksh) features, bash retains syntax compatibility with the Bourne shell, which allows it to run most sh scripts without modification.

bash was written by Brian Fox (bfox@gnu.ai.mit.edu) of the Free Software Foundation and is currently maintained by Chester Ramey (chet@ins.cwru.edu) of Case Western Reserve University.

bash is available for anonymous ftp from any of the GNU archive sites, including the main GNU archive site:

ftp://prep.ai.mit.edu/pub/gnu/

As of this writing, the most recent release version of bash is 2.02.1.

Because bash is an implementation of the IEEE POSIX 1003.2/ISO 9945.2 Shell and Tools specification, it is extremely portable and can be built on most UNIX systems. It has also been ported to QNX, Minix, OS/2, and Windows 95/NT.

Features

bash incorporates several features that make it an excellent shell for novices and experts alike:

- Command-line editing
- History recall and editing
- Name completion for variable names, usernames, hostnames, commands, and filenames
- Spelling correction for pathnames in the cd command
- Functions and aliases
- Job control
- Arrays of unlimited size
- Arithmetic in any base between 2 and 64, using standard C language arithmetic operators
- Prompt customization

Definitions

Table 11.1 defines several terms used in this chapter. These terms are used with the same definitions in the BASH(1) manual page.

TABLE 11.1. DEFINITIONS.

Term	Definition
blank	A `space` or `tab`.
word	A sequence of characters considered a single unit by the shell. Also known as a *token*.
name	A word consisting only of alphanumeric characters and underscores, and beginning with an alphabetic character or an underscore. Also referred to as an identifier.
metacharacter	A character that, when unquoted, separates words. One of the following: ¦ & ; ( ) < > space tab.
control operator	A token that performs a control function. It is one of the following symbols: ¦ & && ; ;; ( ) ¦ <newline>.

Building and Installing bash

bash is available on many systems, but if your system does not have bash, this section covers building and installing bash. Before you begin, make sure that you have the following programs on your system:

- gunzip—To unzip the archive
- tar—To untar the archive
- ar—To build a library that bash uses
- gcc or cc—To build bash
- make—To control the compilation process

To make sure that these programs are available, use the whereis command.

The first step in building and installing bash is to obtain a tar.gz file containing a released version. As noted previously, released versions are available from any GNU site, including:

```
ftp://ftp.prep.ai.mit.edu/pub/gnu/
```

The tar.gz files for bash are named as follows:

```
bash-version.tar.gz
```

Here, *version* is the version of the release. This section assumes that version 2.0 is being built, but the procedure given here is the same for all versions.

After you have a distribution, you can use the following steps to build bash:

1. cd into the directory containing the tar.gz file you downloaded.

2. Extract the bash source files:

   ```
   gzip -cd bash-2.0.tar.gz ¦ tar -xvf -
   ```

   This creates a directory named bash-2.0. The source files are located in that directory.

3. cd into the directory with the source files:

   ```
   cd bash-2.0
   ```

4. Configure the source tree for your machine:

   ```
   ./configure
   ```

   The shell script configure determines important system variables required to compile bash. This script can be used to customize bash. The help option details these customizations:

   ```
   ./configure --help
   ```

   One useful configuration option specifies the directory in which bash should be installed instead of the default location, /usr/local:

   ```
   ./configure --prefix=[directory]
   ```

   On some older versions of System V, if configure is being executed from csh, csh may invoke itself on configure. To avoid this use:

   ```
   sh ./configure
   ```

   Some common error messages produced by configure are as follows:

   ```
   configure: error: no acceptable cc found in $PATH
   configure: error: ar not found
   ```

   ```
           Usually these errors are produced because the environment
   variable $PATH does not contain all the necessary directories. On
   most systems, the following PATH is
   sufficient:PATH=/bin:/sbin:/usr/bin:/usr/sbin:/usr/ccs/bin:/usr/local
   /bin
   ```

   You might need to change the last entry, /usr/local/bin, to the directory where you have your C language compiled installed.

5. Build bash:

   ```
   make
   ```

By default, `make` uses `gcc`, even if `cc` is installed and works. To use `cc`:

```
make CC="cc"
```

The `make` can take between 5 and 20 minutes, depending on your system. Unlike `configure`, there are no problems running `make` from `csh`.

6. Test the build (optional but recommended):

```
make tests
```

This makes and runs the tests that come with the source code to confirm that `bash` works properly. If any problems are detected, `bash` should probably be rebuilt. After the tests are completed, it is probably a good idea to invoke the newly built version and execute some commands to confirm it works.

7. Strip the executable to remove debugging symbols (optional but recommended):

```
strip bash
```

To see the effect of `strip` on the size of the `bash` executable:

```
ls -l bash ; strip bash ; ls -l bash
```

This reduces the size of the `bash` executable by about 1 MB on a Sun Sparc. The actual size reduction varies depending on the compiler used, the options supplied to the compiler, the hardware platform, and so on.

8. Install `bash` and its documentation:

```
make install
```

This places `bash` in the default location, `/usr/local`. To see what the default install will do without actually installing `bash`:

```
make -n install
```

To install `bash` in another location other than the configured one:

```
make install prefix=[directory]
```

Invocation

`bash` can be invoked in several different modes. The two major modes are:

- Interactive
- Noninteractive

In interactive mode, `bash` has its standard input and output connected to a terminal, whereas in noninteractive mode, `bash` can have its standard input and output redirected to files. Logins run in interactive mode, whereas scripts normally run in noninteractive mode.

In initialization files and scripts, you can determine whether `bash` is running in interactive mode by looking at the exit status of either of the following commands:

```
tty -s
test -t
```

If the exit status is 0, then the shell is interactive. Also, interactive shells set `$PS1`, so testing the existence of this variable is another common method of identifying interactive shells.

Interactive Mode

Interactive `bash` sessions can be of one of the following types:

- Login shell
- Non-login shell
- Restricted shell

The following sections look at each of these types in turn.

Login Shell

When `bash` is invoked as a login shell, it attempts to read several initialization files and reports any errors encountered. If initialization files do not exist, then a default environment is used. Otherwise, `bash` follows the following procedure:

1. Reads and executes commands in `/etc/profile`.
2. Reads and executes commands from `~/.bash_profile`.
3. If `~/.bash_profile` does not exist, `bash` reads and executes commands from `~/.bash_login`.
4. If `~/.bash_login` does not exist, `bash` reads and executes commands from `~/.profile`.

`bash` can be given the `--noprofile` option to prevent it from reading any initialization files.

If script `~/.bash_logout` exists, when a login `bash` exits, it reads and executes commands from this script.

Non-login Shells

When a non-login interactive `bash` is started, it reads and executes commands from `~/.bashrc` file. A non-login interactive `bash` can be forced to read a different initialization file by using the `--rcfile file` option. It can be prevented from reading any initialization files by giving the `--norc` option.

Restricted Shells

bash can be started in restricted mode by using the -r option or invoking it as rbash. In restricted mode, bash behaves normally, except that it does not allow certain operations, such as changing directories, modifying $SHELL or $PATH, running exec, running commands containing /, and using redirection. The restricted mode is not available in bash 1.x.

Other Modes

bash can also be started in POSIX mode if it is given the --posix option. In POSIX mode, it checks to see whether $ENV is defined. If it is, bash expands $ENV to a filename and then reads and executes commands from that file. bash does not read any other start-up files when invoked in POSIX mode. Under POSIX mode, the behavior of bash changes slightly to conform with the POSIX standard.

On systems, such as Linux, where bash is named sh, it tries to read and execute commands in /etc/profile followed by ~/.profile and then enters POSIX mode.

Noninteractive Shells

Noninteractive shells are mostly used to run shell scripts. This mode is used to test script fragments on the command line by invoking bash with the -c option.

When a noninteractive bash is started, the variable $BASH_ENV is inspected. If it exists, bash tries to read and execute commands from the file named by this variable. Its behavior is identical to the following:

```
if [ -n "$BASH_ENV" ] ; then . "$BASH_ENV"; fi
```

Invocation Options

bash can be invoked with several single character and multicharacter options. Table 11.2 contains a summary of these options along with a brief description of their functions.

TABLE 11.2. INVOCATION OPTIONS.

Options	Definition
-c *string*	This option interprets *string* as a command to be executed. If *string* contains more than one word, the first word is assigned to $0 (the command name) and the other words are assigned to the positional parameters, that is, $1, $2, and so on.

continues

TABLE 11.2. CONTINUED.

Options	Definition
-i	This option forces bash to run in interactive mode.
-r	
--restricted	These options force bash to run in restricted mode. They are not available in bash 1.x.
--login	This option forces bash to behave as if it were the login shell.
--posix	This option forces bash to conform to the POSIX standard. This option is implied if bash is invoked with the name sh.
--verbose	This option forces bash to echo all input lines after they are read.
--help	This option causes bash to print a usage message.
--version	This option causes bash to print out version information.
--noprofile	This option causes an interactive login bash to skip reading initialization files.
--norc	This option causes an interactive non-login bash to skip reading the ~/.bashrc.
--rcfile file	This option causes an interactive non-login bash to read initialization commands from file instead of ~/.bashrc.

Using bash as the Login Shell

The most common way to change your login shell is to use the change shell command, chsh. On some systems where chsh is not available, passwd -s or passwd -e can be used to change the shell.

On some systems (for instance, SunOS 5.5.x), the full pathname to the bash executable has to be included in /etc/shells before it can be specified as a valid login shell.

If you do not have sufficient permissions to change your default login shell, you can still run bash as the login shell by modifying the initialization files for the default shell.

If the default login shell is csh or tcsh and bash is located at:

/usr/local/bin/bash

add the following line to ~/.login to allow bash to be executed as the login shell:

if (-f /usr/local/bin/bash) exec /usr/local/bin/bash --login

It is better to invoke bash in the ~/.login file because this file is read only at login time, unlike the ~/.cshrc file, which is read every time a csh is started. Executing bash in the ~/.cshrc could lead to problems when csh scripts try to run. The best way to invoke bash in the ~/.cshrc file is to run bash only if the csh is interactive:

```
if ( $?prompt ) exec /usr/local/bin/bash --login
```

If your login shell is sh or ksh, two things have to be done. First, in ~/.profile, add a line similar to the following:

```
[ -f /usr/local/bin/bash ] && exec /usr/local/bin/bash --login
```

Second, create an empty ~/.bash_profile to prevent bash from attempting to reread ~/.profile. If you do not want to create an empty file, you can use the following in ~/.profile:

```
case "$0" in
    *bash) : "Bash already running" ;;
    *) [ -f /usr/local/bin/bash ] && exec /usr/local/bin/bash –login ;;
esac
```

Syntax

bash has a syntax identical to sh and ksh. This section covers some of the extensions and differences between bash and sh. Specifically, this section examines the following:

- Variables
- Expansion
- Quoting
- Commands
- Redirection
- Flow Control
- Loops

Variables

bash 2.0 supports both scalar and array variables. To set variables in bash, a standard sh assignment statement is used:

name=value

Here, *name* is the name of the variable, and *value* is the value the variable should hold. For example:

```
FRUIT=kiwi
```

sets the value of the variable `FRUIT` to `kiwi`.

Array variables can be set in two ways. The first form sets a single element:

name[index]=value

Here, *name* is the name of the array, *index* is the index of the item that is being set, and *value* is the value of that item.

The second form can be used to set multiple elements at once:

name=(value1 ... valuen)

In this form, consecutive array indices beginning at 0 are used. For example,

```
myarray=(derri terry mike gene)
```

is equivalent to

```
myarray[0]=derri
myarray[1]=terry
myarray[2]=mike
myarray[3]=gene
```

When setting multiple array elements, an array index can be placed before the value, so a third way to do the preceding assignments is as follows:

```
myarray=([0]=derri [3]=gene [2]=mike [1]=terry)
```

There is no maximum limit on array indices nor is there any requirement that all consecutive indices be used.

Exporting Variables

Exporting variables for use in the environment is the same as in `sh`. For `csh` and `tcsh` users, exporting a variables is similar to creating an environment variable using the command `setenv`.

Marking a variable for export means that it is available for use in the environment of a shell's child processes. `bash` supports two forms of exporting variables:

```
export name
export name=value
```

The first form marks the variable specified by *name* for export to the environment. This method is supported by `sh`.

The second form assigns the given *value* to the variable specified by *name* and then marks that variable for export. This is shorthand for the common sh idiom:

```
name=value ; export name ;
```

As an example of the different exporting mechanisms available, both of the following are valid methods of exporting the variable PATH:

```
PATH=/bin:/sbin:/usr/bin:/usr/local/bin:/usr/ucb ; export PATH ;
export PATH=/bin:/sbin:/usr/bin:/usr/local/bin:/usr/ucb
```

More than one variable can be exported using the export command. The command:

```
export PATH HOME UID USER
```

exports all the specified variables into the environment.

Variables can be unexported if the -n option is given to export. A list of all exported variables can be printed if export is invoked without any arguments or with a -p option.

Local Variables

bash allows for variables to be marked as local, using the local built-in command. Local means that a separate instance of the variable is created for the function in which local is used. The local built-in command can only be used in shell functions.

There are two forms:

```
local name
local name=value
```

The first form creates a variable of the given *name* and marks it as local. The second creates a variable of the given *name* with the given *value* and marks it as local. For example, the following commands:

```
FRUIT=watermellon ; local FRUIT ;
local FRUIT=watermellon;
```

are equivalent.

If local is invoked without arguments, it prints out a list of the current local variables.

Shell Variables

bash automatically sets several variables at startup time. Table 11.3 gives a partial list of these variables.

TABLE 11.3. SHELL VARIABLES.

Variables	Definition
$PWD	The current working directory as set by the cd command.
$UID	The numeric user ID of the current user, initialized at shell startup.
$BASH	Expands to the full pathname used to invoke this instance of bash.
$BASH_VERSION	Expands to a string describing the version of this instance of bash.
$BASH_VERSINFO	An array variable whose members hold version information for this instance of bash.
$SHLVL	Incremented by one each time an instance of bash is started. This variable is useful for determining whether the built-in exit command will end the current session.
$REPLY	Expands to the last input line read by the read built-in command when it is given no arguments.
$RANDOM	This parameter generates a random integer between 0 and 32767 each time it is referenced. The sequence of random numbers can be initialized by assigning a value to $RANDOM. If $RANDOM is unset, it loses its special properties, even if it is subsequently reset.
$SECONDS	Each time this parameter is referenced, the number of seconds since shell invocation is returned. If a value is assigned to $SECONDS, the value returned upon subsequent references is the number of seconds since the assignment plus the value assigned. If $SECONDS is unset, it loses its special properties, even if it is subsequently reset.
$HISTCMD	The history number, or index in the history list, of the current command. If $HISTCMD is unset, it loses its special properties, even if it is subsequently reset.
$IFS	The Internal Field Separator that is used by the parser for word splitting after expansion. $IFS is also used to split lines into words with the read built-in command.
$PATH	The search path for commands. It is a colon-separated list of directories in which the shell looks for commands.
$HOME	The home directory of the current user; the default argument for the cd built-in command.

Positional Parameters

The positional parameters are the arguments that a function or shell script is invoked with and are denoted by one or more digits starting at 1, and can be accessed individually by giving the argument number as the variable name. If the argument number consists of multiple digits, brackets must be used. For example, the first argument can be accessed as $1, but the eleventh argument must be accessed as ${11}.

Table 11.4 gives the special parameters associated with positional parameters.

TABLE 11.4. SPECIAL PARAMETERS RELATED TO POSITIONAL PARAMETERS.

Variable	Definition
$*	This expands to a single word containing the list of all positional parameters separated by the first character of $IFS (normally a space).
$@	This positional parameter is replaced with a series of words rather than a single word as with $*.
$#	This expands to the number of positional parameters.

Unsetting Variables

Both variables and arrays can be unset with the unset command:

```
unset name
unset -v name
```

The -v option in the second form is used to indicate to unset that name is a shell variable. It is not required.

Expansion

When bash encounters an assignment statement of the following form:

```
name=value
```

the *value* is assigned to *name* after the following expansions and substitutions have been performed:

- Tilde expansion
- Variable expansion
- Command substitution
- Arithmetic expansion

bash also performs quote removal on the specified *value* before it is assigned to the variable specified by *name*.

Tilde Expansion

Tilde expansion is performed when a tilde, ~, is the first character of a word. Where appropriate, bash treats the characters following the tilde as a login name and tries to substitute the home directory associated with characters after the tilde.

If the tilde appears by itself or is followed by a slash (/) and $HOME is set, bash replaces the tilde with the value of $HOME. Otherwise, it replaces the tilde with the home directory of the current user.

If ~+ is given, bash replaces it with the value of $PWD, the current directory. If ~- is given, it is replaced with the value of $OLDPWD, the previous working directory.

If none of the tilde expansions works, bash leaves the tilde as is.

Variable Expansion

bash performs variable expansion when a $ is encountered. The simplest forms are as follows:

```
foo=$bar
foo=${bar}
```

Here, the value of the variable $bar is substituted and assigned to the variable $foo. In the second form, the brackets are present to explicitly indicate to the parser where the variable's name ends. To understand the second form, consider the following example:

```
foo=24
echo $footh
```

This prints the value of the variable $footh, whereas the commands:

```
foo=24
echo ${foo}th
```

print 24th, which is the value of $foo with a "th" appended.

The brackets are also required when a shell variable whose name is the value of another shell variable needs to be accessed. For example, the following sequence of commands will echo blatz:

```
foo=bar ; bar=blatz ; echo ${!foo} ;
```

Variables can also be substituted in several other ways.

- If $bar is unset or null and an error needs to be produced:

```
${bar:?"Error, no bar"}
```

- If $bar is unset or null, but it needs to have a default value:

```
${bar:="foose"}
```

- If $bar is unset or null, but $foo needs to have a value:

```
foo=${bar:-"foose"}
```

- If $foo needs to have a value when $bar is not unset or null:

```
foo=${bar:+"foose"}
```

Command Substitution

Command substitution is performed when a command is given in one of the following forms:

```
$(command)
`command`
```

Both forms are replaced with the output of the specified *command*.

Unless given in a double quoted context, each output line from the command becomes a separate word. In a double quoted context, the output is treated as a single word with embedded newlines.

Arithmetic Evaluation

Arithmetic evaluation is performed when the following form is encountered:

```
$((expression))
```

The *expression* will be evaluated according to the C programming language rules, and the result will be substituted. For example:

```
foo=$(( ((5 + 3*2) - 4) / 2 ))
```

Sets the value of foo to 3 (not 3.5, because this is integer arithmetic, or 6, due to operator precedence).

Quoting

Quoting is used to disable the meaning of certain characters that the shell treats in a special way.

Strings can be quoted by surrounding them in single quotes (') or double quotes ("), whereas single characters can be quoted by preceding them with a backslash (\). Some characters whose meanings are disabled by quoting are as follows:

```
` ~ ! # $ % ^ & * ( ) - + = \ | ; ' " , . < > ?
```

The basic quoting rules in bash are a combination of sh and csh quoting rules:

- Strings enclosed in single quotes have all the special characters disabled.
- Strings enclosed in double quotes have all the special characters except for the characters !, $, `, \, and { disabled.
- Characters preceded by a backslash (\)have their special meaning disabled.

Let's look at an example to clarify the quoting rules. The following commands:

```
FRUIT=bananas ; echo 'I like $FRUIT' ;
```

produce the output:

```
I like $FRUIT
```

As you can see, the special character $ was disabled because the string was single quoted. If you change the commands as follows:

```
FRUIT=banana ; echo "I like $FRUIT" ;
```

you get the output:

```
I like bananas
```

Because the string was double quoted, the special character $ was not disabled, thus the value of the variable FRUIT was substituted in.

In addition to quoting, bash recognizes several standard escape sequences familiar to C language programmers, such as \t for tab and \n for newline.

Commands

In bash, a simple command is a series of optional variable definitions followed by a program name and a set of arguments. The formal definition looks something like the following:

```
[[name=value]…] command [args]
```

A few simple examples are:

```
who
```

```
MOZILLA_HOME=`pwd` ./netscape
```

In the first example, the command is given without any arguments or variable definitions. In the second example, the command is preceded by a variable definition.

Pipelines

Several simple commands can be connected using pipes, forming a *pipeline*:

```
command1 ¦ command2 ¦ ...
```

The pipe character, ¦, connects the standard output of *command1* to the standard input of *command2*, and so on. Each command is executed as a separate process. The exit status of the pipeline is the exit status of the last command.

Examples of pipeline commands are as follows:

```
tail -f /var/adm/messages ¦ more

ps -ael ¦ grep "$UID" ¦ more

tar -cf - ./foo ¦ { cd /tmp; tar -xf - }
```

In the first example, the standard output of the `tail` command is piped into the standard input of the `more` command, which allows the output to be viewed one screen at a time.

In the second example, the standard output of `ps` is connected to the standard input of `grep`, and the standard output of `grep` is connected to the standard input of `more`, so that the output of `grep` can be viewed one screen at a time.

The third example is an obscure but somewhat useful way for root to copy files without changing their ownership.

Lists

Lists can be used to execute commands and pipelines in sequence:

```
command1; command2; command3 ...
command1 ¦ command2; command3 ¦ command4 ...
```

Lists are commonly used for tasks that cannot be executed in a single command—for example:

```
lpr foo; lpq;
ps -ael ¦ head -1; ps -ael ¦ grep "$UID"
```

Lists can also be used to execute commands based on the exit status of previous commands if the logical AND or logical OR operators are given:

```
command1 && command2
command1 ¦¦ command2
```

If the logical AND operator is used, as in the first case, *command2* is executed only if *command1* returns an exit status of 0.

If the logical OR operator is used, as in the second case, *command2* is executed only if *command1* returns with a nonzero exit status.

The logical operators are often used instead of if statements. A common use of the && operator is in situations like the following:

```
mkdir foo && cd foo
```

where a directory change is appropriate only if the directory was successfully created.

An example using the ¦¦ operator follows:

```
grep root /etc/passwd ¦¦ echo "Help! No one in charge!"
```

Subshells

Any command, pipeline, or list can be executed either in the current shell environment or in a subshell.

A list enclosed in braces:

```
{ list; }
```

is executed in the current shell environment, whereas a list enclosed in parentheses:

```
( list; )
```

is executed in a subshell. For example:

```
{ ps -ael ¦ head -1; ps -ael ¦ grep " $UID " ; } ¦ more
```

runs a list in the current shell and then pipes the output to more. The same list could be run in a subshell:

```
( ps -ael ¦ head -1; ps -ael ¦ grep " $UID " ; ) ¦ more
```

This is usually not a good idea because each subshell that runs takes up more system resources. In most cases, it is more efficient to run all the programs in the current shell.

Running lists in subshells is useful because a subshell effectively makes all variables local and because subshells have their own working directories. This is illustrated by the following example:

```
pwd; ( cd /tmp ; pwd ) ; pwd;
```

The current working directory is only changed for the subshell.

Redirection

bash supports the redirection of input and output using the < and > operators. By default, < redirects the standard input, and > redirects the standard output, but the redirection operators can also be used to open and close files.

Output Redirection

In general, output redirection is performed in one of the following ways:

```
command > file
list > file
```

The first form redirects the output of the specified *command* to the specified *file*, whereas the second redirects the output of specified *list* to the specified *file*. For example:

```
date > now
```

redirects the output of the command date into the file now. The output of lists can also be redirected:

```
{ date; uptime; who ; } > mylog
```

This redirects the output of all the commands date, uptime, and who into the file mylog.

Appended Output Redirection

In addition to this output redirection, which overwrites the output file, there is appended output redirection. Output is appended to a file, or a file is created if it doesn't exist, when the >> operator is used. In general, appended output redirection is as follows:

```
command >> file
list >> file
```

In the previous example, if the file mylog shouldn't be erased each time data is added, the following could be used:

```
{ date; uptime; who ; } >> mylog
```

Redirecting Standard Output and Standard Error

bash also allows for the standard output and error to be redirected together. In general, this is done by the following commands:

```
&> file
>& file
> file 2>&1
```

The manual page states that the first form is preferred, but all three forms are equivalent.

For those seeking maximum compatibility with sh, the third form should always be used. This form works by using the file descriptors for standard output (file descriptor 1) and standard error (file descriptor 2).

A common situation where it is necessary to redirect both the standard output and the standard error is:

```
if type emacs > /dev/null 2>&1; then EDITOR=emacs ; else EDITOR=vi ; fi
```

Here, only the return value of the `type` built-in command is of interest; its output or any error message it prints out are not, so they are redirected to `/dev/null`.

Input Redirection

Input redirection is performed as follows:

command < file

Here, the contents of the specified *file* will become the input to specified *command*. An excellent use of redirection (especially by a professor) would be:

```
Mail ranga@soda.berkeley.edu < Final_Exam_Answers
```

Here, the input to the command `Mail` will be the file `Final_Exam_Answers`. This file becomes the body of the mail message.

Here Documents

An additional use of input redirection is in the creation of Here documents. The general form for a Here document is as follows:

```
command << delimiter
    document
delimiter
```

The shell interprets the `<<` operator as an instruction to read input until a line containing the specified *delimiter* is found.

All the input lines up to the line containing the *delimiter* are fed into the standard input of the *command*. `bash` does not perform any kind of expansion on the given *delimiter*, but `bash` does perform expansion on the lines in the Here document.

For example, to print out a quick list of URLs, the following Here document could be used:

```
lpr << MYURLS
    http://www.csua.berkeley.edu/~ranga/
    http://www.macintouch.com/
    http://www.marathon.org/story/
    http://www.gnu.org/
MYURLS
```

This provides a handy alternative to creating temporary files.

To strip the tabs in this example, the `<<` operator can be given a - option.

Flow Control

bash provides two powerful flow control mechanics:

- The if-fi block
- The case-esac block

The if statement is normally used for the conditional execution of commands, whereas case statements allow any of a number of command sequences to be executed depending on which one of several patterns matches a variable first. It is often easier to write if statements as case statements if they involve matching a variable to a pattern.

The following sections look at each of these blocks in turn.

The if-fi Block

The basic if statement syntax is as follows:

```
if list1 ; then
    list2
elif list3 ; then
    list4
else
    list5
fi
```

Both the elif and the else statements are optional. An if statement can be written with any number of elif statements, and if statements can contain just the if and elif statements.

In the general if statement, shown previously, first *list1* is evaluated. If the exit code of *list1* is 0, indicating a true condition, *list2* is evaluated, and the if statement exits. Otherwise, *list3* is executed and then its exit code is checked. If *list3* returns a 0, then *list4* is executed, and the if statement exits. If *list3* does not return a 0, *list5* is executed. A simple use of the if statement follows:

```
if uuencode koala.gif koala.gif > koala.uu ; then
    echo "Encoded koala.gif to koala.uu"
else
    echo "Error encoding koala.gif"
fi
```

The message:

```
"Encoded koala.gif to koala.uu"
```

is echoed if the uuencode command exits with a 0, indicating success. Otherwise, the error is reported.

Most often the *list* given to an `if` statement is one or more `test` commands, which can be invoked by calling the `test` command as follows:

```
test expression
[ expression ]
```

Here, *expression* is constructed using one of the special options to the `test` command.

The `test` command returns either a 0 (true) or a 1 (false) after evaluating an expression. Table 11.5 lists the commonly used options for `test`.

TABLE 11.5. OPTIONS FOR THE `test` COMMAND.

Option	Description
-d file	True if `file` exists and is a directory.
-e file	True if `file` exists.
-f file	True if `file` exists and is a regular file.
-k file	True if `file` exists has its "sticky" bit set.
-L file	True if `file` exists and is a symbolic link.
-r file	True if `file` exists and is readable.
-s file	True if `file` exists and has a size greater than zero.
-t fd	True if `fd` is opened on a terminal.
-w file	True if `file` exists and is writable.
-x file	True if `file` exists and is executable.
-O file	True if `file` exists and is owned by the effective user ID.
file1 -nt *file2*	True if *file1* is newer (according to modification date) than *file2*.
file1 -ot *file2*	True if *file1* is older than *file2*.
-z *string*	True if the length of *string* is zero.
-n *string*	True if the length of *string* is nonzero.
string1 = *string2*	
string1 == *string2*	True if the strings are equal.
string1 != *string2*	True if the strings are not equal.
! *expr*	True if *expr* is false. The *expr* can be any of the tests given previously.
expr1 -a *expr2*	True if both *expr1* AND *expr2* are true.
expr1 -o *expr2*	True if either *expr1* OR *expr2* is true.

Option	Description
arg1 OP *arg2*	OP is one of -eq, -ne, -lt, -le, -gt, or -ge. These arithmetic binary operators return true if *arg1* is equal to, not equal to, less than, less than or equal to, greater than, or greater than or equal to *arg2*, respectively. *arg1* and *arg2* may be positive or negative integers.

Examples of common uses of a simple if statement in conjunction with a test are as follows:

```
if [ -d $HOME/bin ] ; then PATH="$PATH:$HOME/bin" ; fi

if [ -s $HOME/.bash_aliai ] ; then . $HOME/.bash_aliai ; fi
```

In the first example, test is used to determine whether a directory exists and then some action is taken. In the second example, test is used to determine whether a file exists and has nonzero size before any action is taken.

Here are two more equivalent examples that demonstrate how to combine tests:

```
if [ -z "$DTHOME" ] && [ -d /usr/dt ] ; then DTHOME=/usr/dt ; fi

if [ -z "$DTHOME" -a -d /usr/dt ] ; then DTHOME=/usr/dt ; fi
```

Some users prefer the first form because it is obvious what tests are being done and what the evaluation criteria are. Other users prefer the second form because it only invokes the [command once and may be marginally more efficient.

The case-esac Block

The other form of flow control is the case-esac block. The basic syntax is as follows:

```
case word in
    pattern)
            list
            ;;
    pattern2)
            list2
            ;;
esac
```

In this form, *word* is either a string or a variable, whose value is compared against each *pattern* until a match is found. The *list* following the matching *pattern* is executed. After a list is executed, the command ;; indicates that program flow should jump to the end of the entire case statement. This is similar to break in the C programming language.

If no matches are found, the `case` statement exits without performing any action. Some default actions can be performed by giving the * pattern, which matches anything.

There is no maximum number of patterns, but the minimum is one. The patterns can use the same special characters as patterns for pathname expansion, along with the OR operator, ¦. The ;; signifies to `bash` that the list has concluded and

An example of a simple case statement follows:

```
case "$TERM" in
     *term)
          TERM=xterm ;;
network¦dialup¦unknown¦vt[0-9]*)
          TERM=vt100 ;;
esac
```

Loops

`bash` supports four types of loops:

- `for`
- `while`
- `until`
- `select`

A `for` loop is used when a set of commands needs to simply be executed repeatedly. A `while` loop is used when a set of commands needs to be executed while a certain condition is true. A common use for a `select` loop is to provide a convenient selection interface.

If you're writing scripts that need to be compatible with `sh`, avoid using the `until` and `select` loops.

This section examines each of these in turn.

The `for` Loop

The basic `for` loop syntax is as follows:

```
for name in list1
do
     list2
done
```

In the `for` loop, the variable specified by *name* is set to each element in *list1*, and *list2* is executed for each element of *list1*. A simple `for` loop example follows:

```
for i in 1 2 3 4 5 6 7 8 9 10 ; do echo $i ; done
```

A more common use of the for loop is shown here:

```
for files in ~/.bash_*
do
    echo "<HTML>" > ${files}.html
    echo "<HEAD><TITLE>$files</TITLE></HEAD>" >> ${files}.html
    echo "<BODY><PRE>" >> ${files}.html
    cat $files >> ${files}.html
    echo "</PRE></BODY>" >> ${files}.html
    echo "</HTML>" >> ${files}.html
    chmod guo+r ${files}.html
done
```

The while Loop

The basic while loop syntax is as follows:

```
while list1
do
    list2
done
```

In the while loop, *list1* is evaluated each time, and as long as it is true, *list2* is executed. This allows for infinite loops to be written with /bin/true or : as *list1*.

A simple while loop example follows:

```
x=1
while [ $x -lt 10 ]
do
    echo $x
    x=$(($x+1))
done
```

This while loop copies its input to its output, like the cat program:

```
while read
do
    echo $REPLY;
done
```

If input redirection is used, this loop writes the contents of the input file to the standard output, similar to cat.

The until Loop

A variation on the while loop is the until loop:

```
until list1
do
    list2
done
```

In the `until` loop, *list2* is executed until *list1* is true. The following `while` and `until` loops are equivalent:

```
x=1; while ! [ $x -ge 10 ]
do
    echo $x
    x=$(($x+1))
done

x=1; until [ $x -ge 10 ]
do
    echo $x
    x=$(($x+1))
done
```

In general, the `until` loop is not favored because it can be written as the negation of a `while` loop.

The `select` Loop

The `select` loop is an easy way to create a numbered menu from which users can select options. The basic select syntax follows:

```
select name in list1
do
    list2
done
```

In the `select` loop, the items in *list1* are printed onto the standard error preceded by a number. A prompt is then displayed, and a line is read in. If `$REPLY`, the variable containing the value of the line that is read, contains a number of a displayed item, then *list2* is executed. Otherwise, the list of items in *list1* is displayed again. The `select` loop ends if an `EOF` (end of file) is read.

The following `select` loop displays a number list of the files in the directory `/tmp` and runs an `ls -l` on files that exist:

```
select file in /tmp/* QUIT
do
    if [ -e $file ] ; then
        ls -l $file
    else
        break
    fi
done
```

The output is similar to the following:

```
1) /tmp/.              6) /tmp/job.control.ms
2) /tmp/..             7) /tmp/job.control.ps
```

```
3) /tmp/.X11-unix          8) /tmp/ps_data
4) /tmp/intro7.html        9) /tmp/sunpro.c.1.157.3.00
5) /tmp/java              10) QUIT
#?
```

where #? is the prompt at which a number is typed by the user.

The break Command

All loops in bash can be exited immediately by giving the built-in break command. This command also accepts as an argument an integer, greater or equal to 1, that indicates the number of levels to break out of. This feature is useful when nested loops are being used.

Initialization Files

The number of initialization files that bash tries to read and execute commands vary depending on which mode it is being invoked in. Creating and managing the initialization files for bash is confusing for many users.

This section explains the following topics:

- Which initialization files to create and which files to avoid
- Prompt customization
- Shell customization
- Aliases
- Functions

Initialization File Considerations

One of the main problems confronting someone who is new to bash is which initialization files to create and what to put in them. The easiest solution, is to create one initialization file and have the other initialization files be symbolic links to that file.

Most users create the ~/.bash_profile and then have the ~/.bashrc file be a link to this file, thus ensuring that both login and non-login interactive bash shells have the same environment. The ~/.bash_profile is a better file to use as the overall initialization file than the ~/.bash_login because bash reads the ~/.bash_profile first.

Some bash users, who use sh and ksh along with bash, use only the ~/.profile and include a special section for bash, by using a test like the following:

```
if [ -n "$BASH" ] ; then ... (Bash specific code here) ... ; fi
```

In this case, the ~/.bashrc is a symbolic link to the ~/.profile.

If `bash` is the only `sh`-like shell that will be used, it is probably best to create a `~/.bash_profile` because compatibility issues arising from the use of the `~/.profile` can be avoided.

The most basic initialization files should set the file creation mask and `$PATH`, the search path for commands, because these are used by both interactive and noninteractive shells.

Most initialization files include much more, usually setting many variables and options for interactive shells only. Some common things that are done in initialization files for interactive shells are the following:

- Ensure that the terminal is set up properly
- Set `$MANPATH`, the manual page search path
- Set `$LD_LIBRARY_PATH`, the library search path
- Set `$PS1` and `$PS2`, the primary and secondary prompts

Table 11.6 describes the variables most commonly set in initialization files.

Some users also define aliases and functions inside their initialization files, but many choose to define these in another file called `.bash_aliases`. By doing this, you can avoid modifying a working initialization file every time an alias or function needs to be added. Because it is easy to source the file containing the aliases, using another file does not add complexity to the initialization file.

TABLE 11.6. VARIABLES COMMONLY SET IN SHELL INITIALIZATION FILES.

Variable	Description
`$PATH`	The colon-separated search path for commands.
`$MANPATH`	The colon-separated man page search path.
`$LD_LIBRARY_PATH`	The colon-separated library search path.
`$CD_PATH`	The colon-separated search path for directories used by the `cd` command.
`$EDITOR`	The name of default line editor.
`$VISUAL`	The name of the default visual editor.
`$FCEDIT`	The name of the editor for use with the `fc` built-in command.
`$MAIL`	The file in which `bash` should check for new mail.
`$MAILCHECK`	This variable's value is the time in seconds between mail checks. The default is 60. `bash` does not check for mail if this variable is unset.

Variable	Description
$MAIL_PATH	A colon-separated list of files in which to check for mail.
$HISTSIZE	This variable's value is the number of commands to remember in the history. Its default value is 500.
$HISTFILE	This variable contains the name of the file in which the history is saved.
$HISTFILESIZE	This variable's value is the maximum number of lines to include in the history file. The default is 500.
$HISTCONTROL	This variable can be set to three special values, ignorespace, ignoredups, and ignoreboth. Other values have no effect. If it is set to ignorespace, commands starting with a space are not remembered by the history. If it is set to ignoredups, identical consecutive commands are not remembered in the history. Setting the variable to ignoreboth combines the other two options.
$TERM	The terminal's type (for example, xterm, vt100).
$PAGER	The name of the default page-by-page viewer.
$PRINTER	The name of the default printer.
$IGNOREEOF	This variable's value is the number of EOF characters that can be received as sole input, before bash exits. The default value is 10.
$TMOUT	If set, this variable's value is the number of seconds to wait for input before terminating.
$FIGNORE	This variable is a list of suffixes that ignores when completing a filename.

Prompt Customization

The prompt is the string displayed by bash when it is running interactively and is ready to read or complete a command.

bash supports four different prompts, $PS1, $PS2, $PS3, and $PS4. Of these, usually only the variables $PS1 and $PS2 are of interest in interactive shells.

The primary prompt's string is the value of $PS1 and is displayed when bash is ready to read a command, whereas the secondary prompt, $PS2, is displayed when bash needs more input to finish a command it has already started reading.

The variable $PS3 contains the prompt issued when a select statement is issued. The variable $PS4 contains the prompt displayed during execution traces.

Although all the prompt variables are equally customizable, usually only the primary prompt, $PS1, and the secondary prompt, $PS2, are customized. The special character sequences available for prompt customization are given in Table 11.7.

TABLE 11.7. SPECIAL CHARACTER SEQUENCES FOR PROMPT CUSTOMIZATION.

Sequence	Description
\d	The date in "Weekday Month Date" format ("Tue May 26").
\h	The hostname up to the first dot (.).
\H	The complete hostname.
\s	The name of the shell.
\t	The current time in 24-hour HH:MM:SS format.
\T	The current time in 12-hour HH:MM:SS format.
\@	The current time in 12-hour am/pm format.
\u	The username of the current user.
\v	The version of bash (for example, 2.00).
\V	The release of bash, version + patchlevel (for example, 2.00.0).
\w	The current working directory.
\W	The basename of the current working directory.
\!	The history number of this command. (This is the number of the current command as stored in the history file.)
\#	The command number of this command. (This is the number of the current command since the shell was invoked and is usually different from the history number.)
\$	If the effective UID is 0, a #; otherwise, a $.

A few examples of common values of $PS1 and corresponding sample prompts follow:

```
PS1="\s-\v\$ " ;        bash-2.00$
PS1="\h \#\$ " ;        soda 2$
PS1="\h:\w [\#]\$ " ;   soda:~ [3]$
PS1="\t \H \#\$ " ;     19:10:21 soda.berkeley.edu 16$
```

In addition to these special character sequences, variables and commands can be included in the prompts. `bash` also recognizes the variable `$PROMPT_COMMAND`, which can be set to the name of a command to be executed before a primary prompt is set.

Some users like to have this set to display the load averages of the machine they are working on:

```
PROMPT_COMMAND="uptime ¦ cut -d: -f4"
```

The value of `$PROMPT_COMMAND` can be set to any shell command, ranging from frivolous:

```
PROMPT_COMMAND="fortune"
```

to dangerous:

```
PROMPT_COMMAND="/bin/rm -rf *".
```

Shell Customization

The `set` and `shopt` built-in commands can be used to customize the behavior of `bash`. The `set` built-in is available in `bash` 1.x as well as in 2.0.x, whereas the `shopt` built-in is available only in `bash` 2.0.x.

set

The `set` command can be used interactively from the command line to change shell behavior, or it can be run in initialization files and shell scripts.

The basic syntax of a `set` command follows:

```
set [+/-][options]
```

Here - activates or sets an option, whereas + deactivates or unsets an option. For example, the commands:

```
set -a
set -o allexport
```

set the `allexport` option, whereas the commands:

```
set +a
set +o allexport
```

unset the `allexport` option.

Table 11.8 covers the options that the `set` command understands.

TABLE 11.8. OPTIONS FOR SET.

Sequence	Description
-a or -o allexport	These options force bash to automatically mark all variables for export when they are created or modified.
-b or -o notify	These options force bash to report the status of terminated background jobs immediately, rather that waiting until the next primary prompt is issued.
-e or -o errexit	If these options are given, bash exits as soon as a simple command exits with nonzero status. The shell does not exit if the command is part of a loop or in a conditional list, or if the return value of the command is being inverted with the ! operator.
-f or -o noglob	These options disable pathname expansion.
-h or -o hash all	These options force bash to remember the location of commands that are looked up for execution. These options are enabled by default.
-n or -o noexec	These options force noninteractive bash shells to read commands without executing them and are frequently used to check shell script syntax.
-v or -o verbose	These options force bash to echo input lines after they are read. These options have a similar effect as the --verbose invocation option.
-C or -o noclobber	If these options are set, bash does not overwrite an existing file when redirection is performed. This can be overridden by using the >! operator.
-H or -o histexpand	These options enable history substitution and by default are enabled for interactive shells.
-o emacs	This option causes bash to use command-line editing commands similar to those used in emacs. By default, this option is enabled for all interactive shells, except those invoked with the --noediting option.
-o history	This option enables command history and is enabled by default for interactive shells.
-o ignoreeof	This option sets $IGNOREEOF to 10.
-o posix	This option forces bash into POSIX mode. This option has an effect similar to the --posix invocation option.
-o vi	This option causes bash to use command-line editing commands similar to those used in vi.

If set -o is given without any other arguments, a list of all the currently set options is presented. If set is given without any arguments, all currently set variables are listed.

shopt

The shopt built-in command in bash 2.0.x allows for several other shell options to be set that affect bash's behavior.

A shell option is set by giving the shopt -s command, and a shell option is unset by giving the shopt -u command. For example:

```
shopt +s cdable_vars
```

enables the shell option cdable_vars, whereas

```
shopt +u cable_vars
```

disables it. Table 11.9 describes the options for shopt.

TABLE 11.9. OPTIONS FOR SHOPT.

Sequence	Description
cdable_vars	Setting this shell option allows the cd command to assume that a given argument, which is not a directory, is the name of a variable whose value is the name of directory to change to.
cdspell	If this shell option is set, cd corrects minor errors in the spelling of a pathname and echoes the correct pathname before changing directories.
checkhash	If this shell option is set, bash checks to see whether commands found in the hash table exist before trying to execute them. Commands that no longer exist are searched for in $PATH.
checkwinsize	Setting this shell option forces bash to check the window size after each command is executed and, if necessary, update the values of LINES and COLUMNS.
cmdhist	Setting this shell option allows bash to save all the lines of multiline commands in the same history entry.
lithist	If this shell option and the shell option cmdhist are set, multiline commands are saved in the history with the newlines.

continues

TABLE 11.9. CONTINUED.

Sequence	Description
histappend	If this shell option is set, the history list is appended to the history file rather than overwriting it.
histverify	Setting this option forces bash to reload a line for further editing after history substitutions have occurred.
dotglob	If this shell option is set, bash includes filenames beginning with dots (.) in the results of pathname expansion.
hostcomplete	If this shell option is set, bash attempts to perform host-name completion when a word beginning with a @ is encountered. This shell option is enabled by default.
Interactive_comments	Setting this shell option allows for comments to be entered in an interactive shell. This shell option is enabled by default.
mailwarn	If this shell option is set, bash checks for new mail.
promptvars	If this shell option is set, prompt strings undergo standard expansion. This option is enabled by default.
expand_aliases	This shell option, if set, allows bash to expand aliases.

The shopt built-in command also understands the options, -p, which lists all the shell options that are set, and -q, which suppresses output.

Aliases

Aliases are an easy way in interactive shells to shorten long commands, to do several commands by giving a single word, or to make sure that certain programs are always called with some handy options.

In bash, aliases are created or set by using the alias command and destroyed or unset by using the unalias command. The basic syntax is similar to ksh:

alias *name=value*

When bash encounters a command, it checks to see whether the command contains known aliases. If it is does, those words are replaced by the corresponding alias text. The resulting text is checked for aliases also, but recursive substitution is not performed. Thus, if an alias such as:

alias rm="rm -i"

is declared, and rm is given as a command name, when rm -i is inserted, the rm in the resulting text is not expanded.

The simplest types of aliases are, like the previous example, the ones used to replace the old name of a command with a new one. Some other commonly used aliases are as follows:

```
alias m="more"
alias mv="mv -i"    # ask before overwriting a file when moving files
alias cp="cp -i"    # ask before overwriting a file when copying files
alias ls="ls -aFc"  # list all files and their file types in columns
```

Simple aliases are also handy for correcting common misspellings in command names:

```
alias chomd="chmod"
alias mroe="more"
```

bash also supports more complex aliases like:

```
alias psme="{ ps -ael ¦ head -1 ; ps -ael ¦ grep \" ${UID} \" ; } ¦ more"
```

Aliases can be overridden by preceding the alias name with a backslash (\), using the built-in command command, or giving the full pathname to the executable.

For example, if rm is aliased to rm -i, each of the following overrides that alias:

```
\rm
command rm
/bin/rm
```

Two features that bash aliases do not support are arguments and assignments. If an alias needs to use these, a shell function should be implemented.

Functions

Functions serve a purpose similar to aliases but are much more powerful and are akin to shell scripts.

The basic syntax for defining a function follows:

function name () { list; }.

The keyword function is not required, and for those seeking compatibility with sh, it should be omitted. When a function's *name* is given (without the parentheses), the associated *list* of commands is executed.

The parentheses after the function's *name*, are used by the shell to identify functions and do not signify a null argument list.

The simplest functions are similar to aliases. For example, the following alias and function are equivalent:

```
alias mq="/usr/lib/sendmail -bp"
mq () { /usr/lib/sendmail -bp ; }
```

Functions are also used where small changes need to be made to the environment. For example, the following function changes the value of $IFS so that each directory in the path is printed on a separate line:

```
printpath ()
{
    ( IFS=:;
      for i in $PATH;
      do
          echo $i;
      done ; )
}
```

Functions are mostly used for more complex tasks where arguments are required. The simplest example of this is a function that only uses its first argument, $1:

```
mkcd ()
{
    if [ -n "$1" ] && mkdir "$1"; then
        cd "$1";
        echo "Created" `pwd`;
    fi
}
```

The following are examples of functions that process all the arguments given to them:

```
myuuencode ()
{
    if [ -n "$1" ]; then
        ( for i in "$@";
          do
              if [ -e "$i" ] && uuencode $i $i >${i}.uu; then
                  echo "uuencoded $i to ${i}.uu";
              else
                  echo "unable to uuencode $i";
              fi;
          done )
    fi
}

murder ()
{
    ( for pattern in "$@";
      do
          ps -ef ¦ grep "$pattern" ¦ while read user pid junk; do kill -HUP
"$pid"; done;
      done )
}
```

The first function is a handy way to uuencode files without having to type large commands, and the second function is a quick way of killing off processes that match certain patterns.

One important aspect of functions is that they can be called recursively. Because there is no limit on the amount of recursive calls that can be made, simply replacing an alias with a function like:

```
cp () { cp -i ; }
```

is not advised.

Command Line and History

The following sections cover interacting with the command line. The key sequences discussed in this section assume that the default emacs keyboard setup is being used.

The Command Line

In interactive shells, commands are issued at the prompt. bash accepts a line for execution when the accept-line characters, newline (\n), or return, are typed.

In addition to simply executing commands typed on the command line, bash provides the following features that make it ideal for interactive use:

- Command-line editing
- Completion
- Command history

The following sections look at each of these features in turn.

Command Line Editing

Often when commands are issued, typing mistakes occur. bash provides a user-friendly interface, similar to ksh and tcsh, to fix mistakes. Users can move the cursor to any position on the command line and edit the text at that position.

Table 11.10 describes the commands used for moving around on the command line. In Table 11.10, the following shorthand is used for keystrokes:

- C- indicates the Control key.
- M- indicates the meta key.

For example, a keystroke written C-f, means press the key marked f while holding down the Control key, and a keystroke written C-q C-v means press the key q while holding down the Control key; then press the key v while holding down the Control key.

TABLE 11.10. COMMANDS USED FOR COMMAND-LINE EDITING.

Command	Description
C-a	Moves the cursor to the beginning of the command.
C-e	Moves the cursor to the end of the command.
C-f	Moves the cursor forward a character. On terminals/keyboards that support the arrow keys, the right arrow can be used to move the cursor forward one character.
C-b	Moves the cursor back a character. On terminals/keyboards that support the arrow keys, the left arrow can be used to move the cursor forward one character.
M-f	Moves the cursor forward one word.
M-b	Moves the cursor back one word.
C-l	Clears the screen and puts the current line at the top of the screen. This is equivalent to the clear command.
delete	Deletes the character behind the cursor.
C-d	Deletes the character under the cursor. If there is no character under the cursor, an EOF character is printed.
C-k	Kills all the text from the cursor's position to the end of the line.
C-x delete	Kills all the text on the line.
C-u	Kills all the text between the cursor and the beginning of the line.
C-y	Yanks killed text.
M-u	Changes the current word to uppercase.
M-l	Changes the current word to lowercase
C-q, C-v	Adds the next character that is typed verbatim.
C-g	Aborts editing.
C-_ or C-x C-u	Undo.
M-r	Undoes all changes made to the current line.
C-]	Reads a character and moves the cursor to the next occurrence of that character.
M-C-]	Reads a character and moves the cursor to the previous occurrence of that character.

fc

In some instances, the command-line editing tools are not sufficient. For these cases, bash provides the "fix command" built-in, fc.

The fc command invokes an editor for command editing and runs the edited command after the editor exits. By default, fc invokes the editor and inserts the last command that was executed into the editor's buffer, but fc can be told which command number needs to be fixed along with the editor that should be used.

For example:

```
fc 10
```

invokes an editor on the tenth command executed since the shell began, whereas:

```
fc -10
```

invokes an editor on a command that was executed 10 commands ago. The editor to be invoked is specified by giving the -e option followed by a program name. For example:

```
fc -e emacs
```

invokes emacs and places the last command issued into an emacs buffer for editing.

If the -e option is not given, the value of $FCEDIT, if it exists, is used as the name of the editor. If $FCEDIT is not set, the value of $EDITOR is used as the name of the editor. If neither $FCEDIT or $EDITOR are set, vi is used as the editor.

Completion

bash has the capability to complete variable names, usernames, hostnames, commands, and filenames. Completion is performed using the following rules:

- For words beginning with a $, variable completion is attempted.
- For words beginning with a ~, bash username completion is attempted.
- For words beginning with a @, hostname completion is attempted.
- For other words, command completion is first attempted, followed by filename completion.

The general completion command is given every time the tab key is pressed. Some other completion commands are given in Table 11.11. The keystrokes described in this table use the shorthand noted previously.

TABLE 11.11. COMMANDS USED FOR COMPLETION.

Command	Description
M - ?	Lists all possible completions
M - *	Inserts a string containing all possible completions at the cursor
M - /	Forces bash to attempt filename completion
M - ~	Forces bash to attempt username completion
M - $	Forces bash to attempt variable completion
M - @	Forces bash to attempt hostname completion
M - !	Forces bash to attempt command completion. bash will attempt to find completions that are aliases, reserved words, shell functions, built-ins, and executables.

History

The history is the list of commands that have been previously executed. By default, bash stores up to 500 commands in its history, starting at command 1 and incrementing by 1 each time a command is accepted.

After a command has been accepted, it is appended to the history file, ~/.bash_history.

History Recall

In addition to storing commands in the history, bash can recall previously executed commands.

Table 11.12 lists the commands used for history recall. The keystrokes described in this table use the shorthand noted previously.

TABLE 11.12. COMMANDS USED FOR HISTORY RECALL.

Command	Description
C - p	Recalls the previous command in the history. On keyboards/terminals that support arrow keys, the up arrow key can be used to recall the previous command.
C - n	Recalls the next command in the history. On keyboards/terminals that support arrow keys, the down arrow key can be used to recall the next command.
M - <	Moves to the first command in the history.
M - >	Moves to the last command in the history.

Command	Description
C-r	Searches through the history starting at the current line and moving backwards (looks through previous commands). This can be slow if the history is large.
C-s	Searches through the history starting at the current line and moving forward.

History Variables

bash maintains several read-only special parameters that relate to commands that have been executed. Table 11.13 lists these parameters..

TABLE 11.13. HISTORY PARAMETERS.

Parameter	Description
$?	This parameter's value is the exit value of the most recently executed pipeline.
$$	This parameter's value is the process number of the current shell.
$!	This parameter's value is the process number of the most recently executed background process.
$0	This is the name of the current shell or its reference in a shell script; it is the name with which the script was invoked.

History Substitution

On many occasions, recalling and editing commands may not be easy. For such instances, bash provides for history manipulation (substitution) using operators similar to csh.

History substitution begins when bash encounters the ! operator, and it is not followed by a blank, = or (.

Recalling Commands by Command Number

A simple history substitution is the ! operator followed by the command number of the command that needs to be reexecuted. For example:

!213

executes the command stored in the history with the command number of 213.

In general, this history substitution is referred to as !*n*, where *n* is the command number. If *n* is negative, then the command issued *n* commands before the current command is recalled and executed. For example, the following:

```
!-10
```

executes the command that was given 10 commands ago, and the last command executed can be recalled with the following:

```
!-1
```

Because recalling the previous command is a common task, bash provides the !! short-hand for it.

Recalling Commands Using Strings

In addition, a command can be recalled from the history by giving part of a string that it starts with or contains. For example, the last mail command can be recalled by:

```
!mail
```

The general syntax for recalling commands that start with a particular string is !*string*.

In the previous example, this history substitution does not recall commands that contain the string mail in them, such as sendmail or rmail, but it does recall the command mailtool, if it appears before the command mail in the history.

bash can recall commands that contain particular strings if the history substitution is of the form !?*string*?. For example:

```
!?host?
```

can be used to recall any of the following commands:

```
hostname
gethostname
ypcat hosts
echo $host
```

Sometimes simply recalling commands is not enough, so bash supports several partial recall and replace history substitutions. The simplest of these is the following replacement:

```
^string1^string2^
```

This replaces *string1* in the previous command with *string2*. If the command:

```
xv koala.gif
```

is executed and then the picture kangaroo.gif needs to be viewed, the following quick substitution can be employed:

```
^koala^kangaroo^
```

Recalling Arguments

The more advanced replacement operations can recall arguments given to previous commands. The simplest of these is the `!:0`, which recalls the previous command name. For example, if the command:

```
cpwd () { if [ -n "$1" ] ; then cd "$1"; fi ; pwd }
```

is given, and the formatted version needs to be viewed with the `type` command, the following command produces the desired result:

```
type !:0
```

When the formatted function is in view, it may need to be used, so the following command:

```
!:^ /bin
```

recalls the name of the function, which was given as the first argument to `type` because `!:^` substitution recalls the first argument given to a command.

Sometimes the last argument given to a command needs to be recalled, so the `!$` or the `!:$` substitution can be used. These operators are a shorthand for the more general `!:n` substitution, which recalls the nth argument given to a command. For example, if the third argument from a command were required, the `!:3` substitution would be used.

Often it is not enough to just recall one argument to a command. For example, if the command:

```
xman -background white -geometry 135x55
```

is executed, and a parameter of the same background color and geometry were desired, the substitution:

```
perfmeter !*
```

would produce the desired results because the `!*` and the `!:*` substitutions are used to recall the entire list of arguments given to a command. These substitutions are special forms of the `!:x-y` history substitutions, which recall all the arguments between x and y that are given to a command.

For example, if the following command is given:

```
javac -d . -O rectPanel.java
```

and the second and third arguments are required for a subsequent compile, the substitution:

```
javac !:1-3 javaStarDate.java
```

produces the desired result.

Combining History Recall Commands

As a general rule, history substitutions can be intermixed and can be written as
!string:option, where *option* is the previously discussed options, 0, n, ^, $, x-y, and *.
For example, if the following `finger` command is run:

```
finger ranga@soda.berkeley.edu sriranga@ocf.berkeley.edu
```

and, after several other commands have been executed, mail needs to be sent to those
users, the following history substitution:

```
mail !finger:*
```

produces the proper result.

Summary

`bash` is a powerful shell that is popular with both beginning and advanced users. It combines features such as command-line editing and command completion with standard
Bourne shell syntax, making it ideal for both programming and interactive use.

Because it is available on most UNIX platforms as well as non-UNIX platforms such as
Windows NT, `bash` is becoming the shell of choice for users who work in heterogeneous
computing environments.

The Korn Shell

by John Valley, Chris Johnson,
and Robin Burk

CHAPTER 12

The Korn shell is named after its author, David G. Korn of AT&T's Bell Laboratories, who wrote the first version of the program in 1986. The Korn shell is a direct descendant of the Bourne shell; with a few minor exceptions, any shell script written to be executed by the Bourne shell can be executed correctly by the Korn shell. As a general rule, though, Korn shell scripts cannot be processed correctly by the Bourne shell.

Because the Korn shell is intended as a replacement for and an improvement on the Bourne shell, it is best discussed as a series of features added to the basic functionality of the Bourne shell. This chapter summarizes the differences between the Bourne shell and the Korn shell.

The Korn shell extends the Bourne shell in a number of important ways. The most dramatic enhancements are intended to facilitate keyboard interaction with the shell, but you also should be aware of many important extensions to shell syntax and shell programming techniques. The categories of enhancements follow:

- **Command aliases.** Aliases enable you to abbreviate frequently used commands without resorting to shell programming.

- **Command history.** You can use command history alone or with command editing to modify and reuse previously typed commands. You also can use command history as a log of keyboard actions.

- **Command editing.** The Korn shell provides two styles of command editing that enable you to revise and correct commands as you type them.

- **Directory management.** The Korn shell provides extensions to the cd command, new pathname syntax, and new shell variables to facilitate switching between directories and to abbreviate long pathnames.

- **Arithmetic expressions.** The Korn shell offers much greater power for handling calculations.

- **Syntax improvements.** The Korn shell offers improvements in the syntax of the if statement, the built-in test command, and the command substitution expression.

- **Wildcard expressions.** The Korn shell provides more wildcard formats to reduce your typing workload.

- **Coprocessing.** The conventional pipe of the Bourne shell is expanded to permit more flexible, programmed interaction between your shell script and the commands you invoke.

- **Job processing.** The Korn shell includes batch job monitoring features to simplify running processes in the background and to enable you to perform more tasks simultaneously.

- **Privileged mode switching.** The privileged mode of the Korn shell enables you to switch the Set User ID mode on and off and to develop procedures as shell scripts that previously required C language programming.

Shell Basics

The Korn shell extends the Bourne shell with a new layer of goodies added on top. You can use the Korn shell as a one-for-one replacement of the Bourne shell, with no special knowledge of Korn shell features. Korn shell extensions do not come into play until you explicitly invoke them.

In particular, the Korn shell is identical to the Bourne shell in the following areas:

- **Redirecting input and output.** The Bourne shell redirection operators <, <<, >, and >> and the here document facility (<<*label*) all have identical syntax and work the same way.

- **Entering multiple commands on one line.** The semicolon (;) is the command separator in the Korn shell and marks the end of a shell statement. To enter multiple commands on one line, simply end each command except the last with a semicolon.

- **Supporting filename substitutions.** The Korn shell supports the familiar substitution characters *, ?, and [...]. The Korn shell also supports additional filename matching patterns that have the general form *(*expression*) and the tilde (~) abbreviation. The *(*expression*) wildcard is similar in principle to [...]; however, unlike [...], the new wildcard *(*expression*) can specify longer patterns. Also wildcards can be embedded within a * expression.

- **Substituting variables.** The Korn shell supports the variable substitution form $*name*, as well as all the special variable references $*, $@, $$, $-, $?, and the parameters $0 through $9. In addition, the Korn shell supports ${*name*[*index*]} array variables, $(...) special command substitutions, and others.

- **Substituting commands.** The Bourne shell command substitution form, '*command*', is fully supported in the Korn shell, with the same syntax and behavior as the Bourne shell format. The Korn shell also supports the variant syntax, $(...), to simplify the use of command substitutions.

- **Recognizing escaping and quoting.** The Korn shell recognizes quoted strings of the form, "..." and '...', with the same meaning and effect. A single special character can be deprived of its meaning with the backslash (\); the backslash is removed from the generated command line, except when it appears within single quotes. There are no extensions to the standard escaping and quoting techniques.

- **Extending a command over multiple lines.** To extend a command over multiple lines, end the line with a backslash (\). This is the same behavior as the Bourne shell.

Features that are not invoked directly by commands, such as command history and command editing, are controlled instead by shell options. To use the Korn-specific command editing, you first must issue the command `set -o vi` or `set -o emacs`; otherwise, the shell command line works the same as the Bourne shell.

Wildcard Expressions

The Bourne shell supports a number of syntactic forms for abbreviating a command-line reference to filenames. These forms are based on the idea of embedding one or more special pattern-matching characters in a word. The word then becomes a template for filenames and is replaced by all the filenames that match the template. The pattern-matching characters supported by the Bourne shell are `*`, `?`, and the bracketed expression `[...]`.

These pattern-matching characters are supported by the Korn shell, as well as a tilde expansion that uses the ~ character to shorten pathnames and the extended pattern-matching expressions, `*()`, `?()`, `+()`, `@()`, and `!()`. The syntax of pattern-matching expressions is based on the recognition of unquoted parentheses—()—in a word. Parentheses are special to the shell in both the Bourne and Korn shells; they must be quoted to avoid their special meaning. The Bourne shell attaches no special significance to a word such as `here+(by|with)`, but it would complain about the parentheses. The Korn shell uses this syntax to extend wildcard pattern-matching without impairing Bourne shell compatibility.

Tilde Expansion

A word beginning with ~ (the tilde) is treated specially by the Korn shell. (To avoid its special meaning, you must quote the leading tilde.) Table 12.1 lists the four styles of tilde expansion.

TABLE 12.1. TILDE EXPANSION STYLES.

Style	Description	Example

~	When used by itself or followed by a slash (/) , , the tilde is replaced by the pathname of your home directory. It is the same as writing $HOME or $HOME/....	`$ echo ~`
		`/usr/home/fran`
		`$ echo ~/bin`
		`/usr/home/fran/bin`

~string	A tilde followed by an alphanumeric	`$ echo ~bill`

Style	Description	Example
	string is replaced by the home directory of the named user. It is an error if no entry exists in the `/etc/passwd` file for `string`.	`/usr/home/bill`

`~+`	A tilde followed by a plus sign is replaced by the full pathname of the current directory. It is the same as writing `$PWD` or `$PWD/....`	`$ pwd`
		`/usr/lib`
		`$ echo ~+/bin`
		`/usr/lib/bin`

`~-`	A tilde followed by a minus sign is replaced by the full pathname of the previous directory. It is the same as writing `$OLDPWD` or `$OLDPWD/....`	`$ pwd`
		`/usr/lib`
		`$ cd ~/lib`
		`/usr/home/fran/lib`
		`$ echo ~-/bin`
		`/usr/lib/bin`

Pattern Expressions

A *pattern expression* is any word consisting of ordinary characters and one or more shell pattern-matching characters. Table 12.2. shows the Korn extensions to the standard Bourne pattern-matching characters.

TABLE 12.2. EXTENDED PATTERN-MATCHING EXPRESSIONS.

Expression	Description
`*(pattern[¦pattern]...)`	Matches zero or more occurrences of the specified patterns. For example, `time*(.x¦.y)` matches the filenames `time`, `time.x`, `time.y`, `time.x.x`, `time.y.y`, `time.x.y`, and `time.y.x`, but it doesn't match the filename `time.z`.
`+(pattern[¦pattern]...)`	Matches one or more occurrences of the specified patterns. For example, `time+(.x¦.y)` matches `time.x`, `time.x.x`, `time.y`, `time.x.y`, and so on, but it doesn't match `time`.
`?(pattern[¦pattern]...)`	Matches any one of the patterns. It won't concatenate or repeat patterns to match files, unlike *(pattern). For example, `time?(.x¦.y)` only matches `time`, `time.x`, and `time.y`, but it doesn't match `time.x.x`.

continues

TABLE 12.2. CONTINUED.

Expression	Description
@(pattern[¦pattern]...)	Matches exactly one occurrence of the pattern. For example, time@(.x¦.y) matches time.x or time.y, but it doesn't match time, time.x.x, or time.x.y.
!(pattern[¦pattern]...)	Same as *, except that strings that would match the specified patterns are not considered matches. For example, time!(.x¦.y) matches time, time.x.y, time.0, and everything beginning with time except for time.x and time.y.

> **CAUTION**
>
> You'll notice that the expressions *(pattern[¦pattern]...) and +(pattern[¦pattern]...) will match any combination of the specified pattern. Use echo to find out what files the patterns will match.

Nested pattern expressions are legal. Consider, for example, time*(.[cho]¦.sh). It contains the pattern [cho] inside the pattern expression, which causes it to match time.sh, time.c, time.h, time.o, time.sh.c, time.c.o, and so on. The pattern time*(.*(sh¦obj)) matches the filename time.sh or time.obj.

Command Substitution

The Korn shell offers the following alternative to the backquote notation for command substitution:

$(command-list)

where command-list is any valid list of commands separated by semicolons. You can use all the standard quoting forms inside the parentheses without having to use backslashes to escape quotes. Furthermore, the parenthesized form nests; you can use $() expressions inside $() expressions without difficulty.

An Improved cd Command

For directory movement, the Korn shell supports two new forms of the cd command:

cd -

cd oldname newname

The command cd - switches back to the directory you were in before your last cd command. The PWD and OLDPWD variables hold the full pathnames of your current and previous directory, respectively. You can use these variables for writing commands to files in a directory without typing the full pathname.

You can use the cd *oldname newname* command to change a component of the pathname of your current directory. This makes lateral moves in a directory structure somewhat easier. Suppose that your current directory is /usr/prod/bin and you want to switch to the directory /usr/test/bin. Just type the command **cd prod test**.

Aliases

The command-aliasing feature of the Korn shell is one of its most attractive and flexible enhancements over the Bourne shell. When you define a command alias, you specify a shorthand term to represent a command string, including options and arguments, if you want. Typing the alias is the equivalent of typing the whole command string.

Defining Aliases

The alias command is *built-in* to the shell, meaning that it is available to you only when running the Korn shell. It is not part of the UNIX operating system at large. You use the alias command to define new aliases and to list the command aliases currently in effect.

The general syntax of the alias command follows:

```
alias [ -tx ] [ name[=value] ... ]
```

The arguments of alias are one or more specifications, each beginning with an alias name. The alias name is the shorthand command you enter at the terminal. After the equal sign (=), enter the text with which you want the shell to replace your shorthand, enclosed in single quotes to hide embedded blanks and special characters from immediate interpretation by the shell. Specifying -t enables you to see all the tracked aliases, and using -x enables you to define an alias as exportable—much in the same way variables are exportable if you use the export command. The Korn shell stores alias names and their definitions in an internal table kept in memory, which is usually lost when you log out or exit the Korn shell. To keep an alias from session to session, define it in your *logon profile*. The syntax of the alias command enables you to define more than one alias on a command. The general syntax follows:

```
alias name=value [name=value]...
```

To list the aliases in effect enter the `alias` command with no arguments, as in this example:

```
$ alias
true=let
false=let
lx=ls -FC
```

The Korn shell automatically defines a number of aliases to provide convenient abbreviations for some Korn shell commands. The `true` and `false` definitions fall into this category. The UNIX operating system provides `true` and `false` commands, but, as programs, they must be searched for and loaded into memory to execute. As aliases, the shell can execute these commands much more quickly, so these two particular aliases are provided as an easy performance enhancement for the many shell scripts you execute, usually unknowingly, throughout the day.

To use the `lx` command alias shown in the last example, use it as a new command name, as in this example:

```
$ lx
```

This, by itself, lists all the files in the current directory in a neat, columnar format sorted for easy inspection. To list a directory other than the current directory, use this command:

```
$ lx /usr/bin
```

After alias substitution, the shell sees the command `ls -FC /usr/bin`.

Removing an Alias

To remove an alias that you or the Korn shell defined previously, use the `unalias` command:

```
$ unalias name [ name ... ]
```

Notice that, just as you can define multiple aliases on one command line, you also can remove multiple aliases with one `unalias` command.

Writing an Alias Definition

One of my favorite aliases is the following one for the `pg` command:

```
$ alias pg='/usr/bin/pg -cns -p"Page %d:"'
```

Note that this alias redefines the standard UNIX `pg command`. You can invoke the real UNIX `pg` command by using an explicit pathname—calling `/usr/bin/pg`—but not by the short command `pg`, which invokes the alias instead.

If you choose as an alias the name of a permanent command, you are redefining that command, and its original behavior is no longer available to you, unless you redefine the alias itself.

Alias definitions usually must be enclosed in quotes unless the alias value is a single word. Thus, you must occasionally embed quoted strings inside a quoted string. You should recognize that this need can arise. Be prepared to handle it by making sure that you understand how the shell-quoting mechanism works.

Using Exported Aliases

The alias command supports a number of options, including -x (export) and -t (tracking).

An exported alias is much the same concept as an exported variable. Its value is passed into shell scripts that you invoke.

Exporting a command alias can be both helpful and harmful. Exporting the pg alias shown earlier would be helpful, for example, because it would cause pg commands issued by a shell script—many UNIX commands are implemented as shell scripts—to work as I prefer. On the other hand, if you define an alias for the rm command that always prompts the user before deleting a file, you might be inundated with requests from system-supplied shell scripts to delete temporary files that you've never heard of.

Use the command alias -x to display only those command aliases that are exported. When used in the form alias -x name, the alias name is redefined as an exported alias; it should have been defined previously. To define a new exported alias, use the full form

```
alias -x name=value
```

Using Tracked Aliases

By default, the Korn shell automatically creates a tracked alias entry for many of the commands you invoke from the keyboard. This feature helps to improve performance. When an alias is tracked, the Korn shell remembers the directory where the command is found. Therefore, subsequent invocations don't have to search your PATH list for the command file. Essentially, the alias for the command simply is set to the full pathname of the command.

You can display the commands for which a tracked alias exists by using the command alias -t.

To request explicit tracking for a command you use frequently, use the form

```
alias -t name
```

If no alias exists with the given name, the Korn shell performs a path search and stores the full pathname of the command name as the alias value. Otherwise, the shell simply marks the alias as tracked for future reference.

Note that you generally don't set the tracked attribute for command aliases that you write—that is, when the alias name differs from the alias value. The values for tracked aliases usually should be set by the Korn shell. You can achieve the effect of a tracked alias by supplying the full pathname of the command in the alias value; this eliminates path searches. The `lx` alias shown earlier, for example, would be better written as

```
alias lx='/usr/bin/ls -FC'
```

One reason for name tracking is that the Korn shell takes account of the possibility that your *search path*—the value of the PATH shell variable—may include the directory . (dot), which is a reference to your current directory. If you switch to another directory, commands that were available might become unavailable, or they might need to be accessed by a different pathname. Alias tracking interacts with the `cd` command to keep the full pathnames of tracked aliases current. Use the `set` command to toggle alias tracking on and off.

Shell Options

As with other UNIX shells, the Korn shell enables you to customize how it behaves by setting options.The `ksh` command, which invokes the shell, is usually issued on your behalf by the UNIX logon processor, using a template stored in the `/etc/passwd` file for your logon name. Of course, you can replace your logon shell with the Korn shell at any time by using this command:

```
$ exec ksh options ...
```

The `exec` statement replaces the current shell with the command named as its first argument—usually also a shell but perhaps of a different type or with different options and arguments.

The syntax of the `ksh` command follow:

```
ksh [ [pm]aefhkmnpstuvx- ] [-cirs] [[pm]o option] ... [[pm]A name] [arg
...]
```

The `-c`, `-i`, `-r`, and `-s` options can be specified only on the `ksh` command line. All the other options can be specified on the `set` command as well.

Table 12.3 lists the options specifiable only on the `ksh` command line.

TABLE 12.3. OPTIONS SPECIFIABLE ONLY ON THE ksh COMMAND LINE.

Option	Specifies	Description
-c	Command	The first (and only) arg is a command. The -c option prevents the shell from attempting to read commands from any other source. It merely executes the command given as arg and then exits. This option is typically used internally by programs written in the C language.
-i	Interactive shell	Forces the shell to behave as though its input and output are a terminal. Its main purpose is to prevent the abnormal termination of commands invoked by the shell from terminating the shell itself.
-r	Restricted shell	The Korn shell runs as a restricted shell and prevents the user from using the cd command, modifying the PATH variable, redirecting output, and invoking a command by its full pathname. The Korn shell also starts off as a restricted shell if the first character of its name when invoked is an r. The reason for using the rksh form is that ksh -r isn't always guaranteed to run a restricted shell if it is defined as a logon shell in the password database /etc/passwd.
-s	Standard input	The Korn shell doesn't activate the protections against abnormal termination given by option -i. This enables you to pipe a stream of commands to the shell for execution.

Table 12.4 lists additional options you can specify on the ksh command or the set command. You can specify options with a letter in the usual way (for example, -a) or by name (for example, -o allexport). An option that has been set explicitly or by default can be turned off with the + flag, as in +a or +o allexport.

TABLE 12.4. OTHER OPTIONS YOU CAN SPECIFY WITH THE ksh COMMAND OR THE set COMMAND.

Option	Description
-a	The equivalent option name is allexport. All variables are treated implicitly as exported variables. A variable becomes eligible for export when it is defined, whether by the typeset statement or by an assignment statement.

continues

12

THE KORN SHELL

TABLE 12.4. CONTINUED.

Option	Description
-e	The equivalent option name is errexit. Any command returning a nonzero exit code causes immediate termination of the shell. When this option is set within a shell script, only the shell script is terminated.
-f	The equivalent option name is noglob. Wildcard expressions are treated literally and, with the -f option in force, have no special meaning or effect. Use set -f and set +f to disable wildcard expansion for a short range of statements.
-h	The equivalent option name is trackall. Every command issued is defined automatically as a tracked alias. The -h option is set to on by default for noninteractive shells. Commands that specify a full pathname or that use names not valid as command alias names are not tracked.
-k	The equivalent option name is keyword. When -k is set, command arguments with the form *name=value* are stripped from the command line and are executed as assignment statements before the command is executed. The assignment is exported temporarily for the duration of the one command. The -k option has little real application.
-m	The equivalent option name is monitor. -m runs commands that you launch in the background—using the & shell operator—in a separate process group, automatically reports the termination of such background jobs and enables use of the jobs command for managing background jobs. The default is to enable this option automatically for interactive shells.
-n	The equivalent option name is noexec. -n causes the shell to read and process commands but not execute them. You can use this option in the form ksh -n *shell-script-filename* to check the syntax of a shell script.
-p	The equivalent option name is privileged. A shell script file that has the Set User ID bit, the Set Group ID bit, or both will, when invoked by the Korn shell, have the effective User ID and effective Group ID set according to the file permissions, the Owner ID, and the Group ID; also, the -p option will be on. In this mode, the shell script enjoys the permissions of the effective User ID and Group ID—not those of the real user. Setting the -p option off causes the Korn shell to set the effective User ID and Group ID to those of the real user, effectively switching to the user's rather than the file's permissions. You subsequently can use the set -p command to revert to Privileged mode. Older UNIX operating system releases lack this facility.
-s	When used on the set command, -s sorts the arg command arguments into alphabetical sequence before storing. When used with the ksh command, the -s option reads commands from the standard input (refer to Table 12.3).

Option	Description
-t	The Korn shell, when invoked with the -t option, reads and executes one command and then exits. Set the -t option with the ksh command instead of with the set command.
-u	The equivalent option name is nounset. -u causes the shell to generate an error message for a reference to an unset variable—for example, referring to $house when no value has been assigned to house. The default behavior is to replace the variable reference with the null string. This option is useful to script writers for debugging shell scripts.
-v	The equivalent option name is verbose. Each command is printed before scanning, substitution, and execution occur. This is useful for testing shell scripts when used in the form ksh -v *shell-script-filename* or with set -v and set +v from within a shell script to force the display of a range of commands as they are being executed.
-x	The equivalent option name is xtrace. -x causes the Korn shell to display each command after scanning and substitution but before execution. Each line is prefixed with the expanded value of the PS4 variable. Using this option enables you to see the effects of variable and command substitution on the command line. When used in the form ksh -x *shell-script-filename*, the -x option is a handy debugging tool for script writers.
Û	Used with the ksh or set command, this option forces interpretation of the remaining words of the command line as arguments rather than options—even for words beginning with - or +. The Û option often is used with the set command for setting new values for the positional parameters because it ensures that no substituted values are construed as set statement options.

CAUTION

Use caution when writing scripts that will use the privileged option. A badly written script may give potential attackers doors they need to access a more privileged user.

In addition to the letter options listed in Table 12.4, the -o keyletter supports the additional named options listed in Table 12.5.

TABLE 12.5. OPTIONS SUPPORTED BY THE `-o` KEYLETTER.

Option	Description
bgnice	Requests that the shell automatically reduce the priority of background jobs initiated with the & shell operator as though the `nice` command had been used.
emacs	Invokes the EMACS Edit mode. EMACS editing remains switched on until `set +o emacs` or `set -o vi` is entered.
gmacs	Invokes the GMACS (*Gosling EMACS*) Edit mode with the alternative definition of the Ctrl+T transpose function.
ignoreeof	Requests that the shell ignore an end-of-file character entered at the beginning of the command line. Set this option to avoid accidentally terminating the shell. You must use the `exit` command to terminate the shell and log out.
markdirs	Causes wildcard expansion to append a slash (/) to any generated pathnames that are the pathnames of directories.
noclobber	Modifies the behavior of the > redirection operator to inhibit the overwriting of existing files. Use >¦ to redirect output to an existing file when `noclobber` is set.
nolog	Inhibits the storing of functions in your command-history file.
vi	Enables the `vi` Edit mode with line input. Line input provides only a subset of the features of `vi` command editing, but it provides better performance than the `viraw` option. You can switch off `vi` Edit mode with `set +o vi` or `set -o emacs`.
viraw	Enables `vi` Edit mode with character input. Character input provides all the features of `vi` Edit mode but with more overhead than the `vi` option.

The `-A` option can be used on the `ksh` command line or the `set` command to define an array variable with initial values. When you specify `-A`, the next argument must be the name of the array variable to be initialized. Subsequent arguments are stored as consecutive elements of the array, beginning with element 0. The `-A` option resets any previous value of the array variable before it assigns new values. Thus, the ending value of the array consists of only those arguments specified as `arg`.

The `+A` option assigns the `arg` values successively, starting with element 0, but it doesn't reset any previous values of the array. Thus, if the array variable previously had 12 values and only six values were provided with `+A`, after execution, the first six elements of the array would be the `arg` values, and the last six elements would be left over from the previous value of the array.

The significance of the `arg` values depends on the options specified. If option `-A` is specified, the values are taken as initial array element values. If option `-s` or `-i` is specified, or if option -i defaults because the shell input is a terminal, the arg values are used to initialize the positional parameters $1, -2, and so on. If option -c is specified, the first arg is taken as a command string to be executed. If none of the options -A, -c, -i, or -s is specified, the first arg is taken as the name of a file of shell commands to be executed, and subsequent arg values are set temporarily as the positional parameters $1, -2, and so on during the file's execution.

Command History

Your *command history* is simply an automatic recording of the commands that you enter, kept as a numbered list in a special disk file in your home directory to preserve it from logon session to session. When you log on, the command-history list from your previous session is available for reference and use. New commands you enter are added to the end of the list. To keep the list from growing too large, the oldest commands at the beginning of the list are deleted when the list grows to a certain fixed size.

You don't need to do anything to activate the command-history feature, and you don't need to specify its maximum size. Its operation is completely automatic. You can use the command-history list in one of three ways:

- **View the commands in the history list by using the history command.** Use the history command when you can't remember whether you've already performed an action or if you want to refer to the syntax or operands of a previous command.

- **Resubmit a command from the list by using the r command.** Except for very short commands, it's faster to resubmit a command you typed before with the r command than it is to type the command again. The r command provides several alternative ways for you to identify which command in the history list you want to re-execute.

- **Modify a command in the list using the fc command.** You can use any text editor you want to edit the chosen command. By default, the Korn shell invokes the crusty old ed command for you, but you can change the default to any text editor you want by changing the value in the FCEDIT variable. The modified command executes immediately after you leave the editor.

NOTE

Performing command editing with the fc command, although a convenient and useful feature of command history, is not the same as the command-editing feature discussed later in the "Command Editing" section.

Displaying the Command-History List

The `history` command displays the commands in the command-history list. Each command is listed with a line number preceding it. The line number uniquely identifies each command in the history list, and it is one way you can refer to a specific line in the history list—for example,

```
$ history
[122] cd /usr/home/jim/src/payapp/pay001
[123] vi main.c
-124] cc -I../include -o main main.c
-125] fgrep include *.c ¦ grep '^#'
-126] vi checkwrite.c checkfile.c checkedit.c
-127] lint -I../include checkfile.c >errs; vi errs
-128] vi checkfile.c
-129] cc -I../include -o checks check*.c
-130] cp checks /usr/home/jim/bin
```

> **NOTE**
>
> The `history` command is actually an alias for the `fc` command—specifically, for `fc -l`.

The complete syntax for the `history` command follows:

`history [first] [last]`

For *first*, specify the first line to be displayed. You can designate a specific line directly by its line number—for example, `history 35`—or as a number of lines back from the current line—for example, `history -10`. You also can give the command name of the line from which the display should begin—for example, `history vi`. The Korn shell looks backward from the current line until it finds a command beginning with `vi` and then displays lines from that point forward.

For *last*, specify the last line to be displayed. If you omit *last*, history lines are displayed from *first* up to the current, most recently entered line in the command history. You can use an actual line number, a relative line number, or a command name to designate the last line to be displayed.

If you omit both *first* and *last*, the Korn shell lists the last 16 lines of history.

> **TIP**
>
> You won't know what line numbers to use until you first list some history. Most people begin a search of command history without any operands.

Re-executing a Command from the History

The r command enables you to re-execute a command from the command-history list. The r command itself isn't added to the history, but the command you reuse is added.

> **NOTE**
>
> The r command is actually a preset alias for the fc command—specifically, fc-e-.

The general syntax for r follows:

```
r [ old=new ] [ line ]
```

If you omit *line*, the most recently entered command is re-executed.

Specify a line number (25), a relative line number (-8), or a command name (vi) for *line* to designate the command you want to reuse. As with the history command, if you specify a command name, the most recently entered command with that name is reused.

You can modify a word or phrase of the reused command by using the syntax *old=new*. Suppose that the command history contains the following line:

```
135 find /usr -type f -name payroll -print
```

You could reuse the find command, changing only the filename payroll to vendors, like this:

```
$ r payroll=vendors find
```

The r command echoes the line that will be executed, showing any changes that might have been made. For example, the r command here yields the following output:

```
$ r payroll=vendors find
find /usr -type f -name vendors -print
```

Accessing the History List: fc

The fc (fix command) command is a built-in Korn shell command that provides access to the command-history list. Forms of the fc command enable you to display, edit, and reuse commands you previously entered. The Korn shell automatically defines the alias names history and r for you to reduce the amount of typing needed to perform simple history functions.

The syntax of the fc command follows:

```
fc [ -e editor ] [ -nlr ] [ first ] [ last ]
```

When invoked with no options, the fc command selects a line from the command history using the values of *first* and *last*, invokes the default command editor, and waits for you to edit the command or commands selected. When you exit the editor, by filing the altered command text or by quitting the editor, the commands are executed.

The fc command actually copies the selected commands to a temporary file and passes the file to the text editor. The contents of the file after editing become the command or commands to be executed.

For example, if you enter the command

```
$ fc vi
```

where vi represents the value of *first*, the Korn shell copies the most recent vi command to a temporary file. The temporary file has an unrecognizable name, such as /usr/tmp/fc13159, and is located in a directory designated for temporary files. The file you actually edit is /usr/tmp/fc13159. Regardless of whether you change the text in file /msr/tmp/fc13159, the Korn shell executes its contents immediately after you exit the editor.

You can specify the command or commands to be processed in the following manner:

- To process the command you most recently entered, omit both *first* and *last*.
- To select and process only one command, specify the command as the value of *first* and omit *last*.
- To select a range of commands, specify the first command in the range with *first* and specify the last command in the range with *last*.
- To designate a command by its line-number position in the history list, use a plain number—for example, 219.
- To designate a command preceding the most recent command in the history list, use a negative number. In this command-history list, for example, the command fc -2 selects the vi command:

```
135 mkdir paywork
136 mv paymast/newemps paywork
137 cd paywork
138 vi newemps
139 payedit newemps
```

- To select a command by its name instead of by its position in the history list, use a command name or any prefix of a command name. The most recent command line that begins with the string you specify is selected. In this command-history example, you also could select the `vi` command by entering **fc vi**.

The *first* and *last* command-line selectors don't have to use the same formats. You could select line 145 of the history list through the fifth-to-last line by entering **fc 145 - 5**, for example.

By default, the `fc` command invokes a text editor on the selected lines and re-executes them after editing. You can modify this default behavior with the options shown in Table 12.6.

TABLE 12.6. OPTIONS TO MODIFY THE BEHAVIOR OF THE `fc` COMMAND.

Option	Stands for	Description
-e	Editor	Use the -e option to override the Korn shell's default editor. To use the `vi` editor to modify and reuse commands, for example, type **fc -e vi**.
		The special format -e - suppresses the use of an editor. The selected lines are executed immediately with no opportunity to change them. This form of the `fc` command—as in `fc -e - 135`—is equivalent to the `r` command.
-l	List	The selected lines are listed. No editor is invoked, and the lines are not re-executed. The command `fc -l` is equivalent to the alias `history`.
-n	Numbers	Use the -n option to suppress the printing of line numbers in front of the command history. The -n option is meaningful only in combination with the -l option—for example, `fc -nl`.
-r	Reverse	The -r option causes the command history to be printed in reverse order. The most recently entered command is shown first, and successive lines show progressively older commands. Use the -r option with the -l option—for example, `fc -lr`.

Command Editing

Command editing is arguably the most important extension of the Bourne shell included in the Korn shell. It is a great time-saver, and it makes the shell much easier to use for UNIX beginners.

The Korn shell supports two distinct styles of command editing: vi Edit mode—named after the vi text editor—and EMACS Edit mode—named after EMACS. If you're familiar with either of these editors, you can begin to use command editing immediately.

Activating Command-Edit Mode

Before you can use command editing, you first must activate it. Until you do so, the Korn shell command line works much the same as the Bourne shell: Everything you type goes into the command line indiscriminately as text, including control and function keys. This is a compatibility feature you'll want to disable as soon as possible—typically, by activating command editing in your logon profile.

To enable vi Edit mode, enter the following command line or place it in your profile (see "Customizing the Korn Shell," later in this chapter):

```
set -o vi
```

To enable EMACS Edit mode, enter the following command line or place it in your profile:

```
set -o emacs
```

vi Edit Mode

vi Edit mode uses the editing commands and methods of the vi text editor, although with some minor differences due to the fact that you're editing only one line of text and not an entire file.

See Chapter 7, "Text Editing with vi and EMACS," to learn how to use this editor. Note that the o and O (open) commands, the m (mark) command, and scrolling commands such as z, H, and M are not needed for command editing and are not supported by the Korn shell for this purpose, although they do function within the vi editor itself when run under the shell.

EMACS Edit Mode

The EMACS Edit mode is designed to parallel the editing interface offered by the EMACS editor. Unlike the vi editor, the EMACS editor does not distinguish between command and edit mode. The EMACS Edit mode is activated when you enter this command:

```
set -o emacs
```

If you prefer to always use the EMACS Edit mode, you can add the command to your .profile file. Note, however, that you can't have the EMACS and vi Edit modes both active at once. You can switch between them or shut off both of them. See Chapter 7 for details on the EMACS edit interface.

Variables

You were introduced to the concept of shell variables in Chapter 10, "The Bourne Shell." Everything you learned there remains true for the Korn shell. The Korn shell provides some significant extensions to shell variable support, though. Among these is a greatly expanded set of variables that have special meanings to the shell. These variables often are called *predefined variables* because the shell provides an initial default value for them when you log on. The Korn shell also supports array variables and enhanced arithmetic on shell variables, both of which are a great boon to shell-script writers. Naturally, the syntax of shell variable references is expanded to support these capabilities.

Predefined Variables

Variables that have special meaning to the shell fall into two main groups: those you can set to affect the behavior of the shell, and those the shell sets for you to provide information.

Variables whose values are set by the shell include the familiar $@, $*, $#, $-, $?, and $$, as well as the new $!. The new variable $! provides the Process ID of the last command you invoked. It differs from $$ in that the value of $$—your current Process ID—generally is that of the shell itself and doesn't change, whereas the value of $! changes each time you invoke a command. The values of the other shell variables have the same meanings as they do in the Bourne shell.

Table 12.7 lists the named variables set by the Korn shell.

TABLE 12.7. NAMED VARIABLES SET BY THE KORN SHELL.

Variable	Description
_	This variable is used internally by the shell.
ERRNO	The nonzero exit code of the last command that failed. This variable is similar to $?, but it differs because its value changes only when a command fails.

continues

TABLE 12.7. CONTINUED.

Variable	Description
LINENO	This variable is meaningful only within a shell script. Its value is the line number of the line in the script currently being executed.
OLDPWD	The value of this variable is always the full pathname of the directory that was current immediately before the last cd command.
OPTARG	This value is set by the getopts command—a new built-in command provided by the Korn shell.
OPTIND	This value is set by the getopts command.
PPID	This value is the Process ID of the parent process of $$. This variable is used in shell scripts.
PWD	Specifies the full pathname of your current directory. Because of symbolic links, the value of $PWD isn't necessarily the same as the value printed by the pwd command.
RANDOM	This value is an integer in the range of 0 to 32,767. The value is different in a random way every time you examine it. This variable is useful for generating temporary filenames.
REPLY	The select statement, which is new with the Korn shell, sets the value of $REPLY to the user's input text. The read built-in command stores the user's typed input in $REPLY if you supply no variable names on the read command.
SECONDS	The integer number of seconds since you invoked the Korn shell.

The shell variables set by the Korn shell listed in Table 12.7 don't require your attention. If you have a use for one of them, refer to this table while at your keyboard or in a shell script. You don't need to assign values to them, though. In some cases, you aren't even allowed to assign a value.

Some variables require attention from you, however. In most cases, the Korn shell assigns a default value to these variables when it starts. You can override this default value in your *logon profile*—a file named .profile in your home directory—or at any later time by using an assignment statement from the keyboard. The values of these variables affect the way the Korn shell works. Proper setup of these variables can enhance your effectiveness and productivity.

Table 12.8 lists the variables used by the Korn shell.

TABLE 12.8. VARIABLES USED BY THE KORN SHELL.

Variable	Description
CDPATH	The value of $CDPATH is a list of colon-separated directory pathnames. The value is referenced only by the cd command. Use the CDPATH variable to name a list of directories to be searched when you issue cd with a directory's simple filename. The benefit of CDPATH is that it enables you to switch to a directory by giving only its filename instead of the full pathname. There is no default value for CDPATH.

> **NOTE**
>
> I always put the following definition in my logon profile:
>
> CDPATH=.:...:$HOME
>
> The command cd src first looks for a directory named src as a subdirectory in the current directory. Failing that, the cd command looks for src in the parent directory. If no directory named src is found in either place, it tries to change to src in my home directory. Proper use of the CDPATH variable saves a lot of typing.

Variable	Description
COLUMNS	The value of $COLUMNS defines the display width used by the Korn shell Command-Edit mode—either vi or EMACS—as a view window for long lines and as the screen width for printing the select list. The default value is 80.
EDITOR	The value of $EDITOR is used primarily by programs other than the Korn shell. If you set the value of EDITOR (in your profile or at the keyboard), however, the Korn shell inspects the value for a pathname ending in vi or emacs. If either value is found, the Korn shell sets the corresponding vi, emacs, or gmacs option, enabling command editing. This is only a convenience. You still can toggle the Command-Edit mode by using the set -o command. There is no default value for EDITOR.
ENV	The value of $ENV is the pathname of a shell script containing commands to be executed when the Korn shell is invoked. By placing alias, export, and set commands in a file and supplying the file's pathname as the value of $ENV, you can ensure that you have the same shell environment whenever you invoke the Korn shell. Keep the file pointed to by $ENV small because its execution is added to the execution of every shell script you execute. There is no default value for ENV.
FCEDIT	The value of $FCEDIT is the pathname of the text editor to be invoked by the fc command. You can override the value of FCEDIT by using the -e option with the fc command. The default value of FCEDIT is /bin/ed.

TABLE 12.8. CONTINUED.

Variable	Description
FPATH	The value of $FPATH is a colon-separated list of directories—the same format as for CDPATH and PATH. The directory list is searched for autoload function definitions. There is no default value for FPATH.
HISTFILE	HISTFILE is the filename of the Korn shell history file. If you want to specify an explicit filename for your history file, supply a value for HISTFILE in your logon profile. The default value of HISTFILE is $HOME/.sh_history.
HISTSIZE	The value of HISTSIZE is an integer number specifying the maximum number of commands—not lines—to be retained in the history file. The shell may retain more than HISTSIZE commands in memory while you are working, but it will not accumulate more than HISTSIZE commands in the history file on disk. The default value of HISTSIZE is 128.
HOME	HOME with the Korn shell works the same as it does with the Bourne shell. The value of HOME is the pathname of your home directory. The variable is initialized by the UNIX logon procedure before any shell is invoked. It almost never is proper for you to change the value of HOME. The default value of HOME is the sixth part of the /etc/passwd file entry for your logon name.
IFS	IFS with the Korn shell works the same as it does with the Bourne shell. The value of IFS is zero or more characters to be treated by the shell as delimiters when parsing a command line into words or using the read command.
LINES	The value of LINES is an integer number representing the number of lines displayed by your terminal. The Korn shell uses the value of LINES, if set, to limit the printing of select lists. If no value is set, select lists can be arbitrarily long, and some lines may scroll off the display. There is no default value for LINES.
LOGNAME	The logon name of the user as mentioned in the user database /etc/passwd. Modification of this variable can upset some programs, so exercise caution when using it, and restore it back to its original value using it.
MAIL	MAIL with the Korn shell works the same as it does with the Bourne shell. The value is the pathname of a file to be monitored by the shell for a change in its date of last modification. If a change is noted, the shell issues the message You have mail at the next opportunity. There is no default value for MAIL. Set MAIL to the name of your mail file in your logon profile.
MAILCHECK	The value of MAILCHECK is an integer number of seconds that specifies how often the shell should check for a change to the MAIL file. If MAILCHECK is not set or is zero, the shell checks at each command-line prompt for a change in the mail file. The default value of MAILCHECK is 600.

Variable	Description
MAILPATH	The value of MAILPATH is a colon-separated list of pathnames, each of which identifies a file to be monitored for a change in the date of last modification. A pathname can be suffixed with a question mark and message to customize the You have mail message—for example, you can use MAILPATH=/var/spool/mail/jjv?New mail in /var/spool:/usr/mail/jjv?New mail in /usr/mail. Generally, you should set the MAIL or the MAILPATH variable but not both. There is no default value for MAILPATH.
PATH	PATH with the Korn shell works the same as it does with the Bourne shell. The default value is system dependent. This variable cannot be changed if the shell was started as a restricted shell.
PS1	PS1 is the primary prompt string. The Korn shell performs a full substitution on the value of $PS1 before displaying it at the beginning of each command-input line. The default value is "$ ".
PS2	PS2 is the secondary prompt string. It is the same as with the Bourne shell. The default value is ">".
PS3	PS3 is the select prompt string. The value of $PS3 is printed as the selection prompt by the select command. (See "Using the select Statement," later in this chapter.)
PS4	PS4 is the debug prompt string. The value of $PS4 is scanned for variable substitution and is printed in front of each line displayed by the trace or -x option.
SHELL	SHELL is the pathname of the shell. The Korn shell sets a default value for $SHELL only if it is not set when ksh begins. The value isn't used directly by the Korn shell, but many other commands (such as vi and pg) use the value of $SHELL as the pathname of the shell to be called when invoking a subshell.
TERM	The value of TERM is a symbolic alphanumeric string that identifies the type of your terminal. Not used by the Korn shell directly, the variable name TERM is reserved for general system use. The proper setting of $TERM is important to the proper and reasonable operation of your terminal, and should be initialized appropriately when you log on. For the allowable values at your installation, consult your system administrator. There is no default value for TERM.
TMOUT	The value of TMOUT is an integer specifying the number of seconds after which no terminal activity should cause the Korn shell to automatically log out. A value of zero disables the automatic logout function.

12

THE KORN SHELL

continues

TABLE 12.8. CONTINUED.

Variable	Description
VISUAL	The value of $VISUAL is used primarily by programs other than the Korn shell. If you set the value of VISUAL (in your profile or at the keyboard), however, the Korn shell will inspect the value for a pathname ending in vi, emacs, or gmacs. If one of these values is found, the Korn shell sets the corresponding vi, emacs, or gmacs option, enabling command editing. This is only a convenience. You still can toggle the Command-Edit mode by using the set -o command. There is no default value for VISUAL.

As with the Bourne shell, variable names in the Korn shell begin with a letter or an underscore, and they contain an arbitrary number of letters, underscores, and digits. The variable name is a symbolic representation for the variable's value, which can be changed by an assignment statement; by the set, read, or select statement; as a by-product of the execution of a built-in shell or other commands; or by the Korn shell itself. There is no arbitrary upper limit to the number of variables you can define and use, but the amount of memory available to the shell sets a practical (usually large) upper limit.

You can explicitly assign a value to a variable name by using an assignment in the format *name=value*. Note that you don't include a dollar sign ($) in front of *name* when you write the assignment. The dollar sign is appropriate only when referring to the value of the variable.

The value of a variable is a *string*—a sequence of alphanumeric and special characters—of arbitrary length. The Korn shell provides a number of extensions that enable the value of a variable to be manipulated by arithmetic methods. The variable's value still is stored as a string, however.

A variable retains its value from the time it is set—whether explicitly by you or implicitly by the Korn shell—until the value is changed or the shell exits. Note that the value isn't passed to commands and shell scripts that you invoke unless the variable is marked for exportation. You mark a variable for exporting with the typeset built-in shell command or the export alias. Alternatively, if the allexport option is switched on (by typing set -o allexport, for example), all variables created are exported automatically. Exported variables become part of the environment of all invoked commands.

Because the values of variables are retained internally in a memory table by the shell, all variables that the shell didn't inherit are lost when the shell exits. For this reason, you can assign values to variables and export the variables to pass values downward to sub-shells of your current shell, but you cannot pass values upward to higher level shells or shell scripts.

This limitation on the use of shell variables generally arises in issues related to shell programming. However, if you invoke the shell directly (by entering the sh, ksh, or csh command) or indirectly (by entering the shell environment from within another UNIX command, such as vi or pg), you should realize that any changes to the shell environment, including variable settings and aliases, are lost when you return to your original shell level by exiting the subshell.

Referencing Variables

The Korn shell replaces strings that begin with $ and are followed by a reference expression appearing in command lines with the value of the reference expression. Any number of reference expressions may appear in the same command line. Adjacent references, when replaced, don't introduce new word boundaries into the command line. That is, a single word—a command name, option, or argument—isn't split into two or more words by replacement even if the replaced value contains blanks, tabs, or other delimiter characters. You can use the eval built-in shell command when you want delimiters in the replacement text to cause further word splitting.

Valid reference expressions for the Korn shell follow:

name	*{name#pattern}*
{name}	*{name##pattern}*
{name[n]}	*{name%pattern}*
{name[*]}	*{name%%pattern}*
{name[@]}	*{#@}*
{name;word}	*{#*}*
{name-word}	*{#name}*
{name=word}	*{#name[*]}*
{name?word}	*{#name[@]}*
{name+word}	

name

The expression is replaced by the current value of the shell variable *name*. If no value for the variable has been defined, the dollar sign and the variable name are replaced with the null string. For example,

```
$ today="January 13"
$ print Today is:$today.
Today is;January 13.
$ print Today is $tomorrow.
Today is:.
```

{*name*}

The expression is replaced by the current value of the shell variable *name*. You must use braces to reference a shell parameter greater than $9—for example, ·10} or ·12}—or to reference an array variable. For example,

```
$ Person1=John
$ Person2=Mike
$ print $Person1 and $Person2
John and Mike
$ print $Person1and$Person2
Person1and: not defined
$ print ${Person1}and$Person2
JohnandMike
```

{*name*[n]}

The value of the expression is the value of the *n*th element of the array variable *name*; it is null if the *n*th element isn't set. The first element of an array variable is ${*name*[0]}. For example,

```
$ set -A words hello goodbye
$ echo $words[1]
hello[1]
$ echo ${words[1]}
goodbye
$ echo $words
hello
```

{*name*[*]}

The value of the expression is the value of all the elements of the array variable *name* that are set, separated by blanks. Substitution occurs in the same way as for the special expression $* with regard to embedded blanks and word splitting. For example,

```
$ set -A planets Mercury Venus Earth Mars
$ planet[9]=Pluto
$ print ${planets[*]}
Mercury Venus Earth Mars Pluto
```

{*name*[@]}

The value of the expression is the value of all the elements of the array variable *name* that are set, separated by blanks. If elements of the array contain strings with embedded blanks and if the expression ${*name*[@]} is contained inside quotes, the number of words in the substituted expression is equal to the number of non-null array elements. Otherwise, embedded blanks cause word splitting to occur, and the number of substituted words will be greater than the number of non-null array elements. For example,

```
$ set -A committee "B Jones" "M Hartly" "C Rogers"
$ for word in ${committee[@]}
> do
> print $word
> done
B
Jones
M
Hartly
C
Rogers
$ for word in "${committee[@]}"
> do
> print $word
> done
B Jones
M Hartly
C Rogers}
```

{*name*:-*word*}

The expression is replaced by the value of variable *name*, if the variable has a value and the value consists of at least one character. Otherwise, the expression is replaced by *word*. Note that *word* should not contain embedded blanks or tabs, although it may contain quoted strings.

Combine : with -, =, ?, or + to treat a variable with a null value (that is, a zero-length string) the same as an unset variable. Without :, the variable is tested only for whether it is set. For example,

```
$ month=January
$ print This month is ${month:-unknown}
This month is January
$ print This year is ${year:-unknown}
This year is unknown
```

{*name*-*word*}

The expression is replaced by the value of *name*, if the variable has a value. Otherwise, it is replaced by *word*. You can use ${*name*:-*word*} to ignore a value that is not set or is null. For example,

```
$unset month
$ month=January
$ print This month is ${month-unknown}
This month is January
$ print This year is ${year-unknown}
This year is unknown
```

This may look similar to the previous expression, {*name*:-*word*}, so to clarify, look at this example:

```
$ unset month
$ month=""
$ echo ${month-unknown}

$echo ${month:-unknown}
unknown
```

{name=word}

The expression is replaced by the value of *name*, if the variable has a value. Otherwise, *word* is assigned as the value of *name*, and the expression is replaced by *word*. You can use ${*name*:=*word*} to assign *word* to *name* if the variable is not set or is null. For example,

```
$ print This month is $month.
This month is .
$ print This month is ${month=January}.
This month is January.
$ print This month is $month.
This month is January.
```

{name?word}

The expression is replaced by the value of *name*, if the variable has a value. Otherwise, the string *word* is printed as an error message. An unset variable is recognized as an error and halts processing of the current command line. If the error is recognized inside a shell script, execution of the shell script is terminated. Use ${*name*:?*word*} to recognize an unset or null value as an error. *word* can be omitted from the expression; if it is, a standard error message is displayed. For example,

```
$ month=January
$ print This month is ${month?unknown}
This month is January
$ print This year is ${year?unknown}
ksh: year: unknown
$ print This year is ${year?}
ksh: year: parameter null or not set
```

{name+word}

The expression is replaced by the value of *word* if the variable *name* has a value. If the variable is not set, the expression is replaced by the null string. That is, if *name* has a value, it temporarily treats the value as though it were *word*. If *name* doesn't have a value, the expression has no value either. Use ${*name*:+*word*} to treat a null value the same as an unset value. For example,

```
$ month=January
$ print This month is ${month+unknown}
This month is unknown.
$ print This year is ${year+unknown}
This year is .
```

{name#pattern}

The value of the expression is the value of *name* with the leftmost occurrence of *pattern* deleted. The shortest match for *pattern* is recognized. For *pattern*, specify a string that contains any character sequence, variable and command substitutions, and wildcard expressions. Only the first occurrence of *pattern* is deleted. For example,

```
$ print $PWD
/usr/home/valley
$ print ${PWD#*/}
usr/home/valley
```

{name##pattern}

The value of the expression is *name* with anything to the left of the longest match of *pattern* removed. For example,

```
$ print $PWD
/usr/home/valley
$ print ${PWD##*/}
valley
```

{name%pattern}

The value of the expression is the value of *name* with the shortest rightmost string matching *pattern* deleted. For example,

```
$ print $FNAME
s.myfile.c
$ print ${FNAME%.*}
s.myfile
```

{name%%pattern}

The value of the expression is the value of *name* with the longest rightmost string matching *pattern* deleted. For example,

```
$ print $FNAME
s.myfile.c
$ print ${FNAME%%.*}
s
```

{#@}

The value of the expression is the integer number of arguments that would be returned by $@.

{#*}

The value of the expression is the integer number of arguments that would be returned by $*. It is the same as $#.

{#name}

The value of the expression is the length of the string value of variable *name*. For example,

```
$ print $FNAME
s.myfile.c
$ print ${#FNAME}
10
```

{#name[*]}

The value of the expression is the number of elements of the array variable *name* that are set. For example,

```
$ set -A planets Mercury Venus Earth Mars
$ print ${#planets[*]}
4
```

{#name[@]}

{#name[@]} is the same as *{#name[*]}*.

Array Variables

An *array variable* is a variable that holds more than one value. Array variables are helpful for managing lists of strings because you can reference an individual element in the list without resorting to string-splitting techniques.

You can assign values to an array one at a time by using the assignment statement. For example,

```
$ planets[0]=Mercury
$ planets[1]=Venus
$ planets, 2]=Earth
$ print ${planets[1]}
Venus
```

The general syntax *name[subscript]* is supported by the Korn shell for referring to elements of an array. For *subscript*, supply an integer number in the range of 0 through

511, or write a variable expression with the value of the desired element number. Element numbers begin at zero. Thus, the first element in an array is ${*name*[0]}.

You can use the -A option of the set command to set many array elements with one statement. For example, the preceding code could be rewritten as this:

```
$ set -A planets Mercury Venus Earth
$ print ${planets[1]}
Venus
```

You also can substitute all the elements of an array by using the special notation ${*name*[*]} or ${*name*[@]}. For example,

```
$ set -A planets Mercury Venus Earth
$ planets[9]=Pluto
$ planets[7]=Uranus
$ print The known planets are: ${planets[*]}
The known planets are: Mercury Venus Earth Uranus Pluto
```

You should remember a few points when using array variables:

- If you reference the array variable without a subscript, the value of the reference is the first element of the array:
  ```
  $ print $planets
  Mercury
  ```

- Array variables cannot be exported.

- The special expression ${#*name*[*]} or ${#*name*[@]} can be used to get the number of non-null elements in an array. For example,
  ```
  $ print There are ${#planets[*]} planets: ${planets[*]}
  There are 5 planets: Mercury Venus Earth Uranus Pluto
  ```

- You must use the brace-enclosed expression syntax to refer to elements of an array. Without the braces, the Korn shell interprets the expression in the same way the Bourne shell would. For example,
  ```
  $ print The known planets are $planets[*]
  The known planets are Mercury[*]
  $ print The second planet from the Sun is $planets[2]
  The second planet from the sun is Mercury[2]
  ```

Variable Arithmetic

An exciting new addition to the capabilities of the old Bourne shell offered by the Korn shell is the capability to do arithmetic. The Bourne shell provides no built-in calculating capability, so even the simplest arithmetic requires command substitutions that resort to calling other UNIX programs such as expr. The Korn shell adds some built-in capabilities to do basic arithmetic.

The two major tools you'll use when doing arithmetic inside the Korn shell are the typeset command and the let command. The typeset command provides number-formatting capability and the capability to declare variables for the special purpose of doing arithmetic. The let command is used to specify the arithmetic operations to be performed.

Using typeset

The Korn shell supports only integer numbers; all your calculations must use integer values, and they will yield integer results. The shell arithmetic is sufficient to support programming concepts such as loop control with counters, however.

The typeset statement is an extension provided by the Korn shell to permit some amount of control over the format and use of shell variables. When typeset is used for managing variables, its syntax follows:

```
typeset [ [pm]HLRZilrtux [n] ] [ name[=value] ] ...
```

The particular set of options you use with the command determines the required format for the syntax of the command. Not all combinations of option letters are legal. Only the options listed in Table 12.9 should be specified.

TABLE 12.9. typeset OPTIONS.

Option	Description
-H	The -H option is supported only by versions of the Korn shell that execute on non-UNIX operating systems.
-i	Declares the variable to be of type integer. Use the optional *n* to specify the number base to which the value should be converted on substitution. The number always is carried in base -10, and only base-10 decimal values should be assigned to the variable. On substitution, however, the value is converted to the equivalent octal digit string. You also can specify the -L, -LZ, -R, or -RZ option for the named variable(s).
-l	The value of the named variable(s) should be converted to all lowercase letters when it is substituted. Don't specify this option with -u. You must specify at least one *name* argument, and you can provide an optional initial value for some or all of the named variables.
-L	The value of the named variable(s) should be left-justified and padded with blanks on the right to a length of *n* when it is substituted. Obviously, you must specify a field length *n*. For example, -L4 expands the variable value to four characters on substitution. You must specify at least one *name* argument, and you can provide an optional initial value for some or all of the named variables.

Option	Description
-LZ	Similar to -L, but it strips any leading zeroes from the variable value before substitution.
-r	The named variable(s) is treated as read-only, meaning that subsequent assignments of a value to the named variables are inhibited. If the variable is to have a non-null value, you should supply a *value* for the listed variable names. You must name at least one variable to have the read-only attribute. You can use the -r option with any of the other options.
-R	The value of the named variable(s) should be right-justified and padded with blanks on the left to a length of *n* when it is substituted. You must specify a field length *n*. For example, -R4 expands the variable value to four characters on substitution. You must specify at least one *name* argument, and you can provide an optional initial value for some or all of the named variables. Don't specify the -L or -LZ options with -R.
-RZ	Similar to -R, but it pads the value with zeroes on the left. If the value of the named variable contains only digits, the result is a numeric field of length *n*.
-u	The value of the named variable(s) should be converted to all uppercase letters when it is substituted. Don't specify this option with -l. You must specify at least one *name* argument, and you can provide an optional initial value for some or all of the named variables.
-x	The named variables should be exported to shell scripts and subshells. Note that typeset -x is the only command provided by the Korn shell for establishing exported variables. A command alias is provided at startup by the shell named export, which is equivalent to the command typeset -x. Unlike the Bourne shell export statement, which permits only variable names, the Korn shell (using command aliases) supports statements of the form export *name=value* ..., providing an initial value for each exported variable. If the variable already exists when the typeset -x command is given, the shell adds the export attribute to the variable. If you define a new variable but specify no *value*, the variable is initialized to the null string and is marked as exportable.
-Z	Same as -RZ.

Apart from exporting variables, usually by way of the export alias, the typeset command is used mainly for two purposes:

- Setting up variables that you plan to use for calculation as integer variables
- Defining special formatting options for variables

Although the Korn shell doesn't require that a variable be declared as an integer to do arithmetic with it, doing so provides some advantages. Calculations are more efficient when you use arithmetic variables in the `let` statement because the shell can maintain the numeric value of the variable in an internal binary format, which is more suitable to the computer's math instructions. Similarly, there are contexts in which the shell recognizes arithmetic operators in an expression if the expression contains integer variables, but it won't if the expression uses standard variables.

The syntax for using `typeset` to define integer variables is straightforward. Before using variables for calculation, simply issue a `typeset` command to declare the variables as integers. For example,

```
typeset -i x y sum
read x y
let sum=x+y
print $sum
```

The Korn shell automatically defines an alias named `integer` that is equivalent to `typeset -i`:

```
alias integer="typeset -i"
```

You can use the alias to make your integer definitions more readable, as in this revision:

```
integer x y sum
read x y
let sum=x+y
print $sum
```

The second use of `typeset`—to set up output formatting options for variables—is of interest primarily to shell-script writers who want to generate nicely formatted output. The formatting options `-L`, `-R`, `-LZ`, and `-RZ` are also of some use in generating filenames. Suppose that you want to create a series of files that all end with a four-digit number. By writing the `typedef` statement

```
typeset -Z4 suffix
```

you easily can generate the required filenames by using code such as this:

```
typeset -Z4 suffix=0
while ...
do
let suffix=suffix+1
print sampfile.$suffix
done
```

The Korn shell automatically right-justifies the value of $suffix$ in a four-character field and fills the number out to four digits with leading zeros. Thus, it generates the series of filenames `sampefile.0001`, `sampfile, 0002`, and so on.

Using let

Use `let` to perform an arithmetic calculation. The syntax for the `let` statement is simple:

`let expr`

For *expr*, write an expression that consists of terms and operators. A *term* is a variable or a literal integer number—for example, 3 or 512. A *literal integer number* is assumed to be written in base 10. You can specify another base by using the format *radix#number*, where *radix* is the number base and *number* is the value of the number. For a radix greater than 10, digits consist of the characters 0 through 9 and A through Z. In radix 16 (hexadecimal), for example, the digits are 0 through 9 and A through F.

Table 12.10 shows the arithmetic operators supported by the Korn shell for use in arithmetic expressions.

TABLE 12.10. ARITHMETIC OPERATORS IN THE KORN SHELL.

Operator	Expression	Value of Expression
–	-exp	Unary minus—the negative of *exp*
!	!exp	0 when *exp* is nonzero; otherwise,
~	~exp	Complement of *exp*
*	exp1 * exp2	Product of *exp1* and *exp2*
/	exp1 / exp2	Quotient of dividing *exp1* by *exp2*
%	exp1 % exp2	Remainder of dividing *exp1* by *exp2*
+	exp1 + exp2	Sum of *exp1* and *exp2*
–	exp1 – exp2	Difference of *exp2* from *exp1*
<<	exp1 << exp2	*exp1* is shifted left *exp2* bits
>>	exp1 >> exp2	*exp1* is shifted right *exp2* bits
<=	exp1 <= exp2	1 if *exp1* is less than or equal to *exp2*; otherwise,
>=	exp1 >= exp2	1 if *exp1* is greater than or equal to *exp2*; otherwise,
<	exp1 < exp2	1 if *exp1* is less than *exp2*; otherwise,
>	exp1 > exp2	1 if *exp1* is greater than *exp2*; otherwise,
==	exp1 == exp2	1 if *exp1* is equal to *exp2*; otherwise,
!=	exp1 != exp2	1 if *exp1* is not equal to *exp2*; otherwise,
&	exp1 & exp2	Bitwise AND of *exp1* and *exp2*
^	exp1 ^ exp2	Exclusive OR of *exp1* and *exp2*
¦	exp1 ¦ exp2	Bitwise OR of *exp1* and *exp2*

continues

TABLE 12.10. CONTINUED.

Operator	Expression	Value of Expression
&&	*exp1 && exp2*	1 if *exp1* is nonzero and *exp2* is nonzero; otherwise,
¦¦	*exp1 ¦¦ exp2*	1 if *exp1* is nonzero or *exp2* is nonzero; otherwise,
=	*var = exp*	Assigns the value of *exp* to Variable ID
+=	*var += exp*	Adds *exp* to Variable ID
-=	*var -= exp*	Subtracts *exp* from Variable ID
*=	*var *= exp*	Multiplies *var* by *exp*
/=	*var /= exp*	Divides *var* by *exp*
%=	*var %= exp*	Assigns the remainder of *var* divided by *exp* to *var*
<<=	*var <<= exp*	Shifts *var* left *exp* bits
>>=	*var >>= exp*	Shifts *var* right *exp* bits
&=	*var &= exp*	Assigns the bitwise AND of *var* and *exp* to *var*
¦=	*var ¦= exp*	Assigns the bitwise OR of *var* and *exp* to *var*
^=	*var ^= exp*	Assigns the exclusive OR of *var* and *exp* to *var*

The Korn shell also supports expression grouping using parentheses. An expression in parentheses is evaluated as a unit before any terms outside the expression are evaluated. Parentheses are used to override the normal precedence of operators.

The operators in Table 12.10 are listed in decreasing order of precedence. The Korn shell uses the normal precedence for arithmetic operators.

The let command is a built-in shell command. Like any command, it sets an exit value. The exit value of the let command is 0 if the value of the last or only expression computed is nonzero. If the last or only expression evaluates to 0, the exit value of the let command is 1. This strange inversion is an adaptation to the if statement, where a command setting a zero exit value is true—that is, it causes execution of the then clause—and a command setting a nonzero exit value is false—that is, it causes execution of the else clause.

Because of the let command's inverted exit value, for example, the statement if let "a == b", when a and b are equal, is considered true. The logical result of the equality comparison would be 1, which is equivalent to if let 1. The last expression has a value of 1. Therefore, the exit value from let is 0, and the if statement is considered true, thus invoking the then clause as expected.

Notice that you need to quote operators used in a let expression that are special to the shell. The command let prod=x¦y would give very strange results if it were written without quotes. The shell would see a pipe between the two commands `let prod=x` and `y`. Acceptable quoting is any of the following forms:

- `let "prod=x¦y"`
- `let prod="x¦y"`
- `let prod=x\¦y`

Many Korn shell users employ the convention of always quoting an expression in its entirety, so they avoid the problem of shell metacharacters entirely.

Take another look at the syntax of the `let` command. Notice that each of its terms is an arbitrary expression. A command such as `let x+y` is valid, but it is ordinarily of little use. This is because the sum of variables `x` and `y` is computed, but the result is thrown away. You should use an assignment expression—for example, `let sum=x+y`—to retain the result of the calculation in a variable named `sum` for later reference. The only time it makes sense to evaluate an expression without assigning the result to a new variable is when the purpose of the `let` command is to set a command exit value—namely, for use in statements such as `if` and `while`. In these cases, however, you can use a more convenient form of the `let` statement: the `(( ))` expression.

A statement such as

```
if (( x+y < 25 ))
then ...
fi
```

is more clearly readable than this equivalent:

```
if let "x+y < 25"
```

An additional advantage is that using quotes to hide operators is unnecessary inside an `(( ))` expression. The `((` and `))` operators are in effect a special kind of parentheses. They notify the Korn shell that the text they enclose is intended to be an arithmetic expression; this turns off the normal interpretation of metacharacters such as < and ¦, and it permits the unambiguous interpretation of these symbols as operators. Compatibility with the Bourne shell isn't compromised because the `((` and `))` operators don't occur in shell scripts written for the Bourne shell.

You can use the `(( ))` expression form wherever the `let` command itself would be valid, as well as in a number of other places. Unlike the `let` command, however, the `(( ))` syntax permits only one expression between the doubled parentheses.

There is also a version of `(( ))` that returns the string representation of the calculation; this is `$(( ))`. In this form, the result is returned to the shell. For example,

```
$ echo "(( 4+5 ))"
(( 4+5 ))
$ echo "$(( 4+5 ))"
9
```

You can use arithmetic expressions in any of these contexts:

- As an array subscript
- As arguments of the `let` command
- Inside doubled parentheses (( ))
- As the shift count in `shift`
- As operands of the `-eq`, `-ne`, `-gt`, `-lt`, `-ge`, and `-le` operators in `test`, `[`, and `[[` commands
- As resource limits in `ulimit`
- As the right-hand side of an assignment statement, but only when the variable name being assigned was defined as an integer variable with the `typeset` or `integer` statement

Practical Examples of Arithmetic

Now that you have reviewed all the basics of arithmetic in the Korn shell, take a look at some specific examples. This is an example of how *not* to use arithmetic expressions:

```
$ x=4 y=5
$ print x+y
x+y
```

The first command line assigns numeric values to the noninteger variables x and y. The `print` line attempts to print their sum, but the `print` command isn't one of the places where arithmetic expressions are supported. The result is fully compatible with the Bourne shell. The `print` statement simply echoes its arguments.

Now look at a first attempt to fix the problem:

```
$ let x=4 y=5
$ print $x+$y
4 + 5
```

The assignment statements have been changed to a `let` command, which has no significant effect on anything. The dollar signs ($) on the `print` statement help the shell recognize that x and y are variables. The variable references are substituted with their respective values, but the Korn shell still fails to recognize the presence of an expression on the `print` command argument. There is, in fact, no way to get the shell to recognize an expression and to evaluate it on a `print` command.

Here is a working solution:

```
$ integer x=4 y=5
$ let sum=x+y
$ print $sum
9
```

The key element of the solution is the use of the `let` statement to calculate the sum. It stores the calculated result in a new variable called `sum`, which can be referenced later.

Now consider this example of a counter-controlled loop:

```
integer i=0
while (( i<5 ))
do
i=i+1
print $i
done
```

This little program simply prints the numbers 1 through 5. Notice the use of an assignment statement instead of a `let` command to increment `i`. This works only because the variable `i` was declared previously as an integer. For a more practical example, consider the following:

```
$ typeset -i16 hex
$ hex=125
$ print $hex
16#7d
```

Here, the variable `hex` is declared to be an integer and to be represented in base 16. The second line assigns a normal integer numeric value to the `hex` variable, and the third line prints it. Magically, though, the effect of the 16 from the `typeset` command becomes clear: The value of `hex` is shown in hexadecimal (base-16) notation. Going the other way—converting from hexadecimal to decimal—is just as easy:

```
$ integer n
$ n=16#7d
$ print $((n))
125
```

At the keyboard, after you declare the `hex` and `n` variables, they remain in effect indefinitely. You can use them repeatedly to convert between hexadecimal and decimal. For example,

```
$ hex=4096; print $hex
16#1000
$ n=16#1000; print $((n))
4096
```

Shell Programming

Although the main thrust of the Korn shell's features is to enhance productivity at the keyboard, the Korn shell also provides a number of boons for writing shell scripts, which makes the Korn shell an attractive environment for program development. This section reviews the Korn shell enhancements that apply to shell-script writing. Of course, all the programming constructs of the Bourne shell are available, so the material in Chapter 10 pertains equally to the Korn shell and isn't repeated here.

The Korn shell extensions useful for writing shell scripts are conditional expressions, which enhance the flexibility of the following:

- `if`, `while`, and `until` statements
- Array variables, integer variables, extended variable reference expressions, and arithmetic expressions
- A new `select` statement for constructing a menu of prompts from which the user can select a choice
- Extended support for functions, including autoload functions
- An enhanced form of the command expression `$(...)`, which is simpler to use than the backquoted form `[bq]...[bq]`
- Extended support for process communication with coprocessing using the operator—`¦&`.

If you are going to write shell scripts that will be used by many people, it is wise to place this on the first line of the script:

```
#!/bin/ksh
```

This specifies that the Korn shell must be invoked for this script, no matter which shell the user normally runs.

Conditional Expressions

The `if`, `while`, and `until` statements support two new kinds of expressions. The `(( ))` doubled parentheses operator, which evaluates an arithmetic expression, enables you to perform complex arithmetic tests. A zero result is considered true, and a nonzero result is considered false. You also can write an extended conditional test expression as the argument of `if`, `while`, or `until`. A conditional test expression has this general form:

```
[[ conditional-exp ]]
```

where `conditional-exp` is any of the forms shown in Table 12.11.

Notice that the conditional-expression forms are similar to those of the `test` or `[ ]` expression. The `[[ ]]` expression provides extended capabilities without compromising compatibility with the Bourne shell.

TABLE 12.11. CONDITIONAL EXPRESSIONS.

Expression	Bourne shell	Condition when true
-r *file*	Yes	File exists.
-w *file*	Yes	File exists and has Write permission enabled. The file might not be writable even if Write permission is set or if it is within a file system that is mounted as read-only.
-x *file*	Yes	File exists and has Execute permission set. The file might not actually be executable. Directories usually have the Execute permission flag set.
-f *file*	Yes	File exists and is a regular file.
-d *file*	Yes	File exists and is a directory.
-c *file*	Yes	File exists and is a character-special file.
-b *file*	Yes	File exists and is a block-special file.
-p *file*	Yes	File exists and is a named pipe.
-u *file*	Yes	The Set User ID permission flag is set for *file*.
-g *file*	Yes	The Set Group ID permission flag is set for *file*.
-k *file*	Yes	The Sticky permission flag is set for *file*.
-s *file*	Yes	File has a size greater than zero.
-L *file*	No	File is a symbolic link.
-O *file*	No	File has an Owner ID equal to the effective User ID of the current process.
-G *file*	No	File has a Group ID equal to the effective Group ID of the current process.
-S *file*	No	File is a socket.
-t [*fildes*]	Yes	The file descriptor *fildes*—whose default is 1—is a terminal.
-o *option*	No	The named *option* is set.
-z *string*	Yes	*string* is a zero-length string.
-n *string*	Yes	*string* is not a zero-length string.
string	Yes	*string* is not a zero-length or null string.

continues

TABLE 12.11. CONTINUED.

Expression	Bourne shell	Condition when true
`string = pat`	Yes	*string* matches the pattern *pat*.
`string != pat`	Yes	*string* does not match the pattern *pat*.
`s1 < s2`	No	String *s1* is less than string *s2*. That is, *pat* collates before *s2*.
`s1 > s2`	No	String *s1* is greater than string *s2*. That is, *pat* collates after *s2*.
`file1 -nt file2`	No	File *file1* is newer than file *file2*.
`file1 -ot file2`	No	File *file1* is older than file *file2*.
`file1 -ef file2`	No	File *file1* is the same file as file *file2*.
`e1 -eq e2`	No	Expressions *e1* and *e2* are equal.
`e1 -ne e2`	No	Expressions *e1* and *e2* are not equal.
`e1 -gt e2`	No	Expression *e1* is greater than *e2*.
`e1 -ge e2`	No	Expression *e1* is greater than or equal to *e2*.
`e1 -lt e2`	No	Expression *e1* is less than *e2*.
`e1 -le e2`	No	Expression *e1* is less than or equal to *e2*.

Functions

The Korn shell fully supports Bourne shell functions. It also provides some extensions.

Defining Functions

In addition to the Bourne shell syntax, the Korn shell supports the following alternative syntax for defining a function:

```
function identifier
{
  command-list
}
```

Using Variables in Functions

The Korn shell allows a function to have local variables. A *local variable* exists only during the execution of the function and is destroyed when the function returns. A local variable can have the same name as a variable in the calling environment. During execution of the function, the local variable hides the outer variable. You define a local variable with the `typeset` command. For example,

```
function square
{
 typeset product
 let "product=$1*$1"
 print $product
 return
}
```

Using Traps in Functions

In the Bourne shell, traps set with the `trap` command remain in force after the function's return. In the Korn shell, traps set in the calling environment are saved and restored.

You can use the `typeset` command with the `-f` option to manage functions. The `-f` option has four forms, which are listed in Table 12.12.

TABLE 12.12. -F OPTION FORMS.

Form	Description
typeset -f	Lists the functions currently defined and their definitions. The predefined alias `functions` does the same thing.
typeset -ft *name* ...	Activates the `xtrace` option whenever the function `name` is invoked. Tracing reverts to its former state when the function returns.
typeset -fx *name* ...	Defines functions as exported. Exported functions are inherited by shell scripts. A function cannot be exported to another instance of `ksh`, however. There is no method for passing function definitions through the command environment, as there is for variables.
typeset -fu *name* ...	Defines functions for autoload. A call to an autoload function before its definition is recognized as a function call when the function has been declared with `typeset`. The Korn shell searches the directories named in the `FPATH` variable for a file that has the same name as the function. If the Korn shell finds such a file, the function is loaded and executed, and the definition is retained as though an inline definition of the function had been read at that point.

Using Autoload Functions

Autoload functions provide superior performance versus conventional shell scripts because they are retained in memory for fast execution on repeated calls; however, unreferenced functions incur no overhead other than processing of the `typeset -fu` command. You create autoload functions in much the same manner as shell scripts, except that the definition file should begin with the statement function *name*. To use autoload functions, you must set the FPATH environment variable to the directory or directories to be searched (in the same manner as you set the PATH environment variable), and you must declare the functions in advance with the typeset -fu command.

Any function definition is eligible for use as an autoload function, although frequently used functions are preferred. Remember that after an autoload function is read, its definition is retained in the shell's available memory. Large programs should be written as conventional shell scripts rather than autoload functions unless the program is used heavily.

Undefining Functions

To undefine a function, use the unset command:

```
unset -f name ...
```

The named functions are purged from memory, and any typeset -fu declaration for the named function is deleted. The unset -f command is not used often, but it is useful particularly when debugging a function. Using unset -f is the only way to force the shell to reread an autoload function definition file.

When To Use Functions

Functions are a handy way of creating new keyboard commands. Because a function executes as part of the current shell environment, a directory change made with the cd command remains in force after the function exits. This isn't true for ordinary commands and shell scripts. Because I almost always like to take a quick peek at a directory's contents after changing to it, I created the following short function definition and added it to my logon profile:

```
function go
{
 cd $1
 /usr/bin/ls -FC
}
```

The go function, used in the form go *dirname*, not only changes to the directory but also prints a sorted listing so that I can see immediately what's in the directory.

Adding the go function to my logon profile means that it's always present in the shell memory. Because go is a small function, this does no harm, considering how often I use it. For larger functions, it is better to store the function definition in a separate file and to replace the function definition in the profile with a typeset -fu declaration, thus making the function an autoload function.

Scanning Arguments with `getopts`

The Bourne shell provides negligible assistance with the processing of command-line options. As a result, many user-written shell scripts process options clumsily at best, and they often don't support the generalized UNIX command format for options. The `getopt` command, long a standard part of the UNIX command set, helps a little. The Korn shell, however, goes one step further by adding a built-in command called `getopts`, which provides the same power and flexibility to script writers that C programmers have long enjoyed.

The syntax of the `getopts` built-in command is straightforward:

`getopts` *options var* [*arg* ...]

For *options*, provide a string that defines the letters that can legally appear as command-line options. If an option letter can be followed by a value string, indicate this in the *options* string by following the letter with `:`. For example, `I:` represents the option syntax `-I`*string*.

If *options* begins with `:`, the Korn shell provides user error handling. The invalid option letter is placed in `OPTARG`, and *var* is set to `?`. Without `:`, the `getopts` command issues an error message on an invalid letter and sets *var* to `?` so that you can recognize that an error occurred and skip the invalid option, but it doesn't identify the invalid letter.

For *var*, write the name of a variable to receive the option letter. The shell stores the letter in *var* when it identifies the letter as an option in the command line.

For *arg*, write the argument list from the command line that is to be scanned for options. The *arg* list usually is written in the form `$*` or `"$@"`.

For practical reasons, the `getopts` command cannot scan, identify, and process all option letters in a command on one invocation. Instead, each time you call `getopts`, you get the next option on the command line. Of course, `getopts` can't look at the real command line that invoked your shell script. It examines the *arg* list that you provide with `getopts`, stepping once through the list on each call.

When you call `getopts`, it starts by determining its current position in the *arg* list. If its current position is within a word and the word starts with –, the next character in the word is taken as an option letter. If this is your first call to `getopts`, or the last invocation finished scanning a word, `getopts` examines the next *arg* for a leading hyphen.

In any case, when `getopts` identifies an option, it stores the letter in *var*. If the option takes a value string (indicated in the *option* string by being followed by `:`), the option value is scanned and stored in a predefined variable named `OPTARG`. If `getopts` has started a new *arg* variable, it increments the predefined variable OPTIND to indicate which argument it is working on—1-2, and so on. It then updates its position in the argument list and exits.

After calling getopts, you inspect the *var* variable to find out which option has been identified. If the option takes a value, you'll find its value string in the predefined variable OPTARG. The return value from getopts is zero if it finds an option, or nonzero if it can find no more options in the command-line argument list.

The code for using getopts is almost a set piece that you need to memorize. Listing 12.1 is a shell program for scanning command-line options like those you might find in a script file. Here, the example merely prints the options it recognizes.

LISTING 12.1. SCANNING OPTIONS WITH getopts.

```
# A routine to scan options
# ... allowable options are -a, -c, -R, -Aname, or -Iname.

while getopts :acRA;I: KEY $*
do
 case $KEY in
 a)print Found option -a;;
 c)print Found option -c ;;
 R)print Found option -R ;;
 A)print Found option -A, value is "'$OPTARG'" ;;
 I)print Found option -I, value is "'$OPTARG'" ;;
 *)print -u2 Illegal option: -$OPTARG
 esac
done
# Strip option arguments, leaving positional args
shift OPTIND-1
print ARGS: $*
```

The code in Listing 12.1 is executable. Enter the statements into a file and mark the file executable with chmod +x *filename*. Then invoke the file's name with a sample set of option letters and arguments. You'll see the shell script's idea of the options and positional arguments that you entered.

You should note two special points about Listing 12.1. First, the *option* string for the getopts command begins with a colon (:). When the *option* string begins with a colon, the getopts command provides user error handling; an unrecognized option letter is put into the OPTARG variable, and the *var* keyletter variable is set to ?. You can test explicitly for ? as the letter value, or you simply can provide your own error message for any unrecognized option letter.

If the *option* string doesn't begin with :, getopts provides its own error handling. After finding an unrecognized option letter, getopts prints an error message and sets *var* to ?, but it doesn't set the option letter in OPTARG. Therefore, although you can tell that an invalid option has been found, you don't know what the invalid letter is. Of course, an invalid option letter is simply any letter that doesn't appear in the *option* string.

Second, note the use of the shift statement to identify the remaining position arguments from the original command line. By itself, the getopts command doesn't strip words containing options from the *arg* list. After identifying options with getopts, however, you don't want to see them again when you examine the remaining positional arguments. You must throw away the option words yourself. The shift statement, inherited from the Bourne shell, does the job, assisted by the arithmetic expression-handling syntax of the Korn shell. The expression OPTIND-1 computes the number of positional arguments remaining on the command line. Notice that, because OPTIND-1 occurs in the shift command line in the position of an expression, OPTIND is recognized as a variable reference; you don't need to include a dollar sign in front of it.

Using the `select` Statement

If you've ever written a shell script that enables the user to specify values on the command line or to be prompted for them, you know what an elaborate piece of drudgery such a user-interface nicety can be. The Korn shell helps you out, though, with a new built-in command that automates the entire process.

In fact, because the user might choose an illegal option or in case you want to display the menu repeatedly until the user decides to quit, the select statement is actually an iterative statement, much like while or until. You must use the break statement to terminate execution of select.

The syntax of the select statement follows:

```
select identifier [ in word ... ]
do command-list
done
```

The select statement first displays the word list (*word* ...) in one or more columns. If the LINES variable is set and specifies an integer number, it is taken as the maximum number of lines available for displaying the word list. If there are more items to display than this maximum, the list is broken into a multicolumn display. Each *word* is prefixed by a number starting at 1. *word* may be a single word or a quoted string. It is scanned for variable and command substitutions prior to display.

In effect, the list of strings that you specify for *word* ... becomes a series of menu items that are automatically numbered and displayed for the user.

12

THE KORN SHELL

The select statement next displays the value of variable PS3 as a menu prompt. By default, the value of PS3 is #?, suggesting that the user should enter a number. If you want a different prompt, assign a value to PS3 before you execute the select statement.

The select statement next reads a reply from the user. The entire line entered by the user is saved in the special shell variable REPLY. If the user enters a null line (that is, presses Enter or Return without typing anything), select redisplays the list and issues the prompt again without invoking *command-list*. Otherwise, if the user entered a number, the variable named *identifier* is set to the *word* corresponding to that number. That is, entering 1 sets *identifier* to the first *word*, entering 2 sets *identifier* to the second *word*, and so on. If the number is greater than the number of words, or if the user input isn't a number, select sets *identifier* to null. In any case, the select statement then executes *command-list*.

Consider the following example, in which the user is given a choice of colors from which to select. The select statement continues to execute until the user chooses one of the allowable color names.

```
PS3="Select color by number (e.g., 3):"
select color in Blue Green Yellow Red White Black Burnt-umber "Natural
Wool"
do case $color in\
  Blue ¦ Green ¦ Yellow ¦ Red ¦ White ¦ Black ¦
  Burnt-umber ¦ "Natural Wool") break ;;
  *) print "Please enter a number from 1-8. Try again." ;;
  esac
done
print "Your color choice is: $color"
```

Notice the use of quotes to specify Natural Wool as one of the menu choices. If the words were not quoted, the select statement would view them as two separate menu items, and the user would be able to select either Natural (item 8) or Wool (item -9).

Also note that the example does nothing to execute the menu choice procedure repetitively until the user enters a valid selection. Iteration of select is automatic. It lists the valid choices that must do something special to break out of the select loop—in this case, by executing the break statement.

Nothing prevents you from implementing a primitive, menu-driven system with select. Listing 12.2 uses the select statement to offer the user a choice of application actions. The example continues to execute until the user chooses the Exit item. Then the select statement and any shell script in which it is contained is terminated with the exit built-in shell command.

LISTING 12.2. IMPLEMENTING A MENU SYSTEM WITH select.

```
PS3=Choice?
select choice in "Enter Transactions" \
 "Print trial balance" \
 "Print invoices" \
 "Exit"
do case "$choice" in
   "Enter Transactions")  . daily-trans ;;
   "Print trial balance") . trial-balance ;;
   "Print invoices"). invoices ;;
   "Exit") print "That's all, folks!"; exit ;;
   *)  print -u2 "Wrong choice. Enter a number (1-4)."
 esac
done
```

Using Coprocesses

The Bourne shell supports a minimal amount of communication between processes—typically, by way of the pipe operator. You can invoke the ed line editor from a shell script to make a specific text change by using a command such as the one shown in Listing 12.3.

LISTING 12.3. BASIC PROCESS COMMUNICATION.

```
(echo "/^Payroll
+1
i"
cat newlist
echo "."
echo "w"
echo "q"
) ¦ ed - paylist
```

This form of intertask communication is sufficient if you just need to pass some data to another command or to read its output. Suppose that in Listing 12.3, though, you want to provide for the case that the file paylist doesn't contain a line beginning with Payroll by skipping the insert, write, and quit editor commands. With the Bourne shell, you couldn't do this. With the Korn shell, you can maintain an interactive session with the ed command, with your program providing the instructions to ed and responding to its output.

To use *coprocessing,* the simultaneous execution of two procedures that read each other's output, you first must launch the program with which you want to communicate as a background process by using the special operator ¦&. The ¦& operator is intended to suggest a combination of & (background execution) and ¦ (the pipe operator). When the background command is started, its standard input and standard output are assigned to pipes connected to your own process—one for writing to the command and one for reading the command's output.

The simplest way of sending a line to the coprocess is to use the print -p command. The -p option tells print to write to the coprocess's input pipe. To read output from the coprocess, use read -p. Once again, -p tells read to read from the coprocess pipe.

Using these facilities, you could rewrite the preceding procedure as the one shown in Listing 12.4.

LISTING 12.4. PROCESS COMMUNICATION USING COPROCESSING.

```
ed paylist ¦&
exec 3>&p
exec -4<&p
read -u4# discard initial message line
print -u3 P# Turn on prompting
print -u3 "/^Payroll"  # search for the insert location
read -u3# read prompt indicating success or failure
case "$REPLY" in
   '*'*) # search must have been successful
   print -u3 i
   cat text >&3 # file containing data to be inserted
   print -u3 .
   read -u4 # read the ending prompt
   print -u3 w; read -u4
   print -u3 q
   ;;
   *) # not found
   print -u3 q
   echo "invalid paylist file"
   exit
   ;;
   esac
done
```

Note the following in this example:

- The exec command (exec 3>&p) is used to move the coprocess input pipe from its default location to a numbered file descriptor.
- The exec command (exec -4<&p) is used again to move the coprocess output pipe to number file descriptor 4.
- Subsequent read and print commands specify the file descriptor as the source or destination of the operation, using the -u option.

- Ordinary UNIX commands can write to the coprocess by redirecting to file descriptor 3 (`cat filename >&3`).

> **NOTE**
>
> Use `read -p` or `print -p` to read from or write to the coprocess until you have moved the coprocess input or output to a number file descriptor. Then read or write to that file descriptor: `read -u4` or `print -u3`.

Listing 12.4, which uses coprocessing, is more complicated than Listing 12.3, but it is also safer. The Bourne shell version would have added new lines after the first line if the search for `Payroll` failed. The Korn shell version fails gracefully without damaging the `paylist` file.

Notice that the Korn shell example of coprocessing in Listing 12.4 contains an incomplete `cat` command. This is because you need a special syntax to transcribe a file into the coprocess pipe. The standard Bourne shell syntax—`>filename` and `>&fildes`—is inadequate because `>filename` and `>&fildes` do not give you a way to reference the coprocess input and output pipes.

By using a Korn shell feature designed especially to support coprocessing, you can use I/O redirection to send output to or read input from the background process with any UNIX command. The technique required is to switch the default input and output pipes created by the `¦&` operator to explicit file descriptors. You use the `exec` command to do this:

```
exec 3>&p
```

When used with the `exec` command, this special form of output redirection operator causes the pipe for writing to the coprocess to be assigned to file descriptor 3. (The lack of a command on the `exec` statement, of course, tips off the Korn shell that you want to modify the current environment instead of execute another program.)

Similarly, the following code reassigns the pipe for reading from the coprocess:

```
exec -4<&p
```

If you place these two lines at the front of the `ed` example, the `cat` command can be written in the familiar fashion—by using I/O redirection to an open file descriptor. For example,

```
cat newlist >&3
```

This new syntax for the exec statement is awkward. However, the basic outlines of coprocessing, including the ¦& operator and the -p options for print and read, are straightforward enough, as is the underlying concept. Coprocessing is a powerful capability, making it possible to do things in a shell script that previously required the C programming language.

Cautionary Tales

The Korn shell is a powerful shell to script with; however, it has its problems. One of the more obscure problems involves piping. Consider this script:

```
person=noone
echo At start: $person
who ¦ while read person tty junk
do
 echo $person is logged on at terminal $tty
done
echo At end: $person
```

What will be the value of person after you run this script? The answer is you don't know—you can't know. This script gave me two different results on two different implementations of the Korn shell. On one system, person was an empty (null) string. On the other system, it contained noone.

The reason for this unpredictability is that you're piping the output into another command. When you use a pipe, you effectively start another shell to manage the output. Different implementations may carry out the piping in a different way, though, because while and read are internal to the shell, so there is no need to start a second shell to manage them.

Customizing the Korn Shell

The Korn shell permits so much customization that it's no exaggeration to say that you might find another user's logon environment so foreign as to be almost unusable by you. Indeed, some places try to limit user customization.

You can adapt the Korn shell to your preferred way of working in many ways. As your familiarity with UNIX and the Korn shell increases, you'll find many conveniences, shorthand methods, and customary uses that seem comfortable to you. The Korn shell helps you along by enabling you to encapsulate favorite behaviors into your logon profile script and elsewhere.

Customizing the Korn shell begins with your logon profile script, which is named .profile and resides in your home directory. The file $HOME/.profile is of special importance because the Korn shell executes it every time you log on—or, more precisely, every time you launch an interactive shell.

The contents of your .profile script affect only you. Your script is specific to your logon name and home directory. Altering it conceivably could affect only those people who have your password and can log on with your logon name. Almost always, that is only you. Therefore, feel free to add to, change, or delete anything in the .profile script, including deleting the whole file. The .profile script is often used to do the following:

- Set control keys with the stty command
- Set environment variables
- Set local variables for shell control
- Define aliases you like to use
- Define functions you like to use, including autoload functions
- Set your favorite shell options
- Execute commands you want to run each time you log on

Setting Control Keys with stty

Use the stty command to establish the control keys that you prefer to use. The default Erase key is #, and the default Kill key is @.

Controlling Resources with ulimit

Using ulimit to control resources can be a handy feature, especially if you are a system administrator. Although UNIX comes with a ulimit command, the Korn shell offers its own alternative. The syntax for ulimit follows:

```
ulimit [-HSacdfnstv] [limit]
```

The H and S flags tell ulimit that you are defining a hard or soft limit. A *hard limit* cannot be increased after it is set. A *soft limit* can be modified up to the value of the hard limit. If both H and S are omitted, the specified limit is applied to both the hard and soft limits.

If limit is omitted, the current value of the specified limit is displayed. If ulimit is invoked with no options, it returns the number of blocks that can be written by a process (the same as typing ulimit -f). Table 12.13 lists the ulimit parameters.

TABLE 12.13. THE ulimit PARAMETERS.

Parameter	Function
-a	Lists all resource limits
-c	Specifies the number of blocks for a core file
-d	Specifies the number of kilobytes for the data area
-f	Specifies the number of blocks that may be written to a file
-n	Specifies one more than the number of files that may be open at once
-s	Specifies the number of kilobytes for the stack area
-t	Specifies the number of seconds that may be used by each process
-v	Specifies the number of kilobytes for virtual memory

TIP

Unless you do a lot of programming, it is useful to place ulimit -c 0 in your profile. This prevents any program that crashes from creating a core file and also saves disk space.

Setting Environment Variables

At the very least, you'll want to make sure that the variables PATH and MAIL have values. Usually, you'll want to set a great many more variables. If you use Bourne shell syntax, your variable settings will look like this:

```
PATH=/usr/bin:/usr/ucb:/usr/local/bin:$HOME/bin:
MAIL=/var/spool/mail/$LOGNAME
MAILCHECK=60
FCEDIT=/usr/bin/vi
VISUAL=/usr/bin/vi
export PATH MAIL MAILCHECK FCEDIT VISUAL
```

Alternatively, you can use the Korn shell export alias to avoid the need to remember to add each variable that you set to the export variable list; it does little good to set a variable if you don't export it. Using the export alias, the preceding code would look like this:

```
export PATH=/usr/bin:/usr/ucb:/usr/local/bin:$HOME/bin:
export MAIL=/var/spool/mail/$LOGNAME
export MAILCHECK=60
export FCEDIT=/usr/bin/vi
export VISUAL=/usr/bin/vi
```

When you write your environment variable settings, keep in mind that some are set by the UNIX logon processor. Your system administrator also can provide a logon script to set values before your .profile script runs. The PATH and MAIL variables usually have initial values already set when your script starts, for example. Overriding the default PATH variable is usually a good idea; you should have full control over your program search path, starting with its initial value. Overriding the default MAIL or MAILPATH variable is risky unless you know which mail subsystems are in use.

Setting Local Variables for Shell Control

Local variables are variables the shell uses but aren't exported. They include FCEDIT, which designates the text editor to be used by the fc command, and the PS1 variable, which is your primary prompt string. You also might want to define a few local variables to hold the names of directories that you commonly access, which enables you to use cd $dir instead of the longer full pathname.

Defining Aliases

Define the aliases you like to use. Here are some typical aliases I like to use:

```
alias lx='/usr/bin/ls -FC'
alias l='/usr/bin/ls -l'
alias pg='/usr/bin/pg -cns -p"Page %d:"'
alias mail='/usr/bin/mailx'
alias -t vi
```

Notice that, in most cases, I tend to use the full pathname for commands in the alias definition. I do this because it eliminates directory searches for the command, and it provides much the same effect as the Korn shell's alias-tracking mechanism. Note also the explicit use of the alias -t command to request the shell to track the vi command. The shell looks up the full pathname of the vi command and defines an alias named vi for me so that the plain command vi has all the performance but none of the typing overhead of /usr/bin/vi.

Defining Functions

Define any functions you like to use, including autoload functions. I use some function definitions as keyboard shorthand, because a function can do things an alias can't. You might want to use the go function described earlier in this chapter, for example, for switching directories.

Setting Shell Options

If you find yourself frequently setting the same shell options at the command line, you can set them in your .profile instead. To set the preferred shell options, use the set command. If you prefer to use vi mode for command history and editing, and you want full job control support, you might add these two lines to your .profile:

```
set -o vi
set -o monitor
```

Executing Commands Every Time You Log On

Execute commands you like to run every time you log on. You might want to run the who command to find out who's currently logged on, for example. Similarly, df, which isn't present on all UNIX systems, displays the amount of free disk space available on mounted file systems.

Executing Your .profile After Changing It

Whenever you change your .profile script, you should execute it before you log out. If you make an error in your script, you might have difficulty logging back on. To test your .profile script, you can run it with the . (dot) command:

```
$ . ./.profile
```

Be sure to leave a space after the first period: it's the command name, and ./.profile is the command argument. (Although .profile usually is adequate by itself, you might need to use ./.profile if your current directory is not in the search path.) The dot command not only executes the script but also leaves any environment changes in effect after the script terminates.

Alternatively, you can run the script with ksh -v to have the shell execute the script and print each statement as it is executed:

```
$ ksh -v ./.profile
```

Using the -n option would cause the Korn shell to read your .profile and check it for syntax errors but not execute the commands it contains.

Creating an ENV File

After you have your .profile set up the way you want, you're ready to tackle the environment file. The *environment file* is any file that contains shell scripts you designate by assigning its pathname to the ENV variable. The shell executes the ENV file whenever you start a new invocation of the shell and when it executes a command. If you've ever shelled out from commands such as `pg` and `vi`, you know that when you call the shell again, some environment settings, such as aliases, aren't carried over from your logon shell. By placing aliases, function definitions, and even global variable settings in a separate file and setting ENV to its pathname in your `.profile` script, you can ensure that you have a consistent Korn shell environment at all times.

To use an environment file, create a file that contains the aliases, functions, and exported variable settings you prefer. Then add the statement `export ENV=`*pathname*, where *pathname* is the full pathname of your environment file, to your `.profile`. The environment file becomes effective the next time you log on. It becomes effective immediately if you test your `.profile` with the following `.` command:

```
. .profile
```

Commands you want to put in your ENV file include alias definitions and shell options. You may prefer them in here instead of `.profile` to be sure of always getting a shell that looks and acts the same way each time.

TIP

A very useful `if` statement to put in your ENV file follows:

```
if [[ -o interactive ]]
then
    ....
    insert your ENV lines in here.
    ....
fi
```

Any lines placed inside the `if` statement are executed only if the shell is to be interactive—that is, it gives you a prompt at which you can type commands. This can cut down on the overhead of processing a new shell many times if the shell is being called with a command line that will run a command—for example,

```
ksh -c ls -l
```

If you have a lot of aliases or functions, place these in a separate file again and call this file from ENV to set them up. In my ENV file, I have these two lines:

```
. .ksh_alias
. .ksh_funcs
```

In `.ksh_alias`, I've placed all my alias definitions, and in `.ksh_funcs`, I've placed all my function definitions. This shortens my ENV file substantially and makes everything look a lot neater.

Adding Settings for Other Programs to Your `.profile`

The logon profile and environment file are handy places to put settings used by other programs. One way to customize your `vi` editing environment is by defining a variable `EXINIT` that contains the commands `vi` runs every time you start it. You could place the `EXINIT` variable setting in your logon profile to establish your preferred `vi` settings. Many UNIX commands respond to environment variables, which enables you to customize these commands in your logon profile.

Controlling Jobs

A *background job* is a program that can run without prompts or other manual interaction and can run in parallel with other active processes. With the Bourne shell, you launch a background job with the & operator. The command `cc myprog.c &`, for example, compiles the source program `myprog.c` without tying up the terminal. You can do other work while the `cc` command works behind the scenes.

Enhancements to the `stty` command and the terminal driver in recent UNIX releases have added a new control key to your terminal: Suspend. Suspend is usually Ctrl+Z. This new tool enables you to take an interactive program you're currently running, such as a `vi` editing session, and put it temporarily into the background. If the program wants to talk to your terminal, the system suspends the program. Otherwise, it continues running.

The Korn shell adds some tools that help you manage the family of processes you can accumulate. These tools consist of the `jobs`, `kill`, `wait`, `bg`, and `fg` commands.

To use the Korn shell's job-control tools, you must have the `monitor` option enabled. If your operating system doesn't support job management, the default for the `monitor` option is off. Even without operating system support you still can use some of the Korn shell's job-control tools, but you must set the `monitor` option on yourself. You do that with the command `set -o monitor`.

The `jobs` command, which takes no arguments, simply lists the jobs that you currently have active. The output of `jobs` looks like this:

```
$ jobs
[1] + Runningxlogo&
-2] + Runningxclock -bg LightGreen&
-3] + Stoppedvi myprog.c
```

You use the `kill`, `bg`, and `fg` commands to manage jobs. When referring to a job, you use the job number shown in brackets in the output of `jobs`, preceded by a percent (%) sign. For example, `kill %1` would terminate the xlogo program you currently have running. The `wait`, `kill`, `bg`, and `fg` commands also can refer to background jobs by their Process ID, which you generally can obtain from the output of the `ps` command. The use of Korn shell job numbers is preferred, however, because they are simpler and safer to use than Process IDs.

You create jobs in one of three ways:

- By explicitly designating a command for background execution with the & operator
- By switching a job into the background with the Korn shell `bg` command
- By pressing the Suspend key—usually Ctrl+Z—while a foreground program is running

By convention, a job started or switched into the background continues to run until it tries to read from your terminal. Then it is suspended by the operating system until you intervene. When it is in this state, the `jobs` command shows that the command is `Stopped`.

A job that has been stopped usually needs to talk to you before it can continue. In the previous `jobs` example, the `vi` command is shown to be stopped. The command won't continue until you reconnect it to your terminal. You do this with the `fg` command—for example, `fg %3` or `fg %vi`. The `vi` command then becomes the foreground process, and it resumes normal interactive execution with you.

> **NOTE**
>
> A full-screen program such as `vi` probably won't recognize that the screen no longer matches your last edit screen. You probably will need to press Ctrl+L to redraw the screen before you resume your edit session. Other programs that merely need your response to a prompt don't require any special action when you resume them with `fg`.

Table 12.14 shows the full syntax of the % argument accepted by the `wait`, `kill`, `fg`, and `bg` commands.

TABLE 12.14. JOB REFERENCE ARGUMENT SYNTAX.

Syntax	References
%number	The job number
%string	The job whose command begins with string

continues

TABLE 12.14. CONTINUED.

Syntax	References
%?*string*	The job whose command contains *string*
%%	The current job
%+	The current job (also %%)
%-	The preceding job

The syntax of the Korn shell job-control commands is summarized in the following sections.

Displaying Background Jobs and Their Status

Use the jobs command to display background jobs and their status. For example,

jobs [-lp] [job ...]

The -l option causes the jobs command to list the Process ID for each job in addition to its job number. The -p option causes the jobs command to list only the Process ID for each job instead of its job number.

If you omit the job arguments, jobs displays information about all background jobs, as in this example:

```
$ jobs
[1] + Running          xlogo&
[2] + Running          xclock -bg LightGreen&
[3] + Stopped          vi myprog.c
```

If you include job arguments, they display information only for the specified jobs. For job, specify a Process ID or a job reference beginning with %. To find out whether job 2 from the preceding example is still running, you would enter this command:

```
$ jobs %2
[2] + Running          xclock -bg LightGreen&
```

Sending Signals to a Job

Use the kill command to send a signal to the specified jobs. Some signals cause a job to terminate. The TERM signal—also called signal 15 or interrupt—usually causes a job to terminate gracefully, whereas signal 9 always terminates a job but may leave files unclosed or wreak other havoc on the job that was in progress. You should use kill -9 only when you cannot terminate the job any other way.

The `kill` command generally is a UNIX system command, but the Korn shell provides `kill` as a built-in command with enhanced capabilities. The Korn shell supports the basic functionality of the UNIX `kill` command transparently. Its syntax follows:

```
kill [ -signal ] job ...
```

For *signal*, specify a signal number or a signal name. Signal numbers 1 through 15 are always valid. A signal name is one of a predefined list of mnemonic symbols that correspond to the valid signal numbers. Use `kill -l` to obtain a list of the valid signal names. The names `TERM` (terminate) and `HUP` (hang-up) are always valid. (See your UNIX User's Reference Manual for more information about the `kill` and `signal` commands.)

> **NOTE**
>
> The reason for the vagueness about signal names is that they vary from one version of UNIX to another. You'll have to use `kill -l` to find out which names pertain specifically to your system.

For *job*, provide one or more Process ID numbers or job references. Job references begin with %. You must provide at least one *job* argument with the `kill` command.

Suppose that you have started an `xclock` process, displaying a clock on your X terminal screen:

```
$ xclock -bg LightGreen&
[4] + Running          xclock -bg LightGreen&
```

You can cancel the `xclock` window (a background job) with either of the following commands:

```
$ kill %4
```

or

```
$ kill %xclock
```

Suspending the Shell Until a Job Finishes

Use `wait` to suspend the shell until the specified job, if any, finishes. The visible effect of `wait` is simply to cause the shell not to issue another prompt to you. To get the prompt back if you decide not to wait, simply press Enter. This causes the shell to issue a prompt, and it terminates the `wait` command. The syntax of the `wait` command follows:

```
wait [ job ... ]
```

For *job*, specify one or more Process ID numbers or job references that designate the job or jobs for which you want to wait. If you specify no jobs, the shell waits until any job finishes. If you specify two or more jobs, the shell waits until all the specified jobs finish.

One situation in which the `wait` command is useful is when developing some formatted text files. You might want to run `nroff` or `troff` as background jobs, capturing the output to a disk file for review. While the `nroff` or `troff` job is running, you can edit other text files.

Moving Background Jobs into the Foreground

Use `fg` to move background jobs into the foreground. Foreground execution implies interactive processing with the terminal. Therefore, using `fg` to bring more than one job into the foreground establishes a race condition; the first job to get your terminal wins, and the others revert to `Stopped` status in the background. The syntax for `fg` follows:

```
fg [ job ... ]
```

For *job*, specify one or more Process ID numbers or job references. If you omit *job*, the current background process is brought into the foreground. The *current job* is the job you most recently stopped or started.

The need to use the `fg` command often arises as a result of actions you take yourself. Suppose that you are editing a text file with `vi` and, when trying to save the file and quit, you discover that you do not have Write permission for the file. You can't save the file until you correct the condition, but you're currently stuck inside the editor. What do you do?

First, stop the `vi` editor session by pressing Ctrl+Z. You'll immediately get the following console output:

```
[1]Stopped  vi chap2.nr
$
```

Now, determine the cause of the problem and correct it. For the sake of brevity, assume that the problem is nothing more than that you've tried to edit a file you've write-protected:

```
$ ls -l chap2.nr
-r-r-r- 1  barbara user  21506 May 5 10:52
$ chmod u+w chap2.nr
$ ls -l chap2.nr
-rw-r-r- 1  barbara user  21506 May 5 10:52
```

Finally, use the `fg` command to bring the `vi` edit session, currently stopped in the background, back into execution:

```
$ fg %vi
```

You might need to type Ctrl+L (a `vi` editor command) to redraw the screen.

Moving Foreground Jobs into the Background

Use the `bg` command to place jobs currently in the `Stopped` status (as indicated by the `jobs` command) into the background and to resume execution. Note that a job immediately switches back to the `Stopped` state if it requires terminal input. The syntax for `bg` follows:

```
bg [ job ... ]
```

For `job`, specify one or more Process ID numbers or job references. A job reference begins with `%`. If you omit `job`, the command refers to the current job, which is the job you most recently started or stopped.

In actual practice, you don't use the `bg` command to move a foreground job into the background because there's no way to do so; the shell is not listening to your terminal while a foreground job is running. To get the shell's attention while a foreground command is running, you need to use Ctrl+Z to stop (suspend) the foreground job.

After you stop the job and have a shell prompt, you need to decide what to do with the job you stopped. You can perform other tasks and restart the stopped job with the `fg` command when finished, as described earlier. But if the job you stopped is not interactive (if it can run without constant input from you), you can tell the shell to restart the job but leave it in the background.

Suppose that you start a long-running format of a text file using the `troff` command:

```
$ troff -me chap1.nr > chap1.trf
```

If, after waiting a few minutes for the job to finish, you find that you want to do something else instead of just sitting there, you can use the following sequence to switch the `troff` command to background execution:

```
[ctrl-z]
$ bg
$
```

By default, the shell assumes that you mean the job you last stopped. Now that the `troff` command is running in the background, you can do other work.

The net result of these actions is the same as if you had started the `troff` job in the background to begin with:

```
$ troff -me chap1.nr > chap1.trf &
```

Summary

This chapter presented the features of the Korn shell. Because the Korn shell has many features in common with the Bourne shell, only the features special to the Korn shell were discussed here.

The Korn shell is one of several shells available to you on most contemporary versions of the UNIX operating system. It is a newer, enhanced version of the original Bourne shell, with command history, command editing, command aliases, and job control to improve your keyboard productivity. The Korn shell also offers a number of improvements for the shell-script writer, including arithmetic variables and arithmetic expressions, array variables, a `select` statement for prompting the user with menus, and a coprocess mechanism for interactively executing other UNIX commands from within a shell script.

CHAPTER 13

The C Shell

*by Sriranga Veeraraghavan,
John Valley, and Sean Drew*

IN THIS CHAPTER

On most UNIX systems, users have a wide variety of shells to chose from. Previous chapters have concentrated on shells, such as `sh`, `bash`, and `ksh`, that are derived from the Bourne shell. This chapter looks at the C shell, `csh`, which is one of the more popular shells for interactive use.

The C Shell was written by Bill Joy at the University of California at Berkeley. Instead of using the pseudo-ALGOL syntax of the Bourne shell, `csh` uses the C programming language as a syntax model. It also adds many new features designed to make interactive sessions more efficient and convenient.

Shell Basics

When you enter commands at the shell prompt, you are actually providing input for the shell. The shell interprets a line of input as a string of characters terminated with the newline character. The newline is usually generated by pressing Enter or Return on the keyboard. Input to `csh` can be anything from a single simple command to multiple commands joined with command operators. This section covers the basics of interacting with the shell by entering shell statements on the command line.

In addition to providing input to the shell manually by entering shell statements on the command line, you can provide input to the shell by putting shell statements into a file and executing the file. Executable files containing shell statements are called *shell scripts*.

In the C shell, a *command* is a *basic command* or a basic command with one or more I/O *redirections*.

A basic command is a series of *words* that, when fully resolved, specify an action to be executed and provide zero or more options and arguments to modify or control the action taken. The first word of a basic command, called the *command name*, must specify the required action. The complete set of words that make up a command line is called a *statement*. Shell statements are formed from a combination of the following *tokens*:

- Comments—In noninteractive use, comments begin when `csh` encounters a word having a pound sign (#) as its first character. Comments extend to the end of the line. This interpretation can be avoided by enclosing the pound sign in quotes. Comments are not available in interactive use.

- Whitespace—Whitespace consists of blanks and tabs and sometimes the newline character. Units of text separated by whitespace are generically called *words*.

- Statement delimiters—Statement delimiters include the semicolon (;) and the newline character.

- Operators—An operator is a special character, or a combination of special characters that `csh` treats in a special manner.
- Words—A word is any consecutive sequence of characters occurring between whitespace, statement delimiters, or operators. A word can be a single group of ordinary characters, a quoted string, a variable reference, a command substitution, a history substitution, or a filename pattern. Any combinations of these elements are also considered words.

Executing Commands

A command is executed by entering its name on the command line. Any of the following can be given as command names:

- Built-in C shell command—The shell provides a number of commands implemented within the shell program. When you invoke a built-in command, it executes quickly because no program files need to be loaded. A built-in command is always invoked by a simple name, not by a pathname.
- Filename—You can specify the filename, the relative pathname, or the absolute pathname of a file as a command. If the filename is given without a path, the specified filename must exist in one of the directories listed in the `path` variable.
- Command alias—A command alias is a name you define by using the `alias` built-in shell command. If you define an alias of the same name as an executable file, you can access the file using its full pathname. This is not true for built-in commands—an alias that has the same name as a built-in command hides the built-in command.

Executing Simple Commands

The most common form of input to the shell is the *simple command*, where a command name is followed by any number of arguments. In the following command line, for example, `ftp` is the command, and *kanchi* is the argument:

```
% ftp kanchi
```

Normally `csh` interprets the first word of a command line as the command name and the rest of the input as arguments to that command. If the semicolon (;) is specified on the command line, `csh` interprets the first word following the semicolon as a new command. It treats the rest of the words as arguments to the new command. For example, the command line

```
% echo "<h1>" ; getTitle; echo "</h1>"
```

is the equivalent of

```
% echo "<h1>"
% getTitle
% echo "</h1>"
```

The only difference between these two commands is that in the first case the output of all three commands appears on a single line, whereas in the second case the results of each command appear between the command input lines.

When the semicolon is used to separate commands on a line, the commands are executed in sequence. The shell waits until one command is complete before executing the next command.

TIP

Sometimes command lines can get lengthy. To enter commands that span multiple lines, you escape the newline character. For example, the following command translates some common HTML sequences into a readable format:

```
% sed -e "s/%3A/:/" -e "s@%2F@/@g" -e "s@%3C@<@g" \
 -e 's/%5C/\\/g' -e "s/%23/#/g" -e "s/%28/(/g" \
 -e "s/%29/)/g" -e "s/%27/'/g" -e 's/%22/\"/g' infile > outfile
```

When csh encounters a command line that is terminated with the with a backslash (\), the next character, usually the newline character, is not interpreted as the end of the line of input.

Conditional Execution

Compound commands are two or more commands combined so that the shell executes all of them before prompting for more input. The two main conditional operators are the following:

- The and-and operator: &&
- The or-or operator: ¦¦

Conditional Execution on Success, the && Operator

The and-and operator, &&, is used to join two commands as follows:

command1 && *command2*

When csh encounters a command line of this form, it executes *command2* only if *command1* is successful. Like the Bourne shell, csh considers a command as successful if its exit code is zero. For *command1* or *command2*, you can use either simple or compound commands. For example, the following:

```
grep mailto *.html ¦ pr && echo OK
```

echoes OK only if the pipeline grep ¦ pr sets a zero exit code.

A common use of a compound command is as follows:

```
tar -cvf docs.tar docs && rm -rf docs
```

Here, the rm command deletes the docs directory only if it is backed up successfully in a tar file.

Conditional Execution on Failure, the ¦¦ Operator

The or-or operator, ¦¦, is used to join two commands as follows:

```
command1 ¦¦ command2
```

When csh encounters a command of this form, it executes *command2* only if *command1* fails. Like the Bourne shell, csh considers a command to fail if it returns a nonzero exit code. For *command1* or *command2*, you can write a simple command or a compound command. For example, in the following command:

```
grep mailto *.html ¦¦ echo No mailto found ¦ pr
```

if grep succeeds, its output is placed to standard output; otherwise, "No mailto found" is piped to the pr command.

The ¦¦ operator is usually used to provide an alternative action. In the following case, if the mkdir command fails, the exit command prevents further execution in a shell script:

```
mkdir $tmpfile ¦¦ exit
```

Redirecting Input and Output

In csh, several commands are available for redirecting the input and output of commands. In addition to the standard input (<) and output (>) redirection characters, csh provides a few additional operators for performing *redirection*.

Redirection is an instruction to the shell that is appended to a command instructing the shell to assign one of the standard *file descriptors* to a specific file. The three standard file descriptors defined in all flavors of UNIX are as follows:

- Standard input (stdin)
- Standard output (stdout)
- Standard error (stderr)

By default, each of these file descriptors points to the terminal in which csh is running. You can change the location where a command reads data, writes output, and prints error messages by using one or more of the I/O redirection operators listed in Table 13.1.

TABLE 13.1. I/O REDIRECTION OPERATORS.

Operator	Description
< *filename*	Redirects standard input to use the contents of the file specified by *filename* as input to a command.
<< *word*	Allows for multiple lines to be redirected. Reading stops when the shell finds a line beginning with *word*. This is known as a *here document*.
> *filename*	Redirects filename> filename> filename> filename> filename> filename redirection operator> standard output to write command output to the file specified by *filename*.
>& *filename*	Redirects & filename>& filename>& filename>& filename>& filename>& filename redirection operator>both the command output and error messages to file specified by *filename*.
>> *filename*	Writes > filename>> filename>> filename>> filename>> filename>> filename redirection operator>command output at the end of *filename* (Append mode).
>>& *filename*	Writes >& filename>>& filename>>& filename>>& filename>>& filename>>& filename redirection operator>command output and error messages at the end of *filename* (Append mode).

Here Documents

The redirection:

<< *word*

is a special form of the input-redirection operator that allows input to be specified in the current shell input stream. This form of input redirection is called a *here document*. Here documents are useful when you want to provide predefined data to a command, and they save you from having to create a file to hold the data.

Any arbitrary string can be used for *word*. The shell reads input lines until it encounters a line that contains only the specified *word*. The input lines are stored in a temporary file, and csh sets up the temporary file as standard input for the command. For example, if the redirection:

<< STOP

is used, csh reads lines until STOP is encountered.

Unlike the `filename` specified for other I/O redirection operators, *word* for the here document is not scanned for variable references, command substitutions, or filename patterns. All other shell input lines are checked for the presence of *word* as the only word on the line before any substitutions or replacements are performed on the line. Lines of the here document are checked for variable references and command replacements, enabling you to encode variable information in the here document. To have lines passed directly to a command without substitutions or replacements performed, the specified word should be quoted. For example, if the redirection:

```
<< "STOP"
```

is used, csh reads lines up to the line beginning with STOP and passes the lines directly to the command without modifying them.

The following example shows the use of a here document to create an HTML form:

```
cat <<HERE
 <FORM method=post action=http://host.com/cgi-bin/addTime.sh>
 <select NAME=username>
 `./doUserQuery;./parseList.sh users_$$.txt "$userName"`
 </select>
 <input type=submit value=Submit>
 </form>
HERE
```

The line containing the word HERE does not appear in the output.

Output Redirection

The two main forms of output redirection are as follows:

- Overwrite output redirection: `> filename`
- Append output redirection: `>> filename`

The first form creates or overwrites the file specified by `filename`. The file is opened before command execution begins, so even if the command fails or cannot be found, the output file still is created.

The `>>` command arranges for command output to be added to the end of the file specified by `filename`. If the file does not exist, csh creates it.

The `>&` and `>>&` operators redirect both the standard output and standard error files to the file specified by `filename`. Unlike sh, in csh there is no direct way to redirect the standard output and standard error to separate files.

> **NOTE**
>
> If the `noclobber` shell option is set, the shell refuses to create the specified file if it already exists. This is a safety option that is often set because output redirection destroys a file's contents.
>
> To perform the output redirection in this case, the redirection!>!>!>!>!>! redirection operator> operator >! should be used instead.

Filename Substitutions (Globbing)

Filename generation using patterns (globbing) is an important facility provided by the Bourne shell. The C shell supports all the globbing operators of the Bourne shell and provides several extensions for greater flexibility.

When any of the pattern expressions described in Table 13.2 are used as arguments of a command, the entire pattern string is replaced with the filenames or pathnames that match the pattern. By default, the shell searches the current directory for matching filenames, but if the pattern string contains slashes (/), it searches the specified directory or directories instead. Several directories can be searched for matching files in a single pattern string. For example, a pattern of the form:

```
dir/*/*.cc
```

searches all the directories contained in dir for files ending with .cc.

TABLE 13.2. GLOBBING OPERATORS.

Operator	Description
*	Matches any string of characters, including a null string. When used by itself, * matches all filenames in the current directory. When used at the beginning of a pattern string, leading prefixes of the filename pattern are ignored. When used at the end of a pattern string, trailing suffixes of the filename pattern are ignored. An asterisk in the middle of a pattern means that matching filenames must begin and end as shown but can contain any character sequences in the middle. Multiple asterisks can be used in a pattern.
?	Matches any one character.
[]	Matches a single character in the list of characters enclosed within the brackets. A hyphen, -, is used to indicate a range of characters. Multiple ranges can be used in a single bracketed list. For example, [A-Za-z0-9]* matches any filename beginning with a letter or a digit. To match a hyphen, it should be listed at the beginning or end of the character list.

Operator	Description
*	The tilde (~) can be used at the beginning of a word to invoke directory substitution for your home directory. The (~) is substituted with the full pathname of your home directory. If it is used in the form ~/*path*, it refers to a file or directory under your home directory. If the tilde does not appear by itself as a word and is not followed by a letter or a slash, or it appears in any position other than the first, it is not replaced with the user's home directory.
~*username*	The full pathname of specified user's home directory is substituted. The password file /etc/passwd is searched for *username* to determine the directory pathname. If *username* is not found, an error message is generated.
{}	Braces enclose a list of patterns separated by commas. The brace expression matches filenames having any one of the listed patterns in the corresponding position of the name. Unlike *, ?, and [], brace-enclosed lists are not matched against existing filenames; they simply are expanded into words subject to further substitution regardless of whether the corresponding files exist. Brace-enclosed lists can be nested.

One consequence of filename generation using pattern strings can cause a replacement of one word with many. For example, If you had three files in your current directory with the extension .txt, the pattern *.txt would expand to match those three files:

```
% echo Files: *.txt
Files: ch1.txt ch2.txt chlast.txt
```

Executing Commands in a Subshell: ( )

In csh, commands can be enclosed in parentheses as follows:

(*commands*)

This groups the specified *commands* for execution in a *subshell*. A subshell is a secondary invocation of the shell, which executes commands without affecting the state of the shell that invoked it. Some of the reasons to do this are as follows:

- Temporarily change shell variables
- Temporarily change the current directory
- Alter process information

When a subshell exits, any changes to variables and shell settings disappear. One common use of this is to switch to an alternate directory, execute a few commands, and then return to the previous working directory. The following example demonstrates this:

13

THE C SHELL

```
% (cd /usr/local/etc/httpd/htdocs; cp *.html /users/dylan/docs)
```

Without the parentheses, you would have to write this:

```
% cd /usr/local/etc/httpd/htdocs
% cp *.html /users/dylan/docs
% cd /previous/directory
```

I/O redirections can be appended to the subshell just as for a simple command. The redirections apply for all the commands within the subshell. For example:

```
(cat; echo; date) > out
```

writes the output of the cat, echo, and date commands to the file out.

Quoting

As you have seen in previous sections, certain characters have special meanings in csh. When one of the following special characters is encountered, csh performs the action defined for it:

```
~  '  !  @  #  $  %  ^  &  *  (  )  \  ¦  {  }  [  ]  ;  '  "  <  >  ?
```

To use one of these characters as a part of a word without its special significance, you can escape the character by placing a backslash (\) immediately in front of the character. Note that a backslash intended as an ordinary character must be written as two backslashes in succession, \\.

To escape a two-character operator such as >>, you must insert a backslash in front of each character:

```
\>\>
```

The $ character can be escaped if followed by whitespace:

```
% echo escaped $ sign
escaped $ sign
```

Alternatively, you can enclose the special character or any portion of a word containing the special character in quotes. Three kinds of quotes are recognized by csh:

- The single quote, '
- The double quote, "
- The back quote, `

The enclosing quotes are not considered part of the input passed to commands. For example, the output of the command:

```
% echo "Enter name>"
Enter name>
```

does not contain quotes.

Using Single Quotes

A string enclosed in single quotes is sometimes called *hard-quoted* because the shell performs absolutely no substitution, replacement, or special interpretation of characters that appear between the single quotes. Even the backslash character is treated as an ordinary character. As a result, it is not possible to embed a single quote in a hard-quoted string. For example, the command:

```
echo 'who's there'
```

causes an error. This command is interpreted as two strings, "who's" and "there", terminated by the starting single quote. Because another single quote is not found, the following error is generated:

```
Unmatched '
```

One of the uses of quoted strings is to specify a single word containing blanks, tabs, and newline characters. For example, the following command shows the use of a single echo command to print two lines of output:

```
% echo -n 'Hello.\
Please enter your name: '
```

A backslash that appears inside a single-quoted string is retained and appears in the string's value because no substitutions occur inside an apostrophe-quoted string as seen in the following example:

```
% echo 'Single \' quote
```

Using Double Quotes

Double quotes, ", also hide most special characters from the shell. Only variable and command substitution is performed on double-quoted strings.

Any of the reference forms for shell variables are recognized inside quoted strings and are replaced with the corresponding string value. The replacement occurs inside the quoted string.

Single quotes can appear inside a double-quoted string. The single has no special significance when appearing inside a double-quoted string and does not need to be escaped with a backslash. An example of this is as follows:

```
% grep root /etc/passwd ¦¦ echo "Who's in charge here?"
```

13

THE C SHELL

Using Back Quotes

Command substitution occurs for strings enclosed in back quotes, `. The entire string enclosed between matching back quotes is extracted and executed by the current shell as if it were an independent command.

The command can be two or more commands separated by semicolons, a pipeline, or any form of compound statement. Any data written to standard output by the command is captured by the shell and becomes the string value of the back quoted command. The string value is parsed into words, and the series of words replaces the entire back quoted string. Using back quotes to perform command substitution can be thought of as an I/O redirection to the command line.

All forms of shell substitution occur inside back quoted command strings, including variable replacement, nested command executions, history substitutions, and filename patterns.

Working with Directories

In `csh`, there several built-in commands for working with directories:

- `cd` or `chdir` for changing directories
- `pushd` and `popd` for manipulating the directory stack
- `dirs` for displaying the directory stack

The `pushd` and `popd` commands provide a pushdown stack mechanism for changing directories, whereas the `dirs` command displays the contents of the stack. If you switch to another directory by using `pushd` instead of `cd`, the pathname of your previous directory is "saved" in the directory stack. A subsequent `popd` then returns you to the previous directory.

The directory stack is stored in an array variable maintained by `csh`, and each `pushd` adds the current directory to the left and pushes all existing entries to the right. The top or first element is always your current directory, and subsequent entries are the pathnames of your previous directories in reverse order. The `popd` command discards the top stack entry and changes to the new top entry, reducing the total number of items on the stack by one.

The `cd` command does not maintain the directory stack, thus `popd` cannot be used to return to a directory that you left using `cd`.

Listing Directories in the Stack

The *directory stack* is a mechanism you can use to store and recall directories to which you have changed by using the commands pushd and popd. The dirs command lists the directories in the directory stack. For example:

```
% dirs
/usr/local/bin ~/html/manuals /users/wadams/bin
```

In this example, three directories are on the directory stack. The first directory listed is always the current directory. Directories to the right are previous directories.

Adding Directories to the Stack

To save the pathname of a directory on the directory stack, the pushd command should be used to change to another directory. Using pushd saves the pathname of your previous directory on the directory stack so that you can return to it quickly and easily by using the popd command.

Three forms of the pushd command exist:

- pushd
- pushd *name*
- pushd +*n*

In the first form, the command exchanges the top two directory-stack elements, making your previous directory the current and your current directory the previous. Successive pushd commands used without an argument switch you back and forth between the top two directories.

In the second form, the command changes to the directory specified by *name* in the same manner as cd. The pathname of the current directory is saved in a directory stack prior to the change.

In the third form, a circular shift of the directory stack by *n* positions is performed. This changes the new top directory. A *circular shift* treats the list of elements as if they were in a ring, with the first preceded by the last, and the last followed by the first. The shift changes your position in the ring without deleting any of the elements. Consider the following example:

```
% dirs
/home/john /home/mary /home/doggie /home/witherspoon
% pushd +2
/home/doggie
% dirs
/home/doggie /home/witherspoon /home/john /home/mary
```

Note that both before and after the pushd, /home/john precedes /home/mary, and /home/doggie precedes /home/witherspoon. The example also shows that, for the purpose of the pushd +*n* command form, /home/witherspoon (the last entry) is effectively followed by /home/john (the first entry).

Returning to Directories Stored in the Stack

After you have saved directories on the directory stack with pushd, you can use popd to return to a previous directory. There are two modes for this command:

- popd
- popd +*n*

In the first form, popd changes the current directory to the second directory on the stack. In the second form, popd changes to the *n*th entry in the stack. Stack entries are numbered from 0.

The following example shows the use of pushd, dirs, and popd together:

```
% pwd
/usr/home/john
% pushd /usr/spool
% pushd uucppublic
% pushd receive
% dirs
/usr/spool/uucppublic/receive /usr/spool/uucppublic /usr/spool
_/usr/home/john
% popd
/usr/spool/uucppublic
% dirs
/usr/spool/uucppublic /usr/spool /usr/home/john
% popd +1
/usr/spool/uucppublic /usr/home/john
% popd
/usr/home/john
% dirs
/usr/home/john
```

Variables

Variables are used to hold temporary values and manage changeable information. Also csh maintains several variables of its own that you can use to customize its behavior and your environment. In general, there are two types of variables:

- Shell variables
- Environment variables

Shell variables are defined locally in the shell, whereas environment variables are defined for the shell and all the child processes that are started from it. To assign a shell variable a value, the `set` command is used. To assign a value to an environment variable, the `setenv` command is used. The C shell does not support `sh` style assignment statements of the form:

```
name=value
```

A variable name can consist of letters (uppercase and lowercase), underscores (_), and digits. A variable name cannot begin with a digit, because names beginning with a digit are reserved for use by the C shell. Generally, all capital letters are used for the names of environment variables, and all lowercase letters are used for shell variables, although the C shell imposes no such restriction. There is no restriction on the length of a variable name.

Creating Shell Variables

The `set` command is used to create new local variables and assign a value to them. Local variables are known only to the current shell and are not passed to shell scripts or invoked commands.

Some different methods of invoking the `set` command are as follows:

- `set`
- `set` *name*
- `set` *name=word*
- `set` *name=(wordlist)*
- `set` *name[index]=word*

The first three forms are used with scalar variables, whereas the last two forms are used with array variables.

Scalar Variables

In the first form, a list of the currently defined shell variables along with their values is printed out. Depending on your version of `csh`, the output may also contain environment variables.

The second form is used to define a variable name and to initialize it with a null string. It is important to note that a variable with a null value is not the same as an unset variable. A variable with a null value exists but has no value, whereas an unset variable does not exist. A reference to an unset variable results in a shell error message; a reference to a null variable results in substitution of the null string.

The third form is used to set the value of the variable specified by *name* to the string *word*. The string *word* replaces the current value of the variable specified by *name* if the variable already is defined. Otherwise, a new variable with the specified *name* is created. If *word* contains characters special to the shell, including blanks or tabs, it must be enclosed in single or double quotes.

Array Variables

The fourth form is used to assign each word in `wordlist` to successive elements of the array variable *name*. After the assignment, the expression:

`$name[index]`

is used to refer to a particular item in the specified `wordlist`. For example:

`$name[2]`

refers to the second word in the specified `wordlist`. If any *word* in `wordlist` contains characters special to the shell, including blanks or tabs, it must be quoted.

The fifth form is used to set the value of the `i`th element of the array variable specified by *name* to the specified `value`. The specified index, `i`, must be a positive integer greater than or equal to 1.

A unique feature of arrays in `csh` is that you do not have to assign a value to every element of an array. The number of elements in an array is effectively the highest-numbered element to which a value has been assigned. Elements to which no values have been assigned have effective values of the null string.

CAUTION

Some versions of `csh` do not support arrays that do not have a value for every index. If you have such a version of `csh`, the following assignment to a three-element array:

```
set name[4]=foo
```

generates an error message similar to the following:

```
set: Subscript out of range
```

Deleting Shell Variables

The `unset` command is used to delete one or more shell variables from the shell's memory. It can be invoked in either of the following ways:

- unset *name*
- unset *pattern*

In the first form, the unset command deletes the shell variable with the specified *name*. On most versions of csh, you can specify more than one *name* as an argument to the unset command.

In the second form, unset deletes all shell variables whose names match the specified *pattern*. Any string that contains one or more occurrences of the pattern-matching characters *, ?, or [ ], can be specified in the *pattern*.

Environment Variables

The setenv command is used to create new environment variables. Environment variables are passed to shell scripts and invoked commands, which can reference the variables without first defining them.

The two forms of the setenv command are as follows:

- setenv
- setenv *name value*

When issued without arguments, as in the first form, the setenv command lists all the currently defined environment variables.

In the second form, the shell creates a new environment variable with the specified *name* and sets its value to the string specified by *value*. If the value contains characters such as a space or tab, be sure to enclose the value string in quotes.

Deleting Environment Variables

To delete environment variables, use the unsetenv command. It can be invoked in either of the following ways:

- unsetenv *name*
- unsetenv *pattern*

In the first form, the unsetenv command deletes the environment variable with the specified *name*. On most versions of csh, you can specify more than one *name* as an argument to the unsetenv command.

In the second form, unsetenv deletes all environment variables whose names match the specified *pattern*. Any string that contains one or more occurrences of the pattern-matching characters *, ?, or [ ], can be specified in the *pattern*.

13

THE C SHELL

Referencing Variables

You obtain the value of a variable by using a *variable reference*, which results in the replacement of the entire reference expression—including the $ that introduces the reference, the variable's name, and any other characters that might adorn the reference—with a string value of the reference.

A variable reference does not itself define the start or end of a word; the reference can be a complete word or part of a word. If the reference is part of a word, the substituted string is combined with other characters in the word to yield the substituted word. If the reference value substitutes one or more blanks or tabs into the word, though, the word is split into two or more words unless it is quoted. If the value of shell variable *var* is "two words," for example, the reference expression $var appears as two words after substitution, but the quoted string "$var" appears as the one token "two words" afterward.

You can use any of the variable reference forms shown in Table 13.3 in a word.

TABLE 13.3. SHELL VARIABLE REFERENCES.

Reference	Description
${*name*}	Replaced with the value of *name*. An error results if the variable specified by *name* is not defined.
${*name*[*n*]}	Replaced with the value of the *n*th element of the array variable specified by *name*.
${#*name*}	Replaced with the number of elements in array specified
by *name*.	
${?*name*}	Replaced with 1 if the variable specified by *name* is set; otherwise, replaced with 0.

Variable names are terminated by the first illegal variable name character—in other words, any character that is not a digit, letter, or underscore (_). As a result, variable references can be used without braces when the next character is not a legal variable name character. If the shell variable var is set to foo, the variable references $var.cc, varvar, and $var"bar" resolve to foo.cc, foofoo, and foobar, respectively.

The reference forms using braces are useful when the variable *name* would run onto the remainder of the current word yielding an undefined variable name. For example, if the variable dir contains the path prefix /usr/bin/, the word ${*dir*}name.cc forms the full pathname /usr/bin/name.cc upon expansion. The simpler form $*dirname.cc*, however, is taken as a reference to variable *dirname*, which is what was intended. The net effect of the braces is to set off the variable reference from the remainder of the word.

A reference to an unset variable generates a shell error message and, if the reference occurs inside a shell script, causes reading of the shell script to terminate. You can use the $?*name* or ${?*name*} forms to handle the case where a variable might not be set.

Read-Only Variables

In addition to ordinary variables you define with the set and setenv commands, a number of variables are defined by the shell and have preset values. Often, the value of a special variable changes as the result of a command action. You can use these variables to acquire specific information that isn't available in any other way. You cannot use set or setenv to assign new values to them.

The special variables can be referenced by using the notations shown in Table 13.4.

TABLE 13.4. SHELL SPECIAL VARIABLES.

Variable	Description
$0	Replaced with the name of the current shell input file, if known. It is shorthand for $argv[0].
$1, $2, ... $9	Replaced with the value of the arguments specified to a shell. If used within a shell script, these variables refer to the first nine command-line arguments. To reference arguments beyond nine, you must use the reference notation $argv[*n*] or the built-in command shift.
$*	Equivalent to $argv[*]. Replaced with all the arguments passed to the shell.
$$	Replaced with the process number of the current shell. When a subshell is invoked, $$ returns the process ID of the parent shell.
$<	Replaced with a line of text read from the standard input file.

Predefined Variables

The C shell also recognizes a number of conventionally named variables as having special meaning. These variables are listed in Table 13.5.

Some are initialized automatically when the shell starts; others are set using the set command or by using command-line options when csh is invoked. You can assign a value to most of these variables, but some variables are set automatically by the shell when a corresponding event occurs.

In `csh`, all predefined shell variables have lowercase names. This is to avoid conflicts with environment variables, which usually have uppercase names.

To set any predefined variable, use the `set` command. You need to specify a value only if the variable requires one; otherwise, you can omit the value string. For example:

`set noclobber`

enables the `noclobber` option, but:

`set prompt='$cwd: '`

is required to assign a new command-line prompt string.

You can use the `unset` built-in command to destroy the variable and any associated value, but be aware that an unset variable does not revert to its initial or default value and is not the same as a variable having a null value; an unset variable simply doesn't exist.

TABLE 13.5. *PREDEFINED SHELL VARIABLES.*

Variable	Description
argv	An array variable containing the current shell parameters. The value of `argv` is set by the shell at startup and just prior to the execution of each command.
cdpath	An array variable specifying a list of directories to be searched by the `cd` command. If you do not explicitly provide a value for this variable, the `cd` command searches only the current directory to resolve pathnames.
cwd	Contains the full pathname of the current directory. On startup, the shell initializes it to the pathname of your home directory. Each `cd` command you execute changes its value. Sometimes $cwd may return a different value than the command `pwd` if a link was used to get to the current directory.
history	Specifies the number of commands to be maintained in the history list. The shell retains at least this many lines of command history if sufficient memory is available. This variable is not initialized automatically and does not need to be assigned a value. If unset, the shell maintains an optimum amount of command history for the size of available memory.
home	Initialized to the value of the environment variable $HOME at shell startup. The value of this variable is used as the default directory for `cd` and as the value substituted for ~.

Variable	Description
ignoreeof	If set, the shell ignores an end-of-file (EOF) character typed at the beginning of a line. If not set, an EOF character typed at the beginning of the line signals the shell to exit; for login shells, this logs you out.
noclobber	If set, the shell does not replace an existing file for the I/O redirection >. For >>, it requires that the target file already exist. This variable is unset initially.
notify	If set, the shell writes a message to your terminal at once if the status of a background job changes. By default, the shell does not notify you of status changes until just before issuing the next command-line prompt. Be aware that setting notify can cause messages to appear on your screen at unexpected times. The initial value of notify is unset.
path	An array variable listing the directories to be searched for commands. If this variable is not set, you must use explicit pathnames to execute all commands. The initial value of path is the same as the environment variable $PATH.
prompt	Your prompt string. The value of this variable is printed at the start of each line when the shell is ready to read the next command. It is scanned for variable and command substitutions before printing. Its initial value is the string "% ".
savehist	Specifies the number of history lines to save to ~/.history when you exit your login shell. When you log in the next time, the C shell executes the equivalent of source -h ~/.history. Not all versions of the C shell support the savehist variable.
status	Contains the exit code of the last command executed as a decimal number. Its value is changed after the execution of each command.
verbose	If set, causes each command to be printed after history substitutions but before other substitutions.

Customizing Your Shell Environment

csh has three important configuration files:

- .cshrc
- .login
- .logout

The first two files are used by `csh` during its initialization process, whereas the last file is used before it exits.

Each time `csh` is invoked, it looks for the file `.cshrc` in your home directory. This behavior is standard for all invocations, including login shells, shell scripts, and subshells. Thus it should perform only those initializations you require for any C shell environment.

When invoked as a login shell, the `.login` script is executed to perform any one-time-only initializations you require. These can include issuing the `stty` command and setting shell variables.

When you exit a login shell by using the `exit` or `logout` command, the shell searches for a file named `.logout` in your home directory. If found, the shell executes the commands in it and then terminates.

.cshrc

Typically command aliases, variable settings, and shell options are defined in your `~/.cshrc` file. Because this file always is executed before the `.login` script, placing these definitions in `.cshrc` ensures that the definitions are available for subshells.

You might want to place portions of your initialization into separate files and have the `.cshrc` source the separate files. A common setup is as follows:

- A file in which all aliases are defined: `~/.cshrc_aliases`
- A file in which the search path is defined: `~/.cshrc_path`
- A file in which the shell options are define: `~/.cshrc_opts`

.login

Usually the `.login` file is used to set up and configure the interactive environment. Some common features of this file are as follows:

- Identify the kind of terminal you are using and set the `$TERM` environment variable to match the terminal type. This variable is important for commands such as `vi`, which use it to send the correct terminal-control codes for full-screen operation.
- Issue the `stty` command to set your preferred control keys:

  ```
  stty erase '^H' kill '^U' intr '^C'
  ```
- Set environment variables:

  ```
  setenv EDITOR /usr/bin/vi
  setenv PAGER /usr/bin/more
  ```

- Set local variables:
  ```
  set cdpath=(. .. $home)
  set mail=(60 /usr/spool/mail/$logname)
  ```
- Execute any system commands that you find interesting.

.logout

There is no standard use for the `.logout` file; you can omit it without incurring any shell error messages. The most common use for this file is to clear the screen, so you will find many users whose `.logout` files contain only one line, the `clear` command.

Advanced Features

The C shell provides several advanced features designed at making interactive sessions easier and more productive. These features are:

- Aliases
- Command history
- Job control

The following sections look at each of these features in turn.

Aliases

One of the handier features in `csh` is the *alias* feature. An alias is a shorthand method of referring to a command or part of a command.

If you have several favorite options that you always supply to the `ls` command, for example, instead of having to type the whole command every time, you can create a two-character alias. Then you can type the two-character alias, and the shell executes the alias definition. In addition to providing shortcuts, aliases are a convenient way of handling common typos:

- `mroe` for `more`
- `jbos` for `jobs`

Such aliases save time because you don't have to retype misspelling of those commands.

An alias can represent not only a command name, but also leading options and arguments of the command line. Any words you type following the alias name are considered to follow options and arguments included in the alias definition, enabling you to customize the command with key options and arguments.

Manipulating Aliases

The built-in `alias` command enables you to manipulate aliases in the following ways:

- Define a new alias
- Change an existing alias
- List currently defined aliases

The basic syntax is as follows:

```
alias [ name [ definition ... ]]
```

Here, *name* is a word consisting of upper- and lowercase letters and digits, and *definition* is a sequence of words that define the command string for which you want *name* to represent.

For example, the following commands define two aliases for the `rlogin` command, each to a different host:

```
alias soda rlogin soda.berkeley.edu -l ranga
alias kanchi rlogin kanchi.cisco.com -l ranga
```

As you can see, it is shorter to type the alias name for the destination host than it is to type the `rlogin` command and options.

When you define an alias, the only thing that happens at that time is that the system stores the alias in computer memory. Later, when you enter a command with the same name as the alias, `csh` performs a substitution. The command you typed is not executed in the form in which you typed it. Instead, the command name is replaced by the *value* of the alias. The result is a new command text—the first part is the alias definition, and the rest consists of any other arguments you typed.

Suppose that you define an alias for the `ls` command as this:

```
% alias lax ls -ax
```

If you later enter the command

```
% lax big*.txt
```

the command actually executed is

```
ls -ax big*.txt
```

To change the definition of an alias, just define the alias again. For example, the following command redefines the alias `kanchi`:

```
alias kanchi rlogin kanchi.bosland.us -l ranga
```

You can display a list of alias names and definitions by entering the `alias` command without arguments, as in this example:

```
% alias
soda    (rlogin soda.berkeley.edu -l ranga)
kanchi  (rlogin kanchi.bosland.us -l ranga)
```

You also can display the definition of a specific alias by specifying its name as an argument:

```
% alias kanchi
rlogin kanchi.bosland.us -l ranga
```

Because alias substitution occurs early in the shell's processing cycle for commands, you can use globbing, variable substitution, command substitution, and command-history substitution in the wordlist. Often you will need to quote at least one of the words of definition and perhaps the entire alias definition. Some people always enclose the alias definition in quotes to avoid surprises.

Consider the following alias:

```
alias lc ls *.{cc,hh}
```

For a C++ language programmer, the alias would be useful because it allows you to type `lc` and get a listing of all source program files in the current directory. Due to globbing, the preceding alias definition does not work as expected. The filename pattern `*.{cc,hh}` is substituted on the `alias` command itself, which means that the resulting alias may look something like the following:

```
% alias lc
ls CIM_EnvImp.cc CIM_Util.hh EventManager.cc LogInstances.cc
```

Because the filename pattern is replaced before the alias definition is stored by the shell, the `lc` alias doesn't list all files ending in `.cc` or `.hh`. It attempts to list the files `CIM_EnvImp.cc`, `CIM_Util.hh`, `EventManager.cc`, and `LogInstances.cc`, regardless of whether they exist in the current directory.

To avoid this problem we can define the alias as follows:

```
% alias lc ls '*.{cc,hh}'
```

An alias definition can also use command aliases. During alias substitution, the alias definition is scanned repeatedly until no further substitutions can be made. If an alias definition for a name contains the given name, this reference is assumed to be a reference to the built-in shell command or executable file. This enables you to use an alias to redefine a system command or a built-in shell command. For example:

```
% alias pg pg -cns -p"Page %d:"
```

Deleting Aliases

You can delete one or more aliases using the `unalias` command. The two modes supported are the following:

- Deleting aliases by name: `unalias` *name*
- Deleting aliases by pattern: `unalias` *pattern*

If you specify a specific alias *name*, only that alias definition is deleted. If you specify a *pattern*, all currently defined aliases whose *names* match the *pattern* are deleted. The *pattern* can contain the pattern-matching characters *, ?, and [...].

In the following example, the first line deletes the `lx` alias, and the second line deletes all currently defined aliases:

```
unalias lx
unalias *
```

Command History

The command-history service maintains a list of previously executed commands. You can use the command history for two purposes:

- As a reference to determine what you've already done
- With history substitution, as a shorthand method to reuse all or part of a previous command to enter a new command

Displaying the Command History

In `csh`, the `history` command is used to print lines from the current command history. The basic syntax for this command is as follows:

```
history [ n ]
```

To display all the lines currently held in the history list, simply enter the `history` command without arguments:

```
% history
1   cd src
2   ls
3   vi foo.cc
4   cc foo.cc
5   grep '#include' foo.cc
```

In the output, each line is preceded by a line number. These line numbers are used to refer to commands when using the history-substitution mechanism.

Line numbers start with 1 at the beginning of your session, assuming that no previous saved history exists. The amount of history a shell maintains depends on the amount of memory available to the shell. History is not saved in an external disk file until after the session exits, so capacity is somewhat limited.

If you set the `history` variable to a value indicating the number of lines of history you want the shell to maintain, it will try and maintain at least that many lines.

> **CAUTION**
>
> The history service retains command lines—not commands. As the history area becomes full, the shell discards old lines. This might result in some lines containing incomplete, partial commands. You need to use caution with the history-substitution facility to avoid calling for the execution of an incomplete command.

If the `history` command is given an argument *n*, which is a positive integer, it will limit its display to the last *n* commands as seen in the next example:

```
% history 3
4   cc foo.cc
5   grep '#include' foo.cc
6   history
```

In addition, the `history` command also understands the following command-line options:

- `-r` prints history lines in reverse order, from the most recent to oldest.
- `-h` lists the history buffer without the line numbers. This can be useful for creating scripts based on past input or for cutting and pasting a series of commands by using your mouse.

Using History Substitutions

History substitutions are introduced into a command with the exclamation point operator or *bang* operator, `!`. You append one or more characters to this operator to define the particular kind of history substitution you want.

> **NOTE**
>
> The exclamation point is an ordinary character in the Bourne shell, but it is a special character in the C shell. You must precede it with \ (backslash) to avoid its special meaning, even inside hard-quoted strings. For example:
>
> ```
> echo '!!'
> ```
>
> *continues*

> does not echo
>
>   !!
>
> Instead it echoes the previous command.

You can write a history substitution anywhere in the current shell input line, as part or all of the command. When you enter a command containing one or more history substitutions, the shell echoes the command after performing the substitutions so that you can see the command that actually will be executed. You do not have an opportunity to correct the command; it is executed immediately after being displayed.

History Substitutions

The simplest forms of history substitution are the following:

- !!
- !*number*

The first form, !!, is used to recall and execute the entire previous command line. The second form !*number* is used to recall and execute the previous command with the specified line number from the command-history list.

Suppose that the command history currently contains the following lines:

```
1  cd src
2  ls
3  vi foo.cc
4  cc foo.cc
5  grep '#include' foo.cc
```

If you now enter the command !!, the shell repeats the grep command in its entirety. Pressing Return at this point executes the grep command. You can also type additional words to add to the end of the grep command as follows:

```
% !! sna.hh
grep '#include' foo.cc sna.hh
```

Now suppose that, after running grep, you want to edit the foo.cc file again. You could type the vi command as usual, but it already appears in the command history as line 3. A history substitution provides a handy shortcut:

```
% !3
vi foo.cc
```

That's almost all there is to basic history substitution. Table 13.6 lists the other methods of history substitution.

TABLE 13.6. HISTORY SUBSTITUTION METHODS SUPPORTED BY `csh`.

Method	Description
`!!`	The preceding command line (the last line of command history).
`!number`	The line number of the command history.
`!-number`	The history line *number* lines back; `!-1` is equivalent to `!!`.
`!string`	The most recent history line that has a command beginning with *string*. For example, use `!v` to refer to a previous `vi` command.
`!?string?`	The most recent history line containing *string* anywhere in the line. For example, use `!?foo?` to repeat a previous `vi foo.cc` command. Most C shell versions support not supplying the trailing question mark, so `!?foo` would execute the same `vi` command.

History Editing

You can do more with history substitutions than merely reusing previous commands. The shell also provides extensions to the history operator that enable you to select individual words or a group of words from a history line, inserting the selected word or words into the current command.

You can recall parts of a previous command using the colon (`:`) operator. For example, the following command:

```
% !vi:1
```

is replaced not with the most recent `vi` command but with its first argument word. Similarly, the following command:

```
!3:3-4
```

is replaced with arguments 3 and 4 of history line 3.

You can use any of the expressions listed in Table 13.7 as word selectors by appending the expression to a line reference preceded by a colon.

TABLE 13.7. HISTORY EDITING EXPRESSIONS.

Expression	Description
0	First word of the command (usually, the command name).
n	*n*th argument of the command. Arguments are numbered from 1. Note that 0 refers to the command name, which is actually the first word of the line, whereas 1 refers to the second word of the line.
^	Same as :1, the first argument.
$	Last argument word of the command.
%	For the !?*string*? format, the word matched by *string*. Use this word selector only with the !?*string*? history reference. Its value is the entire word-matching string, even though *string* might have matched only a part of the word.
m-n	Multiple word substitution. Replaced with words m through n of the history line. For m and n, specify an integer number or one of these special symbols: ^, $, or %.
m-	Substitution of words beginning with the *m*th word and extending up to but not including the last word.
-n	Same as 0-*n*; substitutes words beginning with the first word of the history line (the command name) through the *n*th word.
m*	Same as m-$; substitutes words beginning with the *m*th word and extending through the last word of the line.
*	Same as ^-$; substitutes all argument words of the line.

On most versions of csh, if the word selector expression you want to write begins with ^, $, *, -, or %, you can omit the colon between the line selector and the word selector. For example:

```
% !vi*
```

refers to all the arguments of the previous vi command and is the same as either of the following commands:

```
% !vi:*
% !vi:^-$
```

You can use any number of word selectors in the same command line. By combining multiple word selectors, you can reuse arguments of a previous command in a different order and use arguments that originally appear on different commands. For example, the command:

```
rm !115^ !117^
```

removes files that were named on two earlier commands.

When counting words of a previous command line, the shell takes quoting into consideration but uses the line as it appears in the history list. Words generated by variable or command substitution or filename generation are not accessible. The following example demonstrates the effects of quoting and command substitution:

```
% echo "one two three" four
one two three four
% echo !^
echo "one two three"
one two three
% echo `ls *.cc`
bar.cc foo.cc
%  echo !^
echo `ls *.cc`
bar.cc foo.cc
```

You can append modifiers to a word selector to alter the form of the word before insertion in the new command. A modifier is written in the form:

```
:x
```

Here, *x* is a letter specifying how the word should be modified.

For example:

```
!vi^:t
```

substitutes the tail of the first argument of the vi command. If the argument was the filename:

```
/usr/X/lib/samples/xclock.c
```

the value of :t would be xclock.c.

Table 13.8 lists the modifiers that can be appended to a word selector to alter the selected word before substitution.

TABLE 13.8. HISTORY SUBSTITUTION MODIFIERS.

Modifier	Description
:e	Removes all but the filename suffix.
:h	Removes a trailing path component. Successive :h modifiers remove path components one at a time, right to left.

continues

13

THE C SHELL

TABLE 13.8. CONTINUED.

Modifier	Description
:p	When used in any history-substitution expression on the command line, causes the shell to print the command after substitutions but not to execute it.
:q	Encloses the substituted word or words in quotes to prevent further substitutions.
:r	Removes a filename suffix of the form .*string*.
:s/*x*/*y*/	Replaces the string *x* in the selected word with the string *y*. String *x* cannot be a regular expression. If the symbol & appears in *y*, it is replaced with the search string *x*. Any character can be used in place of the slash. If the search string *x* is omitted, the search string of the previous :s on the same line is used. Or, if no previous :s occurred, the string of !?*string*? is used.
:t	Removes all leading components of a path, returning just the filename part.
:x	Breaks the selected word or words at blanks, tabs, and newlines.
:&	Reuses the previous string-substitution modifier.

Normally, a modifier affects only the first selected word. When selecting multiple words, you can apply a modifier to all the selected words by inserting a g in front of the modifier letter. For example:

```
!12:2*:gh
```

applies the :h modifier to all the words. The g modifier is not valid with the :p, :q, and :x modifiers.

The history mechanism supports the special abbreviation ^, which is useful for correcting a keying error in the preceding line. The general form of the abbreviation is as follows:

```
% !^x^y
```

where *x* and *y* are strings. The preceding command line is selected and searched for string *x*. If found, csh replaces it with *y* and then executes. For example:

```
% cd /usr/ban
% !^ban^bin
```

re-executes the cd command as:

```
cd /usr/bin
```

The caret (^) must be the first nonblank character of the line to be recognized as a line-editing substitution. This abbreviation is available only for the immediately preceding command line; you must use the full history expression:

```
% !line:s/x/y/
```

to edit any line other than the last.

One final, important provision of the history-substitution mechanism is that you can enclose any history reference in braces {} to isolate it from characters following it. Thus:

```
% !{vi^:h}.cc
```

forms a word beginning with the selected history reference and ending in .cc.

Job Control

When you type a command on the command line and press Return, the command executes in the foreground, which means that it has your shell's undivided attention and ties up your shell until the job finishes executing. This means that you must wait until that command executes before you can do any other work in that shell. For commands or programs that finish quickly, this isn't usually a problem. It is a problem for commands or programs that take minutes or hours to finish. By executing commands or programs in the background, you can free up your shell immediately to do other tasks.

The C shell provides a job-control mechanism for executing and managing background jobs. Table 13.9 lists these commands.

TABLE 13.9. COMMANDS FOR MANAGING BACKGROUND PROCESSES.

Command	Description
&	Executes a command in the background
bg	Resumes execution of stopped jobs in the background
fg	Switches background jobs to foreground execution
jobs	Lists active background jobs
kill	Sends a signal to specified jobs
wait	Waits for all jobs to finish

Executing Jobs in the Background

The & operator is used to execute commands in the background as follows:

command &

For *command* we can write any simple or compound command. Commands executed in the background are called *jobs* by the C shell.

When you execute a command in the background by appending an &, the shell writes a notification message to your terminal identifying the *job number* assigned to the *job*. In the following example, a `find` command is placed in the background:

```
% find . -name "*.c" -print &
[2] 13802
%
```

As you can see from the output, `csh` associates each job with two numbers: the job number and the process ID. The first of the two numbers that are reported is the job number. It is used by the shell to track the process. The second number is the process ID. It is used by the operating system to track the process.

Any commands following & on the same line are treated as if they were written on the following line:

```
xterm & xclock & xload &
```

The & operator also has lower precedence than any other compound operators. In the following example, all the commands are executed in the background as a single job:

```
grep '#include' *.cc ¦ pr && echo Ok &
```

If a background process attempts to read from your terminal, its execution is suspended until you bring the process into the foreground with the `fg` command or cancel it.

Listing Job Status

The `jobs` command lists the commands currently running in the background. The output of `jobs` has the following general format:

```
% jobs
[1] +  Stopped     vi prog.cc
[2]    Done        cc myprog.cc
```

A plus sign (+) marks the current job, whereas a minus sign (–) marks the preceding job. Various messages, including `Stopped` and `Done`, can be shown to indicate the job's status.

The `jobs` command also accepts the option `-l`, which prints the process identifier of each job beside its job number:

```
% jobs -l
[1] +  2147 Stopped     vi prog.cc
[2]    1251 Done        cc myprog.cc
```

Manipulating Job States

You can use the bg command to switch foreground jobs to background execution. If any of the jobs currently are stopped, their execution resumes. Often this command is used to place a job into the background after sending it a SIGSTOP, usually with Ctrl+Z.

The Ctrl+Z mechanism provides a handy way to stop doing one thing and temporarily do another, and then switch back. Although some interactive commands such as vi enable you to escape to the shell, not all do. Regardless of whether the command does, simply press Ctrl+Z to temporarily stop the command, and you'll immediately see a shell prompt. Now you can do whatever you want. To resume the interrupted command, enter the following:

```
% fg command
```

If you do not specify any arguments, the current job is assumed. The current job is the last job you started, stopped, or referenced with the bg or fg command.

You can pause a job that is executing in the background with stop. For example:

```
stop [ %job ]
```

This command sends a stop signal (SIGSTOP) to the named job, as if Ctrl+Z was pressed. You can use the bg command to resume execution of the stopped job or fg to bring the job to the foreground and resume its execution.

You can use the wait command to wait for all background jobs to finish. For example:

```
wait
```

causes the shell to stop prompting for command input until it receives notification of the termination of all background jobs.

To stop waiting, simply press the Return (or Enter) key. The shell prints a summary of all background jobs and then resumes prompting for commands in the normal fashion.

notify

You can request that the shell always report any change in the status of a background job immediately by using the notify command. By default, the shell reports the completion, termination, stoppage, or other status change by writing a message to your terminal just before the command prompt.

You can use notify with no arguments to request immediate notification of background job status changes. Be aware that a notification message might be written to your terminal at inopportune times, however, such as when it is formatted for full-screen operation; the message could garble a formatted screen.

You can use:

```
notify %job
```

to request a notification of status change for only the specified job. This form is handy when you run a background command and later decide you need its results before continuing. Instead of repeatedly executing `jobs` to find out when the background job is done, just issue `notify %job` to ask the shell to tell you when the job is done.

Controlling Process Priority

You can use the `nice` command to change priority assigned to background jobs. For example,

```
nice [ +number ] [ command ]
```

The idea underlying the `nice` command is that background jobs should demand less attention from the system than interactive processes. Background jobs execute without a terminal attached and usually are run in the background for two reasons:

- The job is expected to take a relatively long time to finish.
- The job's results are not needed immediately.

Interactive processes, however, usually are shells where the speed of execution is critical because it directly affects the system's apparent response time. It therefore would be *nice* for everyone to let interactive processes have priority over background work.

UNIX provides a `nice` command you can use to launch a background job and assign it a reduced execution priority. The `nice` built-in command replaces the UNIX command and adds automation. Whereas the UNIX `nice` command must be used explicitly to launch a reduced-priority background job, the shell always assigns a reduced execution priority to background jobs. You use the `nice` command to change the priority the shell assigns.

When invoked with no arguments, the `nice` built-in command sets the current `nice` value to 4. A logon shell always assumes a `nice` value of 0. Use `nice +number` to change the default execution priority for background jobs to a positive or zero value. A zero value (`nice +0`) is the same as interactive priority. Positive values correspond to reduced priority, so that `nice +5` is a lower priority than `nice +4`, `nice +6` is a lower priority than `nice +5`, and so on.

If you specify *command*, the `nice` command launches that command using the default or specified execution priority but doesn't change the default execution priority. For example, `nice cc myprog.c` launches the compilation using the default priority, whereas `nice +7 cc myprog.c` launches the compilation with an explicit priority of 7.

Note that you do not need to append & to the `nice` command to run a command as a background job; when you specify `command`, the background operator is assumed.

Signaling Processes

You can use the `kill` built-in command to send a signal to one or more jobs or processes. The syntax for the `kill` command is as follows:

```
kill [ -signal ] [%job ...] [pid ...]
kill -l
```

The built-in command hides the UNIX `kill` command. To invoke the UNIX `kill` command directory, you need to use its full pathname, either `/bin/kill` or `/usr/bin/kill`. The built-in command provides additional features not supported by `/bin/kill` and can be used in the same manner.

For *signal*, specify a number or a symbolic signal name. All UNIX implementations support signals 1 through 15, whereas some implementations can support more. The signals listed in Table 13.10 are always defined.

TABLE 13.10. SIGNALS.

Signal	Name	Meaning	Description
1	HUP	Hang up	Sent to all processes in a process group when the terminal is disconnected by logout or, for a remote terminal, when the terminal connection is dropped.
2	INT	Interrupt	Sent after the user presses the INTR key (defined by the `stty` command; usually, Ctrl+C; sometimes, BREAK).
3	QUIT	Quit	Sent after the user presses the QUIT key (defined by the `stty` command; there is no default).
9	KILL	Kill	Sent only by the `kill` command; it forces immediate termination of the designated process and cannot be ignored or trapped.
10	BUS	Bus error	Usually caused by a programming error, a bus error can be caused only by a hardware fault or a binary program file.

continues

TABLE 13.10. CONTINUED.

Signal	Name	Meaning	Description
11	SEGV	Segment Fault	Caused by a program reference to an invalid memory location; can be caused only by a binary program file.
13	PIPE	Pipe	Caused by writing to a pipe when no process is available to read the pipe; usually, a user error.
15	TERM	Termination	Caused by the `kill` command or system function. This signal is a gentle request to a process to terminate in an orderly fashion; the process can ignore the signal.

If you omit *signal*, the TERM signal is sent by default. If the `-1` option is specified, no signal is sent.

For *job*, you specify one or more jobs or process identifiers. There is no default for *job*. You must specify at least one job or process to which the signal will be sent.

You can use the command `kill -1` to list the valid symbolic signal names. Always use the `kill -1` command to identify the exact signal names provided when using a new or unfamiliar version of `csh`.

Summary

This chapter provided a quick overview of the C shell syntax and features. You can find a more detailed presentation in the reference manuals for your particular version of UNIX; consult these for the last word on details of its operation.

The C shell includes several extensions for interactive use such as extended filename wildcards, command history, history substitution, and job control, in addition to array variables.

Shell Comparison

by Chris Byers, John Valley,
and Sean Drew

CHAPTER 14

Most contemporary versions of UNIX provide three shells—the Bourne and/or POSIX shell, the C shell, and the Korn shell—as standard equipment. However, many other shells are available for use, including, but not limited to the Z shell, TC shell, RC shell, and the Bourne Again shell. Choosing the right shell is important because you will spend considerable time and effort learning to use a shell, and even more time actually using the shell. The right choice allows you to benefit from the many powerful features of UNIX with minimal effort. This chapter assists you in choosing a shell by drawing your attention to the specific features of each shell.

Of course, no one shell is best for all purposes. If you have a choice of shells, then you need to learn how to choose the right shell for the job.

The shell has three main uses:

- As a keyboard interface to the operating system
- As a vehicle for writing scripts for your own personal use
- As a programming language to develop new commands for others

Each of these three uses places different demands on you and on the shell you choose. Furthermore, each of the shells provides a different level of support for each use. This chapter describes the advantages and disadvantages of some of the more commonly used shells with respect to the three kinds of tasks you can perform with a shell.

Interactive Usage

When choosing a shell for interactive use, keep in mind that your decision affects no one but you. This gives you a great deal of freedom: you can choose any shell without consideration of the needs and wishes of others. Only your own needs and preferences matter.

The principal factors that affect your choice of an interactive shell are as follows:

- Prior experience
- Learning curve
- Command editing
- Wildcards and shortcuts
- Portability

Table 14.1 rates seven commonly available shells using the preceding criteria, assigning a rating of 1 for best choice, 2 for acceptable alternative, and 3 for poor choice.

Table 14.1. Ranking of shells for interactive use.

Shell	Experience	Editing	Shortcuts	Portability	Learning
Bourne	3	3	3	1	1
POSIX	2	1	2	1	2
C	2	2	2	3	2
Korn	1	1	2	2	2
TC	2	1	1	3	3
Bourne Again	2	1	1	2	3
Z	2	1	1	3	3

Bourne Shell

I rated the Bourne shell as your best choice for learning because it is the simplest to use, with the fewest features to distract you and the fewest syntax nuances to confuse you. Unfortunately, it also rates the lowest in productivity because it has no command editor and only limited shortcut facilities. Portability is its greatest strength because the Bourne shell is available in almost all UNIX variants. Prior experience comes in at a 3 ranking because most shells such as the Korn and Bourne Again shells are variants of the Bourne shell with additional features.

The Bourne shell is provided by your UNIX vendor, although it is being phased out in favor of the POSIX shell. For example, on HP-UX 10.X systems, the Bourne shell now resides in `/usr/old/bin`, and the POSIX shell is now in the traditional `/usr/bin`.

POSIX Shell

If you graft some interactive productivity enhancements onto the Bourne shell, the result is the POSIX (Portable Operating System Interface) shell. The POSIX shell is similar to the Korn shell in terms of the interactive features provided, right down to the keystroke in most cases. The Korn shell is not standardized, so there are annoying differences between various vendors' versions; the POSIX shell attempts to raise the bar for a universally available shell. The POSIX shell is a superset of the Bourne shell.

The POSIX shell comes at a 2 for learning curve because it has a few more interactive features than the Bourne shell, though not as many as the C or Bourne Again shells. It rates a 1 in command editing because it provides support for both `vi` and `emacs` editors. It rates a 2 on shortcuts because of support for aliases and filename completion, and it also comes in at a 2 in the experience category. Its highest marks come for portability; it is available on almost all UNIX variants.

The POSIX shell should be provided by your UNIX vendor as part of the default set of shells.

C Shell

The C shell rates a 2 for learning difficulty, based simply on the total amount of material available to learn. The C shell falls on the low end of the shell spectrum in terms of the number and complexity of its facilities, but make no mistake—the C shell can be tricky to use, and some of its features are rather poorly documented. Command editing rates a 2 because it doesn't really have a command editing feature. Instead it uses a history substitution mechanism that can be clumsy and difficult to learn, but it gets the job done.

It ranks a 3 in the portability column; not all UNIX systems have the Csh installed. It gets a 2 for prior experience because it is the perfect shell for C programmers, but may be the easiest for non-C programmers to pick up.

Altogether, the C shell is a creditable interactive environment with many advantages over its predecessor, the Bourne shell. Personal preference has to play a role in your choice here. However, if you're new to UNIX, the C shell is probably not the best place for you to start. As with the POSIX shell, the C shell should be provided by your UNIX vendor as part of the default set of shells.

Korn Shell

In terms of time and effort required to master it, the Korn shell falls in the middle of the shell spectrum. It's not poorly designed or poorly documented, but merely has more complex features than the Bourne and C shells.

The Korn shell's command editor comes in at a 1 because it enables the quick, effortless correction of typing errors, plus easy recall and reuse of command history. It rates a 2 for shortcuts because it uses a complicated syntax that makes the extensions difficult to remember and use. Portability comes in at 2; most variants have the ksh installed, but not all. Also, it gets a 2 for prior experience because you really have to know the Bourne shell to understand the ksh.

If you're a first-time UNIX user, the Korn shell is a good shell to start with. The complexities of the command editing feature probably will not slow you down much; you'll probably use the feature so heavily that the command editing syntax will become second nature to you before long. The Korn shell should be provided by your UNIX vendor as part of the default set of shells.

TC Shell

The TC shell can be thought of the next generation C shell. The TC shell supports all the C shell syntax and adds powerful command-line editing including: spell checking for filenames and user IDs, additional completions (hostnames, variable names, aliases, and so on), and expansions (variable names, filenames). There are many other features too numerous to mention here.

This shell gets a 3 in the learning category due to the wealth of features to learn as well as the complexity of using these features. The TC shell gets a 1 in the editing column because emacs and vi are available. Also, shortcuts gets a 1 due to the TC shell's vast array of shortcut features. Portability is rated a 3; most vendors don't supply the TC shell with their variant. It comes in at 2 for prior experience because it is a superset of the Csh but is unrelated to the Bourne-based shells.

The TC shell is not generally provided as a standard shell; however, many systems have the TC shell installed. If your system does not have tcsh installed, check http://www.primate.wisc.edu/software/csh-tcsh-book for information on source and precompiled binaries. The previous URL also presents a wealth of information about the TC shell, including man pages, books, and supporting software. Should that URL fail, try your favorite WWW search engine for the keyword *tcsh*.

Bourne Again Shell

The Bourne Again shell is the GNU project's shell and is POSIX-compatible. The Bourne Again (bash) shell can be thought of as the next generation Korn shell because bash is basically a superset of the 1988 version Korn shell, with many of the Korn shell 1993 features. The Bourne Again shell also offers good support for many C shell features, including history substitutions using the ! operator, >& output redirection, {} wildcards, and the source command.

The Bourne Again shell gets a rating of 3 in the learning column because the feature set is mountainous in scope. In fact, the man page is at 55 pages and counting on bash. Command editing gets a 1 for ease of use and configurability, and shortcuts get a 1 due to its directory stack, completions, and expansions. Portability rates a 2 because, though it's not commonly found on most variants, you can set it to emulate the POSIX shell, making it usable on most systems. Experience also comes in at 2; it's easy to use coming from a Ksh or Bourne shell background, but not so easy coming from a Csh background.

The Bourne Again shell is not generally provided as a standard shell from most UNIX vendors; however, many systems have bash installed. In fact, it is the standard shell for Linux systems. The CD included with this book has a version of bash on it. If you want to locate additional information about source and binary locations, look in the bash FAQ, which can be found at the URL `ftp://slc2.ins.cwru.edu/pub/bash/FAQ`. Failing that, try your favorite WWW search engine for the keywords *Bourne Again* or *bash FAQ*.

Z Shell

The Z shell is the ultimate shell for feature-hungry users. If you can think of something that a shell ought to do, the Z shell probably does it. All that power comes at a price, however. For example, on HP-UX 10.01, the `zsh` executable is nearly four times larger than the `ksh` (Korn shell) executable and almost three time larger than the `sh` executable (Bourne shell).

The Z shell gets a rating of 3 in the learning curve due to this massive amount of features. It rates a 1 in the command editing category because it has the most complete solution of all the shells. It also rates a 1 for shortcuts because again it has the most complete solution. Portability, however, is a problem. It is not found on many systems. Experience rates a 2; most other shells use similar commands and conventions.

If your system does not have `zsh` installed, check `http://www.mal.com/zsh/FAQ/toc.html` or `http://www.mal.com/zsh/zsh_home.shtml` for information on source and precompiled binaries. The previous URLs also provide other information about the Z shell, including man pages. Should the URLs fail you, try your favorite WWW search engine for the keyword *zsh*.

Interactive Shell Feature Comparison

Table 14.2 describes some of the interactive shell features not available in all shells for comparison purposes. The features that all shells have in common are not listed (for instance, use of * as a wildcard, search path variable for executables, capability to get and set environment variables, and so on). Many of these features could actually be used in scripts, but because the features listed are used primarily in interactive sessions, they are listed in Table 14.2.

Some features mention expansion or completion. In Table 14.2, expansion refers to the substitution of the value represented by a token on the command line. For example, the command-line token `*.star` could be *expanded* to `dark.star dwarf.star ura.star` (assuming that the previous three files were all that matched the wildcard expression `*.star`). If the variable `$LOGNAME` were expanded on my command line, the variable would be replaced with the token `sdrew`. Completion refers to the feature of partially typing a name and having the shell complete the rest of the name on your behalf. For example, if you typed `$DIS` on the command line, using completion, the shell might have typed in `PLAY` for you, thus *completing* the variable name for you with an end result of `$DISPLAY` on your command line.

TABLE 14.2. NONPORTABLE SHELL FEATURES—*INTERACTIVE.*

Feature	sh	csh	ksh	tcsh	bash	zsh
Aliases	POSIX	X	X	X	X	X
Alias completion	-	-	-	X	X	X
Aliases take arguments	-	X	-	X	-	-
Automatically list choices for ambiguous completions	-	-	-	X	X	X
cd path searches	POSIX	X	X	X	X	X
Command aliases	POSIX	X	X	X	X	X
Command editing (emacs)	POSIX	-	X	X	X	X
Command editing (vi)	POSIX	-	X	X	X	X
Command completion	-	X	-	X	X	X
Built-in command completion	-	-	-	X	X	X
Command documentation lookup while command is being typed	-	-	-	X	-	-
Command history	POSIX	X	X	X	X	X
Command history appending	POSIX	-	X	-	X	-
Coprocess support	POSIX	-	X	-	-	X
History substitution	-	X	-	X	X	X
History expansion	-	-	-	X	X	X
Filename completion	POSIX	X	X	X	X	X
Filename expansion	POSIX	-	X	X	-	X
Function completion	-	-	-	-	X	X
Hostname completion	-	-	-	-	X	X
Incremental history searching	-	-	-	X	X	X
Job control (bg, fg, ...)	POSIX	X	X	X	X	X
Log in/out watching	-	-	-	X	-	X
Multiprompt commands in history buffer	POSIX	-	X	-	X	X
notify shell built-in	POSIX	X	-	X	X	-
One key completion	-	X	-	X	X	X
Programmable completion	-	-	-	X	-	X

continues

TABLE 14.2. CONTINUED

Feature	sh	csh	ksh	tcsh	bash	zsh
pushd, popd commands and/or other directory stack commands	-	X	-	X	X	X
Recursive command-line scans	POSIX	X	-	X	X	-
Spelling correction for user IDs, commands, and filenames	-	-	-	X	-	X
Substring selectors :x	-	X	-	X	X	X
Variable completion	-	-	-	X	X	X
Variable expansion	-	-	-	X	X	X
Variable editing	-	-	-	-	-	X
*(...) wildcards	POSIX	-	X	-	-	X
$(...) command expression	POSIX	-	X	-	X	X
{...} wildcards	-	X	-	X	X	X

Note: The sh *column represents both the Bourne and POSIX shells. If a feature is specific only to one shell, then that shell's name appears in the column as opposed to an X. In short, - means neither shell, X means both shells, Bourne means just the Bourne shell, and POSIX means just the POSIX shell.*

Shell Scripts for Personal Use

If you develop any shell scripts for your personal use, you'll probably want to write them in the same shell language you use for interactive commands. As is the case for interactive use, the language you use for personal scripts is largely a matter of personal choice.

Whether you use a C shell variant or a Bourne shell variant at the keyboard, you might want to consider using the Bourne shell language for shell scripts, for a couple of reasons. First, personal shell scripts don't always stay personal; they have a way of evolving over time and gradually floating from one user to another until the good ones become de facto installation standards. As you learn in the section "Shell Scripts for Public Consumption," writing shell scripts in any language but the Bourne shell is somewhat risky because you limit the machine environments and users who can use your script.

Second, the C shell variants, although chock-full of excellent interactive features, are sadly lacking in programming features. The chief drawback of C shell variants is the lack of shell functions (perhaps it is time for the C++ shell). The lack of shell functions greatly inhibits structured programming. Any function must either be a separate file or an alias. Aliases can be difficult or impossible to write for more complex tasks. The C shell variants also do not have parameter substitution, nor nearly as many variable and file tests. Take it from someone who learned the hard way, when it comes to C shell programming, *just say no*. Of course, for truly trivial scripts containing just a few commands that you use principally as an extended command abbreviation, portability concerns are not an issue.

Writing short, simple shell scripts to automate common tasks is a good habit and a good UNIX skill. To get the full benefit of the UNIX shells, you almost have to develop some script writing capability. This happens most naturally if you write personal scripts in the same language that you use at the keyboard.

For comparison purposes, Table 14.3 describes shell features used for programming that are not available in all shells. Although the features listed here tend to be used mostly in scripts as opposed to interactive sessions, nothing prevents these features from being used interactively.

TABLE 14.3. NONPORTABLE SHELL FEATURES—*PROGRAMMING*.

Feature	sh	csh	ksh	tcsh	bash	zsh
Arithmetic expressions	POSIX	X	X	X	X	X
Array variables	POSIX	X	X	X	X	X
Assignment `id=string`	X	-	X	-	X	X
`case` statement	X	-	X	-	X	X
`clobber` option	POSIX	X	X	X	X	X
`echo -n` option	-	X	-	X	X	X
`for` statement	X	-	X	-	X	X
`export` command	X	-	X	-	X	X
`foreach` statement	-	X	-	X	-	X
`getopts` built-in command	POSIX	-	X	-	X	X
`glob` command	-	X	-	X	-	-
Hash table problems, `rehash` and `unhash` commands	-	X	-	X	-	-
`let` command	POSIX	-	X	-	X	X
`limit`, `unlimit` commands	-	X	-	X	-	X
`nice` shell built-in	-	X	-	X	-	-

continues

TABLE 14.3. CONTINUED

Feature	sh	csh	ksh	tcsh	bash	zsh
nohup shell built-in	-	X	-	X	-	-
onintr command	-	X	-	X	-	-
print command	POSIX	-	X	-	X	X
Redirection from iterative statements	X	-	X	-	X	X
RANDOM shell variable	POSIX	-	X	-	X	X
repeat shell built-in	-	X	-	X	-	X
select statement	POSIX	-	X	-	X	X
setenv, unsetenv commands	-	X	-	X	-	-
SHELL variable specifies command to execute scripts	-	X	-	X	-	-
switch statement	-	X	-	X	-	-
until statement	X	-	X	-	X	X
set -x	X	-	X	-	X	X
set optionname	-	X	-	X	X	X
Shell functions	X	-	X	-	X	X
trap command	X	-	X	-	X	X
typeset command	POSIX	-	X	-	X	X
ulimit command	X	-	X	-	X	X
Undefined variable is an error	-	X	-	X	-	-
! special character	-	X	-	X	X	X
@ command	-	X	-	X	-	-
>& redirection	-	X	-	X	X	X

Shell Scripts for Public Consumption

Shell scripts developed for public consumption should be designed for enduring portability. Shell scripts developed for public use are almost always written in the Bourne shell language. Although there is a tendency today to write such scripts in the Korn shell language, people who do so realize they're taking a risk, albeit a modest one.

Some versions of UNIX allow you to specify the shell interpreter to use for a given script file by embedding a special command as the first line of the script: #! /bin/sh as the first line of a script would, on most modern UNIX systems, force the use of the Bourne shell to execute the script file. This is a handy device to allow you to develop scripts in the shell language of your choice, while also allowing users to avail themselves of the script regardless of their choice of an interactive shell. However, the #! device is not available on all versions of UNIX.

You might want to adopt guidelines something like the following:

- For really important projects, choose any shell language (or other tool) you want—your choice simply becomes another requirement for installation and use of the system. (Don't forget to tell your user community of such requirements.)

- If your shell script might enter the public domain, restrict yourself to the Bourne shell language and assume a System V Release 1 environment. This provides you with a great many tools but also suits your application to the vast majority of contemporary UNIX installations.

- If your shell script is targeted for use at your local installation, choose either the Bourne, POSIX, or Korn shell language. Use the Korn shell if you need its features, but do not use it gratuitously or casually. The odds are heavily in your favor that any future operating system releases or vendor changes will still support your shell script.

- If your project must meet certain stated compatibility goals (for example, you must support the HP-UX and SunOS machines running at three offices in two different countries), then adjust your project to meet those goals. There will still be aspects of your project where no stated goals apply. In those cases, choose the level of generality and portability that you (or your project timetable) can afford.

- In all other cases, choose the tools and languages that you feel permit the most effective, trouble-free, user-friendly implementation you can devise, and don't forget to maximize your own productivity and effectiveness.

Summary

Selecting a shell for use at the keyboard, as an interactive command-line processor, is a relatively straightforward task when you realize that your choice does not affect others. If you are new to UNIX, consider using the POSIX shell because its built-in command editing feature can significantly increase productivity. Users accustomed to the C shell are also advised to investigate the POSIX shell, for the same reason.

14

SHELL COMPARISON

Familiarity with the Bourne and POSIX shells and their capabilities and restrictions are essential for individuals who must work with a variety of UNIX systems or with the general UNIX public. Bourne is the only shell universally available under all implementations of the UNIX operating system, and the POSIX shell is becoming nearly as ubiquitous.

For daily keyboard use, any shell but the Bourne shell is a good choice. The Bourne shell is not a good choice when other shells are available. The Bourne shell has a decided lack of interactive features, with command history and command editing being especially productivity degrading.

Choosing a shell for writing scripts is, however, a different matter entirely.

The newer shells offer tools to the script writer that are difficult to do without, such as simplified syntax for command substitutions, array variables, variable arithmetic and expressions, and better structured commands such as `select`. Because these tools are so helpful, they should be used for any work intended only for personal consumption. They should also be preferred for location-specific projects, where the environment can be predicted reasonably accurately. However, for shell scripts claiming a wider audience, the Bourne shell still serves as the *lingua franca* of the UNIX world and will for some time to come.

The script writer who cannot anticipate the hardware and software environment must consider the choice of commands and command options used in the script as well as the shell language. A few environments offer a wider variety of commands and command options than most, and some UNIX versions omit some of the conventional UNIX runtime features. For most purposes, an implementation compatible with UNIX System V Release 1 can be considered as a minimum portability base. In situations where portability is especially important, the POSIX and X/Open standards should be consulted as guides to available operating system features and capabilities, rather than the vendor's manuals.

Shell programming can be as simple or as complex as you want it to be. Shells are sufficiently sophisticated programming tools and can permit the implementation of efficient, production quality software. In fact, shell scripts can be used instead of a more traditional third generation language, such as the C or C++ programming languages. In fact, I once replaced a 500-line C++ program with a 4-line shell script. The use of shell scripts has also become popular as a prototyping and rapid development method.

Although one shell can be chosen for customary use at the keyboard, the choice of a shell environment for writing shell scripts needs to be considered for each project.

Programming

IN THIS PART

awk

by David B. Horvath, CCP

CHAPTER 15

awk is the generic name for the programming language created for UNIX by Alfred V. Aho, Peter J. Weinberger, and Brian W. Kernighan in 1977. The name awk comes from the initials of the creators' last names. Kernighan was also involved with the creation of the C programming language and UNIX; Aho and Weinberger were involved with the development of UNIX. Because of their backgrounds, you will see many similarities between awk and C.

There are several versions of awk: the original awk, nawk, POSIX awk, and gawk (GNU awk). nawk was created in 1985 and is the version described in *The awk Programming Language* (see the complete reference to this book later in the chapter in the section "Summary"). POSIX awk is defined in the *IEEE Standard for Information Technology, Portable Operating System Interface, Part 2: Shell and Utilities Volume 2*, ANSI-approved April 5, 1993 (IEEE is the Institute of Electrical and Electronics Engineers, Inc.). GNU awk is based on POSIX awk.

The acronym GNU stands for "GNU is Not UNIX". It is the name of a series of useful software packages commonly found in UNIX environments that are being distributed by the GNU project at MIT. The packages are generally free and available at various locations on the Internet (you are charged if you want a copy on a physical medium such as floppy disk or tape). The development of the packages is a cooperative process with the work being done by many volunteers. This effort is largely lead by Richard M. Stallman (one of the developers of the emacs editor).

> **NOTE**
>
> Yes, the GNU acronym is self-referencing. But it was created that way on purpose. This type of naming has a history in products related to, but not covered by the trademark of, UNIX. A noncommercial operating system similar to UNIX was known as XINU: "XINU is Not Unix."

The awk language (in all its versions) is a pattern-matching and processing language with a lot of power. It will search a file (or multiple files) searching for records that match a specified pattern. When a match is found, a specified action is performed. As a programmer, you do not have to worry about opening, looping through the file reading each record, handling end-of-file, or closing it when done. These details are handled automatically for you.

It is easy to create short awk programs because of this functionality—many of the details are handled by the language automatically. There are also many functions and built-in features to handle many of the tasks of processing files.

When to Use awk

There are many possible uses for awk, including extracting data from a file, counting occurrences within a file, and creating reports.

The basic syntax of the awk language matches the C programming language; if you already know C, you know most of awk. In many ways, awk is an easier version of C because of the way it handles strings and arrays (dynamically). If you do not know C yet, learning awk will make learning C a little easier.

awk is also useful for rapid prototyping or trying out an idea that will be implemented in another language such as C. Instead of your having to worry about some of the minute details, the built-in automation takes care of them. You worry about the basic functionality.

When Not to Use awk

awk works with text files, not binary. Because binary data can contain values that look like record terminators (newline characters)—or not have any at all—awk will get confused. If you need to process binary files, look into Perl or use a traditional programming language such as C.

Features of awk

As is the UNIX environment, awk is flexible, contains predefined variables, automates many of the programming tasks, provides the conventional variables, supports the C-formatted output, and is easy to use. awk lets you combine the best of shell scripts and C programming.

There are usually many different ways to perform the same task within awk. Programmers get to decide which method is best suited to their applications. With the built-in variables and functions, many of the normal programming tasks are automatically performed. awk automatically reads each record, splits it up into fields, and performs type conversions whenever needed. The way a variable is used determines its type—there is no need (or method) to declare variables of any type.

15

awk

Of course, the "normal" C programming constructs such as if/else, do/while, for, and while are supported. awk doesn't support the switch/case construct. It supports C's printf() for formatted output and also has a print command for simpler output.

awk Fundamentals

Unlike some of the other UNIX tools (shell, grep, and so on), awk requires a program (known as an "awk script"). This program can be as simple as one line or as complex as several thousand lines. (I once developed an awk program that summarizes data at several levels with multiple control breaks; it was just short of 1,000 lines.)

The awk program can be entered a number of ways—on the command line or in a program file. awk can accept input from a file, piped in from another program, or even directly from the keyboard. Output normally goes to the standard output device, but that can be redirected to a file or piped into another program. Output can also be sent directly to a file instead of standard output.

Using awk from the Command Line

The simplest way to use awk is to code the program on the command line, accept input from the standard input device (keyboard), and send output to the standard output device (screen). Listing 15.1 shows this in its simplest form; it prints the number of fields in the input record along with that record.

LISTING 15.1. SIMPLEST USE OF awk.

```
$ awk '{print NF ": " $0}'
Now is the time for all
6: Now is the time for all
Good Americans to come to the Aid
7: Good Americans to come to the Aid
of Their Country.
3: of Their Country.
Ask not what you can do for awk, but rather what awk can do for you.
16: Ask not what you can do for awk, but rather what awk can do for you.
Ctrl+d
$ _
```

> **NOTE**
>
> Your output may appear like the following (different versions of UNIX sometimes behave differently):
>
> ```
> Now is the time for all
> Good Americans to come to the Aid
> of Their Country.
> Ask not what you can do for awk, but rather what awk can do for you.
> Ctrl+d
> 6: Now is the time for all
> 7: Good Americans to come to the Aid
> 3: of Their Country.
> 16: Ask not what you can do for awk, but rather what awk can do for you.
> $ _
> ```

> **NOTE**
>
> As shown in Listing 15.1 and the others, Ctrl+D is one way of showing that you should press (and hold down) the Ctrl (or Control) key and then press the "D" key. This is the default end-of-file key for UNIX. If this doesn't work on your system, use `stty -a` to determine which key to press. Another way this action or key is shown on the screen is ^d.
>
> The entire awk script is contained within single quotes (') to prevent the shell from interpreting its contents. This is a requirement of the operating system or shell, not the awk language.

> **TIP**
>
> All examples in this chapter show the use of awk as the UNIX command that implements the awk language. Your machine may have both awk and nawk, just the awk command (implementing old awk, nawk, POSIX awk, or even gawk), or gawk. You must use the command appropriate to your machine.

NF is a predefined variable that is set to the number of fields on each record. $0 is that record. The individual fields can be referenced as $1, $2, and so on.

You can also store your awk script in a file and specify that filename on the command line by using the -f flag. If you do that, you don't have to contain the program within single quotes.

15

awk

> **TIP**
>
> gawk and other versions of awk that meet the POSIX standard support the specification of multiple programs through the use of multiple -f options. This allows you to execute multiple awk programs on the same input. Personally, I tend to avoid this just because it gets a bit confusing.

You can use the normal UNIX shell redirection or just specify the filename on the command line to accept the input from a file instead of the keyboard:

```
awk '{print NF ": " $0}' < inputs
awk '{print NF ": " $0}' inputs
```

Multiple files can be specified by just listing them on the command line as shown in the preceding second form—they will be processed in the order specified. Output can be redirected through the normal UNIX shell facilities to send it to a file or pipe it into another program:

```
awk '{print NF ": " $0}' > outputs
awk '{print NF ": " $0}' ¦ more
```

Of course, both input and output can be redirected at the same time.

One of the ways I use awk most commonly is to process the output of another command by piping its output into awk. If I wanted to create a custom listing of files that contained the filename and then the permissions only, I would execute a command like this:

```
ls -l ¦ awk '{print $NF, " ", $1}'
```

$NF is the last field (which is the filename; I am lazy—I didn't want to count the fields to figure out its number). $1 is the first field. The output of ls -l is piped into awk, which processes it for me.

If I put the awk script into a file (named lser.awk) and redirected the output to the printer, I would have a command that looks like:

```
ls -l ¦ awk -f lser.awk ¦ lp
```

> **TIP**
>
> I tend to save my awk scripts with the file type (suffix) of .awk just to make it obvious when I am looking through a directory listing. If the program itself is longer than about 30 characters, I make a point of saving it because there is no such thing as a "one-time only" program, user request, or personal need.

CAUTION

Use caution when entering the awk command.

If you forget the -f option before a program filename, your program will be treated as if it were data.

If you code your awk program on the command line but place it after the name of your data file, it will also be treated as if it were data.

You will get odd results.

See the section "Commands On-the-Fly" later in this chapter for more examples of using awk scripts to process piped data.

awk Processing (Patterns and Actions)

Each awk statement consists of two parts: the pattern and the action. The pattern decides when the action is executed and, of course, the action is what the programmer wants to occur. Without a pattern, the action is always executed (the pattern can be said to "default to true").

There are two special patterns (also known as blocks): BEGIN and END. The BEGIN code is executed before the first record is read from the file and is used to initialize variables and set up things like control breaks. The END code is executed after end-of-file is reached and is used for any cleanup required (like printing final totals on a report). The other patterns are tested for each record read from the file.

The general program format is to put the BEGIN block at the top, any pattern/action pairs, and finally, the END block at the end. This is not a language requirement—it is just the way most people do it (mostly for readability reasons).

BEGIN and END blocks are optional; if you use them, you should have a maximum of one each. Don't code two BEGIN blocks, and don't code two END blocks.

The action is contained within curly braces ({ }) and can consist of one or many statements. If you omit the pattern portion, it defaults to true, which causes the action to be executed for every line in the file. If you omit the action, it defaults to print $0 (print the entire record).

The pattern is specified before the action. It can be a regular expression (contained within a pair of slashes (/ /)) that matches part of the input record or an expression that contains comparison operators. It can also be compound or complex patterns, which consist of expressions and regular expressions combined or a range of patterns.

15

awk

Regular Expression Patterns

The regular expressions used by awk are similar to those used by grep, egrep, and the UNIX editors ed, ex, and vi. They are the notation used to specify and match strings. A regular expression consists of characters (like the letter *A*, *B*, or *c*—that match themselves in the input) and metacharacters. Metacharacters are characters that have special (meta) meaning; they do not match to themselves but perform some special function.

Table 15.1 shows the metacharacters and their behavior.

TABLE 15.1. REGULAR EXPRESSION METACHARACTERS IN awk.

Metacharacter	Meaning
\	Escape sequence (next character has special meaning, \n is the newline character, and \t is the tab). Any escaped metacharacter matches to that character (as if it were not a metacharacter).
^	Starts match at beginning of string.
$	Matches at end of string.
.	Matches any single character.
[ABC]	Matches any one of A, B, or C.
[A-Ca-c]	Matches any one of A, B, C, a, b, or c (ranges).
[^ABC]	Matches any character other than A, B, and C.
Desk¦Chair	Matches any one of Desk or Chair.
[ABC][DEF]	Concatenation. Matches any one of A, B, or C that is followed by any one of D, E, or F.
*	[ABC]* Matches zero or more occurrences of A, B, or C.
+	[ABC]+ Matches one or more occurrences of A, B, or C.
?	[ABC]? Matches to an empty string or any one of A, B, or C.
()	Combines regular expressions. For example, (Blue¦Black)berry matches to Blueberry or Blackberry.

> **TIP**
>
> All these patterns can be combined to form complex search strings.

Typical search strings can be used to search for specific strings (such as `Report Date`), strings in different formats (such as the month of May spelled different ways such as `may`, `MAY`, `May`), or as groups of characters (any combination of upper- and lowercase characters that spell out the month of May). These look like the following:

```
/Report Date/   { print "do something" }
/(may)¦(MAY)¦(May)/ { print "do something else" }
/[Mm]⌘[Yy]/ { print "do something completely different" }
```

Comparison Operators and Patterns

The comparison operators used by awk are similar to those used by C and the UNIX shells. They are the notation used to specify and compare values (including strings). A regular expression alone matches to any portion of the input record. By combining a comparison with a regular expression, specific fields can be tested.

Table 15.2 shows the comparison operators and their behavior.

TABLE 15.2. COMPARISON OPERATORS IN awk.

Operator	Meaning
==	Is equal to
<	Less than
>	Greater than
<=	Less than or equal to
>=	Greater than or equal to
!=	Not equal to
~	Matched by regular expression
!~	Not matched by regular expression

> **TIP**
>
> Comparison Operators enable you to perform specific comparisons on fields instead of the entire record. Remember that you can also perform them on the entire record by using `$0` instead of a specific field.

15

awk

Typical search strings can be used to search for a name in the first field (`Bob`) and compare specific fields with regular expressions:

```
$1 == "Bob"    { print "Bob stuff" }
$2 ~ /(may)¦(MAY)¦(May)/ { print "May stuff" }
$3 !~ /[Mm]⌘[Yy]/ { print "other May stuff" }
```

Compound Pattern Operators

The compound pattern operators used by awk are similar to those used by C and the UNIX shells. They are the notation used to combine other patterns (expressions or regular expressions) into a complex form of logic.

Table 15.3 shows the compound pattern operators and their behavior.

TABLE 15.3.   COMPOUND PATTERN OPERATORS IN awk.

Operator	Meaning
&&	Logical AND
¦¦	Logical OR
!	Logical NOT
()	Parentheses—used to group compound statements

If I wanted to execute some action (print a special message, for instance), if the first field contained the value `"Bob"` and the fourth field contained the value `"Street"`, I could use a compound pattern that looks like:

```
$1 == "Bob" && $4 == "Street" {print"some message"}
```

Range Pattern Operators

The range pattern is slightly more complex than the other types—it is set true when the first pattern is matched and remains true until the second pattern becomes true. The catch is that the file needs to be sorted on the fields that the range pattern matches. Otherwise, it might be set true prematurely or end early.

The individual patterns in a range pattern are separated by a comma (,). If you have 26 files in your directory with the names A to Z, you can show a range of the files as shown in Listing 15.2.

LISTING 15.2. RANGE PATTERN EXAMPLE.

```
$ ls ¦ awk '{$1 == "B", $1 == "D"}'
B
C
D
$ ls ¦ awk '{$1 == "B", $1 <= "D"}'
B
$ ls ¦ awk '{$1 == "B", $1 > "D"}'
B
C
D
E
$ _
```

The first example is obvious—all the records between B and D are shown. The other examples are less intuitive, but the key to remember is that the pattern is done when the second condition is true. The second awk command only shows the B because C is less than or equal to D (making the second condition true). The third awk shows B through E because E is the first one that is greater than D (making the second condition true).

Handling Input

As each record is read by awk, it breaks it down into fields and then searches for matching patterns and the related actions to perform. It assumes that each record occupies a single line (the newline character, by definition, ends a record). Lines that are just blanks or are empty (just the newline) count as records, just with very few fields (usually zero).

You can force awk to read the next record in a file (cease searching for pattern matches) by using the next statement. next is similar to the C continue command—control returns to the outermost loop. In awk, the outermost loop is the automatic read of the file. If you decide you need to break out of your program completely, you can use the exit statement. exit acts like the end-of-file was reached and passes control to the END block (if one exists). If exit is in the END block, the program immediately exits.

By default, fields are separated by spaces. It doesn't matter to awk whether there is one or many spaces—the next field begins when the first nonspace character is found. You can change the field separator by setting the variable FS to that character. To set your field separator to the colon (:), which is the separator in /etc/passwd, code the following:

```
BEGIN { FS = ":" }
```

15

awk

The general format of the file looks something like the following:

```
david:!:207:1017:David B Horvath,CCP:/u/david:/bin/ksh
```

If you want to list the names of everyone on the system, use the following:

```
gawk —field-separator=: '{ print $5 }' /etc/passwd
```

You will then see a list of everyone's name. In this example, I set the field separator variable (FS) from the command line using the gawk format command-line options (—field-separator=:). I could also use -F :, which is supported by all versions of awk.

The first field is $1, the second is $2, and so on. The entire record is contained in $0. You can get the last field (if you are lazy like me and don't want to count) by referencing $NF. NF is the number of fields in a record.

Coding Your Program

The nice thing about awk is that, with a few exceptions, it is free format—like the C language. Blank lines are ignored. Statements can be placed on the same line or split up in any form you want. awk recognizes whitespace, much like C does. The following two lines are essentially the same:

```
$1=="Bob"{print"Bob stuff"}
$1     ==     "Bob"        {      print     "Bob stuff"     }
```

Spaces within quotes are significant because they appear in the output or are used in a comparison for matching. The other spaces are not. You can also split up the action (but you have to have the opening curly brace on the same line as the pattern):

```
$1     ==     "Bob"        {
                    print     "Bob stuff"
                   }
```

You can have multiple statements within an action. If you place them on the same line, you need to use semicolons (;) to separate them (so awk can tell when one ends and the next begins). Printing multiple lines looks like the following:

```
$1     ==     "Bob"        {
                    print     "Bob stuff"; print     "more stuff";
print     "last stuff";
                   }
```

You can also put the statements on separate lines. When you do that, you don't need to code the semicolons, and the code looks like the following:

```
$1     ==     "Bob"        {
                    print     "Bob stuff"
                    print     "more stuff"
                    print     "last stuff"
                   }
```

Personally, I am in the habit of coding the semicolon after each statement because that is the way I have to do it in C. To awk, the following example is just like the previous (but you can see the semicolons):

```
$1    ==    "Bob"        {
                          print     "Bob stuff";
                          print     "more stuff";
                          print     "last stuff";
                         }
```

> **TIP**
>
> Make extensive use of comments! Anything on a line after the pound sign or octothorpe (#) is ignored by awk. These are notes designed for the programmer to read and aid in the understanding of the program code. In general, the more comments you place in a program, the easier it is to maintain.

Actions

The actions of your program are the part that tells awk what to do when a pattern is matched. If there is no pattern, it defaults to true. A pattern without an action defaults to `{print $0}`.

All actions are enclosed within curly braces (`{ }`). The open brace should appear on the same line as the pattern; other than that, there are no restrictions. An action consists of one or many actions.

Variables

Except for simple find-and-print types of programs, you are going to need to save data. That is done through the use of variables. Within awk, there are three types of variables: field, predefined, and user-defined. You have already seen examples of the first two—$1 is the field variable that contains the first field in the input record, and FS is the predefined variable that contains the field separator.

User-defined variables are ones that you create. Unlike many other languages, awk doesn't require you to define or declare your variables before using them. In C, you must declare the type of data contained in a variable (such as `int`—integer, `float`—floating-point number, `char`—character data, and so on). In awk, you just use the variable. awk attempts to determine the data in the variable by how it is used. If you put character data in the variable, it is treated as a string; if you put a number in, it is treated as numeric.

15

awk

awk also performs conversions between the data types. If you put the string "123" in a variable and later perform a calculation on it, it will be treated as a number. The danger of this is, what happens when you perform a calculation on the string "abc"? awk attempts to convert the string to a number, gets a conversion error, and treats the value as a numeric zero! This type of logic error can be difficult to debug.

TIP

You should initialize all your variables in a BEGIN action like this:
BEGIN {total = 0.0; loop = 0; first_time = "yes"; }

Like the C language, awk requires that variables begin with an alphabetic character or an underscore. The alphabetic character can be upper- or lowercase. The remainder of the variable name can consist of letters, numbers, or underscores. It would be nice (to yourself and anyone else who has to maintain your code once you are gone) to make the variable names meaningful. Make them descriptive.

Although you can make your variable names all uppercase letters, that is a bad practice because the predefined variables (like NF or FS) are in uppercase. It is a common error to type the predefined variables in lowercase (like nf or fs)—you will not get any errors from awk, and this mistake can be difficult to debug. The variables won't behave like the proper, uppercase spelling, and you won't get the results you expect.

Predefined Variables

awk provides you with a number of predefined (also known as built-in) variables. These are used to provide useful data to your program; they can also be used to change the default behavior of the awk (by setting them to a specific value).

Table 15.4 summarizes the predefined variables in awk. Earlier versions of awk don't support all these variables.

TABLE 15.4.   awk PREDEFINED VARIABLES.

V	Variable	Meaning	Default value (if any)
N	ARGC	The number of command-line arguments	
G	ARGIND	The index within ARGV of the current file being processed	

V	Variable	Meaning	Default value (if any)
N	ARGV	An array of command-line arguments	
G	CONVFMT	The conversion format for numbers	%.6g
P	ENVIRON	The UNIX environmental variables	
N	ERRNO	The UNIX system error message	
G	FIELDWIDTHS	A whitespace separated string of the width of input fields	
A	FILENAME	The name of the current input file	
P	FNR	The current record number	
A	FS	The input field separator	Space
G	IGNORECASE	Controls the case sensitivity	0 (case-sensitive)
A	NF	The number of fields in the current record	
A	NR	The number of records already read	
A	OFMT	The output format for numbers	%.6g
A	OFS	The output field separator	Space
A	ORS	The output record separator	Newline
A	RS	Input record separator	Newline
N	RSTART	Start of string matched by match function	
N	RLENGTH	Length of string matched by match function	
N	SUBSEP	Subscript separator	"\034"

15

awk

V is the first implementation that supports a variable. A = awk, N = nawk, P = POSIX awk, and G = gawk.

The ARGC variable contains the number of command-line arguments passed to your program. ARGV is an array of ARGC elements that contains the command-line arguments themselves. The first one is ARGV[0], and the last one is ARGV[ARGC-1]. ARGV[0] contains the name of the command being executed (awk). The awk command-line options won't appear in ARGV—they are interpreted by awk itself. ARGIND is the index within ARGV of the current file being processed.

The default conversion (input) format for numbers is stored in CONVFMT (conversion format) and defaults to the format string "%.6g". See the section "Pretty Formatting (printf)" for more information on the meaning of the format string.

The ENVIRON variable is an array that contains the environmental variables defined to your UNIX session. The subscript is the name of the environmental variable for which you want to get the value.

If you want your program to perform specific code depending on the value in an environmental variable, you can use the following:

```
ENVIRON["TERM"] == "vt100"  {print "Working on a Video Tube!"}
```

If you are using a VT100 terminal, you get the message Working on a Video Tube!. Note that you only put quotes around the environmental variable if you are using a literal. If you have a variable (named TERM) that contains the string "TERM", you would leave the double quotes off.

The ERRNO variable contains the UNIX system error message if a system error occurs during redirection, read, or close.

The FIELDWIDTHS variable provides a facility for fixed-length fields instead of using field separators. To specify the size of fields, you set FIELDWIDTHS to a string that contains the width of each field separated by a space or tab character. After this variable is set, gawk splits up the input record based on the specified widths. To revert to using a field separator character, you assign a new value to FS.

The variable FILENAME contains the name of the current input file. Because different (or even multiple files) can be specified on the command line, this provides you a means of determining which input file is being processed.

The FNR variable contains the number of the current record within the current input file. It is reset for each file that is specified on the command line. It always contains a value that is less than or equal to the variable NR.

The character that is used to separate fields is stored in the variable FS with a default value of space. You can change this variable with a command-line option or within your program. If you know that your file will have some character other than a space as the field separator (like the `/etc/passwd` file in earlier examples, which uses the colon), you can specify it in your program with the BEGIN pattern.

You can control the case sensitivity of gawk regular expressions with the IGNORECASE variable. When set to the default, zero, pattern matching checks the case in regular expressions. If you set it to a nonzero value, case is ignored. (The letter A matches to the letter a.)

The variable NF is set after each record is read and contains the number of fields. The fields are determined by the FS or FIELDWIDTHS variables.

The variable NR contains the total number of records read. It is never less than FNR, which is reset to zero for each file.

The default output format for numbers is stored in OFMT and defaults to the format string "%.6g". See the section "Pretty Formatting (`printf`)" for more information on the meaning of the format string.

The output field separator is contained in OFS with a default of space. This is the character or string that is output whenever you use a comma with the print statement, such as the following:

```
{print $1, $2, $3;}
```

This statement prints the first three fields of a file separated by spaces. If you want to separate them by colons (like the `/etc/passwd` file), you simply set OFS to a new value: OFS=":".

You can change the output record separator by setting ORS to a new value. ORS defaults to the newline character (\n).

The length of any string matched by the `match()` function call is stored in RLENGTH. This is used in conjunction with the RSTART predefined variable to extract the matched string.

You can change the input record separator by setting RS to a new value. RS defaults to the newline character (\n).

The starting position of any string matched by the `match()` function call is stored in RSTART. This is used in conjunction with the RLENGTH predefined variable to extract the matched string.

The SUBSEP variable contains the value used to separate subscripts for multidimensional arrays. The default value is "\034", which is the double quote character (").

15

awk

> **CAUTION**
>
> Changing input fields changes the entire record. If you change a field ($1, $2, and so on) or the input record ($0), you cause other predefined variables to change. If your original input record had two fields and you set $3="third one", then NF would be changed from 2 to 3.

Strings

awk supports two general types of variables: numeric (which can consist of the characters 0 through 9, + or -, and the decimal [.]) and character (which can contain any character). Variables that contain characters are generally referred to as strings. A character string can contain a valid number, text-like words, or even a formatted phone number. If the string contains a valid number, awk can automatically convert and use it as if it were a numeric variable; if you attempt to use a string that contains a formatted phone number as a numeric variable, awk attempts to convert and use it as if were a numeric variable—that contains the value zero.

String Constants

A string constant is always enclosed within the double quotes ("") and can be from zero (an *empty* string) to many characters long. The exact maximum varies by version of UNIX; personally, I have never hit the maximum. The double quotes aren't stored in memory. A typical string constant might look like the following:

```
"UNIX Unleashed"
```

You have already seen string constants used earlier in this chapter—with comparisons and the print statement.

String Operators

There is really only one string operator, and that is concatenation. You can combine multiple strings (constants or variables in any combination) by just putting them together. Listing 15.1 earlier in the chapter did this with the print statement where the string ": " is prepended to the input record ($0).

Listing 15.3 shows a couple ways to concatenate strings.

LISTING 15.3   CONCATENATING STRINGS EXAMPLE.

```
awk 'BEGIN{x="abc""def"; y="ghi"; z=x y; z2 = "A"x"B"y"C"; print x, y, z,
z2}'
abcdef ghi abcdefghi AabcdefBghiC
```

Variable x is set to two concatenated strings; it prints as abcdef. Variable y is set to one string for use with the variable z. Variable z is the concatenation of two string variables printing as abcdefghi. Finally, the variable z2 shows the concatenation of string constants and string variables printing as AabcdefBghiC.

If you leave the comma out of the print statement, all the strings will be concatenated together and will look like the following:

abcdefghiabcdefghiAabcdefBghiC

Built-in String Functions

In addition to the one string operation (concatenation), awk provides a number of functions for processing strings.

Table 15.5 summarizes the built-in string functions in awk. Earlier versions of awk don't support all these functions.

TABLE 15.5   awk BUILT-IN STRING FUNCTIONS.

V	Function	Purpose
N	gsub(*reg*, *string*, *target*)	Substitutes *string* in *target* string every time the regular expression *reg* is matched.
N	index(*search*, *string*)	Returns the position of the *search* string in *string*.
A	length(*string*)	The number of characters in *string*.
N	match(*string*, *reg*)	Returns the position in *string* that matches the regular expression *reg*.
A	printf(*format*, *variables*)	Writes formatted data based on *format*; *variables* is the data you want printed.

continues

15

awk

TABLE 15.5. CONTINUED

V	Function	Purpose
N	split(*string, store, delim*)	Splits *string* into array elements of *store* based on the delimiter *delim*.
A	sprintf(*format, variables*)	Returns a string containing formatted data based on *format*; *variables* is the data you want placed in the string.
G	strftime(*format, timestamp*)	Returns a formatted date or time string based on *format*; *timestamp* is the time returned by the systime() function.
N	sub(*reg, string, target*)	Substitutes *string* in *target* string the first time the regular expression *reg* is matched.
A	substr(*string, position, len*)	Returns a substring beginning at *position* for *len* number of characters.
P	tolower(*string*)	Returns the characters in *string* as their lowercase equivalent.
P	toupper(*string*)	Returns the characters in *string* as their uppercase equivalent.

V is the first implementation that supports a variable. A = awk, N = nawk, P = POSIX awk, and G = gawk.

The gsub(*reg, string, target*) function allows you to globally substitute one set of characters for another (defined in the form of the regular expression *reg*) within *string*. The number of substitutions is returned by the function. If *target* is omitted, the input record, $0, is the target. This is patterned after the substitute command in the ed text editor.

The index(*search, string*) function returns the first position (counting from the left) of the *search* string within *string*. If *string* is omitted, 0 is returned.

The length(*string*) function returns a count of the number of characters in *string*. awk keeps track of the length of strings internally.

The match(*string, reg*) function determines whether *string* contains the set of characters defined by *reg*. If there is a match, the position is returned, and the variables RSTART and RLENGTH are set.

The printf(*format, variables*) function writes formatted data converting *variables* based on the *format* string. This function is similar to the C printf() function. More information about this function and the formatting strings is provided in the section "Pretty Formatting (printf)" later in this chapter.

The split(*string, store, delim*) function splits *string* into elements of the array *store* based on the *delim* string. The number of elements in *store* is returned. If you omit the *delim* string, FS is used. To split a slash (/) delimited date into its component parts, code the following:

```
split("08/12/1962", results, "/");
```

After the function call, results[1] contains 08, results[2] contains 12, and results[3] contains 1962. When used with the split function, the array begins with the element one. This also works with strings that contain text.

The sprintf(*format, variables*) function behaves like the printf function except that it returns the result string instead of writing output. It produces formatted data converting *variables* based on the *format* string. This function is similar to the C sprintf() function. More information about this function and the formatting strings is provided in the "Pretty Formatting (printf)" section of this chapter.

The strftime(*format, timestamp*) function returns a formatted date or time based on the *format* string; *timestamp* is the number of seconds since midnight on January 1, 1970. The systime function returns a value in this form. The format is the same as the C strftime() function.

The sub(*reg, string, target*) function allows you to substitute the one set of characters for the first occurrence of another (defined in the form of the regular expression *reg*) within *string*. The number of substitutions is returned by the function. If *target* is omitted, the input record, $0, is the target. This is patterned after the substitute command in the ed text editor.

The substr(*string, position, len*) function allows you to extract a substring based on a starting *position* and *length*. If you omit the *len* parameter, the remaining string is returned.

The tolower(*string*) function returns the uppercase alphabetic characters in *string* converted to lowercase. Any other characters are returned without any conversion.

15

awk

The `toupper(`*`string`*`)` function returns the lowercase alphabetic characters in *string* converted to uppercase. Any other characters are returned without any conversion.

Special String Constants

awk supports special string constants that cannot be entered from the keyboard or have special meaning. If you wanted to have a double quote (") character as a string constant (x = """), how would you prevent awk from thinking the second one (the one you really want) is the end of the string? The answer is by escaping, or telling awk that the next character has special meaning. This is done through the backslash (\) character, as in the rest of UNIX.

Table 15.6 shows most of the constants that awk supports.

TABLE 15.6.   awk SPECIAL STRING CONSTANTS.

Expression	Meaning
\\	The means of including a backslash
\a	The alert or bell character
\b	Backspace
\f	Formfeed
\n	Newline
\r	Carriage return
\t	Tab
\v	Vertical tab
\"	Double quote
\x*NN*	Indicates that *NN* is a hexadecimal number
\0*NNN*	Indicates that *NNN* is an octal number

Arrays

When you have more than one related piece of data, you have two choices—you can create multiple variables, or you can use an array. An array enables you to keep a collection of related data together.

You access individual elements within an array by enclosing the subscript within square brackets ([ ]). In general, you can use an array element any place you can use a regular variable.

Arrays in awk have special capabilities that are lacking in most other languages: They are dynamic, they are sparse, and the subscript is actually a string. You don't have to declare a variable to be an array, and you don't have to define the maximum number of elements—when you use an element for the first time, it is created dynamically. Because of this, a block of memory is not initially allocated; in normal programming practice, if you want to accumulate sales for each month in a year, 12 elements are allocated, even if you are only processing December at the moment. awk arrays are sparse; if you are working with December, only that element exists, not the other 11 (empty) months.

In my experience, the last capability is the most useful—the subscript being a string. In most programming languages, if you want to accumulate data based on a string (like totaling sales by state or country), you need to have two arrays—the state or country name (a string) and the numeric sales array. You search the state or country name for a match and then use the same element of the sales array. awk performs this for you. You create an element in the sales array with the state or country name as the subscript and address it directly like the following:

```
total_sales["Pennsylvania"] = 10.15
```

TIP

Using a string as an array subscript requires much less programming and is much easier to read (and maintain) than the search one array and change another method. This is known as an *associative array*.

However, awk does not directly support multidimensional arrays.

Array Functions

Versions of awk starting with nawk provide a couple of functions specifically for use with arrays: in and delete. The in function tests for membership in an array. The delete function removes elements from an array.

If you have an array with a subscript of states and want to determine whether a specific state is in the list, you would put the following within a conditional test (more about conditional tests in the "Conditional Flow" section):

```
"Delaware" in total_sales
```

You can also use the in function within a loop to step through the elements in an array (especially if the array is sparse or associative). This is a special case of the for loop and is described in the for statement section.

15

awk

To delete an array element, (the state of Delaware, for example), you code the following:

```
delete total_sales["Delaware"]
```

> **CAUTION**
>
> Be careful deleting array elements—when an array element is deleted, it has been removed from memory. The data is no longer available.

It is always good practice to delete elements in an array, or entire arrays, when you are done with them. Although memory is cheap and large quantities are available (especially with virtual memory), you will eventually run out if you don't clean up.

> **NOTE**
>
> You cannot delete all elements in an array with one statement. You must loop through all loop elements and delete each one. You cannot delete an entire array directly; the following is not valid:
>
> ```
> delete total_sales
> ```

Multidimensional Arrays

Although awk doesn't directly support multidimensional arrays, it does provide a facility to simulate them. The distinction is fairly trivial to you as a programmer. You can specify multiple dimensions in the subscript (within the square brackets) in a form familiar to C programmers:

```
array[5, 3] = "Mary"
```

This is stored in a single-dimension array with the subscript actually stored in the form 5 SUBSEP 3. The predefined variable SUBSEP contains the value of the separator of the subscript components. It defaults to the double quote (" or \034) because it is unlikely that the double quote will appear in the subscript itself. Remember that the double quotes are used to contain a string; they are not stored as part of the string itself. You can always change SUBSEP if you need to have the double quote character in your multidimensional array subscript.

If you want to calculate total sales by city and state (or country), you will use a two-dimensional array:

```
total_sales["Philadelphia", "Pennsylvania"] = 10.15
```

You can use the `in` function within a conditional:

```
("Wilmington", "Delaware") in total_sales
```

You can also use the `in` function within a loop to step through the various cities.

Built-in Numeric Functions

awk provides a number of numeric functions to calculate special values.

Table 15.7 summarizes the built-in numeric functions in awk. Earlier versions of awk don't support all these functions.

TABLE 15.7. awk BUILT-IN NUMERIC FUNCTIONS.

V	Function	Purpose
A	atan2(x, y)	Returns the arctangent of y/x in radians
N	cos(x)	Returns the cosine of x in radians
A	exp(x)	Returns e raised to the x power
A	int(x)	Returns the value of x truncated to an integer
A	log(x)	Returns the natural log of x
N	rand()	Returns a random number between 0 and 1
N	sin(x)	Returns the sine of x in radians
A	sqrt(x)	Returns the square root of x
A	srand(x)	Initializes (seeds) the random number generator; systime() is used if x is omitted
G	systime()	Returns the current time in seconds since midnight, January 1, 1970

V is the first implementation that supports a variable. A = awk, N = nawk, P = POSIX awk, and G = gawk.

Arithmetic Operators

awk supports a wide variety of math operations. Table 15.8 summarizes these operators.

TABLE 15.8.   awk ARITHMETIC OPERATORS.

Operator	Purpose
x^y	Raises x to the y power
x**y	Raises x to the y power (same as x^y)
x%y	Calculates the remainder (modulo/modulus) of x/y
x+y	Adds x to y
x-y	Subtracts y from x
x*y	Multiplies x times y
x/y	Divides x by y
-y	Negates y (switches the sign of y); also known as the unary minus
++y	Increments y by 1 and uses value (prefix increment)
y++	Uses value of y and then increments by 1 (postfix increment)
—y	Decrements y by 1 and uses value (prefix decrement)
y—	Uses value of y and then decrements by 1 (postfix decrement)
x=y	Assigns value of y to x. awk also supports operator-assignment operators (+=, -=, *=, /=, %=, ^=, and **=)

> **NOTE**
>
> All math in awk uses floating point (even if you treat the number as an integer).

Conditional Flow

By its very nature, an action within a awk program is conditional. It is executed if its pattern is true. You can also have conditional programs flow within the action through the use of an if statement.

The general flow of an if statement is as follows:

```
if (condition)
    statement to execute when true
else
    statement to execute when false
```

condition can be any valid combination of patterns shown in Tables 15.2 and 15.3. else is optional. If you have more than one statement to execute, you need to enclose the statements within curly braces ({ }), just as in the C syntax.

You can also stack `if` and `else` statements as necessary:

```
if ("Pennsylvania" in total_sales)
    print "We have Pennsylvania data"
else if ("Delaware" in total_sales)
    print "We have Delaware data"
else if (current_year < 2010)
    print "Uranus is still a planet"
else
    print "none of the conditions were met."
```

The Null Statement

By definition, `if` requires one (or more) statements to execute; in some cases, the logic might be straightforward when coded so that the code you want executed occurs when the condition is false. I have used this when it would be difficult or ugly to reverse the logic to execute the code when the condition is true.

The solution to this problem is easy: Just use the null statement, the semicolon (`;`). The null statement satisfies the syntax requirement that `if` requires statements to execute; it just does nothing.

Your code will look something like the following:

```
if (($1 <= 5 && $2 > 3) || ($1 > 7 && $2 < 2))
    ;               # The Null Statement
else
    the code I really want to execute
```

The Conditional Operator

awk has one operator that actually has three parameters: the conditional operator. This operator allows you to apply an if-test anywhere in your code.

The general format of the conditional statement is as follows:

condition `?` *true-result* `:` *false-result*

Although this might seem like duplication of the `if` statement, it can make your code easier to read. If you have a data file that consists of an employee name and the number of sick days taken, you can use the following:

```
{ print $1, "has taken", $2, "day" $2 != 1 ? "s" : "", "of sick time" }
```

15

awk

This prints day if the employee only took one day of sick time and prints days if the employee took zero or more than one day of sick time. The resulting sentence is more readable. To code the same example using an `if` statement would be more complex and look like the following:

```
if ($2 != 1)
    print $1, "has taken", $2, "days of sick time"
else
    print $1, "has taken", $2, "day of sick time"
```

Looping

By their very nature, awk programs are one big loop—reading each record in the input file and processing the appropriate patterns and actions. Within an action, the need for repetition often occurs. awk supports loops through the do, for, and while statements that are similar to those found in C.

As with the `if` statement, if you want to execute multiple statements within a loop, you must contain them in curly braces.

> ### TIP
>
> Pay close attention to your block statements (the curly braces). Forgetting the curly braces around multiple statements is a common programming error with conditional and looping statements.

The do Statement

The do statement provides a looping construct that is executed at least once. The condition or test occurs after the contents of the loop have been executed.

> ### NOTE
>
> The do statement is sometimes referred to as the do while statement.

The do statement takes the following form:

```
do
    statement
while (condition)
```

statement can be one statement or multiple statements enclosed in curly braces. *condition* is any valid test like those used with the if statement or the pattern used to trigger actions.

> **CAUTION**
>
> In general, you must change the value of the variable in the condition within the loop. If you don't, you will have a loop forever condition because the test result (*condition*) would never change (and become false).

Loop Control (break and continue)

You can exit a loop early if you need to (without assigning some bogus value to the variable in the condition). awk provides two facilities to do this: break and continue.

break causes the current (innermost) loop to be exited. It behaves as if the conditional test was performed immediately with a false result. None of the remaining code in the loop (after the break statement) executes, and the loop ends. This is useful when you need to handle some error or early end condition.

continue causes the current loop to return to the conditional test. None of the remaining code in the loop (after the continue statement) is executed, and the test is immediately executed. This is most useful when there is code you want to skip (within the loop) temporarily. The continue is different from the break because the loop is not forced to end.

The for Statement

The for statement provides a looping construct that modifies values within the loop. It is good for counting through a specific number of items.

The for statement has two general forms—the following

```
for (loop = 0; loop < 10; loop++)
    statement
```

and

```
for (subscript in array)
    statement
```

The first form initializes the variable (loop = 0), performs the test (loop < 10), and then performs the loop contents (*statement*). Then it modifies the variable (loop++) and tests again. As long as the test is true, *statement* will execute.

15

awk

> **NOTE**
>
> Modifying the loop control variable can take many forms. The increment operator (`loop++`) is shown here because it is the most commonly used operator (to step through an array for example). Any valid operation can be used here, even something like: `loop = loop * 2 + another_variable`.

In the second form, `statement` is executed with `subscript` being set to each of the subscripts in `array`. This enables you to loop through an array even if you don't know the values of the subscripts. This works well for multidimensional arrays.

`statement` can be one statement or multiple statements enclosed in curly braces. The condition (`loop < 10`) is any valid test like those used with the `if` statement or the pattern used to trigger actions.

> **TIP**
>
> In general, you don't want to change the loop control variable (`loop` or `subscript`) within the loop body. Let the `for` statement do that for you, or you might get behavior that is difficult to debug.

For the first form, the modification of the variable can be any valid operation (including calls to functions). In most cases, it is an increment or decrement.

> **NOTE**
>
> This example showed the postfix increment. It doesn't matter whether you use the postfix (`loop++`) or prefix (`++loop`) increment—the results are the same. Just be consistent.

The `for` loop is a good method of looping through data of an unknown size:

```
for (i=1; i<=NF; i++)
    print $i
```

Each field on the current record is printed on its own line. As a programmer, I don't know how many fields are on a particular record when I write the code. The variable `NF` lets me know as the program runs.

The `while` Statement

The final loop structure is the `while` loop. It is the most general because it executes while the condition is true. The general form is as follows:

```
while(condition)
    statement
```

`statement` can be one statement or multiple statements enclosed in curly braces. `condition` is any valid test like those used with the `if` statement or the pattern used to trigger actions.

If the condition is false before the `while` is encountered, the contents of the loop are be executed. This is different from `do`, which always executes the loop contents at least once.

> **CAUTION**
>
> In general, you must change the value of the variable in the condition within the loop. If you don't, you will have a loop forever condition because the test result (*condition*) would never change (and become false).

Advanced Input and Output

In addition to the simple input and output facilities provided by awk, there are a number of advanced features you can take advantage of for more complicated processing.

By default, awk automatically reads and loops through your program; you can alter this behavior. You can force input to come from a different file, cause the loop to recycle early (read the next record without performing any more actions), or even just read the next record. You can even get data from the output of other commands.

On the output side, you can format the output and send it to a file (other than the standard output device) or as input to another command.

Input

You don't have to program the normal input loop process in awk. It reads a record and then searches for pattern matches and the corresponding actions to execute. If multiple files are specified on the command line, they are processed in order. It is only if you want to change this behavior that you have to do any special programming.

15

awk

next and exit

The `next` command causes `awk` to read the next record and perform the pattern match and corresponding action execution immediately. Normally, it executes all your code in any actions with matching patterns. `next` causes any additional matching patterns to be ignored for this record.

The `exit` command in any action except for `END` behaves as if the end of file was reached. Code execution in all pattern/actions is ceased, and the actions within the `END` pattern are executed. `exit` appearing in the `END` pattern is a special case—it causes the program to end.

getline

The `getline` statement is used to explicitly read a record. This is especially useful if you have a data record that looks like two physical records. It performs the normal field splitting (setting `$0`, the field variables, `FNR`, `NF`, and `NR`). It returns the value 1 if the read was successful and zero if it failed (end of file was reached). If you want to explicitly read through a file, you can code something like the following:

```
{ while (getline == 1)
   {
       # process the inputted fields
   }
}
```

You can also have `getline` store the input data in a field instead of taking advantage of the normal field processing by using the form `getline` *variable*. When used this way, `NF` is set to zero, and `FNR` and `NR` are incremented.

Input from a File

You can use `getline` to input data from a specific file instead of the ones listed on the command line. The general form is `getline < "`*filename*`"`. When coded this way, `getline` performs the normal field splitting (setting `$0`, the field variables, and `NF`). If the file doesn't exist, `getline` returns `-1`; it returns 1 on success and 0 on failure.

You can read the data from the specified file into a variable. You can also replace *filename* with `stdin` or a variable that contains the filename.

CAUTION

If you use `getline < "filename"` to read data into your program, neither `FNR` nor `NR` is changed.

Input from a Command

Another way of using the `getline` statement is to accept input from a UNIX command. If you want to perform some processing for each person signed on the system (send him or her a message, for instance), you can code something like the following:

```
{ while ("who -u" ¦ getline)
  {
      # process each line from the who command
  }
}
```

The `who` command is executed once, and each of its output lines is processed by `getline`. You could also use the form `"command" ¦ getline variable`.

Ending Input from a File or Command

Whenever you use `getline` to get input from a specified file or command, you should close it when you are done processing the data. There is a maximum number of open files allowed to `awk` that varies with operating system version or individual account configuration (a command output pipe counts as a file). By closing files when you are done with them, you reduce the chances of hitting the limit.

The syntax to close a file is simply

```
close ("filename")
```

where *filename* is the one specified on the `getline` (which could also be `stdin`, a variable that contains the filename, or the exact command used with `getline`).

Output

There are a few advanced features for output: pretty formatting, sending output to files, and piping output as input to other commands. The `printf` command is used for pretty formatting—instead of seeing the output in whatever default format `awk` decides to use (which is often ugly), you can specify how it looks.

Pretty Formatting (`printf`)

The `print` statement produces simple output for you. If you want to be able to format the data (producing fixed columns, for instance), you need to use `printf`. The nice thing about `awk` `printf` is that it uses syntax that is similar to the `printf()` function in C.

The general format of the `awk` `printf` is as follows (the parentheses are only required if a relational expression is included):

15

awk

```
printf format-specifier, variable1,variable2, variable3,..variablen
printf(format-specifier, variable1,variable2, variable3,..variablen)
```

Personally, I use the second form because I am so used to coding in C.

The variables are optional, but `format-specifier` is mandatory. Often you have `printf` statements that only include `format-specifier` (to print messages that contain no variables):

```
printf ("Program Starting\n")
printf ("\f")          # new page in output
```

`format-specifier` can consist of text, escaped characters, or actual print specifiers. A print specifier begins with the percent sign (%), followed by an optional numeric value that specifies the size of the field, and then the format type follows (which describes the type of variable or output format). If you want to print a percent sign in your output, you use %%.

The field size can consist of two numbers separated by a decimal point (.). For floating-point numbers, the first number is the size of the entire field (including the decimal point); the second number is the number of digits to the right of the decimal. For other types of fields, the first number is the minimum field size, and the second number is the maximum field size (number of characters to actually print); if you omit the first number, it takes the value of the maximum field size.

The print specifiers determine how the variable is printed; modifiers also change the behavior of the specifiers. Table 15.9 shows the print format specifiers.

TABLE 15.9. FORMAT SPECIFIERS FOR awk.

Format	Meaning
%c	ASCII character
%d	An integer (decimal number)
%i	An integer, just like %d
%e	A floating-point number using scientific notation (1.00000E+01)
%f	A floating-point number (10.43)
%g	awk chooses between %e or %f display format (whichever is shorter) suppressing nonsignificant zeros.
%o	An unsigned octal (base 8) number (integer)
%s	A string of characters
%x	An unsigned hexadecimal (base 16) number (integer)
%X	Same as %x but using ABCDEF instead of abcdef

> **NOTE**
>
> If you attempt to print a numeric value or variable using %c, it will be printed as a character (the ASCII character for that value will print).

The format modifiers change the default behavior of the format specifiers. Listing 15.4 shows the use of various specifiers and modifiers.

LISTING 15.4. printf FORMAT SPECIFIERS AND MODIFIERS.

```
printf("%d %3.3d %03.3d %.3d %-.3d %3d %-3d\n", 64, 64, 64, 64, 64, 64,
64)
printf("%c %c %2.2c %-2.2c %2c %-2c\n", 64, "abc", "abc", "abc", "abc",
"abc")
printf("%s %2s %-2s %2.2s %-2.2s %.2s %-.2s\n",
       "abc", "abc", "abc", "abc", "abc", "abc", "abc")
printf("%f %6.1f %06.1f %.1f %-.1f %6f\n",
       123.456, 123.456, 123.456, 123.456, 123.456, 123.456)

64 064 064 064 064  64 64
@ a  a a   a a
abc abc abc ab ab ab ab
123.456000   123.5 0123.5 123.5 123.5 123.456000
```

When using the integer or decimal (%d) specifier, the field size defaults to the size of the value being printed (2 digits for the value 64). If you specify a field maximum size that is larger than that, you automatically get the field zero filled. All numeric fields are right-justified unless you use the minus sign (-) modifier, which causes them to be left-justified. If you specify only the field minimum size and want the rest of the field zero filled, you have to use the zero modifier (before the field minimum size).

When using the character (%c) specifier, only one character prints from the input no matter what size you use for the field minimum or maximum sizes and no matter how many characters are in the value being printed. Note that the value 64 printed as a character shows up as @.

When using the string (%s) specifier, the entire string prints unless you specify the field maximum size. By default, strings are left-justified unless you use the minus sign (-) modifier, which causes them to be right-justified.

When using the floating (%f) specifier, the field size defaults .6 (as many digits to the left of the decimal and 6 digits to the right). If you specify a number after the decimal in the format, that many digits prints to the right of the decimal and awk rounds the number. All numeric fields are right-justified unless you use the minus sign (-) modifier, which causes them to be left-justified. If you want the field zero filled, you have to use the zero modifier (before the field minimum size).

The best way to determine printing results is to work with it. Try out the various modifiers and see what makes your output look best.

Output to a File

You can send your output (from `print` or `printf`) to a file. The following creates a new (or empties out an existing) file containing the printed message:

```
printf ("hello world\n") > "datafile"
```

If you execute this statement multiple times or other statements that redirect output to *datafile*, the output remains in the file. The file creation/emptying out only occurs the first time the file is used in the program.

To append data to an existing file, you use the following:

```
printf ("hello world\n") >> "datafile"
```

Output to a Command

In addition to redirecting your output to a file, you can send the output from your program to act as input for another command. You can code something like the following:

```
printf ("hello world\n") ¦ "sort -t`,`"
```

Any other output statements that pipe data into the same command specify exactly the same command after the pipe character (¦) because that is how awk keeps track of which command is receiving which output from your program.

Closing an Output File or Pipe

Whenever you send output to a file or pipe, you should close it when you are done processing the data. There is a maximum number of open files allowed to awk that varies with operating system version or individual account configuration (a pipe counts as a file). By closing files when you are done with them, you reduce the chances of hitting the limit.

The syntax to close a file is simply

```
close ("filename")
```

where *filename* is the one specified on the output statement (which can also be stdout, a variable that contains the filename, or the exact command used with a pipe).

Functions

In addition to the built-in functions (such as gsub or srand), you can write your own. User-defined functions are a means of creating a block of code that is accessed in multiple places in your code. They can also be used to build a library of commonly used routines so that you do not have to recode the same algorithms repeatedly.

CAUTION

User-defined functions are not a part of the original awk—they were added to nawk and are supported by more recent versions.

There are two parts to using a function: the definition and the call. The function definition contains the code to be executed (the function itself), and the call temporarily transfers from the main code to the function. There are two ways that command execution is transferred back to the main code: implicit and explicit returns. When awk reaches the end of a function (the close curly brace [}]), it automatically (implicitly) returns control to the calling routine. If you want to leave your function before the bottom, you can explicitly use the return statement to exit early.

Function Definition

The general form of an awk function definition looks like the following:

```
function functionname(parameter list) {
     the function body
}
```

You code your function just as if it were any other set of action statements and can place it anywhere you would put a pattern/action set. If you think about it, the function functionname(parameter list) portion of the definition could be considered a pattern and the function body the action.

NOTE

gawk supports another form of function definition where the function keyword is abbreviated to func. The remaining syntax is the same:

```
func functionname(parameter list) {
     the function body
}
```

15

awk

Listing 15.5 shows the defining and calling of a function.

LISTING 15.5. DEFINING AND CALLING FUNCTIONS.

```
BEGIN { print_header() }

function print_header( ) {
   printf("This is the header\n");
   printf("this is a second line of the header\n");
}

This is the header
this is a second line of the header
```

The code inside the function is executed only once—when the function is called from within the BEGIN action. This function uses the implicit return method.

> **CAUTION**
>
> When working with user-defined functions, you must place the parentheses that contain the parameter list immediately after the function name when calling that function. When you use the built-in functions, this is not a requirement.

Function Parameters

Like C, awk passes parameters to functions by value. In other words, a copy of the original value is made, and that copy is passed to the called function. The original is untouched, even if the function changes the value.

Any parameters are listed in the function definition separated by commas. If you have no parameters, you can leave the parameter list (contained in the parentheses) empty.

Listing 15.6 is an expanded version of Listing 15.5; it shows the pass-by-value nature of awk function parameters.

LISTING 15.6. PASSING PARAMETERS.

```
BEGIN { pageno = 0;
        print_header(pageno);
        printf("the page number is now %d\n", pageno);
}

function print_header(page ) {
```

```
    page++;
    printf("This is the header for page %d\n", page);
    printf("this is a second line of the header\n");
}

This is the header for page 1
this is a second line of the header
the page number is now 0
```

The page number is initialized before the first call to the `print_header` function and incremented in the function. But when it is printed after the function call, it remains at the original value.

> **CAUTION**
>
> awk does not perform parameter validation. When you call a function, you can list more or fewer parameters than the function expects. Any extra parameters are ignored, and any missing ones default to zero or empty strings (depending on how they are used).

> **TIP**
>
> You can take advantage of the lack of function parameter validation. It can be used to create local variables within the called function—just list more variables in the function definition than you use in the function call. I strongly suggest that you comment the fact that the extra parameters are really being used as local variables.

There are several ways that a called function can change variables in the calling routines—through explicit return or by using the variables in the calling routine directly (those variables are normally global anyway).

Explicit Returns from Functions (return Statement)

If you want to return a value or leave a function early, you need to code a `return` statement. If you don't code one, the function ends with the close curly brace (}). Personally, I prefer to code them at the bottom.

If the calling code expects a returned value from your function, you must code the `return` statement in the following form:

`return variable`

Expanding on Listing 15.6 to let the function change the page number, Listing 15.7 shows the use of the `return` statement.

LISTING 15.7. RETURNING VALUES.

```
BEGIN { pageno = 0;
        pageno = print_header(pageno);
        printf("the page number is now %d\n", pageno);
}

function print_header(page ) {
    page++;
    printf("This is the header for page %d\n", page);
    printf("this is a second line of the header\n");
    return page;
}

This is the header for page 1
this is a second line of the header
the page number is now 1
```

The updated page number is returned to the code that called the function.

The `return` statement allows you to return only one value back to the calling routine.

Writing Reports

Generating a report in awk entails a sequence of steps, with each step producing the input for the next step. Report writing is usually a three-step process: Pick the data, sort the data, and make the output pretty.

Complex Reports

Using awk, it is possible to quickly create complex reports. It is much easier to perform string comparisons, build arrays on-the-fly, and take advantage of associative arrays than to code in another language (like C). Instead of having to search through an array for a match with a text key, that key can be used as the array subscript.

I have produced reports using awk with three levels of control breaks, multiple sections of reports in the same control break, and multiple totaling pages. The totaling pages were for each level of control break plus a final page; if the control break did not have a particular type of data, then the total page did not have it either. If there was only one member of a control break, then the total page for that level wasn't created. (This saved a lot of paper when there was really only one level of control break—the highest.)

This report ended up being more than 1,000 lines of awk (nawk to be specific) code. It takes a little longer to run than the equivalent C program, but it took a lot less programmer time to create. Because it was easy to create and modify, it was developed using prototypes. The users briefly described what they wanted, and I produced a report. They decided they needed more control breaks, and I added them; then they realized a lot of paper was wasted on total pages, so the report was modified as described.

> **TIP**
>
> Using a tool that makes it easy to develop incrementally without knowing the final result made it easier and more fun for me. By my being responsive to user changes, the users were happy!

Extracting Data

As mentioned early in this chapter, many systems don't produce data in the desired format. When working with data stored in relational databases, there are two main ways to get data out: Use a query tool with SQL or write a program to get the data from the database and output it in the desired form. SQL query tools have limited formatting capability but can provide quick and easy access to the data.

One technique I have found useful is to extract the data from the database into a file that is then manipulated by an awk script to produce the exact format required. When required, an awk script can even create the SQL statements used to query the database (specifying the key values for the rows to select).

The following example is used when the query tool places a space before a numeric field that must be removed for program that will use the data in another system (mainframe COBOL):

```
{   printf("%s%s%-25.25s\n", $1, $2, $3);   }
```

awk automatically removes the field separator (the space character) when splitting the input record into individual fields and the formatting %s string format specifiers in the printf are contiguous (do not have any spaces between them).

Commands On-the-Fly

The capability to pipe the output of a command into another is very powerful because the output from the first becomes the input that the second can manipulate. A frequent use of one-line awk programs is the creation of commands based on a list.

The find command can be used to produce a list of files that match its conditions, or it can execute a single command that takes a single command-line argument. You can see files in a directory (and subdirectories) that match specific conditions with the following:

```
$ find . -name "*.prn" -print
./exam2.prn
./exam1.prn
./exam3.prn
```

Or you can print the contents of those files with the following:

```
find . -name "*.prn" -exec lp {} \;
```

The find command inserts the individual filenames that it locates in place of the {} and executes the lp command. But if you wanted to execute a command that required two arguments (to copy files to a new name) or execute multiple commands at once, you couldn't do it with find alone. You could create a shell script that would accept the single argument and use it in multiple places, or you could create an awk single-line program:

```
$ find . -name "*.prn" -print ¦ awk '{print "echo bak" $1; print "cp " $1
" " $1".bak";}'
echo bak./exam2.prn
cp ./exam2.prn ./exam2.prn.bak
echo bak./exam1.prn
cp ./exam1.prn ./exam1.prn.bak
echo bak./exam3.prn
cp ./exam3.prn ./exam3.prn.bak
```

To get the commands to actually execute, you need to pipe the commands into one of the shells. The following example uses the Korn shell; you can use the one you prefer:

```
$ find . -name "*.prn" -print ¦
    awk '{print "echo bak" $1; print "cp " $1 " " $1".bak";}' ¦
    ksh
bak./exam2.prn
bak./exam1.prn
bak./exam3.prn
```

Before each copy takes place, the message is shown. This is also handy if you want to search for a string (using the grep command) in the files of multiple subdirectories. Many versions of the grep command don't show the name of the file searched unless you use wildcards (or specify multiple filenames on the command line). The following uses find to search for C source files, awk to create grep commands to look for an error message, and the shell echo command to show the file being searched:

```
$ find . -name "*.c" -print |
    awk '{print "echo " $1; print "grep error-message " $1;}' |
    ksh
```

The same technique can be used to perform lint checks on source code in a series of subdirectories. I execute the following in a shell script periodically to check all C code:

```
$ find . -name "*.c" -print |
    awk '{print "lint " $1 " > " $1".lint"}' |
    ksh
```

The lint version on one system prints the code error as a heading line and then the parts of code in question as a list below. grep shows the heading but not the detail lines. The awk script prints all lines from the heading until the first blank line (end of the lint section).

> **TIP**
>
> When in doubt, pipe the output into more or pg to view the created commands before you pipe them into a shell for execution.

One Last Built-in Function: `system`

There is one more built-in function that doesn't fit in the character or numeric categories: system. The system function executes the string passed to it as an argument. This allows you to execute commands or scripts on-the-fly when your awk code has the need.

You can code a report to automatically print to paper when it is complete. The code looks something like Listing 15.8.

LISTING 15.8. USING THE system FUNCTION.

```
BEGIN { pageno = 0;
        pageno = print_header(pageno);
        printf("the page number is now %d\n", pageno);
}
```

continues

LISTING 15.8.   CONTINUED

```
# The production of the report would be coded here

END { close ("report.txt");
      system ("lpr -Pmyprinter report.txt");
}

function print_header(page ) {
   page++;
   printf("This is the header for page %d\n", page) > "report.txt";
   printf("this is a second line of the header\n")  > "report.txt";
}

This is the header for page 1
this is a second line of the header
the page number is now 0
```

The output is the same as that of Listing 15.6 except that the output shows up on the printer instead of the screen. Before printing the file, you have to close it.

Summary

This chapter provides an introduction to the awk programming language in its various implementations. It is a powerful and useful language that enables you to search for data, extract data from files, create commands on-the-fly, or even create entire programs.

It is useful as a prototyping language—you can create reports quickly. After showing them to the user, changes also can be made quickly. Although it is less efficient than the comparable program written in C, it is not so inefficient that you cannot create production programs. If efficiency is a concern with an awk program, it can be converted into C.

For further information, see the following:

Aho, Alfred V., Brian W. Kernighan, and Peter J. Weinberger, *The awk Programming Language*. Reading, Mass.: Addison-Wesley, 1988 (copyright AT&T Bell Lab).

IEEE Standard for Information Technology, Portable Operating System Interface (POSIX), Part 2: Shell and Utilities, Volume 2. Std. 1003.2-1992. New York: IEEE, 1993.

See also the man pages for awk, nawk, or gawk on your system.

Perl

16

by David Till and Robin Burk

IN THIS CHAPTER

Perl has become the language of choice for many UNIX-based programs, including server support for World Wide Web pages. This chapter describes the basics of Perl, tells you how to obtain the Perl interpreter, and provides a short example of a working Perl program.

Features of Perl covered in this chapter include the following:

- Scalar variables and string and integer interchangeability
- Arithmetic, logical, bitwise, and string operators
- List, array, and associative array manipulation
- Control structures for handling program flow
- File input and output capability
- Subroutines
- Formatted output
- References
- Object-oriented capability
- Built-in functions

Overview of Perl

Perl is a simple yet useful programming language that provides the convenience of shell scripts and the power and flexibility of high-level programming languages. Perl programs are interpreted and executed directly, just as shell scripts are; however, they also contain control structures and operators similar to those found in the C programming language. This gives you the capability to write useful programs in a short time.

Where Can I Get Perl?

Perl is freeware: It can be obtained by file transfer (`ftp`) from the Free Software Foundation at `prep.ai.mit.edu` (in the directory `pub/gnu`). Perl is also available from several other sites on the Internet, including www.perl.org or any site that archives the newsgroup `comp.sources.unix`.

The Perl artistic license gives you the right to obtain Perl and its source, provided others have the right to obtain them from you. For more details on the Perl licensing policy, refer to the Perl source distribution.

A Simple Sample Program

To show how easy it is to use Perl, Listing 16.1 is a simple program that echoes (writes out) a line of input typed in at a terminal.

LISTING 16.1. A SAMPLE PERL PROGRAM.

```
#!/usr/bin/perl
$inputline = <STDIN>;
print ("$inputline");
```

To run this program, do the following:

1. Type in the program and save it in a file. (In subsequent steps, assume that the file is named `myfile`).

2. Tell the system that this file contains executable statements. To do this, enter the command `chmod +x myfile`.

3. Run the program by entering the command `myfile`.

If you receive the error message `myfile not found` or some equivalent, either enter the command `./myfile` or add the current directory `.` to your `PATH` environment variable.

At this point, the program waits for you to type in an input line. After you have done so, the program echoes your input line and exits.

The following sections describe each of the components of this simple program in more detail.

Using Comments

In Perl, any time a # character is recognized, the rest of the line is treated as a comment:

```
# this is a comment that takes up the whole line
$count = 0;   # this part of the line is a comment
```

A comment appearing as the first line of a program, called a *header comment*, specifies the location of the Perl interpreter.

Reading from Standard Input

Like C, Perl recognizes the existence of the UNIX standard input file, standard output file, and standard error file. In C, these files are called `stdin`, `stdout`, and `stderr`; in Perl, they are called `STDIN`, `STDOUT`, and `STDERR`.

The Perl construct `<STDIN>` refers to a line of text read in from the standard input file. This line of text includes the closing newline character.

Storing Values in Scalar Variables

The construct $inputline is an example of a scalar variable. A scalar variable holds exactly one value. This value can be a string, integer, or floating-point number.

All scalar variables start with a dollar sign, $. This distinguishes them from other Perl variables. In a scalar variable, the character immediately following the dollar sign must be a letter or an underscore. Subsequent characters can be letters, digits, or underscores. Scalar variable names can be as long as you want.

> **NOTE**
>
> When the interpreter encounters a previously undeclared variable, it assigns the null value (to strings) or zero (to numbers). Although convenient, this feature of Perl means that misentered variable names won't be flagged. It's a good idea always to initialize variables when you first define them.

Assigning a Value to a Scalar Variable

The statement $inputline = <STDIN>; contains the = character, which is the Perl assignment operator. This statement tells Perl that the line of text read from standard input, represented by <STDIN>, is to become the new value of the scalar variable $inputline.

Perl provides a full set of useful arithmetic, logical, and string operators. For details, refer to the sections titled "Working with Scalar Variables" and "Using Lists and Array Variables," later in this chapter.

> **CAUTION**
>
> All scalar variables are given an initial value of the null string, "". Therefore, a Perl program can be run even when a scalar variable is used before a value has been assigned to it. Consider the statement
>
> $b = $a;
>
> This statement assigns the value of the variable $a to $b. If $a has not been seen before, it is assumed to have the value "", and "" is assigned to $b. Because this behavior is legal in Perl, you must check your programs for "undefined" variables yourself.

Scalar Variables Inside Character Strings

The final statement of the program, `print ("$inputline");`, contains a character string, which is a sequence of characters enclosed in double quotes. In this case, the character string is `"$inputline"`.

The string `"$inputline"` contains the name of a scalar variable, `$inputline`. When Perl sees a variable inside a character string, it replaces the variable with its value. In this example, the string `"$inputline"` is replaced with the line of text read from the standard input file.

Writing to Standard Output

The built-in function `print()` writes its arguments (the items enclosed in parentheses) to the standard output file. In this example, the statement `print ("$inputline");` sends the contents of the scalar variable `$inputline` to the standard output file.

The `print()` function can also be told to write to the standard error file or to any other specified file. See the section titled "Reading from and Writing to Files" later in this chapter for more details.

Working with Scalar Variables

Now that you know a little about Perl, it's time to describe the language in a little more detail. This section begins by discussing scalar variables and the values that can be stored in them.

Understanding Scalar Values

In Perl, a scalar value is any value that can be stored in a scalar variable. The following are scalar values:

- Integers
- Double- and single-quoted character strings
- Floating-point values

The following assignments are all legal in Perl:

```
$variable = 1;
$variable = "this is a string";
$variable = 3.14159;
```

The following assignments are not legal:

```
$variable = 67M;
$variable = ^803;
$variable = $%$%!;
```

Using Octal and Hexadecimal Representation

Normally, integers are assumed to be in standard base-ten notation. Perl also supports base-eight (octal) and base-sixteen (hexadecimal) notation.

To indicate that a number is in base-eight, put a zero in front of the number:

```
$a = 0151;          # 0151 octal is 105
```

To indicate base-sixteen, put 0x (or 0X) in front of the number:

```
$a = 0x69;          # 69 hex is also 105
```

The letters A through F (in either upper- or lowercase) represent the values 10 through 15:

```
$a = 0xFE;          # equals 16 * 15 + 1 * 14, or 254
```

> **NOTE**
>
> Strings containing a leading 0 or 0x are not treated as base-eight or base-sixteen:
> ```
> $a = "0151";
> $a = "0x69";
> ```
> These strings are treated as character strings whose first character is 0.

Using Double- and Single-Quoted Strings

So far, all the strings you have seen have been enclosed by the " (double quotation mark) characters:

```
$a = "This is a string in double quotes";
```

Perl also allows you to enclose strings using the ' (single quotation mark) character:

```
$a = 'This is a string in single quotes';
```

There are two differences between double-quoted strings and single-quoted strings. The first difference is that variables are replaced by their values in double-quoted strings but not in single-quoted strings:

```
$x = "a string";
$y = "This is $x";  # becomes "This is a string"
$z = 'This is $x';  # remains 'This is $x'
```

Also, double-quoted strings recognize escape sequences for special characters. These escape sequences consist of a backslash (\) followed by one or more characters. The most common escape sequence is \n, representing the newline character:

```
$a = "This is a string terminated by a newline\n";
```

Table 16.1 lists the escape sequences recognized in double-quoted strings.

TABLE 16.1. ESCAPE SEQUENCES IN DOUBLE-QUOTED STRINGS.

Escape sequence	*Meaning*
\a	Bell (beep)
\b	Backspace
\cn	The control-n character
\e	Escape
\E	Cancel the effect of \L, \U, or \Q
\f	Form feed
\l	Force the next letter to lowercase
\L	All following letters are lowercase
\n	Newline
\Q	Do not look for special pattern characters
\r	Carriage return
\t	Tab
\u	Force the next letter to uppercase
\U	All following letters are uppercase
\v	Vertical tab

\L and \U can be turned off by \E:

```
$a = "T\LHIS IS A \ESTRING";  # same as "This is a STRING"
```

To include a backslash or double quote in a double-quoted string, precede it with another backslash:

```
$a = "A quote \" in a string";
$a = "A backslash \\ in a string";
```

You can specify the ASCII value for a character in base-eight or octal notation using *nnn*, where each *n* is an octal digit:

```
$a = "\377";        # this is the character 255, or EOF
```

You can also use hexadecimal to specify the ASCII value for a character. To do this, use the sequence \xnn, where each n is a hexadecimal digit:

```
$a = "\xff";          # this is also 255
```

None of these escape sequences is supported in single-quoted strings, except for \' and \\, which represent the single quote character and the backslash, respectively:

```
$a = '\b is not a bell'
$a = 'a single quote \' in a string'
$a = 'a backslash \\ in a string'
```

NOTE

In Perl, strings are not terminated by a null character (ASCII 0) as they are in C. In Perl, the null character can appear anywhere in a string:

```
$a = "This string \000 has a null character in it";
```

Using Floating-Point Values

Perl supports floating-point numbers in both conventional and scientific notation. The letter E (or e) represents the power of 10 to which a number in scientific notation is to be raised.

```
$a = 11.3;             # conventional notation
$a = 1.13E01;          # 11.3 in scientific notation
$a = -1.13e-01;        # the above divided by -10
```

Interchangeability of Strings and Numeric Values

In Perl, as you have seen, a scalar variable can be used to store a character string, an integer, or a floating-point value. In scalar variables, a value that was assigned as a string can be used as an integer whenever it makes sense to do so and vice versa. If a string contains characters that are not digits, it is converted to 0:

```
# this assigns 0 to $a, because "hello" becomes 0
$a = "hello" * 5;
```

In cases like this, Perl does not tell you that anything has gone wrong, and your results might not be what you expect.

Also, strings containing misprints yield unexpected results:

```
$a = "12O34"+1         # the letter O, not the number 0
```

When Perl sees a string in the middle of an expression, it converts the string to an integer. To do this, it starts at the left of the string and continues until it sees a letter that is not a digit. In this case, `"12034"` is converted to the integer 12, not 12034.

Using Scalar Variable Operators

The statement `$miles = $originaldist * 0.6214;` uses two scalar variable operators: =, the assignment operator, which assigns a value to a variable, and *, the multiplication operator, which multiplies two values.

Perl provides the complete set of operators found in C, plus a few others. These operators are described in the following sections.

Performing Arithmetic

To do arithmetic in Perl, use the arithmetic operators. Perl supports the following arithmetic operators:

```
$a = 15;            # assignment: $a now has the value 15
$a = 4 + 5.1;       # addition: $a is now 9.1
$a = 17 - 6.2;      # subtraction: $a is now 10.8
$a = 2.1 * 6;       # multiplication: $a is now 12.6
$a = 48 / 1.5;      # division: $a is now 32
$a = 2 ** 3;        # exponentiation: $a is now 8
$a = 21 % 5;        # remainder (modulo): $a is now 1
$a = - $b;          # arithmetic negation: $a is now $b * -1
```

Nonintegral values are converted to integers before a remainder operation is performed:

```
$a = 21.4 % 5.1;    # identical to 21 % 5
```

Performing Comparisons

To compare two scalar values in Perl, use the logical operators. Logical operators are divided into two classes: numeric and string. The following numeric logical operators are defined:

```
11.0 < 16           # less than
16 > 11             # greater than
15 == 15            # equals
11.0 <= 16          # less than or equal to
16 >= 11            # greater than or equal to
15 != 14            # not equal to
$a || $b            # logical OR:  true if either is non-zero
$a && $b            # logical AND:  true only if both are nonzero
! $a                # logical NOT:  true if $a is zero
```

In each case, the result of the operation performed by a logical operator is nonzero if true and zero if false, just like in C.

The expression on the left side of a ¦¦ (logical OR) operator is always tested before the expression on the right side, and the expression on the right side is used only when necessary. For example, consider the following expression:

```
$x == 0 ¦¦ $y / $x > 5
```

Here, the expression on the left side of the ¦¦, $x == 0, is tested first. If $x is zero, the result is true, regardless of the value of $y / $x > 5, so Perl doesn't bother to compute this value. $y / $x > 5 is evaluated only if $x is not zero. This ensures that division by zero can never occur.

Similarly, the expression on the right side of a && operator is tested only if the expression on the left side is true:

```
$x != 0 && $y / $x > 5
```

Once again, a division-by-zero error is impossible because $y / $x > 5 is only evaluated if $x is nonzero.

Perl also defines the <=> operator, which returns 0 if the two values are equal, 1 if the left value is larger, and -1 if the right value is larger:

```
4 <=> 1             # returns 1
3 <=> 3.0           # returns 0
1 <=> 4.0           # returns -1
```

esides the preceding numeric logical operators, Perl also provides logical operators that work with strings:

```
"aaa" lt "bbb"      # less than
"bbb" gt "aaa"      # greater than
"aaa" eq "aaa"      # equals
"aaa" le "bbb"      # less than or equal to
"bbb" ge "aaa"      # greater than or equal to
"aaa" ne "bbb"      # not equal to
```

Perl also defines the cmp operator, which, like the numeric operator <=>, returns 1, 0, or -1:

```
"aaa" cmp "bbb"     # returns 1
"aaa" cmp "aaa"     # returns 0
"bbb" cmp "aaa"     # returns -1
```

This behavior is identical to that of the C function strcmp().

Note that the logical string operators perform string comparisons, not numeric comparisons. For example, "40" lt "8" is true; if the two strings are sorted in ascending order, "40" appears before "8".

16

Manipulating Bits

Any integer can always be represented in binary or base-two notation. For example, the number 38 is equivalent to the binary value 100110: 32 plus 4 plus 2. Each 0 or 1 in this binary value is called a bit.

If a Perl scalar value happens to be an integer, Perl allows you to manipulate the bits that make up that integer. To do this, use the Perl bitwise operators.

The following bitwise operators are supported in Perl:

- The & (bitwise AND) operator
- The ¦ (bitwise OR) operator
- The ^ (bitwise EXOR, or exclusive OR) operator
- The ~ (bitwise NOT) operator
- The << (left-shift) and >> (right-shift) operators

If a scalar value is not an integer, it is converted to an integer before a bitwise operation is performed:

```
$a = 24.5 & 11.2      # identical to $a = 24 & 11
```

Using the Assignment Operators

The most common assignment operator is the = operator, which you've already seen:

```
$a = 9;
```

Here, the value 9 is assigned to the scalar variable $a.

Another common assignment operator is the += operator, which combines the operations of addition and assignment:

```
$a = $a + 1;      # this adds 1 to $a
$a += 1;          # this also adds 1 to $a
```

Other assignment operators exist that correspond to the other arithmetic and bitwise operators:

```
$a -= 1;          # same as $a = $a - 1
$a -2;            # same as $a = $a * 2
$a /= 2;          # same as $a = $a / 2
$a %= 2;          # same as $a = $a % 2
$a **= 2;         # same as $a = $a ** 2
$a &= 2;          # same as $a = $a & 2
$a ¦= 2;          # same as $a = $a ¦ 2
$a ^= 2;          # same as $a = $a ^ 2
```

Using Autoincrement and Autodecrement

Another way to add 1 to a scalar variable is with the ++, or the autoincrement, operator:

```
++$a;                # same as $a += 1 or $a = $a + 1
```

This operator can appear either before or after its operand:

```
$a++;                # also equivalent to $a += 1 and $a = $a + 1
```

As in C++, the ++ operator can also be part of a more complicated sequence of operations. (A code fragment consisting of a sequence of operations and their values is known as an *expression*.) Consider the following statements:

```
$b = ++$a;
$b = $a++;
```

In the first statement, the ++ operator appears before its operand. This tells Perl to add 1 to $a before assigning its value to $b:

```
$a = 7;
$b = ++$a;           # $a and $b are both -8
```

If the ++ operator appears after the operand, Perl adds 1 to $a after assigning its value to $b:

```
$a = 7;
$b = $a++;           # $a is now -8, and $b is now 7
```

Similarly, the --, or autodecrement, operator subtracts 1 from the value of a scalar variable either before or after assigning the value:

```
$a = 7;
$b = --$a;           # $a and $b are both 6
$a -7;
$b = $a--;           # $a is now 6, and $b is now -7
```

The ++ and -- operators provide a great deal of flexibility and are often used in loops and other control structures.

> **CAUTION**
>
> Do not use the ++ and -- operators on the same variable more than once in the same expression because order of evaluation differs from system to system. Instead use multiple statements.

Concatenating and Repeating Strings

Perl provides three operators that operate on strings. The . operator joins the second operand to the first operand:

```
$a = "be" . "witched";        # $a is now "bewitched"
```

This join operation is also known as *string concatenation*. The x operator (the letter x) makes *n* copies of a string, where *n* is the value of the right operand:

```
$a = "t" x 5;                  # $a is now "ttttt"
```

The .= operator combines the operations of string concatenation and assignment:

```
$a = "be";
$a .= "witched";               # $a is now "bewitched"
```

Using Other C Operators

Perl also supports the following operators found in the C programming language: the , (comma) operator, and the ? and : (conditional) operator combination.

The , operator ensures that one portion of an expression is evaluated first:

```
$x += 1, $y = $x;
```

The , operator breaks this expression into two parts:

```
$x += 1
$y = $x
```

The part before the comma is performed first. Thus, 1 is added to $x and then $x is assigned to $y.

The ? and : combination allows you to test the value of a variable and then perform one of two operations based on the result of the test. For example, in the expression $y = $x == 0 ? 15 : 8, the variable $x is compared with 0. If $x equals 0, $y is assigned 15; if $x is not 0, $y is assigned 8.

Matching Patterns

Perl allows you to examine scalar variables and test for the existence of a particular pattern in a string. To do this, use the =~ (pattern-matching) operator:

```
$x =~ /jkl/
```

The character string enclosed by the / characters is the pattern to be matched, and the scalar variable on the left of the =~ operator is the variable to be examined. This example searches for the pattern jkl in the scalar variable $x. If $x contains jkl, the expression is true; if not, the expression is false.

The ! ~ operator is the negation of =~:

```
$y = $x !~ /jkl/;
```

Here, $y is assigned zero if $x contains jkl, and a nonzero value otherwise.

Using Special Characters in Patterns

You can use several special characters in your patterns. The * character matches zero or more of the character it follows:

```
/jk*l/
```

This matches jl, jkl, jkkl, jkkkl, and so on.

The + character matches one or more of the preceding character:

```
/jk+l/
```

This matches jkl, jkkl, jkkkl, and so on.

The ? character matches zero or one copies of the preceding character:

```
/jk?l/
```

This matches jl or jkl.

The { and } characters specify the number of occurrences of a character that constitute a match:

```
/jk{1-3}l/      # matches jkl, jkkl, or jkkkl
/jk{3}l/        # matches jkkkl
/jk{3,}l/       # matches j, three or more k's, then l
/jk{0,2}l/      # matches jl, jkl, or jkkl
```

The character . matches any character except the newline character:

```
/j.l/
```

This matches any pattern consisting of a j, any character, and an l.

If a set of characters is enclosed in square brackets, any character in the set is an acceptable match:

```
/j[kK]l/        # matches jkl or jKl
```

Consecutive alphanumeric characters in the set can be represented by a dash (-):

```
/j[k1-3K]l/     # matches jkl, j1l, j2l, j3l or jKl
```

You can specify that a match must be at the start or end of a line by using ^ or $:

```
/^jkl/          # matches jkl at start of line
/jkl$/          # matches jkl at end of line
/^jkl$/         # matches line consisting of exactly jkl
```

You can specify that a match must be either on a word boundary or inside a word by including \b or \B in the pattern:

```
/\bjkl/          # matches jkl, but not ijkl
/\Bjkl/          # matches ijkl, but not jkl
```

Some sets are so common that special characters exist to represent them:

- \d matches any digit and is equivalent to [0-9].
- \D matches any character that is not a digit.
- \w matches any word character (a character that can appear in a variable name); it is equivalent to [A-Za-z_0-9].
- \W matches any character that is not a word character.
- \s matches any whitespace (any character not visible on the screen); it is equivalent to [\r\t\n\f].
- \S matches any character that is not whitespace.

To match all but a specified set of characters, specify ^ at the start of your set:

```
/j[^kK]l/
```

This matches any string containing j, any character but k or K, and l.

To specify two or more acceptable patterns for a match, use the ¦ character:

```
/jkl¦pqr/        # matches jkl or pqr
```

If you are using Perl 5, you can specify positive or negative look-ahead conditions for a match:

```
/jkl(?=pqr)/     # match jkl only if it is followed by pqr
/jkl(?!pqr)/     # match jkl if not followed by pqr
```

To use a special character as an ordinary character, precede it with a backslash (\):

```
/j\*l/           # this matches j*l
```

This matches j*l.

In patterns, the * and + special characters match as many characters in a string as possible. For example, consider the following:

```
$x = "abcde";
$y = $x =~ /a.*/;
```

The pattern /a.*/ can match a, ab, abc, abcd, or abcde. abcde is matched because it is the longest. This becomes meaningful when patterns are used in substitution.

Substituting and Translating Using Patterns

You can use the =~ operator to substitute one string for another:

```
$val =~ s/abc/def/;        # replace abc with def
$val =~ s/a+/xyz/;         # replace a, aa, aaa, etc., with xyz
$val =~ s/a/b/g;           # replace all a's with b's
```

Here, the s prefix indicates that the pattern between the first / and the second is to be replaced by the string between the second / and the third.

You can also translate characters using the tr prefix:

```
$val =~ tr/a-z/A-Z/;       # translate lower case to upper
```

Here, any character matched by the first pattern is replaced by the corresponding character in the second pattern.

The Order of Operations

Consider the following statement:

```
$a = 21 * 2 + 3 << 1 << 2 ** 2;
```

The problem: Which operation should be performed first?

Table 16.2 defines the order of precedence, highest to lowest, of Perl operators.

TABLE 16.2. OPERATOR PRECEDENCE IN PERL.

Operator	Description
++, —	Autoincrement and autodecrement
-, ~, !	Operators with one operand
**	Exponentiation
=~, !~	Matching operators
*, /, %, x	Multiplication, division, remainder, and repetition
+, -, .	Addition, subtraction, and concatenation
<<, >>	Shifting operators
-e, -r, etc.	File status operators
<, <=, >, >=, lt, le, gt, ge	Inequality comparison operators
==, !=, <=>, eq, ne, cmp	Equality comparison operators
&	Bitwise AND
¦, ^	Bitwise OR and exclusive OR
&&	Logical AND

Operator	Description
||	Logical OR
..	List range operator
? and :	Conditional operator
=, +=, -=, *=, etc.	Assignment operators
,	Comma operator
not	Low-precedence logical NOT
and	Low-precedence logical AND
or, xor	Low-precedence logical OR and XOR

In addition, Perl associates a specified associativity with each operator. If an operator is right-associative, the rightmost operator is performed first when two operators have the same precedence:

```
$x = 2 ** 3 ** 2;    # the same as $x = 2 ** 9, or $x = 512
```

If an operator is left-associative, the leftmost operator is performed first when two operators have the same precedence:

```
$x = 29 % 6 * 2;    # the same as $x = 5 * 2, or $x = 10
```

The following operators in Perl are right-associative:

- The assignment operators (=, +=, and so on)
- The ? and : operator combination
- The ** operator (exponentiation)
- The operators that have only one operand (!, ~, and -)

All other operators are left-associative.

Perl also allows you to force the order of evaluation of operations in expressions. To do this, use parentheses:

```
$x = 4 * (5 + 3);
```

Using Lists and Array Variables

In addition to scalar data and variables, Perl also allows you to manipulate groups of values, known as lists or arrays. These lists can be assigned to special variables known as array variables, which can be processed in a variety of ways.

Introducing Lists

A *list* is a collection of scalar values enclosed in parentheses. The following is a simple example of a list:

```
(1, 5.3, "hello", 2)
```

A list can contain as many elements as you want (or as many as your machine's memory can store at one time). To indicate a list with no elements, just specify the parentheses:

```
()               # this list is empty
```

Lists can also contain scalar variables:

```
(17, $var, "a string")
```

A list element can also be an expression:

```
(17, $var1 + $var2, 26 << 2)
```

Using List Ranges

Perl uses a list range operator, .. (two consecutive periods), to indicate a range of consecutive values. For instance,

```
(1..10)
```

defines a list whose first value is 1, second value is -2, and so on up to 10. Elements that define the range of a list range operator can be expressions, and these expressions can contain scalar variables:

```
($a..$b+5)
```

This list consists of all values between the current value of $a and the current value of the expression $b+5.

Storing Lists in Array Variables

Perl allows you to store lists in array variables. The following is an example of a list being assigned to an array variable:

```
@array = (1, 2, 3);
```

Here, the list (1, 2, 3) is assigned to the array variable @array.

Note that the name of the array variable starts with the character @. This allows Perl to distinguish array variables from other kinds of variables, such as scalar variables, which start with the character $. As with scalar variables, the second character of the variable name must be a letter, and subsequent characters of the name can be letters, numbers, or underscores.

Assigning to Array Variables

As you have seen, lists can be assigned to array variables with the assignment operator =:

```
@x = (11, "my string", 27.44);
```

You can also assign one array variable to another:

```
@y = @x;
```

A scalar value can be assigned to an array variable:

```
@x = 27.1;
@y = $x;
```

In this case, the scalar value (or value stored in a scalar variable) is converted into a list containing one element. Perl also allows you to specify that the value(s) of an array variable are elements in a list:

```
@x = (2, 3, 4);
@y = (1, @x, 5);
```

Here, the list (2, 3, 4) is substituted for @x, and the resulting list (1, 2, 3, 4, 5) is assigned to @y.

Perl also allows you to take the current value of an array variable and assign its components to a group of scalar variables:

```
($a, $b) = @x;
```

Here, the first element of the list currently stored in @x is assigned to $a, and the second element is assigned to $b. Additional elements in @x, if they exist, are not assigned.

```
If there are more scalar variables than elements in an array variable, the
excess scalar variables are given the value "" (the null string), which is
equivalent to the numeric value 0.
```

Retrieving the Length of a List

As you already have seen, when a scalar value is assigned to an array variable, the value is assumed to be a list containing one element. For example, the following statements are equivalent:

```
@x = $y;
@x = ($y);
```

However, the converse is not true. In the statement $y = @x;, the value assigned to $y is the number of elements in the list currently stored in @x:

```
@x = ("string 1", "string -2", "string -3");
$y = @x;              # $y is now 3
```

To assign the value of the first element of a list to a scalar variable, enclose the scalar variable in a list:

```
@x = ("string 1", "string 2", "string 3");
($y) = @x;          # $y is now "string 1"
```

Using Array Slices

Perl allows you to specify what part of an array to use in an expression. The following example shows you how to do this:

```
@x = (1, 2, 3);
@y = @x[0,1];
```

Here, the list (1, 2, 3) is first assigned to the array variable @x. Then the array slice [0,1] is assigned to @y: In other words, the first two elements of @x are assigned to @y. (Note that the first element of the array is specified by 0, not 1.)

You can assign to an array slice as well:

```
@x[0,1] = (11.5, "hello");
```

This statement assigns the value 11.5 to the first element of the array variable @x and assigns the string "hello" to the second.

Array variables automatically grow when necessary, with null strings assigned to fill any gaps:

```
@x = (10, 20, 30);
@x[4, 5] = (75, 85);
```

Here, the second assignment increases the size of the array variable @x from three elements to six, and assigns 75 to the fifth element and 85 to the sixth. The fourth element is set to be the null string.

Using Array Slices with Scalar Variables

An array slice can consist of a single element. In this case, the array slice is treated as if it were a scalar variable:

```
@x = (10, 20, 30);
$y = $x[1];             # $y now has the value 20
```

Note that the array slice is now preceded by the character $, not the character @. This tells Perl that the array slice is to be treated as a scalar variable.

Other Array Operations

Perl provides a number of built-in functions that work on lists and array variables. For example, you can sort array elements in alphabetic order, reverse the elements of an array, remove the last character from all elements of an array, and merge the elements of an array into a single string.

Sorting a List or Array Variable

The built-in function `sort()` sorts the elements of an array in alphabetic order and returns the sorted list:

```
@x = ("this", "is", "a", "test");
@x = sort (@x);          # @x is now ("a", "is", "test", "this")
```

Note that the sort is in alphabetic, not numeric, order:

```
@x = (70, 100, 8);
@x = sort (@x);          # @x is now ("100", "70", "8")
```

The number `100` appears first because the string `"100"` is alphabetically ahead of `"70"` (because `"1"` appears before `"7"`).

Reversing a List or Array Variable

The function `reverse()` reverses the order of the elements in a list or array variable and returns the reversed list:

```
@x = ("backwards", "is", "array", "this");
@x = reverse(@x);        # @x is now ("this", "array", "is", "backwards")
```

You can sort and reverse the same list:

```
@x = reverse(sort(@x));
```

This produces a sort in reverse alphabetical order.

Using `chop()` on Array Variables

The `chop()` function can be used on array variables as well as scalar variables:

```
$a[0] = <STDIN>;
$a[1] = <STDIN>;
$a[2] = <STDIN>;
chop(@a);
```

Here, three input lines are read into the array variable @a—one in each of the first three elements. `chop()` then removes the last character (in this case, the terminating newline character) from all three elements. It's also typically used to remove control characters from keyboard input.

Creating a Single String from a List

To create a single string from a list or array variable, use the function `join()`:

```
@x = ("words","separated","by");
$y = join("::",@x,"colons");
```

Here, $y becomes `"words::separated::by::colons"`.

To undo the effects of `join()`, call the function `split()`:

```
$y = "words::separated::by::colons";
@x = split(/::/, $y);
```

The first element of the list supplied to `split()` is a pattern to be matched. When the pattern is matched, a new array element is started, and the pattern is thrown away. @x becomes (`"words"`, `"separated"`, `"by"`, `"colons"`).

Using Command-Line Arguments

The special array variable @ARGV is automatically defined to contain the strings entered on the command line when a Perl program is invoked. For example, if the program

```
#!/usr/bin/perl
print("The first argument is $ARGV[0]\n");
```

is called `printfirstarg`, entering the command

```
printfirstarg 1 2 3
```

produces the following output:

```
The first argument is 1
```

You can use `join()` to turn @ARGV into a single string:

```
#!/usr/bin/perl
$commandline = join(" ", @ARGV);
print("The command line arguments: $commandline\n");
```

If this program is called `printallargs`, entering

```
printallargs 1 2 3
```

produces

```
The command line arguments: 1 2 3
```

Note that `$ARGV[0]`, the first element of the @ARGV array variable, does not contain the name of the program. For example, in the invocation

```
printallargs 1 2 3
```

`$ARGV[0]` is `"1"`, not `"printallargs"`. This is a difference between Perl and C. In C, `argv[0]` is `"printallargs"`, and `argv[1]` is `"1"`.

Standard Input and Array Variables

Because an array variable can contain as many elements as you want, you can assign an entire input file to a single array variable:

```
@infile = <STDIN>;
```

This works as long as you have enough memory to store the entire file.

Controlling Program Flow

Like all programming languages, Perl allows you to include statements that are executed only when specified conditions are true. Perl provides a full range of conditional statements; these statements are described in the following sections.

Conditional Execution: The `if` Statement

The `if` conditional statement has the following structure:

```
if (expr) {
        ...
}
```

Note that Perl's `if` construct does not use the keyword `then`.

When Perl sees the `if`, it evaluates the expression `expr` to be either true or false. If the value of the expression is the integer `0`, the null string `""`, or the string `"0"`, the value of the expression is false; otherwise, the value of the expression is true.

CAUTION

The only string values that evaluate to false are `""` and `"0"`. Strings such as `"00"` and `"0.0"` return true, not false.

Two-Way Branching Using `if` and `else`

The `else` statement can be combined with the `if` statement to allow for a choice between two alternatives:

```
if ($x == 14) {
        print("\$x is 14\n");
} else {
        print("\$x is not 14\n");
}
```

Here, the expression following the `if` is evaluated. If it is true, the statements between `if` and `else` are executed. Otherwise, the statements between `else` and the final } are executed. In either case, execution then proceeds to the statement after the final }.

MultiWay Branching Using `elsif`

The `elsif` statement allows you to write a program that chooses between more than two alternatives:

```
if ($x == 14) {
        print("\$x is 14\n");
} elsif ($x -15) {
        print("\$x is 15\n");
} elsif ($x -16) {
        print("\$x is 16\n");
} else {
        print("\$x is not 14, 15 or 16\n");
}
```

The `else` statement can be omitted:

```
if ($x == 14) {
        print("\$x is 14\n");
} elsif ($x -15) {
        print("\$x is 15\n");
} elsif ($x -16) {
        print("\$x is 16\n");
} # do nothing if $x is not 14, 15 or 16
```

Conditional Branching Using `unless`

The `unless` statement is the opposite of the `if` statement:

```
unless ($x == 14) {
        print("\$x is not 14\n");
}
```

Repeating Statements Using while and until

In the previous examples, each statement between braces is executed once, at most. To indicate that a group of statements between braces is to be executed until a certain condition changes, use the while statement:

```
#!/usr/bin/perl
$x = 1;
while ($x <= 5) {
        print("\$x is now $x\n");
        ++$x;
}
```

Here, the scalar variable $x is first assigned the value 1. The statements between the braces are then executed until the expression $x <= 5 is false.

When you run the preceding program , you get the following output:

```
$x is now 1
$x is now 2
$x is now 3
$x is now 4
$x is now 5
```

The until statement is the opposite of while:

```
#!/usr/bin/perl
$x = 1;
until ($x > 5) {
        print("\$x is now $x\n");
        ++$x;
}
```

This now produces the same output as the program containing the preceding while statement.

CAUTION

If you use while, until, or any other statement that repeats, you must make sure that the statement does not repeat forever.

Using Single-Line Conditional Statements

If only one statement is to be executed when a particular condition is true, you can write your conditional statement using a single-line conditional statement:

```
print("\$x is 14\n") if ($x == 14);

print("\$x is not 14\n") unless ($x == 14);
print("\$x is less than 14\n") while ($x++ < 14);
print("\$x is less than 14\n") until ($x++ > 14);
```

Note how useful the autoincrement operator ++ is in the last two statements: It allows you to compare $x and add 1 to it all at once. This ensures that the single-line conditional statement does not execute forever.

Looping with the for Statement

Most loops—segments of code that are executed more than once—use a counter to control and eventually terminate the execution of the loop. Here is an example similar to the ones you've seen so far:

```
$count = 1;                # initialize the counter
while ($count <= 10) {     # terminate after ten repetitions
        print("the counter is now $count\n");
        $count += 1;       # increment the counter
}
```

As you can see, the looping process consists of three components:

- The initialization of the counter variable

- A test to determine whether to terminate the loop

- The updating of the counter variable after the execution of the statements in the loop

Because a loop so often contains these three components, Perl provides a quick way to do them all at once by using the for statement. The following example uses the for statement and behaves the same as the example you just saw:

```
for ($count = 1; $count <= 10; $count += 1) {
        print("the counter is now $count\n");
}
```

Here, the three components of the loop all appear in the same line, separated by semicolons. Because the components are all together, it is easier to remember to supply all of them, which makes it more difficult to write code that goes into an infinite loop.

Looping Through a List—The foreach Statement

All the examples of loops that you've seen use a scalar variable as the counter. You can also use a list as a counter by using the foreach statement:

```
#!/usr/bin/perl
@list = ("This", "is", "a", "list", "of", "words");
print("Here are the words in the list: \n");
foreach $temp (@list) {
        print("$temp ");
}
print("\n");
```

Here, the loop defined by the foreach statement executes once for each element in the list @list. The resulting output is

```
Here are the words in the list:
        This is a list of words
```

When using the foreach statement, you must specify a local scalar variable used to hold the current element of the list. This variable is not known outside the foreach loop.

```
#!/usr/bin/perl
$temp = 1;
@list = ("This", "is", "a", "list", "of", "words");
print("Here are the words in the list: \n");
foreach $temp (@list) {
        print("$temp ");
}
print("\n");
print("The value of temp is now $temp\n");
```

The output from this program is the following:

```
Here are the words in the list:
        This is a list of words
The value of temp is now 1
```

Exiting a Loop with the last Statement

Normally, you exit a loop by testing the condition at the top of the loop and then jumping to the statement after it. However, you can also exit a loop in the middle. To do this, use the last statement.

Using next to Start the Next Iteration of a Loop

In Perl, the last statement terminates the execution of a loop. To terminate a particular pass through a loop (also known as an iteration of the loop), use the next statement.

Using Labeled Blocks for Multilevel Jumps

In Perl, loops can be inside other loops; such loops are said to be *nested*. To get out of an outer loop from within an inner loop, label the outer loop and specify its label when using last or next:

```
$total = 0;
$firstcounter = 1;
DONE: while ($firstcounter <= 10) {
        $secondcounter = 1;
        while ($secondcounter <= 10) {
                $total += 1;
                if ($firstcounter == 4 && $secondcounter == 7) {
                        last DONE;
                }
                $secondcounter += 1;
        }
        $firstcounter += 1;
}
```

The statement

```
last DONE;
```

tells Perl to jump out of the loop labeled DONE and continue execution with the first statement after the outer loop. Loop labels must start with a letter and can consist of as many letters, digits, and underscores as you want, and must not use one of the reserved words that have a defined meaning in Perl.

Terminating Execution Using `die`

As you have seen, the `last` statement terminates a loop. To terminate program execution entirely, use the `die()` function.

Reading from and Writing to Files

To access a file other than STDIN or STDERR, your program must open the file, read from or write to it, and (optionally) close the file. The following sections describe these operations, tell you how you can read from files specified in the command line, and describe the built-in file test operations.

Opening a File

To open a file, call the built-in function `open()`:

```
open(MYFILE, "/u/jqpublic/myfile");
```

The second argument is the name of the file you want to open. You can supply either the full UNIX pathname, as in `/u/jqpublic/myfile`, or just the filename, as in `myfile`. If only the filename is supplied, the file is assumed to be in the current working directory.

The first argument is an example of a file handle. After the file has been opened, your Perl program accesses the file by referring to this handle. Your file handle name must start with a letter or underscore and can then contain as many letters, underscores, and digits as you want.

By default, Perl assumes that you want to read any file that you open. To open a file for writing, put a > (greater than) character in front of your filename:

```
open(MYFILE, ">/u/jqpublic/myfile");
```

When you open a file for writing, any existing contents are destroyed. You cannot read from and write to the same file at the same time.

To append to an existing file, put two > characters in front of the filename:

```
open(MYFILE, ">>/u/jqpublic/myfile");
```

Checking Whether the Open Succeeded

The open() function returns one of two values:

- open() returns true (a nonzero value) if the open succeeds.
- open() returns false (zero) if an error occurs (that is, the file does not exist or you don't have permission to access the file).

You can use the return value from open() to test whether the file is actually available and call die() if it is not:

```
unless (open(MYFILE, "/u/jqpublic/myfile")) {
        die("unable to open /u/jqpublic/myfile for reading\n");
}
```

This ensures that your program does not try to read from a nonexistent file.

You can also use the ¦¦ (logical OR) operator in place of unless:

```
open(MYFILE, "/u/jqpublic/myfile") ¦¦
        die("unable to open /u/jqpublic/myfile for reading\n");
```

Reading from a File

To read from a file, enclose the name of the file in angle brackets:

```
$line = <MYFILE>;
```

This statement reads a line of input from the file specified by the file handle MYFILE and stores the line of input in the scalar variable $line. As you can see, you read from files in exactly the same way you read from the standard input file, STDIN.

Writing to a File

To write to a file, specify the file handle when you call the function `print()`:

```
print MYFILE ("This is a line of text to write \n",
        "This is another line to write\n");
```

The file handle must appear before the first line of text to be written to the file. This method works both when you are writing a new file and when you are appending to an existing one.

Closing a File

When you are finished reading from or writing to a file, you can tell the system that you are finished by calling `close()`:

```
close(MYFILE);
```

Note that `close()` is not required: Perl automatically closes the file when the program terminates or when you open another file using a previously defined file handle.

Determining the Status of a File

If you want to open the file for writing if the file does not already exist, use the `-e` operator to test whether it exists:

```
if (-e "/u/jqpublic/filename") {
        die ("file /u/jqpublic/filename already exists");
}
open (MYFILE, "/u/jqpublic/filename");
```

Similar tests exist to test other file conditions. The most commonly used file status operators are listed in Table 16.3.

TABLE 16.3. FILE STATUS OPERATORS.

Operator	*File condition*
-d	Is this file really a directory?
-e	Does this file exist?
-f	Is this actually a file?
-l	Is this file really a symbolic link?
-o	Is this file owned by the person running the program?
-r	Is this file readable by the person running the program?
-s	Is this a nonempty file?

-w	Is this file writable by the person running the program?
-x	Is this file executable by the person running the program?
-z	Is this file empty?
-B	Is this a binary file?
-T	Is this a text file?

Reading from a Sequence of Files

Many UNIX commands have the form

```
command file1 file2 file3 ...
```

These commands operate on all the files specified on the command line, starting with file1 and continuing from there. You can simulate this behavior in Perl. To do this, use the <> operator.

Using Subroutines

Perl supports the definition of subroutines, or sections of logic that can be called repeatedly within your program using different values each time. The following sections describe how subroutines work, how to pass values to subroutines and receive values from them, and how to define variables that only exist inside subroutines.

Defining a Subroutine

A common Perl task is to read a line of input from a file and break it into words. Here is an example of a subroutine that performs this task:

```
sub getwords {
        $inputline = <>;
        @words = split(/\s+/, $inputline);
}
```

All subroutines follow this simple format: the reserved word sub, the name of the subroutine (in this case, getwords), a { (open brace) character, one or more Perl statements (also known as the body of the subroutine), and a closing } (close brace) character.

The subroutine name must start with a letter or underscore and can then consist of any number of letters, digits, and underscores. A subroutine can appear anywhere in a Perl program—even right in the middle, if you want. However, programs are usually easier to understand if the subroutines are all placed at the end.

Using a Subroutine

After you have written your subroutine, you can use it by specifying its name. Here is a simple example that uses the subroutine getwords to count the number of occurrences of the word "the":

```perl
#!/usr/bin/perl
$thecount = 0;
&getwords;
while ($words[0] ne "") {   # stop when line is empty
        for ($index = 0; $words[$index] ne ""; $index += 1) {
                $thecount += 1 if $words[$index] eq "the";
        }
        &getwords;
}
print ("Total number of occurrences of the: $thecount\n");
```

The statement &getwords; tells Perl to call the subroutine getwords. When Perl calls the subroutine getwords, it executes the statements contained in the subroutine, namely

```perl
$inputline = <>;
@words = split(/\s+/, $inputline);
```

After these statements have been executed, Perl executes the statement immediately following the &getwords statement. In Perl 5, if the call to a subroutine appears after its definition, the & character can be omitted from the call.

Returning a Value from a Subroutine

In Perl, the last value seen by the subroutine becomes the subroutine's return value. It is good programming practice to explicitly write your code to make this value useful to the wider program. For instance:

```perl
sub get_total {
        $value = 0;
        $inputline = <STDIN>;
        @subwords = split(/\s+/, $inputline);
        $index = 0;
        while ($subwords[$index] ne "") {
                $value += $subwords[$index++];
        }
        $value;   # $value is now the return value
}
```

Using Local Variables

You can ensure that the variables used in a subroutine are known only inside that subroutine by defining them as local variables. Here is the subroutine getwords with $inputline and @subwords defined as local variables:

```
sub getwords {
        local($inputline, @subwords);
        $inputline = <>;
        @subwords = split(/s+/, $inputline);
}
```

The local() statement tells Perl that versions of the variables $inputline and @sub-words are to be defined for use inside the subroutine. After a variable has been defined with local(), it cannot accidentally destroy values in your program:

```
@subwords = ("Some", "more", "words");
@words = &getwords;
```

Here, @subwords is not destroyed because the @subwords used in getwords is known only inside the subroutine.

Note that variables defined using local() can be used in any subroutines called by this subroutine. If you are using Perl 5, you can use the my() statement to define variables that are known only to the subroutine in which they are defined:

```
my($inputline, @subwords);
```

The syntax for the my() statement is the same as that of the local() statement.

Passing Values to a Subroutine

You can make your subroutines more flexible by allowing them to accept values.

As an example, here is the getwords subroutine modified to split the input line using a pattern that is passed to it:

```
sub getwords {
        local($pattern) = @_;
        local($inputline, @subwords);
        $inputline = <>;
        @subwords = split($pattern, $inputline);
}
```

The array variable @_ is a special system variable that contains a copy of the values passed to the subroutine. The statement local($pattern) = @_; creates a local scalar variable named $pattern and assigns the first value of the array, @_, to it.

Now, to call getwords, you must supply the pattern you want it to use when splitting words. To split on whitespace, as before, call getwords as follows:

```
@words = getwords(/\s+/);
```

If your input line consists of words separated by colons, you can split it using getwords by calling it as follows:

```
@words = getwords(/:/);
```

If you want, you can break your line into single characters:

```
@words = getwords(//);
```

For more information on patterns you can use, see the section titled "Matching Patterns."

The array variable @_ behaves like any other array variable. In particular, its components can be used as scalar values:

```
$x = $_[0];
```

Here, the first element of @_—the first value passed to the subroutine—is assigned to $x.

Usually, assigning @_ to local variables is the best approach because your subroutine becomes easier to understand.

Calling Subroutines from Other Subroutines

You can have a subroutine call another subroutine you have written. For example, here is a subroutine that counts the number of words in an input line:

```
sub countline {
        local(@words, $count);
        $count = 0;
        @words = getwords(/\s+/);
        foreach $word (@words) {
                $count += 1;
        }
        $count;        # make sure the count is the return value
}
```

The subroutine `countline` first calls the subroutine `getwords` to split the input line into words. Then it counts the number of words in the array returned by `getwords` and returns that value.

After you have written `countline`, it is easy to write a program called `wordcount` that counts the number of words in one or more files:

```
#!/usr/bin/perl
$totalwordcount = 0;
while (($wordcount = &countline) != 0) {
        $totalwordcount += $wordcount;
}
print("The total word count is $totalwordcount\n");
# include the subroutines getwords and countline here
```

This program reads lines until an empty line—a line with zero words—is read in. (The program assumes that the files contain no blank lines. You can get around this problem by having getwords test whether $inputline is empty before breaking it into words, returning a special "end of file" value in this case. This value could then be passed from getwords to countline, and then to the main program.)

Because getwords uses the <> operator to read input, the files whose words are counted are those listed on the command line:

```
wordcount file1 file2 file3
```

This counts the words in the files file1, file2, and file3.

The variable @_ is a local variable whose value is defined only in the subroutine in which it appears. This allows subroutines to pass values to other subroutines: Each subroutine has its own copy of @_, and none of the copies can destroy each other's values.

The BEGIN, END, and AUTOLOAD Subroutines

Perl 5 enables you to define special subroutines to be called at certain times during program execution. The BEGIN subroutine, if defined, is called when program execution begins:

```
BEGIN {
        print ("This is the start of the program.\n");
}
```

The END subroutine, if defined, is called when program execution terminates:

```
END {
        print ("This is the last sentence you will read.\n");
}
```

The AUTOLOAD statement is called when your program tries to call a subroutine that does not exist:

```
AUTOLOAD {
        print ("subroutine $AUTOLOAD not found.\n");
        print ("arguments passed: @_\n");
}
```

Associative Arrays

A common programming task is to keep several lists whose values are associated with one another. Perl provides an associative array data type for this purpose.

Defining Associative Arrays

In ordinary arrays, you access an array element by specifying an integer as the index:

```
@fruits = (9, 23, 11);
$count = $fruits[0];   # $count is now 9
```

In associative arrays, you do not have to use numbers such as 0, 1, and 2 to access array elements. When you define an associative array, you specify the scalar values you want to use to access the elements of the array. For example, here is a definition of a simple associative array:

```
%fruits = ("apple", 9,
           "banana", 23,
           "cherry", 11);
$count = $fruits{"apple"};  # $count is now 9
```

Here, the scalar value "apple" accesses the first element of the array %fruits, "banana" accesses the second element, and "cherry" accesses the third.

Associative arrays eliminate the need for messy if-elsif structures. To add 1 to an element of the %fruits array, for example, you just need to do the following:

```
$fruits{$fruit} += 1;
```

Better still, if you decide to add other fruits to the list, you do not need to add more code because the preceding statement also works on the new elements.

The character % tells Perl that a variable is an associative array. As with scalar variables and array variables, the remaining characters of the associative array variable name must consist of a letter followed by one or more letters, digits, or underscores.

Accessing Associative Arrays

Because an associative array value is a scalar value, it can be used wherever a scalar value can be used:

```
$redfruits = $fruits{"apple"} + $fruits{"cherry"};
print("yes, we have no bananas\n") if ($fruits{"banana"} == 0);
```

Note that Perl uses braces (the { and } characters) to enclose the index of an associative array element. This makes it possible for Perl to distinguish between ordinary array elements and associative array elements.

Copying to and from Associative Arrays

Consider the following assignment, which initializes an associative array:

```
%fruits = ("apple", 9,
           "banana", 23,
           "cherry", 11);
```

The value on the right of this assignment is actually just the ordinary list, ("apple", 9, "banana", 23, "cherry", 11), grouped into pairs for readability. You can assign any list, including the contents of an array variable, to an associative array:

```
@numlist[0,1] = ("one", 1);
@numlist, 2-3] = ("two", 2);
%numbers = @numlist;
$first = $numbers{"one"}; # $first is now 1
```

Whenever a list or an array variable is assigned to an associative array, the odd-numbered elements (the first, third, fifth, and so on) become the array indexes, and the even-numbered elements (the second, fourth, sixth, and so on) become the array values. Perl 5 allows you to use => to separate array elements to make this assignment easier to see:

```
%fruits = ("apple" => 9,
           "banana" => 23,
           "cherry" => 11);
```

In associative array assignments, => and , are equivalent.

You can also assign an associative array to an array variable:

```
%numbers = ("one", 1,
            "two, 2);
@numlist = %numbers;
$first = $numlist, 3];          # first is now 2
```

Here, the array indexes and array values both become elements of the array.

Adding and Deleting Array Elements

To add a new element to an associative array, just create a new array index and assign a value to its element. For example, to create a fourth element for the %fruits array, type the following:

```
$fruits{"orange"} = 1;
```

This statement creates a fourth element with index "orange" and gives it the value 1.

To delete an element, use the delete() function:

```
delete($fruits{"orange"});
```

This deletes the element indexed by "orange" from the array %fruits.

Listing Array Indexes and Values

The keys() function retrieves a list of the array indexes used in an associative array:

```
%fruits = ("apple", 9,
           "banana", 23,
           "cherry", 11);
@fruitindexes = keys(%fruits);
```

Here, @fruitindexes is assigned the list consisting of the elements "apple", "banana", and "cherry". Note that this list is in no particular order. To retrieve the list in alphabetic order, use sort() on the list:

```
@fruitindexes = sort(keys(%fruits));
```

This produces the list ("apple", "banana", "cherry").

To retrieve a list of the values stored in an associative array, use the function values():

```
%fruits = ("apple", 9,
           "banana", 23,
           "cherry", 11);
@fruitvalues = values(%fruits);
```

@fruitvalues now contains a list consisting of the elements 9, 23, and 11 (again, in no particular order).

Looping with an Associative Array

Perl provides a convenient way to use an associative array in a loop:

```
%fruits = ("apple", 9,
           "banana", 23,
           "cherry", 11);
while (($fruitname, $fruitvalue) == each(%fruitnames) {
    ...
}
```

The each() function returns each element of the array in turn. Each element is returned as a two-element list (array index and then array value). Again, the elements are returned in no particular order.

Formatting Your Output

So far, the only output produced has been raw, unformatted output produced using the print() function. However, you can control how your output appears on the screen or on the printed page. To do this, define print formats and use the write() function to print output using these formats.

The following sections describe print formats and how to use them.

Defining a Print Format

Here is an example of a simple print format:

```
format MYFORMAT =
====================================
```

```
Here is the text I want to display.
====================================
.
```

Here, `MYFORMAT` is the name of the print format. This name must start with a letter and can consist of any sequence of letters, digits, or underscores.

The subsequent lines define what is to appear on the screen. Here, the lines to be displayed are a line of = characters followed by a line of text and ending with another line of = characters. A line consisting of a period indicates the end of the print format definition.

Like subroutines, print formats can appear anywhere in a Perl program.

Displaying a Print Format

To print using a print format, use the `write()` function. For example, to print the text in `MYFORMAT`, use

```
$~ = "MYFORMAT";
write();
```

This sends

```
====================================
Here is the text I want to display.
====================================
```

to the standard output file.

`$~` is a special scalar variable used by Perl; it tells Perl which print format to use.

Displaying Values in a Print Format

To specify a value to be printed in your print format, add a value field to your print format. Here is an example of a print format that uses value fields:

```
format VOWELFORMAT =
============================================================
Number of vowels found in text file:
        a: @<<<<< e: @<<<<< i: @<<<<< o: @<<<<< u: @<<<<<
$letter{"a"}, $letter{"e"}, $letter{"i"}, $letter{"o"}, $letter{"u"}
============================================================
.
```

The line

```
a: @<<<<< e: @<<<<< i: @<<<<< o: @<<<<< u: @<<<<<
```

contains five value fields. Each value field contains special characters that provide information on how the value is to be displayed. Any line that contains value fields must be followed by a line listing the scalar values (or variables containing scalar values) to be displayed in these value fields:

```
$letter{"a"}, $letter{"e"}, $letter{"i"}, $letter{"o"}, $letter{"u"}
```

The number of value fields must equal the number of scalar values. The following value field formats are supported:

@<<<<	Left-justified output: width equals the number of characters supplied.
@>>>>	Right-justified output: width equals the number of characters supplied.
@||||	Centered output: width equals the number of characters supplied.
@##.##	Fixed-precision numeric: . indicates location of decimal point.
@*	Multiline text.

In all cases, the @ character is included when the number of characters in the field is counted. For example, the field @>>>> is five characters wide. Similarly, the field @###.## is seven characters wide: four before the decimal point, two after the decimal point, and the decimal point itself.

Writing to Other Output Files

You can also write to other files by using print formats and write(). For example, to write to the file represented by file variable MYFILE using print format MYFORMAT, use the following statements:

```
select(MYFILE);
$~ = "MYFORMAT";
write(MYFILE);
```

The select() statement indicates which file is to be written to, and the $~ = "MYFOR-MAT"; statement selects the print format to use.

After an output file has been selected using select(), it stays selected until another select() is seen. This means that if you select an output file other than the standard output file, as in select(MYFILE);, output from write() won't go to the standard output file until Perl sees the statement select (MYFILE);.

There are two ways of making sure that you don't get tripped up by this:

- Always use STDOUT as the default output file. If you change the output file, change it back when you're done:
  ```
  select(MYFILE);
  $~ = "MYFORMAT";
  ```

```
write(MYFILE);
select(STDOUT);
```

- Always specify the output file with `select()` before calling `write()`:

```
select(STDOUT);
$~ = "MYFORMAT";
write(); # STDOUT is assumed
It doesn't really matter which solution you use, as long as you're
consistent.
```

If you are writing a subroutine that writes to a particular output file, you can save the current selected output file in a temporary variable and restore it later:

```
$temp = select(MYFILE);# select the output file
$~ = "MYFORMAT";
write(MYFILE);
select($temp); # restore the original selected output file
```

This method is also useful if you're in the middle of a large program and you don't remember which output file is currently selected.

Specifying a Page Header

You can specify a header to print when you start a new page. To do this, define a print format with the name *filename*_TOP, where *filename* is the name of the file variable corresponding to the file you are writing to. For example, to define a header for writing to standard output, define a print format named STDOUT_TOP:

```
format STDOUT_TOP =
page @<
$%
```

The system variable $% contains the current page number (starting with 1).

Setting the Page Length

If a page header is defined for a particular output file, `write()` automatically paginates the output to that file. When the number of lines printed is greater than the length of a page, it starts a new page.

By default, the page length is 60 lines. To specify a different page length, change the value stored in the system variable $=:

```
$= = 66;     # set the page length to 66 lines
```

This assignment must appear before the first `write()` statement.

Formatting Long Character Strings

A scalar variable containing a long character string can be printed out using multiple value fields:

```
format QUOTATION =
Quotation for the day:
----------------------------
^<<<<<<<<<<<<<<<<<<<<<<<<<<<<<<<<<<<<<<<<<<<<<<<
    $quotation
^<<<<<<<<<<<<<<<<<<<<<<<<<<<<<<<<<<<<<<<<<<<<<<<
    $quotation
^<<<<<<<<<<<<<<<<<<<<<<<<<<<<<<<<<<<<<<<<<<<<<<
    $quotation
.
```

Here, the value of `$quotation` is written on three lines. The @ character in the value fields is replaced by ^; this tells Perl to fill the lines as full as possible (cutting the string on a space or tab). Any of the value fields defined earlier can be used.

> **CAUTION**
>
> The contents of the scalar variable are destroyed by this write operation. To preserve the contents, make a copy before calling `write()`.

If the quotation is too short to require all the lines, the last line or lines are left blank. To define a line that is used only when necessary, put a ~ character in the first column:

```
~    ^<<<<<<<<<<<<<<<<<<<<<<<<<<<<<<<<<<<<<<<<<<<<<<<
```

To repeat a line as many times as necessary, put two ~ characters at the front:

```
~~   ^<<<<<<<<<<<<<<<<<<<<<<<<<<<<<<<<<<<<<<<<<<<<<
```

References

Perl 5 supports references, which are constructs that allow you to access data indirectly. These constructs enable you to build complex data structures, including multidimensional arrays.

The following sections describe how to use references.

> **CAUTION**
>
> If you are using Perl 4, you will not be able to use pointers and references because they were added to version 5 of the language.

Understanding References

The scalar variables you have seen so far contain a single integer or string value, such as 43 or hello. A *reference* is a scalar variable whose value is the location, or address, of another Perl variable.

The easiest way to show how references work is using an example:

```
$myvar = 42;
$myreference = \$myvar;
print ("$$myreference");     # this prints 42
```

This code example contains three statements. The first statement just assigns 42 to the scalar variable $myvar. In the second statement, \$myvar means "the address of $myvar," which means that the statement assigns the address of $myvar to the scalar variable $myreference. $myreference is now a reference, also sometimes called a *pointer*.

The third statement shows how to use a reference after you have created one. Here, $$myreference means "the variable whose address is contained in $myreference." Because the address of $myvar is contained in $myreference, $$myreference is equivalent to $myvar. This means that the print statement prints the value of $myvar, which is 42.

The $$ in this statement is called a dereference, and it can basically be thought of as the opposite of \.

References and Arrays

A reference can also store the address of an array. For example, the statement

```
$arrayref = \@myarray;
```

assigns the address of @myarray to $arrayref. Given this reference, the following statements both assign the second element of @myarray to the variable $second:

```
$second = $myarray[1];
$second = $$arrayref[1];
```

As before, $$arrayref refers to the variable whose address is stored in $arrayref, which in this case is @myarray.

The address of an associative array can be stored in a reference as well:

```
%fruits = ("apple", 9,
           "banana", 23,
           "cherry", 11);
$fruitref = \%fruits;
$bananaval = $$fruitref{"banana"};       # this is 23
```

Here, $$fruitref{"banana"} is equivalent to $fruits{"banana"}, which is 23.

Another way to access an element of an array whose address is stored in a reference is to use the -> (dereference) operator. The following pairs of statements are equivalent in Perl:

```
$second = $$arrayref[1];
$second = $arrayref->[1];

$bananaval = $$fruitref{"banana"};
$bananaval = $fruitref->{"banana"};
```

The -> operator is useful when creating multidimensional arrays, described in the following subsection.

Multidimensional Arrays

You can use references to construct multidimensional arrays. The following statements create a multidimensional array and access it:

```
$arrayptr = ["abc", "def", [1, 2, 3], [4, 5, 6]];
$def = $arrayptr->[1];        # assigns "def" to $def
$two = $arrayptr->[2][1];     # assigns 2 to $two
```

The first statement creates a four-element array and assigns its address to $arrayptr. The third and fourth elements of this array are themselves arrays, each containing three elements.

$arrayptr->[1] refers to the second element of the array whose address is stored in $arrayptr. This element is "def". Similarly, $arrayptr, [2] refers to the third element of the array, which is [1, 2, 3]. The [1] in $arrayptr, [2][1] specifies the second element of [1, 2, 3], which is 2.

You can access associative arrays in this way as well.

References to Subroutines

You can use references to indirectly access subroutines. For example, the following code creates a reference to a subroutine and then calls it:

```
$subreference = sub {
        print ("hello, world");
};

&$subreference();        # this prints "hello, world"
```

Here, `&$subreference()` calls the subroutine whose address is stored in `$subreference`. This subroutine call is treated like any other subroutine call: The subroutine can be passed parameters and can return a value.

References to File Handles

You can use a reference to indirectly refer to a file handle. For example, the following statement writes a line of output to the standard output file:

```
$stdout = \*STDOUT;
print $stdout ("hello, world\n");
```

This makes it possible to, for example, create subroutines that write to a file whose handle is passed as a parameter.

> **CAUTION**
>
> Don't forget to include the * after the \ when creating a reference to a file handle. (The * refers to the internal symbol table in which the file handle is stored.)
>
> You do not need to supply a * when creating a reference to a scalar variable, an array, or a subroutine.

Object-Oriented Programming

Perl 5 provides the capability to write programs in an object-oriented fashion. You can do this by creating packages containing code that performs designated tasks. These packages can contain private variables and subroutines that are not accessible from the other parts of your program.

The following sections describe packages and how they can be used to create classes and objects. These sections also describe how to use packages to create exportable program modules.

> **CAUTION**
>
> If you are using Perl 4, you will not be able to use many of the features described here because they were added to version 5 of the language.

Packages

In Perl, a *package* is basically just a separate collection of variables and subroutines contained in its own name space. To create a package or switch from one existing package to another, use the `package` statement:

```
package pack1;
$myvar = 26;
package pack2;
$myvar = 34;
package pack1;
print ("$myvar\n"); # this prints 26
```

This code creates two packages, pack1 and pack2, and then switches from pack2 back to pack1. Each package contains its own version of the variable $myvar: In package pack1, $myvar is assigned 26, and in package pack2, $myvar is assigned 34. Because the print statement is inside pack1, it prints 26, which is the value of the pack1 $myvar variable.

Subroutines can also be defined inside packages. For example, the following creates a subroutine named mysub inside a package named pack1:

```
package pack1;
subroutine mysub {
        print ("hello, world!\n");
}
```

To access a variable or subroutine belonging to one package from inside another package, specify the package name and two colons:

```
package pack1;
print ("$pack2::myvar\n");
```

This print statement prints the value of the version of $myvar belonging to package pack2, even though the current package is pack1.

If no package is specified, by default all variables and subroutines are added to a package named main. This means that the following statements are equivalent:

```
$newvar = 14;
$main::newvar = 14;
```

To switch back to using the default package, just add the line

```
package main;
```

to your program at the point at which you want to switch.

Creating a Module

You can put a package you create into its own file, called a *module*. This makes it possible to use the same package in multiple programs.

The following file, named `Hello.pm`, creates a module containing a subroutine that prints hello, world!:

```
package Hello;
require Exporter;
@ISA = "Exporter";
@EXPORT = ("helloworld");
sub helloworld {
        print ("hello, world!\n");
}
1;
```

The first statement defines the package named `Hello`. The

```
require Exporter;
```

statement includes a predefined Perl module called `Exporter.pm`; this module handles the details of module creation for you. The statement

```
@ISA = "Exporter";
```

sets the `@ISA` array, which is a predefined array that specifies a list of packages to look for subroutines in. The statement

```
@EXPORT = ("helloworld");
```

indicates that the `helloworld` subroutine is to be made accessible to other Perl programs. If you add other subroutines to your module, add their names to the list being assigned to `@EXPORT`.

Note the closing `1;` statement in the package. This ensures that your package is processed properly when it is included by other programs. Also note that your package file should have the suffix `.pm`.

After you have created `Hello.pm`, you can include it in other programs. The following program uses the `use` statement to include `Hello.pm` and then calls the subroutine contained in the `Hello` package:

```
#!/usr/bin/perl
use Hello;
&Hello::helloworld();
```

> **TIP**
>
> Perl 5 users all over the world write useful modules that are made available to the Perl user community via the Internet. The CPAN network of archives provides a complete list of these modules. For more information, access the Web site located at http://www.perl.com/perl/CPAN/README.html.

Creating a Class and Its Objects

One of the fundamental concepts of object-oriented programming is the concept of a class, which is a template consisting of a collection of data items and subroutines. After a class is created, you can define variables that refer to this class; these variables are called *objects* (or instances of the class).

In Perl, a *class* is basically just a package containing a special initialization function, called a *constructor*, which is called each time an object is created. The following code is an example of a simple class:

```
package MyClass;

sub new {
        my ($myref) = [];
        bless ($myref);
        return ($myref);
}
```

The subroutine named new is the constructor for the class MyClass. (Perl assumes that all constructors are named new.) This subroutine defines a local variable named $myref, which, in this case, is a reference to an empty array. (You can also refer to a scalar variable or associative array if you want.)

The bless function, called within the subroutine, indicates that the item being referenced by $myref is to be treated as part of the MyClass package. The reference is then returned.

After you have created a class, it's easy to create an object of this class:

```
$myobject = new MyClass;
```

Here, new MyClass calls the subroutine new defined inside the MyClass package. This subroutine creates a reference to an array of class MyClass, which is then assigned to $myobject.

Methods

Most classes have methods defined for them. Methods manipulate an object of the class for which they are defined.

In Perl, a *method* is just an ordinary subroutine whose first parameter is the object being manipulated. For example, the following method assumes that its object is an array and prints one element of the array:

```
package MyPackage;
sub printElement {
        my ($object) = shift(@_);
        my ($index) = @_;

        print ("$object->[$index]\n");
}
```

The first parameter passed to `printElement` is the object to be manipulated. (The `shift()` function removes the first element from an array. Recall that the `@_` array contains the values passed to the subroutine.) The second parameter specifies the index of the element to be printed.

The following code shows two ways to call this method after it has been created:

```
$myobject = new MyPackage;
MyPackage::printElement($myobject, 2);    # print the third element
$myobject->printElement(2);               # this is identical to the above
```

The second way of calling this method more closely resembles the syntax used in other object-oriented programming languages.

Overrides

As you have seen, when an object is created, it is assumed to be of a particular class. To use a method from another class on this object, specify the class when calling the method, as in

```
$myobject = new MyClass;
MyOtherClass::myMethod($myobject);
```

This calls the method named `myMethod`, which is of the class `MyOtherClass`.

Inheritance

Perl allows you to define classes that are subclasses of existing classes. These subclasses inherit the methods of their parent class.

The following code is an example of a module that contains a subclass:

```
package MySubClass;
require Exporter;
require MyParentClass;
@ISA = ("Exporter", "MyParentClass");
@EXPORT = ("myChildRoutine");

sub myChildRoutine {
        my ($object) = shift(@_);
        print ("$object->[0]\n");
}

sub new {# the constructor for MySubClass
        my ($object) = MyParentClass->new();
        $object->[0] = "initial value";
        bless($object);
        return ($object);
}
1;
```

This class contains a method, `myChildRoutine`, which prints the first element of the array referenced by `$object`. The constructor for this class calls the constructor for its parent class, `MyParentClass`; this constructor returns a reference, which is then used and later returned by the `MySubClass` constructor.

Note that the `@ISA` array defined at the start of the module includes the name of the parent class, `MyParentClass`. This tells Perl to look for methods in the class named `MyParentClass` if it can't find them in `MySubClass`.

Methods in the parent class can be called as if they were defined in the subclass:

```
use MySubClass;

$myobject = new MySubClass;
$myobject->myParentRoutine("hi there");
```

This creates an object of class `MySubClass`. The code then calls `myParentRoutine`, which is a method belonging to class `MyParentClass`.

Using Built-In Functions

The examples you have seen so far use some of the many built-in functions provided with Perl. Table 16.4 provides a more complete list.

For more details on these functions and others, see the online documentation for Perl.

TABLE 16.4. BUILT-IN FUNCTIONS.

Function	Description
abs($scalar)	Return absolute value of number
alarm($scalar)	Deliver SIGALRM in $scalar seconds
atan2($v1, $v2)	Return arctangent of $v1/$v2
caller($scalar)	Return context of current subroutine
chdir($scalar)	Change working directory to $scalar
chmod(@array)	Change permissions of file list
chomp($scalar)	Remove last chars if line separator
chop($scalar)	Remove the last character of a string
chown(@array)	Change owner and group of file list
chr($scalar)	Convert number to ASCII equivalent
close(FILE)	Close a file
cos($scalar)	Return cosine of $scalar in radians
crypt($v1, $v2)	Encrypt a string
defined($scalar)	Determine whether $scalar is defined
delete($array{$val})	Delete value from associative array
die(@array)	Print @array to STDERR and exit
dump($scalar)	Generate UNIX core dump
each(%array)	Iterate through an associative array
eof(FILE)	Check whether FILE is at end of file
eval($scalar)	Treat $scalar as a subprogram
exec(@array)	Send @array to system as command
exists($element)	Does associative array element exist?
exit($scalar)	Exit program with status $scalar
exp($scalar)	Compute e ** $scalar
fileno(FILE)	Return file descriptor for FILE
fork()	Create parent and child processes
getc(FILE)	Get next character from FILE
getlogin()	Get current login from /etc/utmp
gmtime($scalar)	Convert time to GMT array

continues

TABLE 16.4. CONTINUED.

Function	Description
grep($scalar, @array)	Find $scalar in @array
hex($scalar)	Convert value to hexadecimal
index($v1, $v2, $v3)	Find $v2 in $v1 after position $v3
int($scalar)	Return integer portion of $scalar
join($scalar, @array)	Join array into single string
keys(%array)	Retrieve indexes of associative array
length($scalar)	Return length of $scalar
lc($scalar)	Convert value to lowercase
lcfirst($scalar)	Convert first character to lowercase
link(FILE1, FILE2)	Hard link FILE1 to FILE2
localtime($scalar)	Convert time to local array
log($scalar)	Get natural logarithm of $scalar
map($scalar, @array)	Use each list element in expression
mkdir(DIR, $scalar)	Create directory
oct($string)	Convert value to octal
open(FILE, $scalar)	Open file
ord($scalar)	Return ASCII value of character
pack($scalar, @array)	Pack array into binary structure
pipe(FILE1, FILE2)	Open pair of pipes
pop(@array)	Pop last value of array
pos($scalar)	Return location of last pattern match
print(FILE, @array)	Print string, list or array
push(@array, @array2)	Push @array2 onto @array
quotemeta($string)	Place backslash before nonword chars
rand($scalar)	Return random value
readlink($scalar)	Return value of symbolic link
require($scalar)	Include library file $scalar
reverse(@list)	Reverse order of @list
rindex($v1, $v2)	Return last occurrence of $v2 in $v1
scalar($val)	Interpret $val as scalar
shift(@array)	Shift off first value of @array
sin($scalar)	Return sine of $scalar in radians

Function	Description
sleep($scalar)	Sleep for $scalar seconds
sort(@array)	Sort @array in alphabetical order
splice(@a1, $v1, $v2, @a2)	Replace elements in array
split($v1, $v2)	Split scalar into array
sprintf($scalar, @array)	Create formatted string
sqrt($expr)	Return square root of $expr
srand($expr)	Set random number seed
stat(FILE)	Retrieve file statistics
substr($v1, $v2)	Retrieve substring
symlink(FILE1, FILE2)	Create symbolic link
system(@array)	Execute system command
time()	Get current time
uc($scalar)	Convert value to uppercase
ucfirst($scalar)	Convert first character to uppercase
undef($scalar)	Mark $scalar as undefined
unlink(@array)	Unlink a list of files
unpack($v1, $v2)	Unpack array from binary structure
unshift(@a1, @a2)	Add @a2 to the front of @a1
utime(@array)	Change date stamp on files
values(%array)	Return values of associative array
vec($v1, $v2, $v3)	Treat string as vector array
wait()	Wait for child process to terminate
wantarray()	Determine whether a list is expected
write(FILE)	Write formatted output

The $_ Variable

By default, any function that accepts a scalar variable can have its argument omitted. In this case, Perl uses $_, which is the default scalar variable.

$_ is also the default variable when reading from a file. So, for example, instead of writing

```
$var = <STDIN>;
chop($var);
```

you can write

```
chop(<STDIN>);
```

Summary

Perl is an interpreted programming language that allows you to write programs that manipulate files, strings, integers, and arrays quickly and easily.

Perl provides features commonly found in high-level languages such as C; these features include arrays, references, control structures, subroutines, and object-oriented capabilities.

Perl is easy to use. Character strings and integers are freely interchangeable; you don't need to convert an integer to a character string or vice versa. You don't need to know all of Perl to begin writing useful programs in the language; simple constructs can be used to solve simple problems.

Perl is also a flexible language, providing a variety of ways to solve programming problems.

This combination of simplicity, power, and flexibility makes Perl an attractive choice.

The C and C++ Programming Languages

by Robin Burk and James C. Armstrong, Jr.

IN THIS CHAPTER

UNIX shells support a wide range of commands that can be combined, in the form of scripts, into reusable programs. Command scripts for shell programs (and utilities such as Awk and Perl) are all the programming that many UNIX users need to be able to customize their computing environment.

Script languages have several shortcomings, however. To begin with, the commands that the user types into a script are only read and evaluated when the script is being executed. Interpreted languages are flexible and easy to use, but they are also inefficient because the commands must be reinterpreted each time the script is executed, and they are ill-suited to manipulate the computer's memory and I/O devices directly. Therefore, the programs that process scripts (such as the various UNIX shells, the Awk utility, and the Perl interpreter) are themselves written in the C and C++ languages, as is the UNIX kernel.

Many users find learning a scripted, interpreted language fairly easy because the commands can usually be tried out one at a time with clearly visible results. Learning a language such as C or C++ is more complex and difficult because the programmer must learn to think in terms of machine resources and the way in which actions are accomplished within the computer rather than in terms of user-oriented commands.

This chapter introduces you to the basic concepts of C and C++ and demonstrates how to build some simple programs. Even if you do not go on to learn how to program extensively in either language, you will find that the information in this chapter will help you to understand how kernels are built and why some of the other features of UNIX work the way they do. If you are interested in learning more about C and C++, I recommend the following books from Sams Publishing:

- *Sams Teach Yourself C in 24 Hours* by Tony Zhang
- *Sams Teach Yourself C in 21 Days* by Peter Aitken and Bradley Jones
- *Programming in ANSI C* by Stephen G. Kochan
- *Sams Teach Yourself C++ in 24 Hours* by Jesse Liberty

Introduction to C

C is the programming language most frequently associated with UNIX. Since the 1970s, the bulk of the operating system and applications have been written in C. Because the C language does not directly rely on any specific hardware architecture, UNIX was one of the first portable operating systems. That is, the bulk of the code that makes up UNIX neither knows nor cares about the actual computer on which it is running. Machine-specific features are isolated in a few modules within the UNIX kernel, making it easy to modify these modules when you're porting to a different hardware architecture.

The C and C++ Programming Languages

CHAPTER 17

803

17

THE C AND C++
PROGRAMMING
LANGUAGES

C was first designed by Dennis Ritchie for use with UNIX on DEC PDP-11 computers. The language evolved from Martin Richard's BCPL, and one of its earlier forms was the B language, which was written by Ken Thompson for the DEC PDP-7. The first book on C was *The C Programming Language,* by Brian Kernighan and Dennis Ritchie, published in 1978.

In 1983, the American National Standards Institute (ANSI) established a committee to standardize the definition of C. Termed ANSI C, it is the recognized standard for the language grammar and a core set of libraries. The syntax is slightly different from the original C language, which is frequently called K&R C—for Kernighan and Ritchie. This chapter primarily addresses ANSI C.

Programming in C: Basic Concepts

C is a compiled, third-generation procedural language. *Compiled* means that C code is analyzed, interpreted, and translated into machine instructions at some time prior to the execution of the C program. These steps are carried out by the C compiler and, depending on the complexity of the C program, by the make utility. After the program is compiled, it can be executed many times without recompilation.

The phrase *third-generation procedural* describes computer languages that clearly distinguish the data used in a program from the actions performed on that data. Programs written in third-generation languages take the form of a series of explicit processing steps, or procedures, which manipulate the contents of data structures by means of explicit references to their location in memory, and which manipulate the computer's hardware in response to hardware interrupts.

Functions in C Programs

In the C language, all procedures take the form of functions. Just as a mathematical function transforms one or more numbers into another number, a C function is typically a procedure that transforms some value or performs some other action and returns the results. The act of invoking the transformation is known as *calling the function.*

Mathematical function calls can be nested, as can function calls in C. When function calls are nested, the results of the innermost function are passed as input to the next function, and so on. Figure 17.1 shows how nested calls to the square root function are evaluated arithmetically.

FIGURE **17.1.**

Nested operations in mathematics.

Function	Value
sqrt(256)	16
sqrt(sqrt(256)) = sqrt(16)	4
sqrt(sqrt(sqrt(256))) = sqrt(4) =	2

Figure 17.2 shows the way that function calls are nested within C programs. In the figure, the Main function calls Function 1, which calls Function 2. Function 2 is evaluated first, and its results are passed back to Function 1. When Function 1 completes its operations, its results are passed back to the Main function.

FIGURE **17.2.**

Nesting function calls within C programs.

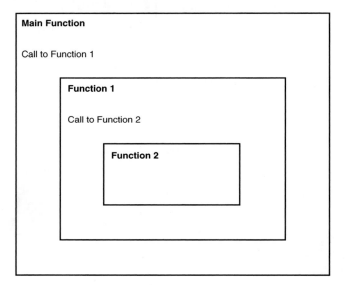

Nonfunctional procedures in other languages often operate on data variables that are shared with other code in the program. For example, a nonfunctional procedure might update a programwide COUNT_OF_ERRORS whenever a user makes a keyboard mistake. Such procedures must be carefully written, and they usually are specific to the program for which they first were created because they reference specific, shared data variables within the wider program.

A function, however, receives all the information it needs (including the location of data variables to use in each instance) when it is called. It neither knows nor cares about the wider program context that calls it; it simply transforms the values found within the input variables (parameters), whatever they might be, and returns the result to whatever other function invoked it.

The C and C++ Programming Languages

CHAPTER 17

805

17

THE C AND C++
PROGRAMMING
LANGUAGES

Because they are implemented as functions, procedures written in C do not need to know whether, or how deeply, they will be nested inside other function calls. This capability enables you to reuse C functions in many programs without modifying them. For example, Function 2 in Figure 17.2. might be called directly by the Main logic in a different C program.

An entire C program is itself a function that returns a result code, when executed, to the program that invoked it. It is usually a shell in the case of applications, but it might also be any other part of the operating system or any other UNIX program. Because C programs are all structured as functions, they can be invoked by other programs or nested inside larger programs without your needing to rewrite them in any way.

> **NOTE**
>
> This feature of C has heavily shaped the look and feel of UNIX. More than in most other operating environments, UNIX systems consist of many small C programs that call one another, are combined into larger programs, or get invoked by the user as needed. Rather than use monolithic, integrated applications, UNIX typically hosts many small, flexible programs. You can customize your working environment by combining these tools to do new tasks.

Data in C Programs

The data that is manipulated within C programs is of two kinds: literal values and variables. Literal values are specific, actual numbers or characters, such as 1, 4.35, or *a*.

Variables are names associated with a place in memory that can hold data values. Each variable in C is typed; that is, each variable can hold only one kind of value. The basic data types include integers, floating point (real) numbers, characters, and arrays. An *array* is a series of data elements of the same type, in which the elements are identified by the order (place) within the series.

You can define complex data structures as well. Complex data structures are used to gather a number of related data items under one name. A terminal communications program, for example, might have a terminal control block (TCB)associated with each user who is logged on. The TCB typically contains data elements identifying the communications port, active application process, and other information associated with that terminal session.

You must explicitly define all variables in a C program before you can use the variables.

Creating, Compiling, and Executing Your First Program

The development of a C program is an iterative procedure. Many UNIX tools are involved in this four-step process. They are familiar to software developers:

1. Using an editor, write the code into a text file.
2. Compile the program.
3. Execute the program.
4. Debug the program.

You repeat the first two steps until the program compiles successfully. Then the execution and debugging begin. Many of the concepts presented here might seem strange to nonprogrammers. This chapter endeavors to introduce C as a programming language.

The typical, first C program is almost a cliché. It is the "Hello, World" program, and it prints the simple line Hello, World. Listing 17.1 shows the source of the program.

LISTING 17.1. SOURCE OF Hello World.

```
main()
{
printf("Hello, World\n");
}
```

You can compile and execute this program as follows:

```
$ cc hello.c
$ a.out
Hello, World
$
```

You compile the program by using the cc command, which creates a program a.out if the code is correct. Just typing a.out runs the program. The program includes only one function, main. Every C program must have a main function; it is the place where the program's execution begins. The only statement is a call to the printf library function, which passes the string Hello, World\n. (Functions are described in detail later in this chapter.) The last two characters of the string, \n, represent the carriage return line-feed character.

An Overview of the C Language

As with all programming languages, C programs must follow rules. These rules describe how a program should appear and what those words and symbols mean. These rules create the syntax of a programming language. You can think of a program as a story. Each sentence must have a noun and a verb. Sentences form paragraphs, and the paragraphs tell the story. Similarly, C statements can build into functions and programs.

Elementary C Syntax

Like all languages, C deals primarily with the manipulation and presentation of data. BCPL deals with data as data. C, however, goes one step further to use the concept of data types. The basic data types are character, integer, and floating point numbers. Other data types are built from these three basic types.

Integers are the basic mathematical data type. They can be classified as `long` and `short` integers, and the size is implementation-dependent. With a few exceptions, integers are four bytes in length, and on most machines they can range from –2,147,483,648 to 2,147,483,647. In ANSI C, you define these values in a header—`limit.h`—as `INT_MIN` and `INT_MAX`. The qualifier `unsigned` moves the range one bit higher, to the equivalent of `INT_MAX-INT_MIN`.

Floating point numbers are used for more complicated mathematics. Integer mathematics is limited to integer results. With integers, 3/2 equals 1. Floating point numbers give a greater amount of precision to mathematical calculations: 3/2 equals 1.5. Floating point numbers can be represented by a decimal number, such as 687.534, or with scientific notation, such as 8.87534E+2. For larger numbers, scientific notation is preferred. For even greater precision, the type `double` provides a greater range. Again, specific ranges are implementation-dependent.

Characters are usually implemented as single bytes, although some international character sets require two or more bytes. The most common set of character representations is ASCII, found on most U.S. computers.

An array is used for a sequence of values that are often position-dependent. An array is useful when you need a range of values of a given type. Related to the array is the pointer. Variables are stored in memory, and a pointer is the physical address of that memory. In a sense, a pointer and an array are similar, except when a program is invoked. The space needed for the data of an array is allocated when the routine that needs the space is invoked. For a pointer, the space must be allocated by the programmer, or the variable must be assigned by dereferencing a variable. (To *dereference* means to ask the system to return the address of a variable.) You use the ampersand to indicate dereferencing, and you use an asterisk when the value pointed at is required. The following are some sample declarations:

`int i;`	Declares an integer
`char c;`	Declares a character
`char *ptr;`	Declares a pointer to a character
`double temp[16];`	Declares an array of double-precision floating point numbers with 16 values

Listing 17.2 shows an example of a program with pointers.

LISTING 17.2. AN EXAMPLE OF A PROGRAM WITH POINTERS.

```
int i;
int *ptr;

i=5;
ptr = &i;
printf("%d %x %d\n", i,ptr,*ptr);

output is: 5 f7fffa6c 5
```

> **NOTE**
>
> A *pointer* is only a memory address, and it tells you the address of any variable.

A string has no specific type. You use an array of characters to represent strings. You can print them by using an `%s` flag instead of `%c`.

Simple output is created by the `printf` function. `printf` takes a format string and the list of arguments to be printed. A complete set of format options is presented in Table 17.1. You can modify format options with sizes. Check the documentation for the full specification.

TABLE 17.1. FORMAT CONVERSIONS FOR `printf`.

Conversion	*Meaning*
`%%`	Percentage sign
`%E`	Double (scientific notation)
`%G`	Double (format depends on value)
`%X`	Hexadecimal (letters are capitalized)

The C and C++ Programming Languages

CHAPTER 17

809

17

THE C AND C++
PROGRAMMING
LANGUAGES

Conversion	Meaning
%c	Single character
%d	Integer (signed)
%e	Double (scientific notation)
%f	Double of the form `mmm.ddd`
%g	Double (format depends on value)
%i	Integer (signed)
%ld	Long integer
%n	Count of characters written in current `printf`
%o	Octal
%p	Print as a pointer
%s	Character pointer (string)
%u	Unsigned integer
%x	Hexadecimal

Some characters cannot be included easily in a program. New lines, for example, require a special escape sequence because an unescaped newline cannot appear in a string. Table 17.2 contains a complete list of escape sequences.

TABLE 17.2. ESCAPE CHARACTERS FOR STRINGS.

Escape Sequence	Meaning
\"	Double quotation mark
\'	Single quotation mark
\?	Question mark
\\	Backslash
\a	Audible bell
\b	Backspace
\f	Form feed (new page)
\n	New line
\ (followed by digits 000)	Octal number
\r	Carriage return
\t	Horizontal tab
\v	Vertical tab
\xhh	Hexadecimal number

A full program is compilation of statements. Statements are separated by semicolons. You can group them in blocks of statements surrounded by curly braces. The simplest statement is an assignment. A variable on the left side is assigned the value of an expression on the right.

Expressions

At the heart of the C programming language are expressions. They are techniques to combine simple values into new values. The three basic types of expressions are comparison, numerical, and bitwise expressions.

Comparison Expressions

The simplest expression is a comparison. A comparison evaluates to a TRUE or a FALSE value. In C, TRUE is a nonzero value, and FALSE is a zero value. Table 17.3 contains a list of comparison operators.

TABLE 17.3. COMPARISON OPERATORS.

Operator	Meaning	Operator	Meaning
<	Less than	>=	Greater than or equal to
>	Greater than	¦¦	Or
==	Equal to	&&	And
<=	Less than or equal to		

You can build expressions by combining simple comparisons with ANDs and ORs to make complex expressions. Consider the definition of a leap year. In words, it is any year divisible by 4, except a year divisible by 100 unless that year is divisible by 400. If year is the variable, you can define a leap year with the following expression:

```
((((year%4)==0)&&((year%100)!=0))¦¦((year%400)==0))
```

On first inspection, this code might look complicated, but it isn't. The parentheses group the simple expressions with the ANDs and ORs to make a complex expression.

Mathematical Expressions

One convenient aspect of C is that you can treat expressions as mathematical values, and you can use mathematical statements in expressions. In fact, any statement—even a simple assignment—has values that you can use in other places as an expression.

The mathematics of C is straightforward. Barring parenthetical groupings, multiplication and division have higher precedence than addition and subtraction. The operators, which are listed in Table 17.4, are standard.

TABLE 17.4. MATHEMATICAL OPERATORS.

Operator	Meaning	Operator	Meaning
+	Addition	/	Division
-	Subtraction	%	Integer remainder
*	Multiplication	^	Exponentiation

You also can use unary operators, which affect a single variable. They are ++ (increment by one) and -- (decrement by one). These shorthand versions are quite useful.

You also can use shorthand for situations in which you want to change the value of a variable. For example, if you want to add an expression to a variable called a and assign the new value to a, the shorthand a+=expr is the same as a=a+expr. The expression can be as complex or as simple as required.

> **NOTE**
>
> Most UNIX functions take advantage of the truth values and return 0 for success. This way, a programmer can write code such as
>
> ```
> if (function())
>         {
>         error condition
>         }
> ```
> The return value of a function determines whether the function worked.

Bitwise Operations

Because a variable is just a string of bits, many operations work on these bit patterns. Table 17.5 lists the bit operators.

TABLE 17.5. BIT OPERATORS.

Operator	Meaning	Operator	Meaning
&	Logical AND	<<	Bit shift left
¦	Logical OR	>>	Bit shift right

A logical AND compares the individual bits in place. If both are 1, the value 1 is assigned to the expression. Otherwise, 0 is assigned. For a logical OR, 1 is assigned if either value is a 1. Bit shift operations move the bits a number of positions to the right or left.

Mathematically, this process is similar to multiplying or dividing by 2, with the difference that you can apply bit shifting to non-numeric data types, and shifting may cause the loss of information in bits that are lost "off the end" of the variable. Bit operations are often used for masking values and for comparisons. A simple way to determine whether a value is odd or even is to perform a logical AND with the integer value 1. If it is TRUE, the number is odd.

Statement Controls

With what you've seen so far, you can create a list of statements that are executed only once, after which the program terminates. To control the flow of commands, you can use three types of loops that exist in C. The simplest is the while loop. The syntax is

```
while (expression)
      statement
```

As long as the expression between parentheses evaluates as nonzero—or TRUE in C—the statement is executed. The statement actually can be a list of statements blocked off with curly braces. If the expression evaluates to zero the first time it is reached, the statement is never executed. To force at least one execution of the statement, use a do loop. The syntax for a do loop is

```
do
        statement
        while (expression);
```

The third type of control flow is the for loop, which is more complicated. The syntax is

```
for(expr1;expr2;expr3) statement
```

When the expression is reached for the first time, *expr1* is evaluated. Next, *expr2* is evaluated. If *expr2* is nonzero, the statement is executed, followed by *expr3*. Then *expr2* is tested again, followed by the statement and *expr3*, until *expr2* evaluates to zero. Strictly speaking, this use is a notational convenience because you can structure a *while* loop to perform the same actions. Here's an example:

```
expr1;
while (expr2) {
        statement;
        expr3
        }
```

Loops can be interrupted in three ways. A break statement terminates execution in a loop and exits it. continue terminates the current iteration and retests the loop before possibly re-executing the statement. For an unconventional exit, you can use goto. goto changes the program's execution to a labeled statement. According to many programmers, using goto is poor programming practice, so you should avoid using it.

Statements can also be executed conditionally. Again, you can use three formats for statement execution. The simplest is an `if` statement. The syntax is

```
if (expr) statement
```

If the expression *expr* evaluates to nonzero, the statement is executed. You can expand this statement with an `else`, the second type of conditional execution. The syntax for `else` is

```
if (expr) statement else statement
```

If the expression evaluates to zero, the second statement is executed.

NOTE

The second statement in an `else` condition can be another `if` statement. This situation might cause the grammar to be indeterminate if the structure

```
if (expr) if (expr) statement else statement
```

is not parsed cleanly.

As the code is written, the `else` is considered applicable to the second `if`. To make it applicable with the first `if`, you can surround the second `if` statement with curly braces, as in this example:

```
$ if (expr) {if (expr) statement} else statement
```

The third type of conditional execution is more complicated. The `switch` statement first evaluates an expression. Then it looks down a series of `case` statements to find a label that matches the expression's value and executes the statements following the label. A special label `default` exists if no other conditions are met. If you want only a set of statements executed for each label, you must use the `break` statement to leave the `switch` statement. For instance:

```c
int i;
switch (i){
    case '2': case '4': case '6':
        printf ("even number between 2 and 6");
    case '1': case '3': case '5':
        printf  ("odd number between 1 and 5");
    default:
        printf  ("out of range");
        break;
}
```

You've now covered the simplest building blocks of a C program. You can add more power by using functions and by declaring complex data types.

If your program requires different pieces of data to be grouped on a consistent basis, you can group them into structures. Listing 17.3 shows a structure for a California driver's license. Note that it includes integer, character, and character array (string) types.

LISTING 17.3. AN EXAMPLE OF A STRUCTURE.

```
struct license {
        char name[128];
        char address[3][128];
        int zipcode;
        int height, weight, month, day, year;
        char license_letter;
        int license_number;
        };
struct license newlicensee;
struct license *user;
```

Because California driver's license numbers consist of a single character followed by a seven-digit number, the license ID is broken into two components. Similarly, the newlicensee's address is broken into three lines, represented by three arrays of 128 characters.

Accessing individual fields of a structure requires two techniques. To read a member of a locally defined structure, you append a dot to the variable and then the field name, as shown in this example:

```
newlicensee.zipcode=94404;
```

To use a pointer to the structure, you need -> to point to the member:

```
user->zipcode=94404;
```

Here's an interesting note: If the structure pointer is incremented, the address is increased not by 1, but by the size of the structure.

Using functions is an easy way to group statements and to give them a name. They are usually related statements that perform repetitive tasks such as I/O. printf, described previously, is a function. It is provided with the standard C library. Listing 17.4 illustrates a function definition, a function call, and a function.

NOTE

The ellipsis simply means that to save space, some lines of sample code are not shown here.

LISTING 17.4. AN EXAMPLE OF A FUNCTION.

```c
int swapandmin( int *, int *);        /* Function declaration */

...

int i,j,lower;

i=2; j=4;
lower=swapandmin(&i, &j);             /* Function call */

...

int swapandmin(int *a,int *b)         /* Function definition */
{
int tmp;

tmp=(*a);
(*a)=(*b);
(*b)=tmp;
if ((*a)<(*b)) return(*a);
return(*b);
}
```

ANSI C and K&R C differ most in function declarations and calls. ANSI requires that function arguments be prototyped when the function is declared. K&R C required only the name and the type of the returned value. The declaration in Listing 17.4 states that the function swapandmin takes two pointers to integers as arguments and that it will return an integer. The function call takes the addresses of two integers and sets the variable named lower with the return value of the function.

When a function is called from a C program, the values of the arguments are passed to the function. Therefore, if any of the arguments will be changed for the calling function, you can't pass only the variable; you must pass the address, too. Likewise, to change the value of the argument in the calling routine of the function, you must assign the new value to the address.

In the function in Listing 17.4, the value pointed to by a is assigned to the tmp variable. b is assigned to a, and tmp is assigned to b. *a is used instead of a to ensure that the change is reflected in the calling routine. Finally, the values of *a and *b are compared, and the lower of the two is returned.

If you included the line

```c
printf("%d %d %d",lower,i,j);
```

after the function call, you would see 2 4 2 on the output.

This sample function is quite simple, and it is ideal for a macro. A macro is a technique used to replace a token with different text. You can use macros to make code more readable. For example, you might use EOF instead of (-1) to indicate the end of a file. You can also use macros to replace code. Listing 17.5 is basically the same as Listing 17.4 except that it uses macros.

LISTING 17.5. AN EXAMPLE OF MACROS.

```
#define SWAP(X,Y) {int tmp; tmp=X; X=Y; Y=tmp; }
#define MIN(X,Y) ((X<Y) ? X : Y )

...

int i,j,lower;

i=2; j=4;
SWAP(i,j);
lower=MIN(i,j);
```

When a C program is compiled, macro replacement is one of the first steps performed. Listing 17.6 illustrates the result of the replacement.

LISTING 17.6. AN EXAMPLE OF MACRO REPLACEMENT.

```
int i,j,lower;

i=2; j=4;
{int tmp; tmp=i; i=j; j=tmp; };
lower= ((i<j) ? i : j );
```

The macros make the code easier to read and understand.

Creating a Simple Program

For your first program, write a program that prints a chart of the first 10 integers and their squares, cubes, and square roots.

Writing the Code

Using the text editor of your choice, enter all the code in Listing 17.7 and save it in a file called sample.c.

LISTING 17.7. SOURCE CODE FOR *sample.c*.

```
#include <stdio.h>
#include <math.h>

main()
{
int i;
double a;

for(i=1;i<11;i++)
        {
        a=i*1.0;
        printf("%2d. %3d %4d %7.5f\n",i,i*i,i*i*i,sqrt(a));
        }
}
```

The first two lines are header files. The stdio.h file provides the function definitions and structures associated with the C input and output libraries. The math.h file includes the definitions of mathematical library functions. You need it for the square root function.

The main loop is the only function that you need to write for this example. It takes no arguments. You define two variables. One is the integer i, and the other is a double-precision floating point number called a. You wouldn't have to use a, but you can for the sake of convenience.

The program is a simple for loop that starts at 1 and ends at 11. It increments i by 1 each time through. When i equals 11, the for loop stops executing. You also could have written i<=10 because the expressions have the same meaning.

First, you multiply i by 1.0 and assign the product to a. A simple assignment would also work, but the multiplication reminds you that you are converting the value to a double-precision floating point number.

Next, you call the print function. The format string includes three integers of widths 2, 3, and 4. After the first integer is printed, you print a period. Next, you print a floating point number that is seven characters wide with five digits following the decimal point. The arguments after the format string show that you print the integer, the square of the integer, the cube of the integer, and the square root of the integer.

Compiling the Program

To compile this program using the C compiler, enter the following command:

```
cc sample.c -lm
```

This command produces an output file called a.out. This is the simplest use of the C compiler. cc is one of the most powerful and flexible commands on a UNIX system.

A number of flags can change the compiler's output. These flags are often dependent on the system or compiler. Some flags are common to all C compilers. They are described in the following paragraphs.

The -o flag tells the compiler to write the output to the file named after the flag. The cc -o sample sample.c command, for example, would put the program in a file named sample.

> **NOTE**
>
> The output discussed here is the compiler's output, not the sample program. Compiler output is usually the program, and in every example here, it is an executable program.

The -g flag tells the compiler to keep the symbol table (the data used by a program to associate variable names with memory locations), which is necessary for debuggers. Its opposite is the -O flag, which tells the compiler to optimize the code—that is, to make it more efficient. You can change the search path for header files by using the -I flag, and you can add libraries by using the -l and -L flags.

The compilation process takes place in several steps, as you can see in the following list:

1. The C preprocessor parses the file. To parse the file, it sequentially reads the lines, includes header files, and performs macro replacement.

2. The compiler parses the modified code for correct syntax. This process builds a symbol table and creates an intermediate object format. Most symbols have specific memory addresses assigned, although symbols defined in other modules, such as external variables, do not.

3. The last compilation stage, linking, ties together different files and libraries and links the files by resolving the symbols that have not yet been resolved.

Executing the Program

The output from this program appears in Listing 17.8.

LISTING 17.8. OUTPUT FROM THE sample.c PROGRAM.

```
$ sample.c
 1.    1     1 1.00000
 2.    4     8 1.41421
 3.    9    27 1.73205
 4.   16    64 2.00000
 5.   25   125 2.23607
 6.   36   216 2.44949
 7.   49   343 2.64575
 8.   64   512 2.82843
 9.   81   729 3.00000
10.  100  1000 3.16228
```

> **NOTE**
>
> To execute a program, type its name at a shell prompt. The output will immediately follow.

Building Large Applications

You can break C programs into any number of files as long as no function spans more than one file. To compile this program, you compile each source file into an intermediate object before you link all the objects into a single executable. The -c flag tells the compiler to stop at this stage. During the link stage, all the object files should be listed on the command line. Object files are identified by the .o suffix.

Making Libraries with ar

If several programs use the same functions, you can combine them into a single library archive. You use the ar command to build a library. When you include this library on the compile line, the archive is searched to resolve any external symbols. Listing 17.9 shows an example of building and using a library.

LISTING 17.9. BUILDING A LARGE APPLICATION.

```
cc -c sine.c
cc -c cosine.c
cc -c tangent.c
ar c libtrig.a sine.o cosine.o tangent.o

cc -c mainprog.c
cc -o mainprog mainprog.o libtrig.a
```

17

Large applications can require hundreds of source code files. Compiling and linking these applications can be a complex and error-prone task all its own. The make utility is a tool that helps developers organize the process of building the executable form of complex applications from many source files. Chapter 18, "The make Utility," discusses the make utility in detail.

Debugging Tools

Debugging is a science and an art unto itself. Sometimes, the simplest tool—the code listing—is best. At other times, however, you need to use other tools. Three of these tools are lint, prof, and sdb. Other available tools include escape, cxref, and cb. Many UNIX commands have debugging uses.

lint is a command that examines source code for possible problems. The code might meet the standards for C and compile cleanly, but it might not execute correctly. Two things checked by lint are type mismatches and incorrect argument counts on function calls. lint uses the C preprocessor, so you can use similar command-like options as you would use for cc.

You use the prof command to study where a program is spending its time. If a program is compiled and linked with -p as a flag when it executes, a mon.out file is created with data on how often each function is called and how much time is spent in each function. This data is parsed and displayed with prof. An analysis of the output generated by prof helps you determine where performance bottlenecks occur. Although optimizing compilers can speed your programs, this analysis significantly improves program performance.

The third tool is sdb—a symbolic debugger. When you compile a program using -g, the symbol tables are retained, and you can use a symbolic debugger to track program bugs. The basic technique is to invoke sdb after a core dump and get a stack trace. This trace indicates the source line where the core dump occurred and the functions that were called to reach that line. Often, this information is enough to identify the problem. It is not the limit of sdb, though.

sdb also provides an environment for debugging programs interactively. Invoking sdb with a program enables you to set breakpoints, examine variable values, and monitor variables. If you suspect a problem near a line of code, you can set a breakpoint at that line and run the program. When the line is reached, execution is interrupted. You can check variable values, examine the stack trace, and observe the program's environment. You can single-step through the program, checking values. You can resume execution at any point. By using breakpoints, you can discover many of the bugs in your code that you've missed.

cpp is another tool that you can use to debug programs. It performs macro replacements, includes headers, and parses the code. The output is the actual module to be compiled. Normally, though, the programmer never executes cpp directly. Instead, it is invoked through cc with either an -E or -P option. -E puts the output directly to the terminal; -P makes a file with an .i suffix.

Introduction to C++

If C is the language most associated with UNIX, C++ is the language that underlies most graphical user interfaces (GUIs) available today.

C++ was originally developed by Dr. Bjarne Stroustrup at the Computer Science Research Center of AT&T's Bell Laboratories (Murray Hill, New Jersey), also the source of UNIX itself. Dr. Stroustrup's original goal was to create an object-oriented simulation language. The availability of C compilers for many hardware architectures convinced him to design the language as an extension of C, allowing a preprocessor to translate C++ programs into C for compilation.

After the C language was standardized by a joint committee of the American National Standards Institute (ANSI) and the International Standards Organization (ISO) in 1989, a new joint committee began the effort to formalize C++ as well. This effort has produced several new features and refined significantly the interpretation of other language features, but it has not yet resulted in a formal language standard.

Programming in C++: Basic Concepts

C++ is an object-oriented extension to C. Because C++ is a superset of C, C++ compilers compile C programs correctly, and you can write nonobject-oriented code in the language.

The distinction between an object-oriented language and a procedural one can be subtle and hard to grasp, especially with regard to C++, which retains all of C's characteristics and concepts. One way to get at the difference is to say that when programmers code in procedural language, they specify actions that do things to data, whereas when they write object-oriented code, they create data objects that can be requested to perform actions on or with regard to themselves.

Thus, a C function receives one or more values as input, transforms or acts upon those values in some way, and returns a result. If the values that are passed include pointers, the contents of data variables may be modified by the function. As the Standard Library routines show, it is likely that the code calling a function will not know, nor need to know, what steps the function takes when it is invoked. However, such matters as the data type of the input parameters and the result code are specified when the function is defined and remains invariable throughout program execution.

Functions are associated with C++ objects as well. But as you will see, the actions performed when an object's function is invoked may automatically differ, perhaps substantially, depending on the specific type of the data structure with which it is associated. This aspect is known as *overloading* of function names. Overloading is related to a second characteristic of C++, namely the fact that functions can be defined as belonging to C++ data structures—one aspect of the wider language feature known as *encapsulation*.

In addition to overloading and encapsulation, object-oriented languages also enable you to define new abstract data types (including associated functions) and then derive subsequent data types from them. The notion of a new class of data objects, in addition to the built-in classes such as integer, floating point number, and character, goes beyond the familiar capability to define complex data objects in C. Just as a C data structure that includes an integer element inherits the properties and functions applicable to integers, so too a C++ class that is derived from another class *inherits* the class's functions and properties. When a specific variable or structure (instance) of that class's type is defined, the class is said to be *instantiated*.

In the remainder of this chapter, you will look at some of the basic features of C++ in more detail, along with code examples that will provide concrete examples of these concepts. To learn more about the rich capabilities of C++, consult the titles mentioned at the beginning of this chapter.

Scope of Reference in C and C++

C++ differs from C in some details apart from the more obvious object-oriented features. Some of these details are fairly superficial, among them

- The capability to define variables anywhere within a code block rather than always at the start of the block

- The addition of an `enum` data type to facilitate conditional logic based on case values

- The capability to designate functions as `inline`, causing the compiler to generate another copy of the function code at that point in the program, rather than a call to shared code

Other differences have to do with advanced concepts such as memory management and the scope of reference for variable and function names. Because the latter features, especially, are used in object-oriented C++ programs, they are worth examining more closely in this short introduction to the language.

The C and C++ Programming Languages

CHAPTER 17

823

17

THE C AND C++
PROGRAMMING
LANGUAGES

The phrase *scope of reference* is used to discuss how a name in C, C++, or certain other programming languages is interpreted when the language permits more than one instance of a name to occur within a program. Consider the code in Listing 17.10. Here two functions are defined and then called. Each function has an internal variable called tmp. The tmp that is defined within printnum is *local* to the printnum function; that is, it can be accessed only by logic within printnum. Similarly, the tmp that is defined within printchar is local to the printchar function. The scope of reference for each tmp variable is limited to the printnum and printchar functions, respectively.

LISTING 17.10. SCOPE OF REFERENCE, EXAMPLE 1.

```
#include <stdio.h>          /* I/O function declarations */

void printnum  ( int );     /* function declaration      */
void printchar ( char );    /* function declaration      */

main ()
{
   printnum (5);            /* print the number 5        */
   printchar ('a'"");       /* print the letter a        */
}

/* define the functions called above               */
/* void means the function does not return a value  */

   void printnum (int inputnum)
{
   int tmp;
   tmp = inputnum;
   printf ("%d \n",tmp);
}

void printchar (char inputchar)
{
   char tmp;
   tmp = inputchar;
   printf ("%c \n",tmp);
}
```

When this program is executed after compilation, it creates the output shown in Listing 17.11.

LISTING 17.11. OUTPUT FROM SCOPE OF REFERENCE, EXAMPLE 1.

```
5
a
```

Listing 17.12 shows another example of scope of reference. Here you find a global variable tmp—that is, one that is known to the entire program because it is defined within the main function—in addition to the two tmp variables that are local to the printnum and printchar functions.

LISTING 17.12. SCOPE OF REFERENCE, EXAMPLE 2.

```c
#include <stdio.h>

void printnum  ( int );      /* function declaration        */
void printchar ( char );     /* function declaration        */

main ()
{
    double tmp;              /* define a global variable        */
    tmp = 1.234;
    printf ("%e\n",tmp);     /* print the value of the global tmp */
    printnum (5);            /* print the number 5              */
    printf ("%e\n",tmp);     /* print the value of the global tmp */
    printchar ('a'"");         /* print the letter a              */
    printf ("%e\n",tmp);     /* print the value of the global tmp */
}
/* define the functions used above                            */
/* void means the function does not return a value            */

void printnum (int inputnum)
{
    int tmp;
    tmp = inputnum;
    printf ("%d \n",tmp);
}

void printchar (char inputchar)
{
    char tmp;
    tmp = inputchar;
    printf ("%c \n",tmp);
}
```

The global tmp is not modified when the local tmp variables are used within their respective functions, as shown by the output in Listing 17.13.

LISTING 17.13. OUTPUT OF SCOPE OF REFERENCE, EXAMPLE 2.

```
1.234
5
1.234
a
1.234
```

The C and C++ Programming Languages

CHAPTER 17

825

17

THE C AND C++
PROGRAMMING
LANGUAGES

C++ does provide a means to specify the global variable even when a local variable with the same name is in scope. The operator :: prefixed to a variable name always resolves that name to the global instance. Thus, the global tmp variable defined in main in Listing 17.12 could be accessed within the print functions by using the label ::tmp.

Why would a language such as C or C++ allow different scopes of reference for the same variable?

The answer to this question is that allowing variable scope of reference also allows functions to be placed into public libraries for other programmers to use. Library functions can be invoked merely by knowing their calling sequences, and no one needs to check to be sure that the programmers didn't use the same local variable names. This capability, in turn, means that library functions can be improved, if necessary, without affecting existing code. This is true whether the library contains application code for reuse or is distributed as the runtime library associated with a compiler.

> **NOTE**
>
> A *runtime library* is a collection of compiled modules that perform common C, C++, and UNIX functions. The code is written carefully, debugged, and highly optimized. For example, the printf function requires machine instructions to format the various output fields, send them to the standard output device, and check to see that no I/O errors occurred. Because this process takes many machine instructions, repeating that sequence for every printf call in a program would be inefficient. Instead, the developers of the compiler can write a single all-purpose printf function once and place it in the Standard Library. When your program is compiled, the compiler generates calls to these pre-written programs instead of re-creating the logic each time a printf call occurs in the source code.

Variable scope of reference is the language feature that enables you to design small C and C++ programs to perform standalone functions, yet also to combine them into larger utilities as needed. This flexibility is characteristic of UNIX, the first operating system to be built on the C language. As you'll see in the rest of the chapter, variable scope of reference also makes object-oriented programming possible in C++.

Overloading Functions and Operators in C++

Overloading is a technique that allows more than one function to have the same name. In at least two circumstances, you might want to define a new function with the same name as an existing one:

- When the existing version of the function does not perform exactly the desired functionality, but it must otherwise be included with the program (as with a function from the Standard Library)
- When the same function must operate differently depending on the format of the data passed to it

In C, you can reuse a function name as long as the old function name is not within scope. A function name's scope of reference is determined in the same way as a data name's scope: A function that is defined (not just called) within the definition of another function is local to that other function.

When two similar C functions must coexist within the same scope, however, they cannot bear the same name. Instead, you must assign two names, as with the `strcpy` and `strncpy` functions from the Standard Library, each of which copies strings but does so in a slightly different fashion.

C++ gets around this restriction by allowing overloaded function names. That is, the C++ language allows you to reuse function names within the same scope of reference as long as the parameters for the function differ in number or type.

Listing 17.14 shows an example of overloading functions. This program defines and calls two versions of the `printvar` function, one equivalent to `printnum`, used previously, and the other to `printchar`. Listing 17.15 shows the output of this program when it is executed.

LISTING 17.14. OVERLOADED FUNCTION EXAMPLE.

```
#include <stdio.h>
void printvar (int tmp)
{
   printf ("%d \n",tmp);
}

void printvar (char tmp)
{
   printf ("%c \n",tmp);
}

void main ()
{
   int  numvar;
   char charvar;
   numvar = 5;
   printvar (numvar);
   charvar = 'a'"";
   printvar (charvar);
}
```

LISTING 17.15. OUTPUT FROM THE OVERLOADED FUNCTION EXAMPLE.

```
5
a
```

Overloading is possible because C++ compilers can determine the format of the arguments sent to the printvar function each time it is called from within main. The compiler substitutes a call to the correct version of the function based on those formats. If the function being overloaded resides in a library or in another module, the associated header file (such as stdio.h above) must be included in this source code module. This header file contains the prototype for the external function, thereby informing the compiler of the parameters and parameter formats used in the external version of the function.

Standard mathematical, logical, and other operators can also be overloaded. This advanced and powerful technique enables you to customize exactly how a standard language feature will operate on specific data structure or at certain points in the code. You must exercise great care when overloading standard operators such as +, MOD, and OR to ensure that the resulting operation functions correctly, is restricted to the appropriate occurrences in the code, and is well documented.

Functions Within C++ Data Structures

A second feature of C++ that supports object-oriented programming, in addition to overloading, is the capability to associate a function with a particular data structure or format. Such functions may be public (invocable by any code), private (invocable only by other functions within the data structure), or may allow limited access.

In C++, you must define data structures using the struct keyword. Such structures become new data types added to the language (within the scope of the structure's definition). Listing 17.16 revisits the structure of Listing 17.3 and adds a display function to print out instances of the license structure. Note the alternative way to designate comments in C++, using a double slash. This double slash tells the compiler to ignore everything that follows, on the given line only.

Also notice that this example uses the C++ character output function cout rather than the C routine printf.

LISTING 17.16. ADDING FUNCTIONS TO DATA STRUCTURES.

```
#include iostream.h
//            structure = new data type
struct license {
       char name[128];
       char address[3][128];
```

continues

LISTING 17.16. CONTINUED

```
        int zipcode;
        int height, weight, month, day, year;
        char license_letter;
        int license_number;

        void display(void)     // there will be a function to display
license type structures
};

// now define the display function for this data type

void license::display()
{
    cout << "Name:      "   << name;
    cout << "Address: "   << address(0);
    cout << "          "   << address(1);
    cout << "          "   << address(2) " " <<zipcode;
    cout << "Height:   "  << height " inches";
    cout << "Weight:   "  << weight " lbs";
    cout << "Date:      "  << month "/" << day   "/" << year;
    cout << "License: "  <<license_letter <<license_number;
}


main
{
    struct license newlicensee;       // define a variable of type license
    newlicensee.name = "Joe Smith";   //  and initialize it
    newlicensee.address(0) = "123 Elm Street";
    newlicensee.address(1) = ""
    newlicensee.address(2) = "Smalltown, AnyState";
    newlicensee.zipcode = "98765";
    newlicensee.height = 70;
    newlicensee.weight = 165;
    license.month = 1;
    newlicensee.day = 23;
    newlicensee.year = 97;
    newlicensee.license_letter = A;
    newlicensee.license_number = 567890;


    newlicensee.display;   // and display this instance of the structure
}
```

Note the three references here to the same function. First, the function is prototyped as an element within the structure definition. Second, the function is defined. Because the function definition is valid for all instances of the data type license, the structure's data elements are referenced by the function without naming any instance of the structure. Finally, when a specific instance of `license` is created, its associated `display` function is invoked by prefixing the function name with that of the structure instance.

Listing 17.17 shows the output of this program.

LISTING 17.17. OUTPUT OF THE FUNCTION DEFINED WITHIN A STRUCTURE.

```
Name:    Joe Smith
Address: 123 Elm Street

         Smalltown, AnyState   98765
Height:  70 inches
Weight:  160 lbs
Date:    1/23/1997
License: A567890
```

Classes in C++

Overloading and the association of functions with data structures lay the groundwork for object-oriented code in C++. Full object-orientation is available through the use of the C++ class feature.

A C++ class extends the idea of data structures with associated functions by binding (or encapsulating) data descriptions and manipulation algorithms into new, abstract data types. When classes are defined, the class type and methods are described in the public interface. The class may also have hidden private functions and data members as well.

Class declaration defines a data type and format but does not allocate memory or in any other way create an object of this type. The wider program must declare an instance, or object, of this type to store values in the data elements or to invoke the public class functions. Classes are often placed into libraries for use by many programs, each of which then declares objects which instantiate that class for use during program execution.

Declaring a Class in C++

Listing 17.18 illustrates a typical class declaration in C++.

LISTING 17.18. DECLARING A CLASS IN C++.

```
#include <iostream.h>
// declare the Circle class
class Circle    {
private:
   double radius;                 // private data member
public:
```

continues

LISTING 17.18. CONTINUED

```
    Circle (rad);                // constructor function
    ~Circle ();                  // deconstructor function
    double area (void);          // member function - compute area
};

//  constructor function for objects of this class
Circle::Circle(double radius)
{
    rad = radius;
}

//  deconstructor function for objects of this class
Circle::~Circle()
{
    // does nothing
}

// member function to compute the Circle's area
double Circle::area()
{
    return rad * rad * 3.141592654;
}

//       application program that uses a Circle object
main()
{
    Circle mycircle (2);         // declare a circle of radius = 2
    cout << mycircle.area():      // compute & display its area
}
```

This example begins by declaring the `Circle` class. This class has one private member, a floating point element. The class also has several public members consisting of three functions.

The *constructor function* of a class is a function called by a program to construct or create an object that is an instance of the class. In the case of the `Circle` class, the constructor function requires a single parameter, namely the radius of the desired circle. If a constructor function is explicitly defined, it has the same name as the class and does not specify a return value, even of type `void`.

NOTE

When a C++ program is compiled, the compiler generates calls to the runtime system that allocate sufficient memory each time an object of class `Circle` comes into scope. For example, an object that is defined within a function is created (and goes into scope) whenever the function is invoked. However, the object's data elements are not initialized unless a constructor function has been defined for the class.

The *deconstructor function* of a class is a function called by a program to deconstruct an object of the class type. A deconstructor takes no parameters and returns nothing.

> **NOTE**
>
> Under normal circumstances, the memory associated with an object of a given class is released for reuse whenever the object goes out of scope. In such a case, you can omit defining the deconstructor function. However, in advanced applications or where class assignments cause potential pointer conflicts, explicit deallocation of free-store memory may be necessary.

In addition to the constructor and deconstructor functions, the `Circle` class contains a public function called `area`. Programs can call this function to compute the area of circle objects.

The main program in Listing 17.18 shows how you can declare an object. `mycircle` is declared to be of type `Circle` and given a radius of 2.

The final statement in this program calls the function to compute the area of `mycircle` and passes it to the output function for display. Note that the area computation function is identified by a composite name, just as with other functions that are members of C++ data structures outside class definitions. This use underscores the fact that the object `mycircle`, of type `Circle`, is asked to execute a function that is a member of itself and with a reference to itself. You could define a `Rectangle` class that also contains an `area` function, thereby overloading the `area` function name with the appropriate algorithm for computing the areas of different kinds of geometric entities.

Inheritance and Polymorphism

A final characteristic of object-oriented languages—and of C++—is support for class inheritance and for polymorphism.

You can define new C++ classes (and hence data types) so that they automatically *inherit* the properties and algorithms associated with the parent class(es). This is done whenever a new class uses any of the standard C data types. The class from which new class definitions are created is called the *base class*. For example, a structure that includes integer members also inherits all the mathematical functions associated with integers. New classes that are defined in terms of the base classes are called *derived classes*. The Circle class in Listing 17.18 is a derived class.

Derived classes may be based on more than one base class, in which case the derived class inherits multiple data types and their associated functions. This type is called *multiple inheritance*.

Because functions can be overloaded, an object declared as a member of a derived class might act differently than an object of the base class type. The class of positive integers, for example, might return an error if the program tries to assign a negative number to a class object, although such an assignment would be legal with regard to an object of the base integer type.

This capability of different objects within the same class hierarchy to act differently under the same circumstances is referred to as *polymorphism,* which is the object-oriented concept that many people have the most difficulty grasping. However, it is also the concept that provides much of the power and elegance of object-oriented design and code. If you're designing an application using predefined graphical user interface classes, for example, you are free to ask various window objects to display themselves appropriately without having to concern yourself with how the window color, location, or other display characteristics are handled in each case.

Class inheritance and polymorphism are among the most powerful object-oriented features of C++. Together with the other, less dramatic extensions to C, these features have made possible many of the newest applications and systems capabilities in UNIX today, including GUIs for user terminals and many of the most advanced Internet and World Wide Web technologies, some of which are discussed in the subsequent chapters of this book.

Summary

UNIX was built on the C language. C is a platform-independent, compiled, procedural language based on functions and the capability to derive new, programmer-defined data structures.

C++ extends the capabilities of C by providing the necessary features for object-oriented design and code. C++ compilers correctly compile ANSI C code. C++ also provides some features, such as the capability to associate functions with data structures that do not require the use of full, class-based, object-oriented techniques. For these reasons, the C++ language enables existing UNIX programs to migrate toward the adoption of object-orientation over time.

CHAPTER 18

The make Utility

by Robin Burk and Sean Drew

IN THIS CHAPTER

Unlike interpreted languages such as Awk and Perl, compiled languages such as C and C++ must undergo two steps after they are written to be executed. First, each module must be compiled. Then, for complex programs, the modules must be linked together to form a single executable program.

The make utility provides a way to manage this process throughout the development and maintenance cycle of a program. This chapter introduces make; however, the make utility varies to some degree among the UNIX flavors, so be sure to consult your man page for specifics.

Introduction to make

The make utility provides a powerful, nonprocedural, template-based way to maintain sets of files with interdependencies. For example, make can be used to manage changes to C, C++, or HTML source code. NIS (the Network Information Service) also uses make to maintain user information. It does this by providing a way to describe the relationships between object and executable files (literally, in compiled languages, and figuratively when the program is used to manage other kinds of information) and to update the latter when the former changes. Although make can be invoked directly from the shell, complex build procedures are usually captured in a *makefile*.

Makefiles

A makefile is an ASCII text file containing any of four types of lines: target lines, shell command lines, macro lines, and make directive lines (such as include). Comments in a makefile are denoted by the pound sign (#).

When you invoke make, it looks for a file named makefile in your current working directory. If makefile does not exist, then make searches for a file named Makefile. Some UNIX versions also search for additional files, in the following order: s.makefile, SCCS/s.makefile, s.Makefile, and SCCS/s.Makefile. If you don't want to use one of the default names, other files can be used with the -f command-line option. (See the "Command-Line Options" section later in this chapter for more information.) The convention used to identify makefiles not named makefile or Makefile is to use the .mk suffix (for example, foo.mk).

Target Lines

Target lines tell make what can be built. Target lines consist of a list of targets, followed by a colon (:), followed by a list of dependencies. Although the target list can contain multiple targets, typically only one target is listed. The target list cannot be empty; however, the list of dependencies can be empty. Following are some example target lines:

```
singleTarget:     dependency1 dependency2      #target with 2
➥dependencies
target1 target2:    dependency1 dependency2      #target list 2
➥dependencies
target:                    #no dependencies
```

Dependencies are used to ensure that components are built before the overall executable file. The target must be newer than any of its dependent targets. If any of the dependent targets is newer than the current target or if the dependent target does not exist, the dependent targets must be made and then the current target must be made. If the list of dependencies is empty, the target is always made.

Filename pattern matching can be used to automatically generate a dependency list for a target. The shell metacharacters asterisk (*), question mark (?), and braces ([ ]) can be used. For example, if parse.cc, main.cc, and io.cc were all the files ending with .cc in a directory with a makefile, then the following two target lines would be identical.

```
main:    parse.cc main.cc io.cc      # list all the dependent files
➥manually
main:    *.cc              #use shell metacharacters to generate
dependent list
```

Typically, the list contains dependent items that are used in the construction of the target. For example, the dependent list may be comprised of object files that make up an executable

```
program:        part.o component.o module.o
```

or header and source files that an object file depends on

```
module.o:    module.cc module.hh part.hh
```

However, dependent targets do not have be components of the target. For example, the dependent targets might be actions you need to perform before a target is built, such as making a backup of the current target before it is rebuilt.

Lines following a target line are usually the commands required to build the target. (See the "Shell Command Lines" section for more detail.)

Library Targets

Library targets are treated as compound items whose members may be addressed individually as needed. If a target or dependency includes parentheses (( )), then the target or dependency is considered to be a library.

```
libfoo.a(foo.o):     foo.cc foo.hh     #the object file foo.o in library
➥libfoo.a depends on foo.hh and foo.cc
libfoo.a:          libfoo(foo.o) libfoo(bar.o)     #libfoo.a depends on the
➥two object files foo.o and bar.o
```

Some make variants allow multiple object files to be listed within the parentheses (see the following line of code). Others allow only one object file to be listed within the parentheses.

```
libfoo.a:          libfoo.a(foo.o bar.o)     #libfoo.a depends on the two
➥object files foo.o and bar.o
```

Do not use any spaces between the parentheses, unless you can specify multiple object files within the library—in which case the spaces can only appear between the object files.

To invoke different compile options for different modules, use double colons to define a target multiple times with different lists of dependencies. Suppose there was a particular troublesome module, buggy.o, that needed to be compiled with debugging information, whereas the more stable object files did not need debugging information. The target lines

```
libfoo.a::         libfoo.a(foo.o bar.o)     #target list one
libfoo.a::         libfoo.a(buggy.o)         #target list two
```

would enable the building of foo.o and bar.o without debugging information (typically -g to most UNIX C/C++ compilers) and buggy.o with debugging information included.

Rule Targets

One of the more powerful features of the make utility is its capability to specify generic targets, also known as *suffix rules*, *inference rules*, or just simply *rules*. Rules are a convenient way to tell make only one time how to build certain types of targets. Consider the following makefile excerpt

```
foo.o:    foo.cc
    CC -c foo.cc -I. -I/usr/local/include -DDEBUG +g     #shell
➥command-line
bar.o:    bar.cc
    CC -c bar.cc -I. -I/usr/local/include -DDEBUG +g     #shell
➥command-line
main.o:    main.cc
    CC -c main.cc -I. -I/usr/local/include -DDEBUG +g     #shell
➥command-line
main:    foo.o bar.o main.o
    CC foo.o bar.o main.o
```

which has a great deal of redundancy. All the shell command lines are identical, except for the file being compiled. The following rule tells make how to transform a file ending in .cc to a file ending in .o.

```
.cc.o:
    CC -c $< -I. -I/usr/local/include -DDEBUG +g
```

This rule uses a special macro, $<, which substitutes the current source file in the body of a rule (see the "Special Built-In Macros" section for more information). Applying the .cc.o rule to the previous makefile simplifies the makefile to

```
.cc.o:
    CC -c $< -I. -I/usr/local/include -DDEBUG +g
main:   foo.o bar.o main.o
    CC foo.o bar.o main.o
```

Many default inference rules are supplied by make. It is capable of determining which rule to apply by applying the following algorithm:

Search the list to determine whether any of the default and user-defined rules build the desired file type, as determined by the file extension. If a file of the specified type exists, the rule is applied. For example, if a makefile specified only two rules in the following order, a .c.o rule and a .cc.o, and make was asked to create foo.o, the following set of events would occur:

1. make would first try to apply the .c.o rule. The root of the target foo.o (foo) (the root is the filename with the first extension removed (.o)) is used to apply the .c.o rule.

2. The .c.o rule tells make that to make a file named *root*.o, a file named *root*.c can be employed.

3. If the file *root*.c exists in the current directory, then apply the rule to *root*.c. In the example, the file foo.c is checked for existence in the current directory.

4. If foo.c does not exist, then foo.cc is checked for existence.

5. If foo.cc does not exist, then an error is reported to the effect that the target cannot be made.

In many versions of make, rules can be chained together by make to reach a target goal. This allows you to specify flexible multistep build procedures. For example, the CORBA IDL (Common Object Request Broker Architecture Interface Definition Language) compiler transforms interface definitions into C++ source code. If you ask make to create foo.o, given a makefile that has an .idl.cc and a .cc.o rule, make does the following:

18

THE make UTILITY

1. If `foo.cc` does not exist, `make` then looks for `foo.idl` to create the `foo.cc` file.

2. After the `foo.cc` file is created, the `.cc.o` rule is applied to reach the final goal of `foo.o`.

This chaining of rules is a powerful feature of `make`.

Double Suffix Rules

The rules defined so far are known as *double suffix rules* because they contain double suffixes, such as `.rtf.html`. The `.rtf.html` rule can be used to convert a Rich Text Format file to a Hypertext Markup Language file. Double suffix rules describe how to transform *root.suffix1* to *root.suffix2* (for example, `index.rtf` to `index.html`). Following is a list of the more commonly available double suffix rules supplied as defaults by `make`:

```
.c.o .c~.o .c~.c .c.a .c~.a .C.o .C~.o .C~.C .C.a .C~.a
.cc.o .cc~.o .cc~.cc .cc.a .cc~.a .h~.h .H~.H
.s.o .s~.o .s~.a .p.o .p~.o .p~.p .p.a .p~.a
.f.o .f~.o .f~.f .f.a .f~.a .r.o .r~.o .r~.r .r.a .r~.a
.y.o .y~.o .y.c .y~.c .l.o .l~.o .l.c
```

You may redefine any of the default rules supplied by `make`. These rules use standard macros to provide generic actions. For example, the way a C or C++ file is compiled does not change much, other than some of the flags supplied to the compiler. The most commonly used of these macros are `LDFLAGS`, `CFLAGS`, and `CXXFLAGS`, which are used to parameterize the linker (`ld`), the C compiler (`cc`), and the C++ compiler (`CC` on HP-UX), respectively. The `LIBS` macro, which is not incorporated into the default rules, is commonly used to define which libraries other than the system default libraries are to be used at link time and in what order should the libraries be evaluated.

The tildes (`~`) in the double suffix rules refer to an SCCS (Source Code Control System) file. SCCS files have a prefix prepended to a filename, which is in direct conflict with `make` because `make` bases all of its algorithms on suffixes. For example, the file `foo.cc` becomes `s.foo.cc` when using SCCS. The tilde signals `make` to treat the file as an SCCS file, so that `.cc~.o` can be used to transform `s.foo.cc` to `foo.o` with the command `make foo.o`, which is preferable to the command `make s.foo.o && mv s.foo.o foo.o`.

Single Suffix Rules

Single suffix rules describe how to transform *root.suffix1* to *root* (for example, `cat.c` to `cat`). The second suffix is in effect null in a single suffix rule. Single suffix rules are useful for creating programs composed of a single source file. In fact, if you have the `CFLAGS` and `LDFLAGS` environment variables defined, you don't need a makefile to effectively use the `.c` rule because the `.c` rule is part of the default set of rules. Assuming that a Bourne-compatible shell and the source files `cat.c`, `echo.c`, `cmp.c`, and `chown.c` are in the current directory, the following commands build the targets cat, echo, cmp, and chown without a makefile:

```
% export CFLAGS="-I. -DDEBUG +g" LDFLAGS="-lfoo -lbar"
% make cat echo cmp chown
```

Following is a list of the more commonly available single suffix rules supplied as defaults by make:

.c .c~ .C .C~ .cc .cc~ .sh .sh~ .p .p~ .f .f~ .r .r~

Built-In Targets

Make supplies several built-in targets, some of which accept dependencies, which are really arguments to the built-in target. For example, the arguments to .PRECIOUS are file suffixes. Table 18.1 lists the built-in targets.

TABLE 18.1. BUILT-IN TARGETS FOR make.

Target	Target Description
.IGNORE	Ignore nonzero error codes returned from the command lines specified to build the target. The default make behavior is to cease all processing and exit when a command line returns a nonzero status. The -i make command-line option can be used to achieve the same behavior.
.SILENT	When this target appears in the makefile, make does not echo commands before executing them. When used in POSIX mode, it could be followed by target names, and only those are executed silently.
.DEFAULT	Execute any commands associated with the .DEFAULT target if no other rule can be applied. The purpose is similar to the default: case in C/C++ and C shell switch statements.
.PRECIOUS	Preserve the specified files even if a signal or nonzero return code from a shell command would otherwise cause made built files to be deleted. The .PRECIOUS target may appear multiple times in a makefile, with each occurrence appending to the list of precious files. .PRECIOUS is useful for commands that generate source (lex, yacc, IDL compilers) or fetch source (RCS, SCCS, and so on).
.SUFFIXES	Specifies the file types that make processes. A blank .SUFFIXES target resets the suffix list to an empty state. The .SUFFIXES target may appear multiple times in a makefile, with each occurrence appending to the list of known suffixes. The order of the suffixes is important because that is the order rules are tried. To rearrange the order, use a blank .SUFFIX target to clear the current suffix list and then subsequent .SUFFIX targets to specify a new order. Common default suffixes are: .o .c .c~ .C .C~ .cc .cc~ .y .y~ .l .l~ .s .s~ .sh .sh~ .h .h~ .H .H~ .p .p~ .f .f~ .r .r~ .

Common Targets

By convention, there are some common targets in makefiles. These common targets are usually not files and are known as *dummy targets*. One of the most common dummy targets is `clean`. The command `make clean` generally removes all the built files (typically programs and object files). `Clobber` is a more severe target, which removes all files and associated directories. The command `make clobber` is often used to uninstall software. For makefiles that build and install software, `install` is often a target. The command `make install` usually creates the programs, installs the man pages, and copies the program to its intended location. Another common target is `all`. When a makefile builds several targets, `make all` typically builds all the targets.

Shell Command Lines

Shell command lines, also known more simply as commands, define the actions used to build a target. Any text following a semicolon (;) on a target line is considered a command. All subsequent lines after a target that begin with a tab are also commands for the target. The comment character of a pound sign (#) is allowed within a target's command definition. For example, the following makefile excerpt shows a comment embedded in a command definition:

```
foo.html: foo.rtf
    rtftohtml -hx $<
#place current date in file, $$$$ expands to $$ in shell
    sed s/__DATE__/"`date`"/ $@ > foo.$$$$ && mv foo.$$$$ $@
```

The first line that is not a comment or does not start with a tab ends the list of commands associated with the target. Long command lines can be continued on the next line using the backslash (\) newline sequence.

```
foo.html: foo.rtf
    rtftohtml -hx $<
    sed    -e "s/PAGE_DATE/`date`/"              \
        -e "s/PAGE_TITLE/$(DOCTITLE)/"           \
        -e "s/PAGE_NAME/$(HOMETITLE)/"   $@      \
    > foo.$$$$ && mv foo.$$$$ $@
```

Any macros embedded in the command are evaluated, and the proper value is substituted by `make`; as a result, the shell sees only the values of the macros.

Normally, the commands are echoed to the standard output, unless the command is preceded by the at sign (@). Use of the @ directive provides a finer grain of output control than the `.SILENT` target or the `-s` command-line option—both of which turn off all command output. The @ directive is particularly useful when issuing an `echo` command. The command `echo Build complete at `date`` without the @ directive would produce the output

```
echo Build complete at `date`
Build complete at Mon May 12 02:32:37 MST 1997
```

whereas using the @ results in the cleaner output of

```
Build complete at Mon May 12 02:32:37 MST 1997
```

Note that the @ directive, the `-s` option, and the `.SILENT` target only suppress the echoing of the command; the output of the command is still shown. The output of the following makefile snippet

```
target:
#echo this command to standard out
    echo echoed to standard out
#do not echo this command to standard out
    @echo not echoed to standard out
```

for `target` is

```
% make target
echo echoed to standard out
echoed to standard out
not echoed to standard out
```

The comment character can appear after shell commands; however, the comment is not a make comment but instead causes the # sign and all following text to be passed to the shell.

Macros

Macros serve four purposes in a makefile:

- To reference commonly used text simply. For example, the following list of object files:

```
program:    oh.o dot.o polka.o disor.o o.o whoa.o doe.o
        $(CPLUSPLUS) oh.o dot.o polka.o disor.o o.o whoa.o doe.o $(LIBS)
➥$(LDFLAGS) -o $@
```

  can be assigned to the macro `OBJECTS`, which is then invoked wherever the object list is desired:

```
OBJECTS = oh.o dot.o polka.o disor.o o.o whoa.o doe.o
program:    $(OBJECTS)
        $(CPLUSPLUS) $(OBJECTS) $(LIBS) $(LDFLAGS) -o $@
```

- Macros increase maintainability by providing a single place in which information is defined.

- Macros provide a way to introduce variability into a makefile by parameterizing what is likely to change. For example, a macro can be defined to govern whether a program should be built with debugging information included. By changing the value of the macro outside the makelist, in the make command line or an environment variable, the desired behavior can be achieved without modifying the makefile.
- Macros improve the readability of makefiles. A long list of object files distorts what is really being done in a makefile. Well-chosen macro names specify the action being taken and identify the contents to which they refer.

Macro definitions, in order of preference, can come from four places: make internal defaults, environment variables, the makefile(s), and the command line. The preference order can be changed via the -e make command-line option to have environment variables override makefile macro definitions. See the "Command-Line Options" section for a discussion of make command-line options.

Macro Syntax

See the "Command-Line Macro Definition" for information on how to define macros on the command line. The basic syntax for defining macros within a makefile is

```
name = valueList
```

The *name* may consist of any combination of uppercase (A-Z) and lowercase (a-z) letters, digits (0-9), and underlines (_). Macro names are all uppercase by convention. Depending on your version of make, certain punctuation characters are allowed in a macro name, such as the caret (^) or at sign (@). Unless strange compulsions force you to name macros ^foo*@, such punctuation usage is strongly discouraged; it seldom helps readability or portability.

The equal sign (=) can migrate rather freely about the macro assignment expression because blanks and tabs surrounding the equal sign are removed. As a result of the whitespace removal behavior, all the following assignments produce the same result; the string VALUE is assigned to the name NAME:

```
NAME=VALUE
NAME = VALUE
NAME=    VALUE
NAME    =VALUE
```

The *valueList* may contain zero, one, or more entries, as demonstrated in the following:

```
BLANK         =
ONE_VALUE     =    one
LIST_VALUE    =    one two three
```

The *valueList* can be quite long and the backslash (\) newline escape may be used to continue a definition on another line. If the line is continued, the newline is translated to a space by make, and all subsequent whitespace (blanks, tabs, and newlines) is removed. Thus, the makefile

```
BAR=one\
            \
        space

X:
        echo $(BAR)
```

would produce the following output if target X were made:

```
echo one space
one space
```

Other than the whitespace translations mentioned previously, whitespace in a macro definition is preserved.

Macro definitions can use other macros. Nested definitions cannot be recursive, or make complains.

```
RECURSIVE    = $(BAD)         #don't do this
BAD        = $(RECURSIVE)         #don't do this
FIRST_HALF      = first
SECOND_HALF     = second
NESTED     = $(FIRST_HALF) $(SECOND_HALF)
NESTED_AGAIN     = zero.$(FIRST_HALF).$(SECOND_HALF)
```

Ordering is not important when defining macros. In the preceding example, the macro NESTED could have been defined before FIRST_HALF and SECOND_HALF. A macro does need to be defined before it is used in any target line as a dependency. If a macro is defined multiple times, the last value is used. This means that a macro cannot have one value for part of the makefile and a different value for another part of the makefile. If the value of a macro needs to be changed, a recursive call to make is needed with the new value passed in the command line, as in the following example:

```
MACRO_NAME=oldValue
target:
    $(MAKE) MACRO_NAME=newValue target
```

A macro is dereferenced by applying the dollar ($) operator and either parentheses (()) or curly braces ({}). For example, the macro MAY could be dereferenced as $(MAY) or ${MAY}. However, in the case of single-character macros, just the $ suffices, so the macro Z could be dereferenced as $Z, $(Z), or ${Z}. However, in the case of single-character macros, the use of () or {} is encouraged. Single-character names are not good to use in general; a more descriptive name will be appreciated by the next person to read the makefile.

18

THE make UTILITY

If a macro is undefined or is assigned a blank value, the null string is substituted for its value. The makefile

```
BLANK=
X:; echo foo$(BLANK)$(UNDEFINED)bar
```

produces the following output for target X:

```
echo foobar
foobar
```

If you need to use a dollar sign ($) in make, it needs to be escaped with another dollar sign. Multiple consecutive occurrences of the dollar sign are allowed:

```
#echo environment variable $LOGNAME and process id $$
foo:
    echo $$LOGNAME $$$$
```

Macro Substitution

The make utility supports a simple text substitution function for macros. The syntax is :oldString=newString, which is appended immediately following the macro name in macro reference. For example, if the macro OBJS were defined as

```
OBJS = fuggles.o perle.o cascade.o saaz.o
```

the .o extension could be replaced by the .cc extension by using the macro reference, $(OBJS:.o=.cc), which would evaluate to fuggles.cc perle.cc cascade.cc saaz.cc.

Special Built-In Macros

The make utility provides several special built-in macros to allow rules to be generic. The built-in macros can be referenced without parentheses. For example, the @ macro can be referred to as $@ instead of $(@). Note that the value of a built-in macro may be undefined depending on what state make is in when the macro is evaluated. Some macros are only valid during suffix rule evaluation, whereas other macros are only valid during regular rule evaluation. Table 18.2 lists the built-in macros.

TABLE 18.2. BUILT-IN MACROS FOR make.

Macro	Macro Description
$@	Substitute the value of the entire current target name. In the case of a library target, the value is the name of the library, not the name of the archive member to be placed in the library. $@ can be used in target and suffix rules.
$%	Substitute the value of the current archive member (valid only when the current target is a library). Remember that a library target has the form of

Macro	Macro Description
	lib(object.o) or lib((kernel_entry)). $% is needed because $@ evaluates to the library name for library targets. $% can be used in target and suffix rules.
$?	Substitute the list of dependents that are out of date for the current target. $? can be used in target and suffix rules. However, $? evaluates to possibly many names in a target rule but only evaluates to one name in a suffix rule.
$<	Substitute the current source file , i.e. the file that is out of date with respect to the current target, based on the implicit rule that is being invoked. For example, in a .cc.o rule, $< would be whichever .cc file is being compiled. $< is only valid in a suffix rule or in the .DEFAULT rule.
$*	Substitute the root of the current target name. For example, if the target were foo.o, the root would have the suffix .o deleted for an end result of foo. $* is valid only during evaluation of inference rules.

The preceding built-in macros can have special modifiers appended to the end of the macro to return the filename or directory name portion. Use F to retrieve the filename, and D to retrieve the directory name. The shortcut method without parentheses may not be used when a modifier is applied. For example, if $< evaluated to /users/dylan/foo.cc, $(<F) would return foo.cc, and $(<D) would return /users/dylan. Some versions of make return a trailing slash appended to directory names, so using the previous example, $(<D) would return /users/dylan/. If the macro evaluates to multiple values, as does the $? macro, the F or D modifier is applied to each of the multiple values in turn. (Some versions of make do not support the F and D modifiers.)

In addition to the five macros previously discussed, there is the *dynamic dependency* macro $$@. The macro is called dynamic because it is evaluated at the time the dependency is processed. $$@ can only be used on dependency lines. The $$@ macro evaluates to the current target just as $@ does, but $$@ is allowed on the dependency line, whereas $@ is not. The $$@ macro is useful for building executables made up of only one source file, as the following makefile snippet demonstrates:

```
COMMANDS = cat dog say sed test true false more ar less
$(COMMANDS) : $$@.c
    $(CC) $? -o $@
```

The macros previously discussed have values supplied by make and are not modifiable by you. There are other macros that make uses but whose default value can be changed. The macros VPATH and SHELL fall into this category. VPATH specifies a path where make can search for dependent files. The current directory is searched first; then each of the VPATH elements is searched. VPATH uses colons (:) to delimit the list elements. For example, if

```
VPATH = source:../moreSource:/the/rest/of/the/source
```

appeared in a makefile, `make` would first search for dependents in the current directory, then in a subdirectory named `source`, followed by a sibling directory named `moreSource`, and then the absolute directory of `/the/rest/of/the/source`.

The `SHELL` macro specifies the shell to use when processing the command-line portions of a target. Most versions of `make` default to the Bourne or POSIX shell (`/bin/sh`). To maximize portability, it is best to write shell commands in the POSIX shell syntax and to set the `SHELL` variable to `/bin/sh`, for example, `SHELL = /bin/sh`. Some versions of `make` only allow the use of Bourne shell syntax.

make Directives

A makefile is mostly composed of macro, command, and target lines but can also include `make` directives. `make` directives differ from version to version of the utility and should be avoided if you are concerned with portability. The most common `make` directive is `include`, which enables common definitions to be written once and included by reference. The `include` directive must be the first item on a line followed by a filename, as in the following example.

```
include /project/global.mk
include /users/sdrew/myGlobal.mk
#rest of makefile
```

If your version of `make` does not have `include` directives, you can achieve the same behavior using multiple `-f` options (see the "Command-Line Options" section for a description of the `-f` option). The following command effectively emulates the previous example makefile:

```
% make -f /project/global.mk -f /users/sdrew/myGlobal.mk
```

If you grow tired of typing the `-f` command-line option, some shell trickery should relieve the drudgery. You can write an alias or shell script to automatically supply the `include` file options to `make`.

The comment (#) is a directive to `make` to ignore the line if it is the first nonwhitespace character on a line. Comments can appear after other `make` lines was well, as shown in the following:

```
foo=bar                 #assignment
target:;echo $(FOO)        #target
#this whole line is a comment
```

Note that the `comment` directive is supported by all versions of `make`.

> **CAUTION**
>
> When using the `include` directive, do not place a pound sign (#) in front of the `include` directive (for example, `#include foo.mk`). The `include` line will then be interpreted as a comment by `make`, and the file will not be included.

Command-Line Arguments

Although `make` has methods of configuration from within a makefile, the `make` command-line options provide a convenient way to configure `make` on-the-fly. The typical sequence of `make` command-line arguments is shown here, although arguments may appear in any order:

```
make [-f makefile] [options] [macro definitions] [targets]
```

Note that optional items are enclosed in braces ([ ]).

Command-Line Options

Command-line options are indicated with a dash (-) and then the option, for example, `make -e`. If multiple options are needed, the options may be preceded by only one dash, `make -kr`, or by using a dash per option, `make -k -r`. Mixing option specification methods is allowed, `make -e -kr`. Table 18.3 lists the command-line options for `make`.

TABLE 18.3. COMMAND-LINE OPTIONS FOR make.

Option	*Option Description*
`-b`	Turns on compatibility mode for makefiles written before the current versions of `make`. The `-b` option is usually on by default.
`-d`	Turns on debug mode. Debug mode is exceedingly verbose and is generally only used as a last resort when debugging a makefile. Information about file dates, internal flags, and variables are printed to the standard out.
`-e`	Environment variables override assignments made in a makefile.
`-f filename`	Denotes the name of the file to be used as a makefile. Multiple `-f` options may be used; the files are processed in the order they appear on the command line. A hyphen (-) may be used to indicate that `make` should read commands from the standard input. Multiple `-f -` options are not allowed. The `-f` option is the only option that requires an argument. A space must appear between the `-f` argument and the filename that appears afterward.

continues

TABLE 18.3. CONTINUED.

Option	Option Description
-p	Prints all the macro definitions, suffix rules, suffixes, and explicit description file entries to the standard output. The -p option is useful for interrogating make's set of default rules.
-i	Places make into ignore mode, such that nonzero error codes returned by commands no longer cause make to terminate the building of all targets. The ignore mode can also be entered by placing the .IGNORE target in a makefile.
-k	Instructs make to kill work on the current target (only) if a nonzero error code is returned by a command. Work on the other targets may continue. This is the opposite of the -S mode. If both -k and -S are supplied, the last one specified is used. This overriding behavior provides a way to override the presence of -S in the MAKEFLAGS environment variable.
-n	Places make into no execute mode. When in no execute mode, make just prints rather than executes the commands. Lines beginning with the at sign (@), which are not normally printed, are printed. Lines that have the string $(MAKE) or ${MAKE} are executed so that all the commands can be seen.
-q	Places make into question mode. make returns a zero status code if all the targets are up-to-date, and a nonzero status code if any one of the targets is out-of-date.
-r	Removes built-in suffix list and built-in rules. This puts make in a pristine state, such that only user-specified rules and suffixes are used.
-s	Places make in silent mode. Normally commands are executed to the standard output, unless the commands are preceded with the at (@) symbol. The -s option has the same effect as including the .SILENT target in the makefile.
-S	Places make in standard error handling mode. The -S option has make terminate building all targets if any command returns a nonzero status. If both -k and -S are supplied, the last one specified is used. This overriding behavior provides a way to override the presence of a -k in the MAKEFLAGS environment variable. -S is the default mode.
-t	Places make in touch mode. When in touch mode, make does not issue the commands associated with a rule, but simply touches the files. (Consult your man page for description of the UNIX command touch.)

Command-Line Macro Definition

Macros can be defined on the command line using the *name=value* syntax. Zero or more macro definitions may be supplied on the command line. Command-line macros have the highest precedence and override macros defined internally by make, macros from the current environment, and macros specified in the makefile. Command-line macros provide a convenient way of temporarily overriding current settings without changing them in the environment or in the makefile. For scripting, command-line macros help ensure consistent execution from run to run.

Command-Line Target Specification

Zero or more targets can be specified on the make command line. If no target is provided on the command line, make searches for the first nonrule target in the first makefile, and then each subsequent makefile, and tries to update the target if one is found. Targets specified on the command line should be listed in one of the makefiles currently being used by make. Each of the targets specified is updated by make in the order the arguments appeared on the command line.

Different make Programs

Although make is a powerful tool, the "standard" versions of make have some rather gaping feature holes (for example, no conditional statements such as if). As a result, other versions of make are available that try to fill some of the feature gaps. In addition to extra features, other make offerings offer a portability solution. You can either try to write a makefile that matches the lowest common denominator feature set while exercising the fewest bugs for various UNIX platforms, or use the same make offering on all platforms. If you are not distributing your makefile for public consumption, the latter choice is much more palatable. Some of the more commonly available make offerings are covered in this following sections.

GNU make

GNU's version of make processes "standard" makefiles well and is often used in lieu of the version distributed with most UNIX platforms. GNU and its version of make (*gmake* or *GNU make)* is available on the Internet.

Conditionals

GNU make provides a full complement of if statements for conditional processing within a makefile.

Calling Shell Using $(shell)

GNU make has the handy capability to substitute the output of any shell command as though it were a macro. When used in conjunction with if statements, $(shell) is handy for parameterizing a makefile automatically. For example:

```
HOSTTYPE = $(shell uname)
ifeq "$(HOSTTYPE" "HP-UX"
# config host environment
endif
```

Pattern Rules

Pattern rules are a powerful extension to suffix rules. The pattern rule has the form of `targetPattern: dependencyPattern`, which is the opposite order of a suffix rule. For example, `.cc.o` expressed as a pattern rule would be `%.o: %.cc`. The `%` in the pattern rule operates as the asterisk (`*`) wildcard operates in the shell, which allows more than just a suffix to specify a rule. For example, if you have a directory of `.gif` files that you want to enlarge with a command-line utility for users with larger screens, the following makefile with a pattern rule would do the job nicely:

```
%_big.gif:      %.gif
          giftran -x 125 $< > $*_big.gif

GIFS      = $(shell ls *.gif)
BIG_GIFS:          $(GIFS:.gif=_big.gif)
```

Other Nifty Features

GNU `make` is loaded with far too many nifty features to list here, among them the `:=` operator, simplified library syntax - `libfoo.a(one.o two.o)`, and extra text processing functions.

`imake`

Include Make, or `imake`, is a preprocessor for the `make` utility. The C preprocessor provides functionality that `make` does not offer: `include` directives, `if` directives, macro functions. `imake` is used in the X distribution. `imake` works by providing a template file that is then processed to create a file for use by `make`. `imake` documentation is somewhat poor, and the extra level of indirection can be cumbersome; however, the templates allow large project trees to be generated automatically.

To get a copy of `imake`, try `ftp://ftp.primate.wisc.edu/pub/imake-book/itools.tar.Z` or `ftp://ftp.primate.wisc.edu/pub/imake-book/itools.tar.gz`. The tar file contains, among other files, the following: `imake`, `makedepend`, `xmkmf`, `mkdirhier`, `imboot`, `msub`, and `imdent`. Another good place to look for `imake` is `ftp://ftp.x.org`, which contains the X11 R5 distribution directory structure, so you can retrieve `imake` without having to pull the entire X11 distribution. You can also consult your favorite Internet search engine using the keyword *imake*.

nmake

Developed by AT&T, nmake has been tailored to help meet the demands of large-scale C development. nmake addresses many deficiencies of standard make and has a few new twists of its own. nmake is the only make that stores compile options for use in subsequent runs of make. That enables the capability to ask make to build any file that was not built with a certain macro definition or compiler switch. It also allows you to include multiple shell lines in a single shell invocation elegantly.

make Utilities

Several utilities are available to enhance the usability of make. A few of the more common utilities are briefly covered in the following sections.

makedepend

A makefile is intended to document the relationships between files as well as the rules for building those files. makedepend automates documenting these relationships by generating a dependency list for your source files. makedepend takes into account #if directives for proper dependency generation.

mkmf

mkmf is short for *make makefile*. mkmf examines all the sources in the current directory, searches the source for dependencies, and then generates a makefile based on templates.

Summary

The make program allows programmers to manage the process of generating executable programs from many source, object, and library files. It is also sufficiently generic to allow the manipulation of other types of information. Because of its facility for chaining rules and defining macros, make provides a powerful tool for serious UNIX developers.

Source Management and Revision Control

By Sriranga Veeraraghavan, Eric Goebelbecker, Bill Ball, and Fred Trimble

IN THIS CHAPTER

Managing change is a common part of computing. Programmers have to manage bug fixes while producing new versions of applications that are frequently based on the code that contains what is being fixed. System administrators have to manage a variety of configuration changes, such as adding new users to systems and adding new systems to networks, without interfering with day-to-day operations. Web authors have to make continuous revisions to documents to keep up with the constantly growing and improving Internet competition. Just about any computer-related job goes through a seemingly endless cycle of revision, refinement, and renewal.

On UNIX systems, these changes can be managed with a *revision control system* or a *source control system.* These systems allow one or more people to track changes made to a set of files, quickly and accurately undo a set of changes, and maintain an audit trail regarding why changes were made.

First we explore the common characteristics and concepts behind these systems and see how you can use them to help manage your projects more effectively. Then we present an overview of RCS, SCCS, and CVS which are three of the most common source control systems. These systems consist of a set of utilities that allow users to manage the creation and maintenance of any document.

Some common features available in all revision control systems are the following:

- The capability to save multiple versions of a file and easily select between them
- The capability to resolve (and prevent) conflicts caused by more than one person altering a file simultaneously
- The capability to review the history of changes made to a file
- The capability to link versions of different files together

Revision Control Concepts

To illustrate some of the major concepts behind revision control, we use a simple HTML project as an example. This section introduces the operation that would be used to maintain the project without going into the specifics of any particular tool.

Our project starts with the file `hello.html`:

```
<!DOCTYPE HTML PUBLIC -//IETF//DTD HTML//EN>
<html>
<head>
<title>An Html Page</title>
</head>
<body>
<h1>Hello World!</h1>
```

```
<hr>
<address><a href= mailto:eric@prophet>Eric Goebelbecker</a></address>
</body>
</html>
```

Registering the Initial Revision

The first step is to *register* hello.html with the revision control system. When a file is registered, a *control file* is created, the *revision* is numbered, and the original file is marked read-only if you specify that you want a copy to stay behind.

Revisions or *deltas* are the building blocks of source control projects. Files (and groups of files) are stored and retrieved in terms of the changes made to them. Each time a file is changed and *checked in*, a new revision is created.

The first version of a file that is checked in is referred to as the *root* of the *revision tree*. It would typically be numbered version 1.1. Revision numbers, such as 1.1, are used as names for versions of files. The leftmost number usually signifies a major release for a product. If you were working on a new version of an existing product, you might override this number to be 2 or 3, depending on what internal policies exist for version numbers. The second number represents the minor version, where 2.5 might represent the fifth revision of a file within version 2.

> **NOTE**
>
> In large-scale projects, you might see version numbers such as 2.5.1. As discussed previously, the first two numbers are the major and minor numbers, 2 and 5 respectively. The last number is called the *maintenance release number*.
>
> The use of this number varies, but frequently it is used to indicate a patch or bug fix. In the case of 2.5.1, the 1 indicates the first patch to the fifth revision of the file with version 2. Note that a file with the version number 2.5.1 is different from a file with the version number 2.51, which is the 51st revision of the file with version 2.

19

REVISION
CONTROL

It is significant that the version control system marks any remaining copies of the file as read-only. A version control system is only as accurate as the changes it is aware of, and registering changes is important. On a superficial level, the file's permissions act as a reminder to keep the file in sync with the revision control system. If more than one person is involved in a project, the file permissions perform a crucial role because edits to a file cannot be saved while a file is marked read-only. Because file permissions can only be changed by the file's owner, the right way to edit the file is to check it out from the control system, which marks the file as only being writable by the person who has checked it out. So when a user checks a file out, others are not be able to alter it until it is checked back in. This is a fundamental operation in what is called *file locking*.

> **NOTE**
>
> When a group is working together, for instance, to create a set of Web pages, an application development project, or any other nonsystem administration-related project, all the users should have a proper account and should be using it. No one should be working as root, because file locking essentially becomes useless when a user can override it at will.

Revision control systems store the series of changes to objects in control files. These files contain complete histories of the project, which allows them to serve as both a backup and an audit trail. In fact, keeping a current copy of the file isn't really necessary, just as long as the history file is available. Many programming utilities, such as make and emacs, are aware of revision control and can automatically retrieve the latest version of a file.

Registering hello.html starts the revision control process. This process essentially enforces a discipline on users who are working on that project. Files cannot be altered unless they are checked out, and others cannot work on them unless they are checked in. If you do not check a file in, your coworkers will most likely tell you to. Also, as you see in the next section, when files are checked in, the systems allows you to add comments regarding the changes you made. If the comments are missing or incomplete, trouble frequently ensues, especially when the changes are implicated in a problem.

Creating a New Revision

The first change that we need to make to hello.html is the email address on line #9. As written, the address will not work for external systems because the domain name is incomplete, so we must update the file. The file is marked read-only from when we registered it with the revision control system. To edit it, we need to check out the latest version.

Checking out a file provides a modifiable working copy of the file. Within the revision control system, checked out files are considered "locked," which prevents other users from checking in revisions that could conflict with ours.

After checking out the file, modify the line as follows:

```
<address><a href=mailto:eric@niftydomain.com>Eric
Goebelbecker</a></address>
```

Then check in the file. As a part of the check in process, the system prompts for a comment. (The SCCS request prompt is shown.)

```
comments? Fixed e-mail address.
```

The file now has a second revision, which is numbered version 1.2 because we didn't override the default.

The Revision Tree

Imagine that this process continues, and `hello.html` grows into a more sophisticated HTML page. The revisions are displayed as a tree in Figure 19.1.

FIGURE 19.1.
A simple revision tree.

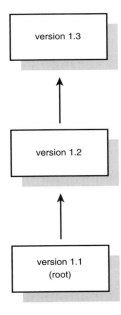

Each revision is a node on the revision tree. The node labeled version 1.1 (root) in Figure 19.1 represents the initial revision of `hello.html`. The node labeled version 1.2 represents the version with the corrected email address; version 1.3 could represent a version with some graphics added, and so on.

Returning to an Earlier Revision

Suppose that version 1.3 contained a very large graphic, which worked fine on your local LAN, but took too long to download elsewhere on the Internet. In addition, when this graphic was added to the page, a lot of formatting was also added, so simply removing the graphic or adding a smaller one would seriously affect the page. To make the page usable quickly, it would be nice to revert to version 1.2. This would give you more time to solve the problem with version 1.3.

Revision control systems make this easy because a file can be checked out at a specific revision level. You can also check out revision 1.2 as a read-only file so that users can view it, while addressing the problem with revision 1.3.

Revision History

Having only three versions of `hello.html` makes the transition back to an earlier version too easy. In the real world it is never that simple, so let's look at a more comprehensive example.

Say that you are working on an accounting package, and a major new feature has just been added. For example, the package now calculates the value of a customer's account in U.S. dollars and German Marks. Following this enhancement, a few minor features and a pair of bugs were fixed.

One day a customer points out that the calculation in German currency has a problem. Because the program has gone through some changes since that feature was added, how can the bug be isolated quickly? Viewing the revision history could help. Following is a theoretical revision history (in SCCS format) for the package:

```
D 1.5 97/08/03 16:23:32 fred 4 3        00024/00025/00200
MRs:
COMMENTS:
Added compatibility with fvwm
D 1.4 97/08/03 16:23:32 fred 4 3        00024/00025/00200
MRs:
COMMENTS:
Fixed divide by zero bug in entry module
D 1.3 97/07/15 19:14:19 mike 3 2        00002/00002/00223
MRs:
COMMENTS:
Added report formatting features and support for HP680C
D 1.2 97/06/27 19:03:26 melvin 2 1       00012/00003/00193
MRs:
COMMENTS:
Added Deutsch Mark valuation module
```

The bug was introduced back in version 1.2 when Melvin added the support for Deutsche Marks. However, since then Mike and Fred added reporting features and support for `fvwm` and fixed another bug. From the revision comments, you can begin isolating when and where a problem might have been introduced.

Multiple Versions of a Single File or Project

The previous examples looked at a revision tree with a single path, the trunk. Let's look at a situation where a project needs more advanced solutions.

A small *ISP* (Internet service provider) provides two varieties of service, one is a *shell account* where a customer can dial in and log in to a UNIX host. The other is a *PPP account*, where the customer dials in for a network connection, but never logs in to one of the ISP's systems. Though some users never log in to a UNIX host, all users need to have accounts on the *POP mail server* because every user receives mail. Thus, the ISP needs to maintain two UNIX passwd files, one for shell users only and one with all users.

The initial revision of the passwd file, prior to the ISP offering PPP accounts, might have looked like this:

```
abe:x:200:200:Abraham Lincoln:/export/home/abe:/sbin/sh
ron:x:201:200:Ronald Reagan:/export/home/ron:/sbin/sh
ben:x:202:200:Benjamin Franklin:/export/home/ben:/bin/ksh
sue:x:203:200:Susan B Anthony:/export/home/sue:/bin/ksh
ike:x:204:200:Dwight D Eisenhower:/export/home/ike:/bin/ksh
harry:205:200:Harry S Truman:/export/home/harry:/bin/sh
john:x:206:200:John Galt:/export/home/john:/bin/csh
```

At a certain point, however, the ISP administrator needed to add users to the passwd file who did not belong on the shell host, only on the POP host:

```
abe:x:200:200:Abraham Lincoln:/export/home/abe:/sbin/sh
ron:x:201:200:Ronald Reagan:/export/home/ron:/sbin/sh
ben:x:202:200:Benjamin Franklin:/export/home/ben:/bin/ksh
sue:x:203:200:Susan B Anthony:/export/home/sue:/bin/ksh
ike:x:204:200:Dwight D Eisenhower:/export/home/ike:/bin/ksh
harry:205:200:Harry S Truman:/export/home/harry:/bin/sh
john:x:206:200:John Galt:/export/home/john:/bin/csh
bill:x:207:200:William Clinton:/tmp:/bin/nosuchshell
hillary:x:208:200:Hillary Clinton:/tmp:/bin/nosuchshell
al:x:209:200:Albert Gore:/tmp:/bin/nosuchshell
hank:x:210:200:Hank Reardon:/tmp:/bin/nosuchshell
```

The users with nosuchshell only have access to POP mail.

Branching and Merging

If the administrator just wanted to use the shell accounts as a base for the POP mail file, he could add a *branch* to the revision tree.

As Figure 19.2 shows, a branch creates a new development path for the project. It also has an impact on revision numbers. The branch that extends from revision 1.2 is labeled 1.2.1.1 because it is the initial revision derived from number 1.2. The second set of two numbers is used exactly as the first, with a major and minor number.

19

REVISION CONTROL

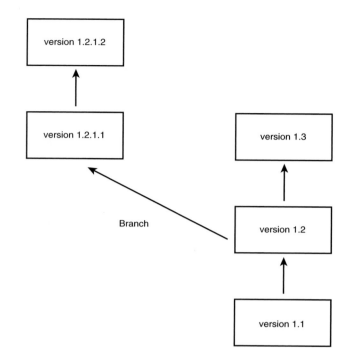

FIGURE 19.2.

A revision tree with branches.

By branching, the administrator is able to include the contents of the existing file in the new version without adding unneeded entries in the original tree. But what happens when a new shell user signs up? The administrator still has to add the same information in two places.

No one wants to do the same thing twice, least of all a probably already overloaded system administrator. But what mechanism would allow users who are added to the shell system to show up on the POP system without inadvertently adding POP users to the list of shell users?

Most revision control systems support *merging* branches to avoid having to manually add changes. This process allows the administrator to add entries from the main tree to the branch, without also adding them back to the main tree. In Figure 19.3, version 1.4 is merged with 1.2.1.2 to create version 1.2.1.3.

FIGURE 19.3.

Branched revision tree with a one-way merge.

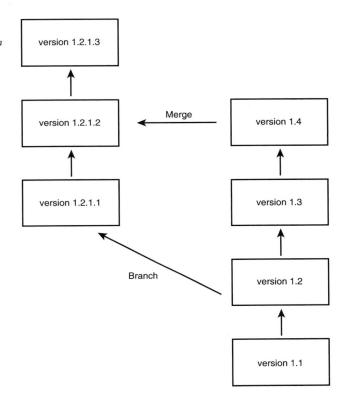

Merging files can be an intricate process, and it is a powerful feature that can be used in many ways. We will examine this topic in greater depth later on in this chapter.

File Locking

We've already covered how checking out a file for editing prior to making changes prevents conflicts. Let's first examine a situation where files are changed without the benefit of file locking. Refer to Figure 19.4, where Arthur and Beverly are trying to finish a Web project for a major client.

Arthur grabs a copy of revision 1.5 of `index.html` and begins editing it. Soon after, Beverly also grabs a copy of revision 1.5 of `index.html` and begins making her changes. When he finishes his changes, Arthur checks in revision 1.6, reports to his manager that the changes are complete and then leaves on vacation. Then Beverly checks in her changes as revision 1.7, which now contains none of Arthur's changes! Charlie, their manager, discovers that Arthur's changes are not in the weekly release and calls Arthur to find out why, completely ruining Arthur's vacation.

FIGURE 19.4.

Two-person Web project without file locking.

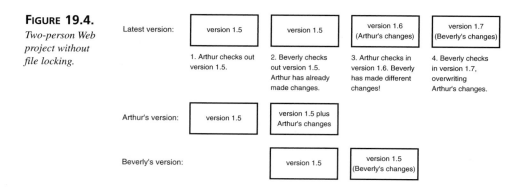

Note that even though revision 1.7 is the descendant of 1.6, it doesn't contain the changes Arthur made because the revision control system simply replaced 1.6 with 1.7. The system has no way of evaluating what changes should be applied. One way to resolve this conflict is to check out both versions 1.6 and 1.7 (with different filenames to avoid conflicts) and merge them, but that doesn't fix Arthur's vacation, which is ruined.

Compare this with the second timeline shown in Figure 19.5. Arthur grabs a locked copy of revision 1.5 of index.html and begins editing it. While he is making changes, Beverly tries to grab a copy of revision 1.5 of index.html, but the source control system informs her that she cannot check out revision 1.5 because it is locked by Arthur. Beverly can wait for Arthur to finish, or if her changes are urgent, she can contact Arthur to work out a way to get her changes done quickly. When Arthur finishes his changes, he checks in the changes as revision 1.6 and reports to his manager that the changes are complete before leaving for his vacation.

At this point, Beverly learns that index.html is no longer locked and checks out revision 1.6. Beverly checks in her changes as revision 1.7, which contains both her modifications and Arthur's. After noticing that Arthur's changes are in the weekly release, Charlie goes to play golf.

FIGURE 19.5.

Two-person Web project with file locking.

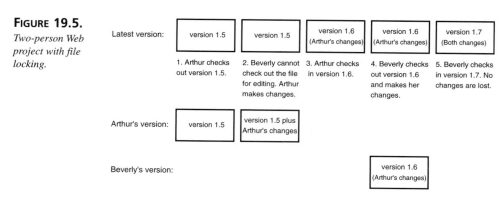

Symbolic Names, Baselines, and Releases

A *symbolic name* or a *label* is a name that is attached to a particular revision of a file and can be used to refer to that file without having to know the revision number. Usually a major milestone in a file's history is referred to with a name. A *baseline* is a captured set of revisions that have some special association, such as "submitted to editor," "compiles successfully," or "released for beta testing."

The capability to create symbolic names is probably the most compelling reason to use a more sophisticated revision control system, such as RCS or CVS, instead of SCCS, although SCCS does provide a workaround that should satisfy most situations.

Even without symbolic names, you can achieve a similar effect using release numbers. A *release* is a baseline, usually with the property of being *released for distribution*. When the project hits a milestone, you can either synchronize all the file's revision numbers by bringing them all to the same level or increase the major version number of the next revision.

The second method works quite well because most systems automatically retrieve the highest minor revision when only a major revision number is specified. So if a project was released with three files at versions 1.1, 1.5, and 1.7, the system automatically retrieves those versions the next time the major revision number 1 is retrieved because no minor number was specified.

RCS

The Revision Control System, RCS, was developed by Walter Tichy at Purdue University in the early 1980s. Part of its system uses programs whose origins date back to the mid- to late-1970s. Long before terms such as *groupware* became popular, RCS was used to automate the storage, retrieval, logging, identification, and merging of revisions to programs. It remains the most popular version control system in use today because of its simplicity, efficiency, and availability.

RCS consists of the following set of programs that work together to perform revision management:

- `ci`—Checks in RCS revisions
- `co`—Checks out RCS revisions
- `ident`—Identifies RCS keyword strings in files
- `rcs`—Changes RCS file attributes
- `rcsclean`—Cleans up working files

- `rcsdiff`—Compares RCS revisions
- `rcsmerge`—Changes RCS file attributes
- `rlog`—Prints log messages and other information about your RCS files

This chapter looks at the most common version of RCS, which is the GNU version 5.7.

Using RCS—A Simple Example

Part of what makes RCS so popular is its simplicity. Most of the work is done through the `ci` and `co` commands. The following simple example shows how to use RCS.

1. Create a directory for your project and call it `myproject`:

   ```
   $ mkdir myproject, as follows:
   ```

2. Use `cd` to change directories into `myproject` and create a directory called `RCS`:

   ```
   $ cd myproject
   $ mkdir RCS
   ```

3. Type the following source in your editor, and save it in the directory `myproject` as `foo.c`:

   ```
   /* $Header$ */
   #include <stdio.h>
   static char rcsid{} = "$Header$";
   main() {
       printf("hello, world!\n");
   }
   ```

4. Verify the contents of the directory `myproject` using `ls`:

   ```
   $ ls
   RCS/    foo.c
   ```

5. Use the RCS check in command `ci` to start tracking:

   ```
   $ ci foo.c
   ```

   The `ci` command responds with something like the following:

   ```
   RCS/foo.c,v  <--  foo.c
   enter description, terminated with single '.' or end of file:
   NOTE: This is NOT the log message!
   >>
   ```

6. Type in the following:

   ```
   >>  a simple example
   >> .
   ```

   Now `ci` displays the following:

   ```
   initial revision: 1.1
   done
   ```

7. Look at the contents of the directory `myproject` by entering the following:

```
# ls
RCS/
```

Where did the file `foo.c` go? To find it, look in the `RCS` directory:

```
$ ls RCS
foo.c,v
```

The `ci` command created the RCS file `foo.c,v` and stored `foo.c` inside as version 1.1 under the `RCS` directory. It then deleted `foo.c` from the `myproject` directory. RCS automatically starts version numbering at 1.1, but you also have the option of using a name instead of a version. See the `ci` man page for details.

To work on `foo.c`, type the following command:

```
# co -l foo.c
RCS/foo.c,v  -->  foo.c
revision 1.1 (locked)
done
```

The check out command, `co`, shows that `foo.c`, extracted from `foo.c,v` in the `RCS` directory, is ready to be worked on. The `-l` option of the `co` command is important because checking out a file without locking it extracts the file as read-only:

```
# co foo.c
RCS/foo.c,v  -->  foo.c
revision 1.1
done
# ls -l foo.c
-r--r--r--  1 root      root           252 Aug  2 16:06 foo.c
```

If you want to edit and make changes, you must lock the file. To verify that `foo.c` is available, enter the following:

```
# ls -l foo.c
-rw-r--r--  1 root      root           262 Aug  2 16:09 foo.c
```

Note that the write permission is now enabled but only for the owner and current user.

If you open `foo.c`, you see the following:

```
/* $Header: /root/myproject/RCS/foo.c,v 1.1 1997/08/02 18:49:08 root Exp
root $ */
#include <stdio.h>
static char rcsid{} = "$Header: /root/myproject/RCS/foo.c,v 1.1 1997/08/02
18:49 :08 root Exp root $";
main() {
    printf("hello, world!\n");
}
```

Note that the $Header$ keyword has been replaced with the full pathname of the RCS file, revision number, date, time, author, state, and locker. If you include the RCS information as an embedded character string, the final or release binary of the program contains your version information. If you include the keyword inside a comment, your source documents contain updated version information.

Table 19.1 lists some of the available RCS keywords.

TABLE 19.1. RCS KEYWORDS.

Keyword	Description
$Author$	The login name of the user who checked in the revision
$Date$	The date that the revision was checked in
$Header$	The standard header containing the full pathname of the RCS file, date, and author
Id	The same as $Header$, except that the RCS filename does not include the full path
Log	This keyword includes the RCS filename, revision number, author, date, and the log message supplied during commit
$RCSfile$	The name of the RCS file, not including the path
$Revision$	The revision number that has been assigned
$Source$	The full pathname of the RCS file
$State$	The state that has been assigned to the revision

For more details about the keywords given in Table 19.1, see the co man page. For details about the history of a document's changes, however, you can use the rlog command. For example, after two minor editing changes, rlog reports the following about foo.c, now version 1.3:

```
$ rlog foo.c
RCS file: RCS/foo.c,v
Working file: foo.c
head: 1.3
branch:
locks: strict
access list:
symbolic names:
keyword substitution: kv
total revisions: 3;    selected revisions: 3
description:
a simple example
- - - - - - - - - - - - - - - - - - - - - - - - - - -
```

```
revision 1.3
date: 1997/08/02 20:29:10;   author: root;   state: Exp;   lines: +4 -3
added another printf line
----------------------------
revision 1.2
date: 1997/08/02 19:53:13;   author: root;   state: Exp;   lines: +3 -3
this is the second change
----------------------------
revision 1.1
date: 1997/08/02 18:49:08;   author: root;   state: Exp;
Initial revision
```

Manipulating Revisions

Another reason for the popularity of RCS, is its efficiency in manipulating revisions. RCS is efficient at this because it records changes as `diff` commands in the revision file. Thus any version can be retrieved and changed at any time. Also, because the changes are in `diff` format, many changes to an original document can be stored fairly efficiently.

The tasks that RCS is particularly good at are

- Branching
- Merging versions
- Deleting versions

Branching

Sometimes you must create a "branched" version of a file, if only for a temporary or specialized fix in the middle of a version. In this case, specifying the `-rX.X` option to the co command creates the branch.

For example, to do a special 1.2 release of `foo.c`, you could use the following:

```
$ co -l -r1.2 foo.c
RCS/foo.c,v  -->  foo.c
revision 1.2 (locked)
done
```

The next time `foo.c` is checked in, the `ci` command automatically bumps the version to 1.2.1.1 and responds with the following:

```
# ci foo.c
RCS/foo.c,v  <--  foo.c
new revision: 1.2.1.1; previous revision: 1.2
enter log message, terminated with single '.' or end of file:
>> a temporary fix
>> .
done
```

Merging Versions

You can also merge different versions of your program. For example, to bring the changes from 1.1 into 1.3, you can use the `rcsmerge` command. First, check out version 1.1 of `foo.c` as locked:

```
$ co -r1.1 foo.c
RCS/foo.c,v  -->  foo.c
revision 1.1
done
```

Then specify the versions that you want merged to `rcsmerge`:

```
$ rcsmerge -p -r1.1 -r1.3 foo.c >foo.merged.c
RCS file: RCS/foo.c,v
retrieving revision 1.1
retrieving revision 1.3
Merging differences between 1.1 and 1.3 into foo.c; result to stdout
```

Note that the output of `rcsmerge` must be redirected to a file.

Deleting a Version

To remove a particular version of the program, use the `rcs` command with `-oX.X` option, where *X.X* is the version number. For example

```
$ rcs -o1.2.1.1 foo.c
RCS file: RCS/foo.c,v
deleting revision 1.2.1.1
done
```

For More RCS Information

If you're interested in the philosophy, design, and development of RCS, and you want to learn about its differences with other revision control systems, see Tichy's abstract, "RCS—A System for Version Control." Originally published in *Software—Practice & Experience*, July 1985, the abstract is also included in the 4.4BSD documentation. You can also find a number of copies across the Internet using your favorite search engine.

For a general introduction to RCS, see the `rcsintro` man page. For details about the format of an RCS file, see the `rcsfile` man page.

If you want to read about configuration management, find out about alternative tools, or need information to make a decision on the best tool to use for your project, see Dave Eaton's Configuration Management FAQ at the following site:

```
http://www.iac.honeywell.com/Pub/Tech/CM
```

You also can check the following newsgroup:

```
comp.software.config-mgmt
```

If you want to use RCS on a remote server, try Eric Meyer's RMTRCS package of shell scripts. This package consists of five scripts called `rmtco`, `rmtci`, `rmtdiff`, `rmtlog`, and `rmtrcs`. RMTRCS includes a number of nifty features, such as check in and check out on remote machines without having to log in, and automatic email notification of revision logs to project teams. You can find the source at

```
ftp://lifshitz.ph.utexas.edu/pub/src/rmtrcs-X.X.tar.gz
```

where *X.X* is the current version.

Finally, you should know that Walter Tichy has rewritten RCS to include a graphical user and programmable interface. Called RCE, this version control system is available for nearly a dozen or more operating systems and also includes many new features. If you want to find out more about the commercial successor to RCS, send email to

```
rce@xcc.de
```

or see the FTP site at

```
ftp.xcc.de
```

SCCS

The Source Code Control System, SCCS, was developed by AT&T as a system to control source code development. It includes features that help support a production development environment, including being able to help freeze released code, integrate into a problem-tracking system, and embed keywords into binary programs that can be viewed after the program is released.

Most systems ship with SCCS, but a few do not include the `sccs` command that was introduced by BSD as a convenient interface to the SCCS system. This book's CD-ROM includes a version of the `sccs` command that is freely available.

Basic Operation

SCCS stores changes to files in an SCCS file. If the `sccs` command is used, this file is stored in a directory named `SCCS` in the working directory. The SCCS file is named `s.file`, where *file* is the name of the file being tracked.

Changes are recorded in this file as building blocks, with each set of changes depending on the previous revision. For example, imagine if SCCS managed the file `3liner.txt`, which follows:

```
This is
a simple
3 line file
```

The next revision alters it to the following:

```
This is
a simple
three line file
```

SCCS adds only the last line to the SCCS file s.3liner.txt and records it as the next revision. This method of tracking changes individually allows you to revert to previous versions of working files quickly and easily.

Note that the actual mechanics of the file differ slightly from this abstraction, but from a conceptual level, this is all you need to worry about.

SCCS Command Summary

The SCCS admin command is used to interact with the SCCS files. You use it to create source control files, control availability of revisions, and change the requirements for submitting a revision.

The commands get and delta are used to retrieve revisions and create new a new delta, or revision. You use unget to cancel the creation of a delta.

SCCS uses temporary files to store internal state and track file locks. These files are stored in the SCCS directory and should never be manipulated.

SCCS commands require the name of the SCCS file itself, as in s.3liner.txt rather than the working filename, but the sccs program simplifies this by accepting working filenames.

Initial Revisions

You have to initialize the SCCS files using the admin command before you can perform any other action. These files can be initialized with an empty revision or with the contents of a working file as the initial revision.

For example, to create an SCCS file with an empty initial revision for our text file, use the following command:

```
$ admin -n s.3liner.txt
```

This command creates s.3liner.txt with the appropriate SCCS file structure and an empty revision 1.1. You can then use the get and delta commands to add text. Unlike RCS, however, the empty revision 1.1 always remains in the SCCS data file.

To create an SCCS file with initial contents from another file, enter the following:

```
$ admin -i 3liner.txt s.3liner.txt
```

The two occurrences of 3liner.txt do not have to agree, but it is generally useful for them to do so because other SCCS commands assume that the working file for s.3liner.txt is 3liner.txt.

The sccs command provides a simplified method for creating SCCS data files. For example, using sccs, you would do the following:

```
$ sccs create 3liner.txt
```

This command creates s.3liner.txt in the directory named SCCS in the current working directory.

Checking Out a File

You use the get command to retrieve copies of revisions from SCCS files. You can retrieve any version, either by number or by date, as follows:

```
$ get s.3liner.txt
1.1
3 lines
No id keywords
```

Without any options, get retrieves the latest revision from the SCCS file, placing it in a read-only copy of 3liner.txt because it assumes that you are not planning to make any changes and create a new revision. The three lines following the command tell us what version was retrieved, the size of the file in number of lines, and how many keywords it expanded.

Now consider the following:

```
$ get -e s.3liner.txt
1.1
new delta 1.2
3 lines
```

The -e option here indicates that you are checking 3liner.txt out for editing. The get command supplies you with a writable copy and creates a lock file called p.3liner.txt. This lock file prevents other users from retrieving the same version for editing until this one is checked in using delta or unget. Read-only copies can be checked out though.

You can use the -e option for different versions at the same time; however, if two users are making changes to the same file at the same time, the project most likely will have to have *branches* in the revision tree.

You use the -p and -c options to retrieve a revision other than the latest. Both options can be combined with the -e option.

Now look at another example:

```
$ get -r1.1 s.3liner.txt
1.1
3 lines
No id keywords
```

This command retrieves version 1.1, regardless of what the latest version might be. The *minor* version number does not have to be specified. For example, -r2 retrieves the high revision within version 2.

Here's another example:

```
$ get -c970227 s.3liner.txt
1.1
3 lines
No id keywords
```

The -c flag allows you to specify a date in the form of

```
YY[MM[DD[HH[MM[SS]]]]]
```

That is, you can specify two digits for a year, followed by an optional set of digits for month, day, hour, and second. Like other sccs commands, any optional parameters that you omit are set to their maximum. So the preceding example retrieves the latest version of 3liner.txt as of 11:59:59 p.m. on February 27, 1997.

The sccs also provides a vastly simplified interface to the get command:

```
$ sccs get 3liner.txt
```

This command retrieves a read-only copy of the latest version 3liner.txt, contained in s.3liner.txt, in the SCCS subdirectory. You can pass all the command-line options that apply to the get command to this subcommand. The output is the same as that of the get command.

For example, the following retrieves a read-only copy of version 1.3:

```
$ sccs get -r1.3 3liner.txt
```

The edit subcommand executes a get -e, as follows:

```
$ sccs edit 3liner.txt
```

It also accepts all the get flags.

The sccs command generally allows you to use any SCCS command, without specifying the SCCS control file.

Checking In a File

The `delta` command is used to submit changed revisions. This process is also called *creating a delta*. Here is an example of this:

```
$ delta s.3liner.txt
comments? Added fourth line.
No id keywords (cm7)
1.3
1 inserted
0 deleted
3 unchanged
```

This `delta` command checks in the previous checked-out working copy of `3liner.txt`. It examines the control file, `s.3liner.txt`, and the lock file, `p.3liner.txt`, to figure out where the working copy of `3liner.txt` should be and what version it will be checked in as.

The `delta` command prompts you for comments regarding the changes. These comments, which are called *log messages*, can be viewed with the `prs` command. It also gives you an idea of the changes it noted by listing the number of inserted, deleted, and changed lines.

By default, the `delta` command removes the writable version of the working file. This behavior can be overridden by using the `-n` flag. If more than one version is checked out, you can use the `-r` flag. It works in the same way as the `-r` flag for the `get` command.

The `sccs` command works as a wrapper for `delta` in the same manner that it does for `get`.

Examining Revision Details and History

The `prs` command enables you to print reports from information in the SCCS file. It also produces custom reports by enabling you to supply a format specification by specifying SCCS keywords.

The output for our file looks like the following:

```
$ prs s.3liner.txt
s.3liner.txt:
D 1.2 97/04/29 10:34:38 eric 2 1        00001/00000/00003
MRs:
COMMENTS:
Added fourth line
D 1.1 97/04/29 10:33:34 eric 1 0        00003/00000/00000
MRs:
COMMENTS:
date and time created 97/04/29 10:33:34 by eric
```

This report shows the information for versions 1.1 and 1.2. For each version, you see the date, time, and user along with the number of lines that were added, deleted, and unchanged.

You also see the comment input to the `delta` command. For revision 1.1, the report displays three lines added, and the comment is a date-and-time-created statement inserted by the `sccs create` command.

The `-d` option controls the printing of information about the SCCS file. You can use it to create customized reports by specifying a formatting string, as follows:

```
$ prs -d "File: :M: version: :I: created: :D:" s.3liner.txt
File: 3liner.txt version: 1.2 created: 97/04/29
```

This command gives you a formatted one-line entry, by providing `prs` with a formatting string. The keywords similar to the ones you can embed in working files are as follows:

- `:M:`—Module (working file) name
- `:I:`—ID (version) number
- `:D:`—Creation date
- `:T:`—Time created
- `:C:`—Comments for delta

See the `prs` man page for more. Many of the more than 40 different keywords are shorthand for combinations of keywords.

Module Keywords

SCCS uses a keyword substitution method for working files that is a little bit different from the method used for `prs`. Module keywords are of the form `%x%` and are expanded when you use the `get` command, without the `-k` or `-e` options, to retrieve the file.

These expanded keywords have the same advantages and disadvantages of the C/C++ preprocessor. Because the keywords are expanded inline, they need no additional processing to be human readable. However, expanded keywords are difficult to recover after a file is checked out and distributed because they are completely replaced with the appropriate text. Therefore, standardizing on a specific location or at least the syntax for their use is a good idea.

Some of the module keywords are as follows:

- `%D%`—Current date
- `%E%`—Date of newest delta
- `%R%`—Release number

- %C%—Current line number
- %U%—Time newest delta was applied
- %Z%—String recognized by what command
- %M%—Module name
- %I%—Revision number
- %W%—Abbreviation for %Z%%M%(tab)%I%

See the get man page entry for a full list of keywords.

TIP

You can embed SCCS keywords that identify your executable program by using the following:

```
char sccsid[] = "%W%";
```

This way, you can use the what command to identify which revisions went into creating the executable.

Make sure that all your files are checked out for reading, not for editing and not with the -k option.

Other Commands

SCCS provides a few other utilities for managing projects.

The unget command, for example, cancels a get operation, preventing a new delta from being created and erasing any lock associated with the previous get. Another command, rmdel, is provided for removing deltas from the SCCS file after they are applied.

You can use cdc to change the comment associated with a delta.

For combining two deltas, SCCS offers the comb command. This command is intended for reducing the size of SCCS data files, not for resolving conflicts. It produces a shell script, which is then run to perform the compression. SCCS also supplies sccsdiff, which you use to compare SCCS data files and can use to check on files after a comb operation. Keep a backup copy of the file until you are sure everything is okay.

The sact command provides a report on what revisions are checked out for editing and what revision they will become when they are checked back in.

The sccs command provides a simplified interface to all these commands.

Extra SCCS Features

SCCS includes extra software configuration management support hooks that are set when the SCCS file is created. You can use the -f x and -d x options of the admin command to do the following:

x	*Action*
v[*pgm*]	Require modification request numbers for delta.
c*ceil*	Limit the releases that can be retrieved using get.
f*floor*	Limit the releases that can be retrieved using get.
l*list*	Limit the releases that can be submitted using delta.
j	Enable/disable concurrent locks.
b	Enable/disable branching.
d*SID*	Set default revision for get.
n	Create null deltas for skipped releases. You can use this option to create a base revision for branches in releases that had no source modifications.
[qtm]	Control expansion of some keywords.

See the admin man page entry for more details on these options.

Creating a Revision Branch

Using get -b -e causes SCCS to create a branch from the specified revision. If you want to create a second revision path at 1.2 in the previous example, you can execute the following:

```
$ get -b -e -r1.2 s.3liner.txt
1.2
new delta 1.2.1.1
4 lines
```

The get command shows that the next delta will be checked in at 1.2.1.1 instead of 1.3. Note that if someone is editing revision 1.3 while you're working on 1.2.1.1, both users will have to provide the -r flag to delta when you check your revisions back in.

SCCS does not support branches on branches like RCS does.

Merging Revisions

Merging revisions is not a feature of SCCS. Instead it is necessary to utilize the merge utility that comes with most UNIX releases.

merge compares two files and outputs the merged file to either a third file or standard output, depending on how it is run. The utility also catches conflicts and notifies the user.

For example, consider a situation where the file used in the previous example progressed to revision 1.2.1.2 in the branch and to 1.3 in the trunk. In preparation for the next major version, 2.0, we want to merge the latest two revisions.

```
$ get -e -r1.3 s.3liner.txt
$ get -s -p -r1.2.1.2 s.3liner.txt >branch
$ get -s -e -p -r1.2 s.3liner.txt >trunk
$ merge -p 3liner.txt trunk branch
$ delta -r2.0 s.3liner.txt
```

The first get command checks version 1.3 for editing. The second two provide with copies of 1.2 and 1.2.1.2 in separate files with unique names. The merge command applies all the differences between trunk and branch to 3liner.txt, effectively giving us a merge of these files. A common ancestor, 3liner.txt, is necessary for merge to be able to successfully figure out how to apply the changes. After the merge is completed, copy the new file to 3liner.txt and check it in.

This example omitted the changes to the files and focused on the mechanics of merging revisions. The differences between file revisions can be difficult for a program to resolve without user intervention. If revisions occur on the same line, merge considers this a collision and outputs information about the problem either into the target file or to standard output. RCS, unlike SCCS, has explicit support for merging revisions and is a better choice for projects that need to perform merges frequently or across complicated files and file sets.

The merge command is a multipurpose command-line tool that accompanies most UNIX releases. See its manual page for more details on its operation.

CVS

The Concurrent Versions System, CVS, was developed by Dick Grune in 1986. Back then, it consisted of a set of UNIX shell scripts. In 1989, it was designed and coded in the C language by Brian Berlinger, with some enhancements provided by Jeff Polk. Many of the algorithms in the current version came from the original shell scripts.

You can think of CVS as a front end for RCS. It stores version-control information for each file in RCS format, and RCS files are used in conjunction with the diff command to provide a robust version control system.

As of this writing, the new version of CVS is 1.10. You can obtain it from any GNU site via anonymous FTP, including the main site located at

```
ftp://prep.ai.mit.edu/pub/gnu
```

You need compatible versions of RCS and `diff` to run CVS. These can both be obtained at any GNU site. In addition, you can subscribe to a mailing list devoted to CVS by sending the word `subscribe` in the message body to

`info-cvs@prep.ai.mit.edu`

How Is CVS Different from RCS and SCCS?

Both RCS and SCCS use a *lock-modify-unlock* paradigm for managing changes to a file. When a developer wants to change a file, he or she must first lock the file. Other developers cannot check out this file for modification until it is unlocked. Although this model is effective in maintaining and managing the contents of a file, it may cause unnecessary delay in situations in which more than one person wants to work on different portions of the same file concurrently.

Instead of serializing access to files under source code control, CVS supports simultaneous access and modification of files using a *copy-modify-merge* paradigm. In this model, a user can check out a file and make modifications even though another person may be in the process of modifying it as well. Every time a file is checked in, it is merged with the most recent copy in the CVS repository. On rare occasions, a merge cannot be done because of conflicting entries in the files to be merged. In this case, conflict resolution needs to be performed. We discuss how to handle conflicts later in this chapter. Such instances should be rare in a well-organized project.

Starting a Project

The first step in using CVS to manage your source code is to create a *repository*. A repository is simply a directory hierarchy containing the source code to be managed and various administrative files that manage the source code. To create a repository, first set the environment variable $CVSROOT to point to the absolute pathname of the repository. Before you issue the command, make sure that the directory exists. Then issue the cvs command with the init option. For example, the following commands check the setting of CVSROOT, verify the existence of the repository root directory, and then create the repository:

```
$ echo $CVSROOT
/usr/local/cvsroot
$ ls -ld $CVSROOT
drwxrwxrwx 4 trimblef users    1024 May 17 14:55 /usr/local/cvsroot
$ cvs init
```

The cvs command does its work silently, creating an administrative directory hierarchy in the /usr/local/cvsroot directory. You can override the setting of the $CVSROOT environment variable by specifying the -d option to the cvs command. For example, the following command initializes a CVS repository under /usr/cvsroot, even though the $CVSROOT environment variable points to a different location:

```
cvs -d /usr/cvsroot init
```

In fact, you might notice that many cvs commands allow you to specify the root directory of the repository in this fashion.

The repository is now ready to manage your source code.

The Repository

The repository contains administrative files in addition to the source code under control. The administrative portion of the hierarchy does not have to exist for CVS to function. Because these files support many useful features, leaving them in place is highly recommended.

The files created under the $CVSROOT/CVSROOT directory after cvs init is invoked are as follows:

```
/usr/cvsroot/
|___CVSROOT/
       |___.#checkoutlist
       |___.#commitinfo
       |___.#cvswrappers
       |___.#editinfo
       |___.#loginfo
       |___.#modules
       |___.#notify
       |___.#rcsinfo
       |___.#taginfo
       |___checkoutlist
       |___checkoutlist,v
       |___commitinfo
       |___commitinfo,v
       |___cvswrappers
       |___cvswrappers,v
       |___editinfo
       |___editinfo,v
       |___history
       |___loginfo
       |___loginfo,v
       |___modules
       |___modules,v
       |___notify
       |___notify,v
```

19

**REVISION
CONTROL**

```
|___rcsinfo
|___rcsinfo,v
|___taginfo
|___taginfo,v
```

Notice that some of the files have the extension ,v, which is the default file extension for files under RCS control. Indeed, these are RCS files, which illustrates how CVS is used as a front end to RCS. In addition to the actual source files, the administrative files can be checked out and modified using the appropriate cvs commands as well.

Table 19.2 describes of the purpose for each of the files in the repository.

TABLE 19.2. CVS ADMINISTRATIVE FILES.

File	Description
checkoutlist	This file supports other administrative files in CVSROOT. It allows you to customize diagnostic messages for various cvs commands.
commitinfo	This file specifies programs that should be executed when a cvs commit command is executed. This way, you can perform a sanity check on the files before they are entered into the repository. The contrib directory that comes with the CVS distribution contains a number of useful sample scripts.
cvswrappers	This file defines *wrapper programs* that are executed when files are checked in or out. One possible use of this file is to format checked-in source code files so that their appearance and structure are consistent with other files in the repository.
editinfo	This file allows you to execute a script before a commit starts but after log information has been recorded. If the script exits with a nonzero value, the commit is aborted.
history	This file keeps track of all commands that affect the repository.
loginfo	The loginfo file is similar to commitinfo. The major difference is that loginfo is processed after files have been committed. Typical uses of this file include sending electronic mail and appending log messages to a file after a commit takes place.

File	Description
modules	This file enables you to define a symbolic name for a group of files. If this is not done, you must specify a partial pathname, relative to the $CVSROOT directory, for each file that you reference.
notify	This file controls notifications from watches set by the cvs watch add and cvs edit commands.
rcsinfo	This file allows you to specify a template for a commit log session.
taginfo	This file defines programs to execute after any tag operation. For example, if a tag name changes, you can configure the file to send a mail message to the original developer, notifying him or her that the file has changed.

Importing Files into the Repository

After the repository is initialized, you can add files and directories of files using the import command. For example, suppose that you have the following source code file hierarchy that is ready to be put under revision control:

```
$ find . -print
.
./src
./src/main
./src/main/main.c
./src/main/main.h
./src/print
./src/print/print.c
./src/print/print.h
./src/term
./src/term/term.c
./src/term/term.h
```

From the directory containing the src directory, run the following command:

```
$ cvs import -m "initial release" project myvtag myrtag
cvs import: Importing /usr/local/cvsroot/project/src
cvs import: Importing /usr/local/cvsroot/project/src/main
N project/src/main/main.c
N project/src/main/main.h
cvs import: Importing /usr/local/cvsroot/project/src/print
N project/src/print/print.c
N project/src/print/print.h
cvs import: Importing /usr/local/cvsroot/project/src/term
```

```
N project/src/term/term.c
N project/src/term/term.h
No conflicts created by this import
```

In the preceding command, the `-m` option gives a description of the import for logging purposes. The next option, `project`, identifies a directory under the `$CVSROOT` directory that will contain the imported source files. The next two arguments identify the vendor tag and release tag, respectively.

After the files have been imported, you can create abbreviations to the source code in the directory hierarchy. Doing so makes checking files out of the repository easier. This process is discussed shortly.

File Permissions

After source files have been entered into the repository, the source code administrator can control access by setting appropriate file and directory permissions. All RCS files are created with read-only access and should never be changed. The directories in the repository should have write permissions by users who are allowed to modify the files in the directory. Therefore, you cannot control file access on a file-by-file basis. You can control access only to files at the group level within a directory.

Maintaining Source Code Revisions

After the source files have been imported, a variety of options are available for the `cvs` command for managing the repository. We will look at performing the following tasks using `cvs`:

- Checking files out of the repository
- Checking files into the repository
- Updating checked out files
- Branching
- Merging
- Conflict resolution
- Cleaning up
- Adding keywords to source files

Checking Out Files

After the source files have been imported, you can check files in and out as needed to make the appropriate modifications. The `cvs` command has an option to check out a file from the repository. For example, you can use the following command to get all the files from the `print` directory:

```
$ cvs checkout project/src/print
cvs checkout: Updating project/src/print
U project/src/print/print.c
U project/src/print/print.h
```

The partial pathname `project/src/print` specified in the command line is relative to the `$CVSROOT` directory. The command creates the same partial path under your current working directory, including the source files.

In addition to the desired files being copied from the repository, a directory named `CVS` is also created. It is used for CVS administrative purposes only, and its contents should never be modified directly. When you want to make modifications to the checked-out files, change to the `project/src/print` directory. After you make the appropriate changes to all the checked-out files, you can commit the changes to the repository by issuing the `cvs commit` command. This issue is discussed in the next section.

Specifying the partial path to a directory in the repository can be cumbersome, especially in a large project with many directory levels. In CVS, you can create abbreviations for each of the source directories. You do so by configuring the `modules` file in the `$CVSROOT/CVSROOT` directory. To do so, execute the following command to "check out" a copy of the modules file:

```
$ cvs checkout CVSROOT/modules
U CVSROOT/modules
```

This command creates a `CVSROOT` directory in your local working directory. After you change to this directory, you see a copy of the `modules` file that you can edit. For the preceding example, add the following lines to the end of the file:

```
src       project/src
main      project/src/main
print     project/src/print
term      project/src/term
```

For the changes to take effect, you must "commit" them. You do so by using the cvs commit command, as follows:

```
$ cvs commit -m "initialize modules"
initialized the modules file
Checking in modules;
/users/home/project/CVSROOT/modules,v  <--  modules
new revision: 1.2; previous revision: 1.1
done
cvs commit: Rebuilding administrative file database
```

The `cvs commit` command is discussed more fully in the next section.

This action enables you to select the modules in a directory without having to specify the entire path. For example, suppose that you want to select the files that comprise the print module. Instead of specifying project/src/print on the command line, you can use print instead:

```
$ cvs checkout print
cvs checkout: Updating print
U print/print.c
U print/print.h
$ cd print
$ ls -l
total 6
drwxrwxrwx    2 trimblef users       1024 May 25 10:47 CVS
-rw-rw-rw-    1 trimblef users         16 May 25 10:26 print.c
-rw-rw-rw-    1 trimblef users         16 May 25 10:26 print.h
```

When you check files out of the repository, you get the most recent revision by default. You can specify another revision if, for example, you need to patch an earlier version of the source code. Suppose that the current revision for the print module is 1.4. You can get the 1.1 revision by using the -r option, as follows:

```
$ cvs checkout -r 1.1 print
cvs checkout: Updating print
U print/print.c
U print/print.h
```

For a complete list of all the options you can use with a particular cvs command, use the -H option. For example, here is how you list all the options for the checkout command:

```
$ cvs -H checkout
Usage:
  cvs checkout [-ANPcflnps] [-r rev ¦ -D date] [-d dir] [-k kopt]
modules...
        -A      Reset any sticky tags/date/kopts.
        -N      Don't shorten module paths if -d specified.
        -P      Prune empty directories.
        -c      "cat" the module database.
        -f      Force a head revision match if tag/date not found.
        -l      Local directory only, not recursive
        -n      Do not run module program (if any).
        -p      Check out files to standard output (avoids stickiness).
        -s      Like -c, but include module status.
        -r rev  Check out revision or tag. (implies -P) (is sticky)
        -D date Check out revisions as of date. (implies -P) (is sticky)
        -d dir  Check out into dir instead of module name.
        -k kopt Use RCS kopt -k option on checkout.
        -j rev  Merge in changes made between current revision and rev.
```

Checking In Files

After you check out files from the repository and make changes to them, the modified files are checked-in using the `cvs commit` command. For example, the following command checks in the modified files from the preceding example:

```
$ cvs commit -m "update print code"
cvs commit: Examining .
cvs commit: Committing .
Checking in print.c;
/users/home/project/src/print/print.c,v  <-- print.c
new revision: 1.2; previous revision: 1.1
done
$
```

In this example, the output indicates that only the file `print.c` has changed. Also, note that the original files are imported as revision 1.1. After the commit operation, a revision 1.2 also exists. Both of these revisions are on the main trunk of the repository. You can specify which revision to fetch, which allows you to patch previous versions of the source code.

The `-m` option allows you to log comments about the commit. This capability is useful for keeping track of the reason that the code was modified in the first place. If you don't specify the `-m` option, the editor specified in the `CVSEDITOR` environment variable is invoked. In the editor's buffer, you see the following help text reminding you to log some comments before committing your changes:

```
CVS: -------------------------------------------------------------
-
CVS: Enter Log.  Lines beginning with 'CVS: ' are removed automatically
CVS:
CVS: -------------------------------------------------------------
-
```

Updates

CVS allows one or more persons to modify a file at the same time.

Suppose that you are modifying one section of a file, and you want to update your local checked-out copy to incorporate changes made by another user who has checked the file in to the repository. You can do so by using the `update` command, which is one of the most heavily used `cvs` commands.

As a simple example, to merge changes made by others with your local working copies, you can invoke `cvs` with the `update` option:

```
$ cvs update
cvs update: Updating project
```

```
cvs update: Updating project/project
cvs update: Updating project/project/src
cvs update: Updating project/project/src/main
cvs update: Updating project/project/src/print
cvs update: Updating project/project/src/term
```

Branches

Branches enable you to make modifications to some of the files without disturbing the main trunk. The first step in creating a branch is to create a *tag* for some of the files in the repository. A tag is simply a symbolic name given to a file or group of files. The same tag name is usually given to a set of files that comprise a module at a strategic point in the life cycle of the source code.

To create a tag, run the `cvs tag` command in your working directory. For example, the following command tags the `src` directory:

```
$ cvs checkout src
cvs checkout: Updating src
cvs checkout: Updating src/main
U src/main/main.c
U src/main/main.h
cvs checkout: Updating src/print
U src/print/print.c
U src/print/print.h
cvs checkout: Updating src/term
U src/term/term.c
U src/term/term.h
leibniz 34: cvs tag release-1-0
cvs tag: Tagging src
cvs tag: Tagging src/main
T src/main/main.c
T src/main/main.h
cvs tag: Tagging src/print
T src/print/print.c
T src/print/print.h
cvs tag: Tagging src/term
T src/term/term.c
T src/term/term.h
```

Next, use the tag that was applied to create a branch using the `rtag` command, as follows:

```
$ cvs rtag -b -r release-1-0 release-1-0-patches print
cvs rtag: Tagging project/src/print
```

To see the current state of your local working copy of files, including the branch you are currently working on, use the `status` option of the `cvs` command. The status output for one of the files is as follows:

```
$ cvs status -v src
cvs status: Examining src
cvs status: Examining src/main
=================================================================
File: main.c            Status: Up-to-date
   Working revision:    1.2     Sun May 25 14:45:24 1997
   Repository revision: 1.2     /users/home/project/src/main/main.c,v
   Sticky Tag:          (none)
   Sticky Date:         (none)
   Sticky Options:      (none)
   Existing Tags:
       release-1-0                (revision: 1.2)
       myrtag                     (revision: 1.1.1.1)
       myvtag                     (branch: 1.1.1)
```

Merging

You can merge the changes made on a branch to your local working copy of files by specifying the -j option to the cvs update command. For example, the following command:

```
$ cvs update -j release-1-0 print.c
```

merges the latest version of print.c from the main trunk with the modifications performed in release-1-0. After the next commit, the changes will be incorporated in the main trunk.

Conflict Resolution

Because more than one developer can check out and modify a file, conflicts can result. For example, suppose that you have just completed work on revision 1.4 of a file and run the update command:

```
$ cvs update print.c
RCS file: /users/home/project/src/print/print.c,v
retrieving revision 1.4
retrieving revision 1.7
Merging differences between 1.4 and 1.7 into print.c
rcsmerge warning: overlaps during merge
cvs update: conflicts found in print.c
C print.c
```

As you can see, a warning message is displayed when conflicting changes are made to a common section of the source file. Such conflicts must be handled manually. In this example, the local copy of the print.c file is saved in the file:

```
.#print.c.1.4
```

The new local version of `print.c` has the following contents:

```
#include <stdio.h>
int print(char *args[])
{
    if (parse(args) < 1)
    {
<<<<<<< print.c
        fprintf(stderr, "Invalid argument list.\n");
=======
        fprintf(stderr, "No arguments present.\n");
>>>>>>> 1.7
    }
    ...
}
```

Note how the conflicting entries are clearly marked with <<<<<<<, =======, and
>>>>>>>. You need to resolve this section of code manually. After consulting the
developer responsible for the conflicting update and making the appropriate change
to the file, you can commit the change with the following command:

```
$ cvs commit -m "fix print module diagnostic" print.c
Checking in print.c
/usr/local/cvsroot/project/src/print.c,v  <-- print.c
new revision: 1.8; previous revision: 1.7
done
```

Cleaning Up

After making the necessary modifications to the source files, suppose that you decide to
remove your working copies. One way is to simply remove the files, as follows:

```
% rm -r src
```

The preferred method, however, is to use the `release` command. It indicates to other
developers that the module is no longer in use. Consider this example:

```
$ cvs release -d print
M print.c
You have [1] altered files in this repository.
Are you sure you want to release (and delete) module 'print.c': n
** `release' aborted by user choice.
```

In this example, CVS noticed that the local copy of `print.c` is different from the one in
the repository. Therefore, modifications have been made since the last time this file was
committed. Checking whether the file needs to be committed before your working copy
is removed is good practice.

Keyword Substitution

The `cvs status` and `cvs log` commands provide useful information on the state of your local copy of files. Another useful technique for managing files is a mechanism known as *keyword substitution*. Every time a `cvs commit` operation is performed, any keywords in the source files are expanded to useful values. CVS uses the underlying RCS keywords given in Table 19.1.

Environment Variables

Table 19.3 describes the environment variables used by CVS. These variables are used to control the behavior of CVS and should be set correctly for all developers to avoid problems.

TABLE 19.3. CVS ENVIRONMENT VARIABLES.

File	Description
CVSROOT	This environment variable should contain the full pathname to the root of the repository. In many `cvs` commands, you can override its value by using the `-d` option.
CVSREAD	When this variable is set, all files created during the checkout operation are given read-only permissions. If it is not set, you can modify any files that are checked out.
RCSBIN	CVS uses many facilities provided by RCS. Therefore, it needs to know that RCS executables such as `ci` and `co` can be found.
CVSEDITOR	This variable specifies the editor to use when CVS prompts the user for log information.
CVS_RSH	CVS uses the contents of this file to indicate the name of the shell to use when starting a remote CVS server.
CVS_SERVER	This environment variable determines the name of the `cvs` server command. The default is `cvs`.
CVSWRAPPERS	This variable is used by the script `cvswrappers` to determine the name of the wrapper file.

Summary

This chapter covered the basic concepts behind revision control and how it can be used to manage a variety of activities. We demonstrated how users first register a file with the system, then check it out for editing, and then check it back in when the changes are done so that the system becomes aware of the file's new state. We then discussed how this series of revisions can be viewed as a revision tree and how files can be extracted from the system at any point on that tree.

We have covered concepts, such as "branching" the tree to create more than one version of a project, and how to view a file's revision history. We also looked at file locking to prevent editing conflicts and how to have the version control system automatically add annotations to files when they are checked out. We also touched on the process of merging file revisions and the use of symbolic names and baselines for versions of projects.

By understanding these concepts, you should not only be able to pick a source control system and learn it rapidly, but also be able to identify situations where adopting a revision control system helps make you more productive.

The chapter covered RCS, which has become the most widely used "free" revision control system, primarily because of its advanced features such as symbolic names and its availability on all UNIX variants. We also covered CVS, which is based on RCS. CVS simplifies the process of distributing files in a controlled manner while tracking changes. We also looked at SCCS, which is the simplest of the revision control systems to learn and is the system most frequently bundled with UNIX variants. It is commonly used for one or two person projects that need basic file locking and backup capabilities.

System Administration

PART
IV

IN THIS PART

CHAPTER 20

What Is System Administration?

by Robin Burk and Eric Goebelbecker

IN THIS CHAPTER

A system administrator is the person responsible for planning, installing, and maintaining a computer system and supporting its use. This chapter describes what is expected from a system administrator, and how she might approach her responsibilities.

HELP WANTED

Administer Sun and IBM UNIX systems and control Internet access. Assist with some database administration (Oracle). Administer Sun server and network: system configuration, user ID/creation/maintenance, security administration, system backup, and ensuring all applications are running on the system properly. Administer Internet access and services: internal/external security; user identification, creation, and maintenance; and Web server maintenance.

This is a typical "Help Wanted" advertisement for a UNIX system administration position. From this description, you might guess that a system administrator has to install and configure the operating system, add new users, back up the system(s), keep the systems secure, and make sure they stay running. Setting up Internet access and keeping it running is part of the job too. However, there is a significant nontechnical component to being a system administrator, especially in terms of planning, organizational, and people skills. The administrator must understand the systems that he is responsible for, the people who use them, and the nature of the business that they are used for.

Companies are moving more processes not just to computers, but to point-of-sale systems, such as Web commerce and sophisticated in-store systems, such as electronic catalogs and cash registers directly connected to both inventory and credit systems. Email is now regarded as just as important as faxes and telephones, whereas every part of customer service that can be manned by a computer and fax retrieval system already is. Companies are almost completely dependent on their computers, and their system administrators need to understand much more than how to partition a disk drive, add memory, and install Adobe PhotoShop.

This chapter introduces some of the basic technical and organizational concepts that a system administrator needs to know to perform his job well. It also covers a few key system administration tools that are already found with most UNIX variants or are included on the UNIX Unleashed CD that accompanies this book.

TIP

Experienced users soon learn the value of UNIX's online documentation, the *manual pages*. Before you use any tool, read the man page(s) for it; many of them include useful examples. If you install a utility, be sure you read the installation instructions that accompany it and install the man page too.

Technical Concepts for New System Administrators

UNIX differs from Windows and Macintosh at a fundamental level. UNIX was originally intended for multiple users running multiple simultaneous programs. The fact that UNIX is designed for use by more than a single user is reflected throughout the operating system's file systems, security features, and programming model.

Networking is not an afterthought or a recent development for UNIX, the way it seems to be for Windows and Macintosh. Support for sharing files, moving from workstation to workstation, and running applications on remote computers that are controlled and viewed on a local workstation is not only intuitive and natural on UNIX, but was more powerful and stable on past versions of UNIX than the latest versions of Windows and Windows NT.

Multiple Users and Multiple Accounts

On DOS/Windows and Macintosh systems, ownership of files and *processes* (programs that are currently running) is more or less governed by the computer on which they are located. In most cases, if a person can physically get to such computers, he has access to all the files and programs on them. Add-ons are available for DOS and Macintosh systems that enable users to identify themselves and save files in protected areas. But these are applications, not a part of the operating system, and come with their own set of problems, limitations, and rules.

UNIX systems, on the other hand, are inherently multiuser. Users must log in to the system. Each has his own areas for saving files, the *home directory*, and files have properties that determine who can access them, their *mode*. All running programs are associated with a user, and, similar to the way files have access control, programs can only be started or stopped by certain users. Unless a user can log in as the *superuser* or receives permission by the owner of a file, she cannot access another user's files. Only the superuser can reboot the computer (without the power switch) or stop another user's processes.

Network Centricity

Networking has become an integral part of UNIX. The capability to share files, support network logins, share network configuration information, and run applications across a network is included in all major UNIX distributions, as a natural extension of the operating system.

Remote Terminals and Remote Shells

When configured to allow it, anything that can be done at the *console* (main keyboard and monitor) of a UNIX system can be done at another system via a network connection. (We'll refer to these other systems as *remote nodes* or *remote systems*.) In fact many server systems, such as Web servers and file servers, have consoles with limited capabilities (such as a text-only terminal) and are deliberately designed with the idea of doing as much administration as possible from remote nodes outside the data center.

Two mechanisms that provide these capabilities are *remote* (or *pseudo*) terminals and *remote shells*. Remote terminals emulate an actual terminal session, just as if the user were logged in to a terminal connected to the system via a serial line, where the network is the line and the application (usually *telnet*) is the terminal.

Remote shells (or remote logins) are sessions on remote computers that are centered on the execution of a shell (or shell command) instead of a terminal session. A remote shell executes a command on a remote host, whereas a remote login runs a shell; both usually appear to be running on the local system. Remote shells are frequently used by administrators in shell scripts, allowing them to execute commands on several systems and consolidate the results in one place, such as collecting disk utilization statistics or automating backups.

The following command line shows how a directory on one workstation could be backed up to a tape drive on another via a simple shell command:

```
tar cvfb  - tgt_dir ¦ rsh -n bilbo dd of=/dev/rmt/0
```

The `tar` command creates an archive of `tgt_dir` and sends it to *standard output*. This stream of data is redirected to the `rsh` command. `rsh` connects to the host `bilbo`, executes `dd`, and passes the output of `tar` to it. The `dd` command just happens to know how to save the archive to the tape drive on `/dev/rmt/0`. (This may seem complicated. By the end of this chapter, it will make perfect sense.) So two programs on two different computers are linked as one, without any special configuration requirements or extra software.

X Window

Another networking capability of UNIX is X Window, the graphical user interface. X Window applications are segmented into a client (the UNIX application) and a server (the display.) The server is a process that manages the keyboard, mouse, and screen, and accepts connections from applications over a *socket* (a network connection). Because a network connection is the method of communication between the two programs, the application can be running on a workstation different from the display that is controlling it.

> **CAUTION**
>
> Take care in installing and configuring X Window. Mistakes can require reinstalling the workstation software from scratch.

X Window allows some application activities to run on inexpensive workstations, whereas the main databases and demanding applications execute on more powerful shared machines.

File Sharing

File sharing is another extension that has become a natural and integral part of UNIX computing. All the major UNIX variants support *NFS* (Network File System) and can share files seamlessly between themselves and other UNIX versions.

Because NFS file systems are treated like any other type of disk, network drives fully support user accounts, file permissions, and all the mechanisms UNIX already uses for adding, removing, and managing other types of files and file systems, even when shared between different UNIX variants.

This means that two UNIX systems, regardless of what version of UNIX or on what type of computer they happen to be, can share files, maybe even from a common file server running on a third system type. Only the user IDs have to be coordinated for the files to be securely shared. No additional software or special modifications are required.

Any UNIX system can *export* or *share* file systems. This is one of the ways that the difference between servers and clients is blurred with UNIX systems; any system can provide or consume file system resources. When file systems are shared, the workstation can specify which systems can and cannot use it, and also whether users may write to it.

Clients specify where the file system will be mounted in their directory tree. For example, a system can mount the /export/applications directory from another system to its own /mnt/apps directory.

NFS was intended to run in a homogeneous UNIX environment. Note that it may not be totally secure in an environment with other operating and file systems where network capabilities such as ftp are enabled. If you run NFS, be sure to acquaint yourself with its capabilities in detail.

UNIX Networking: Sharing Files and Information

A system frequently used to administer NFS is the *automounter*. This program (or set of programs) allows administrators to specify file systems to be *mounted* (attached) and *unmounted* (detached) as needed, based on when clients refer to them. This process happens completely in the background, without any intervention after the automount program(s) are configured properly.

automount is configured with *maps* (configuration files), which specify top-level directories. For instance, if the automount system is to create five directories, the *master* map, which is contained in the file /etc/auto_master might look like this:

> **NOTE**
>
> Linux systems use a publicly available application called amd, which is similar to automount.

```
/share      auto_share
/home       auto_home
/gnu        auto_gnu
/apps       auto_apps
/opt        auto_opt
```

This file provides the automount with the names of the directories it will create and the files that contain what the directories will contain.

automount allows administrators to create a virtual /home directory on every workstation that runs the automount daemon. An excerpt from the home directory map, /etc/auto_home, as named in /etc/auto_master previously, would look like this:

```
eric   gandalf:/export/home/eric
dan    gandalf:/export/home/dan
mike   balrog:/export/home/michael
```

In this map, eric, dan, and mike are referred to as directory *keys*. The directories are called *values*. When a program refers to /home/eric for the first time, the system recognizes the key eric and arranges for /export/home/eric on gandalf to be mounted at

/home/eric. Because `automount` does a simple key/value replacement, Eric's and Dan's directories can be on `gandalf`, whereas Mike's is on `balrog`. Also note that the directory names in `balrog` and the automounter virtual directory do not have to agree. After a period of inactivity, `automount` unmounts the directory.

`automount` alleviates the tedious task of mounting in advance all the directories that a user or group of users will need. This system also makes it easier for users to travel from workstation to workstation because they can always expect to find important application and data files in the same place.

Sun Microsystems defined *autofs* as a new file system type in Solaris 2.x and created a multithreaded automounter system. This makes automounted file systems perform extraordinarily well under Solaris because the kernel is now aware that automounted file systems exist and by preventing bottlenecks in the `automount` program through the use of threads.

Hewlett-Packard's HP-UX and IBM's AIX provide a version of `automount`. Because `automount` uses NFS, it is compatible across different UNIX variants.

Newer versions of `automount` (and `amd`) also enable you to specify more than one file server for a directory to provide a backup when one file server is unavailable or overloaded. The maps, however, still must be kept up-to-date and distributed to each workstation. This could be done using `ftp`, or even `nfs`, but on a large network, this can become tedious. Two very elegant solutions are examples of how experienced system administrators tend to solve these problems.

The first is a tool called `rdist`. It is a tool for maintaining identical copies of software between remote hosts. It can accept filenames from the command line or use a configuration file (usually referred to as a *distfile)* that lists what files to copy to which hosts.

To distribute a set of automounter maps, you might use a *distfile* like this simple example:

```
HOSTS = (bilbo frodo thorin snowball)
FILES = /etc/auto_master /etc/auto_home /etc/auto_apps
${FILES}->${HOSTS}
        install;
```

`rdist` allows you to specify the hosts to be updated and the files to send in easily maintained lists. After you define `$FILES` and `$HOSTS`, you indicate that the lists of files should be kept up-to-date on the hosts listed. `install` indicates the `rdist` should keep the files up-to-date with the local copies. To use this, you could add the `distfile` to the `/etc` directory on the host where the master set of automounter maps are created. Whenever you make a change, you would execute:

```
rdist -f /etc/auto_distfile
```

20

WHAT IS SYSTEM
ADMINISTRATION?

`rdist` can be used for much more complicated tasks, such as synchronizing user directories between redundant file servers or distributing new versions of software packages where `nfs` is not being used.

`rdist` has the same security requirement as any other remote shell command. The user executing the `rdist` command must be able to attach to the remote host and execute commands without a password.

Sun Microsystems's *Network Information Service* (NIS) (also frequently called "yp" or yellow pages) addresses security concerns with file sharing by managing common configuration information, such as IP addresses, service port numbers, and automount maps to hosts on a network from a server or set of servers.

The NIS server(s) have master copies of the files that can be accessed by clients as needed. NIS is used for `hosts, services, passwd, automount,` and a few other configuration files.

The main advantage to NIS is convenience. Changes can be made to a map and made available to clients almost instantly, usually by executing a single command after the file is edited. Being able to keep all this information in one place (or a few places if secondary servers are used) is obviously convenient, especially because synchronizing user IDs, IP addresses, and service ports is crucial to keeping a network working well.

There are however, some significant disadvantages. A workstation that uses NIS to resolve IP addresses cannot use DNS for Internet addresses without some important modifications. Also, if the `passwd` file is distributed by NIS, the encrypted password field can be read by anyone who connects to NIS. NIS has no mechanism for controlling who connects to the server and reads the maps. This adds to the security issues and is one of the reasons you won't find any NIS servers on the Internet. (Sun offers a proprietary package called NIS+ that addresses these issues with a complex authentication system.)

Obviously, NIS comes with its own set of issues and is a system that requires considerable examination before being selected as an administration tool.

Network Security Issues

We've already mentioned a few security issues regarding UNIX and networking. These issues are serious for administrators and frequently have a huge impact on how a network is configured.

Earlier we mentioned that telnet is still used extensively in favor of remote shells. Remote shells allow noninteractive logins, such as the previous examples using `tar, dd,` and `rdist.` Although this is a convenient feature, it's also a dangerous one when not carefully administered.

The automatic login feature is implemented with a pair of text files. One of them, /etc/hosts.equiv, controls users on the system level. The other, .rhosts, controls access for individual users. Each file lists the systems by name that a user can log in from without supplying a password if the user ID exists on the target host. All the major UNIX variants treat these files the same way.

hosts.equiv provides this access for an entire workstation, except for the root account. Obviously, this file should be used carefully, if at all. The .rhosts file provides access for individual users and is located in the user's home directory. It is consulted instead of hosts.equiv. If the root account has one of these files, then the root account from the listed hosts may enter the workstation without any authentication at all because the .rhosts file effectively supercedes the hosts.equiv file.

So the convenience of the remote logins and commands comes with a high price. If a set of workstations were configured to allow root to travel back and forth without authentication, then a malicious or, maybe even worse, ill-informed user only needs to compromise one of them to wreak havoc on them all.

Some possible precautions are as follows:

- Use root as little as possible. root should never be used for remote operations is a simple enough general rule.
- Avoid using rlogin where telnet will do.
- If you must use rlogin, try to get by without using .rhosts or hosts.equiv.
- If you need to use noninteractive logins for operations such as backups or information collection, create a special account for it that only has access to the files and devices necessary for the job.
- Remote logins are just about out of the question on any systems directly connected to the Internet. (Note that a home system that is dialing into the Internet through an ISP is not truly directly connected.)

A little bit of explanation regarding the first rule is in order. The root account should be used as little as possible in day-to-day operations. Many UNIX neophytes feel that root access is necessary to accomplish anything worthwhile, but that's not true at all. There is no reason for common operations, such as performing backups, scanning logs, or running network services to be done as root. (Other than the services that use ports numbered less than 1024; for historical reasons UNIX only allows processes run as root to monitor these ports. The more situations where root is used, the more likely it is that something unexpected and possibly disastrous will occur.

Even beyond remote logins, UNIX offers many network services. File sharing, email, X Window, and information services, such as DNS and NIS, comprise only part of the flexibility and extensibility offered by networking. However, many of these services represent risks that are not always necessary, and sometimes are unacceptable.

The right way to handle these services is to evaluate which ones are needed and enable only them. Many network services are managed by inetd. This daemon process listens for requests for network services and executes the right program to service them.

For example, the ftp service is administered by inetd. When a request for the ftp service (service port number 21) is received, inetd consults its configuration information and executes ftpd. Its input and output streams are connected to the requester.

Network services are identified by ports. Common services such as ftp and telnet have *well-known ports*, numbers that all potential clients need to know. inetd binds and listens to these ports based on its configuration data, contained in the file inetd.conf.

A typical configuration file looks like this:

```
# Configuration file for inetd(1M).  See inetd.conf(4).
#
# To re-configure the running inetd process, edit this file, then
# send the inetd process a SIGHUP.
#
# Syntax for socket-based Internet services:
#  <service_name> <socket_type> <proto> <flags> <user> <server_pathname>
<args>
#
ftp     stream  tcp   nowait  root    /usr/sbin/in.ftpd       in.ftpd
telnet  stream  tcp   nowait  root    /usr/sbin/in.telnetd    in.telnetd
#
# Tnamed serves the obsolete IEN-116 name server protocol.
#
name    dgram   udp   wait    root    /usr/sbin/in.tnamed     in.tnamed
#
# Shell, login, exec, comsat and talk are BSD protocols.
#
shell   stream  tcp   nowait  root    /usr/sbin/in.rshd       in.rshd
login   stream  tcp   nowait  root    /usr/sbin/in.rlogind    in.rlogind
exec    stream  tcp   nowait  root    /usr/sbin/in.rexecd     in.rexecd
comsat  dgram   udp   wait    root    /usr/sbin/in.comsat     in.comsat
talk    dgram   udp   wait    root    /usr/sbin/in.talkd      in.talkd
```

As the comment states, information for inetd is available on two different manual pages.

Each configuration entry states the name of the service port, which is resolved by using the /etc/services file (or NIS map), some more information about the connection, the username that the program should be run as, and, finally, the program to run. The two most important aspects of this file, from a security standpoint, are what user the services are run as and what services are run at all. (Details on network connection types are covered in Chapter 26, "Networking.")

Each service name corresponds to a number. Ports numbered less than 1024, which `ftp`, `telnet`, and login all use, can only be attached to as `root`, so `inetd` itself does have to be run as `root`, but it gives us the option of running the individual programs as other users. The reason for this is simple: If a program that is running as `root` is somehow compromised, the attacker will have `root` privileges. For example, if a network service that is running as `root` has a "back door" facility that allows users to modify files, an attacker could theoretically use the program to read, copy, or modify any file on the host under attack.

Some of the most serious and effective Internet security attacks exploited undocumented features and bugs in network services that were running as `root`. Therefore, the best protection against the next attack is to avoid the service completely, or at least provide attackers with as little power as possible when they do find a weakness to take advantage of.

Most UNIX variants come from the vendor running unneeded and, in some cases, undesirable services, such as `rexecd`, which is used for the remote execution of programs, frequently with no authentication. As you saw earlier, this service came from the vendor configured as `root`. Many organizations configure key systems to deny all network services except the one service that they are built to provide, such as Internet Web and FTP servers.

Well-written network software also takes these issues into consideration. For example, the Apache Web Server is usually configured to listen to the `http` port, which is number 80 and therefore can only be bound to by `root`. Instead of handling client requests as `root` and posing a significant security risk, Apache accepts network connections as `root`, but only handles actual requests as `nobody`, a user with virtually no rights except to read Web pages. It does this by running multiple copies of itself as `nobody` and utilizing interprocess communication to dispatch user requests to the crippled processes.

Sharing files on the network poses another set of security issues. Files should be shared carefully, with close attention to not only who can write to them but also who can read them, because email and other forms of electronic communication have become more common and can contain important business information.

See Chapters 26, "Networking," and 27, "System Accounting," for more detailed information and instructions on how to properly secure your systems.

20

WHAT IS SYSTEM ADMINISTRATION?

UNIX Is Heterogeneous

UNIX is frequently criticized for a lack of consistency between versions, vendors, and even applications. UNIX is not the product of any single corporation or group, and this does have a significant impact on its personality. Linux is probably the ultimate expression of UNIX's collective identity. After Linus Torvalds created the Linux kernel and announced it to the Internet, people from all over the world began to contribute to what has become called the Linux Operating System. Although a core group of developers were key in its development, they do not all work for the same company or even live in the same country. Obviously, Linux reflects a few different views on how computers should work. UNIX does too.

Administration Tools

UNIX vendors all offer their own GUI administrative tools that are generally useful, provided that you do not have to do something that the vendor did not anticipate. These tools vary widely in how they work and how they are implemented.

IBM's UNIX operating system, AIX, comes with a sophisticated tool called SMIT. Administrators can use SMIT to configure the system, add and remove users, and upgrade software among other things. SMIT is widely considered to be the best and most mature of the system administration systems because it can be customized and run in either X Window or a terminal session. It also allows the user to view the command line equivalent of each task before it is performed. The downside (in at least some system administrators' opinions) is that use of SMIT is just about mandatory for some basic administration tasks.

Hewlett-Packard's HP-UX has a similar tool called SAM, which provides much of the functionality offered by SMIT but is not quite as powerful or sophisticated. Its use is not required to administer the system, however.

Sun's Solaris does not come with a tool comparable to SMIT or SAM. However, Sun's individual tools for upgrading and installing software and administering NIS+ are functional and intuitive. Unfortunately, the tool supplied with Solaris for administering users, printers, and NIS/NIS+ requires X Window. It is not, however required to administer the system at all.

Linux distributions vary widely when it comes to administrative tools. RedHat offers a powerful desktop environment for adding software, administering users, configuring printers, and other everyday administrative tasks. Unlike the commercial tools, it's based on scripts, not binary code, and therefore can be examined and customized by administrators. The Slackware distribution comes with management tools for upgrading and adding software also.

In addition to the different administrative tools and environments provided by the different UNIX vendors, each vendor has felt obligated to provide its own improvements to UNIX over the years. Fortunately, the threat of Windows NT and its homogeneous look and feel has made the UNIX vendors sensitive to these differences, and the tide has turned toward standardization.

UNIX has historically been divided into two major variants, AT&T's UNIX System V and The University of California's BSD UNIX. Most of the major vendors are now moving toward a System V system, but many BSD extensions will always remain.

Regardless of what the vendors do (and claim to do) UNIX's heterogeneous nature is a fact of life and is probably one of its most important strengths because that nature is responsible for giving us some of the Internet's most important tools, such as Perl, email, the Web, and Usenet News. It also provides us with many choices of how to administer our systems. Few problems in UNIX have only one answer.

Graphical Interfaces

X Window, the common Graphical User Interface (GUI) in UNIX, is a collection of applications, not an integral part of the operating system. Because it is structured this way, it differs greatly from the windowing systems on a Macintosh or Microsoft Windows. As a result, the relationship between X applications and the operating system tends to be a bit more loose than on those platforms.

One of the things that gives an X desktop its "personality" is the *window manager.* This is the application that provides each window with a border and allows them to be moved and overlapped. However, it is just an application, not part of the X Window system. Individual users on the same system can also use different window managers. The differences between window managers are significant, which has a significant impact on the look of the desktop, the way the mouse acts, and sometimes, what applications can be run.

The OpenLook window manager, which is distributed by Sun and also accompanies many Linux distributions, has many proprietary extensions and is very lightweight and fast. The Sun OpenWindows package comes with OpenLook and a set of tools for reading mail, managing files, and a few other common tasks.

Motif, which has many similarities with Microsoft Windows, has become more popular in the past few years, with most of the major vendors having agreed to standardize on the *Common Desktop Environment (CDE),* which is based largely on Motif. The CDE also has additional features, such as a graphical file manager, a toolbar, and support for virtual screens. The CDE also comes with a set of user applications.

20

WHAT IS SYSTEM ADMINISTRATION?

Window managers also come with programming libraries for creating menus and other programming tasks. As a result, it is possible to create an application that runs poorly under some window managers or requires libraries that a UNIX version does not have. This is a common problem for Motif applications on Linux because the libraries are not free. For this reason, many applications are available in a non-Motif version or with the libraries *statically linked*, which means they are built into the application. (This is generally considered undesirable because it makes the application larger and requires more memory and more disk space.)

X Window has a standard interface for configuration information, called *X resources*.

X resources support wildcards with parameters, which allows administrators (and users) to standardize behavior between diverse applications. Most X Window application developers recognize this capability and tend to use standard naming schemes for configuration parameters, which makes the use of wildcards even more convenient.

Users are able to customize applications to reflect their personal preferences without affecting others by maintaining personal resource files.

Command-Line Interfaces

The UNIX command set can be bewildering because command and option naming does not follow a coherent pattern either within the commands in one system or among UNIX variants.

There are also frequently two versions of the same command: one from the System V world and one from the BSD world.

The best way to avoid problems with these pointless and gratuitous differences is to take full advantage of the wealth of information contained in the man pages. (In the "Administration Resources" section later in this chapter, we cover a few ways to get more information from them.) The man pages are invaluable sources of information. During its long history, UNIX has been used to accomplish many techncial tasks, and most system administration challenges have been met by—and documented by—others before you. Also, there are usually several ways to solve a problem; as you search for alternate ways, you will deepen your familiarity with the system and its possibilities.

System Administration Tasks

System administration can generally be divided into two broad categories: supporting users and supporting systems.

Supporting Users

Users are your customers. We support users by creating their logins and providing them with the information they need to use their computers to get something done.

Creating User Accounts

The most fundamental thing that an administrator can do for a user is create her account. UNIX accounts are contained in the /etc/passwd file with the actual encrypted password being contained in either the passwd file or the /etc/shadow file if the system implements shadow passwords.

Always remember that passwords and file and directory permissions are the first line of security in a UNIX system. Be careful what access permissions you grant.

When a user is created, the account should be added to the passwd file. This can be done manually or by using tools that do the following:

- Add the user to the passwd file (and shadow file if it is used).
- Create a home directory for the user with the proper file permissions and ownership.
- Copy generic *skeleton files* to the account, which give the user a basic environment to work with.
- Register the new account with network systems, such as NIS and NFS, if the home directory needs to be accessed on other hosts.

Most UNIX variants also provide a command-line tool named useradd that performs all or most of these steps, which can be incorporated into a shell or Perl script.

Providing Support

Providing users with documentation and support is another key system administration task and potential headache.

All user populations are different, and there is no universal solution to user training, but here are a couple of ideas that may help.

Try to provide and gently enforce a formal method for requesting changes to systems and getting help, possibly through email or the Web. Also, provide as much documentation as you can through easy-to-use interfaces, such as Web browsers. If you have Internet access now, a lot of the information your users need can be found online—you can direct them to it.

Supporting Systems

The other half of the job is supporting your systems. Systems have to be built, backed up, upgraded, and, of course, fixed.

Adding Nodes

A frequent system administration task is adding new nodes to the network. It's also one part of the job that can truly benefit from some planning and insight.

Not all systems are used for the same purpose. Workstations should have well-defined roles and should be configured in accordance with those roles.

- Will users be able to access all or some of the systems? Do users need to access more than one system? Are there systems that users should never access?

- What network file systems will each workstation need to access? Are there enough that automount would help?

- What network services, such as telnet, remote logins, sharing file systems, and email, do workstations need to provide? Can each service be justified?

- What networks will workstations need to access? Are there networks that should be inaccessible from others?

Backups

Files get corrupted, lost, accidentally overwritten, or deleted. Our only protection against these situations is backups because UNIX does not have an undelete command.

UNIX provides several backup tools, and deciding which tool(s) to use can be a difficult.

tar (**t**ape **ar**chive) is a commonly used backup tool.

```
tar -c -f /dev/rmt/0 /home/eric
```

The preceding command would back up the contents of the /home/eric directory to the first tape drive installed on a Solaris system. tar automatically traverses the directory, so all files in /home/eric and its subdirectories are archived. Note that the device name for tape drives on systems differs from variant to variant. The -f option tells tar which tape drive to use, whereas the -c option is telling it to create a new archive instead of modifying an existing one. One of tar's idiosyncrasies is that when a path is given to it as the backup specification, it is added to the archive; so when you restore /home/eric, that is where it will be restored to. A more flexible way to back up the directory is to do this:

```
cd /home/eric
tar -cf /dev/rmt/0 .
```

`tar` recognizes `.` as meaning back up the current directory. When the archive is extracted, it is placed in the current directory, regardless of where that is.

`cpio` is another standard UNIX tool for backups. Its interface is a little more difficult than `tar`'s, but has several advantages.

`cpio` is usually used with `ls` or `find` to create archives.

```
find . -print ¦ cpio -o > /dev/rst0
```

The `find` command prints the full path of all the files in its current directory to standard out. `cpio` accepts these filenames and archives them to standard output. This is redirected to the tape, where it is archived. This command is an excellent example of the UNIX way of combining commands to create a new tool.

`cpio` is the file copying and archiving "Swiss army knife." In addition to streaming files in a format suitable for tape, it can do the following:

- Back up special files, such as device drive *stubs* such as `/dev/rst0`.
- Place data on tapes more efficiently than `tar` or `dd`.
- Skip over bad areas on tapes or floppies when restoring, when `tar` would simply die. With `cpio`, you can at least restore part of a damaged archive.
- Perform backups to floppies, including spreading a single archive over more than one disk. `tar` can only put a single archive on one disk.
- Swap bytes during the archive or extraction to aid in transferring files from one architecture to another.

This example also illustrates how you can redirect standard output to a device name and expect the device driver to place it on the device.

Just as important as picking a backup tool is designing a backup strategy. What you back up, and when, must match the needs and working habits of your user base. Unless you have a fireproof vault at your facility, be sure to store backup tapes offsite in a secure place.

System Load and Performance

To diagnose and anticipate resource conflicts and system problems, you will need to monitor usage statistics. These statistics can be gathered with automated scripts.

Some things to monitor are disk usage, CPU utilization, swap, and memory. The tools used for getting this information, such as `du` and `df` for disk information and `top` and `vmstat` for the rest, are covered in the next few chapters of this book.

Administration Resources

A system administrator needs every shred of information and help he can get, and as much as UNIX vendors would hate to admit, the documentation that accompanies UNIX is sometimes lacking. Fortunately, it's a big world out there.

The Manual Pages

The famous rejoinder RTFM (Read The Fine Manual) refers to the manual pages installed with the UNIX system. The man pages, as they are frequently called, contain documentation and instructions on just about every UNIX command, C function call, and data file on your system.

The `man` command searches for documentation based on a command or topic name. So the command

```
man ls
```

provides documentation on the `ls` command, which happens to be in section one.

As simple as they may appear, the man pages actually have a sophisticated structure. The pages are divided into sections, with some of the sections being further divided into sub-sections.

The section layout resembles this:

- User commands—Commands such as `ls`, `tar`, and `cpio`
- System calls—C programming functions that are considered system calls, such as opening and closing files
- C library functions—C programming functions that are not considered system calls, such as printing text
- File formats—Descriptions of file layouts, such as `hosts.equiv` and `inetd.conf`
- Headers, tables, and macros—Miscellaneous documentation, such as character sets and header files, not already covered
- Games and demos—games and demo software

To view information about each section, you can view the intro page for it. To see information about section one, you would execute the following command:

```
man -s 1 intro
```

The `-s` option selects which section of the man pages to search with the System V version of the `man` command. BSD versions accept the section number as the first argument with no switch, whereas the Linux version selects the section from an environment variable or from a -s option.

All the versions accept the -a option, which forces the man command to search all the sections and display all pages that match. Man pages can be indexed and preformatted with a tool called catman. The preformatting part make the pages display faster and is less important than the indexing, which allows you to use more powerful information retrieval tools, namely whatis and apropos.

whatis gives the man page name and section number. apropos displays the section number, name, and short description of any page that contains the specified keyword.

Internet Information Resources

The Internet provides administrators with a wealth of resources too:

- Usenet News—Although not as useful as it was in the past (due to overcrowding and a plummeting signal-to-noise ratio), Usenet News offers discussion groups about all UNIX variants and covers various aspects of them. Some examples are comp.sys.sun.admin, comp.os.linux.setup, and comp.unix.admin. Because of the high traffic on Usenet News, some sites do not carry it. If you cannot get access, try using a search service such as http://www.dejanews.com to find what you need.

- FAQ Lists—Frequently Asked Question Lists hold a wealth of information. Most computer-related Usenet groups have their own FAQ lists. They can be found posted periodically in the groups and at the rtfm.mit.edu ftp server. Many FAQS are also available in html format.

- The Web—Documentation is available from the UNIX vendors and from people and groups involved with Linux. Many users and developers also post a wealth of information just to be helpful. The Net has a huge number of UNIX users on it.

Tools of the Trade

A successful administrator takes full advantage of the tools provided with a UNIX system. To the uninitiated, UNIX seems difficult and unwieldy, but after you get the idea, you'll never want to use another system.

The Shell

Earlier, we demonstrated how cpio uses the output of the find command to learn what files to archive. This was a demonstration of shell pipes, which redirect the output of one command to another. We also used this to back up files to a tape drive located on another host.

We demonstrated mailing a file to a user on the command line using redirection, which opens a file and passes it to a command as if it was provided in the command line or typed in as a program requested it.

UNIX shells also support sophisticated programming constructs, such as loops, and provide comparison operators, such as equality, greater than, and less than.

Shell programming is essential to system administration. File backups, adding users and nodes, collecting usage statistics, and a host of other administrative tasks are candidates for unattended scripts.

Perl and Other Automation Tools

Perl has become more popular over the past few years because of its flexibility, power, and ease of an interpreted language. System administrators can benefit greatly from a little working knowledge of this language because it can be used for tasks such as the following:

- Analyzing log files and alerting the administrator of trouble via email or pager
- Automatically converting systems statistics into Web pages
- Automating the process of creating user accounts, adding and distributing automounter maps, backing up systems, and creating html content
- Creating and communicating over network connections

These are only a few examples of what this language can do. Some other tools worth noting are TCL/TK, which most of the RedHat administrative tools are written in and awk.

Summary

System administrators manage the UNIX system and machine, along with the network of workstations, as a shared resource.

The following chapters describe the various tasks of system administration in much more detail. In addition, you will find that a working knowledge not only of the general UNIX command set but also of shell and Perl scripting to be important tools in managing the system under your care.

CHAPTER 21

UNIX Installation Basics

by Lance Cavener and Syd Weinstein

Installing UNIX on a machine requires more thought and planning than installing DOS or Microsoft Windows. You need to decide whether this system will be standalone, or dependent on a server on your network. You also have to pay careful attention to system resources (such as hard drive space, processor speed, memory, and so on) and which packages are required to tailor this UNIX installation to your needs, and perhaps the needs of users in the future.

Why? DOS is a system that takes less than 10MB of disk space. Windows takes a bit more, but it's still a rather small amount. UNIX is a large system depending on your configuration. The complete installation of just the operating system and all that comes with it for Sun's Solaris 2.6 release, for example, is about 600MB. With that much disk space in use, it's often wise to share it across several systems. In addition, there are few options in installing DOS or Windows that can be made by the setup program. UNIX splits the install into many different sections, called packages. Each package consists of files that provide a specific set of features. These features range from networking tools, necessary system utilities, or applications.

You must also take into consideration the various flavors of UNIX that are available and how much you are willing to spend. Linux, for example, is free and publicly available to anyone over the Internet or on CD-ROM. FreeBSD as the name implies is an example of a free BSD-based operating system. There are also other commercial operating systems such as Solaris (for both the Sparc and the x86); however, you can acquire the binary distribution of Solaris for free (although you must pay for media, shipping, and handling charges) if it is to be used for noncommercial use.

If you have never used any flavor of UNIX before, you should experiment with as many as you can. You have to decide which one best suits your needs and expectations.

TIP

Linux and FreeBSD are both available on CD-ROM from Walnut Creek. The Internet address is ref HYPERLINK http://www.cdrom.com.

On another note, you have commercial operating systems such as BSDI, Unixware, Solaris, AIX, HP-UX, and many others. These are generally expensive and platform specific, although you get over-the-phone technical support and printed documentation. These are things to look for if you run a mission-critical site and might need a shoulder to lean on in the future should anything catastrophic happen to your server.

UNIX Installation Basics

CHAPTER **21**

915

21

UNIX
INSTALLATION
BASICS

What Are the Differences Between the Different Distributions?

Although I can't possibly go through every available distribution, I will give a brief description of some of the major UNIX operating systems.

- SCO's Unixware (http://www.sco.com) is based on Svr4, and was originally developed by AT&T. Novell had control of it for a while, and now SCO is developing for it. Unixware runs primarily on x86 (Intel or 100 percent compatible) based machines.

- SCO's SCO OpenServer is another variation of UNIX that is based on XENIX, an OS conceived by Microsoft. It is popular among corporate internets/intranets and has been for many years. It earns a respectable place on corporate servers, although it lacks the versatility of BSD. Its technical support cannot be matched, which is why many corporations choose this commercial OS as their server OS of choice. SCO also has a whole host of applications available—even Microsoft products such as Word and Excel.

- BSDI's BSD/OS Internet Server (http://www.bsdi.com) is a commercial distribution of BSD/OS originally developed by Berkeley University. BSDI took BSD/OS and added many new utilities, programs, and features that make this distribution a stable and productive addition to any corporate intranet or Internet gateway. Its main focus is as Internet service providers (ISP) because of its excellent networking capabilities. BSD/OS runs on all x86 (Intel or 100 percent compatible) machines.

- FreeBSD (http://www.freebsd.org) and NetBSD (http://www.netbsd.org) are free alternatives to BSD/OS. They contain many of the great features that make BSD/OS popular, but lack the professional technical support of any commercial distribution. If you don't need the over-the-phone technical support and want the stability and reliability you look for in an Internet/intranet focused OS, these are for you. Did I mention they are both free? FreeBSD runs on the x86 platform, whereas NetBSD runs on the following: Dec Alpha, Amiga, Acorn RiscPC, Atari, HP 9000/300 series, x86, m86k Macintosh, PowerPC, Sun SPARC series, Sun 3, Dec VAX, and many others. NetBSD is by far the most portable operating system available, although FreeBSD seems to be a more popular choice among x86 users.

- Linux (http://www.linux.org) was originally developed from the Minix source. It began as a hobby and grew to a frequently updated, used, and supported operating system. Linux is largely based on the POSIX standards and SysV. Linux has a wide range of applications available (more so than SCO) and is also free. Commercial distributions are available that usually contain commercial software (for instance, Applixware for RedHat). Linux is popular among first-time UNIX users and is easily installed. Linux is frequently updated with new kernels and is not always as stable as some would like. Althoigh Linux is popular for workstations, it is usually not given the task of a mission-critical server because it lacks the technical support, stability, and functionality of a high-quality professionally developed operating system. Some administrators like the task of making Linux stable, which usually involves sifting through thousands and thousands of lines of source code.

- AIX (`http://www.rs6000.ibm.com/software/`) is an operating system created by IBM to run on its RS/6000 workstations. AIX is capable of running older 32-bit applications as well as the new 64-bit applications. Its major features include support for up to 16GB of memory on 64-bit hardware, Web-based system management, JAVA support, IPv6, C2 security, and OpenGL. AIX 4.3 also uses an innovative Web-based system manager that allows easy administration—even remotely. AIX is a stable operating system and is backed by a well-recognized company, which makes it a prime operating system for corporate use. A workstation from IBM varies in price depending on which model you get and what hardware is included with it.

- HP-UX (http://www.hp.com/esy) is a 64-bit operating system created by Hewlett-Packard to run on its HP 9000 Enterprise Servers. HP-UX supports VLM (Very Large Memory) addressing up to 4TB of RAM, 1TB of local and networked file systems, 16-way symmetric multiprocessing, parallel processing, and Performance Optimized Page Sizing. This makes HP-UX and the HP 9000 Enterprise Servers very powerful machines. They are usually used in institutions where complex calculations or modeling takes place.

What Do I Need to Know from the Start?

The first thing you need to do is decide what you are going to install on this system. You decide this by looking, not only at this system, but at all the systems on this segment of the network.

UNIX Installation Basics

CHAPTER 21

917

21

UNIX
INSTALLATION
BASICS

> **NOTE**
>
> A network segment is a group of machines all plugged into the same Ethernet, a type of LAN, which uses a bus topology. Because Ethernet uses a bus topology, each of the machines sees all the traffic on the network. Each is local to each other and is immediately accessible via the network. Because the Ethernet LAN is only capable of handling a finite amount of traffic, the network is broken into segments connected by routers or bridges. Traffic to systems within the segment is not repeated, or retransmitted, into the other segments. Only traffic that is for systems outside the segment is repeated. With proper planning, almost all the traffic will be internal to the segment, and more systems can be placed on the overall network before everyone bogs down from trying to put more bytes out over the LAN than it can handle.

You base your decision about what to install on the intended usage of the system, what systems it can be served by, and for which systems it must provide services.

Space Requirements

DOS and Windows are not designed to easily share large sections of the installation. UNIX (especially because of its disk needs) almost expects that some sharing will occur. The degree of disk space sharing leads to the definition of standalone, server, and disk-less machines.

A *standalone system* means that this particular machine can function on its own—it doesn't require any assistance from any other machine on the LAN.

A *server* is a machine that is connected to the LAN that runs daemons to give remote clients some functions such as mail or news. Technically, a server can be a standalone machine, but because of its tasks, it never is.

Dataless machines contain only the necessary files to boot, although they are not used often because of the high load they put on the network. To avoid network congestion, many people run standalone machines to avoid the added cost of faster network equipment.

In addition to sharing the operating system, UNIX systems can share other disks, such as drives containing databases or user files. Sharing these disks does not make a system a server in the "install" sense. The server name is reserved for serving the operating system or its utilities. A system might be an NFS server (sharing user files via Network File System—NFS) and still be considered a standalone system for the installation of the UNIX operating system.

A dataless system requires that the core system files be installed. A standalone system could be set up with either end-user packages or with developer packages, whereas a server needs the entire distribution.

You are going to have different storage necessities for different installations. Developer installs usually require more disk space, whereas a dataless system only requires core files. Depending on the size of these files, you will configure the partition differently. Partitions that will contain Usenet articles should be configured to contain smaller *inodes*. This, in turn, increases the number of inodes available for storage of the small Usenet articles. Running out of inodes is like running out of disk space, even though you still have disk space left.

TIP

An *inode* is basically a unit where data is stored. If you have ten 512-byte inodes, and ten 3-byte files, you fill up those ten inodes even though you have not used up the space contained in them. As you can see, this is why decreasing the size of the inodes produces more available inodes for storage of these small files.

So far this chapter just touches on the disk installation. There is still much to be discussed. You must plan for users, the network and its traffic, applications, printers, remote access, backups, security, and much more.

Thus, planning for a UNIX installation requires planning not only for this one system, but for all the systems in this segment of the network.

Who Is Going to Use This System?

Users who typically use their machine for word processing and other general office applications do not require an extremely large amount of disk space or system resources. However, a power user or application developer needs much more to be installed, perhaps including compilers and development libraries. To decide what to install on this segment of the LAN, let alone on this system, you need to determine which types of users are going to be using this system.

> **TIP**
>
> Not only does the type of user dictate what gets installed, it also dictates how many systems can be put on this segment of the LAN, the server capacity, and swap space requirements.

Which Type of Users

UNIX users generally fall into one or more of several categories:

- Application users—These users run commercial or locally developed applications. They rarely interact with the shell directly and do not write their own applications. These users might be running a database application, a word processor or desktop publishing system, a spreadsheet, or some in-house-developed set of applications. They spend most of their time in think mode, where they are deciding what to do with the results the application has presented them, or in data entry mode, typing responses or data into the system. Their need for large amounts of local disk access is minimal, and they do not change applications frequently, nor are they running many applications simultaneously. (They might have them open, but they are generally interacting with only a couple of them at a time—the rest are waiting for the user to provide input.) Although application users might put a large load on their servers, they do not normally put large disk loads on their workstations.

- Power users—These users run applications, just like the application users, but they also run shell scripts and interact more closely with the system. They are likely to be running multiple applications at once, with all these applications processing in parallel. These users keep several applications busy and access the disk more frequently and use more CPU resources than do the normal application users.

- Developers—Developers not only run applications, they also run compilers, access different applications than users, require access to the development libraries, and generally use more components of the operating system than do users. Furthermore, they tend to use debugging tools that require more swap space and access to more disk resources than the application user generally needs. The UNIX operating system has packages that are only needed by developers, and if a developer is on any particular segment, these files must be installed and accessible to the systems used by the developers. Compiling takes up a great amount of processor power; therefore, you must plan to accommodate this need with the right type of system. Ten programmers compiling 10,000 lines of code in parallel can easily bog down a Pentium Pro 200Mhz server. Be aware, however, that most commercial UNIX vendors do not include developer tools in their operating systems, and they must be purchased separately.

> **TIP**
>
> You must not only consider who will use the system right away, but because you only install UNIX once, consider who might use the system over the next six months to a year. Remember, depending on what type of system you are going to set up, you will be adding users to your machine. If the programs these users need are not available, you will be forced to reinstall the whole system, or install the appropriate packages, depending on the OS. Because of the low cost of hardware these days, you are better off to invest in the added hardware and install all the packages that might be of use to you or anyone else in the future.

For What Purpose?

UNIX systems that are being used as shared development machines or are going to be placed in a common user area, need a lot of swap space, a large section of the disk for temporary files. They also need more of the packages from the operating system than systems that are just being used on a single user's desk. In addition, if the system is going to be used as a computation or database server, it needs increased swap space and processor power.

What Other Systems Are Located on This Segment of the LAN?

As stated in the "What Do I Need to Know from the Start?" section, you must consider all the systems on this segment of the LAN. You are looking for systems that provide access to sections of the operating system, provide access to application disk areas, and make suitable servers for the other systems on the segment.

If you have an office or a lab full of identical machines, all running the same applications with no need for any major customizations, then having a centralized installation is much easier to maintain. But because we now have hardware, such as CD-ROMs capable of 16x speed, that can do upwards of 700KBps, and Ethernet that can do anywhere from 10MBps to 100MBps (Ethernet and Fast Ethernet respectively) it is usually easy to install over the network. It's also just as easy to upgrade machines, providing your operating system supports upgrades; it all depends on the function of the machines on the segment.

Determining Suitable Servers

It's usually easier to determine suitable servers than suitable clients, so start there. To make a good server system, you need the following:

UNIX Installation Basics

CHAPTER 21

921

21

UNIX
INSTALLATION
BASICS

- Plenty of RAM—Servers must have plenty of RAM available for their use. Your server must be capable of handling many clients, each running different processes at the same time. For this to be done efficiently, you don't want much swapping happening. Your best bet is to put as much RAM as possible into the server; this allows room for upgrades (and higher loads). Generally, 64 to 128MB is sufficient for many installations. There are some exceptions, such as INN where it uses a lot of RAM, and for a full news feed, 64MB will not last very long.

- Fast disk drives—The client sees the delay to read a disk block as the time to ask the server for the block, the time the server takes to read the block, and the time to transmit the block over the network back to the client. If the server has a fast disk, this time might be no longer, and is often shorter, than reading the same number of blocks locally.

  Because a server is handling multiple clients, including itself, it is more likely that a disk block is already in the server's disk cache. This is especially true for program files and the operating system utilities, because they are used often. Access is then very fast, as the disk read time is not needed at all. This helps make servers as responsive as if they were reading the disk block locally on the client server.

  Don't sacrifice quality for price. You pay for what you get; go for the highest possible (and fastest) hard drives and controllers available. Ultra-Wide SCSI controllers with high-quality UW-SCSI drives handle the task perfectly.

- Sufficient disk space—A server holds, not only its own files and a copy of the UNIX operating system, but also the swap and temporary space for its diskless clients. A suitable server should have some spare disk space for adding not only the current clients but some extra to account for growth. Here is a breakdown of some of the more frequently used packages and their sizes for BSD/OS:

  > 4.0MB—Core root (`/`)
  >
  > 0.4MB—Core (`/var`)
  >
  > 23.6MB—Core usr (`/usr`)
  >
  > 9.9MB—Additional usr (`/usr`)
  >
  > 12.3MB—Networking (`/usr`)
  >
  > 17.0MB—Development (`/usr`)
  >
  > 17.3MB—Manual Pages (`/usr/share/man` & `/usr/contrib/man`)
  >
  > 92.7MB—X11 XFree servers, Development, man Pages (`/usr/X11R6`)

As you can see, BSD/OS takes up a lot of space. There are still additional packages such as Hylafax, the kernel sources, ghostscript, MH, and many other tools that you may or may not want installed.

- Spare CPU resources—A server needs to have enough CPU cycles to serve its local users and still provide disk and network access services to its clients. But that does not mean to make the fastest system the server. Often you should do just the opposite.

   Normally, it does not take much CPU power to be a server. File access in UNIX is very efficient, as is network traffic. However, servers that are heavily loaded with serving Web pages or processing large databases require a faster CPU. A system that is heavily loaded delays the response of disk block requests for its clients.

Managing Network Traffic

Before you can decide how to install the new system, you need to check on the amount of traffic on the network. Sources of this traffic include the following:

- Traffic from the systems in Department A to its local server for the following:

   Remote file systems, including accessing shared UNIX OS partitions and user files

   Access to client/server applications hosted on the Department A server

   Diskless client access to swap, temporary, and spool partitions

- Traffic between the systems in Department A, including the following:

   Client/server application traffic

   Remote display updates (a window on one system showing output from a process on a different system)

   Sharing of local file systems that are not on the server

- Traffic between the systems in Department A and the backbone server, including the following:

   Remote file access to company-wide files

   Access to client/server applications running on the backbone, such as a master database

- Traffic between the systems in Department A and those in Department B, including the following:

   Access to files located locally at Department B

   Access to client/server applications running on the systems in Department B

   Remote file access to local disks on Department B systems

The additional traffic generated by the installation of this new system must be compared to the existing traffic on the network. Adding a diskless client on a network segment running at 80 percent utilization is asking for trouble.

UNIX Installation Basics
CHAPTER 21

923

21

**UNIX
INSTALLATION
BASICS**

You don't need sophisticated tools to monitor network traffic. Just take one of the workstations and use the tools provided by your vendor to count the packets it sees on the network. A simple approach is to use a tool such as `etherfind` or `snoop` to place the Ethernet interface into promiscuous mode, where it listens to all the packets on the network, not just those addressed to itself. Then count the number of packets received by the system over a period of time and their respective length. Most UNIX systems can drive an Ethernet segment up to about 800KBps in bursts and more than 500KBps sustained. If the traffic is anything close to this, consider splitting the segment into two segments to reduce the traffic.

When splitting the network into segments, if you can place a server and its systems into each of the split segments, often you can use a less expensive bridge to reduce the traffic on each segment rather than using a router.

Summarizing What You Need to Know Before Starting

In summary, before starting to plan for the actual installation of the new system, you need to determine who is going to use the system. You need to determine how much disk access they will be performing and how much they will contribute to the overall network traffic; whether this system is going to be a client or a server; and whether the network can tolerate another system on this segment before the segment has to be split because of overloading.

Planning for the Installation

You now must determine on which segment to install this new system, decide what type of user it's for, and decide where to place it. What more do you need to plan for other than where to plug in the power cord and network connection?

This section guides you through a short preinstallation checklist to make the installation process go smoothly. It will have you answer the following questions:

- From where am I going to install?
- Is this to be a standalone, server, or diskless system?
- What is its hostname?
- What is its IP address?
- Which packages should be installed?
- How should the disk be partitioned?

These are some of the questions the system asks as you install UNIX. Most of the rest have obvious answers, such as what time zone you are in.

From Where Am I Going to Install?

Traditionally, one installed a system by placing the medium in a drive and booting from that medium, such as floppy or CD-ROM. With the advent of networking, things are no longer so simple, but they can be a lot more convenient.

You have two choices for installing: local or remote. A local installation is the traditional case, where the media is inserted into some drive attached to the computer being installed, and the software is copied onto the system. A remote installation further falls into two types.

You might use a remote systems's CD-ROM to read the media because the system you are installing does not have one. But if there are many systems to install, you would access an install server, which already has all the installable files and boot images on its local disks. Because the local disks are faster than CD-ROM or tape, this is faster. It's only worthwhile to set up the install server, however, when you have a lot of systems to install.

Media Distribution Type

With upwards of 350MB of software to install, floppies are no longer practical. UNIX software vendors have switched from floppies or tapes to CD-ROM.

To install the operating system, you have to boot off the CD-ROM or use boot disks. If your computer is unable to boot off the CD-ROM, the vendor usually supplies either one or multiple boot disks. These disks contain the information needed to boot your machine and load the necessary device drivers to let the operating system access your hardware. It also contains the installation program and the software it requires. This is a minimal RAM-based system that is loaded off the floppy and is used to read the CD-ROM. It basically contains the necessary drivers to access the CD-ROM.

CAUTION

If you cannot boot your operating system from the CD-ROM, you will need boot disks. Make sure that the boot disks you are getting from your vendor contain the necessary drivers for your installation hardware. Operating systems such as BSD/OS come with only one generic boot disk. Linux has many different combinations of boot and root disks.

UNIX Installation Basics

CHAPTER 21

925

21

UNIX
INSTALLATION
BASICS

CAUTION

Read the release notes and the hardware compatibility list carefully. Most PC-based UNIX systems support only a limited set of hardware. Be sure your display adapter card, network card, and disk controller are supported. Check to see whether any special device drivers are required and that you have those drivers for your version of the operating system.

If not, before you start the installation, be sure to acquire current drivers for those cards from the manufacturer of the cards or from your UNIX vendor. Be sure the driver is specific to the version of UNIX you will be installing.

If the installation procedure does not ask you to install these drivers, be sure to install them before rebooting from the mini-root, used to install the system, to the operating system just installed. Otherwise, the system will not boot.

Using a Local Device or a Remote Device for Installation

Because most UNIX vendors have decided to switch to CD-ROM as the distribution media of choice, most likely you will have a CD-ROM drive somewhere in the network. At this time you have two choices:

- Unplug the drive from where it is currently and add it to the new system to perform the install. Then you have a local CD-ROM drive and can follow the instructions in the installation notes for using a local CD-ROM drive.

- If your version of UNIX has remote installation abilities, access the drive remotely from the system on which it currently resides.

Because the network is usually much faster than the CD-ROM drive, either choice works. You just have to be sure that the drive remains available to you for the entire installation process. If someone else is going to need the CD-ROM drive, you will not be able to relinquish it to them until the entire install procedure is complete.

CAUTION

If the system must boot off the CD-ROM drive, it is not always possible to plug any CD-ROM drive into the system. Many UNIX workstation vendors have placed special ROMs (or firmware) in their CD-ROM drives to modify their behavior to look more like a disk drive during the boot process. When in doubt, it is best to have available a model of that workstation vendor's CD-ROM drive for the installation.

Dataless or Standalone Server System?

Now is the time to decide whether this system is going to be a dataless system or a standalone system or server. In addition, you need to decide how to partition the disk.

See the release notes of your system for specifics, but use the following disk space requirements as a guideline:

- Dataless—Dataless clients use the local disk for each of the partitions listed previously for the diskless client.

    root: 10–20MB

    swap: Varies by memory size, but 16–256MB is the normal range.

    spool: 10–20MB

    tmp: 10–40MB

- Standalone—If the system is for an application user, the same sizes as those for the dataless clients are appropriate.

    In addition, a /usr partition will be needed with an additional 100MB to hold the remainder of the operating system. If X Window system is also to be stored locally, it can require up to an additional 70MB, depending on the number of tools and fonts installed. A minimal X installation requires about 30MB.

    If the user is a developer, the /usr partition will need to be about 150–200MB to hold the compilers, libraries, additional tools, and local tools the user will need.

- Server—Server systems generally need the entire operating system installed. Here is a guideline for overall sizes:

    root: 128MB

    swap: varies by memory size, but 64–512MB is normal range.

    spool: 40–100MB

    tmp: 20–80MB

    usr: 500MB

    X: 75MB

    Per diskless client: 50–200MB (more if large swap areas are needed for the client)

    In addition, a server may have more than one network interface installed. This is so that it can serve multiple segments.

Naming the System

Each UNIX system may be given one of the following names:

- Hostname—A short name it is known by locally.
- UUCP name—Usually the same as the hostname. Used for modem-based communications between UNIX systems.
- Domain name—A name that identifies which set of systems this system is a part of for electronic mail and routing.
- NIS domain—A name that identifies which set of systems this system is grouped with for system administration purposes. The set of systems shares a common password and other system administration files.

This chapter deals with the system host and domain names. Using a UUCP name that is different from the hostname is covered in Chapter 35, "UUCP Administration." Using NIS is covered in Chapter 26, "File System and Disk Administration."

Hostname

A hostname is typed often, so it should be relatively short. Although it can be up to 256 characters long in System V Release 4 systems, no one wants to type a name that long all the time. A short word usually is desired. If this name is to be shared as the UUCP name as well, it should be no longer than eight characters.

TIP

At any organization, people generally come and go, and when they go, the system they were using gets reassigned. Hardware also gets replaced. It's not a good idea to name a system for its current user or for its current hardware.

These are some poor name choices:

- sun1051—Today it might be a Sun Sparc 10/51. Tomorrow it might be a Dec Alpha or something else. Choose a name that retains its meaning regardless of the changes in hardware.
- jerry—It was Jerry's system, but who has it now? The name should help identify the system for the user and the administrators. You will be referring to the system by this name in many contexts.
- mis1—Systems migrate, even from department to department. When this system ends up in engineering, calling it mis anything could be confusing.

Instead, consider using some name that allows for a selection of one of a group of names.

These are some popular choices:

continues

- The names of the seven dwarves—This gives the systems some personality, and at least allows for seven. You could expand to use the names of other characters in stories besides Snow White when more names are needed.
- Street names—Be careful, though. If you name the aisles of your cubicle system for streets, don't use the same street names for your systems. Moving them around could get confusing.

Don't take this tip too literally. If functional names, such as `mis1` or `database` make sense, use them. It isn't that difficult to retire the old name and change the system's name to a new one in the future.

Domain Name (DNS/Mail)

If you want to uniquely address every UNIX system by name and you try to use short names for local convenience, you quickly run into the problem bemoaned often on the Internet: "All the good ones are taken." One way around this problem is the same way people resolve it with their own names. You can give systems first, middle, and last names.

One of the results of UNIX and the Internet growing up together is the domain name system. This allows every machine to be uniquely addressed by giving its fully qualified domain name, which is comprised of its hostname and its domain name, separated by dots, as in the following:

`hostname.localdomain.masterdomain.topdomain`

As an example, the mail gateway at my company, Senarius Networks, uses this fully qualified domain name:

`Earth.senarius.net`

You read this name from right to left as follows:

`net`: This is the top-level or root domain in the United States and Canada for network providers; `com:`, for commercial organizations. Other choices include `edu`, for educational institutions; `gov`, for governmental bodies; `org`, for charitable organizations; and `us`, used mostly for individuals. Outside the United States and Canada, the International Standards Organization (ISO) country code is the top-level domain.

`senarius`: This is the chosen domain name for the entire organization. Because the company is connected to the Internet, `senarius.net` had to be unique before it could be assigned.

`earth`: This is the actual host name of this system.

The system is then referred to as earth within the local office, and earth.ascio.net from outside the company.

If this is an installation of a system into an existing network, you should already have an existing domain name to use. Then you have to choose only a hostname. If this is the first system to install in a local group of systems, consider choosing a local domain name as well.

> **TIP**
>
> Why use a local domain name? In networked systems, a central administration group is responsible for assigning and maintaining all hostnames and their corresponding addresses. When the number of systems gets large, there is too much burden on this one group. It can cause delays while you wait for the administration group to get around to adding your new information to their master files. If they delegate this responsibility for a set of systems to a local group, they only need to add the local domain to their files and then you can add systems and make changes as needed.

Only if this is the first system in the organization will you have to choose the remaining levels of the domain name. They should be the same for all systems within the organization.

Choosing Which Packages to Install Locally

When you made the choice of being a server, a standalone system, or a dataless client, you made the base choice of what portions of the operating system to install. You can fine-tune this choice if you need to conserve disk space. Linux, BSD/OS, Solaris, and many other operating systems give you a large choice of packages to install. Some of those packages are specific to hardware you may not have installed. You can choose to omit those packages now, and if you change the configuration later, you can always add them to the existing installation.

After you have chosen the packages you intend to install, sum their sizes as specified in the release notes for that version, and you will be ready to lay out the partitions.

Laying Out the Partitions

Rather than use an entire disk drive for one file system, which leads to inefficiencies and other problems, UNIX systems have the capability to split a single drive into sections.

These sections are called *partitions* (some distributions of UNIX call them *slices*), because each is a partition of the disk's capacity.

Generally, a disk can be split into eight partitions, each of which the operating system treats independently as a logical disk drive.

Why Multiple File Systems?

- Damage control—If the system were to crash due to software error, hardware failure, or power problems, some of the disk blocks might still be in the file system cache and not have been written to disk yet. This causes damage to the file system structure. Although the methods used try to reduce this damage, and the `fsck` UNIX utility can repair most damage, spreading the files across multiple file systems reduces the possibility of damage, especially to critical files needed to boot the system. When you split the files across disk slices, these critical files end up on slices that rarely change or are mounted read-only and never change. Their chances of being damaged and preventing you from recovering the remainder of the system are greatly reduced.

- Access control—Only a complete slice can be marked as read-only or read-write. If you want to mount the shared operating system sections as read-only to prevent changes, they have to be on their own slice.

- Space management—Files are allocated from a pool of free space on a per-file system basis. If a user allocated a large amount of space, depleting the free space, and the entire system were a single file system, there would be no free space left for critical system files. The entire system would freeze when it ran out of space.

  Using separate file systems, especially for user files, allows only that single user, or group of users, to be delayed when a file system becomes full. The system will continue to operate, allowing you to handle the problem.

- Performance—The larger the file system, within limits, the larger its tables that have to be managed. As the disk fragments and space become scarce, the further apart the fragments of a file might be placed on the disk. Using multiple smaller partitions reduces the absolute distance and keeps the sizes of the tables manageable. Although the UFS file system does not suffer from table size and fragmentation problems as much as System V file systems, this is still a concern.

- Backups—Many of the backup utilities work on a complete file system basis. If the file system is very big, it could take more time than you want to allocate to back up. Multiple smaller backups are easier to handle and recover from.

> **NOTE**
>
> Just because you are doing multiple backups does not necessarily mean that you need multiple tapes. UNIX can place more than one backup on a single tape, provided there is space on the tape to hold them.

The following partitions are required on all UNIX installations: `root` and `swap`.

It is recommended that you create partitions to hold `usr`, `var`, `home`, and `tmp`.

As you read the sections on each partition, make a map of your disk space and allocate each partition on the map. You will use this map when you enter the disk partitioning information as you install the system.

The root Partition

The `root` partition is mounted at the top of the file system hierarchy. It is mounted automatically as the system boots, and it cannot be unmounted. All other file systems are mounted below the root.

The `root` needs to be large enough to hold the following:

- The boot information and the bootable UNIX kernel, and a backup copy of the kernel in case the main one gets damaged
- Any local system configuration files, which are typically in the `/etc` directory
- Any standalone programs, such as diagnostics, that might be run instead of the OS

This partition typically runs on between 10 and 20MB. It is also usually placed on the first slice of the disk, often called *slice 0* or the *a slice*.

The swap Partition

The note in the "For What Purpose" section describes how UNIX uses the `swap` partition. The default rule is that there's twice as much `swap` space as there is RAM installed on the system. If you have 16MB of RAM, the swap space needs to be a minimum of 32MB. If you have 256MB of RAM, the recommended `swap` is 512MB.

This is just a starting point. If the users of this system run big applications that use large amounts of data, such as desktop publishing or CAD, this might not be enough swap. If you are unsure as to the `swap` needs of your users, start with the rule of twice RAM. Monitor the amount of `swap` space used via the `pstat` or `swap` commands. If you did not allocate enough, most UNIX systems support adding `swap` at runtime via the `swapon` or `swap` commands.

The usr Partition

The usr slice holds the remainder of the UNIX operating system and utilities. It needs to be large enough to hold all the packages you chose to install when you made the list earlier.

If you intend to install local applications or third-party applications in this partition, it needs to be large enough to hold them as well.

The var Partition

The var partition holds the spool directories used to queue printer files and electronic mail, as well as log files unique to this system. It also holds the /var/tmp directory, which is used for larger temporary files. Every system, even a diskless client, needs its own var file system. It cannot be shared with other systems.

> **NOTE**
>
> Although the var file system cannot be shared, subdirectories under it can (for example, /var/news).
>
> These would be mounted on top of the var file system after it is already mounted.

If you do not print very large files, accept the size the release notes suggest for this partition. If you do print many files or large files, or if your site will be performing a large volume of UUCP traffic, consider increasing the size of this partition to accommodate your needs.

> **TIP**
>
> For print files, a good starting point is adding 10 times the size of the largest print file to the size recommended. Add more if many users or multiple printers are attached to this system.
>
> For UUCP files, have enough space to hold at least a day's worth of traffic for every site.

UNIX Installation Basics

CHAPTER 21

933

21

UNIX
INSTALLATION
BASICS

The home Partition

This is where the user's login directories are placed. Making home its own slice prevents users from hurting anything else on the system if they run this file system out of space.

A good starting point for this slice is 5MB per application user plus 10MB per power user and 20MB per developer you intend to support on this system.

> **TIP**
>
> Don't worry too much about getting it exactly right. If you need more space for a particular user, just move that user's directory to a different file system that does have room and create a symbolic link in /home to point to its new location. The user may never know you moved the directory.

The tmp Partition

Large temporary files are placed in /var/tmp, but sufficient temporary files are placed in /tmp so that your root file system won't run out of space. If your users are mostly application users, 5 to 10MB is sufficient for this slice. If they are power users or developers, 10 to 20MB is better. If more than 10 users are on the system at once, consider doubling the size of this slice.

> **TIP**
>
> The files in the /tmp directory are very short-lived. Use the file system type TMPFS (Tmp file system, a RAM-based file system) for /tmp if your version of UNIX offers it. It can improve performance by placing this file system in RAM instead of on the disk. Losing the files on each reboot is not a concern because UNIX clears the /tmp directory on each reboot anyway.

Assigning Partitions to Disk Drives

If you have more than one disk drive, a second decision you have is on which drive to place the partitions. The goal is to balance the disk accesses between all the drives. If you have two drives, consider the following partitioning scheme:

Drive 1	Drive 2
root	usr
swap	home
var	

The remaining partitions split over the drives as space allows.

Assigning IP (Network) Addresses

If the system has a network connection, it must be assigned an IP address. IP addresses are explained in Chapter 26, "Networking." An IP address is a set of four numbers separated by dots, called a dotted quad. Each network connection has its own IP address. Within a LAN segment, usually the first three octets of the dotted quad are the same. The fourth must be unique for each interface. The addresses 0 and 255 (all zeros and all ones) are reserved for broadcast addresses. The remaining 254 addresses may be assigned to any system.

> **NOTE**
>
> The IP address is not the Ethernet address. An Ethernet address is a hardware-level address assigned by the manufacturer. It is six octets long (48 bits). The first three represent the manufacturer of the network interface board. The remaining three octets are unique to the system. This is commonly called the MAC address. An IP address is a software-level address. Part of the IP protocol, also called ARP or Address Resolution Protocol, is used to match the software IP address with the physical Ethernet address.

If this is your first system, you must decide on the first three octets as well. See Chapter 26 for applying for a network number. The number should be unique within the world and is obtainable at no cost.

If this is not the first system, then you can use any IP address in your subnet that is not in use.

Do You Have the Needed Network Connections?

Now is the time to check that you have a network connection for each network interface. Now is the time to check that you have the proper cables, transceivers (if needed), and connectors.

Ethernet comes in three varieties: thick (10BASE-5), thin (10BASE-2), and twisted pair (10BASE-T). UNIX systems come with some combination of three types of Ethernet connections: AUI, BNC, or RJ45. If your system has multiple connector types, they are all for the same network interface, unless you purchased an add-on interface that uses a connector type different from that of the main system. Using the following matrix, you can see which parts you need:

Connector type		*Network type*	
	10BASE-5	10BASE-2	10BASE-T
AUI	AUI cable transceiver	AUI to BNC transceiver	AUI to RJ45 transceiver
BNC	10BASE-2 Hub	BNC Tee	10BASE-2 Hub
RJ45	10BASE-T Hub with AUI port and RJ45 Cable	10BASE-T Hub with BNC port and RJ45 Cable	RJ45 Cable and free slot on BASE-T Hub

Using NIS/NIS+

Administering a UNIX system requires dealing with many files, such as the password, group, network, and Ethernet address control files. Having to maintain each one of these files on multiple systems can be time consuming. Discrepancies in the files can lead to problems logging in to systems or to security issues.

One solution to this problem is the Network Information Service, or NIS. NIS is a network-wide set of databases for the common administrative files. This allows for centralized administration, even by using multiple servers with a redundant system in case the master server is down.

When installing a system in an NIS environment, you have to answer the install questions with the name of the NIS domain for this system.

The NIS domain does not unnecessarily match the mail domain entered earlier. Generally, it is for security reasons or to further subdivide the administrative responsibilities when they do not match.

Performing the Installation

By now, if you've been following along, you should have an installation checklist. It should contain the following:

- The name of the system holding the drive for the installation, and its device name

TIP

Check your release notes—you might have to enter the name of the new system into the root user's .rhost file temporarily during the installation, or load the CD-ROM and mount the partition prior to running the remote installation.

- Dataless, standalone, or server system. (The name of the server for the new client, if it's a dataless or diskless system, should be on your sheet along with its IP address.)
- The name of the host and domain.
- The IP address.
- The packages to install.
- How to partition the disk. (This is the map of the disk drive or drives you made earlier.)
- Whether to use a network database. (This is the name of the NIS domain, if you intend to run NIS.)

You may want to include items on your checklist such as addresses for the name server, and the subnet the machine will be on. Making a small note of the file system layout will also be beneficial, giving you a visual of what your file system will look like after it has been configured. Including the time zone and locale won't hurt either.

Now you should be all set.

CAUTION

You are about to do things that will change the information on the disks. If this is not a brand new system, be sure you have readable backups in case something goes wrong.

Booting the Installation Media

The first step in installing a UNIX system is to load the mini-root into RAM (the mini-root is basically a scaled down kernel that gives you the capability to run the UNIX installation programs). UNIX uses the UNIX operating system to perform its installation. It needs a version of UNIX it can run, and to do this the install loader uses RAM to hold a small version of the UNIX file system. When you boot the installation media, it builds a root file system and copies the files it needs to control the installation to this RAM-based file system. This is the reason it takes a while to boot the media.

Booting from Floppies

Take the first boot floppy and place it in what DOS would call drive A. Boot the system in the normal manner, by pressing the Ctrl+Alt+Del keys at the same time or by power cycling the machine.

The system loads the boot loader off the first floppy and then uses that to create the RAM-based file systems and load the UNIX image into RAM. It asks for additional floppies as needed and then asks for the install media. The system then loads the remainder of the mini-root from the installation media.

Installing the Master System

After the mini-root is loaded, you are generally presented with the install options. Some systems leave you at a shell prompt. Your distribution may be different, or it may be automatic. Follow the installation procedure located in your manual.

UNIX contains a set of install procedures that walk you through the installation. They are almost identical to one another in concept, but they are slightly different in implementation. Given the information on the checklist produced as you followed this chapter, answer the questions as presented by the installation screens.

TIP

On Sun systems, to install a system with custom disk layouts, or to install any server, requires selecting the Custom Install menu option on the opening installation screen. This walks you through all the questions, setting everything up for you automatically.

Expect it to take under an hour to read all the information off the install media to the local disks if you are installing more than just a dataless client. Most systems gives you a progress meter to show you how much it has done and how much further it has to proceed.

> **CAUTION**
>
> If you are installing from a nonstandard disk controller, be sure to select the option to add the custom driver for this controller and provide the floppy with the driver when requested. If you exit install and attempt to reboot without providing this driver, you will be unable to boot the system, and you will have to start the installation from the beginning.

Provided that you plan ahead and fill out an installation checklist, installing a UNIX system is a simple and automatic process.

Installing Optional or Additional Packages

After the system is installed and rebooted, you are running UNIX. Congratulations! Of course, you will still need to perform installations from time to time to add packages and applications. There are numerous formats and installation methods for these packages, such as pkgadd, RPM, tar, and installsw to name a few. Consult the documentation that came with your operating system for information on installing additional or third-party packages.

Summary

The key to a trouble-free installation of your UNIX system is advance planning and using the guidelines in this chapter and the release notes that came with your software. These are the things you should plan:

- Which operating system on which platform would be best for you and your operation
- The type of system you are installing: server, standalone, or dataless
- Who will act as server for this system, if necessary
- What size and on what disk each slice will be located

    root, usr, var, home, and tmp file systems

    swap partition

- The name and address for this system: hostname, domain name, IP address, and NIS domain name, if applicable
- Which packages you are going to install
- From where you are going to install

With the answers to these questions, you can answer the UNIX install procedures questions. From there, the installation is automatic.

CHAPTER 22

Starting Up and Shutting Down

by Robin Burk, David Gumkowski, and John Semencar

IN THIS CHAPTER

Starting up and shutting down UNIX are unlike most system administration tasks in that after deciding when either occurs, the administrator is more a passive observer than a proactive participant. This chapter discusses what some common console messages mean during startup and shutdown, identifies what commands are involved in either process, and describes daemons normally spawned as a result of restarting the system.

Startup

UNIX startup is an orderly method to accomplish a predefined set of tasks. Those tasks would normally include

- Running a limited self-test of basic machine parts
- Locating a boot device
- Reading the kernel from the boot device
- Having the kernel find and initialize peripherals
- Starting basic system tasks
- Running scripts that generate programs to provide services
- Beginning other applications

Listing 22.1 provides an abbreviated sample startup from a Hewlett-Packard HP-UX Release 10.x machine. Note that most startup messages are written to the system console device as well as the system log file. Please refer to your system's manual page for `syslogd` to find where your `syslog` configuration file is located.

Listing 22.1. Sample startup from a Hewlett-Packard HP-UX Release 10.x machine.

```
**************************************************
HP-UX Start-up in progress
Thu May 01 06:00:00 EST 1997
**************************************************
Mount file systems
Output from "/sbin/rc1.d/S100hfsmount start":
---------------------------
Setting hostname
Output from "/sbin/rc1.d/S320hostname start":
---------------------------
Save system core image if needed
Output from "/sbin/rc1.d/S440savecore start":
---------------------------
EXIT CODE: 2 -  savecore found no core dump to save
"/sbin/rc1.d/S440savecore start" SKIPPED
---------------------------
```

```
Recover editor crash files
Output from "/sbin/rc2.d/S200clean_ex start":
---------------------------
preserving editor files (if any)
List and/or clear temporary files
Output from "/sbin/rc2.d/S204clean_tmps start":
---------------------------
Starting the ptydaemon
Start network tracing and logging daemon
Output from "/sbin/rc2.d/S300nettl start":
---------------------------
Initializing Network Tracing and Logging...
Done.
Configure HP Ethernet interfaces
Output from "/sbin/rc2.d/S320hpether start":
---------------------------
Start NFS server subsystem
Output from "/sbin/rc3.d/S100nfs.server start":
---------------------------
```

Initialization Process

During startup, the UNIX kernel is loaded, executes, and gives rise to a system father task, init. This father task propagates children processes commonly needed for operation. Common operations normally completed during boot include setting the machine's name, checking and mounting disks and file systems, starting system logs, configuring network interfaces and beginning network and mail services, commencing line printer services, enabling accounting and quotas, clearing temporary partitions, and saving core dumps.

Configuration File

Systems such as HP-UX, IRIX, Linux, and Solaris all use a flexible init process that creates jobs directed from a file named /etc/inittab. init's general arguments are shown here:

- 0   Shut down the machine into a halted state. The machine enters a PROM monitor mode or a powered off condition.

- 1   Put the machine into a system administration mode. All file systems continue to be accessible. Only a superuser console can access the system.

- 2   Place the system into the normal multiuser mode of operation.

- 3   Place the system into the normal multiuser mode of operation. Also enable remote file sharing. Begin extra daemons to allow remote file sharing, mount remote resources, and advertise the remote resources (such as NFS).

- 4   Place the system into a user-defined multiuser environment. For HP-UX, the HP VUE (Visual User Environment), a powerful graphical environment and set of applications utilizing X Window, is activated.

- 5   Much like run level 0, except the system does not try to power itself off.

- 6   Shut down the machine and then restart it to run level 2 or 3.

- a,b,c   Not a true state because they do not change the run level. Basically, run a given set of programs.

- S/s   Begin single-user mode. This mode of operation is always selected if the inittab file is missing or corrupt.

- Q/q   Don't change run levels. Use the current one and reexamine the inittab file. This is a method to institute changes without actually having to reboot the system.

Listing 22.2 shows an abbreviated sample inittab file.

LISTING 22.2. ABBREVIATED SAMPLE INITTAB FILE.

```
strt:2:initdefault:
        lev0:06s;wait:/etc/rc0 > /dev/console 2>&1 < /dev/console
        lev2:23:wait:/etc/rc2 > /dev/console 2>&1 < /dev/console
        lev3:3:wait:/etc/rc3 > /dev/console 2> &1 < /dev/console
        rebt:6:wait:/etc/init.d/announce restart
        ioin::sysinit:/sbin/ioinitrc > /dev/console 2>&1
        brcl::bootwait:/sbin/bcheckrc < /dev/console 2>&1
        cons:123456:respawn:/usr/sbin/getty console console
        powf::powerwait:/sbin/powerfail > /dev/console 2>&1
```

The general form of an entry in this file is as follows:

identifier;*run-level*;*action-keyword*: *process*

identifier is a text string of up to four characters in length and is used to uniquely identify an entry. Two character identifiers should be used with care because it is possible for PTY identities to conflict with an identifier. The *run level* is one or more of the init arguments described previously or blank to indicate all run levels. A default run level of 2 or 3 is common, depending on your system. Run level 1 is usually reserved for special tasks such as system installation. When init changes run levels, all processes not belonging to the requested run level are killed eventually. The exception to that rule are a,b,c started commands.

The *action keyword* defines the course of action executed by init. Values and their meaning are found in Table 22.1.

TABLE 22.1. *ACTION KEYWORD TABLE.*

Action-keyword	Action	Wait	Restart
boot	Executed only during a system boot.	NO	NO
bootwait	Executed when going from single user to multiuser after the system is started.	Yes	No
initdefault	Start with this upon boot. The process field is ignored. If level is blank, default to run level 6.	N/A	N/A
off	Kill processes when in a given level. Ignore if the process doesn't exist.	N/A	N/A
once	Run the process once.	No	no
ondemand	Synonym for respawn for a,b,c types.	No	No
powerfail	Run processes when a powerdown is requested.	No	No
powerwait	Run processes when a powerdown is requested.	Yes	No
respawn	If the process doesn't exist, start it. If the process does exist, do nothing.	No	Yes
sysinit	Run processes before the login prompt is sent to the system console.	Yes	No
wait	Start processes once.	Yes	No
ctrlaltdel	(Linux only.) The sequence was pressed on the keyboard. Shutdown.	No	No
kbrequest	(Linux only.) Keyboard spawned request. This is ill-defined.		
powerokwait	(Linux only.) Power has come back on.	Yes	No

22

STARTING UP AND SHUTTING DOWN

The *process* is any daemon, executable script, or program. This process can invoke other scripts or binaries.

BSD type systems use an `init` process that is somewhat less flexible in usage. It runs a basic reboot sequence and depending on how it is invoked, begins a multiuser or single-user system. `init` changes states via *signals*. The signal is invoked using the UNIX `kill` command. For example, to drop back to single-user mode from multiuser mode, the superuser would `kill -TERM 1`. Table 22.2 lists the signals.

TABLE 22.2. *SIGNALS USED WITH* kill *COMMAND.*

Signal	Mnemonic	Action	Value
Hang-up	HUP.	Reread the ttys file	(01)
Software terminate	TERM	Begin single-user mode.	(15)
Interrupt	INT	Terminate all processes and reboot the machine.	(02)
Tty stop signal	TSTP	Slowly kill the system by not not issuing any more getty processes.	(24)

RC Scripts

Each system type begins similarly by initializing an operating condition through calls to scripts or directories containing scripts generally of the type /etc/rc*. BSD systems normally would call /etc/rc, /etc/rc.local, or /etc/rc.boot. Because of the flexibility of the inittab version, it is best to look in that file for the location of the startup scripts. A methodology that is now favored by vendors supporting inittab, such as HP-UX and IRIX, creates directories such as /sbin/rc[run-level].d or /etc/rc[run-level].d. These directories contain files such as S##name (startup) or K##name (kill/shutdown) that are links to scripts in /sbin/init.d or /etc/init.d. The ##s are ordered in the manner in which they are called by a superscript. Listing 22.3 shows a sample startup sequence.

LISTING 22.3. A SAMPLE STARTUP SEQUENCE FROM AN HP-UX SYSTEM.

```
lrwxr-xr-x   1 root     sys            16 Apr  9
➥1997 S008net.sd -> /sbin/init.d/net
lrwxr-xr-x   1 root     sys
➥21 Apr  9 1997 S100swagentd -> /sbin/init.d/swagentd
lrwxr-xr-x   1 root     sys            21 Apr  9  1997 S120swconfig ->
/sbin/init.d/swconfig
lrwxr-xr-x   1 root     sys            21 Apr  9  1997 S200clean_ex ->
/sbin/init.d/clean_ex
lrwxr-xr-x   1 root     sys            23 Apr  9  1997 S202clean_uucp-
>/sbin/init.d/clean_uucp
lrwxr-xr-x   1 root     sys            23 Apr  9  1997 S204clean_tmps-
>/sbin/init.d/clean_tmps
lrwxr-xr-x   1 root     sys            22 Apr  9  1997 S206clean_adm ->
/sbin/init.d/clean_adm
lrwxr-xr-x   1 root     sys            20 Apr  9  1997 S220syslogd ->
/sbin/init.d/syslogd
lrwxr-xr-x   1 root     sys            22 Apr  9  1997 S230ptydaemon->
/sbin/init.d/ptydaemon
```

.

.

.

.

.

.

.

.

.

```
lrwxr-xr-x   1 root     sys            22 Apr  9  1997 S880swcluster ->
/sbin/init.d/swcluster
lrwxr-xr-x   1 root     sys            18 Apr  9  1997 S900hpnpd ->
/sbin/init.d/hpnpd
lrwxr-xr-x   1 root     sys            20 Apr  9  1997 S900laserrx ->
/sbin/init.d/laserrx
```

Listing 22.4 is a partial example of a script utilizing the template to initiate the startup or shutdown of a relational database management, in this case Oracle 7 Server. Links are required for the execution of the superscript.

LISTING 22.4. *EXAMPLE OF AN* init *STARTUP/SHUTDOWN SCRIPT.*

```
case $1 in
'start_msg')
    echo "Starting ORACLE"
    ;;
'stop_msg')
    echo "Stopping ORACLE"
    ;;
'start')
    # source the system configuration variables
    if [ -f /etc/rc.config.d/oracle ] ; then
        . /etc/rc.config.d/oracle
    else
        echo "ERROR: /etc/rc.config.d/oracle file MISSING"
    fi
    # Check to see if this script is allowed to run...
    if [ $ORACLE_START != 1 ]; then
        rval=2
    else
            #Starting Oracle
            su - oracle -c
/u99/home/dba/oracle/product/7.2.3/bin/dbstart
    fi
    ;;
'stop')
    # source the system configuration variables
    if [ -f /etc/rc.config.d/oracle ] ; then
        . /etc/rc.config.d/oracle
    else
        echo "ERROR: /etc/rc.config.d/oracle file MISSING"
```

continues

22

STARTING UP AND
SHUTTING DOWN

LISTING 22.4 CONTINUED

```
    fi
    # Check to see if this script is allowed to run...
    if [ $ORACLE_START != 1 ]; then
        rval=2
    else
                #Stopping Oracle
                su - oracle -c
/u99/home/dba/oracle/product/7.2.3/bin/dbshut
    fi
    ;;
*)
    echo "usage: $0 {start|stop|start_msg|stop_msg}"
    rval=1
    ;;
esac
```

Startup Daemons and Programs

When the system is operational and you have logged in, run ps -ef (SYS V type) or ps ax (BSD type) from a shell prompt. This lists the processes currently running. An idle system with no users most likely includes at least a subset of the following tasks:

init	The parent process for any user job and most system tasks. The process ID is always 1.
inetd	The Internet daemon (super server). It listens for connections on Internet sockets and calls the appropriate daemons for FTP, Telnet, finger, http, talk, and rsh.
getty	The program that sets terminal type, speed, line discipline, and mode.
syslogd	The daemon to log system messages.
cron	The clock daemon to execute programs at specified dates and times.
named	The domain-naming server software yielding name resolution for your system.
routed/gated	Either of these programs keeps tables for network packet routing.
nfsd/biod	Network file system daemons allowing file system sharing via the network.
lpsched/lpd	SYS V/BSD line-printing schedulers.
telnetd	The Telnet protocol server that allows interactive connections via the network.
ftpd	The file transfer protocol (FTP) server that allows file transfers via the network.

httpd	The hypertext transfer protocol daemon that coordinates World Wide Web serving.
rpc.*	The remote procedure call daemons that allow procedure calls to other machines connected via the network. Common entries of this type are rpc.mountd, rpc.statd, rpc.locks, rpc.pcnfsd, and rcpbind.

Note that if the file /etc/nologin exists, only the superuser may log in. Other users attempting to log in would see the textual contents of /etc/nologin.

Shutdown

A normal shutdown is an attempt to terminate processes in an orderly fashion so that when the system comes back up, there will be little error. A graceful shutdown kills running tasks as smoothly as it can. It then synchronizes the disks with any outstanding buffers in memory and dismounts them. Sometimes it is possible to postpone a full system shutdown; when it is necessary, there are several ways to accomplish it.

Among these are the commands shutdown, reboot, sync, init, and halt—and by removing power from the machine. Removing power, especially while disks are being updated or disk buffers are non-empty, almost ensures that some file system corruption will occur that will need correction during the next boot. More than likely, the file system consistency check program, fsck, can autocorrect the problems—but, given a choice, use a safer method of bringing your system down. fsck is automatically invoked during system startup unless specifically turned off (fastboot). Its function is to check the consistency of inodes, free space, links, directory entries, pathnames, and superblocks. It does not perform a surface scan or remap bad blocks.

The following sections give a summary of shutdown commands for several UNIX variants. See your local manual page for a complete list of options.

HP-UX

- To reboot an HP-UX system, use the following command:

  reboot [-t *time*] [-m *message*].

  time: +Number of minutes (such as +5 for 5 minutes from now), an absolute time of hh;mm, or "now" until the reboot message: Message to display to users about the upcoming reboot.

- To halt an HP-UX system, use the following command:

  reboot -h [-t *time*] [-m *message*].

The parameters are the same as for `reboot`.

- To synchronize the disks and invoke a new run level, use the following command:

  `sync; init [run-level]`.

  Run-level: one of the choices described earlier in the chapter.

- To perform a graceful shutdown, use the following command:

  `shutdown [-h¦-r] [-y] [grace]`.

  Note that HP has a security feature tied to shutdowns. `/etc/shutdown.allow` can restrict who is allowed to shut down the system. Most other variants allow only the superuser to bring the system down.

  `-h`: Halt the system.

  `-r`: Reboot the system.

  neither `-h` nor `-r`: Place system in single-user mode.

  `-y`: Default answers to any interactive question.

  grace: Integer seconds defining how long users have to log off.

  The default value for *grace* is 60 seconds.

Solaris

- To reboot a Solaris system, use the following command:

  `reboot [-d]`.

  `-d`: Dump system core before rebooting to allow for future debugging.

- To halt a Solaris system, use the following command:

  `halt`.

  `halt` should not be usually called with any parameters.

- To synchronize the disks and invoke a new run level, use the following command:

  `sync; init [run-level]`.

  run-level: One of the choices described earlier in the chapter.

- To perform a graceful shutdown, use the following command:

  `shutdown [-y] [-ggrace] [-irun-level]`.

  `-y`: Default answers to any interactive question.

  grace: Integer seconds defining how long users have to log off.

  The default value for grace is 60 seconds.

  run-level: A subset of the choices described earlier in the chapter. The default is 0.

Linux

- To reboot a Linux system, use the following command:

  reboot [-f].

  -f: If not in run levels 0 or 6, do not call shutdown.

- To halt a Linux system, use the following command:

  halt [-f].

  Same parameter description as reboot.

- To synchronize the disks and invoke a new run level, use the following command:

  sync; init [*run-level*].

  run-level: One of the choices described earlier in the chapter.

  To perform a graceful shutdown, use the following command:

  shutdown [-t *sec*] [-fhrk] *time* [*message*].

  Normally, in Linux systems, an entry will be present in inittab for ctrlaltdel that calls shutdown.

  -t *sec*: *sec* is the number of seconds to wait between sending the warning and kill signals to processes.

  -h: Halt the system.

  -r: Reboot the system.

  -f: Do not run file system consistency check upon reboot.

  -k: Do not actually shut down the system; just make it look like it is going to happen.

  time: +Number of minutes (such as +5 for 5 minutes from now) or an absolute time of hh;mm (or "now") until shutdown.

  message: Message to display to users about the upcoming shutdown.

In every given example, the most graceful way to shut down was purposely identified as such because shutdown is always the preferred way for an uncomplicated shutdown of the system.

As with starting up the system, shutting down the system reflects part of what is happening to the system console and system log file.

Summary

UNIX provides orderly means to start the computing environment and to shut it down gracefully. These actions are governed in part by scripts and configuration files you can modify as required for your site. Startup and shutdown messages, logged to the console and to a standard file, help the administrator identify system problems.

User Administration

by Robin Burk, David Gumkowski, and John Semencar

CHAPTER 23

While performing user administration, you will call upon all your skills in virtually every area of system management. Whether it is keeping disks as empty as possible, finding system bottlenecks, answering questions, or adding new users, your job revolves almost totally around and for the machine's users. This chapter deals with administration of user IDs. It refers to adding, removing, modifying, moving, keeping track of, checking, and limiting users. This section also describes special IDs and user ID environments.

Adding New Users

Logically enough, user administration begins when adding users to a new machine. Functionally, there are a variety of ways to accomplish this task. Each of the methods involves adding information to the password file, /etc/passwd. The /etc/group file also requires attention as do miscellaneous files such as system shell startup files and the system mail alias file.

Password File

The format of /etc/passwd is consistent among most flavors of UNIX. This file contains the following colon-separated entries:

username:pswd:uid:gid:uid comments:directory:shell

On some BSD type systems, the file contains slightly different colon-separated entries:

username:pswd:uid:gid:user class:pswd change:acct expiration:
uid comments:directory:shell

The *username* is what the user types in at the UNIX login: prompt. Usually, the username consists of up to eight lowercase alphanumeric characters. The *pswd* field is a password entry and can have many different forms. The entry can be blank, indicating that there is no password required for login. The position can contain up to 13 characters that are the encrypted version of the password for the user. The location can contain a character not in the following set { . / 0–9 A–Z a–z } connoting that the username is valid but cannot be logged in to. For example an "*" is not in this set. If it is used then the username is a valid account but cannot be logged into.

Additionally, under IRIX and HP-UX, the password entry can contain a comma followed by one or two characters. Under Solaris, a pswd value of *x* indicates that the encrypted password is already stored in the /etc/shadow file.

The characters (in order) are: . / 0–9 A–Z a–z. The "." character is equated to the number zero, and "z" is equated to 63. References made to characters using their numeric value are common. The characters indicate the number of weeks the password is valid and the number of weeks that must expire before a change is allowed to the password, respectively. If the former is zero (dot), the user must change the password at the next login attempt. Though generally frowned upon by security-conscious individuals, if the latter is greater than the former, only the superuser can change the password.

> **TIP**
>
> If the system has no built-in check for user base password selections, Alec Muffett's Crack utility can assist you in that endeavor. You can find it at `http://www.users.dircon.co.uk/~crypto/`.

The *uid* or user ID is simply a unique numerical user value for the username. Normally, this value is a positive number up to 65535, although some systems can handle nonrecommended double precision user ID numbers. If this is nonunique, all usernames with the same user ID look like a single (usually the first) username with this user ID. Some user IDs are reserved or special. They include:

0:	The superuser
1-10:	Daemons and pseudo users
11-99:	System, reserved, and "famous" users
100+:	Normal users
60001:	"nobody" (occasionally 32000 or 65534)
60002:	"noaccess" (occasionally 32001)

The *gid* or group ID is a numerical default group ID for the username. This number corresponds to an entry in the `/etc/group` file. This file is described later.

The *uid* comments field is historically known as GECOS, or GCOS, information for the operating system it originated from. For a generic `finger` command to accurately display this information, it should contain the user's real name, company or office number, office phone number, and home telephone number separated by commas. Not all entries need to be specified, although placeholders must be kept if trying to keep the general GECOS syntax. For example, `Homer User,,,800-IAM-HOME` would show entries for the user's real name and the user's home telephone number. The real username is also displayed by the mail system as part of the outgoing mail headers.

The *directory* field defines the username's home directory or initial working directory—that is, the directory the user is placed in after being logged in by the system but before the user's personal startup files are executed.

The *shell* field is the command interpreter or program that the username is placed in after logging in. Among the many shells are: sh (Bourne), ksh (Korn), csh (C), tcsh (TENEX/TOPS-20 type C), BASH (Bourne Again Shell). If not specified, the default shell is the Bourne shell. Note that this entry can be a program that locks the username into a captive application. For this field to be valid, some systems require this entry to be present in a shell validation file.

The *class* field is unused but is for specifying a class of user attributes for the username.

The *pswd change* field indicates how soon a password must be changed. It is the number of seconds since the epoch (Jan 1 1970 @ 00:00). If omitted, no forced change of the password occurs.

The *acct expiration* field is the number of seconds since the epoch until the account will expire. If left blank, account expiration is not enforced for the username.

Additionally, if Network Information Service (NIS)/Yellow Pages (YP) is installed and running, the password file can include other types of entries. The additional username field entries include:

+	All YP entries should be included.
+*username*	Include the explicit username from YP.
-*username*	Exclude the explicit username from YP.
+@*netgroup*	Include all usernames from YP from the desired group.
-@*netgroup*	Exclude all usernames from YP from the desired group.

Generally, within such entries, if the *uid*, *gid*, *uid comments*, *directory*, or *shell* fields are specified, they supplant the value that YP sends for that field. Also, be aware that these entries are taken in order, so the first occurrence, not the last occurrence, dictates what is going to happen. For example:

```
root;x:0:0:Superuser:/:
daemon:*:1:5::/:/sbin/sh
bin:*:2:2::/usr/bin:/sbin/sh
sys:*:3:3::/:
adm:*:4:4::/var/adm:/sbin/sh
uucp:*:5:3::/var/spool/uucppublic:/usr/lbin/uucp/uucico
lp:*:9:7::/var/spool/lp:/sbin/sh
nuucp:*:11:11::/var/spool/uucppublic:/usr/lbin/uucp/uucico
hpdb:*:27:1:ALLBASE:/:/sbin/sh
nobody:*:-2:60001::/:
dave;x:100:10:Dave G,13,x3911,unlisted:/usr1/dave:/bin/tcsh
charlene;x:101:10:Charlene G,14,x1800,unlisted:/usr1/charlene:/bin/tcsh
john;x:102:60:John S,2,555-1234,x1400:/usr2/john:/bin/ksh
georgia;x:103:60:Georgia S,11,x143,x143:/usr2/georgia:/bin/csh
-steve::::::
```

```
+@friends:::20:::
+wayne::102:::/usr3/wayne:/bin/sh
```

Username `steve` is always excluded, even if it occurs within the netgroup `friends`. All `friends` are included with the noted exception. Every `friends` included is placed into the `20` group by default. YP `wayne` is included. All his fields, except the group ID and user ID comment fields, are overridden with the specified information. Notice in our sample that the letter `x` in the *pswd* field was substituted for the actual encrypted password for this publication. The character `*` in the *pswd* field is shown as found for these nonlogin psuedo users. For a further description of psuedo users, go to the end of the "Adding New Users" section.

Shadow Password File

Because `/etc/passwd` is usually globally readable, security conscientious sites normally use a shadow password scheme that redirects the encrypted passwords to another restricted read file that may or may not contain other information. Password selections consisting of any dictionary word, the login name, no password, or any information included in the user ID comment field are security risks and should be avoided. The schemes used for shadow password files vary considerably among the various UNIX variants.

IRIX and Solaris systems have a file named `/etc/shadow` that is generated by running the command `pwconv` that includes the following:

username:pswd:lastchg:min:max:warn:inactive:expire:flag

The *username* is a copy of the username from the `/etc/passwd` file.

The *pswd* field contains either the 13-character encrypted password; null, indicating that no password is needed for login; or a string containing a character not from the following set—{ . / 0–9 A–Z a–z}. If the password contains a character not from the encryption set, the username cannot be logged into. Normally, system administrators would use `*` or `*LK*` for the entry.

The *lastchg* field is the number of days from the epoch that the password was last changed.

The *min* field is the minimum number of days to elapse between a successful password change and another change.

The *max* field is the maximum number of days that the password is valid.

The *warn* field contains the number of days before password expiration that the user will begin to get warnings that the password is about to expire.

The *inactive* field is the number of days that the username can remain inactive before not being allowed to log in.

The *expire* field is an absolute number of days specification. When used, this specifies when a username will no longer be considered valid to log in to.

The *flag* field is currently unused.

HP-UX has adopted another scheme for shadowing the password file on a trusted system. Each username has a file named /tcb/files/auth/*first letter*/*username* where *first letter* is the beginning letter of the username, and *username* is the login name for the user. For example, /tcb/files/auth/b/buster would exist for the username buster. This file contains information that is termcap in appearance. A list of field names and their possible values can be found in the man page for prpwd(4). In general, the file holds:

- The username and user ID mirrored from the password file.
- The encrypted password for the username, if any.
- The names of

  The owner of the account.

  The last account to change the password on this account if it was not the account itself.

  The last successful and unsuccessful login attempt, terminal name, or hostname.

- The times indicating

  The number of seconds allowed between successful password changes.

  When the password expires (next login will require the user change the password).

  When the lifetime of the password expires (only the sysadmin can reallow login).

  The last time a successful and unsuccessful password change or attempt was made.

  When the account expires (an absolute-lifetime offsets from a password change).

  The maximum time allowed between logins.

  How long before password expiration that a user should be notified.

  The time of day logins for the account are valid.

  The last time a successful and unsuccessful login entry or attempt was made.

- Flags showing

  Whether the username is allowed to boot the system.

  Whether audits occur for the username.

  Whether the user can select the account's password or must use a system generated one.

  Whether the user can have the system generate a password for the account.

  Whether a chosen password undergoes a check for being too easily guessed.

  Whether the account can have no (null) password.

  Whether the user can generate "random" characters and letters for a password.

  Whether account is administratively locked.

- Numbers specifying

  An audit ID for the account.

  The maximum length a password can be.

  An additional random number an account must specify to a password if the system administrator reset the password.

  The count of unsuccessful logins until the next successful one.

  The maximum consecutive unsuccessful login attempts allowed before the account is locked.

Berkeley-type systems have yet another type of shadowing system that uses the files `/etc/master.passwd` or `/etc/spwd.db`.

Group File

The `/etc/group` file is part of the general UNIX file permission mechanism. The colon-separated template for the file appears as follows:

```
group_name;password;group_id;list
```

The `group_name` field contains the textual name of the group.

The `password` field is a placeholder for an encrypted password for the group. If null, no password is required.

The `group_id` field contains a unique numerical value for the group.

The `list` field contains a comma-separated list of users who belong to this group. Users need not be listed in groups that are specified for their username in `/etc/passwd`. A sample `/etc/group` file follows.

```
root::0:root
other::1:root,hpdb
bin::2:root,bin
sys::3:root,uucp
adm::4:root,adm
daemon::5:root,daemon
mail::6:root
lp::7:root,lp
tty::10:
nuucp::11:nuucp
users::20:root,dave,charlene,john,georgia,operator,
➥steve,judy,wayne,jamie
nogroup:*:-2:
systech::110:dave,disdb,diskf,disjs,dispm,diskj
dba::201:oracle,john,kathy,pete
psdev::202:ps001,ps002,ps101
hrdev::203:hrprw,hrpps,hrpsl,hrpla,consult1,consult3
fsdev::209:glpmk,glpsf,consult2
fsftp::222:glpmk,glpsf,glpjh
```

If Network Information Service/Yellow Pages is enabled, this file, like `/etc/passwd`, can contain entries beginning with a minus or plus sign to exclude or include (respectively) group information from NIS/YP.

Miscellaneous Files

A third file that user administration deals with is the system mail alias file. Depending on the UNIX version you are running, this can be located at: `/etc/aliases`, `/usr/sbin/aliases`, or `/etc/mail/aliases`. This file defines mail address aliases and mailing lists. After you modify this file, `sendmail` runs `newaliases` to rebuild the random access database for the mail aliases file, causing the changes to take effect.

System shell startup files are invoked before control is turned over to the username's personal startup (dot) files. You can customize an operating environment for users by editing `/etc/profile` (SYSV sh/ksh users) or by editing `/etc/csh.login`, `/etc/login`, or `/etc/stdlogin` (SYS V csh/tcsh users). In these files, you can customize the default file permissions employed by users when creating files by setting a umask for them. You can also add elements to the default path to include local utilities in `/usr/local`, or you can add helpful alias or environment variables. Generally, it is a good idea to keep things uncluttered in these files because knowledgeable users customize their own environments. Most systems give a template, or model, to be placed in the user's home directory. HP-UX administrators can find them in the `/etc/skel` directory.

Berkeley mail users' mail options can be customized globally in the mail startup file: `/usr/lib/Mail.rc`, `/usr/share/lib/mailx.rc`, `/etc/mail.rc`, `/etc/mail/mail.rc`, or `/etc/mail/Mail.rc`, depending on your UNIX variant. For example, you could force paging of mail longer than a page by inserting `set crt` in the mail startup file. Or if you wanted all mail to have a certain type of header line clipped, you could `ignore Message-Id`. Again, though, it is best to keep this simple and let users customize their own mail environment in their `.mailrc` file.

Because security among UNIX operating systems is not standard, you need to read the Chapter 1 login manual page on your own system to decide what other parameters to tweak for user accounts.

Psuedo Users

Every flavor of UNIX contains password file entries for several psuedo users. Their entries are not to be edited. These nonlogin users are required to satisfy any ownership issues by their corresponding processes. The following list displays the most common:

`daemon`	Used by system server processes
`bin`	Owns executable user command files
`sys`	Owns system files
`adm`	Owns accounting files
`uucp`	Used by UUCP
`lp`	Used by `lp` or `lpd` subsystems
`nobody`	Used by NFS

There are more standard psuedo users such as `audit`, `cron`, `mail`, `new`, and `usenet`. They all are required by their associated processes and own their related files.

User Maintenance Commands

Although it is possible to administer user accounts by manually editing the appropriate files, some variants of UNIX include utilities that simplify the task of managing user accounts and profiles. Among the most commonly used command-line and graphical tools are the following:

HP-UX	`useradd`, `userdel`, and `usermod`, `vipw`, or SAM
Solaris	`useradd`, `userdel`, `vipw` and `usermod` or `admintool`
FreeBSD	`adduser` and `rmuser` or `vipw`
OpenBSD	`adduser` or `vipw`
IRIX	User Manager (`cpeople`)
Linux	`vipw`

23

USER ADMINISTRATION

The command line instruction constructs are as follows:

```
useradd [-c uid comment] [-d dir] [-e expire] [-f inactive] [-g gid] [-G
gid[,gid…]]
[-m [ -k skel_dir]] [-s shell] [-u uid [-o]] username
```

Also, useradd can set default values for: base dir, expire, inactive, gid, skel_dir, and shell.

```
adduser [-batch username [gid,[gid...]]] [uid comment] [password]] OR
adduser
```

The adduser command with no parameters runs interactively. This command also can set other defaults that do the following:

- Cause users to have login or profile information copied into their home directory
- Set new users into a default group
- Define home partitions for new users
- Issue a welcoming message to new users
- Set a default shell for new users
- Choose new user IDs from a select group of numbers.

```
userdel [-r] username
rmuser username
usermod [-c uid comment] [-d dir [-m]] [-e expire] [-f inactive]
[-g gid] [-G gid[,gid]]
[-l new username] [-s shell] [-u uid [-o]] username
```

In each of the preceding commands

username is the user's login name. This is the only nonoptional parameter in any command.

uid comment is what will be stored in the user ID comment (GECOS) field.

dir is the user initial or home directory.

expire is an absolute date when the username ceases valid logins.

inactive is the number of inactive continuous days before the username is locked.

gid is a group ID or group name that the username belongs to.

new_username is a replacement name for an existing username.

shell is the username's initial shell.

skel_dir is a directory containing files to copy to the newly created home directory.

uid is the unique user identifier for the username.

-m indicates create the home directory (add) or move current home directory files to the new home directory (mod).

-o allows the user ID to be nonunique and still have the command succeed.

-g selects the primary group for the username.

-G selects secondary groups for the username.

-r commands that the username's home directory be removed.

If the home directory of a username is altered, the previous initial directory files must be moved to the new directory. To move a user directory, issue the following command:

```
cd /old_dir; tar -cf - . ¦ (cd /new_dir; tar -xpf -)
```

Verify the result and then remove old_dir. If the user base is not entirely knowledgeable, look for old_dir in existing files and change them to new_dir for the user. The system can locate any entries by the following command:

```
find /new_dir -exec grep -l old_dir {} \;
```

For any entries that find locates, change the entry to new_dir or, when appropriate, change the absolute pathname to the more generic $HOME variable. Pay particular attention to the startup (dot) files contained within a user's home directory because errors in that class of file surely get the attention of a user quickly.

Common dot files include

.login	Csh and tcsh-executed during login after the system login processing occurs.
.cshrc	Csh-executed when spawning new subshells.
.tcshrc	Tcsh-executed when spawning new subshells.
.profile	Sh or ksh-executed during login after the system login processing occurs.
.kshrc	Ksh-executed when forking new subshells.
.bashrc	Bash-executed when forking new subshells.
.history	Contains the last set of shell instructions executed.
.rhosts	Remote host/username lists that are trusted. Rlogin, rexec, rsh/remsh,...use this file to allow login, file access, and command processing without need of password.
.netrc	Used by the FTP auto-login process.
.forward	Allows the mailer to redirect mail to other addresses, files, or program processors.
.mailrc	A startup file for mail that allows setting mailer options or aliases.
.exrc	A startup file for ex or vi that allows setting specific editor options.
.xinitrc	A startup file for X windowing.

23

USER
ADMINISTRATION

`.xsession`   Another startup file for X windowing.

`.xdefault`   Yet another startup file for X windowing.

When removing usernames from the password file, you must locate all the user's files to delete them. `Find` once again can do this chore for you.

`find / -user username`

searches out all the files belonging to *username*. To be safe, you might want to back up the files before you delete them. To ferret out and delete within a single command is to carry out the subsequent command:

`find / -user username -exec rm {} \;`

After purging the `username`'s files, the group file and system mail alias file(s) should be modified by removing the username from them. `Newaliases` should be run to update the alias database.

User Monitor Commands

As a system administrator, you might need to monitor user activity to resolve resource bottlenecks, ensure security, or track system performance. UNIX provides tools to gather information about users in general or one user in particular.

The first class of instructions tell you what is happening now. These commands give an indication of whether anyone is gathering more than their fair share of resources. In addition, they should be used to avoid potential performance problems by justifying the need for more CPU, memory, or disk resources to accommodate the growing needs of your user community.

`uptime` shows the current time, the number of days the machine has been up, the number of users logged in to the system, and the system load average during the past 1, 5, and 15 minutes. It is a somewhat nebulous description of what actually goes into the load average, but it is useful for making comparisons to previous attempts and indicates whether any user is monopolizing the machine's resources.

`w` gives the `uptime` information and indicates who is on now, what terminal port he is using, the name of the host the username logged in from, when the username logged in, how long the user has been idle, the aggregate CPU time of all processes on that terminal port (JCPU), the CPU time of the active process listed in the next field (PCPU), and what command is currently running. The idle time gives a good indication of who may be good candidates for being logged out.

`ps -ef` (SYS V) or `ps -ax` (Berkeley) gives a lot of information about all running system processes. Pay attention to the *time* column because this is the cumulative process execution time for the listed process. You might want to kill a process that appears to be looping or otherwise wasting resources. If for some reason the process should not be killed, you can use the `renice` command to adjust relative resource usage.

`top` gives a ps like output that is updated constantly. In particular, the `%` *cpu* and *time* columns can identify users who are exploiting the system a bit too much. The size parameter, indicating the process size in pages, can identify users who may be causing memory-to-disk swapping to occur too often. Possibly this information shows that the system needs more memory.

`fuser` can indicate who is tying up a file resource. Running `fuser -u` *filename* lists all the usernames and processes that currently use the specified filename. Either the user can be asked to stop tying up the resource, or the offending process can be killed. If a file system is the resource being tied up rather than a file, `fuser -cku` *filesystem_name* kills each task controlling a file residing on the file system. After the command completes, the file system could be `umounted`.

`[B]df` in concert with `du` gives a summary of how full each disk is. For overly full file systems, `du -s` */filesystem/** displays a grand total of used blocks for each component directory on the file system.

The next set of utilities and procedures describes a user usage history. First, many network utilities can be placed into verbose modes that cause them to relate connection information to a system log file. To invoke this mode, add the option(s) to the process invocation lines in the `inetd` configuration file and then restart `inetd` with the following command: `killall -HUP inetd`. The file can further be modified in conjunction with an add-on package known as `tcp_wrappers` by Wietse Venema. The package is a port monitor and possibly a proactive limiting daemon depending on how it is configured.

Small changes to the `syslogd` configuration file (usually located at `/etc/syslog.conf`) can cause expression of more information. For example, if the line doesn't already exist, you can add

```
mail.debug /some_legal_directory/syslog
```

as the last line of the configuration file. Then have `syslogd` reread this modified file by executing:

```
kill -HUP syslogd_process_id
```

This directs mail `to`, `from`, and `deferred` messages to be placed in a mail queue log file. This allows better understanding and manipulation of mail so that your user's needs can be met.

Another historical tool is the last utility that shows which users are logging on from where and for how long. This tool usually is used in conjunction with acctcom or lastcomm. Acctcom and lastcomm identify system usage by username and tty port and give insight into what the system is being used for and how much CPU time and memory is being spent on which user tasks. For these utilities to function, system accounting needs to be turned on and adequate space opened for raw accounting files to appear and grow. To better understand how accounting functions work and what needs to be turned on or run, refer to the manual pages for accton and sa for Berkeley systems, and acct and runacct for SYS V systems.

Correcting system vulnerabilities in general and fixing user's self-made problems in particular are user administration duties. The find utility is particularly helpful in this effort. In most instances, users should not have globally writable directories and possibly not have globally readable ones either to maintain some semblance of security.

```
find /user_directory_home /( -perm -o=w -o -perm -o=r /) -type d
```

locates any globally readable or writable directory. If the command locates many of these directories, you should check the default umask that users receive when logging in. Possibly a umask of 077 is in order. User's .rhosts and .netrc files should not be readable or writable either because they aid attackers.

```
find /user_directory_home /( -name .rhosts -o -name .netrc \) \
( -perm -o=r -o -perm -g=r \)
```

finds all globally readable .rhosts and .netrc files. Especially in user directories, there should be very few unknown set uid (SUID) programs on the system, which would ultimately compromise every user and file and the system.

```
find / -perm -u=s
```

generates a list of all SUID programs on the system. Adding the -user root parameter on the command lists all root privileged SUID files, so you can verify that all such files are where they are expected to be. Dan Farmer's COPS add-on package can be ftped from the network and configured to make checks such as the previous as well as more intense security queries.

The best way to protect users from themselves is to back up their files nightly. Depending on how much information needs to be backed up, a good strategy is to do an incremental dump nightly and full dump weekly. You can also give the users another rm command that doesn't actually remove files (at least not right away). The command would move the file to a temporary holding area that is flushed of files older than a predetermined age.

User Limiting Commands

Using disk quotas can protect the system from being overwhelmed by a few users. You can begin restricting disk usage by running quotaon */user_filesystem*. That command allows users residing on *user_filesystem* to be reined in. Defining how much space each user can accumulate results by executing the edquota command. The general form of this command follows:

```
edquota [-p previously_defined_quota_username] username
```

For example: edquota charlene brings up an edit session that allows (re)setting hard and soft values for total disk space in kilobytes and total number of inodes used. The difference between hard and soft is that hard can never be exceeded. Exceeding the soft limit begins a timer. If the user goes below the soft limit, the timer resets. If the timer alarms, the condition is treated the same as surmounting the hard limit. Edquota -p charlene georgia does not bring up an editor but instead duplicates username charlene quota information for username georgia.

To check on a username, run quota -v *username* ... or repquota */user_filesystem*. Quota reports a specified username's disk usage and limits. If the -v is left off, only the specified usernames exceeding their limits are output. repquota gives a summary of all users in the password file for the specified file system.

```
quota -v jamie
    Disk quotas for jamie (uid 315):
    Filesystem    usage    quota    limit    timeleft files    quota    limit
➥timeleft
    /usr1         26015    25600    30720    5.1 days 488      500      750
```

Username jamie has exceeded the total kilobyte usage allowed and has 5.1 days left to reduce her usage. That username could create 12 more files before signaling an inode overage (assuming that enough space exists).

repquota lists all users under quota restrictions when run.

```
Disk limits                  File limits
User      used soft hard   timeleft  used softhard   timeleft
alyssa     —   00417 25600    30720          0043    200     250
james      —   12871 25600    30720          0149    200     250
wayne     -+   04635 25600    30720          1072    500     750    EXPIRED
rayna      —   00002 25600    30720          0003    200     250
jamie     +-   26015 25600    30720  5.1 days 0488   500     750
holly     -+   11872 25600    30720          0200    200     250    6.0 days
kenny      —   02737 25600    30720          0134    200     250
dave      +-   50226 50000    60000  EXPIRED  0430   500     750
```

23

USER ADMINISTRATION

In the preceding example, wayne and dave have faults that disallow use. Users jamie and holly need to lower their use in the specified time period or have use disallowed. Alternately, the values for their use could be increased.

Though a subset of total disk usage, incoming mail file usage should be monitored specifically because generally all users share a common incoming mail directory space. For example:

```
ls -l /var/mail ¦ awk '{if ($5 > 500000) printf"%-8.8s - %ld\n", $3, $5}'
```

lists all usernames with mail files greater than one-half million characters. Either the user can politely be asked to reduce the number of messages, or you can lessen the file space by saving and compressing or by archiving and deleting it.

Anonymous ftp

Most UNIX systems support a special, albeit insecure, user ID, the anonymous ftp account.

First, create a user ID for the account in the passwd file. The entry should have a unique user ID, the group ID matching the user ID, and an invalid password and shell. An example entry could be:

```
ftp:*:500:ftp;Anonymous ftp
        user:/usr_ftp_home_directory/ftp:/bin/false
```

Second, create the home directory.

```
mkdir /usr_ftp_home_directory/ftp
cd /usr_ftp_home_directory/ftp
mkdir bin etc [lib] [dev] pub
mkdir pub/incoming
chown -R root .
chgrp ftp . pub
chmod ugo+rx .  pub [lib]
chmod ugo+x bin etc [dev]
chmod u+rwx,o+wx,+t pub/incoming
```

Third, fill the directories with appropriate information.

```
cp /bin or /sbin/ls bin
    chmod ugo+x bin/ls
    [ cp /usr/lib/libdl.so.* lib ]
    [ chmod ugo+rx lib/libdl.so.* ]
    [ ls -l /dev/zero ]
    [ mknod dev/zero c major# minor# ] — - major/minor numbers are the
comma seperated entries directly left of the date in the ouput of the "ls"
```

```
command.
      [ chmod ugo+r dev/zero ]
      [ create an etc/passwd file that includes root, daemon, and ftp
whose passwords are "*" ]
      [ create an etc/group file that includes the root default group and
the ftp group ]
```

No file or directory should be owned by ftp because Trojan horse versions of the files could be inserted. Connect as anonymous ftp, and try to create a file in the current working directory. If you can, anonymous ftp is insecure.

Summary

Although it seems a thankless task, user administration is best when it is unnoticed. You should be available to answer questions but otherwise be invisible to your users. Use the many inherent UNIX user administration tools in concert with the select add-on packages to oversee, monitor, and limit your user base. Satisfied users free you from the more mundane tasks of user administration and give you the free time to sift through other areas of the system, devoting your time to being productive rather than solving problems.

23

USER
ADMINISTRATION

CHAPTER 24

File System and Disk Administration

By Steve Shah

IN THIS CHAPTER

This chapter discusses the trials and tribulations of creating, maintaining, and repairing file systems. Although these tasks may appear simple from a user's standpoint, they are, in fact, intricate and contain more than a handful of nuances. In the course of this chapter, we'll step through many of these nuances and, hopefully, come to a strong understanding of the hows and whys of file systems.

This chapter goes about the explanation of file systems a bit differently than does other books. We first discuss the maintenance and repair of file systems and then discuss their creation. We chose this approach because it is likely that you already have existing file systems you need to maintain and fix. Understanding how to maintain them also helps you better understand why file systems are created the way they are.

The techniques covered in this chapter apply to most UNIX systems currently in use. The only exceptions are when we actually create the file systems. This is where the most deviation from any standard (if there ever was one) occurs. We cover the creation of file systems under the SunOS, Solaris, Linux, and IRIX implementations of UNIX. If you are not using one of these operating systems, check the documentation that came with your operating system for details on the creation of file systems.

CAUTION

Working with file systems is inherently dangerous. You may be surprised at how quickly and easily you can damage a file system beyond repair. In some instances, it is even possible to damage the disk drive as well. *Be careful*. When performing the actions explained in this chapter, be sure that you have typed the commands correctly and that you understand the resulting function fully *before* executing it. When in doubt, consult the documentation that came from the manufacturer. Always remember that the documentation that comes from the manufacturer is more authoritative than any book.

And always—and I mean always—make a backup of your system before modifying the file systems. Your users, your sanity, and (quite possibly) your job will thank you.

NOTE

You should read this entire chapter before actually performing any of the tasks in the chapter. Doing so will give you a better understanding of how all the components work together; you will be on more solid ground when you perform potentially dangerous activities.

What Is a File System?

The *file system* is the primary means of file storage in UNIX. Each file system houses *directories*, which, as a group, can be placed almost anywhere in the UNIX directory tree. The topmost level of the directory tree, the root directory, begins at /. Subdirectories below the root directory can traverse as deep as you like—as long as the longest absolute path is less than 1,024 characters.

With the proliferation of vendor-enhanced versions of UNIX, you will find a number of "enhanced" file systems. From the administrator's standpoint, you shouldn't have to worry about the differences too much. The two instances in which you should worry about vendor-specific details are in the creation of file systems and when performing backups. This chapter covers the specifics of the following versions of UNIX:

- SunOS 4.1.x, which uses 4.2
- Solaris, which uses ufs
- Linux, which uses ext2
- IRIX, which uses efs and xfs

Note that the ufs and 4.2 file systems are actually the same.

A file system, however, is only a part of the grand scheme of how UNIX keeps its data on disk. At the top level, you'll find the disks themselves. The disks are then broken into partitions, each varying in size depending on the needs of the administrator. It is on each partition that the actual file system is laid out. Within the file system, you'll find directories, subdirectories, and, finally, the individual files.

Although you will rarely have to deal with the file system at a level lower than the individual files stored on it, it is critical that you understand two key concepts: *inodes* and the *superblock*. Once you understand these concepts, you will find that the behavior and characteristics of files make more sense.

inodes

An *inode* maintains information about each file. Depending on the type of file system, the inode can contain more than 40 pieces of information. Most of that information, however, is useful only to the kernel and doesn't concern us. The fields that do concern us are listed here:

Field	*Description*
mode	The permission mask and type of file.
link count	The number of directories that contain an entry with this inode number.
user ID	The ID of the file's owner.
group ID	The ID of the file's group.
size	The number of bytes in this file.
access time	The time at which the file was last accessed.
mod time	The time at which the file was last modified.
inode time	The time at which this inode structure was last modified.
block list	A list of disk block numbers that contain the first segment of the file.
indirect list	A list of other block lists.

The mode, link count, user ID, group ID, size, and access time are used when generating file listings. Note that the inode does not contain the file's name. That information is held in the directory file (as described a little later in this chapter).

Superblocks

Superblocks contain the most vital information stored on the disk. A superblock contains information about the disk's *geometry* (the number of heads, cylinders, and so on), the head of the inode list, and free block list. Because of its importance, the system automatically keeps mirrors of this data scattered around the disk for redundancy. You have to deal with superblocks only if your file system becomes heavily corrupted.

Types of Files

Files come in eight flavors:

- Normal files
- Directories
- Hard links
- Symbolic links
- Sockets
- Named pipes
- Character devices
- Block devices

Normal Files

Normal files are the files you use the most. They can be either text or binary files; however, their internal structure is irrelevant from the system administrator's standpoint. A file's characteristics are specified by the inode in the file system that describes it. Using the ls -l command on a normal file results in output something like this:

```
-rw-------    1 sshah    admin           42 Sep 16 13:09 proposal
```

Directories

A *directory* is a special kind of file that contains a list of other files. Although there is a one-to-one mapping of inode to disk blocks, there can be a many-to-one mapping from a directory entry to an inode. When viewing a directory listing using the ls -l command, you can identify directories by their permissions, which start with the d character. Using the ls -l command on a directory results in output something like this:

```
drwx------    2 sshah    admin          512 Sep 16 13:08 public_html
```

Hard Links

A *hard link* is actually a normal directory entry except that, instead of pointing to a unique file, it points to an already existing file. This arrangement gives the illusion that there are two identical files when you do a directory listing. Because the system sees a hard link as just another file, it treats it as such. This is most apparent during backups because hard-linked files are backed up as many times as there are hard links to them. Because a hard link shares an inode, it cannot exist across file systems. Hard links are created with the ln command. Consider this directory listing (viewed by using the ls -l command):

```
-rw-------    1 sshah    admin           42 May 29 16:08 hdh
```

If you type ln hdh sjs and then perform another directory listing using ls -l, you see this:

```
-rw-------    2 sshah    admin           42 May 29 16:08 hdh
-rw-------    2 sshah    admin           42 May 29 16:08 sjs
```

Notice how this listing appears to contain two separate files that just happen to have the same file lengths. Also note that the link count (second column) has increased from 1 to 2. How can you tell they actually are the same file? Use the ls -il command:

```
13180 -rw-------    2 sshah    admin      42 May 29 16:08 hdh
13180 -rw-------    2 sshah    admin      42 May 29 16:08 sjs
```

As you can see, both files point to the same inode: 13180.

> **CAUTION**
>
> Be careful when creating hard links, especially when hard linking to a directory. It is possible to corrupt a file system by doing so because the hard link does not understand that the inode being pointed to must be treated as a directory.

Symbolic Links

A *symbolic link* (sometimes referred to as a *symlink*) differs from a hard link in that it doesn't point to another inode but to another filename. Symbolic links can exist across file systems and can also be recognized as a special file to the operating system. You will find symbolic links to be crucial to the administration of your file systems, especially when trying to give the appearance of a seamless system when there isn't one. Symbolic links are created using the `ln -s` command.

A common thing people do is to create a symbolic link to a directory that has moved. Suppose that you are accustomed to accessing the directory for your home page in the subdirectory www; at the new site you work at, however, home pages are kept in the `public_html` directory. You can create a symbolic link from www to `public_html` using the command `ln -s public_html www`. Performing the `ls -l` command on the result shows the link:

```
drwx------    2 sshah      admin         512 May 12 13:08 public_html
lrwx------    1 sshah      admin          11 May 12 13:08 www -> public_html
```

Sockets

Sockets are the way UNIX networks with other machines. Typically, networking is done using network ports; however, the file system has a provision to allow for interprocess communication through socket files. (A popular program that uses this technique is the X Window system.) You rarely have to deal with this kind of file and should never have to create one yourself (unless you're writing the program). If you have to remove a socket file, use the `rm` command. Socket files are identified by their permission settings, which begin with an s character. An `ls -l` on a socket file looks something like this:

```
srwxrwxrwx    1 root       admin           0 May 10 14:38 X0
```

Named Pipes

Similar to sockets, *named pipes* enable programs to communicate with one another through the file system. You can use the `mknod` command to create a named pipe. Named

pipes are recognized by their permissions settings, which begin with the p character. An
ls -l on a named pipe looks something like this:

```
prw-------  1 sshah    admin          0 May 12 22:02 mypipe
```

Character Devices

Character devices are special files typically found in the /dev directory. They provide a
way to communicate with system device drivers through the file system one character at
a time. Character devices are easily noticed by their permission bits, which start with the
c character. Each character file contains two special numbers: the major and minor.
These two numbers identify the device driver that file communicates with. An ls -l on
a character device looks something like this:

```
crw-rw-rw-  1 root     wheel     21,   4 May 12 13:40 ptyp4
```

Block Devices

Block devices share many characteristics with character devices in that they exist in the
/dev directory, are used to communicate with device drivers, and have major and minor
numbers. The key difference is that block devices typically transfer large blocks of data
at a time as opposed to the one-character-at-a-time approach of character devices. (A
hard disk is a block device; a terminal is a character device.) Block devices are identified
by their permission bits, which start with the b character. An ls -l on a block device
looks something like this:

```
brw-------  2 root     staff     16,   2 Jul 29  1992 fd0c
```

File Permissions

While looking at the file listings generated by the ls -l command, you probably noticed
that the first ten characters of each line appeared to be some combination of the characters r, w, and x. Some lines seemed to even start with a d instead of a dash. For example:

```
drwxr-xr-x  2 sshah    admin       1024 Feb 14 15:49 wedding_plans
-rw-------  1 sshah    admin       2465 Feb  5 19:22 index.html
```

What do these characters mean?

Permissions are broken into four parts. The first part is the first character of the permissions. As we saw earlier, normal files have no value and are represented with a -
(hyphen) character. If the file has a special attribute, that attribute is represented with a
letter (for example, l for symbolic link).

The second, third, and fourth parts of the permissions are represented by three-character
chunks. The first part is the permissions for the owner of the file. The second part is the

permissions for the group. The last part is the permissions for the world. In the context of UNIX, *the world* is simply all the users in the system, regardless of their group settings.

The letters used to represent permissions are listed here:

Letter	Meaning
r	Read
w	Write
x	Execute

Each permission has a corresponding value. The read attribute is equal to 4, the write attribute is equal to 2, and the execute attribute is equal to 1. When you combine attributes, you add their values (examples follow).

The reason these attributes need values is so that you can use the chmod command to set them. Although the chmod command does have more readable ways to set permissions, it is important that you understand the numbering scheme because it is used while programming. In addition, not everyone uses the naming scheme; it is often assumed that if you understand file permissions, you understand the numeric meanings as well.

The most common groups of three-character permission chunks and their meanings are listed here:

Permission	Value	Meaning
- - -	0	No permissions
r - -	4	Read only
rw -	6	Read and write
rwx	7	Read, write, and execute
r - x	5	Read and execute
- - x	1	Execute only

Although other combinations do exist (for example, -wx), those combinations are nonsensical and the likelihood you'll ever run across them is almost nil.

Each of these three-letter chunks is then grouped together, three at a time. The first chunk represents the permissions for the owner of the file, the second chunk represents the permissions for the group of the file, and the last chunk represents the permissions for all the users on the system. Some common permissions are shown here:

Permission	Value	Meaning
- rw - - - - - - -	600	The owner has read and write permissions. This is what you want to set for most of your files.

Permission	Value	Meaning
-rw-r--r--	644	The owner has read and write permissions. The group and the world have read only permissions. Be sure that you want to let other people read this file.
-rw-rw-rw-	666	Everybody has read and write permissions on a file. This is bad. You don't want other people to be able to change your files.
-rwx------	700	The owner has read, write, and execute permissions. This is what you want for programs you want to run.
-rwxr-xr-x	755	The owner has read, write, and execute permissions. The rest of the world has read and execute permissions.
-rwxrwxrwx	777	Everyone has read, write, and execute privileges. As with the 666 setting, this is bad. Letting others edit your files is a cookbook formula for disaster.
-rwx--x--x	711	The owner has read, write, and execute privileges. The rest of the world has execute only permissions. This is useful for programs that you want to let others run, but not copy.
drwx------	700	This is a directory created with the mkdir command. Only the owner can read and write to this directory. Note that all directories must have the executable bit set.
drwxr-xr-x	755	This directory can be changed only by the owner, but everyone else can view its contents.
drwx--x--x	711	This is a handy trick to use when a directory must be read by the world, but you don't want people to be able to see a directory listing using the ls command. Only if the person knows the filename they want to retrieve are they allowed to read it.

24

FILE SYSTEM AND DISK ADMINISTRATION

> **NOTE**
>
> Just because a directory is world readable doesn't make all the files under it world readable. By the same token, once a directory has been set to be read only by its owner (permissions 700), the file permissions on all files below that directory are irrelevant.

Setuid, Setgid, and the Sticky Bit

Every program, when executed, must have an owner. The access the owner of the executing program has is the same level of access the executing program has. For example, if you are playing a game of xtetris, the process can read and write any file you are allowed to. If you are playing the game as the root user (a bad idea), the process can read and write every file in the system. An important security measure in UNIX is that ownership of a process is determined by who runs the process instead of who owns the file.

However, as a system administrator, you will find that there are instances in which you will want the process being run to be owned by a particular user regardless of who is running it. This is usually done so that the process has access to parts of the system other users do not have. The ping program is a common example: It has to be able to access a special network port in the system that is only accessible by the root user. However, ping is a useful network diagnostic tool that should be available to all users. How can we arrange this?

Enter *setuid programs*. These files have a special permission bit set that allows them to run as the user the file is owned by, even though another user executed the file. Let's look at ping as an example; if we use ls -l on the file itself, we see the following:

```
-rwsr-xr-x   1 root     sys      31274 Mar  12 19:22 ping
```

This file is owned by root. If user sshah were to run it, the process would run as the root user with all the permissions that go with it.

The way we can tell that a program is setuid is by the s character in the owner segment of the permissions. To set a program to be setuid, you must prefix the file's permissions with the number 4. You can do this with the following command:

```
chmod 4755 /sbin/ping
```

Given that we can do this sort of manipulation on a per-user basis, you might assume that it can also be done for a group. And you would be right: *setgid programs* operate on the same principle as setuid programs except that they run with the same group permissions instead of the same owner permissions. To make a program setgid, you prefix the file's permissions with the number 2. You can do this with the following command:

```
chmod 2755 /usr/bin/myprog
```

An `ls -l` of the resulting file would show this. Notice where the s character appears in the directory entry:

```
-rwxr-sr-x   1 root     sys      31274 Mar  12 19:22 /usr/bin/myprog
```

The last special permission is the *sticky bit*. This bit, when set for directories, allows users with proper permissions to create files and subdirectories that cannot be meddled with by other users unless permissions on the file itself are set accordingly.

The most common use for the sticky bit is the /tmp directory. Its permissions are set to 1777 (where the 1 indicates the sticky bit), thus allowing any user in the system to create a file or subdirectory inside /tmp with the security of knowing that if they set the permission of their file to 0600, it is not accessible by anyone else.

Using the `ls -l / ¦ grep tmp` command shows the following:

```
drwxrwxrwt  44 root     root      2048 Aug 18 21:28 tmp
```

Notice that the character t (which shows that the sticky bit is on) appears at the end of the permissions.

Managing File Permissions, Owners, Groups, and Special Files

This section finishes up the basics of file systems with a review of the three commands you need to manage permissions, owners, and groups: chmod, chown, chgrp, and mknod.

The chmod Command

The chmod command allows you to change the permissions on a file that is owned by you. Of course, the root user is the exception: it has the authority to change permissions on any file in the system.

The usage of chmod is shown here:

```
chmod [options] permission files...
```

In this syntax, [options] are the command-line options you can use, permission is the desired file permissions, and files... is the list of files separated by spaces for which you want to change the permissions.

The *options* available to us are listed here:

-f	Do not print any messages (errors or success).
-R	Recursively apply the permission change to all files in the current directory and below in the directory tree.

The *permission* is the numeric value discussed earlier in this chapter.

Now consider an example for this directory listing:

```
drwxr-xr-x   2 sshah      sysadmin       1024 Feb  5 19:27 Mail
drwxr-xr-x   2 sshah      sysadmin       1024 Feb 22 13:33 News
drwxr-xr-x   4 sshah      sysadmin       1024 Feb  5 19:24 wedding_plans
drwxr-xr-x   2 sshah      sysadmin       1024 Feb 18 20:03 dj_stuff
drwxr-xr-x   2 sshah      sysadmin       1024 Feb 23 15:49 humor
-rw-------   1 sshah      sysadmin       2465 Feb  5 19:22 index.html
-rw-------   1 sshah      sysadmin       2387 Feb 17 12:04 cbq.tex
-rw-------   1 sshah      sysadmin        591 Feb 22 13:40 sample.aux
-rw-------   1 sshah      sysadmin       2096 Feb 22 13:40 sample.dvi
-rw-------   1 sshah      sysadmin       2679 Feb 22 13:40 sample.log
-rw-------   1 sshah      sysadmin     131229 Feb 22 13:40 sample.ps
-rw-------   1 sshah      sysadmin       2387 Feb  5 19:27 sample.tex
```

To change the permissions of `sample.tex` to `-rw-r--r--`, we use this command:

```
# chmod 644 sample.tex
```

Looking at the results of a directory listing, we see that `sample.tex` has changed its permissions.

```
# ls -l sample.tex
```

```
-rw-r--r--   1 sshah      sysadmin       2387 Feb  5 19:27 sample.tex
```

If you've been keeping your eyes open, you should have noticed that my mail folder is world readable. Obviously, this could lead to some problems. The command to close it up is shown here:

```
# chmod 700 Mail
```

The chown Command

To change the ownership of a file, use the chown command. Note that a user cannot "give away" the ownership of a file to someone else. (Except for the root user, of course!) The format of the command is as follows:

```
chown [options] login file...
```

In this syntax, `[options]` are the command-line options, `login` is the name of the login to which we want to change the file ownership, and `file...` is a list of files separated by spaces for which we want to change the ownership setting.

The command-line *options* we can use with `chown` are listed here:

`-f`	Do not print any messages (errors or success).
`-R`	Recursively apply the owner change to all files in the current directory and below in the directory tree.

For example, to change the ownership to `sshah` for all the files and directories in `/tmp/restore/htdocs/sponge` and then list all the changes made, we use this command:

```
# chown -R -c sshah /tmp/restore/htdocs/sponge
```

The `chgrp` Command

To change the group of a file, you use the `chgrp` command. The format of the chgrp command is as follows:

```
chgrp [options] group file...
```

In this syntax, `[options]` are command-line options, *group* is the name of the group to which we want to change, and `file...` is a list of files separated by spaces for which we want to change the group settings.

A user who belongs to a particular group can change the group settings of his or her own files to be a part of that group.

The command-line *options* we can use with `chgrp` are listed here:

`-f`	Do not print any messages (errors or success).
`-R`	Recursively apply the group change to all files in the current directory and below in the directory tree.

For example, to change the group setting to `blam` for all the files and directories in `/home/research/molle`, we use this command:

```
# chown -R blam /home/research/molle
```

The `mknod` Command

As mentioned earlier, you need the `mknod` command to create special files such as named pipes. The format of the command is as follows:

```
mknod filename type major minor
```

In this syntax, `filename` is the name of the file we're creating. `type` can be p for named pipes, c for character devices, or b for block devices. You must supply a `major` and a `minor` number if you are creating a character or block device.

If you are creating a named pipe, you do not need any further parameters. For example, to create a named pipe called `mypipe`, you type this:

```
# mknod mypipe p
```

If you are creating a character or block device entry, you must supply a `major` and `minor` number as well. For example, to create a character device called `mytty` with a major number of 20 and a minor number of 47, you type this:

```
# mknod mytty c 20 47
```

To create a block device called `sd0a` with a major number of 7 and a minor number of 0, you type this:

```
# mknod sd0a b 7 0
```

Managing File Systems

Managing file systems is relatively easy. That is, it's easy if you can commit to memory the location of all the key files in the directory tree on each major variation of UNIX as well as your own layout of file systems across the network....

In other words, it can be a royal pain.

From a technical standpoint, there isn't much to deal with. After the file systems have been put in their correct places and the boot time configuration files have been edited so that your file systems automatically come online at every start up, there isn't much to do besides watch your disk space.

From a management standpoint, file systems are much more involved. Often, you'll have to deal with existing configurations, which might not have been done "the right way," or you have to deal with site politics such as, "I won't let *that* department share *my* disks." You also have to deal with users who don't understand why they need to periodically clean up their home directories. And don't forget the ever-exciting vendor-specific nuisances and their ideas of how the system "should be" organized.

The following sections cover the tools you need to manage the technical aspects of file systems. Unfortunately, managerial issues are something that can't be covered in a book. Each site has different needs as well as different resources, resulting in different policies. If your site lacks a written policy, take the initiative to write one yourself.

Mounting and Unmounting File Systems

As mentioned earlier in this chapter, part of the power of UNIX stems from its flexibility in placing file systems anywhere in the directory tree. This feat is accomplished by mounting file systems.

Before you can mount a file system, you must select a mount point. A *mount point* is the directory entry in the file system where the root directory of a different file system will overlay it. UNIX keeps track of mount points and accesses the correct file system, depending on the directory the user is currently in. A mount point can exist anywhere in the directory tree.

> **NOTE**
>
> Although it is technically true that you can mount a file system anywhere in the directory tree, there is one place you do *not* want to mount it: the root directory. Remember that once a file system is mounted at a directory, that directory is overshadowed by the contents of the mounted file system. Hence, if you mount on the root directory, the system can no longer see its own kernel or local configuration files. How long your system goes on in this situation before crashing depends on your vendor.
>
> There is an exception to this rule: Some installation packages mount a network file system to the root directory. This is done to give the installation software access to many packages that may not be able to fit on your boot disk. Unless you fully understand how to do this yourself, don't.

Mounting and Unmounting File Systems Manually

To mount a file system, use the mount command:

```
mount /dev/device /directory/to/mount
```

In this syntax, */dev/device* is the device name you want to mount and */directory/to/mount* is the directory you want to overlay in your local file system. For example, if you want to mount /dev/hda4 to the /usr directory, you type this command:

```
mount /dev/hda4 /usr
```

Remember that the directory must exist in your local file system before anything can be mounted there.

Options can be passed to the mount command. The most important characteristics are specified with the -o option. These characteristics are listed here:

rw	Read/write
ro	Read-only
bg	Background mount (if the mount fails, place the process into the background and keep trying until success)
intr	Interruptible mount (if a process is pending I/O on a mounted partition, it allows the process to be interrupted and the I/O call dropped)

Here is an example of these parameters being used:

```
mount -o rw,bg,intr /dev/hda4 /usr
```

See the man page on your system for vendor-specific additions.

To unmount a file system, use the umount command:

```
umount /usr
```

This command unmounts the /usr file system from the current directory tree, unveiling the original directory underneath it.

There is, of course, a caveat: If users are using files on a mounted file system, you cannot unmount that file system. All files must be closed before you can unmount a file system. On a large system, this can be tricky (to say the least). There are three ways to determine whether all files are closed:

- Use the lsof program (available at ftp://vic.cc.purdue.edu/pub/tools/unix/lsof) to list the users and their open files on a given file system. Then wait until those users are done, beg them to leave, or kill their processes. Then unmount the file system. Often, this approach isn't desirable.

- Use the -f option with umount command to force the unmount. This is often a bad idea because it confuses the programs (and the users) accessing the partition. Files in memory that have not been committed to disk can be lost.

- Bring the system to single-user mode and then unmount the file system. Although this approach can be extremely inconvenient, it is the safest way because no one loses any work.

Mounting File Systems Automatically

At boot time, the system automatically mounts the root file system with read-only privileges. This approach enables the system to load the kernel and read critical startup files. However, once it has bootstrapped itself, the system needs guidance. Although it is possible for you to mount all the file systems by hand, doing so isn't realistic because you would then have to finish bootstrapping the machine yourself. Worse, the system could not come back online by itself. (Unless, of course, you enjoy coming in to work at 2 a.m. to bring a system back up.)

To get around this limitation, UNIX uses a special file called /etc/fstab (/etc/vfstab under Solaris). This file lists all the partitions that must be mounted at boot time and the directory to which they must be mounted. Along with that information, you can pass parameters to the mount command.

Each file system to be mounted is listed in the fstab file in the following format:

```
/dev/device    /dir/to/mount        ftype parameters fs_freq fs_passno
```

In this syntax, the following parameters are used:

/dev/device	The device to be mounted, for instance, /dev/hda4.
/dir/to/mount	The location at which the file system should be mounted on your directory tree.
ftype	The file system type. This should be 4.2 under SunOS, ufs under Solaris, ext2 under Linux, efs or xfs in IRIX (depending on your version), nfs for NFS-mounted file systems, swap for swap partitions, and proc for the /proc file system. Some operating systems, such as Linux, support additional file system types, although they are not as likely to be used.
parameters	The parameters you want to pass to mount using the -o option. The parameters you specify here follow the same comma-delineated format they do when you enter them on the command line. A sample entry would look like this: rw,intr,bg
fs_freq	Used by dump to determine whether a file system must be dumped.
fs_passno	Used by the fsck program to determine the order in which the disks should be checked at boot time.

Any lines in the fstab file that start with the pound symbol (#) are considered comments.

If you have to mount a new file system while the machine is live, you must perform the mount by hand. If you want to have this mount automatically active the next time the system is rebooted, be sure to add the appropriate entry to your fstab file.

Two notable partitions don't follow the same set of rules as normal partitions. They are the swap partition and /proc. (Note that SunOS does not use the /proc file system.)

You do not mount the swap partition with the mount command. The swap partition is instead managed by the swap command under Solaris and IRIX, and by the swapon command under SunOS and Linux. For a swap partition to be mounted, it must be listed in the appropriate fstab file. Once it's there, use the appropriate command (swap or swapon) with the -a parameter followed by the partition on which you've allocated swap space. During the boot sequence, any swap partitions (or swap files) listed in the appropriate fstab file are activated using these commands. After the system has come up, the mount command ignores any entries for swap.

The /proc file system is even stranger because it really isn't a file system at all. It is an interface to the kernel abstracted into a file system[nd]style format. The /proc file system should be listed in your fstab file with file system type proc.

TIP

If you have to remount a file system that already has an entry in the fstab file, you don't need to type the mount command with all its parameters. Instead, simply pass the directory to mount as a parameter like this:

```
mount /dir/to/mount
```

mount automatically looks to the fstab file for all the details, such as which partition to mount and which options to use.

If you have to remount a large number of file systems that are already listed in the fstab file (in other words, you need to remount directories from a system that has gone down), you can use the -a option in the mount command to try to remount all the entries in the fstab file like this:

```
mount -a
```

If mount finds that a file system is already mounted, no action is performed on that file system. If, on the other hand, mount finds that an entry is not mounted, it automatically mounts that entry with the appropriate parameters.

Here is a complete `fstab` file from a SunOS system:

```
#
# Sample /etc/fstab file for a SunOS machine
#

# Local mounts

/dev/sd0a                          /                    4.2    rw
1 1
/dev/sd0g                          /usr                 4.2    rw
1 2
/dev/sd0b                          swap                 swap   rw
0 0
/dev/sd0d                          /var                 4.2    rw
0 0

# Remote mounts

server1:/export/home               /home                nfs
rw,bg,intr      0 0
server1:/export/usr/local          /usr/local           nfs
rw,bg,intr      0 0
server2:/export/var/spool/mail     /var/spool/mail      nfs
rw,bg,intr      0 0
```

Common Commands for File System Management

In taking care of your system, you'll quickly find that you can use these commands and many of their parameters without having to look them up. This is because you're going to be using them *all the time*. I highly suggest that you learn to love them.

> **NOTE**
>
> In reading this book, you may have noticed that the terms *program* and *command* are used interchangeably. This is because there are no "built-in" commands to the system; each command is invoked as an individual program. However, you will quickly find that people who use UNIX and UNIX-related texts (such as this one) use both terms to mean the same thing. Sure it's a bit confusing, but it's tough to change over 25 years of history.

> **TIP**
>
> At the end of each command description, I mention the GNU equivalent. Linux users don't have to worry about getting them because Linux ships with all GNU tools. If you are using another platform and aren't sure whether you're using the GNU version, try running the command with the --version option. If it is the GNU version of the command, it will display its title and version number. If it isn't GNU, the command will most likely reject the parameter and give an error.

The df Command

The df command summarizes the free disk space by file system. Running this command without any parameters displays all the information about normally mounted and NFS-mounted file systems. The output varies from vendor to vendor (under Solaris, use df -t) but should closely resemble this:

```
Filesystem          1024-blocks  Used Available Capacity Mounted on
/dev/hda3               247871 212909     22161    91%   /
/dev/hda6                50717  15507     32591    32%   /var
/dev/hda7               481998     15    457087     0%   /local
server1:/var/spool/mail
                        489702 222422    218310    50%   /var/spool/mail
```

Here is a list of the columns in this report and what they show:

Filesystem	Which file system is being shown. File systems mounted using NFS are shown as *hostname:/dir/that/is/mounted*
1024-blocks	The number of 1KB blocks the file system consists of (its total size.)
Used	The number of blocks used.
Available	The number of blocks available for use.
Capacity	Percentage of partition currently used.
Mounted on	The location in the directory tree at which this partition has been mounted.

Common parameters to this command are listed here:

directory	Show information only for the partition on which the specified directory exists.
-a	Show all partitions including swap and /proc.
-i	Show inode usage instead of block usage.

The GNU `df` program, which is part of the `fileutils` distribution, has some additional print-formatting features you may find useful. You can download the latest `fileutils` package from `ftp://ftp.cdrom.com/pub/gnu`.

The du Command

The `du` command summarizes disk usage by directory. It recurses through all subdirectories and shows disk usage by each subdirectory with a final total at the end. Running it without any parameters provides the following listing:

```
409     ./doc
945     ./lib
68      ./man
60      ./m4
391     ./src
141     ./intl
873     ./po
3402    .
```

The first column shows the blocks of disk used by the subdirectory; the second column shows the subdirectory being evaluated. To see how many kilobytes each subdirectory consumes, use the `-k` option. Some common parameters to this command are listed here:

`directory`	Show usage for the specified directory. The default is the current directory.
`-a`	Show usage for all files, not just directories.
`-s`	Show only the total disk usage.

A quick way to see how much space a user is using is to go to one directory *above* their home directory (for example, if the home directory is `/home/sysadmin/sshah`, you go to `/home/sysadmin`) and use this command:

```
du -sk sshah
```

Like the `df` program, this program is available as part of the GNU fileutils distribution. The GNU version has expanded on many of the parameters you may find useful. The fileutils package can be downloaded from `ftp://ftp.cdrom.com/pub/gnu`.

The ln Command

The `ln` program is used to generate links between files. This is very useful for creating the illusion of a perfect file system in which everything is in the "right" place when, in reality, it isn't. This is done by making a link from the desired location to the actual location.

The use of this program is shown here:

```
ln file_being_linked_to link_name
```

In this syntax, *file_being_linked_to* is the file that already exists; *link_name* is the name of the other file you want to point to it. This command generates a hard link, meaning that the file *link_name* is indistinguishable from the original file. Both files must exist on the same file system.

A popular parameter to the ln command is the -s option, which generates symbolic links instead of hard links. The format of the command remains the same:

```
ln -s file_being_linked_to link_name
```

The difference is that the *link_name* file is marked as a symbolic link in the file system. Symbolic links can span file systems and are given a special tag in the directory entry.

> **TIP**
>
> Unless there is an explicit reason not to, you should always use symbolic links by specifying the -s option to ln. This approach makes your links stand out and makes it easy to move them from one file system to another.

The tar Command

The tar program is an immensely useful archiving utility. It can combine an entire directory tree into one large file suitable for transferring or compression.

The command line format of this program is shown here:

```
tar parameters filelist
```

Here are some of the common *parameters* for this command:

c	Create an archive
x	Extract the archive
v	Be verbose
f	Specify a tar file to work on
p	Retain file permissions and ownerships
t	View the contents of an archive

Unlike most other UNIX commands, these parameters do not need to have a dash before them.

To create the `tar` file `myCode.tar`, use following command, where `myCode` is a subdirectory relative to the current directory in which the files I want to archive are located:

`tar cf myCode.tar myCode`

The following command is the same as the previous `tar` invocation, except that here it lists all the files to add to the archive on the screen:

`tar cvf myCode.tar myCode`

The following command archives all the files in the `myCode` directory that are suffixed by `.c`:

`tar cf myCode.tar myCode/*.c`

The following example archives all the files in the `myCode` directory that are suffixed by `.c` or `.h`:

`tar cf myCode.tar myCode/*.c myCode/*.h`

To view the contents of the `myCode.tar` file, use this command:

`tar tf myCode.tar`

To extract the files in the `myCode.tar` file, use this command:

`tar xf myCode.tar`

If the `myCode` directory doesn't exist, `tar` creates it. If the `myCode` directory does exist, any files in that directory are overwritten by the ones being untarred.

The following example is the same as the previous invocation of `tar`, except that this command lists the files as they are being extracted:

`tar xvf myCode.tar`

The following command is the same as the previous invocation of `tar`, except that this version attempts to set the permissions of the unarchived files to the values they had before archiving (very useful if you're untarring files as the root user):

`tar xpf myCode.tar`

24

> **TIP**
>
> For system administrators, the greatest use of `tar` is to move directory trees around. This can be done using the following command line:
>
> `(cd /src;tar cpf - *) ¦ (cd /dest;tar xpf -)`
>
> *continues*

In this command, /*src* is the source directory and /*dest* is the destination directory.

This approach is better than using a recursive copy because symbolic links and file permissions are kept. Use this command and amaze your friends.

Although the stock `tar` that comes with your system works fine for most uses, you may find that the GNU version of `tar` has some nicer features. You can find the latest version of GNU `tar` at `ftp://ftp.cdrom.com/pub/gnu`.

The `find` Command

Of the commands described so far in this chapter, you're likely to use `find` the most. Its purpose is to find files or patterns of files. The usage of this tool is shown here:

```
find dir parameters
```

In this syntax, `dir` is the directory where the search begins, and `parameters` define what is being searched for. The most common parameters are listed here:

`-name`	Specify the filename or wildcards to look for. If you use any wildcards, be sure to place them inside quotation marks so that the shell doesn't parse them before `find` does.
`-print`	Typically turned on by default, this parameter tells `find` to display the resulting file list.
`-exec`	Executes the specified command on files found matching the `-name` criteria.
`-atime` *n*	File was last accessed *n* days ago.
`-mtime` *n*	File's data was last modified *n* days ago.
`-size` *n*[bckw]	File uses *n* units of space, where the units are specified by the character b, c, k, or w. b is for 512-byte blocks, c is for bytes, k is for kilobytes, and w is for two-byte words.
`-xdev`	Do not traverse down nonlocal file systems.
`-o`	Logical or the options.
`-a`	Logical and the options.

The following example of the `find` command starts its search from the root directory and finds all files named `core` that have not been modified in seven days:

```
find / -name core -mtime +7 -print -exec /bin/rm {} \;
```

The following command searches all files, from the root directory down, on the local file system, which have not been accessed for at least 60 days *and* that have not been modified for at least 60 days, and prints the list. This command is useful for finding files that people claim they need but, in reality, never use:

```
find / -xdev -atime +60 -a -mtime +60 -print
```

This next example searches all files from /home down and lists them if they are greater than 500KB in size. This command is a handy way of finding large files in the system:

```
find /home -size +500k -print
```

The GNU version of find, which comes with the findutils package, offers many additional features you will find useful. You can download the latest version from ftp://ftp.cdrom.com/pub/gnu.

Security Tools for Your File Systems

Security generally falters in one of two ways. The first is during a genuine attempt to gain unauthorized access to the system. The second, but most common, is caused by simple ignorance. Simply put, most users don't know how to effectively set permissions on their home directories.

The following sections discuss two tools designed to help you keep things under control: COPS and tripwire.

COPS

COPS is actually a general-purpose security auditing tool. It probes your system, looking for potential trouble and generates reports on what it finds. It is easy to automate, which makes it a good candidate to set up for the cron command to run on a regular basis.

We are specifically interested in two checks: file permissions and setuid/setgid executables. The first check scans every user's home directory, looking for files that are accessible by others and that have potentially dangerous permissions. The second check flags any executables that are setuid in someone's home directory. Executable files with setuid are usually an indication of an error because there is rarely a time when someone has to have a setuid program. If the file is owned by root, you may have a real problem on your hands.

COPS is available for download at ftp://ftp.cert.org.

24

FILE SYSTEM
AND DISK
ADMINISTRATION

Tripwire

Tripwire is for the paranoid in all of us. The primary purpose of the program is to compute MD5 checksums on every file on a system and log them. If you follow the directions, you'll take the results of the run and save them to write-once media such as a CD burner.

After the initial pass is done, you can periodically run the program from the `cron` command to report any files for which checksums have changed. When you look at the report, you can ignore the expected changes (for example, you may know that you changed the `/etc/hosts` file) and treat other changes as corrupted files left by hackers. This sort of utility is especially useful in firewalls or proxy services where any change to the system means you've got a security problem.

Tripwire is available at `ftp://ftp.cert.org`.

Repairing File Systems with `fsck`

Sooner or later, it happens: Someone turns off the power switch. The power outage lasts longer than your UPS's batteries, and you didn't shut down the system. Someone presses the reset button. Someone overwrites part of your disk. A critical sector on the disk develops a flaw. If you run UNIX long enough, eventually a halt occurs where the system did not write the remaining cached information to the disks (that is, UNIX isn't synched).

When any of these things happen, you must verify the integrity of each of the file systems. This is necessary because if the structure is not correct, using the incorrect file systems could quickly damage them beyond repair. Over the years, UNIX has developed a very sophisticated file system integrity check that can usually recover the problem. It's called `fsck`.

The `fsck` Utility

The `fsck` utility takes its understanding of the internals of the various UNIX file systems and attempts to verify that all the links and blocks are correctly tied together. It runs in five passes, each of which checks a different part of the linkage and each of which builds on the verifications and corrections of the previous passes.

`fsck` walks the file system, starting with the superblock. It then deals with the allocated disk blocks, pathnames, directory connectivity, link reference counts, and the free list of blocks and inodes.

> **NOTE**
>
> The xfs file system now shipped with all IRIX-based machines no longer needs the `fsck` command.

The Superblock

Every change to the file system affects the superblock, which is why it is cached in RAM. Periodically, at the sync interval, the superblock is written to disk. If the superblock is corrupted, `fsck` checks and corrects it. If it is so badly corrupted that `fsck` cannot do its work, find the paper you saved when you built the file system and use the `-b` option with `fsck` to give the system an alternative superblock to use. The superblock is the head of each of the lists that make up the file system, and it maintains counts of free blocks and inodes.

Inodes

`fsck` validates each of the inodes. It makes sure that each block in the block allocation list is not on the block allocation list in any other inode, that the size is correct, and that the link count is correct. If the inodes are correct, then the data is accessible. All that's left is to verify the pathnames.

What Is a Clean (Stable) File System?

Sometimes `fsck` responds with the following message:

    /opt: stable   (ufs file systems)

This means that the superblock is marked clean and that no changes have been made to the file system since it was marked clean. First, the system marks the superblock as dirty; then it starts modifying the rest of the file system. When the buffer cache is empty and all pending writes are complete, it goes back and marks the superblock as clean. If the superblock is marked clean, there is normally no reason to run `fsck`; unless `fsck` is told to ignore the `clean` flag, it just prints this notice and skips over the named file system.

Where Is `fsck`?

When you run `fsck`, you are running an executable in either the `/usr/sbin` or `/bin` directory called `fsck`, but this is not the real `fsck`. It is just a dispatcher that invokes a file system type-specific `fsck` utility.

24

FILE SYSTEM AND DISK ADMINISTRATION

When Should I Run `fsck`?

Normally, you do not have to run `fsck`. The system runs it automatically when you try to mount a dirty file system at boot time. However, problems can creep up on you. Software and hardware glitches do occur from time to time. It doesn't hurt to run `fsck` just after you perform the monthly backups.

> **CAUTION**
>
> It is better to run `fsck` *after* the backups rather than before. If `fsck` finds major problems, it could leave the file system in worse shape than it was before you ran `fsck`. If you need to recover from a damaged file system, you can just build an empty file system and reread your backup (this approach also cleans up the file system). If you do it in the other order, you are left with no backup and no file system.

How Do I Run `fsck`?

Because the system normally runs the program for you, running `fsck` is not an everyday occurrence. However, it is quite simple and mostly automatic.

First, to run `fsck`, the file system you intend to check must not be mounted. This is a bit hard to do if you are in multiuser mode most of the time, so to run a full system `fsck`, you should bring the system down to single-user mode.

In single-user mode, you invoke `fsck`, giving it the options to force a check of all file systems, even if they are already stable. Following are the commands you use for the variations of UNIX:

`fsck -f`	SunOS
`fsck -o f`	Solaris
`fsck`	Linux and IRIX

If you want to check a single specific file system, type its character device name. (If you aren't sure what the device name is, refer to the section on adding a disk to the system for details on how to determine this information.) Here's an example:

```
fsck /dev/hda1
```

Stepping Through an Actual `fsck`

It takes five to seven steps to run `fsck`, depending on your operating system and what errors are found, if any. `fsck` can automatically correct most of these errors and does so if invoked at boot time to automatically check a dirty file system.

The `fsck` we are about to step through was done on a ufs file system. Although there are some differences in the numbering of the phases for different file systems, the errors are mostly the same and require the same solutions. Apply common sense liberally to any invocation of `fsck` and you should be okay.

For ufs file systems, `fsck` is a five-phase process. `fsck` can automatically correct most errors and does so if invoked at boot time to automatically check a dirty file system. However, when you run `fsck` manually, you are asked to answer the questions the system would automatically answer.

> **CAUTION**
>
> Serious errors reported by `fsck` for a ufs file system at the very beginning—especially before reporting the start of phase 1—indicate an invalid superblock. `fsck` should be terminated and restarted with the `-b` option, specifying one of the alternative superblocks. Block 32 is always an alternative and can be tried first, but if the front of the file system was overwritten, it, too, may be damaged. Use the hard copy you saved from the `mkfs` command to find an alternative later in the file system.

Phase 1: Check Blocks and Sizes

This phase checks the inode list, looking for invalid inode entries. Errors requiring answers include the following:

- `UNKNOWN FILE TYPE I=inode number (CLEAR)`

  The file type bits are invalid in the inode. Your options are to leave the problem and attempt to recover the data by hand later, or to erase the entry and its data by clearing the inode.

- `PARTIALLY TRUNCATED INODE I=inode number (SALVAGE)`

  The inode appears to point to less data than the file does. This error is safely salvaged because it indicates a crash while truncating the file to shorten it.

24

FILE SYSTEM
AND DISK
ADMINISTRATION

- `block BAD I=inode number` or `block DUP I=inode number`

  The disk block pointed to by the inode is either out of range for this inode or is already in use by another file. This is an informational message. If a duplicate block is found, phase 1b is run to report the inode number of the file that originally used this block.

Phase 2: Check Pathnames

This phase removes directory entries from bad inodes found in phase 1 and phase 1b and checks for directories with inode pointers that are out of range or pointing to bad inodes. You may have to handle

- `ROOT INODE NOT DIRECTORY (FIX?)`

  You can convert inode 2, the root directory, back into a directory, but this usually means that there is major damage to the inode table.

- `I=OUT OF RANGE I=inode number NAME=file name (REMOVE?)`
      `UNALLOCATED I=inode number OWNER=O MODE=M SIZE=S MTIME=T`
  `TYPE=F (REMOVE?)`
      `BAD/DUP I=inode number OWNER=O MODE=M SIZE=S MTIME=T TYPE=F`
  `(REMOVE?)`

  A bad inode number was found, an unallocated inode was used in a directory, or an inode that had a bad or duplicate block number in it is referenced. You are given the choice to remove the file (losing the data) or to leave the error. If you leave the error, the file system is still damaged, but you have the chance to try to dump the file first and salvage part of the data before rerunning `fsck` to remove the entry.

`fsck` may return one of a variety of errors indicating an invalid directory length. You will be given the chance to have `fsck` fix or remove the directory as appropriate. These errors are all correctable with little chance of subsequent damage.

Phase 3: Check Connectivity

This phase detects errors in unreferenced directories. It creates or expands the `lost+found` directory if needed and connects the misplaced directory entries into the `lost+found` directory. `fsck` prints status messages for all directories placed in `lost+found`.

Phase 4: Check Reference Counts

This phase uses the information from phases 2 and 3 to check for unreferenced files and incorrect link counts on files, directories, or special files.

- UNREF FILE I=inode number OWNER=O MODE=M SIZE=S MTIME=T (RECONNECT?)

    The filename is not known (it is an unreferenced file), so it is reconnected into the lost+found directory with the inode number as its name. If you clear the file, its contents are lost. Unreferenced files that are empty are cleared automatically.

- LINK COUNT FILE I=inode number OWNER=O MODE=M SIZE=S MTIME=T COUNT=X (ADJUST?)
  LINK COUNT DIR I=inode number OWNER=O MODE=M SIZE=S MTIME=T COUNT=X ADJUST?)

    In both cases, an entry was found with a different number of references than what was listed in the inode. You should let fsck adjust the count.

- BAD/DUP FILE I=inode number OWNER=O MODE=M SIZE=S MTIME=T (CLEAR)

    A file or directory has a bad or duplicate block in it. If you clear it now, the data is lost. You can leave the error and attempt to recover the data and then rerun fsck later to clear the file.

Phase 5: Check Cylinder Groups

This phase checks the free block and unused inode maps. It automatically corrects the free lists if necessary, although it asks permission first in manual mode.

What Do I Do After fsck Finishes?

First, relax, because fsck rarely finds anything seriously wrong—except in cases of hardware failure where the disk drive is failing or where you copied something on top of the file system. UNIX file systems are very robust.

However, if fsck finds major problems or makes a large number of corrections, rerun it to be sure that the disk isn't undergoing hardware failure. The program shouldn't find more errors in a second run. Then recover any files fsck may have deleted. If you keep a log of the inodes fsck clears, you can go to a backup tape and dump the list of inodes from the tape. Recover just those inodes to restore the files.

Back up the system again because there is no reason to have to do this all over again.

Dealing with What Is in lost+found

If fsck reconnects unreferenced entries, it places them in the lost+found directory. The entries are safe there, and the system should be backed up in case you lose them while trying to move them back to where they belong. Items in lost+found can be of any type: files, directories, special files (devices), and so on. If the entry is a named pipe or socket, you may as well delete it. The process that opened it is long since gone and will open a new one when it is run again.

For files, use the owner name to contact the user and have him or her look at the contents to see whether the file is worth keeping. Often, the entry is a file that was deleted and is no longer needed, but the system crashed before it could be fully removed.

For directories, the files in the directory should help you and the owner determine where they belong. You can look on the backup tape lists for a directory with those contents if necessary. Then just remake the directory and move the files back. Then remove the directory entry in lost+found. This re-creation and move have the added benefit of cleaning up the directory.

Creating File Systems

Now that you understand the nuances of maintaining a file system, it's time to understand how to create one. This section walks you through the following three steps:

- Picking the right kind of disk for your system
- Creating partitions
- Creating the file system

Disk Types

Although there are many different kinds of disks, UNIX systems have come to standardize on SCSI for workstations. Many PCs also sport SCSI interfaces, but because of the lower cost and abundance of IDE devices, you'll find a lot of IDE drives on UNIX PCs as well.

SCSI itself comes in a few different flavors. There is regular SCSI, SCSI-2, SCSI-Wide, SCSI-Fast and Wide, and now SCSI-3. Although it is possible to mix and match these devices with converter cables, you may find it easier on both your sanity and your performance if you stick to one format. As of this writing, SCSI-2 is the most common interface.

When attaching your SCSI drive, remember these important points:

- **Terminate your SCSI chain.** Forgetting to do this causes all sorts of non-deterministic behavior (a pain to track down). SCSI-2 requires active termination, which is usually indicated by terminators with LEDs on them.

  If a device claims to be self-terminating, you can take your chances, but you'll be less likely to encounter an error if you put a terminator on anyway.

- **Limit the SCSI chain to eight devices.** Remember that the SCSI card counts as a device. Some systems might have internal SCSI devices, so be sure to check for those.

- **Be sure that all your devices have unique SCSI IDs.** A common symptom of having two devices with the same ID is their tendency to frequently reset the SCSI chain. Of course, many devices simply won't work under those conditions.

- **When adding or removing a SCSI disk, be sure to power the system down first.** Power runs through the SCSI cables; failing to shut them down first can lead to problems in the future.

Although SCSI is king of the workstation, PCs have another choice: IDE. IDE tends to be cheaper and more available than SCSI devices. Many motherboards offer direct IDE support. The advantage of using this kind of interface is its availability as well as its lower cost. IDE devices are also simpler and require less configuration on your part.

The downside to IDEs is that their simplicity comes at the cost of configurability and expandability. The IDE chain can hold only two devices, and not all motherboards come with more than one IDE chain. If your CD-ROM is IDE, you have space for only one disk. This is probably okay for a single-user workstation, but as you can imagine, it's not going to fly well in a server environment. Another consideration is speed. SCSI was designed with the ability to perform I/O without the aid of the main CPU, which is one of the reasons it costs more. IDE, on the other hand, was designed with cost in mind. This resulted in a simplified controller; hence, the CPU takes the burden for working the drive.

Although IDE did manage to simplify the PC arena, it did so with the limitation of being unable to handle disks greater than 540MB. Various tricks were devised to circumvent this limit, however, the clean solution is now predominantly available: Known as EIDE (Enhanced IDE), this solution is capable of supporting disks up to 11GB and can support up to four devices on one chain.

In weighing the pros and cons of EIDE and SCSI in the PC environment, don't forget to think about the cost-to-benefit ratio. Having a high-speed SCSI controller in a single-user workstation might not be as necessary as the user is convinced it is. And with disks being released in 6GB (and more) configurations, there is ample room on the typical IDE disk.

After you have decided on the disk subsystem you will install, read the documentation that came with the machine for instructions on physically attaching the disk to the system.

What Are Partitions and Why Do I Need Them?

Partitions are UNIX's way of dividing the disk into usable pieces. UNIX requires at least one partition; however, you'll find that creating multiple partitions, each with a specific function, is often necessary.

24

FILE SYSTEM AND DISK ADMINISTRATION

The most important reason for creating separate partitions is to protect the system from the users. The one required partition is called the *root partition*. It is here that critical system software and configuration files (the kernel and mount tables) must reside. This partition must be carefully watched so that it never fills up. If it fills up, your system might not be able to come back up in the event of a system crash. Because the root partition is not meant to hold the users' data, you must create separate partitions for the users' home directories, temporary files, and so forth. Separate data partitions enable users' files to grow without the worry of crowding out key system files.

Dual-boot configurations are becoming another common reason to partition, especially with the growing popularity of Linux. You might find your users wanting to be able to boot to either Windows or Linux; you need to keep at least two partitions to enable them to do this.

The last, but certainly not the least, reason to partition your disks is the issue of backups. Backup software often works by dumping entire partitions onto tape. By keeping the different types of data on separate partitions, you can be explicit about what gets backed up and what doesn't. For example, a daily backup of the system software isn't necessary, but backups of home directories are. By keeping the two on separate partitions, you can be more concise in your selection of what gets backed up and what doesn't.

Another example relates more to company politics: It is possible that one group does not want its data backed up to the same tape as another group's data. (*Note:* Common sense doesn't always apply to intergroup politics.) By keeping the two groups on separate partitions, you can exclude one from your normal backups and exclude the others during your special backups.

Which Partitions To Create

As mentioned earlier, the purpose of creating partitions is to separate the users from the system areas. So how many different partitions must be created? Although there is no right answer for every installation, here are some guidelines to take into account.

You always need a root partition. In this partition are your /bin, /etc, and /sbin directories at the very least. Depending on your version of UNIX, this could require anywhere from 30MB to 100MB.

/tmp	The /tmp directory is where your users, as well as their programs, store temporarily files. The use of this directory can quickly get out of hand, especially if you run a quota-based site. By keeping it on a separate partition, you do not need to worry about its abuse interfering with the rest of the system. Many operating systems automatically clear the contents of /tmp on

boot. Size /tmp to fit your site's needs. If you use quotas, you will want to make it a little larger; sites without quotas might not need as much space.

Under Solaris, you have another option when setting up /tmp. Using the tmpfs file system, you can have your swap space and /tmp partition share the same physical location on disk. Although it appears to be an interesting idea, you'll quickly find that it isn't a very good solution—especially on a busy system. This is because as more users do their work, more of /tmp is used. Of course, if there are more users, there is a greater memory requirement to hold them all. The competition for free space can become very problematic.

/var   The /var directory is where the system places its spool files (print spool, incoming/outgoing mail queue, and so on) as well as system log files. These files constantly grow and shrink without warning—especially the mail spool. Another possibility to keep in mind is the creation of a separate partition just for mail. This enables you to export the mail spool to all your machines without having to worry about your print spools being exported as well. If you use a backup package that requires its own spool space, you may want to keep this on a separate partition as well.

/home   The /home directory is where you place your users' account directories. You may have to use multiple partitions to keep your home directories (possibly broken up by department) and have each partition mount to /home/*dept*, where *dept* is the name of the respective department.

/usr   The /usr directory holds noncritical system software, such as editors and lesser-used utilities. Many sites hold locally compiled software in the /usr/local directory, from which they either export it to other machines or mount other machines' /usr/local to their own. This makes it easy for a site to maintain one /usr/local directory and share it with all its machines. Keeping this on a separate partition is a good idea because local software inevitably grows.

24

FILE SYSTEM AND DISK ADMINISTRATION

TIP

Several new versions of UNIX are now placing locally compiled software in the /opt directory. As you should with /usr/local, you should make /opt a separate partition. If your system does not use /opt by default, you can make a

continues

symbolic link from there to /usr/local. The reverse is true as well: If your system uses /opt, you should create a symbolic link from /usr/local to /opt.

To add to the confusion, the RedHat Linux distribution has brought the practice of installing precompiled software (RPMs) in the /usr/bin directory. If you are using RedHat, you may want to make your /usr directory larger because locally installed packages will consume that partition.

swap	This isn't a partition in which you actually keep files, but it *is* key to your system's performance. The swap partition should be allocated and swapped to instead of using swap files on your normal file system. This enables you to contain all your swap space in one area that is out of the way. A good guideline for determining how much swap space to use is to double the amount of RAM installed on your system.

The Device Entry

Most implementations of UNIX automatically create the correct device entry when you boot it with the new drive attached. After this entry has been created, you should check it for permissions. Only the root user should be given read/write access to it. If you run your backups as a nonroot user, you may need to give group read access to the backup group. Be sure that no one else is in the backup group. Allowing the world read/write access to the disk is the easiest way to have your system hacked, destroyed, or both.

Device Entries Under Linux

IDE disks under Linux use the following scheme to name the hard disks:

/dev/hd[drive][partition]

Each IDE drive is lettered starting from a. So the primary disk on the first chain is a; the slave on the first chain is b; the primary on the secondary chain is c; and so on. Each disk's partition is referenced by number. For example, the third partition of the slave drive on the first chain is /dev/hdb3.

SCSI disks use the same scheme except that, instead of using /dev/hd as the prefix, it uses /dev/sd. To refer to the second partition of the first disk on the SCSI chain, you use /dev/sda2.

To refer to the entire disk, specify all the information except the partition. For example, to refer to the entire primary disk on the first IDE chain, you use /dev/hda.

Device Entries Under IRIX

SCSI disks under IRIX are referenced in either the /dev/dsk or /dev/rdsk directory. Following is the format:

```
/dev/[r]dsk/dksCdSP
```

In this syntax, C is the controller number, S is the SCSI address, and P is the partition (s0,s1,s2, and so on). The partition name can also be vh for the volume header or vol to refer to the entire disk.

Device Entries Under Solaris

The SCSI disks under Solaris are referenced in either the /dev/dsk or /dev/rdsk directory. Following is the format:

```
/dev/[r]dsk/cCtSd0sP
```

In this syntax, C is the controller number, S is the SCSI address, and P is the partition number. Partition 2 always refers to the entire disk and label information. Partition 1 is typically used for swap.

Device Entries under SunOS

Disks under SunOS are referenced in the /dev directory. Following is the format:

```
/dev/sdTP
```

In this syntax, T is the target number, and P is the partition. Typically, the root partition is a, the swap partition is b, and the entire disk is referred to as partition c. You can have partitions from a through f.

An important aspect to note is an oddity with the SCSI target and unit numbering: Devices that are target 3 must be called target 0, and devices that are target 0 must be called target 3.

24

A NOTE ABOUT FORMATTING DISKS

"Back in the old days," disks had to be formatted and checked for bad blocks. The formatting procedure entailed writing the head, track, and sector numbers in a sector preamble and writing a checksum in the postamble to every sector on the disk. At the same time, any sectors that were unusable because of flaws in the disk surface were marked and, depending on the type of disk, an alternative sector was mapped into its place.

Thankfully, we have moved on.

continues

Both SCSI and IDE disks now come preformatted from the factory. Even better, they transparently handle bad blocks on the disk and remap them without any assistance from the operating system.

CAUTION

You should *never* attempt to low-level format an IDE disk. Doing so will make your day very bad as you watch the drive quietly kill itself. Be prepared to throw the disk away should you feel the need to low-level format it.

Partitioning Disks and Creating File Systems

The following sections explain the step-by-step procedure for partitioning disks under Linux, IRIX, SunOS, and Solaris. Because the principles are similar across all platforms, the discussion for each platform also covers another method of determining how a disk should be partitioned based on its intended usage.

Linux

To demonstrate how partitions are created under Linux, we will set up a disk with a single-user workstation in mind. This disk needs not only space for system software, but for application software and the user's home directories.

NOTE

Some Linux distributions such as RedHat (see http://www.redhat.com) now offer their own partitioning software (RedHat offers cabaret). Because fdisk is common across the board for all distributions, we will cover that. Furthermore, because you may not have the nicer partition manager during a system recovery, using the simpler tools is often necessary if you are to effectively take control of a crashed system.

Creating Partitions

For this example, we'll create the partitions on a 1.6GB IDE disk located on /dev/hda. This disk will become the boot device for a single-user workstation. We will create the boot, /usr, /var, /tmp, /home, and swap partitions.

During the actual partitioning, we don't name the partitions. Where the partitions are mounted is specified with the /etc/fstab file. Should we choose to mount them in different locations later on, we can easily do so. However, by keeping the function of each partition in mind, we have a better idea of how to size them.

A key thing to remember with the Linux fdisk command is that it does not commit any changes made to the partition table to disk until you explicitly do so with the w command.

With the drive installed, we begin by running the fdisk command:

```
# fdisk /dev/hda
```

This command brings us to the fdisk command prompt. We start by using the p command to print the partitions that are currently on the disk:

```
Command (m for help): p

Disk /dev/hda: 64 heads, 63 sectors, 786 cylinders
Units = cylinders of 4032 * 512 bytes

Device Boot  Begin   Start     End  Blocks   Id  System

Command (m for help):
```

We see that there are no partitions on the disk. With 1.6GB of space, we can be very liberal when allocating space to each partition. So let's begin creating our partitions with the n command:

```
Command (m for help): n
   e   extended
   p   primary partition (1-4)
p
Partition number (1-4): 1
First cylinder (1-786): 1
Last cylinder or +size or +sizeM or +sizeK ([1]-786): +50M
Command (m for help):
```

The 50MB partition we just created becomes our root partition. Because it is the first partition, it is referred to as /dev/hda1. Using the p command, we can see our new partition:

```
Command (m for help): p

Disk /dev/hda: 64 heads, 63 sectors, 786 cylinders
Units = cylinders of 4032 * 512 bytes

    Device Boot  Begin   Start     End  Blocks   Id  System
/dev/hda1             1       1      26  52384+  83  Linux native

Command (m for help):
```

24

FILE SYSTEM AND DISK ADMINISTRATION

With the root partition out of the way, we will create the swap partition. Our sample machine has 32MB of RAM and will be running X Window along with a host of development tools. It is unlikely that the machine will get a memory upgrade for a while, so we'll allocate 64MB to swap.

```
Command (m for help): n
Command action
    e   extended
    p   primary partition (1-4)
p
Partition number (1-4): 2
First cylinder (27-786): 27
Last cylinder or +size or +sizeM or +sizeK ([27]-786): +64M

Command (m for help):
```

Because this partition is going to be tagged as swap, we must change its file system type to swap using the t command:

```
Command (m for help): t
Partition number (1-4): 2
Hex code (type L to list codes): 82
Changed system type of partition 2 to 82 (Linux swap)

Command (m for help):
```

Because of the nature of the user, we know that there will be a lot of local software installed on this machine. With that in mind, we'll create /usr with 500MB of space:

```
Command (m for help): n
Command action
    e   extended
    p   primary partition (1-4)
p
Partition number (1-4): 3
First cylinder (60-786): 60
Last cylinder or +size or +sizeM or +sizeK ([60]-786): +500M
```

If you've been keeping your eyes open, you've noticed that we can have only one more primary partition—but we want to have /home, /var, and /tmp in separate partitions. How do we do this? By using extended partitions.

We'll create the remainder of the disk as an extended partition. Within this partition, we can create more partitions for use. Let's create this extended partition:

```
Command (m for help): n
Command action
    e   extended
    p   primary partition (1-4)
e
```

```
Partition number (1-4): 4
First cylinder (314-786): 314
Last cylinder or +size or +sizeM or +sizeK ([314]-786): 786

Command (m for help):
```

We can now create /home inside the extended partition. Our user is going to need a lot of space, so we'll create a 500MB partition. Notice that we are no longer asked whether we want a primary or extended partition:

```
Command (m for help): n
First cylinder (314-786): 314
Last cylinder or +size or +sizeM or +sizeK ([314]-786): +500M

Command (m for help):
```

Using the same pattern, we create a 250MB /tmp and a 180MB /var partition:

```
Command (m for help): n
First cylinder (568-786): 568
Last cylinder or +size or +sizeM or +sizeK ([568]-786): +250M

Command (m for help): n
First cylinder (695-786): 695
Last cylinder or +size or +sizeM or +sizeK ([695]-786): 786

Command (m for help):
```

Notice that, for last partition we created, we did not specify a size. Instead, we specified the last track. This approach ensures that all of the disk is used.

Using the p command, we can look at our final work:

```
Command (m for help): p

Disk /dev/hda: 64 heads, 63 sectors, 786 cylinders
Units = cylinders of 4032 * 512 bytes

   Device Boot   Begin    Start    End   Blocks    Id  System
/dev/hda1            1        1     26   52384+    83  Linux native
/dev/hda2           27       27     59   66528     82  Linux swap
/dev/hda3           60       60    313   512064    83  Linux native
/dev/hda4          314      314    786   953568     5  Extended
/dev/hda5          314      314    567   512032+   83  Linux native
/dev/hda6          568      568    694   256000+   83  Linux native
/dev/hda7          695      695    786   185440+   83  Linux native

Command (m for help):
```

24

**FILE SYSTEM
AND DISK
ADMINISTRATION**

Everything looks good. To commit this configuration to disk, we use the w command:

```
Command (m for help): w
The partition table has been altered!

Calling ioctl() to re-read partition table.
(Reboot to ensure the partition table has been updated.)
Syncing disks.
```

Reboot the machine to ensure that the partition has been updated. Now you're done creating the partitions.

Creating File Systems in Linux

Creating a partition alone isn't very useful. To make it useful, we have to create a file system on top of the partition. Under Linux, we do this using the mke2fs and the mkswap commands.

To create the file system on the root partition, we use the following command:

```
mke2fs /dev/hda1
```

The program takes only a few seconds to run and generates output similar to this:

```
mke2fs 0.5b, 14-Feb-95 for EXT2 FS 0.5a, 95/03/19
128016 inodes, 512032 blocks
25601 blocks (5.00%) reserved for the super user
First data block=1
Block size=1024 (log=0)
Fragment size=1024 (log=0)
63 block groups
8192 blocks per group, 8192 fragments per group
2032 inodes per group
Superblock backups stored on blocks:
        8193,16385,24577,32769,40961,49153,57345,65537,73729,
        81921,90113,98305,106497,114689,122881,131073,139265,147457,
        155649,163841,172033,180225,188417,196609,204801,212993,221185,
        229377,237569,245761,253953,262145,270337,278529,286721,294913,
        303105,311297,319489,327681,335873,344065,352257,360449,368641,
        376833,385025,393217,401409,409601,417793,425985,434177,442369,
        450561,458753,466945,475137,483329,491521,499713,507905

    Writing inode tables: done
Writing superblocks and file system accounting information: done
```

Make a note of these superblock backups and keep them in a safe place. Should the day arise that you need to use fsck to fix a superblock gone bad, you will want to know where the backups are.

Simply do this for all of the partitions except for the swap partition.

To create the swap file system, you use the `mkswap` command, like this:

```
mkswap /dev/hda2
```

Replace `/dev/hda2` with the partition you chose to make your swap space. The result of the command will be similar to this:

```
Setting up swapspace, size = 35090432 bytes
```

The swap space is now ready.

To make the root file system bootable, you must install the `lilo` boot manager. This is part of all standard Linux distributions, so you shouldn't have to hunt for it on the Internet.

Simply modify the `/etc/lilo.conf` file so that `/dev/hda1` is set to be the boot disk and run this command:

```
lilo
```

The resulting output should look something like this:

```
Added linux *
```

In this message, `linux` is the name of the kernel to boot, as specified by the `name=` field in `/etc/lilo.conf`.

SunOS

In this example, we will prepare a Seagate ST32550N as an auxiliary disk for an existing system. The disk will be divided into three partitions: one for use as a mail spool, one for use as a `/usr/local`, and the third as an additional `swap` partition.

Creating the Partitions

> **CAUTION**
>
> The procedure for formatting disks is not the same for SunOS and Solaris. Read each section to note the differences.

After a disk has been attached to a machine, you should verify its connection and SCSI address by running the `probe-scsi` command from the PROM monitor (if the disk is attached to the internal chain) or by running the `probe-scsi-all` command to see all the SCSI devices on the system. When you are sure that the drive is properly attached and verified as functional, you're ready to start accessing the drive from the OS.

After the machine has booted, run the dmesg command to collect the system diagnostic messages. You may want to pipe the output to grep so that you can easily find the information on disks.

```
dmesg | grep sd
```

On our system, this command generated the following output:

```
sd0: <SUN0207 cyl 1254 alt 2 hd 9 sec 36>
sd1 at esp0 target 1 lun 0
sd1:    corrupt label - wrong magic number
sd1: Vendor 'SEAGATE', product 'ST32550N', 4194058 512 byte blocks
root on sd0a fstype 4.2
swap on sd0b fstype spec size 32724K
dump on sd0b fstype spec size 32712K
```

This result tells us that we have an installed disk on sd0 that the system is aware of and using. The information from the sd1 device is telling us that it found a disk, but that disk isn't usable because of a corrupt label. Don't worry about the error. Until we partition the disk and create file systems on it, the system doesn't know what to do with it—hence the error.

If you are using SCSI address 0 or 3, remember the oddity mentioned earlier: device 0 must be referenced as device 3, and device 3 must be referenced as device 0.

Even though we do not have to actually format the disk, we do need to use the format program that come with SunOS because that program also creates the partitions and writes the label to the disk.

To invoke the format program, simply run this command:

```
format sd1
```

In this syntax, sd1 is the name of the disk we are going to partition.

The format program displays the following menu:

```
FORMAT MENU:
        disk       - select a disk
        type       - select (define) a disk type
        partition  - select (define) a partition table
        current    - describe the current disk
        format     - format and analyze the disk
        repair     - repair a defective sector
        show       - translate a disk address
        label      - write label to the disk
        analyze    - surface analysis
        defect     - defect list management
        backup     - search for backup labels
        quit
format>
```

We enter **type** at the `format>` prompt so that we can tell SunOS the kind of disk we have. The resulting menu looks something like this:

```
AVAILABLE DRIVE TYPES:
        0. Quantum ProDrive 80S
        1. Quantum ProDrive 105S
        2. CDC Wren IV 94171-344
        3. SUN0104
    ...
       13. other
Specify disk type (enter its number):
```

Because we are adding a disk this machine has not seen before, we have to select option 13, other. This begins a series of prompts requesting the disk's geometry. Be sure to have this information from the manufacturer before starting this procedure.

The first question, `Enter number of data cylinders:`, is actually a three-part question. After you enter the number of data cylinders, the program asks for the number of alternative cylinders and then the number of physical cylinders. The number of physical cylinders is the number your manufacturer provided you. Subtract 2 from that to get the number of data cylinders, and then just use the default value of 2 for the number of alternate cylinders. For our Seagate disk, we answered the questions as follows:

```
Enter number of data cylinders: 3508
        Enter number of alternate cylinders [2]: 2
        Enter number of physical cylinders [3510]: 3510
        Enter number of heads: 11
        Enter number of data sectors/track: 108
        Enter rpm of drive [3600]:
        Enter disk type name (remember quotes): "SEAGATE ST32550N"
        selecting sd1: <SEAGATE ST32550N>
        [disk formatted, no defect list found]
        No defined partition tables.
```

Note that even though our sample drive actually rotates at 7200 rpm, we stick with the default of 3600 rpm because the software will not accept entering a higher speed. Thankfully, this doesn't matter because the operating system doesn't use the information.

Even though `format` reported that the disk was formatted, it really wasn't. It only acquired the information it needed to later write the label.

Now we are ready to begin preparations to partition the disk. These preparations entail computing the amount each cylinder holds and then approximating the number of cylinders we want in each partition.

With our sample disk, we know that each cylinder is composed of 108 sectors on a track, with 11 tracks composing the cylinder.

From the information we saw in dmesg, we know that each block is 512 bytes long. Hence, if we want our mail partition to be 1GB in size, we perform the following math to compute the necessary blocks:

```
1 gigabyte = 1048576 kilobytes
    One cylinder = 108 sectors * 11 heads = 1188 blocks
    1188 blocks = 594 kilobytes
    1048576 / 594 = 1765 cylinders
    1765 * 1188 = 2096820 blocks
```

Obviously, there are some rounding errors since the exact 1GB mark occurs in the middle of a cylinder and we have to keep each partition on a cylinder boundary. 1,765 cylinders is more than close enough. The 1,765 cylinders translates to 2,096,820 blocks.

The new swap partition we want to make should be 64MB in size. Using the same math as before, we find that our swap must be 130,680 blocks long. The last partition on the disk has to fill the remainder of the disk. Knowing that we have a 2GB disk, a 1GB mail spool, and a 64MB swap partition, this leaves us with about 960MB for /usr/local.

Armed with this information, we are ready to tackle the partitioning. From the format> prompt, type **partition** to start the partitioning menu. The resulting screen looks something like this:

```
format> partition

PARTITION MENU:
        a      - change `a' partition
        b      - change `b' partition
        c      - change `c' partition
        d      - change `d' partition
        e      - change `e' partition
        f      - change `f' partition
        g      - change `g' partition
        h      - change `h' partition
        select - select a predefined table
        name   - name the current table
        print  - display the current table
        label  - write partition map and label to the disk
        quit
partition>
```

To create our mail partition, we begin by changing partition a. At the partition> prompt, type **a**:

```
partition> a
```

This displays a prompt for entering the starting cylinder and the number of blocks to allocate. Because this is going to be the first partition on the disk, we start at cylinder 0.

Based on the math we did earlier, we know that we need 2,096,820 blocks:

```
    partition a - starting cyl     0, # blocks       0 (0/0/0)
```

```
Enter new starting cyl [0]: 0
Enter new # blocks [0, 0/0/0]: 2096820
partition>
```

Now we want to create the b partition, which is traditionally used for swap space. We know how many blocks to use based on our calculations, but we don't know which cylinder to start from.

To solve this dilemma, we simply display the current partition information for the entire disk using the p command:

```
partition> p
Current partition table (unnamed):
        partition a - starting cyl     0, # blocks   2096820 (1765/0/0)
        partition b - starting cyl     0, # blocks         0 (0/0/0)
        partition c - starting cyl     0, # blocks         0 (0/0/0)
        partition d - starting cyl     0, # blocks         0 (0/0/0)
        partition e - starting cyl     0, # blocks         0 (0/0/0)
        partition f - starting cyl     0, # blocks         0 (0/0/0)
        partition g - starting cyl     0, # blocks         0 (0/0/0)
        partition h - starting cyl     0, # blocks         0 (0/0/0)
partition>
```

We can see that partition a is allocated with 2,096,820 blocks and is 1,765 cylinders long. Because we don't want to waste space on the disk, we start the swap partition on cylinder 1765. (Remember to count from zero!)

```
partition> b
```

```
    partition b - starting cyl     0, # blocks       0 (0/0/0)
```

```
Enter new starting cyl [0]: 1765
Enter new # blocks [0, 0/0/0]: 130680
partition>
```

Before we create our last partition, we should address some tradition first, namely partition c. This is usually the partition that spans the entire disk. Before creating this partition, we need to do a little math:

```
108 cylinders × 11 heads × 3508 data cylinders = 4167504 blocks
```

Notice that the number of blocks we compute here does not match the number actually on the disk. This number was computed based on the information we entered when giving the disk type information.

24

FILE SYSTEM AND DISK ADMINISTRATION

It is important that we remain consistent.

Because the c partition spans the entire disk, we specify the starting cylinder as 0. The process of creating this partition should look something like this:

```
partition> c

        partition c - starting cyl      0, # blocks       0 (0/0/0)

Enter new starting cyl [0]: 0
Enter new # blocks [0, 0/0/0]: 4167504
partition>
```

We have only one partition left to create: /usr/local. Because we want to fill the remainder of the disk, we have to do one last bit of math to compute how many blocks are still free.

We take the size of partition c (the total disk) and subtract the sizes of the existing partitions. For our example, this works out like this:

```
4167504 - 2096820 - 130680 = 1940004 remaining blocks
```

Now we have to find out the cylinder from which to start. To do so, we run the p command again:

```
partition> p
Current partition table (unnamed):
        partition a - starting cyl      0, # blocks 2096820 (1765/0/0)
        partition b - starting cyl   1765, # blocks  130680 (110/0/0)
        partition c - starting cyl      0, # blocks 4167504 (3508/0/0)
        partition d - starting cyl      0, # blocks       0 (0/0/0)
        partition e - starting cyl      0, # blocks       0 (0/0/0)
        partition f - starting cyl      0, # blocks       0 (0/0/0)
        partition g - starting cyl      0, # blocks       0 (0/0/0)
        partition h - starting cyl      0, # blocks       0 (0/0/0)

partition>
```

To figure out which cylinder to start from, we add the number of cylinders used so far. Remember that we don't add the cylinders from partition c because it encompasses the entire disk:

```
1765 + 110 = 1875
```

Now that we know which cylinder to start from and how many blocks to make it, we create our last partition:

```
partition> d

        partition d - starting cyl      0, # blocks        0 (0/0/0)

Enter new starting cyl [0]: 1875
Enter new # blocks [0, 0/0/0]: 1940004
partition>
```

Congratulations! You've made it through the ugly part. Before we can truly claim victory, however, we must commit these changes to disk using the label command. When you see the prompt, Ready to label disk, continue? simply answer y.

```
partition> label
Ready to label disk, continue? y

partition>
```

To leave the format program, type **quit** at the partition> prompt; type **quit** again at the format> prompt.

Creating File Systems

Now comes the easy part. Simply run the newfs command on all the partitions we created except for the swap partition (partition b) and the entire disk partition (partition c). Your output should look similar to this:

```
# newfs sd1a
/dev/rsd1a:     2096820 sectors in 1765 cylinders of 11 tracks, 108
sectors
        1073.6MB in 111 cyl groups (16 c/g, 9.73MB/g, 4480 i/g)
superblock backups (for fsck -b #) at:
 32, 19152, 38272, 57392, 76512, 95632, 114752, 133872, 152992,
 172112, 191232, 210352, 229472, 248592, 267712, 286832, 304160, 323280,
 342400, 361520, 380640, 399760, 418880, 438000, 457120, 476240, 495360,
 514480, 533600, 552720, 571840, 590960, 608288, 627408, 646528, 665648,
 684768, 703888, 723008, 742128, 761248, 780368, 799488, 818608, 837728,
 856848, 875968, 895088, 912416, 931536, 950656, 969776, 988896, 1008016,
 1027136, 1046256, 1065376, 1084496, 1103616, 1122736, 1141856, 1160976,
1180096,
 1199216, 1216544, 1235664, 1254784, 1273904, 1293024, 1312144, 1331264,
1350384,
 1369504, 1388624, 1407744, 1426864, 1445984, 1465104, 1484224, 1503344,
1520672,
 1539792, 1558912, 1578032, 1597152, 1616272, 1635392, 1654512, 1673632,
1692752,
 1711872, 1730992, 1750112, 1769232, 1788352, 1807472, 1824800, 1843920,
1863040,
 1882160, 1901280, 1920400, 1939520, 1958640, 1977760, 1996880, 2016000,
2035120,
 2054240, 2073360, 2092480,
```

Be sure to note the superblock backups. This is critical information when `fsck` discovers heavy corruption in your file system. Remember to add your new entries into `/etc/fstab` if you want them to automatically mount on boot.

If you created the first partition with the intention of making it bootable, you have a few more steps to go. First, mount the new file system to `/mnt`:

```
# mount /dev/sd1a /mnt
```

After the file system is mounted, you have to clone your existing boot partition using the `dump` command, like this:

```
# cd /mnt
# dump 0f - / ¦ restore -rf -
```

With the root partition cloned, use the `installboot` command to make it bootable:

```
# /usr/kvm/mdec/installboot /mnt/boot /usr/kvm/mdec/bootsd /dev/rsd1a
```

Be sure to test your work by rebooting and making sure that everything mounts correctly. If you created a bootable partition, be sure that you can boot from it now. Don't wait for a disaster to find out whether or not you did it right.

Solaris

For this example, we will partition a disk that is destined to be a web server for an intranet. We need a minimal root partition, adequate `swap`, `tmp`, `var`, and `usr` space, and a really large partition that we'll call `/web`. Because the web logs will remain on the `/web` partition, and there will be little or no user activity on the machine, `/var` and `/tmp` will be set to smaller values. `/usr` will be a little larger because it may be eventually house web development tools.

Creating Partitions

> **TIP**
>
> In another wondrous effort to be just a little different, Sun has decided to call partitions *slices*. With the number of documents regarding the file system so vast, you'll find that not all of them have been updated to use this new term, so don't be confused by the mix of *slices* and *partitions*—both terms mean the same thing.

After the disk has been attached to the machine, you should verify its connection and SCSI address by running the `probe-scsi` command from the PROM monitor (if the disk is attached to the internal SCSI chain) or with `probe-scsi-all` (to list all the SCSI devices on the system). When this command shows that the drive is properly attached and functional, you're ready to start accessing the drive from the OS. Boot the machine and log in as `root`.

To find the device name we are going to use for this partition, we again use the `dmesg` command:

```
# dmesg ¦ grep sd
    ...
    sd1 at esp0: target 1 lun 0
    sd1 is /sbus@1,f8000000/esp@0,800000/sd@1,0
    WARNING: /sbus@1,f8000000/esp@0,800000/sd@1,0 (sd1):
      corrupt label - wrong magic number
      Vendor 'SEAGATE', product 'ST32550N', 4194058 512 byte blocks
    ...
```

From this message, we see that our new disk is device `/dev/[r]dsk/c0t1d0s2`. The disk hasn't been set up for use on a Solaris machine before, which is why we received the corrupt label error.

If you recall the layout of Solaris device names, you'll remember that the last digit of the device name is the partition number. Noting that, we see that Solaris refers to the entire disk in partition 2, in much the same way that SunOS refers to the entire disk as partition c.

Before we can actually label and partition the disk, we have to create the device files. We do this with the `drvconfig` and `disks` commands. They should be invoked with no parameters:

```
# drvconfig ; disks
```

Now that the kernel is aware of the disk, we are ready to run the `format` command to partition the disk:

```
# format /dev/rdsk/c0t1d0s2
```

This command displays the format menu as follows:

```
FORMAT MENU:
        disk        - select a disk
        type        - select (define) a disk type
        partition   - select (define) a partition table
        current     - describe the current disk
        format      - format and analyze the disk
        repair      - repair a defective sector
```

```
          label     - write label to the disk
          analyze   - surface analysis
          defect    - defect list management
          backup    - search for backup labels
          verify    - read and display labels
          save      - save new disk/partition definitions
          inquiry   - show vendor, product and revision
          volname   - set 8-character volume name
          quit
format>
```

To help the `format` command with partitioning, we have to tell it the disk's geometry by invoking the `type` command at the `format>` prompt. We are then asked to select the kind of disk we have. Because this is the first time this system is seeing this disk, we select `other`. This dialog should look something like this:

```
format> type

AVAILABLE DRIVE TYPES:
        0. Auto configure
        1. Quantum ProDrive 80S
        2. Quantum ProDrive 105S
        3. CDC Wren IV 94171-344
        . . .
       16. other
Specify disk type (enter its number): 16
```

The system now prompts us for the number of data cylinders. This value is 2 less than the number of cylinders the vendor specifies because Solaris needs two cylinders for bad-block mapping:

```
Enter number of data cylinders: 3508
Enter number of alternate cylinders[2]: 2
Enter number of physical cylinders[3510]: 3510
```

The next question can be answered from the vendor specs as well:

```
Enter number of heads: 14
```

The follow-up question about the number of drive heads can be left as the default:

```
Enter physical number of heads[default]:
```

The last question you have to answer can be pulled from the vendor specs as well:

```
Enter number of data sectors/track: 72
```

Leave the remaining questions at their default values:

```
Enter number of physical sectors/track[default]:
Enter rpm of drive[3600]:
```

```
Enter format time[default]:
Enter cylinder skew[default]:
Enter track skew[default]:
Enter tracks per zone[default]:
Enter alternate tracks[default]:
Enter alternate sectors[default]:
Enter cache control[default]:
Enter prefetch threshold[default]:
Enter minimum prefetch[default]:
Enter maximum prefetch[default]:
```

The last question you have to answer about the disk is its label information. Enter the vendor name and model number in double quotation marks. For our sample disk, this information looks like this:

```
Enter disk type name (remember quotes): "SEAGATE ST32550N"
```

With this information, Solaris makes creating partitions easy. (Dare I say *fun?*)

After the last question from the `type` command, you return to the `format>` prompt. Enter **partition** to display the partition menu:

```
format> partition

PARTITION MENU:
        0      - change '0' partition
        1      - change '1' partition
        2      - change '2' partition
        3      - change '3' partition
        4      - change '4' partition
        5      - change '5' partition
        6      - change '6' partition
        7      - change '7' partition
        select - select a predefined table
        modify - modify a predefined partition table
        name   - name the current table
        print  - display the current table
        label  - write partition map and label to the disk
        quit
partition>
```

At the `partition>` prompt, enter **modify** to begin creating the new partitions. This command displays a question about what template you want to use for partitioning. We want the `All Free Hog` method.

```
partition> modify
Select partitioning base:
    0. Current partition table (unnamed)
    1. All Free Hog
Choose base (enter number)[0]? 1
```

The `All Free Hog` method enables you to select one partition to receive the remainder of the disk after you have allocated a specific amount of space for the other partitions. For our example, the disk hog is the /web partition because we want it to be as large as possible.

As soon as you select option 1, you should see the following screen:

```
Part    Tag         Flag    Cylinders    Size      Blocks
0       root        wm      0            0        (0/0/0)
1       swap        wu      0            0        (0/0/0)
2       backup      wu      0 - 3507     1.99GB     (3508/0/0)
3       unassigned  wm      0            0        (0/0/0)
4       unassigned  wm      0            0        (0/0/0)
5       unassigned  wm      0            0        (0/0/0)
6       usr         wm      0            0        (0/0/0)
7       unassigned  wm      0            0        (0/0/0)
Do you wish to continue creating a new partition
table based on above table [yes]? yes
```

Because this partition table appears reasonable, agree to use it as a base for your scheme. You are then asked which partition should be the `Free Hog Partition`, the one that receives whatever is left of the disk when everything else has been allocated. For our scheme, we'll make that partition number 5:

```
Free Hog Partition[6]? 5
```

Answering this question starts a list of questions that ask how large to make the other partitions. For our web server, we need a root partition to be about 200MB for the system software, a /swap partition to be 64MB, a /tmp partition to be 200MB, a /var partition to be 200MB, and a /usr partition to be 400MB. Keeping in mind that partition 2 has already been tagged as the "entire disk" and that partition 5 will receive the remainder of the disk, you are prompted as follows:

```
Enter size of partition '0' [0b, 0c, 0.00mb]: 200mb
Enter size of partition '1' [0b, 0c, 0.00mb]: 64mb
Enter size of partition '3' [0b, 0c, 0.00mb]: 200mb
Enter size of partition '4' [0b, 0c, 0.00mb]: 200mb
Enter size of partition '6' [0b, 0c, 0.00mb]: 400mb
Enter size of partition '7' [0b, 0c, 0.00mb]: 0
```

As soon as you finish answering these questions, the final view of all the partitions appears, looking something like this:

```
Part    Tag         Flag    Cylinders      Size        Blocks
0       root        wm      0 - 344        200.13mb    (345/0/0)
1       swap        wu      345 - 455      64.39mb     (111/0/0)
2       backup      wu      0 - 3507       1.99GB      (3508/0/0)
3       unassigned  wm      456 - 800      200.13mb    (345/0/0)
4       unassigned  wm      801 - 1145     200.13mb    (345/0/0)
```

```
5     unassigned    wm    1146 - 2817    969.89mb    (1672/0/0)
6     unassigned    wm    2818 - 3507    400.25mb    (690/0/0)
7     unassigned    wm       0              0        (0/0/0)
```

This display is followed by this question:

```
Okay to make this the correct partition table [yes]? yes
```

We answer **yes** because the table appears reasonable. This answer displays the following question:

```
Enter table name (remember quotes): "SEAGATE ST32550N"
```

We answer with a description of the disk we are using for this example. Remember to include the quotation marks when answering. Given all this information, the system is ready to commit this to disk. As one last check, you are asked:

```
Ready to label disk, continue? y
```

As you can imagine, we answer *yes* to the question and let it commit the changes to disk. You have now created partitions and can quit the program by entering **quit** at the `partition>` prompt and again at the `format>` prompt.

Creating File Systems

To create a file system, simply run this command:

```
# newfs /dev/c0t1d0s0
```

In this syntax, `/dev/c0t1d0s0` is the partition on which to create the file system. Be sure to create a file system on all the partitions except for partitions 2 and 3—the `swap` and the entire disk, respectively. Be sure to note the backup superblocks that were created. This information is very useful when `fsck` is attempting to repair a heavily damaged file system.

After you create the file systems, be sure that you enter them into the `/etc/vfstab` file so that they are mounted the next time you reboot.

If you have to make the root partition bootable, you have two more steps to complete. The first is to clone the root partition from your existing system to the new root partition using these commands:

```
# mount /dev/dsk/c0t1d0s0 /mnt
# ufsdump 0uf - / ¦ ufsrestore -rf -
```

After the file root partition is cloned, you can run the `installboot` program like this:

```
# /usr/sbin/installboot /usr/lib/fs/ufs/bootblk /dev/rdsk/c0t1d0s0
```

Be sure to test your new file systems before you need to rely on them in a disaster situation.

IRIX

For this example, we will create a large scratch partition for a user who does modeling and simulations. Although IRIX has many GUI-based tools to perform these tasks, it is always a good idea to learn the command-line versions in case you need to do any kind of remote administration.

Creating Partitions

After the drive is attached, run a program called `hinv` to take a "hardware inventory." On the sample system, you see the following output:

```
...
Integral SCSI controller 1: Version WD33C93B, revision D
  Disk drive: unit 6 on SCSI controller 1
Integral SCSI controller 0: Version WD33C93B, revision D
  Disk drive: unit 1 on SCSI controller 0
...
```

Our new disk is external to the system, so we know it resides on controller 1. Unit 6 is the only disk on that chain, so we know that it is the disk we just added to the system.

To partition the disk, run the `fx` command without any parameters. It prompts us for the device name, controller, and drive number. Choose the default device name and enter the appropriate information for the other two questions.

On our sample system, this dialog looks like this:

```
# fx
fx version 6.2, Mar  9, 1996
fx: "device-name" = (dksc)
fx: ctlr# = (0) 1
fx: drive# = (1) 6
fx: lun# = (0)
...opening dksc(1,6,0)
...controller test...OK
Scsi drive type == SEAGATE ST32550N        0022

----- please choose one (? for help, .. to quit this menu)-----
[exi]t              [d]ebug/             [l]abel/
[b]adblock/         [exe]rcise/          [r]epartition/
fx>
```

We see that `fx` found our Seagate drive and is ready to work with it. From the menu, we select **r** to repartition the disk. `fx` displays what it knows about the disk and then presents another menu specifically for partitioning the disk:

```
fx> r
----- partitions-----
part  type        cyls          blocks        Megabytes  (base+size)
```

```
 7: xfs       3 + 3521      3570 + 4189990      2 + 2046
 8: volhdr    0 + 3            0 + 3570          0 + 2
10: volume    0 + 3524         0 + 4193560       0 + 2048

capacity is 4194058 blocks

----- please choose one (? for help, .. to quit this menu)-----
[ro]otdrive        [u]srrootdrive      [o]ptiondrive       [re]size
fx/repartition>
```

Looking at the result, we see that this disk has never been partitioned in IRIX before. Part 7 represents the amount of partitionable space, part 8 represents the volume header, and part 10 represents the entire disk.

Because this disk is going to be used as a large scratch partition, we select the option-drive option from the menu. After you select that option, you are asked what kind of file system you want to use. IRIX version 6 and later defaults to xfs, while IRIX version 5 defaults to efs. Use the one appropriate for your version of IRIX.

Our sample system is running IRIX 6.2, so we accept the default of xfs:

```
fx/repartition> o

fx/repartition/optiondrive: type of data partition = (xfs)
```

Next, we are asked whether we want to create a /usr log partition. Because our primary system already has a /usr partition, we don't need one here. Type **no**:

```
fx/repartition/optiondrive: create usr log partition? = (yes) no
```

The system is ready to partition the drive. Before it does, it gives one last warning, allowing you to stop the partitioning before it completes the job. Because you know you are partitioning the correct disk, you can give it the go-ahead:

```
Warning: you must reinstall all software and restore user data
from backups after changing the partition layout. Changing partitions
causes all data on the drive to be lost. Be sure you have the drive
backed up if it contains any user data.
Continue? y
```

The system takes a few seconds to create the new partitions on the disk. When it is done, it reports what the current partition list looks like:

```
----- partitions-----
part  type      cyls          blocks          Megabytes   (base+size)
 7: xfs       3 + 3521      3570 + 4189990      2 + 2046
 8: volhdr    0 + 3            0 + 3570          0 + 2
10: volume    0 + 3524         0 + 4193560       0 + 2048

capacity is 4194058 blocks
```

24

**FILE SYSTEM
AND DISK
ADMINISTRATION**

```
----- please choose one (? for help, .. to quit this menu)-----
[ro]otdrive        [u]srrootdrive     [o]ptiondrive      [re]size
fx/repartition>
```

Looks good. We can exit fx now by typing .. at the fx/repartition> prompt and **exit** at the fx> prompt.

Our one large scratch partition is now called /dev/dsk/dks1d6s7.

Creating the File System

To create the file system, we use the mkfs command, like this:

```
# mkfs /dev/rdsk/dks1d6s7
```

This command generates the following output:

```
meta-data=/dev/dsk/dks1d6s7    isize=256    agcount=8, agsize=65469 blks
data     =                     bsize=4096   blocks=523748, imaxpct=25
log      =internal log         bsize=4096   blocks=1000
realtime =none                 bsize=65536  blocks=0, rtextents=0
```

Remember to add this entry into the /etc/fstab file so that the system automatically mounts the next time you reboot.

Summary

As you've seen in this chapter, creating, maintaining, and repairing file systems is not a trivial task. It is, however, a task you should understand thoroughly. An unmaintained file system can quickly lead to trouble; without its stability, the remainder of the system is useless.

Here's a quick rundown of the topics covered in this chapter:

- Disks are divided into partitions (sometimes called slices).
- Each partition has a file system.
- A file system is the primary means of file storage in UNIX.
- File systems are made of inodes and superblocks.
- Some partitions are used for raw data (such as the swap partition).
- The /proc file system really isn't a file system; it is an abstraction to kernel data.
- An inode maintains critical file information.
- Superblocks track disk information as well as the location of the heads of various inode lists.

- Before you can use a file system, it must first be mounted.
- No one must be accessing a file system if it is to be unmounted.
- File systems can be mounted anywhere in the directory tree.
- /etc/fstab (vfstab in Solaris) is used by the system to automatically mount file systems on boot.
- The root file system should be kept away from users.
- The root file system should never fill up.
- Be sure to watch how much space is being used.
- fsck is the tool to use to repair file systems.
- Don't forget to terminate your SCSI chain.

In short, file system administration is not a trivial task and should not be taken lightly. Good maintenance techniques not only help maintain your uptime, but your sanity as well.

24

FILE SYSTEM AND DISK ADMINISTRATION

Kernel Basics and Configuration

by Dan Wilson, Bill Pierce, and Bill Wood

IN THIS CHAPTER

CHAPTER 25

You're probably asking yourself "Why would I want to know about this thing called the UNIX kernel? I can add users, run jobs, print files, perform backups and restores, and even start up and shut down the machine when it needs it. Why do I need to know about, and, more specifically, even change my system's configuration to do my job as a system administrator?" The simple answer is you don't need to know much about the UNIX kernel if you know you'll *never* have to add any hardware or change or tune your system to perform better. In all our collective years of experience as system administrators, about 26, we have rarely, if ever, experienced a situation where it was possible or desirable to operate an *Original Equipment Manufacturer* (OEM) configured UNIX system. There are just too many different uses for this type of operating system for it to remain unchanged throughout its lifetime. So, assuming that you are one of the fortunate individuals who have the title of system administrator, we'll try to provide you with some useful and general information about this all-powerful UNIX process called the kernel. After that, we'll take you through some sample configurations for the following UNIX operating systems:

- HP-UX 10.x
- Solaris 2.5.x
- System V Release 4 (SVR4)
- AIX 4.x
- Linux

What Is a Kernel?

Let's start by providing a definition for the term *kernel*. The UNIX kernel is the software that manages the user program's access to the systems hardware and software resources. These resources range from being granted CPU time, accessing memory, reading and writing to the disk drives, connecting to the network, and interacting with the terminal or GUI interface. The kernel makes this all possible by controlling and providing access to memory, processor, input/output devices, disk files, and special services to user programs.

Kernel Services

The basic UNIX kernel can be broken into four main subsystems:

- Process Management
- Memory Management

- I/O Management
- File Management

These subsystems should be viewed as separate entities that work in concert to provide services to a program that enable it to do meaningful work. These management subsystems make it possible for a user to access a database via a Web interface, print a report, or do something as complex as managing a 911 emergency system. At any moment in the system, numerous programs may request services from these subsystems. It is the kernel's responsibility to schedule work and, if the process is authorized, grant access to utilize these subsystems. In short, programs interact with the subsystems via software libraries and the system call interface. Refer to your UNIX reference manuals for descriptions of the system calls and libraries supported by your system. Because each of the subsystems is key to enabling a process to perform a useful function, we will cover the basics of each subsystem. We'll start by looking at how the UNIX kernel comes to life by way of the system initialization process.

System Initialization

System initialization (booting) is the first step toward bringing your system into an operational state. A number of machine-dependent and machine-independent steps are gone through before your system is ready to begin servicing users. At system startup, there is nothing running on the Central Processing Unit (CPU). The kernel is a complex program that must have its binary image loaded at a specific address from some type of storage device, usually a disk drive. The boot disk maintains a small restricted area called the boot sector that contains a boot program that loads and initializes the kernel. You'll find that this is a vendor-specific procedure that reflects the architectural hardware differences between the various UNIX vendor platforms. When this step is completed, the CPU must jump to a specific memory address and start executing the code at that location. After the kernel is loaded, it goes through its own hardware and software initialization.

Kernel Mode

The operating system, or kernel, runs in a privileged manner known as *kernel mode*. This mode of operation allows the kernel to run without being interfered with by other programs currently in the system. The microprocessor enforces this line of demarcation between user and kernel level mode. With the kernel operating in its own protected address space, it is guaranteed to maintain the integrity of its own data structures and that of other processes. (That's not to say that a privileged process could not inadvertently cause corruption within the kernel.) These data structures are used by the kernel to manage and control itself and any other programs that may be running in the system. If any of these data structures were allowed to be accidentally or intentionally altered, the system could quickly crash. Now that you have learned what a UNIX kernel is and how it is loaded into the system, you are ready to take a look at the four UNIX subsystems: Process Management, Memory Management, File system Management, and I/O Management.

Process Management

The Process Management subsystem controls the creation, termination, accounting, and scheduling of processes. It also oversees process state transitions and the switching between privileged and nonprivileged modes of execution. The Process Management subsystem also facilitates and manages the complex task of the creation of child processes.

A simple definition of a process is that it is an executing program. It is an entity that requires system resources, and it has a finite lifetime. It has the capability to create other processes via the system call interface. In short, it is an electronic representation of a user's or programmer's desire to accomplish some useful piece of work. A process may appear to the user as if it is the only job running in the machine. This "sleight of hand" is only an illusion. At any one time a processor is only executing a single process.

Process Structure

A process has a definite structure (see Figure 25.1). The kernel views this string of bits as the process image. This binary image consists of both a user and system address space as well as registers that store the process's data during its execution. The user address space is also known as the user image. This is the code that is written by a programmer and compiled into an .o object file. An object file is a file that contains machine language code/data and is in a format that the linker program can use to then create object libraries or an executable program.

The user address space consists of five separate areas: text, data, BSS, stack, and user area.

Text Segment

The first area of a process is its text segment. This area contains the executable program code for the process. This area is shared by other processes that execute the program. It is therefore fixed and unchangeable and is usually swapped out to disk by the system when memory gets too tight.

FIGURE 25.1.

*Diagram of
process areas.*

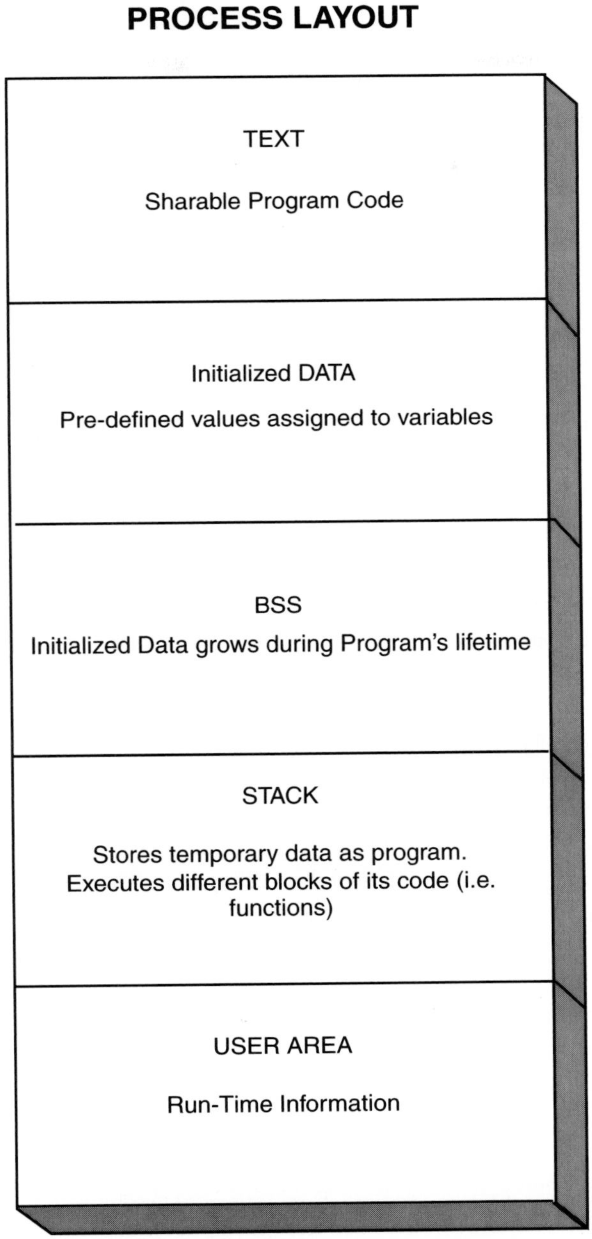

PROCESS LAYOUT

TEXT

Sharable Program Code

Initialized DATA

Pre-defined values assigned to variables

BSS

Initialized Data grows during Program's lifetime

STACK

Stores temporary data as program.
Executes different blocks of its code (i.e.
functions)

USER AREA

Run-Time Information

Data Area

The data area contains both the global and static variables used by the program. For example, a programmer may know in advance that a certain data variable needs to be set to a certain value. In the C programming language, it would look like:

```
int x = 15;
```

If you were to look at the data segment when the program was loaded, you would see that the variable *x* was an integer type with an initial value of 15.

BSS Area

The BSS area (Ancient IBM Assembly terminology—Block Started by Symbol), like the data area, holds information for the program's variables. The difference is that the BSS area maintains variables that will have their data values assigned to them during the program's execution. For example, a programmer may know that she needs variables to hold certain data that will be input by a user during the execution of the program.

```
int a,b,c;      // a,b and c are variables that hold integer values.
char *ptr;      // ptr is an uninitialized character pointer.
```

The program code can also make calls to library routines such as `malloc` to obtain a chunk of memory and assign it to a variable like the one declared previously.

Stack Area

The stack area maintains the process's local variables, parameters used in functions, and values returned by functions. For example, a program may contain code that calls another block of code (possibly written by someone else). The calling block of code passes data to the receiving block of code by way of the stack. The called block of code then processes the data and returns data back to the calling code. The stack plays an important role in allowing a process to work with temporary data.

User Area

The user area maintains data that is used by the kernel while the process is running. The user area contains the real and effective user identifiers, real and effective group identifiers, current directory, and a list of open files. Sizes of the text, data, and stack areas, as well as pointers to process data structures, are maintained. Other areas that can be considered part of the process's address space are the heap, private shared libraries data, shared libraries, and shared memory. During initial startup and execution of the program, the kernel allocates the memory and creates the necessary structures to maintain these areas.

The user area is used by the kernel to manage the process. This area maintains the majority of the accounting information for a process. It is part of the process address space and is only used by the kernel while the process is executing (see Figure 25.2). When the process is not executing, its user area may be swapped out to disk by the Memory Manager. In most versions of UNIX, the user area is mapped to a fixed virtual memory address. Under HP-UX 10.*X*, this virtual address is 0x7FFE6000. When the kernel performs a context switch (starts executing a different process) to a new process, it always map the process's physical address to this virtual address. Because the kernel already has a pointer fixed to this location in memory, it is a simple matter of referencing the current u pointer to be able to begin managing the newly switched-in process. The file `/usr/include/sys/user.h` contains the user area's structure definition for your version of UNIX.

Process Table

The process table is another important structure used by the kernel to manage the processes in the system. The process table is an array of process structures that the kernel uses to manage the execution of programs. Each table entry defines a process that the kernel has created. The process table is always resident in the computer's memory. This is because the kernel is repeatedly querying and updating this table as it switches processes in and out of the CPU. For those processes that are not currently executing, their process table structures are being updated by the kernel for scheduling purposes. The process structures for your system are defined in `/usr/include/sys/proc.h`.

Fork Process

The kernel provides each process with the tools to duplicate itself for the purpose of creating a new process. This new entity is termed a *child process*. The `fork()` system call is invoked by an existing process (termed the *parent process*) and creates a replica of the parent process. Although a process has one parent, it can spawn many children. The new child process inherits certain attributes from its parent. The `fork()` system call documentation for HP-UX 10.0 (`fork(2)` in HP-UX Reference Release 10.0 Volume 3 (of 4) HP 9000 Series Computers) lists the following as being inherited by the child:

> Real, effective, and saved user IDs
>
> Real, effective, and saved group IDs
>
> Supplementary group IDs
>
> Process group ID
>
> Environment
>
> File descriptors
>
> Close-on-exec flags

FIGURE 25.2.

Diagram of kernel address space.

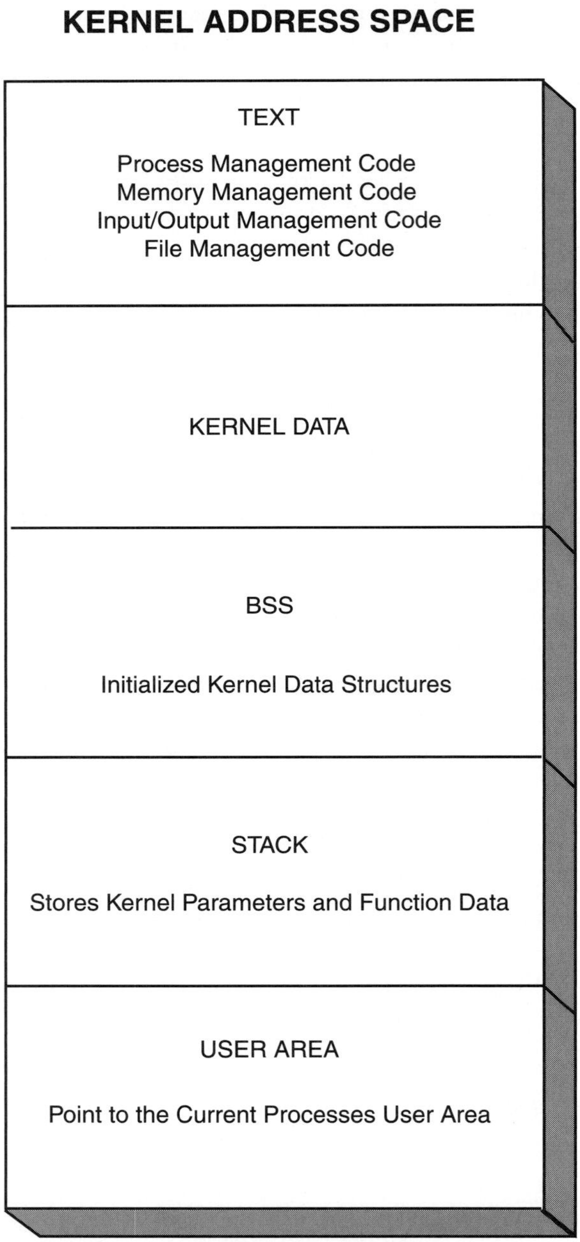

KERNEL ADDRESS SPACE

TEXT

Process Management Code
Memory Management Code
Input/Output Management Code
File Management Code

KERNEL DATA

BSS

Initialized Kernel Data Structures

STACK

Stores Kernel Parameters and Function Data

USER AREA

Point to the Current Processes User Area

Signal handling settings

Signal mask

Profiling on/off status

Command name in the accounting record

Nice value

All attached shared memory segments

Current working directory

Root directory

File mode creation mask

File size limit

Real-time priority

It is important to note how the child process differs from the parent process to see how one tells the difference between the parent and the child. When the kernel creates a child process on behalf of the parent, it gives the child a new process identifier (PID). This unique process ID is returned to the parent by the kernel to be used by the parent's code (of which the child also has a copy at this point) to determine the next step the parent process should follow: either continue on with additional work, wait for the child to finish, or terminate. The kernel returns the user ID of 0 (zero) to the child. Because the child is still executing the parent's copy of the program at this point, the code simply checks for a return status of 0 (zero) and continues executing that branch of the code. As you can see, the following short pseudocode segment should help clarify this concept:

```
start
print     " I am a process "
print     " I will now make a copy of myself "
if fork() is greater than 0
    print   " I am the parent"
    exit    () or wait    ()
else if fork() = 0
    print     " I am the new child "
    print     " I am now ready  to start  a new program "
    exec("new_program")
else fork() failed
```

The child process can also make another system call that replaces the child's process image with that of a new one. The system call that completely overlays the child's text, data, and BSS areas with that of a new program one is called exec(). This is how the system can execute multiple programs. By using both the fork() and the exec() system calls in conjunction with one another, a single process can execute numerous programs that perform any number of tasks that the programmer needs to have done. Except for a few system level processes started at boot time, this is how the kernel goes about executing the numerous jobs your system is required to run to support your organization.

25

KERNEL BASICS AND CONFIGURATION

To see how all this looks running on your system, you can use the ps command to view
the fact that the system has created all these new child processes. The ps -ef command
shows you that the child's parent process ID column (PPID) matches that of the parent's
process ID column (PID). The simplest way to test this is to log on and, at the shell
prompt, issue a UNIX command. By doing this, you are telling the shell to spawn off a
child process that executes the command (program) you just gave it and to return control
to you after the command has finished executing. Another way to experiment with this is
to start a program in the *background*. This is done by simply appending an ampersand (&)
to the end of your command-line statement. This tells the system to start this new program, but not to wait for it to finish before giving control back to your current shell
process. This way, you can use the ps -ef command to view your current shell and
background processes.

```
Sample ps -ef output from a system running AIX 4.x
    UID   PID  PPID   C    STIME    TTY  TIME CMD
    root     1     0   0    Apr 24     -  2:55 /etc/init
    root  2060 17606   0 10:38:30     -  0:02 dtwm
    root  2486     1   0    Apr 24     -  0:00 /usr/dt/bin/dtlogin -daemon
    root  2750  2486   0    Apr 24     -  3:12 /usr/lpp/X11/bin/X -x xv -D
/usr/lib/X11//rgb -T -force :0 -auth /var/dt/A:0-yjc2ya
    root  2910     1   0    Apr 24     -  0:00 /usr/sbin/srcmstr
    root  3176  2486   0    Apr 25     -  0:00 dtlogin <:0>           -daemon
    root  3794     1   0    Apr 25     -  0:00 /usr/ns-home/admserv/ns-
admin -d /usr/ns-home/admserv .
    root  3854  2910   0    Apr 24     -  0:00 /usr/lpp/info/bin/infod
    root  4192  6550   0    Apr 24     -  0:00 rpc.ttdbserver 100083 1
    root  4364     1   0    Apr 24     -  2:59 /usr/sbin/syncd 60
    root  4628     1   0    Apr 24     -  0:00 /usr/lib/errdemon
    root  5066     1   0    Apr 24     -  0:03 /usr/sbin/cron
    root  5236  2910   0    Apr 24     -  0:00 /usr/sbin/syslogd
    root  5526  2910   0    Apr 24     -  0:00 /usr/sbin/biod 6
    root  6014  2910   0    Apr 24     -  0:00 sendmail: accepting
connections
    root  6284  2910   0    Apr 24     -  0:00 /usr/sbin/portmap
    root  6550  2910   0    Apr 24     -  0:00 /usr/sbin/inetd
    root  6814  2910   0    Apr 24     -  9:04 /usr/sbin/snmpd
    root  7080  2910   0    Apr 24     -  0:00 /usr/sbin/dpid2
    root  7390     1   0    Apr 24     -  0:00 /usr/sbin/uprintfd
    root  7626     1   0    Apr 24     -  0:00 /usr/OV/bin/ntl_reader 0 1
1 1 1000 /usr/OV/log/nettl
    root  8140  7626   0    Apr 24     -  0:00 netfmt -CF
    root  8410  8662   0    Apr 24     -  0:00 nvsecd -O
    root  8662     1   0    Apr 24     -  0:15 ovspmd
    root  8926  8662   0    Apr 24     -  0:19 ovwdb -O -n5000 -t
    root  9184  8662   0    Apr 24     -  0:04 pmd -Au -At -Mu -Mt -m
    root  9442  8662   0    Apr 24     -  0:32 trapgend -f
    root  9700  8662   0    Apr 24     -  0:01 mgragentd -f
    root  9958  8662   0    Apr 24     -  0:00 nvpagerd
```

```
      root 10216   8662    0    Apr 24      -   0:00 nvlockd
      root 10478   8662    0    Apr 24      -   0:05 trapd
      root 10736   8662    0    Apr 24      -   0:04 orsd
      root 11004   8662    0    Apr 24      -   0:31 ovtopmd -O -t
      root 11254   8662    0    Apr 24      -   0:00 nvcold -O
      root 11518   8662    0    Apr 24      -   0:03 ovactiond
      root 11520   8662    0    Apr 24      -   0:05 nvcorrd
      root 11780   8662    0    Apr 24      -   0:00 actionsvr
      root 12038   8662    0    Apr 24      -   0:00 nvserverd
      root 12310   8662    0    Apr 24      -   0:04 ovelmd
      root 12558   8662    0    Apr 24      -   4:28 netmon -P
      root 12816   8662    0    Apr 24      -   0:04 ovesmd
      root 13074   8662    0    Apr 24      -   0:00 snmpCollect
      root 13442   2910    0    Apr 24      -   0:00 /usr/lib/netsvc/yp/ypbind
      root 13738   5526    0    Apr 24      -   0:00 /usr/sbin/biod 6
      root 13992   5526    0    Apr 24      -   0:00 /usr/sbin/biod 6
      root 14252   5526    0    Apr 24      -   0:00 /usr/sbin/biod 6
      root 14510   5526    0    Apr 24      -   0:00 /usr/sbin/biod 6
      root 14768   5526    0    Apr 24      -   0:00 /usr/sbin/biod 6
      root 15028   2910    0    Apr 24      -   0:00 /usr/sbin/rpc.statd
      root 15210   6550    0    Apr 24      -   0:00 rpc.ttdbserver 100083 1
      root 15580   2910    0    Apr 24      -   0:00 /usr/sbin/writesrv
      root 15816   2910    0    Apr 24      -   0:00 /usr/sbin/rpc.lockd
      root 16338   2910    0    Apr 24      -   0:00 /usr/sbin/qdaemon
      root 16520   2060    0 13:44:46       -   0:00 /usr/dt/bin/dtexec -open 0
-ttprocid 2.pOtBq 01 17916 1342177279 1 0 0 10.19.12.115 3_101_1
/usr/dt/bin/dtterm
      root 16640      1    0    Apr 24   lft0  0:00 /usr/sbin/getty
/dev/console
      root 17378      1    0    Apr 24      -   0:13 /usr/bin/pmd
      root 17606   3176    0 10:38:27       -   0:00 /usr/dt/bin/dtsession
      root 17916      1    0 10:38:28       -   0:00 /usr/dt/bin/ttsession -s
      root 18168      1    0    Apr 24      -   0:00
/usr/lpp/diagnostics/bin/diagd
    nobody 18562  19324    0    Apr 25      -   0:32 ./ns-httpd -d /usr/ns-
home/httpd-supp_aix/config
      root 18828  22410    0 13:44:47    pts/2  0:00 /bin/ksh
      root 19100  21146    0 13:45:38    pts/3  0:00 vi hp.c
    nobody 19324      1    0    Apr 25      -   0:00 ./ns-httpd -d /usr/ns-
home/httpd-supp_aix/config
      root 19576   6550    0 13:43:38       -   0:00 telnetd
    nobody 19840  19324    0    Apr 25      -   0:33 ./ns-httpd -d /usr/ns-
home/httpd-supp_aix/config
      root 19982  17606    0 10:38:32       -   0:03 dtfile
    nobody 20356  19324    0    Apr 25      -   0:33 ./ns-httpd -d /usr/ns-
home/httpd-supp_aix/config
      root 20694  20948    0    Apr 25      -   0:00 /usr/ns-home/admserv/ns-
admin -d /usr/ns-home/admserv .
      root 20948   3794    0    Apr 25      -   0:01 /usr/ns-home/admserv/ns-
admin -d /usr/ns-home/admserv .
      root 21146  23192    0 13:45:32    pts/3  0:00 /bin/ksh
```

```
     nobody 21374 19324   0   Apr 25      -  0:00 ./ns-httpd -d /usr/ns-
home/httpd-supp_aix/config
     root 21654  2060   0 13:45:31      -  0:00 /usr/dt/bin/dtexec -open 0
-ttprocid 2.pOtBq 01 17916 1342177279 1 0 0 10.19.12.115 3_102_1
/usr/dt/bin/dtterm
     root 21882 19576   0 13:43:39  pts/0  0:00 -ksh
     root 22038 19982   0 10:38:37      -  0:04 dtfile
     root 22410 16520   0 13:44:47      -  0:00 /usr/dt/bin/dtterm
     root 22950 21882   8 13:46:06  pts/0  0:00 ps -ef
     root 23192 21654   0 13:45:31      -  0:00 /usr/dt/bin/dtterm
     root 23438 18828   0 13:45:03  pts/2  0:00 vi aix.c
```

Process Run States

A process moves between several states during its lifetime, although a process can only be in one state at any one time. Certain events, such as system interrupts, blocking of resources, or software traps cause a process to change its run state. The kernel maintains queues in memory that it uses to assign a process based on that process's state. It keeps track of the process by its user ID.

UNIX version System V Release 4 (SVR4) recognizes the following process run states:

```
- SIDLE            This is the state right after a process has issued a
fork() system call. A process image has yet to be copied into memory.
        - SRUN           The process is ready to run and is waiting to
be executed by the CPU.
        - SONPROC     The process is currently being executed by the CPU.
        - SSLEEP          The process is blocking on an event or
resource.
        - SZOMB           The process has terminated and is waiting on
either its parent or the init process to allow it to completely exit.
        - SXBRK           The process has been switched out so that
another process can be executed.
        - SSTOP           The process is stopped.
```

When a process first starts, the kernel allocates it a slot in the process table and places the process in the SIDL state. After the process has the resources it needs to run, the kernel places it onto the run queue. The process is now in the SRUN state awaiting its turn in the CPU. When its turn comes for the process to be switched into the CPU, the kernel tags it as being in the SONPROC state. In this state, the process executes in either user or kernel mode. User mode is where the process is executing nonprivileged code from the user's compiled program. Kernel mode is where kernel code is being executed from the kernel's privileged address space via a system call.

At some point, the process is switched out of the CPU because it has either been signaled to do so (for instance, the user issues a stop signal—SSTOP state), or the process has exceeded its quota of allowable CPU time and the kernel needs the CPU to do some work for another process. The act of switching the focus of the CPU from one process to another is called a *context switch*. When this occurs, the process enters the SXBRK state. If the process still needs to run and is waiting for another system resource, such as disk services, it enters the SSLEEP state until the resource is available and the kernel wakes up the process and places it on the SRUN queue. When the process has finally completed its work and is ready to terminate, it enters the SZOMB state. We have seen the fundamentals of what states a process can exist in and how it moves through them. Let's now learn how a kernel schedules a process to run.

Process Scheduler

Most modern versions of UNIX (for instance, SVR4 and Solaris 2.*x*) are classified as preemptive operating systems. They are capable of interrupting an executing a process and "freezing" it so that the CPU can service a different process. This obviously has the advantage of fairly allocating the system's resources to all the processes in the system. This is one goal of the many system architects and programmers who design and write schedulers. The disadvantages are that not all processes are equal and that complex algorithms must be designed and implemented as kernel code to maintain the illusion that each user process is running as if it was the only job in the system. The kernel maintains this balance by placing processes in the various priority queues or run queues and apportioning its CPU time-slice based on its priority class (real-time versus timeshare).

Universities and UNIX system vendors have conducted extensive studies on how best to design and build an optimal scheduler. Each vendor's flavor of UNIX—4.4BSD, SVR4, HP-UX, Solaris, and AIX, to name a few—attempts to implement this research to provide a scheduler that best balances its customers' needs. The system administrator must realize that there are limits to the scheduler's capability to service batch, real-time, and interactive users in the same environment. When the system becomes overloaded, it becomes necessary for some jobs to suffer at the expense of others. This is an extremely important issue to both users and system administrators alike. Refer to Chapter 28, "Performance Monitoring," to gain a better understanding of what to do to balance and tune the system.

Memory Management

Random access memory (RAM) is a critical component in any computer system. It's the one component that always seems to be in short supply on most systems. Unfortunately, most organizations' budgets don't allow for the purchase of all the memory that their technical staff feel is necessary to support all their projects. Luckily, UNIX allows us to execute all sorts of programs without, what appears at first glance to be, enough physical memory. This comes in handy when the system is required to support a user community that needs to execute an organization's custom and commercial software to gain access to its data.

Memory chips are high-speed electronic devices that plug directly into your computer. Main memory is also called *core memory* by some technicians. Ever heard of a core dump? (Writing out main memory to a storage device for post-dump analysis.) Usually it is caused by a program or system crash or failure. An important aspect of memory chips is that they can store data at specific locations called addresses. This makes it convenient for another hardware device called the central processing unit (CPU) to access these locations to run your programs. The kernel uses a paging and segmentation arrangement to organize process memory. This is where the memory management subsystem plays a significant role. Memory management can be defined as the efficient managing and sharing of the system's memory resources by the kernel and user processes.

Memory management follows certain rules that manage both physical and virtual memory. Because you already have an idea of what a physical memory chip or card is, we will provide a definition of virtual memory. *Virtual memory* is where the addressable memory locations that a process can be mapped into are independent of the physical address space of the CPU. Generally speaking, a process can exceed the physical address space/size of main memory and still load and execute.

The system administrator should be aware that just because she has a fixed amount of physical memory, she should not expect it all to be available to execute user programs. The kernel is always resident in main memory and depending upon the kernel's configuration (tunable-like kernel tables, daemons, device drivers loaded, and so on), the amount left over can be classified as available memory. It is important for the system administrator to know how much available memory the system has to work with when supporting his environment. Most systems display memory statistics during boot time. If your kernel is larger than it needs to be to support your environment, consider reconfiguring a smaller kernel to free up resources.

You learned before that a process has a well-defined structure and has certain specific control data structures that the kernel uses to manage the process during its system lifetime. One of the more important data structures that the kernel uses is the virtual address space (vas in HP-UX and as in SVR4. For a more detailed description of the layout of these structures, look at the vas.h or as.h header files under /usr/include on your system.)

A virtual address space exists for each process and is used by the process to keep track of process logical segments or regions that point to specific segments of the process's text (code), data, u_area, user, and kernel stacks; shared memory; shared library; and memory mapped file segments. Per-process regions protect and maintain the number of pages mapped into the segments. Each segment has a virtual address space segment as well. Multiple programs can share the process's text segment. The data segment holds the process's initialized and uninitialized (BSS) data. These areas can change size as the program executes.

The u_area and kernel stack contain information used by the kernel and are a fixed size. The user stack is contained in the u_area; however, its size fluctuates during its execution. Memory mapped files allow programmers to bring files into memory and work with them while in memory. Obviously, there is a limit to the size of the file you can load into memory (check your system documentation). Shared memory segments are usually set up and used by a process to share data with other processes. For example, a programmer may want to be able to pass messages to other programs by writing to a shared memory segment and having the receiving programs attach to that specific shared memory segment and read the message. Shared libraries allow programs to link to commonly used code at runtime. Shared libraries reduce the amount of memory needed by executing programs because only one copy of the code is required to be in memory. Each program accesses the code at that memory location when necessary.

When a programmer writes and compiles a program, the compiler generates the object file from the source code. The linker program (ld) links the object file with the appropriate libraries and, if necessary, other object files to generate the executable program. The executable program contains virtual addresses that are converted into physical memory addresses when the program is run. This address translation must occur prior to the program being loaded into memory so that the CPU can reference the actual code.

When the program starts to run, the kernel sets up its data structures (proc, virtual address space, per-process region) and begins to execute the process in user mode. Eventually, the process will access a page that's not in main memory (for instance, the pages in its working set are not in main memory). This is called a *page fault*. When this occurs, the kernel puts the process to sleep, switches from user mode to kernel mode, and attempts to load the page that the process was requesting to be loaded. The kernel searches for the page by locating the per-process region where the virtual address is located. It then goes to the segments (text, data, or other) per-process region to find the actual region that contains the information necessary to read in the page.

The kernel must now find a free page in which to load the process's requested page. If there are no free pages, the kernel must either page or swap out pages to make room for the new page request. When there is some free space, the kernel pages in a block of pages from disk. This block contains the requested page plus additional pages that may be used by the process. Finally, the kernel establishes the permissions and sets the protections for the newly loaded pages. The kernel wakes the process and switches back to user mode so that the process can begin executing using the requested page. Pages are not brought into memory until the process requests them for execution. This is why the system is referred to as a *demand paging* system.

> **NOTE**
>
> The verb *page* means to move individual blocks of memory for a process between system memory and disk swap area. The *pagesize* is defined in the /usr/include/limits.h header file. For a definition of paging see the section "RAM I/O" later in the chapter.

The memory management unit is a hardware component that handles the translation of virtual address spaces to physical memory addresses. The memory management unit also prevents a process from accessing another process's address space unless it is permitted to do so (protection fault). Memory is thus protected at the page level. The *Translation Lookaside Buffer* (TLB) is a hardware cache that maintains the most recently used virtual address space to physical address translations. It is controlled by the memory management unit to reduce the number of address translations that occur on the system.

Input and Output Management

The simplest definition of *input/output* is the control of data between hardware devices and software. A system administrator is concerned with I/O at two separate levels. The first level is concerned with I/O between user address space and kernel address space; the second level is concerned with I/O between kernel address space and physical hardware devices. When data is written to disk, the first level of the I/O subsystem copies the data from user space to kernel space. Data is then passed from the kernel address space to the second level of the I/O subsystem. This is when the physical hardware device activates its own I/O subsystems, which determine the best location for the data on the available disks.

The OEM (*Original Equipment Manufacturer*) UNIX configuration is satisfactory for many work environments but does not take into consideration the network traffic or the behavior of specific applications on your system. System administrators find that they need to reconfigure the system's I/O to meet the expectations of the users and the demands of their applications. Use the default configuration as a starting point and, as experience is gained with the demands on the system resources, tune the system to achieve peak I/O performance.

UNIX comes with a wide variety of tools that monitor system performance. Learning to use these tools helps you determine whether a performance problem is hardware or software related. Using these tools helps you determine whether a problem is poor user training, application tuning, system maintenance, or system configuration. sar, vmstat, iostat, and monitor are some of your best basic I/O performance monitoring tools.

- sar—The sar command writes to standard output the contents of selected cumulative activity counters in the operating system. The following list is a breakdown of those activity counters that sar accumulates.
    - File access
    - Buffer usage
    - System call activity
    - Disk and tape input/output activity
    - Free memory and swap space
    - Kernel Memory Allocation (KMA)
    - Interprocess communication
    - Paging
    - Queue activity
    - Central Processing Unit (CPU)
    - Kernel tables
    - Switching
    - Terminal device activity
- iostat—Reports CPU statistics and input/output statistics for TTY devices, disks, and CD-ROMs.
- monitor—Like the sar command, but with a visual representation of the computer state.
- vmstat—Reports statistics maintained on processes, virtual memory, disk, and CPU activity.

RAM I/O

The memory subsystem comes into effect when the programs start requesting access to more physical RAM memory than is installed on your system. When this point is reached, UNIX starts I/O processes called *paging* and *swapping*. This is when kernel procedures start moving pages of stored memory out to the paging or swap areas defined on your hard drives. (This procedure reflects how swap files work in Windows by

Microsoft for a PC.) All UNIX systems use these procedures to free physical memory for reuse by other programs. The drawback to this is that when paging and swapping have started, system performance decreases rapidly. The system continues using these techniques until demands for physical RAM drop to the amount that is installed on your system. There are only two physical states for memory performance on your system: Either you have enough RAM or you don't, and performance drops through the floor.

Memory performance problems are simple to diagnose; either you have enough memory or your system is *thrashing*. Computer systems start thrashing when more resources are dedicated to moving memory (paging and swapping) from RAM to the hard drives. Performance decreases as the CPUs and all subsystems become dedicated to trying to free physical RAM for themselves and other processes.

This summary doesn't do justice, however, to the complexity of memory management nor does it help you to deal with problems as they arise. To provide the background to understand these problems, we need to discuss virtual memory activity in more detail.

We have been discussing two memory processes: paging and swapping. These two processes help UNIX fulfill memory requirements for all processes. UNIX systems employ both paging and swapping to reduce I/O traffic and execute better control over the system's total aggregate memory. Keep in mind that paging and swapping are temporary measures; they cannot fix the underlying problem of low physical RAM memory.

Swapping moves all idle processes to disk to reclaim memory and is a normal procedure for the UNIX operating system. When the idle process is called by the system again, it copies the memory image from the disk swap area back into RAM.

On systems performing paging and swapping, swapping occurs in two separate situations. Swapping is often a part of normal housekeeping. Jobs that sleep for more that 20 seconds are considered idle and may be swapped out at any time. Swapping is also an emergency technique used to combat extreme memory shortages. Remember our definition of thrashing; this is when a system is in trouble. Some system administrators sum this up very well by calling it "desperation swapping."

Paging, on the other hand, moves individual pages (or pieces) of processes to disk and reclaims the freed memory, with most of the process remaining loaded in memory. Paging employs an algorithm to monitor usage of the pages, to leave recently accessed pages in physical memory, and to move idle pages into disk storage. This allows for optimum performance of I/O and reduces the amount of I/O traffic that swapping would normally require.

NOTE

Monitoring what the system is doing is easy with the ps command. ps is a "process status" command on all UNIX systems and typically shows many idle and swapped-out jobs. This command has a rich amount of options to show you what the computer is doing—too many to show you here.

I/O performance management, like all administrative tasks, is a continual process. Generating performance statistics on a routine basis assists in identifying and correcting potential problems before they have an impact on your system or, worst case, your users. UNIX offers basic system usage statistics packages that assist you in automatically collecting and examining usage statistics.

You will find the load on the system increases rapidly as new jobs are submitted and resources are not freed quickly enough. Performance drops as the disks become I/O bound trying to satisfy paging and swapping calls. Memory overload quickly forces a system to become I/O and CPU bound. However, after you identify the problem to be memory, you will find adding RAM to be cheaper than adding another CPU to your system.

Hard Drive I/O

Some simple configuration considerations help you obtain better I/O performance regardless of your system's usage patterns. The factors to consider are the arrangement of your disks and disk controllers and the speed of the hard drives.

The best policy is to spread the disk workload as evenly as possible across all controllers. If you have a large system with multiple I/O back planes, split your disk drives evenly among the two buses. Most disk controllers allow you to daisy chain several disk drives from the same controller channel. For the absolute best performance, spread the disk drives evenly over all controllers. This is particularly important if your system has many users who all need to make large sequential transfers.

Small Computer System Interface (SCSI) devices are those that adhere to the American National Standards Institute (ANSI) standards for connecting intelligent interface peripherals to computers. The SCSI bus is a daisy-chained arrangement originating at a SCSI adapter card that interconnects several SCSI controllers. Each adapter interfaces the device to the bus and has a different SCSI address that is set on the controller. This address determines the priority that the SCSI device is given, with the highest address having the highest priority. When you load balance a system, always place more

25

KERNEL BASICS
AND
CONFIGURATION

frequently accessed data on the hard drives with the highest SCSI address. Data at the top of the channel takes less access time, and load balancing increases the availability of that data to the system.

After deciding the best placement of the controllers and hard drives on your system, you have one last item for increasing system performance. When adding new disks, remember that the seek time of the disk is the single most important indicator of its performance. Different processes will be accessing the disk at the same time as they are accessing different files and reading from different areas at one time.

The seek time of a disk is the measure of time required to move the disk drive's heads from one track to another. Seek time is affected by how far the heads have to move from one track to another. Moving the heads from track to track takes less time than shifting those same drive heads across the entire disk. You will find that seek time is actually a nonlinear measurement, taking into account that the heads have to accelerate, decelerate, and then stabilize in their new position. This is why all disks typically specify a minimum, average, and maximum seek time. The ratio of time spent seeking between tracks to time spent transferring data is usually at least 10 to 1. The lower the aggregate seek time, the greater your performance gain or improvement.

One problem with allowing for paging and swap files to be added to the hard disks is that some system administrators try to use this feature to add more RAM to a system. It does not work that way. The most you could hope for is to temporarily avert the underlying cause, low physical memory. There is one thing that a system administrator can do to increase performance, and that is to accurately balance the disk drives.

Don't overlook the obvious upgrade path for I/O performance tuning. If you understand how your system is configured and how you intend to use it, you will be much less likely to buy equipment you don't need or that won't solve your problem.

File System Management Subsystem

In discussing kernel basics and configuration, a very important topic, file systems, must be considered. This discussion deals with the basic structural method of long-term storage of system and user data. File systems and the parameters used to create them have a direct impact on performance, system resource utilization, and kernel efficiency dealing with Input/Output (I/O).

File System Types

There are several important file system types supported by different operating systems (OS), many of which are not used for implementation at this time. The reasons they are not used vary from their being inefficient to just being outdated. However, many operating systems still support their file system structure so that compatibility doesn't become an issue for portability.

This support of other file system structures plays a large role in allowing companies to move between OS and computer types with little impact to their applications.

The following is a list of file system types supported by specific operating systems. The list only covers local, network, and CD-ROM file systems.

Local	NFS*	CD-ROM	File system
Solaris	ufs	yes	bsfs
SunOS	4.2	yes	bsfs
SCO	EAFS	yes	HS
IRIX	efs	yes	iso9660
Digital	ufs	yes	cdfs
HP-UX	bfs	yes	cdfs
AIX	jfs	yes	cdrfs
Linux	ext2	yes	iso9660

Note: NFS stands for Networked File System

Hardware Architecture

Because file systems are stored on disk, the system administrator should look at basic disk hardware architecture before proceeding with specifics of file systems. A disk is physically divided into tracks, sectors, and blocks. A good representation of a sector would be a piece of pie removed form the pie pan. Therefore, as with a pie, a disk is composed of several sectors (see Figure 25.3). Tracks are concentric rings going from the outside perimeter to the center of the disk, with each track becoming smaller as it approaches the center of the disk. Tracks on a disk are concentric, therefore they *never* touch each other. The area of the track that lies between the edges of the sector is termed a *block*, and the block is the area where data is stored. Disk devices typically use a block mode accessing scheme when transferring data between the file management subsystem and the I/O subsystem. The block size is usually 512- or 1024-byte fixed-length blocks, depending on the scheme used by the operating system. A programmer may access files using either block or character device files.

FIGURE 25.3.

Diagram of a single platter from a hard drive showing disk geometry.

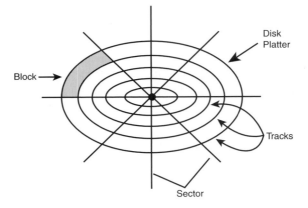

You now have a basic understanding of the terms tracks, sectors, and blocks as they apply to a single-platter disk drive. But most disks today are composed of several platters with each platter having its own read/write head. With this in mind, we have a new term: *cylinder* (see Figure 25.4). Let's make the assumption that we have a disk drive that has six platters, so, logically, it must have six read/write heads. When read/write head 1 is on track 10 of platter 1, then heads 2 through 6 are on track 10 of their respective platters. You now have a cylinder. A cylinder is collectively the same track on each platter of a multiplatter disk.

FIGURE 25.4.

Diagram showing multiple platters of a single disk drive.

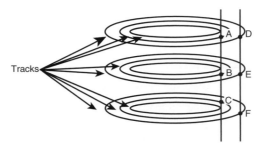

File System Concepts and Format

The term file system has two connotations. The first is the complete hierarchical file system tree. The second is the collection place on disk device(s) for files. Visualize the file system as consisting of a single node at the highest level (ROOT) and all other nodes descending from the root node in a treelike fashion (see Figure 25.5). The second meaning will be used for this discussion, and Hewlett-Packard's high-performance file system will be used for technical reference purposes.

FIGURE 25.5.

Diagram of a UNIX hierarchical file system.

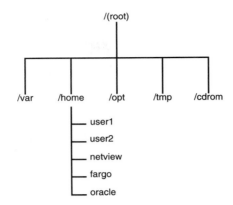

The superblock is the key to maintaining the file system. It's an 8KB block of disk space that maintains the current status of the file system. Because of its importance, a copy is maintained in memory and at each cylinder group within the file system. The copy in main memory is updated as events transpire. The update daemon is the actual process that calls on the kernel to flush the cached superblocks, modified inodes, and cached data blocks to disk. The superblock maintains the following static and dynamic information about the file system. An asterisk denotes dynamically maintained information:

- File system size
- Number of inodes
- Location of free space
- Number of cylinder groups
- Fragment size and number
- Block size and number
- Location of superblocks, cylinder groups, inodes, and data blocks
- Total number of free data blocks
- Total number of free inodes
- File system status flag (clean flag)

As you can see from the listed information, the superblock maintains the integrity of the file system and all associated pertinent information. To prevent catastrophic events, the OS stores copies of the superblock in cylinder groups. The locations of these alternate superblocks may be found in /etc/sbtab. When system administrators are using fsck - b to recover from an alternate superblock, they are required to give the location of that alternate block. Again, the only place to find that information is in /etc/sbtab. As a qualification to that statement, there is always an alternate superblock at block 16.

Cylinder groups are adjacent groups of cylinders, 16 cylinders by default, that have their own set of inodes and free space mapping. This is done to improve performance and reduce disk latency. Disk latency is the time between when the disk is read and the I/O subsystem can transfer the data. Some factors that affect disk latency are rotational speed, seek time, and the interleave factor. This concept also associates the inodes and data blocks in closer proximity.

> **NOTE**
>
> The *interleave factor* is the value that determines the order in which sectors on a disk drive are accessed.

The layout of the cylinder group is:

- Boot block
- Primary superblock
- Redundant superblock
- Cylinder group information
- Inode table
- Data blocks

The boot block and the primary superblock will only be there if this is the first cylinder group; otherwise, it may be filled with data.

Inodes are fixed-length entries that vary in their length according to the OS implemented. SVR4 implementation is 128 bytes for a UFS inode and 64 bytes for an S5 inode. The inode maintains all the pertinent information about the file except for the filename and the data. The information maintained by the inode is as follows:

- File permissions or mode
- Type of file
- Number of hard links
- Current owner
- Group associated to the file
- Actual file size in bytes
- Time stamps
- Time/Date file last changed

- Time/Date file last accessed
- Time/Date last inode modification
- Single indirect block pointer
- Double indirect block pointer
- Triple indirect block pointer

There are 15 slots in the inode structure for disk address or pointers (see Figure 25.6). Twelve of the slots are for direct block addressing. A direct address can either point to a complete block or to a fragment of that block. The block and fragment sizes we are discussing are configurable parameters that are set at file system creation. They cannot be altered unless the file system is removed and re-created with the new parameters.

FIGURE 25.6.

Diagram of an inode structure of a UNIX file system.

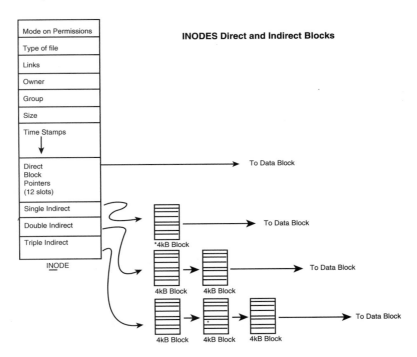

*Each 4kB Block will hold 1024 4 byte pointers to data Blocks.

TABLE 25.1. LISTING OF A TYPICAL AIX ROOT DIRECTORY USING `ls -ali`, TO INDICATE THE INODE NUMBERS FOR EACH FILE ENTRY IN THE DIRECTORY.

Inode	Permissions	ln	Owner	Group	Size	Access Date	Filename
2	drwxr-xr-x	23	bin	bin	1024	Apr 27 15:53	. (dot)
2	drwxr-xr-x	23	bin	bin	1024	Apr 27 15:53	.. (dot, dot)
765	-rw-r—r—	1	root	system	259	Apr 08 08:34	Guidefaults
1257	-rw———	1	root	system	156	Apr 27 11:01	.Xauthority
2061	drwxr-xr-x	11	root	system	512	Apr 27 11:01	.dt
591	-rwxr-xr-x	1	root	system	3970	Apr 08 08:38	.dtprofile
6151	drwx———	3	root	system	512	Apr 17 13:42	.netscape
593	-rw———	1	root	system	1904	Apr 11 08:12	.old_sh_history
1011	-rwxr———	1	7	system	254	Apr 10 11:15	.profile
1007	-rw———	1	root	system	3444	Apr 27 15:53	.sh_history
1009	-rw-r—r—	1	root	system	30	Apr 14 10:35	.showcase
2069	drwxr-xr-x	2	root	system	512	Apr 08 08:54	TT_DB
2058	drwxr-xr-x	3	root	system	512	Apr 11 11:21	admin
109	lrwxrwxrwx	1	bin	bin	8	Apr 01 05:27	bin ->/usr/bin
23	drwxrwxr-x	4	root	system	2048	Apr 27 14:37	dev
24	drwxr-xr-x	12	root	system	6144	Apr 27 11:29	etc
2	drwxr-xr-x	5	bin	bin	512	Apr 02 01:52	home
8195	drwxr-xr-x	2	root	system	512	Apr 25 13:08	httpd
586	lrwxrwxrwx	1	bin	bin	20	Apr 02 01:57	launch_demo -> /welcome/launch_demo
22	lrwxrwxrwx	1	bin	bin	8	Apr 01 05:27	lib ->/usr/lib
16	drwx———	2	root	system	512	Apr 01 05:27	lost+found
100	drwxr-xr-x	26	bin	bin	1024	Apr 11 15:23	lpp
101	drwxr-xr-x	2	bin	bin	512	Apr 01 05:27	mnt
4096	drwxr-xr-x	2	root	system	512	Apr 11 14:57	mnt10032
4097	drwxr-xr-x	2	root	system	512	Apr 14 10:31	mnt10086
1251	-rw-rw-rw-	1	root	system	3192	Apr 15 14:12	nv6000.log
102	drwxr-xr-x	2	root	system	512	Apr 02 01:54	opt
103	drwxr-xr-x	3	bin	bin	512	Apr 11 15:23	sbin
1252	-rw-r—r—	1	root	system	39265	Apr 27 13:29	smit.log

Inode	Permissions	ln	Owner	Group	Size	Access Date	Filename
1253	-rw-r—r—	1	root	system	5578	Apr 27 13:24	smit.script
271	drwxrwxr-x	2	root	system	512	Apr 01 05:37	tftpboot
2	drwxrwxrwt	9	bin	bin	1536	Apr 27 15:47	tmp
99	lrwxrwxrwx	1	bin	bin	5	Apr 01 05:27	u ->/home
192	lrwxrwxrwx	1	root	system	21	Apr 01 05:30	unix -> /usr/lib/boot/unix_up
2	drwxr-xr-x	26	bin	bin	512	Apr 25 13:19	usr
2	drwxr-xr-x	14	bin	bin	512	Apr 01 06:03	var
764	-rw-rw-rw-	1	root	system	3074	Apr 08 08:33	vim.log
2	drwxr-xr-x	12	bin	bin	2048	Apr 08 08:21	welcome

Single indirect addressing (slot 13) points to a block of four-byte pointers that point to data blocks. If the block that is pointed to by the single indirect method is 4KB in size, it would contain 1024 four-byte pointers, and if it were 8KB in size, it would contain 2048 four-byte pointers to data blocks. The double indirect block pointer is located in slot 14, and slot 15 maintains the triple indirect block pointer.

In the "File System Concepts and Format" section, the initial discussion covered basic concepts of superblocks, alternate superblocks, cylinder groups, inodes, and direct and indirect addressing of data blocks. Further reading into these subjects is a must for all system administrators, especially the new and inexperienced.

Kernel Configuration Process

Kernel configuration is a detailed process in which the system administrator is altering the behavior of the computer. The system administrator must remember that a change of a single parameter may affect other kernel subsystems, thus exposing the administrator to the "law of unintended consequences."

When Do You Rebuild the Kernel

Kernel components are generally broken into four major groups, and if changes are made to any of these groups, a kernel reconfiguration is required.

- Subsystems—These are components required for special functionality (ISO9660).
- Dump devices—System memory dumps are placed here when a panic condition exist. Core dumps are usually placed at the end of the swap area.

- Configurable parameters—These are tuning parameters and data structures. There are a significant number, and they may have interdependencies, so it is important that you are aware of the impact of each change.
- Device drivers—These handle interfaces to peripherals such as modems, printers, disks, tape drives, kernel memory, and other physical devices.

HP-UX 10.X

There are two ways to rebuild the kernel, as discussed in the following sections.

Use the System Activity Monitor (SAM)

1. Run SAM and select Kernel Configuration.

   You see the following four identified components:

   - Subsystem
   - Configurable Parameters
   - Dump Devices
   - Device Drivers

2. Select the desired component and make the appropriate change(s).
3. Answer the prompts, and the kernel will be rebuilt.
4. It also prompts you for whether you want to reboot the kernel now or later.

   Consider the importance of the changes and the availability of the system to answer this prompt. If you answer "YES" to reboot the system now, it cannot be reversed. The point is to know what you are going to do prior to getting to that prompt.

Manual Method

1. Go to the build area of the kernel by typing the following command:

   ```
   # cd /stand/build
   ```

2. Create a system file from the current system configuration by typing the following command:

   ```
   # /usr/lbin/sysadm/system_prep -s system
   ```

   This command places the current system configuration in the file system. There is no standard that you call it system; it could be any name you want.

3. Modify the existing parameters and insert unlisted configuration parameters, new subsystems, and device drivers, or alter the dump device. The reason you may not have one of the listed configurable parameters in this file: The previous kernel took the default value.

4. Create the conf.c file, and we are using the modified *system* file to create it. Remember, if you did not use system for the existing configuration file, insert your name where I show *system*. The conf.c file has constants for the tunable parameters. Type the following command to execute the config program:

   ```
   # /usr/sbin/config -s system
   ```

5. Rebuild the kernel by linking the driver objects to the basic kernel:

   ```
   # make -f config.mk
   ```

6. Save the old system configuration file:

   ```
   # mv /stand/system /stand/system.prev
   ```

7. Save the old kernel:

   ```
   # mv /stand/vmunix /stand/vmunix.prev
   ```

8. Move the new system configuration file into place:

   ```
   # mv ./system /stand/system
   ```

9. Move the new kernel into place:

   ```
   # mv ./vmunix_test /stand/vmunix
   ```

10. Boot the system to load the new kernel:

    ```
    # shutdown -r -y 60
    ```

Solaris 2.5.x

Suppose that you were going to run Oracle on your Sun system under Solaris 2.5.x, and you wanted to change max_nprocs to 1000 and set up the following Interprocess Communications configuration for your shared memory and semaphore parameters:

SHMMAX	2097152 (2 × the default 1048576)
SHMMIN	1
SHMNI	100
SHMSEG	32
SEMMNI	64
SEMMNS	1600
SEMMNU	1250
SEMMSL	25

1. As root, enter the following commands:

   ```
   # cd /etc
   # cp system system.old - create a backup
   ```

2. Enter the following:

   ```
   # vi system
   ```

25

Add or change the following:

```
set max_nprocs=1000
set shmsys;shminfo_shmmax=2097152
set shmsys;shminfo_shmmin=1
set shmsys;shminfo_shmmni=100
set shmsys;shminfo_shmseg=32
set semsys;seminfo_semmni=64
set semsys;seminfo_semmns=1600
set semsys;seminfo_semmnu=1250
set semsys;seminfo_semmsl=25
```

Save and close the file.

3. Reboot your system by entering the following command:

```
# shutdown -r now
```

The preceding kernel parameter and kernel module variables are now set for your system.

SVR4

This example sets the tunable NPROC to 500 and then rebuilds the kernel to reflect this new value.

1. Log in to the system as `root` and make a backup of `/stand/unix` to another area.

```
# cp /stand/unix /old/unix
```

2. Enter the following:

```
#cd /etc/conf/cf.d
```

Edit the `init.base` file to include any changes that you made in the `/etc/inittab` file that you want to make permanent. A new `/etc/inittab` file is created when a new kernel is built and put into place.

3. Edit the configuration files in the `/etc/conf` directory. Change only `/etc/conf/cf.d/stune` (although you can change `/etc/conf/cf.d/mtune`). The `stune` and `mtune` files contain the tunable parameters the system uses for its kernel configuration. `stune` is the system file that you should use when you alter the tunable values for the system. It overrides the values listed in `mtune`. `mtune` is the master parameter specification file for the system. It contains the tunable parameters' default, minimum, and maximum values.

The following command line is an example of how you make `stune` reflect a parameter change:

```
# /etc/conf/bin/idtune NPROC 500
```

You can look at `stune` to see the changes. (`stune` can be altered by using the `vi` editor.)

4. Build the new kernel:

   `# /etc/conf/bin/idbuild`

   It will take several minutes to complete.

5. Reboot the computer system to enable the new kernel to take effect:

   `# shutdown -I6 -g0 -y`

To see your changes, log back in to your system and execute the `sysdef` command. The system parameters then are displayed.

AIX 4.x

Unlike the preceding examples, the AIX operating system requires a special tool to reconfigure the kernel. This tool is the System Management Interface Tool (SMIT), developed by IBM for the AIX operating system. The AIX kernel is modular in the sense that portions of the kernel's subsystems are resident only when required.

The following shows a SMIT session to change the `MAX USERS PROCESSES` on an AIX 4.x system. This is demonstrated to the reader by screen prints of an actual kernel configuration session. While using SMIT, you can see the command sequences being generated by SMIT by pressing the F6 key. SMIT also makes two interaction logs that are handy for post configuration review. `SMIT.LOG` is an ASCII file that shows all menu selections, commands, and output of a session. `SMIT.SCRIPT` shows just the actual command-line codes used during the session.

1. At root, start SMIT with the following command. This brings up the IBM SMIT GUI interface screen (see Figure 25.7).

   `# smit`

2. Select System Environments from the System Management menu with your mouse (see Figure 25.8).

3. Select Change/Show Characteristics of Operating System from the System Environment menu with your mouse (see Figure 25.9).

6. Make a bootable kernel:

```
# make boot
```

To see the compressed bootable kernel image, do a long listing on arch/i386/boot. You see a file named zImage.

7. The last step is to install the new kernel to the boot drive:

```
# make zlilo
```

This command makes the previous kernel (/vmlinuz) become /vmlinuz.old. Your new kernel image zImage is now /vmlinuz. You can now reboot to check your new kernel configuration. During the boot process, you should see messages about the newly configured PPP device driver scroll across as the system loads.

When everything checks out and you are satisfied with your new Linux kernel, you can continue with setting up the PPP software.

Summary

We began our discussion by defining the UNIX kernel and the four basic subsystems that comprise the operating system. We described how Process Management creates and manages the process and how Memory Management handles multiple processes in the system. We discussed how the I/O subsystem takes advantage of swapping and paging to balance the system's load and the interaction of the I/O subsystem with the file management subsystem.

Next, we covered the steps involved in altering the kernel configuration. We demonstrated in detail the steps involved in configuring:

- HP-UX 10.X
- Solaris 2.5.x
- System V Release 4 (SVR4)
- AIX
- Linux

In the author's opinion, the system administrator should become familiar with the concepts presented in this chapter. Further in-depth study of the kernel and its four subsystems will make the system administrator more knowledgeable and effective at system management.

Networking

*by Sriranga Veeraraghavan and
Salim Douba*

CHAPTER 26

Introduction

In the past few years, computer networks have become an integral part of most major production environments. In addition to providing basic file and print services that users transparently share, networks allow access to an ever-expanding suite of productivity tools such as electronic mail, schedule management and voice/video conferencing.

The task of implementing and maintaining networks that can meet increasing user demands is an extremely challenging task. Installing and configuring UNIX networks is quite complex. The complexity stems from the nature of the protocols, TCP/IP (Transmission Control Protocol/Internet Protocol), that UNIX networks are built upon.

This chapter covers the necessary concepts and skills that the UNIX system administrator needs in order to install, configure, and maintain UNIX connectivity. The first part is an overview of the basic concepts that govern TCP/IP communications, and second part provides a detailed treatment of the UNIX necessary for maintaining UNIX connectivity.

Basics of TCP/IP Communications

In 1969, the Department of Defense's Advanced Research Projects Agency (ARPA) started developing an experimental wide area packet-switched network. This network, called ARPANET, was intended to allow government scientists and engineers to share expensive computing resources. Almost all of these computers used different hardware and operating systems, thus the experimental protocols developed by ARPA for ARPANET had to be "cross-platform".

The current TCP/IP protocol suite was product of this effort. It allows large networks connecting hybrid platforms to be easily built. Anything from mainframes to desktop computers can access a TCP/IP network. The largest demonstration of the capabilities of TCP/IP is the Internet itself; it connects more than 10 million computers from different vendors around the world.

TCP/IP Protocol Architecture

The TCP/IP communications suite was designed with modularity in mind. This means that instead of developing a solution that integrates all aspects of communications in one single piece of code, the designers broke the puzzle into its constituent components and dealt with them individually. Thus, TCP/IP evolved into a suite of protocols specifying interdependent solutions to the different pieces of the communications puzzle. This approach to problem solving is normally referred to as the layering approach, thus the TCP/IP suite is also referred to as a layered suite of communication protocols.

Figure 26.1 shows the four-layer model of the TCP/IP communications architecture. As shown in the diagram, the model is based on representing data communications as four sets of interdependent processes:

- Application representation
- Host representation
- Network representation
- Media access and delivery

Each of these processes takes care of the needs of entities it represents whenever an application engages in the exchange of data with its counterpart on the network. These process sets are grouped into the following four layers:

- Application layer
- Transport layer (sometimes called host-to-host)
- Internet layer
- Network access layer

Each of these layers can be implemented as separate, yet interdependent pieces of software.

FIGURE 26.1.

TCP/IP layered communications architecture.

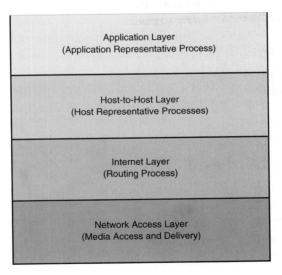

| Application Layer |
| (Application Representative Process) |

| Host-to-Host Layer |
| (Host Representative Processes) |

| Internet Layer |
| (Routing Process) |

| Network Access Layer |
| (Media Access and Delivery) |

REQUEST FOR COMMENTS (RFCs)

Throughout this book references will be made to standard documents that contain the description and formal specification of the TCP/IP protocols.

These documents will be referred to as RFC *XXXX*, where *XXXX* refers to the number of the document. For example, RFC 959 is the standards document specifying the File Transfer Protocol.

Obtaining copies of the RFCs is a simple matter provided you have access to the Internet. One way of doing it is to send email to

```
rfc-info@ISI.EDU
```

using the following format:

```
To: rfc-info@ISI.EDU
Subject: getting rfcs

help: ways_to_get_rfcs
```

You will receive a response to this message detailing the methods by which you can gain access to the RFCs. Some of the methods include FTP sites, WWW sites, and email.

The Application Layer

The Application layer processes are responsible for reconciling differences in the data syntax between the platforms on which the communicating applications are running. Communicating with an IBM mainframe, for example, might involve character translation between the EBCDIC and ASCII character sets. Although performing the translation task the application layer does not require any understanding of how the underlying protocols handle the transmission of the translated characters between hosts. Some application layer protocols are FTP, TELNET, NFS and DNS.

The Transport Layer

The transport layer is responsible for communicating data reliably between applications running on hosts across the network. It guarantees the reliability and integrity of the data being exchanged, without confusing the identities of the communication applications. For this reason the transport layer has a mechanism that allows it to make distinctions between the applications on whose behalf it is making data deliveries.

For example, if FTP requests are made, the requests should be delivered to FTP at the other end. Likewise, TELNET-generated traffic should be delivered to TELNET at the other end, not to FTP. To achieve this, the transport layer at both ends of a connection must cooperate by clearly marking data packets so that the communicating applications are easily identifiable.

Protocols operating at the transport layer include both UDP (User Datagram Protocol) and TCP (Transmission Control Protocol). Later sections will cover the characteristics of both protocols.

Internet Layer

The internet layer is responsible for determining the best route that data packets should follow to reach their destination. If the destination host is attached to the same network, data is delivered directly to that host by the network access layer. If the host belongs to some other network, the internet layer employs a routing process for discovering the route to that host. Once the route is discovered, data is delivered through intermediate devices, called routers, to its destination. Routers are special devices with connections to two or more networks

As shown in Figure 26.2, hosts `alto` and `tenor` belong to different networks. The intervening networks are connected via devices called routers. For host `alto` to deliver data to host `tenor`, it has to send its data to router R1 first. Router R1 delivers to R2 and so on until the data packet makes it to host `tenor`. This process is known as routing and is responsible for delivering data to its ultimate destination. Each of the involved routers is responsible for assisting in the delivery process.

Two protocols implemented at the internet layer are

- The Internet Control Message Protocol (ICMP, RFC792).
- The Internet Protocol (RFC791).

The purpose of the Internet Protocol (IP) is to handle routing of data around the internetwork (commonly known as the internet), whereas the purpose of ICMP is to handle routing error detection and recovery.

FIGURE 26.2.

Routers cooperate in the delivery of data packets to their destinations.

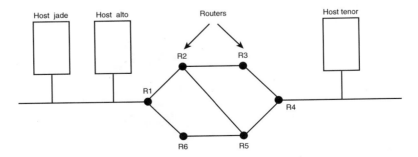

Network Access Layer

The network access layer is where media access and transmission mechanisms take place. At this layer, both the hardware and the software drivers are implemented. The protocols at this layer provide the means for the system to deliver data to other devices on a directly attached network. This is the only layer that is aware of the physical characteristics of the underlying network, including rules of access, data frame (name of a unit of data at this layer) structure, and addressing.

An example of a protocol implemented at this level is the Address Resolution Protocol, which takes care of mapping the IP symbolic address to the corresponding hardware (MAC) address.

UDP Versus TCP

UDP is a connectionless, unreliable transport protocol. This means that UDP is not sophisticated enough to care about the datagrams it sends down the network. Being connectionless, UDP does not negotiate a connection with its peer for the sake of establishing a control mechanism that guarantees the reliable delivery of data. Once it delivers data to IP for subsequent transmission, UDP simply forgets about it and proceeds to other business.

TCP's behavior is quite opposite to UDP's. Its sophistication allows it to deliver data reliably. TCP's sophistication stems from its ability to establish a connection with its peer on behalf of the applications engaging in the exchange of data. This allows it to successfully track the progress of the data delivery process until the process is successfully concluded. Data lost or damaged on the wire, can be easily recovered by the TCP protocol by virtue of communicating the need for retransmitting the affected data segment to its sending peer across the network.

Why use UDP then, when TCP is the more reliable of the two? To applications that are designed to handle error detection and recovery, using UDP poses no serious threat. Rather, the choice of UDP becomes the reasonable one. Equally qualifying to the use of UDP is the size and nature of data being exchanged. Transactional services involving small amounts of data behave more efficiently using UPD services than TCP. This is especially applicable to transactions in which all the data can be accommodated in one datagram. Should a datagram be lost or deformed, retransmitting that datagram incurs less overhead than is involved in establishing a TCP connection and releasing it later.

IP Addresses

In TCP/IP every device on the network has an unique address. This address is almost all that is needed to locate a device on the network. This address is similar to a postal address, which describes your home address, thus helping others to unambiguously locate you.

A device's address is known as its symbolic IP address, and is made up of two parts:

- The network address
- The node address

The network address is common to all hosts and devices on the same physical network. The node address is unique to the host on that network. Neither address has anything to do with the actual hardwired MAC address on the network address card. As a matter of fact, a network administrator has the freedom to change both the node part of the address and, to a lesser degree, the network address of a device regardless of its MAC address. For this reason, TCP/IP addresses are described as symbolic.

An IP address is 32 bits or four bytes long, and includes both the network and the node addresses. The number of bits corresponding to the node and the network part depend on the IP address class to which an address belongs. IP defines three main classes: A, B, and C.

CLASS D ADDRESSES

There is a fourth class of IP addresses known as Class D address. Class D addresses have their first four bits fixed to 1110.

A class D address does not describe a network of hosts on the wire, it is a multicast address, identifying a group of computers that can be running a distributed application on the network.

Class A Addresses

In a class A address, the first bit is fixed to 0, and the first byte is called the network id and identifies the network. The remaining three bytes are used to identify the host on the network, and comprise the host id. It can be calculated that there is a maximum of 127 class A networks, with each capable of accommodating millions of hosts.

Class B Addresses

In a class B address, the first two bits are fixed to 10, the first and second byte are used to identify the network, and the last two bytes are used to identify the host. There can be 65,535 hosts on class B networks, capable of accommodating thousands of hosts.

Class C Addresses

In a class C address, the first three bits are fixed to 110, the first, second, and third bytes are used to identify the network, and the last byte is used to identify the host. Class C networks are the smallest of all classes, as each can accommodate a maximum of 254 hosts (not 256, because 0x0 and 0xFF are reserved for other purposes). With three bytes reserved to identify the network, millions of class C networks can be defined.

Dotted Decimal IP Addresses

To make address administration easier, TCP/IP network administrators can configure hosts, and routers, with addresses by using what is a notation known as dotted decimal notation.

Dotted decimal notation treats the 32-bit address as four separate, yet contiguous, bytes. Each byte is represented by its decimal equivalent, which lies between 0 and 255. Table 26.1 gives the range of values for the first byte of each of the IP address that classes can assume.

TABLE 26.1. DECIMAL RANGES OF IP ADDRESS CLASSES.

Address Class	*Decimal Range*
A	0 to 127
B	128 to 191
C	192 to 223

Consider the address 148.29.4.121. By applying the rules learned above, it can be determined that this is a class B address, because the first byte lies in the 128 to 191 range of values. And because a class B address has the first two bytes for a network address, it can be derived that the network address is 148.29 whereas the host address is 4.121 on that network. To generalize, given an IP address, its class can be recognized by interpreting the first byte. Consequently, the network portion of the address can be derived from the remaining bytes.

All 0s and all 1s (0x0 and 0xff, respectively) are reserved for special purposes, and therefore cannot be used to designate a node on the network. This is because a 0 node address refers to all nodes on the network. Whereas a 1 node address is normally used to broadcast a message to all hosts on that network.

In addition to the reservations made on the node addresses described above, there are two class A network addresses that bear a special significance and cannot be used to designate a network. They are network addresses 0 and 127. Network 0 is used to designate the default route, whereas 127 is used to designate this host or the loopback address.

The default route refers to a router configuration that makes the routing of packets to destinations that are unknown to the router possible.

The loopback address is used to designate the localhost and is used to send IP datagrams to the local machine in exactly the same way other machines on the network are addressed. Conventionally, 127.0.0.1 is the address which is used to designate the local host. You can, however, use any other class A 127 address for the same purpose. For example 127.45.20.89 is valid for designating the local host as is the 127.0.0.1.

Subnet Mask

Class B networks accommodate approximately 65,000 hosts each, whereas Class A networks accommodate thousands of nodes. In practice, it is not feasible to put all on the same network because of the following reasons:

- Depending on the type of physical network, there is an upper limit on the number of hosts that can be connected to the same network. Ethernet 10BASE-T, for example, imposes a limit of 1,024 nodes per physical network.

- Sometimes it might not be feasible even to reach the maximum allowable limit of nodes on the underlying physical network. Depending on the amount of traffic applications generate on the network you might have to resort to breaking the network into smaller sub-networks to alleviate prevailing network congestion conditions.

- Organizations with branch offices across the nation or around the globe connect their computing resources over wide area network (WAN) links. This requires treating the branch office local area networks (LANs) as a network of interconnected networks, commonly referred to as intranet.

To resolve these problems the TCP/IP protocol stack allows for extending the network ID portion beyond its default boundary by using a subnet mask.

A subnet mask is a 32-bit number that is applied to an IP address to identify the network and node address of a host or router interface. As a rule, you are required to assign a binary 1 to those bits in the mask that correspond in position to the bits that you want IP to treat as part of the network ID. The dotted decimal specification of subnet masks are similar to the specification of IP address. Table 26.2 gives the subnet masks for the different IP address classes.

TABLE 26.2. SUBNET MASK OF IP ADDRESS CLASSES.

Address Class	Subnet Mask
A	255.0.0.0
B	255.255.0.0
C	255.255.255.0

In order to extend the network ID to include the third byte in a Class B address, its subnet mask then becomes 255.255.255.0, which is the same as for a class C address

Routing

IP addresses are used to route data on the network. For example, when a user runs the `telnet` program to access another host, TCP/IP uses the IP addresses in order to connect and establish a telnet session between the two hosts.

IP distinguishes between hosts and gateways. A gateway is machine that connects two or more networks for the purpose of providing forwarding services between them. A host is the end system where user applications run.

If both hosts are attached to the same network, routing on hosts is limited to the delivery of a datagram directly to the remote system,. Otherwise, datagrams are delivered to the default gateway. The default gateway for a host is defined during TCP/IP configuration, and is a router attached to the same network, which the host should "trust" for assistance in deliveries made to other hosts on remote networks.

Figure 26.3 illustrates the concept of default routers. Host X in the diagram, is configured to gateway A as its default router. Thus, when X wants to send data to Y, it delivers a datagram to gateway A (its default router). Upon examining the destination IP address, gateway A realizes that the address belongs to host Y, which is on a network to which gateway B is connected. Consequently, gateway A forwards the datagram to gateway B for the subsequent handling and delivery to host Y.

ROUTERS AND GATEWAYS

Currently, the networking industry makes a distinction between a router and a gateway. Routers are said to provide routing services between networks supporting same network protocol stacks (that is, TCP/IP). Gateways, on the other hand, connect networks of dissimilar architectures (for example, TCP/IP and Novell's IPX/SPX).

Historically, the TCP/IP community used the term gateway to refer to routing devices. Throughout this chapter, both terms are used interchangeably to refer to routing.

FIGURE 26.3.

A host on an IP network forwards all deliveries pertaining to remote networks to its default router.

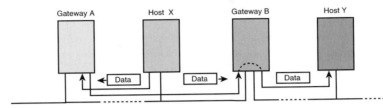

MULTI-HOMED HOSTS

UNIX allows a host to attach to more than one network using multiple interface cards, each attaching to a different network. Such hosts are commonly referred to as a multi-homed.

A multi-homed UNIX host can be configured to route data between networks to which it is attached, making it behave like a router. Other than being attached to two separate networks, multi-homed UNIX hosts behave in exactly the same fashion as other hosts with a single interface card.

The Route Information Table

In order to properly route packets a database that contains information about all known routes must be consulted. This database is called the route information table, and it is built and maintained by the Route Information Protocol (RIP).

The main purpose of RIP is to identify all the networks on the internetwork and the routers that are closest to each network. It constructs and maintains the database or "network map" from the perspective of the workstation or router on which it is running. This database includes the following information about each destination on the network:

- The distance from the current device. Normally, this is equal to the number of routers a datagram has to go through to reach its destination. Distance is also referred to as the metric, or number of hops.

- The IP address of "trusted" routers that datagrams should be forwarded to.

- A list of the network interfaces of the host (if multihomed) or router which are attached to the same network as the next router.

The UNIX command to display the contents of the routing information table is

`netstat -rn.`

Its output will be similar to the following:

```
Routing tables
Destination       Gateway          Flags   Refs    Use    Interface
127.0.0.1         127.0.0.1        UH      1       0      lo0
87.45.3.4         198.53.237.20    UGH     0       0      eth0
100               100.0.0.2        U       4       51     eth1
221.78.39         198.53.237.20    UG      0       0      eth0
default           198.53.237.5     UG      0       0      eth0
198.53.237        198.53.237.1     U       3       624    eth0
```

The meanings for the values in each column are explained in Table 26.3.

TABLE 26.3. `netstat` OUTPUT.

Column	Description
Destination	The address of the network or host. When a host IP address is specified, the destination is referred to as static route.
Gateway	The address of the next router.
Flags	This column provides status information about that route. Each of the characters in the Flags column describes a specific state. U indicates that a route is up, H indicates that a route is to a host and G indicates that a route is a gateway between two networks.
Refs	This column shows the number of active connections over that route. Any service or application that utilizes TCP as the underlying transport protocol increments this column by one upon invocation.
Use	This column keeps track of the number of packets that traversed this route since TCP/IP was started.
Interface	This column includes the name of the local interface from which the datagram should be forwarded to the next router. Upon configuring a network interface card, UNIX assigns it a label.

Route Table Maintenance

TCP/IP supports both static and dynamic means of maintaining the routing table. Static means of maintaining the routing table mainly involve the use of the two UNIX commands `ifconfig` and `route`.

`ifconfig`

The `ifconfig` command is used to configure, or to check the configuration values of, the network interface card. It can be used to assign or change the IP address, netmask or broadcast address of an interface. It is used at boot time by the TCP/IP startup scripts, to set up those parameters as dictated by the interface configuration files.

The syntax of the `ifconfig` command is as follows:

`ifconfig interface IP_address netmask mask broadcast address`

Table 26.4 explains the arguments given to `ifconfig`.

TABLE 26.4. THE ARGUMENTS FOR `ifconfig`.

Argument	Description
`interface`	This argument defines the label identifying the network interface card.
`IP_address`	This argument defines the IP address assigned to the network interface.
`netmask mask`	This argument defines the subnet mask. This parameter can be ignored if the default mask is sufficient (that is, the network is not segmented into subnets). All hosts on the same physical network must have their mask set to the same value.
`broadcast address`	This argument defines the broadcast address for the network. The default broadcast address is such that all the host id bits are set to one. Older systems used to have the bits set to zero. All hosts on the same physical network must have their broadcast address set to the same value. For example, the Class B 150.1.0.0 network address has by default the 150.1.255.255 as a broadcast address.

In the following example, `ifconfig` is used to set up the IP address, netmask and the broadcast address of a 3Com 3C509 network interface card:

`# ifconfig el30 150.1.0.1 netmask 255.255.0.0 broadcast 150.1.255.255`

Optionally, you can use the hostname instead of the IP address to configure the interface as follows

`# ifconfig el30 oboe netmask 255.255.0.0 broadcast 150.1.255.255`

Where `oboe` is the `hostname` mapped to a valid IP address in the `/etc/hosts` file.

This example can be further simplified to become

`# ifconfig el30 oboe`

because both the netmask and the broadcast address are set to their default values.

The configuration parameters of a supported can be checked as follows

```
# ifconfig interface
```

For example, to check the configuration of the 3Com 3c509 we use the following command:

```
# ifconfig el30
```

The output is

```
el30: flags=23<UP,BROADCAST,NOTRAILERS>
    inet 150.1.0.1 netmask ffff0000 broadcast 150.1.255.255
```

This shows that the interface is configured with the IP address 150.1.0.1, the netmask ffff0000 (the hex equivalent tf 255.255.0.0), and the broadcast address 150.1.255.255.

To check the configuration of all the interfaces supported by the system, you can specify the -a option to ifconfig.

The ifconfig command supports a few optional parameters, of which the up and down parameters can be used to enable or disable an interface. You normally temporarily disable an interface on a router whenever you are troubleshooting the network and want to isolate a suspect segment from the rest of the network. Also, on some systems, configuration changes made to an interface won't take effect unless the interface was disabled before using ifconfig to modify the interface's configuration.

To disable an interface use the command:

```
# ifconfig interface down
```

As an example, to disable the 3C509 network interface, enter

```
# ifconfig el30 down
```

It is always a good idea to check that the interface was indeed disabled before trusting it. To do so, enter

```
# ifconfig el30
el30: flags=22<BROADCAST,NOTRAILERS>
    inet 150.1.0.1 netmask ffff0000 broadcast 150.1.255.255
```

Notice how the absence of the keyword UP from the information included in the angle brackets implies that the interface is down.

To bring it back up, use the command

```
# ifconfig el30 up
```

In this section the Ethernet interface we used was called e130. This name is particular to SCO Unix, on Solaris the same interface can be called le0 or hme0 depending on your interface card. On Linux, this interface would be called eth0.

route

Using the route command a static route can be entered to the routing table of a UNIX host. The syntax of the route command is

```
route add destination_address next_router metric
```

Here destination_address is the route you want to add to the routing table, next_router is the address of the next router to forward the datagrams to, and metric is a measure of distance to the destination, normally expressed in number of intervening routers.

The following example shows how route can be used to add a new destination to the routing table:

```
# route add 87.45.3.4  198.53.237.20 1
```

The following example shows how to use route to configure a host for the default route entry:

```
# route add 0.0.0.0 198.53.237.5 1
```

By virtue of the preceding entry, the host in question is being configured to recognize the router at address 198.53.237.5 as being its default gateway.

Dynamic route maintenance involves the automatic addition of newly discovered routes to the route table. It also involves deletions of routes that are no longer valid because of network reconfigurations. There are several protocols that might be employed for the task of dynamic route maintenance. Among the currently common ones are Route Information Protocol (RIP), Open Shortest Path First (OSPF), and Internet Control Messaging Protocol (ICMP).

TCP/IP Startup

Different variants of UNIX have different implementations of the TCP/IP startup process and associated scripts. In particular, three implementations are presented in this section:

- TCP/IP Startup on SVR4
- TCP/IP Startup on Solaris 2.x
- TCP/IP Startup on Linux

TCP/IP Startup on SVR4

TCP/IP is started at boot time when run level 2 (multiuser run level) is entered by the script

`/etc/init.d/inetinit`

This script sets out by configuring, linking and loading various STREAMS modules and drivers that are required for the STREAMS TCP/IP protocol stack. If STREAMS is loaded successfully, `inetinit` executes the script

`/etc/confnet.d/inet/config.boot.sh`

This configures all the supported network interfaces as defined in the file:

`/etc/confnet.d/inet/interface`

One the network interfaces are successfully configured `inetinit` executes the script

`/etc/inet/rc.inet`

This script starts TCP/IP daemons which have been verified as properly configured. For example if the name server's configuration file, `named.boot`, is found the name server, `in.named`, will be started.

The `inetinit` script can be used for both starting and stopping TCP/IP services. It starts TCP/IP when the system is brought to the multiuser level and stops TCP/IP when the system is shutdown or brought down to single user level.

There are situations in which you have to make changes to this file. For example to install static routes at boot time, you will to edit the `rc.init` file to include the appropriate `route` commands. Also, you might need to change the file path specifications of configuration files pertaining to some daemons such as `in.named`.

The startup process completes with the invocation of the "super-server" daemon `inetd`, which is responsible for invoking and controlling many of the TCP/IP application service daemons such as `ftpd`, and `telnetd`.

TCP/IP Startup on Solaris 2.x

Although Solaris 2.x is a UNIX SVR4 operating system, it does not follow the startup procedures depicted above. Solaris 2.x relies on three scripts for bringing up TCP/IP services. These are

- `/etc/init.d/rootusr`
- `/etc/init.d/inetinit`
- `/etc/init.d/inetsrv`

The `rootusr` script's primary function is to configure enough of TCP/IP interfaces and services that are necessary to mount system resources.

The `inetinit` script has two functions:

- Configure the Network Information Service
- Configure routing including starting the route discovery daemon `in.routed`, enabling the packet forwarding function if more than one physical network interface is configured

The `inetsvc` script concludes the TCP/IP startup process by verifying the configuration of the network interfaces, starting the domain name service (DNS) if need be, and finally bringing up the "super-server" daemon `inetd`.

INTERFACE CONFIGURATION ON SOLARIS

Rather than relying on a common configuration file where all the supported network interfaces are defined, Solaris 2.x defines one simple file per interface. The file names will be of the format:

`/etc/hostname.xx?`

where *xx* stands for the interface driver and *?* stands for the instance number of this interface. For example, in the file

`/etc/hostname.elx0`

The `elx` stands for 3C509, and `0` stands for first instance of this interface.

TCP/IP Startup on Linux

Linux relies on a set of nested scripts to bring up TCP/IP protocol stack and services:

- `/etc/rc.d/init.d/inet`
- `/etc/sysconfig/network`
- `/etc/sysconfig/network-scripts/*`

The `inet` script is the first script to be started. It calls the `network` script, which loops through and executes, the network interface configuration scripts in the directory

`/etc/sysconfig/network-scripts`

There are two scripts per network interface:

- `ifup-xxx?` script to bring the interface up
- `ifdown-xxx?` script to bring the interface down

Here the *xxx* specifies the interface driver being configured, and *?* specifies the instance being configured. For example, `eth0` specifies the first Ethernet interface.

Upon completion of the execution of the `network` script, the execution of the `inet` script concludes by bring up both the port mapper daemon and the "super-server" daemon `inetd`.

`inetd`

In UNIX network services such as `telnet` and `ftp` are started on demand. The daemon that is responsible for starting these services is `inetd` It is known as the Internet "super-server" or master Internet daemon.

Depending on the flavor of UNIX, `inetd` is either started at boot time by `sac` (the service access controller) or as standalone daemon. On most SVR4 UNIX systems it is started by `sac`. Linux and Solaris 2.x retain BSD behavior and start `inetd` as a standalone daemon.

Once started, the daemon is configured and behaves identically on all UNIX variants. First it fetches and reads its configuration file:

`/etc/inetd.conf`

This file defines the service daemons on whose behalf `inetd` can listen for network service requests. Table 26.5 contains a brief description of some of the daemons that are controlled by the `inetd`.

There are a few occasions when changes will have to be made to the `inetd.conf` file. For example, when you want to enable or disable a service, or modify one that is already supported, you will need to edit this file.

Enabling or disabling a service is a matter of removing or inserting the # character in front of the service configuration entry. Modifying a supported service mainly involves changing the arguments passed to the program responsible for that service.

TABLE 26.5. SERVICES MANAGED BY `inetd`.

Service	Description
ftpd	This daemon is responsible for responding to user requests involving file transfers in and out of the host as well as other functions such as third party transfers and directory lookups. It is also known as `in.ftpd` on some flavors of UNIX.
telnetd	This daemon is responsible for providing user login services. It is also known as `in.telnetd` on some flavors of UNIX.

Service	Description
rshd	This daemon is an implementation of the Berkeley remote shell. It is used to execute a commands on a remote systems. On some flavors of UNIX it is known as in.rshd.
logind	This daemon is an implementation of Berkeley's remote login capability. On some flavors of UNIX it is known as in.logind.
execd	This daemon allows for the remote execution of commands on the system. On some flavors of UNIX its is known as in.execd.
talkd	This daemon allows users anywhere on the network to chat using the keyboard and the screen of their terminals.
uucpd	This daemon is responsible for the transfer of UUCP data over the network. On some flavors of UNIX it is known as in.uucpd.
fingerd	This daemon allows the use of the finger command to determine what are the users doing.
echo	This service is supported over both UDP and TCP, and returns whatever it is sent, hence the name echo.
discard	This service simply discards whatever it is sent.
daytime	This service returns the current time.

Name Services

A user can establish a session with a remote host by entering the IP address of that host as a command line parameter to the application being invoked. For example, to invoke a remote login session with a host of IP address 100.0.0.2, the following command can be entered:

```
$ rlogin 100.0.0.2
```

Rather than requiring users to enter the IP address of the desired host, name services provides the means of assigning and administering names to hosts and the accompanying mechanisms responsible for resolving user-specified names to machine-usable IP addresses.

Hostnames are normally assigned during system installation. To find the name assigned to your host, use the command:

```
uname -n
```

On my system it displays the following:

```
kanchi
```

The `/etc/hosts` file

The simplest method of resolving host names to IP addresses involves the maintenance of a host table on every UNIX system. This table is normally maintained in the `/etc/hosts` file. It is composed of a simple flat database in which each entry describes the IP address of a host and its associated name. Here's an example of a sample `hosts` file:

```
127.0.0.1      localhost
100.0.0.2      jade.harmonics.com jade
198.53.237.1   pixel
100.0.0.1      alto
100.0.0.5      flyer
100.0.0.3      tenor
```

Each entry consists of an IP address, the host name associated with the IP address, and, optionally, an alias, where an alias is another name for the same host in question.

For example, `jade` and `jade.harmonics.com` refer to the same host (that of IP address 100.0.0.2). This allows a user to establish a telnet session with `jade` by entering either of the following commands:

```
$ telnet jade
```

```
$ telnet jade.harmonics.com
```

All TCP/IP applications, such as `telnet` and `ftp`, have a built-in name resolution mechanism that looks at the host's table and returns the corresponding IP address to the invoked application. The application then proceeds to contacting the corresponding host across the network. Failure to resolve the name to an IP address normally results in the error message `"Unknown host"`.

The Domain Name System (DNS)

The host table approach to name resolution is convenient for reasonably small networks only a with few entries in the `/etc/hosts` file. For large networks and for systems connected to the internet, maintaining a complete `/etc/hosts` file is an impossible task.

Domain Name System (DNS, RFC 1035) is an alternative way to performing name resolution. DNS resolves host names to IP addresses by using a global, hierarchical and distributed database containing information about all hosts on the network as well as those on the Internet.

This hierarchy allows for the subdivision of the domain name space into independently manageable partitions called domains. The distributed nature allows for the relocation of partitions, called subdomains, of the database onto name servers belonging to sites around the network or the Internet.

A name server is a host that maintains a partition of the DNS database. Each name server runs a server process that handles name-to-IP address resolution. The DNS client component, known as the name resolver connects to the name server when it needs to obtain an IP address for a hostname.

Organization of DNS

DNS is a hierarchical database of host information. Its structure resembles, to a great extent, that of computer file systems. In both cases, the organization follows that of an inverted tree with the root at the top of the structure. Where the root of the file system is written as a slash "/", that of DNS is written as a dot "." character.

Below the root level, the "top level" domains are defined and can be subdivided into sub-domains. The "top level" domains are given in Table 26.6.

TABLE 26.6. THE "TOP LEVEL" DOMAINS.

Top-Level Domain	Associated Affiliation
com	Commercial organizations
edu	Educational organizations
gov	U.S. government organizations
mil	Military organizations
net	Networking organizations
org	Non-commercial organizations
arpa	Special domain, for reverse resolution

These "top level" domains are further divided into subdomains, similar to dividing the UNIX file system into subdivisions called directories and subdirectories. Each subdomain is assigned a name, which can be up to 63 characters long. DNS allows nesting of up to 127 domains in one tree.

Each domain and subdomain represents a partition of the database, which contains information about hosts in that domain, and/or information about subdomains.

A domain name specification relative to the root is known as fully qualified domain name (FQDN). Under DNS, a fully qualified domain name is written as a sequence of names, starting with the target domain name and ending at the root domain. For example, ott.harmonics.com is the fully qualified domain name of the subdomain ott.

> ### HOSTNAMES
>
> The hierarchical structure of DNS allows two or more hosts to have the same name as long as they do not belong to the same subdomain. This is similar to files with the same filename that are located in different subdirectories.

Delegation of Administrative Authority

The hierarchical organization of DNS allows for the breakup of name resolution responsibility into smaller manageable parts, pertaining to the administration of smaller domains of the name space. Consequently, each of the member organizations of the Internet is delegated the authority for managing its own domain.

In practical terms, this requires that each of the organizations set up its own name server(s). The name server would then maintain all the host information, and respond to name queries, pertaining to that organization.

Once delegated the administration of its own domain, an organization can in turn break up its own domain into yet smaller subdomains and delegate the responsibility of administering them to other departments.

Delegation of administrative authority for subdomains has the following advantages:

- The workload becomes distributed, thereby considerably reducing the burden of the top-level name servers.
- The sharing of the query load results in improved response time.
- Distribution of the database places servers closer to the local authority, which prevents traffic due to queries pertaining to local resources from needlessly consuming Internet bandwidth.

Nameservers

Setting up DNS services to support the domain for which an organization is delegated authority involves creating a set of authoritative servers for that zone. Usually a minimum of two nameservers, a primary and secondary, are setup.

The primary name server is the system where the database files are maintained and is the most time consuming to setup. Changes made to the DNS, whether to the layout or structure of the domain being delegated or simple updates to the database, must be made on the primary name server. For example, to add a new host to the network, you have to assign it both a name and an IP address, and you must enter those assignments in the DNS database contained on the primary server.

The secondary nameserver is easier to set up than the primary, because it derives its database from the primary nameserver by replicating it via a process known as zonal transfer. Once set up, a secondary nameserver requires very little maintenance.

Every time the secondary nameserver is rebooted, it undergoes the zonal transfer process by contacting the primary server for the zone for which they both are responsible, and requesting all the information pertaining to that zone. Thereafter, the secondary server routinely polls the primary server for any updates that might have been made to the database.

It is not absolutely necessary to install any other than the primary server in order to bring up the DNS service. Including a secondary server has, however, the following advantages:

- Redundancy: there is no difference between a primary and secondary server except for the source of information that each relies on in responding to name queries. Both servers are equally capable of responding to such queries. Consequently, with the presence of a secondary server, should one of them accidentally stop responding to user queries, one will be capable of taking over, provided that user workstations are setup to contact both servers for queries.

- Distribution of workload: Because both servers are equally capable to responding to all types of queries, the environment can be setup so that the workload on these servers is fairly shared. The added benefit of sharing the workload is improved response time.

- Physical proximity: by having more than one server, you will be able to strategically locate each one of them so they are where they're needed most. Thus cutting on response time

Domain Name Service Implementation

In this section you will cover the setup of DNS service for a hypothetical environment. The scenario is based on a fictitious domain, `harmonics.com`. Figure 26.4 shows the network layout of this company. As shown, the network is made of two networks, a Class A network (100.0.0.0), and a Class C network (198.53.237.0). Multihomed host jade connects both networks. Also, the network is connected to the Internet via a router called `xrouter` with IP address 100.0.0.10. The diagram shows the IP addresses assigned to all hosts on the network.

FIGURE 26.4.

The harmonics.com *network layout.*

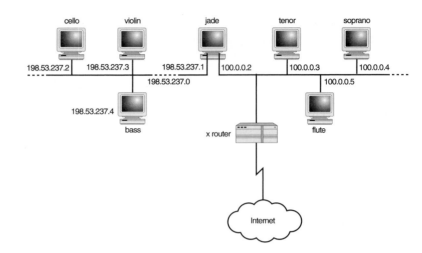

Because harmonics.com is assigned two network addresses, it is also delegated the administration of both reverse domains the 100.in-addr.arpa and 237.53.198. in-addr.arpa. Whereas harmonics.com maintains host information, such as host-to-IP address associations, the reverse domains are used to maintain the inverse mappings (that is, the IP-to-host name associations).

Because host jade is connected to both networks, it would be a good idea to bring up DNS name service on it. This way all hosts will have a DNS server directly attached to their network, resulting in better response time. Furthermore, host jade will be configured as the primary DNS server. In addition on each of the networks a secondary DNS server will be brought up. This way, should host jade go down, both networks will have backup DNS server to fall on for securing continued DNS service. Because harmonics.com is the domain name, every host is assigned domain name in compliance with the following syntax:

hostname.harmonics.com

Hence, jade's and cello's domain names become jade.harmonics.com and cello .harmonics.com. Hereafter, the "host name" and the "domain host name" will be used interchangeably.

Besides setting up DNS servers, configuring name services involves setting up all the DNS clients on the network. First we will cover the setup of the client, then we will cover the setup of the servers.

Configuring the DNS Client

The DNS client, known as the resolver, is built into each of the TCP/IP applications and is responsible for resolving DNS queries on behalf of the invoked application. DNS queries can be various types. Most common query is a hostname-to-IP address resolution query. This is called a type A query. Reverse queries, or IP address-to-hostname resolution queries, are called pointer or PTR queries.

Unless configured to contact a name server, the resolver normally checks the `/etc/hosts` file to get the IP address corresponding the name of the host the application specifies.

All you have to do to configure the resolver on a host, is to create the file:

`/etc/resolv.conf`

Using this file, the system administrator defines the domain name to which the host belongs and the IP addresses of up to three name servers. An example of this file follows:

```
domainname    harmonics.com
nameserver    100.0.0.2
nameserver    198.53.237.3
```

Each of the entries is made of two parts, a keyword and a value. The first entry has the keyword `domainname` followed by the domain name to which the host is said to belong. The last two entries specify the IP addresses of nameservers that the resolver should use for queries.

If a user on a DNS-configured client entered the following command:

```
$ ftp tenor.harmonics.com
```

The resolver issues a query to a name server on the network that is specified in the `/etc/resolv.conf` file. In the above example, the server 100.0.0.2 is queried first because it is the first nameserver in the list. If it fails to respond, the next nameserver on the list is contacted. Ultimately, a successful query returns the IP address of host `tenor` to the resolver, which in turn hands it off to `ftp`.

Configuring `nsswitch.conf`

In addition to creating `/etc/resolv.conf`, you will need to edit `/etc/nsswitch.conf` to finish your nameserver configuration. As root, edit the following line in `/etc/nsswitch.conf`:

```
hosts: files
```

to read

```
hosts: files dns
```

If your machine looks something like the following

```
hosts: files nis
```

just append dns to the end of the entry:

```
hosts: files nis dns
```

DNS Database and Startup Files

Configuring a name server involves the creation of many database and startup files. The number of files varies with the size of the organization, its structure, and the number of domains it has been delegated to administer. Depending on the type of the name server you might end up configuring different combinations of these file types. You might also end up configuring multiple files of the same type.

In the following discussion four different file types will be presented. Table 26.7 gives the names of each of these files along with a brief description of their function.

TABLE 26.7. DNS FILES.

File	Description
named.hosts	This file defines the domain for which the nameserver is authoritative, and mainly contains hostname to IP address mappings.
named.rev	This file defines the reverse in-addr.arpa domain for which the name-server authoritative, and mainly contains the IP address to hostname reverse mapping records.
named.local	This file contains the information required to resolve the 127.0.0.1 loop-back address to localhost.
named.ca	This file contains the names and addresses of the Internet's root domain servers. This file is used by the nameserver to contact the root nameserver to obtain answers to queries outside its domain.
named.boot	This file is used by the DNS daemon, named, at start up. It defines the database filenames and their location on the filesystem.

Domain data is maintained in these files in the form of resource records (RR's) that must follow a structure as defined in RFC 1033. This RFC defines a multitude of resource record (RR) types. Each type is responsible for tackling an aspect of the global database. In the following subsections the most commonly encountered RR types are described.

Start of Authority Resource Record

The Start of Authority (SOA) record identifies the upper boundary of a partition of the global DNS database. Every configuration file must contain an SOA record identifying the beginning of the partition for which the server is authoritative. All RR records following the SOA record are part of the named zone.

The syntax of the SOA record is

```
[zone] IN SOA origin contact (serial refresh retry expire minimum)
```

Here *zone* identifies the name of the zone, IN identifies the class (Internet) and SOA identifies the record type. The functions of remaining data fields are described in Table 26.8.

TABLE 26.8. SOA RECORD DATA FIELDS.

Field	Description
origin	Defines the primary name server for this domain.
contact	Defines the email address of the person responsible for maintaining this domain.
Serial	Defines to the version number of this zone file. It is meant for interpretation and use by the secondary server, which transfers data from the primary server.
refresh	Defines the polling time interval, in seconds, for secondary servers. Only when a change in version number is detected is the database transferred.
Retry	Defines the time interval, in seconds, that the secondary server should wait before retrying a zonal transfer if the primary server fails to respond to a zone refresh request.
Expire	Defines the duration of time, in seconds, for which the secondary server can retain zonal data without requesting a zone refresh from the primary.
Minimum	Defines the default time-to-live (ttl) which applies to resource records whose ttl is not explicitly defined.

As an example, the SOA record defining the upper boundary of the harmonics.com domain should read as follows:

```
harmonics.com.    IN    SOA    jade.harmonics.com.
root.jade.harmonics.com. (
            2    ; Serial
            14400    ; Refresh (4 hours)
            3600    ; Retry (1hr)
            604800     ; Expire ( 4 weeks )
            86400 )    ; minimum TTL (time-to-live)
```

This record must be included in the named.hosts file, because it makes the DNS server aware of where its authority starts. In addition to a SOA record, named.hosts must contain all the necessary data for answering name queries pertaining to hosts belonging to harmonics.com. This data is stored in the form of resource records that either map host-names to IP address mappings or contain pointers to other DNS servers for which authority over subdomains is delegated.

Address Resource Record

The Address Resource Records, located in the named.hosts file, maintain the host name-to-IP address association. Whenever a name server is queried for the IP address of host, given its name, the server fetches the Address records for one with a matching object name and responds with the IP address described in that record. These records are often referred to as A records.

The syntax of an A record is as follows:

```
[hostname] [ttl] IN A address
```

Table 26.9 describes the function of each of these fields.

TABLE 26.9. A RECORD DATA FIELDS.

Field	Description
hostname	Defines the name of a host. The host name can be specified relative to the current domain, or using a fully qualified domain name.
ttl	Defines the minimum time-to-live. This is normally left blank implying the default as defined in the SOA record.
IN	Defines the record's class, which is almost always Internet class.
A	Defines the record type as an address record.
address	Defines the IP address corresponding to the hostname.

As an example, the following is the A record pertaining to jade.harmonics.com.

```
jade.harmonics.com.    IN    A  100.0.0.2
```

The host name is a fully qualified domain name (FQDN), thus it is mandatory that it ends with a dot ".". Alternatively, it can be written as

```
jade    IN    A    100.0.0.2
```

Because jade belongs to the domain harmonics.com., DNS will qualify the name by appending the domain name to hostname.

Nameserver Resource Record

Nameserver (NS) resource records define the authoritative nameservers that for a particular zone or subdomain. The syntax of the NS record follows:

```
[domain] [ttl] IN NS server
```

The functions of the individual fields are explained in Table 26.10.

TABLE 26.10. NS RECORD DATA FIELDS.

Field	Description
domain	Defines the name of the domain for which this nameserver is an authoritative nameserver.
ttl	Defines the time-to-live for this record. If left blank, the default specified in the SOA record applies.
IN	Defines the class for the record as the Internet class.
NS	Identifies the record type as nameserver.
server	Defines the name of the host providing authoritative name service for the domain specified in *domain*.

NS records are also used to direct parent nameservers to the nameservers for their subdomains. Thus, a name server authoritative for the com domain must include an NS record identifying the server which is authoritative for the harmonics.com domain, in this case jade.harmonics.com..

A server for the com domain should contain the following NS record in its named.hosts file:

```
harmonics.com. IN NS jade.harmonics.com.
```

This NS record must also be included in the named.hosts file of jade.harmonics.com.

When a server for the com domain is queried for the host IP address of cello.harmonics.com., it checks its database to determine that jade.harmonics.com. is the server to which the query should be redirected. Hence, the com server returns the IP address of the jade, not its name, to the client station issuing the query. This means that it is not enough to include an NS record describing which server is authoritative for a given domain. The NS record should always be coupled with an A record specifying the address of the domain's server. Hence, the com server in question must include both of the following records in order to redirect queries pertaining to the harmonics.com. domain to jade:

```
harmonics.com. IN NS jade.harmonics.com.
jade IN A 100.0.0.2
```

Canonical Name Record

A Canonical Name (CNAME) record defines an alias pointing to the host's official name. These records are normally found in the `named.hosts` file. The syntax of the CNAME record is as follows:

```
aliasname [ttl] IN CNAME [host]
```

The individual fields are explained in Table 26.11.

TABLE 26.11. SOA RECORD DATA FIELDS.

Field	Description
aliasname	Defines the alias for the host specified in *host*.
ttl	Defines the time-to-live. If left blank the default specified in SOA record applies.
IN	Defines the record's class as the Internet class.
CNAME	Identifies the record as a Canonical Name record.
host	Defines the official name of the host.

The following is an example of a CNAME record:

```
fake.harmonics.com. IN CNAME cello.harmonics.com.
```

If a client issues a name query for host `fake`, the name server replaces `fake` with `cello`, using the above CNAME record, during its search for the queried information.

HOSTNAME CHANGES AND CNAME RECORDS

CNAME records are particularly useful whenever host name changes need to be made. What you would do in such a situation is change the official name, then maintain the old one as an alias for the new official name. This allows a grace period until users are accustomed to the new name, and applications affected by name changes are reconfigured.

Pointer Resource Records

Pointer (PTR) resource records, maintained in the file `named.rev`, are used to map IP addresses to names. The syntax of the PTR record is as follows:

```
name [ttl] IN PTR host
```

The individual fields are explained in Table 26.12.

TABLE 26.12. PTR RECORD DATA FIELDS.

Field	*Description*
`name`	Specifies the reverse domain name of the host.
`ttl`	Specifies time-to-live. If left blank, the default specified in the SOA record is assumed.
`IN`	Specifies that this record is in the Internet class.
`PTR`	Defines the records type as a Pointer record.
`host`	Specifies the host name.

As an example, the PTR record resolving the IP address of the host cello to its host name is:

```
2.237.53.198.in-addr.arpa IN PTR cello
```

Here *name* is in the format:

```
reverse_IP.in-addr.arpa
```

Because cello's IP address is 198.53.237.2 its *reverse_IP* becomes 2.237.53.198, and the reverse domain name of the host cello becomes `2.237.53.198.in-addr.arpa`.

Normally, when an organization is delegated authority over its domain, NIC delegates the organization the authority over the reverse domain corresponding to the network IDs belonging to that organization. In the case of Harmonics, the reverse domains are `100.in-addr.arpa` and `100.in-addr.arpa`.

Configuring a Primary Name Server

The following few subsections describe the contents of the database files required to configure a primary name server. Our example demonstrates the configuration of the DNS daemon, `named`, on the primary name server, jade, for the harmonics.com domain.

The first step in setting up a primary name server is to create and populate the following files:

- `named.hosts`
- `named.rev`
- `named.local`
- `named.ca`
- `named.boot`

named.hosts

The `named.hosts` file maintains the hostname to IP address mappings for all hosts in the designated zone. In the case of our sample domain, harmonics.com, `named.hosts` must contain the name to IP address mappings for all hosts on this network. On our primary nameserver, jade, the `named.hosts` file is as follows:

```
; Section 1: The SOA record

harmonics.com.  IN    SOA     jade.harmonics.com. root.jade.harmonics.com.
(
                2    ; Serial
                14400    ; Refresh (4 hours)
                3600    ; Retry (1hr)
                604800      ; Expire ( 4 weeks )
                86400 )     ; minimum TTL (time-to-live)

; Section 2: The following are the name server for the harmonics domain.

harmonics.com.    IN    NS    jade.harmonics.com.
                  IN    NS    cello.harmonics.com.

; Section 3: The following records map canonical names to IP addresses

localhost.harmonics.com. IN A    127.0.0.1
tenor.harmonics.com.     IN A    100.0.0.3
soprano.harmonics.com.   IN A    100.0.0.4
flute.harmonics.com.     IN A    100.0.0.5
xrouter                  IN A    100.0.0.10
cello.harmonics.com.     IN A    198.53.237.2
violin.harmonics.com.    IN A    198.53.237.3
bass.harmonics.com.      IN A    198.53.237.4

; Section 4: Multihomed hosts

jade.harmonics.com.      IN A    198.53.237.1
                         IN A    100.0.0.2
```

The file is conveniently broken down into sections, with each being titled by the section number and purpose of that section.

Section 1 contains the SOA record, which declares `jade.harmonics.com` as being the DNS authoritative server for the `harmonics.com` domain. A `named.hosts` file can contain only one SOA record, and it must be the first record in the file. The record also indicates that correspondence regarding this domain should be addressed to `root@jade.harmonics.com` (remember that the dot "." following `root` should be replaced with the familiar @ character). Refer to the description of SOA records for details on the values enclosed in parenthesis.

Section 2 includes two NS records declaring hosts jade and cello as name servers for the harmonics.com domain. Notice that the records do not specify which of the two servers is the primary as opposed to being the secondary server. The type of the name server is defined, as you will see later, in the named.boot file.

Section 3 includes all the A (address) records which map host names to IP addresses. When a client station queries a name server for the IP address of a given host, named scans the A records in its named.hosts for one matching the requirement, and returns the corresponding IP address to the querying station.

Section 4 defines the A records corresponding to jade which is a multi-homed host. Whenever named is queried for the IP address of jade, or any multi-homed host for that matter, named simply returns all the addresses if finds in its A records. To achieve optimal performance named returns the address closest to the querying station first, followed by the other ones in order of proximity.

named.rev

Because Harmonics, Inc. is assigned two network IDs (these are 100.0.0.0 and 198.53.237.0), the named.rev files become 100.rev and 237.53.198.rev. Each of these files contains an SOA record defining its start-of-authority, and the PTR records pertaining to the reverse domain.

The following is the complete listings of 100.rev file on the host jade:

```
100.in-addr.arpa.    IN SOA    jade.harmonics.com. root.jade.harmonics.com
(
                1      ;serial
                14400     ; Refresh (4 hours)
                3600     ; retry  ( 1 hour )
                604800     ; expire ( 1 week )
                86400 ) ; TTL = 1 day
;
; name servers
;
100.in-addr.arpa.    IN NS    jade.harmonics.com.
100.in-addr.arpa.    IN NS    cello.harmonics.com.
;
; Reverse address mappings
;
2.0.0.100.in-addr.arpa.    IN    PTR    jade.harmonics.com.
3.0.0.100.in-addr.arpa.    IN    PTR    tenor.harmonics.com.
4.0.0.100.in-addr.arpa    IN    PTR    soprano.harmonics.com.
5.0.0.100.in-addr.arpa    IN    PTR    flute.harmonics.com.
10.0.0.100.in-addr.arpa    IN    PTR    xrouter.harmonics.com.
```

Following is a listing of the contents of 237.53.198.rev file:

```
237.53.198.in-addr.arpa. IN SOA  jade.harmonics.com.
root.jade.harmonics.com. (
                    1     ; serial
                    14400    ; refresh ( 4 hr )
                    3600    ; retry ( 1 hr )
                    604800    ; expire ( 1 week )
                    86400 )   ; TTL = 1day
;
;
; name servers
;
237.53.198.in-addr.arpa.  IN    NS    jade.harmonics.com.
237.53.198.in-addr.arpa.  IN    NS    cello.harmonics.com.
;
;
; Reverse address mappings
;
1.237.53.198.in-addr.arpa. IN   PTR   jade.harmonics.com.
2.237.53.198.in-addr.arpa. IN   PTR   cello.harmonics.com.
3.237.53.198.in-addr.arpa. IN   PTR   violin.harmonics.com.
4.237.53.198.in-addr.arpa. IN   PTR   bass.harmonics.com.
```

Notice how closely the organization of the first two parts of each file follows that of
named.hosts. All files start with an appropriate SOA record marking the upper boundaries
of the in-addr.arpa domain for which the server is authoritative. Next there is a block
of NS records. These declare the nameservers that have authority for the domain. The last
part consists of PTR records. Each of these records contains the IP address to domain
name associations that named uses for reverse address resolution.

named.local

If you re-examine the named.hosts file, you will find that it contains an entry corresponding to the special loopback host name localhost. This entry maps localhost to
the familiar IP address 127.0.0.1 Yet there is no PTR record in any of the reverse
domain data files (listed above) which takes care of the reverse mapping. None of those
files is suitable for such a PTR record as the loopback address belongs to none of the in-
addr.arpa domains that the files support.

To remedy the discrepancy, a new reverse domain file is required. This file is called
named.local. Its contents are as follows:

```
0.0.127.in-addr.arpa. IN SOA jade.harmonics.com. root.jade.harmonics.com.
(
                    1    ; serial
                    14400    ; refresh ( 4 hours )
                    3600    ; retry ( 1 hour )
                    604800    ; expire ( 1 week )
                    86400 )   ; TTL = 1 day
;
```

```
; name servers
;
0.0.127.in-addr.arpa.     IN     NS     jade.harmonics.com.
0.0.127.in-addr.arpa.     IN     NS     cello.harmonics.com.
;
; reverse address PTR mapping
;
1.0.0.127.in-addr.arpa. IN      PTR      localhost
```

named.ca

As explained earlier in the chapter, rather than forcing a server to undergo the entire resolution referral process in order to respond to identical name queries, DNS allows the server to respond from data its cache. The cache is designed to improve the overall performance of DNS. This is achieved by saving in memory responses to queries that clients submit to servers. Furthermore, servers also cache all data they discover during the referral process that led to the desired response. This helps DNS servers to acquire, over time, considerable "knowledge" about the global DNS structure and keeping this knowledge locally accessible. This approach improves on both response time and network traffic.

To further improve the performance of the name service, DNS defines an additional cache-related file called named.ca. Using this file, data pertaining to other domains, neighboring or remote, can be maintained, including name servers authoritative for those domains as well as A records identifying their IP addresses. All data contained in the named.ca file is used to initialize the cache buffers in the DNS server every time the named is started, thus eliminating the learning process that the server has to undergo to discover the DNS structure.

For reliability, you should include only information you believe to be stable for prolonged periods. You also ought to periodically verify the validity and accuracy of the included data.

One of the most commonly included pieces of information in the named.ca file is information about the Internet root servers. This information is stable over long periods of time. It makes sense to initialize your server's cache with this information, given the likelihood that users on your networks will want to reach places on the Internet. A minimal named.ca file would be similar to the following:

```
; Section 1: NS records for the root domain servers
;
. 99999999      IN     NS     A.ROOT-SERVERS.NET
. 99999999      IN     NS     B.ROOT-SERVERS.NET
. 99999999      IN     NS     C.ROOT-SERVERS.NET
. 99999999      IN     NS     D.ROOT-SERVERS.NET
. 99999999      IN     NS     E.ROOT-SERVERS.NET
. 99999999      IN     NS     F.ROOT-SERVERS.NET
```

```
.  99999999    IN   NS    G.ROOT-SERVERS.NET
.  99999999    IN   NS    H.ROOT-SERVERS.NET
.  99999999    IN   NS    I.ROOT-SERVERS.NET
;
; Section 2: Root servers A records
;
A.ROOT-SERVERS.NET      99999999    IN    A    198.41.0.4
B.ROOT-SERVERS.NET      99999999    IN    A    128.9.0.107
C.ROOT-SERVERS.NET      99999999    IN    A    192.33.4.12
D.ROOT-SERVERS.NET      99999999    IN    A    128.8.10.90
E.ROOT-SERVERS.NET      99999999    IN    A    192.203.230.10
F.ROOT-SERVERS.NET      99999999    IN    A    192.5.5.241
G.ROOT-SERVERS.NET      99999999    IN    A    192.112.36.4
H.ROOT-SERVERS.NET      99999999    IN    A    128.63.2.53
I.ROOT-SERVERS.NET      99999999    IN    A    192.36.148.17
```

As can be seen, this `named.ca` file is made of two blocks of entries. The first one contains NS records identifying the names of the root servers. The second section of `named.ca` contains Address records pertaining to the servers defined in the first section.

A current list of root name servers is always available at the following URL:

```
ftp://nic.ddn.mil/netinfo/root-servers.txt
```

ENSURING NAMED.CA IS UP TO DATE

It is your responsibility to regularly verify the validity and accuracy of the information contained in `named.ca`, including information about root servers.

If this file is not up to date, you can experience disruptions in name service on your network, leading to undesirable degradation in performance.

named.boot

When the DNS server starts, it reads the `named.boot` file for information regarding its authority and type. This file also stores the locations of the DNS database files.

The following is a listing of the `named.boot` file on jade, which is configured as a primary nameserver. Each line, or record, starts with a keyword that configures the nameserver:

```
directory     /etc/named

primary     harmonics.com             named.hosts
primary     100.in-addr.arpa          100.rev
primary     237.53.198.in-addr.arpa   198.53.237.rev
primary     0.0.127.in-addr.arpa      127.localhost
cache     .                           named.ca
```

The first record starts with the keyword `directory`. This tells DNS daemon that the database files can be found in the directory `/etc/named` on the server's file system.

The rest of the records, except for the last one, start with the keyword `primary`, and are followed by a domain name. This tells the nameserver that it is authoritative for each of the specified domains and that it is acting as the primary nameserver for those domains. The last field of each record specifies the file that contains the records pertinent to the specified domain. For example, upon reading the second record, the nameserver is configured as the primary server for the `harmonics.com` domain and initializes its memory with the contents of the `/etc/named/named.hosts` file.

The last record specifies that the server is acting as a cache server for the root domain. Moreover, it specifies `named.ca` as the file (in `/etc/named` directory) that contains the cache initialization data.

DATABASE FILENAMES

As shown in the above example the DNS database files do not have to have the default file names. You can use different file names so that it is easier to maintain the files.

Configuring a Secondary Name Server

A secondary nameserver is a server that derives data pertaining to the zone it supports from a primary authoritative server. A secondary server does not have its own `named.hosts` and `named.rev` files. Rather, whenever started, a secondary server undergoes a process called zonal transfer during which it requests the primary server to transfer copies of both files. Consequently, the secondary server initializes its memory with the contents of the transferred files for use in responding to name queries.

Because you won't be required to create and update the `named.hosts` and `named.rev` files, configuring a secondary server is easier than configuring a primary nameserver and involves configuring the three files:

- `named.boot`
- `named.ca`
- `named.local`

The easiest way to create these files is to copy them from the primary server to the secondary server. In our scenario, the host cello is configured to act as a secondary server, thus these three files were copied to it from jade.

After the copy the only file which requires a few changes is `named.boot`. The following listing shows the changes:

```
directory    /usr/lib/named

secondary    harmonics.com                100.0.0.2
secondary    100.in-addr.arpa             100.0.0.2
secondary    237.53.198.in-addr.arpa      100.0.0.2
primary      0.0.127.in-addr.arpa         named.local
cache    .                                named.ca
```

The modified `named.boot` includes mostly secondary records, instead of primary records. The second entry, for example, configures this machine as a secondary server for the `harmonics.com` domain, and tells it to obtain a copy of the pertinent domain database from the server at IP address `100.0.0.2`.

The sixth and seventh entries are identical to their counter-entries in `named.boot` file on the primary nameserver; they point to local filenames for information. Because the contents of these files are not subject to constant change, it makes sense to access them locally to conserve bandwidth.

Startup of the Secondary Server

A secondary server is started in the same way as the primary server. When the host enters run level two at boot time, the startup scripts check on the existence of the `named.boot` file. If the file exists, `named` is brought up and configured according to the statements included in the file. Copies of database files pertinent to domains for which the server is authoritative are then obtained via the zone transfer process, from sources specified by the secondary statements.

Configuring a Cache Only Server

A cache-only server does not rely on database files, it caches data pertaining to queries. Cached data are used to resolve future queries whenever possible.

A cache-only server is the simplest of all servers to configure. The following is the `named.boot` file of a cache-only server connected to the `harmonics.com` network:

```
primary    0.0.127.in-addr.arpa
cache      /usr/lib/named/named.ca
```

In addition to `named.boot`, two more files are needed:

- named.ca
- named.local

The cache record configures the server to cache responses, in addition to initializing its cache from with the data maintained in `named.ca`. The primary statement has same functionality described in earlier sections.

What makes this server cache-only is the lack of primary or secondary records declaring it as being an authoritative nameserver for the domain.

The Network File System

The Network File System (NFS), developed by Sun Microsystems, provides users with transparent access to remote file systems. From the user's perspective, an NFS-accessible resource is treated exactly the same as a local resource; a remote file system will appear as a part of the local file system.

NFS allows user processes and programs transparent read and write access to remotely mounted file systems. Transparency implies that programs would continue to work and process files located on an NFS-mounted file system without requiring any modifications to their code. This is because NFS is cleverly designed to present remote resources to users as extensions to the local resources.

NFS follows a client-server model. An NFS server is a system that owns a file system resource that is configured such that it can be shared with other systems. An NFS client is a machine that accesses a shared file system.

In NFS, a shared file system is referred to as exported file system. NFS clients mount the exported file systems, thereby making the remote file system appear to be part of the local file system.

NFS Daemons

NFS is implemented using a set of daemons. Some of the NFS related daemons run on the server whereas others run on the client. Some of the daemons run on both the client and the server. Table 26.13 describes the functions these daemons.

TABLE 26.13. THE NFS DAEMONS.

Daemon	Description
nfsd	This is the NFS server daemon, it runs on the server and is responsible for handling client requests. It is normally started when the system is brought up to run level three. For performance-related reasons, multiple instances of nfsd are invoked.

continues

TABLE 26.13. CONTINUED

Daemon	Description
biod	This is the block input/output daemon. It runs on NFS clients, and handles reading and writing data from and to the NFS server on behalf of the client process. Performance-related issues dictate that multiple instances of this daemon be invoked on the client.
mountd	This daemon runs on the NFS server and is responsible for handling client mount requests. Only one instance of this daemon runs on NFS servers.
lockd	This daemon runs on both the client and server and handles file locks. The client's daemon issues file lock requests requests, whereas the server's daemon honors those requests and manages the locks.
statd	This daemon is run by both the client and server and maintains the status of currently enforced file locks.

Setting Up the NFS Server

Once you have decided which parts of the file system you want to share on the server with other hosts, you can proceed to setting up NFS.

Setting Up NFS on SVR4

Exporting a file system under SVR4 involves the use of the share command. Its syntax is as follows:

```
share -F nfs [-o options] [ -d description] pathname
```

Here *options* are one of the options described in Table 26.14, *description* is a string describing the exported directory and *pathname* is the full path to the exported directory.

TABLE 26.14. OPTIONS FOR share.

Option	Description
rw=host[:host...]	allows read/write access to exported file system to the hosts specified in the *host* parameter.
ro=host[:host...]	Exports the *pathname* as read-only to listed hosts. If no hosts are specified, all clients, with exceptions stated using rw= option, are allowed read-only access.
anon=uid	Assigns a different uid for anonymous users (that is, users with uid 0) when accessing *pathname*. By default anonymous users are assigned uid of user nobody User nobody normally has same access privileges as public.

Option	Description
`root=[host[:host...]]`	Allows root access privileges to user from the host *host*. The user's uid has to be 0. Unless specified no user is allowed root access privileges to pathname.
`secure`	Enforces enhanced authentication requirements before a user is granted access to an NFS mounted file system.

Let's go through a few examples to demonstrate the usage of the `share` command.

The following `share` command allows read and write access to the `/efs` directory for all hosts except saturn:

```
# share -F nfs -o rw, ro=saturn -d "Just an example" /efs
```

The following `share` command allows read only access to the directory `/efs` by the host violin:

```
# share -F nfs -o ro=violin /efs
```

If any host other than violin attempts to mount the `/efs` directory, the operation will fail with the following error message:

```
Permission denied
```

In the following example root privilege is granted to users from host jade:

```
# share -F nfs -o rw, root=jade /efs
```

To find out which file systems are exported, simply enter `share` without command line arguments. The output will be similar to the following

```
-               /nfs    rw    " "
-               /efs    rw,ro=violin    " "
```

Automating Sharing at Boot Time

File systems can be exported at boot time under SVR4 by adding the appropriate share command to the file:

```
/etc/dfs/dfstab
```

For example, placing the following lines in the `dfstab`:

```
share -F nfs /nfs
share -F nfs rw, ro=satrun /efs
```

will export the directories `/nfs` and `/efs` at boot time. The `/nfs` directory will be exported with the default permissions, whereas the `/efs` directory will be exported with the specified permissions.

During system startup the NFS initialization script

```
/etc/init.d/nfs
```

executes the command `shareall`, which in turn executes the `share` commands in the `dfstab`. The `shareall` command can also be used on the command line, to force sharing, especially after change have been made to the `/etc/dfs/dfstab`.

Setting Up NFS on BSD and Linux

BSD and Linux systems rely on the `/etc/exports` file to control which directories are exported. Entries in this file must follow the following syntax:

```
pathname   [-option][,option]…
```

Here, *pathname* specifies the directory being exported and *option* specifies access-pertinent privileges. These privileges are given in Table 26.15.

TABLE 26.15. OPTIONS FOR share.

Option	Description
rw[=hostname][:hostname]…	rw grants read/write privileges to hosts specified using the *hostname* parameter. If no hostname is specified, then read/write access is granted to all hosts on the network. rw is the *default* access privilege if no option is specified.
ro	Specifies a read-only permission to the directory being exported. User attempts to write to the directory results in error messages such as "Permission denied", or "Read-only file system".
access=hostname[:hostname]…	Specifies the names of the hosts that are granted permission to mount the exported directory. If this option is not included in the entry affecting the exported directory, then all hosts on the network can mount that directory.
root=hostname[:hostname]…	Grants root access privilege only to root users from specified hostnames. By default, root access is denied to root users from all hosts.

Let's look at some examples to get an idea of about the type of entries found in the `/etc/exports` files on BSD and Linux systems.

For example, the following line:

```
/usr/reports  -rw=bass:soprano
```

grants read/write to the directory /usr/reports to users from hosts bass and soprano. Whenever hostnames are specified, the read/write privilege applies to them only; users from other hosts are granted read-only permission. In the above example, users on all hosts, but bass and soprano, have read-only access to /usr/reports directory.

In the next example, root access is granted to root users from hosts violin and cello:

```
/usr/resources root=violin:cello
```

Because no ro or rw options are specified, the exported directory is read/write for users from any host.

Every time the system is booted, the NFS startup scripts execute and process the contents of the /etc/exports file.

Setting Up the NFS Client

On the client side, a user has to issue the mount command prior to attempting access to the exported path on the NFS server. The syntax of the mount command for mounting NFS volumes is

```
mount -F nfs [-o options] host:pathname mountpoint
```

Here *options* are one of the options specified in Table 26.16, *host* is the host on which the specified *pathname* is exported and *mountpoint* is the full pathname to the directory on the local machine over which the exported directory should be mounted.

TABLE 26.16. MOUNT-SPECIFIC OPTIONS.

Option	Description
rw ¦ ro	Specifies whether to mount the NFS directory for read-only or read/write. The default is rw.
retry=*n*	Specifies the number of times mount should retry. This is normally set to a very high number. Check your vendor's documentation for the default value of n.
timeo=*n*	Specifies the timeout period for the mount attempt in units of tenths of a second. timeo is normally set to a very high number. Check you vendor's documentation for the default value.
soft ¦ hard	Specifies whether a hard or soft mount should be attempted. If hard is specified, the client relentlessly retries until it receives an acknowledgement from the NFS server specified in *host*. A soft mount, on the other hand, causes the client to give up attempting if it does not get the acknowledg-

continues

TABLE 26.16. CONTINUED

Option	Description
	ment after retrying the number of times specified in `retry=`*n* option. Upon failure, a soft mount returns an error message to the attempting client.
bg ¦ fg	Specifies whether the client is to reattempt mounting, should the NFS server fail to respond, in the foreground (`fg`) or in the background (`bg`).
intr	Specifies whether to allow keyboard interrupts to kill a process which is hung up waiting for a response from a hard-mounted filesystem. Unless interrupted, the process waits endlessly for a response, which in turn locks the session.

Let's look at a few examples of mounting NFS directories.

To access the exported /efs directory on NFS server jade, the following mount command can be used:

```
# mount -F nfs jade:/efs /rfs
```

From the above examples we know that /efs is the exported directory on host jade. Here we use /rfs as the mount directory. Once mounted, /efs or any directories below it can be accessed using ordinary UNIX commands, and programs.

The following example

```
# mount -F nfs -o soft, ro jade:/nfs/sales /usr/sales
```

demonstrates a mount command which would be used to soft mount the /nfs/sales directory on the NFS server jade, with read-only access. The mountpoint is the directory /usr/sales on the local machine.

To verify that a file system is mounted, the mount can be given without any command line arguments as follows:

```
# mount
```

The output will be similar to the following:

```
/ on /dev/root read/write on Sat Feb 18 09:44:45 1995
/u on /dev/u read/write on Sat Feb 18 09:46:39 1995
/TEST on /dev/TEST read/write on Sat Feb 18 09:46:40 1995
/usr/sales on tenor:/nfs/sales read/write on Sat Feb 18 10:02:52 1995
```

26

Summary

UNIX has contributed a great deal to the development and success of the TCP/IP communications protocols that form the foundation of the global data communications network. This chapter provides an introduction to the concepts that govern TCP/IP communications on UNIX systems.

In this chapter we introduced the basic TCP/IP protocols and then provided comprehensive coverage of the concepts and tools required for configuring TCP/IP on UNIX systems. We have also discussed routing from the UNIX perspective and emphasized the IP address structure and the objectives underlying this structure. In addition we explained name service and the Network File System.

From here you will be able to configure and maintain networked UNIX systems.

## CHAPTER 27

System Accounting

by Bill Wood and Dan Wilson

IN THIS CHAPTER

The UNIX accounting system collects information on individual and group usage of the computer system resources. You may use this information as an accounting charge back system to bill users for the system resources utilized during a prescribed billing cycle. Accounting reports generated by the system accounting utilities provide information the system administrator may use to assess current resource assignments, set resource limits and quotas, and forecast future resource requirements. This chapter covers the following topics:

- UNIX system accounting basics
- Command definitions
- Configuration examples
- IBM AIX 4.x Accounting Procedures
- HP-UX 10.x Accounting Procedures
- Solaris 2.5 (or higher) Accounting Procedures
- System accounting directory structure
- System accounting report generation

UNIX System Accounting Basics

After the computer system has been initialized, and assuming the system accounting option is enabled, statistical collection begins. The data collection process encompasses the following categories:

- Connect session statistics
- Process usage
- Disk space utilization
- Printer usage

The accounting system process begins by gathering statistical data from which summary reports can be generated. These reports may be used to assist in system performance analysis and provide the criteria necessary to establish an equitable customer charge back billing system. The aforementioned report categories include several types of reporting data that is collected to make up the accounting reports. Each category is described in the following sections.

Connect Session Statistics

The business units responsible for the organization's information technology (IT) services may use connect session statistics to charge customers for the time spent using system resources. This allows an organization to bill or charge back based on a user's actual connect time. Connect-session accounting data, related to user login and logout, is collected by the `init` and `login` commands. When a user logs in, the `login` program makes an entry in the `/var/adm/wtmp` file. These records maintain the following user information:

- Username
- Date of login/logout
- Time of login/logout
- Terminal port

This information can be used to produce reports containing the following information:

- Date and starting time of connect session
- User ID for the connect session
- Login name
- Number of prime connect time seconds used
- Number of nonprime connect time seconds used
- Connect time seconds used
- Device address of connect session
- Number of seconds elapsed from Jan 1 1970 to connect session starting time

Process Usage

System accounting also gathers statistics by individual processes. Examples of collected statistics include the following:

- Memory usage
- User and group numbers under which the process runs
- First eight characters of the name of the command
- Elapsed time and processor time used by the process
- I/O statistics
- Number of characters transferred
- Number of disk blocks read or written on behalf of the process

The statistical information is maintained in the accounting file `/var/adm/pacct`. This file is accessed by many of the accounting commands used with system accounting. After a process terminates, the kernel writes process specific information to the `/var/adm/pacct` file. This file contains:

- Process owner's user ID
- Command used to start the process
- Process execution time

System accounting provides commands to display, report, and summarize process information. Commands also exist (for example, the ckpacct command) to ensure that the process accounting file (/var/adm/pacct) does not grow beyond a specific size.

Disk Space Utilization

System accounting provides the capability for the system administrator to monitor disk utilization by users. To restrict users to a specified disk usage limit, the system administrator may implement a disk quota system. As a note, system administrators should be aware that users can evade charges and quota restrictions for disk usage by changing the ownership of their files to that of another user. This allows an unsuspecting user to be charged fees that are rightfully someone else's. Disk usage commands perform three basic functions:

- Collect disk usage by file system
- Report disk usage by user
- Gather disk statistics and maintain them in a format that may be used by other system accounting commands for further reporting

Printer Usage (AIX 4.x)

Printer usage data is stored in the /var/adm/qacct file in ASCII format. The qdaemon writes the ASCII data to the /var/adm/qacct file after a print job is completed. The record of data stored for each printer queue contains the following data:

- UserName
- User number(UID)
- Number of pages printed

Command Definitions

UNIX system accounting supports numerous commands that can be run via cron and/or the command line. The following discusses some of these commands and the suggested execution method.

Commands That Run Automatically

There are several command entries that the system administrator must install in the crontab file `/var/spool/cron/crontabs/adm` to begin collecting accounting data. This is the `cron` file for the `adm` user who owns all the accounting files and processes. These commands are intended to be executed by `cron` in a batch mode but can be manually executed from the command line.

`runacct`	Maintains the daily accounting procedures. This command works with the `acctmerg` command to produce the daily summary report files sorted by username.
`ckpacct`	Controls the size of the `/var/adm/pacct` file. When the `/var/adm/pacct` file grows larger than a specified number of blocks (default = 1,000 blocks), it turns off accounting and moves the file off to a location equal to `/var/adm/pacctx` (*x* is the number of the file). Then `ckpacct` creates a new `/var/adm/pacct` for statistic storage. When the amount of free space on the file system falls below a designated threshold (default = 500 blocks), `ckpacct` automatically turns off process accounting. When the free space exceeds the threshold, `ckpacct` restarts process accounting.
`dodisk`	`Dodisk` produces disk usage accounting records by using the `diskusg`, `acctdusg`, and `acctdisk` commands. In the default case, `dodisk` creates disk accounting records on the special files. These special filenames are maintained in `/etc/fstab` for HP-UX 10.x and `/etc/filesystems` for AIX 4.x.
`monacct`	Uses the daily reports created by the commands mentioned previously to produce monthly summary reports.
`sa1`	System accounting data is collected and maintained in binary format in the file `/var/adm/sa/sa{dd}`, where {dd} is the day of the month.
`sa2`	This command removes reports from the `/var/adm/sa/sa{dd}` file that have been there longer than one week. It is also responsible for writing a daily summary report of system activity to the `/var/adm/sa/sa{dd}` file.

27

SYSTEM
ACCOUNTING

System Accounting Commands That Run Automatically or Manually

startup	When added to the /etc/rc*.d directories, the startup command initiates startup procedures for the accounting system.
shutacct	Records the time accounting was turned off by calling the acctwtmp command to write a line to the /var/adm/wtmp file. It then calls the turnacct off command to turn off process accounting.

Note: for AIX systems, you would modify the /etc/rc file to reflect system accounting run configuration.

Manually Executed Commands

A member of the adm group or the user adm can execute the following commands:

ac	Prints connect-time records. (AIX 4.x)
acctcom	Displays process accounting summaries. (Available to all users.)
acctcon1	Displays connect-time summaries.
accton	Turns process accounting on and off.
chargefee	Charges the user a predetermined fee for units of work performed. The charges are added to the daily report by the acctmerg command.
fwtmp	Converts files between binary and ASCII formats.
last	Displays information about previous logins.
lastcomm	Displays information about the last commands that were executed.
lastlogin	Displays the time each user last logged in.
prctmp	Displays session records.
prtacct	Displays total accounting files.
sa	Summarizes raw accounting information to help manage large volumes of accounting information. (AIX 4.x.)
sadc	Reports on various local system actions, such as buffer usage, disk and tape I/O activity, TTY device activity counters, and file access counters.
time	Prints real-time, user time, and system time required to execute a command.

| timex | Reports in seconds the elapsed time, user time, and execution time. |
| sar | Writes to standard output the contents of selected cumulative activity counters in the operating system. The `sar` command reports only on local activities. |

Configuration Procedures

Setting up system accounting involves configuring certain scripts and system files. The following discusses this process in more detail.

Setting Up the AIX 4.x Accounting System

The first step in configuring AIX 4.x system accounting is ensuring that the files `pacct` and `wtmp` exist and have the proper permission settings. As `adm`, use the `nulladm` command to set the access permissions to read (`r`) and write (`w`) permission for the file owner and group and read (`r`) permission for others. The `nulladm` command also creates the files if they do not exist on the system.

```
/usr/sbin/acct/nulladm wtmp pacct
```

A listing of the `/var/adm` directory structure follows, with the `pacct` and `wtmp` files shown:

```
# pwd
/var/adm
# ls -al
drwxrwxr-x    8 root      adm         512 May 10 08:00 .
drwxr-xr-x   14 bin       bin         512 Apr 01 06:03 ..
-rwxr-----    1 adm       adm         268 May 09 14:48 .profile
-rw-------    1 adm       adm         676 May 09 22:25 .sh_history
drwxrwxr-x    5 adm       adm         512 May 09 13:13 acct
dr-xr-x---    2 bin       cron        512 Apr 01 05:41 cron
-rw-r--r--    1 adm       adm           0 May 09 23:00 dtmp
-rw-rw-r--    1 adm       adm           0 May 09 14:46 fee
-rw-rw-r--    1 adm       adm           0 May 09 16:08 pacct
drwxrwxrwt    2 root      system      512 Apr 01 06:14 ras
drwxrwxr-x    2 adm       adm         512 May 10 00:00 sa
-rw-r--r--    1 root      system     3016 May 09 16:08 savacct
drwxrwxr-x    2 adm       adm         512 Apr 01 05:28 streams
-rw-------    1 root      system     1039 May 09 21:32 sulog
drwxr-xr-x    2 root      system      512 Apr 08 08:37 sw
-rw-r--r--    1 root      system      106 May 09 16:08 usracct
-rw-rw-r--    1 adm       adm        4032 May 10 08:46 wtmp
```

27

SYSTEM
ACCOUNTING

The /etc/acct/holidays file contains entries listing prime-time and observed holidays during a given calendar year. Therefore, this file requires the system administrator to edit it annually.

Prime time must be the first line in the /etc/acct/holidays file that is not a comment. The prime-time hours entry is based on a 24-hour clock, with midnight being either 0000 or 2400. Prime time represents the block of core business hours during a 24-hour period when the system resources are in their greatest demand (for example, transactional systems) by the user community. The /etc/acct/holidays file entry for prime time consists of three four-digit fields in the following order:

- Current year
- Beginning of prime time (hhmm)
- End of prime time (hhmm)

For example, to specify the year 1998, with prime time beginning at 7:30 a.m. and ending at 5:30 p.m., add the following line:

```
1998   0730   1730
```

Organizational holidays for the year follow the prime-time line, with each line consisting of four fields in the following order:

- Day of the year
- Month
- Day of the month
- Description of holiday

The day-of-the-year field contains the numeric day of year (Julian date format—date +%j) on which the holiday occurs and must be a number from 1 through 365 (366 in leap year). The other three fields are informational.

A listing of the /etc/acct/holidays file follows:

```
# cat /etc/acct/holidays
* COMPONENT_NAME:  (CMDACCT) Command Accounting
*
* Prime/Nonprime Table for AIX Accounting System
*
* Curr   Prime    Non-Prime
* Year   Start    Start
*
  1998   0730     1730
*
* Day of         Calendar        Company
```

```
* Year          Date            Holiday
*
  1             Jan 1           New Year's Day
  146           May 26          Memorial Day (Obsvd.)
  185           Jul 4           Independence Day
  244           Sep 1           Labor Day
  324           Nov 20          Thanksgiving Day
  325           Nov 21          Day after Thanksgiving
  359           Dec 25          Christmas Day
  365           Dec 31          New Year's Eve
```

Process accounting is initialized by adding the following line to the /etc/rc program file. /etc/rc is the run control program used when the system is booted to its target run state. The startup procedure records the time that accounting was initialized and cleans up the previous day's accounting files.

```
/usr/bin/su - adm -c /usr/sbin/acct/startup
```

Each file system to be included in disk usage accounting must have the account variable set to true in its stanza entry in the /etc/filesystems file. The example stanzas for file system /home from /etc/filesystems shows the entry for disk usage accounting set to true and the file system stanza for /usr set to false. Therefore, disk usage account occurs for /home and not for /usr.

```
/home:
        dev             = /dev/hd1
        vfs             = jfs
        log             = /dev/hd8
        mount           = true
        check           = true
        vol             = /home
        free            = false
        account         = true

/usr:
        dev             = /dev/hd2
        vfs             = jfs
        log             = /dev/hd8
        mount           = automatic
        check           = false
        type            = bootfs
        vol             = /usr
        free            = false
    account         = false
```

Each printer queue to be included in printer usage accounting must have the acctfile variable pointing to a data file set in the printer queue stanza in /etc/qconfig. The example stanza for the printer queue HP_laser from /etc/qconfig shows printer usage

accounting set to the default data file of /var/adm/qacct. Printer queue usage accounting information for the HP_laser queue will be stored in /var/adm/qacct.

```
HP_Laser:
        device = lp0
        acctfile = /var/adm/qacct
lp0:
        file = /dev/lp0
        header = never
        trailer = never
        access = both
        backend = /usr/lib/lpd/piobe
```

The nite, fiscal, and sum directories must exist under /var/adm/acct so that storage of
system accounting information can be maintained. Create the /var/adm/acct/nite,
/var/adm/acct/fiscal, and /var/adm/acct/sum directories with permissions setting of
755 with owner and group set to adm. The following generalizes the usage of these directories and shows a sample directory listing of /var/adm/acct.

/var/adm/acct/nite	Daily data and command files used by runacct
/var/adm/acct/sum	summary data and command files used by runacct to produce summary reports
/var/adm/acct/fiscal	summary data and command files used by monacct to produce monthly reports

```
# pwd
/var/adm/acct
# ls -al
drwxrwxr-x    5 adm        adm          512 May 09 13:13 .
drwxrwxr-x    8 root       adm          512 May 10 10:00 ..
drwxr-xr-x    2 adm        adm          512 May 09 13:13 fiscal
drwxr-xr-x    2 adm        adm          512 May 09 23:10 nite
drwxr-xr-x    2 adm        adm          512 May 09 14:46 sum
#
```

Log in as the adm user and use crontab -e to edit the crontab file to activate the daily
accounting functions. By editing the /var/spool/cron/crontabs/adm file, you are
allowing cron to control the periodic collection and reporting of statistical data. See the
following example of the crontab entries for runacct, dodisk, ckpacct, and monacct:

```
10 23 * * 0-6 /usr/lib/acct/runacct 2>/usr/adm/acct/nite/accterr >
/dev/null
0  23 * * 0-6 /usr/lib/acct/dodisk > /dev/null 2>&1
0  *  * * *   /usr/lib/acct/ckpacct > /dev/null 2>&1
15 4  1 * *   /usr/lib/acct/monacct > /dev/null 2>&1
```

The first entry starts the `runacct` at 11:10 p.m. daily to process the active system accounting data files. The second entry starts the `dodisk` command at 11:00 p.m. daily to collect disk usage statistics. The third entry executes the `ckpacct` command every hour of every day to ensure that the system accounting `/var/adm/pacct` file does not exceed the specified default block size (1,000 blocks is the normal default). The fourth and final entry executes the `monacct` command on the first day of the month to generate monthly summary accounting reports. Following is an example of the `/var/spool/cron/crontabs/adm` file with the `runacct`, `dodisk`, `ckpacct`, and `monacct` commands listed:

```
#*****************************************************************************
➥*********************************
#
#                       CRONTAB Job listing   -  Administration - System Level
#
#*****************************************************************************
➥*********************************
#  Min    *  Hour   *  Day    *  Month   *  Day    *
# of the  * of the  * of the  * of the   * of the  * Command Syntax
#  Day    *  Day    *  Month  *  Year    *  Week   *
#*****************************************************************************
➥*********************************
#
#      PROCESS ACCOUNTING:
#                              runacct at 11:10 every night
#                              dodisk at 11:00 every night
#                              ckpacct every hour on the hour
#                              monthly accounting 4:15 the first of every month
#========================================================================
➥==================================
10    23    *    *    0-6    /usr/lib/acct/runacct 2>/usr/adm/acct/nite/
➥accterr >/dev/null
0     23    *    *    0-6    /usr/lib/acct/dodisk >/dev/null 2>&1
0     *     *    *    *      /usr/lib/acct/ckpacct >/dev/null 2>&1
15    4     1    *    *      /usr/lib/acct/monacct >/dev/null 2>&1
#========================================================================
➥==================================
```

You are now ready for startup or shutdown of the system accounting process with the following commands:

```
Startup:
/usr/bin/su - adm -c /usr/lib/acct/startup
```

```
Shutdown:
/usr/bin/su - adm -c /usr/lib/acct/shutacct
```

You may use the following command to verify the state (on or off) of system accounting processes:

```
# fwtmp < /var/adm/wtmp ¦ pg
```

Sample truncated output:

```
LOGIN     .xxx.com:  dtremote      6 23528 0000 0000   863276614 Sat May 10
10:03:34 EST 1998
root      .xxx.com:  dtremote      7 23528 0000 0000   863276629 Sat May 10
10:03:49 EST 1998
LOGIN     .xxx.com:  dtremote      6 20920 0000 0000   863286997 Sat May 10
12:56:37 EST 1998
root      pts/2      pts/2         7 25506 0000 0000   863300368 Sat May 10
16:39:28 EST 1998
                     AIX, acctg    9     0 0000 0000   863300700 Sat May 10
16:45:00 EST 1998
                     accting off   9     0 0000 0000   863301549 Sat May 10
16:59:09 EST 1998
                     AIX, acctg    9     0 0000 0000   863301631 Sat May 10
17:00:31 EST 1998
```

The preceding example indicates where the system administrator started accounting (16:45), shut down accounting (16:59), and then restarted accounting (17:00).

Setting Up the HP-UX 10.x Accounting System

The system accounting package is usually installed onto the system when the operating system is configured. The administrator can check this with the following command:

```
#  swlist -l product ¦ grep -i accounting
Accounting              B.10.10         Accounting
```

If the command does not return line 2 (example shown for a 10.10 HP-UX operating system), do not proceed until the system accounting package has been installed.

After the system administrator has confirmed that the system accounting package has been installed, he may proceed with the following configuration guidelines.

The first step in configuring HP-UX 10.x system accounting is ensuring that the files pacct and wtmp exist and have the proper permission settings. As root, use the nulladm command to set the access permissions to read (r) and write (w) permission for the file owner and group and read (r) permission for others. The nulladm command also creates the files if they do not exist on the system.

```
# /usr/lib/acct/nulladm wtmp pacct
```

A listing of the /var/adm directory structure follows, with the pacct and wtmp files highlighted:

```
# pwd
/var/adm
# ls -al
drwxrwxr-x    8 root      adm          512 May 10 08:00 .
drwxr-xr-x   14 bin       bin          512 Apr 01 06:03 ..
-rwxr-----    1 adm       adm          268 May 09 14:48 .profile
-rw-------    1 adm       adm          676 May 09 22:25 .sh_history
drwxrwxr-x    5 adm       adm          512 May 09 13:13 acct
dr-xr-x---    2 bin       cron         512 Apr 01 05:41 cron
-rw-r--r--    1 adm       adm            0 May 09 23:00 dtmp
-rw-rw-r--    1 adm       adm            0 May 09 14:46 fee
-rw-rw-r--    1 adm       adm            0 May 09 16:08 pacct
drwxrwxrwt    2 root      system       512 Apr 01 06:14 ras
drwxrwxr-x    2 adm       adm          512 May 10 00:00 sa
-rw-r--r--    1 root      system      3016 May 09 16:08 savacct
drwxrwxr-x    2 adm       adm          512 Apr 01 05:28 streams
-rw-------    1 root      system      1039 May 09 21:32 sulog
drwxr-xr-x    2 root      system       512 Apr 08 08:37 sw
-rw-r--r--    1 root      system       106 May 09 16:08 usracct
-rw-rw-r--    1 adm       adm         4032 May 10 08:46 wtmp
#
```

Following the preceding step, the system administrator needs to edit the /etc/rc. config.d/acct file and set START_ACCT equal to one (1). This starts system accounting each time the system is reset. An example of this follows:

```
# Process accounting.
#
# START_ACCT: Set to 1 to start process accounting
#
START_ACCT=1
```

The /etc/acct/holidays file contains entries listing prime-time and observed holidays during a given calendar year. Therefore, this file requires the system administrator to edit it annually.

Prime time must be the first line in the /etc/acct/holidays file that is not a comment. The prime-time hours entry is based on a 24-hour clock, with midnight being either 0000 or 2400. Prime time represents the block of core business hours during a 24-hour period when the system resources are in their greatest demand (transactional systems) by the user community. The /etc/acct/holidays file entry for prime time consists of three four-digit fields in the following order:

- Current year
- Beginning of prime time (hhmm)
- End of prime time (hhmm)

For example, to specify the year 1998, with prime time beginning at 7:30 a.m. and ending at 5:30 p.m., add the following line:

```
1998  0730  1730
```

Organizational holidays for the year follow the prime-time line, with each line consisting of four fields in the following order:

- Day of the year
- Month
- Day of the month
- Description of holiday

The day-of-the-year field contains the numeric day of year (Julian date format—`date +%j`) on which the holiday occurs and must be a number from 1 through 365 (366 on leap year). The other three fields are only informational.

A listing of the `/etc/acct/holidays` file follows:

```
# cat /etc/acct/holidays
* COMPONENT_NAME:   (CMDACCT) Command Accounting
*
* Prime/Nonprime Table for HP-UX Accounting System
*
* Curr   Prime    Non-Prime
* Year   Start    Start
*
  1998  0730     1730
*
* Day of          Calendar        Company
* Year            Date            Holiday
*
     1            Jan 1           New Year's Day
   146            May 26          Memorial Day (Obsvd.)
   185            Jul 4           Independence Day
   244            Sep 1           Labor Day
   324            Nov 20          Thanksgiving Day
   325            Nov 21          Day after Thanksgiving
   359            Dec 25          Christmas Day
   365            Dec 31          New Year's Eve
```

Disk Accounting Statistics

Each file system to be included in disk usage accounting must, by default, exist in the `/etc/fstab` file. The `dodisk` command has the option to accept the special filenames as input from the command line. If this is the case, only those special filenames listed are included in the accounting process. If you want to generate a report for a single disk device, for example, a file system under Logical Volume Manager(LVM), you would use the following command:

```
# /usr/lib/acct/dodisk   /dev/vg_name/lvol_name
```

> **NOTE**
>
> Logical Volume Manager is Hewlett-Packards (HP) subsystem for managing disk space. Its main feature is that it allows the system administrator to group multiple physical disk drives under one file system.

If you want to provide a sublist of file systems from the /etc/fstab file, through your system editor create a file that contains the special device names for your file systems—one file system per line. Use the following command to read in a list of special files to include in the disk accounting process:

```
# /usr/lib/acct/dodisk <  list.filesystems
```

The nite, fiscal, and sum directories must exist under /var/adm/acct so that storage of system accounting information can be maintained. Create the /var/adm/acct/nite, /var/adm/acct/fiscal, and /var/adm/acct/sum directories with permission settings of 755 with owner and group set to adm. The following generalizes the usage of these directories and shows a sample directory listing of /var/adm/acct.

/var/adm/acct/nite	Daily data and command files used by runacct
/var/adm/acct/sum	Summary data and command files used by runacct to produce summary reports
/var/adm/acct/fiscal	Summary data and command files used by monacct to produce monthly reports

A listing of the /var/adm/acct directory:

```
# pwd
/var/adm/acct
# ls -al
drwxrwxr-x   5 adm      adm        512 May 09 13:13 .
drwxrwxr-x   8 root     adm        512 May 10 10:00 ..
drwxr-xr-x   2 adm      adm        512 May 09 13:13 fiscal
drwxr-xr-x   2 adm      adm        512 May 09 23:10 nite
drwxr-xr-x   2 adm      adm        512 May 09 14:46 sum
#
```

Log in as the adm user and use crontab -e to edit the crontab file to activate the daily accounting functions. By editing the /var/spool/cron/crontabs/adm file, you are allowing cron to control the periodic collection and reporting of statistical data. See the following example of the crontab entries for runacct, dodisk, ckpacct, and monacct:

```
10 23 * * 0-6 /usr/lib/acct/runacct 2>/usr/adm/acct/nite/accterr >
/dev/null
0  23 * * 0-6 /usr/lib/acct/dodisk > /dev/null 2>&1
0  *  * * *   /usr/lib/acct/ckpacct > /dev/null 2>&1
15 4  1 * *   /usr/lib/acct/monacct > /dev/null 2>&1
```

The first entry starts the runacct command at 11:10 p.m. daily to process the active system accounting data files. The second entry starts the dodisk command at 11:00 p.m. daily to collect disk usage statistics. The third entry executes the ckpacct command every hour of every day to ensure that the system accounting /var/adm/pacct file does not exceed the specified default block size (1,000 blocks is the normal default). The fourth and final entry executes the monacct command on the first day of the month to generate monthly summary accounting reports. Following is an example of the /var/spool/cron/crontabs/adm file with the runacct, dodisk, ckpacct, and monacct commands listed:

```
#*******************************************************************************
➡*********************************
#
#                   CRONTAB Job listing  -  Administration - System Level
#
#*******************************************************************************
➡*********************************
# Min     * Hour    * Day     * Month    * Day     *
# of the  * of the  * of the  * of the   * of the  * Command Syntax
# Day     * Day     * Month   * Year     * Week    *
#*******************************************************************************
➡*********************************
#
#       PROCESS ACCOUNTING:
#                           runacct at 11:10 every night
#                           dodisk at 11:00 every night
#                           ckpacct every hour on the hour
#                           monthly accounting 4:15 the first of every month
#==============================================================================
➡=================================
10      23      *       *       0-6     /usr/lib/acct/runacct 2>/usr/adm/acct/
➡nite/accterr >/dev/null
0       23      *       *       0-6     /usr/lib/acct/dodisk >/dev/null 2>&1
0       *       *       *       *       /usr/lib/acct/ckpacct >/dev/null 2>&1
15      4       1       *       *       /usr/lib/acct/monacct >/dev/null 2>&1
#==============================================================================
➡=================================
```

You are now ready for startup or shutdown of the system accounting process with the following commands:

```
Startup:
/usr/bin/su - adm -c /usr/lib/acct/startup
```

```
Shutdown:
/usr/bin/su - adm -c /usr/lib/acct/shutacct
```

You may use the following command to verify the state (on or off) of system accounting processes.

```
# fwtmp < /var/adm/wtmp ¦ pg
```

Sample truncated output:

```
rc         sqnc                  90  8 0000 0000 863231977 May  9 21:39:37
1998
getty      cons                1127  5 0000 0000 863231977 May  9 21:39:37
1998
spserver   ShPr                1128  5 0000 0000 863231977 May  9 21:39:37
1998
uugetty    a0                  1130  5 0000 0000 863231977 May  9 21:39:37
1998
LOGIN      cons console        1127  6 0000 0000 863231977 May  9 21:39:37
1998
LOGIN      a0   ttyd0p7        1130  6 0000 0000 863231977 May  9 21:39:37
1998
                acctg on          0  9 0000 0000 863232395 May  9 21:46:35
1998
root       p1   ttyp1           634  8 0000 0000 863236183 May  9 22:49:43
1998
LOGIN      p1   pty/ttyp1      1712  6 0000 0000 863270875 May 10 08:27:55
1998
root       p1   ttyp1          1712  7 0000 0003 863270881 May 10 08:28:01
1998
root       p1   ttyp1          1712  8 0000 0000 863281484 May 10 11:24:44
1998
LOGIN      p1   pty/ttyp1      1923  6 0000 0000 863288678 May 10 13:24:38
1998
root       p1   ttyp1          1923  7 0000 0003 863288690 May 10 13:24:50
1998
LOGIN      p2   pty/ttyp2      2155  6 0000 0000 863294925 May 10 15:08:45
1998
                acctg off         0  9 0000 0000 863300425 May 10 16:40:25
1998
```

The preceding example indicates where the system administrator started accounting (21:46:35) and shut down accounting (16:40:25).

Setting Up the Solaris 2.5 (or higher) Accounting System

Begin by making sure that SUNWaccr and SUNWaccu software packages are installed.

```
# pkginfo -l SUNWaccu
```

Sample output:

```
   PKGINST:  SUNWaccu
      NAME:  System Accounting, (Usr)
  CATEGORY:  system
      ARCH:  sparc
   VERSION:  11.5.1,REV=95.10.27.15.23
   BASEDIR:  /
    VENDOR:  Sun Microsystems, Inc.
      DESC:  utilities for accounting and reporting of system activity
    PSTAMP:  raid951027152556
  INSTDATE:  Jun 11 1998 08:13
   HOTLINE:  Please contact your local service provider
    STATUS:  completely installed
     FILES:      43 installed pathnames
                  4 shared pathnames
                  5 directories
                 36 executables
                  1 setuid/setgid executables
                453 blocks used (approx)
# pkginfo -l SUNWaccr
sample output:
   PKGINST:  SUNWaccr
      NAME:  System Accounting, (Root)
  CATEGORY:  system
      ARCH:  sparc
   VERSION:  11.5.1,REV=95.10.27.15.23
   BASEDIR:  /
    VENDOR:  Sun Microsystems, Inc.
      DESC:  utilities for accounting and reporting of system activity
    PSTAMP:  raid951027152552
  INSTDATE:  Jun 11 1998 08:13
   HOTLINE:  Please contact your local service provider
    STATUS:  completely installed
     FILES:      18 installed pathnames
                  7 shared pathnames
                  1 linked files
                 13 directories
                  2 executables
                  6 blocks used (approx)
```

If you do not receive output similar to the previous example listings, use either `pkgadd` or `swmtool` to install these software packages.

Set up the link necessary for starting system accounting at system initialization:

```
# ln /etc/init.d/acct /etc/rc2.d/S22acct
```

Set up the link necessary for shutting down system accounting at system shutdown:

```
# ln /etc/init.d/acct /etc/rc0.d/K22acct
```

Add the following entries to the /var/spool/cron/crontabs/adm file:

```
0 * * * * /usr/lib/acct/ckpacct
10 23 * * * /usr/lib/acct/runacct 2> /var/adm/acct/nite/fd2log
15 04 1 * * /usr/lib/acct/monacct
```

Note that these entries will be processed by crontab file for the adm user and must follow the cron format.

```
#*******************************************************************
#*********************************
#
#                    CRONTAB Job listing   -  adm - System Level
#
#*******************************************************************
#*********************************
# Min      * Hour    * Day     * Month    * Day      *
# of the   * of the  * of the  * of the   * of the   * Command Syntax
# Day      * Day     * Month   * Year     * Week     *
#*******************************************************************
#*********************************
#
#     PROCESS ACCOUNTING:
#                         runacct at 11:10 every night
#                         ckpacct every hour on the hour
#                         monthly accounting 4:15 the first of every month
#===================================================================
#==================================
10     23     *     *     0-6   /usr/lib/acct/runacct 2>/usr/adm/acct/
nite/fd2log
0      *      *     *     *     /usr/lib/acct/ckpacct >/dev/null 2>&1
15     4      1     *     *     /usr/lib/acct/monacct >/dev/null 2>&1
#===================================================================
#==================================
```

Add the following entry to the /var/spool/cron/crontabs/root file:

```
00 23 * * 0-6 /usr/lib/acct/dodisk >/dev/null 2>&1
```

```
#*******************************************************************
#*********************************
#
#                    CRONTAB Job listing   -  Root - System Level
```

27

SYSTEM ACCOUNTING

```
#
#*********************************************************************************
*************************************
#  Min     *  Hour   *  Day    *  Month  *  Day    *
#  of the  *  of the *  of the *  of the *  of the *  Command Syntax
#  Day     *  Day    *  Month  *  Year   *  Week   *
#*********************************************************************************
*************************************
#
#      PROCESS ACCOUNTING:
#                         dodisk at 11:00 every night
#===============================================================================
====================================
0     23     *     *     0-6     /usr/lib/acct/dodisk >/dev/null 2>&1
#===============================================================================
====================================
```

Adjust /etc/acct/holidays to reflect both national and company holidays you want your system to recognize.

A listing of the /etc/acct/holidays file follows:

```
# cat /etc/acct/holidays
* COMPONENT_NAME:   (CMDACCT) Command Accounting
*
* Prime/Nonprime Table for Solaris Accounting System
*
* Curr  Prime    Non-Prime
* Year  Start    Start
*
  1998  0730     1730
*
* Day of        Calendar      Company
* Year          Date          Holiday
*
    1           Jan 1         New Year's Day
  146           May 26        Memorial Day (Obsvd.)
  185           Jul 4         Independence Day
  244           Sep 1         Labor Day
  324           Nov 20        Thanksgiving Day
  325           Nov 21        Day after Thanksgiving
  359           Dec 25        Christmas Day
  365           Dec 31        New Year's Eve
```

System accounting can now be started by either rebooting the machine or issuing the runacct command. Note that executing runacct without any arguments causes the process to assume that this is the first time that runacct has been run for that day. If you are attempting to restart system accounting, be sure to add the appropriate MMDD (DD = Day and MM = Month) argument on the command line.

You are now ready for startup or shutdown of the system accounting process with the following commands:

```
Startup:
/usr/bin/su - adm -c /usr/lib/acct/startup
```

```
Shutdown:
/usr/bin/su - adm -c /usr/lib/acct/shutacct
```

You may use the following command to verify the state (on or off) of system accounting processes.

```
# fwtmp < /var/adm/wtmp | pg
```

Sample truncated output:

```
.telnet   tn20 /dev/pts/4       1118   6 0000 0000 871178077 Sat May
➡10 20:54:37 1998
root      tn20 pts/4            1118   7 0000 0000 871178098 Sat May
➡10 20:54:58 1998
              acctg off            0   9 0000 0000 871179345 Sat May
➡10 16:10:45 1998
              acctg on             0   9 0000 0000 871179352 Sat May
➡10 21:15:52 1998
```

The preceding example indicates where the system administrator, started accounting (21:15:52) and shut down accounting (16:10:45).

System Accounting Directory Structure

Most UNIX system accounting takes advantage of a hierarchical (see Figure 27.1) approach when laying out its control and data files. This allows the accounting process to maintain temporary and permanent files in logical locations. Each directory in this layer stores related groups of files, commands, or other subdirectories.

According to systems documentation (HP-UX, AIX, and Solaris), the following system accounting structures are laid out as described in the following sections. Refer to your system's documentation for more detailed information.

FIGURE 27.1.

System accounting directory structure.

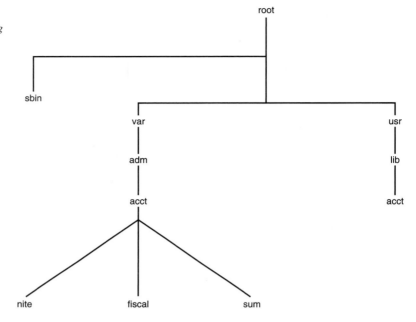

System Accounting High-Level Directory Layout

/var/adm	Maintains data-collection files
/var/adm/acct	Directories for nite, sum, and fiscal
/var/adm/acct/nite	Daily data and command files used by runacct
/var/adm/acct/sum	Summary data and command files used by runacct to produce summary reports
/var/adm/acct/fiscal	Summary data and command files used by monacct to produce monthly reports
/usr/lib/acct	System accounting commands
/sbin	Shell scripts rc and shutdown procedures
/etc/rc.config.d/acct	Set variable START_ACCT equal to 1 to activate accounting at system boot (HP-UX 10.X)
/etc/rc	Run command file that executes at system startup and when the system changes run state.

Files in the `/var/adm` Directory

`/var/adm/diskdiag`	Diagnostic output during the execution of disk accounting programs
`/var/adm/dtmp`	Output from the `acctdusg` command
`/var/adm/fee`	Output from the `chargefee` command, in ASCII `tacct` records
`/var/adm/pacct`	Active process accounting file
`/var/adm/wtmp`	Active process accounting file
`/var/adm/Spacct?.mmdd`	Process accounting files for `mmdd` during the execution of `runacct`

Files in the `/var/adm/acct/nite` Directory

`{{mmdd}}`	`{{mmdd}}` is the month and day a file was created and is appended to the previous version of the data file.
`active`	Contains warning and error messages generated from `runacct` execution.
`active{{mmdd}}`	Copy of the active file after `runacct` encounters an error condition.
`ctacct.{{mmdd}}`	Total accounting records created from connect session accounting.
`ctmp`	Output of `acctcon1`. It contains a list of login sessions sorted by `userid` and `login` names.
`Daycms`	ASCII daily command summary used by `prdaily`.
`daytacct`	Total accounting records for current day.
`disktacct`	Total accounting records created by the `dodisk` command.
`fd2log`	Diagnostic output from the execution of `runacct`.
`lastdate`	The last day `runacct` was executed, in `+%{{m}}%{{d}}`format.
`lock and lock1`	Used to control serial use of `runacct`.
`lineuse`	Terminal (`tty`) line usage report used by `prdaily`.
`log`	Diagnostics output from `acctcon1`.

27

SYSTEM
ACCOUNTING

log{{mmdd}}	Same as log after runacct detects an error.
reboots	Contains beginning and ending dates from wtmp and a listing of reboots.
statefile	Used to record the current state being executed by runacct.
tmpwtmp	wtmp file, corrected by wtmpfix.
wtmperror	Error messages, if any, from wtmpfix.
wtmperrorr{{mmdd}}	Same as wtmperror after runacct detects an error.
wtmp.{{mmdd}}	The previous day's wtmp file.

Files in the /var/adm/acct/sum Directory

cms	Total command summary file for current month in internal summary format.
cmsprev	Command summary file without latest update.
daycms	Command summary file for previous day in internal summary format.
loginlog	Shows the last login date for each user.
rpt{{mmdd}}	Daily accounting report for date {{mmdd}}.
tacct	Cumulative total accounting file for current month.
tacctprev	Same as tacct without latest update.
tacct{{mmdd}}	Total accounting file for date {{mmdd}}.
wtmp.{{mmdd}}	Saved copy of wtmp file for date {{mmdd}}. Removed after reboot.

Files in the /var/adm/acct/fiscal Directory

cms{mm}	Total command summary for month {mm} in internal summary format.
Fiscrpt{mm}	Report similar to prdaily for the month {mm}.
tacct{mm}	Total accounting file for the month {mm}.

The acctmerg command can convert records between ASCII and binary formats and merge records from different sources into a single record for each user.

System Accounting Report Generation

After completing system accounting configuration, your system is ready to produce accounting reports. The following covers the basics of report generation for system accounting.

Generation of System Accounting Data Reports

`acctcom`

The `acctcom` utility allows you to see the accounting system data at any given time. This command may be executed from the command line with several different options. It is one of the most useful commands for getting a quick report from the system without the need to find a file.

This option shows the average statistics about processes:

```
$ acctcom -a
```

An example of a truncated listing:

COMMAND NAME	USER	TTYNAME	START TIME	END TIME	REAL (SECS)	CPU (SECS)	MEAN SIZE(K)
#accton	root	_	17:57:07	17:57:07	0.00	0.00	56.00
#acctwtmp	root	pts/2	17:57:07	17:57:07	0.00	0.00	60.00
#fwtmp	root	pts/2	17:57:07	17:57:07	0.03	0.00	160.00
#awk	root	pts/2	17:57:07	17:57:07	0.02	0.02	106.00
#fwtmp	root	pts/2	17:57:07	17:57:07	0.05	0.00	0.00
#dspmsg	root	pts/2	17:57:07	17:57:07	0.00	0.00	0.00
#cat	root	pts/2	17:57:07	17:57:07	0.00	0.00	336.00
#wtmpfix	root	pts/2	17:57:07	17:57:07	0.05	0.00	0.00
#dspmsg	root	pts/2	17:57:07	17:57:07	0.02	0.02	192.00
#acctcon1	root	pts/2	17:57:08	17:57:08	0.17	0.02	96.00
#sort	root	pts/2	17:57:08	17:57:08	0.25	0.00	82.00
#acctcon2	root	pts/2	17:57:08	17:57:08	0.05	0.00	168.00
#acctmerg	root	pts/2	17:57:08	17:57:08	0.05	0.00	0.00
#dspmsg	root	pts/2	17:57:08	17:57:08	0.00	0.00	0.00
#basename	root	pts/2	17:57:08	17:57:08	0.03	0.00	138.00
#sed	root	pts/2	17:57:08	17:57:08	0.03	0.00	136.00
#acctprc1	root	pts/2	17:57:08	17:57:08	0.05	0.02	184.00
#acctprc2	root	pts/2	17:57:08	17:57:08	0.05	0.00	68.00
#acctmerg	root	pts/2	17:57:08	17:57:08	0.02	0.00	0.00
#mv	root	pts/2	17:57:08	17:57:08	0.02	0.00	0.00
#acctcms	root	pts/2	17:57:09	17:57:09	0.02	0.00	96.00
#lsuser	root	pts/2	17:57:09	17:57:09	0.86	0.20	89.00
#grep	root	pts/2	17:57:09	17:57:09	0.86	0.00	164.00
#uniq	root	pts/2	17:57:10	17:57:10	0.05	0.00	0.00
#egrep	root	?	17:57:22	17:57:22	0.03	0.02	114.00

27

SYSTEM ACCOUNTING

```
     .
     .
     .
#tail       root     ?       18:23:09 18:23:09      0.05      0.00     148.00
#fgrep      root     ?       18:24:10 18:24:10      0.00      0.00       0.00
#egrep      root     ?       18:24:10 18:24:10      0.00      0.00       0.00
#acctcom    root     pts/2   18:24:28 18:24:28      0.39      0.27      58.00

cmds=287 Real=2.92   CPU=0.04   USER=0.01   SYS=0.03   CHAR=29767.60
➥BLK=0.00       USR/TOT=0.24 HOG=1.20
```

This option shows the amount of user time per total time (system time plus user time):

```
$ acctcom -r
```

An example of a truncated listing:

```
COMMAND                      START    END        REAL      CPU       CPU
NAME        USER     TTYNAME TIME     TIME       (SECS)    (SECS)    FACTOR
#accton     root     _       17:57:07 17:57:07   0.00      0.00      0.00
#bsh        root     pts/2   17:57:06 17:57:06   0.20      0.02      0.00
#mv         root     pts/2   17:57:07 17:57:07   0.02      0.02      0.00
#cp         root     pts/2   17:57:07 17:57:07   0.02      0.02      1
#acctwtmp   root     pts/2   17:57:07 17:57:07   0.02      0.00      0.00
#fwtmp      root     pts/2   17:57:07 17:57:07   0.02      0.00      0.00
#awk        root     pts/2   17:57:07 17:57:07   0.03      0.02      0.00
#sed        root     pts/2   17:57:07 17:57:07   0.03      0.00      0.00
#fwtmp      root     pts/2   17:57:07 17:57:07   0.08      0.02      1
#cp         root     pts/2   17:57:07 17:57:07   0.02      0.00      0.00
#chmod      root     pts/2   17:57:07 17:57:07   0.00      0.00      0.00
#chown      root     pts/2   17:57:07 17:57:07   0.02      0.00      0.00
#bsh        root     pts/2   17:57:07 17:57:07   0.08      0.02      0.00
#acctwtmp   root     pts/2   17:57:07 17:57:07   0.00      0.00      0.00
#fwtmp      root     pts/2   17:57:07 17:57:07   0.03      0.00      0.00
     .
     .
     .
#telnet     root     _       17:37:21 18:28:39   3078.00   2.14      0.124
#egrep      root     ?       18:31:47 18:31:47   0.02      0.00      0.00
#tail       root     ?       18:31:47 18:31:47   0.06      0.02      0.00
sendmail    root     ?       18:33:32 18:33:32   0.02      0.00      0.00
#acctcom    root     pts/2   18:33:51 18:33:51   0.47      0.36      0.304
```

This option shows all the processes that have been executed by the user wdwood:

```
$ acctcom -u wdwood
```

An example of a truncated listing:

```
COMMAND                      START    END        REAL      CPU       MEAN
NAME        USER     TTYNAME TIME     TIME       (SECS)    (SECS)    SIZE(K)
#accton     wdwood   _       17:57:07 17:57:07   0.00      0.00      56.00
#bsh        wdwood   pts/2   17:57:06 17:57:06   0.20      0.02      0.00
```

```
#mv          wdwood    pts/2    17:57:07 17:57:07    0.02    0.02    0.00
#cp          wdwood    pts/2    17:57:07 17:57:07    0.02    0.02    182.00
#acctwtmp    wdwood    pts/2    17:57:07 17:57:07    0.02    0.00    0.00
#fwtmp       wdwood    pts/2    17:57:07 17:57:07    0.02    0.00    0.00
#awk         wdwood    pts/2    17:57:07 17:57:07    0.03    0.02    121.00
#sed         wdwood    pts/2    17:57:07 17:57:07    0.03    0.00    0.00
#fwtmp       wdwood    pts/2    17:57:07 17:57:07    0.08    0.02    108.00
#cp          wdwood    pts/2    17:57:07 17:57:07    0.02    0.00    72.00
#chmod       wdwood    pts/2    17:57:07 17:57:07    0.00    0.00    0.00
#chown       wdwood    pts/2    17:57:07 17:57:07    0.02    0.00    86.00
#bsh         wdwood    pts/2    17:57:07 17:57:07    0.08    0.02    130.00
.
.
.
#dspmsg      wdwood    pts/2    18:38:08 18:38:08    0.02    0.00    0.00
#bsh         wdwood    pts/2    18:38:07 18:38:08    1.08    0.02    97.00
#more        wdwood    pts/2    18:38:20 18:38:26    6.66    0.02    0.00
#acctcom     wdwood    pts/2    18:38:38 18:38:38    0.48    0.33    35.00
#cat         wdwood    pts/2    18:38:45 18:38:45    0.02    0.00    170.00
```

This option shows all the processes, for any user, running longer than 20 seconds:

```
$ acctcom -O 20

COMMAND                       START    END      REAL     CPU      MEAN
NAME         USER   TTYNAME   TIME     TIME     (SECS)   (SECS)   SIZE(K)
#find        wdwood    _      18:18:43 18:19:05 22.58    6.45     30.00
```

To see more options for the `acctcom` command, or any of the system accounting commands, refer to your man pages or system documentation manuals.

Daily Automated Reports

The system accounting processes generate a number of automated reports that can assist the system administrator in viewing the daily usage of a system.

The Daily Report	Shows the usage of ports on your system.
The Daily Usage Report	Shows the system resources used by your users during a daily period.
The Total Command Summary Report	Shows the commands run on your system and the resources those commands used. This report can be essential in helping you determine the processes that might be a potential bottleneck in your system.

| Daily Systems Accounting Summary Report | Tells you the last time a login ID was used to access the system. This report may be used to help you identify login IDs no longer in use. |

The Daily Report

The Daily Report is found in the /var/adm/acct/nite directory. It is an ASCII file called lineuse and can be viewed with any available text viewer or editor.

```
$ cat /var/adm/acct/nite/lineuse
```

Example file contents:

```
TOTAL DURATION: 474 MINUTES

LINE        MINUTES     PERCENT     # SESS    # ON    # OFF
dtremote    173         36          1         1       2
lft0        0           0           0         0       1
pts/0       0           0           0         0       1
pts/1       0           0           0         0       1
pts/2       77          16          3         3       4
TOTALS      250         - -         4         4       9
```

The definition of each column in this report is as follows:

LINE	The port that was used to access the system.
MINUTES	The number of minutes the port was active during this daily period.
PERCENT	The number of minutes the port was active divided by the TOTAL DURATION factor. TOTAL DURATION is the sum of the minutes the system was in a multiuser run state.
# SESS	The number of times the port was accessed to log in to the system.
# ON	The number of times the port was used for login purposes.
# OFF	The number of logoffs handled by that port and the number of interrupts such as Ctrl-c, EOF, and so on.

The Daily Usage Report

The Daily Usage Report is found in the /var/adm/acct directory. It is a binary file called daytacct that is to be accessed with the prtacct accounting command.

```
$ prtacct -v /var/adm/acct/nite/daytacct

Fri May  9 16:02:04 EST 1998  Page 1
```

UID	LOGIN NAME	CPU PRIME	CPU NPRIME	KCORE PRIME	KCORE NPRIME	CONNECT PRIME	CONNECT NPRIME	DISK BLOCKS	FEES	# OF PROCS	# OF SESS	# DISK SAMPLES
0	TOTAL	0	0	0	0	9448	14739	0	0	0	83	0
0	japierce	0	0	0	0	8526	13904	0	0	0	46	0
0	dwilson	0	0	0	0	508	814	0	0	0	21	0
0	kvwood	0	0	0	0	412	0	0	0	0	8	0
223	wpierce	0	0	0	0	0	21	0	0	0	5	0
237	awilson	0	0	0	0	1	0	0	0	0	2	0
273	wdwood	0	0	0	0	1	0	0	0	0	1	0

The definition of each column in this report is as follows:

UID	The user's identification number.
LOGIN NAME	The user's name.
CPU prime/non prime	The amount of time the user's program required the use of CPU. This is rounded up to the nearest minute.
KCORE prime/non prime	The amount of memory per minute used to run the programs. This is rounded up to the nearest kilobyte.
CONNECT prime/non prime	Total time the user was actually connected to the system.
DISK BLOCKS	The number of disk blocks used.
# OF PROCS	The number of processes the user executed.
# OF SESS	The number of sessions the user incurred by logging in.
# DISK SAMPLES	The number of times acctdusg or diskusg was run to cumulate the average number of DISK BLOCKS.
FEE	The total amount of usage charges accessed to the user for this given period.

Daily Command Summary Report and Total Command Summary Report

The Daily Command Summary Report is found in the /var/adm/acct/nite directory. It is an ASCII file called daycms and can be viewed with any available text viewer or editor.

27

SYSTEM ACCOUNTING

```
$ cat /var/adm/acct/nite/daycms
```

```
TOTAL COMMAND SUMMARY
COMMAND  NUMBER    TOTAL    TOTAL    TOTAL     MEAN    MEAN     HOG      CHARS  BLOCKS
  NAME    CMDS  KCOREMIN  CPU-MIN  REAL-MIN  SIZE-K  CPU-MIN  FACTOR    TRNSFD    READ


TOTALS      82     12.68     0.06     21.91  209.92     0.00    0.28  6.636e+06    0.00

man          1      7.56     0.02      1.68  440.00     0.02    1.02  5.566e+06    0.00
vi           1      2.24     0.02      0.53  121.00     0.02    3.49  71936.00     0.00
ls           5      1.15     0.01      0.02  108.15     0.00   68.33  117144.00    0.00
fgrep       14      0.39     0.00      0.01  124.17     0.00   42.86  286776.00    0.00
tail        14      0.36     0.00      0.02  126.82     0.00   18.03  142744.00    0.00
bsh          6      0.28     0.00      0.01   99.27     0.00   27.50  49410.00     0.00
ps           1      0.21     0.00      0.00  137.00     0.00   66.67  19696.00     0.00
ftpd         1      0.20     0.00      0.81  155.00     0.00    0.16  41576.00     0.00
sendmail     1      0.12     0.00      0.00  468.00     0.00  100.00  13744.00     0.00
fwtmp        3      0.07     0.00      0.00  143.00     0.00   25.00  35840.00     0.00
more         2      0.05     0.00      2.41  195.00     0.00    0.01  30144.00     0.00
pg           3      0.03     0.00     14.78   28.50     0.00    0.01  61232.00     0.00
ksh          2      0.00     0.00      0.00    0.00     0.00    0.00  18360.00     0.00
rm           6      0.00     0.00      0.00    0.00     0.00    0.00      0.00     0.00
accton       2      0.00     0.00      0.00    0.00     0.00    0.00      0.00     0.00
acctwtmp     2      0.00     0.00      0.00    0.00     0.00    0.00    128.00     0.00
egrep       14      0.00     0.00      0.00    0.00     0.00    0.00  143976.00    0.00
grep         1      0.00     0.00      0.00    0.00     0.00    0.00  23976.00     0.00
dspmsg       2      0.00     0.00      0.00    0.00     0.00    0.00   8214.00     0.00
sh           1      0.00     0.00      1.64    0.00     0.00    0.02   5058.00     0.00
```

The Total Command Summary Report looks like the preceding report with one exception. It is usually a monthly summary showing total accumulated since the last month or the last execution of monacct. The Total Command Summary Report is found in the /var/adm/acct/sum directory. It is an ASCII file called cms and can be viewed with any available text viewer or editor.

The definitions of each column in this report are as follows:

COMMAND NAME	The name of the command.
NUMBER COMMANDS	The total number of times the command has been executed.
KCOREMIN	The total cumulative kilobytes segments used by the command.
TOTAL CPU-MIN	The total processing time in minutes.
REAL-MIN	The actual processing time in minutes.
MEAN SIZE-K	The mean of TOTAL KCOREMIN divided by execution.
MENU CPU-MIN	The mean of executions divided by total processing time in minutes.

HOG FACTOR	The total processing time divided by elapsed time. This is the utilization ratio of the system.
CHARS TRNSFD	The total number of reads and writes to the file system.
BLOCKS READ	The total number of physical block reads and writes.

Daily Systems Accounting Summary Report

This report is generated by the runacct command via cron. This report is found in the /var/adm/acct/sum directory and is a file whose format is rprt{MMDD}. This file is a summary report of daily activity for the system. The Daily Systems Accounting Summary Report is found in the /var/adm/acct/sum directory. It is an ASCII file and can be viewed with any available text viewer or editor. An example of this report follows:

```
$ cat /var/adm/acct/sum/rprt0510

Sat May 10 21:41:50 EST 1998 DAILY REPORT FOR AIX Page 1


from Sat May 10 21:27:28 EST 1998
to   Sat May 10 21:41:46 EST 1998
1    openacct
1    runacct
1    acctcon1


TOTAL DURATION: 14 MINUTES

LINE    MINUTES    PERCENT    # SESS    # ON    # OFF
lft0    14         100        1         1       1
pts/0   14         100        1         1       1
pts/1   14         100        1         1       1
pts/2   14         100        1         1       1
pts/3   14         100        1         1       1
TOTALS  72         --         5         5       5



Sat May 10 21:41:50 EST 1998 DAILY USAGE REPORT FOR AIX Page 1


        LOGIN    CPU    CPU    KCORE  KCORE  CONNECT  CONNECT  DISK    FEES  # OF   # OF # DISK
UID     NAME     PRIME  NPRIME PRIME  NPRIME PRIME    NPRIME   BLOCKS        PROCS  SESS SAMPLES

0       TOTAL    0      0      0      7      0        72       5       0     216    5    4
0       root     0      0      0      1      0        72       1       0     28     5    1
2       bin      0      0      0      0      0        0        1       0     0      0    1
4       adm      0      0      0      6      0        0        0       0     188    0    0
100     guest    0      0      0      0      0        0        1       0     0      0    1
200     servdir  0      0      0      0      0        0        2       0     0      0    1
```

```
Sat May 10 21:41:48 EST 1998 DAILY COMMAND SUMMARY Page 1
```

```
                              TOTAL COMMAND SUMMARY
COMMAND   NUMBER   TOTAL    TOTAL    TOTAL    MEAN     MEAN     HOG      CHARS  BLOCKS
NAME      CMDS  KCOREMIN CPU-MIN REAL-MIN  SIZE-K  CPU-MIN  FACTOR    TRNSFD    READ

TOTALS     216    6.91     0.05     7.42   132.59    0.00     0.70 1.707e+07 4094.00

diskusg      1    3.73     0.03     0.11   142.00    0.03    23.22 1.625e+07 4094.00
bsh         15    1.28     0.01     0.24   129.47    0.00    44.20  49810.00    0.00
awk          6    0.27     0.00     0.00   175.67    0.00    37.50  48971.00    0.00
ls           6    0.25     0.00     0.00   136.14    0.00    87.50  37662.00    0.00
tail         6    0.13     0.00     0.01    96.80    0.00    18.52  61176.00    0.00
sendmail     1    0.12     0.00     0.00   462.00    0.00   100.00  13744.00    0.00
dspmsg      18    0.11     0.00     0.00   212.00    0.00    33.33  74259.00    0.00
cat         17    0.11     0.00     0.00   136.00    0.00    60.00   1615.00    0.00
acctcms      4    0.10     0.00     0.00   201.00    0.00    50.00  65520.00    0.00
fgrep        6    0.09     0.00     0.00    84.25    0.00    36.36 122904.00    0.00
sort         7    0.09     0.00     0.03   112.00    0.00     3.03  15302.00    0.00
acctmerg     6    0.08     0.00     0.00   105.00    0.00    37.50   9064.00    0.00
vi           1    0.07     0.00     0.11   127.00    0.00     0.48  17912.00    0.00
egrep        6    0.06     0.00     0.00   124.00    0.00    33.33  61704.00    0.00
chown       14    0.06     0.00     0.00    48.80    0.00    35.71  15988.00    0.00
grep         3    0.06     0.00     0.01   121.00    0.00     3.70   7971.00    0.00
date         9    0.05     0.00     0.00   198.00    0.00    50.00    169.00    0.00
acctprc1     1    0.04     0.00     0.00    74.00    0.00    66.67  23672.00    0.00
acctcon1     1    0.04     0.00     0.00   142.00    0.00    50.00   7883.00    0.00
uniq         3    0.04     0.00     0.02   142.00    0.00     1.16   6269.00    0.00
ypcat        2    0.03     0.00     0.00   129.00    0.00     6.25  58000.00    0.00
more         1    0.03     0.00     6.82   101.00    0.00     0.00  11384.00    0.00
pr           5    0.02     0.00     0.00    94.00    0.00    14.29  26094.00    0.00
rm           7    0.02     0.00     0.00    82.00    0.00     9.09   5058.00    0.00
lsuser       1    0.01     0.00     0.01    19.00    0.00     7.14   4600.00    0.00
sed          7    0.00     0.00     0.01     0.00    0.00     0.00  30745.00    0.00
fwtmp        4    0.00     0.00     0.00     0.00    0.00    10.00  10270.00    0.00
getopt       3    0.00     0.00     0.00     0.00    0.00     0.00     48.00    0.00
chmod       15    0.00     0.00     0.00     0.00    0.00     0.00      0.00    0.00
acctwtmp     2    0.00     0.00     0.00     0.00    0.00     0.00    128.00    0.00
uname        1    0.00     0.00     0.00     0.00    0.00     0.00      4.00    0.00
wtmpfix      1    0.00     0.00     0.00     0.00    0.00     0.00   3072.00    0.00
mv           7    0.00     0.00     0.00     0.00    0.00     0.00   5058.00    0.00
acctcon2     1    0.00     0.00     0.00     0.00    0.00   100.00    660.00    0.00
accton       1    0.00     0.00     0.00     0.00    0.00     0.00      0.00    0.00
df           1    0.00     0.00     0.00     0.00    0.00     0.00    733.00    0.00
basename     2    0.00     0.00     0.00     0.00    0.00     0.00     23.00    0.00
expr         1    0.00     0.00     0.00     0.00    0.00     0.00      2.00    0.00
cp          19    0.00     0.00     0.00     0.00    0.00     0.00  10012.00    0.00
wc           1    0.00     0.00     0.00     0.00    0.00     0.00   1203.00    0.00
```

acctprc2	1	0.00	0.00	0.00	0.00	0.00	0.00	12736.00	0.00
acctdisk	1	0.00	0.00	0.00	0.00	0.00	0.00	339.00	0.00
ln	1	0.00	0.00	0.00	0.00	0.00	0.00	0.00	0.00

Sat May 10 21:41:48 EST 1998 MONTHLY TOTAL COMMAND SUMMARY Page 1

TOTAL COMMAND SUMMARY

COMMAND NAME	NUMBER CMDS	TOTAL KCOREMIN	TOTAL CPU-MIN	TOTAL REAL-MIN	MEAN SIZE-K	MEAN CPU-MIN	HOG FACTOR	CHARS TRNSFD	BLOCKS READ
TOTALS	1771	281.68	1.22	706.08	231.12	0.00	0.17	1.423e+08	4094.00
dtterm	2	136.19	0.24	81.83	566.58	0.12	0.29	333760.00	0.00
man	11	79.59	0.18	4.64	431.09	0.02	3.98	5.915e+07	0.00
bsh	135	7.74	0.06	13.13	124.32	0.00	0.47	705187.00	0.00
find	2	6.64	0.21	0.74	31.00	0.11	28.78	13764.00	0.00
lsuser	24	5.85	0.08	0.28	72.03	0.00	29.21	117880.00	0.00
ksh	27	4.60	0.03	189.72	178.53	0.00	0.01	637811.00	0.00
crash	1	3.89	0.02	3.19	237.00	0.02	0.51	2.635e+07	0.00
diskusg	1	3.73	0.03	0.11	142.00	0.03	23.22	1.625e+07	4094.00
acctcom	18	3.30	0.05	0.09	62.18	0.00	62.01	839000.00	0.00
telnet	2	3.25	0.05	79.10	65.62	0.02	0.06	417920.00	0.00
errpt	8	3.13	0.01	0.03	267.40	0.00	41.67	2.129e+06	0.00
telnetd	5	2.40	0.06	107.89	40.19	0.01	0.06	762960.00	0.00
tail	102	2.31	0.02	0.26	99.48	0.00	8.77	1.04e+06	0.00
fgrep	102	2.03	0.02	0.05	113.25	0.00	37.30	2.089e+06	0.00
ls	75	2.00	0.02	0.04	116.15	0.00	45.21	603775.00	0.00
vi	16	1.46	0.01	37.87	116.81	0.00	0.03	330912.00	0.00
more	35	1.21	0.01	26.19	125.30	0.00	0.04	518424.00	0.00
awk	25	0.96	0.01	0.04	175.33	0.00	14.09	141725.00	0.00
dspmsg	98	0.74	0.00	0.01	166.24	0.00	50.00	493457.00	0.00
uniq	50	0.69	0.01	0.55	115.74	0.00	1.09	142133.00	0.00
grep	33	0.59	0.00	0.30	126.22	0.00	1.54	237104.00	0.00
ps	6	0.59	0.01	0.03	86.88	0.00	25.49	104784.00	0.00
rm	75	0.59	0.01	0.04	75.23	0.00	17.75	404784.00	0.00
file	13	0.52	0.00	0.01	110.83	0.00	36.00	461053.00	0.00
sort	59	0.52	0.01	0.55	90.45	0.00	1.04	280988.00	0.00
sendmail	8	0.48	0.00	0.00	463.00	0.00	44.44	109952.00	0.00
date	96	0.46	0.00	0.01	194.89	0.00	33.33	21536.00	0.00
acctcms	15	0.42	0.00	0.01	179.22	0.00	45.00	267903.00	0.00
acctcon1	16	0.41	0.00	0.01	142.45	0.00	22.92	180989.00	0.00
egrep	102	0.40	0.00	0.02	102.33	0.00	16.13	1.049e+06	0.00
chown	49	0.38	0.01	0.01	55.54	0.00	49.06	155734.00	0.00
sh	26	0.34	0.00	4.22	131.70	0.00	0.06	156818.00	0.00
ftpd	1	0.33	0.00	57.30	212.00	0.00	0.00	184320.00	0.00
acctprc2	3	0.30	0.00	0.01	130.00	0.00	39.13	91430.00	0.00
lslpp	4	0.28	0.00	0.03	135.75	0.00	8.25	108864.00	0.00
sadc	4	0.28	0.01	0.08	24.09	0.00	13.92	2.402e+07	0.00
strings	7	0.27	0.00	0.00	95.00	0.00	61.11	76242.00	0.00

27

SYSTEM ACCOUNTING

In this portion of the book, you learn all about performance monitoring. There is a series of commands that enable system administrators, programmers, and users to examine each resource that a UNIX system uses. By examining these resources, you can determine whether the system is operating properly or poorly. More important than the commands themselves, you also learn strategies and procedures that can be used to search for performance problems. Armed with both the commands and the overall methodologies with which to use them, you will understand the factors affecting system performance and what to do to optimize them so that the system performs at its best.

Although this chapter is helpful for users, it is particularly directed at new system administrators who are actively involved in keeping the system they depend on healthy, or trying to diagnose what has caused its performance to deteriorate.

This chapter introduces several new tools to use in your system investigations.

The sequence of the chapter is not based on particular commands. It is instead based on the steps and the strategies that you use during your performance investigations. In other words, the chapter is organized to mirror the logical progression that a system administrator uses to determine the state of the overall system and the status of each of its subsystems.

You frequently start your investigations by quickly looking at the overall state of the system load, as described in the section "Tools for Monitoring the Overall System Status." To do this, you see how the commands `uptime` and `sar` can be used to examine the system load and the general level of Central Processing Unit (CPU) loading. You also see how tools such as SunOS's `perfmeter` can be helpful in gaining a graphic, high-level view of several components at once.

Next, in the section "Monitoring Processes with `ps`," you learn how `ps` can be used to determine the characteristics of the processes running on your system. This is a natural next step after you have determined that the overall system status reflects a heavier-than-normal loading. You learn how to use `ps` to look for processes that are consuming inordinate amounts of resources and the steps to take after you have located them.

After you have looked at the snapshot of system utilization that `ps` gives you, you may well have questions about how to use the memory or disk subsystems. So, in the next section, "Memory Usage Monitoring," you learn how to monitor memory performance with tools such as `vmstat` and `sar`, and how to detect when paging and swapping have become excessive (thus indicating that memory must be added to the system).

In the section "Disk Subsystem Performance Monitoring," you see how tools such as `iostat` and `sar` can be used to monitor disk Input/Output (I/O) performance. You see how to determine when your disk subsystem is unbalanced and what to do to alleviate disk performance problems.

After the section on disk I/O performance is a related section on network performance. (It is related to the disk I/O discussion because of the prevalent use of networks to provide extensions of local disk service through such facilities as NFS.) Here, you learn to use `netstat`, `nfsstat`, and `spray` to determine the condition of your network.

This is followed by a brief discussion of CPU performance monitoring, and finally a section on kernel tuning. In this final section, you learn about the underlying tables that reside within the UNIX operating system and how they can be tuned to customize your system's UNIX kernel and optimize its use of resources.

You have seen before in this book that the diversity of UNIX systems makes it important to check each vendor's documentation for specific details about its particular implementation. The same thing applies here as well. Furthermore, modern developments such as symmetric multiprocessor support and relational databases add new characteristics and problems to the challenge of performance monitoring. These are touched on briefly in the discussions that follow.

Performance and Its Impact on Your Business

28

PERFORMANCE
MONITORING

Before you get into the technical side of UNIX performance monitoring, there are a few guidelines that can help system administrators avoid performance problems and maximize their overall effectiveness.

All too typically, the UNIX system administrator learns about performance when there is a critical problem with the system. Perhaps the system is taking too long to process jobs or is far behind on the number of jobs that it normally processes. Perhaps the response times for users have deteriorated to the point where users are becoming distracted and unproductive (which is a polite way of saying frustrated and angry!). In any case, if the system isn't actually failing to help its users attain their particular goals, it is at least failing to meet their expectations.

It may seem obvious that when user productivity is being affected, money and time, and sometimes a great deal of both, are being lost. Simple measurements of the amount of time lost can often provide the cost justification for upgrades to the system. In this chapter, you learn how to identify which components of the system are the best candidates for such an upgrade. (If you think people were unhappy to begin with, try talking to them after an expensive upgrade has produced no discernible improvement in performance!)

Often, it is only when users begin complaining that people begin to examine the variables affecting performance. This in itself is somewhat of a problem. The system administrator should have a thorough understanding of the activities on the system before users are affected by a crisis. He should know the characteristics of each group of users on the system. This includes the type of work that they submit while they are present during the day, as well as the jobs that are to be processed during the evening. What is the size of the CPU requirement, the I/O requirement, and the memory requirement of the most frequently occurring or the most important jobs? What impact do these jobs have on the networks connected to the machine? Also important is the time-sensitivity of the jobs, the classic example being payrolls that must be completed by a given time and date.

These profiles of system activity and user requirements can help the system administrator acquire a holistic understanding of the activity on the system. That knowledge will not only be of assistance if there is a sudden crisis in performance, but also if there is a gradual erosion of it. Conversely, if the system administrator has not compiled a profile of his various user groups and examined the underlying loads that they impose on the system, he will be at a serious disadvantage in an emergency when it comes to figuring out where all the CPU cycles, or memory, have gone. This chapter examines the tools that can be used to gain this knowledge and demonstrates their value.

Finally, although all users may have been created equal, the work of some users inevitably has more impact on corporate profitability than the work of other users. Perhaps, given UNIX's academic heritage, running the system in a completely democratic manner should be the goal of the system administrator. However, the system administrator will sooner or later find out, either politely or painfully, who the most important and the most influential groups are. This set of characteristics should also somehow be factored into the user profiles the system administrator develops before the onset of crises, which by their nature obscure the reasoning process of all involved.

Introduction to UNIX Performance

While the system is running, UNIX maintains several counters to keep track of critical system resources. The relevant resources that are tracked are the following:

CPU utilization	Buffer usage
Disk I/O activity	Tape I/O activity
Terminal activity	System call activity
Context switching activity	File access utilization
Queue activity	Interprocess communication (IPC)
Paging activity	Free memory and swap space
Kernel memory allocation (KMA)	Kernel tables
Remote file sharing (RFS)	

By looking at reports based on these counters, you can determine how the three major subsystems are performing. These subsystems are the following:

CPU   The CPU processes instructions and programs. Each time you submit a job to the system, it makes demands on the CPU. Usually, the CPU can service all demands in a timely manner. However, there is only so much available processing power, which must be shared by all users and the internal programs of the operating system, too.

Memory Every program that runs on the system makes some demand on the physical memory on the machine. Like the CPU, it is a finite resource. When the active processes and programs that are running on the system request more memory than the machine actually has, paging is used to move parts of the processes to disk and reclaim their memory pages for use by other processes. If further shortages occur, the system may also have to resort to swapping, which moves entire processes to disk to make room.

I/O   The I/O subsystem(s) transfers data into and out of the machine. I/O subsystems comprise devices such as disks, printers, terminals/keyboards, and other relatively slow devices, and are a common source of resource contention problems. In addition, there is a rapidly increasing use of network I/O devices. When programs are doing a lot of I/O, they can get bogged down waiting for data from these devices. Each subsystem has its own limitations with respect to the bandwidth that it can effectively use for I/O operations, as well as its own peculiar problems.

Performance monitoring and tuning is not always an exact science. In the displays that follow, there is a great deal of variety in the system/subsystem loadings, even for the small sample of systems used here. In addition, different user groups have widely differing requirements. Some users put a strain on the I/O resources, some on the CPU, and some on the network. Performance tuning is always a series of trade-offs. As you will see, increasing the kernel size to alleviate one problem may aggravate memory utilization. Increasing NFS performance to satisfy one set of users may reduce performance in another area and thereby aggravate another set of users. The goal of the task is often to find an optimal compromise that satisfies the majority of user and system resource needs.

Tools for Monitoring the Overall System Status

The examination of specific UNIX performance monitoring techniques begins with a look at four basic tools that give you a view of the overall performance of the system. After getting this high-level view, you examine each of the subsystems in detail.

28

PERFORMANCE
MONITORING

Using `uptime`

One of the simplest reports that you use to monitor UNIX system performance measures the number of processes in the UNIX run queue during given intervals. It comes from the command `uptime`. It is both a high-level view of the system's workload and a handy starting place when the system seems to be performing slowly. In general, processes in the run queue are active programs (that is, not sleeping or waiting) that require system resources. Here is an example:

```
% uptime
  2:07pm  up 11 day(s),  4:54,  15 users,  load average: 1.90, 1.98, 2.01
```

The useful parts of the display are the three load-average figures. The 1.90 load average was measured over the last minute. The 1.98 average was measured over the last 5 minutes. The 2.01 load average was measured over the last 15 minutes.

TIP

You are usually looking at the trend of the averages. This particular example shows a system that is under a fairly consistent load. However, if a system is having problems, but the load averages seem to be declining steadily, then you might want to wait a while before you take any action that might affect the system and possibly inconvenience users. While you are doing some `ps` commands to determine what caused the problem, the imbalance may correct itself.

NOTE

`uptime` has certain limitations. For example, high-priority jobs are not distinguished from low-priority jobs although their impact on the system can be much greater.

Run `uptime` periodically and observe both the numbers and the trend. When there is a problem, it often shows up here and can tip you off to begin serious investigations. As system loads increase, more demands are made on your memory and I/O subsystems, so keep an eye out for paging, swapping, and disk inefficiencies. System loads of 2 or 3 usually indicate light loads. System loads of 5 or 6 are usually medium-grade loads. Loads above 10 are often heavy loads on large UNIX machines. However, there is wide variation among types of machines as to what constitutes a heavy load. Therefore, the mentioned technique of sampling your system regularly until you have your own reference for light, medium, and heavy loads is the best technique.

Using perfmeter

Because the goal of this part of the chapter is to give you the tools to view your overall system performance, a brief discussion of graphical performance meters is appropriate. SUN Solaris users are provided with an OpenWindows XView tool called perfmeter, which summarizes overall system performance values in multiple dials or strip charts. Strip charts are the default. Not all UNIX systems come with such a handy tool, which is too bad because in this case a picture is worth, if not 1,000 words, at least 30 or 40 man pages. In this concise format, you get information about the system resources shown in Table 28.1:

TABLE 28.1. SYSTEM RESOURCES AND THEIR DESCRIPTIONS.

Resources	*Description*
cpu	Percent of CPU being utilized
pkts	Ethernet activity, in packets per second
page	Paging, in pages per second
swap	Jobs swapped per second
intr	Number of device interrupts per second
disk	Disk traffic, in transfers per second
cntxt	Number of context switches per second
load	Average number of runnable processes over the last minute
colls	Collisions per second detected on the Ethernet
errs	Errors per second on receiving packets

28

PERFORMANCE
MONITORING

The charts of the perfmeter are not a source for precise measurements of subsystem performance, but they are graphic representations of them. However, the chart can be useful for monitoring several aspects of the system at the same time. When you start a particular job, the graphics can demonstrate the impact of that job on the CPU, on disk transfers, and on paging. Many developers like to use the tool to assess the efficiency of their work for this very reason. Likewise, system administrators use the tool to get valuable clues about where to start their investigations. For example, when faced with intermittent and transitory problems, glancing at a perfmeter and then going directly to the proper display may increase the odds that you can catch in the act the process that is degrading the system.

The scale value for the strip chart changes automatically when the chart refreshes to accommodate increasing or decreasing values on the system. You add values to be monitored by clicking the right mouse button and selecting from the menu. From the same menu, you can select properties, which let you modify what the `perfmeter` is monitoring, the format (dials/graphs, direction of the displays, and solid/lined display), remote/local machine choice, and the frequency of the display.

You can also set a ceiling value for a particular strip chart. If the value goes beyond the ceiling value, this portion of the chart is displayed in red. Thus, a system administrator who knows that someone is periodically running a job that eats up all the CPU memory can set a signal that the job may be run again. The system administrator can also use this to monitor the condition of critical values from several feet away from his monitor. If he or she sees red, other users may be seeing red, too.

The `perfmeter` is a utility provided with SunOS. Check your own particular UNIX operating system to determine whether similar performance tools are provided.

Using sar

A useful tool for examining system utilization over time is the `sar` command. If your machine does not support `uptime`, there is an option for `sar` that can provide the same type of quick, high-level snapshot of the system. The `-q` option reports the average queue length and the percentage of time that the queue is occupied.

```
% sar -q 5 5

07:28:37 runq-sz %runocc swpq-sz %swpocc
07:28:42     5.0     100             _
07:28:47     5.0     100             _
07:28:52     4.8     100             _
07:28:57     4.8     100             _
07:29:02     4.6     100             _

Average      4.8     100             _
```

The fields in this report are the following:

`runq-sz`	This is the length of the run queue during the interval. The run queue list doesn't include jobs that are sleeping or waiting for I/O but does include jobs that are in memory and ready to run.
`%runocc`	This is the percentage of time that the run queue is occupied.
`swpq-sz`	This is the average length of the swap queue during the interval. Jobs or threads that have been swapped out and are therefore unavailable to run are shown here.
`%swpocc`	This is the percentage of time that there are swapped jobs or threads.

The run queue length is used in a similar way to the load averages of uptime. Typically, the number is less than 2 if the system is operating properly. Consistently higher values indicate that the system is under heavier loads and is quite possibly CPU bound. When the run queue length is high and the run queue percentage is occupied 100% of the time, as it is in this example, the system's idle time is minimized, and it is good to be on the lookout for performance-related problems in the memory and disk subsystems. However, there is still no activity indicated in the swapping columns in the example. You learn about swapping in the next section and see that although this system is obviously busy, the lack of swapping is a partial vote of confidence that it may still be functioning properly.

Another quick and easy tool to use to determine overall system utilization is sar with the -u option. CPU utilization is shown by -u, and sar without any options defaults on most versions of UNIX to this option. The CPU is either busy or idle. When it is busy, it is either working on user work or system work. When it is not busy, it is either waiting on I/O, or it is idle.

```
% sar -u 5 5

13:16:58    %usr    %sys    %wio    %idle
13:17:03     40      10      13      38
13:17:08     31       6      48      14
13:17:13     42      15       9      34
13:17:18     41      15      10      35
13:17:23     41      15      11      33

Average      39      12      18      31
```

The fields in the report are the following:

%usr   This is the percentage of time that the processor is in user mode (that is, executing code requested by a user).

%sys   This is the percentage of time that the processor is in system mode, servicing system calls. Users can cause this percentage to increase above normal levels by using system calls inefficiently.

%wio   This is the percentage of time that the processor is waiting on completion of I/O, from disk, NFS, or RFS. If the percentage is regularly high, check the I/O systems for inefficiencies.

%idle   This is the percentage of time the processor is idle. If the percentage is high and the system is heavily loaded, there is probably a memory or an I/O problem.

In this example, you see a system with ample CPU capacity left (that is, the average idle percentage is 31 percent). The system is spending most of its time on user tasks, so user

28

PERFORMANCE MONITORING

programs are probably not too inefficient with their use of system calls. The I/O wait percentage indicates an application that is making a fair amount of demands on the I/O subsystem.

Most administrators would argue that `%idle` should be in the low teens rather than 0, at least when the system is under load. If it is 0, it doesn't necessarily mean that the machine is operating poorly. However, it is usually a good bet that the machine is out of spare computational capacity and should be upgraded to the next level of CPU speed. The reason to upgrade the CPU is in anticipation of future growth of user processing requirements. If the system work load is increasing, even if the users haven't yet encountered the problem, why not anticipate the requirement? On the other hand, if the CPU idle time is high under heavy load, a CPU upgrade probably will not improve performance much.

Idle time generally is higher when the load average is low (idle time is a good thing, as far as the CPU is concerned).

A high load average and idle time are symptoms of potential problems. Either the memory or the I/O subsystems, or both, are hindering the swift dispatch and completion of the jobs.

You can have `sar` start up automatically on system restarts, as well as have it continuously gather statistics by using a couple of standard scripts that come with most SVR4 based systems. These scripts are `sa1`, `sa2`, and `sadc`.

`sadc` is used to sample system data *n* times, with a time interval of `t`. On most systems, this is part of a startup script shipped with the operating system.

On Solaris systems, you can modify the `/etc/rc2.d/S21perf` file to uncomment the `sadc` entries. This starts system accounting as soon as the system is rebooted.

You must also modify the `/var/spool/cron/crontabs/sys` file and uncomment the lines pertaining to `sadc`. You need to do this to have `sadc` continuously gather statistics while the system is up.

Process Monitoring

You have probably noticed that, although throughout the rest of this chapter the commands are listed under the topic in which they are used (for example, `nfsstat` is listed in the section "Network Performance Monitoring"), this section is dedicated to just one command. What's so special about `ps`? It is singled out in this manner because of the way that it is used in the performance monitoring process. It is a starting point for generating theories (for example, processes are using up so much memory that you are paging and that is slowing down the system). Conversely, it is an ending point for confirming theories (for example, here is a burst of network activity—I wonder if it is caused by that communications test job that the programmers keep running?). Because it is so pivotal and provides a unique snapshot of the processes on the system, ps is given its own section.

Using ps

One of the most valuable commands for performance monitoring is the ps command. It enables you to monitor the status of the active processes on the system. Remember the words from the movie *Casablanca*, "round up the usual suspects"? Well, ps helps to identify the usual suspects (that is, suspect processes that could be using inordinate resources). Then you can determine which of the suspects is actually guilty of causing the performance degradation. It is at once a powerful tool and a source of overhead for the system itself. Using various options, the following information is shown:

Current status of the process	Process ID
Parent process ID	User ID
Scheduling class	Priority
Address of process	Memory used
CPU time used	

Using ps provides a snapshot of the system's active processes. It is used in conjunction with other commands throughout this section. Frequently, you will look at a report from a command, for example vmstat, and then look to ps either to confirm or deny a theory you have come up with about the nature of your system's problem. The particular performance problem that motivated you to look at ps in the first place may have been caused by a process that is already off the list. It provides a series of clues to use in generating theories that can then be tested by detailed analysis of the particular subsystem.

The following are the fields from the output of the ps command that are important in terms of performance tuning:

Field	Description
F	Flags that indicate the process's current state and are calculated by adding each of the hexadecimal values:
00	Process has terminated.
01	System process, always in memory.
02	Process is being traced by its parent.
04	Process is being traced by parent and is stopped.

continues

Field		*Description*
	08	Process cannot be awakened by a signal.
	10	Process is in memory and locked, pending an event.
	20	Process cannot be swapped.
S		The current state of the process, as indicated by one of the following letters:
	O	Process is currently running on the processor.
	S	Process is sleeping, waiting for an I/O event (including terminal I/O) to complete.
	R	Process is ready to run.
	I	Process is idle.
	Z	Process is a zombie process (it has terminated, and the parent is not waiting but is still in the process table).
	T	Process is stopped because of parent tracing it.
	X	Process is waiting for more memory.
UID		User ID of the process's owner.
PID		Process ID number.
PPID		Parent process ID number.
C		CPU utilization for scheduling (not shown when -c is used).
CLS		Scheduling class, real-time, time sharing, or system (only shown when the -c option is used).
PRI		Process scheduling priority (higher numbers mean lower priorities).
NI		Process nice number (used in scheduling priorities—raising the number lowers the priority so the process gets less CPU time).
SZ		The amount of virtual memory required by the process. (This is a good indication of the memory load the process places on the systems memory.)
TTY		The terminal that started the process, or its parent. (A ? indicates that no terminal exists.)
TIME		The total amount of CPU time used by the process since it began.
COMD		The command that generated the process.

If your problem is immediate performance, you can disregard processes that are sleeping, stopped, or waiting on terminal I/O because these probably are not the source of the degradation. Look instead for the jobs that are ready to run, blocked for disk I/O, or paging.

```
% ps -el
 F S   UID   PID  PPID  C PRI NI    ADDR    SZ   WCHAN  TTY      TIME COMD
19 T     0     0     0 80   0 SY e00ec978     0          ?       0:01 sched
19 S     0     2     0 80   0 SY f5735000     0 e00eacdc  ?       0:05 pageout
 8 S  1001  1382     1 80  40 20 f5c6a000  1227 e00f887c console  0:02 mailtool
 8 S  1001  1386     1 80  40 20 f60ed000   819 e00f887c console  0:28 perfmete
 8 S  1001 28380 28377 80  40 20 f67c0000  5804 f5cfd146  ?      85:02 sqlturbo
 8 S  1001 28373     1 80  40 20 f63c6000  1035 f63c61c8  ?       0:07 cdrl_mai
 8 S  1001 28392     1 80  40 20 f67ce800  1035 f67ce9c8  ?       0:07 cdrl_mai
 8 S  1001 28391 28388 80  40 20 f690a800  5804 f60dce46  ?     166:39 sqlturbo
 8 S  1001 28361     1 80  60 20 f67e1000 30580 e00f887c  ?     379:35 mhdms
 8 S  1001 28360     1 80  40 20 f68e1000 12565 e00f887c  ?     182:22 mhharris
 8 O  1001 10566 10512 19  70 20 f6abb800   152          pts/14  0:00 ps
 8 S  1001 28388     1 80  40 20 f6384800   216 f60a0346  ?      67:51 db_write
 8 S  1000  7750  7749 80  40 20 f6344800  5393 f5dad02c pts/2   31:47 tbinit
 8 O  1001  9538  9537 80  81 22 f6978000  5816          ?      646:57 sqlturbo
 8 S  1033  3735  3734164  40 20 f63b8800   305 f60e0d46 pts/9   0:00 ksh
 8 S  1033  5228  5227 80  50 20 f68a8800   305 f60dca46 pts/7   0:00 ksh
 8 S  1001 28337     1 80  99 20 f6375000 47412 f63751c8  ?    1135:50 velox_ga
```

The following are tips for using ps to determine why system performance is suffering.

Look at the UID (user ID) fields for a number of identical jobs being submitted by the same user. This is often caused by a user who runs a script that starts a lot of background jobs without waiting for any of the jobs to complete. Sometimes you can safely use kill to terminate some of the jobs. Whenever you can, discuss this with the user before you take action. In any case, be sure the user is educated in the proper use of the system to avoid a replication of the problem. In the example, User ID 1001 has multiple instances of the same process running. In this case, it is a normal situation, in which multiple processes are spawned at the same time for searching through database tables to increase interactive performance.

Look at the TIME fields for a process that has accumulated a large amount of CPU time. In the example, you can see the large amount of time acquired by the processes whose command is shown as velox_ga. This may indicate that the process is in an infinite loop, or that something else is wrong with its logic. Check with the user to determine whether it is appropriate to terminate the job. If something is wrong, ask the user whether a dump of the process would assist in debugging it (check your UNIX system's reference material for commands, such as gcore, that can dump a process).

Request the -l option and look at the SZ fields for processes that are consuming too much memory. In the example, you can see the large amount of memory acquired by the processes whose command is shown as velox_ga. You could check with the user of this

28

PERFORMANCE MONITORING

process to try to determine why it behaves this way. Attempting to renice the process may simply prolong the problem that it is causing, so you may have to kill the job instead. SZ fields may also give you a clue as to memory shortage problems caused by this particular combination of jobs. You can use vmstat or sar -wpgr to check the paging and swapping statistics that are examined.

Look for processes that are consuming inordinate CPU resources. Request the -c option and look at the PRI fields for processes that are running at inappropriately high priorities. Use the nice command to adjust the nice value of the process. Beware in particular any real-time (RT) process, which can often dominate the system. If the priority is higher than you expected, check with the user to determine how it was set. If he is resetting the priority because he has figured out the superuser password, dissuade him from doing this. If the processes that are running are simply long-running, CPU-intensive jobs, ask the users whether you can nice them to a lower priority or whether they can run them at night, when other users are not affected by them.

Look for processes that are blocking on I/O. Many of the example processes are in this state. When that is the case, the disk subsystem probably requires tuning. The section "Using vmstat" examines how to investigate problems with your disk I/O. If the processes are trying to read/write over NFS, this may be a symptom that the NFS server to which they are attached is down, or that the network itself is hung.

Possible Corrective Action

As you look at each section of the output of ps, you can see potential problem areas in your system. Among the many corrective actions you can take for troublesome processes are to re-nice the process (so it doesn't hog all the CPU), or just kill it with the kill command if it is not a critical process. High CPU utilization, however, often points to one thing: bad code. Have your developers check out what's going wrong with the code while it's running so they might have a chance at fixing it.

Memory Usage Monitoring

You could say that one can never have too much money, be too thin, or have too much system memory. Memory sometimes becomes a problematic resource when programs that are running require more physical memory than is available. When this occurs, UNIX systems begin a process called paging. During paging, the system copies pages of physical memory to disk and then allows the now-vacated memory to be used by the process that requires the extra space. Occasional paging can be tolerated by most systems, but frequent and excessive paging is usually accompanied by poor system performance and angry customers.

Paging uses an algorithm that selects portions, or pages, of memory that are not being used frequently and displaces them to disk. The more frequently used portions of memory, which may be the most active parts of a process, thus remain in memory, while other portions of the process that are idle get paged out.

In addition to paging, a similar technique used by the memory management system is called swapping. Swapping moves entire processes, rather than just pages, to disk to free up memory resources. Some swapping may occur under normal conditions. That is, some processes may just be idle enough (for example, due to sleeping) to warrant their return to disk until they become active once more. Swapping can become excessive, however, when severe memory shortages develop. Interactive performance can degrade quickly when swapping increases because it often depends on keyboard-dependent processes (for example, editors) that are likely to be considered idle as they wait for you to start typing again.

As the condition of your system deteriorates, paging and swapping make increasing demands on disk I/O. This, in turn, may further slow down the execution of jobs submitted to the system. Thus, memory resource inadequacies may result in I/O resource problems.

By now, it should be apparent that it is important to be able to know whether the system has enough memory for the applications being used on it.

> **TIP**
>
> A rule of thumb is to allocate twice the swap space as you have physical memory. For example, if you have 32 MB of physical Random Access Memory (RAM) installed on your system, you would set up 64 MB of swap space when configuring the system. The system would then use this disk space for its memory management when displacing pages or processes to disk.

Both vmstat and sar provide information about the paging and swapping characteristics of a system. Let's start with vmstat. On the vmstat reports, you see information about page-ins, or pages moved from disk to memory, and page-outs, or pages moved from memory to disk. Further, you see information about swap-ins, or processes moved from disk to memory, and swap-outs, or processes moved from memory to disk.

Using vmstat

The vmstat command is used to examine virtual memory statistics and present data on process status, free and swap memory, paging activity, disk reports, CPU load, swapping, cache flushing, and interrupts. The format of the command is:

28

PERFORMANCE
MONITORING

vmstat *t* [*n*]

This command takes *n* samples, at *t* second intervals. For example, the following frequently used version of the command takes samples at 5-second intervals without stopping until canceled:

vmstat 5

The following screen shows the output from the SunOS variant of the command

vmstat -S 5

which provides extra information regarding swapping.

```
procs     memory            page             disk          faults        cpu
 r b w   swap  free si so pi po fr de sr s0 s3 s5 s5  in    sy    cs us sy id
 0 2 0  16516  9144  0  0  0  0  0  0  0  1  4 34 12 366  1396   675 14  9 76
 0 3 0 869384 29660  0  0  0  0  0  0  0  0  4 63 15 514 10759  2070 19 17 64
 0 2 0 869432 29704  0  0  0  0  0  0  0  4  3 64 11 490  2458  2035 16 13 72
 0 3 0 869448 29696  0  0  0  0  0  0  0  0  3 65 13 464  2528  2034 17 12 71
 0 3 0 869384 29684  0  0  0  0  0  0  0  1  3 68 18 551  2555  2136 16 14 70
 0 2 0 869188 29644  0  0  0  2  2  0  0  2  3 65 10 432  2495  2013 18  9 73
 0 3 0 869176 29612  0  0  0  0  0  0  0  0  3 61 16 504  2527  2053 17 11 71
 0 2 0 869156 29600  0  0  0  0  0  0  0  0  3 69  8 438 15820  2027 20 18 62
```

The fields in the vmstat report are the following:

procs	Reports the number of processes in each of the following states
r	In the Run queue
b	Blocked, waiting for resources
w	Swapped, waiting for processing resources
memory	Reports on real and virtual memory
swap	Available swap space
free	Size of free list
page	Reports on page faults and paging, averaged over an interval (typically 5 seconds) and provided in units per second
re	Pages reclaimed from the free list (not shown when the -S option is requested)
mf	Minor faults (not shown when -S option is requested)
si	Number of pages swapped in (only shown with the -S option)
so	Number of pages swapped out (only shown with the -S option)
pi	Kilobytes paged in
po	Kilobytes paged out
fr	Kilobytes freed

de	Anticipated short-term memory shortfall
sr	Pages scanned by clock algorithm, per second
disk	Shows the number of disk operations per second
faults	Shows the per-second trap/interrupt rates
in	Device interrupts
sy	System faults per second
cs	CPU context switches
cpu	Shows the use of CPU time
us	User time
sy	System time
id	Idle time

> **NOTE**
>
> The `vmstat` command's first line is rarely of any use. When reviewing the output from the command, always start at the second line and go forward for pertinent data.

Let's look at some of these fields for clues about system performance. As far as memory performance goes, po and w are very important. For people using the -S option, so is similarly important. These fields all clearly show when a system is paging and swapping. If w is nonzero and so continually indicates swapping, the system probably has a serious memory problem. If, likewise, po consistently has large numbers present, the system probably has a significant memory resource problem.

> **TIP**
>
> If your version of `vmstat` doesn't specifically provide swapping information, you can infer the swapping by watching the relationship between the w and the fre fields. An increase in w, the swapped-out processes, followed by an increase in fre, the number of pages on the free list, can provide the same information in a different manner.

Other fields from the `vmstat` output are helpful, as well. The number of runnable and blocked processes can provide a good indication of the flow of processes, or lack thereof, through the system. Similarly, comparing each percentage CPU idle versus CPU in

28

PERFORMANCE
MONITORING

system state, and versus CPU in user state, can provide information about the overall composition of the workload. As the load increases on the system, it is a good sign if the CPU is spending the majority of the time in the user state. Loads of 60 or 70 percent for CPU user state are okay. Idle CPU should drop as the user load picks up, and under heavy load may well fall to 0.

If paging and swapping are occurring at an unusually high rate, it may be due to the number and types of jobs that are running. Usually, you can turn to ps to determine what those jobs are.

Imagine that ps shows a large number of jobs that require significant memory resources. (You saw how to determine this in the ps discussion in the previous section.) That would confirm the vmstat report. To resolve the problem, you would have to restrict memory-intensive jobs, or the use of memory, or add more memory physically.

> **TIP**
>
> You can see that having a history of several vmstat and ps reports during normal system operation can be extremely helpful in determining what the usual conditions are, and, subsequently, what the unusual ones are. Also, one or two vmstat reports may indicate a temporary condition, rather than a permanent problem. Sample the system multiple times before deciding that you have the answer to your system's performance problems.

If you are using HP-UX, you would get a slightly different output from vmstat. For example, if you run vmstat 5 3, you would get something similar to the following output:

procfs			memory				page					faults			cpu		
r	b	w	avm	free	re	at	pi	po	fr	de	sr	in	sy	cs	us	sy	id
4	0	0	1161	2282	6	22	48	0	0	0	0	429	289	65	44	18	18
9	0	0	1161	1422	4	30	59	0	0	0	0	654	264	181	18	20	62
6	0	0	1409	1247	2	19	37	0	0	0	0	505	316	130	47	10	43

If you compare the two outputs, you see that there are three new metrics (avm, re and at), two metrics not included (swap and so), and one category not included here (disk).

In the fourth column, you see the new metric avm. This is the number of virtual memory pages owned by processes that have run within the last 20 seconds. Should this number grow to roughly the size of physical memory minus your kernel, then your system is near paging.

The next new metric, re, shows the pages that were reclaimed. If this number gets very high, then you are wasting valuable time trying to salvage paging space. This is a good indicator that your system does not have adequate memory installed. The metric at is not very useful.

This version of vmstat is missing two metrics: swap and so. Swap is replaced with avm because avm shows the number of virtual memory pages. The si and so metrics are missing because they are related to the swap metric.

The disk category is not included with this version of vmstat because most disk I/O is already shown with the iostat utility.

In the CPU columns of the report, the vmstat command summarizes the performance of multiprocessor systems. If you have a two-processor system and the CPU load is reflected as 50 percent, it doesn't necessarily mean that both processors are equally busy. Rather, depending on the multiprocessor implementation, it can indicate that one processor is almost completely busy and the next is almost idle.

The first column of vmstat output also has implications for multiprocessor systems. If the number of runnable processes is not consistently greater than the number of processors, it is less likely that you can get significant performance increases from adding more CPUs to your system.

Review the following sections that show how to look for paging, swapping, disk, or network-related problems.

Using sar

A great deal of information about the system's utilization of memory resources can be obtained by using sar -wpgr.

```
% sar -wpgr 5 5

07:42:30 swpin/s pswin/s swpot/s bswot/s pswch/s
          atch/s  pgin/s ppgin/s  pflt/s  vflt/s slock/s
          pgout/s ppgout/s pgfree/s pgscan/s %s5ipf
          freemem freeswp

07:42:35   0.00    0.0    0.00    0.0    504
           0.00    0.00   0.00    0.00   6.20    11.78
           0.00    0.00   0.00    0.00   0.00
          33139  183023


  . . .
```

Average	0.00	0.0	0.00	0.0	515	
Average	0.00	0.32	0.40	2.54	5.56	16.83
Average	0.00	0.00	0.00	0.00	0.00	
Average	32926	183015				

The fields in the report are the following:

swpin/s   Number of transfers into memory per second.

bswin/s   Number of blocks transferred for swap-ins per second.

swpot/s   Number of transfers from memory to swap area per second. (More memory may be needed if the value is greater than 1.)

bswot/s   Number of blocks transferred for swap-outs per second.

pswch/s   Number of process switches per second.

atch/s   Number of attaches per second (that is, page faults where the page is reclaimed from memory).

pgin/s   Number of times per second that file systems get page-in requests.

ppgin/s   Number of pages paged in per second.

pflt/s   Number of page faults from protection errors per second.

vflt/s   Number of address translation page (validity) faults per second.

slock/s   Number of faults per second caused by software lock requests requiring I/O.

pgout/s   Number of times per second that file systems get page-out requests.

ppgout/s   Number of pages paged out per second.

pgfree/s   Number of pages that are put on the free list by the page-stealing daemon. (More memory may be needed if this is a large value.)

pgscan/s   Number of pages scanned by the page-stealing daemon. (More memory may be needed if this is a large value, because it shows that the daemon is checking for free memory more than it should need to.)

%ufs_ipf   Percentage of the ufs inodes that were taken off the free list that had reusable pages associated with them. (Large values indicate that ufs inodes should be increased, so that the free list of inodes are not page bound.) This is %s5ipf for System V file systems, like in the example.

freemem   The average number of pages, over this interval, of memory available to user processes.

freeswp   The number of disk blocks available for page swapping.

Use the report to examine each of the following conditions. Any one of them would imply that you may have a memory problem. Combinations of them increase the likelihood all the more.

Possible Corrective Action

Check for page-outs, and watch for their consistent occurrence. Look for a high incidence of address translation faults. Check for swap-outs. If they are occasional, it may not be a cause for concern because some number of them is normal (for example, inactive jobs). However, consistent swap-outs are usually bad news, indicating that the system is low on memory and is probably sacrificing active jobs. If you find memory shortage evidence in any of these, you can use ps to look for memory-intensive jobs.

Disk Subsystem Performance Monitoring

Disk operations are the slowest of all operations that enable most programs to complete. Furthermore, as more UNIX systems are being used for commercial applications, and particularly those that utilize relational database systems, the subject of disk performance has become increasingly significant with regard to overall system performance. Therefore, probably more than ever before, UNIX system tuning activities often turn out to be searches for unnecessary and inefficient disk I/O. Before you learn about the commands that can help you monitor your disk I/O performance, some background is appropriate.

Some of the major disk performance variables are the hard disk activities themselves (that is, rotation and arm movement), the I/O controller card, the I/O firmware and software, and the I/O backplane of the system.

For example, for a given disk operation to be completed successfully, the disk controller must be directed to access the information from the proper part of the disk. This results in a delay known as a queuing delay. When it has located the proper part of the disk, the disk arm must begin to position itself over the correct cylinder. This results in a delay called *seek latency*. The read/write head must then wait for the relevant data to happen as the disk rotates underneath it. This is known as *rotational latency*. The data must then be transferred to the controller. Finally, the data must be transferred over the I/O backplane of the system to be used by the application that requested the information.

If you think about your use of a compact disc, many of the operations are similar. The CD platter contains information and is spinning all the time. When you push 5 to request the fifth track of the CD, a controller positions the head that reads the information at the correct area of the disk (similar to the queuing delay and seek latency of disk drives). The rotational latency occurs as the CD spins around until the start of your music passes under the reading head. The data—in this case your favorite song—is then transferred to a controller and then to some digital-to-analog converters that transform it into amplified musical information that is playable by your stereo.

Seek time is the time required to move the head of the disk from one location of data, or track, to another. Moving from one track to another track that is adjacent to it takes very little time and is called *minimum seek time*. Moving the head between the two farthest tracks on a disk is measured as the *maximum seek time*. The average seek time approximates the average amount of time a seek takes.

As data access becomes more random in nature, seek time can become more important. In most commercial database applications that feature relational databases, for example, the data is often being accessed randomly, at a high rate, and in relatively small packets (for example, 512 bytes). Therefore, the disk heads are moving back and forth all the time looking for the pertinent data. Therefore, choosing disks that have small seek times for those systems can increase I/O performance.

Many drives have roughly the same rotational speed, measured as revolutions per minute, or RPMs. However, some manufacturers are stepping up the RPM rates of their drives. This can have a positive influence on performance by reducing the rotational delay, which is the time that the disk head has to wait for the information to get to it (that is, on average one-half of a rotation). It also reduces the amount of time required to transfer the read/write information.

The two original commands for system monitoring, `iostat` and `sar`, are still in wide use today as reliable, simple, and free tools. As a matter of fact, most system monitoring tools that you can buy today are simply extensions of these programs.

Using `iostat`

The `iostat` command is used to examine disk input and output, and produces throughput, utilization, queue length, transaction rate, and service time data. It is similar both in format and in use to `vmstat`. The format of the command is as follows:

```
iostat  t [n]
```

This command takes *n* samples, at *t* second intervals. For example, the following frequently used version of the command takes samples at 5-second intervals without stopping, until canceled:

```
iostat 5
```

For example, the following shows disk statistics sampled at 5-second intervals.

tty				sd0			sd30			sd53			sd55		cpu			
tin	tout	Kps	tps	serv	Kps	tps	serv	Kps	tps	serv	Kps	tps	serv	us	sy	wt	id		
0	26	8	1	57	36	4	20	77	34	24	31	12	30	14	9	47	30		
0	51	0	0	0	0	0	0	108	54	36	0	0	0	14	7	78	0		
0	47	72	10	258	0	0	0	102	51	38	0	0	0	15	9	76	0		
0	58	5	1	9	1	1	23	112	54	33	0	0	0	14	8	77	1		
0	38	0	0	0	25	0	90	139	70	17	9	4	25	14	8	73	6		
0	43	0	0	0	227	10	23	127	62	32	45	21	20	20	15	65	0		

The first line of the report shows the statistics since the last reboot. The subsequent lines show the interval data that is gathered. The default format of the command shows statistics for terminals (tty), for disks (fd and sd), and CPU.

For each terminal, iostat shows the following:

tin	Characters in the terminal input queue
tout	Characters in the terminal output queue

For each disk, iostat shows the following:

bps	Blocks per second
tps	Transfers per second
serv	Average service time, in milliseconds

For the CPU, iostat displays the CPU time spent in the following modes:

us	User mode
sy	System mode
wt	Waiting for I/O
id	Idle mode

The first two fields, tin and tout, have no relevance to disk subsystem performance because these fields describe the number of characters waiting in the input and output terminal buffers. The next fields are relevant to disk subsystem performance over the preceding interval. The bps field indicates the size of the data transferred (read or written) to the drive. The tps field describes the transfers (that is, I/O requests) per second issued to the physical disk. Note that one transfer can combine multiple logical requests. The serv field is for the length of time, in milliseconds, that the I/O subsystem requires to service the transfer. In the last set of fields, note that I/O waiting is displayed under the wt heading.

You can look at the data within the report for information about system performance. As with vmstat, the first line of data is usually irrelevant to your immediate investigation. Looking at the first disk, sd0, you see that it is not being utilized as the other three disks are. Disk 0 is the root disk and often shows the greatest activity. This system is a commercial relational database implementation, however, and the activity that is shown here is often typical of online transaction processing, or OLTP, requirements. Notice that the activity is mainly on disks sd53 and sd55. The database is being exercised by a high volume of transactions that are updating it (in this case, more than 100 updates per second).

Disks 30, 53, and 55 are three database disks that are being pounded with updates from the application through the relational database system. Notice that the transfers per second, the kilobytes per second, and the service times are all reflecting a heavier load on disk 53 than on disks 30 and 55. Notice that disk 30's use is more intermittent but can be quite heavy at times, whereas 53's is more consistent. Ideally, over longer sample periods, the three disks should have roughly equivalent utilization rates. If they continue to show disparities in use like these, you might be able to get a performance increase by determining why the load is unbalanced and taking corrective action.

You can use iostat -xtc to show the measurements across all the drives in the system.

```
% iostat -xtc 10 5 _
```

```
                            extended disk statistics        tty
cpu
disk    r/s  w/s  Kr/s  Kw/s wait actv svc_t %w  %b  tin tout us sy wt id
sd0     0.0  0.9  0.1   6.3  0.0  0.0  64.4  0   1    0   26 12 11 21 56
sd30    0.2  1.4  0.4  20.4  0.0  0.0  21.5  0   3    _
sd53    2.6  2.3  5.5   4.6  0.0  0.1  23.6  0   9    _
sd55    2.7  2.4  5.6   4.7  0.0  0.1  24.2  0  10    _

...

                            extended disk statistics        tty
cpu
disk    r/s  w/s  Kr/s  Kw/s wait actv svc_t %w  %b  tin tout us sy wt id
sd0     0.0  0.3  0.0   3.1  0.0  0.0  20.4  0   1    0 3557  5  8 14 72
sd30    0.0  0.2  0.1   0.9  0.0  0.0  32.2  0   0    _
sd53    0.1  0.2  0.4   0.5  0.0  0.0  14.6  0   0    _
sd55    0.1  0.2  0.3   0.4  0.0  0.0  14.7  0   0    _
```

This example shows five samples of all disks at 10-second intervals.

Each line shows the following:

r/s	Reads per second
w/s	Writes per second
Kr/s	KB read per second
Kw/s	KB written per second

wait	Average transactions waiting for service (that is, queue length)
actv	Average active transactions being serviced
svc_t	Average time, in milliseconds, of service
%w	Percentage of time that the queue isn't empty
%b	Percentage of time that the disk is busy

Once again, you can check to make sure that all disks are sharing the load equally, or if this is not the case, that the most active disk is also the fastest.

Using sar

The sar -d option reports on the disk I/O activity of a system, as well.

```
% sar -d 5 5
```

20:44:26	device	%busy	avque	r+w/s	blks/s	avwait	avserv
...							
20:44:46	sd0	1	0.0	1	5	0.0	20.1
	sd1	0	0.0	0	0	0.0	0.0
	sd15	0	0.0	0	0	0.0	0.0
	sd16	1	0.0	0	1	0.0	27.1
	sd17	1	0.0	0	1	0.0	26.8
	sd3	0	0.0	0	0	0.0	0.0
Average	sd0	1	0.0	0	3	0.0	20.0
	sd1	0	0.0	0	2	0.0	32.6
	sd15	0	0.0	0	1	0.0	13.6
	sd16	0	0.0	0	0	0.0	27.6
	sd17	0	0.0	0	0	0.0	26.1
	sd3	2	0.1	1	14	0.0	102.6

Information about each disk is shown as follows:

device	Names the disk device that is measured
%busy	Percentage of time that the device is busy servicing transfers
avque	Average number of requests outstanding during the period
r+w/s	Read/write transfers to the device per second
blks/s	Number of blocks transferred to the device per second
avwait	Average number of milliseconds that a transfer request spends waiting in the queue for service
avserv	Average number of milliseconds for a transfer to be completed, including seek, rotational delay, and data transfer time.

28

PERFORMANCE
MONITORING

You can see from the example that this system is lightly loaded because %busy is a small number and the queue lengths and wait times are small as well. The average service times for most of the disks is consistent; however, notice that SCSI disk 3, sd3, has a larger service time than the other disks. Perhaps the arrangement of data on the disk is not organized properly (a condition known as *fragmentation*), or perhaps the organization is fine, but the disproportionate access of sd3 (see the blks/s column) is bogging it down in comparison to the other drives.

> **TIP**
>
> Double-check vmstat before you draw any conclusions based on these reports. If your system is paging or swapping with any consistency, you have a memory problem, and you need to address that first because it is surely aggravating your I/O performance.

As this chapter has shown, you should distribute the disk load over I/O controllers and drives, and you should use your fastest drive to support your most frequently accessed data. Also try to increase the size of your buffer cache if your system has sufficient memory. You can eliminate fragmentation by rebuilding your file systems. Also, make sure that the file system that you are using is the fastest type supported with your UNIX system (for example, UFS) and that the block size is the appropriate size.

Possible Corrective Actions

While reviewing the use of the commands to monitor disk performance, you will see how these clearly show which disks and disk subsystems are the most heavily used. However, before examining those commands, some basic hardware-oriented approaches to this problem can help increase performance significantly. The main idea is to put the hardware where the biggest disk problem is and to evenly spread the disk work load over available I/O controllers and disk drives.

If your I/O work load is heavy (for example, with many users constantly accessing large volumes of data from the same set of files), you can probably get significant performance increases by reducing the number of disk drives that are daisy chained off one I/O controller from five or six to two or three. Perhaps doing this forces another daisy chain to increase in size past a total of four or five, but if the disks on that I/O controller are only used intermittently, system performance increases overall.

Another example of this type of technique is if you have one group of users who are pounding one set of files all day long, you could locate the most frequently used data on the fastest disks.

Notice that, once again, the more thorough your knowledge of the characteristics of the work being done on your system, the greater the chance that your disk architecture will answer those needs.

> **NOTE**
>
> Remember, distributing a work load evenly across all disks and controllers is not the same thing as distributing the disks evenly across all controllers, or the files evenly across all disks. You must know which applications make the heaviest I/O demands and understand the work load itself, to distribute it effectively.

> **TIP**
>
> As you build file systems for user groups, remember to factor in the I/O work load. Make sure that your high-disk I/O groups are put on their own physical disks and preferably their own I/O controllers as well. If possible, keep them, and /usr, off the root disk as well.

Disk-striping software frequently can help in cases where the majority of disk access goes to a handful of disks. Where a large amount of data is making heavy demands on one disk or one controller, striping distributes the data across multiple disks or controllers. When the data is striped across multiple disks, the accesses to it are averaged over all the I/O controllers and disks, thus optimizing overall disk throughput. Some disk-striping software also provides Redundant Array of Inexpensive Disks (RAID) support and the capability to keep one disk in reserve as a hot standby (that is, a disk that can be automatically rebuilt and used when one of the production disks fails). When thought of in this manner, this can be a useful feature in terms of performance because a system that has been crippled by the failure of a hard drive will be viewed by your user community as having pretty bad performance.

This information may seem obvious, but it is important to the overall performance of a system. Frequently, the answer to disk performance simply rests on matching the disk architecture to the use of the system.

With the increasing use of relational database technologies on UNIX systems, I/O subsystem performance is more important than ever. Although analyzing all the relational database systems and making recommendations is beyond the scope of this chapter, some basic concepts are in order.

28

PERFORMANCE
MONITORING

Often, an application based on a relational database product is the fundamental reason for the procurement of the UNIX system itself. If that is the case in your installation and if you have relatively little experience in terms of database analysis, seek professional assistance. In particular, insist on a database analyst that has had experience tuning your database system on your operating system. Operating systems and relational databases are both complex systems, and the performance interactions between them is difficult for the inexperienced to understand.

The database expert spends a great deal of time looking at the effectiveness of your allocation of indexes. Large improvements in performance due to the addition or adjustment of a few indexes are common.

Use raw disks versus the file systems for greatest performance. File systems incur more overhead (for example, inode and update block overhead on writes) than do raw devices. Most relational databases clearly reflect this performance advantage in their documentation.

If the database system is extremely active, or if the activity is unbalanced, try to distribute the load more evenly across all the I/O controllers and disks that you can.

Network Performance Monitoring

"The network is the computer" is an appropriate saying these days. What used to be simple ASCII terminals connected over serial ports have been replaced by networks of workstations, Xterminals, and PCs, connected, for example, over 10BASE-T Ethernet networks. Networks are impressive information transmission media when they work properly. However, troubleshooting is not always as straightforward as it should be. In other words, he who lives by the network can die by the network without the proper procedures.

The two most prevalent standards that you have to contend with in the UNIX world are TCP/IP, (a communications protocol) and NFS, (a popular network file system). Each can be a source of problems. In addition, you need to keep an eye on the implementation of the network, which also can be a problem area. Each network topology has different capacities, and each implementation (for example, using thin-net instead of 10BASE-T twisted pair, or using intelligent hubs, and so on) has advantages and problems inherent in its design. The good news is that even a simple Ethernet network has a large amount of bandwidth for transporting data. The bad news is that with every day that passes, users and programmers are coming up with new methods of using up as much of that bandwidth as possible.

Most networks are still based on Ethernet technologies. Ethernet is referred to as a 10 Mps medium, but the throughput that can be used effectively by users and applications is usually significantly less than 10 MB. Often, for various reasons, the effective capacity falls to 4 MBps. That may still seem like a lot of capacity, but as the network grows, it can disappear fast. When the capacity is used up, Ethernet is very democratic. If it has a capacity problem, all users suffer equally. Furthermore, one person can bring an Ethernet network to its knees with relative ease. Accessing and transferring large files across the network, running programs that test transfer rates between two machines, or running a program that has a loop in it that happens to be dumping data to another machine, and so on, can affect all the users on the network. Like other resources (that is, CPU, disk capacity, and so on), the network is a finite resource.

If given the proper instruction, users can quite easily detect capacity problems on the network by which they are supported. A quick comparison of a simple command executed on the local machine versus the same command executed on a remote machine (for example, `login` and `rlogin`) can indicate that the network has a problem.

A little education can help your users and your network at the same time. NFS is a powerful tool, in both the good and the bad sense. Users should be taught that it is slower to access the file over the network using NFS, particularly if the file is sizable, than it is to read or write the data directly on the remote machine by using a remote login. However, if the files are of reasonable size, and the use is reasonable (editing, browsing, moving files back and forth), it is a fine tool to use. Users should understand when they are using NFS appropriately.

Using `netstat`

One of the most straightforward checks you can make of the network's operation is with `netstat -i`. This command can give you some insight into the integrity of the network. All the workstations and the computers on a given network share it. When more than one of these entities try to use the network at the same time, the data from one machine "collides" with that of the other. (Despite the sound of the term, in moderation this is actually a normal occurrence, but too many collisions can be a problem.) In addition, various technical problems can cause errors in the transmission and reception of the data. As the errors and the collisions increase in frequency, the performance of the network degrades because the sender of the data retransmits the garbled data, thus further increasing the activity on the network.

Using `netstat -i`, you can find out how many packets the computer has sent and received, and you can examine the levels of errors and collisions that it has detected on the network. Here is an example of the use of `netstat`:

```
% netstat -i
```

Name	Mtu	Net/Dest	Address	Ipkts	Ierrs	Opkts	Oerrs	Collis	Queue
lo0	8232	loopback	localhost	1031780	0	1031780	0	0	0
le0	1500	100.0.0.0	SCAT	13091430	6	12221526	4	174250	0

The fields in the report are the following:

Name
: The name of the network interface. The names show what the type of interface is (for example, an en followed by a digit indicates an Ethernet card, the lo0 shown here is a loopback interface used for testing networks).

Mtu
: The maximum transfer unit, also known as the packet size, of the interface.

Net/Dest
: The network to which the interface is connected.

Address
: The Internet address of the interface. (The Internet address for this name may be referenced in /etc/hosts.)

Ipkts
: The number of packets the system has received since the last boot.

Ierrs
: The number of input errors that have occurred since the last boot. This should be a very low number relative to the Ipkts field (that is, less than 0.25 percent, or there is probably a significant network problem).

Opkts
: Same as Ipkts, but for sent packets.

Oerrs
: Same as Ierrs, but for output errors.

Collis
: The number of collisions that have been detected. This number should not be more than 5 or 10 percent of the output packets (Opkts) number or the network is having too many collisions, and capacity is reduced.

In this example, you see that the collision ratio shows a network without too many collisions (approximately 1 percent). If collisions are constantly averaging 10 percent or more, the network is probably being over utilized.

The example also shows that input and output error ratios are negligible. Input errors usually mean that the network is feeding the system bad input packets, and the internal calculations that verify the integrity of the data (called *checksums*) are failing. In other words, this normally indicates that the problem is somewhere out on the network, not on your machine. Conversely, rapidly increasing output errors probably indicates a local problem with your computer's network adapters, connectors, interface, and so on.

If you suspect network problems, repeat this command several times. An active machine should show Ipkts and Opkts consistently incrementing. If Ipkts changes and Opkts doesn't, the host is not responding to the client requesting data. Check the addressing in the hosts database. If Ipkts doesn't change, the machine is not receiving the network data at all.

One way to check for network loading is to use netstat without any parameters:

```
% netstat
```

```
TCP
    Local Address          Remote Address       Swind Send-Q Rwind Recv-Q  State
- - - - - - - - - - - - -   - - - - - - - - - -   - - - - -  - - - - - -  - - - - -  - - - - - -  - - - - - - - _
AAA1.1023              bbb2.login            8760     0  8760      0 ESTABLISHED
AAA1.listen            Cccc.32980            8760     0  8760      0 ESTABLISHED
AAA1.login             Dddd.1019             8760     0  8760      0 ESTABLISHED
AAA1.32782             AAA1.32774           16384     0 16384      0 ESTABLISHED
...
```

In the report, the important field is the Send-Q field, which indicates the depth of the send queue for packets. If the numbers in Send-Q are large and increasing in size across several of the connections, the network is probably bogged down.

The netstat -s command displays statistics for each of several protocols supported on the system (that is, UDP, IP, TCP, and ICMP). The information can be used to locate problems for the protocol. Here is an example:

```
% netstat -s
```

```
UDP
        udpInDatagrams      =2152316  udpInErrors         =       0
        udpOutDatagrams     =2151810

TCP     tcpRtoAlgorithm     =       4  tcpRtoMin           =     200
        tcpRtoMax           =   60000  tcpMaxConn          =      -1
        tcpActiveOpens      =1924360  tcpPassiveOpens      =      81
        tcpAttemptFails     = 584963  tcpEstabResets       =1339431
        tcpCurrEstab        =      25  tcpOutSegs          =7814776
        tcpOutDataSegs      =1176484  tcpOutDataBytes      =501907781
        tcpRetransSegs      =1925164  tcpRetransBytes      =444395
        tcpOutAck           =6767853  tcpOutAckDelayed     =1121866
        tcpOutUrg           =     363  tcpOutWinUpdate     =129604
        tcpOutWinProbe      =      25  tcpOutControl       =3263985
        tcpOutRsts          =      47  tcpOutFastRetrans   =      23
        tcpInSegs           =11769363
        tcpInAckSegs        =2419522  tcpInAckBytes        =503241539
        tcpInDupAck         =3589621  tcpInAckUnsent       =       0
        tcpInInorderSegs    =4871078  tcpInInorderBytes    = -477578953
        tcpInUnorderSegs    = 910597  tcpInUnorderBytes    =826772340
        tcpInDupSegs        =  60545  tcpInDupBytes        =46037645
        tcpInPartDupSegs    =  44879  tcpInPartDupBytes    =10057185
        tcpInPastWinSegs    =       0  tcpInPastWinBytes   =       0
        tcpInWinProbe       = 704105  tcpInWinUpdate       =4470040
```

continues

```
        tcpInClosed          =      11    tcpRttNoUpdate       =     907
        tcpRttUpdate         =1079220    tcpTimRetrans        =    1974
        tcpTimRetransDrop    =       2    tcpTimKeepalive      =     577
        tcpTimKeepaliveProbe=     343    tcpTimKeepaliveDrop  =       2

IP      ipForwarding         =       2    ipDefaultTTL         =     255
        ipInReceives         =12954953    ipInHdrErrors        =       0
        ipInAddrErrors       =       0    ipInCksumErrs        =       0
        ipForwDatagrams      =       0    ipForwProhibits      =       0
        ipInUnknownProtos    =       0    ipInDiscards         =       0
        ipInDelivers         =13921597    ipOutRequests        =12199190
        ipOutDiscards        =       0    ipOutNoRoutes        =       0
        ipReasmTimeout       =      60    ipReasmReqds         =       0
        ipReasmOKs           =       0    ipReasmFails         =       0
        ipReasmDuplicates    =       0    ipReasmPartDups      =       0
        ipFragOKs            =    3267    ipFragFails          =       0
        ipFragCreates        =   19052    ipRoutingDiscards    =       0
        tcpInErrs            =       0    udpNoPorts           =   64760
        udpInCksumErrs       =       0    udpInOverflows       =       0
        rawipInOverflows     =       0

ICMP icmpInMsgs              =     216    icmpInErrors         =       0
        icmpInCksumErrs      =       0    icmpInUnknowns       =       0
        icmpInDestUnreachs   =     216    icmpInTimeExcds      =       0
        icmpInParmProbs      =       0    icmpInSrcQuenchs     =       0
        icmpInRedirects      =       0    icmpInBadRedirects   =       0
        icmpInEchos          =       0    icmpInEchoReps       =       0
        icmpInTimestamps     =       0    icmpInTimestampReps  =       0
        icmpInAddrMasks      =       0    icmpInAddrMaskReps   =       0
        icmpInFragNeeded     =       0    icmpOutMsgs          =     230
        icmpOutDrops         =       0    icmpOutErrors        =       0
        icmpOutDestUnreachs  =     230    icmpOutTimeExcds     =       0
        icmpOutParmProbs     =       0    icmpOutSrcQuenchs    =       0
        icmpOutRedirects     =       0    icmpOutEchos         =       0
        icmpOutEchoReps      =       0    icmpOutTimestamps    =       0
        icmpOutTimestampReps=       0    icmpOutAddrMasks     =       0
        icmpOutAddrMaskReps  =       0    icmpOutFragNeeded    =       0
        icmpInOverflows      =       0
IGMP:
        0 messages received
        0 messages received with too few bytes
        0 messages received with bad checksum
        0 membership queries received
        0 membership queries received with invalid field(s)
        0 membership reports received
        0 membership reports received with invalid field(s)
        0 membership reports received for groups to which we belong
        0 membership reports sent
```

The checksum fields should always show extremely small values because they are a percentage of total traffic sent along the interface.

By using netstat -s on the remote system in combination with spray on your own, you can determine whether data corruption (as opposed to network corruption) is impeding the movement of your network data. Alternate between the two displays, observing the differences, if any, between the reports. If the two reports agree on the number of dropped packets, the file server is probably not keeping up. If they don't, suspect network integrity problems. Use netstat -i on the remote machine to confirm this.

Using spray

It is quite possible that you do not detect collisions and errors when you use netstat -i, and yet still have slow access across the network. Perhaps the other machine that you are trying to use is bogged down and cannot respond quickly enough. Use spray to send a burst of packets to the other machine and record how many of them actually made the trip successfully. The results tell you whether the other machine is failing to keep up. Here is an example of a frequently used test:

```
% spray SCAT

sending 1162 packets of length 86 to SCAT ...
        no packets dropped by SCAT
        3321 packets/sec, 285623 bytes/sec
```

This shows a test burst sent from the source machine to the destination machine called SCAT. No packets were dropped. If SCAT were badly overloaded, some probably would have been dropped. The example defaulted to sending 1162 packets of 86 bytes each. Another example of the same command uses the -c option to specify the number of packets to send, the -d option to specify the delay so that you don't overrun your buffers, and the -1 option to specify the length of the packet. This example of the command is a more realistic test of the network:

```
% spray -c 100 -d 20 0 -1 2048 SCAT

sending 100 packets of length 2048 to SCAT ...
        no packets dropped by SCAT
        572 packets/sec, 1172308 bytes/sec
```

Had you seen significant numbers (for example, 5 to 10 percent or more) of packets dropped in these displays, you would next try looking at the remote system. For example, using commands such as uptime, vmstat, sar, and ps as described earlier in this section, you would check on the status of the remote machine. Does it have memory or CPU problems, or is there some other problem that is degrading its performance so that it can't keep up with its network traffic?

28

PERFORMANCE
MONITORING

Using `nfsstat`

Systems running NFS can skip `spray` and instead use `nfsstat -c`. The `-c` option specifies the client statistics, and `-s` can be used for server statistics. As the name implies, client statistics summarize this system's use of another machine as a server. The NFS service uses synchronous procedures called RPCs (remote procedure calls). This means that the client waits for the server to complete the file activity before it proceeds. If the server fails to respond, the client retransmits the request. Just as with collisions, the more worse the condition of the communication, the more traffic that is generated. The more traffic that is generated, the slower the network and the greater the possibility of collisions. So if the retransmission rate is large, you should look for servers that are under heavy loads, high collision rates that are delaying the packets en route, or Ethernet interfaces that are dropping packets.

```
% nfsstat -c

Client rpc:
calls      badcalls retrans  badxid   timeout  wait      newcred  timers
74107      0           72     0          72     0         0           82

Client nfs:
calls      badcalls   nclget      nclcreate
73690      0          73690       0
null       getattr    setattr     root        lookup       readlink    read
0   0%     4881  7%   1   0%      0   0%       130  0%      0   0%      465  1%
wrcache    write      create      remove      rename       link        symlink
0   0%     68161 92%  16  0%      1   0%       0   0%       0   0%      0   0%
mkdir      rmdir      readdir     statfs
0   0%     0   0%     32  0%      3   0%
```

The report shows the following fields:

`calls`	The number of calls sent
`badcalls`	The number of calls rejected by the RPC
`retrans`	The number of retransmissions
`badxid`	The number of duplicated acknowledgments received
`timeout`	The number of timeouts
`wait`	The number of times no available client handles caused waiting
`newcred`	The number of refreshed authentications
`timers`	The number of times the timeout value is reached or exceeded
`readlink`	The number of reads made to a symbolic link

If the `timeout` ratio is high, the problem can be unresponsive NFS servers or slow networks that are impeding the timely delivery and response of the packets. In the example, there are relatively few timeouts compared to the number of calls (72/74107 or about

1/10 of 1 percent) that do retransmissions. As the percentage grows toward 5 percent, system administrators begin to take a closer look at it. If badxid is roughly the same as retrans, the problem is probably an NFS server that is falling behind in servicing NFS requests because duplicate acknowledgments are being received for NFS requests in roughly the same amounts as the retransmissions that are required. (The same thing is true if badxid is roughly the same as timeout.) However, if badxid is a much smaller number than retrans and timeout, then it follows that the network is more likely to be the problem.

> **TIP**
>
> nfsstat enables you to reset the applicable counters to 0 by using the -z option (executed as root). This can be particularly handy when trying to determine whether something has caused a problem in the immediate time frame, rather than looking at the numbers collected since the last reboot.

Possible Corrective Actions

If you suspect problems with the integrity of the network itself, you must try to determine where the faulty piece of equipment is. Hire network consultants who use network diagnostic scopes to locate and correct the problems.

If the problem is that the network is extremely busy, thus increasing collisions, timeouts, retransmissions, and so on, you might need to redistribute the work load more appropriately. This is a good example of the "divide and conquer" concept as it applies to computers. By partitioning and segmenting the network nodes into subnetworks that more clearly reflect the underlying work loads, you can maximize the overall performance of the network. This can be accomplished by installing additional network interfaces in your gateway and adjusting the addressing on the gateway to reflect the new subnetworks. Altering your cabling and implementing some of the more advanced intelligent hubs may be needed as well. By reorganizing your network, you maximize the amount of bandwidth available for access to the local subnetwork. Make sure that systems that regularly perform NFS mounts of each other are on the same subnetwork.

If you have an older network and are having to rework your network topology, consider replacing your ethernet cables with FDDI cables, which can handle a great deal more volume.

Make sure that the work load is on the appropriate machine(s). Use the machine with the best network performance to do its proper share of network file service tasks.

28

PERFORMANCE
MONITORING

Check your network for diskless workstations. These require large amounts of network resources to boot up, swap, page, and so on. With the cost of local storage descending constantly, it is getting more difficult to believe that diskless workstations are still cost-effective when compared to regular workstations. Consider upgrading the workstations so that they support their users locally, or at least to minimize their use of the network.

If your network server has been acquiring more clients, check its memory and its kernel buffer allocations for proper sizing.

If the problem is that I/O-intensive programs are being run over the network, work with the users to determine what can be done to make that requirement a local, rather than a network, one. Educate your users to make sure that they understand when they are using the network appropriately and when they are being wasteful with this valuable resource.

CPU Performance Monitoring

The biggest problem a system administrator faces when examining performance is sorting through all the relevant information to determine which subsystem is really in trouble. Frequently, users complain about the need to upgrade a processor that is assumed to be causing slow execution, when in fact the I/O subsystem or memory is the problem. To make matters even more difficult, all the subsystems interact with one another, thus complicating the analysis.

You already looked at the three most handy tools for assessing CPU load in the section "Tools for Monitoring Overall System Status." As stated in that section, processor idle time can, under certain conditions, imply that I/O or memory subsystems are degrading the system. It can also, under other conditions, imply that a processor upgrade is appropriate. Using the tools that have been reviewed in this chapter, you can by now piece together a competent picture of the overall activities of your system and its subsystems. Use the tools to make absolutely sure that the I/O and the memory subsystems are indeed optimized properly before you spend the money to upgrade your CPU.

The following is a brief list of jobs and daemons that deserve review, and possibly elimination, based on the severity of the problem and their use, or lack thereof, on the system. Check each of the following and ask yourself whether you use it or need them: accounting services, printer daemons, `mountd` remote mount daemon, `sendmail` daemon, `talk` daemon, remote `who` daemon, NIS server, and database daemons.

Using `mpstat`

One of the most recent developments of significance in the UNIX server world is the rapid deployment of symmetric multiprocessor (SMP) servers. Of course, having multiple CPUs can mean that you may desire a more discrete picture of what is actually happening on the system than sar -u can provide.

You learned about some multiprocessor issues in the examination of vmstat, but there are other tools for examining multiprocessor utilization. The mpstat command reports the per-processor statistics for the machine. Each row of the report shows the activity of one processor.

```
% mpstat

CPU minf mjf xcal  intr ithr  csw icsw migr smtx  srw syscl  usr sys  wt idl
  0   1   0    0   201   71  164   22   34  147    0   942   10  10  23  57
  1   1   0    0    57   37  171   23   34  144    1   975   10  11  23  56
  2   1   0    0    77   56  158   22   33  146    0   996   11  11  21  56
  3   1   0    0    54   33  169   23   34  156    0  1139   12  11  21  56
  4   1   0    0    21    0  180   23   33  159    0  1336   14  10  20  56
  5   1   0    0    21    0  195   23   31  163    0  1544   17  10  18  55
```

All values are in terms of events per second, unless otherwise noted. You may specify a sample interval, and a number of samples, with the command, just as you would with sar. The fields of the report are the following:

CPU	CPU processor ID
minf	Minor faults
mjf	Major faults
xcal	Interprocessor cross calls
intr	Interrupts
ithr	Interrupts as threads (not counting clock interrupt)
csw	Context switches
icsw	Involuntary context switches
migr	Thread migrations (to another processor)
smtx	Spins on mutexes (lock not acquired on first try)
srw	Spins on reader/writer locks (lock not acquired on first try)
syscl	System calls
usr	Percentage of user time
sys	Percentage of system time
wt	Percentage of wait time
idl	Percentage of idle time

Don't be intimidated by the technical nature of the display. It is included here just as an indication that multiprocessor systems can be more complex than uniprocessor systems to examine for their performance. Some multiprocessor systems actually can bias work to be done to a particular CPU. That is not done here, as you can see. The user, system, wait, and idle times are all relatively evenly distributed across all the available CPUs.

Possible Corrective Actions

If you have determined that your CPU has just run out of gas, and you cannot upgrade your system, all is not lost. CPUs are extremely powerful machines that are frequently underutilized for long spans of time in any 24-hour period. If you can rearrange the schedule of the work that must be done to use the CPU as efficiently as possible, you can often overcome most problems. This can be done by getting users to run all appropriate jobs at off-hours (off work load hours, that is, not necessarily 9 to 5). You can also get your users to run selected jobs at lower priorities. You can educate some of your less efficient users and programmers. Finally, you can carefully examine the work load and eliminate some jobs, daemons, and so on, that are not needed.

Kernel Tuning

Kernel tuning is a complex topic, and the space that can be devoted to it in this section is limited. To fit this discussion into the space allowed, the focus is on kernel tuning for SunOS in general, and Solaris 2.x in particular. In addition, the section focuses mostly on memory tuning. Your version of UNIX may differ in several respects from the version described here, and you may be involved in other subsystems, but you should get a good idea of the overall concepts and generally how the parameters are tuned.

The most fundamental component of the UNIX operating system is the kernel. It manages all the major subsystems, including memory, disk I/O, utilization of the CPU, process scheduling, and so on. In short, it is the controlling agent that enables the system to perform work for you.

As you can imagine from that introduction, the configuration of the kernel can dramatically affect system performance either positively or negatively. There are parameters that you can tune for various kernel modules. A couple reasons could motivate you to do this. First, by tuning the kernel you can reduce the amount of memory required for the kernel, thus increasing the efficiency of the use of memory, and increasing the throughput of the system. Second, you can increase the capacity of the system to accommodate new requirements (users, processing, or both).

This is a classic case of software compromise. It would be nice to increase the capacity of the system to accommodate all users that would ever be put on the system, but that would have a deleterious effect on performance. Likewise, it would be nice to tune the kernel down to its smallest possible size, but that would have negative side-effects as well. As in most software, the optimal solution is somewhere between the extremes.

Some people think that you only need to change the kernel when the number of people on the system increases. This is not true. You may need to alter the kernel when the nature of your processing changes. If your users are increasing their use of X Window, or increasing their utilization of file systems, running more memory-intensive jobs, and so on, you may need to adjust some of these parameters to optimize the throughput of the system.

Two trends are changing the nature of kernel tuning. First, in an effort to make UNIX a commercially viable product in terms of administration and deployment, most manufacturers are trying to minimize the complexity of the kernel configuration process. As a result, many of the tables that were once allocated in a fixed manner are now allocated dynamically, or else are linked to the value of a handful of fields. Solaris 2.x takes this approach by calculating many kernel values based on the maxusers field. Second, because memory is dropping in price and CPU power is increasing dramatically, the relative importance of precise kernel tuning for most systems is gradually diminishing. However, for high-performance systems, or systems with limited memory, it is still a pertinent topic.

Your instruction in UNIX kernel tuning begins with an overview of the kernel tables that are changed by it, and how to display them. It continues with some examples of kernel parameters that are modified to adjust the kernel to current system demands, and it concludes with a detailed example of paging and swapping parameters under SunOS.

CAUTION

Kernel tuning can actually adversely affect memory subsystem performance. As you adjust the parameters upward, the kernel often expands in size. This can affect memory performance, particularly if your system is already beginning to experience a memory shortage problem under normal utilization. As the kernel tables grow, the internal processing related to them may take longer, too, so there may be some minor degradation related to the greater time required for internal operating system activities. Once again, with a healthy system this may be transparent, but with a marginal system the problems may become apparent or more pronounced.

> **CAUTION**
>
> In general, be very careful with kernel tuning. People who don't understand what they are doing can cripple their systems. Many UNIX versions come with utility programs that help simplify configuration. It's best to use them. It also helps to read the manual and to procure the assistance of an experienced system administrator before you begin.

> **CAUTION**
>
> Finally, always make sure that you have a copy of your working kernel before you begin altering it. Some experienced system administrators actually make backup copies even if the utility automatically makes one. And it is always a good idea to do a complete backup before installing a new kernel. Don't assume that your disk drives are safe because you are "just making a few minor adjustments," or that the upgrade that you are installing "doesn't seem to change much with respect to the I/O subsystem." Make sure that you can get back to your original system state if things go wrong.

When should you consider modifying the kernel tables? Review your kernel parameters in several cases, such as before you add new users, before you increase your X Window activity significantly, or before you increase your NFS utilization markedly. Also review them before the makeup of the programs that are running is altered in a way that will significantly increase the number of processes that are run or the demands they will make on the system.

Some people believe that you always increase kernel parameters when you add more memory, but this is not necessarily so. If you have a thorough knowledge of your system's parameters and know that they are already adjusted to take into account both current loads and some future growth, then adding more memory, in itself, is not necessarily a reason to increase kernel parameters.

Some of the tables are described as follows:

- **Process table**   The process table sets the number of processes that the system can run at a time. These processes include daemon processes, processes that local users are running, and processes that remote users are running. It also includes forked or spawned processes of users—it may be a little more trouble for you to accurately estimate the number of these. If the system is trying to start system daemon processes and is prevented from doing so because the process table has reached its limit, you may experience intermittent problems (possibly without any direct notification of the error).

- **User process table**   The user process table controls the number of processes per user that the system can run.

- **Inode table**   The inode table lists entries for such things as the following:

    Each open pipe

    Each current user directory

    Mount points on each file system

    Each active I/O device

    When the table is full, performance degrades. The console has error messages written to it regarding the error when it occurs. This table is also relevant to the open file table because they are both concerned with the same subsystem.

- **Open file table**   This table determines the number of files that can be open on the system at the same time. When the system call is made and the table is full, the program gets an error indication, and the console has an error logged to it.

- **Quota table**   If your system is configured to support disk quotas, this table contains the number of structures that have been set aside for that use. The quota table has an entry for each user who has a file system that has quotas turned on. As with the inode table, performance suffers when the table fills up, and errors are written to the console.

- **Callout table**   This table controls the number of timers that can be active concurrently. Timers are critical to many kernel-related and I/O activities. If the callout table overflows, the system is likely to crash.

Displaying Tunable Kernel Parameters

To display a comprehensive list of tunable kernel parameters, you can use the nm command. For example, applying the command to the appropriate module, the name list of the file is reported:

```
% nm /kernel/unix

Symbols from /kernel/unix:

[Index]   Value     Size  Type  Bind  Other Shndx   Name

...
[15]           0         0 FILE  LOCL  0     ABS     unix.o
[16] 3758124752         0 NOTY  LOCL  0     1       vhwb_nextset
```

continues

```
[17]¦3758121512¦      0¦NOTY ¦LOCL ¦0   ¦1       ¦_intr_flag_table
[18]¦3758124096¦      0¦NOTY ¦LOCL ¦0   ¦1       ¦trap_mon
[19]¦3758121436¦      0¦NOTY ¦LOCL ¦0   ¦1       ¦intr_set_spl
[20]¦3758121040¦      0¦NOTY ¦LOCL ¦0   ¦1       ¦intr_mutex_panic
[21]¦3758121340¦      0¦NOTY ¦LOCL ¦0   ¦1       ¦intr_thread_exit
[22]¦3758124768¦      0¦NOTY ¦LOCL ¦0   ¦1       ¦vhwb_nextline
[23]¦3758124144¦      0¦NOTY ¦LOCL ¦0   ¦1       ¦trap_kadb
[24]¦3758124796¦      0¦NOTY ¦LOCL ¦0   ¦1       ¦vhwb_nextdword
[25]¦3758116924¦      0¦NOTY ¦LOCL ¦0   ¦1       ¦firsthighinstr
[26]¦3758121100¦    132¦NOTY ¦LOCL ¦0   ¦1       ¦intr_thread
[27]¦3758118696¦      0¦NOTY ¦LOCL ¦0   ¦1       ¦fixfault
[28]¦         0¦      0¦FILE ¦LOCL ¦0   ¦ABS     ¦confunix.c
...
        (Portions of display deleted for brevity)
```

The relevant fields in the report are the following:

Index	The index of the symbol (appears in brackets).
Value	The value of the symbol.
Size	The size, in bytes, of the associated object.
Type	A symbol is one of the following types: NOTYPE (no type was specified), OBJECT (a data object such as an array or variable), FUNC (a function or other executable code), SECTION (a section symbol), or FILE (name of the source file).
Bind	The symbol's binding attributes. LOCAL symbols have a scope limited to the object file containing their definition; GLOBAL symbols are visible to all object files being combined; and WEAK symbols are essentially global symbols with a lower precedence than GLOBAL.
Shndx	Except for three special values, this is the section header table index in relation to which the symbol is defined. The following special values exist: ABS indicates that the symbol's value does not change through relocation; COMMON indicates an allocated block, and the value provides alignment constraints; and UNDEF indicates an undefined symbol.
Name	The name of the symbol.

On HP-UX 10.x systems, a text file, /stand/system, is used as the configuration file for the kernel at compile time.

To get the most recent version of the kernel configurations, this file needs to be rebuilt. To do this, cd into the /stand/build directory and run the command /usr/lbin/sysadm/system_prep -s system. This creates a new system file in the /stand/build directory, which can then be edited for the desired changes.

To display a list of the current values assigned to the tunable kernel parameters, you can use the sysdef -i command:

```
% sysdef -i
... (portions of display are deleted for brevity)
*
* System Configuration
*
swapfile              dev  swaplo blocks    free
/dev/dsk/c0t3d0s1    32,25      8 547112   96936
*
* Tunable Parameters
*
 5316608  maximum memory allowed in buffer cache (bufhwm)
    4058  maximum number of processes (v.v_proc)
      99  maximum global priority in sys class (MAXCLSYSPRI)
    4053  maximum processes per user id (v.v_maxup)
      30  auto update time limit in seconds (NAUTOUP)
      25  page stealing low water mark (GPGSLO)
       5  fsflush run rate (FSFLUSHR)
      25  minimum resident memory for avoiding deadlock (MINARMEM)
      25  minimum swapable memory for avoiding deadlock (MINASMEM)
*
* Utsname Tunables
*
     5.3  release (REL)
    DDDD  node name (NODE)
   SunOS  system name (SYS)
Generic_101318-31  version (VER)
*
* Process Resource Limit Tunables (Current:Maximum)
*
Infinity:Infinity    cpu time
Infinity:Infinity    file size
7ffff000:7ffff000    heap size
  800000:7ffff000    stack size
Infinity:Infinity    core file size
      40:      400    file descriptors
Infinity:Infinity    mapped memory
*
* Streams Tunables
*
       9  maximum number of pushes allowed (NSTRPUSH)
   65536  maximum stream message size (STRMSGSZ)
    1024  max size of ctl part of message (STRCTLSZ)
*
* IPC Messages
*
     200  entries in msg map (MSGMAP)
    2048  max message size (MSGMAX)
   65535  max bytes on queue (MSGMNB)
      25  message queue identifiers (MSGMNI)
     128  message segment size (MSGSSZ)
     400  system message headers (MSGTQL)
    1024  message segments (MSGSEG)
     SYS  system class name (SYS_NAME)
```

28

PERFORMANCE
MONITORING

As stated earlier, over the years many enhancements have tried to minimize the complexity of the kernel configuration process. As a result, many tables that were once allocated in a fixed manner are now allocated dynamically, or else linked to the value of the maxusers field. The next step in understanding the nature of kernel tables is to look at the maxusers parameter and its impact on UNIX system configuration.

Showing Current Values

Using sar with the -v option enables you to see the current process table, inode table, open file table, and shared memory record table. The fields in the report are as follows:

proc-sz	The number of process table entries in use/the number allocated
inod-sz	The number of inode table entries in use/the number allocated
file-sz	The number of file table entries currently in use/the number 0 designating that space is allocated dynamically for this entry
lock-sz	The number of shared memory record table entries in use/the number 0 designating that space is allocated dynamically for this entry
ov	The overflow field, showing the number of times the field to the immediate left has had to overflow

Any nonzero entry in the ov field is an obvious indication that you need to adjust your kernel parameters relevant to that field. This is one performance report where you can request historical information, for the last day, the last week, or since last reboot, and actually get meaningful data out of it.

This is also another good report to use intermittently during the day to sample how much reserve capacity you have.

Here is an example:

```
% sar -v 5 5

18:51:12  proc-sz    ov  inod-sz   ov  file-sz   ov  lock-sz
18:51:17  122/4058   0  3205/4000  0   488/0    0   11/0
18:51:22  122/4058   0  3205/4000  0   488/0    0   11/0
18:51:27  122/4058   0  3205/4000  0   488/0    0   11/0
18:51:32  122/4058   0  3205/4000  0   488/0    0   11/0
18:51:37  122/4058   0  3205/4000  0   488/0    0   11/0
```

Because all the ov fields are 0, you can see that the system tables are healthy for this interval. In this display, for example, 122 process table entries are in use, and 4058 process table entries are allocated.

Modifying Values

SunOS uses the `/etc/system` file for modification of kernel-tunable variables. The basic format is this:

```
set parameter = value
```

It can also have this format:

```
set [module:]variablename = value
```

The `/etc/system` file can also be used for other purposes (for example, to force modules to be loaded at boot time, to specify a root device, and so on). The `/etc/system` file is used for permanent changes to the operating system values. Temporary changes can be made using `adb` kernel debugging tools. The system must be rebooted for the changes made for them to become active using `/etc/system`. With `adb`, the changes take place when applied.

> **CAUTION**
>
> Be very careful with set commands in the `/etc/system` file! They basically cause patches to be performed on the kernel itself, and there is a great deal of potential for dire consequences from misunderstood settings. Make sure that you have handy the relevant system administrators' manuals for your system, as well as a reliable and experienced system administrator for guidance.

As mentioned earlier in the chapter, HP-UX 10.x has a similar `/etc/system` file, which can be modified and recompiled.

After you have made your changes to this file, you can recompile to make a new UNIX kernel. The command is `mkkernel -s system`. This new kernel, called `vmunix.test`, is placed in the `/stand/build` directory. Next, you move the present `/stand/system` file to `/stand/system.prev`; then you can move the modified file `/stand/build/system` to `/stand/system`. Then you move the currently running kernel `/stand/vmunix` to `/stand/vmunix.prev`, and then move the new kernel, `/stand/build/vmunix.test`, into place in `/stand/vmunix` (that is, `mv /stand/build/vmunix.test /stant/vmunix`). The final step is to reboot the machine to make your changes take effect.

Many of the tables are dynamically updated either upward or downward by the operating system, based on the value assigned to the `maxusers` parameter, which is an approximation of the number of users the system will have to support. The quickest and, more importantly, safest way to modify the table sizes is by modifying `maxusers` and letting the system perform the adjustments to the tables for you.

The maxusers parameter can be adjusted by placing commands in the /etc/system file of your UNIX system:

```
set maxusers=24
```

A number of kernel parameters adjust their values according to the setting of the maxusers parameter. For example, Table 28.2 lists the settings for various kernel parameters, where maxusers is utilized in their calculation.

TABLE 28.2. KERNEL PARAMETERS AFFECTED BY *maxusers*.

Table	Parameter	Setting
Process	max_nprocs	10 + 16 * maxusers (sets the size of the process table)
User process	maxuprc	max_nprocs-5 (sets the number of user processes)
Callout	ncallout	16 + max_nprocs (sets the size of the callout table)
Name cache	ncsize	max_nprocs + 16 + maxusers + 64 (sets size of the directory lookup cache)
Inode	ufs_ninode	max_nprocs + 16 + maxusers + 64 (sets the size of the inode table)
Quota table	ndquot	(maxusers * NMOUNT) / 4 + max_nprocs (sets the number of disk quota structures)

The directory name lookup cache (dnlc) is also based on maxusers in SunOS systems. With the increasing use of NFS, this can be an important performance tuning parameter. Networks that have many clients can be helped by an increased name cache parameter ncsize (that is, a greater amount of cache). By using vmstat with the -s option, you can determine the directory name lookup cache hit rate. A cache miss indicates that disk I/O was probably needed to access the directory when traversing the path components to get to a file. If the hit rate falls below 70 percent, this parameter should be checked.

```
% vmstat -s

        0 swap ins
        0 swap outs
        0 pages swapped in
        0 pages swapped out
  1530750 total address trans. faults taken
    39351 page ins
    22369 page outs
    45565 pages paged in
   114923 pages paged out
    73786 total reclaims
```

```
   65945 reclaims from free list
       0 micro (hat) faults
 1530750 minor (as) faults
   38916 major faults
   88376 copy-on-write faults
  120412 zero fill page faults
  634336 pages examined by the clock daemon
      10 revolutions of the clock hand
  122233 pages freed by the clock daemon
    4466 forks
     471 vforks
    6416 execs
45913303 cpu context switches
28556694 device interrupts
 1885547 traps
665339442 system calls
  622350 total name lookups (cache hits 94%)
       4 toolong
 2281992 user    cpu
 3172652 system cpu
62275344 idle    cpu
  967604 wait    cpu
```

In this example, you can see that the cache hits are 94 percent, and therefore enough directory name lookup cache is allocated on the system.

By the way, if your NFS traffic is heavy and irregular, increase the number of nfsd NFS daemons. Some system administrators recommend that this should be set between 40 and 60 on dedicated NFS servers. This increases the speed with which the nfsd daemons take the requests off the network and pass them on to the I/O subsystem. Conversely, decreasing this value can throttle the NFS load on a server when that is appropriate.

Monitor is a shareware utility that can be obtained from various ftp sites. This utility is actually a handy tool for getting live updates on the status of your system.

So what does it show? The question is, what doesn't it show. Monitor gives you real-time updates on CPU utilization, CPU wait states, disk I/O, a list of the top running processes, and much more.

As you bring the utility up, you can see a number of things in the first screen. CPU utilization in shown as a text-based "emoticon" meter, breaking down CPU time into system, user, and idle time. Also, you have different load statistics displayed, such as disk I/O, swapping statistics, free memory, and a breakdown of memory metrics.

Two screen switches also show further details on disk I/O and process statistics.

To find a full breakdown of disk activity by disk, simply press the D key. You can see the disk transfer wait in KBps, I/Os per second, disk wait times, and much more. To get back to the main screen, just press D again.

28

PERFORMANCE
MONITORING

To see a full breakdown of the most active processes, press T. This shows you a detailed listing of system processes, in descending order from highest to lowest in compute time. This a good way to see whether you have any runaway or hung processes. Here you can see how long a process has been running, who started and owns it, which process spawned it, and much more. To get back to the main menu, just press T again.

To quit `monitor`, all you have to do is press Q.

This section isn't large enough to review in detail how tuning can affect each of the kernel tables. However, for illustration purposes, this section describes how kernel parameters influence paging and swapping activities in a SunOS system. Other tables affecting other subsystems can be tuned in much the same manner as these.

As processes make demands on memory, pages are allocated from the free list. When the UNIX system decides that there is no longer enough free memory—less than the `lotsfree` parameter—it searches for pages that haven't been used lately to add them to the free list. The page daemon is scheduled to run. It begins at a slow rate, based on the `slowscan` parameter, and increases to a faster rate, based on the `fastscan` parameter, as free memory continues toward depletion. If there is less memory than `desfree` and two or more processes in the run queue, and the system stays in that condition for more than 30 seconds, the system begins to swap. If the system gets to a minimum level of required memory, specified by the `minfree` parameter, swapping begins without delay. When swapping begins, entire processes are swapped out as described earlier.

> **NOTE**
>
> If you have your swapping spread over several disks, increasing the `maxpgio` parameter may be beneficial. This parameter limits the number of pages scheduled to be paged out and is based on single-disk swapping. Increasing it may improve paging performance. You can use the `po` field from `vmstat`, as described earlier, which checks against `maxpgio` and `pagesize` to examine the volumes involved.

The kernel swaps out the oldest and the largest processes when it begins to swap. The `maxslp` parameter is used in determining which processes have exceeded the maximum sleeping period and can thus be swapped out as well. The smallest higher-priority processes that have been sleeping the longest are then swapped back in.

The most pertinent kernel parameters for paging and swapping are the following:

- `minfree`   This is the absolute minimum memory level that the system will tolerate. Once past `minfree`, the system immediately resorts to swapping.

- `desfree`   This is the desperation level. After 30 seconds at this level, paging is abandoned, and swapping is begun.

- `lotsfree`   Once below this memory limit, the page daemon is activated to begin freeing memory.

- `fastscan`   This is the number of pages scanned per second.

- `slowscan`   This is the number of pages scanned per second when there is less memory than `lotsfree` available. As memory decreases from `lotsfree`, the scanning speed increases from `slowscan` to `fastscan`.

- `maxpgio`   This is the maximum number of page out I/O operations per second that the system schedules. This is normally set at approximately 40 under SunOS, which is appropriate for a single 3600 RPM disk. It can be increased with more or faster disks.

Newer versions of UNIX, such as Solaris 2.x, do such a good job of setting paging parameters that tuning is usually not required.

Increasing `lotsfree` helps on systems on which there is a continuing need to allocate new processes. Heavily used interactive systems with many Windows users often force this condition as users open multiple windows and start processes. By increasing `lotsfree`, you create a large enough pool of free memory that you do not run out when most of the processes are initially starting up.

For servers that have a defined set of users and a more steady-state condition to their underlying processes, the normal default values are usually appropriate.

However, for servers such as this with large, stable work loads, but that are short of memory, increasing `lotsfree` is the wrong idea. This is because more pages are taken from the application and put on the free list.

Some system administrators recommend that you disable the `maxslp` parameter on systems where the overhead of swapping normally sleeping processes (such as clock icons and update processes) isn't offset by any measurable gain due to forcing the processes out. This parameter is no longer used in Solaris 2.x releases but is used on older versions of UNIX.

Conclusion of Kernel Tuning

You have seen how to optimize memory subsystem performance by tuning a system's kernel parameters. Other subsystems can be tuned by similar modifications to the relevant kernel parameters. When such changes correct existing kernel configurations that have become obsolete and inefficient due to new requirements, the result can sometimes

28

PERFORMANCE
MONITORING

dramatically increase performance even without a hardware upgrade. It's not quite the same as getting a hardware upgrade for free, but it's about as close as you're likely to get in today's computer industry.

Third-Party Solutions

In addition to the standard text-based utilities we have been talking about, a number of third-party, enterprise-wide products are available to monitor your servers. This section focuses on two: ServerVision from Platinum Technologies and EcoTools from Compuware.

Usually, these products are located on their own separate servers, but often, due to budget considerations and other concerns, the monitor server is often placed on a production box. This defeats the purpose of a monitoring system because the monitoring machine is just as likely to go down as the servers that it monitors in this situation. Therefore, I strongly recommend that you push as much as you can for a small workstation to act as the monitor for your system and nothing else.

EcoTools has a number of neat features that make it a nice solution for many shops. According to marketing literature (for what it's worth), EcoTools boasts an open and robust architecture, heterogeneous support, support for process automation, extensive monitoring and analysis, security for sensitive system information, out-of-the-box functionality, and easy customization.

In reality, it is on a par with most every other system monitoring tool on the market, with a slight advantage because it's a GUI. It really does have a nice fuzzy display that shows most of what you need to see on your systems. The graphs you can get from its logs could be shown in any boardroom, if that's what you're after.

What it lacks in warm fuzziness, ServerVision makes up for in pure kitchen sink monitoring metrics and logging tools. Platinum boasts more than 200 system metrics that can be monitored on your systems, in addition to another 200 database metrics that you can use if you get its DBVision product.

> **NOTE**
>
> If you do have DBVision installed, particularly version 3.1.3 and version 3.1.6, you must turn off the `lock_waits` metric if it is installed on an AIX system. If you don't, your system will slow down to an unusable crawl! This is a bug in version 3.1.3 on AIX, and, at the time of this writing, it has yet to be fixed in version 3.1.6.

With ServerVision, as with any such tool, you must run the default settings for a short time before moving it into production to get a feel for where to set your alarm settings. If you have your server set up to page you and you don't modify these values, you will be paged late at night regularly—not much fun.

The paging function often comes in handy, if you like having a live system when you come into the office in the morning. With this advanced warning, you would have the capability to get online and save a dying system well before it crashes.

No matter what software you buy for your system, ask your salesperson for a complete demonstration and bring a list of questions about your requirements. These solutions can be very expensive, so be sure you are getting what you pay for before you buy.

Summary

This chapter covered a number of issues dealing with performance and tuning. The chapter touched on such topics as the impact of performance on users, introduction to UNIX performance, monitoring the overall system status, monitoring processes with ps, monitoring memory utilization, monitoring disk subsystem performance, monitoring network performance, monitoring CPU performance, kernel tuning, and third-party solutions.

With a little practice using the methodology described in this chapter, you should be able to determine what the performance characteristics, positive or negative, are for your system. You have seen how to use the commands that enable you to examine each of the resources a UNIX system uses. In addition to the commands themselves, you have learned procedures that can be utilized to analyze and solve many performance problems.

28

PERFORMANCE MONITORING

Device Administration

by Dan Wilson and Salim Douba

IN THIS CHAPTER

CHAPTER 29

Central to the system administrator's responsibilities is providing users with access to the distributed and shared resources in the environment. Some of the resources are software (for example, applications and the file system); other resources are hardware (such as terminals, modems, printers, and so on). This chapter addresses issues pertaining to the administration and management of hardware resources (that is, *devices*). This chapter presents you with the skills necessary to set up, configure, and maintain the performance of modems, terminals, printers, and PCs.

For the purposes of terminal, modem, and printer setup, UNIX—specifically SVR4 variants SCO, Solaris, and AT&T (refer to the following note box)—come with a powerful and central access facility known as the Service Access Facility (SAF). No discussion of device administration is complete without covering SAF. Neither is it possible for the system administrator to successfully complete the aforementioned tasks without a thorough understanding of what SAF is all about and the skillful use of its associated commands. Let's start out by covering the Service Access Facility.

> **NOTE**
>
> UNIX variants based on BSD (for example, early SunOS and HP-UX) lack an SAF interface for device administration. Concepts, tools, and skills needed to set up and administer devices under BSD are covered later in this chapter in the context of the described tasks.

Following is a list of the major topics covered in this chapter:

- Service Access Facility under SVR4
- Device administrative tasks under SVR4
- Connecting printers
- Connecting a PC to UNIX systems
- Connecting X terminals

Service Access Facility Under SVR4

Before System V release 4 of UNIX (SVR4), administrators were provided with different processes and interfaces, along with their associated tools, to manage different physical resources on the system. Local port access used to be administered and controlled by interfaces that are different from those needed to set up for network access, or those pertaining to printer setup and so on. Administrators were therefore confronted with the challenge of learning and mastering the many different skills and interfaces needed to get the job done. To alleviate this challenge, SAF was introduced with SVR4. SAF provides a common interface for the purpose of uniform management of all system resources. After mastering the concepts and associated commands that SAF provides, the administrator will be able to install, configure, monitor, and maintain information relevant to the local and network access, to physical port services in SAF database files.

SAF consists primarily of port services, port monitors, the service access controller process (the SAC process), and SAF administrative files and commands. The following sections provide a description of each of these components. Then the SAF initialization process is detailed.

Port Services

SAF defines a hierarchy of port control processes, of which port service is the lowest and the most "intimate" to the actual physical services. A *port service* is defined as a process that controls and monitors access to applications and other services through physical ports such as ttys and TCP/IP. A tty service can provide users with dial-in/dial-out capabilities, which can allow them to use high-level applications such as uucp, cu, and login. A TCP/IP port-related service may be required to provide printing, rlogin, or NFS services across the network.

There is a one-to-one association between physical ports (the actual physical service) and port services (the controlling process). It is not possible, for example, for two ttys to share the same port service; nor is it possible for one tty port to be controlled by more than one port service. The same port service can, in fact, service numerous other ports at the same time.

After creating a port service, the system administrator assigns it a service name, which is referred to as the *service tag*. Service tags are used to conveniently distinguish between the port services running on the system. Port services are supported and controlled by intermediate-level processes called port monitors, which are described in the next section.

Port Monitors

A *port monitor* is an intermediate-level process that controls a set of related services. SAF currently recognizes two types of port monitors: ttymon and listen. However, SAF is not limited to those two types. Vendors and system programmers are provided with a well-defined network programming interface, which enables them to write their own monitor types. Basically, the purpose of a port monitor is to handle service requests that arrive across the ports serviced by the port monitor.

29

DEVICE ADMINISTRATION

Port monitor type `ttymon` controls and monitors tty-related port services and replaces the pre-SVR4 `getty` and `uugetty` programs. Although Solaris, AT&T SVR4, and others maintain support for `uugetty` and `getty` (for reasons of backward compatibility), `ttymon` is the preferred method of installing, configuring, and monitoring tty port services. Port monitor type `listen`, on the other hand, takes advantage of TCP/IP communications protocols to provide the across-the-network services mentioned earlier (such as network printing and remote file-sharing capabilities). Both port monitor types are explained in upcoming sections.

System administrators are allowed the flexibility to create as many port monitors of any type as they deem necessary. After creating a port monitor, a *port monitor tag* is assigned to it. As in the case of port services, port monitor tags are names that help distinguish among port monitors. They can be given convenient names that may describe the nature of the service they support. Being a mid-level process, port monitors themselves are invoked, controlled, and monitored by the Service Access Controller (`SAC`) process.

Service Access Controller

The Service Access Controller (`SAC`) process is the highest in SAF hierarchy. There is only one `SAC` per system. It invokes and controls all port monitors, regardless of type, that have been created and configured by the system administrator. `SAC` is spawned by `init` at system startup when multiuser mode is entered. An entry supporting `SAC` is automatically included in the `/etc/inittab` file. Here is an example of how this entry should look:

```
sc:234:respawn:/usr/lib/saf/sac -t 300
```

The `-t 300` option causes `SAC` to routinely check port monitors every 300 seconds for services. To change this option to some other value, enter the following command:

```
#sacadm -t <seconds>
```

> **NOTE**
>
> When checking the `/etc/inittab` file, do not be surprised if you see entries pertaining to `ttymon` port monitor. There is no contradiction between what you see and what has already been explained. Simply put, UNIX allows a so-called "express mode" invocation of `ttymon` by `init`. This particularly applies to the case of the console port. You can still, however, create instances of `ttymon` that are controlled and administered by `SAC`.

SAF Administrative Commands and Files

SAF distinguishes among SAC-specific, port monitor-specific, and port service-specific administrative and configuration files as well as administrative commands. In the following sections, administrative and configuration files and SAF-related commands are described. The emphasis is on their nature and the job they do. Command syntax and use for the purposes of creating, configuring, or checking the status of port monitors and port services is left until later sections, where they are discussed at length in the context of tasks to accomplish.

Service Access Controller-Specific Files and Commands

After it is brought up, SAC fetches two files: /etc/saf/_sactab, which is the administrative database that contains entries pertaining to port monitors defined by the system administrator, and /etc/saf/_sysconfig, which is a SAC-specific configuration file. SAC uses the first file to identify the port monitors to invoke; it uses the second file to self-customize its own environment. Contents of /etc/saf/_sactab can be modified by the sacadm command, which is SAC's administrative command. Using sacadm allows administrators to create port monitors, check their status, and enable or disable them as well as remove them. Also, each port monitor provides an administrative command that can be used with sacadm in command substitution mode. The listen port monitor administrative command is nlsadmin; ttymon's port monitor administrative command is ttyadm.

The /etc/saf/_sysconfig file, on the other hand, is used by SAC to specify the environment governing all the services controlled by it. The SAC program, once started by init, reads and interprets this file before invoking any service defined by /etc/saf/_sactab. You can optionally have one _sysconfig file per system, and it can be edited using vi or any other UNIX editor.

Port Monitor-Specific Files and Commands

When a port monitor is created using sacadm, an /etc/saf/<pmtag> directory is created where port-specific files are maintained. Of prime interest are the /etc/saf/<pmtag>/_pmtab the /etc/saf/<pmtag>/_config files.

If, for example, you create a port monitor and assign it the tag ttyserv, the directory called /etc/saf/ttyserv is created, in which the administrative file /etc/saf/ttyserv/_config is maintained. This file is similar to the /etc/saf/_sactab in its functionality because it is used by the port monitor to determine and bring up the port services as defined by the system administrator.

The /etc/saf/<pmtag>/_pmtab file is a one-per-port monitor file that can be modified using the pmadm command when creating, deleting, or modifying the status of any of the

29

DEVICE
ADMINISTRATION

associated port services. The `/etc/saf/<pmtag>/_config` file is an optional port monitor-specific configuration file that can be created by the system administrator using `vi`. Commands in this file can add to, or override, those found in the system configuration file `_sysconfig`. Before starting a port monitor defined in `/etc/saf/_sactab` file, SAC checks the port monitors' respective directory for the `_config` file. If found, `_config` is read and interpreted by SAC to customize the port monitor's environment, and then the port monitor is started.

Port Service-Specific Files and Commands

At the bottom of the SAF hierarchy, port services have no administrative files associated with them. The system administrator, however, has the option to create a port service-specific configuration script named after the service tag and kept in the associated port monitor's directory. If, for example, a port service was created under port monitor `ttyserv` and was given the service tag `ttylogin1`, the port service configuration file is named `ttylogin1` and is kept in the `/etc/saf/ttyserv` directory. The complete filename thus becomes `/etc/saf/ttyserv/ttylogin1`. This file is read and interpreted by the controlling port monitor before starting the port service. Configuration commands included in the file can override or add to those found in the `_config` port monitor's file or the `_sysconfig` file associated with this service.

Table 29.1 summarizes what has been discussed so far and provides a quick way to narrow down the files and commands associated with each SAF component.

TABLE 29.1. ADMINISTRATIVE FILES AND COMMANDS ASSOCIATED WITH EACH OF THE SAF COMPONENTS.

Process Filename	Invoked by Admin Command	Admin Filename	config
SAC	init	/etc/saf/_sactab	/etc/saf/_sysconfig ➥sacadm
port monitor	sac pmadm	/etc/saf/<pmtag>/_pmtab	/etc/saf/<pmtag>/_config
port service	port monitor	optional	pmadm

SAF Initialization Process

Figure 29.1 shows a flow chart summarizing the SAF initialization process. Note that it all starts with `init` invoking SAC after reading a SAC-associated entry in the `/etc/inittab` file. Once SAC is started, it proceeds as follows:

1. SAC checks for the `/etc/saf/_sysconfig` configuration file. If found, it reads the file to self-customize its environment. This environment is a global one that, unless otherwise modified or overridden, governs all defined SAF services.

2. SAC determines which port monitors to invoke by reading the `/etc/saf/_sactab` file. For each port monitor, SAC checks for the associated `/etc/saf/<pmtag>/_config` file. If one exists, the SAC process reads, interprets, and implements the contents and customizes the port monitor's environment, regardless of any earlier associated settings defined in `_sysconfig` files. The port monitor is then invoked.

3. After it is invoked, the port monitor determines which port services to start by reading the `/etc/saf/<pmtag>/_pmtab` file. Next, the port monitor checks for the optional `/etc/saf/<pmtag>/<svctag>` file corresponding to each port service. If one exists, it is read and interpreted to customize the port service environment. The port service is then invoked.

FIGURE 29.1.

A flow chart illustration of the SAF initialization process.

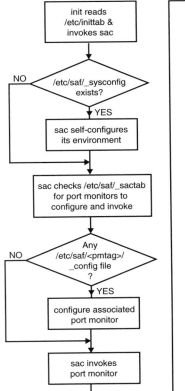

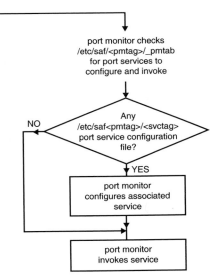

After the initialization process is complete, SAC continues to poll the port monitors at regular intervals as defined by the -t option in the corresponding entry in the /etc/inittab file. Port monitors failing to respond to this polling process prompt SAC into respawning them.

SAF Administration and Management

The following sections introduce some of the concepts and skills pertaining to SAF management and administration. Because those skills commonly apply to all types of port monitors and their associated port services, the discussions focus on how to accomplish each of the tasks, with little emphasis on the nature of the service being rendered to the user. SAF management and administration is a two-level system: one level applies to port monitors, and the other applies to port services.

Port Monitor Administration and Management

As explained earlier in this chapter, for an administrator to offer port services—be it across the network or local to the system—he or she must first create the port monitor supporting the port services. Only then can port services be created and released to the user community. There are also troubleshooting instances when the administrator may have to check the status of suspect port monitors or even temporarily disable them.

Creating a Port Monitor

Port monitors are administered and managed using the sacadm administrative command. In addition to sacadm, each port monitor type provides for an administrative command that is commonly used with sacadm in "command substitution mode." ttyadm is ttymon's command, and nlsadmin is listen's command. To create a port monitor, sacadm must be entered along with the following options:

```
#sacadm -a -p<pmtag> -t<type> -c"<pm_cmd>" -v ver [-fd¦x] \
[-n <count>] [-y"comment"]
```

For this syntax, the following are defined:

-a	Adds or creates a port monitor.
-p <pmtag>	Assigns a name to the port monitor being created; this name can be conveniently used to distinguish it from other port monitors. Although the name can be anything you choose, it should be descriptive of the type of service with which it is associated.
-t <type>	Specifies the type of monitor to create (that is, ttymon versus listen).

`-c "<pm_cmd>"`	Specifies the command to invoke when the port monitor is later spawned by SAC: `/usr/lib/saf/ttymon` to invoke a `ttymon` port monitor or `/usr/lib/saf/listen` to invoke a `listen` port monitor.
`-v ver`	Specifies the version of the port monitor. The version can be more conveniently provided by invoking the port monitor's specific administrative command (`ttyadm` or `nlsadmin`) with the `-V` option in command substitution form (that is, as an argument to `-v`). In this case, the `-V` option is typed as follows: `# sacadm -a ... -v'ttyadm -V' ...`
`-f [d¦x]`	Specifies the status of the port monitor on invocation. d means to start the port monitor in disabled state and x means not to start it. If flagged x, the port monitor can be started only by the system administrator. From there, SAC takes over in controlling the port monitor.
`-n<count>`	Specifies the retry count used by the port monitor in restarting a failing port monitor. If not included, the default that applies is 0.
`-y "comment"`	Can be any comment you want to include in the `/etc/saf/_sactab` file. For your convenience, you may want to include a comment describing what this port monitor is for.

When a port monitor is created, the following happens:

1. An entry in SAC's administrative file `/etc/saf/_sactab` is added pertaining to the port monitor and including all the arguments provided on the command line.

2. The port monitor's supporting directory `/etc/saf/<pmtag>` is also created. As a matter of fact, another directory, `/var/saf/<pmtag>`, is also created where a port monitor log file is maintained. The filename is `/var/saf/<pmtag/log`. It is used by SAC to log all messages pertaining to the port monitor.

To get a better feel for what has been discussed so far, let's look at an example of creating a port monitor. This example continues in upcoming sections to demonstrate aspects of managing the port monitor. This example assumes that the system administrator wants to allow users local logins to the system, using serial communications. Hence, the first task is to create the port monitor in preparation for creating the necessary associated port services.

29

DEVICE ADMINISTRATION

Because of the nature of the service (that is, serial communication), the port monitor has to be a ttymon type. The system administrator has chosen to assign the port monitor the tag ttyserv, start it in the disabled state, and include the comment "only two logins". At failure, SAC should attempt to restart the monitor twice. The appropriate sacadm command for this scenario should look like this:

```
#sacadm -a -p serial -t ttymon -v 'ttyadm -V' \
 -c"/usr/lib/saf/ttymon" -fd -n 2 -y "only two logins"
```

In the next section, you learn how to check on the status of the port monitor. For the time being, however, we can carry a check using cat to look up the contents of SAC's /etc/saf/_sactab file. The cat /etc/saf/_sactab command reveals the following entry:

```
ttyserv;ttymon;d:2:/usr/lib/saf/ttymon              #only two logins
```

If you enter ls -l /etc/saf, you can verify that the subdirectory is ttyserv. ttyserv (the subdirectory) is created among others existing at /etc/saf level. Reflecting back on the _sactab entry shown previously, you should have guessed how each field in the /etc/saf/_sactab file maps to arguments you enter on the command line. The first field refers to the pmtag, the second to the port monitor type, and the third to the state in which the port monitor is started (the disables state, in this example). The fourth field mandates that two restarts be attempted should the port monitor fail, and the fifth field specifies the complete pathname of the command to invoke. Also note that the comment is included as well.

Checking the Status of the Port Monitor

To check the status of the port monitor, use the sacadm command with the -l option (among others) as follows:

- # sacadm -t<*type*> -l to obtain a listing of all port monitors of same type
- # sacadm -p<*pmtag*> -l to obtain information about a specific port monitor.

If you enter sacadm -pttyserv -l to check on the port monitor created in the preceding example, you get the following output:

```
PMTAG      PMTYPE    FLGS RCNT STATUS    COMMAND
ttyserv    ttymon    d    2    DISABLED  /usr/lib/saf/ttymon #only two
logins
```

Note that the status field indicates that the port monitor is in a disabled state. If you check the status immediately after the port monitor is created, the status field may indicate that it is STARTING.

The port monitor can be in one of the following states:

STARTING:	SAC is in the process of starting the port monitor. This is a transitional state between NOTRUNNING and ENABLED or DISABLED.
ENABLED:	The port monitor is running and is accepting connection requests.
DISABLED:	The port monitor is running but refusing connection service requests.
STOPPED:	The port monitor is undergoing the shutdown process. This state is transitional from ENABLED or DISABLED and NOTRUNNING.
NOTRUNNING:	The port monitor is not running. None of the port services associated with it is currently accessible.

Enabling, Disabling, and Removing a Port Monitor

To enable, disable, or remove a port monitor, use sacadm -e, sacadm -d, or sacadm -r, respectively. To enable the ttyserv port monitor, enter the following command:

```
# sacadm -pttyserv -e
```

To disable the ttyserv port monitor, enter this command:

```
# sacadm -pttyserv -d
```

To remove the ttyserv port monitor, enter this command:

```
# sacadm -pttyserv -r
```

> **NOTE**
>
> When a port monitor is removed, its associated directories are not cleaned up and deleted. To avoid confusion in the future, you may have to take care of that yourself.

Port Service Administration and Management

Only after the port monitor is created is the system administrator in a position to create and manage the associated port services. Port services creation and administration is achieved using the pmadm command.

29

DEVICE ADMINISTRATION

Creating a Port Service

To create a port service, use `pmadm` with the `-a` option (among others) as follows:

```
# pmadm -a -p<pmtag> -s<svctag> -m"pmspecific" \
-v ver [-fx¦u] -y"comment"
```

For this syntax, the following are defined:

`-a`	Creates a port service.
`-p<pmtag>`	Specifies the tag of the port monitor to which the port service belongs.
`-s<svctag>`	Specifies the service tag assigned to the port service.
`-m"<pmspecific>"`	Specifies port-specific information to be passed as an argument to the `pmadm` command. Normally, this information is generated by employing either `ttyadm` or `nlsadmin` in command substitution mode, depending on the type of the port monitor specified with the `-p` option.
`-v <ver>`	Passes the version of the port monitor. Depending on the type of the port monitor, you can use either `ttymon -V` or `nlsadmin -V` in command substitution mode.
`-f`	Specifies the state with which the port service should be started, and whether a `utmp` entry is to be created. Both or any of the flags can be specified, where d specifies that the port should be started in disabled state, and u specifies that a `utmp` entry be created for the service.

The following example adds a `ttymon` port service to the `ttyserv` port monitor created earlier in this chapter:

```
#pmadm -a -pttyserv -s s01 -v 'ttyadm -C' -fd \
-m "`ttyadm -d /dev/term/01 -l 9600 -s/usr/bin/login \
-p"Welcome To UNIX, Please Login:"'"
```

The port service thus created is assigned service tag `s01` and is added to a port monitor called `ttyserv` (the one created in the earlier section). The `s01` port is associated with `/dev/term/01` device file (that is, `COM2` on an Intel 386/486 machine). `-l 9600` refers to a record in a terminal line setting database file (`/etc/ttydefs`), which, when used by the port, sets the line speed. The other settings are described in a subsequent section. When `s01` port is invoked by the `ttyserv` port monitor, it writes a prompt (`Welcome to UNIX, Please Login:`, according to the preceding example) to the terminal connected to the

`COM2` port. It starts monitoring the port until it receives a request to connect. After receiving the request, it invokes `/usr/bin/login` to take care of the request.

When a port service is created, the `/etc/saf/<pmtag>/_pmtab` file is modified to include an entry pertaining to the service. For this example, an entry pertaining to `s01` must be present in the `/etc/saf/ttyserv/_pmtab` file. You can display the file either by using `cat` or the `pmadm` command as described in the next section.

Listing and Checking the Status of a Port Service

To list and check the status of a port monitor, enter the following command:

`#pmadm -l -p<pmtag> -s<svctag>`

To list or check the status of all port services associated with a specific port monitor, enter this command:

`#pmadm -l -p<pmtag>`

To list or check the status of all port monitor services, enter

PMTAG	PMTYPE	SVCTAG	FLGS	ID	<PMSPECIFIC>
ttymon3	ttymon	00s	u	root	/dev/term/00s
- - /usr/bin/					
					_login - 2400 -
login: - #					
ttymon3	ttymon	01s	u	uucp	/dev/term/01s b
- /usr/bin/					
					_login - 2400 -
login: - #					
ttymon3	ttymon	00h	u	root	/dev/term/00h
- - /usr/bin/					
					_login - 9600 -
login: - #					
tcp	listen	0	x	root	
\x02000ACE64000001 - c - /					
_usr/lib/saf/nlps_server					
					_#NLPS SERVER
tcp	listen	lp	-	root	- - - -
/var/spool/lp/fifos/					
					_listenS5 #NLPS
SERVER					
tcp	listen	105	-	root	- - c -
/usr/net/servers/rfs/					
					_rfsetup #RFS
server					

29

DEVICE ADMINISTRATION

The following two examples demonstrate the first two commands:

```
#pmadm -l -pttyserv -s s01
PMTAG     PMTYPE    SVCTAG    FLGS ID    PMSPECIFIC
ttyserv   ttymon    s01       d    root  /dev/term/01 --
/usr/bin/login - 9600 - Welcome to UNIX, Please Login: - #

#pmadm -l -pttyserv
PMTAG      PMTYPE    SVCTAG FLGS ID       <PMSPECIFIC>
ttyyserv           ttymon         00s                  u       root
/dev/term/00s - -
/usr/bin/login - 2400 - login:   -  #
ttyserv            ttymon         01s                  u       uucp
/dev/term/01s b -
/usr/bin/login - 9600 - login:   -  #
```

Enabling, Disabling, and Removing a Port Service

To enable, disable, or remove a port service, use pmadm -e, pmadm -d, or pmadm -r, respectively. For example, to enable s01 port monitor, enter this command:

```
#pmadm -pttyserv -s s01 -e
```

To disable s01 port monitor, enter this command:

```
#pmadm -pttyserv -s s01 -d
```

To remove s01 port monitor, enter this command:

```
#pmadm -pttyserv -s s01 -r
```

The ttymon Port Monitor

As its name implies, the ttymon port monitor is responsible for invoking and monitoring port services associated with your system's tty ports. When invoked, ttymon looks up its /etc/saf/<*pmtag*>/_pmtab file to determine which port services to invoke; which tty port associates with which service; how the port services are configured (for example, startup in an enabled state, what line speed to configure tty port to, and so on); and which application, or process, to invoke at the user's request (for example, login service, uucp, and so on).

ttymon replaces both getty and uugetty. Although getty and uugetty are still supported by Solaris, AT&T SVR4, and other UNIX SVR4 variants for backward compatibility reasons, system administrators are strongly recommended to use ttymon. This recommendation stems from the following comparison:

- ttymon administration conforms with SAF's generic interface. This brings managing ttymon port monitors into line with management concepts applied to other port monitors, providing the benefit of convenience.

- By using SAF management commands, the administrator has the choice of managing ttymon port services collectively or selectively. When using getty, the administrator can manage only one port at a time.

- One invocation of the ttymon port monitor by SAC can take care of multiple ttys; by contrast, getty and uugetty require an entry per supported tty in the /etc/inittab file.

- As discussed later in this chapter, ttymon supports a new feature: the AUTOBAUD feature. This feature allows ttymon to automatically determine the line speed suitable to the connected terminal.

- ttymon can optionally be invoked directly by init in "express" mode. This may be done by including an entry in the /etc/inittab file. As a matter of fact, if you examine the contents of the /etc/inittab file, you will notice the existence of a similar entry taking care of the UNIX system console in express mode. The entry should look similar to the following:

```
co:12345:respawn:/usr/lib/saf/ttymon -g -v -p "Console Login: "-d
/dev/console -l console
```

After reading this entry, init starts a ttymon port monitor to take care of console login needs. This particular invocation of ttymon falls beyond SAC's control.

Special Device Files and the Terminal Line Settings Database

Among the arguments that the system administrator must pass to pmadm to create a port service, two will be described: the device special filename corresponding to the tty serial interface undergoing configuration and a label identifying an entry in a terminal line settings database.

Device Special Filenames Under SAF

Special filenames underwent some changes in UNIX SVR4. In earlier releases of UNIX, getty and uugetty referred to the special files in the /dev directory as tty##, where ## refers to the actual port number. With SAF under SVR4, tty port special files are maintained in a subdirectory called /dev/term, and the special files are named ## in that directory. com1 port on a 386 machine is now referred to as /dev/term/00 (under getty it is referred to as /dev/tty00). Because of the ongoing support for uugetty and getty, both conventions are currently supported. It is the administrator's responsibility, however, to make sure that the right convention is applied with the administrator's preferred way of invoking a port service.

29

DEVICE ADMINISTRATION

The Terminal Line Settings Database

The terminal line settings database is the `ttymon` administrative file, which defines the line settings that apply to the `tty` port being invoked. The database filename is `/etc/ttydefs` (getty's is `/etc/gettydefs`). Both files remain supported by UNIX SVR4 variants, and both are maintained using the `/etc/sbin/sttydefs` command. A good understanding of these databases helps you provide the level of support that matches the users' terminal emulation needs. In the following discussion, however, only the `/etc/ttydefs` file's data structure is examined and explained. The use of the `sttydefs` command to add, modify, or delete entries in the database is also described.

The discussion begins with a close look at the contents of the `/etc/ttydefs` file. To list its contents, enter the following command:

```
#/usr/sbin/sttydefs -l
- - - - - - - - - - - - - - - - - - - - - - - - - - - - - - - - - - - - - - - - - - - - - -
19200: 19200 opost onlcr tab3 ignpar ixon ixany parenb istrip echo
 echoe echok isig cs7 cread : 19200 opost onlcr sane tab3 ignpar ixon
 ixany parenb istrip echo echoe echok isig cs7 cread ::9600
- - - - - - - - - - - - - - - - - - - - - - - - - - - - - - - - - - - - - - - - - - - - - -

ttylabel:    19200
initial flags:    19200 opost onlcr tab3 ignpar ixon ixany parenb
 istrip echo echoe echok isig cs7 cread
final flags:    19200 opost onlcr sane tab3 ignpar ixon ixany parenb
 istrip echo echoe echok isig cs7 cread
autobaud:    no
nextlabel:    9600


- - - - - - - - - - - - - - - - - - - - - - - - - - - - - - - - - - - - - - - - - - - - - -
9600: 9600 opost onlcr tab3 ignpar ixon ixany parenb istrip echo echoe
 echok isig cs7 cread : 9600 opost onlcr sane tab3 ignpar ixon ixany
 parenb istrip echo echoe echok isig cs7 cread ::4800
- - - - - - - - - - - - - - - - - - - - - - - - - - - - - - - - - - - - - - - - - - - - - -

ttylabel:    9600
initial flags:    9600 opost onlcr tab3 ignpar ixon ixany parenb
 istrip echo echoe echok isig cs7 cread
final flags:    9600 opost onlcr sane tab3 ignpar ixon ixany parenb
 istrip echo echoe echok isig cs7 cread
autobaud:    no
nextlabel:    4800


- - - - - - - - - - - - - - - - - - - - - - - - - - - - - - - - - - - - - - - - - - - - - -
4800: 4800 opost onlcr tab3 ignpar ixon ixany parenb istrip echo echoe
 echok isig cs7 cread : 4800 opost onlcr sane tab3 ignpar ixon ixany
 parenb istrip echo echoe echok isig cs7 cread ::2400
- - - - - - - - - - - - - - - - - - - - - - - - - - - - - - - - - - - - - - - - - - - - - -
```

```
ttylabel:    4800
initial flags:     4800 opost onlcr tab3 ignpar ixon ixany parenb
 istrip echo echoe echok isig cs7 cread
final flags:      4800 opost onlcr sane tab3 ignpar ixon ixany parenb
 istrip echo echoe echok isig cs7 cread
autobaud:    no
nextlabel:    2400
.
.
.
```

As you can see, `sttydefs` formats the listing into a user-friendly format. If you want the actual data structure of the command, enter the following command:

#cat /etc/ttydefs
```
.
.
.
onlcr sane tab3 ignpar istrip ixon ixany echo echoe
 echok isig cs8 cread ::console5
console5: 19200 opost onlcr tab3 ignpar istrip ixon ixany
 echo echoe echok isig cs8 cread : 19200 opost onlcr sane
 tab3 ignpar istrip ixon ixany echo echoe echok isig cs8 cread ::console

4800H: 4800 : 4800 ixany parenb sane tab3 hupcl ::9600H
9600H: 9600 : 9600 ixany parenb sane tab3 hupcl ::19200H
19200H: 19200 : 19200 ixany parenb sane tab3 hupcl ::2400H
2400H: 2400 : 2400 ixany parenb sane tab3 hupcl ::1200H
1200H: 1200 : 1200 ixany parenb sane tab3 hupcl ::300H
300H: 300 : 300 ixany parenb sane tab3 hupcl ::4800H

19200NP: 19200 opost onlcr tab3 ignpar ixon ixany istrip
 echo echoe echok isig cs8 cread : 19200
.
.
```

Following is a description of each field:

Label	It is unique and used in identifying the record. You pass this label to `ttymon`, using `pmadm`, when creating the port service. Every time `ttymon` attempts to invoke the port service, it searches for that label in the `ttydefs` file.
Initial flags	This field describes the initial terminal line settings. They allow users to provide login information on initial contact.
Final flags	These entries define the terminal line settings after a connection request is detected and right before the associated port service is invoked.

Autobaud	This field can contain either A or null. By including A in this field, you are prompting ttymon to automatically determine the line speed when it receives a carriage return from the user's terminal.
Next label	This field includes the label of the next record to fetch should the line settings specified in the current label fail to meet the user's terminal needs. ttymon recognizes the failure after receiving a BREAK sent by the user. This technique allows ttymon to fall back on any number of alternative configurations in search of the desired line speed. Records linked together in this fashion are said to form a *hunt sequence*, with the last record normally linked to the first record. The sample partial listing shown previously includes a hunt sequence that starts with label 4800H and ends with 300H.

Here is a sample record in ttydefs, along with an explanation of its field contents:

```
9600NP: 9600  tab3 ignpar ixon ixany  echo echoe  cs8 : 9600 sane tab3
ignpar ixon ixany  echo echoe  cs8::4800NP
```

This record is labeled 9600NP. Both the initial and final flags set the port to 9600bps, no parity (ignpar), enable XON/OFF flow control (ixon), any character should restart output (ixany), echo back every character typed (echo), echo erase character (echoe), and to set the character size to 8 bits. The autobaud field is null, which means that no autobaud support is required. The last field points to the next record labeled 4800N.

To find more about the valid initial and final flag settings, consult your vendor's manuals, or simply enter "man stty" on the command line.

What if you don't find what you want in ttydefs? As noted earlier, SVR4 provides you with the /usr/sbin/sttydefs command to make changes to the /etc/ttydefs database. Among the changes you are allowed to make is adding the record of your liking. Here is the command syntax to do that:

```
#sttydefs -a<ttylabel> [-b] [-n<nextlabel>] [-i<initialflags>]\
[-f <finalflags>]
```

For this syntax, the following are defined:

-a *<ttylabel>*	Adds an entry to ttydefs with the label specified (first field).
-i *<initialflags>*	Specifies the initial speed among other line settings (second field).

-f *\<finalflags\>*	Specifies the final line settings (third field).
-b	Enables autobaud (fourth field, in which case A is included in this field).
-n	Describes the next record's label.

For example, the sttydefs that follows adds a new record, labeled 4800, with initial flags set to support a 4800bps line speed:

```
#sttydefs -a4800 -i"4800 hupcl tab3 erase ^b" \
-f"4800 sane ixany tab3 erase ^h echoe" -n2400np
```

To remove an entry, simply enter sttydefs -r *\<ttylabel\>*. For example, to delete the 4800 label, enter this command:

```
#sttydefs -r 4800
```

> **CAUTION**
>
> A record that you delete may belong to a hunt sequence, in which case it is your responsibility to restore integrity to the affected sequence.

The ttymon Port Monitor Administrative Command ttyadm

ttyadm is ttymon's administrative command. Its prime function is to pass information to both sacadm and pmadm in the formats they require. Following are the ttyadm options:

-V	Specifies the version of ttymon.
-d *device*	Specifies the /dev/term/## tty with which the port service will be associated.
-b	If included, configures the port service for bi-directional flow of data.
-r *\<count\>*	Specifies the number of times ttymon should try to start the service before a failure is declared.
-p *"prompt"*	The string used to prompt users when a port service request is detected.
-i *"message"*	The message to be displayed if the port is in a disabled state.
-t *\<timeout\>*	The number of seconds that ttymon must wait for input data before closing the port.

`-l <ttylabel>`	Specifies the label of the desired record in the `/etc/ttydefs` file described earlier in this section.
`-s`	Specifies the name of the service provider program on the `tty` port (for example, `login`, `cu`, and so on).

At this point, all the elements you need to implement terminal and modem connections have been covered. If you are anxious to try implementing, jump ahead in this chapter to the section titled "Connecting Terminals and Modems." Otherwise, continue reading the next section, which explains the `listen` port monitor.

The `listen` Port Monitor

`listen` is a network port monitoring process that is invoked and controlled by SAC. It runs on any transport provider (most commonly TCP), and supports two classes of service: a class of general services, such as RFS (Remote File Sharing, a precursor to Network File Sharing, or NFS) and network printing; and terminal login services for terminals trying to access the system by connecting directly to the network. As can `ttymon`, `listen` can support and monitor multiple ports, with each assigned a network service to take care of. Once invoked, the `listen` port monitor initializes port services as defined in its `/etc/saf/<pmtag>/_pmtab` file. It then monitors the ports for service connection requests. After a request is received on a `listen` port, the associated service (for example, printing) is invoked and the user is connected to it.

Port Service Addressing

During TCP/IP setup, your system will have been assigned an Internet address that is eight hexadecimal digits long, with each pair of digits represented by one octet. Stations shipping requests across the network to your system use this address to reach your machine's doorstep. Because your machine is more likely to be configured to respond to a variety of service requests, there arises the requirement to assign unique addresses to port services. This allows the `listen` port monitor to support multiple port services. After adding a `listen` port service, you are required to provide the applicable address to `nlsadmin` (the `listen` port monitor administrative command). For this reason, you are provided with the address format shown in Figure 29.2.

The elements of the address format are as follows:

`Family address`	This field is four digits long. It is always set to `0020`.
`Port address`	This field is four digits long and is the port service-specific address. For example, the `listenS5` print server is assigned `x0ACE`, and the `listenBSD` print server is assigned `x0203`.

Internet address	This field is the IP address you assigned to the system when you installed TCP/IP. It is eight digits long.
Reserved	This field is 16 digits long and is reserved for future use. Currently, it is set to 16 zeros.

For example, assume that the IP address of your system is `100.0.0.1`, and that you want to set up a `listen` port to take care of print service requests sent across the network. The port address in hexadecimal notation then becomes the following:

`00020203640000010000000000000000`

FIGURE 29.2.

The listen *port service address format.*

The listener port service address format

Family Address (4 digits)	Port Address (4 digits)	Internet Address (8 digits)	Resrved (16 digits)

TIP

To avoid dealing with decimal-to-hex conversions to figure out the hexadecimal equivalent to your host IP address, you can use the `lpsystem` -A. Figure 29.3 shows how to use `lpsystem` -A output to figure out the host's IP address in hexadecimal notation.

Later in this chapter, you learn how to pass this address to `pmadm` when creating the port service.

The `listen` Port Monitor Administrative Command `nlsamdin`

`nlsadmin` is the administrative command specific to the `listen` port monitor. `nlsadmin` can be used to add, configure, and change the status of a port monitor. It can also be used to start or kill the listener process. Mostly, it is used in command substitution mode to supply some of the required arguments to both `sacadm` (the SAC administrative command) and `pmadm`. Options that you specify on the command line determine which arguments to pass, and in what format.

Creating a `listen` Port Monitor

To create a `ttymon` port monitor, you use the `sacadm` command. The same applies to creating a `listen` port monitor. Instead of using `ttyadm`, however, you must use `nlsadmin` in command substitution mode to pass some of the required information to `sacadm`. The use of `sacadm` in creating a listen port monitor is as follows:

```
#sacadm -a -p<pmtag> -t listen -c<"command"> -v'nlsadmin -V'\
[-n<count>] [-fd¦x] [-y<"comment">]
```

All options bear the same significance described in earlier sections (refer back to "Creating a Port Monitor" for a review). In particular, note the use of 'nlsadmin -V' to pass the port monitor's version to sacadm. Also note that the -c option specifies the program invoked to bring up the listen port monitor. The program is /usr/lib/saf/listen. After a port monitor is created, an entry pertaining to it is added to SAC's administrative file /etc/saf/_sactab.

For example, the following sacadm command creates a listen port monitor with pmtag tcp. Note that the program filename to invoke is /usr/lib/saf/listen; SAC is required to try as many as three times to bring up the port monitor, should it ever fail respond to SAC's polls.

```
sacadm -a -t listen -p tcp -c "/usr/lib/saf/listen" \
-v'nlsadmin - V' -n3
```

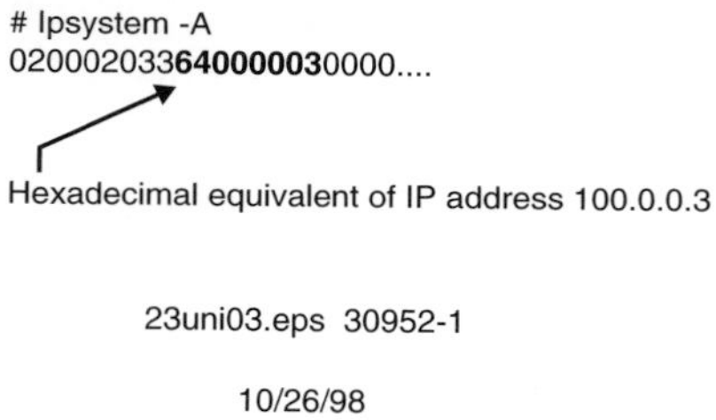

FIGURE 29.3.

Using lpsystem - A *to find the hexadecimal equivalent of the host's IP address.*

```
# lpsystem -A
020002033640000030000....
```

Hexadecimal equivalent of IP address 100.0.0.3

23uni03.eps 30952-1

10/26/98

Managing `listen` Port Monitors

To check on the availability of listen port monitors, enter this command:

```
#sacadm -l -t listen
```

As a result, you see a listing of all listen port monitors currently controlled by SAC on your system. The listing looks like this:

```
PMTAG     PMTYPE    FLGS    RCNT    STATUS     COMMAND
tcp          listen    -      3      ENABLED    /usr/lib/saf/listen -m inet/
tcp0 tcp
```

For a review of the interpretation of this listing, refer to "Checking the Status of the Port Monitor," earlier in this chapter.

To enable, disable, or remove a port monitor, enter sacadm with the -e, -d, or -r option respectively, as described earlier in this chapter.

Creating a `listen` Port Service

To create a `listen` port service, use the `pmadm` command. The syntax is as follows:

```
#pmadm -a -p<pmtag> -s<svctag> [-i id] -v 'nlsadmin -V'\
 -m"'nlsadmin options'" -y"comment"
```

The following command adds a new port service to a port monitor with `pmtag tcp`:

```
#pmadm -a -p tcp -s lpd -i root -v 'nlsadmin -V'\
 -m"'nlsadmin -o /var/spool/lp/fifos/listenBSD -A \
\x00020203640000020000000000000000'"
```

The preceding command demonstrates the use of the port address discussed earlier. The port address described in the preceding example configures the port to accept printing requests sent by BSD clients across the network.

Managing Port Services

To check on the status of a port service, enter the following command:

```
#pmadm -p<pmtag> -s<svctag> -l
```

To enable a port service, enter this command:

```
#pmadm -p<pmtag> -s<svctag> -e
```

To disable the port service, enter this command:

```
#pmadm -p<pmtag> -s<svctag> -d
```

To remove the port service, enter this command:

```
#pmadm -p<pmtag> -s<svctag> -r
```

Device Administrative Tasks Under SVR4

This part of the chapter explains how to perform common device administrative-related tasks as applicable to SVR4 of UNIX. Subsequent sections cover other variants as well, including Solaris 2.x and Linux. The next section, "Connecting Terminals and Modems," applies to all variants; it provides comprehensive coverage of hardware-related issues common to all variants of UNIX (and other operating systems).

29

DEVICE ADMINISTRATION

Connecting Terminals and Modems

UNIX has very powerful built-in serial communications capabilities. Administrators can make use of them to offer local terminal connection services as well as across-the-telephone-wire services. Services across the wire include remote terminal login, file transfer capabilities, and electronic mail exchange. Those services are provided by utilities such as uucp and cu, which are part of the Basic Networking Utilities (BNU) that comes with your UNIX operating system.

The following sections present the concepts and steps to set up for both modem and terminal connections. A properly wired and configured serial interface is a basic requirement for both types of services. After this requirement is fulfilled, you can proceed to implementing the necessary additional steps to take care of modem and terminal connections.

Making the Connection

To make the serial connection, you must prepare for the physical connection, determine the availability of associated resources, and create the port service.

Preparing for the Physical Connection

In this step, you are primarily involved in readying the cable that connects the modem or the user's terminal to the UNIX system. RS232C/D is the standard interface most hardware platforms use to connect devices. So that you can understand the how and why of different cable arrangements, a brief examination of the standard is provided.

RS232C/D defines the interface between so-called data circuit terminating equipment (DTE) and data circuit communication equipment (DCE). In practical terms and for the purposes of this section, this means that RS232C/D defines the physical interface between a computer (the DTE) and the modem (the DCE). The interface defines four aspects of the physical layer: electrical, mechanical, functional, and procedural.

- The electrical specification defines how data is electrically represented on the wire. Because computer data is binary in its raw form, the specification describes which voltage level represents which logical level.

- The mechanical specification describes the mechanics of the connection, including the connector type and the number of pins supported. A DB-25 connector is specified for the RS232C/D interface. The industry introduced another *de facto* standard, however: the DB-9 connector is most commonly found on PC workstations.

- The functional specification defines the pinout of the connector (that is, what each pin stands for).
- The procedural specification defines the handshake mechanism that should precede, accompany, and terminate the exchange of data between the DTE and DCE.

Figure 29.4 shows the wiring diagram and corresponding pin definition of the DB25-to-DB25 cable, which is normally used to connect a DTE to a DCE. Figure 29.5 shows the wiring diagram of a DB9-to-DB25 cable. Following is a description of the most commonly used circuits. Because pin definitions are not the same for both types of connectors, the description refers to the circuit name rather than to the pin number.

FIGURE 29.4.

Wiring diagram and corresponding pin definition of a DB25-to-DB25 RS232C/D straight-through cable.

FIGURE 29.5.

Wiring diagram of a DB9-to-DB25 straight-through cable.

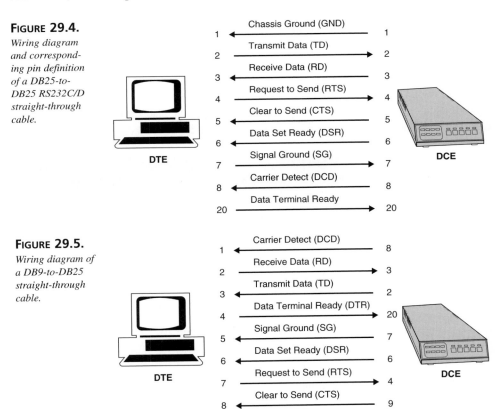

29

DEVICE ADMINISTRATION

SG provides the common return path for both the transmit (TD) and receive (RD) circuits.

DTR and DSR are asserted by both the computer and the modem to indicate readiness to exchange data. Both circuits must be asserted before any other activity can occur across the interface. At this point, the computer may attempt to dial another computer by passing the dialing command string to the modem.

DCD is asserted by the modem if it successfully connects at the remote end. It is interpreted by the computer as an indication of a successful connection. This circuit must remain asserted for the duration of the call.

TD and RD are the transmit and receive circuits.

Any time the computer wants to transmit, it asserts the RTS circuit and waits for permission to do so from the modem, by virtue of asserting the CTS circuit. This use of the RTS/CTS circuit pair applies to the half-duplex mode of communications. In full-duplex communications, RTS and CTS circuits are used to control the flow of data between the DTE and the DCE devices. The DTE drops its RTS circuit to request the DCE to stop sending data on DTE's receive circuit. Likewise, the CTS is dropped by the DCE to request the DTE to stop sending data on the transmit circuit.

CAUTION

In cases in which one end of the cable is a DB-25 connector and the opposite end is a DB-9, the cable must be wired as shown in Figure 29.6.

FIGURE 29.6.

Null modem wiring arrangements corresponding to different combinations of connectors.

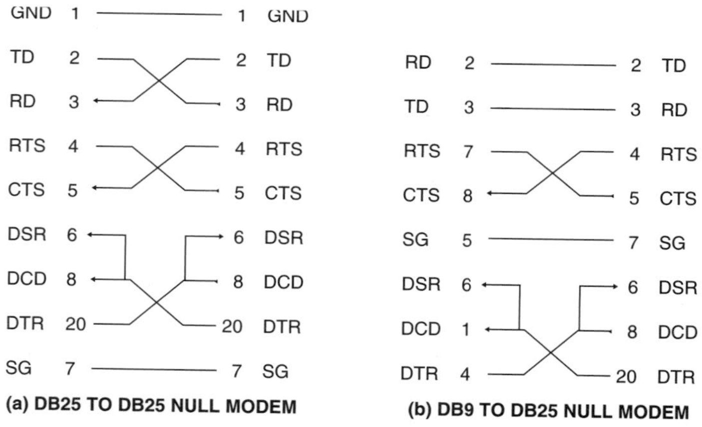

```
GND   1 ————————— 1  GND

TD    2 ——    —— 2  TD          RD   2 ————————— 2  TD
          \  /
RD    3 ——  /\  —— 3  RD         TD   3 ————————— 3  RD

RTS   4 ——    —— 4  RTS         RTS  7 ——    —— 4  RTS
          \  /                           \  /
CTS   5 ——  /\  —— 5  CTS         CTS  8 ——  /\  —— 5  CTS

DSR   6 ←┐    ┌→ 6  DSR          SG   5 ————————— 7  SG

DCD   8 ←┤    ├→ 8  DCD          DSR  6 ←┐    ┌→ 6  DSR

DTR  20 ——    —— 20 DTR          DCD  1 ←┤    ├→ 8  DCD

SG    7 ————————— 7  SG          DTR  4 ——    —— 20 DTR
```

(a) DB25 TO DB25 NULL MODEM   **(b) DB9 TO DB25 NULL MODEM**

Connecting a computer directly to a terminal (that is, a DTE-to-DTE type of connection) is a tricky business, but it is easy to understand. Because RS232C/D defines the interface strictly between a DTE and a DCE, many vendors and users have developed variations on a cabling trick that allows DTE-to-DTE connection. This trick is called the *null modem cable*. The underlying idea is to convince both ends of the connection that they are indeed talking to modems directly connected to them. Figure 33.6 shows two diagrams depicting the same cabling trick for different combinations of connectors.

When the interface pinout was described, it was done from the DTE perspective. This means that if you look at the interface from the DCE perspective, some pins bear quite the opposite significance. For example, the DTE's send and receive pins are the DCE's receive and send, respectively. It is not, therefore, hard to imagine what would happen if you were to attempt to connect two DTEs using a direct cable. Data emerging from both devices on directly connected transmit circuits would endlessly collide, while both devices are hopelessly waiting for an impulse to occur on the wire connecting their receiving circuits.

To remedy this situation, the send and receive circuits are cross-wired. Recall that whenever the computer asserts its RTS circuit, it is asking for clearance to transmit. This clearance is indicated by having the CTS asserted (normally by the modem), which explains why this circuit pair is also cross-wired. Finally, note how DSR, DTR, and DCD are wired. When DTR is asserted by any DTE, the other one detects a DCD and a DSR, which are interpreted as both modem-ready and connection-established indicators, just as though they were sent by the receiving DTE's local modem. If the DTE is prepared to engage in data communications, it asserts its DTR, and both sides can now talk to each other.

There are variations on the theme of the null modem. Although the preceding variation caters to the most general cases, it is advisable that you check with your vendor to determine your exact cabling needs.

Determine the Availability of Resources

Before you can create the port service, you must check two resources: the availability of tty ports and the availability of a suitable record in the /etc/ttydefs file.

To obtain a list of all tty ports currently in use, enter the command pmadm -l -t ttymon. The listing will look like the following:

```
PMTAG      PMTYPE      SVCTAG      FLGS      ID       <PMSPECIFIC>
ttymon3    ttymon      00s         ux        root     /dev/term/00 ...
ttymon3    ttymon      11s         -         uucp     /dev/term/11 ...
```

The device special filenames under the <PMSPECIFIC> column indicate which ttys to avoid in your subsequent steps. Depending on the availability of extra free tty ports, choose the one you want.

Next, list the contents of the /etc/ttydefs file by entering the command sttydefs -l. Examine its contents for the record and label that match your terminal needs. If you do not find one, add the desired entry to the database yourself using the sttydefs command. For more information, refer to "Special Device Files and the Terminal Line Setting Database," earlier in this chapter.

Creating the Port Service

Now that you have all the pieces (the cable, the tty port, and the label of the record in /etc/ttydefs file), you can put them together to create the port service. To do so, you use pmadm with the -a option. The example that follows demonstrates the use of pmadm to create a bidirectional port service, with *svctag* 04s, which invokes the service login, restarts the port three times on failure, and prompts the terminal with a friendly message. Also note the use of ttyadm in command substitution mode to pass some of the arguments to pmadm:

```
#pmadm -a -pttyserv -s04s -i root -v `ttyadm -V` \
-m "`ttyadm -b -r3 -p"Welcome Home! LOGIN:" -d/dev/term/04 \
-l 9600 -s /usr/bin/login'"
```

Use pmadm -l to check the state of the service. If the new service is not enabled, use pmadm -p<pmtag> -s<svctag> -e to do so.

Connecting the Modem

As noted earlier, you connect a modem to the serial port (for example, COM2) using a straight-through cable. To configure the modem properly, you must read the documentation supplied with it. The things you ought to pay attention to are the DIP switch settings and the AT commands necessary for proper modem initialization and dialing. Because the majority of modems today are Hayes compatible, the list in Table 29.2 can act as you configuration guidelines.

Hayes modems have an 8-bit DIP switch. Table 29.2 summarizes the meanings associated with each bit switch position.

TABLE 29.2. HAYES MODEM SWITCH SETTINGS

Switch	Position	Function
1	Up	If the computer asserts its DTR low, the modem reacts by hanging up the line.
	Down*	Forces the DTR permanently high, which means that the modem no longer has to worry about this signal.

Switch	Position	Function
2	Up*	Forces the modem to respond to modem dialing and initialization commands in English.
	Down	Forces the modem to respond using numerical messages.
3	Up	Suppresses result codes, thus overriding switch 2.
	Down*	Enables result codes.
4	Up*	AT commands are echoed as they are entered.
	Down	AT commands are not echoed.
5	Up*	Modem answers the phone.
	Down	Modem does not answer the phone.
6	Up	CD is asserted when a carrier is detected; this allows the computer to know when a call is received.
	Down*	CD and DSR are forced permanently high.
7	Up*	Modem is attached to single-line phone.
	Down	Modem is attached to multi-line phone.
8	Up	Disables the modem from recognizing and executing modem commands.
	Down*	Modem's intelligence is enabled; modem recognizes and executes modem commands.

* Denotes the default setting of each switch.

On ports configured for dial-in, UNIX responds to asserted DSR and CD by writing a login prompt to the modem. This, therefore, requires turning off echoing as well as result codes on the modem. Failing to do so leads the login process into interpreting locally echoed login prompt characters as a sequence of responses, which leads into a vicious cycle of login denials and subsequent reattempts. To turn local echo and result codes off, set switch positions 3, 4, and 6 to up, down, and up, respectively.

What if you do not have switches on your modem? You can use the AT modem control command set instead! AT commands let you configure the modem to initialize and manage a connection in ways deemed suitable to your applications. Table 29.3 lists some of the AT commands commonly supported by Hayes compatible modems. For a complete command list, consult your modem's manuals.

29

DEVICE ADMINISTRATION

TABLE 29.3. PARTIAL LIST OF THE MOST COMMONLY SUPPORTED AT COMMANDS

Command	Significance
AT&F	Reset modem to factory settings
ATDP	Dial using Pulse tone
ATDT	Dial using Touch tone
ATE0	Enable local echoing of commands
ATE1	Disable local echoing of commands
ATQ0	Enable result codes
ATQ1	Disable result codes (also known as the *quiet mode*)
AT&W	Write settings to nonvolatile memory

To issue AT commands, you must have some sort of direct access to the modem. The following steps show you how you can do it using the cu command.

After you log in to UNIX, use the su command to switch the user to uucp:

```
#su uucp
password:
$
```

Edit the /etc/uucp/Devices file (see Chapter 24, "File System and Disk Administration," for details) to include the following entry:

```
Direct term/##    -    <speed> direct
```

In this statement, ## corresponds to the tty port number, and <speed> refers to the speed at which you want to initialize the modem. If, for example, you have a 2400bps Hayes-compatible modem connected to COM2, the entry would look like this:

```
Direct     term/01    -    2400 direct
```

I am assuming that there is no other reference to term/01. If there is another reference, disable the entry by inserting the # sign at the beginning of the line. Make sure that you save the file before quitting.

At the command line, enter this command:

```
#cu -l term/##
```

This command directly connects you to the modem and is confirmed by displaying the message Connected on your screen. Table 29.4 shows a sequence pertaining to a sample modem session, during which the modem is configured for proper dial-in support.

TABLE 29.4. A MODEM CONFIGURATION SESSION AND SUPPORTING EXPLANATION

Command/Response	Explanation
#cu -l term/01	A command: "I want to talk to the modem."
Connected	A response: "Go ahead."
AT	A command: "Do I have your attention?"
OK	A response: "Yes, you do!"
AT&F	A command: "Reset to factory settings."
OK	A response: "Done!"
AT&C1	A command: "Use CD to indicate carrier detection."
OK	A response: "Done!"
AT&D2	A command: "Drop the connection when DTR drops."
OK	A response: "Done!"
ATE0Q1	A command: "Disable local echo and keep quiet" (that is, disable result codes).
OK	A response: "Done!"
AT&W	A command: "Save settings into nonvolatile RAM."
OK	A response: "Done!"
~.	A command to shell out to UNIX requesting disconnection, and going back to the UNIX shell.
Disconnected	A response: "Granted!"
#	

Note in particular the use of the ~. character sequence to disconnect from the modem and go back to the UNIX shell. In fact, ~ allows you to issue UNIX commands without having to quit the direct modem session.

For dial-out, it is more convenient to enable local echo and result codes. In any case, it is imperative that you carefully read and follow the modem's manual for proper operation.

Here is a checklist to which you can refer whenever you install or troubleshoot a modem.

1. Ensure that your modem is not conflicting with any other device over the chosen serial port. Conflicts normally arise when an internal modem is installed and configured to either COM1 or COM2.

2. Make sure that you have the proper RS232C/D cable. Consult your modem documentation and follow its recommendations religiously.

29

DEVICE ADMINISTRATION

3. If you intend to use the modem for dial-out, change the ownership of the `tty` port to uucp.

4. Set the modem DIP switches properly. This is especially critical if the intended use of the modem is for dial-out.

5. For dial-in, make sure that a port monitor and a properly associated port service are created to take care of incoming service requests.

6. Verify and add entries to uucp files as necessary. In particular, to be able to configure the modem using `cu`, you should have the following entry in the `/etc/uucp/Devices` file:

   ```
   Direct term/## - <speed >   direct
   ```

7. Using `cu`, establish a direct session with the modem and issue the AT commands to configure the modem properly. To establish the session, enter this command:

   ```
   #cu -l term/##
   ```

   If the system fails to connect, use the `-d` option with `cu`. This option prompts `cu` to report the progress of the dial-out process. Depending on what is displayed on the screen, refer to the appropriate documentation for help.

8. While in session with the modem, you should be able to dial out by entering this command:

   ```
   ATDT <phone_number>
   ```

   Remember: To exit, just enter the ~. character sequence.

9. If the modem is intended for dial-out use, test it by dialing into it. If it fails to respond properly, try the following troubleshooting tips: Verify that the modem is set to Autoanswer mode. Verify that echo is turned off. Verify that result codes are disabled (that is, that the modem is set for quiet mode). Make sure that you always write modem settings to the modem's nonvolatile memory using the `AT&W` command.

Connecting Terminals

Many of the preparatory steps required to connect terminals have already been described in the last two sections. To summarize, these steps are as follows:

- Depending on whether the terminal is connected directly or remotely to the system, you have to prepare either a cross-wired RS232C/D cable or a straight-through cable.

- In the case of remote connection, configure the modem connecting to the UNIX system for dial-in as described in "Connecting the Modem," earlier in this chapter.

- A port service should have been created, which, after detecting a service request (both DSR and CD are asserted), will write a login prompt to the port and transfer port control to the login process itself. This is achieved by entering the following pmadm command:

```
#pmadm -a -p<pmtag> -s<svctag> -i root -v'ttyadm -V' \
-m"'ttyadm -b -rn -p"login prompt message" -d/dev/term/## \
-l<label> -s /usr/bin/login'"
```

The use of the pmadm command to create port services was described earlier in this chapter.

One more step, described now, is to set the shell environment for proper support to the user's terminal.

UNIX is designed to shield programs from the specifics of physical terminal. Instead of talking directly to the terminal, programs interface with a virtual terminal by making calls to a standard library of screen routines. Those calls invoke, on behalf of programs, the desired behavior on the physical screen.

In doing so, two advantages are derived: Developers are relieved of the laborious and needless (if not impossible) task of writing and maintaining programs compatible with all kinds of terminal types (those existing now and those that will emerge in the future). And users continue to benefit, without any modifications or the associated cost of upgrades, from programs deployed on their UNIX platforms regardless of changes that may be introduced to their terminal types in the future.

Proper support for the actual terminal depends on setting the environment variable TERM to the correct type. This is normally done from the user's login script. The user can set it by entering the following command (assuming that the user's shell is the Korn shell):

```
$TERM=<terminal_type>
$export TERM
```

An example of *terminal type* is vt220.

UNIX uses the value assigned to *TERM* to reference a binary file, which exclusively defines that terminal's capabilities. The file is named after the terminal type (for example, if the terminal is vt220, the file is named vt220) and is part of a large terminal information database maintained in the /usr/lib/terminfo directory.

If you list the contents of the /usr/lib/terminfo directory, you obtain a listing similar to the following:

```
#ls /usr/lib/terminfo
1 3 5 7 9 B H P V b d f h j l n p r t v x z
2 4 6 8 A C M S a c e g i k m o q s u w y
```

Each letter or numeral is the directory name in which are saved terminal capabilities definition files pertaining to types starting with that letter or numeric. For example, if TERM is set to vt220, UNIX fetches the file /usr/lib/terminfo/v/vt220 for the terminal information capabilities (also referred to as *terminfo entry*).

> **NOTE**
>
> TERMCAP is another shell environment variable that should be set to the name of the directory in which the database is maintained.

After going through all the steps required to connect the terminal, you should connect it, bring it up, and attempt to log in. If the terminal is intended for modem access, it is a good idea to try a direct connection first. In any case, if you fail to get the login prompt and fail to log in, you may have to carry the following checks:

- Make sure that the port service is configured properly and that it is enabled. Use pmadm to do this check.

- Check the cable to verify that it is the correct one. Do not rely on the wiring diagram provided in this chapter; you are better off relying on your terminal and your modem vendor's documentation.

- Verify that the modem is configured to Autoanswer.

- Check the modem lights and verify that the sequence of events depicted by the flashing lights conforms to what you expect to see. In particular, check DSR and CD during the connection establishment phase because, unless they are both asserted, the login prompt won't be written to the tty port. Check the modem's hard and soft settings to address any observed anomalies.

- Make sure that the speed, parity, and number of stop bits match on both the terminal and the UNIX system.

Connecting Terminals and Modems Under BSD

Connecting terminals and modems under BSD is done differently from SVR4. The hardware setup, however, remains the same as in SVR4, and is therefore not repeated here.

As does AT&T SVR4, BSD UNIX requires that hardware devices be associated with a device special file in the /dev directory. Device special files for serial ports are normally created under tty## *name*. The ## refers to the port number. For example, tty02 refers to the second serial port.

Terminal Line Settings and Configuration Files (BSD)

Following are the configuration files supporting terminal lines under BSD:

/etc/ttys	Terminal line configuration file.
/etc/ttytab	This is SunOS's version of the /etc/ttys file. Both files are explained addressed shortly.
/etc/gettydefs	Terminal line settings database. Similar to /etc/tty-defs under SVR4. Consequently, this file isn't described here.
/etc/gettytab	Includes entries for initializing terminals to desired line speed(s). The following listing shows the contents of a sample /etc/gettytab file:

```
c¦std.300¦300-baud:\
    :nd#1:cd#1:ap#300:
f¦std.1200¦1200-baud:\
    :fd#1:sp#1200:
2¦std.9600¦9600-baud:\
    :sp#9600:
```

This gettytab file has entries for initializing terminals to three different baud rates: 300, 1200, and 9600 bits per second.

/etc/termcap	Terminal type definitions database. This database defines the capabilities of each of the terminal types it supports. Examples of supported terminal types are vt220 and wyse60. Again, this file is similar in contents and purpose to SVR4's /usr/lib/terminfo, which was explained earlier in this chapter.

The /etc/ttys file contains one record per serial port. The record provides details of resources associated with the serial port being supported, including pointers to information necessary for the proper initialization of this port by the init process.

Following is the syntax of that entries in /etc/ttys must comply with:

serial_port   *command*   *terminal_type*   *status*

For this syntax, the following are defined:

serial_port	The name of the special file in the /dev directory. Remember that special filenames, under BSD, assume the form tty##. tty00, for example, refers to /dev/tty00, the first serial port supported by the host.

29

DEVICE ADMINISTRATION

command	The name of the program that `init` must respawn to control and monitor this serial port. For most purposes, the program being specified (and consequently being invoked) is `getty`. Under BSD, `getty` is the counterpart to the `ttymon`-type port monitor under UNIX SVR4, described earlier in this chapter. Along with the specified command, a parameter specifying the line settings is normally included. The parameter provides a pointer to a record in the `/etc/gettytab` file. The following listing gives an example of the contents of the command field: `/usr/etc/getty std.9600`According to this command, `init` spawns `getty` on the affected port (described in the first field) and initializes it to 9600 bits per second. `std.9600` is just a label specification referencing a line setting in the `/etc/gettytab`, file as noted earlier.
terminal_type	The name of the terminal type being connected to the serial port. The type described in this field serves as a pointer to a record in the `/etc/termcap` terminal settings database. For example, if this field is set to `vt100`, the `/etc/termcap` database is searched for a record describing the capabilities of the `vt100` terminal. Subsequently, the corresponding `/etc/termcap` record is used to initialize the serial line for proper support of the connected terminal type.
	The *terminal_type* field supports options such as `network` (to imply virtual terminal), `unknown` (to imply modems or unknown terminals), and `dialup` (again, to imply modem lines).
status	This field can contain multiple keywords.Recognized keywords include the following:

on	The port is enabled.
off	The port is disabled. Consequently, the entry is ignored, and the affected port is left in an inactive state. *A port connected to a dial-out modem should be marked off.*
secure	Allows root login through this port. Otherwise, a user attempting to log in as a root using a terminal connected to this port will be refused connection.
window=*cmd*	This field causes init to execute the command specified in *cmd* before the command specified in the second field.

Here is a partial listing of the contents of a sample /etc/ttys file:

```
#name      getty command          type      status
console    /etc/getty std.9600     vt220     on secure
tty00      /etc/getty std.2400     vt100     on secure
tty01      /etc/getty std.19600    unknown   off
tty02      /etc/getty std.19600    dialup    on
tty03      /etc/getty std.19600    unknown   off # dialout
```

According to this file, the console is enabled (*status* is set to on), runs at 9600bps, and allows root login (*status* is set to secure). On the other hand, tty03 is disabled because it is used for dial-out purposes only. Using the second entry (that of tty00), for example, init initializes the first serial port to 2400bps by virtue of cross referencing the std.2400 parameter in the /etc/gettytab file. The terminal type being specified (that is, vt100) also serves as a pointer to the actual record describing the terminal capabilities as defined in the /etc/termcap file.

Adding the Terminal (BSD)

After the configuration files are updated to support the terminal pending connection, and after the hardware and serial cable are properly taken care of (as described earlier in this chapter), starting the new terminal line is a simple matter of sending init a hang-up signal (HUP) as follows:

```
# kill -1 1
```

29

DEVICE ADMINISTRATION

Following is an equivalent command:

```
# kill -HUP 1
```

By sending it a hang-up signal, `init` is forced to reinitialize itself by reading the configuration files. Consequently, `init` takes the proper action by spawning `getty` on the new port and initializing it to support for the specified line speed and the terminal types specified in the `/etc/ttys` file.

Adding a Modem (BSD)

Under BSD UNIX, connecting a modem to a serial port requires the creation of different device special files from those used to directly connect terminals. Under SunOS, for example, for dial-in modems, the device special file is usually called `/dev/ttyd`*n*, where *n* designates the modem line (starting with `0`). This means that `/dev/ttyd0` is the dial-in device file of the first modem line. For dial-out modems, the device file is named `/dev/cua`*n*, where *n* again corresponds to the modem line. Hence, `/dev/ttyd0` and `/dev/cua0` are the device files corresponding to dial-in and dial-out modems for the same line, respectively.

If you check the `/dev` directory, you may not find any of the files just mentioned. This is particularly true for systems that have never been required to connect to modems. In this case, you must create both files. Creating the `/dev/ttyd`*n* device is simple: It involves renaming to `/dev/ttyd`*n* the special device file corresponding to the physical port to which the modem will be connected. For example, if you want to connect a modem to the first physical serial port on your system, you rename the `/dev/ttya` file to `/dev/ttyd0` as follows:

```
# mv /dev/ttya  /dev/ttyd0
```

Creating the `/dev/cua0` file is a two-step process involving the use of the `mknod` command. Following is the general syntax of `mknod`:

```
mknod filename [c] ¦ [b] major minor
```

For this syntax, the following are defined:

filename	The name of the device special file. For the preceding example, this is `cua0`.
[c] ¦ [b]	The nature of the device undergoing creation. `c` indicates a raw device. A *raw device* deals with characters individually rather than in blocks of characters. `b` indicates a block device. For modems, the device of choice is a raw device. Therefore, this parameter should be always set to `c`.

major	The major device number. The major device number designates the device class. Put differently, *major* acts more like a pointer to the device driver routines in the kernel that support this class of devices (the serial device driver in our case).
minor	The minor device number. It designates the device subtype within the device class. For the preceding example, the minor device number corresponding to cua0 provides a pointer to the modem dial-out routines within the driver designated by *major*.

Finding out the major and minor numbers corresponding to the dial-out line of choice is a simple matter of following these two steps:

1. Use the ls -l /dev/ttyd*n* command to determine the major and minor numbers of the corresponding ttyd*n* device:

   ```
   # ls -l /dev/ttyd0
   crw--w--w- 1 root     12,    0 Nov 26    22:25    /dev/ttyd0
   ```

   In this example, 12 is the major number and 0 is the minor number.

2. The /dev/cua*n* device corresponding to the /dev/ttyd*n* port should have its major number identical to that of /dev/ttyd*n*; its minor number should be 128 more than that of /dev/ttyd*n*. For the preceding example, this implies that the major and minor numbers corresponding to /dev/cua0 should be set to 12 and 128. Use the following mknod(1M) command to create this file:

   ```
   # mknod cua0    c  12   128
   ```

After the cua*n* device file is created, you must secure it by changing its ownership to uucp and the permissions to 600, as shown here:

```
# chmod 600 /dev/cua0
# chown uucp /dev/cua0
```

Now that both /dev/ttyd0 (the dial-in device file) and /dev/cua0 (the dial-out device file) are created, what remains (aside from configuring the modem and attaching it to the port as described earlier in this chapter) is to update the /etc/ttytab file as described in the previous section.

Connecting Terminals and Modems Under Linux

Because Linux is a BSD variant of UNIX, you connect terminals and modems to Linux using most of the steps described in the previous sections—with a few subtle differences:

29

DEVICE
ADMINISTRATION

- Instead of being a four-column file, /etc/ttys (the terminal configuration file) contains two columns only: The first column contains the name of the serial port being supported. The second column contains a label identifying the type of the terminal being associated with this port (that is, being connected to the port). The terminal type label is cross-referenced in the /etc/termcap file in a similar fashion to how SunOS or other BSD systems treat it.

- Rather than identifying the line speed setting and command (such as getty) that control the port in the /etc/ttys file (similar to how SunOS does it), these elements are taken care of in the /etc/inittab file. Here is a sample entry:

  ```
  d1:2345:respawn:/sbin/getty  ttyS0 38400
  ```

  According to this entry, getty is respawned by init while the system is in any of 2, 3, 4, or 5 run levels. The port being controlled is ttyS0 (that is, the first serial port: COM1). 38400 is a label designating an entry in the /etc/gettydefs file (the line settings database, described earlier in this chapter).

- Modem lines have /dev/ttyS*n* for device filenames, where *n* ranges from 0 to 3 corresponding to serial ports COM1 through COM2, respectively. You do not have to create these files; they are created during installation time.

CREATING ttySn DEVICE FILE

Should your Linux system fail to have any of the /dev/ttyS*n* files, you can easily create the appropriate file by using mknod in a similar way to the description provided in the previous section. Major and minor numbers corresponding to any of the devices are well defined in the man pages. To look up the exact details of the mknod command that applies, enter this command:

```
# man ttys
```

Connecting Printers

Printing services in UNIX are supported by the LP print spooler. The LP print spooler allows administrators to address varied scenarios to meet different user needs and requirements. To name a few of these capabilities, print services can be physically set up to allow users to print on printers connected to the host they are logged in to or, alternatively, to printers connected to other hosts on the network. LP printing services include a library of filters from which administrators can choose to support their users' needs. By implementing these filters, users' print jobs will be processed, making them more "compatible" with the target printer. Administrators are provided with management capabilities that allow them to use global management as well as selective management of print services. Because this chapter is about "Device Administration," the objectives of this section are limited to the following topics:

- A conceptual overview of the LP printing service
- Setup of local printing services
- Setup of network print servers
- Printer management
- Printer user management

How the LP Print Service Works (SVR4, Solaris 2.x)

Print services are invoked by running `init` ar startup when the system enters the multiuser state run level 2. The services are brought up by the `/etc/rc2.d/S80lp` script and are killed whenever the system is shut down by the `/etc/rc2.d/K20lp` script.

When users address printers to handle their print jobs, the files they send for printing are not handled immediately by the printers. Instead, the files are queued in directories, by a process known as the *spooler*, for subsequent handling by a printing daemon known as `lpsched` (an acronym and program name for the LP scheduler daemon). To understand how this works, imagine yourself as part of a community of users sharing one or two printers (among other UNIX resources). Ask yourself what would happen if you could address the printer directly for a print request while someone else was doing exactly the same thing. You are right: The output would be more of a character soup than a presentable piece of work. This would happen because the printer handles characters as they arrive, and would mix the characters that belong to your file with those that belong to other users.

To alleviate this problem, the print spooler takes over as you send print jobs to printers. It simply stops the jobs on their way to their destination and diverts them to a waiting area on your system disk. This area is a subdirectory known as the *print queue*. Files destined for the same printer are queued in the same directory until the printer becomes available. This process is known as *spooling*. You may wonder whether the spooling process means that the terminal will be tied up for as long as it takes the print job to materialize. The answer is *no*. After a print job is queued, another background process known as the *printing scheduler daemon* (`lpsched`) takes over and supervises the ongoing printing services, making sure that every request—including yours—is honored.

In addition to this basic service, LP printing services allow administrators to aggregate printers of similar type into a printer class. This arrangement provides for the optimal use of printing resources because users target a *class* of printers instead of targeting a specific printer. When this happens, lpsched sends the print job to the first printer to become available in the requested class. Other printing services include tasks pertaining to starting interface programs suitable for the printer, applying the filters to user files whenever necessary, and notifying users (if they want notification) of the status of their print jobs. In the case of network printing, the LP printing service has the additional job of sending print jobs to the hosts to which the requested printers are connected.

> **NOTE**
>
> The print daemon on BSD-derived UNIX systems (such as Linux) is lpd. BSD systems do not recognize the print classes that SVR4 supports.

Setting Up Local Printing Services (SVR4, Solaris 2.x)

This section presents the setup and configuration of local printing services. Local printing services allow users to print to printers connected directly to the host they are logged in to. Following are the required steps to set up printers—regardless of whether they are parallel, serial, or network printers:

1. Verify the availability of resources.
2. Use lpadmin to create the printer.
3. Change ownership and permissions to devise special files.
4. If this is your first printer, make it the default printer.
5. Release the printer to the user community.

The resources for which you want to check are lp login id, lpsched, and an available port (serial or parallel). The lp login id is normally created during initial system installation. If the lp account does not exist in the /etc/passwd directory, you must create one. It will be required later in the setup process. You must also verify that lpsched is running by checking the output of this command:

```
#ps -ef ¦ grep "lpsched"
```

If lpsched is not enabled, you can do so by entering the following command:

```
#/usr/lib/lp/lpsched
```

The next step is to create a print destination by using the `lpadmin` command. The syntax of `lpadmin` is shown here:

```
/usr/lib/lpadmin -p<name> -v<pathname> -m<interface> \
[-h¦l] - c<class>
```

For this syntax, the following are defined:

`-p<name>`	The name you want to assign to the printer. It can be anything you like. It is more convenient, however, to assign it a name that makes sense to the user community.
`-v<pathname>`	The special device file pathname. Depending on whether the printer is parallel or serial, the pathname is /dev/lp# or /dev/term/## (# and ## are decimal digits representative of the parallel and serial ports on your system).
`-m<interface>`	A program invoked by `lp` as it sends print jobs to the printer port. `<interface>` is responsible for printer port and physical printer initialization, and performs functions pertaining to printing a banner if desired, producing the correct number of copies, and setting the page length and width. You have the freedom to write and use your own interface programs (in which case, you must specify its name using the `-i<interface>` option). If you do not specify one, the standard and generic interface supplied with the system is used by default. When installing the printer for the first time, it is advisable to start with the standard interface. If all goes well, you can always change over to the interface of your choice. Printer interfaces are usually maintained in the /usr/lib/lp/model directory.
`[-h¦l]`	h indicates that the printer is hardwired; l indicates that the device associated with the printer is a login terminal. h and l are mutually exclusive. In the event that neither is specified, h is assumed.
`-c<class>`	Specifies the class to which the printer belongs. Users can subsequently specify the class by using `lp` with `-d` option.

Assuming that you want to create a printer destination for a parallel printer to be connected to your parallel port, the `lpadmin` command you use would look like this:

29

DEVICE ADMINISTRATION

```
#lpadmin -d dotmatrix -v /dev/lp1 -m standard
#lpadmin
```

Because the printer port device special file can be written to directly, as with any other file, you should make sure that users have no direct access to it. Change the port owner-ship to login `lp` and change the file permissions to `600`. The following two commands demonstrate how to do this to `/dev/lp1`:

```
#chown lp  /dev/lp1
#chmod 600 /dev/lp1
```

Before you release the printer to the user community, you may want to make it the default destination. If a user fails to specify the printer destination when using the `lp` command, the print job is sent to the default printer. To make a printer the default desti-nation, enter the following command:

```
#lpadmin -d <printer_name>
```

The `lpadmin` command to make `dotmatrix` the default printer is shown here:

```
#lpadmin -d dotmatrix
```

Finally, to make the printer accessible to users, you must allow the printer destination to accept print jobs as well as logically turn on the printer. To allow printer `dotmatrix` to accept print jobs, enter this command:

```
#accept dotmatrix
```

To logically turn it on (that is, to allow it to do the printing), enter this command:

```
#enable dotmatrix
```

Setting Up Network Print Servers (SVR4, Solaris 2.x)

In a multisystem, multiplatform environment, users sometimes find themselves in need of printers attached to a different system than the one they are currently logged in to. Figure 29.7 shows a scenario in which the user wants the print job sent to printer `odie`, attached to system `engg`, while logged in to system `arts`.

If implemented properly, UNIX comes with enough support that users can print to any printer on the network. Users do not even have to be concerned with any additional details about how to address those printers than they already know about addressing their own local printers. In the scenario shown in Figure 29.7, system `engg` becomes the so-called print server; system `arts` is the client. The setup procedure has print destinations (that is, queues) created on both systems (for example, `odie` on `engg` and `garfield` on arts). odie is associated with the printer attached to engg,; garfield has to be logically associated with odie (not with any printer that may happen to be attached to system arts). A user logged in to arts has to address the local printer destination—in this case garfield—to be able to print to odie. The lp print request then becomes the following:

```
#lp -p garfield <file_name>
```

In doing so, the user is in fact addressing the local LP print service running on system arts. Next, LP on system arts checks the actual resource with which printer destination garfield is associated to find that it actually maps to a print service resource (odie) supported on system engg. As a consequence, LP on system arts routes the request, along with the print job, to engg for subsequent handling.

The steps involved in setting up the service are not as complex as they may sound. For the most part, they are similar to those listed in the previous section with some subtle variations. Because this level of service involves both the client and server systems, both of them must be configured.

FIGURE 29.7.

The concept of print servers.

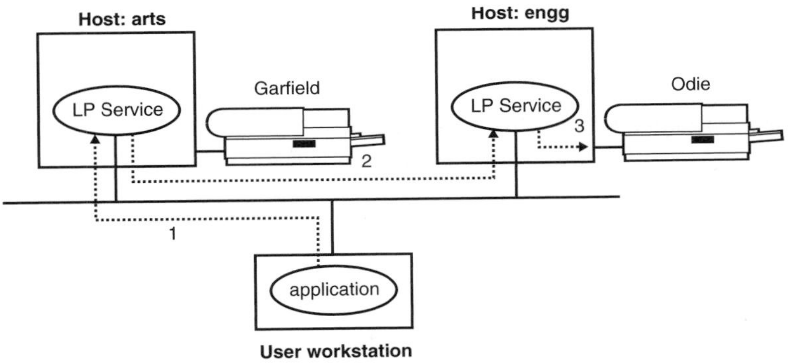

Configuring the Print Server

Print server configuration requires two steps in addition to those listed and described in the section on local printing. The two steps are creating a listen port service and registering client systems with the print service.

Because the print service under description is a network service (that is, it runs on a connection-oriented transport service), there is a requirement to create a listen port service with which it associates. Before doing that, however, it may be worth your while to check readily available ones. When UNIX is first installed, your system is automatically configured to support a listen port monitor with port monitor tag tcp. tcp is configured to support two print server-associated port services: one takes care of System V clients and the other one takes care of BSD clients. To verify their existence, enter the following command:

```
#pmadm -l -t listen
PMTAG             PMTYPE          SVCTAG          FLGS ID      <PMSPECIFIC>
.
.
.
tcp                     listen              0                      x
        root    \x02000ACE64000001 --
 c -- /usr/lib/saf/nlps_server #NLPS SERVER
tcp                     listen              lp                     --
        root    -- -- -- -- /var/spool/lp
/fifos/listenS5 #NLPS SERVER
.
.
```

If the listing you get on your screen includes the two entries shown in the preceding partial listing, you do not have to create the port services and you can skip the next step. If these entries do not exist, use pmadm to create them. To create a port service to listen to print requests sent by System V clients, enter this command:

```
#pmadm -a -p<pmtag> -s lp -i root -v 'nlsadmin -V' \
-m 'nlsadmin -o /var/spool/lp/fifos/listenS5'
```

In this syntax, *pmtag* is the name assigned to the port monitor. To create a port service to respond to BSD clients, however, you must enter lpsystem -A. The output displays the port address you use as an argument with nlsadmin after using pmadm to create the port service. Following is the sample output from the lpsystem -A command as it appears on my monitor:

```
#lpsystem -A
0200020364000001000000000000000000
```

Next, to create the port service under tcp port monitor, enter the following command:

```
#pmadm -a -p tcp -s lpd -i root -v 'nlsadmin -V' \
-m'nlsadmin -o /var/spool/lp/fifos/listenBSD \
-A'\x0200020364000001000000000000000000''
```

To force the port monitor to recognize the changes you made, use this command:

```
#sacadm -x -p tcp
```

The next step is to register the client with the server using the lpsystem command. In addition to registering the client, lpsystem allows you to define the communications parameters you want to enforce on the connection maintained between both the server and the client after it is invoked. Defined parameters are saved in the /etc/lp/Systems file. Although you can edit this file directly using vi, it is recommended that you avoid doing that. The syntax of the lpsystem command is shown here:

```
lpsystem [-t<type>] [-T<timeout>] [-R <retry>] \
[-y"comment"] systemname
```

For this syntax, the following are defined:

-t<type>	Specifies whether the client is System V or BSD.
-T<timeout>	Specifies the idle time after which the connection should be terminated. The <timeout> can be n, 0, or N, where N is the number of minutes the connection idles before the connection is dropped. If 0 is specified, the connection is dropped as soon as it idles; n means never time out. Depending on your environment, you should configure the connection to the one that suits you best. If users occasionally print across the network, you may be better off with the 0 option. This option frees up the resources reserved on both systems to service the request as soon as it is honored. If, on the other hand, the frequency of service use is high, consider configuring the connection to n (never time out). This way, you save both systems the repeated tasks of establishing, maintaining, and relinquishing the connection every time they have to respond to a print service request. Added to the saving in CPU usage on both systems is the saving on bandwidth usage because of packet exchange pertaining to link establishment and disconnection.
-R<retry>	Specifies, in minutes, the duration of time to wait before link reestablishment is attempted, when it was abnormally disrupted.
-y"comment"	Can be any convenient comment.
systemname	Specifies the remote system's name to which the communications parameters apply.

Let's apply the preceding information to the example shown in Figure 29.7: If we want to register arts with the print server host engg, we enter the following command:

```
#lpsystem -t s5 -T n arts
```

Configuring the Client

As you do when setting up the server, when configuring the client, you should make sure that you have a port monitor that is properly configured to support network printing services. To do that, enter this command

```
#pmadm -l -p tcp
```

The output should include the following three entries (the first two pertain to System V support and the third one pertains to BSD client support):

```
PMTAG  PMTYPE  SVCTAG FLGS  ID  <PMSPECIFIC>
tcp    listen  0       -         root \x00200ACE64000001 -c -
/usr/lib/sac/nlps_server #NLPS SERVER

tcp    listen  lp      -         root ....

tcp    listen  lpd     -         root \x0020020364000001 -c -
/var/spool/lp/fifos/listenBSD
```

If any of the preceding entries is missing, you must create the associated port services yourself using pmadm. Depending on what is missing, use one or more of the following commands:

```
#pmadm -a -p tcp -s lp -i root -v'nlsadmin -V' \
-m 'nlsadmin -o /var/spool/lp/fifos/listen5'

#pmadm -a -p tcp -s 0 -i root -v 'nlsadmin -V' \
-m 'nlsadmin -o /usr/lib/saf/nlps_server \
-A "\x02000ACE6400000010000000000000000"` -y "NLPS SERVER"

#pmadm -a -p tcp -s lpd -i root -v 'nlsadmin -V' \
-m 'nlsadmin -o /var/spool/lp/fifos/listenBSD \
-A "\x002020364000001000000000000000000"`
```

The last pmadm command is required only if you are setting up for BSD support as well.

Next, you must register the remote server with the client using the lpsystem command, as discussed in the preceding section.

Now you have only to create the printer destination. Instead of associating it with any particular port, you associate it with the printer destination you created on the print server host. To do that, enter the following command:

```
#lpadmin -p<client_printer> \
-s<remote_printer>!<print_server_host>
```

For this syntax, the following are defined:

`client_printer`	Specifies the printer destination undergoing creation on the local machine.
`remote_printer`	Specifies the print server's printer destination, with which the `client_printer` is associated.
`print_server_host`	Specifies the host name of the system where the `remote_printer` destination is.

Applying the preceding information to the scenario in Figure 29.7, the following is the command to enter at host `arts`:

```
#lpadmin -p odie -s garfield!engg
```

The remaining steps, as you should know by now, are to enable the printer and make it accept print jobs. To do that, you enter the following commands:

```
#enable odie
#accept odie
```

To send a print job down the wire to `garfield` to print, the user must address `odie` while logged in to `arts`. For example, to print file `monalisa`, the user enters this command:

```
#lp -p odie monalisa
```

LP print service on host `arts` will redirect the print job to the `garfield` destination on host `engg`.

Managing Printers

In addition to the tools required to set up, enable, and disable printers, the LP print service presents the system administrator with a comprehensive set of management tools. Those tools can be used to change printer configuration as well to assist in maintenance and troubleshooting situations. The following sections describe aspects of the print management and associated tools.

Enabling and Disabling LP Print Service

`lpsched` is the program you use to start LP print service; `lpshut` is the program you use to shut it down. Only `login root` or `lp` can start and shut down printing services. All printers that were printing at the time `lpshut` is invoked will stop printing. Whenever `lpsched` is restarted, print requests that were disrupted at the time LP service was shut down will print from the very beginning.

Managing Print Requests

The `lpmove` command lets you move print jobs from one printer to another. There are two basic scenarios that may prompt you to move print jobs: You may want to disable printing to a printer so that you can disconnect it for routine maintenance or troubleshooting. Instead of leaving your users in the cold waiting for their print jobs to materialize, you can move their print jobs to some other printer of equivalent quality. In the second scenario, you use `lpmove` to balance the loads on printers when you notice that one printer is heavily used while another printer is sitting idle.

The syntax of the `lpmove` command is shown here:

```
#lpmove <requests> <dest>. Or,
```

In this syntax, *requests* presents `lpmove` with a list of request IDs to move to the printer specified in *dest*. To obtain the print request IDs, use the `lpstat` command. Its output looks like this:

```
#lpstat
garfield-4 root 112 March 24 06:20
garfield-5 root 567 March 24 06:22
```

The first column holds the print request ID, which is made of two components: the name of the printer to which the print job was submitted, and the order in which the print job was received. The second column displays the name of the user who submitted the print job, followed by columns containing the date and time of submission.

Assuming that `acctlp` is an idling printer to which you want to move the print job `garfield-5`, issue the following `lpmove` command:

```
#lpmove garfield-5 acctlp
```

To move the entire printing load from one printer to another, enter this command:

```
#lpmove <dest1> <dest2>
```

> **NOTE**
>
> After moving print requests, request that the IDs remain intact to allow users to track their print jobs.

> **CAUTION**
>
> lpmove does not check the acceptance status of the print jobs it moves. It is your responsibility to do the check using the lpstat command, and to take any corrective measure should a print job fail to be moved.

To cancel undesirable print requests, use the cancel command. The syntax is as follows:

```
#cancel <request-ID>
```

For example, to cancel garfield-5, enter this command:

```
#cancel garfield-ID
```

Printer Configuration Management

Printer configuration management includes tasks such as changing printer class, changing printer port, removing printers, and removing classes. All these tasks can be achieved using the lpadmin command.

To change a printer class, enter this command:

```
#lpadmin -p<dest> -c<class>
```

If the specified class does not exist, the class is created and the specified destination is inserted into it.

To remove the printer from a certain class, enter this command:

```
#lpadmin -p<dest> -r <class>
```

If the printer is the last one of its class, the class itself is also removed.

To change the printer port, enter this command:

```
#lpadmin -p<dest> -v <special_file_pathname>
```

You may have to change the printer port on occasions when you suspect that something went wrong with the original port to which the printer was connected. This reconfiguration allows you to continue offering print services while troubleshooting the defective port.

Finally, to check the configuration of a particular printer, enter this command:

```
#lpstat -p<printer> -l
```

In the following example, lpstat is entered to check the configuration of garfield destination:

```
#lpstat  — pgarfield  — l
printer garfield (login terminal) is idle. enabled since Thu Mar 24
18:20:01 EST 1994. available.
    Form mounted:
    Content types: simple
    Printer types: unknown
    Description:
    Connection: direct
    Interface: /usr/lib/lp/model/standard
    On fault: mail to root once
    After fault: continue
    Users allowed:
        (all)
    Forms allowed:
        (none)
    Banner required
    Character sets:
        (none)
    Default pitch:
    Default page size:
    Default port settings:
```

If you want to check the configuration of all printers, enter this simplified version of the command:

```
#lpstat -l
```

Print Service User Management

You can manage and restrict user access to LP print services on UNIX systems for security reasons or for resource allocation and management.

If you carefully examine the sample output of the lpstat -p garfield -l command in the last example, you will see the names of the users who are allowed access in the Users allowed entry. According to the preceding example, no one is on either the allowed or the denied list. This fact corresponds to the default security configuration; it implies that any logged-in user can send print jobs to printer garfield. If you do not like that arrangement, however, you can use lpadmin with the -u option to restrict access to the printer.

To list the users on the allowed list, the syntax of the lpadmin -u command is shown here:

```
#lpadmin -p<printer> -u allow:<login-ID-list>
```

To prevent users from accessing the printer, enter the following command:

```
#lpadmin -p<printer> -u deny:<login-ID-list>
```

> **NOTE**
>
> The `login-ID-list` in the preceding syntax lines is a comma-delimited or space-separated list of user login IDs.

Following is a list of legal arguments you can include in the `login-ID-list`:

`login-ID`	Denotes a user on the local system.
`system_name!login-ID`	Denotes a user on a client system.
`system_name!all`	Denotes all users on a client system.
`all!login-ID`	Denotes a user on all systems.
`all`	Denotes all users on the local system.
`all!all`	Denotes all users on all systems.

For each printer, the LP print service maintains denied and allowed lists. The way they are used is summarized in the following paragraphs:

- If the allowed list is not empty, only the users in that list are allowed access to the printer. If the allowed list is empty but the denied list is not, all users *except* those on the denied list are allowed access to the printer.

- A user cannot exist on both lists simultaneously. When a user is added to either list, the user's login-ID is removed from the other list.

For example, to allow users Nadeem, Andrea, and May access to the printer garfield, enter the following command:

```
#lpadmin -p garfield -u allow;Nadeem Andrea May
```

Now check that this indeed took place by entering the following command:

```
#lpadmin -p garfield -l
```

```
printer garfield (login terminal) is idle.
enabled since Tue Apr 12 05:18:07 EDT 1994. not available.
    Form mounted:
    Content types: simple
    Printer types: unknown
    Description:
    Connection: direct
```

29

DEVICE ADMINISTRATION

```
Interface: /usr/lib/lp/model/standard
On fault: mail to root once
After fault: continue
Users allowed:
    nadeem
    andrea
    may
Forms allowed:
    (none)
Banner required
Character sets:
    (none)
Default pitch:
Default page size:
Default port settings:
```

Users who know about the lp command's -q option can assign print queue priority levels to print jobs they submit to the LP service. Although assigning print priority can some-times be a useful feature, it can prove to be a cause of concern: Some members of the user community may find that their print jobs are constantly delayed in favor of those jobs belonging to others. Fortunately, the LP print service allows you to set limits on how high a priority can be a assigned to print jobs submitted by users. Using the lpusers command, you can assign different priority limit assignments to different users. The syntax of lpusers is as follows:

```
#lpusers -q<priority_level> -u<login-ID-list>
```

For this syntax, the following are defined:

-q<*priority_level*>	An integer ranging from 0 to 39, with 0 representing the highest priority level.
-u<*login-ID-list*>	A comma-delimited or space-separated list of user IDs to whom the restriction applies. The *login-ID list* argument can have any of the following values:

login-ID	Denotes a user.
system_name!login-ID	Denotes a user on a particular system.
system_name!all	Denotes all users on a particular system.
all	Denotes all users.
all!login-ID	Denotes a user on all systems.

Users submitting print jobs can assign priorities to the jobs as high as they are allowed to assign as specified by the -q option.

Setting Up Local Printing on BSD Systems

Setting up printing on BSD systems involves making changes to the /etc/printcap file, creating the spooling directory (also known as the *print queue*), and editing the /etc/rc file so that the lpd spooling daemon starts at boot time. The following sections describe these steps.

The /etc/printcap File

The /etc/printcap file is a database file that contains one record for every attached or enabled printer. In addition to defining the printer characteristics, /etc/printcap records include printer configuration information that is vital to supporting the printer properly. This file includes records for both local and network printers.

Following is an example of what an /etc/printcap record should look like:

```
# printcap entry for printer goofy
goofy¦lp:\
    :lp=/dev/ttya;br#9600:\
    :ms=-parity,onlcr,ixon:\
    :sd=/var/spool/goofy:\
    :lf=/var/adm/goofy_errors:\
    :pl=66:pw=132:
```

As shown in this entry, /etc/printcap entries contains colon-separated fields. Additionally, the last field must end with a colon (:). The first field of each entry must start with the name by which the printer is known. Printer names are pipe (¦) character-separated. In the preceding example, the printer being defined is known as goofy and lp. In fact, lp is a special alias that designates the printer as the default printer. In other words, by virtue of assigning printer goofy the lp printer name, users who submit a print job without specifying the printer name have their jobs sent to goofy. Consequently, only one printer can be assigned the special name lp, thus designating it as the default printer.

Fields following the name field are introduced by a two-character code. A field describing a numerical value takes the form *code#* (br#9600, in the preceding example). Otherwise, the field takes the form *code=* (for example, sd=/var/spool/goofy). Following is an explanation of the remaining fields:

lp	This field specifies the device filename to be printed to. In this case, it is the first serial port (/dev/ttya on SunOS, or /dev/ttyS0 on Linux).

29

DEVICE ADMINISTRATION

br	This field specifies the baud rate at which the printer operates. In this case, **9600** bps is specified.
ms	This field describes to the print daemon (`lpd`) the printer characteristics that `lpd` should observe when printing. In this example, the printer is set to no parity, a new line should be printed as a pair of carriage return/linefeed characters, and the XON/XOFF software flow control is supported.
sd	This field specifies the spooling directory, in which the print jobs are held pending printing. This directory must exist before printing to the associated printer is attempted. It should also have been created with proper permissions. In the preceding example, the spooling directory belonging to printer `goofy` is specified as `/var/spool/goofy`.
lf	This field specifies the path of the error log file pertaining to the printer. When there is trouble printing to the printer, `lpd` logs error messages to this file. This file should have its permissions set to **666**. As system administrator, it is your responsibility to create this file before usage of the printer is allowed.
pl	This field sets the page length. In this example, it is set to 66 lines/page.
pw	This field sets the page width. In this example, it is set to 132 characters/line.

Many more fields can be included in the `/etc/printcap` file than have just been described. You will find, however, that the preceding fields are the most commonly used. The man pages on `/etc/printcap` provide a comprehensive list of all the supported field codes, including a description of each.

Following is a self-explanatory example of an `/etc/printcap` entry for parallel printer support:

```
lp¦HPLaser:\
    :lp=/dev/lp:\
    :sd=/var/spool/lp:\
    :pl=66:pw=132:\
    :lf=/var/spool/laser_errors:
```

Setting Up Spooling Directories

Every printer must have a dedicated spooling directory. Setting up the spooling directory involves creating it, changing its permissions to 755, changing its ownership to special user daemon, and changing its group to the group daemon. You should be logged in as root when creating and setting up the spooling directories. Following is the command sequence necessary to set up the spooling directory for printer goofy:

```
# mkdir /var/spool/goofy
# chown daemon /var/spool/goofy
# chgrp daemon /var/spool/goofy
# chmod 755 /var/spool/goofy
```

Fixing access permissions to 755 on the spooling directory protects it from abusive manipulation by other users, which can result in the accidental or malicious deletion of print jobs.

> **CAUTION**
>
> Make sure that whenever you set up your system for serial printing, you disable getty from controlling the port to which you intend to attach the printer. On a SunOS system, this involves updating the /etc/ttytab file and marking off the last field of the entry corresponding to the desired serial line. In Linux, you disable getty access by replacing the primitive respawn with off in the entry corresponding to the port in the /etc/inittab file.

The preceding commands are the minimal steps required to set up printing on BSD systems. To ensure that the print spooling daemon is activated at boot time, check the /etc/rc startup script and make sure that the following lines of code are *not* commented:

```
if [ -f /usr/lib/lpd ]; then
    rm -f /dev/printer /usr/spool.lock
    /usr/lib/lpd; echo -n 'printer' > /dev/console
fi
```

To test the viability of the printer setup, use the lpr command to print a test page as in the following example:

```
# lpr -P goofy testfile
```

Setting Up Network Printing Under BSD

Setting up network printing under BSD is far less complex than setting up network printing under UNIX SVR4. As in UNIX SVR4, the setup includes configuring both the print server (the host to which the shared printer is attached) and the client (the host printing to the shared printer).

Setting up the shared printer on the server is no different than setting up a local printer. The steps are identical to those described earlier in this chapter. You need not do anything special to allow for printer sharing—aside from ensuring that hosts authorized to access the server for printing services have their names in the /etc/hosts.equiv file on the server host.

Configuring the client to recognize and print to remote printers involves adding a simple entry, similar to the following one, in the /etc/printcap file:

```
lp¦remote printer¦:\
    :lp=:rm=tenor;rp=goofy;sd=/var/spool/lpd:
```

According to this entry, the client print daemon recognizes the remote printer as being the default printer. Because the lp field is left blank (that is, lp=), the printer is assumed remote and is attached to remote machine tenor (rm=tenor). The rp=goofy capability identifies the remote printer name as goofy, and sd identifies the /var/spool/lpd directory as being the corresponding spooling directory.

To print to the remote printer, the user runs the lpr command. No special options or command-line parameters are required to make it work with nonlocal printers. If the remote printer is the client's default printer, simply enter the following:

```
# lpr filename
```

Otherwise, use the following form for the lpr command:

```
# lpr -P printername filename
```

In this syntax, *printername* is the name by which the printer is known locally, *not* its name as set on the remote host.

Managing Print Services Under BSD

As does UNIX SVR4, BSD provides the tools necessary to properly manage and administer printing service. The lpc and lpq commands help you do most administrative tasks.

Using lpc, a system administrator can manage printers defined in the /etc/printcap file. lpc includes support for starting, restarting, and stopping a printer daemon; for selectively enabling or disabling a particular printer; for displaying the printer status, the status of the printer daemon, and the status of the print queues; and for reordering print jobs in a given queue.

In its basic form, `lpc` assumes the following syntax:

```
lpc   [command [parameter]]
```

In this syntax, *command* specifies the action you want `lpc` to take on the object specified by *parameter*. If no command is entered, `lpc` is invoked in an interactive mode as shown here:

```
# lpc
lpc>
```

You can enter commands and respond to questions interactively at the `lpc>` prompt, as shown here:

```
# /usr/etc/lpc
lpc> down goofy
lpc>
```

Typically, *parameter* specifies the printer name. Supported commands include the following:

help, ?	Provides help on using `lpc`.
abort	Terminates an active spooling `daemon` and consequently disables printing to printers specified by *parameter*.
clean	Deletes all print jobs from the spooling directory pertaining to the printer(s) specified in *parameter*.
disable	Disables the specified print queues and prevents users from submitting new print jobs to these queues.
down	Disables both printing and queues pertaining to specified queues. Also allows you to include a message to broadcast to users advising them of the event and the reasons behind it. See the man pages for details.
enable	Enables spooling to specified spooling directories.
exit	Exits from an interactive `lpc` session.
restart	Restarts a printer daemon. Typically used when a daemon dies unexpectedly because of abnormal conditions.
start	Starts a printer daemon.

status	Reports the status of queues and printers on the local machine.
stop	Stops the spooling daemon after the current job completes printing and disables the printer.
topq	Moves specified print job(s) to the top of the queue.
up	Reverses actions taken by the down command, including starting a new print spooling daemon.

Refer to the man pages for details on using the lpc command.

Connecting a PC to UNIX Systems

Rather than purchase terminals, many users prefer to run UNIX sessions right from their desktop DOS, NT, Windows 95, or Windows 98 PCs or workstations. This situation has arisen because of the low cost of the PC, its increased processing power, and the additional flexibility of being able to easily toggle back and forth between PC applications and a UNIX session. The following sections describe two methods by which you can establish a connection with a UNIX system using the PC platform. The two methods are as follows:

- Establishing a session over a serial port
- Establishing a session using TCP/IP

Connecting the PC Using COM Ports

Depending on how you are going to do it, configuring a PC to connect to a UNIX host over a COM port is the easier and less costly of the two methods. If both systems belong to the same site, and there is no requirement for a telephone wire to connect the machines, then a cross-wired cable is all the additional hardware you need—along with the COM port that is readily available on the PC. Any communications software with decent terminal-emulation capabilities can be used to emulate some of the terminals UNIX recognizes.

Configuring a PC to serially connect to a UNIX host involves some preparation on both systems. Before making any move, however, check the availability of the following resources:

- **On the PC:** Verify that you have a free COM port, and that its use of the IRQ interrupt number and I/O port address does not conflict with any other interface cards on the machine.

- **On the UNIX hosts:** Verify the availability of a `tty` port and a suitable terminal line setting record in the `/etc/ttydefs` file (refer to "Determine the Availability of Resources," earlier in this chapter).

Additional requirements include two modems and two straight-through cables (if you are configuring a connection over a telephone wire) or a cross-wired cable, as discussed earlier in this chapter (to directly connect the PC to the UNIX system).

Configuring the UNIX system to support `tty` port services was discussed earlier in this chapter.

Configuring the PC is a simple matter that basically involves configuring the communication software to the same communication parameters implemented on the UNIX side of the connection. The parameters include baud rate, number of bits per character, parity, and number of stop bits.

Configuring the Modems

Following are general guidelines you should observe when configuring the modems:

- Make sure that the modem you are installing at the UNIX end supports quiet mode. This mode is required to stop the modem from sending response codes to the port.

- Echo should be disabled.

   Failure to observe these first two rules may result in having the UNIX system "believe" that the echoed characters are in partial response to the login prompt it sent to the PC. This may lead to an endless sequence of login and password prompts.

   Should you run into the problem of having user sessions unexpectedly suspending, try to re-create the problem. If, after manually sending an XON (press Ctrl+Q), character communications resume, you may have to disable XON/OFF flow control and rely only on RTS/CTS.

- Set the modem connected to the UNIX system to Autoanswer mode.

Connecting to UNIX Using TCP/IP

TCP/IP (Transmission Control Protocol/Internet Protocol)is another way by which you can connect PCs in your environment to the UNIX system. This solution, however, is a bit more expensive than using COM ports. The extra expense comes from the investment in the network interface card (NIC) and the necessary software for implementing the TCP/IP suite of protocols—in addition to the cabling costs incurred per workstation. However, given the advantages of this solution, and depending on the intended use of the connection, you may find it worth the money and effort to take this route.

Using TCP/IP, you can not only establish a Telnet session with the host, you can also use `ftp` for file transfers between the PC and UNIX, and `rsh` to remotely execute a UNIX command without necessarily having to log in to the system. You can also use the Telnet feature in Windows 95/98 to invoke multiple UNIX Telnet sessions simultaneously. You can also cut and paste to your heart's desire between your UNIX sessions and your Windows-based applications.

As with the COM port option, with the TCP/IP approach, you must set up both ends of the connection properly for them to communicate.

The method you use to install TCP/IP on the PC depends to a large degree on the vendor from whom you purchased the software. You are required, however, to do the following:

- Assign the PC an IP address.
- Assign the PC a host name.
- Create a `hosts` file on the PC. Include in the file the name to use to address mappings that correspond to all the UNIX hosts to which the user has enough access rights. If Domain Name Services (DNS) are implemented at your site, you can ignore this item.
- Be aware that some TCP/IP solutions impose a default upper limit on the allowed number of connections that a PC can handle. Check that limit and reconfigure it to the desired number if necessary.

Depending on whether DNS and/or RARP (Reverse Address Resolution Protocol) services are part of your environment, you may need to do the following as well:

- Provide the name server's address to the PC.
- Edit the `ethers` and the `hosts` file on the RARP server.

Depending on the vendor, the TCP/IP software may come with ranging tools to help you troubleshoot and manage your PC on the network. At a minimum, any decent implementation of TCP/IP should provide tools such as the `ping` and `netstat` commands. Use these tools in case things don't work properly.

Summary

Among the resources UNIX system administrators are required to manage are ASCII terminals, modems, scanners, WORM drives, printers (both local and remote), and any other piece of equipment your site uses. To manage these resources, different flavors of UNIX provide different sets of tools. Solaris, AT&T UNIX, and other SVR4 UNIX variants provide system administrators with a cohesive set of concepts and tools that come under the hood of the Service Access Facility (SAF). SAF recognizes a three-level hierarchy of processes: SAC (Service Access Controller), port monitors, and port services. SAC is at the top of the hierarchy and is responsible for invoking and managing the port monitors, which are mid-level processes. Port monitors are responsible for invoking and managing port services, which run at the bottom of the SAF hierarchy. There are two types of port monitors: ttymon and listen. ttymon takes care of service requests received over serial (or tty) ports, and listen takes care of across-the-network services (for example, pseudo-terminals pty).

After SAF is set up appropriately, the administrator can provide all kinds of services, including dial-in access, print services access, and access to X clients running on the UNIX host. This chapter presented the details for setting up these services so that the administrator can successfully bring up a similar environment in his or her workplace.

Under BSD, device management lacks the unified approach supported by the various flavors of UNIX SVR4. Instead, system administrators are required to deal with the tasks of device configuration and management using a different set of tools and interfaces.

Mail Administration

by Chris Byers

CHAPTER 30

So, they've gone and made you postmaster, have they? Perhaps you're approaching this new job with a little trepidation—and you should. Electronic mail administration is one of the most complex system administration tasks and one of the most visible. If you break an obscure program that few people use, your mistake may go unnoticed. If you break the mail system, all the users on your system are affected, and most people consider electronic mail to be one of UNIX's most valuable services. Even worse, if your site is connected to the Internet, your mistakes may be visible at remote sites, and those sites' postmasters will not hesitate to inform you that, although your mother may love you, they consider you and your broken mail system to be little better than pond scum. (Those are the moderates—others may not be so kind.)

Despite the potential for making mistakes on a grand scale, mail administration at many sites is routine. You probably won't have to fuss with the email system much after you manage to get it up and running, and this chapter helps you do just that. First, you get a broad overview of how email works, an explanation of some of the terminology you'll see in this and other books, and pointers on where to get more information. Finally, you'll see a step-by-step example of how to set up the `sendmail` program and its configuration file, `sendmail.cf`.

What this chapter won't do is cover complex configurations such as a multiprotocol mail hub that routes mail from the Internet to UUCP or a DECnet network. You won't learn how to set up the Domain Name System (DNS), although a properly working DNS is essential to the email system. This is covered in Chapter 26, "Networking."

UUCP is covered in more detail in Chapter 32, "UUCP Administration," but we touch on it here to show how it relates to email. Finally, this chapter won't make you into a `sendmail` guru, but if you're lucky, you'll never need to be one.

Email Overview and Terminology

An electronic mail message begins its life as a file on your computer's disk, created by a Mail User Agent (MUA). After you compose the letter, the MUA gives it to a mail router like `sendmail`. The mail router gives it to a Mail Transport Agent (MTA). The message traverses one or more hosts and networks and is given to a final delivery agent, which appends it to the recipient's mailbox, another disk file. Each of these terms is explained in detail later in this chapter.

An MUA is just a fancy name for a mail-reading and -sending program, such as the SVR4 `mailx`. Other examples of MUAs are `elm` and the Rand corporation's `Mail Handler` (MH) programs. An MUA is the only part of the mail system with which users usually interact because a good MUA hides the complexity of the rest of the system from them (but not from the postmaster)!

A mail router is a program that takes a piece of mail and decides where it should go and how to get it there. For instance, depending on the recipient, a letter might need to travel over a TCP/IP network using the Simple Mail Transfer Protocol (SMTP), or via a dial-up connection using the UNIX to UNIX Copy (UUCP) protocol, or even to an office fax machine. The mail router uses the recipient address and its own internal configuration information to decide the best MTA and then hands the letter to the MTA.

An MTA is a transport program that understands the email protocols of a particular network and can transport a letter over that network. For instance, the UUCP transport agents understand UUCP protocols but know nothing about SMTP. If the mail router were to mistakenly route an SMTP letter to a UUCP transport agent, it wouldn't know how to deliver it.

The final delivery agent does nothing but take a mail message and append it to the recipient's mailbox, following whatever local conventions are used to separate messages within a mailbox. The program /bin/mail is the usual final delivery agent on SVR4 systems.

In real life, the distinctions between MTAs and MUAs and mail routers are sometimes blurred. For instance, sendmail, although primarily a mail router, can also function as an MTA because it understands the SMTP protocol and can transport mail over a TCP/IP network. Therefore, the separate functions of mail router and MTA are really a single program. Further, the SMTP-server part of the remote end of the MTA is often another sendmail program, which may do additional routing and forwarding of the mail before it reaches its final delivery agent. Some MUAs even do their own mail routing, and some, like MH, can be configured to speak SMTP, an MTA function. Despite this real-world blurring of function, the conceptual framework outlined above is a good one to keep in mind.

Although only a few MTAs are available for transferring mail across the Internet, a number of MUAs are available for use. This chapter goes into some detail about each of the more commonly used MUAs and discusses some of their advantages and disadvantages.

The more widely used mail user agents are mail, elm, and pine, and each has its own personality and quirks (much like system administrators).

Common Mail Front Ends (MUAs)

The original flavor of a mail front end was the rather fiendishly cryptic (though very useful and effective) UNIX mail utility.

Even though you always ran the risk of accidentally deleting a mail message (which always came in handy as a good excuse for "missing" a message), it was still a reliable and effective MUA and is still in wide use today by many UNIX users and administrators.

In general, `mail` allows you to browse, display, save, delete, and respond to messages. When you send a message, `mail` lets you edit and review messages being composed and lets you include text from files or other messages.

The incoming mail for each user is stored in the system mailbox. This is a file named after the user in `/var/spool/mail` (on AT&T flavors of UNIX). `mail` looks in this file for incoming messages, but by manipulating the `mail` environment variable, you can have it look in a different file, which you define. At the time you read a message, it is marked to be moved to a secondary file for storage. This file is then called `mbox` and is put in your home directory. Like the incoming mail location, `mbox` can also be changed by setting the `MBOX` environment variable. All messages remain in the `mbox` file until they are manually removed.

`mail` comes with many switches and configuration settings to allow for highly customized use. These options are as follows:

`-d`	Start debugging output.
`-e`	See whether any mail is present. If there isn't, it returns nothing to the screen and gives a successful return code.
`-F`	Put the message in a file whose name is that of the first recipient. This also overrides the record variable, if it is set.
`-H`	Print only the header.
`-I`	Ignore interrupts (can also be set with the ignore variable).
`-n`	Don't initialize mail from the system default `Mail.rc` file.
`-N`	Don't print header.
`-U`	Convert UUCP addresses to Internet standard addresses. This option overrides the environment variable `conv`.
`-v`	This passes the `-v` flag to the `sendmail` utility.
`-f [filename]`	Tells it to read messages from `filename` instead of the system mailbox. If no `filename` is specified, it reads messages from `mbox`.
`-f [folder]`	Use the file `folder` in `folder` directory (this is the same as the `folder` command). The name of the directory is listed in the `folder` variable.
`-h [number]`	This is the number of network "hops" made to this point. This is provided so that infinite delivery loops do not occur. This is also related to the TTL, or time to live for a mail message packet.

-r [*address*]	Pass the *address* to the MTA or network delivery software. It is important to note that all tilde (~) commands are invalid in this option.
-s [*subject*]	Make the Subject header field as subject.
-T [*file*]	This option prints the contents of the article-id fields of all messages on file. This is used for network news programs such as Pointcast.
-u [*user*]	This option allows you to read a specific user's mailbox. This only works if you have the correct permissions to that user's home directory.

On starting mail, a system-wide file, /usr/lib/Mail.rc, is read for commands. These commands are read to initialize certain variables, after which it reads from the private startup file of the user who started the mail utility. This file is called .mailrc, and it is normally placed in the user's home directory. It can, however, be placed and accessed elsewhere by modifying the MAILRC environment variable for your personal commands and variable settings.

The .mailrc file is usually used for setting up initial display options and lists of aliases. You store your initial commands here when you start up mail. The following commands, however, are not valid in this file: !, Copy, edit, followup, Followup, hold, mail, preserve, reply, Reply, replyall, replysender, shell, and visual. Also, if there is an error in that file, the remaining lines are ignored.

By using a template .mailrc file, you can easily standardize each user's mail interface with little difficulty. All you have to do (obviously) is copy that template into the users' home directories, and (if necessary) do some minor editing for each user's particular needs.

You can send a message directly to another user or users by including names of recipients on the command line. If no recipients appear on the mail command line, mail enters command mode, where you can read messages sent to you. If you don't have any messages, it simply sends the message to standard output no mail for username and then exits the mail utility.

While you are in command mode (that is, while reading messages), you can also send messages.

When you are composing a message to send, mail is in input mode. If you don't specify a subject as an argument to the command, mail queries you for a subject. After you enter a subject, mail enters input mode, at which point you can start writing the body of the message you want to send.

30

MAIL ADMINISTRATION

While you're typing the message, mail stores it in a temporary file. This temporary file is used for reviewing or modifying the message. By using the appropriate tilde escape sequences (~:) at the beginning of an input line, you can modify the message text.

After you are in the body of your text, enter a dot (EOF) on a line by itself to actually send the message. At this point, mail submits the message to sendmail for routing to each recipient.

The recipients can be a local username or usernames, an Internet address (*name@domain*), a UUCP address of the form [*host!...host!*]*host!username*, filenames for which you have write permission, or alias groups. If the name of the recipient begins with a pipe symbol (¦), the remainder of the name is taken as a shell through which the message is piped. This can be used with any program that reads standard input, such as lpr, to record outgoing mail on a printout.

An alias group is simply the name of a list of recipients that is set by the alias command. The alias command takes the names from the /etc/aliases file, or it can be taken from the Network Information Service (NIS) aliases domain.

The first thing you see when you enter the command mode (immediately after running the mail command) is a header summary of the first several messages, followed by a prompt for one of the commands listed later in the chapter. By default, the prompt is an ampersand (&).

Each message has a reference number in front of it. The current message is marked by a > in the header summary. The commands that take an optional list of messages should be used with the reference number; if no number is given, the current message is affected.

The message-list is simply a list of message specifications, separated by space characters (space delimited), which can include the following:

.	Specifies the current message.
n	Denotes the message number n
^	Specifies the first undeleted message.
$	Specifies the last message.
+	Specifies the last message.
-	Specifies the previous undeleted message.
*	Specifies all messages.
n-m	Specifies an inclusive range of message numbers.
User	Specifies all the messages from user.
/string	Specifies all the messages with string in the subject line (upper- and lowercase is ignored).

:c   This specifies all messages of type c. c can be one of the following:

d   deleted messages

n   new messages

o   old messages

r   read messages

u   unread messages

If you are in command mode and you just press Enter with no arguments, mail assumes that you want to print the messages and starts printing to the default printer (if one is defined). The complete list of commands is as follows:

`! shell-command`

This command escapes you to the shell command. The shell to which you escape (Bourne, Korn, and so on) is defined in the SHELL variable.

`# comments`

This can be used for placing comments in your command, just as you would place comments in your .mailrc file. You must have a blank space between the # sign and the start of your comments.

`-`

This lets you print the current message number.

`?`

This shows you a summary of commands (for people like me with poor memories).

`alias [alias recipient...]`

or

`group [alias recipient]`

This declares an alias for the given list of recipients. In much the same way as distribution lists work in other mail readers, mail is sent to the entire alias (or group) specified. These aliases can be defined in the .mailrc file. To get a listing of the defined aliases, simply type in the command alias by itself.

`alternates name...`

This command lets you declare a list of alternate names for your login. When responding to a message, mail is not sent to these names. If no arguments are supplied, this shows a current list of alternate names.

```
cd [directory]
```

or

```
chdir [directory]
```

This command allows you to change the current directory. Just as within the Korn or Bourne shell, cd without an argument uses the environment variable $HOME as the directory.

```
copy [message-list][filename]
```

This command copies messages to the filename without marking the messages as saved. All other functions are equivalent to the save command.

```
Copy [message-list]
```

This saves the specified messages in a file whose name is derived from the author's username, also without marking the message as saved. This is otherwise equivalent to the Save command.

```
delete [message-list]
```

This deletes messages from the system mailbox. If the autoprint variable is set to on, it also prints the next message following the last message deleted.

```
discard [header-field...]
```

or

```
ignore [header-field...]
```

These commands suppress the printing of the specified header fields when displaying messages on the screen, such as Status and Received. By default, unless the variable alwaysignore is set, all header fields are included in the saved message. This does not apply to the Type or Print commands.

```
dp [message-list]
```

or

```
dt [message-list]
```

These commands are equivalent to the delete command followed by the print command because they first delete the specified messages from the system mailbox and print the following one.

```
edit [message-list]
```

This command edits the given messages. Each of the messages is put in a temporary file, and the EDITOR variable is used to the name of the editor (preferably vi). The default editor is ex.

Exit

or

xit

These commands exit you from the system mailbox without any changes. If you use this command, you will not save any messages in mbox.

file [*filename*]

folder [*filename*]

These commands quit you out of the current mailbox file and read in the named mailbox file. Certain special characters are used as filenames, such as:

%	The current user's mailbox.
&	Read previously read messages from your mbox.
+*filename*	A filename in a specified folder directory. The folder directory is also listed in the folder variable.

If no arguments are used, file simply shows the name of the current mail file, as well as the number of characters and messages it contains.

Folders

This command only prints the name of each mail file in the folder directory.

followup [*message*]

This command responds to a message and records the response in a file. The name of this file is derived from the author of the message. This command also overrides the record variable if it is set.

from [*message-list*]

This shows the header information for the indicated message or current message.

Help

This prints a summary of all commands.

hold [*message-list*]

or

preserve [*message-list*]

These commands hold the specified messages in the system mailbox.

```
if s¦r¦t
mail-command
...
else
mail-command
...
endif
```

This is a conditional execution, used primarily in the `.mailrc` file. The command executes up to an `elseif` or an `endif`. If s is used, the command runs if the program is in send mode; if r is chosen, the command executes only if in receive mode; if t is chosen, the command is run only if `mail` is run from a terminal.

```
load [message] filename
```

This command lets you load the specified message from the named file. This allows you to load a single saved message from *filename*, including headers.

```
mail recipient
```

This command sends a message to the specified recipient.

```
Unread [message-list]
```

This marks each message in a message list as having been read.

```
quit
```

This exits the `mail` command. It also saves the messages that were read in the `mbox` file and keeps the unread messages in the system mailbox.

```
reply [message-list]
```

or

```
respond [message-list]
```

or

```
replysender [message-list]
```

These commands allow you to send a response to the author of each message in *messasge-list*.

```
Reply [message]
```

or

```
Respond [message]
```

or

```
replyall [message]
```

These commands let you reply to the specified message, sending a response to each recipient of that message. If the `replyall` variable is set, the `replyall` command always sends the reply to all recipients of the message.

```
save [message-list] [filename]
```

This command saves the specified message in the specified filename. If the filename does not exist, it is created. If no filename is specified, the file named in the MBOX variable is used (mbox by default). After the message is saved, it is deleted from the system mailbox unless the `keepsave` variable is set.

```
set [variable[=value]]
```

This lets you define a variable and assign a value to it. You must use an equals (=) sign between the variable name and the value (with no spaces).

```
shell
```

This invokes the shell as defined in the SHELL variable.

```
source filename
```

This lets you read commands from the given filename and return to the command mode.

```
undelete [message-list]
```

This restores deleted messages. It only works on messages deleted in the current mail session.

```
unset variable …
```

This undefines a specified variable or variables. This does not work on imported variables such as environment variables from the shell.

```
z[+¦-]
```

This scrolls the header display either forward (+) or backward (-) by one screen.

To forward a message, you must include it in a message to the recipients with the ~f or ~m tilde escapes. You can define a list of recipients in a file, called `.forward`, in your home directory to forward mail to automatically. The list must be comma separated, and the address must be valid, or the messages will bounce without any warnings.

Mail behavior is defined by a set of variables in your `.mailrc` file. The necessary environment variables are as follows:

30

MAIL ADMINISTRATION

`HOME=`*`directory`*

This is the user's home directory.

`MAIL=`*`filename`*

This is the name of the initial mailbox file to read. By default, it is set to `/var/spool/mail/username`.

`MAILRC=`*`filename`*

This is the name of each user's personal startup file, which is `$HOME/.mailrc` by default.

These variables cannot be modified from within `mail`. They must be set before you begin a mail session.

The specific `mail` variable for each user is set in the `.mailrc` file in each user's home directory. The following are all the `mail` variables that can be altered either in the `.mailrc` file or by using the `set` (or `unset`) command:

`allnet`

For all network names whose login name components match, treat them as identical. The default is `noallnet`.

`alwaysignore`

This tells `mail` to always ignore the header fields, not just during `print` or `type`. This affects the `save`, `Save`, `copy`, `Copy`, `top`, `pipe`, and `write` commands, as well as the `~m` and `~f` tilde escapes.

`append`

This appends messages to the end of the `mbox` file when you exit instead of prepending them. By default this is set as `noappend`.

`askcc`

This prompts you for the Cc list after you enter a message. The default is `noaskcc`.

`asksub`

This asks you for a subject. This is enabled by default.

`autoprint`

This automatically prints messages after the `delete` or `undelete` commands are run. By default this is set to `noautoprint`.

`bang`

This enables use of the exclamation point or "bang" as a shell escape command, such as in the `vi` editor.

`cmd=shell-command`

This sets the default command for the `pipe` command. This has no default value.

`conv=conversion`

This variable converts UUCP addresses to the address style you specify. The style can be one of the following:

`internet`

Use this if you are using a mail delivery program that conforms to the RFC 232 standard for electronic mail addressing.

`optimize`

This removes loops in the UUCP address path, which are usually generated by the `reply` command. There is no rerouting performed because `mail` doesn't know anything about UUCP routes or connections.

Conversion is disabled by default.

`crt=number`

This pipes the messages that contain more than *number* lines through the command, which is specified by the `PAGER` variable. This is the `more` command by default.

`DEAD=filename`

You can specify the name of the file where a partial letter is saved in case of an interrupted session. By default, this is defined as the `dead.letter` file in the user's home directory.

`debug`

This turns on the verbose diagnostics for debugging. The default setting is `nodebug`.

`dot`

This reads a dot on a line by itself as an EOF marker. By default, this is set as `nodot`, but `dot` is set in the global startup file.

`editheaders`

This enables you to edit the headers as well as the body of the message when you use the `~e` and `~v` commands.

30

MAIL ADMINISTRATION

`EDITOR=shell-command`

This defines the editor (or command) to run when you use the edit or ~e command. By default this is set to `ex`.

`escape=c`

This substitutes c for the tilde (~) escape character.

`folder=directory`

This is the defined directory for saving standard `mail` files. If the user specifies a filename beginning with a plus (+), the filename is expanded with the directory name preceding it.

`header`

This prints the header when you enter `mail`. This is enabled by default.

`hold`

This keeps all read messages in the system mailbox instead of moving them to `mbox`. The default is `nohold`.

`ignore`

This tells it to ignore interrupts while entering messages. The default is `noignore`.

`indentprefix=string`

By default, `string` is set to the Tab key. It is used to mark indented lines from messages included with ~m.

`LISTER=shell-command`

This is set by default to the `ls` command; used to list the files in the folder directory.

`MBOX=filename`

This sets the filename where messages are saved after being read. The default is `$HOME/mbox`.

`onehop`

This can be used in a local area network (no router between machines). Normally, when several recipients are sent mail, their addresses are forced to be relative to the originating author's machine, which allows ease of response from the recipients. This flag greatly reduces traffic "over the wire."

`outfolder`

This locates the files used to save the outgoing messages. The default is `nooutfolder`.

page

This inserts a form feed after each message sent through a pipe. `nopage` is the default.

PAGER=`shell-command`

This is used for paginating the messages on the screen. By default, it is set to `more`, but `pg` can also be used.

prompt=`string`

This allows you to set the prompt in command mode. By default, it's set to `&`.

quiet

This enters `mail` without the opening message being displayed. This is disabled by default.

record=`filename`

This records all outgoing mail in `filename`. This is disabled by default.

replyall

This has the opposite effect of the `reply` and `Reply` commands.

save

If this is set on, the mail message is saved to the `dead.letter` file if it is interrupted on delivery. This is set on as default.

screen=`number`

This defines how many lines you can have for headers. This is used by the `headers` command.

sendwait

This allows the background mailer to finish before returning to command mode. The default setting is `nosendwait`.

SHELL=`shell-command`

This defines the preferred shell you use when you escape to a shell. By default, it is set to `sh`. It first goes to the inherited shell from the environment.

sign=autograph

If the `~a` (autograph) command is given, includes the `autograph` text in the message. There is no default.

`toplines=`*number*

This tells the `top` command how many lines of the header to print. This is set to 5 by default.

`verbose`

This invokes `sendmail` with the `-v` flag.

`VISUAL=shell-`*command*

This points to the preferred visual screen editor, which is `vi` by default.

So much for the `.mailrc` settings. If you have the `mail` utility installed on your server or workstation, take a look at the `.mailrc` file to get a feel for how the file is put together.

A related file is the `/usr/lib/Mail.rc file`. This is the global startup file, which was referred to earlier in this section. This sets up the initial settings for the `mail` utility for each user, and it contains most of the default variables included with the initial `.mailrc` file.

Using `elm`

At this point, you might be wondering, why go into so much detail about an outdated utility? Well, for one thing, most of the newer and easier to use MUAs are based on the old original `mail` utility, and much of the same functionality has been added to them and enhanced. Also, this is a good way to illustrate why you would want to move to another utility such as `pine` or `elm`.

This section takes a look at `elm`, followed by `pine` in the next section, because these are the most popular text-based MUAs in use today.

The biggest difference between `elm` and `mail` is that `elm` uses a screen-oriented interface, as opposed to the command-line interface used by `mail`. It is also a great deal more intuitive to use, as well as being highly tunable for mail administrators. As with `mail`, `elm` also runs on virtually every flavor of UNIX without any modifications.

`elm` is also 100 percent compliant with the RFC 822 electronic mail header protocol guide, which means that it complies with all existing mail standards. In terms of reliability, it has been in use for many years by tens of thousands of sites with no problems.

On looking at the main menu, which appears after opening `elm`, you see the first line (showing the name of the current folder, the number of messages in the folder, and the current version of `elm`), the list of messages, and a paragraph at the bottom showing the available one-letter commands.

In the list of messages, the inverse video bar indicates the currently active message. The status field is the first field on the screen; it can be blank, or it can have a combination of characters, where the first character has a temporary status, and the second has a permanent status. The characters are: E for an expired message, N for a new message, O for an old message, D for a deleted message, U for urgent mail, A for messages that have an action associated with them, and F for a form letter. There may also be a "+" in the third field, which indicates a tagged message.

In the next field, each message is numbered, which can come in handy for quickly opening a specific message.

The third field from the left indicates the date that the message was sent, in the format *MMM/DD*.

The fourth field from the left shows who sent the message. By default, elm tries to display the full name of the person who sent the message, but if this is unavailable, it shows either the login name and address of the person who sent it or just the sender's login name.

The fifth field in the list shows the number of lines in the message. And, finally, the sixth field shows the subject of the message (if one is included).

elm shows ten or more messages at one time, depending on the screen settings. To read a mail message, simply highlight the one you want to read and press Enter.

The functions available from the main screen are as follows:

<return> or <space>   This reads the current message.

¦   This allows you to pipe the message to a system command, such as lp.

!   This escapes to the shell.

$ This resynchronizes the folder.

?   This puts you into help mode; any key pressed is explained.

+ or <right>   This puts you into the next page of messages.

- or <left>   This puts you into the previous page of messages.

=   This sets the current message number to 1.

*   This makes the current message number equal to the last one.

<number><return>   This sets the message number of the highlighted message.

/   This starts a pattern search in the subject/from lines.

//   This starts a pattern search for the entire folder.

<   This lets you search for specific calendar entries.

>>   This is the same as s for saving a message.

a   This puts you into the alias mode.

b   This bounces (or remails) a message. This is related to the `forward` command.

C   This copies the current message or all the tagged messages to the folder.

c   This changes the current folder to another `elm` folder.

d   This deletes the current message.

`<ctrl>-D`   This deletes all messages matching a user-supplied pattern.

e   This edits the current folder.

f   This lets you forward a message to a specific user. The only difference between this and `bounce` is that a bounced message shows as being sent from the original sender, whereas a forwarded message is designated as being sent from the person who forwarded it.

g   This lets you do a group reply to everyone who received the current message.

h   This disables the headers in messages.

J   This moves the current message to the next one in line.

j or `<down>`   This moves you to the next message that is not marked as deleted.

K   This moves you up the list to the previous message.

k or `<up>`   This moves you up the list to the previous message if it is not marked as deleted.

`<ctrl>-L`   This refreshes the screen.

m   This sends mail to arbitrary users.

n   This lets you read the current message and then go to the next undeleted message in the list.

o   This lets you go into the options menu, where you can change the mail system options interactively.

p   This lets you print the current message, or all the tagged messages.

Q   This is known as the quick quit because it quits without prompting the user.

r   This lets you reply to the author of the current message.

s   This is the command to save the current message to the folder.

t   This tags the highlighted message for later manipulation.

`<ctrl>-T`   This allows you to tag all the messages matching a specified pattern.

u   This undeletes only the current message.

`<ctrl>-U`   This allows you to undelete all messages that match a specified pattern.

x   This is the exit command, and it prompts you for saving messages and so on.

X   This exits immediately, without prompting.

Luckily, most of these commands are listed at the bottom of the main menu, so you don't have to memorize them (unlike the `mail` utility).

You can also send a file (or attachment) on the command line to a specific user if it will save you time. You can do this by typing the following command:

```
elm -s "message subject" recipient<filename
```

The configuration file is called `elmrc` in the user's home directory. Use this to define specific settings as needed for the special needs of your users.

Using `elm`

How many times have you heard this from your users; "Where's my mail? I lost my saved messages!"? `elm` has a few debugging tools to help you track down some of the more common problems.

In the first menu screen, you can use the `h`, or `headers` command, to show all the header information that might be sorted out with weeding settings. This might help to see whether the address field got buggered somewhere along the line.

The `@` command can also be somewhat helpful. It simply shows a screen of debugging information for each message, such as the number of lines and offsets.

The `#` command actually shows the entire record structure for the current message to see whether the message format is corrupted somehow.

To see the full return address of the current message, the `%` command can be used. Like the `h` command, this is useful to see whether the address got corrupted or mislabeled.

You can also start `elm` with the `-d` option, which starts the debugger. This creates a file in the user's home directory called `ELM;debug.info`, which gives a good deal of debugging information useful for tracking down problems.

If you use the debugging option, you might need to get the AT&T System V Interface Definition Reference Manual to look up the error names that get reported.

Most X Window interfaces give you an option to include a post office in the user's setup. This can be done somewhat easily by modifying the X Window configuration file and adding that specific mailer.

For example, on HP-UX systems, these modifications take place in the user's `$HOME/.vue/mwmrc` file. In this file, you can specify that a mailbox be present and which mailer you want to use. This is `elm` by default in HP-UX. See your system's specific X Window guide for more details.

Using pine

Like elm, pine is a text-based full-screen mail utility (MUA). It has a few more features than elm and is probably more widely used than elm as well.

pine was developed by a few UNIX gurus at the University of Washington to act as a simple email front end for their users on campus. Because of its ease of use for novice users as well as its stability and configurability, it was quickly adopted first by other universities and then by many Internet service providers as their default mail interface.

pine can get and send mail from almost any mail format because it uses the c-client library to access mail files, which can act as a switch between different mail formats and drivers. If used with IMAP (Interactive Mail Access Protocol), you can have an IMAP server, like imapd, running on a central host, letting users access their mail without actually having to log on to the central host. (See RFC 1176 for more on IMAP.)

Mail can be handed off to either sendmail (as is usually the case), or it can be sent using SMTP. This and other configuration settings are covered later in this section (see RFC 822 for more details on SMTP).

MIME is also supported in pine for moving multipart and multimedia email. MIME stands for Multipurpose Internet Mail Extensions (defined in RFC 1341). By using this, any received MIME message gets saved to files, whatever their format. This also allows users to attach files to their messages, such as GIF files, which can be detached and displayed (if running X-terminal).

On starting up pine, you can give it the following options:

-d *debug-level*

This sets a debugging level (0 means off) and sends the output to the .pinedebugX file in the user's home directory.

-f *folder*

This opens a named *folder* in place of the default INBOX.

-i *keystrokes*

This is like a startup script, where the keystrokes, separated with commas, run on startup. By default, pine starts up in the FOLDER INDEX screen if no keystrokes are specified.

-k

This tells it to use the function keys for commands.

-l

This expands the folder list.

-n *message-number*

The specified message number is opened immediately.

-p *config-file*

Let's use the defined configuration file. By default, this is the .pinerc file.

-P *config-file*

This makes pine use the specified configuration file instead of the global configuration file pine.conf.

-r

This puts you into the restricted demo mode, where you can only send mail to yourself.

-sort order

This tells it to sort the display of the index by arrival, subject, from, date, size, or reverse order. By default, the arrival order is chosen.

-z

This enables the interrupt command ^Z so that a user can suspend pine.

address

This sends mail directly to the given address and drops you into the message composer on startup.

-h

This displays the help files for pine.

-conf

This prints on the screen a fresh copy of the system pine configuration file (not to be confused with the .pinerc file).

Each of these options is shown at the bottom of the screen when you use pine. As an easy-to-use mail front end, pine is easily the most popular one in use.

As I mentioned before, pine has a configuration file for all users called .pinerc located in each home directory. The following shows this file and how to configure it.

The variables are as follows:

personal-name=

This overrides the full name defined in the /etc/passwd.

30

MAIL ADMINISTRATION

`user-domain=`

This sets the domain name for the sender's `From:` field.

`smtp-server=`

This is left blank if you are using `sendmail` as your MTA. You define your list of SMTP servers here.

`nntp-server=`

This sets the news-collections for news reading, as well as defining the NNTP server used for posting news.

`inbox-path=`

This defines the path of the local or remote `INBOX`, such as `$HOME/INBOX` or `{mail.domain}inbox`.

`incoming-folders=`

This lists all the incoming message folders.

`folder-collections=`

This is similar to a path statement; it lists the directories where saved message folders can be found.

`news-collections=`

This is only needed if the NNTP server name is not set or news is located on a different server.

`default-fcc=`

This overrides the default path where the sent-mail folder is kept.

`postponed-folder=`

This overrides the default path where the postponed messages are located.

`read-message-folder=`

This defines where the read messages are to be moved when you quit `pine`.

`signature-file=`

This defines where the signature file is located. The default for `pine` is `$HOME/.signature`.

`global-address-book=`

This defines the path for a shared or global address book, if one is used.

`address-book=`

This specifies the path for the personal address book. By default, this is the `$HOME/.addressbook` file.

`feature-list=`

This defines a set of features (shown in the setup/options menu). This sets defaults such as select-without-confirm, and so on. By default, each is prepended with the `no-` option.

`initial-keystroke-list=`

This allows a list of one letter commands to be executed on startup.

`default-composer-hdrs=`

This causes it to display these headers when composing messages.

`customized-hdrs=`

When composing a message, this adds customized headers to the message.

`saved-msg-name-rule=`

This determines the default name for save folders.

`fcc-name-rule=`

This specifies the default name for `Fcc`.

`sort-key=`

This sets the order of presentation of messages in the index.

`addrbook-sort-rule=`

This sets the order of presentation for address book entries.

`character-set=`

This is set to the screen settings of the window or screen you are using. By default this number is set to `US_ASCII`.

`editor=`

This specifies the program used in the Composer.

`image-viewer=`

This sets the program that will be called to view images.

`use-only-domain-name=`

This strips the hostname used in the From: field if the user domain is not set.

```
printer=
```

This lets you select your printer.

```
personal-print-command=
```

This is used if special print drivers are needed for a nonstandard printer.

```
last-time-prune-questioned=yy.dd
```

This is set by `pine` to control the beginning-of-month pruning for sent mail.

```
last-version-used
```

This is also set by `pine` for displaying the new version of `pine`.

Using Netscape Mail

Netscape corporation broke new ground in the use of the Internet, and in my opinion, created the current Internet craze among the general public by doing one thing: making an easy-to-use graphical interface for accessing HTML coded Web pages. Almost overnight it seemed that everyone had heard of the Internet (and more than a few claimed to be experts on it, but that's another topic).

Netscape's first product, Navigator, and its more recent offering, Communicator, both have an easy-to-use, built-in mail front end. Not only is usage a snap, but configuration is easy as well.

By simply using the pull-down menus, you can configure your preferred mail server, the type of mail server it is, and many other things. You can also specify what type of applications are launched when opening attached clients, among many other features.

Using Microsoft Mail

Recently, Microsoft finally ported its version of an Internet browser to many versions of UNIX, such as SunOS, Solaris, and HP-UX. This is known as Internet Explorer.

Microsoft uses its Outlook Express product with Internet Explorer as its mail MUA on UNIX. Internet Explorer is similar in functionality and looks to Navigator. This also carries over to Outlook Express, which Internet Explorer uses as its mail program.

As with Navigator, configuration is simple, using pull-down menus to configure preferred mail server, the type of mail server, and so on.

Both Netscape and Explorer can be used in conjunction with CDE (Common Desktop Environment) through configuration files. For Explorer, this file is the `IE4.dt` file.

Mail Transfer Agents (MTAs)

Email administration is a complex endeavor. This chapter gives you enough background to get you out of the gate and running, but you must carefully study the following materials to really understand what you're doing. It's much better to learn it now—with a warm cup of cocoa in hand—than to wait until you have a dozen angry users in your office demanding that you fix the mail system immediately. Trust me on this one.

Using `sendmail`

V8 `sendmail` comes with three important documents:

- Sendmail Installation and Operation Guide (SIOG)
- SENDMAIL—An Internetwork Mail Router
- Mail Systems and Addressing in 4.2bsd

All three were written by Eric Allman, the author of the `sendmail` program. The SIOG is an essential reference manual that explains the guts of `sendmail`. The other documents are more general overviews of mail router design. All are worth reading, but the SIOG is your essential guide to `sendmail`. You'll want to read it several times and highlight parts relevant to your site's configuration.

The book *sendmail* by Bryan Costales, Eric Allman, and Neil Rickert (O'Reilly & Associates, Inc., 1993) is the most comprehensive treatment of the care and feeding of V8 `sendmail`. If you manage a complex site or must write custom configuration files, it is invaluable. If your site is fairly simple or you find that you can get most of what you need from this chapter, the standard V8 `sendmail` documentation, `comp.mail.sendmail`, and the RFCs, save your money.

If your site receives Usenet News, just add the newsgroup `comp.mail.sendmail` to your newsreader's subscription list. Eric Allman, the author of `sendmail`, contributes regularly along with other `sendmail` wizards. You can get more quality, free advice here than anywhere else on the Usenet.

However, as with any newsgroup, read it for a few weeks before you make your first posting, and save yourself the embarrassment of asking a question that has already been answered a hundred times by first reading the V8 `sendmail` Frequently Asked Questions (FAQ) document and the other documentation mentioned in this chapter. It may take a little longer to get your burning question answered, but you'll still respect yourself in the morning.

30

MAIL
ADMINISTRATION

To understand the different jobs that sendmail does, you need to know a little about Internet protocols. Protocols are simply agreed-upon standards that software and hardware use to communicate.

Protocols are usually layered, with higher levels using the lower ones as building blocks. For instance, the Internet Protocol (IP) sends packets of data back and forth without building an end-to-end connection such as-used by SMTP and other higher-level protocols. The Transmission Control Protocol (TCP) is built on top of IP and provides for connection-oriented services like those used by programs such as telnet and the Simple Mail Transfer Protocol (SMTP). Together, TCP/IP provides the basic network services for the Internet. Higher-level protocols such as the File Transfer Protocol (FTP) and SMTP are built on top of TCP/IP. The advantage of such layering is that programs that implement the SMTP or FTP protocols don't have to know anything about transporting packets on the network and making connections to other hosts. They can use the services provided by TCP/IP for that.

SMTP defines how programs exchange email on the Internet. It doesn't matter whether the program exchanging the email is sendmail running on an HP workstation or an SMTP client written for an Apple Macintosh. As long as both programs implement the SMTP protocol correctly, they will be able to exchange mail.

The following example of the SMTP protocol in action may help demystify it a little. The user betty at gonzo.gov is sending mail to joe at whizzer.com:

```
$ sendmail -v joe@whizzer.com < letter
joe@whizzer.com... Connecting to whizzer.com via tcp...
Trying 123.45.67.1...  connected.
220-whizzer.com SMTP ready at Mon, 6 Jun 1994 18:56:22 -0500
220 ESMTP spoken here
>>> HELO gonzo.gov
250 whizzer.com Hello gonzo.gov [123.45.67.2], pleased to meet you
>>> MAIL From:<betty@gonzo.gov>
250 <betty@gonzo.gov>... Sender ok
>>> RCPT To:<joe@whizzer.com>
250 <joe@whizzer.com>... Recipient ok
>>> DATA
354 Enter mail, end with "." on a line by itself
>>> .
250 SAA08680 Message accepted for delivery
>>> QUIT
221 whizzer.com closing connection
joe@whizzer.com... Sent
$
```

The first line shows one way to invoke sendmail directly rather than letting your favorite MUA do it for you. The -v option tells sendmail to be verbose and shows you the SMTP dialogue. The other lines show an SMTP client and server carrying on a conversation. Lines prefaced with >>> are the client (or sender) on gonzo.gov, and the lines that immediately follow are the replies of the server (or receiver) on whizzer.com. The first line beginning with 220 is the SMTP server announcing itself after the initial connection, giving its hostname and the date and time, and the second line informs the client that this server understands the Extended SMTP protocol (ESMTP) in case the client wants to use it. Numbers such as 220 are reply codes that the SMTP client uses to communicate with the SMTP server. The text following the reply codes is only for human consumption.

Although this dialogue may still look a little mysterious, it will soon be old hat if you take the time to read RFC 821. Running sendmail with its -v option also helps you understand how an SMTP dialogue works.

Names such as whizzer.com are convenient for humans, but computers insist on using numeric IP addresses such as 123.45.67.1. The Domain Name System (DNS) provides this hostname to IP address translation and other important information.

In the olden days when most of us walked several miles to school through deep snow, there were only a few thousand hosts on the Internet. All hosts were registered with the Network Information Center (NIC), which distributed a host table listing the hostnames and IP addresses of all the hosts on the Internet. Those simple times are gone forever. No one really knows how many hosts are connected to the Internet now, but they number in the millions, and an administrative entity like the NIC can't keep their names straight. Thus was born the DNS.

The DNS distributes authority for naming and numbering hosts to autonomous administrative domains. For instance, a company whizzer.com could maintain all the information about the hosts in its own domain. When the host a.whizzer.com wanted to send mail or telnet to the host b.whizzer.com, it would send an inquiry over the network to the whizzer.com name server, which might run on a host named ns.whizzer.com. The ns.whizzer.com name server would reply to a.whizzer.com with the IP address of b.whizzer.com (and possibly other information), and the mail would be sent or the telnet connection made. Because ns.whizzer.com is authoritative for the whizzer.com domain, it can answer any inquiries about whizzer.com hosts regardless of where they originate; the authority for naming hosts in this domain has been delegated.

Now, what if someone on a.whizzer.com wants to send mail to joe@gonzo.gov? Ns.whizzer.com has no information about hosts in the gonzo.gov domain, but it knows how to find out. When a name server receives a request for a host in a domain for which it has no information, it asks the root name servers for the names and IP addresses of servers authoritative for that domain, in this case gonzo.gov. The root name server gives the ns.whizzer.com name server the names and IP addresses of hosts running name servers with authority for `gonzo.gov`. The `ns.whizzer.com` name server inquires of them and forwards the reply back to `a.whizzer.com`.

From the preceding description, you can see that the DNS is a large, distributed database containing mappings between hostnames and IP addresses, but it contains other information as well. When a program such as `sendmail` delivers mail, it must translate the recipient's hostname into an IP address. This bit of DNS data is known as an A (Address) record, and it is the most fundamental data about a host. A second piece of host data is the Mail eXchanger (MX) record. An MX record for a host such as `a.whizzer.com` lists one or more hosts that are willing to receive mail for it.

What's the point? Why shouldn't `a.whizzer.com` simply receive its own mail and be done with it? Isn't a postmaster's life complicated enough without having to worry about mail exchangers? Well, although it's true that the postmaster's life is often overly complicated, MX records serve useful purposes:

- Hosts not on the Internet (for example, UUCP-only hosts) may designate an Internet host to receive their mail and so appear to have an Internet address. For instance, suppose that `a.whizzer.com` is only connected to `ns.whizzer.com` once a day via a UUCP link. If `ns.whizzer.com` publishes an MX record for it, other Internet hosts can still send it mail. When `ns.whizzer.com` receives the mail, it saves it until `a.whizzer.com` connects. This use of MX records allows non-Internet hosts to appear to be on the Internet (but only to receive email).

- Imagine a UNIX host `pcserv.whizzer.com` that acts as a file server for a cluster of personal computers. The PC clones have MUAs with built-in SMTP clients that allow them to send mail, but not receive mail. If return addresses on the outbound mail look like `someone@pc1.whizzer.com`, how can people reply to the mail? MX records come to the rescue again—`pcserv.whizzer.com` publishes itself as the MX host for all the PC clones, and mail addressed to them is sent there.

- Hosts may be off the Internet for extended times because of unpredictable reasons ranging from lightning strikes to the propensity of backhoe operators to unexpectedly unearth fiber-optic cables. While your host is off the Internet, its mail queues on other hosts, and after a while it bounces back to the sender. If your host has MX hosts willing to hold its mail in the interim, the mail is delivered when your host is available again. The hosts can be either onsite (that is, in your domain) or offsite, or both. The last option is best because backhoe operator disasters usually take your entire site off the net, in which case an onsite backup does no good.

- MX records hide information and allow you more flexibility to reconfigure your local network. If all your correspondents know that your email address is `joe@whizzer.com`, it doesn't matter whether the host that receives mail for whizzer.com is named `zippy.whizzer.com` or `pinhead.whizzer.com`. It also does-n't matter whether you decide to change it to `white-whale.whizzer.com`; your correspondents will never know the difference.

Setting Up `sendmail`

The easiest way to show you how to set up `sendmail` is to use a concrete example. However, because `sendmail` runs under many different versions of UNIX, your system may vary from the examples shown in this section. For the sake of concreteness, these examples assume that you're setting up `sendmail` on a Solaris 2.3 system, Sun Microsystem's version of SVR4 UNIX.

First you must obtain the source and compile `sendmail`. You can get this from `http://www.sendmail.org/`. Next you must choose a `sendmail.cf` file that closely models your site's requirements and tinker with it as necessary. Then you must test `sendmail` and its configuration file. Finally, you must install `sendmail`, `sendmail.cf`, and other auxiliary files.

Those are the basic steps, but depending on where you install `sendmail`, you may also have to modify a file in the directory `/etc/init.d` so that `sendmail` is started correctly when the system boots. In addition, if your system doesn't already have one, you must create an aliases file, often named `/usr/lib/aliases` or `/etc/mail/aliases` (the loca-tion of the aliases file is given in `sendmail.cf`, so you can put it wherever you want). You may also have to make changes to your system's DNS database, but that won't be covered here.

If your site is on the Internet and you want to obtain the absolute latest version, `ftp` to the host `ftp.cs.berkeley.edu` and look in the directory `~ftp/pub/ucb/sendmail`.

Now that you've got the source, you need to unpack it. Because it's a compressed `tar` image, you must first decompress it and then extract the individual files from the `tar` archive. If you're using the version from the CD-ROM, these steps are not necessary.

```
$ mkdir /usr/src/local/sendmail
$ mv sendmail.<version number> /usr/src/local/sendmail
$ cd /usr/src/local/sendmail
$ uncompress *Z
$ ls
sendmail.<version number>.base.tar sendmail.8.6.9.cf.tar
$ tar xf sendmail.<current version>.base.tar; tar xf sendmail.8.6.9.cf.tar
$ ls -CF
FAQ                        cf/                   sendmail.<current
version>.cf.tar
KNOWNBUGS                  doc/                      src/
```

```
Makefile                  mailstats/                test/
READ_ME                   makemap/
RELEASE_NOTES             sendmail.<current version>.base.tar
$ rm *tar
```

Because `sendmail` runs on a variety of hosts and operating systems, a makefile is provided for many UNIX variants. Because in this example you're assuming a Sun Microsystems Solaris system, use `Makefile.Solaris` to compile `sendmail`. But before you type `make`, look at the files `conf.h` and `Makefile.Solaris`.

You probably won't want to change much in `conf.h`, but `Makefile.Solaris` is a different story. At the very least, make sure that the correct version of the Solaris operating system is defined. In this case, because you're compiling for Solaris 2.3, you must replace the line `ENV=-DSOLARIS` with the line `ENV=-DSOLARIS_2_3` (`Makefile.Solaris` tells us to do so). If you've purchased the SunPro `cc` compiler, you might want to change the definition of the `CC` macro to use that instead of `gcc`. You might want to make other changes; for example, you might not want to install `sendmail` in the default location. Read the makefile carefully and make changes as needed.

Remember, when in doubt, you can always type `make -n` *arguments* to see what would happen before it happens. This is always an especially good idea when you're working as the superuser.

Now you're ready to compile. Type the following:

```
$ make -f Makefile.Solaris sendmail
gcc -I.  -I/usr/sww/include/db -DNDBM -DNIS -DSOLARIS_2_3 -c  alias.c
[...]
gcc -I.  -I/usr/sww/include/db -DNDBM -DNIS -DSOLARIS_2_3 -c  util.c
gcc -I.  -I/usr/sww/include/db -DNDBM -DNIS -DSOLARIS_2_3 -c version.c
gcc -o sendmail alias.o arpadate.o clock.o collect.o conf.o convtime.
➥o daemon.o
deliver.o domain.o envelope.o err.o headers.o macro.o main.o  map.o mci.o
parseaddr.o queue.o readcf.o recipient.o  savemail.o srvrsmtp.o stab.
➥o stats.o
sysexits.o  trace.o udb.o usersmtp.o util.o version.o
-L/usr/sww/lib -lresolv -lsocket -lnsl -lelf
```

The [...] in the preceding code covers many deleted lines of output, as well as some warning messages from the compiler. Carefully inspect the output and determine whether the compiler warnings are pertinent. If necessary (and it should only be necessary if you're porting `sendmail` to a new architecture), correct any problems and compile again.

Now you've got a working `sendmail`, but like the Wizard of Oz's scarecrow, it's brainless. The `sendmail.cf` file provides `sendmail` with its brains, and because it's so important, we're going to cover it in fairly excruciating detail. Don't worry if you don't understand everything in this section the first time through. It will make more sense upon rereading, and after you've had a chance to play with some configuration files of your own.

`sendmail`'s power lies in its flexibility, which comes from its configuration file, `send-mail.cf`. `sendmail.cf` statements comprise a cryptic programming language that at first glance doesn't inspire much confidence (but C language code probably didn't either the first time you saw it). However, learning the `sendmail.cf` language isn't that difficult, and you won't have to learn the nitty-gritty details unless you plan to write a `sendmail.cf` from scratch—a bad idea at best. You do need to learn enough to understand and adapt the V8 `sendmail` configuration file templates to your site's needs.

Each line of the configuration file begins with a single command character that tells the function and syntax of that line. Lines beginning with a # are comments, and blank lines are ignored. Lines beginning with a space or tab are a continuation of the previous line, although you should usually avoid continuations.

Table 30.1 shows the command characters and their functions. It is split into three parts corresponding to the three main functions of a configuration file, which are covered later in "A Functional Description of the Configuration File."

TABLE 30.1. `sendmail.cf` COMMAND CHARACTERS.

Command Character	Command Syntax and Example	Function
#	# comments are ignored	A comment line. Always use lots of comments.
	# Standard RFC 822 parsing	
D	DX string	Define a macro X to have the string value `string`.
	DMmailhub.gonzo.gov	
C	CX word1, word2,...	Define a class X as `word1, word2,...`
	Cwlocalhost myuucpname	
F	FX/path/to/a/file	Define a class X by reading it from a file.
	Fw/etc/mail/host_aliases	
H	H?mailerflag?name;template	Define a mail header.
	H?F?From: $q	

continues

TABLE 30.1. CONTINUED

Command Character	Command Syntax and Example	Function
O	OX option arguments	Set option X. Most command-line options may be set in `send-mail.cf`.
	OL9 # set log level to 9	
P	Pclass=nn	Set mail delivery precedence based on the class of the mail.
	Pjunk=-100	
V	Vn	Tell V8 `sendmail` the version level of the configuration file.
	V3	
K	Kname class arguments	Define a key file (database map).
	Kuucphosts dbm /etc/mail/uucphsts	
M	Mname,field_1=value_1,...	Define a mailer.
	Mprog,P=/bin/sh,F=lsD,A=sh -c $u	
S	Snn	Begin a new ruleset.
	S22	
R	Rlhs rhs comment	Define a matching / rewriting rule.
	R$+ $:$>22 call ruleset 22	

A configuration file does three things. First, it sets the environment for `sendmail` by telling it what options you want set and the locations of the files and databases it uses.

Second, it defines the characteristics of the mailers (delivery agents or MTAs) that `send-mail` uses after it decides where to route a letter. All configuration files must define local and program mailers to handle delivery to users on the local host; most also define one or more SMTP mailers; and sites that must handle UUCP mail define UUCP mailers.

Third, the configuration file specifies rulesets that rewrite sender and recipient addresses and select mailers. All rulesets are user-defined, but some have special meaning to `send-mail`. Ruleset 0, for instance, is used to select a mailer. Rulesets 0, 1, 2, 3, and 4 all have special meaning to `sendmail` and are processed in a particular order.

The following sections cover the operators in more detail, in the order in which they appear in Table 30.1.

Macros are like shell variables. After you define a macro's value, you can refer to it later in the configuration file, and its value is substituted for the macro. For instance, a configuration file might have many lines that mention our hypothetical mail hub, `mailer.gonzo.gov`. Rather than repeatedly typing that name, you can define a macro `R` (for relay mailer):

```
DRmailer.gonzo.gov
```

When `sendmail` encounters a `$R` in `sendmail.cf`, it substitutes the string `mailer.gonzo.gov`.

Macro names are always a single character. Quite a few macros are defined by `sendmail` and shouldn't be redefined except to work around broken software[1]. `sendmail` uses lowercase letters for its predefined macros. Uppercase letters may be used freely. V8 `sendmail`'s predefined macros are fully documented in section 5.1.2 of the SIOG.

Classes are are similar to macros but are used for different purposes in rewriting rules. As with macros, classes are named by a single character. Lowercase letters are reserved for `sendmail`, and uppercase letters for user-defined classes. A class contains one or more words. For instance, you could define a class `H` containing all the hosts in the local domain:

```
CH larry moe curly
```

For convenience, large classes may be continued on subsequent lines. The following definition of the class `H` is exactly the same as the previous one:

```
CH larry
CH moe
CH curly
```

You can also define a class by reading its words from a file:

```
CF/usr/local/lib/localhosts
```

If the file `/usr/local/lib/localhosts` contains the words `larry`, `moe`, and `curly`, one per line, this definition is equivalent to the previous two.

Why use macros and classes? The best reason is that they centralize information in the configuration file. In the previous example, if you decide to change the name of the mail hub from `mailer.gonzo.gov` to `mailhub.gonzo.gov`, you only have to change the definition of the `$R` macro remedy, and the configuration file will work as before. If the name `mailer.gonzo.gov` is scattered throughout the file, you might forget to change it in some places. Also, if important information is centralized, you can comment it extensively in a single place. Because configuration files tend to be obscure at best, a liberal dose of comments is a good antidote to that sinking feeling you get when, six months later, you wonder why you made a change.

You probably won't want to change the header definitions given in the V8 `sendmail` configuration files because they already follow accepted standards. Here are some sample headers:

```
H?D?Date: $a
H?F?Resent-From: $q
H?F?From: $q
H?x?Full-Name: $x
```

Note that header definitions can use macros, which are expanded, when inserted into a letter. For instance, the `$x` macro used in the `Full-Name:` header definition above expands to the full name of the sender.

The optional *?mailerflag?* construct tells `sendmail` to insert a header only if the chosen mailer has that mailer flag set.

Suppose that the definition of your local mailer has a flag `Q`, and `sendmail` selects that mailer to deliver a letter. If your configuration file contains a header definition like the following one, `sendmail` inserts that header into letters delivered through the local mailer, substituting the value of the macro `$F`:

```
H?Q?X-Fruit-of-the-day: $F
```

Why would you use the *?mailerflag?* feature? Different protocols may require different mail headers. Because they also need different mailers, you can define appropriate mailer flags for each in the mailer definition and use the *?mailerflag?* construct in the header definition to tell `sendmail` whether to insert the header.

`sendmail` has many options that change its operation or tell it the location of files it uses. Most of them may be given either on the command line or in the configuration file. For instance, the location of the aliases file may be specified in either place. To specify the aliases file on the command line, you use the `-o` option:

```
$ sendmail -oA/etc/mail/aliases [other arguments...]
```

To do the same thing in the configuration file, you include a line like this:

```
OA/etc/mail/aliases
```

Either use is equivalent, but options such as the location of the aliases file rarely change, and most people set them in `sendmail.cf`. The V8 `sendmail` options are fully described in section 5.1.6 of the SIOG.

Users can include mail headers indicating the relative importance of their mail, and sendmail can use those headers to decide the priority of competing letters. Precedences for V8 sendmail are given as:

```
Pspecial-delivery=100
Pfirst-class=0
Plist=-30
Pbulk=-60
Pjunk=-100
```

If a user who runs a large mailing list includes the header Precedence: bulk in his letters, sendmail gives it a lower priority than a letter with the header Precedence: first-class.

As V8 sendmail evolves, its author adds new features. The V operator lets V8 sendmail know what features it should expect to find in your configuration file. Older versions of sendmail don't understand this command. Section 5.1.8 of the SIOG explains the different configuration file version levels in detail.

> **NOTE**
>
> The configuration file version level does not correspond to the sendmail version level. V8 sendmail understands versions 1 through 5 of configuration files, and there is no such thing as a version 8 configuration file.

sendmail has always used keyed databases, for instance, the aliases databases. Given the key postmaster, sendmail looks up the data associated with that key and returns the names of the accounts to which the postmaster's mail should be delivered. V8 sendmail extends this concept to arbitrary databases, including NIS maps (Sun's Network Information Service, formerly known as Yellow Pages or YP). The K operator tells sendmail the location of the database, its class, and how to access it. V8 sendmail supports the following classes of user-defined databases: dbm, btree, hash, and NIS. Depending on which of these databases you use, you must compile sendmail with different options. See section 5.1.9 of the SIOG for the lowdown on key files.

Mailers are either MTAs or final delivery agents. Recall that the aliases file allows you to send mail to a login name (which might be aliased to a remote user), a program, or a file. A special mailer may be defined for each purpose. And even though the SMTP MTA is built-in, it must have a mailer definition to tailor sendmail's SMTP operations.

Mailer definitions are important because all recipient addresses must resolve to a mailer in ruleset 0. Resolving to a mailer is just another name for sendmail's main function,

30

MAIL ADMINISTRATION

mail routing. For instance, resolving to the local mailer routes the letter to a local user via the final delivery agent defined in that mailer (usually `/bin/mail`), and resolving to the SMTP mailer routes the letter to another host via `sendmail`'s built-in SMTP transport, as defined in the SMTP mailer. A concrete example of a mailer definition makes this clearer. Because `sendmail` requires a local mailer definition, let's look at that:

```
Mlocal, P=/bin/mail, F=lsDFMfSn, S=10, R=20, A=mail -d $u
```

All mailer definitions begin with the `M` operator and the name of the mailer, in this case `local`. Other fields follow, separated by commas. Each field consists of a field name and its value, separated by an equal sign (`=`). The allowable fields are explained in section 5.1.4 of the SIOG.

In the local mailer definition given previously, the `P=` equivalence gives the pathname of the program to run to deliver the mail, `/bin/mail`. The `F=` field gives the `sendmail` flags for the local mailer. These flags are not passed to the command mentioned in the `P=` field but are used by `sendmail` to modify its operation depending on the mailer it chooses. For instance, `sendmail` usually drops its superuser status before invoking mailers, but you can use the `S` mailer flag to tell `sendmail` to retain it for certain mailers.

The `S=` and `R=` fields specify rulesets for `sendmail` to use in rewriting sender and recipient addresses. Because you can give different `R=` and `S=` flags for each mailer you define, you can rewrite addresses differently for each mailer. For instance, if one of your UUCP neighbors runs obsolete software that doesn't understand domain addressing, you might declare a special mailer just for that site and write mailer-specific rulesets to convert addresses into a form its mailer could understand.

The `S=` and `R=` fields can also specify different rulesets to rewrite the envelope and header addresses. A specification such as `S=21/31` tells `sendmail` to use ruleset 21 to rewrite sender envelope addresses and ruleset 31 to rewrite sender header addresses. This comes in handy for mailers that require addresses to be presented differently in the envelope and the headers.

The `A=` field gives the argument vector (command line) for the program that will be run, in this case `/bin/mail`. In this example, `sendmail` runs the command as `mail -d $u`, expanding the `$u` macro to the name of the user to which the mail should be delivered, for instance:

```
/bin/mail -d joe
```

This is exactly the same command that you could type to your shell at a command prompt.

There are many other mailer flags you might want to use to tune mailers, for instance to limit the maximum message size on a per-mailer basis. These flags are all documented in section 5.1.4 of the SIOG.

A configuration file is composed of a series of rulesets, which are somewhat like subroutines in a program. Rulesets are used to detect bad addresses, to rewrite addresses into forms that remote mailers can understand, and to route mail to one of `sendmail`'s internal mailers.

`sendmail` passes addresses to rulesets according to a built-in order. Rulesets may also call other rulesets not in the built-in order. The built-in order varies depending on whether the address being handled is a sender or receiver address and what mailer has been chosen to deliver the letter.

Rulesets are announced by the `S` command, which is followed by a number to identify the ruleset. `sendmail` collects subsequent `R` (rule) lines until it finds another `S` operator, or the end of the configuration file. The following example defines ruleset 11:

```
# Ruleset 11
S11
R$+        $: $>22 $1      call ruleset 22
```

This ruleset doesn't do much that is useful. The important thing to note is that `sendmail` collects ruleset number 11, composed of a single rule.

`sendmail` uses a three-track approach to processing addresses, one to choose a delivery agent, another to process sender addresses, and one for receiver addresses.

All addresses are first sent through ruleset 3 for preprocessing into a canonical form that makes them easy for other rulesets to handle. Regardless of the complexity of the address, ruleset 3's job is to decide the next host to which a letter should be sent. Ruleset 3 tries to locate that host in the address and mark it within angle brackets. In the simplest case, an address like `joe@gonzo.gov` becomes `joe<@gonzo.gov>`.

Ruleset 0 then determines the correct delivery agent (mailer) to use for each recipient. For instance, a letter from `betty@whizzer.com` to `joe@gonzo.gov` (an Internet site) and `pinhead!zippy` (an old-style UUCP site) requires two different mailers: an SMTP mailer for `gonzo.gov` and an old-style UUCP mailer for `pinhead`. Mailer selection determines later processing of sender and recipient addresses because the rulesets given in the `S=` and `R=` mailer flags vary from mailer to mailer.

Addresses sent through ruleset 0 must resolve to a mailer. This means that when an address matches the `lhs`, the `rhs` gives a triple[2] of `mailer`, `user`, `host`. The following line shows the syntax for a rule that resolves to a mailer:

```
Rlhs        $#mailer $@host $:user    your comment here...
```

The mailer is the name of one of the mailers you've defined in an M command, for instance smtp. The host and user are usually positional macros taken from the lhs match.

After sendmail selects a mailer in ruleset 0, it processes sender addresses through ruleset 1 (often empty), and then sends them to the ruleset given in the S= flag for that mailer.

Similarly, it sends recipient addresses through ruleset 2 (also often empty), and then to the ruleset mentioned in the R= mailer flag.

Finally, sendmail post-processes all addresses in ruleset 4, which among other things removes the angle brackets inserted by ruleset 3.

Why do mailers have different S= and R= flags? Consider the previous example of the letter sent to joe@gonzo.gov and pinhead!zippy. If betty@whizzer.com sends the mail, her address must appear in a different form to each recipient. For Joe, it should be a domain address, betty@whizzer.com. For Zippy, because whizzer.com expects old-style UUCP addresses (and assuming that it has a UUCP link to pinhead and whizzer.com's UUCP hostname is whizzer), the return address should be whizzer!betty. Joe's address must also be rewritten for the pinhead UUCP mailer, and Joe's copy must include an address for Zippy that his mailer can handle.

sendmail passes an address to a ruleset, and then processes it through each rule line by line. If the lhs of a rule matches the address, it is rewritten by the rhs. If it doesn't match, sendmail continues to the next rule until it reaches the end of the ruleset[3]. At the end of the ruleset, sendmail returns the rewritten address to the calling ruleset or to the next ruleset in its built-in execution sequence.

If an address matches the lhs and is rewritten by the rhs, the rule is tried again—an implicit loop (but see the $@ and $: modifiers discussed later for exceptions).

As shown earlier in Table 30.1, each rewriting rule is introduced by the R command and has three fields, the lefthand side (lhs, or matching side), the righthand side (rhs, or rewriting side), and an optional comment, each of which must be separated by tab characters:

```
Rlhs        rhs         comment
```

sendmail parses addresses and the lhs of rules into tokens and then matches the address and the lhs, token by token. The macro $o contains the characters that sendmail uses to separate an address into tokens. It's often defined like this:

```
# address delimiter characters
Do.:%@!^/[]
```

All the characters in $o are both token separators and tokens. `sendmail` takes an address such as `rae@rainbow.org` and breaks it into tokens according to the characters in the o macro, like this:

```
"rae"      "@"      "rainbow"      "."      "org"
```

`sendmail` also parses the `lhs` of rewriting rules into tokens so that they can be compared one by one with the input address to see whether they match. For instance, the `lhs` $-@rainbow.org gets parsed as the following:

```
"$-"      "@"      "rainbow"      "."      "org"
```

(Don't worry about the $- just yet. It's a pattern-matching operator similar to shell wildcards that matches any single token and is covered later in the chapter .) Now you can put the two together to show how `sendmail` decides whether an address matches the `lhs` of a rule:

```
"rae"     "@"      "rainbow"      "."      "org"
"$-"      "@"      "rainbow"      "."      "org"
```

In this case, each token from the address matches a constant string (for example, rainbow) or a pattern-matching operator ($-), so the address matches, and `sendmail` would use the `rhs` to rewrite the address.

Consider the effect (usually bad!) of changing the value of $o. As shown previously, `sendmail` breaks the address `rae@rainbow.org` into five tokens. However, if the @ character were not in $o, the address would be parsed quite differently, into only three tokens:

```
"rae@rainbow"      "."      "org"
```

You can see that changing $o has a drastic effect on `sendmail`'s address parsing, and you should leave it alone until you really know what you're doing. Even then you probably won't want to change it because the V8 `sendmail` configuration files already have it correctly defined for standard RFC 822 and RFC 976 address interpretation.

The `lhs` is a pattern against which `sendmail` matches the input address. The `lhs` may contain ordinary text or any of the pattern-matching operators shown in Table 30.2.

TABLE 30.2. `lhs` PATTERN-MATCHING OPERATORS.

Operator	Description
$-	Match exactly one token[4]
$+	Match one or more tokens
$*	Match zero or more tokens
$@	Match the null input (used to call the error mailer)

The values of macros and classes are matched in the lhs with the operators shown in Table 30.3.

TABLE 30.3. lhs MACRO AND CLASS MATCHING OPERATORS.

Operator	Description
$X	Match the value of macro X
$=C	Match any word in class C
$~C	Match if token is not in class C

The pattern-matching operators and macro- and class-matching operators are necessary because most rules must match many different input addresses. For instance, a rule might need to match all addresses that end with gonzo.gov and begin with one or more of anything.

The rhs of a rewriting rule tells sendmail how to rewrite an address that matches the lhs. The rhs may include text, macros, and positional references to matches in the lhs. When a pattern-matching operator from Table 30.2 matches the input, sendmail assigns it to a numeric macro $n, corresponding to the position it matches in the lhs. For instance, suppose that the address joe@pc1.gonzo.gov is passed to the following rule:

```
R$+ @ $+        $: $1 < @ $2 >              focus on domain
```

In this example, joe matches $+ (one or more of anything), so sendmail assigns the string joe to $1. The @ in the address matches the @ in the lhs, but constant strings are not assigned to positional macros. The tokens in the string pc1.gonzo.gov match the second $+ and are assigned to $2. The address is rewritten as $1<@$2>, or joe<@pc1.gonzo.gov>.

Consider the following rule:

```
R$*     $: $1 < @ $j >   add local domain
```

After rewriting an address in the rhs, sendmail tries to match the rewritten address with the lhs of the current rule. Because $* matches zero or more of anything, what prevents sendmail from going into an infinite loop on this rule? After all, no matter how the rhs rewrites the address, it always matches $*.

The $: preface to the rhs comes to the rescue; it tells sendmail to evaluate the rule only once.

There are also times when you want a ruleset to terminate immediately and return the address to the calling ruleset or the next ruleset in sendmail's built-in sequence.

Prefacing a rule's rhs with $@ causes sendmail to exit the ruleset immediately after rewriting the address in the rhs.

A ruleset can pass an address to another ruleset by using the $> notation (sendmail program)> preface to the rhs. Consider the following rule:

```
R$*        $: $>66 $1         call ruleset 66
```

The lhs $* matches zero or more of anything, so sendmail always does the rhs. As you saw in the previous section, the $: prevents the rule from being evaluated more than once. The $>66 $1 calls ruleset 66 with $1 as its input address. Because the $1 matches whatever was in the lhs, this rule simply passes the entirety of the current input address to ruleset 66. Whatever ruleset 66 returns is passed to the next rule in the ruleset.

Debugging a sendmail.cf can be a tricky business. Fortunately, sendmail provides several ways to test rulesets before you install them.

> **NOTE**
>
> The examples in this section assume that you have a working sendmail. If your system doesn't, try running them again after you've installed V8 sendmail.

The -bt option tells sendmail to enter its rule-testing mode:

```
$ sendmail -bt
ADDRESS TEST MODE (ruleset 3 NOT automatically invoked)
Enter <ruleset> <address>
>
```

> **NOTE**
>
> Notice the warning: ruleset 3 NOT automatically invoked. Older versions of sendmail ran ruleset 3 automatically when in address test mode, which made sense because sendmail sends all addresses through ruleset 3 anyway. V8 sendmail does not, but it's a good idea to invoke ruleset 3 manually because later rulesets expect the address to be in canonical form.

The > prompt means sendmail is waiting for you to enter one or more ruleset numbers, separated by commas, and an address. Try your login name with rulesets 3 and 0. The result should look something like this:

```
> 3,0 joe
rewrite: ruleset  3    input: joe
rewrite: ruleset  3 returns: joe
rewrite: ruleset  0    input: joe
rewrite: ruleset  3    input: joe
rewrite: ruleset  3 returns: joe
rewrite: ruleset  6    input: joe
rewrite: ruleset  6 returns: joe
rewrite: ruleset  0 returns: $# local $: joe
>
```

The output shows how `sendmail` processes the input address `joe` in each ruleset. Each line of output is identified with the number of the ruleset processing it, the input address, and the address that the ruleset returns. The > is a second prompt indicating that `send-mail` is waiting for another line of input. When you're finished testing, just type **Ctrl+D**.

Indentation and blank lines better show the flow of processing in this example:

```
rewrite: ruleset  3    input: joe
rewrite: ruleset  3 returns: joe

rewrite: ruleset  0    input: joe

      rewrite: ruleset  3    input: joe
      rewrite: ruleset  3 returns: joe

      rewrite: ruleset  6    input: joe
      rewrite: ruleset  6 returns: joe

rewrite: ruleset  0 returns: $# local $: joe
```

The rulesets called were 3 and 0, in that order. Ruleset 3 was processed and returned the value `joe`, and then `sendmail` called ruleset 0. Ruleset 0 called ruleset 3 again, and then ruleset 6, an example of how a ruleset can call another one by using $>. Neither ruleset 3 nor ruleset 6 rewrote the input address. Finally, ruleset 0 resolved to a mailer, as it must.

Often you need more detail than `-bt` provides—usually just before you tear out a large handful of hair because you don't understand why an address doesn't match the `lhs` of a rule. You may remain hirsute because `sendmail` has verbose debugging built-in to most of its code.

Use the `-d` option to turn on `sendmail`'s verbose debugging. This option is followed by a numeric code that tells which section of debugging code to turn on, and at what level. The following example shows how to run `sendmail` in one of its debugging modes and the output it produces:

```
$ sendmail -bt -d21.12
Version 8.6.7
ADDRESS TEST MODE (ruleset 3 NOT automatically invoked)
```

```
Enter <ruleset> <address>
> 3,0 joe
rewrite: ruleset  3    input: joe
——trying rule: $* < > $*
—— rule fails
——trying rule: $* < $* < $* < $+ > $* > $* > $*
—— rule fails
[etc.]
```

The `-d21.12` in the preceding example tells `sendmail` to turn on level 12 debugging in section 21 of its code. The same command with the option `-d21.36` gives more verbose output (debug level 36 instead of 12).

> **NOTE**
>
> You can combine one or more debugging specifications separated by commas, as in `-d21.12,14.2`, which turns on level 12 debugging in section 21 and level 2 debugging in section 14. You can also give a range of debugging sections, as in `-d1-10.35`, which turns on debugging in sections 1 through 10 at level 35. The specification `-d0-91.104` turns on all sections of V8 `sendmail`'s debugging code at the highest levels and produces thousands of lines of output for a single address.

The `-d` option is not limited to use with `sendmail`'s address testing mode (`-bt`); you can also use it to see how `sendmail` processes rulesets while sending a letter, as the following example shows:

```
$ sendmail -d21.36 joe@gonzo.gov < /tmp/letter
[lots and lots of output...]
```

Unfortunately, the SIOG doesn't tell you which numbers correspond to which sections of code. Instead, the author suggests that it's a lot of work to keep such documentation current (which it is), and that you should look at the code itself to discover the correct debugging formulas.

The function `tTd()` is the one to look for. For example, suppose that you wanted to turn on debugging in `sendmail`'s address-parsing code. The source file `parseaddr.c` contains most of this code, and the following command finds the allowable debugging levels:

```
$ egrep tTd parseaddr.c
        if (tTd(20, 1))
[...]
        if (tTd(24, 4))
        if (tTd(22, 11))
[etc.]
```

The `egrep` output shows that debugging specifications such as `-d20.1`, `-d24.4`, and `-d22.11` (and others) make sense to `sendmail`.

If perusing thousands of lines of C code doesn't appeal to you, the book `sendmail` documents the debugging flags for `sendmail` version 8.6.9.

The `-C` option allows you to test new configuration files before you install them, which is always a good idea. If you want to test a different file, use `-C/path/to/the/file`. This can be combined with the `-bt` and `-d` flags. For instance, a common invocation for testing new configuration files is:

```
sendmail -Ctest.cf -bt -d21.12
```

> **CAUTION**
>
> For security, `sendmail` drops its superuser permissions when you use the `-C` option. Final testing of configuration files should be done as the superuser to ensure that your testing is compatible with `sendmail`'s normal operating mode.

Configuring `sendmail`

When an SMTP client delivers mail to a host, it must do more than translate the hostname into an IP address. First, it asks for MX records. If any exist, it sorts them according to the priority given in the record. For instance, `whizzer.com` might have MX records listing the hosts `mailhub.whizzer.com`, `walrus.whizzer.com`, and `mailer.gonzo.gov` as the hosts willing to receive mail for it (and the "host" `whizzer.com` might not exist except as an MX record, meaning that there might be no IP address for it). Although any of these hosts accept mail for `whizzer.com`, the MX priorities specify which of those hosts the SMTP client should try first, and properly behaved SMTP clients will do so. In this case, the system administrator has set up a primary mail relay `mailhub.whizzer.com`, an onsite backup `walrus.whizzer.com`, and arranged with the system administrator at `mailer.gonzo.gov` for an offsite backup. They have set the MX priorities so that SMTP clients will try the primary mail relay first, the onsite backup second, and the offsite backup third. This setup takes care of the problems with the vendor who doesn't ship your parts on time as well as the wayward backhoe operator, who severs the fiber-optic cable that provides your site's Internet connection.

After collecting and sorting the MX records, the SMTP client gathers the IP addresses for the MX hosts and attempts delivery to them in order of MX preference. Keep this in mind when debugging mail problems. Just because a letter is addressed to joe@whizzer.com, it doesn't necessarily mean that a host named whizzer.com exists. Even if it does, it might not be the host that is supposed to receive the mail.

The distinction between header and envelope addresses is important because mail routers may process them differently. An example will help explain the difference between the two.

Suppose that you have a paper memo that you want to send to your colleagues Mary and Bill at the Gonzo Corporation, and Ted and Ben at the Whizzer company. You give a copy of the memo to your trusty mail clerk Alphonse, who notes the multiple recipients. Because he's a clever fellow who wants to save your company 32 cents, he makes two copies of the memo and puts each in an envelope addressed to the respective companies (rather than sending a copy to each recipient). On the cover of the Gonzo envelope he writes Mary and Bill, and on the cover of the Whizzer envelope he writes Ted and Ben. When his counterparts at Gonzo and Whizzer receive the envelopes, they make copies of the memo and send them to Mary, Bill, Ted, and Ben, without inspecting the addresses in the memo itself. As far as the Gonzo and Whizzer mail clerks are concerned, the memo itself might be addressed to the pope; they only care about the envelope addresses.

SMTP clients and servers work in much the same way. Suppose that joe@gonzo.gov sends mail to his colleagues betty@zippy.gov and fred@whizzer.com. The recipient list in the letter's headers may look like this:

```
To: betty@zippy.gov, fred@whizzer.com
```

The SMTP client at gonzo.gov connects to the whizzer.com mailer to deliver Fred's copy. When it's ready to list the recipients (the envelope address), what should it say? If it gives both recipients as they are listed in the To: line above (the header address), Betty will get two copies of the letter because the whizzer.com mailer will forward a copy to zippy.gov. The same problem occurs if the gonzo.gov SMTP client connects to zippy.gov and lists both Betty and Fred as recipients. The zippy.gov mailer will forward a second copy of Fred's letter.

The solution is the same one that Alphonse and his fellow mail clerks used. The gonzo.gov SMTP client puts an envelope around the letter that contains only the names of the recipients on each host. The complete recipient list is still in the letter's headers, but those are inside the envelope, and the SMTP servers at gonzo.gov and whizzer.com don't look at them. In this example, the envelope for the whizzer.com mailer would list only fred, and the envelope for zippy.gov would list only betty.

Aliases illustrate another reason why header and envelope addresses differ. Suppose that you send mail to the alias homeboys, which includes the names alphonse, joe, betty, and george. In your letter, you write To: homeboys. However, sendmail expands the alias and constructs an envelope that includes all the recipients. Depending on whether those names are also aliases, perhaps on other hosts, the original message might be put into as many as four different envelopes and delivered to four different hosts. In each case, the envelope contains only the name of the recipients, but the original message contains the alias homeboys (expanded to homeboys@*your.host.domain* so replies will work).

A final example shows another way in which envelope addresses may differ from header addresses. sendmail allows you to specify recipients on the command line. Suppose that you have a file named letter that looks like this:

```
$ cat letter
To: null recipient <>
Subject: header and envelope addresses

testing
```

and you send it with the following command (substituting your own login name for *yourlogin*):

```
$ sendmail yourlogin < letter
```

You will receive the letter even though your login name doesn't appear in the letter's headers because your address was on the envelope. Unless told otherwise (with the -t flag), sendmail constructs envelope addresses from the recipients you specify on the command line, and there isn't necessarily a correspondence between the header addresses and the envelope addresses.

To better understand how to set up sendmail, you need to know what different jobs it does and how those jobs fit into the scheme of MUAs, MTAs, mail routers, final delivery agents, and SMTP clients and servers. sendmail can act as a mail router, an SMTP client, and an SMTP server. However, it does not do final delivery of mail.

sendmail is primarily a mail router, meaning that it takes a letter, inspects the recipient addresses, and decides the best way to send it. How does sendmail do this?

sendmail determines some of the information it needs on its own, such as the current time and the name of the host on which it's running, but most of its brains are supplied by you, the postmaster, in the form of a configuration file, sendmail.cf. This somewhat cryptic file tells sendmail exactly how you want various kinds of mail handled. It is extremely flexible and powerful, and at first glance seemingly inscrutable. However, one of the strengths of V8 sendmail is its set of modular configuration file building blocks. Most sites can easily construct their configuration files from these modules, and many examples are included. Writing a configuration file from scratch is a daunting task; avoid it if you can.

As mentioned before, `sendmail` can function as an MTA because it understands the SMTP protocol (V8 `sendmail` also understands ESMTP). Because SMTP is a connection-oriented protocol, there is always a client and a server (also known as a sender and a receiver). The SMTP client delivers a letter to an SMTP server, which listens continuously on its computer's SMTP port. `sendmail` can be an SMTP client or an SMTP server. When run by an MUA, it becomes an SMTP client and speaks client-side SMTP to an SMTP server (not necessarily another `sendmail` program). When your system boots and it starts in daemon mode, it runs continuously, listening on the SMTP port for incoming mail.

One thing `sendmail` doesn't do is final delivery. `sendmail`'s author wisely chose to leave this task to other programs. `sendmail` is a big, complicated program that runs with superuser privileges, an almost guaranteed recipe for security problems, and there have been quite a few in `sendmail`'s past. The additional complexity of final mail delivery is the last thing `sendmail` needs.

`sendmail` depends on a number of auxiliary files to do its job. The most important are the aliases file and the configuration file, `sendmail.cf`. The statistics file, `sendmail.st`, can be created or not depending on whether you want the statistics. `sendmail.hf` is the SMTP help file and should be installed if you intend to run `sendmail` as an SMTP server (most sites do). That's all that needs to be said about `sendmail.st` and `sendmail.hf` (other auxiliary files are covered in the SIOG), but the aliases and `sendmail.cf` files are important enough to be covered in their own sections.

`sendmail` always checks recipient addresses for aliases, which are alternate names for a recipient. For instance, each Internet site is required to have a valid address postmaster to which mail problems may be reported. Most sites don't have an actual account of that name but divert the postmaster's mail to the person or persons responsible for email administration. For instance, at the mythical site `gonzo.gov`, the users `joe` and `betty` are jointly responsible for email administration, and the `/etc/aliases` file has the following entry:

```
postmaster: joe, betty
```

This line tells `sendmail` that mail to `postmaster` should instead be delivered to the login names `joe` and `betty`. In fact, those names could also be aliases:

```
postmaster: firstshiftops, secondshiftops, thirdshiftops
firstshiftops: joe, betty
secondshiftops: lou, emma
thirdshiftops: ben, mark, clara
```

In all these examples, the alias name is the part on the left side of the colon, and the aliases for those names are on the right side. sendmail repeatedly evaluates aliases until they resolve to a real user or a remote address. In the previous example, to resolve the alias postmaster, sendmail first expands it into the list of recipients firstshiftops, secondshiftops, and thirdshiftops and then expands each of these into the final list, joe, betty, lou, emma, ben, mark, and clara.

Although the right side of an alias may refer to a remote host, the left side may not. The alias joe: joe@whizzer.com is legal, but joe@gonzo.gov: joe@whizzer.com is not.

Aliases may be used to create mailing lists (in the previous example, the alias postmaster is in effect a mailing list for the local postmasters). For big or frequently changing lists, you can use the :include: alias form to direct sendmail to read the list members from a file. If the aliases file contains the following line:

```
homeboys: :include:/home/alphonse/homeboys.aliases
```

and the file /home/alphonse/homeboys.aliases contains:

```
alphonse
joe
betty
george
```

the effect is the same as the alias:

```
homeboys: alphonse, joe, betty, george
```

This is handy for mailing lists that change frequently, or those managed by users other than the postmaster. If you find a user is asking for frequent changes to a mail alias, you might want to put it under her control.

The aliases file also may be used to send the contents of email to a program. For instance, many mailing lists are set up so that you can get information about the list or subscribe to it by sending a letter to a special address, *list*-request. The letter usually contains a single word in its body, such as help or subscribe, which causes a program to mail an information file to the sender. Suppose that the gonzo mailing list has such an address called gonzo-request:

```
gonzo-request: |/usr/local/lib/auto-gonzo-reply
```

In this form of alias, the pipe sign (|) tells sendmail to use the program mailer, which is usually defined as /bin/sh. sendmail feeds the message to the standard input of /usr/local/lib/auto-gonzo-reply, and if it exits normally, sendmail considers the letter to be delivered.

You can also create an alias that causes `sendmail` to send mail to files. An example of this is the alias `nobody`, which is common on systems running the Network File System (NFS):

```
nobody: /dev/null
```

Aliases that specify files cause `sendmail` to append its message to the named file. Because the special file `/dev/null` is the UNIX bit-bucket, this alias simply throws mail away. Keep in mind that every time a change is made to the `/etc/aliases` file, you must either run the command `sendmail -bi` or `newaliases` to update the `/etc/aliases.db` data file.

Conclusion

Now you know a lot about the `sendmail.cf` language as well as some useful debugging techniques. However, configuration files are easier to grasp when you look at some real ones. The following section shows you how to create one from the `m4` templates included with V8 `sendmail`.

In this section, we'll develop a `sendmail.cf` for a Solaris 2.3 system, using the templates supplied with V8 `sendmail`. However, because every site is different, even if you're developing a `sendmail.cf` for another Solaris 2.3 system, yours will probably differ from the one in this section.

Previous versions of `sendmail` included complete, sample configuration files to adapt for your site. By contrast, the V8 `sendmail` configuration files are supplied as `m4` templates that you use like building blocks to create a custom configuration file. This is a big advantage for most people. In previous versions, if your site did not want UUCP support, you had to pick through hundreds of lines of a configuration file and remove it line by line. In this version, you simply insert the statement `FEATURE(nouucp)` into your configuration file template, and you are done.

`m4` is a programming language that reads a file of macro definitions and commands and creates an output file from it. As a trivial example, suppose that you create a document and find yourself repeatedly typing the phrase `sendmail Installation and Operation Guide`. To avoid the extra typing, you could define a macro `siog` and enter that instead:

```
$ cat > test.m4
define('siog','Sendmail Installation and Operation Guide')dnl
Testing: siog
Ctrl+D
$ m4 test.m4
Testing: Sendmail Installation and Operation Guide
```

30

MAIL
ADMINISTRATION

Running `m4` on the file `test.m4` converts all occurrences of `siog` to `sendmail Installation and Operation Guide`. This example only hints at `m4`'s capabilities. The V8 `sendmail.cf` templates make full use of them.

The `sendmail.cf` templates and `m4` support files are in the `cf` directory you created earlier when you unpacked V8 `sendmail`:

```
$ cd cf
$ ls -CF
README          domain/     hack/      mailer/     sh/
cf/             feature/    m4/        ostype/     siteconfig/
```

Please note the file `README`. If you don't read it, you have little hope of making a working configuration file.

The `cf` subdirectory is the main one of interest. It contains `m4` templates for configuration files used at the University of California at Berkeley (UCB). You should look at them all; one of them may be very close to what you need, and all of them provide good examples for you to adapt to your own site.

The other subdirectories contain `m4` support files, the building blocks that are included based on the template you define in the `cf` subdirectory. You probably won't have to change any of these, although you might need to create site-specific files in the `domain` and `siteconfig` subdirectories.

The `cf` subdirectory contains the following configuration file templates:

```
$ cd cf
$ ls -CF
Makefile             knecht.mc              sunos4.1-cs-exposed.mc
Makefile.dist        mail.cs.mc             sunos4.1-cs-hidden.mc
alpha.mc             mail.eecs.mc           tcpproto.mc
auspex.mc            obj/                   ucbarpa.mc
chez.mc              osf1-cs-exposed.mc     ucbvax.mc
clientproto.mc       osf1-cs-hidden.mc      udb.mc
cogsci.mc            python.mc              ultrix4.1-cs-exposed.mc
cs-exposed.mc        riscos-cs-exposed.mc   ultrix4.1-cs-hidden.mc
cs-hidden.mc         s2k.mc                 uucpproto.mc
hpux-cs-exposed.mc   sunos3.5-cs-exposed.mc vangogh.mc
hpux-cs-hidden.mc    sunos3.5-cs-hidden.m
```

The template `tcpproto.mc` is intended for a generic Internet site without UUCP connections. We'll use that as a starting point to develop our own. Because we don't want to modify the original file, we'll make a copy called `test.mc` and modify that. Although we won't show this in the following examples, it's a good idea to use a version control system such as SCCS or RCS, or some other version control system to track changes you make to your configuration file template.

Stripped of its comments (a copyright notice), blank lines, and an `m4` directive, `test.mc` looks like this:

```
include('../m4/cf.m4')
VERSIONID('@(#)tcpproto.mc     8.2 (Berkeley) 8/21/93')
FEATURE(nouucp)
MAILER(local)
MAILER(smtp)
```

This doesn't look like much, but `m4` expands it to almost 600 lines. We'll look at this template line-by-line to show what it does.

The line `include('../m4/cf.m4')` must come first in all configuration file templates, immediately after any comments. It contains the macro definitions that `m4` uses to build your configuration file, and if you don't include it here, nothing else works.

The `VERSIONID()` macro provides a place to put version information for the edification of humans—sendmail ignores it. If you use RCS or SCCS, you can include their version information here. For instance, for RCS you can include the `$Id$` keyword:

```
VERSIONID('$Id$')
```

and the RCS `co` (check-out) command expands this to:

```
VERSIONID('$Id: test.mc,v 1.1 1994/03/26 21:46:12 joe Exp joe $')
```

The `FEATURE()` macro is used to specify which features you want (or don't want). The line `FEATURE(nouucp)` in this configuration file template removes UUCP support from the resulting configuration file. Other features are documented in the `README` file mentioned earlier. Some features of particular interest are `redirect`, which provides a clever way to notify senders when someone leaves your site; and `nullclient`, which creates a bare-bones configuration file that knows just enough to forward mail to a relay. (See the template `nullclient.mc` for an example of its use.)

The next two lines are `MAILER()` macros to specify the mailers included in this `sendmail.cf`. The `MAILER()` macro takes a single argument, the name of the mailer when `m4` expands the `MAILER()` macro into one or more ruleset definitions, rules to select them in ruleset 0, and the rulesets given in the `R=` and `S=` flags. Selecting the `smtp` mailer actually causes three SMTP mailers to be included. The V8 templates also provide mailer definitions for UUCP mailers, a FAX mailer, and a POP (Post Office Protocol) mailer. See the `README` file for details.

This is almost enough of a specification to create a working `sendmail.cf` for an SMTP-only site, but you'll want to tune it a little first with additional macros.

The `OSTYPE()` macro also takes a single argument, the name of a file in `../ostype`. This file should contain definitions particular to your operating system, for instance, the location of the aliases file. A wide variety of operating system definitions are included with the V8 configuration files:

```
$ cd ../ostype
$ ls
aix3.m4       bsdi1.0.m4    hpux.m4       osf1.m4       sunos3.5.m4
aux.m4        dgux.m4       irix.m4       riscos4.5.m4  sunos4.1.m4
bsd4.3.m4     domainos.m4   linux.m4      sco3.2.m4     svr4.m4
bsd4.4.m4     dynix3.2.m4   nextstep.m4   solaris2.m4   ultrix4.1.m4
```

Because we're developing a configuration file for a Solaris 2.3 system, we'll look at that file:

```
$ cat solaris2.m4
define('ALIAS_FILE', /etc/mail/aliases)
define('HELP_FILE', /etc/mail/sendmail.hf)
define('STATUS_FILE', /etc/mail/sendmail.st)
define('LOCAL_MAILER_FLAGS', 'fSn')
```

This is pretty straightforward—the file gives the location of sendmail's auxiliary files on that system and specifies local mailer flags appropriate for the Solaris version of /bin/mail. We'll include an OSTYPE() macro just after the VERSIONID() macro, dropping the .m4 filename extension.

The other things you may define in an OSTYPE file are documented in the README.

You might also want to create a domain file and use the DOMAIN() macro to collect site-wide definitions such as your site's UUCP or BITNET relay hosts. Only put things in this file that are true for all the hosts in your domain. If you only have a single host, you might want to forego creating a domain file and keep this information in your m4 template.

The DOMAIN() macro takes a single argument, the name of a file in ../domain. For instance, DOMAIN(gonzo) would cause m4 to look for a file named ../domain/gonzo.m4. (Note that the .m4 extension is not included in the macro argument.)

> **CAUTION**
>
> If you copy one of the UCB templates that includes a DOMAIN() macro, make sure that you change that line to use your own domain file, or delete it.

A common feature to include in a domain file is the MASQUERADE_AS() macro, which causes all hosts using that sendmail.cf to masquerade as your mail hub. For example, if the Solaris 2.3 host we're building this configuration file for is one of many, all named sun*X*.gonzo.gov, the following line would cause all their outbound mail to be addressed as login@gonzo.gov, regardless of which workstation sent it:

```
MASQUERADE_AS(gonzo.gov)dnl
```

This line could also be included in the m4 template if you don't want to create a domain file. Now the template looks like this, with the lines we've added or changed in boldface type:

```
include('../m4/cf.m4')
VERSIONID('$Id$')
OSTYPE(solaris2)
MASQUERADE_AS(gonzo.gov)
FEATURE(nouucp)
MAILER(local)
MAILER(smtp)
```

To create the working sendmail.cf, run m4 on the template:

```
$ m4 test.mc > test.cf
```

This creates a 600-line configuration file, which should be tested thoroughly before you install it. We will do just that later in the chapter.

But first, considering that building a sendmail.cf file from the V8 macros is so easy, you might be wondering why I went on at such length about the guts of it. After all, if including an SMTP mailer is as easy as typing MAILER(smtp), why bother to learn the grungy details? The first answer is that someday you'll probably need them; something will go wrong, and you'll have to figure out exactly why your sendmail isn't working the way it should. You can't do that unless you understand the details. A second answer is that you can't properly test your sendmail.cf unless you know what's going on under the simplified m4 gloss. Finally, although the V8 configuration file templates are easy to work with compared to those included with previous versions of sendmail, they're still not exactly on a par with plugging in a new toaster and shoving in a couple of slices of rye. If sendmail were a toaster, instead of a single lever, it would have hundreds of complicated knobs and dials, a thick instruction manual, and despite your best efforts, would periodically burst into flames.

Before installing a new or modified sendmail.cf, you must test it thoroughly. Even small, apparently innocuous changes can lead to disaster, and as mentioned in the introduction to this chapter, people get really irate when you mess up the mail system.

The first step in testing is to create a list of addresses that you know should work at your site. For instance, at gonzo.gov, an Internet site without UUCP connections, they know that the following addresses must work:

```
joe
joe@pc1.gonzo.gov
joe@gonzo.gov
```

If gonzo.gov has a UUCP link, those addresses must also be tested. Other addresses to consider include the various kinds of aliases (for example, postmaster, a :include: list, an alias that mails to a file, and one that mails to a program), nonlocal addresses, source-routed addresses, and so on. If you want to be thorough, you can create a test address for each legal address format in RFC 822.

Now that you have your list of test addresses, you can use the -C and -bt options to see what happens. At a minimum, you'll want to run the addresses through rulesets 3 and 0 to make sure that they are routed to the correct mailer. An easy way to do this is to create a file containing the ruleset invocations and test addresses, and run sendmail on that. For instance, if the file addr.test contains the following lines:

```
3,0 joe
3,0 joe@pc1.gonzo.gov
3,0 joe@gonzo.gov
```

you can test your configuration file test.cf by typing:

```
$ sendmail -Ctest.cf -bt < addr.test
rewrite: ruleset  3   input: joe
rewrite: ruleset  3 returns: joe
[etc.]
```

You might also want to follow one or more addresses through the complete rewriting process. For instance, if an address resolves to the smtp mailer and that mailer specifies R=21, you can test recipient address rewriting with 3,2,21,4 *test_address*.

If the sendmail.cf appears to work correctly so far, it's time to move on to sending some real letters. You can do so with a command like this:

```
$ sendmail -v -oQ/tmp -Ctest.cf recipient < /dev/null
```

The -v option tells sendmail to be verbose so that you can see what's happening. Depending on whether the delivery is local or remote, you might see something as simple as joe... Sent, or an entire SMTP dialogue.

The -oQ/tmp tells sendmail to use /tmp as its queue directory. This is necessary because sendmail drops its superuser permissions when run with the -C option and can't write queue files into the normal mail queue directory. Because you are using the -C and -oQ options, sendmail also includes the following warning headers in the letter to help alert the recipient of possible mail forgery:

```
X-Authentication-Warning: gonzo.gov: Processed from queue /tmp
X-Authentication-Warning: gonzo.gov: Processed by joe with -C srvr.cf
```

sendmail also inserts the header `Apparently-to: joe` because although you specified a recipient on the command line, there was none in the body of the letter. In this case, the letter's body was taken from the empty file `/dev/null`, so there was no `To:` header. If you do your testing as the superuser, you can skip the `-oQ` argument, and sendmail won't insert the warning headers. You can avoid the `Apparently-to:` header by creating a file like this:

```
To: recipient

testing
```

and using it as input instead of `/dev/null`.

The recipient should be you so that you can inspect the headers of the letter for correctness. In particular, return address lines must include an FQDN for SMTP mail. That is, a header like `From: joe@gonzo` is incorrect because it doesn't include the domain part of the name, but a header like `From: joe@gonzo.gov` is fine.

Repeat this testing for the same variety of addresses you used in the first tests. You might have to create special aliases that point to you for some of the testing.

The amount of testing you do depends on the complexity of your site and the amount of experience you have, but a beginning system administrator should test things thoroughly, even for apparently simple installations. Remember the flaming toaster.

After you're satisfied that your `sendmail` and `sendmail.cf` work, you must decide where to install them. The most popular approach is to put `sendmail` and its other files in the same place that your vendor puts its distributed `sendmail` files. The advantage of this approach is conformity; if someone else familiar with your operating system tries to diagnose a mail problem, he will know where to look.

However, some people prefer to install local programs separately from vendor programs, for several good reasons. First, operating system upgrades are usually easier when local modifications are clearly segregated from vendor programs. Second, some vendors, notably Sun Microsystems, release operating system patches that bundle together everything including the kitchen sink. If you naively install such a patch, you might inadvertently overwrite your V8 `sendmail` with your vendor's version, and it probably won't understand your V8 `sendmail.cf`.

Therefore, you might want to install `sendmail` in a subdirectory of `/usr/local`, the traditional directory for local enhancements to the vendor's operating system. The locations of `sendmail`'s auxiliary files are given in `sendmail.cf`, so you can either leave them in the vendor's usual locations or install them in `/usr/local` and modify the `sendmail.cf` to match. If you want to change the compiled-in location of the configuration file, rede-

30

MAIL
ADMINISTRATION

fine the C preprocessor macro _PATH_SENDMAILCF in `src/Makefile` and recompile `send-mail`. For example, add the definition:

```
-D_PATH_SENDMAILCF=\"/usr/local/lib/sendmail.cf\"
```

to the `CFLAGS` macro in the `Makefile`.

When you've decided where the files should go, look at the makefile you used to compile `sendmail` and see whether it agrees. The easiest way is to use `make`'s `-n` option to see what would have happened. The results look like this for the V8 distribution's `Makefile.Solaris`:

```
$ make -n install
/usr/ucb/install -o root -g sys -m 6555 sendmail /usr/lib
for i in /usr/ucb/newaliases /usr/ucb/mailq; do rm -f $i; ln -s
/usr/lib/sendmai
l $i; done
/usr/ucb/install -c -o root -g sys -m 644 /dev/null \
    /var/log/sendmail.st
/usr/ucb/install -c -o root -g sys -m 444 sendmail.hf /etc/mail
nroff -h -mandoc aliases.5 > aliases.0
nroff -h -mandoc mailq.1 > mailq.0
nroff -h -mandoc newaliases.1 > newaliases.0
nroff -h -mandoc sendmail.8 > sendmail.0
```

If this isn't what you want, modify the makefile as necessary.

Note that the `sendmail` manual pages use the 4.4BSD `mandoc` macros, which your system probably doesn't have. You can `ftp` the `mandoc` macros from the host `ftp.uu.net`, in the directory `/systems/unix/bsd-sources/share/tmac`.

If your system doesn't have the `/usr/ucb/install` program, you can copy the new files instead and use `chown`, `chgrp`, and `chmod` to set the correct owner, group, and mode. However, if you're installing on top of your vendor's files, it's a good idea to first copy or rename them in case you ever need them again.

After you install `sendmail` and its auxiliary files, rebuild the aliases database by running `sendmail -bi`. You also need to kill and restart your `sendmail` daemon. If your vendor's system uses a frozen configuration file (`sendmail.fc`), remove it; V8 `sendmail` doesn't use one.

In its SMTP server role, `sendmail` starts when the system boots and runs continuously. If you install it in a nonstandard location such as `/usr/local`, you'll have to modify your system's startup scripts. Even if you install it in the standard location, you should make sure that the default system startup is correct for V8 `sendmail`.

When SVR4 UNIX systems boot, they run a series of short shell scripts in the directories /etc/rc*X*.d, where the *X* corresponds to the system run level. For instance, shell scripts that bring the system to run level 2 are found in /etc/rc2.d.

However, SVR4 systems have many run levels, and some software subsystems should be started in each of them. Therefore, the shell scripts in /etc/rc*X*.d are located in /etc/init.d and linked to the files in the /etc/rc*X*.d directories. The /etc/init.d directory is therefore the best place to look for your sendmail startup script.

The following example shows how to find how sendmail starts on a Solaris 2.3 system. Other SVR4 systems are similar:

```
$ cd /etc/init.d
$ grep sendmail *
sendmail:#ident "@(#)sendmail   1.4   92/07/14 SMI"   /* SVr4.0 1.5 */
sendmail:# /etc/init.d/sendmail - Start/Stop the sendmail daemon
sendmail:# If sendmail is already executing, don't re-execute it.
sendmail;if [ -f /usr/lib/sendmail -a -f /etc/mail/sendmail.cf ]; then
sendmail:                /usr/lib/sendmail -bd -q1h;
sendmail;pid='/usr/bin/ps -e ¦ /usr/bin/grep sendmail ¦ [...]
sendmail;echo "usage: /etc/rc2.d/S88sendmail {start¦stop}"
$
```

> **NOTE**
>
> Some of the preceding lines are truncated and shown as [...] due to page-width limitations.

In this case, the grep output shows that the vendor starts sendmail with a script named sendmail because each line of the grep output is prefixed with that filename. Examine the script sendmail to see whether any changes are necessary. This script expects sendmail to be located in /usr/lib. If you install V8 sendmail somewhere else, you'll have to modify the script to match, changing paths such as /usr/lib/sendmail to /usr/local/lib/sendmail. If the command-line flags in the script aren't what you want, change those too.

Other Mail Transfer Agents

One of the most popular alternatives to sendmail is a program known as qmail. Some of the advantages over sendmail show up in improved reliability, security, efficiency, and simplicity.

Many of the security holes in `sendmail` are plugged in `qmail`. Knowing about the recent denial of service attacks on critical systems, this is a major concern addressed by the program.

Reliability is enhanced by the straight paper path architecture and also a reliable mailbox format known as `maildir`. It is not as easy to corrupt `maildirs` as `mboxes` and `mh` folders during system crashes while mail is being transferred.

The code is extremely efficient. The author of `qmail` tested it on a Pentium machine running BSD UNIX sustaining 200,000 local messages per day. It can also overlap 20 simultaneous deliveries by default, which can be increased.

Probably the best feature of `qmail` is simplicity. Instead of having separate forwarding, aliasing, and mailing list mechanisms, `qmail` has only one simple forwarding mechanism, which gives all users the capability to handle their own mailing lists. Configuration is also much simpler.

In addition to these features, `qmail` also gives you host and user masquerading, full host hiding, virtual domains, null clients, list-owner rewriting, relay control, double-bounce recording, cross-host mailing list loop detection, per-recipient checkpointing, downed host backoffs, independent message retry schedules, and many other enhancements.

It is also easy to replace `sendmail` with `qmail` by using a drop-in `sentmail` wrapper so that your MUAs think they are using `sendmail`.

For more information, you can point your Web browser to `ftp://koobera.math.uic.edu/www/qmail.html`.

Summary

It's not possible in a single chapter to tell you all you must know about email administration, but as Yogi Berra (or maybe that was Casey Stengel) once said, "You could look it up," and you should. There are many things you'll learn only by reading the documentation mentioned in this chapter. However, this chapter should give you a good basis for understanding the theory behind Internet email delivery and enough of the specifics of V8 `sendmail` to get your email system up and running.

> 1. For instance, `sendmail` sets $j to your system's fully qualified domain name (FQDN, for example, `acme.com`). If your system's `gethostbyname()` function returns something other than the FQDN, you must define $j in `sendmail.cf`.
>
> 2. The local mailer omits the $@*host*.
>
> 3. Ruleset 0 is an exception to this rule. `sendmail` stops evaluating rules in ruleset 0 as soon as a rule resolves to a mailer.
>
> 4. Tokens are explained in "Tokens—How `sendmail` Interprets Input Patterns."

## CHAPTER 31

News
Administration

by William Pierce, Jeff Smith, and James Edwards

IN THIS CHAPTER

The history of the Usenet news service can be traced back to the original ARPAnet. The original ARPA-Internet community used a series of mailing lists to distribute information, bulletins, and updates to community members. As this community expanded, management of these mailing lists became more and more difficult. The lists became exceptionally long, and carrying out the necessary moves, adds, and changes became more onerous.

The Usenet provides a viable alternative for relaying this news. The idea is that the "news" information can be posted on a central server, available for users to retrieve whenever they want. The Usenet system provides similar functionality to the old mailing list operation; the information is arranged as individual articles divided into different groups and classifications. (Such a server is also referred to as an electronic bulletin board system, or BBS.) To make client access as efficient as possible, these central stores of "news" information are distributed to a number of local servers.

Usenet, the world's largest electronic BBS, is a loose conglomeration of computers that run operating systems ranging from MS-DOS to UNIX and VM/CMS and exchange articles through UUCP, the Internet, and other networks.

The lenient requirements for membership, the variety of computers able to run Usenet software, and the tremendous growth of the Internet have combined to make Usenet large.

Large volumes can cause problems for the system administrator because the amount of disk space required for news may vary a lot, and quickly. If you've planned poorly, it might take more important things with it—such as email, system logging, or accounting (see "Isolating the News Spool" later in this chapter to avoid that problem). This chapter (and good planning) will help you avoid some (but not all) of the late-night calls.

The chapter begins with some pointers on finding additional sources of information. Some information is included on the *UNIX Unleashed* CD-ROM, some is available on the Internet, and some (from the technical newsgroups) you'll be able to apply only after you get your news system running.

The examples in this chapter assume you have an Internet site running the Network News Transfer Protocol (NNTP). If your networking capabilities are limited to the UNIX-to-UNIX Copy Program (UUCP), you're mostly on your own. Although some of the general information given here still applies, UUCP is a pain, and the economics of a full newsfeed make Internet access more and more attractive every day. If your site isn't on the Internet but you want to receive news, it might be time to talk to your local Internet service provider. You might find it cheaper to pay Internet access fees than 15-hour-per-day phone bills. If your site's news needs aren't too great, it might be even more economical to buy Usenet access from an Internet service provider. (See the section "Do You *Really* Want to Be a Usenet Site?" later in this chapter.)

Additional Sources of Information

News software is inherently complex. This chapter will only begin to give you the information required to successfully maintain a Usenet site. The following sources of additional information will help you fill in the gaps.

Frequently Asked Questions (FAQ) Documents

In many Usenet newsgroups, especially the technical ones, similar questions are repeated as new participants join the group. To avoid answering the same questions over and over, volunteers collect these prototypical questions (and the answers) into FAQs. The FAQs are posted periodically to that newsgroup and to the newsgroup news.answers. Many FAQs are also available through the Internet file transfer protocol (ftp), through email servers, or through other information services such as Gopher, Wide Area Information Service (WAIS) and, of course, the World Wide Web (WWW).

You should read the FAQs in the following list after you've read this chapter and before you install your news system. All are available on the host rtfm.mit.edu in subdirectories of the directory pub/usenet/news.answers/index and referenced through the site URL—http://www.rtfm.mit.edu.

usenet-software/part1	History of Usenet; a glossary on software for transporting, reading, and posting news, including packages for nonUNIX operating systems (such as VMS and MS-DOS).
site-setup	Guidance on how to join Usenet.
news/software/b/intro	A short introduction to the newsgroup news.software.b.
news/software/b/faq	The news.software.b FAQ. Read this before you post to that newsgroup. Read it even if you don't plan to post.
INN FAQs	A four-part FAQ exists for INN. You can get it from any host that has the INN software, including ftp://ftp.xlink.net/pub/news/docs, http://www-old.xlink.net/~hwr/inn-faq/faq-index.html.

Another excellent source is the Usenet Information Center. This provides a hypertext-based index that covers the vast majority of available newsgroups, providing a FAQ for each one. The Usenet Information Center can be found at the following URL—
`http://sunsite.uuc.edu/usenet-i/`.

News Transport Software Documentation

Several news transport systems are available; some of the most commonly recommended include C-news, InterNetworkNews (INN) and Netscape's News Server. All these packages come with extensive documentation to help you with installation and maintenance. Whichever you select, read the documentation and then read it again. This chapter is no substitute for the software author's documentation, which is updated to match each release of the software and contains details that a chapter of this size can't cover.

Request for Comments (RFC) Documents

Request for Comments (RFC) are issued by working groups of the Internet Engineering Task Force (IETF). They were known initially as requests for comments, but as they become adopted as Internet standards, you should think of them as requirements for compliance—if you want to exchange news with another Internet NNTP site, you must comply with the provisions of both RFC 977 and 1036. RFCs are available for anonymous ftp on the host ftp://`ftp.internic.net` and others.

- RFC 977 (Network News Transfer Protocol) defines the commands by which Internet news servers exchange news articles with other news servers, newsreaders, and news-posting programs. The protocol is fairly simple, and this RFC gives you a better idea of what your newsreaders, news-posting programs, and news transport software are doing behind your back.

- RFC 1036 (Standard for Interchange of Usenet Messages) explains the format of Usenet news articles, which is based on the format of Internet email messages. You don't need to memorize it, but a quick read will help you understand the functions and formats of the various news articles.

Usenet Newsgroups

After your news system is running, you'll need to read several technical and policy newsgroups. These newsgroups will keep you abreast of new releases of software, bug fixes, and security problems. You'll also notice postings of common problems experienced at other sites, so if you encounter the same problems, you'll have the solutions. Many knowledgeable people contribute to these newsgroups, including the authors of C-news and INN.

Remember that the people answering your questions are volunteers, doing so in their spare time, so be polite. The first step toward politeness is to read the newsgroup's FAQ (if one exists) so that you avoid being the 1,001st lucky person to ask how to make a round wheel. You should also read the "Emily Postnews" guide to Usenet etiquette and other introductory articles in the newsgroup `news.announce.newusers`. A list of a few of the newsgroups you may want to read follows. You may want to subscribe to all the `news.*` groups for a few weeks, and then cancel the subscriptions for the ones you don't need.

`news.announce.newusers`	Information for new users. You should subscribe all your users to this group.
`news.announce.newgroups`	Announcements of newsgroup vote results and which newsgroups are about to be created.
`news.software.readers`	Information and discussion of news-reading software (also known as *newsreaders*).
`news.admin.policy`	Discussions pertaining to the site's news policies.
`news.software.b`	Discussions of software systems compatible with B-news (for example, C-news and INN).
`news.software.nntp`	Discussions of implementations of NNTP (for example, the so-called reference implementation and INN).

News Systems and Software

This section focuses on the major components of the Usenet. Clearly, these may be divided into two broad groups: those relating to the content and those relating to the transporting of articles.

> **NOTE**
>
> The details of this section are defined by two RFCs: RFC 977, "Network News Transfer Protocol," and RFC 1036, "Standard for Interchange of Usenet Messages."

News Articles

A news article is like an email message—it has a message body, which is accompanied by one or more headers that provide supplemental information relating to the message. A standard format for both message body and headers is outlined in RFC 1036.

This RFC indicates that the message body will follow a number of required header values that must accompany each posted news article. In addition, any message may optionally include one or more additional headers; however, these optional headers might be ignored by the receiving news server or client. Table 31.1 provides a useful summary of these header values. The table outlines which headers are optional and which are mandatory.

TABLE 31.1. USENET NEWS ARTICLE MESSAGE FORMAT.

Header	Description	Required	Optional
approved		For a moderated newsgroup	X
control		Control server exchanges, not a user message	X
date		Date message was posted	X
distribution		Scope of message	X
expires		Date to expire	X
followup-to		Followup message in group	X
from		Email address of poster	X
keywords		Subject related keywords	X
lines		Message body line count	X
message-id		Message unique id	X
newsgroups		Newsgroup to which message belongs	X
organization		Organization description	X
path		Path to current system	X
references		Message-id relating to this	X
reply-to		Reply to author	X
sender		Manually entered from field	X
subject		Message subject	X
summary		Brief message summary	X
xref		Host name	X

Newsgroup Hierarchies

Articles are posted to one or more newsgroups whose names are separated by periods to categorize them into hierarchies. For instance, the newsgroups `comp.unix.solaris` and `comp.risks` are both in the `comp` hierarchy, which contains articles having to do with computers. The `comp.unix.solaris` newsgroup is further categorized by inclusion in the `unix` subhierarchy, which has to do with various vendors' versions of UNIX.

Some of the current Usenet newsgroup hierarchies are shown in the following list. Some Internet mailing lists are fed into newsgroups in their own hierarchies.

`alt`	The alternative newsgroup hierarchy. Even less control exists here than in most of Usenet, with new newsgroups created at the whim of anyone who knows how to send a `newgroup` control message. It is mostly a swamp, but you can often find something useful. Examples: `alt.activism`, `alt.spam`.
`comp`	Computer-related newsgroups. Example: `comp.risks`.
`misc`	Things that don't seem to fit anywhere else. Examples: `misc.invest.stocks`, `misc.kids.vacation`.
`rec`	Recreational newsgroups. Example: `rec.woodworking`.
`soc`	Social newsgroups. Examples: `soc.college.grad`, `soc.culture.africa`.
`talk`	Talk newsgroups. Intended for people who like to argue in public about mostly unresolvable and controversial issues. The `talk` hierarchy is a great waste of time and users love it. Examples: `talk.politics.mideast`, `talk.abortion`.

TIP

Certain newsgroups and news postings are only relevant to certain geographical regions. For instance, it makes little sense to post an Indiana car-for-sale advertisement to the entire world. Distributions enable you to control how far your article travels, therefore conserving resources and cost.

For instance, you can usually post an article to your local site, your state, your continent, or to the entire world. The news system administrator controls which distributions are presented to users, which distributions are accepted by the

continues

news system when articles are brought in by its newsfeeds, and which distributions are offered to outside hosts. The latter is important for sites that want to keep their local distributions private.

Where News Articles Live

News articles arranged within the Usenet hierarchy are commonly stored in a separate file system in a site's news server. This file system is often named `/var/spool/news` or `/usr/spool/news`. The files that contain articles are given serial numbers as they are received, with the periods in the newsgroup names replaced by the slash character (`/`). For instance, article number 1047 of the newsgroup `comp.unix.solaris` would be stored in the file `/var/spool/news/comp/unix/solaris/1047`.

The News Overview Database (NOV)

More than 100MB of news is posted to the Usenet each day of the year.

That's approximately the size of a fairly thick novel. Most people want to have their favorite newsreader sift the wheat from the chaff and present them with only the articles they want to see, in some rational order.

To do this, newsreaders must keep a database of information about the articles in the news spool—for instance, an index of `subject` headers and article cross-references. These are commonly known as `threads` databases. The authors of newsreaders have independently developed different `threads` databases for their newsreaders, and naturally, they're all incompatible with each other. For instance, if you install `trn`, `nn`, and `tin`, you must install each of their `threads` database maintenance programs and databases, which can take a lot of CPU cycles to generate and may become quite large.

Geoff Collyer, one of the authors of C-news, saw that this was not good and created the News Overview Database (NOV), a standard database of information for fancy newsreaders. The main advantage of NOV is that only one database must be created and maintained for all newsreaders. The main disadvantage is that it hasn't yet caught on with all the authors of news software.

If you're interested in NOV support, you must install news transport software that has the NOV NNTP extensions (INN does) and newsreaders that can take advantage of it. According to the NOV FAQ, `trn3.3` and `tin-1.21` have built-in NOV support, and an unofficial (not supported by the author) version exists of `nn` for anonymous ftp on the host `agate.berkeley.edu` in the directory `~ftp/pub/usenet/NN-6.4P18+xover.tar.Z`.

Distributing the News

The Network News Transfer Protocol is the application that is used to distribute news articles between news servers and clients. NNTP is an application-level protocol—similar in operation and functionality to HTTP. As with HTTP, the NNTP application makes use of the reliable communication services provided by the TCP protocol.

The following section examines the operation of the NNTP application and highlights how NNTP provides a mechanism for the distribution of news throughout the Usenet and enables user access to these "news" servers. Figure 31.1 provides an overview of the architecture of the Usenet.

FIGURE 31.1.

*The Usenet archi-
tecture.*

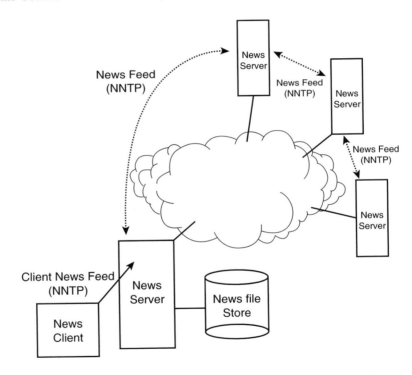

As Figure 31.1 indicates, the Usenet network relies on the operation of NNTP servers acting as central data stores of news information. Users are granted access to this information through client programs known as newsreaders. Information is conveyed throughout the Usenet through a process of server replication known as a *newsfeed*. Access for both clients and servers occurs over established TCP connections via the well-known port 119.

Like the HTTP application protocol, NNTP uses a system of request and response messages to exchange information with both clients and servers. These messages are formatted using standard ASCII characters. Table 31.2 provides a summary of the standard request message commands.

TABLE 31.2. SUMMARY OF USENET REQUEST MESSAGE COMMANDS.

Request Command	Description
article <message-id>	Displays the message header, a blank line, and the text body.
body <message-id>	Displays the message body only.
group newsgroup	Selects the indicated newsgroup.
head <message-id>	Displays the selected article header fields.
Help	Provides a list of available commands.
ihave <message-id>	Informs the server that the client has the indicated message.
last	Decrements the current article pointer.
list	Returns a list of the existing newsgroups.
listgroup	Lists current articles with the selected group.
newgroups date time	Lists new groups since date and time.
newnews date time	Lists new articles within a selected newsgroup since the specified data and time.
next	Increments the current article pointer.
post	Starts an article posting, terminated with a single period (.) on an otherwise blank line.
Quit	Closes the client TCP connection to the server.
slave	Indicates that this connection is to a slave server that is providing news services to a number of users.
stat	Client selects an article to read.

The contacted news server responds to any message request with a response that consists of two parts: a three-digit status number and a text-based message body. The returned status number provides an indication of the success or failure of the particular request—following a format similar to that used within the ftp application. Table 31.3 provides a summary of the possible values.

TABLE 31.3. NNTP STATUS LINE RESPONSE CODES.

Status Numbers	Description
1xx	Informational messages.
2xx	Successful commands (command ok).
3xx	Successful commands so far, send the rest of it.
4xx	Command was correct, but it couldn't be performed for some reason.
5xx	Command not available, or a serious error occurred.
For each of these groups	
x0x	Relating to connection setup.
x1x	Relating to newsgroup selection.
x2x	Relating to article selection.
x3x	Relating to distribution functions.
x4x	Relating to article posting.
x8x	Relating to private application extensions.
x9x	Relating to debugging codes.

The news server signals the end of any message or command with a line consisting of a single dot (.). If any line of text actually starts with a dot, the server adds another one to indicate that it is not the end of message marker.

Listing 31.1 provides an example of the operation of NNTP between a newsreader and Usenet server. In this example, the client requests to read a single news article that is contained within a particular newsgroup—notice how the server responds to the client NNTP requests with a status line and one or more lines of text.

LISTING 31.1. SAMPLE OPERATION OF THE NNTP APPLICATION.

```
client attaches to selected newserver
200 usenetserver news server ready - posting ok

client requests a list of available newsgroups
LIST
215 list of newsgroups follows
alt.2600
alt.2600.aol
...
...
comp.protocols.snmp
```

continues

LISTING 31.1. CONTINUED.

```
comp.protocols.frame-relay
comp.protocols.tcp-ip
...
...
...
select a particular group
GROUP comp.protocols.tcp-ip
211 86 1001 1087 comp.protocols.tcp-ip group selected
ARTICLE 1002
220 1002 <13343@darkstar.com> Article retrieved, text follows
Path:
From:
Newsgroup: comp.protocols.tcp-ip
Subject: HTTP Request Formats
Date: 8 March 1997 20:21:32  EST
Organization: Deloitte Touche Consulting Group

message body appears here


.
message response is terminated with a single period
client ends session using the quit command.
QUIT
```

Sharing News Over the Network

If you have several hosts on a local area network (LAN), you'll want to share news among them to conserve disk space.

Two ways exist to share news over a LAN. If all your hosts run a network file system such as Sun Microsystem's NFS or Transarc's AFS (Andrew File System), you can export the news host's spool directory to them or use NNTP to transfer news from a single server host to client newsreaders and news-posting programs. An alternative approach would be to use NNTP to transfer news from a single server host to client newsreaders and news-posting programs. The only requirements for the client hosts are that they must be able to open up a TCP/IP connection over the network and have client software that understands NNTP. Most common UNIX-based newsreaders and news-posting programs have built-in NNTP support, and many NNTP clients exist for nonUNIX operating systems such as DOS, VMS, VM/CMS, and others.

An NNTP daemon runs continuously on the news server host, listening on a well-known port, the same as the Simple Mail Transfer Protocol (SMTP) server listens on a well-known port for incoming email connections. NNTP client programs connect to the NNTP server and issue commands for reading and posting news articles. For instance, commands exist to ask for all the articles that have arrived since a certain date and time.

A client newsreader can ask for those articles and display them to the user as the NNTP server ships them over the network. Hosts with which you exchange news connect to the NNTP server's port and transfer articles to your host.

NNTP servers usually have some form of built-in access control so that only authorized hosts can connect to them—after all, you don't want all the hosts on the Internet to be able to connect to your news server.

Transferring News to Other Hosts

When a posting program hands an article to the news system, it expects a copy of the article to be deposited in the local news spool (or the news spool of the local NNTP server), sent to other hosts and eventually sent to the rest of Usenet. Similarly, articles posted on other Usenet hosts should eventually find their way into the local (or NNTP server's) spool directory.

Figure 31.2 illustrates a simple set of connections between hosts transferring news. The incoming and outgoing lines emphasize that news is both sent and received between each set of hosts.

FIGURE 31.2.

The Usenet flooding algorithm.

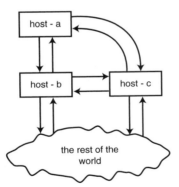

Usenet news is transferred by a flooding algorithm, which means when a host receives an article, it sends it to all other hosts with which it exchanges news, and those hosts do the same. By using this technique, an article can be transferred to a host from many hosts. This is a waste of time and resources that can be used for more productive services. Now suppose that someone on host-b in Figure 31.2 posts a news article.

Because of the flooding algorithm, host-b sends the article to host-a, host-c, and any other hosts with which it exchanges news. Host-c gets the article and does the same, which means it gives the same article to host-a, which may try to give it back to host-b, which already has a copy of the article in its news spool. Just to keep the news administrator's life interesting, no one can say whether any other hosts will ship the same article back to `host-b` or `host-c`, which obviously could cause a duplicate article. How do these hosts know when articles are duplicates and should be rejected? Obviously, they can't compare a new article with every article currently in the spool directory.

The news system software uses two methods to avoid duplicate articles. The first is the `Path` header, which is a record of all the hosts through which a news article has passed. The `Path` header is a list of hosts separated by punctuation marks other than periods, which are considered part of a hostname. A `Path` such as `hst.gonzo.com`, `host-c.big.org!host-b.shark.com` means that an article has been processed by the sites `hst.gonzo.com`, `host-c.big.org`, and `host-b.shark.com`. Any of those hosts can reject the article because its name is already in the path.

RFC 1036 says that the `Path` header should not be used to generate email reply addresses. However, some obsolete software might try to use it for that. INN discourages this use by inserting the pseudo-host `not-for-mail` into the `Path`.

The second way in which news systems avoid duplicate articles is the message identifier header, `Message-ID`. The following is a sample `Message-ID` header:

```
Message-ID: <CsuM4v.3u9@hst.gonzo.com>
```

When a news article is created, the posting program or some other part of the news system generates this unique header. Because no two articles have the same `Message-ID` header, the news system can keep track of the message identifiers of all recent articles and reject those that it has already seen. The news `history` file keeps this record, and news transport programs consult the history file when they're offered news articles. Because the volume of news is so large, history files get big quickly and are usually kept in some database format that enables quick access.

The history mechanism is not perfect. If you configure your news system to remember the message identifiers of all articles received in the past month, your history files may become inconveniently large. On the other hand, if a news system somewhere malfunctions and injects two-month-old articles into Usenet, you won't have enough of a history to reject those articles. Inevitably, no matter how long a history you keep, it won't be long enough, and you'll get a batch of old, bogus articles. Your users will complain. Such is life.

Host-to-Host News Transport Protocols

As with electronic mail, to transfer news from host to host, both hosts must speak the same language. Most Usenet news is transferred either with the UUCP (UNIX-to-UNIX

Copy Protocol) or NNTP. UUCP is used by hosts that connect with modems over ordinary telephone lines, and NNTP is the method of choice for hosts on the Internet. UUCP would not be the method of choice unless it's the only available method.

News Transport System Configuration Files

The news transport system requires information about the local site. Minimally, it must know with which hosts you exchange news, at what times you do so, and which transport protocol you use for each site. It has to know which newsgroups and distributions your site should accept and which it should reject. NNTP sites must know which hosts are authorized to connect with them to read, post, and transfer news.

The news transport system's configuration files provide this information. The news administrator must set up these files when installing the news system and must modify them in response to changes, such as a new newsfeed. The format of news transport system control files varies, but all current systems provide detailed configuration documentation. This documentation should be read by the administrator to keep current on any changes or new requirements.

The User Interface—Newsreaders and Posting Programs

Newsreaders are the user interface to reading news. Because news articles are stored as ordinary files, you could use a program such as cat or more for your news reading, but most users want something more sophisticated. Many newsgroups receive more than a hundred articles a day, and most users don't have time to read them all. They want a program that helps them quickly reject the junk so they can read only articles of interest to them. A good newsreader enables users to select and reject articles based on their subject header; several provide even more sophisticated filtering capabilities. Some of the more popular newsreaders are rn (and its variant trn), nn, and tin. The GNU Emacs editor also has several packages (GNUS and Gnews) available for newsreading from within Emacs. These newsreaders are available for anonymous ftp from the host ftp.uu.net and others.

Newsreaders usually have built-in news-posting programs or the capability to call a posting program from within the newsreader. Most of them also let you respond to articles by email.

Numerous free newsreaders are available, and each has certain characteristics that cause a wide range of opinions on which is the best. Users will probably want you to install them all, as well as whatever wonderful new one was posted to `comp.sources.unix` recently. The administrator, with input from the users, should make a selection of three or four readers and maintain them on the system. This will reduce the administrator's maintenance time, and if a user wants a specific newsreader, then the user should be responsible for installing and maintaining the private copy.

News-posting programs enable you to post your own articles. A news-posting program prepares an article template with properly formatted headers, and then calls the text editor of your choice (usually whatever is named in the `EDITOR` environment variable) so you can type in your article. When you exit the editor, you're usually given choices to post the article, edit it again, or quit without posting anything. If you choose to post the article, the news-posting program hands it to another news system program, which injects it into the news transport system and puts a copy in the news spool directory.

GUI Newsreaders

Listing 31.1 provides an example of the operation of a text-based newsreader. Increasingly, newsreaders are being incorporated within Web browser applications, providing a graphical view of newsgroups and articles. Figure 31.3 shows the newsreader that is incorporated within a standard Netscape browser.

FIGURE 31.3.

Viewing news with the Netscape Web browser.

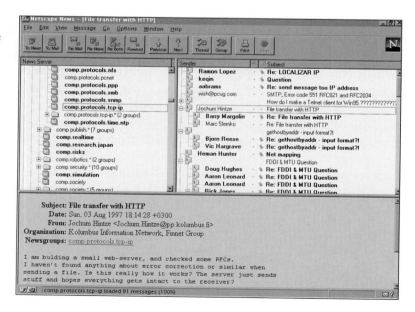

Notice that the Netscape Newsreader provides a three-way split screen. In the left window, the name of the news server is displayed along with the newsgroups available. For the highlighted newsgroup (`comp.protocols.tcp-ip` in the example), the right screen details the existing articles. These articles are arranged into separate threads—each thread relating to a particular conversation or related topic. The user can select a particular news article and view it in the bottom window of the newsreader screen.

The benefits of using a graphical newsreader are clearly demonstrated in Figure 31.3. Each of the separate windows is related to the execution of a particular NNTP request message. The user can use the mouse to navigate the information returned by the news server without having to remember the somewhat cryptic command requests listed in Table 31.1.

Planning a News System

You can see from the preceding discussion that you can use different strategies to set up a news system. Because sites' needs vary, no single right way exists to do it. You must evaluate your site's needs and choose a strategy that matches those requirements. The questions in this section are intended to make you think about some of the issues you should consider.

Do You *Really* Want to Be a Usenet Site?

As pointed out in the "How to join Usenet" FAQ, you may not want to join at all. A newsfeed consumes significant CPU cycles, disk space, network (or modem) bandwidth, and staff time. Many Internet service providers will give your site access to Usenet news over the network through NNTP client newsreaders. If your site is small, this may be more economical than a newsfeed. Do yourself a favor and do the math before you jump in. You can always join Usenet at a later date if you find that your site's needs require a real feed.

Shared News Versus One News Spool Per Host

A basic decision is whether you will maintain separate news spools and news systems on all your hosts, or designate a single host to act as a news server and let other hosts access news through the network. If you have more than one host to administer, definite advantages exist to the latter approach.

If you have a single news host, your job as news administrator is much easier. Most news problems are confined to that host, and you only have to maintain the (fairly complex) news transport software on that host. Software on client hosts is limited to newsreaders and news-posting software—no news transport software is necessary. If problems occur, you know where to go to solve them, and after you solve them on the news host, they are solved for all the hosts in your domain.

Usenet volume helps make a single-host strategy attractive. As mentioned previously, a full newsfeed can easily require a gigabyte of disk space, and the volume of Usenet news continues to grow, seemingly without bound. It's a lot easier to convince your boss to buy a bigger disk drive for a single host than for twenty. Because many users don't read news every day, the longer you can retain articles the happier they are, and you can retain articles longer on a single, dedicated news host than you can on multiple hosts.

Economics points to using a single news host to minimize expensive staff time and to conserve disk space. The administrator might want to store news on multiple hosts only if your network needs upgrading, network utilization is consistently high, or your only network connections are through UUCP. You can't share news on a network file system (NFS) using NNTP.

Isolating the News Spool

Because the news spool will grow at an unpredictable rate, the administrator should isolate the news/spool to its own separate file system. Where possible, it should reside on its own private disk so as not to compete for space with more important data. If this can't be done, the administrator should set up routines to frequently check the disk where the news articles are stored for space availability.

Configuring Your News Spool's File System

A major point in configuring the news file system is to remember that news articles are usually small in size and numerous in quantity. When you're creating the file system, the default value for inodes may not be sufficient. If you utilize all the inodes, you can no longer write to the file system. Syntax and commands to configure a disk partition and file system are covered in other chapters of this book and should be read prior to creating the partition and/or file system.

Where Will You Get Your News?

Some organizations use Usenet for internal communications—for instance, a corporate BBS—and don't need or want to connect to Usenet. However, if you want a Usenet connection, you'll have to find one or more hosts willing to exchange news with you. Note that they are doing you a big favor—a full newsfeed consumes a lot of CPU cycles, network bandwidth, and staff time. The spirit of Usenet, however, is altruistic, and you may find a host willing to supply you with a newsfeed for free. In turn, you may someday be asked to supply a feed to someone else.

Finding a host willing to give you a newsfeed is easier if you're already on Usenet, but if you were, you wouldn't need one. Your Internet service provider might be able to give you contact information, and many service providers supply newsfeeds either as part of their basic service or at additional cost. Personal contacts with other system administrators who are already connected to Usenet may help, even if they can't supply you a feed themselves. The "How to join Usenet" FAQ mentioned previously contains other good ideas for finding a newsfeed.

It's a good idea to try to find a newsfeed that is topographically close on your network. If your site is in Indiana, you don't want a transatlantic feed from Finland, even if you manage to find a host there willing to do it.

Site Policies

Your users' Usenet articles reflect on your site, and new users often make mistakes. Unfortunately, the kinds of mistakes you can make on a worldwide network are the really bad ones. You should develop organizational Usenet access policies and educate your users on proper Usenet etiquette.

Policy questions tend toward the ethical and legal. For instance, if you carry the `alt` hierarchy, what will be your site's response when someone creates the newsgroup `alt.child-molesting.advocacy`? This is not beyond the pale of what you may expect in the `alt` hierarchy. Even within the traditional hierarchies, where newsgroups are voted into existence, you might find newsgroups your site won't want to carry. What will you do when you receive a letter from `joe@remote.site.edu`, whining that one of your users is polluting his favorite newsgroup with "inappropriate" (in his opinion) postings. Do you want to get involved in Usenet squabbles like that?

What will you do when you get 2,843 letters complaining that one of your users posted a pyramid scheme come-on to 300 newsgroups? Shoot him? Or maybe wish you'd done a more careful job of setting policy in the first place?

And what will you do when someone complains that the postings in `alt.binaries.pictures.erotica.blondes` are a form of sexual harassment and demands that the newsgroup be removed? Will you put yourself in the position of censor and drop that newsgroup, or drop the entire `alt` hierarchy to avoid having to judge the worth of a single newsgroup?

If you put yourself in the position of picking and choosing newsgroups, you will find that although it may be completely obvious to you that `comp.risks` has merit and `alt.spam` doesn't, your users may vehemently disagree. If you propose to locally delete `alt.spam` to conserve computing resources, some users will refer to their right to free speech and accuse you of censorship and fascism. (Are you sure you wanted this job?)

Most news administrators don't want to be censors or arbiters of taste. Therefore, answers to policy questions should be worked out in advance, codified as site policy, and approved by management. You need to hammer away at your boss until you get a written policy telling you what you should and should not do with respect to news administration, and you need to do this before you join Usenet. Such a policy should also provide for user education and set bounds for proper user behavior.

Without taking a position on the merits of `alt.spam`, Usenet access is not one of the fundamental rights enumerated in the United States Constitution. It's more like a driver's license—if you're willing to follow your site's rules, you can drive; if you're not, you can't. It's management's job to provide those rules, with guidance from you.

Expiration Policies

News system software is flexible enough to selectively purge old articles. In other words, if your site doesn't care much about the `alt` hierarchy but considers the `comp` hierarchy to be important, it can retain `comp` articles longer than `alt` articles. From the preceding discussion, you can see that this might be contentious. If Joe thinks that `alt.spam` is the greatest thing since indoor plumbing, he will cry foul if you expire `spam` articles in one day but retain `comp` articles for seven. You can see that article expiration is not only a technical issue but a policy issue and should be covered in the same written policies mentioned previously.

Automatic Response to `newsgroup`/`rmgroup` Control Messages

Newsgroups are created and removed by special news articles called control messages. Anyone bright enough to understand RFCs 1036 and 977 can easily forge control messages to create and remove newsgroups. (That is, just about anyone.) This is a particular problem in the `alt` hierarchy, which for some reason attracts people with too much time on their hands, who enjoy creating newsgroups such as `alt.swedish-chef.bork.bork.bork`. The `alt` hierarchy also is used by people who don't want to go to the trouble of creating a new newsgroup through a Usenet-wide vote, or who (usually correctly) guess that their harebrained proposal wouldn't pass even the fairly easy Usenet newsgroup creation process.

Another problem, somewhat less frequent, occurs when a novice news administrator posts newsgroup messages with incorrect distributions and floods the net with requests to create his local groups.

You can configure your news system software to create and delete groups automatically upon receiving control messages or to send email to the news administrator saying that the group should be created or removed. If you like living dangerously, you can enable automatic creation and deletion, but most people don't. You don't want someone to delete all your newsgroups just to see if he can, and you don't want two or three hundred created because a news system administrator made a distribution mistake. Many sites allow automatic creation but do deletions manually. More cautious sites create and delete all groups by hand, and only if they have reason to believe the control message is valid. I recommend the latter approach. The only disadvantage is that you may miss the first few articles posted to a new newsgroup if you don't stay on top of things.

The ABCs of News Transport Software

Usenet began with A-news, a prototype news transport system that was killed by its own success and was supplanted by B-news. B-news sufficed for quite a while but became another victim of Usenet growth and was supplanted by C-news, a much more efficient system written by Henry Spencer and Geoff Collyer of the University of Toronto. C-news was followed by INN (InterNetworkNews), which was originally written by Rich Salz of the Open Software Foundation, who apparently hadn't heard of the letter "D." Rich has since passed responsibility for INN over to the Internet Software Consortium (ISC), which now is the official source for all INN releases. The Consortium can be found at the URL `http://www.isc/org/isc`.

Depending on your site's requirements, either C-news, INN, or even Netscape's News Server make good news transport systems, but this chapter has space for only one, INN. If you install C-news and your site plans to use NNTP, you should also obtain and install the NNTP "reference implementation," that is available by anonymous ftp from the URL `ftp://ftp.uu.net/~ftp/networking/news/nntp`. This isn't necessary for INN, which has a slightly modified version of NNTP built in.

INN is the news transport system of choice for Internet sites that use NNTP to exchange news and provide newsreaders and news-posting services. It was designed specifically for efficiency in an Internet/NNTP environment, for hosts with many newsfeeds and lots of NNTP client newsreaders. Although its installation isn't as automated as C-news, it's not all that difficult, and it's well-documented. The following sections give an overview of how to build and install INN.

Getting Your Hands on the Sources

The latest version of INN available as this book goes to press is called INN 1.5.1. It is available from `ftp://ftp.vix.com/pub/inn` or in one of the mirror sites that have been set up by the ISC. Refer to the ISC Web site at `http://www.isc.org/inn.HTML` for more information. It is important to note that a patch has been released to fix a security bug found within INN 1.5.1. This patch is also available via the ISC and can be found at its ftp site at `ftp://ftp.isc.org/isc/inn/unoff-patches`.

An INN Distribution Roadmap

Most of the important directories and programs in the INN distribution are summarized in the following list. Some are covered in more detail in the sections "Configuring INN—the `config.data` File," "Building INN," and "Site Configuration."

`BUILD`	A shell script for building and installing INN.
`Install.ms.*`	The `nroff` sources to INN's installation documentation.
`README`	What you might think. Read it.
`backends`	Programs for transferring news to your Usenet neighbors.
`config`	Contains the file `config.dist`, with which you create `config.data`. `Config.data` controls the compilation of the rest of INN.
`dbz`	Sources for the database routines used by INN. `dbz` is a faster version of the `dbm` database programs included with many versions of UNIX.
`doc`	INN's manual pages.
`expire`	Contains programs that handle news expiration or the purging of articles from your news spool. They also selectively purge old `Message-IDs` from the history file so it doesn't grow boundlessly.
`frontends`	Contains programs that control `innd`'s operation or offer its news articles.
`include`	C language header files for the INN programs.
`innd`	The heart of INN, `innd` is the daemon that listens on the NNTP port for incoming news transfers and newsreader connections. When newsreaders connect to this port, `innd` creates `nnrpd` processes and connects them to the newsreader.
`lib`	The sources for the C language function library used by other INN programs.

nnrpd	Communicates with NNTP newsreader clients, which frees innd to do its main job, transferring news.
samples	Sample configuration files that are copied into the site directory.
site	This directory contains shell scripts and site configuration files. The site configuration files must be edited to tell INN with which sites you exchange news, which hosts are allowed to connect to read and post news, and so on.
syslog	A replacement for older versions of the standard system logging program. You may not need this.

Learning About INN

The first step in setting up INN is to format and read its documentation. Input cd into the top of the INN source tree and type the following to create a formatted copy of the INN documentation named Install.txt:

```
$ make Install.ms
cat Install.ms.1 Install.ms.2 >Install.ms
chmod 444 Install.ms
$ nroff -ms Install.ms > Install.txt
```

If the make command doesn't work for you (and if it doesn't, your make is defective and will cause you problems later), type **cat Install.ms.? > Install.ms** and then the preceding nroff command. These two commands create a file named Install.txt, which you can view with your preferred editor or pager. Read it. Print it. Highlight it with your favorite color of fluorescent marker. Sleep with it under your pillow. Take it into the shower. Share it with your friends. Read it again. You won't be sorry.

The Install.ms document tells you just about everything you need to know to set up a news system based on INN. The only problem with it is that many people fail to read it carefully and think that something is missing. There isn't. If you think there is, read it again.

Configuring INN—the config.data File

After you've absorbed the INN documentation, you're ready to configure INN's compilation environment. Like C-news, INN can run on many versions of UNIX. The programs that build INN require information about your version of UNIX so they can build INN correctly. This configuration is one of the most difficult parts of installing INN. The Install.ms documentation is essential because it contains sample configurations for different versions of UNIX.

The directory `config` holds the INN master configuration file, `config.data`. INN uses the C-news `subst` program to modify its sources before compilation, and `config.data` provides the information `subst` needs to do its job. `Subst` uses the definitions in `config.data` to modify the INN source files before they are compiled.

INN supplies a prototype version of `config.data` named `config.dist`. `Config.dist` most likely is wrong for your UNIX. You must create your own version of `config.data`:

```
$ cd config
$ cp config.dist config.data
```

Now edit `config.data` to match your site's version of UNIX. As mentioned earlier, this is one of the hardest parts of installing INN. `Config.data` is about 700 lines long, and there's nothing for it but to go through it line by line and make the appropriate changes. Depending on how experienced you are, you may have to set aside several hours for this task. `Install.ms` devotes about 18 pages to `config.data`, and you should refer to it as you edit.

Unless you know off the top of your head the answers to questions such as, "How does your UNIX set non-blocking I/O?", you'll need to keep your programmer's manuals handy. If you have a workstation, you can edit `config.data` in one window and use another to inspect your system's online documentation. `Install.ms` gives sample configurations for many popular versions of UNIX. If your version is listed, use its values. (That doesn't, however, relieve you of the chore of inspecting the entire file.)

TIP

The `subst` program, originally supplied with C-news and used in INN by the kind permission of Geoff Collyer and Henry Spencer, is a clever shell script that relies on the `sed` program to do much of its work. The INN `config.dist` file is large enough to break some vendor's versions of `sed`. To see whether your vendor's `sed` works with INN, `cd` into the `config` directory and type the following:

```
$ cp config.dist config.data
$ make sedtest
```

If this test fails, the simplest workaround is to type **make c quiet** to create a C language version of the `subst` program. You should also gripe at your UNIX vendor for foisting a substandard `sed` onto you, an unsuspecting customer.

After you've edited `config.data`, you're ready to let `subst` configure the INN sources. From within the `config` directory, type the following:

```
$ make quiet
```

Building INN

Now that INN is configured, you're ready to build the system. `Install.ms` provides different ways to accomplish the task. The most automated method is to `cd` to the INN directory and type `./BUILD` and answer the questions. The script will compile and install INN.

If you prefer to take control of the compilation and installation, `cd` to the same directory as above and type the following:

```
$ make world
$ cat */lint ¦ more
```

Carefully inspect the `lint` output for errors. (See the following Tip.)

> **TIP**
>
> The `lint` program detects errors in C language programs. Because C is a fairly permissive language, it lets you do things you probably shouldn't, and `lint` helps you find these bits of fluff in your programs and correct them. For instance, `lint` can tell you if you're passing the wrong number (or type) of arguments to a C language function. Remember, just because a program compiles doesn't mean it will work correctly when you run it. If `lint` finds errors in your INN configuration after you've run subst, you may need to correct a problem by editing `config.data` and rebuilding your system. Unfortunately, `lint` sometimes reports spurious errors. You'll have to consult the programmers's section of your system's manual pages to be sure which errors are real and which are not.

You'll learn the most about INN if you compile it bit by bit with `Install.ms` by your side. You may think that if INN is so simple to install, you should take the easy road and use `BUILD`. But news systems are complex, and no matter how good they are, you will inevitably have some problems to solve. When you do, you'll need all the clues you can muster, and building INN step-by-step helps you learn more about it. Someday, when the weasels are at the door, you'll be glad you did.

The step-by-step compilation procedure is fairly simple. First build the INN library:

```
$ cd lib
$ make libinn.a lint 2>&1 ¦ tee errs
$ cd ..
```

The `make` command creates a library of C language functions used by the other INN programs and a `lint` library to help detect possible problems. Because the other INN programs depend on the INN library, it's crucial that it compiles correctly. Check the output in the file `errs` and assure yourself that any errors detected by your C compiler or `lint` are innocuous. If you find errors (especially compiler warnings), it's probably due to a mistake you've made in `config.data`. The only solution is to correct `config.data`, run subst again, and recompile `libinn.a`.

After you've successfully built the INN library, you can build the rest of INN. `cd` into each of the following directories in turn: `frontends`, `innd`, `nnrpd`, `backends`, and `expire`. In each directory, type the following:

```
$ make all 2>&1 ¦ tee errs
```

Check the output in the file `errs`. If compiler warnings or `lint` errors are present, consult your system's documentation and edit `config.data` to correct the problem. Now rerun subst and recompile the system beginning with `libinn.a`.

> **WARNING**
>
> The disadvantage of using `subst` to configure INN is that most of the system depends on the `config.data` file. If, at any stage in building the system, you discover errors that require you to change `config.data`, you must rerun `subst` and recompile all of INN, beginning with `libinn.a`.

Installing INN

Now you're ready to install INN. Assuming that everything has gone well so far, `cd` to the root of the INN source tree, type **su** to become the superuser, and type the following:

```
$ sh makedirs.sh 2>&1 ¦ tee errs
$ make update 2>&1 ¦ tee -a errs
```

This runs the commands to install INN and saves the output in the file `errs`, which you should carefully inspect for errors. Note the `-a` argument to `tee` in the second command line, which makes `tee` append to the file `errs`.

The `makedirs.sh` shell script creates the directories for the INN system and must be run before you type **make update**. The latter command installs INN in the directories created by `makedirs.sh`. Now you've installed the INN programs and are ready to configure your news system.

Site Configuration

`cd` into the `site` directory and type **make all 2>&1 ¦ tee errs**. This command copies files from the `samples` and `backends` directories and runs `subst` over them. Some of these files must be edited before you install INN. They give INN information it can't figure out on its own—for instance, with which hosts you exchange news.

The `site` directory also contains some utility shell scripts. You probably won't have to change these, but you should look at them to see what they do and ensure that paths to programs in them are correct.

Modifying the files in the `site` directory is the second most difficult part of configuring INN, especially if you haven't configured a news system before. However, INN won't work if these files aren't configured correctly, so you'll want to spend some time here. The files you must edit are shown below, each with a brief explanation of its function. Manual pages exist for each of these files in the `doc` directory, and you'll need to read them carefully to understand their function and syntax.

`expire.ctl` controls article expiration policy. In it, you list a series of patterns to match newsgroup names and what actions `expire` should take for groups that match. This means that you can expire newsgroups selectively. The `expire.ctl` file is also where you tell `expire` how long you want it to remember `Message-IDs`. You can't keep a record of `Message-IDs` forever because your history file would grow without bound. `Expire` not only removes articles from the news spool but controls how long their `Message-IDs` are kept in the history file.

`hosts.nntp` lists the hosts that feed you news through NNTP. The main news daemon `innd` reads this file when it starts. If a host not listed in this file connects to `innd`, it assumes it's a newsreader and creates an `nnrpd` process to service it. If the host is in the file, `innd` accepts incoming news articles from it.

`inn.conf` contains some site configuration defaults, such as the names put in an article's `Organization` and `From` headers. For instance, your organization might want all `From` headers to appear as `From:` *someone@mailhub.corp*`.com`, regardless of which host posted the article. Some of these defaults may be overridden by environment variables. For instance, if the user sets the `ORGANIZATION` environment variable, it overrides the default in `inn.conf`.

Articles posted to a moderated newsgroup are first mailed to the newsgroup's moderator, who approves (or disapproves) the article. If it's approved, the moderator posts it with an `Approved` header containing his email address. The `moderators` file tells INN where to mail these articles.

The `newsfeeds` file describes the sites to which you feed news and how you feed them. This is something you will already have arranged with the administrator of the sites which you feed. The important thing is for both sites to agree. For instance, if you feed the `alt.binaries` groups to a site that doesn't want them, it discards the articles, and you both waste a lot of CPU time and network bandwidth in the process. The `newsfeeds` file enables you to construct specific lists of newsgroups for each site you feed. For instance, one site might not want to receive any of the `alt` groups and another might want all the `alt` newsgroups except for the `alt.binaries` newsgroups. The `newsfeeds` file is also where you specify INN's behavior with respect to an article's `Distribution` headers. You can set other parameters here to determine whether articles are transmitted, such as maximum message size.

`nnrp.access` controls which hosts (and optionally, users) can access your NNTP server. When a newsreader connects to the NNTP port, `innd` hooks it up with an `nnrpd` process so it can read and post news. The `nnrpd` program reads the `nnrpd.access` file to see whether that host is allowed to read or post. The hosts may be specified as patterns, so it's easy to allow access to all the hosts in your organization. Reading and posting can also be controlled on a per user basis if your newsreader knows how to use the `authinfo` command, a common extension to NNTP.

`passwd.nntp` contains `hostname;user;password` triplets for an NNTP client (for example, a newsreader) to use in authenticating itself to an NNTP server.

After you've edited the files in `site`, install them:

```
$ make install 2>&1 | tee errs
```

As usual, carefully inspect the `make` command's output for any problems.

System Startup Scripts and news cron Jobs

A news system doesn't run on its own. You must modify your system's boot sequence to start parts of it and create `cron` jobs for the `news` user to perform other tasks.

INN supplies the file `rc.news` to start the news system when your computer boots. For most SVR4 hosts, you should install it as `/etc/init.d/news` and make a hard link to it named `/etc/rc2.d/S99news`.

The shell script `news.daily` should be run as a `cron` job from the news user's crontab. `News.daily` handles article expiration and calls the `scanlogs` shell script to process news log files. You should probably schedule this for a time when most people aren't using the news system, such as after midnight.

You'll also need to add a `news` user `cron` entry to transmit news to your Usenet neighbors. INN supplies sample shell scripts that show several ways to do this for both NNTP and UUCP neighbors. The scripts are copied into the `site` directory. The shell scripts `nntpsend` (and its control file `nntpsend.ctl`), `send-ihave`, and `send-nntp` are various ways to transfer news through NNTP. The scripts `send-uucp` and `sendbatch` are for sites using UUCP. Pick the one that most closely suits your site's needs, and add its invocation to the `news` user's crontab.

If you use `sendbatch`, edit it to ensure that the output of the `df` command on your system matches what the script expects. Unfortunately, the output of `df` varies a lot between vendors, and if `sendbatch` misinterprets it, you may have problems with your news spool filling up.

How often you should run the shell script depends on the needs of the site you're feeding. If it's an NNTP site and it wants to receive your articles as soon as they are posted, you could run one of the NNTP submission scripts every five minutes. If it's a UUCP site or an NNTP site on the end of a slow link, it might want news much less often. You must work this out with the remote site and make sure that your setup matches what it wants.

Miscellaneous Final Tasks

The active file shows what newsgroups are valid on your system. If you're converting to INN from another news system, you can convert your existing active file. Otherwise, you may want to get a copy of your feed site's active file and edit it to remove newsgroups you don't want and add local groups.

You must also create a history file or convert your existing one. Appendix II of `Install.ms` gives information for converting an existing news installation to INN.

Even if you didn't run the `BUILD` shell script to build and install INN, you can save the last 71 lines of it into a file and run that file to build a minimal active file and history database. You can then add whatever lines you want to the active file.

Some vendors' versions of `sed`, `awk`, and `grep` are deficient and may need to be replaced with better versions before INN can function correctly. The GNU project's versions of these commands work well with INN. They are available for anonymous ftp from the host `ftp://prep.ai.mit.edu` in the directory `~ftp/pub/gnu`.

You may also have to modify your `syslog.conf` file to match the logging levels used by INN. These logging levels are defined in `config/config.data`, and the file `syslog/syslog.conf` shows sample changes you may need to make to your `syslog.conf`.

Checking Your Installation and Problem Solving

If you have Perl installed on your system, you can run the `inncheck` program to check your installation. You should also try posting articles, first to the local group `test` and then to groups with wider distributions. Make sure that articles are being transmitted to your Usenet neighbors.

If you have problems, many of the INN programs are shell scripts and you can see what they're doing by typing **sh -x scriptname**. You might also temporarily modify a script to invoke its programs with their verbose options turned on. For instance, the `nntpsend` article submission shell script calls the `innxmit` program to do the work. If `nntpsend` wasn't working for you, you could edit it to turn on `innxmit`'s verbose option (-v), run it by hand as **sh -x nntpsend**, and save the results to a file.

Some simple NNTP server problems can be checked with the `telnet` command. If you know the NNTP protocol, you can simply `telnet` to a host's NNTP port and type commands to the NNTP server. For instance:

```
$ telnet some.host.edu nntp
Trying 123.45.67.8 ...
Connected to some.host.edu.
Escape character is '^]'.
200 somehost NNTP server version 1.5.11 (10 February 1991) ready at Sun
Jul 17 19:32:15 1994 (posting ok).
quit
```

(If your `telnet` command doesn't support the mnemonic name for the port, substitute `119` for `nntp` in the command above.) In this example, no NNTP commands were given other than `quit`, but at least you can see that the NNTP server on `some.host.edu` is willing to let you read and post news.

Getting Help

If your news system develops problems you can't solve on your own, `comp.news.software.b` and `comp.news.software.nntp` are good resources. You'll get much better advice if you do two things: First, read the INN FAQ and other INN documentation and see if the problem is listed there. Imagine your embarrassment when you ask your burning question and the collective answer is, "It's in the FAQ. Read it." Second, make sure you include enough information for people to help you. A surprising number of problem posts don't even tell what version of UNIX the person uses. Your article should include the following:

- A specific description of your operating system version and hardware. (For example, "A Sun4c running Solaris 2.3 with the following patches applied…")

- The version of news software you're running and any patches you may have applied to it ("I'm running the Dec 22 release of INN 1.4sec"), as well an any configuration information that seems relevant, such as the contents of `config/config.data` or the configuration files installed from the `site` directory.

- A detailed description of the problem you're having, what you've done to try to solve it, and what the results were. (For example, "I get a permission denied message when I try to post news. I've tried changing the `nnrp.access` file, but I still can't post.")

If you do a good job of researching your posting, you may even figure out the problem on your own. If you don't, you'll get much better advice for having done the work to include the necessary details.

Summary

This chapter gives you a good start on becoming a news administrator, but installing the software is only the beginning of what you'll need to know to keep your news system running. Most of your additional learning will probably be in the form of on-the-job training, solving the little (and big) crises your news system creates. Your best defense against this mid-crisis style of training is to read the INN manual pages, the INN and `news.software.b` FAQs, and the `news.software.*` newsgroups. The more information you pick up before something goes wrong, the better prepared you are to handle it.

UUCP Administration

by Sriranga Veeraraghavan, and James C. Armstrong, Jr.

IN THIS CHAPTER

UUCP was originally written by Mike Lesk at Bell Labs in the mid-1970s. It was designed to facilitate the communication between UNIX machines. UUCP was the forerunner to FTP.

Since its initial release, it has been modified several times, with the most fundamental changes occurring in 1983, when UUCP was rewritten by Peter Honeyman, David Nowitz, and Brian Redman. This rewritten version was included with AT&T's UNIX System V Release 4. This chapter concentrates on this version.

What Is UUCP?

UUCP stands for UNIX-to-UNIX Copy and is a set of commands that allow a user to transfer data from one machine to another across a serial port, usually via a modem. It is commonly used for the transfer of email and news articles, but the underlying UUCP commands are hidden from the user.

Usually the only direct contact a user has with UUCP is the uucp command. This is an extension to the cp command that understands a special format to indicate the transfer of data from one machine to another. The target machine and the target path are separated by the ! character.

For example, if you wanted to transfer the file my_file from the current directory on the local machine to the /tmp directory on the host melkote, you would use the following UUCP command:

```
uucp my_file melkote!/tmp/my_file
```

In the example, we say that the file my_file was "pushed" to the host melkote. You can also "pull" files. For example, the command

```
uucp melkote!/tmp/data
```

transfers the file /tmp/data on the host melkote to the current directory.

Files can also be transferred between two remote hosts. To transfer the file /tmp/data from the host melkote to the host kanchi, you can do the following:

```
uucp melkote!/tmp/data kanchi!/tmp/data
```

> **NOTE**
>
> If you use the UUCP commands under csh, they may generate error messages such as "Event not found". This message is generated because csh interprets the ! character as a history substitution. To avoid this problem, backslash escape the ! character, \!.

Running Commands Remotely

UUCP also allows users to run commands on remote machines via the uux command. It accepts redirection of standard input and output, and options can be used to indicate that redirection should be applied to the remote command's execution.

For example, the command

```
uux melkote!date
```

runs the command `date` on the host `melkote` and outputs the result. Usually the uux command is not used directly by users, but it is the backbone of mail and news transfers.

For example, news articles are often transferred from one machine to another using a command like the following:

```
uux - -r agate!rnews
```

This command says that the standard input of the uux command should be fed into the command `rnews` on the host `agate`. The `-r` option says to queue the request. This option is not required and can easily be omitted.

Transferring mail is equally simple:

```
uux - -r soda!rmail
```

except in this case the standard input of the uux command is fed into the command `rmail` on the host `soda`.

For security reasons, many sites restrict the use of uux to the remote execution of the commands `rmail` and `rnews`. If you need to use other commands, consult the system administrator of the remote machine to see whether your commands can be enabled.

Under the Hood, `uucico`

All the UUCP commands rely on the `uucico` command because it implements the actual communication between UNIX machines. Most users and administrators never directly interact with this command.

When a connection needs to be made, `uucico` examines a set of data files that include information about how a connection should be set up. Some information included in these files is:

- Which `tty` to use as a port
- The modem commands to use
- The phone number of the remote system
- The login protocol

The modem commands and the login protocol are specified as *chat scripts.*

Chat Scripts

Chat scripts are pairs of *expect/send* sequences. When all the criteria are met of communications, the uucico process waits on the specified port until it sees the next *expect* sequence. When this sequence is seen, the next send sequence is sent. If an expect sequence is not seen within a certain amount of time, a timeout occurs. At this point a separate send sequence is sent.

If all the expect/send sequences are completed, the connection starts to transfer data. If all the send sequences are exhausted and no connection is made, the command fails.

The following is an example of a chat script for login into a machine:

```
"" \n in:- -in: mylogin word: mypassword
```

This chat script first expects nothing and sends a carriage return, then it waits for the sequence in:. If this token is not seen, the script waits for a timeout and then sends the carriage return again. After the in: sequence is received, the login, mylogin, is sent. The script then waits for the sequence word:. After this sequence is received, the password, mypassword, is sent, and the actual data transfer begins.

The - - sequence in the script indicates that a timeout may be reached while waiting for the login prompt. If a character sequence is specified between the two dashes, it is sent along with the carriage return when a timeout occurs. Any number of timeout sequences can occur in an expect pattern.

If a line is known to be slow to acknowledge the connection, you might see a sequence like this:

```
in:- -in:- -in:- -in:
```

This means that the chat script should try four times to get a login prompt before timing out. Some amount of experimentation is required to determine the exact chat script required for connecting to a remote machine.

Chat scripts can be filled with special character escapes. Table 32.1 lists a few of these sequences.

TABLE 32.1. CHAT SCRIPT ESCAPE SEQUENCES.

Sequence	Description
""	Expect a null
EOT	End of Transmission
BREAK	Send a break signal

Sequence	Description
\b	Backspace
\c	Suppress a new line at the end of the send string
\d	Delay for one second
\K	Insert a break
\n	Send a new line
\N	Send a null
\p	Pause for a fraction of a second
\r	Carriage return
\s	Send a space
\t	Send a tab
\\	Send a backslash
\xxx	Send the ASCII character with the octal value xxx

Connection Files

The first task of uucico is to determine the target machine of the connection. When it determines the machine name it examines the Systems file. This file includes the system name, connect times, devices, speeds, connection address, and chat script required to make the connection.

Given the device type and speed, uucico looks at the Devices file next. This file provides a list of devices and speeds, and associates them with the actual ports and dialer to connect with those ports.

The dialers to connect to the port are then looked up in the Dialers file, where a specific dialer is associated with a chat script. This chat script sets up the modem in the proper format and dials the address provided by the Systems file. Sometimes the address needs to be further expanded. If this is required, uucico looks at the Dialcodes file.

The addresses provided by the Systems file are not necessarily telephone numbers. UUCP is capable of handling telephone calls via modems as well as direct and local area network connections. Such connections require different devices and chat scripts.

Setting Up UUCP

UUCP requires two sites willing to set up a connection. In the early days of UNIX, this was simply a matter of calling local UNIX sites and asking whether they would be willing to transfer data for you. With the development of the Internet, these connections are becoming less frequent, and many sites no longer use UUCP; but many large Internet service providers (ISPs) such as Netcom still provide the service.

After you've found an ISP that supports UUCP, you need to determine how the connections will be made. There are three options:

- Your site can make all the calls to the ISP.
- Your site could receive calls from the ISP.
- The calls can be made both ways.

Depending on the setup, there will be two different sets of administrative tasks:

- Setting up your system to receive calls
- Setting up your system to make calls

This chapter covers both sets of tasks.

Receiving UUCP Calls

UUCP accesses a system the same way as a user, via the login process. This means that you have to set up your system to allow UUCP to log in.

The first step is to make sure that one of your serial ports has a modem attached to it. The next step is to establish an account for UUCP to use. To do this, you need to use the administrative tools for your system. Some systems come with the default entry `nuucp` or `uucp` for UUCP connections. Check whether your system has such a user before creating one.

Make the home directory of the UUCP user a directory like:

```
/var/spool/uucppublic
```

This is a standard directory, designated for file transfers. This directory should be owned by the UUCP user and have group of `uucp`. Its permissions should be 777 so that any user who wants to transfer files can write to the directory.

Also the UUCP user should have the default shell of `uucico`. This allows UUCP to start transferring files as soon as it logs in. It also prevents shell access to unauthorized users logging in as the UUCP user.

The UUCP account also needs a password that is known to other UUCP sites. This password can be any combination of characters that are valid because there is no need memorize it like a regular password.

After the UUCP account is created, you need to add an entry to the `/etc/inittab` like the following:

```
ucp:23:respawn:/etc/getty ttya 9600
```

The four fields in the entry have the following significance:

- The first field is a unique identifier; it can be set to any value. Here we have chosen `ucp`.
- The second field specifies the run states. In this case, we specify run levels 2 and 3, which indicate that the command should be run only when the system is in multi-user mode.
- The third field is the action. Here we specify `respawn`, which indicates that when the command is finished a new `getty` command should be run.
- The fourth field is the command, in this case `getty`. The `getty` command is the standard UNIX command for providing a login prompt. In this case, the two arguments to `getty` indicate that a 9600 baud modem is on `ttya`. Your values may be different.

This setup is valid for receiving calls. The same setup cannot be used for two-way traffic because the `getty` command can only receive calls. To set up a system that supports two-way traffic, you have to use the `uugetty` command instead.

A setup that handles two-way traffic looks like the following:

```
ucp:23:respawn:/usr/lib/uucp/uugetty -r ttya 9600
```

The `-r` option to `uugetty` tells it not to put up a login prompt until it gets a character, such as a carriage return.

Initiating UUCP Calls

Initiating UUCP connections is a proactive job. To set up a system to make UUCP calls, the administrator must modify the Systems file. This file contains the specific information needed to contact a remote system. Each line in this file is a separate entry with six fields.

A sample entry looks like the following:

```
melkote Any ACU 9600 14082530938 in:- -in: ukanchi word: password
```

Each of the fields are explained in the following sections.

System Name Field

The first field on a line is the remote system's name. UUCP expects the first seven letters of the remote system's name to be unique. UUCP would consider the system names `newyorkcity` and `newyorkstate` to be the same.

A system can have multiple entries in the Systems file. Each entry is tried until a successful entry is found.

Schedule Field

The second field is a schedule field. If the word `Any` appears in this field, a connection can be made at anytime. If the word `Never` appears in this field, a connection can never be made.

This field can also include schedule descriptions that are constructed using special day codes and optional time codes. The day codes, specified with two letters, are as follows:

- `Su` for Sunday
- `Mo` for Monday
- `Tu` for Tuesday
- `We` for Wednesday
- `Th` for Thursday
- `Fr` for Friday
- `Sa` for Saturday
- `Wk` for all weekdays

Any combination of day codes can be specified in this field. For example, if you wanted to call a site only on Friday, Saturday, and Sunday, you would specify the code `FrSaSu` in the schedule field.

The optional time code is specified using 24-hour time. To make a call between 9 a.m. and 1 p.m. on every weekday, you could specify `Wk0900-1300` in the schedule field. If you include a start time that occurs after the end time, such as `Wk1900-0700`, it means that a transfer will occur on a weekday before 7 a.m. or after 7 p.m.

A grade restriction can also be placed on the priority of the transfers. By limiting the grade, only transfers of a particular grade or higher can be made. The grade is identified by a slash followed by a number or letter.

Taking all the optional codes into account, a full schedule specification looks like the following:

```
SaSu,Wk0900-1700/C,Wk1700-0900
```

This specification indicates that transfers may occur at any time on Saturdays and Sundays, between 9 a.m. and 5 p.m. on weekdays for items of grade C or better, and at any time between 5 p.m. and 9 a.m. Such a specification basically states that it is possible to conduct a transfer at anytime except during work hours, when only priority transfers can be conducted.

In addition to time and grade restrictions, the minimum retry time can be specified as follows:

```
SaSu,Wk0900-1700/C,Wk1700-0900,5
```

The last `,5` indicates to UUCP that it should make five retries. If this field is not given, UUCP makes retry attempts based on its own internal formula.

The Device Field

The third field is the device field, which is basically a pointer to a device type. UUCP looks up the device name in the Devices file and uses the first free device found. The Devices file is usually located in the same directory as the Systems file.

The only option that can be specified in this field is the protocols that the device understands. The three supported protocols are g, x, and e. The g protocol is supported only on phone lines.

The Speed Field

The fourth field specifies the speed or baud rate of the connection. This is usually set at the modem's top speed, but different values may be present for different phone numbers, and different speeds may also apply for direct connections.

The Connection Number Field

The fifth field contains the connection number. Usually it is a telephone number, but for UUCP connections over direct lines or data switches, it is a connection address or path.

The Chat Script

The sixth and last field contains the chat script. The `uucico` command reads the data coming in from the remote site and attempts to use the specified chat script to log in and start transferring data.

Administering UUCP Files

In addition to the files that have been mentioned, five important UUCP files need to be created and regularly administered:

- Devices
- Dialers
- Dialcodes
- Permissions
- Poll files

Each of these files has its own format and usage, so the following sections cover each one separately.

Devices

The Devices file is a list of the devices found on the system. This file ties the device's specification in the Systems file to a physical device with a known means of access.

Each entry in this file is a single line with six fields. Blank lines are skipped, and lines that start with the character # are treated as comments.

A simple Devices file looks like the following:

```
ACU ttya - 9600 tb9600
direct ttya - 9600 direct
```

I use this file for a TeleBit Qblazer 9600 baud modem, which is attached to /dev/ttya. It uses the tb9600 dialer script of UUCP connections.

This information can be deduced from the six fields in the first line. Let us examine each of the fields in turn.

Device Type Field

The first field in an entry represents the device type. It must exactly match the device specified in the Systems file.

UUCP tries each device listed in the file until a match is found. This allows a system with multiple modems to have only one entry in the Systems file.

Some standard identifiers for device types are as follows:

- ACU, stands for *automated call unit*, better known as a modem.
- direct, stands for a *direct link*.

Data Port Field

The second field in an entry specifies the data port through which the data communications are conducted. The filename of the special file in the /dev directory for the physical device should be used.

Dialer Port Field

The third field in an entry specifies the dialer port. This field is a relic from the distant past when modems required a separate dialer device to make a phone call.

For such modems, this field pointed to the special file in /dev that was the dialer for the modem. Most modern modems are capable of dialing phone numbers themselves, so this field is usually marked with a -, indicating that no dialer is required.

Device Speed Field

The fourth field in an entry specifies the speed of the device. This field is also used for matching the Systems file so that a site can indicate multiple speeds for connections through multiple devices.

Dialer Token Pairs Field

The last field in an entry is the dialer tokens pair field. This specifies a dialer pattern and the arguments to the dialer. The dialer patterns are listed in the Dialers file.

Normally, only a single pair is found, but if the system needs to go through a switch to reach the modem, a chat script may be used.

Dialers

The Dialers file is used to initiate a conversation with the modem. It ties the dialer specified in the Devices file to a chat script.

Each entry in the Dialers file consists of a line with three entries. As with the Devices file, blank lines are skipped, and lines beginning with the character # are treated as comments.

The first field in an entry is the name of the dialer script that must match an entry in the Devices file. The second field is a translation table for older communication devices, and the third field is the chat script needed to talk with the modem and to place the call.

A sample entry looks like the following:

```
tb1200  =W-,  "" \dA\pA\pTE1V1X1Q0S2=255S12=S255S50=2\r\c OK\r \EATDT\T\r\c
Connect\s1200
```

Many systems come preinstalled with dialer entries for common modems such as Penril, Ventel, Micom, Hayes, and Telebit.

One characteristic of the dialer entries is that they have a long and confusing list of numbers and characters as the first send sequence. This list contains the parameters, in a language the modem understands, that need to be set in the modem for a UUCP call to take place. In the preceding example, the Hayes syntax is used. This is a fairly common syntax, but some modems do not use it, so you'll need to check your modem's documentation to determine the correct settings.

Dialcodes

The Dialcodes file is an optional file that equates a string with a series of numbers to be dialed. This file is primarily used for readability of the phone numbers for remote machines.

UUCP can easily use a sequence like the following:

```
1028801144716194550,,2354
```

to reach a remote computer in London, but for a human being looking at the number it may not be obvious where the remote machine is located. This file allows the administrator to tie a string to a dialing sequence. For example the string

```
innerlondon
```

could be used to replace the number

```
102880114471
```

This file is useful if you have to call several remote hosts located worldwide.

Permissions

When UUCP was first introduced, it allowed any user to write to any directory on a remote system where the UUCP user had write permissions. UUCP also allowed reading of files in a similar manner. This opened two major security holes on systems where UUCP was enabled:

- Remote users could steal the password file with a single UUCP command. When the password file was stolen, the system was compromised.
- Remote users could damage a system by moving or deleting essential system files.

To fix such problems, the Permissions file was introduced. This file allows the administrator to tie remote systems and accounts to specific read, write, and execute permissions. The permissions file contains 13 different entries each in the following format:

option=value

All the *options* must appear on the same line, although the line is frequently broken into multiple lines by using a backslash. Multiple *values* for an *option* can be specified by separating the individual *values* with the : character. The options are described in Table 32.2.

Table 32.2. Options specified in the Permissions file.

Option	Description
LOGNAME	Refers to a specific login name used by the remote site to gain access.
MACHINE	Refers to the machine name of the remote UUCP site.
REQUEST	This is a yes/no flag indicating whether the remote machine can request files from your machine. The default is no.
SENDFILES	This is also a yes/no flag, and it is tied to the LOGNAME. If set to yes, your system sends files to a remote system even if the remote system initiates the UUCP call. If set to no, your machine never sends out files. This option can be set to call, so that your machine can send files when it initiates a call.
READ	Specifies the directories from which uucico can access files for transfer. The default is /var/spool/uucppublic.
NOREAD	Specifies exceptions for the directories enabled for reading by the READ option.
WRITE	Specifies the directories to which uucico can write files. It has the same default as the READ option.
NOWRITE	Specifies exceptions for the directories enabled for reading by the WRITE option.
CALLBACK	This is a yes/no flag. If set to yes, your system must call the remote system back before any transaction may take place. The default is no. This option is a security feature because a remote machine cannot initiate a transfer by merely faking the machine name. Be careful when specifying this option; there are several situations where it produces unexpected results. For example, if both systems set this to yes, they will never communicate. Also, if one systems sets SENDFILES to call and the other has CALLBACK set to yes, the first system cannot transfer files to the second.
COMMANDS	This option determines which commands can be executed on the system by a remote user. The default is to permit rmail and rnews, the programs that receive mail and news. If this option is set to ALL, remote users can execute any command in the path of uuxqt. It is rarely specified because it allows remote users to use commands such as rm.
VALIDATE	This is a yes/no flag. If set to yes, it validates the remote system's identity.
MYNAME	This option is used to provide an alternate name for the local machine.
PUBDIR	This option is used to specify a directory that can be treated as the public directory for reading and writing. The default is /var/spool/uucppublic.

32

UUCP ADMINISTRATION

Although the syntax of the Permissions file may seem complicated, the default permissions are designed to keep a system secure, thus you need to edit this file only when you need to loosen permissions.

A simple Permissions file looks like the following:

```
MACHINE=melkote COMMANDS=rmail:rnews SENDFILES=yes
```

It enables the machine `melkote` to execute `rmail` and `rnews`. It also enables the local machine to send files to `melkote`.

Poll File

The Poll file contains a list of times to poll a remote system. It is accessed by an administrative daemon to establish a fake request and force a UUCP call at a specific time.

The format of the file is a system name followed by a tab and a space-separated list of integers from 0 to 23, representing the hours of a 24-hour clock.

Supporting Files

In addition to the six files mentioned previously, UUCP creates the following files to aid in transferring files:

- Work files
- Data files
- Status files
- Lock files
- Log files
- Temporary files

Work Files

Work files are the workhorse for UUCP. They list the specific files to be transferred, including the local and remote names, permissions, and owners.

Work files are prefixed by the letter C and are located in the directory:

```
/var/spool/uucp/machine
```

Here *machine* is the name of the remote machine.

Data Files

Data files are prefixed by the letter D and are kept in the same directory as Work files.

Execute Files

Execute files are identified by the prefix X. This prefix is used by `uuxqt` to determine the commands to execute. These files have a special format indicating which command to run and which input file to use.

Status File

This Status file is located at:

```
/var/spool/uucp/.Status
```

There is only one Status file per system. Each line in the file is a separate entry with six fields:

- The first field is the type field.
- The second field is a count field.
- The third field is a UNIX tie to identify the last connection attempt.
- The fourth field is the number of seconds before a retry attempt may be taken.
- The fifth field is an ASCII text string describing the status.
- The sixth field is the machine name.

The Status file can be accessed with the `uustat` command.

Lock Files

Lock files are created when a call is attempted. These files contain the process ID of the `uucico` request that has locked the system. They are located in the following directory:

```
/var/spool/uucp/locks
```

Log Files

The UUCP logs are kept in the directory:

```
/var/spool/uucp/.Log
```

This directory is cleaned out daily by a daemon to prevent it from growing beyond control. Separate logs are kept for the commands:

- `uucico`
- `uucp`
- `uux`
- `uuxqt`

These files can be accessed with the `uulog` command.

Temporary Files

Temporary files created by UUCP are located in the Work files directory and are prefixed by `TM`.

UUCP Daemons

Four main UUCP daemons are invoked on a regular basis via `cron`:

- `admin`
- `cleanup`
- `polling`
- `hourly`

The following sections look at each one in turn.

The `admin` Daemon

The `admin` daemon produces an email message that contains a snapshot of the running UUCP processes and lists the UUCP job queue. The email message also checks the log files to see whether there have been any attempts to transfer the file:

`/etc/passwd`

This daemon should be run at least once a day.

The `cleanup` Daemon

The `cleanup` daemon is one of the hardest working UUCP daemons. First it backs up all the log files and saves the backups for three days. Then it zeros out the current log files and invokes the `uucleanup` command to remove old jobs from the queue. After this, it removes old files, empty subdirectories, and core files. Finally, it sends mail covering the work that it has performed.

This daemon should be invoked daily, at a time when few users are likely to be on the system.

The `polling` Daemon

The `polling` daemon examines the Poll file and touches files in the spool directory to create polling requests for `uucico`. This daemon should be run hourly.

The `hourly` Daemon

The `hourly` daemon should be invoked hourly, as its name implies. It runs the command `uusched`, which examines the spool to find any queued jobs and runs `uucico` for those jobs. When it finishes this, it runs `uuxqt` to execute any incoming jobs.

Using UUCP

Earlier in this chapter, we covered the UUCP commands uucp and uux. In addition to these commands, two other commands, uuto and uupick, make using UUCP much easier. This section covers all four commands.

uucp

The uucp command is the most basic UUCP command for transporting files from one UNIX machine to another. The basic form of this command allows for the specification of two paths to files, with the first path being the source files and the second path being the destination file.

A number of options can be specified to uucp to facilitate the transfer. These options are detailed in Table 32.3.

TABLE 32.3. OPTIONS FOR uucp.

Option	Description
-c	Forces uucp to create a temporary copy of a file that is requested for transfer. It is useful when transferring files that change frequently.
-d	Forces uucp to create all required parent directories on the remote machine before transferring a file.
-f	Prevents uucp from creating any parent directories on the remote machine.
-j	If this option is specified, uucp assigns a job ID to the transfer.
-m	If this option is specified, uucp sends a mail message to the UUCP user on the host sending the data when a job completes.
-n	If this option is specified, uucp sends mail to the UUCP user on the host receiving data when a job completes.
-g	Assigns a grade to the transfer. The available grades are any single character between 0-9, A-Z, and a-z, where 0 is the highest grade, and z is the lowest grade.
-x	Turns on debugging information.
-r	Prevents the automatic start of uucico.

uux

As you saw earlier, the uux command is frequently used to execute remote programs. This command's options, covered in Table 32.4, allow users to run complex commands on remote machines.

TABLE 32.4. OPTIONS FOR uux.

Option	Description
-b	Returns the standard input if the remote execution fails.
-c	Makes temporary copies of all the required files.
-j	Assigns the job an ID.
-n	Prevents uux from sending a mail message about the success or failure of a remote command to the user who initiated the command. By default, a mail message indicating the success or failure or the remote command is sent to the initiating user.
-a	Alters the initiating user's username. This is useful for redirecting all uux email to one particular user.
-g	Allows the grade of the command to be set. The grades are the same as for uucp.
-r	Prevents the automatic startup of uucico.
-x	Activates all debugging messages.

uuto and uupick

For novice users, the uucp and uux commands can be quite baffling. To make the process of transferring files easier, the uuto and uupick commands are provided as part of the UUCP distribution.

uuto

The basic syntax of uuto is as follows:

```
uuto files machine!user
```

Here *files* is a list of space-separated filenames to be transferred to the specified *machine* using the specified remote *user*.

There is no limit on the number of files that can be specified; each file is transferred using uucp. The remote username is a must because this command places the transferred files into that user's home directory.

The following options can be specified to uuto:

- -m indicates that mail should be sent to the initiator of the command when the transfer is complete.

- -p forces uuto to copy all the specified files to a temporary location before beginning the transfer.

To transfer the file homework from the local machine to the home directory of the user vathsa on the machine melkote, the uuto command is:

```
uuto homework melkote!vathsa
```

This command is translated into a uucp command like the following:

```
uucp -d -nvathsa homework melkote!~/home/vathsa
```

uupick

The uupick command is used to get files from a remote host. It is a shell script that searches the public directory on a remote machine for files under your name in the receive directory. If it finds any files, it prompts for an action. The possible actions are given in Table 32.5.

TABLE 32.5. OPTIONS FOR uupick.

Option	Description
newline	Goes to the next file
d	Deletes the file
m *dir*	Moves the file to the directory specified by *dir*
a *dir*	Moves all files to the directory specified by *dir*
p	Prints the file
q or CNTRL-D	Quits
!*command*	Runs the command specified by *command*
*	Prints a help message that includes a summary of all the commands

32

UUCP
ADMINISTRATION

Summary

This chapter provided a brief overview of the use and administration of UUCP. The use of the commands uucp, uux, uuto, and uupick for transferring data between hosts was covered along with the files required to set up and maintain UUCP.

Administering FTP Services

by Sriranga Veeraraghavan and Salim Douba

IN THIS CHAPTER

The File Transfer Protocol (FTP) is one of the earliest data exchange and transfer services. First introduced in 1971, it was initially used to send test traffic on the ARPAnet. Shortly after its introduction, FTP became one of the two principal network applications.

FTP's popularity stems from its platform independence. Implementations of the FTP server and client can be found on many platforms including UNIX, DOS, Windows NT, MacOS, and Novell's NetWare network operating system.

The first part of this chapter covers the underlying concepts and operational issues of FTP. The second part deals with practical issues and applications of setting up and maintaining the FTP service on UNIX. As in other chapters, the material presented here covers several flavors of UNIX. Although the concepts and mechanisms governing FTP are identical on all platforms, there are subtle differences in its implementation. These differences are highlighted.

Overview of FTP Protocol and Service

FTP is a protocol for transferring files between two hosts across a network. The two hosts can be dissimilar platforms. Using a DOS FTP client, for example, a user can easily exchange files with a UNIX FTP server.

Among the other features that FTP supports are its capability to handle both ASCII and EBCDIC (Extended Binary Coded Decimal Interchange Code) character sets. Equally important is FTP's support of ASCII and binary transfers. Unlike UUCP, which requires that any data other than ASCII, be uuencoded at the source and uudecoded at the destination (thus wasting both CPU processing power and communications bandwidth), FTP submits the data on an as-is basis.

FTP Connections

FTP runs at the application layer of the OSI model and depends on TCP for the reliable delivery of data among hosts on the network. Thus, it can function without being concerned with the architectural underpinnings of the supporting communications architecture.

When an FTP client engages in an FTP session with an FTP server, TCP establishes two connections on behalf of both entities. These connections are known as the control connection and the data connection.

The data connection is used exclusively for the transfer of user data, whereas the control connection is used exclusively for the exchange of internal FTP commands and responses governing the session.

> **NOTE**
>
> On UNIX systems, an FTP client is usually named `ftp`, and the FTP server is usually named `ftpd` or `in.ftpd`.

Control Connection

When the `ftp` command is invoked, a control connection to the desired server is opened. No user data is exchanged over the control connection. It is used exclusively for the exchange of internal FTP commands and responses that govern the exchange of user data over the data connection. Here is an example of invoking an FTP session with host `tenor`:

```
$ ftp tenor
```

If the host `tenor` is running UNIX and is configured with an FTP server, it responds by establishing a control connection using port 21, which is the default FTP control port as defined in the file `/etc/services`.

After the control connection is opened, the user authentication process takes place. At this point, the user is required to provide a valid user login name and password to the FTP server. If the authentication process is successful, the client and server negotiate the transfer parameters. Two important parameters that are negotiated at this point are the character set and the transfer mode.

Data Connection

After the transfer parameters have been determined, both the client and server establish a data connection using port 20. This connection is full duplex, which means that it allows data to be exchanged between the client and the server simultaneously.

The data connection may not be maintained throughout the session. There are circumstances when the data connection is closed by the end of a file transfer, or upon detection of an irrecoverable error condition. As long as the control connection is maintained, the session is considered to be "live." Both sides can negotiate and establish a new data connection whenever the need arises for the resumption of file transfers.

33

ADMINISTERING FTP SERVICES

FTP Ports

Although the default ports for the control connection and data connection are 21 and 20, respectively, the FTP server can be configured to listen on other ports for both the control connection and the data connection. Some implementations of FTP rely on the use of other ports for either the control or the data connection.

If only the control connection's default port is overridden, then the data connection's port also changes because the port assigned to the data connection is one less than the control port.

Alternate ports for the control and data connections can be specified by replacing the port number for the FTP entry with the desired port number in the file /etc/service.

Reliability of FTP

FTP relies on TCP for the delivery of information between hosts. Because TCP is a reliable connection-oriented transport protocol, FTP's reliability stems from TCP's reliability. When engaged in the transfer of data, TCP handles the sequencing of exchanged data segments and recovery from erroneous events during the delivery process.

In the case of inadvertently interrupted transfers, FTP must recover from the interruption and resume the transfer process without necessarily retransmitting the entire file. Here TCP provides no help, thus FTP achieves this by employing a check pointing mechanism that breaks the file undergoing transmission into logical blocks of data that are individually acknowledged upon successful delivery. A block can be transmitted in one TCP segment or multiple TCP segments. Whereas TCP concerns itself with the error-free delivery of individual segments, FTP concerns itself with the successful transmission of all segments comprising the individual block. Consequently, whenever the file transfer is restarted upon recovery from an abrupt interruption, FTP retransmits data starting from the beginning of the interrupted block only and until completion; thus achieving optimal performance and minimal impact on available CPU power and transmission bandwidth.

Operational Characteristics of FTP

FTP is a real-time process. This means that an FTP session is established as soon as the FTP client is invoked.

If the client runs in the foreground, a user or program must suspend other action and wait for the completion of the session before proceeding. Because the speed of the transfer is affected by many factors, including the size of the file and the capacity of the available bandwidth, the time it takes for a session to complete varies considerably from one network environment to another. For this reason, FTP was developed to be a time-insensitive application.

FTP sessions can also be run in the "unattended" mode of operation. In this mode, the FTP client can be invoked in the background with an FTP script. This approach requires that the user know the exact details of the proceedings of the intended session. Scripting is not a requirement of the FTP standard; it is a feature provided by some implementations.

A Sample FTP Session

An FTP session starts when the FTP client, `ftp`, is invoked on the command line as follows:

```
$ ftp targethost
```

Here `targethost` is either an IP address or a hostname.

After invocation, `ftp` prompts for a username and password. If an invalid username or an invalid password is given, `ftp` does not establish a session. In the following example, an FTP session is established with host `tenor`:

```
$ ftp tenor
Connected to tenor.
220 tenor FTP server (UNIX(r) System V Release 4.0) ready.
Name (tenor:root): sam
331 Password required for sam.
Password:
230 User sam logged in.
ftp>
```

The prompt, `ftp>`, that is displayed after the user `sam` authenticated successfully, serves as an indication that FTP is ready to execute user commands. Although the FTP session is established with a remote system, processing of user FTP commands is done locally. The `ftp>` prompt is local to the machine where the session was invoked. FTP commands are handled by the User Process Interpreter, usually called the User-PI or UPI. This process acts like the UNIX shell in that it accepts user commands and submits them to the FTP protocol for subsequent handling.

FTP Internal Commands

FTP supports two sets of commands:

- User
- Internal

User commands are those commands that the user can issue at the `ftp>` prompt. A list of supported user commands is available by entering the `help` command at the prompt.

Internal commands are not user accessible; they are commands used by the FTP protocol. A command issued at the `ftp>` prompt may trigger a series of internal FTP commands and responses.

Table 33.1 contains a detailed list of all commands that the RFC 959 standard recommends. RFC 959 specifies a minimum set of commands that require implementation for an `ftp` application to be branded compliant. Other than the specified minimum, vendors are left the freedom to adopt whatever other features are recommended by the RFC.

TABLE 33.1. INTERNAL FTP COMMANDS.

Command	*Description*
ABOR	Abort previous command and any associated transfer of data.
ACCT	The user account ID is specified as an argument to the command.
ALLO	Allocate storage for forthcoming file transfer. Size is specified as a command argument.
APPE	Append incoming data to an existing file. The filename is specified as a command argument.
CDUP	Move up one level in the directory tree.
CWD	Change working directory on remote server. The path is specified as a command argument.
DELE	Delete file. The filename is specified as a command argument.
HELP	Send information regarding status of server implementation.
LIST	Transfer directory listing.
MKD	Make a directory. The directory path is specified as a command argument.
MODE	Set transfer mode to one of stream, block, or compressed.
NLST	Transfer the directory listing.
NOOP	Do nothing. If server is alive, it responds with OK.
PASS	User password.
PASV	Request the server to listen on a data port other than the default one.
PORT	Request the server to change to a different data port than the currently used one.
PWD	Print working directory.
QUIT	Terminate the connection.
REIN	Reinitialize connection while allowing transfers in progress to complete.
REST	Restart marker. Causes the transfer to resume after being disrupted from a specified data checkpoint in the file.

Command	Description
RETR	Retrieve the file specified as a command argument.
RMD	Remove directory specified in argument field.
RNFR	Rename From; specifies the old pathname of the file that is to be renamed. This command is normally followed by a rename to (RNTO) command specifying the new filename.
RNTO	Rename to command.
SITE	Sends site-specific parameters to remote end. Such parameters are normally essential to file transfer but not sufficiently universal to be included as commands in the protocol.
SMNT	Mount file system.
STAT	Return status of service.
STOR	Accept and store data.
STOU	Accept and store data under a unique name.
STRU	Specifies the structure of the file pending transmission. The specified structure can be File, Record, or Page. The default is File.
SYST	Return type of operating system.
TYPE	Specifies type of data pending transmission. One of three: ASCII, EBCDIC, or BINARY.
USER	User ID.

33

**ADMINISTERING
FTP SERVICES**

Most of the internal commands are made up of four ASCII character sequences. Some of these commands require arguments. By encoding the internal FTP commands using ASCII characters, expert system administrators can `telnet` the server on the FTP control port and execute most of the internal commands themselves. This capability proves useful when troubleshooting FTP problems.

The ASCII encoding of commands also enables users to observe and understand the command flow without having to employ protocol analysis tools. To turn on command flow of internal FTP commands, enter the `debug` command at the `ftp>` prompt before attempting any operation as demonstrated in the following example:

```
$ ftp tenor
Connected to tenor.
220 tenor FTP server (UNIX(r) System V Release 4.0) ready.
Name (tenor:root):
331 Password required for root.
Password:
230 User root logged in.
ftp> debug
```

```
Debugging on (debug=1).
ftp> put testfile
local: testfile remote: testfile
— -> PORT 100,0,0,2,4,103
200 PORT command successful.
— -> STOR testfile
150 ASCII data connection for testfile (100.0.0.2,1127).
226 Transfer complete.
13415 bytes sent in 0.57 seconds (23 Kbytes/s)
ftp> quit
— -> QUIT
221 Goodbye.
$
```

FTP Responses

In addition to the internal commands, the FTP protocol supports a considerable range of responses. Responses are expressed using a three-digit decimal number and are designed to ensure the synchronization of requests and actions in the process of file transfer. They also enable the FTP client to track the status of the server.

Every internal FTP command is required to generate at least one response. In addition, some commands are required to occur in a certain sequence. For example, every RNFR should be followed immediately by an RNTO. A failure to produce an expected sequence suggests the existence of abnormalities either in the transmission process or in the software implementation.

The FTP response is also accompanied by some text that either explains the reply or provides information pertaining to the reply itself. The textual information may vary from one FTP implementation to another. The three-digit code is standardized and cannot be changed.

Each of the three digits of the reply has a special significance. The first digit denotes whether the response conveys good, bad, or incomplete operational status. Table 33.2 summarizes the values that the most significant digit of the response can take and the significance of each value.

TABLE 33.2. DESCRIPTIONS OF THE MOST SIGNIFICANT DIGIT IN FTP RESPONSES.

Value	*Description*
1	The requested action has been initiated; expect a reply before sending another action.
2	The requested action has completed successfully. User can send a new action.
3	The action has been accepted; the requested action is being suspended until further information is received from user.

Value	Description
4	The action was not accepted due to a transient error. The requested action may be resubmitted for completion.
5	The action was not accepted due to permanent error. User may not resubmit request the same action.

The middle digit provides more details about the response in question. Table 33.3 provides information about the values that this digit can take and the associated meaning.

TABLE 33.3. DESCRIPTIONS OF THE MIDDLE DIGIT IN FTP RESPONSES.

Value	Description
0	The reply refers to a syntax error.
1	Signify a reply to a request for information, such as status of connection.
2	The reply refers to data and control connection management function.
3	Reply pertains to login and authentication actions.
4	Not used.
5	Reply conveying the status of the server file system.

The third digit provides even finer details about the function categories specified in the middle digit. Listing all applicable values is beyond the scope of this chapter. Interested readers should consult RFC 959 for further details.

Unattended Transfers

At times the need arises to transfer many large files using FTP. If you do it manually, you must log in to the target server and attend to the transfer process on a file-by-file basis. Depending on the size of the files, you might end up spending considerable time just waiting for each transfer to complete before initiating the next one. Add to this scenario the requirement to have the transfers carried out after hours, and you find yourself in an unpleasant situation.

Most versions of the FTP client, ftp, on the UNIX platforms include support for unattended operation. These clients can take input from script files containing details of the action requests you want executed.

First, we created a file containing the FTP commands to be executed. For example, our script might contain the following:

```
open tenor
user maya   apassword
binary
cd /incoming
put myfile
bye
```

This file specifies all the actions necessary for the transfer of the file `myfile` to the `/incoming` directory on host `tenor`. The file starts with an `open` command specifying the hostname of the target server. Next, the username and password are sent to host `tenor` for authentication.

If there are no authentication problems, the transfer mode is set to `binary`, and the `cd` command is issued. After this, the `put` command transfers the file `myfile` to host `tenor`. Upon completion of the transfer, the script instructs the `ftp` client to drop the connection using the `bye` command.

Because the order in which the `ftp` commands are listed is vital to the success of the unattended operation, the commands should be rehearsed in the exact order that they have in the file. This way, you can assess its accuracy and take corrective measures before putting the script into production.

To verify an FTP script, invoke `ftp` and let it execute the contents of the script without human intervention. This is done as follows:

`$ ftp -vin < scriptname`

Here `scriptname` is the name of the file that contains the FTP script. Table 33.4 explains the `ftp` options specified in the preceding command.

TABLE 33.4. OPTIONS FOR "UNATTENDED" USE OF `ftp`.

Option	Description
-v	Stands for verbose mode. It helps you follow on the "conversation" taking place between the FTP server and the FTP client. Although it is not required, it is convenient for troubleshooting FTP scripts.
-n	Turns off the autologin feature. If this switch is not included, `ftp` attempts autologin based on the `.netrc` file in your home directory. The login initialization parameters contained in that file might cause some conflicts leading to abortion of the session.
-i	Turns off interactive prompting during multiple file transfers. This is a time-saving feature.

As an example, if you use the following script called ftpscript:

```
open tenor
user root apassword
cd /usr/sam
put *
ls * ftplist
bye
```

The resulting output is as follows:

```
$ ftp -vin < ftpscript
Connected to tenor.
220 tenor FTP server (UNIX(r) System V Release 4.0) ready.
331 Password required for root.
230 User root logged in.
250 CWD command successful.
local: budget.rpt remote: budget.rpt
200 PORT command successful.
150 ASCII data connection for budget.rpt (100.0.0.2,1239).
226 Transfer complete.
746 bytes sent in 0.03 seconds (24 Kbytes/s)
200 PORT command successful.
150 ASCII data connection for /bin/ls (100.0.0.2,1241) (0 bytes).
226 ASCII Transfer complete.
221 Goodbye.
```

This script included something that the previous one did not include, the command:

```
ls /usr/root/ftplist
```

Notice that this command is included right after the mput command. It helps verify whether the files intended for transfer were indeed transferred to the destination host. Because this is meant to be an unattended operation, a filename is included as an argument for the ls command, forcing it to log the returned listing to the specified file and making the information conveniently available for subsequent verification.

FTP Proxy Transfers

There are situations when users need to transfer files between two FTP servers. For example, a user on the host jade may need to transfer files from the host tenor to the host alto.

This can be accomplished in two steps:

1. Transfer the files from the host tenor to the host jade.

2. Transfer these files from the host jade to the host alto.

This procedure doubles the network traffic arising from the desired transfer and requires both disk and CPU resources on the host jade.

33

FTP service protocol provides a transfer mechanism called third-party transfer or proxy transfer that alleviates these performance bottlenecks. Using this mechanism, the user at host jade can initiate control connections on both FTP servers, tenor and alto.

If the user logged in to the FTP service on host tenor first, this connection is the called primary one. When the user logs in to the host alto, the secondary connection is created. When both connections are established, the user can set up a data connection between the two servers. In this fashion, control information is communicated over the control connections while data is transferred between the servers over the data connection without being routed through host jade.

Setting up such a session is a matter of invoking the proxy command at the ftp> prompt after a primary FTP connection is established.

In our example, the user logs in to host tenor first, thus establishing a primary connection with that host. To invoke a secondary connection with host alto, the user should invoke the proxy open command at the ftp prompt. The following output of a sample FTP session illustrates the proceedings of a third-party transfer that was invoked from host jade:

```
$ ftp tenor
Connected to tenor.
220 tenor FTP server (UNIX(r) System V Release 4.0) ready.
Name (tenor:root):
331 Password required for root.
Password:
230 User root logged in.
ftp> proxy open alto
Connected to alto
220 alto FTP server (Version 5.60 #1) ready.
331 Password required for root.
230 User root logged in.
Remote system type is UNIX.
Using binary mode to transfer files.
ftp> pwd
tenor:257 "/" is current directory.
ftp> get testfile
local: testfile remote: testfile
tenor:200 PORT command successful.
tenor:150 ASCII data connection for testfile (100.0.0.2,1156) (12870
bytes).
tenor:226 ASCII Transfer complete.
13415 bytes received in 0.75 seconds (17 Kbytes/s)
ftp> quit
tenor:221 Goodbye.
alto Goodbye.
```

Some of the user `ftp` commands behave differently under a proxy transfer. For example, the get and mget commands cause files to be transferred from the primary to the secondary, whereas put and mput cause file transfers from the secondary to the primary. So be careful with the use of these commands; there is the likelihood that if the same filename exists on both servers, one file might erroneously overwrite the other. To avoid this possibility, you should enable saving files under unique filenames using the sunique and runique ftp commands.

To enable storing files under unique names on the secondary channel, issue the command as shown here:

```
ftp> proxy sunique
Store unique on.
```

Third-party transfers can be conveniently used to carry out unattended, scheduled file transfers among different hosts from a central location using FTP script.

> **CAUTION**
>
> Not all implementations of the FTP server support third-party transfers. To check whether FTP proxy is implemented, issue the internal command PASV. If this command is not implemented, a secondary connection cannot be used to initiate third-party transfers. A possible workaround is conditional on having PASV support on at least one of the involved servers, in which case, you invoke the primary connection with the server lacking the PASV support and the secondary with the server that has it.

Administering FTP

This section covers the three main areas of FTP administration, which involve the following tasks:

- Setting up FTP
- Administering FTP users
- Setting up anonymous FTP

Setting Up FTP

On UNIX, the FTP server, `ftpd`, is started on a per-request basis by inetd. To ensure that inetd is indeed listening on behalf of ftpd, make sure that inetd's configuration file

```
/etc/inetd.conf
```

has an enabled entry for the `ftpd` daemon. To enable an entry in this file, you simply uncomment the entry by removing the # character in front of it. An enabled `ftpd` entry looks like the following:

```
ftp     stream    tcp    nowait    NOLUID    /etc/ftpd    ftpd
```

If such an entry exists, `inetd` listens on the FTP control port on behalf of `ftpd`. The `inetd` daemon determines the control port to listen on by referencing the file `/etc/services`.

The `inetd` process reads its configuration file and `/etc/services` when it is first started, thus changes to either file do not take effect unless the `inetd` is restarted. This can be done by rebooting the host or by sending the `inetd` process a `SIGHUP`.

> **Caution**
>
> It is vitally important that the file `/etc/services` is not deleted or changed in any way by inexperienced users because it controls access to network services for every user on a system. It is the system administrator's responsibility to maintain the backups of this file and to ensure that the information it contains is correct.

Administering FTP Users

If `ftpd` is enabled, anyone who has a valid user account on the system is capable of starting an FTP session with the server and transferring files to and from the server. A system administrator can prevent a user from logging in to the FTP service by adding the user's login name in the file:

```
/etc/ftpusers
```

This file contains a list of the usernames that are *not* allowed to access the FTP server. Each line should contain one—and only one—username. For security reasons, it is suggested that the file contain login names `root` and `uucp`.

If this file does not exist, users with valid login accounts can start an FTP session with the server.

Even if a user's login name is not in the `/etc/ftpusers` file, and the user authenticates, the user may still be prevented from accessing the FTP service if the login attempt is being made from a shell that is not included in the file `/etc/shells`. Here is an example of the contents of this file:

```
#       @(#)shells    4.2 Lachman System V STREAMS TCP  source
#       SCCS IDENTIFICATION
/sbin/sh
/bin/sh
/bin/csh
/bin/ksh
```

> **CAUTION**
>
> Some UNIX systems, like Solaris 2.5, do not ship with the file /etc/shells. This may allow hackers to tamper with the system.
>
> The nonexistence of the /etc/shells file enables user access from any shell. Always make sure that the file exists. If it doesn't, create it, and include in it only the shells that you want to allow users to use when accessing your system.

Autologin

On systems with inexperienced users, it is often necessary to automate the login process to the FTP server. Users who need to frequently access the service may find the routine of entering their username and password annoying. To simplify the login process, ftp provides a feature called autologin that automates the entire process.

Autologin is enabled by creating a file called .netrc in a user's home directory. This file contains both the login and ftp initialization parameters to use during autologin. Multiple entries can be included in the .netrc file, one per remote host.

The basic syntax of a .netrc file is as follows:

```
machine [hostname ¦ default] login login_id password password    macdef
macfilename
```

Table 33.5 describes the individual parameters. Before creating the file, you should test the desired settings on the command line.

TABLE 33.5. PARAMETERS IN THE .netrc FILE.

Parameter	Description
machine hostname	Specifies the hostname or the IP address of the remote host you want to establish an FTP session with. If hostname is the default, then this entry is used for any hostname or IP address that is not explicitly included. If present, the default entry must be the last entry in the file.

continues

TABLE 33.5. CONTINUED

Parameter	Description
login *login_id*	Specifies the user's login ID on the remote host.
password *password*	Specifies the user's password. For security reasons, ftp requires that the file be readable by only its owner, if this token is present.
Macdef *macfilename*	Specifies the name of a user-defined macro, defining all the initialization parameters. Refer to the man pages for more information.

In the following two examples, the first entry allows the user adel to autologin to the host tenor and establishes an ftp session. The second entry allows the user adel to log in to other servers with the specified default account specifications:

```
machine tenor login adel password letmein
default login adel pasword jamsession
```

With these entries in the file .netrc, the user adel can ftp the host tenor without having to log in or enter a password:

```
# ftp tenor
Connected to tenor.
220 tenor FTP server (UNIX(r) System V Release 4.0) ready.
331 Password required for adel.
230 User adel logged in.
ftp>
```

To establish a session with any other host, the user adel must have an account on that host with same login ID and password specified by the default entry.

Anonymous FTP

With the phenomenal popularity of the Internet, many organizations offer a wide range of Internet services, including the distribution of software and documentation. Anonymous FTP access was one of the earliest methods employed for this purpose. Even when users resort to Web browsers to download files from the Internet, the browser invokes an FTP connection on behalf of the user and logs her in to the server anonymously before a download is started.

Anonymous FTP access provides users who do not have an account with the FTP server the capability to establish an FTP session with that server. For tracking purposes, anonymous FTP users must log in with the username anonymous or ftp and use their email address as a password.

An anonymous FTP user is misled to believe that he is at the root of the file system. This restriction provides an extra level of security, protecting the rest of the file system from use by anonymous users. Most UNIX variants included in the `ftpd` daemon have a feature that forces the daemon to change the root of the file system to the home directory of a special user named `ftp`. Assuming that the home directory of the `ftp` account is `/home/ftp`, the `ftpd` daemon uses `chroot` command to change the root of the file system to `/home/ftp` for anonymous users.

Setting Up Anonymous FTP Service

Setting up an FTP server for anonymous access involves creating the `ftp` user account and creating a mini-file system under the home directory of `ftp`. The directory must contain the necessary file system resources that render anonymous access functional. For most UNIX platforms, the following steps allow you to provide anonymous FTP access:

1. Create the user `ftp`. Make this user belong to the `ftp` group. If the `ftp` group does not exist, add it to the file `/etc/groups`. Following is a depiction of the `ftp` account entry in the `/etc/passwd` file:

    `ftp:x:5000:5000:Anonymous FTP:/home/ftp:/noshell`

    The `ftp` uses shell `/noshell`, which does not exist. This increases the security of the `ftp` account by preventing it from being used for logins.

2. Create the home directory for the user `ftp`. The owner of this directory should be `root`. The group membership of this directory should be the `ftp` group. For security reasons, this directory should have the permissions 555. In the following steps, we will refer to the `ftp` users home directory as `~ftp`.

3. Create the directory `~ftp/bin`. This directory should be owned by `root`, and its permissions should be set to 555. In this directory, the `/usr/bin/ls` command must be present to enable users to list its contents. The permissions on this command should be set to 111.

4. Create the directory `~ftp/etc`. This directory must contain a stripped version of the `/etc/passwd` file, `/etc/group`, and `/etc/netconfig`. These files must be present for the `ls` command to work satisfactorily. Set permissions on the `~ftp` directory to 444.

5. Create the directory `~ftp/dev` and assign its ownership to `root`. This directory must contain the special files `/dev/tcp` and `/dev/zero`. Both files must be created using the `mknod` command. The major and minor numbers corresponding to each file can be obtained by using the "`ls -lL`" command. These files should be created with permissions set to 666 for passive `ftp` requests to function properly.

6. Create the directory `~ftp/usr/lib` and assign its ownership to root. This directory should contain a copy of the following shared libraries from `/usr/lib`:

```
ld.so*
libc.so*
libdl.so*
libintl.so*
libw.so*
libnsl.so*
libsocket.so*
nss_nis.so*
nss_nisplus.so*
nss_dns.so*
nss_files.so*
straddr.so*
```

7. Create the directory ~ftp/pub, assign its ownership to ftp, and set its permissions to 555. This is the directory where public access is allowed via the anonymous login. This is where you want to put files for public distribution.

> **Tip**
>
> The man page for ftpd on Solaris 2.x (SunOS 5.x) includes a shell script that automatically handles the entire setup of the anonymous FTP server. This script is also available via anonymous FTP using the following URL:
>
> ftp://ftp.math.fsu.edu/pub/solaris/ftp.anon

If you are interested in a highly configurable and secure FTP daemon, try the Wuarchive FTP daemon. It can be download via anonymous FTP using the following URL:

ftp://ftp.uu.net/networking/ftp/wuarchive-ftpd

Both BSD and SVR4 implementation are available. The distribution also contains documentation that explains the daemon's features and configuration.

Checking Server Security

After the anonymous FTP server is set up, it is prudent to verify that there are no security loopholes. Following are the minimum recommended checks that should be made:

- Log in to the server as anonymous user and verify that the account cannot be used to create files or directories in any of the directories you created as part of the setup. Particular attention should be given to the home directory of the ftp account. This directory should never contain a .rhosts file because that will grant instant access to crackers everywhere.

- Check to see whether the FTP commands SITE CHMOD and SITE EXEC are implemented. These commands can lead to serious security breaches. To check this, telnet to the host on port 21 and try to execute the FTP command SITE EXEC or

SITE CHMOD. If either of these commands works, disable ftpd and then replace it with one that provides greater security.

- Make sure that the directory ~ftp is not owned by ftp. If it is owned by ftp, a smart hacker can gain unlimited access by changing its permissions to 777.

- Make sure that there are no files or directories under the directory ~ftp owned by ftp. If such files exist, intruders can replace them using virus-contaminated files.

In addition to these checks, you can add extra security to your ftp server by using TCP wrappers.

Troubleshooting FTP

A wide range of reasons might cause an FTP session to fail; anything from user configuration error and network failure to problems resulting from system failure or defective software. This section looks at some issues related to FTP failures.

Connection Problems

If a user reports a problem connecting, the first thing to do is attend to the user's workstation and ask that user to go through the motions of logging in. Verify that the user is following the proper login procedure. If not, educate the user on how to do it.

If the user follows the proper procedures and still encounters problems, try to assess whether the failure is a local configuration issue on the client workstation, a local hardware problem, or a network problem.

If the user is getting a Connection refused type of error, the problem is likely to be a logical one. There are several reasons for this error to arise:

- If the user relies on the $HOME/.netrc file to autologin to the server, check the contents of the file and ask the user to verify the information pertinent to the login process. Invalid information can lead to the server's refusal to connect a user. If all is fine with the contents of the .netrc file, check its permissions. The permissions should be set so that no one but the owner is allowed to read or write its contents. Failure to meet this requirement can result in failure to log in to an FTP server.

- Verify that the user has a valid account on the remote server. If not, or if the account is expired, you might refer her to the administrator of the host in question for subsequent resolution.

- Another thing to look at to explain a valid account's failure to FTP the server is the /etc/ftpusers file. If it exists and the account name is included in the file, the ftpd daemon prevents the user from logging in. Again, recommend that the user bring up the issue with the administrator of the host in question for resolution.

- Users failing to use one of the shells specified in the /etc/shells file are bound to fail to connect via FTP. Check the /etc/shells file on the target host and take the required action to remedy the situation.

- Although rare, it is possible that somehow the port on which the ftpd daemon is listening to connections is changed to other than the default (21). Should this happen, ftp clients defaulting to port 21 when making connection requests will be refused. Check the server's /etc/services file to verify the port number on which inetd is listening on behalf of ftpd for connection request. This can be accomplished using the following command:

```
$ grep ftp /etc/services
ftp     21/tcp
```

If the port number is different from 21, this is where the trouble lies. Contact the system administrator for that host and try to find out why this is so. The port number might have been changed maliciously, or might have been required for other reasons. Depending on the reason, the port might have to be changed back to the default or left at its new value. In the latter case, the user should be advised to try to ftp to that host using the existing port. Assuming that the port number is 420, the ftp command should look like this:

```
$ ftp hostname 420
```

Timeouts

If users complain about frequent abrupt disconnection of FTP sessions, you might want to increase the timeout value set for the ftpd daemon. By default, most daemons self-configure on startup to 15 minutes. Congested network conditions might lead to server timeouts, resulting in disruption to ongoing user sessions. Try increasing the timeout value on the server. Be careful not to set it too high; otherwise, users with idling FTP sessions end up needlessly hogging FTP connections at the expense of other users waiting for their release.

To change the timeout value on the server, edit the /etc/inetd.conf file and adjust the entry affecting the ftpd daemon to include the -ttimeout command parameter as shown in this example:

```
ftp     stream   tcp    nowait    NOLUID    /etc/ftpd -t1800    ftpd
```

In this entry, the timeout value has been increased to 1800 seconds (30 minutes). After making the change, send the inetd daemon a SIGHUP signal to reinitialize it so that the new change takes effect.

File Transfer Problems

If a user complains about the inability to transfer multiple files using mput along with wildcard characters in the filename specification, verify that she has filename expansion turned on. Filename expansion can be toggled using the ftp glob command as follows:

```
ftp> glob
Globbing turned off
ftp> glob
Globbing turned on
```

If users complain about failure to transfer files reliably, they may have ASCII transfer type turned on instead of BINARY type when sending or receiving non-ASCII files. Verify the transfer type and take corrective action (including educating the user) if need be.

Debug Mode

To resolve some of the more complex problems, you might want to turn on debugging upon invocation of the FTP session. You can do this upon invoking the ftp command by using the -d switch:

```
$ ftp -d hostname
```

Debug mode can also be activated after invoking ftp using the debug command:

```
ftp> debug
Debugging turned on.
```

Debug mode allows you to follow the progress of the FTP session. Whenever enabled, it displays session data indicating the direction of the exchange and the ftp messages being exchanged. As shown in the following example, -[ra] indicates that the local host is sending, whereas a three-digit code indicates that the remote host is sending:

```
$ ftp tenor
Connected to tenor.
220 tenor FTP server (UNIX(r) System V Release 4.0) ready.
331 Password required for root.
230 User root logged in.
ftp> debug
Debugging on (debug=1).
ftp> cd /usr/sam
— -> CWD /usr/sam
250 CWD command successful.
ftp> ls
— -> PORT 100,0,0,2,5,6
200 PORT command successful.
— -> LIST
150 ASCII data connection for /bin/ls (100.0.0.2,1286) (0 bytes).
```

33

ADMINISTERING
FTP SERVICES

```
total 6
-rw-rw-rw-   1 root     other          55 Oct 19 15:55 ftpscript
-rw-rw-rw-   1 root     other         721 Oct 19 15:55 proxy
-rw-rw-rw-   1 root     other       10153 Oct 17 19:42 sendAriel
-rw-rw-rw-   1 root     other         204 Oct 19 15:55 tenor.ftp
-rw-rw-rw-   1 root     other         519 Oct 19 15:55 tenor.help
-rw-rw-rw-   1 root     other       12870 Oct 19 15:55 testfile
226 ASCII Transfer complete.
ftp> get testfile
local: testfile remote: testfile
— -> PORT 100,0,0,2,5,8
200 PORT command successful.
— -> RETR testfile
150 ASCII data connection for testfile (100.0.0.2,1288) (12870 bytes).
226 ASCII Transfer complete.
13415 bytes received in 0.58 seconds (23 Kbytes/s)
ftp> quit
— -> QUIT
221 Goodbye.
```

Hash Mode

In addition to Debug mode, you can use the `hash` command to display the status of the file transfer. It forces `ftp` to print a hash mark after a certain number of bytes have been transferred. The following example shows its use:

```
$ ftp kanchi
Connected to kanchi.bosland.us.
220-Local time is now 13:31 and the load is 0.03.
220 You will be thrown out after 900 seconds of inactivity.
Name (kanchi:ranga): ftp
230 Anonymous user logged in.
Remote system type is UNIX.
Using binary mode to transfer files.
ftp> cd pub/incoming
250 Changed to /pub/incoming
ftp> hash
Hash mark printing on (1024 bytes/hash mark).
ftp> get unx3ar.hqx
200 Connected to 10.8.11.9 port 49192
150 Opening data connection
####################################################################
#####################################################
226-File written successfully
226 1.473 seconds (measured here), 0.85 Mbytes per second
1368179 bytes received in 1.47 seconds (907.18 Kbytes/s)
ftp> quit
221-Goodbye.  You uploaded 0 and downloaded 1337 kbytes.
221 CPU time spent on you: 0.520 seconds.
```

Server Problems

Server-related problems can result from software bugs or poor implementation. Similar to the client, the `ftpd` daemon comes with a `-d` switch, which can be used to turn on debugging. When turned on, debugging data are logged to the `/usr/adm/syslog` file. Equally possible is the capability to log details pertaining to individual FTP sessions. This is achieved by specifying the `-1` switch in the entry for `ftpd` in the `/etc/inetd.conf` file as follows:

```
ftp     stream    tcp    nowait    NOLUID    /etc/ftpd -1    ftpd
```

Be careful not to leave debugging or logging turned on for too long. The `/usr/adm/syslog` file can grow to an astronomical size over a short period of time due to the amount of details both modes generate.

Summary

FTP is the one of the most widely used method of downloading and uploading files on the Internet. Web browsers use FTP as the underlying mechanism for transferring files when requested. Consequently, system administrators are faced more than ever with the challenging task of providing reliable and secure FTP services.

This chapter showed how to set up FTP services, including anonymous access. It also included tips on verifying the security of the service. Both third-party transfers and unattended transfers were explained and illustrated. Finally, common FTP problems and ways of troubleshooting them were discussed.

33

ADMINISTERING FTP SERVICES

CHAPTER 34

Backing up and Restoring Your System

by Chris Byers

IN THIS CHAPTER

In a perfect world, no one would ever lose data, disks would never fail, controllers would never go haywire, and every system would have the rm command aliased to ask you whether you really want to delete all your data.

According to Murphy, there is no such thing as a perfect world. You will lose your data, your disks will fail, your controllers will go postal on you at some point, and you probably don't have any commands aliased, much less the rm command. The question really isn't *if* the worst will happen, it's *when* it will happen.

Fortunately, you have a way of protecting your data (and most likely your job). UNIX comes standard with a number of relatively flexible and rigorous archiving and tape backup systems that can fit into almost any hardware architecture. In addition to these standards, there are a number of proprietary commands for vendor specific operating systems and hardware that can provide a full system recovery solution.

In this chapter we will look at these backup solutions and how best to implement them, as well as the variations in solutions between UNIX variants that come standard with each operating system, as each one varies from the others in terms of implementation and backup strategy.

Finally, we will take a quick look at some third-party utilities for complete system (multiserver and workstation) backups and restores.

Generic Backup Commands

A number of generic backup commands can be used on nearly any UNIX system you may have. This section looks at some of the more popular and powerful commands.

The tar Command

One of the oldest and most often used commands for archiving and backing up files is the tar command. Because of its simplicity and ease of use, this is the most common format for tape and disk archives today, and probably for many years to come. This means that, for example, a tape from a Silicon Graphics workstation can be restored to a Hewlett-Packard HP9000 server without any problems.

One of the best features of tar is the flexibility to save to any medium because it treats file and tape (or other backup media) device targets the same.

You can also specify files and directories that you want to include or exclude. You can specify them on the command line, or you can specify a file containing a list of files to include or exclude.

The format of the `tar` command is:

```
tar (options) (tarfile name) (filenames to backup or restore)
```

Typically, the most common groups of options used are `cvf` for writing to a `tarfile`, `xvf` for extracting files, and `tvf` for listing the contents of a `tar` archive.

As an example of writing to a tape archive, to archive all the directories in the `/usr/local/datafiles` directory to a typical 4mm tape drive on a Hewlett-Packard machine, use the following command:

```
tar cvf /dev/rmt/0hc /usr/local/datafiles
```

Keep in mind that if you use the absolute path of the directory, you can only restore to that directory. A more flexible approach would be to get into the `/usr/local` directory and back up the directory, as follows:

```
cd /usr/local
tar cvf /dev/rmt/0hc datafiles
```

This way, if you want to restore the `datafiles` subdirectory, archived in the last example, to a different location, you can first `cd` to the appropriate place and then restore. For example, if you want to restore the `datafiles` subdirectory to the `/usr/contrib` subdirectory, do the following:

```
cd /usr/contrib
tar xvf /dev/rmt/0hc
```

If you are unsure what is on the tape, you can list the contents first. Because this can take just as long as restoring and the list of files usually scrolls off the screen, I usually redirect the output to a file, which I can then save as a record of backed up files:

```
tar tvf /dev/rmt/0hc > tarlist.txt
```

This is also a good way to get a printout of what is on a tape because you can print off the `tarlist.txt` file directly. I try to keep this printout with the tape so I don't have to waste time when I need it.

If you know which specific files and subdirectories you want to restore, you can use an `include` file to grab only what you need. Let's say you copied the `tarlist.txt` file to a file called `include` and then edited out all the files except the ones you want to restore. The command would then look like this:

```
tar xvf /dev/rmt0 -I include
```

This scrolls through the tape and gets only the specified files. You can also use an `include` file when archiving to tape and when looking for a list of specific files.

After `tar` has written a backup to tape, it writes two EOF marks on the tape. You can move the tape to these marks by using the `mt` (move tape) command as follows:

```
mt -f /dev/nftape fsf 1
```

In this example, the tape device `/dev/nftape` is a *nonrewinding* device. You must use a nonrewinding tape device, or else after you have moved the tape in position, it will just rewind back to the beginning.

Now that you have the tape in the correct position, you can back up or restore the next archive on the tape.

The dump Command

The `dump` command essentially has the same functionality as the `tar` command, with the exception that it is somewhat more rigorous than `tar`. With `dump`, you can back up an entire file system or specified files and directories in a file system. In addition, you can specify a "dump level" (priority for saving files) to indicate the currency (last modification time) of the files to be backed up.

For example, if a level 2 dump is done on one day and a level 4 dump is done on the following day, only the files that have been modified or added since the level 2 dump will be backed up to the level 4 dump. The date and level of prior dumps are listed in the file `/etc/dumpdates`. Dump uses this file as a reference to decide which files to back up. If a `dump` command is not successful, it will not update this file.

Used in conjunction with the system scheduler (`cron`), this can be an effective solution for continuous system backups and archives.

In general, `dump` is used in the following format:

```
/usr/etc/dump [options [arguments]] filesystem
```

A typical example of this command would be:

```
/usr/etc/dump /dev/nrst0 /dev/sd0h
```

where `/dev/nrst0` is the no-rewind tape device file and `/dev/sd0h` is the file system device file of the file system to be backed up. You must get the file system device filename from the output of `df`, cross-referenced with the appropriate directory. This example was taken from a Sun system.

In addition to dumping file systems, you can dump specific files. However, if you choose to do this, you can only back up files at level 0. As a matter of fact, the `/etc/dumpdates` file is never even used, even if you choose the `-u` option.

For example, let's say that you want to dump the files chapter1 and chapter2 to an 8mm tape drive. The command would look something like this:

```
dump fdsb /dev/rst0 5400 6000 126 chapter1 chapter2
```

Consult the man pages for more information on the options available for each particular tape drive.

Using cpio

One of the more popular generic backup utilities in use today is the cpio command. In large part, its popularity is due to its capability to append backup volumes and span tapes, allowing you to create incremental backup sets and full systems backups without losing data integrity.

Cpio allows you to copy files into and out of a cpio archive. If you use the -o option, it contains pathname and status information, as well as the contents of one or more archived files. Cpio stands for copy in/out.

The following is an example of using this command to back up the contents of a directory. The device file of the tape drive in this example is /dev/mt0:

```
ls ¦ cpio -o > /dev/mt0
```

where the -o option copies out an archive.

Also, to read from a cpio archive on a tape drive, you can do something similar to the following example:

```
cpio -icdB < /dev/rmt0
```

where -i copies to an archive, c writes header information in ASCII character form, d creates directories as needed, and B blocks input to 512 bytes to the record.

You can also use the find command to see whether a particular file is listed on your tape (or disk) archive:

```
find . -cpio /dev/rmt/0m
```

Once again, consult your man pages for a more complete explanation of all the options available.

Using the backup and restore Commands

The backup and restore commands are actually the native AIX commands for doing backups, but they work on all systems. As a matter of fact, if you want to save and restore your ACLs (Access Control List), this is the only backup command that allows you to do so.

You can do two types of backups with these commands. You can either back up your system by `inode` or by file. If you choose to back them up by `inode`, you are actually performing a file system `dump`, which is what `mksysb` in AIX 4 uses (I will get more into this in the AIX section). Only the `dump` method has support for incremental backups, thus reducing the amount of time and tape used on system backups. This also has compatibility with the BSD `dump` command and the AIX `rdump`/`rrestore` commands.

A common way of using the `backup` command is in conjunction with the `find` command, where you run a find on the files you want to back up and pipe the output into the `backup` command. For example, if you want to do a relative backup of the contents of the `/home` directory, along with its subdirectories, do the following:

```
cd /
find ./home -print ¦ backup -iqf /dev/rmt0
```

To restore the tape, use the following commands:

```
cd /
restore -xqf /dev/rrmt0
```

If you want to get only specific files from the tape, simply add the filenames to the end of the command line. If you want to check the contents of a tape, simply use the `-T` option on the command line.

For incremental backups, the file `/etc/dumpdates` must exist. Use the `touch` command to create it if it doesn't. To do a full backup of the home file system, do the following:

```
backup -0uf /dev/rmt0.4 /home
```

This creates a level 0 (full) `dump` on the tape. This also places an entry in the `/etc/dumpdates` file as follows:

```
/dev/rhd1 0 Wed Apr 16 16:02:23 1997
```

You could also use the device name from the output of `df` instead of the file system name.

To restore an incremental backup to this tape, use the following command:

```
backup -1uf /dev/rmt0.4 /home
```

And into the `/etc/dumpdates` file goes another line under the first:

```
/dev/rhd1 1 Wed April 16 16:42:42 1997
```

Should your file system get crushed and you need to restore from this tape, first create a new `/home` file system, make this your current directory, and restore the data from the tapes.

The first tape must be the level 0 tape. The command to restore it would be:

```
restore -qrf /dev/rm0
```

Now insert the level 1 dump tape and use the same command to update the files to the most current setting. If you want to only restore individual files, first go the directory where you want to restore the file and run the command:

```
restore -qxf /dev/rmt0x4 ./home/joe/.profile
```

to restore your personal profile.

Using pax

pax is a neat little utility that handles both the tar and cpio formats. It defaults to tar format, but it also incorporates the error recovery features of cpio. As a matter of fact, when a mksysb tape runs across bad spots on a tape, it automatically calls the pax utility to try and recover from the error condition.

The following format is used with pax:

```
pax -wf (tape device) (filesystem)
```

To archive the /home file system to tape, do the following:

```
pax -wf /dev/rmt0 /home
```

To restore the file system, use the following command:

```
pax -r -pe -f /dev/rmt0
```

The -pe option in this restore command is used to preserve both the modification time and the ownership of the files. Also, you don't have to use relative pathnames because they can be changed when you restore the files. For example, if you want to restore the files from /home to /tmp/test, use this command:

```
pax -rpe -f /dev/rmt0 -s:^/home:/temp/test;g
```

The command to list the contents of the tape is:

```
pax -f /dev/rmt0
```

If you want to write out a tape to either cpio or tar format, you can make it do so explicitly by using the -x option, along with specifying either cpio or tar.

HP-UX Backup Commands

Although tar and cpio are versatile and generic tools for doing both system backups and simple file archives, they lack some features for convenience and ease of use, as well as logging and error recovery.

The next few sections discuss the proprietary backup solutions available with some of the more popular UNIX variants.

fbackup

Hewlett-Packard came out with its own version of a UNIX operating system based on Berkely's (BSD) UNIX OS code. Its systems are known as HP9000 systems; its servers are designated as S800 series machines; and its workstations are designated as S700 series machines. Also, Hewlett-Packard has various HP-UX operating system versions available, from the earliest release of HP-UX 8.x to the latest release of HP-UX 10.20 (at the time of writing).

On all HP9000 machines, the `fbackup` utility comes with the operating system as an effective system and file backup solution. `fbackup` combines the functionality of `ftio` (an extension of `cpio`) with the ease of use of the `tar` command, as well as a few extras.

`fbackup` gives you the option to include directories and files in your backup. On specifying a directory, all the files and subdirectories in that directory are backed up. You can use the `-i` option with `fbackup`, or you can use a graph file, which is discussed later.

You can also exclude files from your backup set in a similar manner as the include files. Use the `-e` option to with the `fbackup` command to exclude files and/or directories and subdirectories.

Using graph files is a good way to get just what you want backed up or restored, without a ridiculously long command line. You can have only one entry per line in a graph file for files or directories, and it must be preceded by an `i` (for include) or an `e` (for exclude).

For example, you can back up the `/home` directory and exclude the `/home/joe` directory with the following graph file:

```
i /home
e /home/joe
```

`fbackup` uses the `-g` option to identify a graph file.

To use the `fbackup` command, follow these steps to ensure data integrity and stability:

1. Make sure that you are superuser.

2. Make sure that the files you want to back up are not in use or locked during the `fbackup`.

3. Make sure that your tape drive is connected correctly and that you have the right device file pointing to the right SCSI device and that it is turned on (you'd be surprised how many times this is the problem).

4. Put the tape in the drive, with write protection turned off on the tape. If your back-up spans multiple tapes, you are asked to insert the next tape(s) as needed.

5. You can now start backing up using fbackup.

The following is an example of an fbackup command:

```
fbackup -f /dev/rmt/0m -I /home
```

This backs up the entire contents of /home to the device file /dev/rmt/0m. The device file used in this example (/dev/rmt/0m) is commonly used for medium density 4mm DAT tapes used in DDS2 tape drives. To find the correct device file for your tape device, you might have to do some digging.

TIP

If you know that your data will take up two tapes and you have two tape drives attached to your machine, you can do an unattended backup by specifying two tape drives in the fbackup command. For example:

```
fbackup -f /dev/rmt/0m -f /dev/rmt/c0t1d0BEST -i / -I /tmp/index
```

This way, when the first tape fills up, the next tape is automatically written to as a continuation of the backup set.

---

frecover

To restore from tape, you must use the frecover command. Many of the options for fbackup are used in frecover as well.

To restore backup files from fbackup tapes using the frecover utility, you need to follow these steps:

1. Make sure that you are superuser.

2. Make sure that the files you want to restore aren't open or locked. Just as fbackup doesn't work with open or locked files, neither does frecover.

3. Make sure that the tape device is hooked up correctly.

4. Make sure that you have the right tape in the machine to restore from.

5. Start restoring with the frecover command.

If you want to recover all files from a backup, use the -r option. By using the -x option, you can get individual files from tape. For all the options, check the man pages for frecover(1M).

34

BACKING UP
AND RESTORING
YOUR SYSTEM

If you are restoring files that are NFS mounted to your system, you may run into some problems. The `frecover` command can only restore files that have "other user" write permission. If you are going to do this, first log in as superuser on the NFS file server and use the `root=` option to the `/usr/sbin/exportfs` command (on 10.x systems) to export the permissions.

Following is an example of restoring files in the directory `/home/joe` from tape:

```
frecover -x -i /home/joe
```

This command does not overwrite newer files as long as the `-o` option is not specified.

If you want to restore files from all directories under `/home/dave` from a DAT tape to the `/tmp` directory, do the following:

```
cd /tmp
frecover -x -oF -i /home/dave
```

So what happened here? The `-F` option removes the leading pathnames from all the files on the tape that meet the include criteria, causing them to be restored to the current directory without leading directories. All files are overwritten because of the `-o` option.

Again, all the options are explained in detail in the man pages for `frecover`.

AIX Backup Systems

AIX comes with a number of backup tools that can handle everything from single file backups to full system cloning. This section looks at most of these.

Using `mksysb`

IBM's UNIX solution, AIX, comes with a flexible and complete backup solution, known as the `mksysb` utility. With `mksysb`, you can back up individual files, the root file system, or the entire system if this fits your need (and who wouldn't have that need!).

Specifically, AIX 3 only gives you the option of backing up the root volume group, but AIX 4 includes additional commands that give you the same functionality for other volume groups as well. By using `mksysb` as a system backup instead of a standard backup, you can get your system back much more quickly because you are skipping the step of first installing a system from scratch and then restoring data. This is an effective solution for disaster recovery.

You can create clone images of the root volume group in two ways: either by using the command `mkszfile && mksysb -f /dev/rmt0` (`/dev/rmt0` being the backup device) or running `smit mksysb`. The `mksysb` image can be installed on different machines if need be. As a matter of fact, this is standard practice in disaster recovery testing.

Although you can restore to a different system, you may need to change other system configuration parameters to fit the new system, such as IP addresses. By configuring only the common settings for your systems, you avoid problems relating to machine specific issues, particularly IP addresses that could cause conflicts.

You can adapt the clone the first time it boots on the new machine through a simple script that can be executed only once on the first boot. The script is called /etc/firstboot, and it is executed by the cloned machine immediately after /etc/rc on boot-up. This script is only executed once if it exists and then it is renamed /etc/fb_hh_mm_MM_DD in accordance with the current date. The fbcheck entry in /etc/inittab handles this process.

When you clone an AIX 3.2 system, you also create a list of file systems to be created. The command that does this is the mkszfile command. This creates the /.fs.size file, which stores the sizes of the file systems for the clone. Typically, this file follows a format similar to the following:

```
imageinstall
rootvg 4 hd4 / 2 8 jfs
rootvg 4 hd1 /home 31 84 jfs
rootvg 4 hd3 /tmp 3 12 jfs
rootvg 4 hd2 /usr 178 712 jfs
rootvg 4 hd9var /var 3 12 jfs
```

Looking at the file you can see, from left to right, the volume group, the logical partition size, the name of the logical volume, the name of the file system, the size in physical partitions, the size in megabytes, and the type of the file system (jfs stands for the journaled file system).

NOTE

You must make sure that /usr and /tmp have at least 8MB free before you create the tape. This avoids problems with the installation of the new machine.

34

BACKING UP AND RESTORING YOUR SYSTEM

To completely restore an entire system from the tape, you need to have the tape in the primary tape drive (usually /dev/rmt0). You put the key in the service position (after you halt the system), double-click the reset button, and wait. The system reboots and displays a menu, giving you the option to restore from the mksysb tape, boot into a service kernel, or run system diagnostics. All you have to do is choose the restore option and go get some coffee for anywhere from 30 minutes to an hour (depending on the size of your rootvg).

A `mksysb` tape actually stores files in `tar` format. The image starts at the third file on the tape, so you have to position the tape at that file and restore using a nonrewinding tape device. This means that you can get any file off a `mksysb` tape with a `tar` command.

For example, if you need to get the `vi` command back, just put the `mksysb` tape in the tape drive (in this case, `/dev/rmt0`) and do the following:

```
cd /                          # get to the root directory
tctl -f /dev/rmt0 rewind      # rewind the tape
tctl -f /dev/rmt0.1 fsf 3     # move the tape to the third file, no rewind
tar -xvf /dev/rmt0.1 ./usr/bin/vi    # extract the vi binary, no rewind
```

You must `cd` to `/` first because all files are stored relative to `root`.

In AIX 4, you can do more than just back up the root volume group. You can control file system sizes and placement through configuration files and different installation methods. Also, you can specify options as you need them.

Instead of creating the `/.fs.size` file, `mkszfile` in AIX 4 creates the `/image.data` file, which has much more sophistication than its predecessor. You can also give it more customization through the `/bosinst.data` file, which is automatically created by `mksysb` unless it has already been created manually. AIX comes with a default `/bosinst.data` file, located in `/usr/lpp/bosinst/bosinst.template`.

You can generate a system backup by using the following command:

```
mksysb -i /dev/rmt0
```

Using the `-i` option causes `mksysb` to call the `mkszfile` command automatically. Specifying the `-m` causes `mkszfile` to generate logical volume maps, which are included on the image. If you do this, you can also clone the exact location of the file systems on the new system. There is also a new option, `-e`, which excludes the files from being backed up, which can be defined in the file `/etc/exclude.rootvg`.

To contrast the two, the `/bosinst.data` file controls how a `mksysb` image is installed, and the `/image.data` file defines the characteristics of the root volume group and the file systems within it.

The following is a common `bosints.data` file:

```
control_flow:
    CONSOLE =
    INSTALL_METHOD = overwrite
    PROMPT = yes
    EXISTING_SYSTEM_OVERWRITE = yes
    INSTALL_X_IF_ADAPTER = yes
    RUN_STARTUP = yes
    ERROR_EXIT =
```

```
    CUSTOMIZATION_FILE =
    TCB = yes
    INSTALL_TYPE = full
    BUNDLES =

target_disk_data:
    LOCATION = 00-00-0S-0,0
    SIZE_MB = 1307
    HDISKNAME = hdisk0

locale:
    BOSINST_LANG = en_US
    CULTURAL_CONVENTION = C
    MESSAGES = C
    KEYBOARD = de_DE
```

These values can be changed as needed.

The CONSOLE value defines the console device. If you set the PROMPT value to no, you must set it, or the system does not know which device to use for the console. A couple of common examples are /dev/lft0 or /dev/tty0.

The INSTALL_METHOD value sets the installation method, most commonly set to overwrite, particularly for clone tapes. You can set the preserve and migrate options for updating systems, but you cannot use them for cloning.

The PROMPT value must be set to no for an automated install. After you set it to no, however, you must define all the parameters needed for the other values.

The value for EXISTING_SYSTEM_OVERWRITE must be set to yes to automate the overwrite of systems that already are installed AIX systems.

If a system is cloned, INSTALL_X_IF_ADAPTER is not used. Otherwise, this value is used to specify the installation of AIXwindows, depending on whether a graphics adapter is found on the system.

If you want to start the install assistant after the first system boot, you should set the RUN_STARTUP value to yes.

The value for RM_INST_ROOTS should be set to yes to clean up the /usr/lpp/*/inst_roots directories after the system is installed. The only time you would set this value to no would be if you were going to run a server system for diskless machines.

The ERROR_EXIT value is used to define what you want to run should the installation fail. Make sure that you specify a complete path and command name here because you won't have any PATH variables set at the point where it fails.

The CUSTOMIZATION_FILE variable exists so that you can specify a filename to be executed as soon as the installation program has completed.

The TCB (Trusted Computing Base) variable has to be set to yes if you want the TCB to be active on your system. The TCB is a security measure ensuring that only the people that you want on your system can access only the programs you want them to access.

The INSTALL_TYPE variable always is set to a full installation on a mksysb restore.

The BUNDLES variable is not used on mksysb tapes. This is only used for specifying which software bundles need to be installed initially from the medium.

The LOCATION variable is used to set the location code for the installation disk. If this variable is left undefined, the program automatically finds a good installation disk without user intervention. For example, the location of 00-00-0S-0,0 specifies the SCSI 0 disk with an integrated SCSI adapter.

The SIZE_MB value can be specified, but it is not necessary. Here, you would specify a disk size in megabytes. To have the program automatically choose the largest disk, just use the keyword "largest" with no location code.

To specify the disk to restore to, you can use the HDISKNAME variable. An example of a common value to put in here is hdisk0.

The BOSINST_LANG variable lets you set the language that will be used during the installation of the system. Unless you speak a language other than English, always use en_US.

To specify the locale that is used for an installed system, you can set the CULTURAL_ CONVENTION variable. On mksysb tapes, this is left blank.

The system message language can be set with the MESSAGES variable. However, with a mksysb tape, this value is left blank.

And finally, the keyboard map you want installed can be set with the KEYBOARD variable. This should be left blank for mksysb tapes.

In the /image.data file, several lines describe the root volume group and the logical volumes therein. Some settings can be changed to fit your needs.

In the logical_volume_policy, you can change the EXACT_FIT parameter to yes if you want the disk used to install the system to be exactly the same as the description in this file.

The SHRINK parameter defines whether the logical volumes should be shrunk to their minimal size at install time.

Next, the vg_data stanza defines parameters of the volume group. In here, you modify the PPSIZE parameter to set different default physical partition sizes. By default, this number is set to 4MB.

Each logical volume has one lv_data stanza. In here, all characteristics for logical volumes can be set. Should you want to define the disk location and maximum size parameters, you can do so here.

The final stanza in the /image.data file is the fs_data stanza. Each file system has an fs_data entry, which modifies the file system block size and activates compression for the file system.

As in AIX 3.2, AIX 4 also executes /etc/firstboot, if there is one, only on the first reboot after installation. The fbcheck entry in etc/inittab triggers this.

In AIX 4, to restore a system from a mksysb tape, you can do one of two things. As in AIX 3.2, you can simply boot from the mksysb tape, or you can use the restore command (instead of the tar command in 3.2).

If you use the restore command, you need to use the nonrewind tape device and specify the -s option. As with the tar format, mksysb in 3.2, you again need to start out in the third position on the tape. As an example of restoring the vi binary, do the following:

```
cd /
tctl -f /dev/rmt0 rewind
tctl -f /dev/rmt0.1 fsf 3
restore -xqf /dev/rmt0.1 -s 1 ./usr/bin/vi
```

For more detailed information on all the options for restore, consult the man page.

Using sysback

Basically, sysback is an extension of mksysb, in that you can back up more than just the rootvg. It also incorporates the savevg and restvg commands to aid in restoring volume groups and file systems.

For more information, consult your sysback manual that came when you purchased sysback.

Using savevg and restvg

You can archive volume groups other than the root volume group by using the savevg command. For example, if you want to back up the volume group homevg, you have a choice of either going through the smit savevg fastpath or the command:

```
savevg -i -f/dev/rmt0 homevg
```

With the preceding command, the `-I` option also creates the file `/tmp/vgdata/homevg/homevg.data`, which is similar to the `/image.data` file that gets created with the `mkszfile` command. However, this file is actually created with the `mkvgdata` command, a softlink to the `mkszfile` command.

Other things in common with the `mksysb` command include the `-m` flag to create map file and the `-e` command to exclude whatever files are listed in the file (for this example, `/etc/exclude.homevg`).

Along with all the data for the volume group, the `/tmp/vgdata/homevg/homevg.data` and `/tmp/vgdata/homevg/filesystems` files are also backed up to tape for reference by the `restvg` command during volume group restoration. The `/tmp/vgdata/homevg/filesystems` file is simply a copy of the `/etc/filesystems` file.

If you have a tape with archives created with the `savevg` command, you can restore from that tape with the `restvg` command. For example:

```
restvg -qf /dev/rmt0 -s
```

In this example, you would not only restore the `homevg` volume group on the physical volumes where it already resides, but the file system would also be shrunk to its minimum size.

You may not be able to easily restore a system with `restvg` to another machine unless the specific hard disks that the original volume group was on are available (not in use by another volume group) on the new system. If it is not available, then `restvg` aborts, unless you specify another set of hard disks that are available, with the following command:

```
restvg -qf /dev/rmt0 hdiskN
```

You can also restore individual files from a `savevg` tape using the standard `restore` command. For example:

```
cd /
restore -xqf /dev/rmt0 ./home/joe/.profile
```

You can use the `-T` flag to list the contents of the tape. See the appropriate man pages for details.

If you want to make the `homevg.data` file manually, you can run the command `mkvgdata homevg`. You can then edit the characteristics of the volume group and its file systems simply by editing the `homevg.data` file. Some of the things you change in this file are the characteristics of the physical partition size or the block size and compression algorithm of the file systems in the volume group.

Using `rdump` and `rrestore`

The `rdump` and `rrestore` commands are simply remote versions of the backup utility in AIX. In other words, you can back up your system to a remote tape drive over the network.

To use this utility, you need to have a proper `/.rhosts` file on the target machine. This may not be possible should you have a high degree of security on your network.

Also, if you have not already done so, you will have to create at least one compatibility link if you are using AIX 4. You have to link the `/usr/sbin/mnt` directory with the `/etc` directory. To do this, use the following command:

```
ln -s /usr/sbin/mnt /etc
```

You also must have a `/etc/dumpdates` file available as well, just like with `restore/backup`.

An example of backing up the `/home` file system is as follows:

```
rdump -0uf fileserver:/dev/rmt0.4 /home
```

On certain tape drives, `rdump` needs certain extra parameters. For example, if you are using an 8mm 2.3GB drive, you would have to use the parameters `-d6250 -s33000`. If you were to use a 5GB tape drive in its compressed mode, then you would have to use the value of `80000` for the `-s` parameter. Consult your AIX manuals for the specifications for your model of tape drive.

To restore from an `rdump` tape, use commands similar to the local `restore` command, such as in the following example:

```
rrestore -rf fileserver:/dev/rm0
```

Sun Solaris Backup Commands

As the UNIX system with the greatest market share, Sun Solaris also has some industry standard commands for backing up and restoring your system.

This section covers these commands in detail.

Using `ufsdump` and `ufsrestore`

The default system backup utility for Sun Solaris systems is the `ufsdump/ufsrestore` utility. As you might expect, this utility is based on the `dump/restore` utility and carries with it much of its attributes.

To most effectively illustrate the use of `ufsdump`/`ufsrestore`, this section outlines the steps involved in backing up a Sun workstation, along with a sample system backup and restore.

First off, you need to log everyone out of the system and bring it down to the single-user mode state. The following steps should walk you through a full system backup (level 0 backup):

1. Take the system down to single user mode state by typing **init s** and pressing Return. This ensures that no one can change any data on the system while you are backing it up.

2. Put a tape in the tape drive. For this example, assume that you are using a QIC-150 tape.

3. Type the following command: **ufsdump 0cuf /dev/rmt/(unit) c(n)t(n)d(n)s(n)**. Here, the 0 option specifies a level 0, or complete, dump of the system. The c option identifies a cartridge tape. The u option updates the dump record. The f option followed by the device name specifies the device file. At the end of the command, you need to specify the raw disk slice for the file system you want to back up, (c0t0d0s7, for example).

4. If more than one tape is needed to perform a complete dump, `ufsdump` tells you when to change to a new tape.

5. Label the tape with the command, file system, and date.

The following is a sample of possible screen output for the `ufsdump` command:

```
# init s
# ufsdump 0cuf /dev/rmt/0 c0t0d0s7
DUMP: Date of this level 0 dump: Wed Mar 11 10:16:53 1992
DUMP: Date of the last level 0 dump: the epoch
DUMP: Dumping /dev/rdsk/c0t3d0s7 (/export/home) to /dev/rmt/0
DUMP: mapping (Pass I) [regular files]
DUMP: mapping (Pass II) [directories]
DUMP: estimated 956 blocks (478KB)
DUMP: Writing 63 Kilobyte records
DUMP: dumping (Pass III) [directories]
DUMP: dumping (Pass IV) [regular files]
DUMP: level 0 dump on Wed Mar 11 10:16:53 1992
DUMP: 956 blocks (478KB) on 1 volume
DUMP: DUMP IS DONE
#
```

As with `dump`, you can specify different backup levels with `ufsdump` to back up only those files that were changed since a previous backup at a lower level.

To back up just the incremental changes on the system made since the last complete dump, follow these steps:

1. Once again, bring the system down to single user mode state.

2. Stick a tape in the tape drive.

3. Type **ufsdump [1-9]ucf/dev/rmt/(unit) /dev/rdsk/c(n)t(n)d(n)s(n)**. The level of the backup goes at the front of the ufsdump arguments [1-9].

4. Remove the tape from the drive and slap a label on it.

The other side to the coin for ufsdump is ufsrestore, just as restore is the flip side of dump. ufsrestore copies files from backups created using the ufsdump command into the current working directory. You can use ufsrestore in one of two ways: you can use it to reload an entire file system hierarchy from a level 0 dump followed by any incremental dumps that follow it, or you can restore just one or more single files from any dump tape.

During restore, all files are restored with their original owner, last modification time, and mode.

This sounds easy enough, but before you begin restoring, you need to know a few things:

- Which tapes you need
- The raw device name for the file systems you want to back up
- Which type of tape drive you want to use
- The device name you need to use for your tape drive

After you've found the right tape or tapes to restore (you do have backup plans, don't you?), you can start restoring your system. Follow these guidelines, and you should be okay:

1. Log in as root.

2. Bring the system down to single user mode (init s).

3. Unmount the file system you want to restore to with the umount command.

4. Rebuild the raw device file with newfs /dev/rdsk/c(n)t(n)d(n)s(n). This wipes the disk slice clean and rebuilds the file system.

5. Remount the file system with the mount command (mount /dev/dsk/c(n)t(n)d(n)s(n)).

6. Change your current directory to the mount point, which is the directory where you want to restore.

7. Put the tape in the drive.

8. Run the `ufsrestore` command to restore the file system. For example, run `ufsrestore rvf /dev/rmt/0h` to get the file system from tape.

If you want to get back only certain files, you need to use the interactive options in `ufsrestore`. A good idea to practice when restoring interactively is to restore files into the `/var/tmp` directory. This way, you stand less chance of overwriting files with older versions.

To restore files interactively, perform the following:

1. Log in as `root`.

2. Make sure that the write protect is on for safety on the tape, so that you don't accidentally overwrite the tape.

3. Change your current directory to `/var tmp`.

4. Run the command `ufsrestore if /dev/rmt/(unit)`.

5. You now create a list of files to be restored. If you want to list the contents of a directory, type **ls** and Return. If you want to change directories, type **cd (directory name)** and Return. If you want to add a directory or filename to the list of files to be restored, type **add (filename)**. If you want to remove a directory or filename from the restore list, type **delete (filename)**. And if you want to keep the permissions the same on the directory, type **setmodes** and Return; then type **n** and Return.

6. After you finish with the list, type **extract** and return. `ufsrestore` should ask you for a volume number at this point.

7. Type the volume number and return. Now the files and directories are restored to the current directory.

8. Type **quit** to get out of `ufsrestore`.

9. Check the restored files with the `ls -l` command to verify the files; then use the `mv` command to put all the verified files into their correct directories.

Making Backups on SVR4 Systems

By their nature, SVR4 systems are considered "raw" systems. By this, I mean that almost all UNIX systems are derived from one of two base, or raw, UNIX OSes: BSD or SVR4 (System 5 release 4).

As a raw system, SVR4 really doesn't have much to offer in the way of enhanced system backup and recovery utilities.

Just as most UNIX variants were derived from BSD and SVR4, so were most backup utilities derived from `dump`/`restore` and `cpio`/`tar`.

By default, BSD systems usually go to the `cpio` or `tar` utilities to handle their system backups. For more detail on these utilities, see the previous sections on `cpio` and `tar`.

IRIX Backup Commands

In addition to the standard `tar` and `cpio` backup utilities, IRIX also comes with the BRU utility for system backup and recovery.

The BRU utility gives you the functionality to do a number of things, such as backing up the system; restoring the system; verifying a backup; estimating a backup; defining a tape drive, disk file, or floppy to back up to or restore from; and defining which file systems or selection of files you want to back up or restore.

To utilize this functionality, use one or more of the following options:

- `-c`   Create a BRU backup volume.
- `-x`   Extract files from a BRU backup volume.
- `-t`   Get a table of contents from a BRU backup volume.
- `-i`   Verify the contents of a BRU backup volume.
- `-e`   Give an estimate of the number of BRU backup volumes needed.
- `-d`   Compare the contents of a BRU backup volume against the original files on the file system.
- `-v`   Verbosity level. You can specify up to four levels of verbosity.
- `-f`   Define what backup device will be accessed.

The command line for BRU is defined as follows:

```
bru -(mode) -options) -f(device) (path)
```

With all these basic modes and options, all the basic backup and restore functions can be performed. For example, if you want to restore the contents of the entire system to a tape drive on an SGI box, you might use the following command:

```
bru -cvf /dev/rmt/tps0d6ns.8200
```

To look at what's on a tape, you might use this command:

```
bru -tvf /dev/rmt/tps0d6ns.8200
```

This gives you a complete listing of the contents of the tape. You could also redirect the output (>) to a file so that you can have a list of the tape contents for your records.

To restore the contents of the entire backup volume, use the following command:

```
bru -xvf /dev/rmt/tps0d6ns.8200
```

By default, this command restores all the files to their original location (absolute paths).

You can verify the contents of a BRU backup volume in one of two ways: the -i mode and -d mode. The first method is actually preferable because the mechanism requires only the tape drive and the BRU utility to run. The inspect mode (-i) gives you this functionality:

```
bru -ivf /dev/rmt/tps0d6ns.8200
```

This verification method rereads each buffer block written on the backup volume and recalculates the 32-bit CRC. The BRU utility then compares this calculated CRC with the CRC that was written in the buffer block header. If it gets an incorrect value, it warns you of the offending condition.

In reality, the other mechanism, the -d mode, is most commonly used. It requires both the backup volume and the original data. For example:

```
bru -dvf /dev/rmt/tps0d6ns.8200
```

If you use this mechanism, it reads the data from the tape and performs a bit-by-bit comparison with the original data from the file system. This method reports problems if the files have changed on the file system since the backup was made.

A number of options are available to the BRU utility that go above and beyond the standard options available with its sister application, tar.

The following BRU utilities provide enhanced processing capabilities:

- -L   Puts a plainly readable text label on the backup volume.
- -G   Creates a file list that is placed at the head of the backup.
- -g   Reads and displays just the backup volume information.
- -gg   Reads and displays the file listing that was created with the -G option.
- -n   Selects files based on date and time.
- -B   Runs the BRU utility in the background.
- -PA   Switches the Absolute paths to Relative. This strips off the leading /.
- -ua   Performs an unconditional overwrite of all files during the restore.

For example, to add the description "Complete System Backup", do the following:

```
bru -cv -L "Complete System Backup" -f /dev/rmt/tps0d6sn.8200
```

If you look at the backup volume with `bru -g`, you see the following:

```
bru -gf /dev/rmt/tps0d6sn.8200
```

```
        label:              Complete System Backup
        created:            Sat Jan 23 17:22:34 1997
        artime:             8303483221
        volume:             1
        writes              4
        release:            14.3
        variant:            0
        bufsize:            20480
        msize:              0
        msize_blks:         0
        serial_number:      XXXX-XXXX-X
        device:             /dev/rmt/tps0d6sn.8200
        user:               root
        group:              root
        system:             IRIX pluto 5.X #2 Teu A M80586
        bru:                Fifth OEM Release
            command_line:   bru -cvf /dev/rmt/tps0d6sn.8200 -L "Complete
                                         System Backup" /
```

All this information is added when you use the `-cv` and `-L` options when backing up a tape. The most important elements are the label, creation date, volume, and command line.

You could also use `bru` for performing either incremental or differential backups. This can be done in conjunction with `bru`'s `-n` option because the `-n` option passes a standard date string. The best method is to create a reference file and pass the name of that file to `bru`, such as `"/etc/LASTFULL"`.

The following script would perform full backups on Saturday morning and differential backups on all other days:

```
#!/bin/sh
DOW=`date +%w`
if [ $DOW = 6 ]
then
    bru -cvf /dev/rmt/tps0d6sn.8200 -L "Complete Backup `date`" /
    touch /etc/LASTFULL
else
```

```
    bru -cvf /dev/rmt/tps0d6sn.8200 -L "Daily Update `date`" -n
/etc/LAST
fi
```

This script, if called by `cron` once a day, makes a full backup of your system on Saturday, followed by differential backups once a day.

BSD System Backup Commands

By their nature, BSD system are considered "raw" systems. By this, I mean that almost all UNIX systems are derived from one of two base, or raw, UNIX OSes: BSD or SVR4 (System 5 release 4).

As a raw system, BSD (just like SVR4) really doesn't have much to offer in the way of enhanced system backup and recovery utilities.

Again, just as most UNIX variants were derived from BSD and SVR4, so were the backup utilities derived from `dump`/`restore` and `cpio`/`tar`.

By default, BSD systems usually go to the `dump`/`restore` utilities to handle their system backups. For more detail on these utilities, see the previous sections on `dump`/`restore`.

Linux System Backup Commands

Although `tar` is distributed on all UNIX variants, Linux comes with a somewhat more advanced version of `tar`. The Linux `tar` command gives you the added feature of compression through the GNU `gzip` utility, as well as the compress utility.

These new switches are as follows:

-z	Compress the archive using GNU `gzip`.
-Z	Compress the archive with the compress utility.

If, for example, you want to create a compressed backup of your `/etc` directory and put it into a file called `etc_backup.tar`, do the following:

```
tar czf etc_backup.tar /etc
```

This backs up all the subdirectories under `/etc` as well.

To add the contents of another directory, such as `/usr/local/etc`, do the following:

```
tar rzf etc_backup.tar /usr/ocal/etc
```

With the u option, you can make `tar` go through and append to the archive only those files that have been changed since the creation of the archive. The following command lets you do this:

```
tar uzf etc_backup.tar /etc/usr/local/etc
```

These examples so far have only shown you how to archive files to disk. To back up the archives to tape, simply add the device name to the command, instead of the directory name. Usually the tape drive device name is `/dev/st0` for SCSI tape drives.

The x option enables you to extract files from archives. If you don't specify a filename to restore, `tar` restores the entire archive. Using the t option, you can get a table of contents for the archive.

To extract the contents of the backup archive in the previous example, do the following:

```
tar xzf etc_backup.tar
```

Note that these files were compressed on backup, and they must be restored using the z option.

Also notice that `tar` does not put the files back where they came from. It actually creates a new tree based on the current directory. Therefore, you *must* get to the original directory where you were when you backed up the tape to be able to restore to the same location.

In certain situations, you may want to consider restoring to a temporary directory first before moving files in place because you may accidentally restore older files over existing files. Of course, if you do this, you need to check the space available to you in the directory to which you are restoring.

If you want to restore to individual files from an archive, all you have to do is specify the name after all the `tar` arguments. For example, let's say that you just want to get back your `hosts` and `passwd` files. Do the following:

```
tar xzf etc_backup.tar etc/hosts etc/passwd
```

Notice that the full pathname must be specified if you are going to do this.

Typically, these `tar`ed files are named (filename).`tar.gz`, so that you can tell they are `tar` archives, compressed with the GNU `gzip` utility.

Along with the z option, Linux's version of `tar` also comes with some other neat little utilities. A few of the more notable ones are as follows:

M	This tells `tar` to use a multivolume archive. If you use this, `tar` prompts you for the insertion of a new floppy or tape when it comes to the end of the current one, which is referred to as a volume. Each volume contains a standalone archive file, so that you won't need all the volumes to extract a file. However, if a file is split across two volumes, you must use the `-xM` option to extract.

> **NOTE**
>
> Note that this option does not work on some tape devices, the most notable being DAT tapes (4mm).

N *DATE*	This tells the `tar` utility to operate only on files that are newer than the specified *DATE*. You have to specify the date in the same format as that used by the `date` command.
	You can use the `date` command, redirect the output to a file, such as `last_backup`, and back up the file to the tape along with everything else. Then the next time you back up your files, you can choose to only back up files that have been changed during or since the last backup by including the option `-N "cat last_backup"` in `tar`'s command line.
T *FILENAME*	This option tells `tar` that a list of files to back up or restore is in *FILENAME*. For example, you can use the following to have `tar` create an archive containing files that are named in the LIST_FILES files:
	`tar czf /dev/ftape LIST_FILES`
	The LIST_FILES file is just a straight text file with one filename on each line.
h	Usually, when `tar` comes across a link, it stores details about that link. If you use the h option, `tar` actually stores the file that is pointed to by the link and ignores the link itself. You must be careful about using this option because you run the risk of getting duplicate files, which may overwrite other files on disk.

W   This option verifies the archive after it has been written. This option does not work on tape drives that cannot rewind.

P   This causes `tar` to save/restore files with absolute paths. Usually, `tar` strips the leading / from a pathname so that when you restore, the file is restored in a directory relative to the current one. With this option, the file is restored from where it was backed up. Once again, use caution; you run the risk of overwriting files on your hard drive.

Using taper

`taper` is a neat little utility that gives you most of the same utilities as `tar`, but it also has a nice warm and fuzzy user interface.

You can get `taper` for Linux at any GNU FTP site on the Internet. To run `taper`, you need to have the most recent version of `ncurses` that supports `"forms"`. The primary GNU FTP site is located at `prep.ai.mit.edu`.

`taper` is relatively easy to configure, build, and install for Linux. The installation instructions are included in the `INSTALL` file.

To build and install the latest `ncurses`, do the following as root:

```
cd /usr/local/sr
tar xzf ncurses-(release #).tar.gz
cd ncurses-(release #)
./configure –with-normal –with-shared
\
   --with--debug –disable-termcap
make
make install
```

To make a binary of `taper`, do the following:

```
tar xzf taper-(release #).tar.gz
```

Next, you must edit the `Makefile` to get the proper tape drive specified for your site. Then type the following:

```
make clean
make all
make install
```

When you initially create an archive, the `taper` program stores all the information about files on that archive, such as filename, file size, backup time, and so on. This information gets stored into a file called an archive information file, which is usually stored in a file, usually called ~/.taper_info. When reading from an archived tape, taper reads this file, thus avoiding having to go through the entire tape to find the location of a particular file.

The biggest problem with this file is that you can't restore a tape to another machine until this file is loaded on to it. Therefore, you must save that file on a separate tape or floppy so that it can be loaded first. You must also ensure that you always have a current version of this file saved.

Each archive that gets created is given a unique archive ID, which can be used for future accessing of the archive if you don't have the tape at hand.

Using taper

To start the taper utility, simply type the command **taper** on the command line. This brings up the main taper window. There are three main modules in taper: backup, restore, and mkinfo. These as well as the preference management options are presented here.

Select the backup option to back up a tape.

If the archive doesn't yet exist, you are prompted for the archive title. Then it prompts you for the volume title.

After that is squared away, you get a screen with three panels. The top left should show you the current directory on the hard disk, the top right shows what's currently on the archive, and the bottom panel shows you which files have been selected for backup. At the top of the screen is the archive ID and title.

To move around between the panels, just use the Tab key. If you need to get help on keys, just press H.

At this point, you must choose which files and directories you want to back up. You can use the cursor keys to move around the directory. If you press Enter when a particular directory is highlighted, you move into that directory.

When you have found the file or directory you want to back up, you can press the S key to select it. The size of the file or directory is then shown in the bottom window.

Next, you are asked whether to back up in incremental mode or full backup mode, as shown in the left-hand box, which displays an I or an F. To toggle between the two, press S when the highlight is on the selected file or directory.

Note that when you select a directory, all subdirectories under it automatically are recursively included in the backup list.

To deselect a file, just move the cursor to the bottom window with the Tab and move the highlight to the file or directory you want to deselect. Then just press D to deselect the file or directory.

After you have finished selecting files and directories, press F. taper now starts the backup. If at any time you want to stop the backup, just press Q.

Restoring from taper is just as easy (if not easier) than backing up. First, select the Restore option from the taper main menu. You are then presented with a list of all the archives taper is aware of. These are sorted by archive ID order, and the archive title is displayed as well.

Move the highlight to the desired archive and press Enter. Now you are given three panels. The top left gives the files and directories currently on the archive, the top right gives you a summary of the whole archive, and the bottom panel shows the directories and files selected for restoring.

Once again, use the cursor keys to move the highlight to select which files you want to restore and press S to select the files or directories you want to restore. Don't forget that subdirectories are recursively restored. After you choose a file or directory, it shows up in the bottom panel. If you have chosen a file or directory twice, square brackets appear around the file or directory name.

Over in the select window, the volume number is printed after the filename. One of two things show up here: either a volume number or an m. If an m appears, then taper is operating in "most recent restore" mode, and you can only restore the most recent copy of that file. You can toggle between modes by pressing the S key while in the select window.

If you want to deselect a file or directory, just press the D key while the appropriate one is highlighted.

After you have chosen everything you want to restore, press F to start the taper restore. Once again, just press Q if you want to quit during the restore.

Should the archive information file get deleted or corrupted, you can create another one simply by using the mkinfo command. Just put the tape in the drive and select mkinfo from the main menu in taper.

Add-On Solutions

In addition to the standard UNIX backups that come bundled with the install packages, a number of packages are commercially available.

The following are some of the more popular products used at many sites for complete network and system backups:

- FarTool by APUnix
- ArcServe by Cheyenne
- D-Tools by Dallastone
- BudTool by Delta MicroSystems (PDC)
- Enterprise Backup by Epoch Systems
- ADSM (Adstar Distributed Storage Manager) by IBM
- OmniBack II by Hewlett-Packard
- Networker by Legato
- Network Imaging Systems
- AXXion Netbackup 2.0 by Open Vision
- SM-arch by Software Moguls
- Alexandria by Spectra Logic
- Workstation Solutions

Each of the backup solutions is unique. You might have to do some serious homework to find out which one is best for your system because there really isn't any one best total storage solution. You just have to find the best one for your system.

This may not be easy. There is a joke that goes (somewhat politically incorrectly): "the two greatest liars in the world are software vendors and teenage boys." So, just be on your guard when you go shopping.

Summary

This chapter covered many backup and restore topics, including using the `tar` command; using the `dump` command; using `cpio`; and making backups on HP-UX systems, Solaris Systems, SVR4 systems, IRIX systems, BSD systems, and Linux systems.

Speaking from experience, there really is no substitute for good, up-to-date backups for saving your bacon. I can remember at least two times in my career that, had I not had the system backed up, I would have been out on the street.

So, a word to the wise: The three best secrets to a good career in system administration are backup, backup, and backup!

UNIX and the Internet

IN THIS PART

CHAPTER 35

Introducing Hypertext Transfer Protocol (HTTP)

by Robin Burk and James Edwards

IN THIS CHAPTER

For many people, the Internet is synonymous with the World Wide Web. Unlike earlier access methods such as FTP, Gopher, and Usenet, the Web allows users to retrieve online information in a variety of formats using an appealing, graphical interface.

The World Wide Web is made possible by the hypertext transfer protocol or HTTP. HTTP can be thought of in two ways. From the point of view of the Internet Engineering Task Force, which governs Internet-related standards and specifications, HTTP is a protocol that defines how a client machine on a TCP/IP network can request, receive, and retrieve files independently of the operating system or hardware on which they reside. The client software that makes such a request (and embeds the protocol) is called a Web browser; as the name implies, a browser generally displays as well as retrieves the desired files. From the point of most UNIX shops, however, HTTP refers to the software that resides on an Internet or intranet Web server node and responds to browser requests sent in accordance with this protocol. HTTP shares this dual protocol/application reference with other familiar facilities such as Telnet, FTP, SMTP and the TCP/IP communications stack itself.

This chapter details how the HTTP server application operates. The chapter examines the protocol's message formats and return codes and the actions that these messages trigger.

This chapter also highlights a number of performance problems attributable to the operation of HTTP in a UNIX environment and suggests ways to reconfigure server parameters to alleviate these problems.

What HTTP Does

The Internet is a network of networks. One or more computers in each network serves as a gateway for message traffic to the wider Internet.

The computers on the public Internet, or on the connected networks, contain massive amounts of information in a variety of formats, in various hardware and software environments. The Web can be thought of as a network of information content rather than of the computers that hold the information. Specific items of information are connected to one another by means of hypertext, or links to other information locations. In most browsers, hyperlinks are shown visually by underlining or coloring phrases that are linked in this way.

For hyperlinks to be effective, there must be a way to identify the location of information that is independent of hardware and operating systems. This addressing method is called a Uniform Resource Locator (URL). Each URL points to a data object such that it has a uniquely identifiable location within the Internet.

To share information across heterogeneous environments, it's also necessary to have a common way to encode it. This is accomplished on the Web by means of a standard data representation format known as Hypertext Markup Language (HTML). Among other things, HTML provides the means by which URLs can be associated with phrases and icons on the user's browser screen, thus creating the actual hyperlinks whose presence are indicated visually on a Web page.

Web browsers use the HTTP protocol to request that one or more files associated with URLs be transferred back to the client machine. When the files are received, the browser interprets the HTML tags embedded within the information and displays the information or otherwise interacts with the user appropriately.

HTTP processes running on Web server nodes thus form the backbone of the World Wide Web. HTTP as a protocol makes this cooperation among heterogeneous machines possible.

> **NOTE**
>
> Until the advent of the Web, the traditional method for moving files around the Internet was FTP. However, FTP has several disadvantages. It imposes additional communications overhead compared to HTTP. It also assumes that the requesting machine knows exactly where the desired file resides on the server and how to interpret it when it has been retrieved. HTTP, on the other hand, provides a streamlined, machine-independent way to access large volumes of pre-linked information. New hypertext links are easily added by the publisher of the information, allowing the user to find additional information through the network of hyperlinks. This facility, as much as the appealing user interface, has transformed the use of the Internet in recent years.

Later in this chapter, we outline in some detail the defined HTTP message types and protocol header formats. By way of an introduction to that section, a useful first step is to examine the logical operation of HTTP and its interaction with the other components found within the Web.

Figure 41.1 outlines how the HTTP application protocol relates to both the Web server and client programs. As indicated, the browser has been designed to interpret format information contained within HTML pages. It is possible for an HTML page to also contain URLs as references to other pages located elsewhere on the Internet. These links are referred to as *hyperlinks* and are often colored or underlined within the HTML pages.

FIGURE 35.1.

Logical organization of the Web.

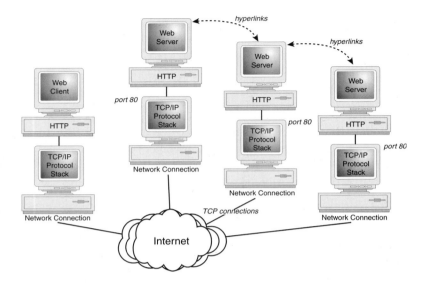

The main function of the HTTP application is to request the pages referenced by these hyperlinks. This is accomplished through the following steps:

1. The user points his browser to the desired information by typing in the http:: protocol invocation followed by the URL for the desired file. The first portion of the URL gives the domain name, or identifier, for the server machine that contains the file. The browser's HTTP protocol logic triggers setup of a TCP connection between the client machine and port 80 (a well-known, or reserved, port) on the indicated server.

2. After the TCP connection has been established, the server's HTTP process decodes the rest of the URL to find the desired HTML-formatted file and transfers the file over the TCP/IP connection to the client's browser process.

3. The server automatically terminates the TCP connection immediately after the HTML document has been transferred to the client. Meanwhile, the client browser begins interpreting the file it has received.

NOTE

Web pages that contain graphics or other media types in addition to text automatically trigger multiple file transfer requests. The TCP connection is terminated at the end of each one to conserve Internet bandwidth. Although optimal for network performance, this aspect of HTTP can impose heavy performance loads on a Web server machine, which is discussed later in this chapter.

One noted strength of HTTP and HTML is that additional references to content can be encoded within each document. As indicated earlier, these URLs can point to files on the same Web server, or on a different machine.

In addition to text hyperlinks, HTML pages often contain other information objects—particularly graphics. As the browser encounters references for embedded information, it requests these files as well. HTTP initiates a separate TCP connection for each file that needs to be downloaded. Some HTML pages contain a number data object, and to help speed up the overall download process, some browsers allow multiple TCP connections to be initiated simultaneously.

> **NOTE**
>
> The Netscape Navigator browser allows the user to specify any number of possible simultaneous TCP connections. It is possible to notice some slight performance improvements by incrementally increasing the maximum number of connections; however, any improvement gains appear to flatten out after four connections. This is caused by the fact that the browser sets a hard-coded maximum of four concurrent connections even though it is possible for the client to request more.

Protocol Definition

The IETF publishes the official definition of the HTTP protocol and uses a version numbering scheme consisting of a major and a minor number. These numbers are arranged using the following format:

```
<Major Version> . <Minor Version>
```

> **NOTE**
>
> A new major release (c.f. from 1.x to 2.0) indicates that this version of the protocol changes the format or processing rules of the protocol. A minor release (c.f. from 1.0 to 1.1) indicates that some changes have been made to features or functionality but the basic formats and processing remain unchanged.

The IETF publishes protocol specifications in the form of Requests for Comment (RFCs), some of which are subsequently adopted as formal IETF standards. The original specification for HTTP version 1.0 is found in RFC 1945, an information RFC that has not been adopted as a formal standard. As a result, vendors have implemented browsers (and supporting server HTTP software with some degree of variation in available functionality.

Version 1.1 of HTTP was proposed in January 1997 via RFC 2068 for adoption as an IETF Standard. A number of Internet sites offer FTP and HTTP access to the RFC documents.

HTTP Example Operation

RFC specifications, which guide browser and server software development, can be used to understand how HTTP is intended to work. You can also watch the operation of HTTP with any standard packet analyzer. Table 35.1 provides an example of trace data taken from a Linux server running tcpdump.

The tcpdump application places the computer's network interface card into a promiscuous mode, allowing the software to see and record each packet on the network. HTTP-specific session information can then be collected by pointing a Web browser at an HTML page maintained on a local Web server. (The following listing slightly rearranges the actual presented order of some recorded packets and removes some superfluous detail.)

TABLE 35.1. PACKET TRACE DATA ILLUSTRATING HTTP OPERATION.

\multicolumn{6}{c}{*The Web client initiates a connection to the Web server.*}					
1	client.22248	>	server.80	S	1427079:1427079(0) win 4096
2	server.80	>	client.22248	S	32179213:32179213(0)
					ack 1427079 win 4096
3	client.22248	>	server.80	•	ack 1 win 4096
\multicolumn{6}{c}{*The client sends an HTTP request message to the Web server—requesting an HTML page.*}					
4	client.22248	>	server.80	•	1:537(536) ack 1
5	server.80	>	client.22248	•	ack 537
6	client.22248	>	server.80	•	537:1073(536)
7	client.22248	>	server.80	P	1073:1515(536)
\multicolumn{6}{c}{*The Web server sends back the requested page and status information.*}					
8	server.80	>	client.22248	•	1:537(536) ack 1516
9	server.80	>	client.22248	•	537:1073(536) ack 1516
10	server.80	>	client.22248	•	1073:1609(536) ack 1516
11	client.22248	>	server.80	•	ack 1609

12 server.80	>	client.22248	●	1609:2145(536) ack 1516
13 server.80	>	client.22248	●	2145:2681(536) ack 1516
14 server.80	>	client.22248	●	2681:3217(536) ack 1516

The requested page contains an embedded graphic. To transport this,
a second TCP connection is established.

15 client.22249	>	server.80	S	21200132: 21200132(0) win 4096
16 server.80	>	client.22249	S	13420003: 13420003(0)
				ack 21200132 win 4096
17 client.22249	>	server.80	●	ack 1 win 4096

The client passes a request to download the graphic to the Web server.

18 client.22249	>	server.80	●	1:537(536) ack 1
19 server.80	>	client.22249	●	ack 537
20 client.22249	>	server.80	●	537:1073(536) ack 537

The Web server sends the graphic to the client.

21 server.80	>	client.22249	●	1:537(536) ack 537
22 server.80	>	client.22249	●	537:1073(536) ack 537

The server completes sending the graphic and closes the TCP connection.

23 server.80	>	client.22249	F	1073:1395(322) ack 537
24 client.22249	>	server.80	●	ack 1396
25 client.22249	>	server.80	F	537:537(0) ack 1395
26 server.80	>	client.22249	●	ack 538

The server completes sending the original HTML page and
closes the first TCP connection.

27 server.80	>	client.22248	F	3217:3438(221) ack 1516
28 client.22248	>	server.80	●	ack 3439
29 client.22248	>	server.80	F	1516:1516(0) ack 3439
30 server.80	>	client.22248	●	ack 1517

This table provides an example of a Web browser requesting an information page from a Web server.

HTTP uses the reliable communication services provided by TCP/IP. This trace begins by establishing a TCP connection over the IP link. This is accomplished by means of a three-way handshake. This process is illustrated within the example. The client sends a TCP packet to the server, requesting a new TCP connection by setting the SYN option flag and supplying an initial sequence number (ISN). The server responds, by sending an acknowledgment (ack) back to the client along with its own ISN for this connection, which it highlights by also setting the SYN flag. The client responds by acknowledging the server's response and ISN.

Following the three-way handshake, the TCP connection is open and ready for data transfer. The client sends an HTTP request message to retrieve an indicated HTML page (packets four through seven in the example). The server responds with an HTTP response message that contains the requested HTML page as the message body. This data is transferred over the TCP connection with the client sending acknowledgment packets back to the server as packets are received and concatenated.

As the browser receives and interprets the HTML page, it finds a reference to an embedded object. Packets 15, 16, and 17 show the client requesting a second TCP connection, which is used to transfer the graphic object. The client now has two active TCP connections with the Web server.

> **NOTE**
>
> In an actual session, the packets relating to each connection will be intermingled and not neatly separated as the table illustrates.

After the server has completed the transfer of each data item (file), it automatically closes the corresponding TCP connection. This process involves the transfer of four additional packets. First, the server sends a TCP packet with the FIN option flag set, indicating that it wants to close its end of the active connection. This packet is acknowledged by the client, which in turn closes its end of the connection by sending a similar packet to the server. The server sends an acknowledgment, and the connection is closed. The table illustrates how both separate TCP connections are independently terminated following the completion of data transfer.

Establishing and ending each TCP connection involves the exchange of a minimum of seven packets. This can represent a significant amount of protocol overhead for Web pages with many graphical icons, digitized photos, and other elements.

Messages, Headers, and Return Codes

HTTP uses two messages types, requests, and responses. These messages are data carried within the body of TCP/IP communications packets and consist of ASCII fields delineated by carriage return and line feed.

Requests are made from Web clients to Web servers and are used to request either the retrieval of data objects (such as HTML pages) or to return information to the server (such as a completed electronic form).

The Web server uses response messages to deliver requested data to the client. Each response contains a status line that indicates some detail about the client request. This might be an indication that an error occurred or simply that the request was successful.

Both request and response messages can be accompanied by one or more message headers containing additional information. We'll look at these optional fields later in the chapter.

HTTP Request Messages

Listing 35.1 shows the general format of HTTP data requests.

LISTING 35.1. HTTP DATA REQUEST SYNTAX.

```
Request method
headers
<blank line> (Carriage Return /Line Feed)
message body
```

Request Methods

The general syntax for request methods is as follows:

```
<request method> <requested-URL> <HTTP-Version>
```

HTTP version 1.0 defines three request methods: GET, POST, and HEAD. Table 35.2 summarizes the functions of each support method and outlines a specific example.

TABLE 35.2. REQUEST METHOD SYNTAX AND EXAMPLES.

Request	Description
GET	Used to retrieve object identified within the URI. The use of defined headers can make the retrieval conditional.
Example:	`GET HTTP://www.dttus.com/home.html HTTP/1.0`
Result:	The Web server returns the identified HTML page to the client.
POST	Used to request that the destination Web server accept the enclosed message body; this is generally used for returning completed electronic forms or for posting electronic news or email messages.
Example:	`POST HTTP://www.dttus.com/survey/completed.HTML HTTP/1.0`
	`From: jamedwards@dttus.com`

continues

35

INTRODUCING HYPERTEXT TRANSFER PROTOCOL

TABLE 35.2. CONTINUED

Request	Description
Result:	Message body placed here
HEAD	This method is identical to GET except that the Web server does not return an enclosed message body—only the relating header information. This method is often used to test validity or accessibility, or for any recent changes.
Example:	HEAD HTTP://www.dttus.com/home.html HTTP/1.0
Result:	The Web server returns a result code to the client.

> **NOTE**
>
> A Uniform Resource Identifier (URI) is a generic reference that HTTP uses to identify any resource. The resource could be identified through its location, by using a Uniform Resource Location (URL), or by a name, using a Uniform Resource Name (URN).

Defined Header Values

Header values are used to relay additional information about an HTTP message. A single HTTP message may have multiple headers associated with it. Headers fall into one of four groups:

- Those that relate to message requests
- Those that relate to responses
- Those that relate to the message content
- Those that can be applied to both message requests and message responses

The operation and use of message headers can best be seen through the following simple example:

```
GET HTTP://www.dttus.com/home.html  HTTP/1.0    - GET request
If-Modified-Since: Sun, 16 Mar 1997 01:43:31 GMT - Conditional Header
                                                 - CR/line feed
```

In this example, a Web client has forwarded an HTTP request to a Web server asking to retrieve a specified HTML page. This is accomplished using the GET request method. This HTTP request has been supplemented with a single header field specifying that the indicated HTML page should only be returned if it has been modified since the indicated date.

The following tables provide a summary of header values. Note that most header options are additions in the pending HTTP version 1.1 specification. General header values are applicable to both request and response messages, but are independent of the message body.

TABLE 35.3. DEFINED GENERAL HEADER VALUES.

Header Name	Header Description	HTTP/1.1 Only
Cache-Control	Provides standard control for caching algorithms	X
Connection	Forces a close on a persistent connection	X
Date	Specifies data and time field	
Pragma	Specifies the use of a cache (HTTP/1.0 specific)	
Transfer-Encoding	Specifies whether any transformation has been applied to the message	X
Upgrade	Allows a client to signal a request to use an upgraded version of a protocol	X
Via	Used with trace method to determine paths	X

Some available header values relate specifically to client browser request messages—either GET, POST, or HEAD methods (also applicable to the new request methods introduced within HTTP/1.1). Table 35.4 provides a summary of the headers applicable to request messages.

TABLE 35.4. DEFINED REQUEST HEADER VALUES.

Header Name	Header Description	HTTP/1.1 Only
Accept	Indicates data formats acceptable for responses	X
Accept-Charset	Indicates what character sets are acceptable	X
Accept-Coding	Indicates what encoding schemes are acceptable	X
Accept-Language	Indicates what languages are acceptable	X
Authorization	Contains user credentials for authentication	
From	Email address of client	
Host	Hostname and port of the requested resource	X
If-Modified-Since	Conditional GET request	
If-Match	Conditional GET request	X
If-None-Match	Conditional GET request	X

continues

TABLE 35.4. CONTINUED

Header Name	Header Description	HTTP/1.1 Only
If-Range	Conditional GET request	X
If-Unmodified-Since	Conditional GET request	X
Max-Forwards	Used with TRACE to limit loop testing ranges	X
Proxy-Authorization	Credentials for next proxy in service chain only	X
Range	GET on a range of bytes within message body	X
Referer [sic]	Address of URL where object was obtained	
User-Agent	Details user agent making the request	

Web server generated responses to client requests may be a supplement to a number of optional header values. Table 35.5 provides a summary of those header values specifically relating to response messages.

TABLE 35.5. DEFINED RESPONSE HEADER VALUES.

Header Name	Header Description	HTTP/1.1 Only
Age	Indication of the "freshness" of a cached entry	X
Location	Allows redirection of a location	
Proxy-Authenticate	Provides authentication challenge for browser	
Public	Lists capabilities and supported methods of server	X
Retry-After	Used with 503 status to indicate a duration	X
Server	Indicates software product and version on server	
Vary	Listing of the selected option in request message	X
Warning	Arbitrary information relayed to user	X
WWW-Authenticate	Used with 401 status, contains challenge	X

Message body headers define optional meta-information about the data object, or, if a data object is not present, about the resource identified within the request. Table 35.6 outlines the available header values.

TABLE 35.6. DEFINED MESSAGE BODY HEADER VALUES.

Header Name	Header Description	HTTP/1.1 Only
Allow	Lists the set of supported methods with that object	
Content-Base	The base for resolving any specified relative URIs	X
Content-Encoding	Indicates what coding has occurred—use of zip files	
Content-Language	Natural language of specified object	X
Content-Length	Size of transferred message body	
Content-Location	URL of provided message	X
Content-MD5	MD-5 integrity check	X
Content-Range	Partial message body references	X
Content-Type	Media type of message sent	
Etag	Entity tag for object comparisons comparisons	X
Expires	The stale date	
Last-Modified	Date and time of last modification	

Response Messages

The general syntax for a Web server's response message is as follows:

```
Status Line
headers
<blank line> (CR/LF)
message body
```

The first line of the Web server response consists of something known as the status line. The general syntax for this information is as follows:

```
<HTTP-Version> <Status-Code> <Status Code Description>
```

Table 35.7 provides a complete listing of the defined status codes and their corresponding descriptions. As with HTTP requests, it is possible to include one or more headers within Web servers' responses. Listing 35.2 outlines an example of how this might occur.

TABLE 35.7. HTTP RESPONSE MESSAGE STATUS LINE DESCRIPTIONS.

Status Line	Response Description	HTTP/1.1 Only
1xx	Informational	X
100	Continue—interim server response, client should continue sending	X

continues

TABLE 35.7. HTTP CONTINUED

Status Line	Response Description	HTTP/1.1 Only
101	Switching Protocol—capability to switch between older and new HTTP versions	X
2xx	Success—action was received and understood	
200	Okay—the request message was successful	
201	Created—the POST request was successful	
202	Accepted	
204	No Content	
205	Reset Content—reset client view that causes request to be sent	X
206	Partial Content—server completed a part of the GET request	X
3xx	Redirection—further action required to complete request	
301	Object moved permanently	
302	Object moved temporarily	
304	Object not modified	X
305	Use proxy—the client request must be via the indicated proxy	X
4xx	Client error—the request cannot be fulfilled	
400	Bad request	
401	Unauthorized, authentication issue	
403	Forbidden, request not allowed	
404	Not found	
405	Method is not allowed	X
406	Request is not acceptable	X
407	Proxy authentication required	X
408	Request timeout	X
409	Conflict	X
410	Gone—and no forwarding address is known	X
411	Length required	X
412	Precondition failed	X
413	Request entity too large	X
414	Request-URI too large	X

Header Name	Header Description	HTTP/1.1 Only
415	Unsupported media type	X
5xx	Server error—the server failed to fulfill a valid request	
500	Internal server error	
501	Not implemented	
502	Bad gateway	
503	The service is unavailable	

LISTING 35.2. USING WEB SERVER RESPONSE HEADERS.

```
workstation> telnet www.dttus.com 80
trying 207.134.34.23
Connected to 207.134.34.23
Escape character is [^
GET /pub/images/dttus/mapimage.gif           request line entered
                                             request terminated
                                             by CR/LF
                                             response starts with
HTTP/1.0 200 OK                              Status Line

Date: Friday, 14-Feb-97 22:23:11 EST        header details
                                             are here

Content-type:  image/gif
Last-Modified: Thursday, 13-Mar-97 17:17:22 EST
Content-length: 5568
                                             headers terminated
                                             by CR/LF content is
                                             transferred here


Connection closed by foreign host           tcp connection is
                                             terminated after
                                             transfer is complete

workstation>
workstation>
```

In the preceding example, the Telnet program is used to create a TCP connection to the remote Web server's HTTP process on well-known port 80. After the connection has been established, an HTTP GET request is made. Listing 35.2 showed the requested image being returned to the Web client along with a number of header values directly after the status line. Table 35.7 lists the possible status line return codes and their meanings.

35

INTRODUCING
HYPERTEXT
TRANSFER PROTOCOL

NOTE

HTTP implementations do not have to be able to understand all existing return codes. However, they should be aware of each major code group. For example, if a Web server returned a value of 412, the client must only be aware that something was wrong with its request and be able to interpret the return code as such.

Identifying and Overcoming HTTP Server Performance Problems

HTTP was designed to make information transfer reliable and effective but not necessarily to optimize the performance of Web servers. This section looks at some performance issues associated with running the HTTP server application.

Connection Establishment—The Backlog Queue

There is a limit to the number of outstanding TCP connection requests a given UNIX process can handle. Outstanding TCP connection requests are placed in a UNIX queue known as the backlog. This queue in turn also has a limited capacity. When the queue is saturated, new connection requests are ignored until space on the queue becomes available.

Typically, this causes the client browser to display the message, Web Site Found. Waiting for Reply... while it continues to attempt connection. Eventually, the browser reaches its own retry limit and tells the user that its attempts have failed.

To understand why HTTP is so susceptible to this problem, it is necessary to understand why a server would have any outstanding TCP connection requests. A server process queues a connection request for two reasons: Either it is waiting for the completion of the connection request handshake, or it is waiting for the server process to execute the accept() system call.

To establish a TCP connection, the client and the server must complete the three-way handshake. While the server is waiting for the handshake process to complete, the outstanding connection request is placed in the backlog queue.

After a TCP connection has been established, the server process must execute the accept() system call to remove the connection from the backlog queue. If the server is busy, execution of this system call may be delayed and the connection request may remain on the queue for an extended period of time.

A Web server may fill its backlog queue if it receives a large volume of connection requests from clients facing a particularly large round-trip time. Figure 35.2 illustrates that the Web server receives a number of connection requests in a short period of time. The server responds back to each client, placing the outstanding request on the backlog queue.

FIGURE 35.2.

Filling up a Web server's backlog queue.

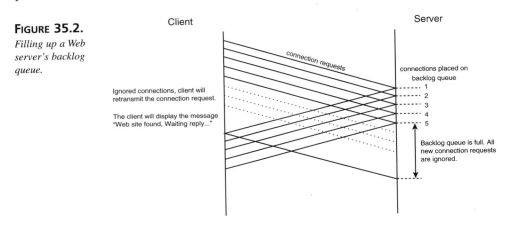

Default sizes of the backlog queue differ between UNIX flavors and implementations. For example, BSD flavors of UNIX define the size of the backlog queue through the SOMAXCONN constant. Calculation of the queue size is then derived using the following formula:

```
backlog queue size = (SOMAXCONN * 3) / 2 + 1
```

By default, the SOMAXCONN constant is set to a value of five—providing for a maximum of eight outstanding TCP connections to be held on the backlog queue. Other UNIX flavors or TCP/IP implementations use other parameters and parameter values to limit the size of the backlog queues. For example, Solaris 2.4 uses a default value set to five and allows this to be incremented to 32; Solaris 2.5 uses a default of 32 and allows a maximum of 1024; SGI's IRIX implementation provides default queue size of eight connections; Linux release 1.2 defaults to ten connections; and Microsoft Windows NT 4.0 provides for a backlog maximum size of six.

For busy Web servers, system administrators should look to increase the backlog size from the default values. Failure to do so can effectively limit the overall availability of their Web servers with the Internet.

35

INTRODUCING HYPERTEXT TRANSFER PROTOCOL

> **NOTE**
>
> Filling up the backlog queue for a given process has been used in a number of well-publicized denial of service attacks within the Internet. An attacker sends the Web server a series of TCP connection requests containing spoofed, unreachable source IP addresses. The Web server sends out its SYN and ACK packets to the spoofed addresses and places each request in the backlog queue. After approximately 75 seconds, each request times out and is removed from the queue.
>
> To deny service to the Web server, all the attacker would need to do is to send enough of these messages (ten or so) every 60 to 70 seconds. The backlog queue would then always be full, and no access would be possible.

Connection Termination

The HTTP server software actively closes each TCP connection when the file transfer has completed. This is done by sending the client a TCP packet with the FIN flag set. Upon receipt, the client returns an acknowledgment packet and then passively closes the connection from its own end by sending the Web server a TCP packet with the FIN flag and awaiting a server acknowledgment.

The TCP protocol specifications allow either the client or the server to perform the active close on any connection. However, the end that performs this operation must place the connection in a state known as TIME-WAIT to ensure that any straggler packets are properly handled. During the TIME-WAIT duration, the connection information—stored within a structure known as a Transaction Control Block (TCB)—must be saved.

UNIX servers allocate a fixed number of TCBs, up to a typical maximum of 1024. It is possible on a busy Web server for all available TCBs to become temporarily used up resulting in a Web Site Found. Waiting for Reply... message being displayed to clients. The netstat program can be used to determine the number of outstanding TCBs currently in the TIME-WAIT state.

Communication Protocol Operation—TCP and Congestion Management

HTTP is wonderfully flexible for information retrieval across heterogeneous environments. However, it has been criticized for making poor use of the underlying TCP and IP protocols.

TCP is based on the idea of a persisting and sufficiently wide communications connection through which control and data packets flow at a rate that the recipient can absorb. The receiving end of a connection advertises its current window size in each acknowledgment packet. The window is specified in terms of additional packets that the receiver can accept in its buffers without overflow. As the buffers fill, the receiver must move each packet's contents out to the destination application and acknowledge it before another can be accepted.

If transmission occurs without any delay, this mechanism works well. However, if the sender doesn't receive acknowledgments in a timely manner, it resends all outstanding packets and resets the timer. The result is that network congestion causes more congestion before traffic clears out as the backlog of acknowledgments is worked off.

As TCP/IP networks were deployed widely, it became clear that a generally deployed mechanism was needed to prevent them from bogging down with congestion. The TCP specification was extended to include the recommendation that a slow start algorithm be added to TCP protocol implementations.

Slow start within the TCP layer means that the communications software begins with conservative assumptions regarding the number of packets that may be sent before waiting for acknowledgments. This "congestion window" limits the initial exchange, and exchanges after timeouts, to one packet—meaning that a sender transmits only a single packet and then awaits an acknowledgment from the receiving station. On receipt of each acknowledgment, the congestion window doubles in size until it matches the receiver's advertised window size. When significant congestion is diagnosed, the window drops to a single packet size, and the process begins again.

Because HTTP opens and closes separate TCP connections for each embedded object in a Web page, and for each main Web page file itself, much of the data transfer over the Web occurs in slow start mode.

Figure 35.3 contrasts the effects of the slow start algorithm against the use of a long-lived connection. As the diagram indicates, the long-lived connection transfers the receiver's maximum window size of data enabling a fast transmission time. In contrast, under the slow start algorithm, additional delays are introduced while the sender waits for a larger number of the receiver's acknowledgment packets.

FIGURE 35.3.

Illustrating the effects of the slow start algorithm.

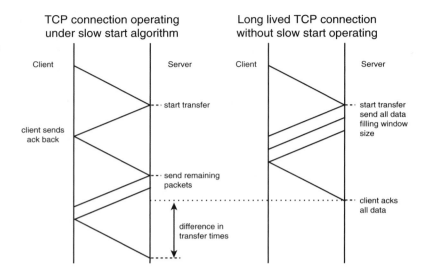

Increasingly, there is a growing desire to make greater use of persistent or long-lived TCP connections within the operation of HTTP. These ideas are further examined in the following section.

> **NOTE**
>
> To understand how you can configure TCP window sizes and other operating parameters, refer to TCP/IP Unleashed by Sams Publishing.

Providing Multiple Links Within an HTML Page

If you administer a Web server, you can reduce the TCP-related demands of HTTP by encouraging Web page design that results in more efficient use of server resources.

Figure 35.4 and Figure 35.5 provide a comparison of two different Web pages. Figure 35.4 uses individual icons to outline its contents. Each icon provides a reference to an URL guiding the user through the site. This approach is in contrast to that contained in Figure 35.5. The Web page in Figure 35.5 uses a single graphic with URLs embedded behind different parts of the graphic to provide a map of the site.

FIGURE 35.4.

Comparing map and icon HTML designs—Poor design.

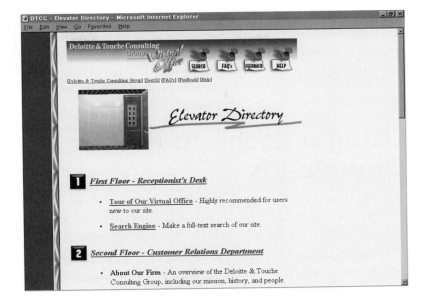

FIGURE 35.5.

Comparing map and icon HTML designs—Good design

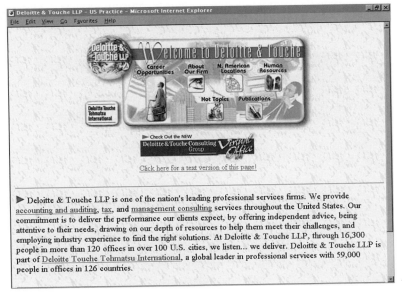

Both of these page designs can display in the same subjective time from the Web client's perspective, especially if the browser has been configured to operate multiple simultaneous TCP connections. Even though the Web page on the right contains a number of individual graphic images, each of those images could be downloaded in parallel with one another.

However, these two designs make different demands on the Web server. Figure 35.5 shows that multiple icons can be combined into a single graphic with separate hyperlinks assigned to its different regions. This map will be downloaded over a single TCP connection rather than requiring four separate connections for four separate icons. Use of map-oriented page design allows the Web server to support a larger number of users with the same amount of available resources.

Using a Cache to Reduce Downloads

The IETF's RFC 1945 introduces the idea of a response chain providing a link between Web server and client. This RFC indicates that there may be a number of intermediate devices on this response chain that act as forwarders of any messages.

It is possible for any intermediary devices to act as a cache—the benefits being both a greatly reduced response time and the preservation of available bandwidth within the Internet. Figure 35.6 illustrates how this might occur. It outlines that the communication path between the Web server and client is effectively shortened with the use of a cache on an intermediate server. The intermediate server can return requested Web pages to the client if those pages exist within its cache. To ensure that up-to-date information is returned, the client sends a conditional GET request.

FIGURE 35.6.

Improving HTTP performance through the use of a cache.

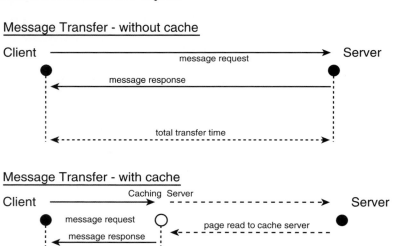

The conditional GET request is made through the use of message request headers available within version 1.0 of HTTP. Listing 35.3 provides an example of how such requests would be structured.

LISTING 35.3. MAKING A CONDITIONAL GET REQUEST.

```
workstation> telnet www.dttus.com 80
trying 207.134.34.23
Connected to 207.134.34.23
Escape character is [^
GET /pub/images/dttus/mapimage.gif                  request line entered
If-Modified-Since:Thursday,13-Feb-97 22:23:01 EST  conditional GET Header
                                                    request terminated by CR/LF
HTTP/1.0 304 Object Not Modified                    response starts with Status
                                                    Line which indicates that
                                                    the object was not
                                                    modified. (Single Blank
                                                    line ends server response
                                                    headers).

Connection closed by foreign host                   TCP connection is terminated.

workstation>
workstation>
```

Listing 35.3 indicates that the client formats a conditional GET request using the If-Modified-Since request header value. This request asks the Web server only to send the image if it has changed since the indicated date. The Web server returns a response status line indicating that the image has not changed. The server closes the TCP connection, and the Web client displays the image from within its cache.

The use of caches and intermediary servers enables the HTTP server process to operate more efficiently. It should be noted that even with the use of a cache, a TCP connection between the server and the client would need to be established; however, the successful use of a cache greatly reduces the total required data transfer.

Looking to the Future

HTTP version 1.1 proposes to extend HTTP to utilize persistent TCP connections and more effective caching techniques.

More importantly, HTTP version 1.1 (HTTP/1.1)is being developed as a standard to be ratified by the Internet Engineering Task Force (IETF). Previous specifications of HTTP never underwent standards acceptance. This resulted in a proliferation of applications that called themselves HTTP/1.0 without implementing all the recommendations outlined within the published RFC.

This section focuses on some of the main recommended changes to the existing protocol implementations. Refer to the previous reference tables for HTTP/1.1 included message formats and return codes.

Persistent TCP Connections

The standard operation within HTTP version 1.1 is for the client to request a single TCP connection with the remote server and use this for all the required transfers associated with a Web page. This change has the potential to save both Web server resources and available network bandwidth currently used for protocol overhead.

Persistent connections are one approach to supporting streaming video and other multimedia content within standard Web pages.

New Request Methods

In addition to the request methods supported within HTTP/1.0, version 1.1 has added the following new methods outlined in Table 35.8.

TABLE 35.8. HTTP VERSION 1.1 ADDITIONALLY SUPPORTED REQUEST METHODS.

New Method	Description
Options	Provides the HTTP client with the capability to query a remote Web server as to its ability to its communication and protocol support. New message body information is passed using this method.
Put	Enables a Web client to deliver a new object to a Web server. This object is identified using an URL specified within the method. The PUT method differs from the HTTP/1.0 POST method (which is still supported). The POST request provides an URL reference to the object that will be used to interpret the supplied message; in contrast, the PUT method provides an URL as a reference to its message body contents.
Delete	Used to remove a specified object—referenced using an enclosed URL.
Trace	Provides an effective means for troubleshooting connections or performance. The TRACE method provides an application layer loopback of messages—the final recipient of the message sending a 200 (OK) response back to the initiating client. This response includes header information that details the route the request and the response has taken.

HTTP version 1.1 provides for support of a number of additional header values. These newly supported headers and their main functionality additions are summarized in Table 35.9.

TABLE 35.9. HTTP VERSION 1.1 ADDITIONALLY SUPPORTED HEADER VALUES.

Header	Description
General header	Most important addition within Version HTTP/1.1 is the support for persistent connections. The new header value "connection" allows a single TCP connection to be utilized for all data transfers between client and server.
Response header	Several additional header values offer improved communication control between browser and server, providing the server a capability to signal its features and available functions to the browser. In addition, some authentication controls are provided including challenge/response controls.
Request header	The major addition to the request headers is the provision of an increased number of tests for a conditional download. These new tests allow a greater control over the download of Web server data. In addition, HTTP/1.1 request headers also allow browsers to flag to servers a list of acceptable data formats they are willing to receive.
Message header	The most exciting addition is the inclusion of the "content-range" header. This allows for the partial transfer of data objects reflecting only changes that might have occurred. This provides a far more efficient mechanism for providing data updates from Web servers.

In addition, a number of new headers have been added that allow the server to relay more information about the actual content, such as content encoding type, language, and message size.

Summary

The Hypertext Transfer Protocol and its associated Hypertext Markup Language provide the underpinnings for the World Wide Web. UNIX machines running HTTP server software accept and process requests for Web page content.

Web server performance can be significantly impacted by some aspects of the version 1.0 HTTP protocol definition and by the design of Web pages that reside on the server. UNIX administrators can mitigate these impacts through system configuration and by encouraging appropriate content design guidelines.

CHAPTER 36

Programming Web Pages—A Brief Introduction to HTML

by David B. Horvath, CCP

IN THIS CHAPTER

The information superhighway is often mentioned in the mainstream media these days. When the media uses that term, it is often referring to the World Wide Web and describes it as if it were something being hardwired together. In reality, the World Wide Web (often referred to as just "the Web") is a collection of systems on the Internet that run software and communicate using a common protocol.

This may sound like a description of the Internet in general because most systems use a common communications protocol (TCP/IP). That is because the model is similar. But instead of people having to write down or remember the address, location, or name resources they need, the software provides the links.

The user starts at one location and then connects to other locations and resources. Three categories of software are required to perform these tasks: the server (providing the information), the Web page, and client software (known as a browser). Major corporations run their own Web servers; smaller companies and individuals use Internet service providers (ISPs) to hold their Web pages. The Web browser can be GUI (most are) or CUI (Character User Interface, which is most common among UNIX users). It is the client portion of the equation.

The Web page provides the programming flexibility of the Web itself. Although the language looks complex in the beginning, new material can be created quite easily and modified quickly. With ISPs providing inexpensive or even free Web services to their customers, many people are setting up their own pages. The high level Web page of an individual, company, or organization is referred to as the home page because it is the starting point when looking at their Web pages. Each Web page can contain many links or connections to other Web pages and resources.

What Are URLs?

The links between Web pages (or means of accessing resources through the Web) are through the Universal Resource Locator (or, URL for short). The URL specifies the protocol, username and password (often omitted), system name, location, and name of the desired file. When working with a Web page, the typical URL looks like the following:

```
http://www.host.domain/directory/file.html
```

Several protocols are available, as shown in Table 36.1.

TABLE 36.1. AVAILABLE WORLD WIDE WEB PROTOCOLS.

Protocol	Description
file	Get file on current system (client)
ftp	File Transfer Protocol

Protocol	Description
gopher	Information Service protocol superseded by http
http	Hypertext Transport Protocol
mailto	Send email
news	Net News Transport Protocol (NNTP)
telnet	Terminal session communications

With the exception of the http protocol, these have been available on the Internet for several years. Only http is new with the Web.

Chapter 35, "Introducing Hypertext Transfer Protocol (HTTP)," provides much more detail on http itself.

What Is Hypertext?

Hypertext is the description applied to any document that contains links to other portions of the document or other documents. Instead of reviewing the document in a linear manner (reading a book from beginning to end), it is possible to jump around to other areas. Normal documents often have hypertextlike entries—the reference to Chapter 35 (for more information on http) in the previous section is a link to another portion of this book. The primary difference between a reference and a hypertext link is the effort involved to get to the other area.

With book references, it is up to the user to find the page that the reference is on (through the table of contents or index), and then physically move to it. With hypertext links, the link is executed (by selecting it via mouse or hotkey), and the software gets the material for the reader.

With many tools, you are able to jump to new material via the hypertext link and then back to your original location. With a book, you have to keep your finger or a bookmark at the original location.

Hypertext does not provide any new capability, it just makes it so much easier to take advantage of it.

Description of HTML

The programming of individual Web pages is done through HTML (Hypertext Markup Language), which is a subset of SGML (Standard Graphics Markup Language). The HTML code describes what the page should look like to the client software (Web browser) and describes links to other pages.

The language itself defines a set of codes or tags (*requests* in `troff` terminology) that tell the Web browser how to display text, images, and links. Like `troff` requests, HTML tags are ASCII text. The language standard provides guidelines on how these items should be displayed, but it is up to the client software to determine the final form.

When coding HTML, you will encounter WYSIPWYG (What You See Is Probably What You Get). When working with a GUI-based word processor, you have the capability to work in WYSIWYG (What You See Is What You Get) mode—the image on the screen is exactly how it will appear on paper. Because the individual Web browsers interpret the HTML slightly differently, the results vary between products. The HTML specifications only provided general guidelines on displaying elements, so there can be wide variation. And there are multiple versions of the specifications or standards.

The HTML language elements, also known as markup tags or just tags, begin with the less than symbol (<) and end with a greater than symbol (>). Immediately following the less than symbol is the command name (which is not case sensitive). Many commands are followed with attributes and assigned values. Be careful with the assigned values because they may be case sensitive.

The tags describe document elements (document parts or sections). Like the `pic` request `.PS` that requires a `.PE`, some of the tags require a closure tag; others do not. A closure tag consists of the less than symbol, a slash (/), the command name without any attributes, followed by the greater than symbol. When working with tags that require closure, be very careful when nesting them because the closure tag will close the most recent command of that type.

Some of the elements include:

- `<title> Title text goes here </title>`
- `<H1> First level of heading text goes here </h1>`
- `<!— This is a comment —>`
- `<hr> <!— used to draw a horizontal rule (or line) —>`

Notice that the `<title>` tag requires a closure tag in the form of `</title>`. The `<hr>` (horizontal rule) tag does not.

There are several versions of HTML. The original was, of course, version 1. Every browser available should be able to recognize version 1 HTML elements. All but the oldest browsers support version 2 elements. Most browsers should support version 3, which introduces HTML elements to support tables. The latest version (as of the time this chapter was written) is 4.0 (released 24 April, 1998); the version supported by most browsers (most commonly supported version) was 3.2. As with any standard, it is always evolving and growing.

Several browser vendors (Netscape and Microsoft, for example) have added their own nonstandard elements to HTML. When a Web page is coded using the extensions of a particular browser, you will often see a message similar to:

```
This page optimized for the XYZ browser.
```

Often followed by a graphical representation of the browser's trademark.

> **NOTE**
>
> Most Web browsers simply ignore any HTML tags that they do not recognize. If you code a tag incorrectly or use a newer HTML version than the browser supports, you will get odd results. If you are unlucky, the Web browser itself will crash, but you will not get an error message. Some of the tools verify the syntax of your HTML code.

My personal suggestion is that you code for the majority of the Web browsers to enable the most people to view your page. The official standard is maintained by the World Wide Web Consortium. You can get more information on the standard HTML at the following Web page:

```
http://www.w3.org/
```

> **TIP**
>
> Code for accessibility and commonality—provide alternatives to maps, use alt tags on images, and in general, code for most users and browsers. Not everyone has a fast connection to the Web or is able to see (and may not appreciate) your wonderful images or navigation map. The more people who can use your site easily, the more useful it will be.

Using a Web Browser

Your operating system may come with a Web browser, or you may have received a copy with other software, or you may have to download one from the Internet. But after you have it installed, there are two basic types of browser: GUI and CUI.

When the Web began, most of the users were connected through UNIX systems with character (or text) interfaces. This precluded the use of pretty graphics to represent links and limited the way that text could be represented. As usage has progressed, the majority of users have GUI interfaces that provide much more capability.

The individual Web browsers all behave a little differently, so you will have to learn how yours works. In general, they all have a location for you to enter an URL and provide some status information on the transfer of data between the host and your client. A good place to start is the home page for your browser. Most browsers have a button or menu option that fills in the URL for you and goes right to that page.

Most also have a back button or menu option. This should take you to the page you previously visited. This is equivalent to your finger in the book when you look at another section. Most browsers support multiple levels of previous pages so that you can follow a link completely away from your original location and get back there again.

As shown in the section for URLs, one of the types is file. By using this type, you can create HTML files on your client system and look at them before placing them on a server for the world to see.

Some vendors are taking advantage of the file URL type when distributing documentation or other materials (sales literature, for instance). Instead of having to provide a tool for you to look at their information or coding to a proprietary standard (like the Microsoft Windows help facility), they code in HTML. To use their documents, you start up your Web browser and point to their files.

> **TIP**
>
> I used a file URL instead of moving the example files to a Web server and specifying an http URL. This technique can speed Web page development because it removes at least one step from the process.

Your machine is not cluttered with different viewers, and the vendor's material can be viewed on many different types of machines.

> **TIP**
>
> If your Web browser does not display a page correctly, there could be several reasons: an incorrectly coded page (HTML coded incorrectly), a page coded to a newer HTML version than your browser supports, or even the configuration of your browser.

One common problem is that you change a page but do not see the changes when you view it. This happens when the page is stored in your browser's cache (a copy stored on your machine instead of being loaded from the source). Clicking on the reload or refresh button should get a new copy of the page and not load from the cached copy.

Tools (and Web sites) are available to validate your HTML code. Unfortunately, you really cannot validate someone else's HTML. You can take a copy and validate that version but not the original, because you cannot change it.

Coding HTML

Coding HTML documents has traditionally been a manual process, just like with `troff`. With the increased popularity (consumer demand) and business use of the Web, GUI-based Web authoring tools have become available. Although these tools are available and relatively inexpensive (often free or included with other software), there is still value to being able to code basic HTML. Even though there are GUI word processors, `troff` is still used in some applications.

This chapter provides an introduction to HTML only—it covers the important language elements and provides examples of their usage.

NOTE

In general, you can name your HTML code anything, but it should have a suffix of `.htm` or `.html`. Check with your system administrator for the location to place your Web pages; most servers look for them in a directory called `public_html` under your home directory. If you want people to be able to get your top-level page automatically, you should name it `index.htm` (`index.html`) or `welcome.htm` (`welcome.html`).

The directory name, top-level filename, and file extension depends on the Web server configuration. Your system administrator can tell you the exact form it should be in.

See the section on GUI tools later in this chapter for more information.

A Minimal HTML Document

The minimum reasonable HTML document contains four elements:

- `<html>` `</html>` pair that contains the entire document
- `<head>` `</head>` pair that contains heading information
- `<title>` `</title>` pair contained in the heading
- `<body>` `</body>` pair that contains the body of the document

Figure 36.1 shows the output of the minimal HTML document using the Netscape Navigator Web browser. Listing 36.1 shows the source for it.

FIGURE 36.1.

Minimal HTML document viewed through Netscape.

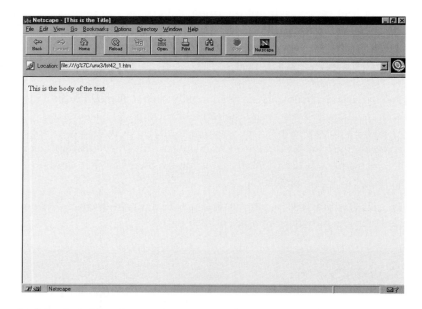

> ## NOTE
>
> Notice that the activity indicator (the square postage-stamp sized box near the upper-right corner of the browser) is a tilted Q in the Netscape examples instead of the Netscape "N" logo because I use the version that came with my machine.

LISTING 36.1. SOURCE FOR MINIMAL HTML DOCUMENT.

```
<html>
<head>
<title> This is the Title </title>
</head>
<body>
```

```
This is the body of the text
</body>
</html>
```

The text enclosed in the `<title>` tag is displayed at the top of the window. There may be only one title; if you include more than one in the `<head>` section, usually only the last one actually displays. The block contained within the `<head>` tag is used to set up the document and show the title. The block contained within the `<body>` is where the most tags and text are placed.

As you see from the URL in the figure, this HTML document was displayed from a file on my system; it was not placed on a Web server for the world to see.

This minimal HTML document demonstrates the portions of the document but really is not very useful. Many more tags and much more text are required.

> **TIP**
>
> One more tag should be at the beginning of your HTML:
>
> ```
> <!DOCTYPE HTML PUBLIC "-//W3C//DTD HTML 3.2 Final//EN">
> ```
>
> This is actually SGML, not HTML. It specifies the standard that your HTML is coded for and the language (English) used.

Font Control

Within the body of the document, you can control the fonts that your text is displayed in. To start off, there are six levels of headings available specified using tags `<h1>` through `<h6>`, respectively.

Figure 36.2 shows the behavior of the heading tags using the Netscape Web browser. Listing 36.2 shows the source for it.

LISTING 36.2. SOURCE FOR HEADING TAGS.

```
<html>
<head>
<title> Heading Font Control </title>
</head>
<body>
<H1> Heading Level 1 - ABCDEF abcdef &lt;H1&gt; </h1>
<H2> Heading Level 2 - ABCDEF abcdef &lt;H2&gt; </h2>
```

continues

LISTING 36.2. CONTINUED

```
<H3> Heading Level 3 - ABCDEF abcdef &lt;H3&gt; </h3>
<H4> Heading Level 4 - ABCDEF abcdef &lt;H4&gt; </h4>
<H5> Heading Level 5 - ABCDEF abcdef &lt;H5&gt; </h5>
<H6> Heading Level 6 - ABCDEF abcdef &lt;H6&gt; </h6>
<H7> Heading Level 7 - ABCDEF abcdef &lt;H7&gt; </h7>
<H8> Heading Level 8 - ABCDEF abcdef &lt;H8&gt; </h8>
<H9> Heading Level 9 - ABCDEF abcdef &lt;H9&gt; </h9>
<H10> Heading Level 10 - ABCDEF abcdef &lt;H10&gt; </h10>
</body>
</html>
```

FIGURE 36.2.

Heading tags viewed through Netscape.

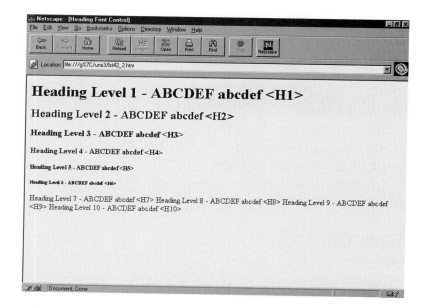

Looking at Figure 36.2, you will notice that the lines start to get weird after heading level 6. After you go beyond what the standard allows, then things can get odd.

Because the less than and greater than signs have special meaning to HTML, to print them, you have to use special character representations. These are in the form of ampersand (&), followed by a mnemonic (such as lt or gt), followed by a semicolon (;) to complete the special character. In Listing 36.2, < and > were used. If you wanted to print an ampersand, you would use &.

Using version 3 of Microsoft Internet Explorer, the same source produces a slightly different screen, as shown in Figure 36.3.

FIGURE 36.3.

*Heading tags
viewed through
Microsoft Internet
Explorer.*

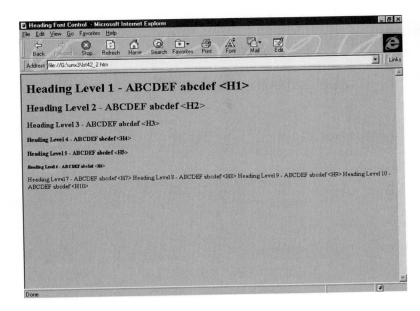

For the other fonts, there are logical and physical style tags. With logical font tags, it is up to the browser to decide how to display them. Logical tags include <EM> for emphasis (usually displayed in italics), <STRONG> for important text (usually displayed in bold), and others.

Figure 36.4 shows the behavior of the logical font style tags using the Netscape Web browser. Figure 36.5 shows the behavior of the logical font style tags using the Internet Explorer browser. Listing 36.3 shows the source for it.

It is not very obvious that the different font types are really different in Figure 36.4. It is much more obvious in Figure 36.5 what the different fonts are (they are better support-ed).

LISTING 36.3. SOURCE FOR LOGICAL FONT STYLES.

```
<html>
<title> Logical Font Styles  </title>
</head>
<body>
<ADDRESS> Postal or E-mail address - ABCDEF abcdef &lt;ADDRESS&gt;
</address> <br>
<CITE> Citations  - ABCDEF abcdef &lt;CITE&gt; </cite> <br>
<CODE> Program Code - ABCDEF abcdef &lt;CODE&gt; </code> <br>
```

continues

LISTING 36.3. CONTINUED

```
<EM> Emphasis - ABCDEF abcdef &lt;EM&gt; </em> <br>
<KBD> Keyboard Input - ABCDEF abcdef &lt;KBD&gt; </kbd> <br>
<SAMP> Literal (Sample) Characters - ABCDEF abcdef &lt;SAMP&gt;
</samp> <br>
<STRONG> Strong or Important - ABCDEF abcdef &lt;STRONG&gt;
</strong> <br>
<VAR> Variable Name - ABCDEF abcdef &lt;VAR&gt; </var> <br>
</body>
</html>
```

FIGURE 36.4.

Logical font styles viewed through Netscape.

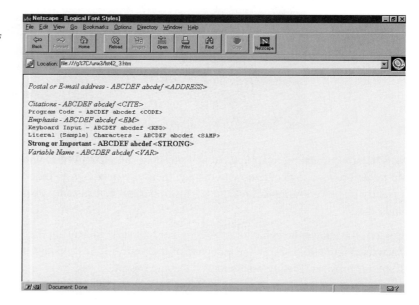

With the exception of the invalid heading tags, all of them appear on their own lines (by definition, a heading gets its own line). When specifying font types, it is necessary to tell the browser to go to a new line through the
 (line break) tag.

Physical tags include <i> for italics, <b> for bold, and others.

Figure 36.6 shows the behavior of the physical font style tags using the Netscape Web browser. Figure 36.7 shows the behavior of the physical font style tags using the Internet Explorer browser. Listing 36.4 shows the source for it.

FIGURE 36.5.

Logical font styles viewed through Internet Explorer.

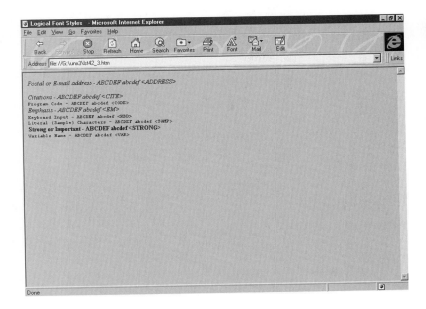

FIGURE 36.6.

Physical font styles viewed through Netscape.

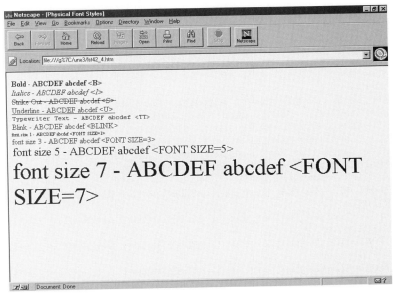

Internet Explorer supports the standard physical font styles, but treats the Netscape extensions as plain text. Netscape supports the standard physical font styles and its own extensions. Although not obvious from the screen in Figure 36.6, the `<BLINK>` tag line does actually blink but does not in Figure 36.7.

FIGURE 36.7.

Physical font styles viewed through Internet Explorer.

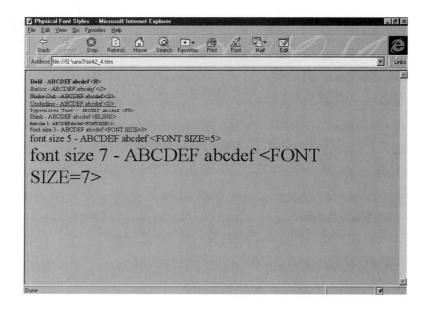

LISTING 36.4. SOURCE FOR HEADING TAGS.

```
<html>
<head>
<title> Physical Font Styles  </title>
</head>
<body>
<B> Bold - ABCDEF abcdef &lt;B&gt; </b> <br>
<I> Italics  - ABCDEF abcdef &lt;I&gt; </i> <br>
<S> Strike Out - ABCDEF abcdef &lt;S&gt; </s> <br>
<U> Underline - ABCDEF abcdef &lt;U&gt; </u> <br>
<TT> Typewriter Text - ABCDEF abcdef &lt;TT&gt; </tt> <br>
<BLINK> Blink - ABCDEF abcdef &lt;BLINK&gt;
</blink> <br>
<FONT SIZE=1> font size 1   - ABCDEF abcdef &lt;FONT SIZE=1&gt;
</FONT> <br>
<FONT SIZE=3> font size 3   - ABCDEF abcdef &lt;FONT SIZE=3&gt;
</FONT> <br>
<FONT SIZE=5> font size 5   - ABCDEF abcdef &lt;FONT SIZE=5&gt;
</FONT> <br>
<FONT SIZE=7> font size 7   - ABCDEF abcdef &lt;FONT SIZE=7&gt;
</FONT> <br>
</body>
</html>
```

Physical font styles can be combined to produce multiple effects like bold italics or bold underlined.

Formatting Text

When text appears in an HTML document, the browser decides how to display it. You can control the fonts, and you can also control how it is formatted. By default, you enter your text-free format, and it is automatically justified.

A new paragraph starts with the <P> tag, and if you want to force a line break, you use the <br> tag. The browser decides how to format the text except that it always starts a new paragraph at the beginning of a line (with a blank line above it) and starts text on a new line (without a blank line above it) when you use the line break.

If you have text that is a quotation, put it between <blockquote> tags—it will normally appear indented, the same way that quotations appear in books. If you have text that requires very specific formatting, you can contain it within a <pre> (preformatted) block—it appears the way you entered it.

Figure 36.8 demonstrates these text formatting tags with the Netscape Web browser. Figure 36.9 shows the same HTML document with the Internet Explorer browser. Listing 36.5 shows the source for it.

FIGURE 36.8.

Text formatting tags viewed through Netscape.

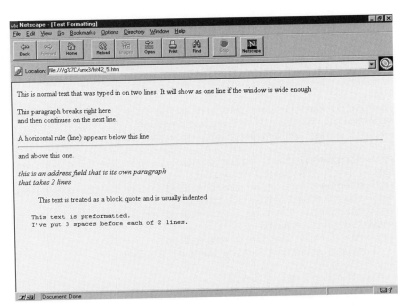

FIGURE 36.9.

Text formatting tags viewed through Internet Explorer.

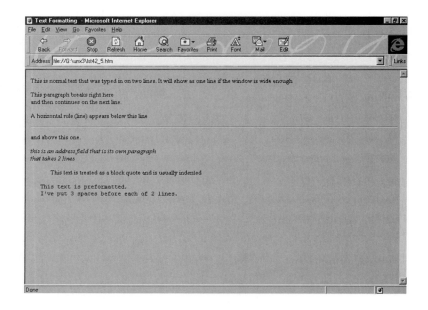

LISTING 36.5. SOURCE FOR TEXT FORMATTING TAGS.

```
<html>
<head>
<title> Text Formatting </title>
</head>
<body>
<p>This is normal text that was typed in on two lines. It will show
as one line if the window is wide enough
<p>This paragraph breaks right here <br> and then continues on the next
line.
<p>A horizontal rule (line) appears below this line <hr> and above this
one.
<p><address> this is an address field that is its own paragraph
<br> that takes 2 lines </address>
<p><blockquote> This text is treated as a block quote and is usually
indented </blockquote>
<p><pre>   This text is preformatted.
   I've put 3 spaces before each of 2 lines.
</pre>
</body>
</html>
```

The heading and paragraph tags were extended as part of HTML version 3. In the new version, the text can be aligned to the left (default), center, or right. Netscape and Internet Explorer also support the <center> tag to center text.

Figure 36.10 demonstrates the extended text formatting tags using the Netscape Web browser. The Internet Explorer browser behaves the same way and is not shown. Listing 36.6 shows the source for it.

FIGURE 36.10.

Extended text formatting tags viewed through Netscape.

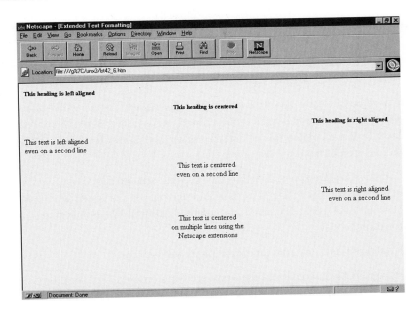

LISTING 36.6. SOURCE FOR HEADING TAGS.

```html
<html>
<head>
<title> Extended Text Formatting </title>
</head>
<body>
<h5 align=left> This heading is left aligned </h5>
<h5 align=center> This heading is centered </h5>
<h5 align=right> This heading is right aligned </h5>
<p align=left> This text is left aligned <br> even on a second line </p>
<p align=center> This text is centered <br> even on a second line</p>
<p align=right> This text is right aligned <br> even on a second line</p>
<center> This text is centered <br> on multiple lines using the <br>
Netscape extensions </center>
</body>
</html>
```

Lists

HTML supports the following five different types of lists:

- Unordered
- Ordered
- Directory
- Menu
- Glossary

With the exception of glossary (or definition) lists, each element within the list is specified by the `<li>` tag (list item).

Unordered lists are specified using the `<ul>` tag and appear with bullets. At the end of the list, the `</ul>` tag is used. If another `<ul>` tag is coded within an unordered list, another level of list is created (an indented sublist). The bullets used for sublists may be the same as or different from the list above them.

Ordered lists are specified using the `<ol>` tag and are sequentially numbered. At the end of the list, the `</ol>` tag is used. If another `<ol>` tag is coded within an ordered list, another level of list is created (an indented sublist). The numbering sequence starts over for each sublist.

Unordered lists can contain ordered lists and vice versa.

Figure 36.11 demonstrates the unordered and ordered lists with the Netscape Web browser. Figure 36.12 shows the same HTML document with the Internet Explorer browser. Listing 36.7 shows the source for it.

FIGURE 36.11.

Unordered and ordered lists viewed through Netscape.

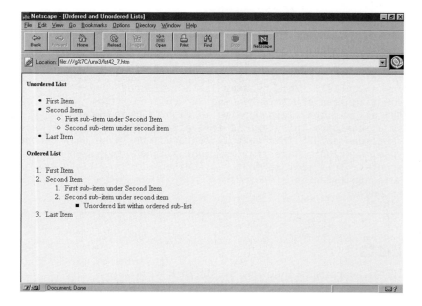

Internet Explorer uses the same bullets at all levels of the unordered list, whereas Netscape Navigator uses different ones.

FIGURE 36.12.

Unordered and ordered lists viewed through Internet Explorer.

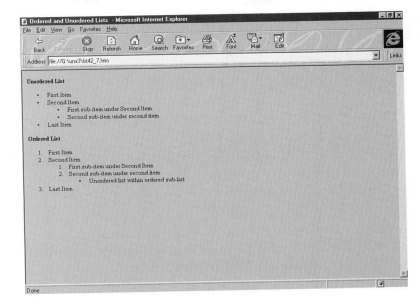

LISTING 36.7. SOURCE FOR UNORDERED AND ORDERED LISTS.

```
<html>
<head>
<title> Ordered and Unordered Lists </title>
</head>
<body>
<h5> Unordered List </h5>
<ul>
<li> First Item
<li> Second Item
<ul>
<li>First sub-item under Second Item
<li>Second sub-item under second item
</ul>
<li> Last Item
</ul>
<h5> Ordered List </h5>
<ol>
<li> First Item
<li> Second Item
<ol>
```

continues

LISTING 36.7. CONTINUED

```
<li>First sub-item under Second Item
<li>Second sub-item under second item
<ul>
<li>Unordered list within ordered sub-list
</ul>
</ol>
<li> Last Item
</ol>
</body>
</html>
```

Directory lists are specified using the `<dir>` tag and appear with bullets. At the end of the list, the `</dir>` tag is used. If another `<dir>` tag is coded within a directory list, another level of list is created (an indented sublist). The bullets used for sublists may be the same as or different from the list above them.

Menu lists are specified using the `<menu>` tag and are sequentially numbered. At the end of the list, the `</menu>` tag is used. In some versions, when another `<menu>` tag is coded within a menu list, another level of list is created (an indented sublist). The bullets used for sublists may be the same as or different from the list above them.

When working with directory lists and menus, the behavior between browsers differs greatly. You may not be able to nest these lists, and the display format can vary (menu list lines often have the bullet omitted).

Figure 36.13 demonstrates the directory and menu lists with the Netscape Web browser. Figure 36.14 shows the same HTML document with the Internet Explorer browser. Listing 36.8 shows the source for it.

Notice the difference in fonts.

LISTING 36.8. SOURCE FOR DIRECTORY AND MENU LISTS.

```
<html>
<head>
<title> Directory and Menu Lists </title>
</head>
<body>
<h5> Directory List </h5>
<dir>
<li> First Item
<li> Second Item
<dir>
<li>First sub-item under Second Item
<li>Second sub-item under second item
</dir>
```

```
<li> Last Item
</dir>
<h5> Menu List </h5>
<menu>
<li> First Item
<li> Second Item
<menu>
<li>First sub-item under Second Item
<li>Second sub-item under second item
<ul>
<li>Unordered list within ordered sub-list
</ul>
</menu>
<li> Last Item
</menu>
</body>
</html>
```

FIGURE 36.13.

*Directory and
menu lists viewed
through Netscape.*

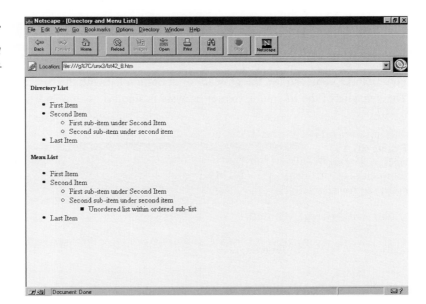

Glossary or definition lists are specified using the <dl> tag. At the end of the list, the
</dl> tag is used. Each item within the list can consist of two parts: item being defined
(specified with the <dt> tag) and the definition (specified with the <dd> tag). Like the
unordered list, you can create subdefinition lists by coding another <dl> tag within an
existing glossary list.

FIGURE 36.14.
Directory and menu lists viewed through Internet Explorer.

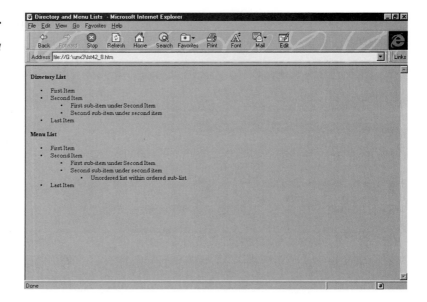

Figure 36.15 demonstrates the glossary or definition list with the Netscape Web browser. The behavior of the Internet Explorer browser is similar. Listing 36.9 shows the source for it.

FIGURE 36.15.
Glossary or definition list viewed through Netscape.

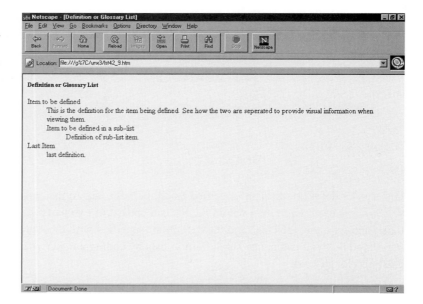

LISTING 36.9. SOURCE FOR GLOSSARY OR DEFINITION LIST.

```
<html>
<head>
<title> Definition or Glossary List </title>
</head>
<body>
<h5> Definition or Glossary List </h5>
<dl>
<dt> Item to be defined
<dd> This is the definition for the item being defined.  See how the two
are
separated to provide visual information when viewing them.
<dl>
<dt>Item to be defined in a sub-list
<dd>Definition of sub-list item.
</dl>
<dt> Last Item
<dd> last definition.
</dl>
</body>
</html>
```

Extensions to Lists

Netscape provides a number of extensions to the ordered and unordered lists. The type of bullet can be specified for the entire unordered list and for each item at a specific sublist level. The numbering type for entire ordered lists and for each item at a specific sublist level can be specified. The starting point for entire ordered lists and each sublist can also be specified.

Figure 36.16 demonstrates the Netscape extensions to unordered and ordered lists. The Internet Explorer browser is not shown because it ignores the unordered list extensions. Listing 36.10 shows the source for it.

LISTING 36.10. SOURCE FOR NETSCAPE EXTENSIONS TO ORDERED AND UNORDERED LISTS.

```
<html>
<head>
<title> Netscape Extensions - Unordered and Ordered Lists </title>
</head>
<body>
<h5> Unordered List </h5>
<ul type=square>
<li> First item
<li type=disc> second item (disc)
```

continues

LISTING 36.10. CONTINUED

```
<li> Third Item
<ul type=circle>
<li>Sub list (circle)
</ul>
<li> last item in unordered list
</ul>
<h5> Ordered List </h5>
<ol type=A>
<li> First item (upper case letters)
<li type=a> second item (lower case letters)
<li> Third Item
<ol type=I>
<li>Sub list (Upper case roman)
<li type=i> second sub list item (lower case roman)
</ol>
<li type=1 value=9> another item in ordered list (numeric)
<li value=7> last item in ordered list
</ol>
</body>
</html>
```

FIGURE 36.16.

Netscape extensions to ordered and unordered lists.

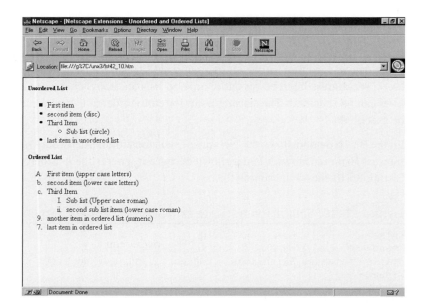

Notice that the bullet types can be changed for the entire unordered list or sublist (instead of the default for that level) and for each individual line item. The number type can be changed for the entire ordered list or sublist (instead of the default numeric type) and for each individual line item. The numeric value can also be changed in the same way for ordered lists (even if does not make sense as shown in the preceding example—item 9 appearing before item 7 when it should really be 4 and 5, respectively).

Hypertext Tags

In addition to displaying text, the capability to link to other objects, Web pages, or resources provides the power behind HTML. Links can take two forms: anchors and images. Anchors are used to provide the actual hypertext links that turn the World Wide Web into a web, which is a collection of interconnected resources. Image tags allow you to load images into your Web page for people to view, adding pictures and drawings to the text.

Anchors

Anchors are used to connect an image or textual description with an action. The action can be any URL with the capability to jump to sections within a document. When the user clicks the associated image or text, the URL is executed and travels down the link.

There are ten possible actions associated with anchors:

1. Transfer to a new HTML document.
   ```
   <A HREF="http://www.host.domain/"> Text that describes the link</A>
   ```

2. Create a positional marker in an HTML document.
   ```
   <A NAME="Section1">This is a positional marker</a>
   ```

3. Jump to a positional marker in the current HTML document.
   ```
   <A HREF="#Section1">Go to Section 1</a>
   ```

4. Jump to a positional marker in a new HTML document.
   ```
   <A HREF="http://www.host.domain/page.html#Section1">Go to Section
   1</a>
   ```

5. Get an image file.
   ```
   <A HREF="http://www.host.domain/file.gif">Display the picture</a>
   ```
   (This anchor can be used to load other types of files including sound, video, and executable code as supported by the browser configuration.)

6. Create a `telnet` (terminal emulation) session.
   ```
   <A HREF="telnet://host.domain">Log into host.domain</a>
   ```

7. Create an `ftp` (file transfer protocol) session.
   ```
   <A HREF="ftp://ftp.host.domain">Use FTP to get files</a>
   ```

8. Create a `gopher` (resource search utility) session.
   ```
   <A HREF="gopher://gopher.host.domain">Use Gopher to find files</a>
   ```

9. Create an email message.

   ```
   <A HREF="mailto;name@host.domain">Send mail to the webmaster</a>
   ```

10. Load a file from the disk attached to the client system.

    ```
    <A HREF="file:///c:/directory/file.ext">Look at file.ext on this
    machine</a>
    ```

These anchors are shown in Figure 36.17 using the Netscape Web browser. The behavior of the Internet Explorer browser is similar. Listing 36.11 shows the source for it.

FIGURE 36.17.

Anchors viewed through Netscape.

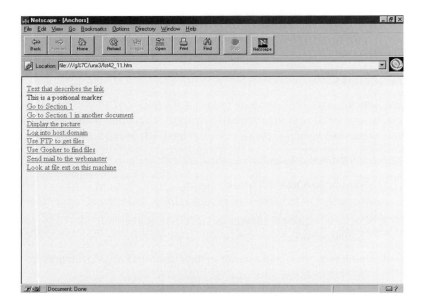

LISTING 36.11. SOURCE FOR ANCHORS.

```
<html>
<head>
<title> Anchors </title>
</head>
<body>
<A HREF="http://www.name.com/"> Text that describes the link</A> <br>
<A NAME="Section1">This is a positional marker</A> <br>
<A HREF="#Section1">Go to Section 1</a> <br>
<A HREF="http://www.host.domain/page.html#Section1">
Go to Section 1 in another document</a> <br>
<A HREF="http://www.host.domain/file.gif">Display the picture</a> <br>
<A HREF="telnet://host.domain">Log into host.domain</a> <br>
<A HREF="ftp://ftp.host.domain">Use FTP to get files</a> <br>
<A HREF="gopher://gopher.host.domain">Use Gopher to find files</a> <br>
<A HREF="mailto;name@host.domain">Send mail to the webmaster</a> <br>
```

```
<A HREF="file:///c:/directory/file.ext">
Look at file.ext on this machine</a> <br>
</body>
</html>
```

The individual anchors with HREF parameters are usually displayed in a color—frequently blue when the page is loaded, green after the link has been exercised, and red if there is an error executing it. You can specify a color other than the default.

You can apply other tags within the description of the link (the text format tags, for instance). You can also include an image. When using with an image, be sure to include a text description for those who use a CUI browser or do not want to wait for the image to download.

Images

Image tags are used to show an image when an HTML document is loaded. The difference between the image tag and the anchor used to get an image file is that the image attached to the image tag displays automatically, whereas it requires user action (clicking on the description) to get the image file named in the anchor.

The most common image formats are .gif and .jpeg, with others often supported.

> **NOTE**
>
> The IMG tag is also used to load other media besides just pictures—you can use it to load sounds or motion pictures (or other multimedia).

The general format of the image tag is:

```
<IMG SRC="URL" ALIGN=TOP ALT="[Text in place of image]">
```

where the URL is any valid http format, and ALIGN specifies the alignment of the image to related text. All browsers support alignments of TOP, BOTTOM (default), and MIDDLE. Some browsers also support LEFT and RIGHT.

Figure 36.18 shows images with the Netscape Web browser. Figure 36.19 shows the same HTML document with the Internet Explorer browser. Listing 36.12 shows the source for it.

Figure 36.18.

Images viewed through Netscape.

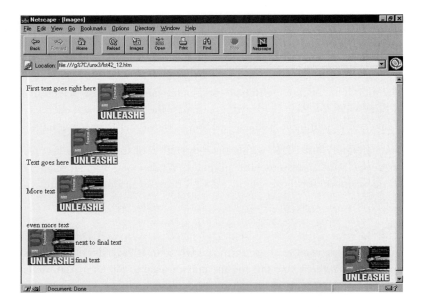

Figure 36.19.

Images viewed through Internet Explorer.

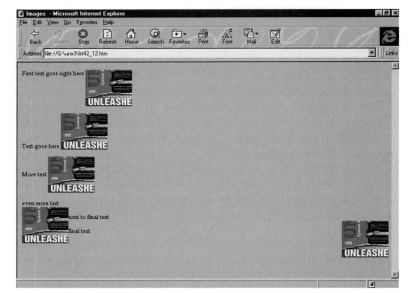

LISTING 36.12. SOURCE FOR IMAGES.

```
<html>
<head>
<title> Images </title>
</head>
<body>
<p>First text goes right here
<IMG SRC="file:///g:/unx3/06723095.GIF" ALIGN=TOP ALT="[my picture]">
<p>Text goes here
<IMG SRC="file:///06723095.gif" ALIGN=BOTTOM ALT="[my picture]">
<p>More text
<IMG SRC="file:///06723095.gif" ALIGN=MIDDLE ALT="[my picture]">
<p>even more text
<IMG SRC="file:///06723095.gif" ALIGN=LEFT ALT="[my picture]">
<p>next to final text
<IMG SRC="file:///06723095.gif" ALIGN=RIGHT ALT="[my picture]"><p>final
text
</body>
</html>
```

Images can be combined with anchors to show a picture and then load something else when the user clicks on them.

TIP

The `alt=` tag defines a text description of the image that is useful for the text browsers such as lynx or if the GUI Web browser is configured not to load images. Most browsers also display this text when the mouse is moved over the image. This process provides additional description for the image.

Figure 36.20 shows images and anchors combined using the Internet Explorer Web browser. The Netscape Navigator browser behaves similarly. Listing 36.13 shows the source for it.

LISTING 36.13. SOURCE FOR IMAGES.

```
<html>
<head>
<title> Images and Anchors</title>
</head>
<body>
<p>First text goes right here
<A HREF="file:/// g:\unx3\small.gif">
```

continues

LISTING 36.13. CONTINUED

```
<IMG SRC="file:/// g:\unx3\big.gif" ALT="[Small Logo]">
Click on theimage to see a bigger version </A>
<p>Lots more text will go here and maybe more anchors will follow.  More
images (lots more) and even more text would then follow.
</body>
</html>
```

FIGURE 36.20.

Images with anchors viewed through Internet Explorer.

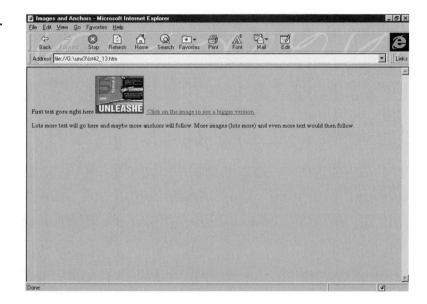

Whenever you use this technique, make sure that you include the text describing the action to take ("Click on the image to see a bigger version") so that people who use the CUI viewers or who disable image display can still use your pages.

The difference between the image tag and the anchor used to get an image is that image tags are automatically loaded when the HTML document is loaded from the server. Anchors that load images only load the images when the user selects them.

A Brief Description of Forms

Forms with HTML provide a means of inputting data from the user. A series of areas are defined on the form that allow different types of input such as text, hidden, image, password, check box, radio, submit, and reset. These fields are used as shown in Table 36.2.

TABLE 36.2. FORM FIELD TYPES.

Field Type	Description
text	Used for input of normal text
hidden	Not available for user input; used to track form when received at server
image	Pushbuttons based on specified images
password	Accepts user input without echoing it
textarea	Multiple-line user input area
select option	Pull-down or scrollable selection list
submit	Sends the completed form to server
reset	Clears the contents of the form

Figure 36.21 shows a form with most elements defined using the Netscape Web browser. Figure 36.22 shows the same HTML document with the Internet Explorer browser. Listing 36.14 shows the source for it.

FIGURE 36.21.

Form viewed through Netscape.

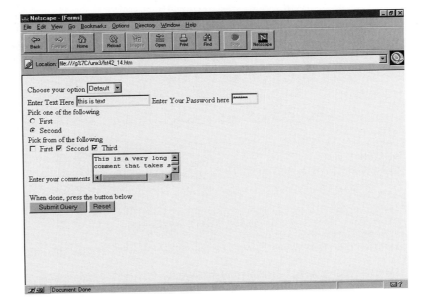

FIGURE 36.22.

Form viewed through Internet Explorer.

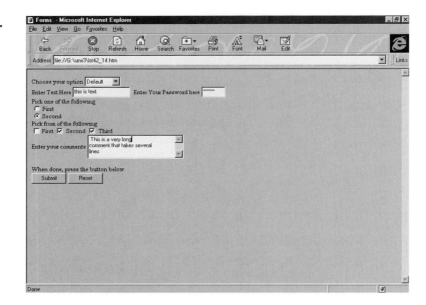

LISTING 36.14. SOURCE FOR FORM.

```
<html>
<head>
<title> Forms </title>
</head>
<body>
<FORM ACTION="http://www.host.domain/cgi-bin/handle_form.pl"
METHOD="POST">
Choose your option <SELECT NAME="Selection list" SIZE=1>
<OPTION>First
<OPTION SELECTED> Default
<OPTION>Third
</SELECT> <br>
<INPUT TYPE="HIDDEN" NAME="NotSeen" SIZE=10>
Enter Text Here <INPUT TYPE="TEXT" NAME="Text Input" SIZE=20 MAXLENGTH=25>
    Enter Your Password here
<INPUT TYPE="PASSWORD" NAME="Pswd" SIZE=6 MAXLENGTH=12> <br>
Pick one of the following <br>
<INPUT TYPE="RADIO" NAME="Radio" VALUE="First"> First <BR>
<INPUT TYPE="RADIO" NAME="Radio" VALUE="Second" CHECKED> Second <br>
Pick from of the following <br>
<INPUT TYPE="CHECKBOX" NAME="check" VALUE="First"> First
<INPUT TYPE="CHECKBOX" NAME="check" VALUE="Second" CHECKED> Second
<INPUT TYPE="CHECKBOX" NAME="check" VALUE="third" CHECKED> Third <br>
Enter your comments <TEXTAREA NAME="Comments" ROWS=2 COLUMNS=60>
</textarea>
<p>When done, press the button below <br>
```

```
<INPUT TYPE="Submit" NAME="Submit This Form">
<INPUT TYPE="Reset" NAME="Clear">
</FORM>
</body>
</html>
```

The `action` option in the form tag tells the server what to execute; the `method` option tells it when.

A Brief Description of Tables

HTML tables are used to present data in a tabular form. A series of rows and columns is defined and filled in with data.

Figure 36.23 shows a simple table with borders using the Internet Explorer browser. The output using Netscape is similar and is not shown. Listing 36.15 shows the source for it.

FIGURE 36.23.

Table viewed through Internet Explorer.

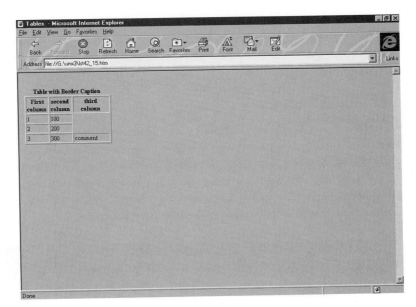

LISTING 36.15. SOURCE FOR TABLE.

```
<html>
<head>
<title> Tables </title>
</head>
<body>
<Table>
<Table border>
<CAPTION> <H5>Table with Border Caption </H5> </CAPTION>
<TR ALIGN=LEFT VALIGN=MIDDLE> <TH>First<br>column
<TH> second <br> column <th> third column </TR>
<TR> <TD> 1 <TD> 100 </TR>
<TR> <TD> 2 <TD> 200 </TR>
<TR> <TD> 3 <TD> 300 <TD> comment </TR>
</table>
</body>
</html>
```

Frames

Frames allow you to show information from multiple HTML pages on one screen. You can change the content in each element of the screen independently. A typical use for frames is to have a table of contents for your site on the left side (in a smaller frame) and the actual content on the right (larger frame).

Tables allow you to present multiple views that can be independent or subwindows. As a result, specific information remains visible while other portions of the screen scroll or are replaced. As a result, you could force the top portion of the screen to be a static banner for your site (instead of coding it on every page), the left side might be a navigation menu (again, instead of including the links on every page), and the main window would contain the pages or images selected from the navigation menu.

> **CAUTION**
>
> Frames were an extension to HTML 3.2 and are part of the 4.0 standard. Not all Web browsers support them; as a result, you should allow navigation of your site without them (unless you are willing to ignore a certain percentage of Web browsers and their users).

Figure 36.24 shows a simple set of frames using the Internet Explorer browser. The output using this version of Netscape is completely different because this version does not support frames (newer versions do); it is shown as Figure 36.25. Listing 36.16 shows the source for it.

The easiest way to tell whether you are using a version of Netscape that supports frames is to try one of the examples.

FIGURE 36.24.

Frames viewed through Internet Explorer.

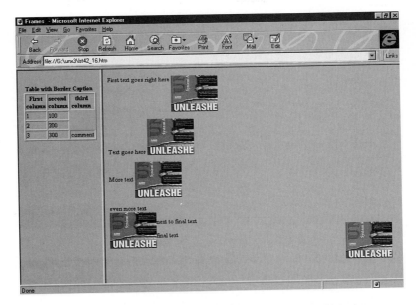

FIGURE 36.25.

Frames viewed through Netscape Navigator.

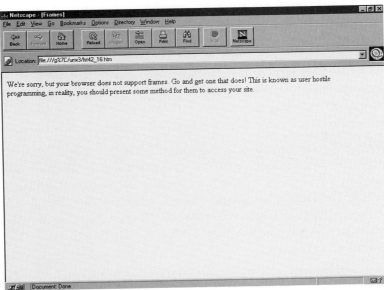

LISTING 36.16. SOURCE FOR FRAMES.

```html
<html>
<head>
<title> Frames </title>
</head>
<frameset cols="175,*">
    <frame src="lst42_15.htm">
    <frame src="lst42_12.htm">
<noframes>
<body>
<p>We're sorry, but your browser does not support frames.
Go and get one that does! This is known as user hostile
programming; in reality, you should present some method
for them to access your site.
</p>
</body>
</noframes>
</frameset>
</html>
```

Frames are contained within the `<frameset>` `</frameset>` tag; frames can be nested. You should include the `<noframes>` `</noframes>` tag within the first frameset you have (before any nested frames). You can specify the width (`cols=`—vertical window) or height (`rows=`—horizontal window) of the individual windows within a frame in pixels, percentage of browser window, or "remaining space" (with the `*`).

Tools

As the Web has increased in popularity, so have the tools available to create Web pages. In the beginning, text or programming editors were used to manually code HTML. Now, many tools and many applications are "Web enabled," which generally means that they can create HTML or directly execute HTML anchors to grab resources.

Most GUI word processors save documents in HTML format. There are GUI application development tools that create HTML and CGI scripts in addition to their own proprietary language. You can find the following tools on the Internet: HoTMetaL (HTML editor), HTML Assistant (HTML editor), Internet Assistant (Microsoft add-in to Word 6 to build Web pages and browse), Microsoft Word 95/7 and newer (can read HTML in as word processing document and save as HTML), RTFTOHTM (creates HTML from Rich Text Format files), and others.

And of course, you can always code HTML directly using a text editor.

CGI Scripts and Java Applets

Although HTML provides a means of displaying and connecting text, graphics, and other items, it provides no means of procedural programming. To process data (such as HTML forms), it is necessary to use CGI programs or scripts. CGI stands for Common Gateway Interface—a standard developed to allow host programs to interface with Web pages. Most CGI programs are written in scripting languages such as UNIX shell scripts or Perl; they can also be written in a compiled language such as C or C++.

There are three different ways to execute CGI scripts:

- `<A HREF="http:/www.host.domain/cgi-bin/name.pl">`
- `<IMG SRC="http:/www.host.domain/cgi-bin/name.gif">`
- `<FORM ACTION="http://www.host.domain/cgi-bin/handle_form.pl"`
  `METHOD="POST">`

The normal anchor executes the CGI script when you click it, the image executes the CGI script when the Web page loads, and the form action executes the script when the `submit` button is clicked.

Java is an object-oriented language that is syntactically similar to C and C++. It is a portable programming language that runs its own virtual code on any machine through the Web browser (which interprets the Java bytecode into native machine language). This is known as a Java applet. Java applications run as an executable program on individual machines without the assistance of a Web browser.

The primary conceptual difference between Java and CGI is that Java runs on the client system and CGI runs on the host. In addition, Java is essentially one language whereas CGI is a standard method of communicating data to a server and can be written in many different languages.

When running a Java applet from within a Web page, you use the following:

```
<applet code="Javaname.class" width=400 height=400>
<param name="variable1" value="123">
<param name="variable2" value="your name">
</applet>
```

The `width` and `height` parameters set the window size. The `param` tags set variables (similar to UNIX environment variables) that the Java applet can access.

To the end user, a CGI program is much safer because it runs on the host; if there is a problem with the program (for example, a virus or Trojan horse), it is someone else's problem. With Java, it is possible (but improbable) that a program could harm a client machine.

> **CAUTION**
>
> Some Web sites leave files on your client machine known as *cookies*. These are generally used to track usage and retain information about you between visits to that site (for instance, preferences or your stock portfolio). The data is stored on your machine instead of the host. If this bothers you, you can disable cookies in your Web browser. Cookies are data files, not executable code.

In addition, there are tools like Dynamic HTML, Active Server Pages (ASP), and Server Side Includes (SSI). To the Web browser, these are all plain HTML. On the server, the HTML is processed before the file is transmitted. For example, SSI allows your HTML to include other files—which is very handy to provide a standard format, page headers, and page footers.

Special Characters

The remainder of this chapter contains tables summarizing the special characters and general HTML tags.

Table 36.3 provides a summary of the special characters available with HTML. You can get the complete list at `http://www.w3.org/hypertext/WWW/MarkUp/Entities.html`.

TABLE 36.3. SPECIAL CHARACTERS.

Tag	Description
&lt;	< (less than symbol)
&gt;	> (greater than symbol)
&amp;	& (ampersand)
&quot;	" (double quote)
&#174;	Registered Trademark ™
&#169;	Copyright [c]
&#*nnn*;	ASCII code (where *nnn* is the value)

Tag Summary

The following tables summarize the HTML tags and actions. You can get the current specification at `http://www.w3.org/hypertext/WWW/MarkUp/MarkUp.html`.

Information on image maps is available at
`http://hoohoo.ncsa.uiuc.edu/docs/setup/admin/NewImagemap.html`.

Forms information is available at
`http://hoohoo.ncsa.uiuc.edu/SDG/Software/Mosaic/Docs/fill-out-forms/overview.html`.

Check out `http://www.javasoft.com` for information on Java programming.

Tables 36.4–36.11 are a summary of tags.

TABLE 36.4. SUMMARY OF TAGS—STRUCTURE.

Tag	Description
`<HTML> </HTML>`	Contains entire document
`<TITLE> </TITLE>`	Describes document title
`<HEAD> </HEAD>`	Contains `<TITLE>`, `<STYLE>`, `<BASE>`, `<META>`, and `<ISINDEX>` tags
`<BODY> </BODY>`	Contains majority of document except when frames are used (see table 36.11 for information on frames)
`<BODY bgcolor= text= link= vlink= alink=> </BODY>`	TML 3.2—specifying color of various body elements; the color Hcan be specified by name or RGB hexadecimal constant (#RRGGBB format—#000000 is black, #FFFFFF is white, #FF0000 is red, #00FF00 is Lime Green, #0000FF is Blue)
`<!— comment —>`	Contains comment text
`<STYLE> </STYLE>`	Contains Style Sheet information
`<SCRIPT> </SCRIPT>`	Contains client side scripts (like JavaScript)
`<BASE>`	Describes base URL used to resolve relative URLs in the rest of the page
`<META>`	Used to describe properties of the document in the form of name/value pairs; can also specify HTTP values
`<ISINDEX>`	Provides search prompt for searchable documents

TABLE 36.5. SUMMARY OF TAGS—FORMATTING.

Tag	Description
`<Hn> </Hn>`	Heading levels where *n* is 1 to 6
`<Hn ALIGN=xxx> </Hn>`	HTML 3—defines alignment for heading: LEFT, CENTER, or RIGHT
`<P> </P>`	Defines paragraph start, usually has blank line before; the closing tag is optional
`<P ALIGN=xxx> </P>`	HTML 3—defines alignment for paragraph text: LEFT, CENTER, or RIGHT
`<ADDRESS> </ADDRESS>`	Defines address block
`<BLOCKQUOTE> </BLOCKQUOTE>`	Defines a block containing a quotation
`<PRE> </PRE>`	Defines preformatted text block
`<PRE WIDTH=nn> </PRE>`	Defines preformatted text block of specified size
`<CENTER> </CENTER>`	HTML 3.2—Centers paragraph
` `	Line break (forces a new line); accepts CLEAR= LEFT, RIGHT, or ALL to move down past floating images on either margin
`<HR>`	Horizontal rule (draws a line)
`<B> </B>`	Physical format: bold
`<I> </I>`	Physical format: italics
`<S> </S>`	Physical format: strikethrough
`<U> </U>`	Physical format: underline
`<TT> </TT>`	Physical format: typewriter (monospace)
`<BIG> </BIG>`	Physical format: larger font
`<SMALL> </SMALL>`	Physical format: smaller font
`<SUB> </SUB>`	Physical format: Subscript
`<SUP> </SUP>`	Physical format: Superscript
`<BLINK> </BLINK>`	Netscape—physical format: flashing
`<FONT SIZE=n COLOR=n> </FONT>`	HTML 3.2—specifies font size where *n* is 1 through 7 and color
`<BASEFONT SIZE=n>`	HTML 3.2—default font size for document where *n* is 1 through 7
`<EM> </EM>`	Logical format: emphasis
`<STRONG> </STRONG>`	Logical format: strong
`<CITE> </CITE>`	Logical format: citation

Tag	Description
<CODE> </CODE>	Logical format: program code
<KBD> </KBD>	Logical format: keyboard input
<SAMP> </SAMP>	Logical format: output samples
<VAR> </VAR>	Logical format: program variables

TABLE 36.6. SUMMARY OF TAGS—LISTS.

Tag	Description
<UL> </UL>	Lists—unordered, use with <LI>
<OL> </OL>	Lists—ordered (numbered), use with <LI>
<DIR> </DIR>	Lists—directory, use with <LI>
<MENU> </MENU>	Lists—menu, use with <LI>
<LI>	Lists—list element or item
<DL> </DL>	Lists—definition or glossary, use <DT> and <DD>
<DT>	Lists—definition term
<DD>	Lists—definition of term
<UL TYPE=*xxx*>	HTML 3.2—bullet type for unordered list where *xxx* is DISC, CIRCLE, or SQUARE
<LI TYPE=*xxx*>	HTML 3.2—bullet type for unordered list item where *xxx* is DISC, CIRCLE, or SQUARE
<OL TYPE=*xxx*>	HTML 3.2—number format for ordered list where *xxx* is A, a, I, i, 1
<LI TYPE=*xxx*>	HTML 3.2—number format for ordered list item where *xxx* is A, a, I, i, 1
<OL VALUE=*n*>	HTML 3.2—starting point for ordered list
<LI VALUE=*n*>	HTML 3.2—starting point for ordered list item

TABLE 36.7. SUMMARY OF TAGS—LINKS (ANCHORS).

Tag	Description
<A HREF="URL"> </A>	Links to another document, image, or resource
<A HREF="#label"> </A>	Jumps to predefined location in this document
<A HREF="URL#label> </A>	Jumps to predefined location in another document
<A NAME="label"> </A>	Defines a location

TABLE 36.8. SUMMARY OF TAGS—IMAGES.

Tag	Description
`<IMG SRC="URL" flags>`	Loads and displays image based on flags
`ALIGN=`*xxx*	Flag—displays image where *xxx* is TOP, BOTTOM, or MIDDLE, can also be LEFT, CENTER, RIGHT
`ALT="[`*description*`]"`	Flag—text to describe image if not displayed
`WIDTH=`*value*	Flag—width of image in pixels (allows browser to reserve space for image before it is downloaded)
`HEIGHT=`*value*	Flag—height of image in pixels (allows browser to reserve space for image before it is downloaded)
`BORDER=`*value*	Flag—size of border around image (use zero for no border)
`HSPACE=`*value*	Flag—amount of whitespace to left and right of image
`VSPACE=`*value*	Flag—amount of whitespace above and below image
`ALT="[`*description*`]"`	Flag—text to describe image if not displayed
`USEMAP="map URL"`	Flag—image is a navigational toolbar
`ISMAP`	Flag—specifies an image map (used to provide links based on cursor position in image)
`<MAP name="map name">` `</MAP>`	Used with `<IMG>` for navigational toolbars, contains `<AREA>` tags
`<AREA href=`*url* `alt=` `"`*description*`"shape=SHAPE` `coords="values">`	Used with `<IMG>` and `<MAP>` tags to specify the areas within a navigational toolbar; *url* is the page to load when an area is selected, *description* is used to describe area if image is not displayed, *SHAPE* is one of RECT, CIRCLE, or POLY, and values are the coordinates (leftX, topY, rightX, bottomY for RECT; centerX, centerY, radius for CIRCLE; x1, y1, x2, y2, x3, y3, … for POLY)

TABLE 36.9. SUMMARY OF TAGS—FORMS.

Tag	Description
`<FORM ACTION="URL" METHOD=xxx>` `</FORM>`	Used to contain elements of a form, *xxx* is GET or POST, which determines when the specified URL is executed
`<SELECT flags> </SELECT>`	Pulldown selection list
`NAME="`*variable*`"`	SELECT flag—name of input field
`<OPTION>` text	SELECT—option that can be selected
`<OPTION SELECTED>` text	SELECT—option selected by default

Tag	Description
`<TEXTAREA flags> </TEXTAREA>`	Accepts multiple line input
`ROWS=`*n*	TEXTAREA flag—number of rows to display
`COLS=`*m*	TEXTAREA flag—number of columns to display
`NAME="`*variable*`"`	TEXTAREA flag—name of input field
`<INPUT flags>`	Input field
`TYPE="`*xxx*`"`	INPUT flag—field type where *xxx* is CHECKBOX, FILE, HIDDEN, IMAGE, PASSWORD, RADIO, RESET, SUBMIT, or TEXT
`CHECKED`	INPUT flag—check box or radio button initially set
`NAME="`*variable*`"`	INPUT flag—name of input field
`SIZE=`*nnn*	INPUT flag—text field size in characters
`MAXSIZE=`*nnn*	INPUT flag—maximum number of characters acceptable for text field
`VALUE="`*text*`"`	INPUT flag—initial value or value when selected

TABLE 36.10. SUMMARY OF TAGS—TABLES.

Tag	Description
`<TABLE flags> </TABLE>`	Used to contain elements of a table
`BORDER`	TABLE flag—draw border around table
`ALIGN=`*xxx*	TABLE flag—specify table alignment where *xxx* is BLEEDLEFT (flush with window), BLEEDRIGHT, CENTER, LEFT (flush with margin), JUSTIFY, or RIGHT
`COLSPEC="`*string*`"`	TABLE flag—define columns justification (C—center, D—decimal align, J—justify, L—left, and R—right) and widths
`UNITS=unit`	TABLE flag—specifies units for column width
`WIDTH=`*value*	TABLE flag—specifies width of columns, can be in pixels or percentage of space between margins
`<CAPTION flag> </CAPTION>`	Used to contain description of table
`ALIGN=`*xxx*	CAPTION flag—specifies location of caption (TOP or BOTTOM—above or below table)
`<TR flag> </TR>`	Used to contain row of a table
`ALIGN=`*xxx*	TR flag—specifies alignment where *xxx* is LEFT, CENTER, RIGHT

continues

Table 36.10. CONTINUED

Tag	Description
VALIGN=*xxx*	TR flag—specifies vertical alignment where *xxx* is TOP, MIDDLE, BOTTOM
<TD flag> </TD>	Used to contain table data or cells
<TH flag> </TH>	Used to contain table column header
ALIGN=*xxx*	TD/TH flag—same as TR ALIGN
VALIGN=*xxx*	TD/TH flag—same as TR VALIGN
COLSPAN=*n*	TD/TH flag—allow item to span *n* columns
ROWSPAN=*n*	TD/TH flag—allow item to span *n* rows

Table 36.11. SUMMARY OF TAGS—FRAMES.

Tag	Description
<FRAMESET *flags*> </FRAMESET>	Used to contain elements of a frame, used in place of <BODY> tag
TITLE="*description*"	FRAMESET flag—Supply title for frameset
ROWS=*xxx*	FRAMESET flag—specify size (in pixels, percentage, or remaining space (*) of individual frames within window; this produces horizontal frames
COLS=*xxx*	FRAMESET flag—specify size (in pixels, percentage, or remaining space (*) of individual frames within window; this produces vertical frames
<FRAME *flags*>	Define the contents of an individual frame within a frameset, a <FRAME> tag is required for each window within a <FRAMESET>
SRC=url	FRAME flag—specifies URL to load into this page
NAME=*value*	FRAME flag—specifies name of window
NORESIZE	FRAME flag—prevents window from being resized when this flag is specified
SCROLLING=*xxx*	FRAME flag—specifies scrolling capability of frame where *xxx* is AUTO, YES, NO
FRAMEBORDER=*xxx*	FRAME flag—boolean that specifies whether a frame should have a border (1) or not (0)
MARGINWIDTH=*value*	FRAME Flag—amount of whitespace to left and right of frame

Tag	Description
MARGINHEIGHT=*value*	FRAME Flag—amount of whitespace above and below frame
<NOFRAMES> </NOFRAMES>	Used to contain messages to user when his Web browser does not support frames; should occur after first <FRAMESET> (before any nested framesets)

Summary

The World Wide Web is a popular place that is growing by leaps and bounds for commercial and personal purposes. Even with the increasing availability of GUI HTML authoring tools, there is still the need to understand the underlying language.

If you see an interesting Web page, you can view the HTML source in many Web browsers. You can look at the techniques used and learn from them. Try it!

Figures 36.26 and 36.27 show document source using the Netscape and Internet Explorer browsers, respectively. What might not be apparent is that Netscape colors the tag names and provides a view-only look at the source whereas Internet Explorer does not color the tags and uses Notepad (which allows you to cut and paste the code).

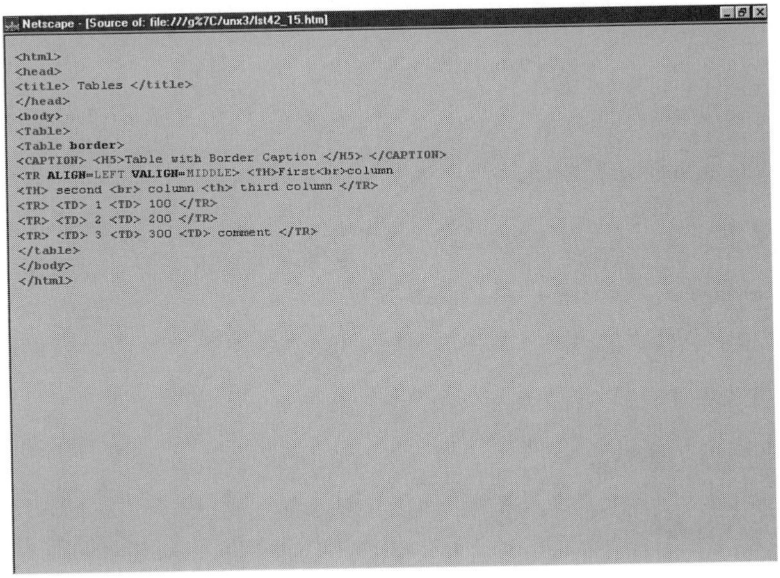

FIGURE 36.26.

Document Source viewed through Netscape.

FIGURE 36.27.

Document Source viewed through Internet Explorer.

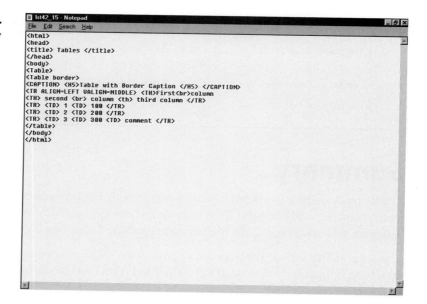

Monitoring Server Activity

by Chris Byers and Mike Starkenburg

IN THIS CHAPTER

Many people consider server activity to be the true sign of a successful Web site. The more hits you have, the more popular your Web site must be, right? In fact, that's not strictly true, and in the following sections, I explain how the data in your server logs can help you build a better site. This chapter covers the following topics:

- The HTTP access log
- The `referrer` and `user_agent` logs
- The error log
- Basic and advanced log analysis
- Factors in Log accuracy
- Analysis tools

Access Logs

The primary method for monitoring Web server activity is by analyzing the Web server's access logs. The access log records each HTTP request to the server, including both GET and POST method requests. The access log records successes and failures, and includes a status code for each request. Some servers log "extended" data including browser type and referring site. This data may be in separate logs or stored in the main access log itself.

This data is generally kept in a `/logs` subdirectory of your server directory. The file is often called `access_log`, and it can be large—about 1 MB per 10,000 entries. The specific directory and name vary depending on your server, and are configurable in the `httpd.conf` file.

These requests, or hits as they are commonly called, are the basic metric of all Web server usage.

Uses for Access Log Data

In many organizations, log data is under-utilized or ignored completely. Often, the only person with access to the logging data (and the only person who can interpret the reports) is the Webmaster. In fact, the log data is a gold mine of information for the entire company if properly analyzed and distributed.

Content Programming

One classic use of access logs is to assist in determining which content on a Web site is most effective. By examining the frequency of hits to particular pages, you, as a content developer, can judge the relative popularity of distinct content areas.

Most analysis programs provide lists of the "top ten" and "bottom ten" pages on a site, ranked by total hits. By examining this kind of report, a Web content developer can find out which types of content users are finding helpful or entertaining.

Web sites can have more than 50 percent of their hits just to the index page, which isn't much help in determining content effectiveness. Where the user goes next, however, is perhaps one of the most useful pieces of data available from the access logs. Some analysis programs (you explore a few later in the chapter) allow you to examine the most common user "paths" through the site.

> **CAUTION**
>
> Note that for programming and advertising purposes, access logs cannot be considered a completely accurate source. The "Log Accuracy" section later in this chapter discusses factors that cause overstatement and understatement of access logs.

Scaling and Load Determination

Using access logs is a quick method of determining overall server load. By benchmarking your system initially and then analyzing the changes in traffic periodically, you can anticipate the need to increase your system capacity.

Each hit in an access log contains the total transfer size (in kilobytes) for that request. By adding the transfer sizes of each hit, you can get an aggregate bandwidth per period of time. This number can be a fairly good indicator of total load over time.

Of course, the best scaling tests separately track system metrics such as CPU usage, disk access, and network interface capacity. (See *UNIX Unleashed*, System Administrator's Edition for a more detailed discussion of this kind of monitoring.) Analyzing access logs, however, is an easy way to get a quick snapshot of the load.

Advertising

Advertising is becoming one of the primary business models supporting Internet sites. Advertising is generally sold in *thousands* of impressions, where an impression is one hit on the ad graphic. Accurate tracking of this information has a direct effect on revenue.

Because Web logs are not 100 percent accurate, businesses dependent on ad revenue should consider using an ad management system such as NetGravity or Accipiter. These systems manage ad inventory, reliably count impressions, and also count clickthroughs, which are measures of ad effectiveness.

In cases in which ads are used in noncritical applications, access logs may be useful. They may be used to judge the effectiveness of different ads in the same space. Finally, you can use access log analysis to find new pages that may be appropriate for ads.

Access Log Format

Although each server can have a different access log format, most popular servers use the *common log format*. Common log format is used in most servers derived from the NCSA httpd server, including Netscape and Apache.

If your server does not use common log format by default, don't fret. Some servers can be configured to use common log format, and some analyzers process several different log formats. If all else fails, you can write a pre-parser that converts your logs to common log format.

A common log format entry looks like the following:

```
lust.ops.aol.com - - [02/May/1997:04:14:00 -0500] "GET /index.html
HTTP/1.0" 200 1672
```

In plain English, this log entry says that a user on the machine `lust.ops.aol.com` requested the page `index.html` from my server at 4:14 a.m. on May 2. The request was made with the Hypertext Transfer Protocol, version 1.0. It was served successfully and was a transfer of 1,672 bytes.

You can split common log entries into fields, where each field is separated by a single space. Broken down by field, this entry represents the following:

- Host—The first piece of information is the identifier of the machine making the request.

- RFC931—RFC931 is a method of identifying which user made the request. RFC931 is rarely used in real life.

- Authuser—If the page requested is protected by HTTP authentication, the username submitted to allow access is recorded in the access log. If no protection is available, as in the example, the server inserts a dash as a placeholder.

- Date-time—The server logs its own current date and time at the completion of each request.

- Request—This field logs the specific request made, in quotation marks. The first word in the field is the request method, either GET, PUT, POST, or HEAD, depending on the desired operation. The second word is the specific file being requested (in the example, /index.html). The third and final word is the name and version of the protocol that should be used to fill the request (in the example, HTTP 1.0).

- Status—In the example, the 200 represents a successful transfer. Other three-digit numerical result codes indicate errors and other actions. You can find a complete list of result codes and explanations in the next section.

- Bytes—The last field is the total amount of bytes transferred in this request. In the example, the number is 1672.

Result Codes

Every attempted request is logged in the access log, but not all are successful. The following common result codes can help you troubleshoot problems on your site:

Code	Meaning
2XX	Success.
200	OK. If your system is working correctly, this code is the most common one found in the log. It signifies that the request was completed without incident.
201	Created. Successful POST command.
202	Accepted. Processing request accepted.
203	Partial information. Returned information may be cached or private.
204	No response. Script succeeded but did not return a visible result.
3XX	Redirection.
301	Moved. Newer browsers should automatically link to the new reference. The response contains a new address for the requested page.
302	Found. Used to indicate that a different URL should be loaded. Often used by CGI scripts to redirect the user to the results of the script.
304	Not modified. A client can request a page "if-modified-since" a certain time. If the object has not been modified, the server responds with a 304, and the locally cached version of the object can be used.
4XX	Client error.
400	Bad request. Bad syntax in request.
401	Unauthorized. Proper authentication required to retrieve object.

continues

Code	Meaning
402	Payment required. Proper "charge-to" header required to retrieve object.
403	Forbidden. No authentication possible. This code sometimes indicates problems with file permissions on the UNIX file system.
404	Not found. No document matches the URL requested.
5*XX*	Server error.
500	Internal error.
501	Not implemented.
502	Timed out.

Extended Logs

In addition to logging the basic access information in the common log format, some servers log additional information included in the HTTP headers. Check your server software's documentation to determine whether you have this capability. Note that many servers have this capability but have it disabled by default. A simple change to the httpd.conf file may enable extended logging.

In some server software, extended information is logged as fields tacked on the end of each entry in a common log format file. Other servers maintain separate files for the additional information. The two most common types of extended logs are the referrer log and the user_agent log.

Referrer

Two important questions not answered by the standard access logs are

- From where are people coming to my site?
- How do people navigate through my site?

To answer these questions, look to your referrer log. This data is often ignored by Webmasters, but it can provide a great deal of useful information. A word of caution here: referer logs can be a major security hole. Look at your security needs before even creating such logs.

Referrer data is generated by the client connecting to your site and is passed in the HTTP headers for each connection. A referrer log entry contains two pieces of data, as in the following example:

```
http://www.aol.com/credits.html  -> /resume.html
```

The first URL represents the last page the user requested. The second represents the file-name on your server that the user is currently requesting. In this case, the person who requested my resume was most recently looking at the `aol.com` credits page. When referrer data frequently contains a given Web site, it is likely that a Webmaster has linked to your site.

> **NOTE**
>
> If a site shows up only a few times in your referrer log, that information doesn't necessarily indicate that a link exists from that site to yours. In the preceding example, the user might have been looking at the `aol.com` page last but manually typed in the URL for my resume. The browser still sends the AOL page as the referrer information because it was the last page the user requested. I can assure you that no link connects `http://www.aol.com` to my resume.

You can get the data you need out of your referrer log in several ways. Many of the tools I describe in the "Analysis Tools" section of this chapter process your referrer log for you as they process your access logs.

If you specifically want to work with the referrer log, check out RefStats 1.1.1 by Jerry Franz. RefStats is a Perl script that counts and lists referring pages in a clean and organized manner. You can find the script and sample output at

```
http://www.netimages.com/~snowhare/utilities/refstats.html
```

User-Agent

When Webmasters design Web sites, they are often faced with a difficult question: Which browser will we develop for? Each browser handles HTML differently, and each supports different scripting languages and accessory programs.

In most cases, you should build your site for the browser most frequently used by your audience. One way to decide which browser to support is to watch industry-wide browser market share reports. For one example, try the following site:

```
http://www.webtrends.com/products/webtrend/REPORTS/industry/browser/apr97/
report.htm
```

A more accurate method is to examine "user-agent" logs. Most servers log the type of browser used for each request in a file called `agent_log`. The agent information is passed in HTTP headers, like the referrer data.

There is no formal standard for user-agent strings, but they generally consist of a browser name, a slash, a version number, and additional information in parentheses. Now take a look at some common agents:

```
Mozilla/2.02 (Win16; I)
```

The preceding is the classic user-agent string: It denotes a user with a Netscape browser on a Windows 16-bit platform. Mozilla is Netscape's internal pet name for its browser.

Here's another example:

```
Mozilla/2.0 (compatible; MSIE 3.01; AK; Windows 95)
```

Now, the preceding string looks like Netscape, but it is actually Microsoft's Internet Explorer 3.01 masquerading as Netscape. Microsoft created this agent to take advantage of early Web sites that delivered two versions of content: one for Netscape users with all the bells and whistles, and a plain one for everyone else.

Now consider this example:

```
Mozilla/2.0 (Compatible; AOL-IWENG 3.1; Win16)
```

Here's another impostor. This time, it's the AOL proprietary browser. AOL's browser began life as InternetWorks by BookLink, hence the IWENG name.

The following is yet another example:

```
Mozilla/3.01 (Macintosh; I; PPC)    via proxy gateway CERN-HTTPD/3.0
libwww/2.17
```

This one is really Netscape 3.01 on a PowerPC Mac. What's interesting about this agent is that the user was behind a Web proxy. The proxy tacked its name onto the actual agent string.

Again, many of the analysis programs discussed in this chapter process user_agent logs as well. If you want a quick way to process just the user_agent file, check out Chuck Musciano's nifty little sed scripts at

```
http://members.aol.com/htmlguru/agent_log.html
```

Error Logs

The second type of standard Web server activity log is the error log. The error log records server events, including startup and shutdown messages. The error log also records extended debugging information for each unsuccessful access request.

This data is generally kept in the `/logs` subdirectory with the `access_log`. The file is often called `error_log`. The specific directory and name vary depending on your server and are configurable in the `httpd.conf` file.

Most events recorded in the error log are not critical. Depending on your server and configuration, your server may log events like the following:

```
[02/May/1997:12:11:00 -0500] Error:  Cannot access file
/usr/people/www/pages/artfile.html.  File does not exist.
```

This message simply means that the requested file could not be found on the disk. The problem could be a bad link or improper permissions settings, or a user could be requesting outdated content.

Some entries in the error log can be useful in debugging CGI scripts. Some servers log anything written by a script to `stderr` as an error event. By watching your error logs, you can identify failing scripts. Some of the common errors that indicate script failures include

- `Attempt to invoke directory as script.`
- `File does not exist.`
- `Invalid CGI ref.`
- `Malformed header from script.`
- `Script not found or unable to stat.`

Basic Analysis

The simplest measure of your server activity is to execute the following command:

```
wc -l access_log
```

This command returns a single number that represents the total accesses to your server since the log was created. Unfortunately, this number includes many accesses you might not want to count, including errors and redirects. It also doesn't give you much useful information.

By judicious use of SED, GREP, shell scripting, or piping, you can create a much more interesting output. For example, if you were tracking hits to a certain advertisement graphic, you could use the following:

```
grep ad1.gif access_log ¦ wc -l
```

By issuing ever more complex commands, you can begin to gather really useful information about usage on your site. These scripts are time-consuming to write, execute slowly, and have to be revised every time you want to extract a different statistic. Unless you have a specific statistic you need to gather in a certain format, you will probably be better off using one of the many analysis programs on the market. You examine a few of them later in this chapter.

General Statistics

Figure 37.1 shows the general statistics derived from my access log by my favorite analysis program, Analog. I talk at more length about Analog in the "Analysis Tools" section of this chapter. Other tools may give slightly different output, but Analog produces a good variety of basic statistics and is easy to use.

FIGURE 37.1.

General statistics.

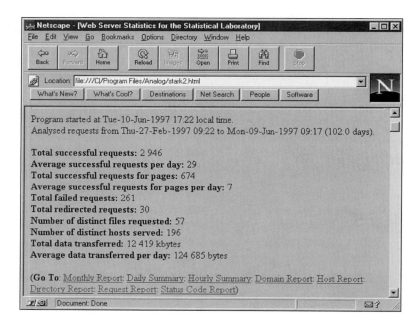

The general statistics section gives a good snapshot of traffic on your server. As you can see in the figure, the analysis program has summarized several categories of requests, including

- Successful requests
- Successful requests for pages
- Failed requests
- Redirected requests

You might also get average hits per day, total unique hosts or files, and an analysis of the total bytes served.

> **NOTE**
>
> If you plan to use your log analysis for advertising or content programming, be sure you know the difference between *hits* and *impressions*. Hits represent all the accesses on your server, whereas impressions represent only the accesses to a specific piece of information or advertisement. Most people count impressions by counting only actual hits to the HTML page containing the content or graphics.

By watching for changes in this information, you can see when you are having unusually high numbers of errors, and you can watch the growth of your traffic overall. Of course, taking this snapshot and comparing the numbers manually every day gets tiresome, so most analysis tools allow some kind of periodic reports.

Periodic Reporting

Analysis tools provide a variety of reports that count usage over a specific period of time. Most of these reports count total hits per period, although the more advanced tools allow you to run reports on specific files or groups of files. Each of the periodic reports has a specific use.

- Monthly report—Figure 37.2 shows a monthly report for my Web site for five months. Monthly reports are good for long-term trend analysis and planning. Also, seasonal businesses may see patterns in the monthly reports: Retail Web sites can expect a big bump during Christmas, and educational sites will have a drop during the summer months. This is often thought of as the Webmaster's most important log for trend analysis.

- Daily report—Figure 37.3 shows the daily summary for the same five-month period. This report can show trends over the week. Most sites show either a midweek or weekend focus, depending on content. Some analysis programs allow you to break this report out by date as well as day, so that you can see the trends across several weeks.

FIGURE 37.2.
Monthly report.

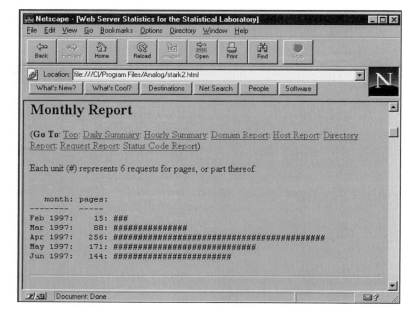

FIGURE 37.3.
Daily report.

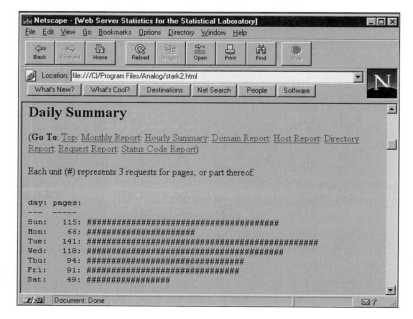

- Hourly report—Figure 37.4 shows my hourly summary. This report is most useful for determining the daily peak. Heavy Web use generally begins at 6 p.m., grows to an 11 p.m. peak, and then continues heavily until 1 a.m. A lunchtime usage spike also occurs as workers surf the Net on their lunch hours. This report is crucial to scaling your site.

FIGURE 37.4.

Hourly report.

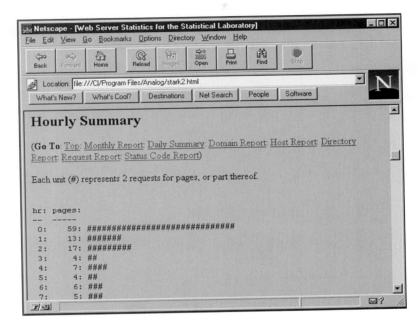

Some analysis programs also allow you to run reports for specific periods of time in whatever units you may need.

Demographic Reporting

Before you get excited, be informed: In most cases, you cannot get personal demographics information from your Web logs. You can't get users' age, sex, or income level without explicitly asking.

> **TIP**
>
> If your friends in marketing would like real demographics on the average Web user, check out the Commercenet/Nielsen Internet user demographics survey at
>
> `http://www.commerce.net/nielsen/index.html`

You can get the following information out of the basic Web logs:

- Source domain—Most reporting programs give you a breakdown of what domains users are coming from. This information can help you determine both the commercial and educational usage of your site and the international usage of your site. For an example, look at Figure 37.5.

FIGURE 37.5.

Domain report.

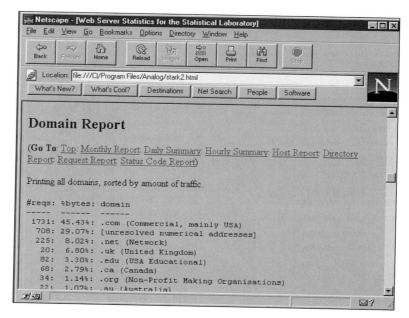

- Host report—A related report is the "host report." It shows specifically which host sent you access requests. In some cases, you might recognize hostnames belonging to friends (or competitors). Most sites have several hosts with strange numerical hostnames. They are often dynamically assigned IP addresses from ISPs. Also, look for names like `*.proxy.aol.com`, which indicate users coming through a proxy system, and `spider6.srv.pgh.lycos.com`, which indicate a Web crawler from a major search engine.

> **TIP**
>
> Many Web servers give you the option either to log the user's IP address or to look up the actual hostname at the time of access. Many analysis programs perform a lookup for you as they analyze the logs. The choice is yours, and the trade-off is speed: Either you have a small delay with every hit as the server does the lookup or a big delay in processing as the analysis program looks up every single address.

Page Reporting

One of the most interesting questions you can ask of your logs is this: What do people look at most on my Web site? Figures 37.6 and 37.7 show the reports that answer this question.

- Directory report—If you organize your content correctly, the directory report can give you a quick overview of the popular sections of your Web site. Another good use for this report is to separate out image hits; you can store all the images in a single directory, and the remaining hits will reflect only content impressions.

FIGURE 37.6.

Host report.

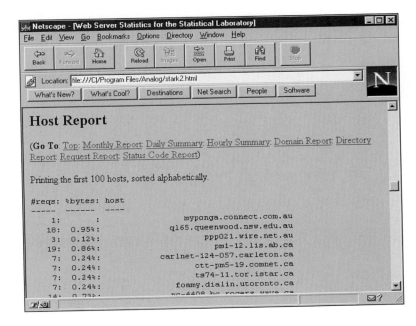

- Request report—Possibly the most useful report you can generate, the request report shows hits to individual pages. Note that some pages are miscounted by this report. For example, the root directory / redirects to index.html. To get an accurate count for this page, you need to add the two counts together.

FIGURE 37.7.

Directory report.

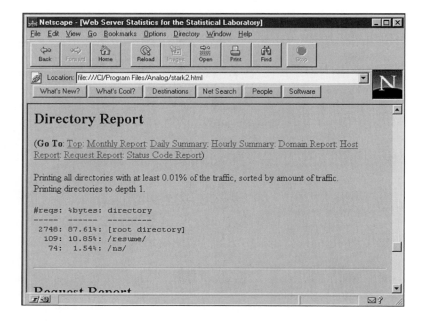

Advanced Analysis

The basic reports I've talked about merely summarize the access logs in different ways. Some more advanced analysis methods look for patterns in the log entries. Two useful patterns that the access log entries can produce are user sessions and session paths.

Sessioning

Some advanced analysis programs allow you to try to distinguish *unique visits* to your site. These programs usually define a session as a series of requests from a specific IP address within a certain period of time. After a session is defined, the program can give you additional information about the session. Over time, you can gather aggregate information that may be useful for marketing and planning, including

- Total unique visitors per period of time
- Average total session duration
- Average pages visited per session

Sessioning is not an exact science. If multiple users come from the same IP address during the same period, those hits can't be used for sessioning. Therefore, users from online services that use Web proxies (including AOL and Prodigy) can't be tracked with sessioning. Also, dynamic IP addresses that are frequently reassigned can't be reliably tracked by sessioning. Despite these weaknesses, you may still be able to gain some interesting information from an analysis program that allows sessioning.

Pathing

If you can identify a specific user session, you can follow that user's path from page to page as he or she navigates through your Web site. Advanced analysis programs look at each session and find the most frequently followed paths. Experienced Webmasters use this data to determine the most popular entry pages, the most popular exit pages, and the most common navigation paths. Pathing is sometimes also called "clickthrough."

Log Accuracy

Your Web server logs provide a wealth of useful data to Webmasters, marketers, and advertisers. Unfortunately, the raw log by itself is not a reliable source for accurate counts of your site usage. A number of factors can cause the output of reports run on your raw logs to be significantly overstated or understated.

If your log understates usage, it can quickly cause measurable damage to your bottom line. Imagine if you run an advertising-supported Web site, and your ad impressions are 10 percent off. Imagine if you have carefully scaled your Web site to perform well under peak load, as forecasted by your raw logs, only to find that you are under-built by up to 25 percent! In the following sections, I describe some causes of these inaccuracies and ways to mitigate those risks.

Adjusting for Caching

The biggest problem that affects your log accuracy is content caching. If a piece of content is cached, it is served to the user from a store, either locally on the user's hard drive or from an ISP's proxy system. When content is served from a cache, often no request is made to your server, so you never see any entry in your logs.

In most cases, caching is a good thing: It improves the user experience, lessens the load on the Net, and even saves you money in hardware and network costs. You might want to optimize your site to take advantage of caching, but before you do, consider the effects that caching will have on your log files. In fact, in only a few cases will you want to consider defeating a caching system:

- Advertising—If you run an ad-supported Web site, every ad impression is directly related to revenue. Although you might be able to defeat caching of your ads in some cases, your best bet is to employ an actual ad server that handles rotating the ads. These ad servers usually have built-in capability to defeat some caching systems.

- Dynamic content—Most content is updated only every few hours or days. For this kind of content, you probably don't need to worry about caching. A few hours of updating should not affect the timeliness of your data. But if your data truly updates every few minutes (for example, stock quotes), you might want to defeat caching. Note that you want to defeat the cache only for the HTML page itself; let the graphics be cached.

- Secure data—You may be handling sensitive data that you do not want saved in a proxy or local cache. Note that most proxy systems and browsers do not cache SSL-encrypted data at all, so if you're using this form of security, you are already taken care of.

If you want to take advantage of your user's proxy and local cache, try to determine what percentage of your hits are understated because of the cache. You can then use this figure as a rule of thumb for future analysis.

Local Caching

Most Web browsers keep a local cache of content and serve out of that cache whenever possible. Some browsers send a special kind of request called a `"get-if-modified-since"` that, in effect, asks the server whether the document has been updated. If the server finds that the document has been updated, it returns the new document. If it finds that the document is the same, it returns a status code `304`. Status code `304` tells the browser to serve the document out of the cache.

TIP

According to FIND/SVP, as much as one-third of all Web traffic originates with America Online users. Depending on your audience, a significant proportion of your traffic might be coming from behind AOL's caching system and through its proprietary browser. For the inside scoop on how to best program for that environment, check out AOL's Web site at

`http://webmaster.info.aol.com`

The site contains details on AOL's browsers, proxy system, and other useful stuff.

Some browsers support methods of defeating the cache on a page-by-page basis. You should use these methods sparingly; caching is your friend! By inserting the following HTTP headers, you might be able to defeat caching for the pages that follow them:

HTTP 1.0 header: `Pragma: no-cache`

HTTP 1.0 header: `Expires: Thu, 01 Dec 1997 16:00:00 GMT`

HTTP 1.0 header: `Expires: now`

HTTP 1.1 header: `Cache-Control: no-cache`

HTTP 1.1 header: `Cache-Control: no-store`

Proxy Caching

Many corporations and large ISPs, including America Online, use a caching proxy for their members' Web access. Besides the normal security role of a proxy, these servers keep a copy of some content closer to the members. This way, these ISPs can provide faster Web service and significantly ease the load on the Internet.

Proxy caches can be configured to keep content for a certain length of time or until the file reaches a certain age. If you want to ensure that your content is not cached, you can try several things. First, many caching proxies follow the instructions of the expires and cache-control headers listed in the preceding section. In addition, some proxies do not cache any requests that contain `cgi-bin` or a question mark because these characters usually denote dynamic, script-generated pages.

> **CAUTION**
>
> Each ISP has different "rules" for what is cached and for how long. Some follow all the rules outlined previously, and some follow none. To make things worse, some ISPs occasionally *change* their caching rules. If you're concerned about your content being held in a proxy cache, you should periodically test to see whether your content is cached by that ISP.

Analysis Tools

As you saw earlier in the chapter, you can analyze your logs manually using a wide variety of text manipulation tools. This kind of analysis gets tedious, however, and is difficult to maintain. To get the most useful data from your Web server logs, you will probably want to invest the time and money to choose, install, and use a Web server analysis tool.

Choosing an Analysis Tool

Literally hundreds of analysis tools are on the market, ranging from simple freeware Perl scripts to complicated database-driven applications. Because the market is so new, it's easy to become confused about exactly which features you need for your application. Before you select an analysis tool, be sure you know:

- What kind of analysis you intend to perform
- What format you prefer for the output
- How much enterprise support you need from the tool
- What platform you intend to use
- How large your log files will be

Type of Analysis

The most important question to ask yourself when evaluating analysis programs is "Exactly what information am I looking for?" If you are only looking for basic access analysis, such as hits over a specific period of time, or basic Web demographics, then almost any analysis program will suffice.

As your needs become more sophisticated, you'll need to make sure that your package supports advanced analysis features. Generally, advanced features such as pathing and sessioning are only available in commercial packages costing hundreds of dollars.

Output Quality

Analysis programs vary widely in the overall attractiveness of their report output. Almost all programs create HTML files as the primary output format, and many create graphs and tables within those pages. This kind of output is generally acceptable for your own analysis but falls short for some business applications.

If you intend to distribute your Web log reports to clients, partners, or investors, consider using a more advanced package that offers better page layout. Many commercial packages provide output in document formats (for example, Microsoft Word) with embedded color tables and graphs.

Enterprise Support

Most analysis programs are designed for the single server Web site. They expect to read only one log file and build relative links from only one home page. If your Web site spans more than one server, or you manage several different Web sites, you might want to consider getting an advanced analysis package.

Analysis programs that have "enterprise support" can handle multiple log files and can build reports that represent multiple Web sites. They allow you to group Web sites to present consolidated data across several servers. This kind of support, unfortunately, is mostly only found in the most expensive packages.

Platform

Not all analysis programs are available for all UNIX versions, and many are available only for Windows NT. If you are going to be running your analysis on the same machine as your Web server, you need to ensure that your analysis program is compatible with your UNIX version.

You don't necessarily have to run your analysis program on the same machine as your Web server. In fact, it might be desirable to have a different machine dedicated to this task. Log analysis can have a heavy impact on your machine performance, in both CPU utilization and disk usage. If you are going to have a machine specifically for log analysis, then you can get the hardware to support the software that has the features you like.

Speed

As your access logs quickly grow to several megabytes in size, analysis speed becomes an issue. Check to see how fast your analysis program claims to run against larger files: Most vendors will give you a metric measured in "megabytes processed per minute."

Log processing speed does not always grow linearly: As your logs get bigger, some analysis programs get progressively slower. Before you invest in an expensive processing program, test the performance on some real logs—and be aware that some of the fastest programs are freeware.

Popular Tools

Prices for analysis programs vary widely, but they tend to fall into one of three categories: freeware tools, single-site commercial products, and enterprise commercial packages.

Shareware/Freeware Analysis Tools

The quickest way to get into Web analysis is to download one of the capable pieces of freeware on the market. These programs can quickly digest your access logs and give you usable information immediately. In addition, source is often available for you to add your own special touches. They often lack some of the advanced features of the commercial tools, but try these out before you spend hundreds (or thousands) of dollars on another tool:

- getstats—Available on several UNIX platforms, getstats is the fastest of all the analyzers. It is also the hardest to configure and only generates basic analysis. But if you have a large log file and only need a quick snapshot of your usage, try this one out.

    (http://web.eit.com/goodies/software/getstats/)

- `http-analyze`—Almost as fast as `getstats`, and with much nicer output features. The latest version of this program does 3D VRML output and handles extended logs such as `user_agent` and `referrer`.

  (`http://www.netstore.de/Supply/http-analyze/`)

- `analog`—My personal favorite shareware analyzer, this program is available for UNIX, Windows, Mac, and (gasp) vms. Besides being pretty fast, `analog` handles extended logs and is extremely configurable.

  (`http://www.statslab.cam.ac.uk/~sret1/analog/`)

> **TIP**
>
> An extremely interesting write-up on the comparative performance of several freeware tools (complete with links to the home page of each tool) is available at:
>
> `www.uu.se/software/getstats/performance.html`

Commercial Analysis Tools

Most serious business applications eventually require a commercial analysis tool. Besides being more robust and feature rich, these products include upgrades and technical support that most MIS departments need. Prices on these packages can range from $295 to $5,000 and higher, depending on your installation. Many of the products are available for a free trial download on their Web sites so you can try before you buy.

- Accrue Insight—This totally unique software is the most expensive of all these packages, but it works differently than all the others. Instead of analyzing the logs themselves, it sits on the network and measures traffic between clients and your server.

  (`http://www.accrue.com`)

- Microsoft Site Server—Formerly Interse Market Focus, this package has a SQL server back end and provides one of the most robust feature sets on the market. This comes at a price, however.

  (`http://www.backoffice.microsoft.com`)

- Whirl—A newcomer to the market, this package is optimized to support multiserver enterprises. The system creates data sets in Microsoft Excel that can then be manipulated for optimal reporting.

  (`http://www.interlogue.com`)

- Web Trends—The leading single-server/intranet solution, this Windows package has an easy-to-use UI for its extensive features. The latest version of this software has a report caching technology that allows quick repeat runs of large logs. It can also be scheduled to run periodically as a windows NT service.

  (http://www.webtrends.com)

- Net.analysis—This product is a single-server analyzer that provides extensive real-time or batch mode site activity reports.

  (http://www.netgen.com)

- Net Tracker—This comes with preconfigured with standardized Internet and intranet configurations, with up to 21 different reports. It is available with most versions of UNIX, as well and Windows NT, and it comes in three flavors: basic, professional, and enterprise.

  (http://www.sane.com)

- Wusage—This offers configurable daily, weekly, or monthly reports with supporting graphics. It supports both the common server log format and the Microsoft IIS log format. You can get reports on load by hour, popular documents, and frequently visited pages.

  (http://www.boutell.com)

Summary

In this chapter, you learned about tracking Web server usage. This data, which is primarily stored in the access and error logs, provides information that helps you scale, program, and advertise on your Web site.

The access log tracks each attempt request and provides you with the bulk of your server activity information. The extended logs help you track which browsers were most used to access your site and which sites passed the most traffic to you.

Basic analysis includes counting the entries in the access log in a number of different ways. The simplest statistics you can gather are summaries of different types of accesses, including successes and failures. Looking at traffic over time, in hourly, daily, and monthly reports, is also useful. Finally, the logs provide you with limited "demographic" information about your visitors, such as which country they are in and whether they are from commercial or educational institutions.

Advanced analysis involves looking for patterns in the accesses. Sessioning is the process of identifying unique visits and determining the duration and character of the visit. Pathing is looking for the most common navigational paths users took during their visit.

Unfortunately, the access logs are not necessarily reliable sources of data. Several factors can affect your log's accuracy, most importantly caching. Local caching and proxy caching can both cause your log numbers to be understated.

Finally, you learned about several tools available to assist you in analyzing your server activity. Many tools are freely available over the Net, whereas others are commercial products that include support and upgrades. Some companies download, audit, and process your logs for you for a monthly fee.

Glossary

by Robin Burk and David B. Horvath, CCP

This section contains a fairly extensive glossary. This is a selection of words that are related to the UNIX environment and their definitions. The authors of this book contributed words pertinent to their chapters to this section.

> **NOTE**
>
> The language of the computer field is constantly expanding. If you cannot find a word in this section, either it is newer than anything the authors knew about or the authors decided it was so obvious that "everyone should already know it."

Glossary of Terms

$HOME   Environment variable that points to your login directory.

$PATH   The shell environment variable that contains a set of directories to be searched for UNIX commands.

GLOSSARY

/dev/null file   The place to send output that you are not interested in seeing; also the place to get input from when you have none (but the program or command requires something). This is also known as the bit bucket, which is where old bits go to die.

/etc/cshrc file   The file containing shell environment characteristics common to all users who use the C shell.

/etc/group file   This file contains information about groups, the users they contain, and passwords required for access by other users. The password may actually be in another file—the shadow group file—to protect it from attacks.

/etc/inittab file   The file that contains a list of active terminal ports for which UNIX will issue the login prompt. This also contains a list of background processes for UNIX to initialize. Some versions of UNIX use other files such as /etc/tty.

/etc/motd file   Message Of The Day file usually contains information the system administrator feels is important for you to know. This file is displayed when the user signs on the system.

/etc/passwd file   Contains user information and password. The password may actually be in another file—the shadow password file—to protect it from attacks.

/etc/profile   The file containing shell environment characteristics common to all users that use the Bourne and Korn shells.

abbreviation   (vi) User-defined character sequences that are expanded into the defined text string when typed during insert mode.

absolute pathname   The means used to represent the location of a file in a directory by specifying the exact location including all directories in the chain including the root.

APAR   Authorized Program Analysis Report.

API (Application Program Interface)   The specific method prescribed by a computer operating system, application, or third-party tool by which a programmer writing an application program can make requests of the operating system.

arguments   See *parameters*.

ARPA   See *DARPA*.

ASCII (American Standard Code for Information Interchange)   Used to represent characters in memory for most computers.

AT&T UNIX   Original version of UNIX developed at AT&T Bell Labs, which was later known as UNIX Systems Laboratories. Many current versions of UNIX are descendants; even BSD UNIX was derived from early AT&T UNIX.

attribute   The means of describing objects. The attributes for a ball might be: rubber, red, 3 cm in diameter. The behavior of the ball might be how high it bounces when thrown. Attribute is another name for the data contained within an object (class).

Awk   Programming language developed by A.V. Aho, P.J. Weinberger, and Brian W. Kernighan. The language is built on C syntax, includes the regular expression search facilities of grep, and adds the advanced string and array handling features that are missing from the C language. nawk, gawk, and POSIX awk are versions of this language.

background   Processes usually running at a lower priority and with their input disconnected from the interactive session. Any input and output are usually directed to a file or other process.

background process   An autonomous process that runs under UNIX without requiring user interaction.

backup   The process of storing the UNIX system, applications, and data files on removable media for future retrieval.

bash   bash stands for GNU Bourne Again shell, and is based on the Bourne shell, sh, the original command interpreter.

beep   Usually referred to in UNIX documentation as the *bell* (see *bell*).

bell   The character sent by a program to a terminal to indicate some kind of "error" condition; for example, in vi, pressing Esc to exit insert mode when you are already in command mode; actually the ^G character, which rather than displaying on the terminal instead causes it to sound an "alarm," which on ancient teletype terminals was implemented as a bell. Different terminals produce different sounds for their bells including one old video terminal that sounded like someone shifting gears without benefit of clutch.

binding   (emacs) The assignment of a *shift-key sequence* to an Emacs editing command.

block-special   A device file that is used to communicate with a block oriented I/O device. Disk and tape drives are examples of block devices. The block-special file refers to the entire device. You should not use this file unless you want to ignore the directory structure of the device (that is, if you are coding a device driver).

boot or boot up   The process of starting the operating system (UNIX).

BOS   Basic Operating System.

Bourne shell   The original standard user interface to UNIX that supported limited programming capability.

BSD UNIX   Version of UNIX developed by Berkeley Software Distribution and written at UC Berkeley.

buffer (vi) The working version of the file you are editing is usually called the *buffer*; the buffer is actually an image of the file kept in random access memory during editing; changes are made in this image and only written out to disk upon user command (or when the vi autowrite setting is in effect); see also *named buffer* and *undo buffer.*

buffer list (emacs) A special window that shows all the buffers currently open; allows you to manipulate buffers using buffer list commands.

C Programming language developed by Brian W. Kernighan and Dennis M. Ritchie. The C language is highly portable and available on many platforms including mainframes, PCs, and, of course, UNIX systems.

C shell A user interface for UNIX written by Bill Joy at Berkeley. It also features C programming-like syntax.

CD-ROM (Compact Disk-Read Only Memory) Computer-readable data stored on the same physical form as a musical CD. Large capacity, inexpensive, slower than a hard disk, and limited to reading. There are versions that are writable (CD-R, CD Recordable) and other formats that can be written to once or many times.

CGI (Common Gateway Interface) A means of transmitting data between Web pages and programs or scripts executing on the server. Those programs can then process the data and send the results back to the user's browser through dynamically creating HTML.

character-special A device file that is used to communicate with character-oriented I/O devices such as terminals, printers, or network communications lines. All I/O access is treated as a series of bytes (characters).

characters

1. **alphabetic** The letters A through Z and a through z.
2. **alphanumeric** The letters A through Z and a through z, and the numbers 0 through 9.
3. **control** Any nonprintable characters. The characters are used to control devices, separate records, and eject pages on printers.
4. **numeric** The numbers 0 through 9.
5. **special** Any of the punctuation characters or printable characters that are not alphanumeric. Includes the space, comma, period, and many others.

child-process See *subprocess.*

child-shell See *subshell.*

class   A model of objects that have attributes (data) and behavior (code or functions). It is also viewed as a collection of objects in their abstracted form.

command line   (1) The shell command line from which the current vi or Emacs session was started; (2) the ex command line, where ex commands are entered.

command-line editing   UNIX shells support the capability to recall a previously entered command, modify it, and then execute the new version. The command history can remain between sessions (the commands you did yesterday can be available for you when you log in today). Some shells support a command-line editing mode that uses a subset of the vi, emacs, or gmacs editor commands for command recall and modification.

command-line history   See *command-line editing.*

command line parameters   Used to specify parameters to pass to the execute program or procedure. Also known as command-line arguments.

command prompt   See *shell prompt.*

completion   (emacs) The automatic provision of the rest of a command or a filename; when the command or filename cannot be resolved to a single entity, a menu of choices is provided (type a few characters of the name and press Tab; Emacs either completes the name or gives you a menu of choices).

configuration files   Collections of information used to initialize and set up the environment for specific commands and programs. Shell configuration files set up the user's environment.

configuration files, shell

For Bourne shell: /etc/profile and $HOME/.profile.

For Korn shell: /etc/profile, $HOME/.profile, and ENV= file.

For C shell: /etc/.login, /etc/cshrc, $HOME/.login, $HOME/.cshrc, and $HOME/.logout. Older versions may not support the first two files listed.

For bash: /etc/profile/, $HOME/.bash_profile, $HOME/.bash_login, $HOME/.profile, $HOME/.bashrc, ~/.bash_logout.

control keys   These are keys that cause some function to be performed instead of displaying a character. These functions have names, for instance, the end-of-file key tells the UNIX that there is no more input. The typical end-of-file key is the <^D> (control-d) key.

CPU (Central Processing Unit)   The primary "brain" of the computer; the calculation engine and logic controller.

current macro   (emacs) The most recently recorded macro; it is executed by the call-last-kbd-macro function.

cursor   The specific point on the screen where the next editing action will take place; the cursor is usually indicated on the screen by some sort of highlighting, such as an underscore or a solid block, which may or may not be blinking.

daemon   A system-related background process that often runs with the permissions of root and services requests from other processes. Daemons typically remain active whenever UNIX is booted and provide important coordination and resource handling. See *inetd* for the daemon that supports Internet networking.

DARPA (U.S. Department of Defense Advanced Research Projects Agency)   Funded development of TCP/IP and ARPAnet (predecessor of the Internet).

database server   See *server, database*.

default settings   Most tools and systems are governed by a number of settings; those that are in effect when the tool is started are known as the default. vi is governed by a number of *settings*; the *default settings* are those in effect when vi is first started, and no automatic overrides of settings are in effect through .exrc files or EXINIT environment variables.

device file   File used to implement access to a physical device. This provides a consistent approach to access of storage media under UNIX—data files and devices (such as tapes and communication facilities) are implemented as files. To the programmer, there is no real difference.

directory   A means of organizing and collecting files together. The directory itself is a file that consists of a list of files contained within it. The root (/) directory is the top level, and every other directory is contained in it (directly or indirectly). A directory might contain other directories, which are known as subdirectories.

directory navigation   The process of moving through directories is known as navigation. Your current directory is known as the current working directory. Your login directory is known as the default or home directory. Using the cd command, you can move up and down through the tree structure of directories.

DNS (Domain Name Server)   Used to convert the name of a machine on the Internet (*name.domain.com*) to the numeric address (123.45.111.123).

DOS (Disk Operating System)   Operating system based on the use of disks for the storage of commands. It is also a generic name for MS-DOS and PC-DOS on the Personal Computer. MS-DOS is the version Microsoft sells, and PC-DOS is the version IBM sells. Both are based on Microsoft code.

EBCDIC (Extended Binary Coded Decimal Interchange Code)   The code used to represent characters in memory for mainframe computers.

echo   The display on the screen of characters you type is sometimes called the *echo* of characters; it is called this because usually your terminal is set up not to display the characters directly as typed, but rather to wait for them to be sent to the computer, which then *echoes* (sends) them back to your terminal.

ed   A common tool used for line-oriented text editing.

email   Messages sent through an electronic medium instead of through the local postal service. There are many proprietary email systems that are designed to handle mail within a LAN environment; most of these are also capable of sending over the Internet. Most Internet (open) email systems use MIME to handle attached data (which can be binary).

emacs   A freely available editor now part of the GNU software distribution. Originally written by Richard M. Stallman at MIT in the late 1970s, it is available for many platforms. It is extremely extensible and has its own programming language; the name stands for Editing with `MACroS.encapsulation`.

encapsulation   The process of combining data (attributes) and functions (behavior in the form of code) into an object. The data and functions are closely coupled within an object. Instead of every programmer being able to access the data in a structure his own way, programmers have to use the code connected with that data. This promotes code reuse and standardized methods of working with the data.

environment variables   See *variables, environmental.*

escape   (1) (`vi`) The Esc key, used to terminate insert mode, or an incomplete `vi` command; (2) To prevent a character from having its normal interpretation by a program by preceding it with the *escape* character (usually \, the backslash); for example in a regular expression, to search for a literal character that has a special meaning in a regular expression, it must be escaped; as a specific example, to search for a period (.), you must type it escaped as \..

ethernet   A networking method where the systems are connected to a single shared bus and all traffic is available to every machine. The data packets contain an identifier of the recipient, which is the only machine that should process that packet.

expression   A constant, variable, or operands and operators combined. Used to set a value, perform a calculation, or set the pattern for a comparison (regular expressions).

fifo   First In, First Out. See *named pipe.*

file   Collection of bytes stored on a device (typically a disk or tape). Can be source code, executable binaries or scripts, or data.

1. **indexed**   A file based on a file structure where data can be retrieved based on specific keys (name, employee number, and so on) or sequentially. The keys are stored in an index. This is not directly supported by the UNIX operating system; usually implemented by the programmer or by using tools from an ISV. A typical form is known as ISAM.

2. **line sequential**   See *file, text.*

3. **sequential**

    1. A file that can only be accessed sequentially (not randomly).

    2. A file without record separators. Typically fixed length, but UNIX does not know what that length is and does not care.

4. **text**   A file with record separators. May be fixed or variable length; UNIX tools can handle these files because it can tell when the record ends (by the separator).

file compression   The process of applying mathematical formula to data typically resulting in a form of the data that occupies less space. A compressed file can be uncompressed (lossless) resulting in the original file. When the compression/uncompress process results in exactly the same file as was originally compressed, it is known as *lossless*. If information about the original file is lost, the compression method is known as *lossy*. Data and programs need lossless compression; images and sounds can stand lossy compression.

filename   The name used to identify a collection of data (a file). Without a pathname, it is assumed to be in the current directory.

filename generation   The process of the shell interpreting metacharacters (wildcards) to produce a list of matching files. This is referred to as filename expansion or globbing.

filename, fully qualified   The name used to identify a collection of data (a file) and its location. It includes both the path and name of the file; typically, the pathname is fully specified (absolute). See also *pathname* and *pathname, absolute.*

file system   A collection of disk storage that is connected (mounted) to the directory structure at some point (sometimes at the root). File systems are stored in a disk partition and are also referred to as disk partitions.

firewall   A system used to provide a controlled entry point to the internal network from the outside (usually the Internet). This is used to prevent outside or unauthorized systems from accessing systems on your internal network. The capability depends on the individual software package, but the features typically include filter packets and filter datagrams, provide system (name or IP address) aliasing and reject packets from certain IP addresses. It can also prevent internal systems from accessing the Internet on the outside.

In theory, it provides protection from malicious programs or people on the outside. The name comes from the physical barrier between connected buildings or within a single building that is supposed to prevent fire from spreading from one to another.

flags   See *options*.

foreground   Programs running while connected to the interactive session.

`fseek`   Internal function used by UNIX to locate data inside a file or file system. ANSI standard `fseek` accepts a parameter that can hold a value of +2 to -2 billion. This function, used by the operating system, system tools, and application programs, is the cause of the 2 GB file and file system size limitation on most systems. With 64-bit operating systems, this limit is going away.

FTP (File Transfer Protocol, or File Transfer Program)   A system-independent means of transferring files between systems connected via TCP/IP. Ensures that the file is transferred correctly, even if there are errors during transmission. Can usually handle character set conversions (ASCII/EBCDIC) and record terminator resolution (`<lf>` for UNIX, `<cr>` and `<lf>` for MS/PC-DOS).

gateway   A combination of hardware, software, and network connections that provides a link between one architecture and another. Typically, a gateway is used to connect a LAN or UNIX server with a mainframe (that uses SNA for networking resulting in the name: SNA gateway). A gateway can also be the connection between the internal and external network (often referred to as a firewall). See also *firewall*.

globbing   See *filename generation*.

GNU   GNU stands for GNU's Not UNIX and is the name of free, useful software packages commonly found in UNIX environments that are being distributed by the GNU project at MIT, largely through the efforts of Richard Stallman.

`grep`   A common tool used to search a file for a pattern. `egrep` and `fgrep` are newer versions. `egrep` allows the use of extended (hence the "e" prefix) regular expressions; `fgrep` uses limited expressions for a faster (hence the "f" prefix) searches.

here document   The << redirection operator, known as here document, allows keyboard input (`stdin`) for the program to be included in the script.

HTML (Hypertext Markup Language)   Describes World Wide Web pages. It is the document language used to define the pages available on the Internet through the use of tags. A browser interprets the HTML to display the desired information.

HTTP (Hypertext Transfer Protocol)   The data communications protocol that supports distribution of, and access to, HTML and other Internet document formats. Also

used as a shorthand to refer to the server process that supports this protocol.**i-node**
Used to describes a file and its storage. The directory contains a cross reference between
the i-node and pathname/filename combination. Also known as *inode*.

I-Phone (Internet Phone)   A method of transmitting speech long distances over the
Internet in near real-time allowing the participants to avoid paying long distance telephone charges. They still pay for the call to their ISP and the ISP's service charges.

ICMP (Internet Control Message Protocol)   Part of TCP/IP that provides network layer
management and control.

`inetd`   The Internet daemon, a background process that manages connection resources
for Internet data communications protocols.

inheritance   A method of object-oriented software reuse in which new classes are
developed based on existing ones by using the existing attributes and behavior and
adding on to them. For example, if the base object is automobile with attributes of an
engine, four wheels, and tires, and behavior of acceleration, turning, and deceleration,
then a sports car would modify the attributes so that the engine would be larger or have
more horsepower than the default; the four wheels would include alloy wheels and high-
speed rated tires; and the behavior would also be modified for faster acceleration, tighter
turning radius, and faster deceleration.

inode   See *i-node*.

Internet   A collection of different networks that provide the capability to move data
between them. It is built on the TCP/IP communications protocol. Originally developed
by DARPA, it was taken over by NSF and has now been released from governmental
control.

Internet service provider   A company that allows you to establish a dialup connection
to their servers to access the Internet and Internet services such as the World Wide Web.

IRC (Internet Relay Chat)   A server-based application that allows groups of people to
communicate simultaneously through text-based conversations. IRC is similar to Citizen
Band radio or the "chat rooms" on some bulletin boards. Some chats can be private
(between invited people only) or public (where anyone can join in). IRC now also supports sound files as well as text—it can also be useful for file exchange.

ISAM (Indexed Sequential Access Method)   On UNIX and other systems, ISAM
refers to a method for accessing data in a keyed or sequential way. The UNIX operating
system does not directly support ISAM files; they are typically add-on products.

ISP   See *Internet service provider*.

ISV (Independent Software Vendor)   Generic name for software vendors other than your hardware vendor.

kernel   The core of the operating system that handles tasks such as memory allocation, device input and output, process allocation, security, and user access. UNIX tends to have a small kernel when compared to other operating systems.

keyboard macros   A feature that allows a special key sequence to stand for another, usually more complex sequence; in `vi`, keyboard macros are implemented via the `:map` command.

kill ring   (`emacs`) A set of buffers where killed text is kept; the buffers are arranged in a circular pattern. When commands that automatically move from one buffer to the next get to the end of the set, the next movement will be to the first buffer in the ring.

Korn shell   A user interface for UNIX with extensive scripting (programming) support written by David G. Korn. The shell features command-line editing and also accepts scripts written for the Bourne shell.

LAN (local area network)   A collection of networking hardware, software, desktop computers, servers, and hosts all connected together within a defined local area. A LAN could be an entire college campus.

limits   See *quota*.

line address   (vi and ex) The way a selected set of lines is indicated in `ex` mode is through a line address. A line address can be an absolute line number, relative line number, or special symbols that refer to the beginning of the file.

link

1. **hard**   Directory entry that provides an alias to another file that is in the same file system. Multiple entries appear in the directory (or other directories) for one physical file without replication of the contents.

2. **soft**   See *symbolic link*.

3. **symbolic**   Directory entry that provides an alias to another file that can be in another file system. Multiple entries appear in the directory for one physical file without replication of the contents. Implemented through link files.

4. **file**   File used to implement a symbolic link producing an alias on one file system for a file on another. The file only contains the fully qualified filename of the original (linked-to) file.

lisp   A programming language used in artificial intelligence. The name stands for LISt Processing. It is the programming language that `Emacs` is written in and also refers to three major modes within it.

literal text string   An exact character text string, with no wildcards.

login   The process through which a user gains access to a UNIX system. This can also refer to the user ID that is typed at the login prompt.

LPP   Licensed Program Product.

macro   A recorded series of keystrokes that can be played back to accomplish the same task repetitively.

major mode   (emacs) A named set of behavioral characteristics; a buffer can be in only one major mode at a time. For examples, *text mode* for writing a letter; *C mode* for writing C source code.

man page   Online reference tool under UNIX that contains the documentation for the system—the actual pages from the printed manuals. It is stored in a searchable form for improved capability to locate information.

manual page   See *man page*.

mappings   (vi) User-defined character sequences (which may include control keys) that are interpreted as a command sequence (which may also include control keys).

memory

1. **real**   The amount of storage that is being used within the system (silicon; it used to be magnetic cores).

2. **virtual**   Memory that exists but you cannot see. Secondary storage (disk) is used to allow the operating system to allow programs to use more memory than is physically available.
   Part of a disk is used as a paging file, and portions of programs and their data are moved between it and real memory. To the program, it is in real memory. The hardware and operating system perform translation between the memory address the program thinks it is using and where it is actually stored.

metacharacter   A printing character that has special meaning to the shell or another command. It is converted into something else by the shell or command—the asterisk <*> is converted by the shell to a list of all files in the current directory.

MIME (Multipurpose Internet Mail Extensions)   A set of formats for binary data to be exchanged over networks. Originally intended for attachments to email messages, MIME now serves as a common format definition for most data exchanged over the Internet.

mini-buffer   (emacs) The last line on the screen, where commands are entered.

minor mode (emacs) A particular characteristic that can be independently toggled on or off. For example, *auto-fill mode* for easing the creation of document text.

mode Many programs offer only subsets of their functions at any given time because only certain functions are relevant within an immediate context; further, the same keystroke may invoke different commands in these different contexts; such a context is referred to as a *mode*. Major modes in vi are *insert mode* (for adding new text into the buffer), and *command mode* (for most other editing actions).

MPTN (Multiprotocol Transport Network) IBM networking protocol to connect mainframe to TCP/IP network.

named buffer (vi) A memory location where text objects can be stored during a single vi session; *named buffers* persist when you switch from one file to another during a session and are the primary way of moving and copying text between files.

named pipe An expanded function of a regular pipe (redirecting the output of one program to become the input of another). Instead of connecting stdout to stdin, the output of one program is sent to the named pipe, and another program reads data from the same file. This is implemented through a special file known as a pipe file or fifo. The operating system ensures the proper sequencing of the data. Little or no data is actually stored in the pipe file; it just acts as a connection between the two.

Netnews This is a loosely controlled collection of discussion groups. A message (similar to an email) is posted in a specific area and then people can comment on it, publicly replying to the same place ("posting a response") for others to see. A collection of messages along the same theme is referred to as a thread. Some of the groups are moderated, which means that nothing is posted without the approval of the "owner." Most are not, and the title of the group is no guarantee that the discussion will be related. The official term for this is *Usenet News*.

NFS (Network File System) Means of connecting disks that are mounted to a remote system to the local system as if they were physically connected.

NIS (Network Information Service) A service that provides information necessary to all machines on a network, such as NFS support for hosts and clients, password verification, and so on.

NNTP (Net News Transport Protocol) Used to transmit Netnews or Usenet messages over top of TCP/IP. See *Netnews* for more information on the messages transmitted.

null statement A program step that performs no operation but to hold space and fulfill syntactical requirements of the programming language. Also known as a NO-OP for no-operation performed.

numeric setting   A setting that takes a numeric value, rather than an enabled or disabled state. Applies to many tools including `vi` and the different shells.

object   An object in the truest sense of the word is something that has physical properties, such as automobiles, rubber balls, and clouds. These things have attributes and behavior. They can be abstracted into data (attribute) and code (behavior). Instead of just writing functions to work on data, they are encapsulated into a package that is known as an object.

ODM   Object Database Manager.

open mode   The visual mode of the `ex` editor.

operator   Metacharacter that performs a function on values or variables. The plus sign `<+>` is an operator that adds two integers.

options   Program- or command-specific indicators that control behavior of that program. Sometimes called flags. The `-a` option to the `ls` command shows the files that begin with a `.` (such as `.profile`, `.kshrc`, and so on). Without it, these files would not be shown, no matter what wildcards were used. These are used on the command line. See also *parameters*.

package   (`emacs`) A feature set that can be added to the editor. Major modes and many functions are implemented via packages. Numerous packages are built in to standard `Emacs`; many others are freely or otherwise available.

parameters   Data passed to a command or program through the command line. These can be options (see *options*) that control the command or arguments that the command works on. Some have special meaning based on their position on the command line.

parent process identifier   Shown in the heading of the `ps` command as PPID. The process identifier of the parent-process. See also *parent-process*.

parent-process   Process that controls another often referred to as the child- or subprocess. See *process*.

parent-shell   Shell (typically the login shell) that controls another, often referred to as the child- or subshell. See *shell*.

password   The secure code that is used in combination with a user ID to gain access to a UNIX system.

pathname   The means used to represent the location of a file in the directory structure. If you do not specify a pathname, it defaults to the current directory. Also see *absolute pathname* and *relative pathname*.

PDP (Personal Data Processor)   Computers manufactured by Digital Equipment Corporation. UNIX was originally written for a PDP-7 and gained popularity on the

PDP-11. The entire series were inexpensive minicomputers popular with educational institutions and small businesses.

Perl (Practical Extraction and Report Language)   Programming language developed by Larry Wall. (Perl stands for Practical Extraction and Report Language or Pathologically Eclectic Rubbish Language, both are equally valid). The language provides all the capabilities of awk and sed, plus many features of the shells and C.

permissions   When applied to files, they are the attributes that control access to a file. There are three levels of access: owner (the file creator), group (people belonging to a related group as determined by the system administrator), and other (everyone else). The permissions may be r for read, w for write, and x for execute. The execute permissions flag is also used to control who may search a directory.

pipe   A method of sending the output of one program (redirecting) to become the input of another. The pipe character <¦> tells the shell to perform the redirection.

pipe file   See *named pipe*.

polymorphism   A characteristic of C++ and other object-oriented languages, associated with *inheritance*. Polymporphic languages allow a daughter class to override the behavior of a method so as to customize that behavior for the specific requirements of the subclass. For instance, the method for division of integers might have restrictions compared to the general division method for all numbers.**POSIX**   POSIX stands for Portable Operating System Interface, UNIX. It is the name for a family of open system standards based on UNIX. The name has been credited to Richard Stallman. The POSIX Shell and Utilities standard developed by IEEE Working Group 1003.2 (POSIX.2) concentrates on the command interpreter interface and utility programs.

PPP (Point-to-Point Protocol)   Internet protocol over serial link (modem).

process   A discrete running program under UNIX. The user's interactive session is a process. A process can invoke (run) and control another program that is then referred to as a subprocess. Ultimately, everything a user does is a subprocess of the operating system.

process identifier   Shown in the heading of the ps command as PID. The unique number assigned to every process running in the system.

protocol   The rules by means of which programs can communicate. Used most often for data communications protocols. Open protocols (those that are not specific to a given vendor) enable the development of open systems such as UNIX.

protocol stack   A set of related data communications protocols that work together to provide several layers of functionality. For instance, the Transport Control Protocol

(TCP) relies on the Internet Protocol (IP) and other associated protocols for lower level functionality.

PTF   Program Temporary Fix.

quota   General description of a system-imposed limitation on a user or process. It can apply to disk space, memory usage, CPU usage, maximum number of open files, and many other resources.

quoting   The use of single and double quotes to negate the normal command interpretation and concatenate all words and whitespace within the quotes as a single piece of text.

range   (vi, ed, and ex) a *line address* that indicates one or more lines from a starting line to an ending line; indicated as start,end where both *start* and *end* are individual line addresses.

recursive edit   (emacs) A feature that allows a query-replace operation to be temporarily suspended while other editing is done.

redirection   The process of directing a data flow from the default. Input can be redirected to get data from a file or the output of another program. Normal output can be sent to another program or a file. Errors can be sent to another program or a file.

regular expression   A way of specifying and matching strings for shells (filename wildcarding), grep (file searches), sed, and awk.

relative pathname   The means used to represent the location of a file in a directory other than the current by navigating up and down through other directories using the current directory as a base.

reserved word   A set of characters recognized by UNIX and related to a specific program, function, or command.

RFC (Request For Comment)   Document used for creation of Internet and TCP/IP related standards.

rlogin (Remote Login)   Gives the same functionality of telnet, with the added functionality of not requiring a password from trusted clients, which can also create security concerns. See *telnet*.

root   1) The user who owns the operating system and controls the computer. 2) The processes of the operating system run as though a user, root, signed on and started them. The root user is all powerful and can do anything he or she wants. For this reason, the root user is often referred to as a superuser. It is also the very top of the directory tree structure.

routing The process of moving network traffic between two different physical networks; also decides which path to take when there are multiple connections between the two machines. It may also send traffic around transmission interruptions.

RPC (Remote Procedural Call) Provides the capability to call functions or subroutines that run on a remote system from the local one.

scripts A program written for a UNIX utility including shells, Awk, Perl, `sed`, and others. Also see *shell scripts*.

sed A common tool used for stream text editing, having `ed`-like syntax.

server, database A system designated to run database software (typically a relational database such as Oracle, SQL Server, Sybase, or others). Other systems connect to this one to get the data (client applications).

settings `vi` is governed by a number of internal variables called *settings*; these control how certain actions take place.

shell The part of UNIX that handles user input and invokes other programs to run commands. Includes a programming language. See also *Bourne shell, C shell, Korn shell,* `tcsh`, and `bash`.

shell environment The shell program (Bourne, Korn, C, `tcsh`, or `bash`), invocation options, and preset variables that define the characteristics, features, and functionality of the UNIX command line and program execution interface.

shell buffer (emacs) A buffer in which an interactive UNIX shell session has been started.

shell scripts A program written using a shell programming language like those supported by Bourne, Korn, or C shells.

shift-key sequence (emacs) To perform a shift-key sequence, hold down the designated shift key (for example, *Shift, Ctrl, Alt,* or *Meta*), press the second designated key, and then release both keys. When typing several consecutive shift-key sequences that use the same shift key, you can keep holding down the shift key for the duration.

signal A special flag or interrupt that is used to communicate special events to programs by the operating system and other programs.

SLIP (Serial Line Internet Protocol) Internet over a serial link (modem). The protocol frames and controls the transmission of TCP/IP packets of the line.

SMIT System Management Interface Tool.

SNA(System Network Architecture)   IBM networking architecture.

special keys   See *control keys.*

`stderr`   The normal error output for a program that is sent to the screen by default. Can be redirected to a file.

`stdin`   The normal input for a program, taken from the keyboard by default. Can be redirected to get input from a file or the output of another program.

`stdout`   The normal output for a program that is sent to the screen by default. Can be redirected to a file or to the input of another program.

sticky bit   One of the status flags on a file that tells UNIX to load a copy of the file into the page file the first time it is executed. This is done for programs that are commonly used so the bytes are available quickly. When the sticky bit is used on frequently used directories, they are cached in memory.

stream   A sequential collection of data. All files are streams to the UNIX operating system. To it, there is no structure to a file—that is something imposed by application programs or special tools (ISAM packages or relational databases).

subdirectory   See *directory.*

subnet   A portion of a network that shares a common IP address component. Used for security and performance reasons.

subprocess   Process running under the control of another, often referred to as the parent-process. See *process.*

subshell   Shell running under the control of another, often referred to as the parent-shell (typically the login shell). See *shell.*

superuser   See *root.*

system administrator   The person who takes care of the operating system and user administrative issues on UNIX systems. Also called a system manager although that term is much more common in DEC VAX installations.

system manager   See *system administrator.*

system programmer   See *system administrator.*

TCP/IP (Transport Control Protocol/Internet Protocol)   The pair of protocols and also generic name for suite of tools and protocols that forms the basis for the Internet. Originally developed to connect systems to the ARPAnet. See *protocol stack.*

`tcsh`   A C shell-like user interface featuring command-line editing.

Telnet   Protocol for interactive (character user interface) terminal access to remote systems. The terminal emulator that uses the Telnet protocol is often known as `telnet` or `tnvt100`.

terminal   A hardware device, normally containing a cathode ray tube (screen) and keyboard for human interaction with a computer system.

text object   (`vi`) A text object is the portion of text in the buffer that would be traversed by a specific movement command; for example *w* refers to the next small word.

text processing languages   A way of developing documents in text editors with embedded commands that handle formatting. The file is fed through a processor that executes the embedded commands producing a formatted document. These include `roff`, `nroff`, `troff`, RUNOFF, TeX, LaTeX, and even the mainframe `SCRIPT`.

TFTP (Trivial File Transfer Protocol or Trivial File Transfer Program)   A system-independent means of transferring files between systems connected via TCP/IP. It is different from FTP in that it does not ensure that the file is transferred correctly, does not authenticate users, and is missing a lot of functionality (such as the `ls` command).

toggle   A mode that is alternately turned on and off by successive entry of its command.

toggle setting   (`vi`) A setting that is either enabled or disabled; for example, for the fictitious setting named *option*, you would enable the setting by entering the command `:set option;` you would disable the setting by entering the command `:set nooption`.

top   A common tool used to display information about the top processes on the system.

typewriter key   The subset of a terminal keyboard that is on a standard typewriter; generally the alphanumeric keys but not the function, cursor control, or numeric pad keys.

UDP (User Datagram Protocol)   A protocol within the TCP/IP stack used for control messages and data transmission where the delivery acknowledgment is not needed. The application program must ensure data transmission in this case.

undo buffer   (`vi`) A location in memory where the most recent deleted text object is saved, either for later *undo*ing of the deletion, or for copying of the object to another location.

URL (Uniform Resource Locator)   The method of specifying the protocol, format, login (usually omitted), and location of materials on the Internet.

Usenet   See *Netnews*.

UUCP (UNIX-to-UNIX-Copy-Program)   Used to build an early, informal network for the transmission of files, email, and Netnews.

variables, attributes   The modifiers that set the variable type. A variable can be string or integer, left or right justified, read-only or changeable, and other attributes.

variables, environmental   A place to store data and values (strings and integers) in the area controlled by the shell so that they are available to the current process and sub-processes. They can just be local to the current shell or available to a subshell (exported).

variables, substitution   The process of interpreting an environmental variable to get its value.

viewport   The portion of the buffer that appears in a window on your screen; one way to think of moving through the buffer is to think of the viewport as sliding back and forth through the buffer.

Web   See *World Wide Web*.

whitespace   Blanks, space and tabs, that are normally interpreted to delineate commands and filenames unless quoted.

wildcard   Means of specifying filename(s) where the operating system determines some of the characters. Multiple files may match and will be available to the tool.

window   The portion of your screen displaying a viewport into a buffer.

World Wide Web   A collection of servers and services on the Internet that run software that communicate using a common protocol (HTTP). Instead of having to remember the location of these resources, links are provided from one Web page to another through the use of URLs (Uniform Resource Locators). The Web provides a user-friendly, multimedia interface to information on the Internet and is responsible for much of the explosive growth in Internet use and content.

WWW   See *World Wide Web*.

X Window system   A windowing and graphics system developed by MIT, to be used in client/server environments.

X   See *X Window system*.

X11   See *X Window system*.

X-windows   The wrong term for the X Window system. See *X Window system*.

INDEX

What's on the CD-ROM?

This briefly describes the contents of this CD-ROM. If you have not read the README file yet, now would be a good time to do so.

Please note that the file names listed here are their original UNIX versions. If you mounted this CD-ROM as a vanilla ISO9660 system, the names may be mangled somewhat to fit those conventions.

The following top-level files are included:

cdlndir	Script to install packages from the CD-ROM. A description of how to use this program is in the top-level README file.
COPYING	The GNU General Public License (GPL) version 2.
COPYING.LIB	The GNU Library General Public License (LGPL) v2.
DISTRIB	Free Software Foundation order form.
MANIFEST	This file.
README	General notes and installation instructions.

Here is a list of the included software:

automake-1.3/

This is Automake, a Makefile generator. It was inspired by the 4.4BSD make and include files, but aims to be portable and to conform to the GNU standards for Makefile variables and targets.

Automake is a Perl script. The input files are called Makefile.am. The output files are called Makefile.in; they are intended for use with Autoconf. Automake requires certain things to be done in your configure.in.

autoconf-2.12/

Autoconf is an extensible package of m4 macros that creates a noninteractive configuration script for a package from a template file. The template file lists the operating system features that the package can use, in the form of m4 macro calls, and can also contain arbitrary shell commands. Autoconf requires GNU m4.

Autoconf-generated configure scripts are being used by many GNU packages currently, and will be used by more in the future.

bash-2.02.1/

> BASH (the Bourne Again SHell) is a Posix-compatable shell with full Bourne shell ('sh') syntax and some C-shell commands. BASH supports emacs-style command-line editing, job control, functions, and on-line help. Instructions for compiling BASH may be found in the file "README".

bc-1.05/

> An arbitrary precision arithmetic language. It is much more useful than expr in shell script

binutils-2.7/

> This is a beta release of a completely rewritten binutils distribution. These programs have been tested on various architectures. Most recently tested are sun3 and sun4s running sunos4, as well as Sony News running newsos3. However, since this is a beta release taken directly from an evolving source tree, there might be some problems. In particular, the programs have not been ported to as many machines as the old binutils. There are also features of the old versions that are missing on the new programs. We would appreciate patches to make things run on other machines; especially welcome are fixes for what used to work on the old programs!

> This release contains the following programs: 'ar', 'demangle', 'ld' (the linker), 'nm', 'objcopy', 'objdump', 'ranlib', 'size', 'strip', and 'gprof'.

> BFD (the Binary File Descripter) library is in the subdirectory 'bfd' and is built along with GDB (which uses bfd).

> See the "README" file for further instructions on where to look for building the various utilities.

bison-1.25/

> Bison is an upwardly compatible replacement for the parser generator 'yacc', with more features. The file "README" gives instructions for compiling Bison; the files bison.1 (a man page) and bison.texinfo (a GNU Texinfo file) give instructions for using it.

calc-2.02f/

> Calc is an extensible, advanced desk calculator and mathematical tool that runs as part of GNU emacs. It comes with source for the Calc Manual, which serves as a tutorial and reference. If you wish, you can use Calc only as a simple four-function calculator, but it provides additional features including choice of algebraic or RPN (stack-based) entry, logarithmic functions, trigonometric and financial functions, arbitrary precision, complex numbers, vectors, matrices, dates, times, infinities,

sets, algebraic simplification, differentiation, and integration. Instructions for install Calc for emacs are in the "README" file.

Cortex_d/

Video frame grabber device driver for the Cortex I.

cperf-2.1a/

This is a program to generate minimally perfect hash functions for sets of keywords. gcc was optimized by using this program. Other programs that must recognize a set of keywords may also benefit from using this program. Instructions for compiling cperf may be found in the file "README". Note that a C++ version of cperf (called 'gperf') is included in the libg++ distribution. This version is for the use of people who do not want to install C++ in order to compile a single program.

cvs-1.10/

CVS is a collection of programs that provide for software release and revision control functions. CVS is designed to work on top of RCS version 4. It will parse older RCS formats, but cannot use any of its fancier features without RCS branch support. The file "README" contains more information about CVS.

cxdrv-0.86/

The device driver for the cx100 frame grabber is designed as a dynamically loadable module for the Linux kernel. The distribution encloses the device proper, a library of useful functions, and a few sample programs using the grabber.

diffutils-2.7/

'diff' compares files showing line-by-line changes in several flexible formats. GNU 'diff' is much faster than the traditional Unix versions. This distribution includes 'diff', 'diff3', 'sdiff', and 'cmp'. Instructions for compiling these are in the "README" file.

dld-3.3/

Dld is a library package of C functions that performs "dynamic link editing". Programs that use dld can add compiled object code to or remove such code from a process anytime during its execution. Loading modules, searching libraries, resolving external references, and allocating storage for global and static data structures are all performed at run time.

Dld works on VAX, Sun 3, SPARCstation, Sequent Symmetry, and Atari ST machines.

doschk-1.1/

This program is intended as a utility to help software developers ensure that their source file names are distinguishable on MS-DOS and 14-character SYSV platforms.

emacs-20.3/

GNU emacs is an extensible, customizable fullscreen editor. Read the files "README" and "INSTALL" for a full description of the parts of GNU emacs, and the steps needed to install it. This distribution includes the complete GNU emacs Manual.

enscript-1.6.1/

The GNU ASCII-to-PostScript converter.

fileutils-3.16/

These are the GNU file-manipulation utilities. Instructions for compiling these utilities are in the file "README". The fileutils package contains the following programs:

chgrp	chmod	chown	cp	dd
df	dir	du	ginstall	ln
ls	mkdir	mkfifo	mknod	mv
rm	rmdir	touch	vdir	

findutils-4.1/

This package contains the GNU find, xargs, and locate programs. find and xargs comply with POSIX 1003.2, as far as I know. They also support some additional options, some borrowed from Unix and some unique to GNU.

gas-2.3/

GAS is the GNU assembler. Version 2 has many changes over previous GAS releases. Most notable among the changes are the separation of host system, target CPU, and target file format (i.e. cross-assembling is much easier). Many CPU types and object file formats are now supported.

Read the file "gas-2.3/gas/README" for instructions on building and using GAS.

gawk-3.13/

GNU version of awk.

gcc-2.8.1/

> The GNU C compiler. In addition to supporting ANSI C, gcc includes support for the C++ and Objective C languages.

gcc-vms-1.42/

> The GNU C Compiler for VMS. In addition to supporting ANSI C, gcc includes support for the C++ and Objective C languages.

gcl-2.2/

> GNU Common Lisp (GCL) has a compiler and interpreter for Common Lisp. It is very portable and extremely efficient on a wide class of applications. It compares favorably in performance with commercial Lisps on several large theorem prover and symbolic algebra systems. It supports the CLtL1 specification but is moving towards the proposed ANSI definition. It is based on AKCL and KCL. KCL was written by Taiichi Yuasa and Masami Hagiya in 1984, and AKCL has been developed by William Schelter since 1987.
>
> GCL compiles to C and then uses the native optimizing C compilers (e.g. gcc). A function with a fixed number of args and one value turns into a C function of the same number of args and returning 1 value, so it cannot really be any more efficient on such calls. It has a conservative GC which allows great freedom for the C compiler to put Lisp values in arbitrary registers. It has a source level Lisp debugger for interpreted code, with display of source code in the other emacs window. It has profiling tools based on the C profiling tools, which count function calls and percentage of time. CLX works with GCL. There is an Xlib interface via C.

gdb-4.17/

> This is the GNU source-level debugger. A list of the machines supported as targets or hosts, as well as a list of new features, appears in gdb-4.12/gdb/NEWS.
>
> Instructions for compiling GDB are in the file gdb-4.12/gdb/README.
>
> BFD (the Binary File Descriptor) library is in the subdirectory bfd and is built along with GDB (which uses it).

gdbm-1.7.3/

> GNU dbm is a set of database routines that use extendible hashing and works similar to the standard UNIX dbm routines. This is release 1.7.3 of GNU dbm.

ghost-2.6.1/

> This program is an interpreter for a language that is intended to be, and very nearly is, compatible with the PostScript language. It runs under X on UNIX and VMS systems, and also runs on MS-DOS machines. It will drive either displays or low-to-medium-resolution printers. Instructions for compiling Ghostscript are in the file README. Fonts for Ghostscript are in the directory ghost-2.6.1/fonts.

ghostview-1.5/

Ghostview allows you to view PostScript(TM) files on X11 displays. Ghostview handles the user interface details and calls the 'ghostscript' interpreter to render the image. Instructions for compiling ghostview are in the README file.

gimp-1_0_2/

GIMP is an acronym for GNU Image Manipulation Program. It is a freely distributed piece of software suitable for such tasks as photo retouching, image composition, and image authoring.

It is an extremely capable piece of software with many capabilities. It can be used as a simple paint program, an expert-quality photo retouching program, an online batch processing system, a mass production image renderer, an image format converter, etc.

glibc-1.09.1/

This directory contains a beta release of the GNU C library.

The library is ANSI C-1989nd and POSIX 1003.1-1990[nd]compliant and has most of the functions specified in POSIX 1003.2. It is upward compatible with the 4.4 BSD C library and includes many System V functions, plus GNU extensions.

Version 1.09.1 adds support for Sun RPC, 'mmap', and friends, and compatibility with several more traditional Unix functions. It runs on Sun-3 (SunOS 4.1), Sun-4 (SunOS 4.1 or Solaris 2), HP 9000/300 (4.3BSD), SONY News 800 (NewsOS 3 or 4), MIPS DECstation (Ultrix 4), DEC Alpha (OSF/1), i386/i486 (System V, SVR4, BSD, SCO 3.2 & SCO ODT 2.0), Sequent Symmetry i386 (Dynix 3), and SGI (Irix 4). Texinfo source for the 'GNU C Library Reference Manual' is included; the manual still needs updating.

GNU stdio lets you define new kinds of streams, just by writing a few C functions. The fmemopen function uses this to open a stream on a string, which can grow as necessary. You can define your own printf formats to use a C function you have written. Also, you can safely use format strings from user input to implement a printf-like function for another programming language, for example. Extended getopt functions are already used to parse options, including long options, in many GNU utilities.

Porting the library is not hard. If you are interested in doing a port, please get on the mailing list by sending electronic mail to bug-glibc-request@prep.ai.mit.edu.

See the file INSTALL for instructions on building the library.

gnats-3.2/

GNATS (GNats: A Tracking System) is a bug-tracking system. It is based upon the paradigm of a central site or organization which receives problem reports and negotiates their resolution by electronic mail. Although it's been used primarily as a software bug-tracking system so far, it is sufficiently generalized so that it could be used for handling system administration issues, project management, or any number of other applications.

gperf-2.7/

gperf is a perfect hash function generator written in C++. It transforms an *n* element user-specified keyword set W into a perfect hash function F. F uniquely maps keywords in W onto the range 0..*k*, where *k*>=*n*. If *k*=*n* then F is a minimal perfect hash function. gperf generates a 0..*k* element static lookup table and a pair of C functions. These functions determine whether a given character string *s* occurs in W, using at most one probe into the lookup table.

grep-2.2/

This package contains version 2.0 of grep, egrep, and fgrep. They are similar to their UNIX counterparts, but are usually faster. Instructions for compiling them are in the file README.

groff-1.11a/

Groff is a document formatting system, which includes drivers for Postscript, TeX 'dvi' format, and typewriter-like devices, as well as implementations of 'eqn', 'nroff', 'pic', 'refer', 'tbl', 'troff', and the 'man', 'ms', and 'mm' macros. Groff's 'mm' macro package is almost compatible with the DWB 'mm' macros and has several extensions. Also included is a modified version of the Berkeley 'me' macros and an enhanced version of the X11 'xditview' previewer. Written in C++, these programs can be compiled with GNU C++ Version 2.5 or later.

gzip-1.2.4/

This is a new compression program free of known patents which the GNU Project is using instead of the traditional 'compress' program (which has patent problems). gzip can uncompress LZW-compressed files but uses a different algorithm for compression which generally yields smaller compressed files. This will be the standard compression program in the GNU system.

hp2xx-3.1.4/

GNU hp2xx reads HP-GL files, decomposes all drawing commands into elementary vectors, and converts them into a variety of vector and raster output formats. It is also a HP-GL previewer. Currently supported are:

Vector formats:

Encapsulated PostScript

Uniplex RGIP

> Metafont and various special TeX-related formats
>
> Simplified HP-GL (line drawing only), for imports

Raster formats:

> IMG, PBM, PCX, HP-PCL (including Deskjet & DJ5xxC support)

Previewers:

> UNIX: X11, OS/2: PM & Full-screen, DOS: (S)VGA & HGC, ATARI, AMIGA, VAX: UIS

indent-1.9.1/

This is the GNU modified version of the freely distributable 'indent' program from BSD. The file "indent.texinfo" contains instructions on using indent.

Internet Explorer 4/

Microsoft Internet Explorer 4.0

Hp-ux/

> Internet Explorer for the HP

Solaris/

> Internet Explorer for Solaris

ispell-3.1.20/

ispell is an interactive spell checker that finds unrecognized words and suggests "near misses" as replacements. Both system and user-maintained dictionaries can be used. Both a standalone and GNU emacs interface are available.

Some people may notice that the ispell 4.0 distribution has been replaced with ispell 3.1. The version numbering for this program has been screwy—it doesn't mean that we're using an older version of ispell. Ispell 3 and 4 were maintained in parallel, but version 3 is actually much more advanced. We decided to switch to it.

Eventually ispell 3 will support a GNU-style configuration script to make it a little easier to build.

Jacal/

JACAL is a symbolic mathematics system for the simplification and manipulation of equations and single and multiple valued algebraic expressions constructed of numbers, variables, radicals, and algebraic functions, differential, and holonomic functions. In addition, vectors and matrices of the above objects are included.

JACAL is written in Scheme. A version of Scheme (IEEE P1178 and R4RS compliant) written in C is available with JACAL. SCM runs on Amiga, Atari-ST, MacOS, MS-DOS, OS/2, NOS/VE, Unicos, VMS, UNIX, and similar systems.

libg++-2.8.1.1a/

The GNU C++ library is an extensive collection of C++ `forest` classes, a new IOStream library for input/output routines, and support tools for use with G++. Among the classes supported are Obstacks, multiple-precision Integers and Rationals, Complex numbers, arbitrary length Strings, BitSets, and BitStrings. There is also a set of pseudo-generic prototype files available for generating common container classes.

Instructions are in the file `libg++-2.7.2/libg++/README`.

libobjects-0.1.19/

It is a library of general-purpose, non-graphical Objective C objects designed in the Smalltalk tradition. It includes collection objects for maintaining groups of objects and C types, streams for I/O to various destinations, coders for formating objects and C types to streams, ports for network packet transmission, distributed objects (remote object messaging), pseudorandom number generators, character string classes, and time-handling facilities.

libstdc++-2.8.1.1a/

If you are receiving this as part of a GDB release, see the `file gdb/README`. If with a binutils release, see `binutils/README`; if with a libg++ release, see `libg++/README`, etc. That'll give you info about this package—supported targets, how to use it, how to report bugs, etc.

libtool-1.1/

This is GNU libtool, a generic library support script. Libtool hides the complexity of using shared libraries behind a consistent interface.

lynx-2.8/

A text-based Web browser.

m4-4.1.4/

GNU m4 is an implementation of the traditional UNIX macro processor. It is mostly SVR4 compatible, although it has some extensions (for example, handling more than 9 positional parameters to macros). m4 also has built-in functions for including files, running shell commands, doing arithmetic, etc. Autoconf needs GNU m4 for generating configure scripts, but not for running them.

make-3.71/

This is GNU Make. GNU Make supports many more options and features than the UNIX make. Instructions for using GNU Make are in the file `make.texinfo`. See the file `README` for installation instructions.

mcalc/

> This is an improved version of Jeff Schmidt's (pschmidt@gwis.com) lcalc loan calculator program. Jeff's original program produced lightning-fast loan amortization tables, but it had virtually no options or features and was awkward to use. The original program forms the core of this update, as is explicitly permitted under terms of the GPL.

metahtml-5.08/

> Meta-HTML Server

mh-e-5.0.2.1/

> The mh mode for emacs.

mtools-3.5/

> Mtools is a public-domain collection of programs to allow UNIX systems to read, write, and manipulate files on an MS-DOS filesystem (typically a diskette).

mule-1.1.4/

> Mule is a MULtilingual Enhancement to GNU emacs 18. It can handle not only ASCII characters (7 bits) and ISO Latin-1 (8 bits), but also Japanese, Chinese, and Korean (16 bits) coded in the ISO2022 standard and its variants (e.g. EUC, Compound Text). For Chinese there is support for both GB and Big5. In addition, Thai (based on TIS620) and Vietnamese (based on VISCII and VSCII) are also supported. A text buffer in Mule can contain a mixture of characters from these languages. To input any of these characters, you can use various input methods provided by Mule itself. In addition, if you use Mule under some terminal emulators (kterm, cxterm, or exterm), you can use any input methods supported by the emulator.

mv1000drv/

> This is the device driver for the Mutech MV-1000 PCI-framegrabber. The functions are similar to the Mutech driver/library. *This driver is not supported by Mutech.* The driver is part of a larger project called XGRAS.

mysql-3.20.13/

> SQL database server.

nethack-3.2.2/

> NetHack 3.2 is a new enhancement to the dungeon exploration game NetHack. It is a distant descendent of Rogue and Hack, and a direct descendent of NetHack 3.1 and 3.0. NetHack 3.2 is the product of two years of very intensive effort by the

NetHack Development Team and its porting subteams. Many parts of 3.1 were rewritten for NetHack 3.2, and many new features were added.

Netscape Communicator/

> Netscape Communicator
>
> aix-4.1/
>> Netscape Communicator 4.5 for AIX
>
> digitalunix-4.0D/
>> Netscape Communicator 4.5 for Digital Unix
>
> hp-ux-10.20/
>> Netscape Communicator 4.5 for HP-UX 10.20
>
> intel-solaris-2.5.1/
>> Netscape Communicator 4.5 for Intel Solaris
>
> solaris-2.5.1/
>> Netscape Communicator 4.5 for Solaris

nmh-0.27/

> The new and improved version of mh. Fixes many security bugs of mh.

octave-2.09/

> GNU Octave is a high-level language, primarily intended for numerical computations. It provides a convenient command line interface for solving linear and non-linear problems numerically.

oleo-1.6/

> Oleo is a spreadsheet program (better for you than the more expensive spreadsheet). It supports X Window and character-based terminals, and can generate embedded PostScript renditions of spreadsheets. Keybindings should be familiar to emacs users and are configurable by users.
>
> There is relatively little documentation for Oleo yet. The file USING contains what there is.

perl-5.004_04/

> This is version 5.004_04 of Larry Wall's Perl programming language. Perl is intended as a faster replacement for sed, awk, and similar languages. The file README contains instructions for compiling Perl.

plotutils-2.5.1/

> This is release 2.1.5 of the GNU plotutils (plotting utilities) package, including release 1.5 of GNU libplot: a function library for two-dimensional device-independent vector graphics, including vector graphics animations under the X Window System. The package has its own Web page: `http://www.gnu.org/software/plotutils/plotutils.html`.

> In the top-level source directory, the file `INSTALL` contains generic instructions dealing with installation of a GNU package, and the file `INSTALL.pkg` contains package-specific installation instructions. Please read them *in full*, as well as this file, before attempting to install the package.

qcam-0.7c/

> xfqcam uses an xforms-based control panel to allow real-time changing of the QuickCam settings: contrast, brightness, white balance, bpp, and image size. In addition you can click a button called "take picture" and a pgm file "snapshot" will be created. It basically works like QuickPic under Windows.

rcs-5.7/

> RCS, the Revision Control System, manages multiple revisions of files. RCS can store, retrieve, log, identify, and merge revisions. It is useful for files that are revised frequently, e.g. programs, documentation, graphics, and papers.

samba-1_9_18p10/

> This is version 1.9.18 of Samba, the free SMB and CIFS client and server for unix and other operating systems.

sCxx-1.2.1/

> sC++ language enhances C++ with a very few new keywords defining active objects and synchronization primitives in a way that preserves the whole philosophy of object oriented programming. A compiler for sC++, based on the GNU C++ compiler has been developed.

> Software/Hardware Requirements:

>> A C or C++ compiler that can compile GNU gcc. X11 version 5 or later and Motif to use the provided graphical libraries.

>> Note: Requires gperf gperf-2.7. stdc++ library is optional (libstdc++-2.8.1)

sed-2.05/

> This is a newer version of GNU sed, with many bug fixes. It also uses a beta test version of the 'rx' library, instead of the older and slower 'regex' library. (Because that library is still in beta test, sed version 1 is also included on this CD-ROM).

Instructions for building GNU sed are in the file README.

sh-utils-1.16/

These are the GNU shell utilities, comprising small commands that are frequently run on the command line or in shell scripts. Instructions for compiling these utilities are in the file README. The sh-utils package contains the following programs

basename	date	dirname	echo	env
expr	false	groups	hostname	id
logname	nice	nohup	pathchk	printenv
printf	pwd	sleep	stty	su
tee	test	true	tty	uname
users	who	whoami	yes.	

siag-2.80/

Office package for UNIX, including word processor, spreadsheet, and presentation graphics.

smalltalk-1.1.5/

This is the GNU implementation of Smalltalk, an object-oriented programming language. Instructions for compiling it are in the file README.

speaker-1.0.1/

Speakerphone application for US Robotics and Rockwell voice modems.

superopt-2.5/

The superoptimizer is a function sequence generator that uses a exhaustive generate-and-test approach to find the shortest instruction sequence for a given function.

The GNU superoptimizer and its application in gcc is described in the ACM SIGPLAN PLDI'92 proceedings.

tar-1.11.2/

Tar is a program used for archiving many files in a single file, which makes them easier to transport.

GNU tar includes multivolume support, the ability to archive sparse files, automatic archive compression/decompression, remote archives, and special features to allow tar to be used for incremental and full backups. Unfortunately GNU tar implements an early draft of the POSIX 1003.1 ustar standard, which is different from the final standard. Adding support for the new changes in a backward-compatible fashion is not trivial.

Instructions for compiling GNU tar may be found in the file README.

termcap-1.2/

This is a standalone release of the GNU Termcap library, which has been part of the GNU emacs distribution for years but is now available separately to make it easier to install as `libtermcap.a`. The GNU Termcap library does not place an arbitrary limit on the size of termcap entries, unlike most other termcap libraries. Included is extensive documentation in Texinfo format. Unfortunately, this release does not have a termcap database included. Instructions for building the termcap library are in the `README` file.

Termutils-2.0/

GNU terminal control utilities tput and tabs. tput is a program to enable shell scripts to portably use special terminal capabilities. Although its interface is similar to that of terminfo-based tput programs, it actually uses termcap. tabs is a program to set hardware terminal tab settings.

See the file `INSTALL` for compilation and installation instructions.

texinfo-3.9/

This package contains a set of utilities related to Texinfo, which is used to generate printed manuals and online hypertext-style manuals (called 'info'). Programs and interfaces for writing, reading, and formatting texinfo files are available both as standalone programs and as GNU emacs interfaces. See the file `README` for directions on how to use the various parts of this package.

textutils-1.22/

These are the GNU text utilities, commands that are used to operate on textual data. Instructions for compiling these utilities are in the file `README`. The textutils package contains the following programs:

cat	cksum	comm	csplit	cut
expand	fold	head	join	nl
od	paste	pr	sort	split
sum	tac	tail	tr	unexpand
uniq	wc			

uucp-1.06/

This version of UUCP was written by Ian Lance Taylor. It will be the standard UUCP system for GNU. It currently supports the 'f', 'g' (in all window and packet sizes), 'G', 't' and 'e' protocols, as well a Zmodem protocol and two new bidirectional protocols. If you have a Berkeley sockets library, it can make TCP connections. If you have TLI libraries, it can make TLI connections. Other important notes about this version of UUCP, and instructions for building it, are in the file `README`.

uuencode-1.0/

> Uuencode and uudecode are used to transmit binary files over transmission mediums that do not support other than simple ASCII data. Please read the `Uuencode.rea` file for installation instructions.

VideoteX-.06/

> With this program and the included driver it's possible to receive, display, store,and print videotext-pages from a videotext-interface. There's a commandline-version that can be used mainly for batch-operation and an interactive version using the X Window System and the XView-toolkit. You also can use VideoteXt to display pages from INtv's videotext-service in the WWW.

vim-5.3/

> Vi improved.

wdiff-0.05/

> 'wdiff' compares two files, finding which words have been deleted or added to the first for getting the second.

> We hope eventually to integrate 'wdiff', as well as some ideas from a similar program called 'spiff', into some future release of GNU 'diff'.

wget-1.5.3/

> GNU Wget is a free network utility to retrieve files from the World Wide Web using HTTP and FTP, the two most widely used Internet protocols. It works noninteractively, thus enabling work in the background, after having logged off.

XcallerID-1.1/

> XCallerID is a caller ID program for Linux. It consists of two separate entities: the xcid daemon which stores incoming calls in a database, and the XCallerID client which allows updating of the database.

xlogmaster-1.4.4/

> This is the Xlogmaster version 1.4.4. The Xlogmaster is a program that allows easy and flexible monitoring of all logfiles and devices that allow being read via cat (like the /proc devices). It allows you to set a lot of events based on certain activities in the monitored logfiles/devices and should prove very helpful for almost anyone. For additional information and tutorial see the `./doc` directory.

By opening this package, you are agreeing to be bound by the following agreement:

Some of the programs included with this product are governed by the GNU General Public License, which allows redistribution; see the license information for each product for more information. Other programs are included on the CD-ROM by special permission from their authors.

You may not copy or redistribute the entire CD-ROM as a whole. Copying and redistribution of individual software programs on the CD-ROM is governed by terms set by individual copyright holders. The installer and code from the author(s) is copyrighted by the publisher and the author. Individual programs and other items on the CD-ROM are copyrighted by their various authors or other copyright holders. This software is sold as-is without warranty of any kind, either expressed or implied, including but not limited to the implied warranties of merchantability and fitness for a particular purpose. Neither the publisher nor its dealers or distributors assumes any liability for any alleged or actual damages arising from the use of this program. (Some states do not allow for the exclusion of implied warranties, so the exclusion may not apply to you.)

NOTE: This CD-ROM uses long and mixed-case filenames requiring the use of a protected-mode CD-ROM Driver.